P9-ECU-714

CLASSICAL AND MEDIEVAL LITERATURE CRITICISM

Guide to Gale Literary Criticism Series

For criticism on	Consult these Gale series
Authors now living or who died after December 31, 1959	*CONTEMPORARY LITERARY CRITICISM (CLC)*
Authors who died between 1900 and 1959	*TWENTIETH-CENTURY LITERARY CRITICISM (TCLC)*
Authors who died between 1800 and 1899	*NINETEENTH-CENTURY LITERATURE CRITICISM (NCLC)*
Authors who died between 1400 and 1799	*LITERATURE CRITICISM FROM 1400 TO 1800 (LC)* *SHAKESPEAREAN CRITICISM (SC)*
Authors who died before 1400	*CLASSICAL AND MEDIEVAL LITERATURE CRITICISM (CMLC)*
Black writers of the past two hundred years	*BLACK LITERATURE CRITICISM (BLC)*
Authors of books for children and young adults	*CHILDREN'S LITERATURE REVIEW (CLR)*
Dramatists	*DRAMA CRITICISM (DC)*
Hispanic writers of the late nineteenth and twentieth centuries	*HISPANIC LITERATURE CRITICISM (HLC)*
Native North American writers and orators of the eighteenth, nineteenth, and twentieth centuries	*NATIVE NORTH AMERICAN LITERATURE (NNAL)*
Poets	*POETRY CRITICISM (PC)*
Short story writers	*SHORT STORY CRITICISM (SSC)*
Major authors from the Renaissance to the present	*WORLD LITERATURE CRITICISM, 1500 TO THE PRESENT (WLC)*

ISSN 0896-0011

Volume 27

CLASSICAL AND MEDIEVAL LITERATURE CRITICISM

Excerpts from Criticism of the Works of World Authors from Classical Antiquity through the Fourteenth Century, from the First Appraisals to Current Evaluations

Jelena O. Krstović
Editor

GALE
DETROIT • LONDON

STAFF

Crook, Jelena Krstović, Daniel G. Marowski, *Editors*
Suzanne Dewsbury, *Associate Editor*
g E. Hutchison, Ira Mark Milne, *Assistant Editors*
Aarti D. Stephens, *Managing Editor*

Susan M. Trosky, *Permissions Manager*
Kimberly F. Smilay, *Permissions Specialist*
Steve Cusack, Kelly A. Quin, *Permissions Associates*
Sandy Gore, *Permissions Assistant*

Victoria B. Cariappa, *Research Manager*
Gary Oudersluys, *Research Specialist*
Norma Sawaya, Tracie A. Richardson, *Research Associates*
Phyllis Blackman, *Research Assistant*

Mary Beth Trimper, *Production Director*
Deborah Milliken, *Production Assistant*

Pamela A. Reed, *Imaging Coordinator*
Randy Bassett, *Image Database Supervisor*
Robert Duncan, Michael Logusz, *Imaging Specialists*
Christine O'Bryan, *Desktop Publisher*

Address until September 15, 1998:
835 Penobscot Building
Detroit, MI 48226-4094
Address after September 15, 1998:
27500 Drake Rd.
Farmington Hills, MI 48331-3535

This book is printed on acid-free paper that meets the minimum requirements of American National Standard for Information Sciences—Permanence Paper for Printed Library Materials, ANSI Z39.48-1984.

Library of Congress Catalog Card Number 88-658021
ISBN 0-7876-2406-3
ISSN 0896-0011
Printed in the United States of America

10 9 8 7 6 5 4 3 2 1

Contents

Preface

Since its inception in 1988, *Classical and Medieval Literature Criticism* has been a valuable resource for students and librarians seeking critical commentary on the writers and works of these periods in world history. Major reviewing sources have assessed *CMLC* as "useful" and "extremely convenient," noting that it "adds to our understanding of the rich legacy left by the ancient period and the Middle Ages," and praising its "general excellence in the presentation of an inherently interesting subject." No other single reference source has surveyed the critical reaction to classical and medieval literature as thoroughly as *CMLC.*

Scope of the Series

CMLC is designed to serve as an introduction for students and advanced readers of the works and authors of antiquity through the fourteenth century. The great poets, prose writers, dramatists, and philosophers of this period form the basis of most humanities curricula, so that virtually every student will encounter many of these works during the course of a high school and college education. By organizing and reprinting an enormous amount of commentary written on classical and medieval authors and works, *CMLC* helps students develop valuable insight into literary history, promotes a better understanding of the texts, and sparks ideas for papers and assignments. Each entry in *CMLC* presents a comprehensive survey of an author's career, an individual work of literature, or a literary topic, and provides the user with a multiplicity of interpretations and assessments. Such variety allows students to pursue their own interests; furthermore, it fosters an awareness that literature is dynamic and responsive to many different opinions.

CMLC continues the survey of criticism of world literature begun by Gale's *Contemporary Literary Criticism (CLC), Twentieth-Century Literary Criticism (TCLC), Nineteenth-Century Literature Criticism (NCLC), Literature Criticism from 1400 to 1800 (LC),* and *Shakespearean Criticism (SC).* For additional information about these and Gale's other criticism series, users should consult the Guide to Gale Literary Criticism Series preceding the title page in this volume.

Coverage

Each volume of *CMLC* is carefully compiled to present:

- criticism of authors and works which represent a variety of genres, time periods, and nationalities

- both major and lesser-known writers and works of the period (such as non-Western authors and literature, increasingly read by today's students)

- 4-6 authors or works per volume

- individual entries that survey the critical response to each author, work, or topic, including early criticism, later criticism (to represent any rise or decline in the author's reputation), and current retrospective analyses. The length of each author or work entry also indicates relative importance, reflecting the amount of critical attention the author, work, or topic has received from critics writing in English, and from foreign criticism in translation.

An author may appear more than once in the series if his or her writings have been the subject of a substantial amount of criticism; in these instances, specific works or groups of works by the author will be covered in separate entries. For example, Homer will be represented by three entries, one devoted to the *Iliad,* one to the *Odyssey,* and one to the Homeric Hymns.

Starting with Volume 10, *CMLC* will also occasionally include entries devoted to literary topics. For example, *CMLC*-10 focuses on Arthurian Legend and includes general criticism on that subject as well as individual entries on writers or works central to that topic—Chrétien de Troyes, Gottfried von Strassburg, Layamon, and the Alliterative *Morte Arthure*. Presocratic Philosophy is the focus of *CMLC*-22, which includes general criticism as well as essays on Greek philosophers Anaximander, Heraclitus, Parmenides, and Pythagoras.

Organization of the Book

An author entry consists of the following elements: author heading, biographical and critical introduction, principal English translations or editions, excerpts of criticism (each preceded by a bibliographic citation and an annotation), and a bibliography of further reading.

- The **Author Heading** consists of the author's most commonly used name, followed by birth and death dates. If the entry is devoted to a work, the heading will consist of the most common form of the title in English translation (if applicable), and the original date of composition. Located at the beginning of the introduction are any name or title variations.

- A **Portrait** of the author is included when available. Many entries also feature illustrations of materials pertinent to the author or work, including manuscript pages, book illustrations, and representations of people, places, and events important to a study of the author or work.

- The **Biographical and Critical Introduction** contains background information that concisely introduces the reader to the author, work, or topic.

- The list of **Principal Works** and **English Translations** or **Editions** is chronological by date of first publication and is included as an aid to the student seeking translated versions or editions of these works for study. The list will focus primarily on twentieth-century translations, selecting those works most commonly considered the best by critics.

- **Criticism** is arranged chronologically in each entry to provide a useful perspective on changes in critical evaluation over the years. All titles by the author featured in the critical entry are printed in boldface type to enable the user to ascertain without difficulty the works being discussed. Also for purposes of easier identification, the critic's name and the publication date of the essay are given at the beginning of each piece of criticism. Anonymous criticism is preceded by the title of the journal in which it appeared. Publication information (such as publisher names and book prices) and parenthetical numerical references (such as footnotes or page and line references to specific editions of works) have been deleted at the editors' discretion to provide smoother reading of the text. Many critical entries in *CMLC* also contain translations to aid the users. Footnotes that appear with previously published pieces of criticism are reprinted at the end of each essay or excerpt. In the case of excerpted criticism, only those footnotes that pertain to the excerpted text are included

- A complete **Bibliographic Citation** provides original publication information for each piece of criticism.

- Critical excerpts are also prefaced by **Annotations** providing the reader with information about both the critic and the criticism, the scope of the excerpt, the growth of critical controversy, or changes in critical trends regarding an author or work. In some cases, these notes include cross-references to excerpts by critics who discuss each other's commentary. Dates in parentheses within the annotation refer to a book publication date when they follow a book title, and to an essay date when they follow a critic's name.

- An annotated bibliography of **Further Reading** appears at the end of each entry and lists additional secondary sources on the author or work. In some cases it includes essays for which the editors could not obtain reprint rights. When applicable, the Further Reading is followed by references to additional entries on the author in other literary reference series published by Gale.

Topic Entries are subdivided into several thematic rubrics in which criticism appears in order of descending scope.

Cumulative Indexes

Each volume of *CMLC* includes a cumulative **author index** listing all authors who have appeared in Gale's Literary Criticism Series, along with cross references to such biographical series as *Contemporary Authors* and *Dictionary of Literary Biography*. For readers' convenience, a complete list of Gale titles included appears on the page prior to the author index. Useful for locating an author within the various series, this index is particularly valuable for those authors who are identified with a certain period but who, because of their death date, are placed in another, or for those authors whose careers span two periods. For example, Geoffrey Chaucer, who is usually considered a medieval author, is found in *Literature Criticism from 1400 to 1800* because he died after 1399.

Beginning with the tenth volume, *CMLC* includes a cumulative index listing all topic entries that have appeared in the Gale Literary Criticism Series *Classical and Medieval Literature Criticism, Contemporary Literary Criticism, Literature Criticism from 1400 to 1800, Nineteenth-Century Literature Criticism,* and *Twentieth-Century Literary Criticism.*

Beginning with the second volume, *CMLC* also includes a cumulative nationality index. Authors and/or works are grouped by nationality, and the volume in which criticism on them may be found is indicated.

Title Index

Each volume of *CMLC* also includes an index listing the titles of all literary works discussed in the series. Foreign language titles that have been translated are followed by the titles of the translations—for example, *Slovo o polku Igorove (The Song of Igor's Campaign)*. Page numbers following these translated titles refer to all pages on which any form of the title, either foreign language or translated, appears. Titles of novels, dramas, nonfiction books, and poetry, short story, or essay collections are printed in italics, while those of all individual poems, short stories, and essays are printed in roman type within quotation marks. In cases where the same title is used by different authors, the author's name or surname is given in parentheses after the title, e.g. *Collected Poems* (Horace) and *Collected Poems* (Sappho).

Critic Index

An index to critics, which cumulates with the second volume, is another useful feature of *CMLC.* Under each critic's name are listed the authors and/or works on whom the critic has written and the volume and page number where criticism may be found.

A Note to the Reader

When writing papers, students who quote directly from any volume in the Literary Criticism Series may use the following general forms to footnote reprinted criticism. The first example pertains to material drawn from a periodical, the second to material reprinted from books.

Rollo May, "The Therapist and the Journey into Hell," *Michigan Quarterly Review,* XXV, No. 4 (Fall 1986), 629-41; excerpted and reprinted in *Classical and Medieval Literature Criticism,* Vol. 3, ed. Jelena O. Krstovic (Detroit: Gale Research, 1989), pp. 154-58.

Dana Ferrin Sutton, *Self and Society in Aristophanes* (University of Press of America, 1980); excerpted and reprinted in *Classical and Medieval Literature Criticism,* Vol. 4, ed. Jelena O. Krstovic (Detroit: Gale Research, 1990), pp. 162-69.

Suggestions Are Welcome

Readers who wish to make suggestions for future volumes, or who have other comments regarding the series, are cordially invited to write or call the editors (1-800-347-GALE, Fax: (313) 961-6815).

Acknowledgments

The editors wish to thank the copyright holders of the excerpted criticism included in this volume and the permissions managers of many book and magazine publishing companies for assisting us in securing reproduction rights. We are also grateful to the staffs of the Detroit Public Library, the Library of Congress, the University of Detroit Mercy Library, Wayne State University Purdy/Kresge Library Complex, and the University of Michigan Libraries for making their resources available to us. Following is a list of the copyright holders who have granted us permission to reproduce material in this volume of CMLC-27. Every effort has been made to trace copyright, but if omissions have been made, please let us know.

COPYRIGHTED EXCERPTS IN *CMLC*, VOLUME 27, WERE REPRODUCED FROM THE FOLLOWING PERIODICALS:

Dumbarton Oaks Papers, n. 18, 1964. Reproduced by permission.—***The Muslim World,*** v. XLI, January, 1951. Reproduced by permission.—***Philosophy and Literature,*** v. 13, October, 1989. (c) 1989. Reproduced by permission of The Johns Hopkins University Press.—***The Review of Metaphysics,*** v. XXXIII, December, 1979 for "On Socrates, with Reference to Gregory Vlastos" by James Haden. Copyright (c) 1979 by The Review of Metaphysics. Reproduced by permission of the publisher.

COPYRIGHTED EXCERPTS IN *CMLC*, VOLUME 27, WERE REPRODUCED FROM THE FOLLOWING BOOKS:

Anderson, David. From an introduction to ***On The Divine Images: Three Apologies Against Those Who Attack the Divine Images.*** Translated by David Anderson. St. Vladimir's Semiary Press, 1980. Translation (c) 1980 St. Vladimir's Semiary Press. Reproduced by permission.—Bryce, Derek. From ***Ch'ung-Hu-Ch'en-Ching or The Treatise of the Transcendent Master of the Void.*** Translated by Leon Wieger. Llanerch Publishers, 1992. Copyright (c) English edition Derek Bryce 1992. Reproduced by permission.—Fry, Paul H. From ***The Reach of Criticism: Method and Perception in Literary Theory.*** Yale University Press, 1983. Copyright (c) 1983 by Yale University Press. All rights reserved. Reproduced by permission.—Gomez-Lobo, Alfonso. From ***The Foundations of Socratic Ethics.*** Hackett Publishing Company, Inc., 1994. Copyright (c) 1994 by Hackett Publishing Company, Inc. All rights reserved. Reproduced by permission of the publisher.—Graham, A. C. From ***The Book of Lieh-tzu.*** Translated by A. C. Graham. John Murray, 1960. (c) A. C. Grahma 1960. Reproduced by permission of the publisher.—Gulley, Norman. From ***The Philosophy of Socrates.*** Macmillan, 1968. Copyright (c) Norman Gulley. Reproduced by permission of Macmillan, London and Basingstoke. In North American by St. Martin's Press, Inc.—Guthrie, W. K. C. From ***A History of Greek Philosophy.*** Cambridge University Press, 1969. (c) Cambridge University Press 1969. Reproduced by permission of the publisher and the author.—McGiffert, Arthur Cushman. From ***A History of Christian Thought: Volume 1 Early and Eastern: From Jesus to John of Damascus.*** Charles Scribner's Sons, 1932. Copyright, 1932, by Charles Scribner's Sons. Copyright renewed (c) 1960 by Gertrude H. Boyce McGiffert. All rights reserved. Reproduced with permission of Scribner, a Division of Simon & Schuster, Inc.—Navia, Luis E. From ***The Socratic Presence.*** Garland Publishing, Inc., 1993. Copyright (c) 1993 Luis E. Navia. All rights reserved. Reproduced by permission.—Noffke, Suzanne. From an introduction to ***Catherine of Siena: The Dialogue.*** Translated by Suzanne Noffke. O. P. Paulist Press, 1980. Copyright (c) 1980 by The Missionary Society of St. Paul the Apostle in the State of New York. All rights reserved. Reproduced by permission of Paulist Press.—Parry, Kenneth. From ***Depicting the Word: Byzantine Iconophile Thought of the Eighth and Ninth Centuries.*** E. J. Brill, 1996. (c) Copyright 1996 by E. J. Brill, Leiden, The Netherlands. All rights reserved. Reproduced by permission of Brill NV.—Sahas, Daniel J. ***From John of Damascus on Islam: The 'Heresy of the Ishmaelites.'*** E. J. Brill, 1972. Copyright 1972 by E. J. Brill, Leiden, Netherlands. All rights reserved. Reproduced by permission of Brill NV.—Scott, Karen. From "'Io Catarina': Ecclesiastical Politics and Oral Culture in the Letters of Catherine of Siena" in ***Dear Sister: Medieval Women and the Epistolary Genre.*** Edited by Karen Cherewatuk and Ulrike Wiethaus. University of Pennsylvania Press, 1993. Copyright (c) 1993 by the University of Pennsylvania Press. All rights reserved. Reproduced by permission of the publisher.-Vlastos, Gregory. From ***Socrates, Ironist and Moral Philosopher.*** Cornell University Press, 1991. Copyright (c) Cambridge University Press and Cornell University Press, 1991. All rights reserved. Reproduced by permission of the publisher, Cornell University Press. All additional uses of this material-including, but not limited to, photocopying and reprinting-are prohibited without the prior written approval of Cornell University Press for rights in the United States, its dependencies, the Philippine Republic and Canada. In the United Kingdom by Cambridge University Press and the Literary Estate for Gregory Vlastos.—Welch, Holmes. From ***The Parting of the Way: Lao Tzu and the Taoist Movement.*** Beacon Press, 1957. (c) 1957, 1965 by Holmes Welch. Renewed 1985 by Nathaniel Welch. Reproduced by permission of Beacon Press, Boston.—Wolfskeel, Cornelia. From "Catherine of Siena" in ***A History of Women Philosophers, Volume II: Medieval, Renaissance and Enlightenment Women Philosophers A. D. 500-1600.*** Edited by Mary Ellen Waithe. Kluwer Academic Publishers, 1989. (c) 1989 by Kluwer Academic Publishers. All rights reserved. Reproduced by permission.—Woozley, A. D. From ***The Philosophy of Socrates: A Critical of Critical Essays.*** University of Notre Dame Press, 1971. Copyright (c) 1971 by University of Notre Dame Press. All rights reserved. Reproduced by permission.

PHOTOGRAPHS AND ILLUSTRATIONS APPEARING IN *CMLC,* VOLUME 27, WERE RECEIVED FROM THE FOLLOWING SOURCES:

A title page for "The Works of Dionysius Longinus, On the Sublime: Or, A Treatise Concerning the Sovereign Perfection of Writing," Translated from Greek by Mr. Welsted, 1712, edition, photograph. Courtesy of the Graduate Library, University of Michigan. Reproduced by permission.—Plato, photograph. The Library of Congress.—Prison of Socrates, Athens, photograph. The Library of Congress.—Socrates, from The Harvard Classics edition, engraving. The Library of Congress.—St. John of Damascus, woodcut. Archive Photos, Inc. Reproduced by permission.—Xenophon, drawing. The Library of Congress.

St. Catherine

1347?-1380

Italian mystic and saint. Also known as Caterina di Giacomo di Benincasa.

INTRODUCTION

One of the most popular of Catholic saints, Catherine of Siena was noted not only for her religious devotion and charitable service to the underprivileged but also for her eloquent, forceful, and controversial involvement in the politics of the Roman Catholic Church and of Italian city-states. Her mysticism was combined with a strong belief in the practical relief of human suffering. During her lifetime she gained legendary status, which only increased after her death due to her considerable following. Her literary work displays her intellectual independence and passionate engagement with both the spiritual and institutional aspects of Christianity.

Biographical Information

Catherine's life experiences were deeply influenced by her spirituality, and the immediacy of this relationship between the worldly and the divine is constantly manifested in her writings. Her life prior to the time that she joined the order of San Domenico at the age of eighteen is somewhat uncertain, due to the difficulty of separating out accurate accounts of this early period from the myths that circulated around her. Her birth date is usually given as 1347, although there is some evidence that this date was fabricated in order to make her thirty-three at her death, the same age as Christ at his death. Catherine was the second youngest of twenty-five children born to Lapa and Jacopomo Benincasa (a wool-dyer by trade), who enjoyed moderate wealth and status in the city of Siena. As a young child, Catherine displayed imagination, independence, and spiritual devotion; a 1374 biography claims that she experienced her first vision during her early childhood. Although she had no formal education, by the time she was an adolescent she had developed, according to Suzanne Noffke, "a passion for the truth of things"—one that led her to reject the more conventional path of marriage in favor of the Church. When Catherine was eighteen, she joined the Dominican order and began a period of extreme isolation. During this time she learned to read, although there is no documentation regarding her schooling or education. In 1368 she felt called to end her solitude in order to perform works of charity for the poor and the sick, as a way of manifesting her devotion to God. With the ultimate goal of helping to unite the Church, she also began to intervene in the political conflicts between the papacy and Italian city-states and to vehemently call for another crusade to the Holy Land; at times this activism put her life in danger, a risk she embraced in the light of her explicit desire to become a martyr. She traveled extensively around Italy in order to counter anti-papal influence. At the same time, her mystical experiences became central to her life: she was frequently unable to sleep or eat, and on one occasion she "died": for several hours she was unconscious and later claimed to have experienced a spiritual union with the divine. Her deteriorating health between 1378 and 1380 reflects in part divine and diabolic visions of increasing frequency that eventually prevented her from eating anything at all. Catherine of Siena died in Rome on April 29, 1380. In 1970 she became one of only two women in the Roman Catholic Church to earn the title of *doctor ecclesiae*.

Major Works

Catherine's political involvement and personal commitments spurred her to write numerous letters, almost four hundred of which are extant; her *Il Dialogo* (*The Dialogue*) is the record of a profoundly mystical experience, in which she described offering four petitions to God and receiving four teachings. Her principal works, therefore, reflect the unique fusion of spiritual contemplation and worldly activity that guided her life. Despite her lack of education, she strongly believed in the power of reason within faith and the importance of truth in the service of the glory of God. Her interpretation of Christian doctrine is highly original—arising out of a faith steeped in ecstatic union with the divine, which intensified the controversy surrounding her life and her subsequent canonization by the Church. One of her most striking interpretive images, in *The Dialogue* is that of the crucified Christ as a bridge between the divine and earthly spheres: three stages (the feet, the heart, and the mouth) correspond to three movements of the soul (by affections, by love that mirrors the love of Christ, and toward peace after its conflicts with sin). *The Dialogue* was, according to legend, dictated during a five-day period of ecstasy; her letters show, however, that she worked on it for somewhere close to one year. The dialogue explains four petitions Catherine offered to God and the elaborate responses she received. This text stands as the most comprehensive account of Catherine's understanding of Christian doctrine, as it explains, among other ideas, the path of salvation, the goal of spiritual contemplation, and the role of the Church in faith. *Le Orazioni* contains transcriptions of what Catherine said during her almost daily states of ecstasy in the last few years of her life. The thoughts documented in this text reflect and explicate some of the ideas in *The Dialogue* and particularly focus on the issue of God's love for humanity. Catherine's letters (her *Epistolario*), in contrast to these writings, are addressed to a wide range of correspondents on a variety of political and religious topics. Written in the Sienese dialect, these letters secured Catherine's place as one of the most important women in early Italian literature. According to Karen Scott, the letters are "characterized by a combination of didactic content, personal tone, and passionate concern to affect public matters and people's lives." Catherine understood her own writing to be infused with divine authority; the letters contain teachings directed at specific individuals and groups in particular circumstances, and often speak of her intensely personal spiritual experiences in order to strengthen the faith of her correspondents. The letters are an extension of her charitable works and provide important insights into her understanding of her spiritual role and of the importance of discourse in the transmission of faith.

Textual History

All of Catherine's writings were dictated to and transcribed by nuns or by her confessors, and have been preserved as church documents, but have appeared in a variety of editions. *The Dialogue*, which was written in 1377-1378 but first published in 1472, survives not in its original form, but in several versions from the fourteenth century; it was edited by Giuliana Cavallini in 1968 according to a thematic organization that reflects the narrative unity of the dialogue rather than the more traditional separation of the text into four sections, corresponding to the four questions. The *Orazioni*, recorded between 1376 and 1380, were originally spoken in the Sienese dialect but were translated into Latin during Catherine's lifetime and survive in several forms. The letters, also dictated in the last decade of her life, were first published in 1500 and form one of the earliest contributions by a woman to canonical fourteenth-century literature.

Critical Reception

Critics who were Catherine's contemporaries generally fall sharply into two groups: detractors and supporters. For centuries after her death, accounts of her life and writings were permeated by the struggle for canonization. Her work was included in various collections of vernacular literature but has had contradictory evaluations. Her style, as Scott contends, is often "confused" and overly didactic, and the letters, in particular, tend towards repetitiveness. However, recent scholarship has focused on Catherine's use of imagery in articulating her spiritual experiences and on her position as an author: a woman who achieved literacy in a mysterious way (her confessor Raymond of Capua wrote that she had been taught all she knew by the Holy Spirit), one who claimed divine authority and commanded a sophisticated understanding of religious and philosophical ideas; and one who dictated much of her work in the vernacular and during periods of ecstatic communion with the divine. Although she inherited a cohesive set of theological doctrines, she contributed a "fresh and vivid expression of the tradition," as Noffke has claimed, through her personal experiences, both worldly and ecstatic.

PRINCIPAL WORKS

**Il Dialogo della Divina Provvidenza ovvero Libro della Divina Dottrina* [*The Dialogue*] (dialogue) 1472

Epistolario (letters) [edited by Aldo Manuzio] 1500

***Le Orazioni* (speeches) [edited by Giuliana Cavallini] 1978

**Il Dialogo* was written during the years 1377-78.

**The speeches contained in *Le Orazioni* were recorded during the years 1376-80.

PRINCIPAL ENGLISH TRANSLATIONS

The Dialogue [translated by Suzanne Noffke] 1980

The Letters of St. Catherine of Siena [translated by Suzanne Noffke] 1988-.

CRITICISM

Edmund G. Gardner (essay date 1907)

SOURCE: "Catherine's Literary Work," in *Saint Catherine of Siena: A Study in the Religion, Literature and History of the Fourteenth Century in Italy,* J. M. Dent and Company and E. P. Dutton and Company, 1907, pp. 353-850.

[*In the excerpt that follows, Gardner places Catherine of Siena's literary work within the context of Christian mysticism as well as within more mainstream theology.*]

> "Anco vi prego che il Libro e ogni scrittura la quale trovaste di me, voi e frate Bartolomeo e frate Tomaso e il Maestro, ve le rechiate per le mani; e fatene quello che vedete che sia più onore di Dio, con missere Tomaso insieme: nel quale io trovava alcuna recreazione."—St. Catherine to Fra Raimondo, Letter 373 (102).

At the end of her life, Catherine took thought for the written word that she was leaving behind her, still to speak with her voice after she had passed away. We have seen her, in her last letter, commend her works to Fra Raimondo and her other literary executors: *il Libro e ogni scrittura la quale trovaste di me.* The literary value of these remains is probably the last thing of which the Saint, "this blessed virgin and mother of thousands of souls," as Barduccio calls her, would have thought; she was not, in any normal sense of the words, a "woman of letters"; but, nevertheless, her spiritual and mystical writings rank among the classics of the language of her beloved native land, and hold, indeed, a position of unique importance in the literature of the fourteenth century.

It was in the brief interval between her leaving Florence and her going to Rome, a few months of comparative peace which she passed at Siena in the late summer and early autumn of 1378, that Catherine had completed her wonderful book: the ***Dialogo,*** or ***Trattato della Divina Provvidenza,*** also known as the ***Libro della Divina Dottrina.***

"When the peace had been announced," writes Fra Raimondo,

> she returned to her own home, and set herself with fresh diligence to the composition of a certain book, which, inspired by the supreme Spirit, she dictated in her vernacular. She had besought her secretaries (who were wont to write the letters which she despatched in all directions) attentively to observe everything when, according to her custom, she was rapt out of her corporeal senses, and carefully to write down whatever she then dictated. This they did heedfully, and compiled a book full of high and most salutary doctrines, which had been revealed to her by the Lord and were dictated by her, by word of mouth, in the vernacular speech.[1]

In her last letter, Catherine simply refers to it as *il libro nel quale io trovava alcuna recreazione,* "the book in which I found some recreation"; and, although her friends and disciples thus describe her as dictating it to her secretaries while "rapt in singular excess and abstraction of mind," it is not clear that she herself would have made any claims of supernatural authority for it, or have regarded it as anything more than the pious meditations of a spirit "athirst with very great desire for the honour of God and the salvation of souls," one who (in her own characteristic phrase) "was dwelling in the cell of knowledge of self, in order better to know the goodness of God."

The book is concerned with the whole spiritual life of man, in the form of a prolonged dialogue, or series of dialogues, between the eternal Father and the impassioned human soul, who is here clearly Catherine herself. It seems to be properly divided into six treatises or *Trattati:* an Introduction (cap. 1 to cap. 8), the *Trattato della Discrezione* (cap. 9 to cap. 64), the *Trattato dell' Orazione* (cap. 65 to cap. 86), the *Trattato delle Lagrime* (cap. 87 to cap. 134), the *Trattato della Divina Provvidenza* (cap. 135 to cap. 153), and the *Trattato dell' Obbedienza* (cap. 154 to cap. 167).[2] It opens with a striking passage on what we may call the essence of mysticism, the possibility of the union of the soul with God in love:—

> When a soul lifts herself up, athirst with very great desire for the honour of God and the salvation of souls, she exercises herself for a while in habitual virtue, and dwells in the cell of knowledge of self, in order better to know the goodness of God; for love follows knowledge, and, when, she loves, she seeks to follow and to clothe herself with the truth·

> But in no way does the creature taste and become illumined by this truth as much as by means of humble and continuous prayer, based on knowledge of self and of God; for prayer, exercising the soul in this way, unites her to God, as she follows the steps of Christ crucified; and thus, by desire and affection and union of love, she is transformed into Him. This it seems that Christ meant when He said: *If a man love Me, he will keep My words;* and again: *He that loveth Me shall be loved of My Father, and I will love him and will manifest Myself to him, and he will be one with Me and I with him.* And in many places we find similar words, by which we can see that it is true that, by affection of love, the soul becomes another He.[3]

The rest of the book is practically an expansion of the revelation that Catherine had in a vision, after receiving Holy Communion on a feast of the Blessed Virgin, in the autumn of the previous year; a revelation which, in a more partial form, she had already set forth in a letter to Fra Raimondo.[4] It is, as it were, a gathering together of the spiritual teachings scattered through her letters. On the whole, it reads somewhat less ecstatically, as though written with more deliberation than the letters, and is in parts drawn out to considerable length, and sometimes moves slowly. The effect is that of a mysterious voice from the cloud, talking on in a great silence; and the result is monotonous, because the listener's attention becomes overstrained. Here and there, it is almost a relief when the Divine Voice ceases, and Catherine herself takes up the word. At other times, however, we feel that we have almost passed behind the veil that shields the Holy of Holies, and that we are, in very truth, hearing Catherine's rendering into finite words of the ineffable things which she has learned by intuition in that half hour during which there is silence in Heaven. The importance of the ***Dialogo*** in the history of Italian literature has never been fully realized. In a language which is singularly poor in mystical works (though so rich in almost every other field of thought), it stands with the *Divina Commedia* as one of the two supreme attempts to express the eternal in the symbolism of a day, to paint the union of the soul with the suprasensible while still imprisoned in the flesh. The whole of Catherine's life is the realization of the end of Dante's poem: "to remove those living in this life from the state of misery, and to lead them to the state of felicity"; and the mysticism of Catherine's book is as practical and altruistic as that of Dante's, when he declares to Can Grande that the whole *Commedia* "was undertaken not for speculation, but for work. For albeit in some parts or passages it is treated in speculative fashion, this is not for the sake of speculation, but for the sake of work."[5] Thus Catherine, in the preliminary chapters of the ***Dialogo,*** "wishing more virilely to know and follow the truth," makes her first petition to the eternal Father for herself, only because "the soul cannot perform any true service to her neighbour by teaching, example, or prayer, unless she first serves herself by acquiring and possessing virtue." By the infinite desire that proceeds from love, the soul can make reparation to God for her neighbour's sins, as well as for her own. Even as charity gives life to all the virtues, so all the vices have their root in self-love, and both are realized in action by means of others. "There can be no perfect virtue, none that bears fruit, unless it be exercised by means of our neighbour."[6]

For virtue to be perfect, it must be exercised with discretion, which discretion is nought else than a true knowledge that the soul should have of herself and of Me, and in this knowledge it has its root." Discretion, which springs from charity and is nurtured in the soil of humility, should be the lamp of the whole spiritual life, directing all the powers of the soul to serve God and to love her neighbour, offering up the life of the body for the salvation of his soul, and her temporal substance for the welfare of his body. The face of the Church, the Spouse of Christ, has grown like that of one smitten with leprosy, through the impurity, the self-love, the pride and avarice of her ministers, "those who feed at her breasts"; but by the prayers, desires, tears, and labours of God's servants, her beauty will be restored to her, for the humanity of the Word still stands as the bridge between earth and Heaven.

This figure of the Word as the bridge from time to eternity, the road to which has been broken by the fall of Adam, is worked out at length, Catherine laying stress upon the doctrine that "the eternal Truth has created us without ourselves, but will not save us without ourselves." The bridge has three steps or grades: the Feet that were nailed to the Cross; the Side, that was pierced to reveal the ineffable love of the Heart; the Mouth, where the bitterness of gall and vinegar is turned to peace. On the bridge (Catherine's imagery suddenly changing form) is the garden of the Church, to minister the bread of life and the blood that is drink, in order that the pilgrims may not faint by the way. These three steps also represent the three powers of the soul: will, memory, and understanding; as likewise the three states of the soul in God's service, by which she passes from servile fear and mercenary obedience to true fidelity and friendship, and, lastly, to perfect filial love. . . .

To this state of perfection in love, the soul comes by perseverance in holy prayer, offered up continually in the house of knowledge of self and of God, inebriated with the blood, clad in the fire of divine charity, fed on the sacramental food. Vocal prayer is but the preparation for mental prayer, in which God visits the soul, and the affection of charity is in itself a perpetual prayer. Souls that love God less for His own sake than for the consolation that they find in Him are easily deceived. When that consolation fails them, they think they offend God; and, for fear of losing their own peace, they do not succour their neighbour in his need, not realizing that "every vocal or mental exercise is ordained by Me, that the soul may practise it to come to perfect charity towards Me and towards her neighbour, and to preserve her in that charity."[8] Such souls are deluded by spiritual self-love, and are easily deceived by false visions that come from the devil. But the soul who has attained to perfect love, and who truly knows herself, does not consider the gifts and graces of her divine Friend, but the charity with which He gives them. Without leaving the cell of self-knowledge, she goes forth in God's name, prepared to endure sufferings, and to put into practice for the service of her neighbour the virtues that she has conceived in her mystical habitation. Thus the soul attains a fourth state, of perfect union in God: "for there is no love of Me without love of man, and no love of man without love of Me, for the one love cannot be separated from the other."[9]

In this state of perfect union, the Saints receive such strength that they not merely bear with patience, but long with panting desire to endure suffering for the glory of God's name. With St. Paul, such as these bear in their bodies the marks of Christ: "that is, the crucified love that they have glows out in their bodies, and they reveal it by despising themselves, and by delighting in insults, enduring troubles and pains from whatever side and in whatever way I concede them." Perfectly dead to their own will, they are never deprived of the presence of God even in feeling: "I continually reside by grace and by feeling in their souls; and whenever they wish to unite their mind with Me through affection of love, they can do so; for their desire has attained to such complete union, through love's affection, that nothing can separate them from Me."[10] But although such souls ever possess God by grace, and realize His presence in feeling, they cannot be uninterruptedly united to Him as long as they are fettered to the body. . . .

Such souls yearn to be delivered from the body, but are perfectly resigned to the will of God, rejoicing in being allowed to suffer for His honour. Their union with Him, thus temporarily interrupted, is ever renewed with increased intimacy: "I ever return with increase of grace and with more perfect union, ever revealing Myself to them anew, with a more lofty knowledge of My truth."[12] It is for such souls as these, with their prayers and sweat and tears, to wash the face of Christ's Spouse, the Church: "for which reason I showed her to thee in the guise of a damosel, whose face was all made filthy, as though of one smitten with leprosy, by the sins of her ministers and of all the Christian community who feed at her breast."

A frightful picture of the corruption of the clergy follows, in the *Trattato delle Lagrime,* after Catherine has touched at some length upon "the infinite variety of tears," and the way of coming to perfect purity. The dignity of the priesthood, and the ineffable mystery of the Sacrament which they have to administer, require a greater purity in the ministers of the Church than in any other creature. They are God's anointed, His Christs, with power over the Lord's sacramental body that even the Angels have not, and He considers all injuries done to them as inflicted upon Himself, as persecution of His blood. But, in contrast with Peter himself, Sylvester, Gregory, Augustine, Jerome, Thomas Aquinas, and the other holy ecclesiastics of olden time, we are shown the modern priests and prelates, whose lives are founded in self-love, and who perform the office of devils. Avarice, lust, and pride are the masters that they serve. The table of the Cross is deserted for the sake of the tavern; the poor are left destitute, while the substance of the Church is squandered upon harlots. Nay, more, the leprosy of unnatural vice, the sin from which even the devils flee in horror because of their angelical nature, has contaminated their minds and bodies. The priests celebrate Mass after a night of sin, and often their mistresses and children join the congregation; others use the Blessed Sacrament of the altar to make love-charms to seduce the little sheep of their flock, or persuade them to commit fornication under pretext of delivering them from diabolical possession. Some priests, realizing their own sinful state sufficiently to fear God's judgments, only pretend to consecrate when they say Mass, and thereby lead the people into idolatry by making them worship as the body of Christ what is no more than a piece of bread. The prelates connive at infamous monks corrupting the nuns in the monasteries under their charge. Ministers of the Church have become usurers; benefices and prelacies are bought and sold, while the poor are left to die of hunger. Spiritual things are abandoned, while the rulers of the Church usurp temporal power and secular government.[13] It is only possible here to touch very slightly upon the contents of these terrible chapters; but the student of the religious life of the fourteenth century is compelled to face the fact that in them we have the testimony of Boccaccio's *Decameron* confirmed by the burning words of a great saint, who does not shrink from putting them into the mouth of God Himself.

From this Catherine turns to the contemplation of the Divine Providence, shown in the creation of man in God's image and likeness, with memory, understanding, and will, for the Beatific Vision; in his redemption by means of the Incarnation; and in the institution of the Blessed Sacrament for his spiritual sustenance. As an instance of this Providence, in a particular case, we have a somewhat mysterious allusion to one whose soul was saved by a violent death.

> I would have thee know that, to save him from the eternal damnation which thou seest he had incurred, I allowed this to happen, in order that by his blood he might have life in the blood of My only-begotten

> Son. For I had not forgotten the reverence and love which he bore to Mary, the most sweet Mother of My only-begotten Son, to whom it is given by My goodness, for reverence of the Word, that whoso holds her in due reverence, be he a just man or a sinner, shall never be taken or devoured by the infernal demon. She is as a bait set by My goodness to take all rational creatures.[14]

Catherine's own miraculous communions, when her Divine Bridegroom intervened to give her the food of Angels which the priests would fain have denied her, show God's providential dealings with souls that hunger for the sweet Sacrament.[15] There are three states of the human soul: those of mortal sin, imperfect love, and perfect charity; and in each God's Providence acts in diverse ways to draw her to Himself.

One of the means He uses to draw the imperfect from their imperfection is an absorbing devotion for a fellow-creature, the *amor amicitiae* of which the Angelical Doctor writes, the kind of love of which Dante had given the supreme exposition in the *Vita Nuova.* By such a love, the soul is exercised in virtue and raised above herself; the heart is stripped of all sensitive passion and disordered affection. By the perfection of this love can be measured the perfection of the soul's love of God. When one who loves in this way sees himself deprived of the delight he used to have in familiar intercourse with the person loved, and sees that person now more intimately associated with another than with himself, the very pain that he feels will teach him to know himself, and will spur him on to hatred of his own selfishness and to love of virtue. He will humbly repute himself unworthy of the desired consolation, and will be assured that the virtue, for which he should chiefly love that person, is not diminished in his regard. This love will have taught him to desire to bear all suffering for the glory of God.[16] For tribulation is the test of true charity, and, with those who have come to the perfect state, God uses the means of suffering and persecution to preserve and augment their perfection. Goaded on by their hunger for the salvation of souls, forgetting themselves, they knock, night and day, at the gate of Divine Mercy. For the more man loses himself, the more he finds God. This truth they read in the sweet and glorious book of the Word, and bring forth the fruit of patience. Although, with St. Paul, they have received the doctrine of truth in the abyss of the Godhead, they have likewise received the thorn in the flesh, to keep them in self-knowledge and humility, and to make them compassionate towards the weaknesses and frailty of others. The anguish that they endure, in seeing the sins that are done against God, purges them from all personal sorrows; and God suffers Himself to be constrained by their panting desires, to have mercy upon the world, and by their endurance to reform His Church: "Verily, such as these can be called another Christ crucified, My only-begotten Son; for they have taken upon themselves the office of Him who came as mediator to end the war, and to reconcile man with Me in peace, by much endurance even unto the shameful death of the Cross."[17]

The whole being of such a saint is attuned to mystical music, and has become one sweet harmony, in which all the powers of the soul and all the members of the body play their parts. This spiritual melody was first heard from the Cross, and those that followed have learnt it from that Master.

> My infinite Providence has given them the instruments, and has shown them the way in which to play upon them. And whatever I give and permit in this life is to enable them to increase the power of these instruments; if they will only know it, and not obscure the light by which they see, with the cloud of self-love and their own pleasure and opinion.[18]

Inebriated with trust in the Divine Providence, these souls embrace the doctrine of voluntary poverty, choosing Lady Poverty, the Queen, as their bride, with whom they become mistresses of all spiritual wealth:—

> Then that soul, as though inebriated and enamoured of true and holy Poverty, passing out of herself into the supreme eternal Greatness, and transformed in the abyss of the sovereign inestimable Providence (in such wise that, while still in the vessel of the body, she saw herself out of the body by the overshadowing and rapture of the fire of Its charity), kept the eye of her understanding fixed upon the Divine Majesty, saying to the supreme and eternal Father: 'O eternal Father, O fire and abyss of Charity, O eternal Beauty, O eternal Goodness, O eternal Clemency, O hope and refuge of sinners, O inestimable Bounty, O eternal and infinite Bliss! Thou that art mad with love, hast Thou any need of Thy creature? Yea, it seemeth to me that Thou dost act as though Thou couldst not live without her, albeit Thou art the life from which all things have life and without which nothing lives. Why, then, art Thou thus mad? Thou art mad, because Thou art enamoured of what Thou hast made. Within Thyself Thou didst take delight in her, and, as drunk with desire of her salvation, Thou dost seek her when she flies from Thee; she shuns Thee, and Thou drawest near her. Nearer to her Thou couldst not come than to clothe Thyself with her humanity. What then shall I say? I will do as one that is tongue-tied, and say: *Ah, Ah;* for there is nought else I can say, since finite speech cannot express the affection of the soul which desires Thee infinitely. Methinks I can say with Paul: *Eye hath not seen, nor ear heard, neither have entered into the heart of man,* the things which I have beheld. I have seen the hidden things of God. My soul, thou hast tasted and seen the abyss of the sovereign and eternal Providence.'[19]

Obedience is the special virtue that ruled Catherine's spiritual life, even as poverty had informed that of St.

Francis and the realization of justice had been the inspiration of that of Dante. She treats it as the key which the Father put into the hand of the Word to unlock the gate of eternal life, and which the Word left with His vicar at the Ascension. All the faith is founded upon it. Each soul receives it into her hand at baptism, and must fasten it, with the cord of detachment, to the girdle of resignation to the will of God. Like poverty, obedience is a bride of souls, a queen enthroned above the tempests of the world. Besides the general obedience to which all are bound, there is the special obedience of the religious life, shown in its perfection in the ideals with which Benedict, Francis, and Dominic founded their orders. The chapter dealing with the Franciscans and Dominicans, the sublime ideals of their two patriarchs who based their rules on poverty and learning, respectively, and the degeneration of their followers, is thoroughly Dantesque in spirit and in expression. Catherine has, however, worse things to record against the friars of her own order than those which the divine poet puts upon the lips of the Angelical Doctor; even the vow of chastity is continually broken, and the light of science perverted by them to darkness. The days of Thomas Aquinas, whom Catherine ever names with profound admiration and marked personal love (he was one of the saints with whom she used to speak in her visions), and of Peter Martyr, whose career appealed to the sterner side of her character, have passed away.[20] The resemblance at times between Catherine's phraseology, as well as her thought, in the ***Dialogo*** as in the Letters, with that of Dante, is not likely to be entirely fortuitous. Although she never mentions the poet, and assuredly had never read the *Divina Commedia,* she must frequently have heard his lines quoted by her followers. Neri di Landoccio, at least, appears to have been a Dante student.[21] It would be pleasant to think of such passages as the mystical espousals of St. Francis with Poverty, the praises of St. Dominic, or St. Bernard's invocation to the Blessed Virgin, being read aloud in Catherine's circle, and Saint and secretaries alike being fired by the music of him who had fought the same battle for righteousness more than half a century before.

From the consideration of her own order, Catherine turns to the religious life in general, the excellence of its ideals, the disastrous results when these are corrupted or neglected. The perfect religious, *il vero obbediente,* he who has humbled himself like a little child to enter into the kingdom of Heaven, is contrasted with the unfaithful and disobedient monk or friar, "who stays in the bark of his order with such great pain to himself and to others, that in this life he tastes the pledge of hell." Midway between the two types is that of the average religious, neither perfect nor corrupt, but lukewarm in his profession, ever in danger of falling, but still with the power of joining the truly obedient in their holy race. After a glowing eulogy of the virtue of obedience, illustrated by the miracles that the saints of old have wrought by its power, and a recapitulation of the whole book, Catherine ends with the impassioned eloquence of what may be called her universal prayer:—

> Thanks, thanks be to Thee, eternal Father, for Thou hast not despised me, Thy creature, nor turned Thy face from me, nor contemned my desires. Thou that art light, hast not considered my darkness; Thou that art life, hast not considered my death; nor hast Thou, the physician, turned from my grievous maladies. Thou art eternal purity, and I am full of the mire of many miseries; Thou art infinite, and I am finite; Thou art wisdom, and I am foolishness; for all these and other infinite evils and defects that are in me, Thy wisdom, Thy goodness, Thy clemency, and Thy infinite blessedness has not despised me; but in Thy light Thou hast given me light, in Thy wisdom I have known the truth, in Thy clemency I have found Thy charity and the love of my neighbour. Who has constrained Thee to this? Not my virtues, but Thy charity alone. May this same love constrain Thee to illumine the eye of my understanding in the light of faith, in order that I may know and comprehend the truth Thou hast revealed to me. Grant that my memory may be capable of retaining Thy benefits, that my will may burn in the fire of Thy charity, and that fire make my body pour forth blood; so that with that blood, given for love of the blood, and with the key of obedience, I may unlock the gate of Heaven. This same grace I crave of Thee for every rational creature, in general and in particular, and for the mystical body of Holy Church. I confess and do not deny that Thou didst love me before I was, and that Thou dost love me ineffably, as mad with love for Thy creature.

> O eternal Trinity, O Godhead, Thou that, by Thy divine nature, didst make the price of the blood of Thy Son avail! Thou, eternal Trinity, art a sea so deep, that the more I enter therein, the more I find, and, the more I find, the more I seek of Thee. Thou art the food that never satiates; for, when the soul is satiated in Thine abyss, it is not satiated, but it ever continues to hunger and thirst for Thee, eternal Trinity, desiring to behold Thee with the light of Thy light. *As the hart panteth after the water brooks,* so does my soul desire to issue from the prison of the darksome body, and behold Thee in truth. O how long shall Thy face be hidden from my eyes? O eternal Trinity, fire and abyss of charity, dissolve henceforth the cloud of my body; the knowledge that Thou hast given me of Thyself, in Thy truth, constrains me to desire to leave the heaviness of my body, and to give my life for the glory and praise of Thy name; because I have tasted and seen, with the light of the understanding in Thy light, Thy abyss, eternal Trinity, and the beauty of Thy creature. Contemplating myself in Thee, I see that I am Thy image; Thou, eternal Father, hast given me of Thy power, and of Thy wisdom in the understanding, which wisdom is assigned to Thy only-begotten Son; the Holy Spirit, which proceeds from Thee and from Thy Son, has given me the will, whereby I am made able to love. Thou, eternal Trinity, art the Maker, and I he work of Thy hands; I have known, by Thy

recreation of me in the blood of Thy Son, that Thou art enamoured of the beauty of what Thou hast made.

O abyss, O eternal Godhead, O deep sea! And what more couldest Thou give me, than give Thyself? Thou art fire that ever burnest and art not consumed; Thou art fire that consumest all self-love in the soul by Thy heat; Thou art fire that destroyest all coldness; Thou dost illumine, and by Thy light Thou hast made me know Thy truth. Thou art that light above all light, with which light Thou givest supernatural light to the eye of the understanding, in such abundance and perfection that Thou dost clarify the light of faith; in which faith I see that my soul has life, and in this light she receives Thee, the Light. In the light of faith, I acquire wisdom, in the wisdom of the Word, Thy Son. In the light of faith, I am strong, constant, and persevering. In the light of faith, I hope; it will not let me faint on the road. This light teaches me the way, and, without this light, I should walk in darkness; and, therefore, I besought Thee, eternal Father, to illumine me with the light of most holy faith. Verily, this light is a sea, for it nourishes the soul in Thee, sea of peace, eternal Trinity; the water of this sea is never stormy, and, therefore, the soul has no fear, because she knows the truth; it is ever clear and reveals things hidden; and thus, where the most abundant light of Thy faith abounds, it, as it were, makes the soul certain about what she believes. It is a mirror, as Thou, eternal Trinity, dost make me know; for, gazing into this mirror, holding it with the hand of love, it shows me myself in Thee, who am Thy creature, and Thee in me, by the union which Thou didst make of the Godhead with our humanity. In this light it reveals Thee to me, and I know Thee, supreme and infinite Good, good above all good, blissful good, incomprehensible good, inestimable good; Beauty above all beauty; Wisdom above all wisdom. Yea, Thou art very Wisdom; Thou, the food of Angels, hast given Thyself to men with fire of love; Thou, the raiment that coverest up my nakedness, dost feed the famished in Thy sweetness; sweet Thou art, without any bitterness.

O eternal Trinity, in Thy light which Thou didst give me, receiving it with the light of most holy faith, I have known (for Thou makest it plain to me by many and wondrous revelations) the way of great perfection, in order that I may serve Thee with light and not with darkness; that I may be a mirror of good and holy life, and thus rise up from my own miserable life; for, through my sins, I have ever served Thee in darkness; I have not known Thy truth, and, therefore, have not loved it. Why did I not know Thee? Because I did not see Thee with the glorious light of most holy faith, for the cloud of self-love darkened the eye of my understanding; and Thou, eternal Trinity, with Thy light didst dissolve that darkness. And who shall reach Thy height, to render Thee thanks for so measureless a gift, and such great benefits as Thou hast granted me, the doctrine of truth which Thou hast given me, which is a special grace beyond the general grace which Thou dost give to other creatures! Thou wishest to condescend to my necessity, and to that of other creatures who will look into it as into a mirror. Do Thou, Lord, answer for me; Thou Thyself hast given, do Thou Thyself answer and make satisfaction, infusing a light of grace into me, in order that with that light I may give Thee thanks. Robe, robe me with Thyself, eternal Truth, so that I may run this mortal life with true obedience and with the light of most holy faith, with which light it seemeth that Thou dost inebriate my soul anew.[22] . . .

The simple, but profound philosophy underlying all Catherine's writings is the same that, put into practice, armed her to pass unsubdued and unshaken through the great game of the world.

Love is the one supreme and all-important, all-embracing, all-enduring, limitless and boundless thing. In a famous passage of the *Purgatorio,* Dante had shown how Creator and every creature is moved by love; how, in rational beings, love is the seed of every virtue and of every vice, because love's natural tendency to good is the material upon which Free Will works for bliss or bane.[42] But Catherine goes a step further than this. Not only God, but man, in a sense, is love. "Think," she writes,

> that the first raiment that we had was love; for we are created to the image and likeness of God only by love, and, therefore, man cannot be without love, for he is made of nought else than very love; for all that he has, according to the soul and according to the body, he has by love. The father and mother have given being to their child, that is, of the substance of their flesh (by means of the grace of God), only by love.[43]

And in another place:

> The soul cannot live without love, but must always love something, because she was created through love. Affection moves the understanding, as it were saying: I want to love, for the food wherewith I am fed is love. Then the understanding, feeling itself awakened by affection, rises as though it said: If thou wouldst love, I will give thee what thou canst love.[44]

Love nurtures the virtues like children at its breast; it robes the soul with its own beauty, because it transforms the beloved and makes her one with the lover.[45]

> Love harmonizes the three powers of our soul, and binds them together. The will moves the understanding to see, when it wishes to love; when the understanding perceives that the will would fain love, if it is a rational will, it places before it as object the ineffable love of the eternal Father, who has given us the Word, His

> own Son, and the obedience and humility of the Son, who endured torments, injuries, mockeries, and insults with meekness and with such great love. And thus the will, with ineffable love, follows what the eye of the understanding has beheld; and, with its strong hand, it stores up in the memory the treasure that it draws from this love.[46]

Then, since the supreme act of Divine Love is seen in the Sacrifice of Calvary, and again in the mystical outpouring of Pentecost, Love's symbols for Catherine are blood and fire—but, above all, blood, and sometimes this finds startling expression. She calls her letters written in blood. Those to whom they are addressed are bidden drink blood, clothe themselves in blood, be transformed and set on fire with blood; they are inebriated with blood; their will, their understanding, and their memory are filled with blood; they are drowned beneath the tide of blood. "Drown yourself in the blood of Christ crucified," she writes to Fra Raimondo,

> and bathe yourself in the blood; inebriate yourself with the blood, satiate yourself with the blood, and clothe yourself with the blood. If you have been unfaithful, baptise yourself again in the blood; if the demon has darkened the eye of your understanding, wash it with the blood; if you have fallen into ingratitude for gifts which you have not acknowledged, be grateful in the blood; if you have been an unworthy pastor, and without the rod of justice tempered with prudence and mercy, draw it from the blood; with the eye of understanding, see it in the blood, and take it with the hand of love, and grasp it with panting desire. Dissolve your tepidity in the heat of the blood, and cast off your darkness in the light of the blood. I wish to robe myself anew in blood, and to strip myself of every raiment which I have worn up to now. I crave for blood; in the blood have I satisfied and shall satisfy my soul. I was deceived when I sought her among creatures; so am I fain, in time of solicitude, to meet companions in the blood. Thus shall I find the blood and creatures, and I shall drink their affection and love in the blood.[47]

And Catherine carries this into actual life; the blood that splashes the streets and palaces of the Italian cities in the fierce faction-fights, the blood that is poured out upon the scaffold at the Sienese place of execution, fires her imagination and seems shed by Love itself. The sight and smell of blood have no horror for her. We find the fullest realization of this in one of the most beautiful and famous of her letters, that to Fra Raimondo describing the end of the young noble of Perugia, Niccolò di Toldo, unjustly doomed to die by the government of Siena:—

> I went to visit him of whom you know, whereby he received such great comfort and consolation that he confessed, and disposed himself right well; and he made me promise by the love of God that, when the time of execution came, I would be with him; and so I promised and did. Then in the morning, before the bell tolled, I went to him, and he received great consolation; I brought him to hear Mass, and he received the holy Communion, which he had never received since the first. That will of his was harmonized with and subjected to the will of God, and there only remained a fear of not being strong at the last moment; but the measureless and inflamed goodness of God forestalled him, endowing him with so much affection and love in the desire of God, that he could not stay without Him, and he said to me: 'Stay with me, and do not abandon me, so shall I fare not otherwise than well, and I shall die content'; and he leaned his head upon my breast. Then I exulted, and seemed to smell his blood, and mine too, which I desire to shed for the sweet Spouse Jesus, and, as the desire increased in my soul and I felt his fear, I said: 'Take heart, sweet brother mine, for soon shall we come to the nuptials; thou wilt fare thither bathed in the sweet blood of the Son of God, with the sweet name of Jesus, which I wish may never leave thy memory, and I shall be waiting for thee at the place of execution.' Now think, father and son, how his heart lost all fear, and his face was transformed from sadness to joy, and he rejoiced, exulted, and said: 'Whence comes such grace to me, that the sweetness of my soul should await me at the holy place of execution?' See, he had reached such light that he called the place of execution *holy,* and he said: 'I shall go all joyous and strong, and it will seem to me a thousand years till I come thither, when I think that you are awaiting me there'; and he spoke so sweetly of God's goodness, that one might scarce sustain it. I awaited him, then, at the place of execution; and I stayed there, waiting, with continual prayer, in the presence of Mary and of Catherine, Virgin and Martyr. But, before he arrived, I placed myself down, and stretched out my neck on the block; but nothing was done to me, for I was full of love of myself; then I prayed and insisted, and said to Mary that I wished for this grace, that she would give him true light and peace of heart at that moment, and then that I might see him return to his end. Then was my soul so full that, albeit a multitude of the people was there, I could not see a creature, by reason of the sweet promise made me. Then he came, like a meek lamb, and, seeing me, he began to laugh, and he would have me make the sign of the Cross over him; and, when he had received the sign, I said: 'Down! to the nuptials, sweet brother mine, for soon shalt thou be in eternal life.' He placed himself down with great meekness, and I stretched out his neck, and bent down over him, and reminded him of the blood of the Lamb. His mouth said nought save *Jesus* and *Catherine;* and, as he spoke thus, I received his head into my hands, closing my eyes in the Divine Goodness, and saying: *I will.*

Then to her ecstatic gaze the heavens seemed to open, and she saw the God made Man, in brightness like the sun, receive the victim's blood into His own open wounds, his desire into the fire of His divine charity, blood into blood, flame into flame, and the soul herself pass into His side, "bathed in his own blood, which availed as though it were the blood of the Son of God." But, as the soul thus entered and began to taste the divine sweetness,

> she turned to me, even as the bride, when she has come to her bridegroom's door, turns back her eyes and her head to salute those who have accompanied her, and thereby to show signs of thanks. Then did my soul repose in peace and quiet, in such great odour of blood that I could not bear to free myself from the blood that had come upon me from him. Alas, miserable and wretched woman that I am, I will say no more; I remained on earth with the greatest envy.[48]

Ordina quest' amore, O tu che m' ami, sang Jacopone da Todi: "Set this love in order, O thou that lovest Me." Following out this Franciscan line, Dante had based his *Purgatorio* (which symbolizes the whole life of man) upon the need of ordering love rightly. And it is the same with Catherine. "The soul," she says, "that loves disordinately becomes insupportable to herself." Only the Creator may be loved for Himself alone and without any measure. Too readily may a spiritual love for a creature become entirely sensual, if the eye is not kept fixed on the blood of Christ crucified.[49] And this love disordered grows up into the monster of self-love, *amore proprio,* which plays the same part in Catherine's doctrine as did the *Lupa,* the she-wolf of Avarice, in the *Divina Commedia.* "Self-love," she writes,

> which takes away charity and love of our neighbour, is the source and foundation of every evil. All scandals, and hatred, and cruelty, and everything that is untoward, proceed from this perverse root of self-love; it has poisoned the entire world, and brought disease into the mystical body of Holy Church and the universal body of the Christian religion.[50]

And she makes magnificent use of this doctrine in addressing the democratic rulers of the Italian republics. "You see, dearest brothers and lords," she writes to the Anziani and Consuls and Gonfalonieri of Bologna, "that self-love is what lays waste the city of the soul, and ravages and overturns earthly cities. I would have you know that nothing has wrought this division in the world save self-love, from which has risen and rises all injustice."[51] Through self-love, she tells the Signoria of Florence, the virtue of justice has died out in monarchies and republics alike:

> The legitimate sovereigns have become tyrants. The subjects of the Commune do not feed at its breast with justice nor fraternal charity; but each one, with falseness and lies, looks to his own private advantage, and not to the general weal. Each one is seeking the lordship for himself, and not the good state and administration of the city.[52]

Similarly, it is to self-love alone that Catherine ascribed the war between the Tuscan communes and the Holy See, no less than the Great Schism itself; self-love had transformed Gregory's legates to ravening wolves, and Urban's cardinals to incarnate demons.

Man, therefore, must draw out the two-edged sword of love and hate, and slay this worm of sensuality with the hand of Free Will. He must utterly cast off servile fear. "Servile fear takes away all power from the soul. I think not that man has any cause to fear, for God has made him strong against every adversary."[53]

> No operation of the soul that fears with servile fear is perfect. In whatever state she be, in small things and in great, she falls short, and does not bring to perfection what she has begun. O how perilous is this fear! It cuts off the arms of holy desire; it blinds man, for it does not let him know or see the truth. This fear proceeds from the blindness of self-love; for, as soon as the rational creature loves itself with sensitive self-love, it straightway fears. And this is the cause for which it fears; it has set its love and hope upon a weak thing, that has no firmness in itself, nor any stability, but passes like the wind.[54]

Whether he be in the cloister or in the world, man must enter the cell of self-knowledge, *la cella del cognoscimento di noi,* and abide therein. At its door he must set the watch-dog, conscience, to rouse the understanding with its voice: the dog whose food and drink are blood and fire.[55] Within that cell, he will know God and man; he will understand God's love, possess His truth, and freely let himself be guided by His will. The cell of self-knowledge is the stable in which the traveller through time to eternity must be born again. "Thou dost see this sweet and loving Word born in a stable, while Mary was journeying; to show to you, who are travellers, that you must ever be born again in the stable of knowledge of yourselves, where you will find Me born by grace within your souls."[56]

In addition to the book and the letters, a certain number of prayers, twenty-six in all, have been preserved, which Catherine uttered on various occasions. One, the shortest, is said to be the first thing that she wrote with her own hand:—

> O holy Spirit, come into my heart; by Thy power draw it to Thee, its God, and grant me love with fear. Guard me, Christ, from every evil thought; warm me and reinflame me with Thy most sweet love, so that every pain may seem light to me. My holy Father and my sweet Master, help me now in all my ministry. Christ Love, Christ Love, Amen.[57]

The others are mystical outpourings, which were taken down at the time by the Saint's disciples, and repeat in similar or slightly varied forms the aspirations that breathe from her other writings. We have the same "sweet enragement of celestial love," the same impassioned contemplation of the sovereign mysteries of the faith, the same devotion to the Blessed Virgin, the same desire of offering up her own life for the salvation of souls and the reformation of the Church. It is, indeed, piteous to watch this exquisitely tender and angelical woman besieging Heaven with prayers for that grim and ruthless man whom she called her "sweet Christ on earth," imploring God to look upon his good will, to hide him under the wings of His mercy so that his enemies, the *iniqui superbi,* may not be able to injure him, to robe him with the purity of the faith, to give him light that all the world may follow him, to temper his "virile heart" with holy humility. In the striking prayer composed on the feast of the Circumcision, probably that of 1380, when those "admirable mysteries" began to work within her that finally delivered her from the world, we find Catherine including not only Urban, but those very schismatics whom she had addressed as incarnate demons, men worthy of a thousand deaths; now her only thought is for the salvation of their souls, and she beseeches the God of sovereign clemency to punish their sins upon her own body. The last of the series consists of the words she uttered when she regained consciousness on the Monday after Sexagesima, when her household were weeping for her as dead. It strikes the keynote of her passion, and seems, as it were, to sum up the aspirations of those weeks of prolonged suffering:—

> O eternal God, O divine Craftsman, who hast made and formed the vessel of the body of Thy creature of the dust of the ground! O most sweet Lovè, Thou hast formed it of so vile a thing, and hast put therein so great a treasure as is the soul, which bears the image of Thee, eternal God. Thou, good Craftsman, my sweet Love, Thou art the potter who dost mar and make again; Thou dost shatter and mend this vessel, as pleases Thy goodness. To Thee, eternal Father, I, wretched woman, offer anew my life for Thy sweet Spouse, that, as often as pleaseth Thy goodness, Thou mayest draw me from the body and restore me to the body, each time with greater pain than the other; if only I may see the reformation of this sweet Spouse, Thy holy Church. I demand this Spouse of Thee, eternal God. Also, I commend to Thee my most beloved children, and I beseech Thee, supreme and eternal Father, if it should please Thy mercy and goodness to draw me out of this vessel and make me no more return, not to leave them orphans, but visit them with Thy grace, and make them live as dead, with true and most perfect light; bind them together in the sweet bond of charity, that they may die of ardent desire in this sweet Spouse. And I beseech Thee, eternal Father, that not one of them may be taken out of my hands. Forgive us all our iniquities, and forgive me my great ignorance, and the great negligence that I have committed in Thy Church, in not having done what I might and should have done. I have sinned, Lord, be merciful unto me. I offer and commend my most beloved children to Thee, because they are my soul. And if it please Thy goodness to make me still stay in this vessel, do Thou, sovereign Physician, heal and sustain it, for it is all torn and rent. Grant, eternal Father, grant us Thy sweet benediction. Amen.

Notes

[1] *Legenda,* III. i. 2 (§332). Cf. III. iii. 1 (§§349, 350). In the Vatican MS., *Cod. Barb. Lat.* 4063, the book is entitled simply: "Il libro facto per divina revelacione de la venerabile et admirabile vergine beata Katherina da Siena."

[2] The arrangement I adopt is a compromise between that of the manuscripts and early editions of the Italian text and that given by Fra Raimondo in his Latin version—a compromise which, as far as making the *Trattato delle Lagrime* a separate treatise, seems justified by Catherine's own reference to it in Letter 154 (63), as well as by internal evidence.

[3] Cap. 1.

[4] Letter 272 (90).

[5] *Epist.* X. 16.

[6] *Dialogo,* cap. 1-cap. 8, cap. 11. Cf. Letters 311 (203), 282 (39). . . .

[8] Cap. 69.

[9] Cap. 74.

[10] Cap. 78. . . .

[12] This is worked out in cap. 83, cap. 84, of which the modern printed editions and translations contain only a mutilated version of what we find in the MSS. and in Fra Raimondo's Latin.

[13] Cap. 121-cap. 130. Cf. Caesarius Heisterbacensis, *Dialogus miraculorum* (ed. Strange, Cologne, 1851), dist. IX. cap. 6; *Revelationes S. Birgittae,* I. 49, IV. 133. An equally appalling picture is given, some years later, by Nicolas de Clémanges, in his *De ruina Ecclesiae,* cap. 15-cap. 23 (*Opera,* Leyden, 1613).

[14] Cap. 139. Cf. the salvation of Buonconte da Montefeltro, *Purg.* v. 100-107. Catherine alludes to this case in similar words in Letter 272 (90). Probably, either Niccolò di Toldo or Trincio Trinci is the person meant.

[15] Cap. 142. Cf. *Legenda,* II. xii. 4-14 (§§316-324).

[16] Cap. 144.

[17] Cap. 145, cap. 146.

[18] Cap. 147.

[19] Cap. 153. Catherine's treatment of holy Poverty, cap. 151, is thoroughly Franciscan. It is curious to notice how loosely she often quotes the Scriptures; Fra Raimondo usually corrects her in his Latin version.

[20] Cap. 158. Cf. Dante, *Par.* xi., xii., and xxii. 73-93. The encyclical letters issued by Fra Elias of Toulouse, as master-general of the order, in 1368, 1370, and 1376, strikingly confirm Catherine's testimony as to the corruption and degeneracy of the Dominicans at this time. "We have come to such a pass," he had written in 1376, "that whoso cares for the ceremonies of the Church is pointed out with the finger, and whoso keeps the rules of the order is reckoned by the others as of singular life." See *Monumenta ordinis Fratrum Praedicatorum historica,* tom. v. pp. 306-312.

[21] Cf. *Lettere dei discepoli,* 18. But Capecelatro, pp. 343, 344, following Ignazio Cantù, much overstates Catherine's possible knowledge of Dante.

[22] Cap. 167, corrected by the Vatican MS., *Cod. Barb. Lat.* 4063, with which Fra Raimondo substantially agrees. . . .

[42] *Purg.* xvii. and xviii.

[43] Appendix, Letter I. Cf. Letter 196 (4).

[44] *Dialogo,* cap. 51.

[45] Letter 108 (172).

[46] Letter 95 (308).

[47] Letter 102 (93).

[48] Letter 273 (97), corrected by the Harleian MS.

[49] Letter 76. Cf. the curiously interesting Letter 245 (122), "to a Genoese of the third order of St. Francis, who had engaged in a spiritual friendship with a woman, whereby he endured much travail." I find in the Casanatense MS. 292 that this tertiary was a certain Fra Gasparo.

[50] *Dialogo,* cap. 7.

[51] Letter 268 (200).

[52] Letter 337 (199).

[53] Appendix, Letter I.

[54] Letter 242 (37), to the Bishop of Florence, Angelo Ricasoli, when he left the city to observe the interdict. Catherine had previously used the same words to Cardinal Pierre d'Estaing, Letter 11 (24).

[55] Cf. Letters 2 (50) and 114 (267).

[56] *Dialogo,* cap. 151. Cf. Botticelli's allegorical picture of the Nativity in the National Gallery.

[57] *Orat.* IV. A slightly different version of this prayer, in Latin, is given by Fra Tommaso Caffarini in the *Processus,* col. 1279, and in the *Supplementum,* MS. *cit.,* f. 9.

Bibliography

Capecelatro, Alfonso. *Storia di S. Caterina da Siena e del Papato del suo tempo.* 4th edition. Siena, 1878.

Suzanne Noffke (essay date 1980)

SOURCE: Introduction to *Catherine of Siena: The Dialogue,* by St. Catherine of Siena, translated by Suzanne Noffke, Paulist Press, 1980, pp. 1-22.

[*In the following excerpt, Noffke examines Catherine of Siena's ecstatic experiences as they are articulated in her writings and recorded by her contemporaries.*]

. . . What, in terms of human inheritance, were the springs of Catherine's knowledge and teaching? She had no formal schooling. Just how extensively she read is not certain, but she was a tireless conversationalist. She never wrote what could be called theology reduced to a system; in fact, it is her lack of an established system that lends her writings their marvelous if sometimes frustrating and tiring style of layer on layer of interwoven development: No thread is ever let go of or left unrelated to every other thread. Yet critics continue to debate her academic pedigree: Her teaching is clearly scholastic and Thomistic (e.g., Cordovani, Taurisano, Paris, Oddasso-Cartotti). Her teaching is clearly *not* Thomistic (e.g., Foster). Her teaching is predominantly Augustinian (e.g., Canet, Hackett). She was most influenced by Ubertino da Casale (Grion). The writings of the Dominicans Jacopo da Voragine and Cavalca exercised the more primary influence on her (D'Urso). This list is certainly not exhaustive. I would lean, however, toward the position of those (e.g., Getto) who are content to recognize multiple influences in Catherine's writings: Augustine, Cassian, Gregory the Great, Bernard, Francis, Thomas, Ubertino, Passavanti, Cavalca, Colombini. Like everything that came her way she absorbed them all and integrated them into her whole knowledge. Theologically there is nothing new or original. Catherine is completely immersed in the main current of Catholic teaching, and she is impeccably orthodox even in subtle distinctions where one might expect her, untrained as she was in formal theology, to have slipped up at least occasionally.

What is original in Catherine is her capacity for fresh and vivid expression of the tradition. The scholars taught and wrote still in Latin. Yet all that she wrote and dictated was in her own Sienese dialect, *nel suo volgare.* True, Passavanti and Cavalca before her had used the vernacular to write of things religious, but they were popularizers. Catherine, though she addressed herself to every imaginable class of people—popes and cardinals; monarchs, princes, and governors; priests, nuns, and pious laity; mercenaries, prisoners, and prostitutes—was not a popularizer. In her own apparently systemless yet close-knit system she developed her arguments and themes in great detail. Her pages are studded with metaphors and compounded metaphors. She repeats, yet always with some new layer of relationship. She explodes into ecstatic prayer. She teaches. Always she teaches.

The Scriptures she heard and read presumably only in Latin are at home in her works, in her own dialect, with a natural sort of familiarity that is strongly reminiscent of the long savoring and fondling of the old Jewish masters. These are no mere recited "proof-texts." They flow in and out of her sentences with such ease and integration that it is more often than not difficult to set them off with quotation marks. She so rearranges and combines passages around a single stream of thought that her own message and that of the Scriptures fuse into one.

Remarkable also, and especially noticeable in the ***Dialogue*** because of its somewhat secondary nature in relation to some of her earlier letters, is Catherine's handling of her own mystical experiences. What she has "heard" in these encounters with God is not her own to tamper with. She may rephrase stories she repeats from the *Lives of the Fathers* or incidents she has related in other contexts, but whenever she lifts the "words of God" from her own first accounting of them she leaves the original wording intact. If clarification is needed she expands with parenthetical inserts, but seldom touches that original wording. In a way not unlike the Scriptures, these words are hers to use but not to change.[17]

While Catherine's letters are the better window to her personality, growth, and relationships with others, the ***Dialogue*** is her crowning work, her bequest of all her teaching to her followers. She called it simply "my book," and in her last letter to Raymond[18] she entrusted its destiny to him: "I ask you also—you and brother Bartolomeo [de' Dominici] and brother Tommaso [della Fonte] and the maestro [Giovanni Tantucci]—to take in hand the book and any of my writings that you find. Together with master Tommaso [Pietra] do with them what you see would be most for the honor of God. I found some recreation in them."

Certain twists in the path by which the tradition has come into English have ended in a rather common belief that Catherine dictated the ***Dialogue*** entirely in the space of a single five-day ecstasy.[19] The total composite of references to the work by Catherine herself and a number of her contemporaries, however, makes it clear that a much longer time was involved, probably close to a year.

Both Raymond and Caffarini set the beginning and immediate motive of the work in a particularly significant mystical experience. Raymond writes:

> So about two years before her death, such a clarity of Truth was revealed to her from heaven that Catherine was constrained to spread it abroad by means of writing, asking her secretaries to stand ready to take down whatever came from her mouth as soon as they noticed that she had gone into ecstasy. Thus in a short time was composed a certain book that contains a dialogue between a soul who asks the Lord four questions, and the Lord himself who replies to the soul, enlightening her with many useful truths.[20]

Caffarini further specifies that she "composed her book and set it in order."[21]

The experience referred to is without a doubt the one Catherine elaborates in a long letter to Raymond, written from Rocca d'Orcia in early October 1377, the letter that was to form the framework and basic content of her book. She tells of having offered four petitions to God (for the reform of the Church, for the whole world, for Raymond's spiritual welfare, and for a certain unnamed sinner), to each of which, in her ecstasy, God had responded with specific teachings.[22]

Catherine probably began the work then and there, while still at Rocca d'Orcia. In the same letter to Raymond she relates how she had suddenly learned to write, and in another to Monna Alessa she tells of God's having given her a diversion from her pains in her writing.[23] In any case, the book must have taken some shape by the time she left on her second peacemaking mission to Florence, for in May or June of 1378 she writes to Stefano Maconi back in Siena:

> I sent a request to the countess [Benedetta de' Salimbeni, with whom she had lived at Rocca d'Orcia] for my book. I have waited several days for it and it hasn't come. So if you go there, tell her to send it at once, and tell anyone who might go there to tell her this.[24]

Almost certainly she spent some time on the manuscript between acts during those tumultuous months in

Florence. She left it behind at her quick departure, and on her return to Siena wrote to the man who had probably been her host there: "Give the book to Francesco . . . for I want to write something in it."[25] And Raymond records, significantly, that "when the peace [between Florence and the Papacy] had been proclaimed, she returned home and attended *more diligently* to the composition of a certain book, which she dictated in her own dialect, inspired by the supernal Spirit."[26]

The book must have been in a form Catherine considered finished before the schism had fully erupted, for there is no allusion to schism in it, though there is much about corruption in the Church and the need for reform. Also, Caffarini states that she had finished the book before she was called to Rome in November of 1378.[27]

The testimony of Catherine's contemporaries is unanimous that the book involved a great deal of dictation on her part while she was in ecstasy.[28] And Caffarini in his testimony in the *Processus* of Venice adds some fascinating details:

> I say also that I have very often seen the virgin in Siena, especially after her return from Avignon, rapt beyond her senses, except for speech, by which she dictated to various writers in succession sometimes letters and sometimes the book, in different times and in different places, as circumstances allowed. Sometimes she did this with her hands crossed on her breast as she walked about the room; sometimes she was on her knees or in other postures; but always her face was lifted toward heaven. Concerning the composition of her book, then: This among other marvels occurred in the virgin: When emergencies would cause several days to pass in which she was kept from pursuing her dictation, as soon as she could take it up again she would begin at the point where she had left off as if there had been no interruption or space of time. Moreover, as is evident in the course of her book, sometimes after she had dictated several pages, she would summarize or recapitulate the main content as if the things she had dictated were (and in fact they were) actually present to her mind.[29]

But the style of the ***Dialogue*** betrays not only such "ecstatic dictation," but also a great deal of painstaking (sometimes awkward) expanding and drawing in of passages written earlier. There is every reason to believe that Catherine herself did this editing. First of all, it is not an editing in the direction of more polished style, which it probably would have been had it been the work of any of her secretaries, for they were men whose own style reflected their learning. And if Raymond's attitude is typical, they considered the saint's writings too sacred to tamper with.[30] Furthermore, besides his reference to Catherine's setting her book in order, Caffarini records having been told by Stefano Maconi that the latter had seen Catherine writing with her own hand "several pages of the book which she herself composed in her own dialect."[31]

It has already been noted how the ***Dialogue*** owes much of its content and structure to the experience Catherine related to Raymond in her letter of October 1377.[32] Dupré-Theseider, in the article already referred to, elaborates further direct parallels between letter 64/65 and chapters 98 to 104 of the ***Dialogue.*** Numerous less spectacular instances of carryover must await further study, but no one can read both letters and ***Dialogue*** without noticing the recurrence of certain themes and images. . . .

Notes

. . . [17] Cf. E. Dupré-Theseider, "Sulla composizione del 'Dialogo' di Santa Caterina da Siena," *Giornale storica della letteratura italiana* 117 (1941): 161-202.

[18] Let. 373, written February 15, 1380.

[19] Cf. especially J. Hurtaud in the Introduction to his French translation of the *Dialogue* (Paris: Lethellieux, 1931) and J. Jorgensen, *Saint Catherine of Siena* (London: Longmans, Green and Co., 1939), p. 311. The latter, however, takes a broader view in note 8, p. 428.

[20] [*Legenda Major. S. Caterina da Siena.* Tr. Giuseppe Tinagli (Siena: Cantagalli, 1934),] III, iii. It is to references such as this that we owe the book's present title. Catherine's early disciples variously called it *The Book of Divine Providence, The Book of Divine Teaching, The Dialogue, The Dialogue of Divine Providence.*

[21] *Legenda Minor* [*di S. Caterina da Siena.* Ed. Francesco Grottanelli (Bologne: Presso Geetano Romagnoli, 1868)], III, iii.

[22] Let. 272. For a detailed presentation of parallels between this letter and the *Dialogue,* see Dupré-Theseider, "Sulla composizione. . . ."

[23] Let. 119.

[24] Let. 365.

[25] Addendum to Let. 179, published by R. Fawtier in *Mélanges d'archéologie et d'histoire* 34 (1914): 7.

[26] *Leg. Maj.* III, i.

[27] *Leg. Min.* III, i.

[28] *Leg. Maj.* III, i; Cristofano di Gano Guidini, *Memorie,* ed. Milanesi, p. 37; testimonies of Stefano Maconi, Francesco Malavolti, Bartolomeo de' Dominici, in *Processus,* cited in Grion, [Aluaro.] *Santa Caterina* [*da Siena: dottrine e fonti* (Brescia: Morcelliana, 1953)],

p. 318; Caffarini, *Libellus de Supplemento,* [Ed. Guiliana Cavallini and Imelda Foralosso (Rome: Edizioni Cateriniane, 1974),] III, vi, 6.

[29] *Processus,* cited in Grion, *Santa Caterina,* p. 318.

[30] *Leg. Maj.* III, iii, Lamb, p. 321: "Meanwhile, so that no one will imagine that . . . I have added anything of my own, I call upon first Truth itself to be my judge and witness. . . . On the contrary, I have tried to keep the same order of words, and have made every effort, insofar as is allowed by the Latin syntax, to translate word for word, though strictly speaking this cannot always be done without adding some kind of interpolation, a conjunction or an adverb for instance, that is not in the original. But this does not mean that I have tried to change the meaning or add anything; it simply means that I have tried to achieve a certain elegance and clarity of utterance."

[31] *Supp.* I, i, 9.

[32] Let. 272. . . .

Cornelia Wolfskeel (essay date 1989)

SOURCE: "Catherine of Siena," in *A History of Women Philosophers, Volume II: Medieval, Renaissance, and Enlightenment Women Philosophers, A.D. 500-1600,* edited by Mary Ellen Waithe, Kluwer Academic Publishers, 1989, pp. 223-60.

[*In the excerpt that follows, Wolfskeel discusses* Il Dialogo *and the* Orazioni, *both of which express Catherine of Siena's unique understanding of her relationship with the divine.*]

. . . *2.* ***Il Dialogo***

Il Dialogo, simply called "my book" by Catherine herself, came to existence in the period 1377-1378.[69] It is a dialogue with God who, questioned by Catherine, instructs her and elaborately answers her questions. ***Il Dialogo*** is a testimony of God's providence and of the revelation of Holy Truth (= Christ). Raimondo da Capua (*Leg.* Maj. III. ch. 3) says that Catherine was forced to write "her book" by Holy Truth Himself, who revealed Himself to her, about two years before her death.

The text of ***Il Dialogo*** is preserved to us in codices, which are present in the Biblioteca Communale of Siena. ***Il Dialogo*** was printed for the first time in Venice in the year 1472. Various editions followed in Italy in the centuries to come. It was edited by Gigli,[70] together with Catherine's other writings, in the eighteenth century. M. Fiorilli prepared an edition of ***Il Dialogo*** in the 20th century.[71] ***Il Dialogo*** was normally edited according to a system of division of the contents into four treatises and 167 chapters, before Giuliana Cavallini[72] edited the text according to a system of division of the contents into ten main themes, in the year 1968. (For reasons of quotation she also maintained the numbers of the chapters of the previous editions). The whole ***Dialogo*** is composed according to a system of demanding, answering and thanksgiving, in Cavallini's opinion. Cavallini, very unsatisfied with the previous way of editing[73] the text, used what she thought to be the underlying system of the ***Dialogo,*** as a key to understand the ***Dialogo*** and to discover its organic structure. Her effort was not without result. It became clear to her that the key she used actually revealed the organic structure and logical division of the contents of the ***Dialogo,*** as Catherine herself had meant it to be. Cavallini became convinced that the old division into four treatises, which had originally been the work of Onofrio Farri in the 16th century, had to be discarded. This revolutionary view of Cavallini was generally accepted by other scholars. Suzanne Noffke follows the thread of Cavallini in her beautiful English translation of ***Il Dialogo.***[74] The ten main themes discovered by Cavallini are:

I Prologue (ch. 1-2)

II The way of perfection (ch. 3-12)

III The Dialogue (ch. 13-25)

IV The Bridge (ch. 26-87)

V The Tears (ch. 88-97)

VI The Truth (ch. 98-109)

VII The Mystical Body of Holy Church (ch. 110-134)

VIII Divine Providence (ch. 135-153)

IX Obedience (ch. 154-165)

X Conclusion (ch. 166-167)

(a) *ad I. Prologue.* The first two chapters introduce the main issues of the whole book: God's Truth and Love, and the dignity of the human being created in God's image and likeness, whose perfection is in the union with God. The work is placed in a setting within Catherine's life. Even petitions Catherine made are mentioned: for herself, for the reform of the Church, for the whole world, for the conversion of rebellious Christians, for divine providence in all things, and especially in regard to a particular case which seems to have troubled Catherine very much. (It is uncertain what this case really was).

(b) *ad II. The Way of Perfection.* In chapters 3 through 12, God instructs Catherine that every offense against

Him, who is "infinite Good" demands infinite satisfaction. Man needs "infinite desire," that is, true contrition of the heart and love of God. The value of suffering and penance is not in suffering or penance itself, but in the soul's desire. Neither desire nor any other virtue has value in life, except through Christ crucified. The way of perfection is the way of following Christ in His footsteps. This way of love of God necessarily implies love of our neighbours, for every virtue and every vice is committed by means of our neighbours. The soul needs discernment: true knowledge of itself and of God, which involves charity. (This part lacks a thanksgiving).

When commenting on the different main themes of ***Il Dialogo*** discovered by Cavallini, we must keep in kind that these themes are all interwoven and closely linked to each other. So "the way of perfection" is closely linked to the doctrine of the Bridge (= Christ), that of Truth (= Christ), that of Tears, and that of Obedience. "The way of perfection," which is the "way of following Christ in His footsteps" is elaborately worked out in connection with the other main themes. Catherine, dealing with the other themes, elucidates what this really meant. She is teaching her audience step by step. In chapters 3-12 she introduces the way of perfection. It becomes clear—and Catherine's discussion of the other themes will make it clearer—that this way of perfection is possible for all and certainly is not a privilege of clergymen, monks or nuns. Like St. Bernard of Clairvaux, Catherine identifies perfection with salvation. Bernard considered "perfectio" the soul's return to God through a purification of the heart given by God Himself and through the process of rehabilitation under God's guidance.[75] In Bernard's opinion, the perfection of man who is the image of God, is in the likeness to God. A conformity of will to the will of God must correspond with the image of God, which is imprinted in the nature of man. This conformity of will is the consequence of grace and at the same time of the free consent of the will. Such a movement of return to God, to man's model, as Bernard puts it, is fulfilled in charitable love. This concept of man's way to perfection as a return to God by God's grace and man's accepting of this grace is very similar to Catherine's concept of the way of perfection. We have already mentioned that in Catherine's doctrine charity underlies all virtues and necessarily belongs to the soul's way of perfection. Thomas Aquinas also considered the way of perfection that of love of God and neighbour. However, Thomas thought that this charitable love could grow if people kept the commandments of Christ. In Thomas' view, people did not necessarily have to keep the counsels of Christ, as well as His commandments, in order to reach perfection. (Thomas considered keeping the counsels as well merely instrumental).[76] Catherine slightly differs from Thomas in this respect. She certainly does not consider it necessary that people keep the counsels in fact in order to attain salvation. Those who keep the commandments in fact, and the counsels in spirit only, will be saved in the end. They are those who are passing through earthly life in ordinary love (ch. 47). Catherine, however, strongly emphasizes the fact that people may attain a greater perfection if they keep the counsels of Christ not only in spirit, but in fact as well. Then they will pass through earthly life most perfectly. Keeping the counsels in spirit and in fact is essential to those who want to pass most perfectly, in Catherine's opinion. Her way of perfection certainly has been submitted to some Franciscan influence in this respect.[77] She obviously follows the Augustinian thread, when she says that the soul must first come to self-knowledge and knowledge of its own misery in order to attain knowledge of God. This process of internalization reminds us of Augustine's *Confessions.*

Knowledge of God is the necessary condition for love of God, which, according to Catherine, includes love of the neighbours. This stress laid on the intellectual aspect of man's conversion to God, which becomes more obvious in the way Catherine deals with the human soul in the following chapters of ***Il Dialogo,*** also indicates Augustinian influence. To Catherine, perfection first of all means a condition of the soul, but one that immediately and necessarily has practical consequences for the way people treat their neighbours. Catherine lays great stress on this aspect of the way of perfection. Her mysticism has a very great, and inherently practical impact. Her way of following Christ and of achieving great perfection is by means of the neighbour. According to Catherine, even in the final state of perfection when the soul experiences God as a peaceful sea, the soul is concerned with the salvation of the neighbour (ch. 89). In this respect Catherine differs from other Dominican mystics of her time, like Eckhart and Suso, whose mysticism is characterized by strong speculative tendencies.

(c) *ad III. The Dialogue.* Chapters 13 through 25 deal with three petitions (partly a repetition of those enumerated before): 1, for mercy for the Church, 2, for mercy for the whole world, and 3, for mercy for an unnamed person (the "certain case"). God answers in correspondence to these petitions. The instruction leads up to the following doctrine: God explains that he has made Christ "the bridge" between heaven and earth. The redemptive blood of Christ sets man free from all his sins, original sin included, if man wants to accept by his own free choice, God's grace offered to him in baptism. Those people who made their choice for a sinful life after they were redeemed are false Christians and enemies of God, worse than pagans. They deserve God's punishment, but God, wanting the salvation of souls, will gracefully accept on their behalf the prayers and tears of His servants, who have a holy desire for the salvation of souls. God's mercy is offered to the whole world, for He created everything, except sin. The unnamed person will have to make his own way "through the bridge," accepting the suffering God grants him. Catherine thanks God (ch. 25) for His answers and courageously asks Him who are those who cross over the bridge, and those who do not. This question leads up to a new answer and instruction.

The concept that God's grace is offered to all mankind reflects Catherine's strong belief in the goodness and providence of God, whom (following Augustine in this respect) she elsewhere calls the Highest Good. She obviously is in accord with Augustine's doctrine when she says that God did not create sin. Like Augustine she considers all moral evil non being. Catherine, however, certainly differs from Augustine when she speaks of God's desire for the salvation of mankind and of His offering grace to all mankind. The absence of the doctrine of predestination we discussed above, undoubtedly underlies this concept. In Catherine's opinion, God offers grace; the only thing man has to do is accept this grace in free choice. We will discuss man's free will and free choice elaborately when commenting on "the Bridge." Catherine pictures Christ Mediator as "the Bridge" between heaven and earth. This picture is part of Catherine's highly figurative language.

(d) *ad IV. The Bridge.* The doctrine of the Bridge,[78] developed in chapters 26 through 87, is the most important part of the book. The Bridge was raised up, when Christ, who was God and man, was crucified. Since man could not pay for his debts to God, and God, the Father could not do penance for the guilt of man, it was Christ, God and man, who had to pay for the debts of mankind through His blood. Christ is the Bridge between heaven and earth, between God and man. Were it not for the Bridge, there would be no salvation for mankind. No one could walk on that Bridge until Christ was raised up from the grave. The Bridge was raised high and it has steps to enable man to mount it more easily. Climbing the Bridge and keeping to it means following the teachings of Holy Truth (= Christ).[79]

Those who pass through earthly life, not keeping to the Bridge, but going through the river beneath it, will drown in the end. They have "blinded the eye of their intelligence (ch. 46) with the infidelity they have drawn over it by their (wrong) self-love." At their baptism "the pupil of faith" was potentially given to the eye of their intelligence, but when they reached the age of discernment, they turned away from God and virtuous life and consequently lost the light of faith. They deluded themselves by their own free choice. They will consequently "drown themselves in the river." They could have been saved, if they had just followed the voice of their conscience instead of their sensuality.

Man has to choose whether he wants to go "through the Bridge" or "through the river." Some people cross the Bridge in ordinary love, others in perfect love. Those who travel in ordinary love keep the commandments of Christ, but they follow His counsels in spirit only, and not in fact. For instance: they need not be poor, but they must possess their riches without any attachment to them. They must lay down all wrong self-love. They must use the three faculties (1, memory and consciousness, 2, intelligence and 3, will) of their soul properly, conforming their will to God's will. They will then have climbed the three stairs.[80] Those who keep Christ's commandments and His counsels in fact as well as in spirit travel through the Bridge in perfect love. They go the way of "great perfection," loving God and their neighbour. The doctrine of the Bridge (summarized in ch. 87) is closely connected to the doctrine of tears. Catherine wanted to be instructed on tears for this reason.

Catherine uses the picture of Christ as the Bridge to express the Christian doctrine of salvation, according to which Christ is the only Saviour of fallen mankind. Christ as the Bridge is Christ Mediator. Christ is the incarnate Word. He could pay off the guilt of mankind, because He was God and man. Were it not for His divinity, His work would not have had the "value of life." If we compare Catherine's doctrine of Christ as the Mediator between God and mankind with Augustine's statements in this matter,[81] we have to notice some slight differences. Augustine considered Christ to be a mediator in His humanity, but not in His divinity. Christ in His humanity gave His life as a sacrifice to redeem the guilt of mankind.[82] Catherine apparently assumes a much closer relationship between the two natures of Christ in the matter of the redemption of mankind by the sacrifice of His "eternal blood."[83] This in particular becomes clear from Chapter 110, where it is said:

> So is this Word, my Son, His most gracious blood is a sun, wholly God and wholly human, for He is one thing with me and I with Him.[84]

To Catherine, Christ, the Bridge is the incarnate word, whose blood brings salvation. As soon as the soul has passed through the narrow gate of the Word, immersed in His blood, it comes to me (God, the Father), the sea of peace" (ch. 131).

Another major difference with Augustine's doctrine of salvation is to be found in the way Catherine deals with human free will. We discussed the latter in the Part II, above. Man must accept God's grace in free choice. Man is capable of free choice, because man's will is the only one of the three capacities (*potenze*) of man's soul which is not affected by original sin. Augustine thought that both body and soul, including the will, were affected by original sin.[85] On the one hand, Augustine says that man is free, on the other he says that man is capable of nothing good except through the grace of God. He reconciles these apparently contradictory statements by means of his concept of God's domination of man's will. Augustine emphatically says in his later writing *De praedestinatione sanctorum,*[86] that every willing of man which is good, is preceded by God's grace, or is the fruit of God's grace. God is capable of changing the will of man. If man wants something which is morally good, it is God's grace that makes man want this good. Fallen man in his own capacity has only a will for the worse, according to Augustine. If man accepts God's grace, it is God's grace that makes man accept this grace, in Augustine's opinion. God is the absolute master of all decisions of human will. Human freedom and human will must be considered from this point of view. From our previous discussion of free will in Catherine's doctrine it will be clear that she differs from Augustine in this matter. This difference is easily explained by the absence of the doctrine of predestination, which we discussed above. In Catherine's view, if people will be damned in the end, it will be their own fault. No divine predestination will have anything to do with their damnation. To Augustine's way of thinking divine omnipotence required a markedly different view of human will and freedom. Catherine never denied God's omnipotence. She believed in it (***Orazioni***). However, convinced as she is of God's great love of mankind, (God's essence is love, in her view), she implicitly denies any divine predestination of those who will be blessed or damned, while stressing human free will. She emphatically says that the only way God draws people to Him is by love. God wants man's salvation, but He never forces man in any way to accept His salvation except by His love. This is the way God chose it to be. Man's free will is a great gift of God. God Himself guaranteed this gift, even in the process of salvation. Free will, being a gift of God, does not affect God's power in any way according to Catherine. Her view reminds us of Bernard of Clairvaux in his writing *De gratia et libero arbitrio.* Like Bernard, she considers free will something belonging to the dignity of man, who is made in the image of God. The essence of will is that it is free.

Man's free will is a great gift of God, and it also is a great responsibility. If man makes the wrong choice, his end will be damnation. If man wants to be saved, he has to make his choice for the Bridge. Without the Bridge there is no salvation for man. Man needs salvation, in order to live a virtuous life. Catherine certainly is in accordance with Augustinian doctrine, in stressing man's need of salvation. Also, her opposition of the voice of conscience to sensuality is not alien to Augustine. The same is true of man's need of baptism, which sets man free from original sin. Man can lose the light of faith given to him in baptism, if he turns away from God and the virtuous life. According to the ***Orazioni,*** man can even become bestial in this way. By this Catherine means that the rational faculty of man's soul can be affected by man's turning away from God. This doctrine reminds us of Augustine's doctrine of illumination in some way.[87] Augustine taught that the human mind functions through illumination by the divine Logos. Man's rational capacity belongs to the image of God in man, or as Augustine puts it, man's rational soul is the image of God in man. Even in man's fallen condition man's reason is exalted by the divine "informing," so that God is the light by which are known whatsoever things are known, temporal or eternal. This general conception of knowledge is employed by Augustine in all areas of science, including physical science, aesthetics and moral values. God, the inward illuminator, is the cause of the certainties of all sciences. The human mind enlightened by God judges corporeal things (*sensibilia*) according to incorporeal and eternal principles (*rationes*), which, unless they were above the human mind, would certainly not be unchangeable.[88] In Augustine's opinion, those principles or *rationes* are the Platonic Ideas, which are in the mind of God, that is, in the divine Logos. The human mind illuminated by the eternal ideas judges everything in accordance with the Ideas, including physical objects (which in their turn are an image of the Ideas). According to Augustine (who bases himself in this respect on the Prologue of the Gospel of St. John), both nature and the human mind are informed "by the Divine Logos."[89] If man accepts God's grace, he may grasp religious truths through his reason. Faith will serve him to achieve these truths, which he would not otherwise have understood. As long as man is alive on earth, man's reason will never be completely blinded. Man will certainly not become bestial by losing his rationality. On the other hand, conversion to God enables man to reach greater knowledge, to wit religious knowledge.

Catherine, considering the capacity for rational thinking the most important capacity of man's soul, and part of the image of God in man, often speaks of the illumination of the soul by Divine Truth. In doing so, she is in accordance with Augustine, as she is when calling God the real object of man's soul. Augustine speaks of the Divine Logos as of Truth (= Veritas). Catherine calls Christ the incarnate Word (= Logos) Truth (= Verita), but she does not relate the Divine Truth to the Platonic ideas. Her doctrine of divine illumination is missing this Augustinian epistemological concept. According to Catherine, Divine Truth enables man to reason well by enlightenment, giving man the light of faith in baptism, without which light man cannot "follow Christian doctrine and the footsteps of the Word" (***Or.*** *X,* 76). Light of faith enables man's intelligence to see and understand religious truth and consequently man's will becomes full of love of that which intelligence has understood. A functioning, discerning intelligence is necessary for following Christ in His footsteps, that is, "to keep to the Bridge." The stress laid on the importance of intelligence certainly is an Augustinian element in Catherine's thought. This also is true of the three capacities of the soul, which, forming the image of God in man, must always work together (***Dial.*** ch. 52 sq). Memory, which includes consciousness, is related to God, the Father; intelligence to the Son; will to the Holy Spirit. This reference to the three Persons of the Trinity elucidates the unity of God's image in man. Ordinary light of faith is needed by man in order to make the capacities of his soul function well. The latter is necessary, whether man passes through earthly life keeping to the Bridge in ordinary love or in perfect love.

(e) *ad V. Doctrine of Tears.* Chapters 88 through 99 discuss five kinds of tears, corresponding to the spiritual levels of the soul's progress. On the lowest level of spiritual improvement for the better, the soul weeps out of fear of punishment, on the highest level, that of the union with God, the soul sheds "sweet tears of charity." (See our discussion of Catherine's doctrine above).

Tears are an accompanying phenomenon of the soul's way of perfection, which is the way of the soul's salvation through Christ, who is the Bridge between heaven and earth.

(f) *ad VI. The Doctrine of Truth.* In chapters 98 through 109, Catherine speaks of Christ as of "Gentle First Truth." Truth is the real object of the soul's contemplation. Truth enlightens the soul in order to make it see the transitory nature of this world. This is ordinary light of faith. Without this enlightenment the soul would be incapable of discerning between good and evil. When the soul is enlightened by ordinary light of faith, it ought not be content, but must desire to advance to a new spiritual stage. The light will give it the will to advance to a greater perfection.

In this second light there are two kinds of perfect souls. The first kind of these perfect souls occupies itself with mortifying the body, rather than with killing wrong self-love. However, those souls are perfect as long as their desire for penance has its roots in Christ and not in pride. They must learn that it is Truth who decides what is necessary for their salvation and perfection, whether this is consolation or trial. The second kind of perfect soul sees that Christ gives everything out of love. These souls accept everything for love of God. Their love has prudence as its counterpart. They consider themselves deserving of suffering, but they also consider themselves unworthy of any benefits that may come to them through their suffering. They conform their will completely to the will of God. They rejoice in everything. They do not judge the degree of perfection of others or constrain them to follow the same way. They do not base themselves on penance, but on Truth Himself. They are given right discernment in order to know whether visions and consolations given to them are from God or not.

Catherine asks God for more mercy for herself and her companions. She also wants to know the sins of the clergy so that she may intensify her prayers for the mystical Body of Christ. God tells her to pray, reminding her of the responsibility of knowledge.

The doctrine of the Truth is an epistemological account of the doctrine of Christ as the Bridge. (See III, 2 (d), above). Catherine's concept of truth is influenced by Augustinian doctrine, although there are also differences. Catherine calls Truth the real object of the soul. This is Augustinian doctrine.[90] Catherine also speaks of "gentle first Truth." This utterance becomes clearer if we compare it to ***Orazione*** *XV,* 4 sq. There it is said that Truth makes, speaks and "works" all things. The meaning is that Truth is the worker and cause of everything. Like Augustine, who identified Truth and the Divine Logos, Catherine (***Or.*** *XV*) considers Truth, the second person of the Trinity, the source of everything created. In her opinion, Truth also is the source of every truth human beings can achieve (***Or,*** *XV*). This concept is also influenced by Augustinian doctrine.[91] Catherine is in accordance with Augustine in ascribing man's achievement of truth, whether this is religious truth or scientific truth, to the illumination of man's intelligence by Truth (***Or.*** *XV*).

We must keep in mind that the Augustinian concept of the Platonic Ideas is missing in Catherine's concept of Truth. (See III, 2 (d)), above. Ordinary light of faith is necessary in order to make man's intelligence function well. We know from ***Le Lettere*** and the ***Orazioni*** that this light is offered man in baptism. This ordinary light of faith can only be acquired by rejection of sensuality (***Or.*** *IX*). Man risks losing his natural light of reason if he rejects the light of faith. The soul is more or less perfect according to its ability to correctly use its natural light of intelligence (***Or.*** *XXI,* 114). This is only possible in the light of faith, for by rejecting this light of faith man even risks losing his natural light of reason. Catherine evidently goes further than Augustine in considering the relationship between faith and intelligence so close. According to Catherine (***Dial.*** 98; ***Or.*** 12) the human soul is endowed with the capacity of (*levare se sopra di se*), elevating itself to the knowledge of God in the light of reason which belongs to the soul by nature, if reason is enlightened by the light of faith. It is the light of reason guided by faith, that enables man to go "the way of Truth (= the Bridge)." The three capacities of the soul (memory, including consciousness, intelligence and will), forming the image of the trinitarian God in man, always work together (***Dial.*** 51). Therefore, if intelligence accepts divine grace and the light of faith, man's will and memory are involved as well. Like Augustine in his

De Trinitate, Catherine relates memory to God the Father; intelligence to the Son; and will to the Holy Spirit (***Or.*** *XII;* ***Or.*** *XIII;* ***Or.*** *XVII;* ***Dial.*** 111). The Father is the Power, the Son Wisdom and the Holy Spirit Mercy (***Dial.*** 140), which also reminds us of Augustine in his *De Trinitate.* The unity of the three persons of the Trinity, always working together, guarantees the unity and cooperation of the three capacities of the soul, which form the trinitarian image of God in man. It is in Christ's eternal blood (***Or.*** *IX*) that the soul knows the light of God's truth (***Or.*** *XII*). Through the Passion of Christ the soul, guided by the light of grace, learns to know God's love of mankind. In the finite time of earthly life it is only by the light of grace that the soul will learn to know the essence of God in the infinite (***Or.*** *XII*). The soul can only learn to know God to the extent that its three faculties (*potenze*) rise from the baseness of humanity, and to the extent that it learns to know God in His light through the light God has given to the soul. Catherine stresses the fact that self knowledge underlies the knowledge of God (***Dial.*** *IV*). If the soul learns to know itself, it becomes humble and filled with hatred of sensuality.[92] In this humility it is united to God. It will then be illuminated by the light of grace. It can go the way of perfection, which is the way of Truth, the Bridge. The soul, going this way, guided by "ordinary light," might even be endowed with supernatural light and reach greater perfection. Catherine is convinced that, during its earthly life, the soul can reach the knowledge of God in His essence (***Or.*** *XII*).

(g) *ad VII. The Mystical Body of the Church.* This section, which includes chapters 110-134, deals with the incarnation of Christ, the grace of God in Christ offered to man, and the place of the ministers in the Church. God has chosen His ministers, in order that through them Christ's holy blood and body would be administered to all members of the Church. Catherine is informed about the terrible sins of the clergy: impurity, pride and greed, but she is also told that no one is allowed to punish clergymen (or religious people) except he who has appointed them. Whatever the sins of the ministers might be, they are entitled to carry out their function as ministers of the blood of Christ. Catherine praises God as "light and fire," asking Him again for mercy for the Church and for the whole world.

In this section Catherine stresses the dignity of the Church, of its ministers (***Dial.*** 120) and of its members as well. The members of the Church have received greater dignity than the angels through the union with mankind which God made in Christ. God became man and humanity became God through the union of divine nature with human nature in Christ. Catherine's language is highly mystical in this section. This explains the deification of humanity. In this context Cavallini refers to Thomas Aquinas in one of his *Sermons,*[93] where it is said that the only begotten Son of God, wanting us to share in His divinity, took our nature, in order to make men gods by the fact that He had become man Himself. The ministers of the Church are sacrosanct as ministers of the Eucharistic mystery, whatsoever their sins may be.

(h) *ad VIII. God's Providence.* Chapters 135 to 153 deal with God's general providence as well as with His special providence. (See our discussion of Catherine's doctrine in part II, 5, above). The latter is especially evident in the way He provides for those who have chosen to be poor, and in the way He will provide in "a certain case." Catherine praises God and asks for instruction on obedience. Catherine was informed in providence in connection with her concern for "a certain case," mentioned in the beginning of the book.

(i) *ad IX. Obedience.* In chapters 154 through 165, obedience is related to the obedience of Christ, who in obedience paid for Adam's sin. Only through obedience can mankind attain eternal life. There is ordinary obedience and a still more perfect obedience of religious people. It is obedience that conforms the soul to God in charity after the example of Christ. A characteristic of obedience is that it is accompanied by patience.

Like Thomas Aquinas in his writing *De perfectione vitae spiritualis,*[94] Catherine relates obedience to the obedience of Christ. She does not discuss obedience only here, but she also discusses it in many of her ***Lettere,*** for instance, Misc. 39; 67; 79 and 215. In her view, obedience is essentially connected with perfection, which is essentially charity. Obedience is the total and complete conformity of man's will to that of Christ. The greater obedience, the greater perfection and vice versa. So, it is by the fruit of obedience that charity enters heaven (ch. 153). Those who follow the commandments and the counsels of Christ in fact as well as in spirit have greater obedience than those who just keep the commandments in fact and in spirit, and follow the counsels not in fact, but in spirit only. Religious people who take the vow of obedience are expected to have a greater obedience than those who are outside a religious order. In all cases the merit of man's obedience is measured by man's love and charity. All human acts fulfilled in obedience have merit. Obedience is nourished by self-knowledge and knowledge of God. Since charity underlies all virtues and all virtues are linked together, (although God gives them differently to different people), it is understandable that obedience is always accompanied by patience.

(j) *ad X. Conclusion.* The last chapters (166-167) are a summary of the contents of the whole book. Catherine thanks the Holy Trinity.

*3. The **Orazioni***

The ***Orazioni*** came to existence in the period 1376-1380. They are preserved in codices in libraries in Rome and Siena, and partly in codices in libraries in Naples and Vienna, whereas ***Orazione*** 25 and ***Orazione*** 26 are preserved on M.S. 1574 in the University Library of Bologna.[95] Catherine spoke her ***Orazioni*** in the Italian dialect of Siena.[96] Her secretaries, including Bartolomeo Dominici and Raimondo da Capua, wrote them down verbatim and translated them into Latin as well.

According to the testimony of Bartolomeo Dominici, Catherine spoke her ***Orazioni*** when she was in a state of ecstasy, having lost the use of her senses.[97] In this state which occurred nearly every day in the period 1376-1380 after she had received Holy Communion, she spoke with God in a clear and loud voice and uttered her ***Orazioni.*** Bartolomeo Dominici says in respect to the ***Orazioni:***

> Those words and their contents did not seem at all to belong to a woman; on the contrary they made the impression of being the doctrine and the memories of a great doctor.

Le Orazioni deal with Catherine's deepest feelings and thoughts on God's love of mankind, manifested in His creation of mankind and in the incarnation of the Word (= Il Verbo). God is considered "love by essence." He created man for no other reason than His love for mankind to be. God, who, as Catherine puts it, knew us all in general and individually even before we were born (***Or.*** 4), knew that man would sin, but this did not prevent Him from creating man. He created man in His image and likeness, giving man the three faculties of the soul: memory, intelligence and will (***Or.*** 1, ***Or.*** 7, ***Or.*** 17), which reflect the Trinity.[98] This trinitarian image in man is damaged by Adam's fall and stained by original sin, but man's will is still free after the fall (***Or.*** 7). Man's will is so strong that neither God nor the Devil can overrule it, if man does not want it to be overruled. God, who created man out of love, wanted man's salvation. This is why Christ (God and man) was incarnated. Man could not pay his own debts, because man's works are finite, and God, the Father could not do penance either (***Or.*** 10). Christ paid for the debts of fallen mankind by his holy blood on the cross (***Or.*** 12).

Christ offers man the light of grace in baptism which sets man free from original sin. Man has to accept this grace, when he has come to the age of discernment (***Or.*** 9). Even fallen man is not totally deprived of the light of intelligence, but man has to use his rational faculty very carefully. Otherwise man risks becoming bestial by losing even the natural light of his intelligence (***Or.*** 5). Fallen man must accept Christ's grace offered to him in baptism, in order to free himself from wrong self-love and sensuality, and to find the real object of his soul, which is God (***Or.*** 21). Since God has created man without man, but is not going to save man without man, man must accept God's grace through his own free choice. God, who has created man for no other reason than His great love for mankind to be wants man's salvation but He does not force man to accept His grace. God, being love by essence, draws man only by His love (***Or.*** 1). If man accepts God's grace, man will be recreated into a real image of God (***Or.*** 21). Then the three faculties of man's soul will function well, because his soul will no longer be darkened by sensuality and wrong self-love (***Or.*** 20). There will then be a reciprocal conformity between man's soul and the Holy Trinity through the light which the Holy Trinity infuses into man's soul. Man's will becomes stronger and stronger in loving God. Then man will reach the destiny he was created for. He will love God and consequently, his neighbour (***Or.*** 8).

IV. Summary

We have discussed the most important themes of ***Le Orazioni,*** many of which are also dealt with in ***Il Dialogo*** and in ***Le Lettere.*** However, Catherine deals with the same subjects from different aspects in her different writings. In ***Il Dialogo*** she deals with the soul's way to spiritual perfection in connection with God's providence (which implies the entire doctrine of salvation), whereas in ***Le Orazioni*** she primarily focusses her attention on God as the Creator of mankind and His salvation of fallen mankind (which implies the doctrine of the soul made in God's image and likeness). ***Le Orazioni*** and the other writings prove Catherine's talent for writing and preaching. Her writing demonstrates her knowledge of and mastery of many topics of religious philosophy: the nature of God, the nature of knowledge of God, the nature of the soul, the relationship of God to man, the relationship between intelligence, faith and virtue, and, the religious foundation of moral action, in particular that exemplified by charity towards our neighbour. Her preaching makes her a true member of the order of St. Dominic. Moreover, her writing and preachings demonstrate that her involvement in Church politics was based on her philosophical and theological conviction that her knowledge imposed on her a duty to act on her beliefs, even at great personal risk. In doing so she is in the company of all those Christian philosophers who were more or less influenced by Plato and Platonism, and whose philosophy always implied a way of life in accordance with the system of their philosophy. The old concept that philosophy was more than an intellectual system and necessarily implied "a way of life" was still alive in the Middle Ages. Catherine, who certainly was longing to be granted martyrdom for Christ's sake, was faithful to the old Platonic tradition of philosophy.

Notes

[69] It was probably finished in the spring of 1378 before Catherine left for Rome. See G. Cavallini, *S. Caterina da Siena, Il Dialogo,* (Edizioni Cateriniane, Roma 1968); Suzanne Noffke, *Catherine of Siena, The Dialogue,* London/New York 1980, (Introduction).

[70] Girolamo Gigli, *Il Dialogo,* in *Opere Cateriniane, IV,* Lucca 1726.

[71] M. Fiorilli, *Il Dialogo,* in *Scrittori d'Italia,* Bari 1912.

[72] Giuliana Cavallini, *S. Caterina da Siena, Il Dialogo della Divina Provvidenza,* Edizioni Cateriniane. Roma 1980. (1. Roma 1968).

[73] In her Introduction to *Il Dialogo* Cavallini gives a survey of all previous text editions.

[74] Suzanna Noffke, *Catherine of Siena, the Dialogue,* London/New York, 1980.

[75] See P. Delfgaauw in *La Doctrine de la perfection selon St. Bernard,* in *Collections Cisterciennes* 40, 1978, 115e-118. (*Collectanea Cisterciensia,* ed. Forges, Abbaye Cistercienze de Scourmont, 1965 sq.)

[76] *Summa Theologiae* II, II, q. 188, a7, ad resp. e ad1. Tanta erit unaquaeque religio secundum paupertatem perfectior, quanto habet paupertatem proportionatam proprio fini. (To Thomas poverty and the other counsels have to serve the goal of man's salvation).

[77] The Franciscan order demanded absolute poverty, chastity and obedience. See *Rule* II (*Regula* II, *bullata of 1223*). St. Francis thought this the way of living in accordance with Christ's claims in the gospel. (See *Testamentum* 14).

[78] In her figurative language Catherine describes a bridge, comparable to the famous (and today still standing) "ponte vecchio" in Florence. For instance in ch. 27, she says that the bridge has walls of stones, so that handlers will not be hindered by rain.

[79] Catherine often speaks of "Gentle first Truth," meaning Christ. St. Augustine also spoke of Truth (Veritas), referring to the divine Logos, in many of his writings.

[80] See above for a more detailed description of the stairs.

[81] See for instance *Confessiones X,* ch. 43.

[82] See *Sermo* 152,9 (*Patrologiae Latinae* cursus 38, 824).

[83] See also *Orazione VI.*

[84] See Noffke. *op. cit.,* p. 206; see also G. Cavallini, *op. cit.,* p. 264. N.B. The comparison of Christ to a sun apparently is of Augustinian origin. The same holds for the image of Christ as heavenly physician in *Or. VI,* which picture appears in Augustine's *Sermones.* (See J. Eykenboom, *Het Christus medicus motief in de preken van S. Augustinus,* Assen 1960. Catherine's speaking of the ineffability of God also reminds us of Augustine in *In Evangelium Johanni,* 1,5.

[85] See *De civitate Dei XII,* 26; *De anima et eius origine,* ch. 12,19.

[86] *De praedestinatione sanctorum,* ch. 17 *Sermo* 177.

[87] *De Trinitate XII,* 10,24.

[88] See for instance *De Trinitate XII,* 2,2.

[89] *De diversis quaestionibus* 83, no. 46.

[90] The concept that the soul must return to God for its own good and happiness is found in all the writings of Augustine, for instance in *De vita beata,* where it underlies the entire argument.

[91] See Augustine in the "Cassiacum Dialogues," passim; for instance *Contra Academicos III,* and in *De Magistro,* passim; *De Trinitate,* passim.

[92] This concept compares with Augustine's doctrine of conversion in his *Confessiones* (passim).

[93] Thomas Aquinas, *Sermo,* in *Opusc.* 57. G. Cavallini, *Santa Caterina da Siena, il Dialogo,* Rome 1980, p. 264.

[94] *De perfectione vitae spiritualis,* ch. 12.

[95] For the history of the manuscripts, see G. Cavallini in the Introduction of her text edition of *Le Orazioni,* Roma 1978.

[96] Catherine's language influenced the literary Italian of later centuries.

[97] See G. Cavallini in the introduction of *Le Orazioni,* Roma 1978, p. XII. Cavallini mentions *Il Processo Castellano a cura di M.H. Laurent* (F.V.S.C.S.H.IX) as her source.

[98] Memory (memoria) refers to God the Father, intelligence to the Son and will to the Holy Spirit. The influence of St. Augustine (*De Trinitate* passim) is very clear. Like the Augustinian "memoria," memory implies consciousness.

Karen Scott (essay date 1993)

SOURCE: "*'Io Catarina'*: Ecclesiastical Politics and Oral Culture in the Letters of Catherine of Siena," in *Dear Sister: Medieval Women and the Epistolary Genre,* edited by Karen Cherewatuk and Ulrike Wiethaus, University of Pennsylvania Press, 1993, pp. 87-121.

[*In the following essay, Scott concentrates on Catherine of Siena's* Epistolario *(her letters) as "examples of female activism," arguing that Catherine used her letters as a means of furthering both her religious and political causes.*]

It is May 6, 1379. Rome is divided by a civil war into camps supporting two contending Popes, Urban VI and Clement VII. The mercenary soldiers of the Company of St. George have just succeeded in recapturing the Castel Sant'Angelo for Urban VI after a long siege. Soon the Antipope Clement VII will have to flee Rome and establish his court in Avignon.[1] That day Catherine of Siena dictated at least four letters concerning the events of the Schism. She sent two letters to supporters of Urban VI—the city government of Rome and the Captain of the Company of St. George; and she sent two letters to the supporters of Clement VII—Queen Giovanna of Naples and King Charles V of France.[2] She had been in Rome since late November 1378, called there officially by Urban to help him reunite the Church, and now she was busy doing so through her prayer, her verbal persuasion, and her voluminous correspondence.

Among Catherine's many activities at the time of the Schism, one must count her attempt to bring to Rome a contingent of holy men to assist Urban VI, her exhortation of the college of cardinals in Rome to remain faithful to him, and her desire to travel to Naples to convince Queen Giovanna to support him.[3] She sent over sixty letters relating to the Schism, most of them to the protagonists of the conflict. But she had too little time for her plans to bear fruit. Catherine would die on April 29, 1380, worn out by her work for Church unity; the Schism continued well into the fifteenth century.

If the Pope called on Catherine of Siena, an uneducated *popolana* of the artisan class and a lay Dominican tertiary, for help in the arduous task of ending the Schism, it was because by 1379 she was Italy's most famous holy woman, known not only for her fasts and her visions but also for her active desire to effect political and ecclesiastical reform. In 1376 Catherine had traveled to Avignon to convince Pope Gregory XI to make peace with a League of Italian cities and to return the seat of his government to Rome; with Papal approval she had preached peace in the Sienese countryside in 1377; and in 1378 she had spent several months trying to persuade the Florentines to end their war with the Papacy. By 1379 she had finished dictating the theological masterpiece which she called her ***Libro*** or Book, and which later editors entitled ***Il Dialogo della divina provvidenza (The Dialogue of Divine Providence).***[4] She also had already sent the majority of her 382 letters to prominent politicians, Church prelates, and ordinary people.

Catherine's correspondence is characterized by a combination of didactic content, personal tone, and passionate concern to affect public matters and people's lives. Her prolific writings manifest her wide circle of human relations, her deep caring for temporal peace and ecclesiastical reform, and her desire to present spiritual issues in thoughtful and convincing ways. Through her epistles she hoped to inspire her correspondents to take specific actions. An overview suggests that Catherine's letters might best be analyzed as examples of female activism and raises the question of how she might have obtained such an outspoken and confident voice in public affairs.[5] This essay argues that the answer to that question lies in the oral culture in which Catherine lived. Significantly, however, recent studies have not emphasized Catherine's actual apostolic endeavors, her self-image as a person called to travel and preach "for the honor of God and the salvation of souls," or her dictation of letters as a means of furthering her political and ecclesiastical causes. Two other interpretations have drawn the most scholarly attention and will need to be examined carefully: first, the letters have been viewed as examples of early Italian literature; and second, they have been considered "prophetic" and "mystical" texts.

*The **Epistolario** as Literature*

Because it cannot boast a modern critical edition and has not yet been translated in its entirety into English, the ***Epistolario*** is often neglected today as a source for Catherine's life and thought.[6] This neglect continues a trend in Catherine studies which began in the Renaissance. Since the sixteenth century scholars who have paid attention to her letters have concentrated not on her apostolic activities, but on her place in the development of the Italian language. The key to Catherine's literary reputation is the first printing of the complete ***Epistolario*** in 1500 by the influential Venetian humanist Aldus Manutius. Though he did not publish the letters for their stylistic merit, the fact that he had published them at all brought them to the attention of prominent humanists.[7]

By the middle of the sixteenth century Catherine's ***Epistolario*** was the only letter collection by a woman to be included in the literary canon set up in Anton Francesco Doni's *Libraria,* a list of books which he believed a scholarly humanist should have in his private library. Doni listed Catherine's name several times, most notably in the category of writer of "Translated letters" (as if she had originally written her letters in Latin, and then had had them translated into Italian):

> Cicerone / Ovidio / Fallaride / Seneca /
>
> Di diversi: Plinio, Petrarca, Pico, Poliziano e altri / San Cipriano / Marsilio Ficino / Papa Pio / Battista Ignazio / San Girolamo / Santo Agostino / Santa Catarina.[8]

By being associated with admired Latin authors from the ancient Roman, early Christian, and Renaissance periods, Catherine acquired the reputation of being a valid and solid literary figure. Her Italian letters could then be appropriated as real stylistic models seminal to the formation of the modern Italian language.

Catherine's inclusion in such sixteenth-century lists of valued letter collections in the vernacular ensured her a prominent place in Italian literary debates. In the early eighteenth century her letters became the focus of an intense controversy in Tuscany, when the Sienese scholar Girolamo Gigli published her complete works and argued in his *Vocabolario cateriniano* that her Sienese language was superior to the Florentine tongue. This claim brought down on him the wrath of the Florentine Academia della Crusca. The Grand Duke of Tuscany had the *Vocabolario* banned and burned, and Gigli was forced into exile.[9]

In more recent literary studies, Catherine's letters have attained dubious honor. The ***Epistolario*** is included among the earliest examples of vernacular Italian literature—Catherine is still considered the first important woman writer in Italy—and then critiqued and practically dismissed, this time not because of its Sienese dialect, but because of its very "imperfect" style. Beginning with pre-determined literary standards about "serenity" and "harmony," clear structure, stylistic variety, grammatical correctness, and sobriety in the use of imagery and redundancy, scholars such as Giovanni Getto and Natalino Sapegno have found Catherine's prose to be far less "artful" than the "genuine" masterpieces by Dante or Petrarch. For example, Sapegno wrote that her letters were works of political propaganda and mysticism, written with a practical and didactic, and not a valid "poetic" intent. He called her style "strange" and "flowery," "spontaneous," and "colloquial" (*dialettale*). Typical is his judgment of the imagery Catherine used so often to make her thinking more appealing: "the mystic's glimmering and carnal metaphor is one thing, and the poet's limpid metaphor . . . is quite another" ("Altra cosa e la metafora fremente, carnale . . . del mistico, e altra la metafora limpida . . . del poeta").[10] Paradoxically, then, Catherine's inclusion in the humanist canon both ensured the survival of her letters, considered basic to the development of Italian literary discourse, and led to their discredit because of their lack of poetic quality, their confused style, and their mystical, didactic, and political content.

Although it is important to evaluate the literary quality of early vernacular letters like Catherine's in order to determine their place in the history of the Italian language, the type of analysis proposed by Getto and Sapegno is misleading and anachronistic. What Italian literary critics since the sixteenth century have not considered sufficiently is that Catherine's letters were oral documents dictated by an uneducated and, at best, only partly literate person whose goals were anything but stylistic or literary. Moreover, these scholars have not focussed on the fact that this author was a woman, in fact the only one included in their anthologies of fourteenth-century Italian literature. It has been argued that religious women, whose culture was still predominantly oral, played an important part in the development of the various vernacular literatures of the late Middle Ages, and that their style of writing reflected their particular background.[11] For Catherine, the question that needs to be posed is not why her style was so "deficient" and "unliterary", but how this uneducated woman was able to develop her particular kind of style and voice.

Catherine's Voice as Supernatural: Holy Women and Hagiography

Catherine's remarkable success as a writer of letters leads one to wonder what factors enabled her to overcome the many obstacles facing women in Trecento Italy and what factors made possible such an extroverted and active epistolary "career." One often assumes that persons such as herself, an uneducated lay woman of the artisan class, had few opportunities to know about or affect decisively the politics of their commune or the life of the Church. They had no official channels to political or religious power. Confessors advised women who desired holiness to live humbly in solitude or in cloistered communities, to pray, and to do penance. Women were usually not encouraged to make political and ecclesiastical affairs the focus of their spirituality, to preach, or to write.[12] Moreover, the fourteenth century was an age of improved literacy in both Latin and the vernacular. In Tuscan cities schooling was relatively common, and Italian society was increasingly dependent on the written word.[13] Modern scholars often assume that people who remained illiterate or barely literate functioned with difficulty within this literate and more bureaucratic system. Such an assumption would seem especially true of lay women like Catherine who had much less access to formal education than did men.

How were Catherine and other uneducated women able to find a voice and exert public influence? One answer scholars have given is that the prophetic and supernatural quality of their speech made their words acceptable to their audiences and gave them the courage to act. From this perspective, women in a patriarchal society and church can acquire an acceptable voice and exert power in religious matters only if the words they speak are considered to be God's words and not their own. Such an approach to Catherine tends to minimize her desire to shape Church and state affairs in a practical way and stresses the more narrowly defined ascetic and mystical sides of her life.[14]

The interpretation of Catherine which emphasizes the supernatural dimension of her life is based less on an analysis of her letters than on the abundant hagiographical sources for her life, especially the *Legenda Major,* written several years after her death by her former confessor Raymond of Capua to help bring about her canonization by the Church. It is important to examine the evidence in this Saint's life because it contains important information about Catherine's composition of the letters and because its portrait of her as a mystic prepared for the establishment of her cult. Moreover, though Catherine's self-presentation in her own letters differs significantly from Raymond's stylization of her, as we shall see, it is his view that has most fascinated devotees and recent historians.

In the *Legenda* Raymond attributes to Catherine a kind of semi-literacy, noting her ability to read certain prayers of the divine office in Latin but not to read ordinary texts or write in Italian or in Latin.[15] His main message is that she was taught all she knew directly by the Holy Spirit and consequently did not attend school or learn anything from teachers or books. Although she worked hard to learn to read in the ordinary way by mastering the alphabet, the task proved impossible. In the context of a story about her custom of walking about her little room praying the Psalms out loud, literally, with Jesus at her side, Raymond inserts an account of how Catherine was miraculously instructed by the Holy Spirit, and learned to "read" the Canonical Hours in Latin "very fast" (*velocissime*). He specifies that her ability to read the Office was truly remarkable because after the miracle occurred she could still not speak Latin, read by separating syllables, or distinguish the letters.[16] Though Raymond's intent is to stress the miraculous dimension of the event and to reinforce his mystical portrayal of her, and not to give precise information concerning her ability to read, this account leads one to doubt whether Catherine really achieved the skills one normally associates with literacy.[17]

In addition, by implying that Catherine did not use her miraculous gifts to peruse books other than the prayers of the Office, Raymond may be hinting that she was unable to read anything she had not heard chanted out loud in a liturgical setting.[18] Another possible interpretation of his remarks is that he is using this story to protect her from a male ecclesiastical audience who assumed that interest in doctrinal matters on the part of uneducated lay women would be easily tainted with misunderstandings and heresy.[19] He wants to make clear that she read out of a desire only to pray better, not to seek special doctrinal instruction or entertainment. Consequently, he implies also, the content of her writing and preaching could not be based on information gained from books but only on divine inspiration.

In his Prologue to the *Vita* Raymond addresses the issue of Catherine's importance as a writer and affirms that she dictated all her letters with God's direct assistance. The fact that she spoke so quickly and self-confidently and could keep in mind what she wanted to say to three or four secretaries at a time, each taking down a different letter, is a sign to him that her writing was a real miracle:

> She dictated these letters quickly and without any interval for thinking, however small; she spoke as if she were reading out of a book placed before her. . . . Many who knew her before I did have told me that very frequently they had seen her dictating to three or four writers at the same time, and with that same speed and power of memory; for me, that this occurred in the body of a woman so weakened by vigils and fasting points more to a miracle and a super-celestial infusion than to any natural capacity of hers. . . . [20]

Raymond finds Catherine's writings to be especially remarkable and filled with supernatural power because they were dictated effortlessly. Perhaps his awe at her capacity to compose letters so easily reflects his inability, as a highly literate man, to understand the process of oral composition. Catherine may have dictated her letters at the speed of oral discourse, one that was ordinary to her, but too quick to be comprehensible to Raymond, accustomed to the laborious process of written composition. In any case, this account of her dictating letters reveals that Raymond is following a supernatural model of holiness that attributes all of the saint's achievements to God's miraculous intervention. Raymond makes the same point when he expresses admiration that the ***Epistolario*** was authored by a holy person so terribly worn down and weakened by ascetic practices. Only divine help could account for the energy she exhibited in the act of dictating so many letters.

Raymond reinforces his emphasis on God by pointing out that it was a mere "woman" who produced these texts. Elsewhere in the *Legenda* Raymond maintains that though women are "ignorant and fragile by their very nature" ("feminas, de sui natura ignorantes & fragiles"), God sometimes chooses them to ensure the success of His salvific mission. Completely "filled" with God because they are by nature so "empty", these female saints teach divine doctrine and reform the hearts of men, "especially those who consider themselves well-educated and wise" ("potissime illorum, qui litteratos & sapientes se reputant"). These women are "fragile but chosen vessels" ("vasa fragilia sed electa"), "gifted with divine power and wisdom, to confound the temerity [of proud men]" ("virtute & sapientia divina dotatas, in confusionem temeritate eorum").[21] Raymond emphasizes Catherine's natural female weakness so as to give all the credit for her achievements to God alone.

As a further proof of the divine origin of Catherine's speech, Raymond pays her the very high compliment of saying that if one were to translate her Italian idiom into Latin, her style would be comparable to the Latin prose of St. Augustine and the Apostle Paul. Modern literary critics do not share this view, but it is nonetheless important that Raymond attributes to her words a kind of supernaturally infused literary style which had Latinate qualities.[22] Though he may have been the first commentator on Catherine to emphasize the beauty of her style and lead readers to think of her as a literary figure, he does so not in order to attribute her success as a writer to her own natural gifts or hard effort to communicate well, but rather to prove that given her low level of instruction and literacy, only God Himself could have been the author of her letters.

Finally, Raymond states in his Prologue that all Catherine's words were so astonishingly wise for a woman as to constitute a sign that God was speaking through her:

> The Lord gave her a most erudite tongue, so that she knew how to utter a speech in every place, and her words burned like flames; and there was no one hearing her who could completely hide from the warmth of her fiery words. . . . Who from these signs would not see that the fire of the Holy Spirit lived in her? What other proof does one need that Christ spoke in her? . . . Where did this little woman get such wisdom? . . . She held the key to the abyss, that is to the depth of supernatural wisdom, and by illuminating darkened minds, she opened to the blind the treasure of eternal light. . . . [23]

Ultimately Raymond links Catherine's success as a writer to the warmth of her spoken words, and not her literary talents. He attributes the effectiveness of those words to the fire of the Holy Spirit and the very power and wisdom of God which lived in this fragile female "vessel."

In the narrative sections of the *Legenda* Raymond uses accounts of Catherine's effective speaking to reiterate his theology of female weakness and divine inspiration. In particular, he tells a significant story about her preaching at the beginning of the Schism to the Pope and his cardinals in Rome. After listening to Catherine's exhorting them to trust in divine providence and not fear for the future of the Church, Raymond says, Urban VI spoke these words to his cardinals:

> "This little woman shames us. I call her a little woman not out of contempt for her, but as an expression of her female sex which is by nature fragile, and for our own instruction. This woman by nature ought to fear, while we ought to be secure: and yet while now we tremble, she is without fear and comforts us with her persuasive words. A great shame must arise in us now." And he added: "What has the Vicar of Jesus Christ to fear, even if the entire world opposes him? The omnipotent Christ is more powerful than the world, and it is not possible that He abandon His holy Church". . . . [24]

Raymond does not conclude from the empirical evidence of Catherine's strength that the female nature might not be so naturally fragile as he had been led to believe. Instead, Urban's surprise at Catherine's superb performance as a preacher reflects Raymond's view that a female voice can emerge only if it is totally controlled by the divine. Under such conditions, however, he hints that even Popes may be converted. "Instructed" by her exceptional and miraculous example and words, Urban can now fulfill the properly male and papal role and confidently exhort his cardinals himself. One notes in passing that Raymond implies that Urban's bold speech is normal, not exceptional or supernatural like Catherine's. Though ending the story with the Pope's words may help Raymond assert the dominance of ecclesiastical over charismatic power and highlights Catherine's obedience to the Church, it also underlines her miraculous effectiveness in her mission of humbling, or "shaming" proud men.

Catherine's Letter to the Government of Rome

If one turns from a study of the hagiography to Catherine's own writings and her references to herself as a letter writer and speaker, one finds that she projects a sense of self that is rather different from Raymond's. First, her correspondence shows that being an uneducated woman may very well have been less of an obstacle to her developing a public apostolate and finding a strong voice than Raymond and subsequent historians imagined. Her letters are self-confident and natural, as if advising important people about spiritual, ecclesiastical, and political affairs were the most normal activity for a simple lay woman. Her presentation of self displays none of Raymond's careful apologetic focus. The ***Epistolario*** indicates that Catherine was well-informed about the main events of her day and formed opinions about them. When she saw an urgent need to find solutions to problems, she had the courage to speak about what she thought and to send letters to the main protagonists telling them what they should do to bring about Church reform and peace.

Second, though she believed that obeying the divine will was essential in any Christian life, including hers, and though she often expressed gratitude to God for her gifts and achievements, rarely did Catherine give a supernatural or prophetic flavor to her statements about her relationship with Him. The tone of most of her letters is so mundane that they hardly qualify as "mystical" or "literary" texts. Rather, her tone most resembles that of other Italian Trecento letters sent by ordinary people about ordinary things.[25] This similarity in tone suggests that Catherine viewed her writing of letters as part of her broader active vocation, which for her was one of ordinary speech and oral communication, and not prophetic or supernatural speech.

Among the letters which Catherine dictated on May 6, 1379, the one she sent to the city government of Rome ("A' Signori Banderesi e quattro Buoni Uomini mantenitori della Repubblica di Roma") is particularly interesting as an example of her epistolary strategy and her degree of involvement in public affairs during the Schism. It shall serve as a starting point for a discussion and explanation of her importance as a writer of letters.[26] The letter begins with a set of formulas which recur often, with slight variations, in all of her correspondence: "In the name of Jesus Christ crucified and sweet Mary. Dear brothers and earthly Lords, in sweet Christ Jesus. I Catherine, slave of the servants of Jesus Christ, write to you in His precious blood, with the desire to see you be grateful . . ." ("Al nome di Gesù Cristo crocifisso e di Maria dolce. Carissimi fratelli e signori in terra, in Cristo dolce Gesù. Io Catarina, schiava de'servi di Gesù Cristo, scrivo a voi nel prezioso sangue suo; con desiderio di vedervi grati . . .").

After this introduction, Catherine devotes the main part of the letter to a long religious lesson on the spiritual and social consequences of ingratitude and gratitude to God. Her message is relatively simple and straightforward. People who are ungrateful to God, she says, offer the love they owe Him to their own sensuality and turn the love they owe their neighbor into hatred, envy, malicious gossip, and injustice. Deprived of charity, their hearts are so narrow that there is no place for God or neighbor within them. With characteristically blunt and passionate language Catherine accuses the ungrateful person "of contaminating justice and selling the flesh of his neighbor. . . . Not only does he blaspheme and speak ill of other creatures; but his mouth treats God and His Saints no better nor worse than he might do with his feet" ("contaminando la giustizia e rivendendo la carne del prossimo suo. . . . Non tanto che bestemmi e dica male delle creature, ma egli pone bocca a Dio e a' Santi suoi nè più nè meno, come se lo avesse fatto co'piedi").[27]

On the contrary, Catherine says that people who are grateful to God look to Christ's humility and purity, and to the abundance of blood He shed out of love for humanity, and they broaden their hearts to offer assistance to all.

> Such a person lives honestly, helping his neighbor in his need whether he be subordinate or lord, . . . small or great, poor or rich, according to true justice. He does not lightly believe in a neighbor's failing, but with a prudent and mature heart he examines very carefully who speaks [about that failing] and who the person is that is spoken of [accused]. He is grateful to who serves him: because he is grateful to God, he is grateful to him. And he does not serve only those who serve him, but he loves and is merciful to whoever disserves him. . . . [28]

Following this didactic section, the last quarter of the letter shifts in tone to a strongly worded request that the Roman officials apply her general moral principles about gratitude to the situation of the moment, and therefore adopt certain policies. The government, she writes with her firm, almost imperious *voglio* ("I want you to . . ."), should recognize that the papal victory is God's doing. Officials should institute public rituals to thank God for saving Rome from danger: they could imitate Urban VI's humble procession barefoot through the streets of the city. The government should also organize better care for the soldiers of the Company of St. George, especially for those who were wounded in the battle for Castel Sant'Angelo, because these men were Christ's instruments and because a show of genuine gratitude would keep these mercenaries on Urban's side.[29]

Furthermore, Catherine asks the government of Rome to put an end to some negative talk about Giovanni Cenci, the Senator who organized the Pope's victory, and to thank him more fully for his selfless and prudent contributions:

> I would not want him or anyone else who is serving you to be treated in this way [with ingratitude and slander], because it would be greatly offensive to God and harmful for you. For the entire community needs wise, mature, and discreet men with a good conscience. No more of this, for the love of Christ crucified! Take whatever remedy your Lordships think best, to keep the simple-mindedness of the ignorant from impeding what is good. . . . [30]

Finally, at the very end of the letter, fearing that her words might have sounded too outspoken, and perhaps knowing that in a time of civil war her suggestions would not be popular with everyone in Rome, Catherine suggests that her correspondents ought to listen to her because she is truly disinterested, caring, and sincere. This closing assumes a quite personal tone:

> I say this to you for your own good, and not out of self-interest, for as you know I am a foreigner and I speak to you for your good, because I value all of you and him [Cenci] as much as my own soul. I know that as wise and discreet men you will look to the affection and purity of heart with which I

> write to you. And so you will forgive the presumption, with which I presume to write. . . . [31]

The letter concludes with a set of formulas which recur very often in the correspondence: "I say no more. Remain in the holy and sweet love of God. Be grateful to God. Jesus sweet, Jesus love" ("Altro non dico. Permanete nella santa e dolce dilezione di Dio. Siate, siate grati e cognoscenti a Dio. Gesù dolce, Gesù amore").[32] In her letter to the government of Rome Catherine gives very practical advice and moves from an abstract to a more personal tone.

*The **Epistolario:** An Overview*

Catherine's remarkable ***Epistolario*** is composed of 382 extant letters dictated and sent to a total of about 220 individuals and 25 groups (governments and religious communities) over the span of about eight years. She engages her correspondents well enough to elicit written answers from some of them and to exchange letters with them over a period of several years.[33] These letters generally follow the pattern exemplified in the one she sent to the government of Rome. An overview of the correspondence allows one to discern the epistolary strategy which Catherine used to persuade people to take the actions she deemed desirable. These letters also carry something of her original voice, and thus they can serve as an introduction to the personality and concerns of the historical Catherine.

The opening formulas ("In the name of Jesus Christ crucified and of sweet Mary" and "I Catherine, servant and slave of the servants of Jesus Christ") indicate that Catherine desires to communicate her views with great authority, both in God's name and in her own. The wording of these formulas is her own, reflecting her Christocentric spirituality and her self-image as loving "servant" to both God and neighbor. These idiosyncratic introductions may function as the equivalent of signatures confirming the authorship of her letters.[34] From the very beginning Catherine also creates intimacy with her correspondents by addressing them as her spiritual relatives—as her "sons" or "daughters" if they are her disciples, and as her "mothers" or "fathers" if they are rulers or members of the clergy to whom she must express respect.[35]

Catherine leaves to a comparatively short end section any mention of the concrete action which she wants to inspire her correspondents to take, and she spends most of each letter teaching in a reasoned and rather impersonal way the spiritual lessons that should persuade them to do as she wishes.[36] She structures these didactic sections around a discussion of a main virtue which she wishes her correspondents to understand and practice better—gratitude, charity, obedience, humility, patience, and so on—or a vocation which she believes they need to live more fully—priest, cloistered nun, pope, knight, political leader, son or daughter of God, and so on. Christ is the central model and theological focus of her teaching, and she relies heavily on imagery of all sorts to make her thinking accessible and appealing.[37] The moral and doctrinal content of her teaching is conventional, ordinary, and mostly unoriginal. The tone is simple and straightforward—usually not mystical or visionary, theological or philosophical, or stylistically artful.

What is more remarkable about these didactic sections, if one examines the entire ***Epistolario,*** is their variety. Catherine has at her disposal a vast repertoire of suggestions and arguments, and her letters advocate and defend many different callings.[38] On the one hand, she writes a community of enclosed nuns in Perugia to do everything to avoid social contact: they should flee the parlor, keep to their cell, and converse only with God.[39] Likewise she advises a prominent Florentine politician to keep away from the Chancery and the Palace, to refuse any new office, and to stay at home to avoid becoming entangled in the world.[40] On the other hand, Catherine can portray in glowing terms the heart-warming joys of good conversation among ordinary God-fearing people.[41] Moreover, she spends much energy attempting to persuade prelates to become less reclusive and to pay attention to Church reform. Since the shepherds of the Church are asleep in their own selfishness, she says, they hardly notice that their sheep are being stolen by infernal wolves. So she exhorts one prelate to awake and cry out with a hundred thousand tongues, and she tells a Cardinal to roar like a lion.[42]

Catherine adapts her spiritual and moral teachings and the imagery she uses to convey her points to her particular audiences. Even her portrayals of Christ can vary: for some correspondents He is the loving bridegroom, while for others He is the immaculate Lamb shedding salvific blood on the cross. He can be a model of humble silence and patience, the spiritual Master, or the eternal Truth and Word of God the Father. This variety reflects Catherine's desire to make her letters personal and unique: she sends her correspondents individually tailored sermons containing those spiritual lessons which she believes they most need to hear or read. The diversity of content in the ***Epistolario*** also means that one should be careful not to generalize about her moral and spiritual thought from what she wrote in any one letter.

In the end sections of her letters Catherine abandons the general approach of the didactic portions and applies her theoretical teachings to the particular circumstances of her correspondents. She usually highlights the distinction between the two main sections of her letters by inserting the customary phrase "I have nothing more to say" ("altro non dico") at the end of her lesson. She implies that she is beginning the least formal and most personal portion of her text. Her tone becomes very ordinary and intimate, especially when she deals with matters pertaining to her "family" of spiritual disciples in Siena.

For example, she writes this message to invite her young friend Neri Pagliaresi into her spiritual family: "You asked me to receive you as my son: so though I be unworthy, lowly, and wretched, I have already received you, and I receive you with affectionate love" ("Domandastemi, che io vi ricevessi per figliuolo: onde io, poniamochè indegna misera e miserabile sia, v'ho già ricevuto e ricevo con affettuoso amore").[43] Another disciple, Francesco Malavolti, has left her group and engaged in a life of sin, and she sends him this note: "I write to you with the desire of putting you back in the sheepfold with your companions. . . . Console my soul; and do not be so cruel to your own salvation as to deny me a visit. Do not let the devil trick you with fear or shame. Break this knot; come, come, dearest son" ("Io scrivo a te con desiderio di rimetterti nell'ovile con li compagni tuoi. . . . Consola l'anima mia; e non essere tanto crudele per la salute tua, di far caro d'una tua venuta. Non ti lassare ingannare, per timore nè per vergogna, al dimonio. Rompi questo nodo; vieni, vieni, figliuolo carissimo").[44] Thus Catherine reassures her friends that she loves them and prays for them.

When her friends are ill, imprisoned, bereaved, or suffering economic difficulty, Catherine writes to express affection and consolation. Her advice manifests a certain concern with the practical side of life. For example, she suggests that the sick temper their ascetic practices. She says to Daniella of Orvieto, "If the body is weak and sick, one should not only stop fasting, but also eat meat; and if once a day is not enough, then four times a day. If one cannot stand up on the ground, then one should go to bed; and if one cannot kneel, then one should sit or lie down if necessary" ("Se il corpo è debile, venuto ad infermità, debbe non solamente lassare il digiuno, ma mangi della carne: e se non gli basta una volta il dì, pigline quattro. Se non può stare in terra, stia sul letto; se non puo inginocchioni, sia a sedere e a giacere, se n'ha bisogno").[45] In other letters, Catherine's desire to assist her friends is reflected in her offer to intervene with the prefect of Rome to ask that he free a prisoner without exacting an enormous ransom, and in her request that friends visit another prisoner.[46] She begs financial assistance for poor nuns, and she tells a prostitute from Perugia that her brother has promised to support her if she renounces her profession.[47]

Because of her focus on the apostolate, Catherine rarely indicates that it is *she* who needs assistance, but on a few occasions she does insert short phrases indicating that she misses the companionship of a friend. Raymond of Capua, her confessor and disciple, was the person whose absence caused her most hardship at the end of her life when her attempts to help resolve the Schism were not meeting with success. She suggests in a parenthetical aside that her apostolic work would be easier if he were present: "I, a wretched slave, put in this field where blood is shed for love of [Christ's] blood (and you have left me here, and have gone off with God), will never stop working for you" ("Io vile schiava, che son posta nel campo, ove è sparto il sangue per amore del sangue (e voi mi ci avete lassata, e setevi andato con Dio), non mi ristarò mai di lavorare per voi").[48] In her last letter to Raymond Catherine expresses again her need for his friendship, but she sets his work for Church unity as a higher priority: "Do not be afflicted because we are physically separated from each other, for though it would be a very great consolation for me [to see you], the joy of seeing the fruit you make in the holy Church is a greater consolation" ("E non pigliate pena perchè corporalmente siamo separati l'uno dall'altro; e poniamochè a me fusse di grandissima consolazione, maggiore consolazione è l'allegrezza di vedere il frutto che fate nella santa Chiesa").[49]

It is usually in these end sections that Catherine discusses events in her own life and places other autobiographical materials, especially issues related to her apostolic activities. In a little less than half of the extant letters (about 160), the end sections show that Catherine's main goal in writing is to persuade her correspondents to take concrete political or ecclesiastical actions.[50] She sent these letters to advance the great causes which she held dear, such as peace in Italy, a crusade, Church reform, or the return of the Pope to Rome. Many of the letters she wrote between November 1378 and her death in April 1380 reflect her strong desire to end the Schism and her search for practical solutions.

For example, it is with reasoned arguments and outright threats that Catherine begs Urban's supporters to remain faithful and his opponents to return to the fold. She sends her disciples on mission to Genova and Naples. She asks nuns, bishops, and members of confraternities to say special prayers. Catherine suggests that Urban VI create good bishops and keep faithful friends at his side and she sends many letters to convince her more "spiritual" followers and acquaintances to join her in Rome for that purpose. In these sections of her letters, her tone also becomes self-assured and uncompromising. Catherine's individual voice emerges distinctly because she highlights the personal quality of her views with such words as *io* and *voglio.*

It is here that she shifts occasionally from offering her strongly opinionated advice to mentioning quite unapologetically her own participation as a protagonist in public affairs, especially her conversations with political and ecclesiastical officials. Particularly significant is her account of her first meeting with Pope

Gregory XI in Avignon several years before the beginning of the Schism, when she worked to mediate a conflict between Florence and the Papacy. She writes the Florentines,

> I have spoken with the holy Father. He heard me graciously, by God's goodness and his own, showing that he has an affectionate love for peace. . . . He took such a special delight in this that my tongue can hardly narrate it. After I had talked a good long time with him, at the conclusion of these words he said that if what I had put before him about you was true, he was ready to receive you as his sons and to do whatever seemed best to me. . . . [51]

Catherine usually keeps such autobiographical materials for the end sections of her letters. An important exception to this rule is a series of short narratives about her personal spiritual experiences which she inserts in the didactic portions of some twenty-five of her letters. Significantly, when she discusses these encounters with God, it is usually not to draw attention to her own uniqueness or supernatural powers; instead, her goal is to teach and encourage her correspondents to accomplish whatever they need to do for their own spiritual progress. While Raymond's *Legenda* highlights all that was miraculous and exceptional about Catherine's life with God, as we saw above, in her letters she describes her own experiences as simple, quite unspectacular dialogues between God and "a soul" or "a servant of God".[52]

In these dialogues God and Catherine talk about mainstream moral, theological, and spiritual matters. For example, Catherine begins a letter to "a great prelate" with an abstract exposition of the idea that the pain of Christ's desire to save humanity was greater than any physical suffering He endured. Then she inserts this more autobiographical passage to confirm and reinforce her idea:

> This reminds me of what the sweet and good Jesus once manifested to a servant of His [Catherine]. She saw in Him the cross of desire and the cross of His body, and she asked: "My sweet Lord, what caused You greater pain, the pain of the body or the pain of desire?" He responded sweetly and benignly, and said, "My daughter, do not doubt. . . . As soon as I, the incarnate Word, was sown in Mary's womb, I began the cross of My desire to obey My Father and fulfil His will for man, that man be restored to grace and receive the end for which he was created. This cross brought Me greater suffering than any other physical pain I endured. . . . "

This conversation continues for several pages. Then Catherine shifts back to the general lesson she wants the prelate to learn:

> So you see well, reverend Father, that the sweet and good Jesus Love, He dies of thirst and hunger for our salvation. I beg you for the love of Christ crucified to take the hunger of this Lamb as your object. This is what my soul desires, to see you die from a holy and true desire, that is from the affection and love which you will have for the honor of God, the salvation of souls, and the exaltation of holy Church. . . . [53]

Though Catherine revealed a great deal about herself thoughout the ***Epistolario,*** she conveyed above all a strong identification with her varied apostolates. Even when she inserted personal dialogues with God in her letters, she wanted less to explore the intricacies of the self, or to write formal autobiography, than to present the self as a general model and source of encouragement to others. Such an extroverted self-portrait is essential also to Catherine's interpretation of her role as a writer of letters. Further analysis will show that Catherine developed her epistolary voice out of a deep need to communicate to others her experience of God and her views about political and ecclesiastical affairs. She believed that God had bestowed upon her a mission to speak. Undoubtedly the oral culture in which she lived facilitated her practice of that call.

"I Catherine write to you": Writing and Orality

Catherine's letters reflect a late fourteenth-century culture that was aware of the literate world but still essentially and self-consciously oral. Access to the public sphere, in her case, was facilitated by her reliance on an epistolary genre that partook of both the oral and the written. Far from representing a serious obstacle to her apostolate, her lack of education in such a context may well have constituted an advantage. Catherine's oral culture sharpened her capacity for speech and helped her to formulate ideas, opinions, and advice in a blunt, passionate, and articulate manner. Moreover, viewed as the written version of spoken words, letters held many advantages for someone like Catherine who felt a strong desire to influence other people. When her words were dictated to secretaries, they became letters which could reach extended audiences. Finally, such letters constituted an important meeting place of literate and oral cultures. Since both educated and uneducated people in the Middle Ages often dictated their letters, this genre enabled Catherine to enter the public sphere and to communicate with political and ecclesiastical leaders almost on a footing of equality.

Moreover, letters of the sort that Catherine sent were considered so ephemeral by her society as to be uncontroversial; they were personal and private documents, neither threatening nor as legally binding to their recipients, unlike official Latin or Italian epistles.[54] The private, oral, and momentary nature of Catherine's kind of letter writing was especially beneficial to women, who were forbidden official channels of communication and influence, but who could not be stopped from sending personal messages. Significantly, while Catherine's writings contain important evidence that her travels and unofficial preaching were criticized in her own day, there is no hint that anyone ever questioned her sending of letters, or that she felt the need to defend the legitimacy of her epistolary activities.[55] Rather, she indicates that dictating her correspondence is an enjoyable and worthy task that is obviously on a continuum with other forms of ordinary speech meant to benefit her neighbors.

In her statements about herself in the ***Epistolario*** Catherine specifies some of the ways in which letter writing was personally rewarding for her. Letters allow her "refreshment" ("recreazione") from the labors of the apostolate.[56] When she is suffering from physical ailments, dictating letters "distracts" her from her pain ("spassare le pene").[57] After she experiences union with God, writing about what she has learned helps her "unburden her heart" ("sfogare il cuore").[58] The most common sentiment which Catherine expresses about her motivations for writing, however, is that letters allow her to express love for her neighbor and that God Himself wants her to help save souls and resolve the problems of her day through her correspondence. For example, this is how she justifies the outspoken nature of a letter to the Queen of Naples: "Because I love you, I have been moved to write you, out of a famished desire for the salvation of your soul and body. . . . Now I have unburdened my conscience" ("Perchè io v'amo, mi sono mossa dall'affamato desiderio della vostra salute dell'anima e del corpo a scrivere a voi. . . . Ho scaricata la coscienzia mia").[59] Catherine's conscience bothered her equally for the Queen's adversary Pope Urban VI. She explains to him that she has written him with such "strong assurance" ("sicurtà") because she "was constrained by the divine Goodness, the general need, and the love I bear for you" ("costretta dall divina Bonta, e dal bisogno che si vede, e dall'amore ch'io porto a voi").[60]

Catherine's statements about herself as a writer reflect an apostolic, not a literary sensitivity. The closest she comes to expressing self-conscious pride in her writings is a note in the last letter she wrote as she was dying in Rome, probably in February 1380, to her confessor Raymond of Capua: "I also ask you to get your hands on my Book [the ***Dialogue***] and every other writing of mine that you can find [presumably her letters], and do with them whatever will best serve the honor of God" ("Anco vi prego che il libro e ogni scrittura la quale trovaste di me . . . ; e fatene quello che vedete sia più onore di Dio").[61] That Catherine wants her works to be preserved and distributed by her confessor and friends reflects her awareness of their value and potential usefulness. But when she states that she hopes to further "the honor of God" she implies that her goal in writing is not literary but religious: she wants her letters to help save souls.

Catherine's lack of formal education ensured that her basic mentality remained that of an illiterate person. Though she was aware of the effects that literacy and study can have on people, Catherine consistently disapproved of these effects or downplayed them. For example, in several letters she delights in the fact that literacy is not a requirement for salvation. Christ crucified is the only "Book" one needs to read, she says. This "Book" was "written" with blood, not ink, and its large illuminated letters [*capoversi*] are Christ's wounds. The content of this Book is Jesus' virtues of humility and meekness. With such a Book, "who will be so illiterate with so low an understanding, that he will not be able to read it?" ("Quale sarà quello idiota grosso, di si basso intendimento che non lo sappia leggere?")[62]

Likewise, Catherine advises people to prefer the spiritual direction of "a humble and unschooled person who has a holy and upright conscience to that of a proud scholar who studies with much knowledge" ("Unde ti dico che molto meglio è ad andare per consiglio della salute dell'anima a uno idioto umile con santa e diritta coscienza, che a uno superbo letterato studiante con molta scienza").[63] Her distrust of formal education is reflected also in her condemnation of excessively rhetorical preaching. In a passage about bad priests in the ***Dialogue,*** Catherine writes that God said to her: "Their sermons are set up to please men and give pleasure to the ear, rather than give honor to Me; for they study not a good life, but very elegant speech" ("Le loro predicazioni sono fatte più a piacere degli uomini e per diletta-re l'orecchie loro che ad onore di me; e però studiano non in buona vita, ma in favellare molto pulito").[64]

The ***Epistolario*** provides important evidence that Catherine "wrote" through dictation, and that letters were an oral medium for her. First, her letters name several of her secretaries. In a letter to the Podestà of Siena, she says: "My female companions who used to write for me are not here now, and so it has been necessary for me to have Frate Raimondo write" ("Non ci sono ora le mie compagne che mi solevano scrivere: e però è stato di bisogno che io abbia fatto scrivere a frate Raimondo").[65] At the end of a letter to her disciple and friend Stefano Maconi, her secretary of the moment adds: "May the negligent and ungrateful writer be recommended to you" ("Il negligente e ingrato scrittore ti sia raccomandato").[66] Many other letters include similar greetings, often somewhat humorous and self-deprecating, which name Catherine's friends who served as her secretaries: "Alessa grassotta" (fatty Alessa Saracini), "Cecca perditrice di tempo (Francesca the time waster), "Giovanna Pazza" (crazy Giovanna Pazzi), "Francesco cattivo e pigro" (naughty and lazy

Francesco Buonconti), "Neri del quattrino" (wealthy Neri Pagliaresi), and "Barduccio cieco" (blind Barduccio Canigiani).[67]

Second, some of the language which Catherine uses at the end of her letters to soften her reproofs of church prelates reflects the fact that she was writing with her tongue and her mouth—that is, that she was dictating. In a letter to Pope Urban VI a few months before her death she refers to her mouth: "Forgive me, most sweet and holy Father, if I say these words to you. . . . Do not despise or disdain them because they come out of the mouth of a most unworthy woman" ("Perdonatemi, dolcissimo e santissimo Padre, che io vi dica queste parole. Confidomi, che l'umiltà e benignità vostra è contenta che elle vi sieno dette, non avendole a schifo nè a sdegno perchè elle escano di bocca d'una villissima femmina").[68] In a cryptic message of a letter to Raymond of Capua concerning the beginning of the Schism and her opinion of Urban VI, she uses an odd mix of language about the mouth and the hand: "Now keep silent, my soul. I do not want to try my hand, dearest father, at saying that which I could not write with a pen or say with my tongue; but let my being silent manifest to you what I want to say" ("Or tieni silenzio, anima mia, e non parlare più. Non voglio mettere mano, carissimo padre, a dire quello che con penna non potrei scrivere nè con lingua parlare; ma il tacere vi manifesti quello ch'io voglio dire").[69] Catherine's wording shows that writing for her was simply a form of speaking.

Third, she views her letters as the written record of an oral discourse of hers which will be delivered orally to her correspondent by a messenger or carrier.[70] She asks Raymond of Capua to "announce to the Pope what I write in this letter, as the Holy Spirit will inspire you to do" ("annunziategli quello che io vi scrivo in questa lettera, secondo che lo Spirito Santo vi ministrerà").[71] Her Sienese disciple Sano di Maco receives a letter containing her request that he "read this letter to all my children" ("Voi prego, Sano, che a tutti i figliuoli leggiate questa lettera").[72] Catherine sends Stefano Maconi a note telling him to read two other letters she had enclosed, to give them to their addressees, that is, to the Government of Siena and to the members of a confraternity, and "to speak to them fully about this matter which is contained in the letters" ("Parla loro pienamente sopra questo fatto che si contiene nelle lettere").[73] In all these cases the written text is actually an oral medium, a means for her message to travel from her mouth to her friend's ear.

Fourth, for Catherine the writing of letters was really a form of speech, in continuity with other kinds of words which she believed God called her to utter, and that is, informal preaching and prayer. At the beginning of the Schism she writes Pope Urban VI about what she sees as the three components of her vocation: "As long as I live, I shall never stop spurring you on with my prayer, and with my live voice or my writing" (Io non mi resterò mai di stimolarvi coll'orazione, e con la voce viva o con scrivere, mentre che io viverò").[74]

Finally, Catherine said to many of her correspondents that she would have preferred direct oral discourse with them to dictating and sending written letters to them. For example, during the Schism she writes King Charles V of France, "It is love for your salvation that makes me say these things; I would much rather say them to you with my mouth and with my presence than in writing" ("L'amore della vostra salute mi costringe a più tosto dirvele a bocca con la presenzia, che per scritta").[75] "Let it not seem hard if I sting you with words, for it is the love of your salvation which has made me write you", she says to three schismatic cardinals. She then adds, "I'd rather sting you with my live voice, if God were to allow me to do so" ("Non vi parrà duro se io vi pungo con le parole, che l'amore della salute vostra m'ha fatto scrivere; e più tosto vi pungerei con voce viva, se Dio m'l permettesse").[76] Letters were only a poor substitute for the warmth of the human voice. Catherine clearly believes that her action would be far more effective if she could visit Urban VI's opponents, see their situation first hand, and address them directly with whatever tone and advice they seemed to need most.

Catherine's emphasis on speech brought her to reflect a great deal on the power and the morality of words, her own and those of her contemporaries. In her view words carry power, not because God grants supernatural effectiveness to the words of a few chosen individuals, but because words which represent strong personal emotions are always effective and persuasive. For her this is as true of the words of sinners as it is of the words of saints. For example, she attributes much of the urban violence she witnessed around her to the inflammatory power of hateful speech. God tells her: "As a result of words you have seen and heard of revolutions, the destruction of cities, and many evils and murders. For the word entered the center of the heart of the person to whom it was said; it entered where the knife could not have passed" ("Per le parole avete veduto e udito venire mutazioni di stati, disfacimento delle città e molti altri mali e omicidi; perchè la parola entrò nel mezzo del cuore a colui a cui fu detta: intrò dove non sarebbe passato il coltello").[77] Insults such as "You are a brute animal" cause an escalation of anger: "One word seems like a knifing, and if they do not answer with four words, they feel their heart will explode with poison!" ("Una parola gli pare una coltellata; e se essi non ne rispondono quattro, pare che il cuore scoppi veleno!").[78] "Sometimes this gives birth to injurious words, and these words are often followed by murder" ("Alcuna volta partorisce parole ingiuriose, dopo le quali parole spesse volte seguita l'omicidio").[79] In Catherine's experience, evil words almost inevitably lead to evil consequences.

Likewise, words that are good and holy cannot fail to pierce and convert the heart of their listeners. The key to holy words is their speaker's sincerity and godliness of purpose. Catherine explains that a sincere and open heart is one which "everyone can understand, for it does not demonstrate one thing on the face and the tongue, while it has another thing inside" ("Ogni uno el può intendere perchè non dimostra una cosa in faccia e in lingua, avendone dentro un'altra").[80] The "voice of the heart" is as effective a force for good as words of hatred are a force for violence and murder. When Catherine writes to the Romans that they should listen to her words because of the "affection and purity of heart with which I write to you" she is really expressing her trust that her letter will bear good fruit in the souls of those who hear it.[81]

Catherine's model for the power of good speech is the Apostles after Pentecost. As she writes to a Dominican preacher, "When the fire of the Holy Spirit came upon them, they climbed into the pulpit of the holy cross, and there they could feel and taste the hunger of the Son of God, and the great love he had for us; and so the words came out of them like a fiery knife out of the furnace, and with this warmth they pierced the hearts of those who listened" ("Perchè il fuoco dello Spirito Santo fu venuto sopra di loro, essi salsero in su'l pulpito dell'affocata croce, ed ine sentivano e gustavano la fame del Figliuolo di Dio, e l'amore che portava all'uomo: onde allora escivano le parole di loro, come esce il coltello affocato dalla fornace; e con questo caldo fendevano i cuori degli uditori").[82] Catherine explains the Apostles' success as preachers through the power of their deep identification with Christ's salvific love for humanity. The fire within their hearts becomes a fire potent enough to pierce through all obstacles in the hearts of their audience. Such is the fire which she wants her Dominican correspondent to communicate through his holy words.

Catherine does not believe that God gives this fire only to priests, however. She calls Mary Magdalene *apostola* and *discepola,* and she identifies personally with Christ's male and female apostles.[83] This apostolic fervor is echoed in a letter which she wrote her mother in 1377 to defend her own informal preaching mission in the Sienese countryside. Catherine asked her mother to treat her with the same understanding which Mary showed her Son's Apostles after Pentecost: "The disciples, who loved her without measure, actually leave joyfully and sustain every pain [of the separation] to give honor to God; and they go among tyrants, bearing many persecutions. . . . You must know, dearest mother, that I, your miserable daughter, have not been put on earth for anything else: my Creator elected me to this" ("I discepoli che l'amavano smisuratamente, anco, con allegrezza si partono, sostenendone ogni pena per onore di Dio; e vanno fra i tiranni, sentendo le molte persecuzioni. . . . Sappiate, carissima madre, che io miserabile figliuola, non son posta in terra per altro. A questo m'ha eletta il mio Creatore").[84] Fortified by the example of the Apostles, Catherine too is willing to travel, preach to the "tyrants" of her day, and bear many "persecutions," for she is convinced that it is her vocation to utter relentlessly earnest, passionate, and ultimately persuasive words.

Catherine's approach to speech provides the key to how she explained her success as an apostle and a writer of letters. She is convinced that if one's words are inspired by a sincere and humble desire to obey the promptings of the Holy Spirit and to help bring salvation to souls, then one's speech cannot fail to effect good. For Catherine this holds true for all kinds of speech: oral discourse is especially effective, but letters are influential to the degree that the power of her original voice dictating those words can be transmitted onto the written page. Moreover, this power and influence are present not only in the exceptional words of a few saints, but also in the ordinary words of all kinds of people, including Popes, ordained priests, politicians, and even well-intentioned lay women like herself.[85]

Conclusion: Women and Oral Culture

It is Catherine's trust that her sincere words would bear fruit in the hearts of her various audiences that propelled her, a woman, into the public sphere as a writer of letters, and that explained, at least to her satisfaction, whatever measure of influence and success she enjoyed in her apostolic work. This understanding of herself is significantly different from the portrayal of her in the hagiographical literature. One recalls that Raymond of Capua emphasized the supernatural quality of her life, including the miraculous components of her writing letters, in order to defend her sanctity as an ignorant and weak female vessel completely filled with divine power. Her being a woman was one of the issues which concerned Raymond the most. Though this view of Catherine may reflect how many of her contemporaries explained the impact of her voice and why they were willing to listen to her, it does not explain how she became confident enough to speak, because this was not her self-understanding.

Catherine did not focus on whatever might have been exceptional in her life. Her main desire was to love her neighbor and advance her various political and ecclesiastical causes through ordinary written and oral speech. Perhaps the most significant characteristic of her approach is her silence about the fact that she was a woman engaging in these activities. Catherine does not mention even once in the ***Epistolario*** that her apostolate was controversial because of her gender. Among the social categories she discusses, male and female distinctions have no place. She does not reflect on what a female "nature" might be: if she believes herself to be a sinner in need of divine mercy and assistance, she does not attribute her failings to a particularly "female weakness." Though it is known that at the time of the Schism she suggested a mode of life somewhat like her own to at least one other woman, she did not found a religious community of female activists.[86] Unlike her near contemporary Christine de Pizan, Catherine did not feel the need to defend the female sex from attack in any way.[87]

Why did Catherine not talk about herself as a woman? Faced with the paradox of an influential activist woman who did not write about gender, one must conclude that she was relatively indifferent to gender, and that God and the success of her apostolic causes mattered to her more. It is likely that Catherine's oral culture was one reason for that indifference. The feminist consciousness of a writer such as Christine de Pizan arose out of a clearer awareness of the classical and medieval intellectual tradition of misogyny than Catherine could ever have achieved. Christine begins her *Book of the City of Ladies* by describing herself seated in her study and in a state of considerable discomfort because she perceives that throughout history so many learned men have insulted women in their books. Her interest in defending women comes from the realization that they have been unjustly attacked. Catherine may have been less vulnerable to negative views of women because she was not used to reading books. Her lack of education may have shielded her from the more virulent and debilitating theories of misogyny prevalent in her time. Instead, she saw other urgent needs in her world and her Church, and she spoke her mind about them in a manner which was very much her own creation.

Notes

[1] For an analysis of the events of the Schism and Catherine's participation in them, see Arrigo Levasti, *S. Caterina da Siena* (Turin: U.T.E.T., 1947), pp. 414-500; Giles Meerseman, "Gli amici spirituali di S. Caterina a Roma alla luce del primo manifesto urbanista," *Bulletino Senese di Storia Patria* 69 (1962): 83-123; André Vauchez, "La sainteté mystique en Occident au temps des papes d'Avignon et du Grand Schisme," in *Genèse et débuts du Grand Schisme d'Occident: Avignon, 25-28 septembre 1978* (Paris: Éditions du Centre National de la Recherche Historique, 1980), pp. 361-68.

[2] The edition of Catherine's letters that I have used here is *Le Lettere di S. Caterina da Siena,* ed. Piero Misciatelli (Florence: Giunti, 1940), 6 vols. The letters Catherine sent on May 6, 1379 are numbers 347, 348, 349 and 350, in *Lettere,* vol. 5, pp. 165-87. All translations in this paper are my own.

[3] In addition to Catherine's letters, one can find much information about her activities during the Schism in her main *vita,* Raymond of Capua's *Legenda Major.* This text is published under the title of *De S. Catharina Sensensi virgine de poenitentia S. Dominici,* in *Acta Sanctorum Aprilis,* vol. 3 (Antwerp, 1675), pp. 853-959. A recent English translation of the *Legenda* is *The Life of Catherine of Siena,* trans. Conleth Kearns (Wilmingon, DE: Michael Glazier, 1980).

[4] S. Caterina da Siena, *Il Dialogo della divina provvidenza ovvero Libro della divina dottrina,* ed. Giuliana Cavallini (Rome: Edizioni cateriniane, 1980). The most recent English translation is *The Dialogue,* trans. Suzanne Noffke (New York: Paulist Press, 1980).

[5] For a full presentation of the evidence, see Karen Scott, "Not Only With Words, But With Deeds: The Role of Speech in Catherine of Siena's Understanding of Her Mission" (Doctoral dissertation, University of California, Berkeley, 1989).

[6] A modern critical edition exists only for the first eighty-eight letters which Catherine sent between the early 1370s and the end of 1376: S. Caterina da Siena, *Epistolario,* ed. Eugenio Dupré Theseider (Rome: Tipografia del Senato, 1940). This volume has been translated recently into English: *The Letters of Catherine of Siena,* trans. Suzanne Noffke (Binghamton, NY: Center for Medieval and Early Renaissance Studies, 1988). Antonio Volpato of the University of Rome is currently working to complete Dupré Theseider's critical edition.

[7] Amadeo Quondam, "Dal 'Formulario' al 'Formulario': cento anni di 'Libri di lettere'," in *Le "carte messaggiere." Retorica e modelli di comunicazione epistolare: per un indice dei libri di lettere del Cinquecento* (Rome: Bulzoni, 1981), pp. 13-156, esp. p. 60. See also Carlo Dionisotti, *Gli umanisti e il volgare fra quattro e cinquecento* (Florence: F. Le Monnier, 1968), pp. 3-5; and Gabriella Zarri, "Le sante vive. Per una tipologia della santità femminile nel primo Cinquecento," *Annali dell'Istituto storico italo-germanico in Trento* 6 (1980): 408-9.

[8] Anton Franceso Doni, *La Libraria,* ed. Vanni Bramanti (Milano: Longanesi, 1972), p. 195. Doni also included Catherine's letters and the *Dialogue* in another list of titles, in the category of texts available in the vernacular: *La Libraria,* pp. 208, 210. The only other female writers mentioned in that second list are Angela of Foligno, Tullia, Olimpia, Terracina, and Isabella Sforza. For a short study of Doni's work, and Catherine's mention in it, see Quondam, "Dal Formulario," p. 59.

[9] *L'Opere di Santa Caterina da Siena, nuovamente pubblicate da Girolamo Gigli* (Siena, 1707-1726). The *Vocabolario cateriniano* constitutes volume 5 of Gigli's work. See Augusta Theodosia Drane, *The History of St. Catherine of Siena and Her Companions* (London: Longmans, Green, 1915), p. xviii.

[10] N. Sapegno, *Il Trecento* (Milan: Vallardi, 1966), p. 495; Giovanni Getto, *Saggio letterario su S. Caterina da Siena* (Florence: G. C. Sansoni, 1939).

[11] An early study of the link between vernacular writing and women is Herbert Grundmann, *Religiose Bewegungen im Mittelalter* (1935); see also the Italian translation *Movimenti religiosi nel Medioevo* (Bologna: il Mulino, 1974), esp. Ch. 8. For an illuminating discussion of stylistic aspects of medieval women's writings, see Elizabeth Alvida Petroff, "Introduction" to *Medieval Women's Visionary Literature* (New York and Oxford: Oxford University Press, 1986), pp. 3-59.

[12] There is a growing historiography on women, politics, and religion in late medieval Italy. See for an example Christiane Klapisch-Zuber, *Women, Family, and Ritual in Renaissance Italy,* trans. Lydia Cochrane (Chicago and London: University of Chicago Press, 1985). For a review of the literature see Scott, "Not Only With Words" (note 5), pp. 117-25, 139-48.

[13] Recent studies of the growth of Italian literacy include Franco Cardini, "Alfabetismo e livelli di cultura nell'età comunale," *Quaderni storici* 13 (1978): 488-522; Peter Burke, "The Uses of Literacy in Early Modern Italy," in *The Historical Anthropology of Early Modern Italy: Essays on Perception and Communication* (Cambridge: Cambridge University Press, 1987), pp. 110-31; and Paul F. Grendler, *Schooling in Renaissance Italy: Literacy and Learning, 1300-1600* (Baltimore: Johns Hopkins University Press, 1989).

[14] Though Catherine's historical significance as an activist and writer has not been explored in depth in recent historical scholarship, her life has usually been subsumed under the category of prophecy and visionary activity. For example, Rudolph Bell, Anna Benvenuti Papi, Caroline Bynum, John Coakley, Richard Kieckhefer, and André Vauchez have recently noted Catherine's extreme fasting, rigorous ascetic practices, and mystical religious experiences, and have used them to explain how she gained fame as a holy woman: see Rudolph M. Bell, *Holy Anorexia* (Chicago and London: University of Chicago Press, 1985), pp. 22-53; Anna Benvenuti Papi, "Penitenza e santità femminile in ambiente cateriniano e bernardiniano," in *Atti del simposio internazionale cateriniano—bernardiniano, Siena, 17-20 aprile 1980,* ed. Domenico Maffei and Paolo Nardi (Siena: Accademia senese degli intronati, 1982), pp. 865-78, esp. 872; Caroline Walker Bynum, *Holy Feast and Holy Fast: The Significance of Food to Medieval Women* (Berkeley and Los Angeles: University of California Press, 1987), pp. 165-80; John Wayland Coakley, "The Representation of Sanctity in Late Medieval Hagiography: The Evidence from *Lives* of Saints of the Dominican Order" (Th.D. dissertation, Harvard University, 1980); Richard Kieckhefer, *Unquiet Souls: Fourteenth Century Saints and Their Religious Milieu* (Chicago and London: University of Chicago Press, 1984); and André Vauchez, "Les Représentations de la sainteté d'après les procès de canonization medièvaux (XIII-XVe siècles)," in *Convegno internazionale. Agiografia nell'occidente cristiano, secoli XIII-XV, Roma (1-2 marzo 1979)* (Rome: Accademia nazionale dei lincei, 1980), pp. 31-43.

[15] Like Raymond of Capua, Catherine's second most important hagiographer Thomas Caffarini believed that she miraculously learned to read and dictated her letters. However, unlike Raymond he stated that toward the end of her life Catherine learned to write in her own hand through a further divine miracle. He limited this claim, though, by stating that she herself had written only two letters, the concluding part of the *Dialogue,* and a prayer, and thus by implying that on the whole she continued to function most comfortably within her oral culture. See *Il Processo Castellano,* ed. M.-H. Laurent, Fontes Vitae S. Catharinae Senensis Historici, vol. 9 (Milan: Bocca, 1942), pp. 51, 62; and *Libellus de Supplemento: Legenda prolixe virginis Beate Catharine de Senis,* ed. Giuliana Cavallini and Imelda Foralosso (Rome: Edizioni Cateriniane, 1974), pp. 77-79. Caffarini's views may be based on Catherine's L. 272, in *Lettere,* vol. 4, p. 172.

[16] *Legenda,* p. 881, col. 1: "Verum, quia mentio facta est hic de psalmodia, scire te, lector, volo, quod virgo haec sacra litteras quidem sciebat, sed eas homine viatore docente nequaquam didicerat: & dico literas, non quod sciret loqui Latinum, sec scivit legere literas & proferre." Unable to learn to read in an ordinary way, Catherine asks God for a miracle: "Antequam de oratione surgeret, ita divinitus est edocta, quod postquam ab ipsa surrexit, omnem scivit litteram legere, tam velociter & expedite, sicut quicumque doctissimus. Quod ego ipse dum fui expertus, stupebam: potissime propter hoc, quod inveni, quia cum velocissime legeret, si jubebatur syllabicare, in nullo sciebat aliquid dicere: imo vix literas cognoscebat: quod aestimo pro signo miraculi ordinatum a Domino tunc fuisse" (*Legenda,* p. 881, col. 1-2).

[17] Overall, the story sounds similar to the achievement of small children who have heard their parents read stories to them so often that they memorize the words and can pretend to read as they recite what they know by heart.

A further indication that Raymond considered Catherine's Latin literacy weak is the fact that though she could "read" Latin in that particular way, she could not use this language fluently for prayer, writing, or direct speech. Throughout her life, he said, she loved to repeat the prayers which begin the divine Office, but she did so not in Latin but in the vernacular. See *Legenda,* p. 881, col 2: "Verbum psalmi, per quod quaelibet hora incipitur, scilicet: Deus in adjutorium meum intende, Domine ad adjuvandum me festina: quod in vulgari reductum, frequentius repetebat." Raymond also mentioned that when Catherine visited Avignon to speak with Pope Gregory XI in 1376, he had to serve as her interpreter because she spoke no French or Latin: *Legenda,* p. 925, col. 2 and p. 956, col. 2. He did not comment at all on any ability of hers to read or write Italian.

[18] *Legenda,* p. 881, col. 2: "Coepit libros quaerere divinum Officium continentes, & in ipsis legere psalmos, hymnos, & reliqua quae pro canonicis Horis sunt deputata."

[19] See Grundmann, *Movimenti religiosi,* pp. 156, 281; and comments by Jean Gerson quoted by Caroline Walker Bynum, "Jesus as Mother and Abbot as Mother: Some Themes in Twelfth-Century Cistercian Writing" in *Jesus as Mother: Studies in the Spirituality of the High Middle Ages* (Berkeley, Los Angeles and London: University of California Press, 1982), pp. 134-35.

[20] *Legenda,* "first prologue," p. 854, col. 2.

[21] See *Legenda,* p. 883, col. 1-2. For an analysis of the place of these passages in the *Legenda* as a whole, see Scott, "Not Only With Words", pp. 161-81. For the view that medieval interpretations of women viewed their "natural" vulnerability and weakness as the female avenue to power and strength, see Bynum, *Holy Feast,* and Barbara Newman, *Sister of Wisdom. St. Hildegard's Theology of the Feminine* (Berkeley and Los Angeles: University of California Press, 1987). I shall argue below that Catherine did not share Raymond's or Hildegard's "theology of the feminine."

[22] *Legenda,* First Prologue, p. 854, col 2: "Quamvis enim proprio sermone vulgari loquatur in eis, quia non cognovit letteraturam: quia tamen introivit in potentias Domini cum clavi profunditatis profundae, stylus eius (si quis diligenter advertit) potius videtur Pauli quam Catharinae, melius alicujus Apostoli quam cujuscumque puellae"; and "Sententiae sunt tam altae pariter & profundae, quod si eas in Latino perceperis prolatas, Aurelii Augustini putes potius fuisse quam cujuscumque alterius."

[23] *Legenda,* p. 885, col. 1.

[24] *Legenda,* p. 937, col. 1-2. Raymond also discusses Catherine's desire to travel to Naples to persuade Queen Giovanna to support Urban VI. His intent in describing her activities during the Schism may be to portray her life as a model for the *vita apostolica.* He mentions that her group of followers in Rome lived together in voluntary poverty, and "chose to travel and beg with the holy virgin" ("eligentes magis cum sacra virgine peregrinari & mendicare"; *Legenda,* p. 937, col. 1.) He gives no hint that such a mode of life involving mendicant itinerant preaching was controversial for lay women and men in his time; he may have had in mind the observant reform he was promoting among friars as Master General of the Dominican Order at the time he was composing the *Legenda.* For Raymond's use of Catherine's life to promote the Urbanist Papacy and his own observant reform, see Coakley, "The Representation of Sanctity," pp. 86-90.

There is another interesting account of Catherine "preaching" to men. Raymond writes that at some unspecified time the prior of the Carthusian monastery on the island of Gorgona, near Pisa, invited her and some twenty companions to come to the island and speak to his monks. The entire community walked to the lodging where she and her female companions (*socia*) were staying. The prior "cunctos Fratres duxit ad eam, rogans aedificationis verbum pro filiis. . . . Tandem aperuit os suum, & locuta est prout Spiritus sanctus dabat . . ." (*Legenda,* p. 927, col. 1).

[25] For example, see the letters published by Lodovico Zdekauer in his *Lettere familiari del Rinascimento senese (1409-1525)* (Siena, 1897) and *Lettere volgari del Rinascimento senese* (Siena, 1897); *Le Lettere di Giovanni Colombini,* ed. Dino Fantozzi (Lanciano, n.d.); "Le Lettere di Margherita Datini a Francesco di Marco," ed. Valeria Rosati, *Archivio storico pratese* XLX (1974): 4-93.

[26] L. 349 in *Lettere,* vol. 5, pp. 219-25. This is one of the few letters of the *Epistolario* which is dated. The rubrics which are found in the first letter collections and were printed in the first editions indicate also that the letter was dictated while Catherine was in a state of ecstacy: "A dì 6 Maggio 1379. In astrazione fatta."

[27] L. 349, p. 177.

[28] L. 349, p. 178.

[29] L. 349, pp. 178-79. Raymond of Capua suggests in the *Legenda* that Urban's decision to walk barefoot in a procession of thanksgiving was due to Catherine's direct influence: see *Legenda,* p. 940, col. 1.

[30] L. 349, pp. 179-80.

[31] L. 349, p. 180.

[32] L. 349, p. 180.

[33] Catherine indicates that she is answering a letter from a correspondent in sixty-six of her letters. She mentions receiving sixty-nine letters from a total of fifty different people or groups of people. Her politically prominent correspondents were Pope Gregory XI, Niccolò Soderini of Florence, Bernabò Visconti the Duke of Milan, Queen Giovanna of Naples, and the governments of Siena and Bologna. None of the letters which Catherine mentions having received is to be found among the four extant letters which were sent to her (by Tommaso Caffarini, Bernabò Visconti's daughter-in-law Elizabeth of Bavaria, the Prior of the Carthusian monastery of Gorgona, and the Abbot of Monte Oliveto); see *Lettere,* vol. 6, pp. 45-53.

[34] Catherine's formula is her original variation on the ordinary salutation one finds at the beginning of other Trecento letters: "In God's name. Amen" ("Al nome di Dio. Amen"). The formulas with which she ended all of her letters are similarly her own.

[35] On the epistolary form as it was used in the Middle Ages, see Giles Constable, *Letters and Letter Collections,* Typologie des sources du Moyen Âge occidental, fasc. 17 (Turnhout: Brepols, 1976); and James J. Murphy, *Rhetoric in the Middle Ages. A History of Rhetorical Theory from St. Augustine to the Renaissance* (Berkeley and Los Angeles: University of California Press, 1974), pp. 194-268. For late medieval Italian letters see Nicola De Blasi, "La lettera mercantile tra formulario appreso e lingua d'uso," *Quaderni di retorica e poetica* 1 (1985): 39-47. In contrast to most medieval writers of letters who used their opening salutations to emphasize the differences in social level of their correspondents, Catherine kept her opening salutations very simple.

[36] Though the content of Catherine's didactic sections is conventional and similar to that found in letters by other religious figures of the Middle Ages, both men and women, the division of each letter into two distinct parts—general and personal—and the ordered structure of the didactic section seem more idiosyncratic.

[37] For example, self-knowledge and humility are a "treasure" one should "buy" and "possess." One should dwell in the "shop," "cavern," "cell," "house" of self-knowledge and love of God. Humility is also one's "armour" and "sword" in the "battle" against spiritual "enemies"; or it is "clothing," a "belt," a "pin." Humility is the charity's "wetnurse" or "mother"; self-knowledge "feeds" the "hungry" soul. It is a "deep abyss," or a "fertile" "ground" upon which all the virtues are "planted." For a "dictionary" of Catherine's imagery, see Gabriella Anodal, *Il linguaggio cateriniano* (Siena: Edizioni Cantagalli, 1983).

[38] For examples of how Catherine's spiritual advice can differ from one letter to another, see Karen Scott, "La tolleranza religiosa nel pensiero di Santa Caterina da Siena," *Nuovi studi cateriniani* 2 (1985): 97-111; and "La pratica della tolleranza religiosa da parte di S. Caterina," *Nuovi studi cateriniani* 3 (1987): 5-26.

[39] L. 217 in *Lettere,* vol. 3, p. 257.

[40] L. 258 in *Lettere,* vol. 4, pp. 96-97.

[41] L. 190 in *Lettere,* vol. 3, p. 143.

[42] L. 16 in *Lettere,* vol. 1, pp. 54-56; and L. 177, vol. 3, pp. 92-93.

[43] L. 99 in *Lettere,* vol. 2, pp. 117-18.

[44] L. 45 in *Lettere,* vol. 1, pp. 180-182.

[45] L. 213 in *Lettere,* vol. 3, p. 233.

[46] L. 89 (XIV) in *Lettere,* vol. 6, p. 36; and L. 254, in *Lettere,* vol. 4, p. 82.

[47] For letters about poor nuns, see L. 88, 129, 170, 198; L. 276 is addressed to the prostitute from Perugia.

[48] L. 344 in *Lettere,* vol. 5, p. 155.

[49] L. 373 in *Lettere,* vol. 5, p. 292.

[50] An even greater proportion of Catherine's letters than this probably contained practical suggestions for political or ecclesiastical action. It is known that some of her early editors cut out the more practical end sections of the letters and published only the moral and spiritual lessons which they considered more useful for the general religious edification of the faithful. It would be a mistake to conclude from this that the early editors substantially altered the content or the wording of those sections of Catherine's letters which they did publish, for the evidence is that they left the didactic lessons intact.

To reconstruct Catherine's political and eclesistical activities from her *Epistolario* is not an easy task. Unfortunately for modern scholars, most of her letters were probably not dated: only three of the eight originals are dated. However, even when dates were originally included, they were usually placed at the end of the end sections, and thus some dates were probably cut out. See Robert Fawtier, *Sainte Catherine de Sienne: Essai de critique des sources,* vol. 2 (Paris: E. de Boccard, 1930), Ch. 7-8.

Five of the original letters are preserved in Ms. T.III.3 of the Biblioteca Comunale of Siena: L. 298, 320, 319, 329, and 332. The other letters are preserved in a Sienese Confraternity (L. 365); at the monastery of San Rocco in Arcireale (L. 192); and at Saint Aloysius church in Oxford. This last letter is not numbered; Robert Fawtier published it in "Catheriniana," *Mélanges d'archéologie et d'histoire* 34 (1914): 31-32.

[51] L. 230 in *Lettere,* vol. 3, p. 312.

[52] Significantly, Catherine uses a very similar dialogue form to convey important theological and spiritual insights in her masterpiece called, appropriately, the *Dialogue of Divine Providence.*

[53] L. 16 in *Lettere,* vol. 1, pp. 52-53.

[54] The fact that only eight of Catherine's original letters survived may reflect the difficulties of the Trecento postal system, as well as the private nature of such an *epistolario.*

[55] See below for examples of Catherine's response to criticism of her itinerant preaching.

[56] L. 373 in *Lettere,* vol. 5, p. 291.

[57] L. 119 in *Lettere,* vol. 2, p. 190.

[58] L. 272 in *Lettere,* vol. 4, pp. 171-72.

[59] L. 312 in *Lettere,* vol. 5, p. 14.

[60] L. 364 in *Lettere,* vol. 5, p. 251.

[61] L. 373 in *Lettere,* vol. 5, p. 291.

[62] L. 309 in *Lettere,* vol. 4, p. 294. See also L. 316 and 318. Catherine's letters show that though she is aware the Christian Scriptures are actually written texts, the Bible she is familiar with is the oral text proclaimed and preached in church. She knows the provenance of certain phrases: "Taste and see" ("Gustate et vedete") comes from the Psalter, and "Come beloved bride" ("Vieni, diletta sposa mia") is part of the Song of Songs ("Cantica"). She has heard of the Old Testament ("Testamento vecchio"). She mentions the "Gospel" quite often, and she notes once that St. Paul communicated in "letters" ("pistola") (*Dialogo,* XI, p. 27). Still, for Catherine Scripture mostly takes the form of short pithy sayings; she does not comment on long Biblical texts or differentiate among the evangelists as writers. She is interested in what Jesus said, or in what God's trumpeter ("banditore") Paul said, not in where and how those spoken words were written.

[63] *Dialogo* LXXXV, pp. 194-95. Significantly, two centuries later the literate Teresa of Avila would advise the opposite to her nuns. See *The Life of Teresa of Jesus. The Autobiography of St. Teresa of Avila,* trans. E. Allison Peers (Garden City, NY: Image Books, 1960), Ch. XIII, pp. 144-47.

[64] *Dialogo* CXXV, p. 316.

[65] L. 135 in *Lettere,* vol. 2, p. 257.

[66] L. 320 in *Lettere,* vol. 5, p. 60.

[67] I have counted over thirty letters with probable references to secretaries. The question of how much these men and women influenced the content of Catherine's letters as they took her dictation or made clean copies of the texts is important and difficult. They certainly controlled details of spelling and punctuation, and it is likely that they inserted something of their own here and there. But they also revered Catherine as their spiritual teacher, and they would have felt that altering her words was sacriligeous. The opening and closing formulas bear Catherine's personal mark; her style and use of imagery are equally idiosyncratic. Overall, the letters do seem to convey Catherine's voice.

[68] L. 370 in *Lettere,* vol. 5, p. 272.

[69] L. 330 in *Lettere,* vol. 5, p. 87.

[70] In some cases Catherine entrusted the carrier with an oral message that was too important to be written down. See L. 295 in *Lettere,* vol. 4, p. 243: "Lasso questo e l'altre cose dire a Cristofano."

[71] L. 267 in *Lettere,* vol. 4, p. 147.

[72] L. 294 in *Lettere,* vol. 4, p. 239.

[73] L. 368 in *Lettere,* vol. 5, p. 265.

[74] L. 364 in *Lettere,* vol. 5, p. 252.

[75] L. 350 in *Lettere,* vol. 5, p. 187.

[76] L. 310 in *Lettere,* vol. 4, p. 306.

[77] *Dialogo,* p. 217.

[78] L. 318 in *Lettere,* vol. 5, p. 52.

[79] *Dialogo,* p. 15.

[80] S. Caterina da Siena, *Le Orazioni,* ed. Giuliana Cavallini (Rome: Edizioni cateriniane, 1978): Orazione III, p. 88.

[81] L. 349 in *Lettere,* vol. 5, p. 180.

[82] L. 198 in *Lettere,* vol. 3, p. 172.

[83] Karen Scott, "St. Catherine of Siena, *'Apostola',*" *Church History* 61 (March 1992): 34-46.

[84] L. 117 in *Lettere,* vol. 2, p. 185.

[85] See also Sharon Farmer, "Persuasive Voices: Clerical Images of Medieval Wives," *Speculum* 61 (1986): 517-43.

[86] L. 316 in *Lettere,* vol. 5, pp. 37-41.

[87] Christine de Pizan, *The Book of the City of Ladies,* trans. Earl Jeffrey Richards (London: Pan Books, 1983).

FURTHER READING

Bell, Rudolph M. "I, Catherine." In *Holy Anorexia,* pp. 22-53. Chicago, Ill.: University of Chicago Press, 1985.

Contends that Catherine's persistent fasting was deeply invested with religious symbolism and in its development followed the major turning points of her life.

Falassi, Alessandro. "Catherine of Siena: Life, Death and Miracles." *New York Folklore* 11, Nos. 1-4 (1985): 109-33.

Discusses the life and thought of Catherine of Siena and describes the strong following she acquired after her death.

Noffke, Suzanne. Introduction to *The Letters of St. Catherine of Siena, Volume I,* pp. 1-31. Binghamton, N.Y.: Medieval and Renaissance Texts and Studies, 1988.

Compares the existing collections, translations, and secondary scholarship of the letters of Catherine of Siena.

Ryley, M. Beresford. "Catherine of Siena: 1347-1380." In *Queens of the Renaissance,* pp. 1-52. London: Methuen & Co., 1907.

Argues that Catherine of Siena "represented a strain of feeling" that properly belongs to the Renaissance, although her life preceded that cultural period.

St. John
700?-752?

Byzantine (Syrian) theologian. Also known as St. John Damascene and St. Johannes Damascenus.

INTRODUCTION

John of Damascus was one of the first of a new generation of Christian theologians—the Scholastics—who attempted to transform a multiplicity of tenets and practices into a coherent and consistent system of beliefs. Although his major theological work was the task of compiling the wisdom of earlier leaders of the Church, John of Damascus is well known for his original contributions to the iconoclastic controversy that fractured the Christian church in the eighth and ninth centuries. His defense of the worship of images also led him to respond to the Muslim accusation that Christianity involved the practice of idolatry; his response took the form of a dialogue and was one of the first theological representations of the "heresy" of Islam to Christians.

Biographical Information

Although there is disagreement about the family background of John of Damascus, it is generally acknowledged that he was born around the end of the seventh century into a prominent Christian family. Damascus at that point in its history was a city ruled by a Muslim caliph (a successor to Mohammed), and John thus had a great deal of exposure to the tensions between the emerging beliefs of Islam and the slightly more well-established ones of Christianity. Fluent in Arabic, he seems to have been familiar with at least part of the *Koran*—the sacred text of Islam—as well as with scholarly interpretations of it. Before becoming a monk at the monastery of Saint Sabbas in Jerusalem, he occupied a hereditary political office in Damascus. He was interested in music and is also famous as a hymnographer. Known for his eloquence, John of Damascus wrote several treatises describing and defending orthodoxy, and is considered by many to be a transitional figure between the Eastern theologians of the early centuries of the Christian church and the European scholastics of the Middle Ages. Even after entering monastic life, he traveled extensively in Syria to defend the worship of images within Christian ritual. This view propelled him into a prominent place in the iconoclastic controversy and brought him sharp disapproval from the Byzantine Emperor Leo III (680?-741), against whose powerful interventions into church policy John of Damascus strenuously argued. John also traveled to Constantinople to meet with Leo's successor, Constantine V (719-775), to discuss the status of images within Christian doctrine. In general, however, John of Damascus did not engage in political activities, concentrating instead on compiling the wisdom of past theologians.

Major Works

John of Damascus took his most important task to be that of collecting and organizing the diversity of Christian thought into a coherent doctrinal system. According to most scholars, his greatest achievement was the *Sources of Knowledge* (written circa 743), also known as the *Fount of Knowledge,* which contains the three major works of *Capita Philosophica* (or *Dialectica*), an explanation of philosophical terms and ideas; *De Haeresibus,* a compilation of Christian and non-Christian heresies; and *De Fide Orthodoxa,* a systematic exposition of the Christian faith. The work is intended to instruct both negatively and positively—the heresies are described in order to reveal the error of those who might stray from the orthodox path. John of Damascus also is credited with writing two dialogues, *Disceptatio Christiani et Saraceni* and *Disputatio Saraceni et Christiani,* which represent the theological tensions between the two major religions of Palestine in the eighth century. Accordingly, John of Damascus is best known for his anti-Islamic polemics and his defense of Christian doctrine against the charge of idolatry, which Islamic scholars directed at Christianity. Islam is discussed as part of the catalogue of heresies in the *Sources of Knowledge:* John of Damascus frequently referred to Muslims as "Ishmaelites," or those who have fallen into the error of "deceptive superstition," an estrangement from orthodox Christianity. In particular, he criticized Islam for the rejection of the divinity of Christ and defended the paradoxical (and paradigmatically Christian) idea that the divine can also be incarnate. In his response to the Muslim accusation that Christians engage in idolatry, John of Damascus referred to the theological distinction between idols and icons: idols are associated with demons or, more generally, are images of beings which have no corporeal existence. Icons, contrastingly, are representations of corporeally existing beings. This difference between true and false images is intended to distinguish the Christian veneration of icons from pagan idolatry. It is Islam, John of Damascus countered, that practices idolatry, manifested in the worship of the "morning star and Aphrodite" (both are designations of the planet Venus, depending on its position in the sky; this worship was a practice preserved from pre-Islamic religion in Arabia), and the veneration of the Ka'ba. Although he recognized that Mohammed returned the Arabic people to monotheism, John of Damascus characterized him as a "false prophet," one who does not accept the tripartite nature of God. In general, John of Damascus sought to introduce Islam, as a nascent system of beliefs, to Christians as a way of deterring them from falling into a heretical understanding of the divine. This task typifies his larger goal of systematizing Christian doctrine.

Textual History

Due to the propensity of John of Damascus to compile the writings of others, as well as to revise extensively his own work, it is difficult to establish precisely what he wrote and what he merely collected. Some critics have contended that the entire list of heresies (*De Haeresibus*) cannot be attributed to John of Damascus, as this part of the *Sources of Knowledge* does not appear in all editions of that work, particularly in early manuscripts. As the other two parts form a coherent unit, it has been suggested that the catalogue of heresies was incorporated later. Its first eighty chapters seem to have been copied from a fourth-century work, the *Panarion,* by Saint Epiphanius of Salamis. Yet most scholars have concluded that *De Haeresibus* is an "integral part," as Sahas claims, of the *Sources of Knowledge,* for it functions as a critical contrast to the exposition of Christian doctrine in the concluding part, *De Fide Orthodoxa.* Another controversy with regard to the authorship of this text is the question of the authenticity of Chapter 101 (as it appears in the nineteenth-century edition), the chapter that deals with the heresy of Islam. It can be distinguished both by its length and its style from the first one hundred chapters: its discussion of Islam is an extended dialogue. As early as the ninth century, however, this chapter was included in editions of the work. Although the issue of the authorship of Chapter 101 remains a subject of debate among scholars, the chapter is still primarily acknowledged to be the work of John of Damascus. Apart from this major theological work, John of Damascus is also generally credited with two dialogues between a "Saracen" (a Muslim) and a Christian, but John Meyendorff has argued that both are actually the work of Theodore Abu-Qurra and were merely compiled by John. All of these texts were preserved under the name of John of Damascus in church documents and were published in the nineteenth-century in J. P. Migne's authoritative *Patrologiae Cursus Completus.*

Critical Reception

John of Damascus is generally considered to have been an important compiler of orthodox Christian doctrine, a function that places him between the early period of Christianity, which involved significant diversity and strife regarding central tenets and practices, and the Scholastic era. His defense of icons also places him at the center of the iconoclastic controversy, a crisis that contributed to theological differences between the Western and Eastern Church. It is his encounter with Islam, however, that has engendered the most critical attention in recent years. There is considerable disagreement about the extent of his knowledge about Islam—how familiar he might have been with all or part of the *Koran*, his understanding of the nature of the divine in Islam, and his grasp of Muslim law. In addition, there is much debate about the adequacy of John's responses to the Muslim charge of idolatry and the cogency of his counter-accusations. Most critics do acknowledge that John of Damascus had some sophisticated understanding of Islamic beliefs and practices, although his interpretation was significantly influenced by his designation of Islam as a heresy. His writings provide significant insights into the theological character of eighth-century Christianity, although Christian practices varied widely, as John's determined attempt to establish a single set of doctrines indicates. His fundamentally conservative approach manifests his belief that knowledge is a form of "spiritual contemplation" and that the greatest knowledge had already been divulged by past theologians. Later scholars within the Christian church have conformed to this approach, and therefore John of Damascus has had a crucial influence on such thinkers as Peter Lombard and Thomas Aquinas. Accordingly, as David Anderson has argued, the questions and tensions that animate John of Damascus's writings remain relevant for contemporary religious thinkers. Specifically, the problem of divine incarnation and the difficult issue of encounters between Christianity and "heresies," both within and outside of the Church, still inform contemporary religious scholarship.

PRINCIPAL WORKS

Disceptatio Christiani et Saraceni (dialogue)

Disputatio Saraceni et Christiani (dialogue)

Sources of Knowledge (philosophy) c. 743

PRINCIPAL ENGLISH TRANSLATIONS

"The Apology of John of Damascus" [translated by John W. Voorhis] 1934

Saint John of Damascus: Writings [translated by Frederic H. Chase] 1958

On the Divine Images [translated by David Anderson] 1980

CRITICISM

Arthur Cushman McGiffert (essay date 1932)

SOURCE: "John of Damascus and the Eastern Church of the Middle Ages," in *A History of Christian Thought, Vol. I: Early and Eastern, from Jesus to John of Da-mascus,* Charles Scribner's Sons, 1949, pp. 308-32.

[*In the essay below, originally published in 1932, McGiffert locates the theological work of John of Damascus within the broader context of the early Christian church. In particular, the critic focuses on the third book of the* Sources of Knowledge—*the* Exposition of the Orthodox Faith—*finding that it provided no new or profound insights, but acknowledging that it significantly influenced the theology of the Eastern church for many ensuing decades.*]

With the third Council of Constantinople which met in 680 the dogmatic development in the eastern church came to a close, except for the dogma of image-worship enunciated in 787 at the second Council of Nicæa, the seventh œcumenical council. In the first half of the eighth century the development was summed up by John of Damascus, the last of the outstanding theologians of the eastern church and the first great scholastic. With him the productive period in theology may be said to have closed so far as the east was concerned. John himself as a matter of fact did not contribute to the development in any significant way. He was a systematizer rather than a creative thinker and he added nothing important of his own. But he summed up all that had gone before and set it out in clear and orderly fashion, thus supplying the Greek communion with an orthodox system of theology which has remained normative ever since.

John came of a prominent Christian family of Damascus and after his father's death held political office there under the Caliph, an office hereditary in his family. After a time however for reasons unknown he abandoned his public career and retired to the monastery of St. Sabas near Jerusalem, where he spent the remainder of his life. While there he was ordained a presbyter in the church of Jerusalem, but he continued to live in the monastery and devoted himself chiefly to studying and writing. He was a great scholar, perhaps the greatest of his age. He was also a voluminous writer and his extant works, including many of doubtful authenticity, cover a wide range of subjects.

He first attracted general notice by his spirited defense of image-worship in opposition to the iconoclastic policy of Emperor Leo the Isaurian. In three successive treatises he set forth in vigorous fashion the familiar arguments for the use of images[1] in churches: that they aid devotion; that they make Christ and the saints more real; that there is the same reason for them as for other sensible signs of spiritual realities; that the prohibition against images in the decalogue has no application since Christ came in the flesh and thus made God visible; that the worship afforded visible things is not the highest form of worship, which is reserved for God alone, but a lower form which amounts to no more than homage or reverence; that it is proper thus to honour every sacred object, pictures of Christ and the saints as well as the eucharistic elements, the cross, the altar and other things of the kind; that it is not the visible object that is really honoured but the one represented by it; and finally that to refrain from venerating things because they are material is to treat matter as evil and thus to fall into the heresy of the Manichæans. John also argued earnestly and boldly for the freedom of the church which he claimed was threatened by the Emperor's effort to force his will upon it and to dictate its policy in spiritual affairs.[2] As was his custom in most of his works he appealed both to the Scriptures and to the Fathers in support of his position. Among the latter he cited Dionysius the Areopagite first of all, referring to him in high terms as holy and divine and an expert in the things of God.

In addition to the treatises on the worship of images John's writings include an extended philosophical and theological work entitled ***The Fount of Knowledge;*** a large thesaurus of passages from Scripture and the Fathers bearing chiefly on ethical topics and known as the Sacra parallela; Christological essays defending the orthodox position against Nestorians, Monophysites and Monothelites; an apology for Christianity against Mohammedanism in the form of a dialogue between a Saracen and a Christian; commentaries, homilies, ascetic tracts, liturgical canons, and hymns. He was much interested in ecclesiastical music and was a famous composer and hymn-writer. Some of his productions are still used in the services of the Greek church, notably at Christmas and Easter.

His most important work and the only one that need engage our attention here is his ***Fount of Knowledge,*** divided into three parts, the first containing philosophical prolegomena, the second a history of heresy, and the third a summary of the orthodox faith. The first part is entitled ***Philosophical Topics*** and is commonly referred to as ***Dialectica.*** It opens with the words "Nothing is more excellent than knowledge," and the third chapter contains six definitions of philosophy. "Philosophy is the knowledge of things as they are, that is, of the nature of things"; "the knowledge of divine and human affairs, that is, the visible and invisible"; "meditation on death"; "imitation of God"; "the art of arts and science of sciences"; "the love of wisdom." Philosophy is divided, John says, into speculative and practical; speculative philosophy into theology, physiology and mathematics, and practical philosophy into ethics, economics (or domestic economy), and politics. There follows a definition of each of these, and the body of the book is devoted to a detailed discussion of a variety of philosophical conceptions: being, substance, accident, genus, species, the individual, identity and difference, form, quantity, quality, time, simultaneity, succession, propositions, syllogisms, and the like. As was natural John was particularly interested in theological and Christological terms, but his discussion is by no means confined to them. In fact it covers a wide range of topics and fulfills capitally the purpose of a philosophical introduction to Christian theology as it was understood in his day. The philosophical presuppositions are in the main Aristotelian, supplemented and modified here and there by Neoplatonic ideas.[3]

The second part of the ***Fount of Knowledge*** deals with heresies, and is little more than an abridgment of Epiphanius' work against heresies with additions from Theodoret and others, supplemented by a few contributions from the pen of the author himself. These last have to do with errors originating since the time of Epiphanius and Theodoret, particularly Mohammedanism which is discussed at considerable length.

The third part of the ***Fount of Knowledge*** is entitled ***Exposition of the Orthodox Faith*** and contains a systematic presentation of the theology of the eastern church. It was not intended to set forth the results of John's own independent thinking but only the truths taught by the Bible and the Fathers. The three Cappadocians, particularly Gregory Nazianzen, are followed most closely, and in certain parts of the work Dionysius the Areopagite. Use is made also of many other Fathers of the fourth and following centuries, among them Athanasius, Chrysostom, Nemesius of Emesa, Cyril of Alexandria and Leontius of Byzantium. Origen, in accordance with the general opinion of his day, John regarded as a heretic and referred to him only to condemn him.

In the strict sense the eastern church of John's age had only two dogmas: the Trinity, promulgated at the Council of Nicæa, and the Person of Christ, formulated at the Council of Chalcedon and later synods. But there was a large circle of beliefs which made up the orthodox faith and were also counted as authoritative. The Nicæno-Constantinopolitan Creed, the great symbol of the eastern church, in addition to the doctrine of the Trinity contains the incarnation of the Son of God for our salvation, the virgin birth, the crucifixion, resurrection, and ascension of Christ and his return for judgment, the Holy Catholic church, baptism for the remission of sins, the resurrection of the dead and life everlasting. All these constituted a part of the church's faith and were esteemed as irrefragable and as binding on the conscience of Christians as the dogmas of the Trinity and the Person of Christ. Beyond these there were still other doctrines generally recognized as orthodox. With them as well as with the dogmas of the church in the narrower sense John dealt in his ***Exposition of the Orthodox Faith.***

It is interesting to compare John's work[4] with Origen's *De principiis,* the first system of theology. While the *De principiis* was an attempt not merely to state the common faith of the church but also to discover the deeper truths involved in or to be deduced from it, the ***Exposition of the Orthodox Faith*** was only a summary of what was already believed. Origen's work was original and creative in no mean degree; John's was quite without new ideas. The latter was more nearly akin to Theodoret's *Epitome of Divine Dogmas,* the fifth and last book of his treatise against heresy in which he supplemented his polemic with a statement of the true Christian faith, to show what ought to be believed in contrast with the false teachings of the heretics. John followed Theodoret somewhat closely but his method was different and his work covered many subjects omitted by the earlier theologian. In fact it was constructed on a larger scale and included the results of the dogmatic development since Theodoret's day especially in Christology.

In spite of its lack of originality the value of John's work was very great. It served an important purpose and was excellently adapted to the existing situation. The author had a marked capacity for systematic thinking and his gift of clear and concise statement was considerable. To be sure the work was not without its repetitions, irrelevancies and obscurities, but on the whole it fulfilled its aim admirably and its reputation was so great that it was never superseded in the eastern church.

The work was divided by John into a hundred chapters; the division into four books, which is followed in all our editions, dates from a later time. The first book, containing fourteen chapters, deals with God. Here John follows Gregory Nazianzen and Dionysius the Areopagite most closely. In agreement with them God is represented as incomprehensible and ineffable and above all being. Not that he does not exist but that he is more than all existing things and even existence itself.[5] Knowledge has to do with what is and if God is above all being he must also be above all knowledge. We can assert what he is not but not what he is.

Nevertheless, though God is above human comprehension, he has not left us in complete ignorance of himself. He has implanted in all men the conviction that he exists. Moreover, the creation of the world and its preservation and government show his power and majesty, and through the law and the prophets and through Jesus Christ he has told us all that it was possible or profitable to acquaint us with. Beyond this we must not go. On the contrary we must be content with what has been revealed and be careful not to overstep tradition.[6]

Notwithstanding all John has to say about the incomprehensibility of God there are really many things we know about him. We know, for instance, that he is eternal, uncreated, unchangeable, uncompounded, incorporeal, invisible, impalpable, infinite, without limits; the creator of all things; almighty, all-controlling, all-seeing; just and good; sovereign and judge. We know too that he is one, that is of one substance (ousia), and that he subsists in three hypostases: Father, Son and Holy Spirit. But what his substance is and how it exists as it does we do not know. Like Gregory of Nyssa and the other Cappadocian Fathers, John thought of abstract being existing in three individuals or persons, rather than of one personal being existing in three relations.[7]

Though the knowledge of God's existence is inborn, Satan has led many to deny it. John therefore repeats the common theistic proofs from a changeable world to an unchanging creator and from an ordered world to an intelligent designer—proofs that had been used by Christian theologians from the beginning. Similarly the familiar arguments are employed to show that God is one not many.[8] There follow chapters on the Logos, on the Holy Spirit, and on the Trinity, in which the traditional positions are set forth clearly and explicitly without addition or subtraction.[9] These chapters constitute an admirably clear and succinct account of the orthodox doctrine of the Trinity. They are supplemented by a discussion of the names of God and the anthropomorphisms of Scripture, which is entirely in the spirit of Dionysius and in which he is referred to and quoted more than once.

The second book, containing more than thirty chapters, deals with the creation. God in his goodness not being content to contemplate himself brought other beings into existence that they might enjoy his benefits. He created everything by thinking of it, the Logos carrying out his thought and the Spirit perfecting it.[10] The account of the creation begins, as was customary, with the angels, who are intelligent, incorporeal beings, endowed with free will and able either to remain good as they were created or to choose evil. However, if they choose evil they are without the power to repent which belongs only to corporeal beings, for man's repentance is due to the weakness of his body. A little later John says that repentance is impossible to the fallen angels because their fall is final, just as death is final for men. Though incorporeal, angels can be and act only in one place at a time, but they are in perpetual motion and are so swift that wherever the divine glance bids them go they are immediately there. They are immortal not by nature but by grace, for everything that has a beginning comes to an end unless preserved by God. God alone is eternal, for he who created time is not subject to time but above it. Angels are the guardians of nations and regions of the earth over which they are set by God, and they govern all human affairs and bring men help as it may be needed. Their duty is to sing God's praise and carry out his will.

The prince of this world, to whom God committed the care of it, was created good and for a good purpose, but with a host of angels who were subject to him he rebelled against his creator. From him and his followers all evil comes, but men are able to withstand them and resist temptation if they will. In agreement with the Areopagite and the Neoplatonists, John says that evil is nothing else than the absence of good, as darkness is only the absence of light.[11] Though he repeated the statement later in his work he did not make earnest with the notion or draw the consequences that naturally follow from it. As a matter of fact the metaphysic on which it was based was not his and the idea itself was out of line with his general attitude. As a rule he spoke of evil not as the mere absence of good but as something very positive, and he followed the common Christian tradition in viewing death as a punishment inflicted on man for his sin rather than a natural consequence of the loss of good and hence of being.

After dealing with the angels, good and bad, John turns to the visible creation. In this part of his work he follows Aristotle and Ptolemy and particularly the Cappadocian Basil, whose Hexæmeron, treating of the early chapters of Genesis, was a standard work among Christians both in east and west. God made the visible universe out of nothing, part of it directly, such as heaven, earth, air, fire, and water, part of it indirectly, as for instance living creatures who are composed of already created substances.[12]

The chapters on the visible creation contain summaries of current ideas on astronomy, physics, geology and geography, which show that the orthodox faith was supposed to include much more than mere theology, though to be sure alternative views are sanctioned in more than one instance, and it was evidently not intended to make a particular scientific opinion obligatory on Christians except in so far as it might be supported by Scripture. Even these scientific subjects were made to serve a religious end. The lesson is drawn, for instance, from the relation of the sun and moon that men should live in an ordered society and should not question the authority of the rulers set over them by God. Eclipses show the changeableness of all created things and the folly of those who worship the creature instead of the creator. Astrology is rejected because it substitutes fate for free will and thus makes God unjust when he gives good things to some and evil things to others.

A considerable part of the second book is devoted to man. Here John followed Aristotle closely, deviating from him only when his views were out of agreement with Christian tradition. Man is a microcosm, connected through his body with the whole visible creation, animate and inanimate, and through his reason with the invisible world of incorporeal and intelligent beings.[13] He is composed of body and soul, the two being created simultaneously. In this connection John rejected with scorn Origen's doctrine of the preëxistence of souls. Though created at the same time with the body the soul, according to John, is wholly independent of it and makes such use of it as it will, for all the powers of the body are under its control. Pleasure, pain, fear, anger, imagination, sensation, thought, memory are discussed at some length. The organ of imagination is placed in the front of the brain, the organ of thought in the middle, and the organ of memory at the back.[14]

The freedom of the will is asserted, freedom being inseparable from rationality. That the will is free is proved by the fact that men deliberate before acting, and to pronounce the fairest and most precious of man's endowments superfluous is the height of absurdity.[15] The book closes with a discussion of providence and predestination and their relation to free will. All things are foreknown but not predetermined by God. He does not cause evil; nevertheless he permits it and overrules it for good. He is the source and cause of all good and without his coöperation we can neither will nor do any good thing, but it is in our power to remain virtuous, as we were created, or to depart from God and fall into wickedness. John's discussion is brief and superficial. Free will is asserted in unequivocal terms, but the problems involved in it, particularly the difficulties inherent in any attempt to reconcile it with divine predestination are not appreciated and are dismissed in a few sentences. Evidently while free will was very important to John, as to the Greek Fathers in general, he did not take divine predestination seriously.

The third book and the first eight chapters of the fourth are devoted to the person and work of Christ, particularly his person, which is dealt with much more carefully and at much greater length than his work. Man, having yielded to the temptation of Satan, was banished from Paradise, condemned to death and made subject to corruption. God, however, did not desert him. On the contrary he had compassion on him and by various means strove to release him from the control of sin, above all by the incarnation of his only-begotten Son, the divine Logos. The incarnation showed both the goodness and the justice of God, his goodness in having compassion on man and his justice in that Satan was overcome not by some alien power but by man himself in the person of Jesus Christ.

Being perfect God the Logos became perfect man and thus Christ had two complete natures, divine and human, neither being absorbed by the other and neither being altered by the union. The result was not one composite nature but two simple natures, divine and human, united in the one person Jesus Christ. To the elucidation and defense of the doctrine of one person in two natures John devotes several chapters.[16] Christ had not only two natures—divine and human—but also two wills and energies, will and energy belonging to nature rather than to person.[17] It is Christ who wills, that is, the willing is done by the one composite person Jesus Christ, but in willing he employs either the divine or the human will, or both of them, the two being always perfectly in harmony one with the other.[18] John laid great emphasis on this doctrine of two wills in Christ—the doctrine officially promulgated at the sixth œcumenical council of 680—and expounded and defended it at considerable length in opposition to the Monothelites who were evidently still formidable. On the whole these Christological chapters (chapters 3 to 19) constitute one of the clearest and best summaries of the orthodox Christology that we have. At the same time John did not succeed in doing away with the ambiguities and resolving the contradictions involved in that Christology any more than those who preceded him.

The account of the orthodox Christology is followed by several chapters on Christ's human nature as exhibited in his earthly career.[19] In these chapters John endeavors, on the one hand, in opposition to the Monophysites, to show that Jesus Christ was a real man possessed of complete human nature with all its passions and limitations, including weakness and fear and ignorance, on the other hand, in opposition to the Nestorians, to show that the union between the divine and human in Christ was perfect and that because of it he was superior to the limitations of humanity: that he was sinless, sin being due not to man's natural desires but wholly to the temptation of the devil who was unable to prevail over the Lord, that he was without fear, except the natural physical shrinking from death, that he knew all things and was in possession of miraculous power, and that he was complete in wisdom and grace from the beginning, so that his apparent growth in them, spoken of in Scripture, meant only their increasing manifestation. Moreover, his praying recorded in the gospels was not because of any need of his own but only that he might set us an example.

These chapters, unlike the preceding, are lame and halting and reveal the increasing difficulties in which the orthodox Christology was involved when it was applied to the actual life of Jesus, in other words when it was brought down from the abstract to the concrete, from the realm of metaphysics to that of psychology. As a matter of fact, as was seen in a previous chapter, the orthodox Christology was built not on the life of the historic figure Jesus Christ, as reflected in the gospels, but on a theory of redemption framed in large part independently of him and translated into the terms of the prevailing philosophy of the age. To bring it into harmony with the life of Jesus was naturally difficult as John's treatment abundantly shows.

John's controlling interest, like that of most of the eastern Fathers for some centuries before his time, was Christological rather than soteriological. The greater part of the third book and several chapters of the fourth were devoted to the person of Christ and even in his philosophical prolegomena he had something to say upon the subject. In comparison he concerned himself little with Christ's saving work. After referring to the incarnation very briefly at the beginning of the third book—where the method of it seems to interest him more than the fact itself—he entered upon a protracted discussion of the person and natures of Christ and only at the end of the book spoke of him in passing as having offered himself to the Father as a ransom, thus freeing men from condemnation. In this connection the old idea shared by Origen and others that the ransom was paid to Satan is repudiated in strong terms.

In the fourth chapter of the fourth book, where John has most to say about the work of Christ, he declares that Christ came to restore the likeness of God, which man had lost by his sin, to free men from corruption and death by granting them communion with himself, to teach them virtue and make virtuous living easier, to redeem them from the tyranny of the devil by giving them a knowledge of God, to break the power of demons and remove the terror of death by implanting the assurance of a resurrection. In chapter nine it is remarked that Christ redeemed man from corruption through his passion, and in chapter thirteen that he took on our nature in order to cleanse us and make us incorruptible, and to give us again a share in his divinity which was lost by the fall. "Through his birth, or incarnation, and his baptism and passion and resurrection, he freed our nature from the sin of our first parent and from death and corruption, and became the first fruits of the resurrection, and made himself a way and image and pattern that we also, following in his footsteps, might become by adoption what he is by nature, sons and heirs of God and joint heirs with him."[20]

In these scattered passages there are traces of various traditional notions about Christ's work, but a clear and definite theory is altogether lacking. Irenæus' idea of the transformation of human nature by its union with the divine, an idea that was shared by Athanasius and underlay his insistence upon the real deity of Christ, is suggested but not stated clearly. The notion of Christ's death as a ransom for sin is also referred to, but only in passing, and the same is true of the common belief that his work was that of a teacher and exemplar, revealing God and inciting to virtue. As a matter of fact the orthodox faith of the eastern church of John's time included no definite doctrine of Christ's saving work. The doctrine of his person had so absorbed the attention of theologians as almost completely to crowd out all interest in anything else. The Nicæno-Constantinopolitan Creed says only that the Son of God became incarnate for our salvation and beyond that the eastern church did not go. It is noticeable also that the connection between Christ's person and saving work, which had meant so much to Paul and Irenæus and Athanasius, was altogether lost sight of by John. The deity of Christ as he viewed it did not depend in any way, as it did to them, upon man's need of redemption by deification. Person and work had fallen completely apart and had become independent and unrelated items of the orthodox faith.

Even more striking than the small amount of attention given to the saving work of Christ is the complete absence of any section dealing with salvation itself and the way of salvation. It is clear from passing remarks that John thought of salvation as involving the deification of man or his participation in the nature of Deity,[21] and that he shared the common notion of a future life of eternal blessedness to be enjoyed by the saved. It is clear too that he regarded both faith and works as necessary to salvation, and also the regeneration and the remission of sins to be had in baptism; but all this appears only by the way and in connection with the discussion of other matters. Whether because he was less interested in it or thought it too well understood to need dwelling upon at any rate John had much less to say about soteriology than about Christology.

After finishing his treatment of Christ, to which the whole of the third book and the first eight chapters of the fourth are devoted, John deals in the remainder of his work with a variety of subjects thrown together with little regard for logical sequence. In these chapters he recurs to matters already discussed in earlier parts of the work, as for instance the person and work of Christ, Mary the Mother of God, the freedom of the will, the nature of evil and God's permission of it. In addition he treats of certain subjects not already touched upon, among them faith, baptism, the eucharist, the worship of saints and images, the Bible, the Sabbath, virginity, Antichrist, and the resurrection. There is little in these chapters that needs mention. Faith, the author says, is of two kinds: the acceptance of the truth taught by the Catholic church and the confident assurance that God will answer our prayers and will fulfill his promises.[22] The latter is a gift of the Spirit, the former is in our own power—an interesting example of the notion current within the church from an early day that belief is a matter of will, and that wrong belief is therefore morally reprehensible. Of the connection of faith with salvation nothing is said.[23] Indeed, as already remarked, the whole subject of salvation and the way of salvation is passed by without discussion.

In a chapter on the Holy and Immaculate Mysteries of the Lord[24] John maintains and defends at some length the theory that the bread and wine in the eucharist are supernaturally changed[25] into the body and blood of Christ or into the body and blood of God as he also phrases it. They are therefore, he insists, not merely figuratively but in reality the deified body of the Lord. The change of bread and wine is complete so that there are in the eucharist body and blood alone, not in addition to bread and wine. In this matter John followed the common opinion of the eastern church. The change of the elements was clearly taught by Cyril of Jerusalem, Gregory of Nyssa, Chrysostom, Theodoret and others and was generally taken for granted in John's day.[26]

The use of bread and wine in the euchrist John explained as due to man's weakness which makes the unfamiliar and unusual repellent to him. Because of this God has appointed common objects both in baptism and the eucharist in order that by employing things that are natural we may rise to a knowledge of the supernatural. In partaking of the eucharist we not only commune with Christ and share in his divine nature,[27] we commune also with our fellow Christians, becoming one body of Christ and members one of another. We must therefore see to it that we do not commune with heretics, for if we do we become one with them and thus share in their condemnation. Nothing is said about our sharing in the condemnation of the wicked if we partake of the eucharist in company with those whose character and conduct are not what they should be.

While John made a great deal of the eucharist as communion with Christ and participation in his divine nature, the sacrificial idea of it, emphasized among other eastern Fathers by Cyril of Jerusalem and Chrysostom, he referred to only in passing and in the most general terms. This was in harmony with his customary attitude, for his interest was rather in the mystical than in the legal aspect of Christianity.

The perpetual virginity of Mary the Mother of God is asserted in chapter fourteen and in chapter twenty-four virginity is extolled as an ideal for all Christians. Marriage to be sure is not wrong, for it has been approved by God, but celibacy is more honourable, as much more honourable than marriage as angels are higher than men. The lack of a reference to monasticism in this connection is surprising, all the more so because John himself was a monk and because Dionysius had so much to say about it in his Ecclesiastical Hierarchy.

The resurrection of the body is dwelt upon in the closing chapter of the work. If there is to be no resurrection, John says, let us live a life of mere pleasure. Except for the resurrection we differ in no way from the brutes and are even more miserable than they, for their lives are free from sorrow. Unless the dead rise there is neither God nor providence, for the good suffer and the wicked prosper in this life. Divine justice demands that there shall be a resurrection and that the righteous shall be rewarded and the wicked punished everlastingly. Why the punishment should be everlasting John does not say. Very likely he never asked himself the question but simply took the traditional opinion for granted. The fire of hell, he maintains, is not material, but what its nature may be is known to God alone. At this point as at some others he takes refuge in a wholesome agnosticism.

Only less surprising than the omission of a section on salvation and the way of salvation, to which allusion has already been made, was John's failure to include any doctrine of the church. The existence of the Catholic church was taken for granted and the necessity of accepting the orthodox faith as taught by it, but nothing is said about the nature of the church, its origin, its purpose, or its place in the divine plan of salvation. Moreover nothing is said about the various orders of the clergy or the distinction between the clergy and the laity. In fact both ecclesiasticism and sacerdotalism are wholly lacking in John's work. There is lacking also all reference to penance[28] which the western church was making much of. Indeed, as already remarked, the legal side of Christianity, from the beginning so prominent in the west, was evidently of less interest to John than the mystical. To be sure he insisted that good works are necessary as well as faith and that without obedience there is no salvation,[29] but his emphasis lay rather on union with God and participation in the divine nature, and in this he was typical of the eastern church in general.

The account that has been given of John's ***Exposition of the Orthodox Faith*** shows that his treatment of the subject was neither profound nor marked by fresh insights. Especially noticeable is the lack of any controlling principle binding the various doctrines together. The subject of Christology, which he regarded as most important and treated at greatest length, was left quite unrelated to everything else, and the same is true of all the other matters dealt with. Most of the beliefs described might have been accepted without involving the acceptance of any others. Thus the systematic character of the work is wholly external. It is a system of theology only in the sense that it describes and expounds a large number of theological beliefs, not in the sense that they are wrought into a concatenated whole. In the latter sense the eastern church of John's day had no system of theology and his work was therefore truly representative. The lack which we may feel in it was not felt by his contemporaries or by those who came after him. To them, as to him, the orthodox faith embraced a multiplicity of doctrines altogether or largely independent of each other, which were to be accepted because taught by the Scriptures and the Fathers. Their acceptance rested wholly upon authority, though in some cases rational grounds existed and might be urged in their support if it were clearly understood that the real and sufficient ground for believing them was not that they were rational or good but that they had been divinely revealed.

I referred above to another of John's works, the ***Sacra parallela,*** a large collection of passages from the Bible and the Fathers bearing upon ethics. What has been said about the lack of a controlling principle, binding together the several parts of the ***Exposition of the Orthodox Faith,*** is true also of the ***Sacra parallela.*** The ethics of the latter is as atomic as the theology of the former. There is no attempt in either work to relate the various items to each other, to show their mutual dependence, or to trace them to a common root. Equally noticeable is the lack of any connection between ethics and theology. If theology, as set forth by John, appears largely unrelated to religion, it appears equally unrelated to moral conduct, except for the fact that it is God's will we should live virtuously and that he will reward us if we do and punish us if we do not. Authority is the last word in both fields. We believe and we do whatever is required by God. In faith as in conduct not what seems good to us, or true and right in itself, but what has been commanded—this is our duty, to be fulfilled humbly and unquestioningly.

John's ***Exposition of the Faith*** (for that matter the ***Sacra parallela*** as well) reflected the spirit of his day. Everywhere it was felt that the age was barren and unproductive and that all wisdom belonged to the past. In philosophy as in theology the attitude was the same. There was no thought of discovering new truth or attaining new points of view. The most that could be done was to reproduce and expound the opinions of the great thinkers of the past. This task John performed admirably. But to learn from his exposition what Christianity really is, or what it was even to John and his contemporaries, would be very difficult if not impossible. His doctrinal work is not a formulation of the religious experience of Christians or of the truths involved therein, nor is it an account of the religious values which were conserved by Christianity. It has indeed very little to do with religion, and still less with the actual experience of religious men. It deals mainly with such matters as the nature of God, the nature of the universe, the nature of man, and the nature of Christ. These fill the greater part of the work and give it its prevailing character. In comparison with what is said of such philosophical and scientific subjects, for they are all philosophical or scientific not religious, the references to religious matters like divine providence, faith, salvation, and union with God, and to Christian ceremonies like baptism and the eucharist, are unimportant and bulk very small.

It may undoubtedly be taken for granted that the Christianity depicted in John's work was not the real Christianity of the eastern church of his day. To be sure the same might be said of much if not most of the theology of the past, which has had as a rule little relation to the religious life of Christians. But the disparity between theology and religion has perhaps never been more clearly seen than in John's work. After all this is not surprising, for the absorption for so many centuries of the leading theologians of the east in speculative Christological questions wholly divorced from the practical religious life made anything else impossible.

The Christians of the east in John's day—and what was true then has been generally true ever since—found their Christianity chiefly in the cultus. Parallel with the doctrinal evolution that has been traced went a development in the matter of worship which touched the people much more nearly. The influence of the Græco-Oriental world was felt as truly in the one as in the other. The ritual of the eastern church with its sacraments and other sacred rites, its elaborate ceremonial, its worship of Mary and the saints, its veneration of relics and the like, was as syncretistic as its theology. There entered into it age-old superstitions and practices which long antedated Christianity itself and which serve to bind the Christian east, not of the Middle Ages alone but of modern times as well, with the pagan east of a remote antiquity.

Moreover, as in the ethnic religions ritual practices meant more than theology to the masses of the people so it was in the Christian church. It is not the place in a history of Christian thought to deal with the cultus in detail or to trace its development; only the underlying principles concern us here. These principles, in the eastern church at least—and it is with that church alone that we have to do at present—were largely identical with those that underlay the pagan mysteries. Through the cultus Christians come into union with God. Participating in the sacraments of the church and sharing in its worship they enjoy communion with him and become partakers of his divinity and heirs of immortality. The worship of the church is made up of a series of sacred and symbolic acts, looking upon which men are lifted above themselves and brought into the presence of the divine. More and more as time passed this seemed to the mass of Christians the whole of Christianity, and more and more to the theologians themselves if not the whole of Christianity at least the major part of it.

Because the cultus included the recitation or the chanting of the creed the latter also had its part in the deification of the Christian; it too was a sacred symbol by means of which union between the Christian and his God is promoted. Dogma gradually lost all independent significance and was regarded as essential only because embodied in the worship of the church. Not as the formulation of truth but as a holy mystery it was of value. To understand it therefore was not important but to preserve it intact. It was this conception of the place of dogma that came to expression in the notorious controversy over the *filioque*.[30] To keep the ancient symbol verbally unchanged was a paramount religious duty.

In this chapter on John of Damascus I have allowed myself to give a more detailed account of his ***Exposition of the Orthodox Faith*** than the interest of the work itself might seem to warrant. My justification is its genuinely representative character and the degree to which it dominated for centuries the theological thinking of the eastern church. In studying it we have in effect been studying the theology of that church as it prevailed throughout the Middle Ages. The divorce between theology and religion, the lack of a controlling principle binding the various items of the orthodox faith into a consistent whole, the scholasticism that marks the treatment—all these are characteristic not simply of John's work, but of the writings of those that came after him. His influence was very great. Few questions were raised by his successors that he had not already discussed, and, if not always at any rate usually, their solutions and his agreed. His position in the east was not unlike that of Thomas Aquinas in the west, though he had fewer rivals and enjoyed a more undivided allegiance. Nor was his influence confined to the east. His ***Exposition of the Orthodox Faith*** was translated into Latin in the twelfth century and was highly regarded by theologians of the west, particularly by Peter Lombard and Thomas Aquinas who made large use of it.

With John our account of Christian thought in the eastern church may fairly be brought to a close. There were theologians after him. Indeed throughout the Middle Ages the greater part of Byzantine literature was theological or religious. But there was little creative thinking and it is not important to follow the subject further here. The Byzantine east was not intellectually stagnant during the Middle Ages as is often said. As a matter of fact until the fourteenth and fifteenth centuries the level of culture was higher there than in the west. But the deference to the past was so great and its authority so complete that little independent thinking was done in any lines, least of all in theology. Some centuries after John's time the Greek church took over from the Roman the latter's doctrine of the sacraments, and in certain other matters the influence of the west was felt to some degree. But all this was of minor importance. The development of Christian thought in the east was already virtually complete when John produced his summary of the orthodox faith.

On the other hand, in the west the development still went on and has not even yet come to an end. In part it paralleled that of the east; many of the questions asked and answered were duplicates, if not echoes, of those discussed by eastern theologians. In still greater part the west expended its efforts in other directions. Its religious leaders faced a frontier of civilization. They inherited a political and cultural empire. They had to deal with a wholly new set of problems arising from the fact that individuals were jolted loose from their ancestral securities as they were not in the east, and needed moral reinforcing and stabilizing. For a time, not long after the conclusion of the productive era of eastern thought, western thinking also appeared doomed to stagnation. But appearances were deceptive, and under the surface its vitality remained unimpaired. Quickened by unfamiliar and challenging situations, and fertilized, among other things, by fresh contacts with Greek philosophy, it flowered anew in the creative work of the leading schoolmen and seemed vigorous and commanding enough to bend the forces of the modern age to its service. Then came the Protestant Reformation and the beginning of changes that are still going on. All this lies beyond the horizon of the present volume and will have to be treated later. But though more intimately connected with our contemporary religion and culture, it cannot be understood without the development that has been already traced. For our modern Christianity, whether Catholic or Protestant, is the heir of both east and west.

Notes

[1] In the east these were chiefly pictures and bas-reliefs.

[2] This was widely regarded as the crux of the matter.

[3] Aristotelianism had already influenced eastern theologians to some extent, but it owed chiefly to John of Damascus the large place which it had in the theology of the east from his time on.

[4] That is, his *Exposition of the Orthodox Faith.* Though it is only the third part of the *Fount of Knowledge,* it often circulated separately, and for convenience sake I refer to it as if it were an independent work.

[5] Bk. I. chap. 4.

[6] Bk. I. chap. 1. Cf. also Bk. IV. chap. 11 where John condemns in unsparing terms carnal curiosity or the desire to know more than has been revealed. This attitude appears over and over again in Christian history, one of many expressions of the age-old dread of infringing on the prerogatives of the gods.

[7] See above, p. 269.

[8] Bk. I. chap. 5.

[9] Bk. I. chaps. 6-8.

[10] Bk. II. chap. 2.

[11] Bk. II. chap. 4.

[12] Bk. II. chap. 5.

[13] Bk. II. chap. 12.

[14] Bk. II. chaps. 17, 19, 20.

[15] Bk. II. chap. 25.

[16] Bk. III. chaps. 3 ff.

[17] Bk. III. chaps. 13 ff.

[18] Bk. III. chaps. 14, 15.

[19] Bk. III. chaps. 20-24.

[20] Bk. IV. chap. 13.

[21] Cf. *e.g.* Bk. IV. chaps. 9 and 13.

[22] Bk. IV. chap. 10.

[23] But in the previous chapter it is said in passing that as faith apart from works is dead, so are works apart from faith (IV. 9).

[24] Bk. IV. chap. 13.

[25] The Greek word is [*metapoieō*].

[26] It is interesting that it does not appear in the Pseudo-Dionysian writings where the symbolism of the elements was emphasized.

[27] The Greek word is [*metalambanō*].

[28] Unless the sixth baptism of repentance and tears mentioned in IV. 9 is to be so interpreted.

[29] Cf. Bk. III. chap. I; Bk. IV. chap. 9.

[30] In the so-called Nicæno-Constantinopolitan Creed the Holy Spirit is spoken of as "proceeding from the Father." Augustine, the great Latin theologian, in his desire to emphasize the equality of Father and Son, taught that the Spirit proceeds from both of them, and later the word *filioque* ("and from the Son") was inserted in the western text of the Creed. This addition was made by the easterners one of the grounds for the break with the western church.

John Ernest Merrill (essay date 1951)

SOURCE: "Of the Tractate of John of Damascus on Islam," in *The Muslim World,* Vol. 41, No. 1 (January 1951): 88-97.

[*In the essay that follows, Merrill discusses the response John of Damascus makes to the Muslim charge that Christianity encourages idolatry and polytheism, and documents the limits of the information about Islam available to John of Damascus.*]

> "The first outstanding scholar to enter the field of polemic against the Moslem was John of Damascus. (He is) known to history as the most honored of the later theologians of the Greek Church. . . . His great dogmatic work on the ***Sources of Knowledge*** includes an important section 'Concerning Heresies,' and it is one chapter under this heading that deals with Moslems.[1] The topics the author selected and the arguments he used have been constantly repeated by similar champions from the eighth century to the twentieth. . . . Throughout all his controversial work John of Damascus displays a thorough knowledge of Islam. Fully at home in the Arabic tongue, he often cites the Koran word for word and shows his

familiarity with the Hadith, or traditions. . . . It is characteristic, in fact, of all the earlier polemic, during the age when Islam and Christendom were in close touch, that the Christian advocate is in full control of his material and knows at first hand what he is talking about."[2]

Dr. Addison is expressing, of course, a typical and not a private estimate. A document held in such high regard and of such wide influence merits careful investigation. Failure some years ago to find Quranic documentation for some of the statements in the Tractate about the "Camel of God" led the present writer to undertake a detailed examination of the entire document. This article embodies the results.

John of Damascus prefixed to his great work ***De Fide Orthodoxa*** a compendium of one hundred heresies. The idea was that, if one read first an account of the errors into which men had strayed, his mind would be the more ready to accept the truth, when it was presented to him. He added at least two other heresies, the first (101st) being Islam. Let us proceed at once to his description of this late "heresy." It will serve our purpose to itemize his statements. In case a statement can be confirmed from the Qur'ān, the passage is indicated in parenthesis, the verse numbers being those of the Royal Egyptian text; a second number indicates that of the verse in the text of Fluegel, if the two are different.

1. There is One God (*cf.* 3.2/1),

2. Maker of all things (2:117/111),

3. Himself not begotten, nor having begotten (*cf.* 112:3).

4. Christ is God's Word and His Spirit (4:171/169),

5. but created (3:59/52)

6. and a servant (4:172/170).

7. He was formed, without seed, from Mary (3:47/42),

8. the sister of Moses and Aaron (3:33-35/30:31; 19:27/28-28/29).

9. For the Word of God and the Spirit entered into Mary, and begat Jesus (4:171/169),

10. a prophet (19:30/31),

11. and a servant of God (4:172/170; 19:30/31).

12. The Jews, acting against the Law, determined to crucify him (*cf.* 3:54/47);

13. and when they seized him,

14. they crucified his shadow (4:157/156),

15. but Christ himself was not crucified (4:157/156),

16. nor did he die (4:157/156),

17. for God took him to be with Himself into heaven (4:158)

18. through loving him (*cf.* by contrast 3:57/50).

19. When Christ came into the heavens (*cf.* 4:158; 5:109/108),

20. God asked him, saying (5:116),

21. "O Jesus, did you say, 'I am Son of God, and God?'" (*cf.* 5:116)

22. and Jesus answered (5:116),

23. "Be merciful to me, Lord. Thou knowest that I did not say it, nor do I count myself above being Thy servant, but erring men wrote that I said this word, and spoke falsely against me, and they have been deceived." (*cf.* 5:116-118).

24. God answered and said to him (5:119),

25. "I know you did not say this thing." (*cf.* 5:119).

The documentations indicated from the Qur'ān show that John of Damascus was not without sources of correct information. However, the textual order in item 3, "begetteth not, . . . is not begotten," is reversed, something of which a Muslim source would seem incapable. "Acting against the Law . . . seized him . . . through loving him" (items 12, 13, 18) are Christian elucidations, and are not found in the Qur'ān. The resemblance of items 19-25 to the text of 5:109/108-119 is evident, but the wording of the supposed conversation differs very considerably from the original. Further, it is to be noted that, except for items 1 and 2, Islam is described as a Christological heresy, an appraisal that is manifestly but partial, and is negative in conception. At the beginning of the Tractate John of Damascus characterizes Islam as a precursor *(prodromos)* of Anti-Christ. The coming of Anti-Christ occupied a prominent place in his own thought, and in that of his times, and seems to have been connected with the Arabs. Mingana describes a Syriac document (Catalogue of Syriac MSS., No. 65) which treats of events at the end of the world, including the apparition of the Arabs from Yathrib and their defeat by the Greeks, and the apparition of Anti-Christ.

The Tractate goes on to tell of discussions between Christians and the adherents of this "heresy." These latter have a prophet who has written a Book. He is said to boast in this Book that the Book was brought down to him from heaven, and his adherents declare his statement to be true. Also they charge Christians with being polytheists, because they say, "Christ is the Son of God, and God," and idolators, because Christians "worship the Cross."

To these assertions the Christians reply. Their answers to the Muslims about their prophet and his Book leave the Muslims confounded. "Who witnessed God's giving of the Book to your prophet?" "What prophet foretold that such a prophet would come?" They are at a loss for a response. "Why did God not provide proofs, as in the case of Moses and of Jesus, so that men could be sure about your prophet?" "God does as He wills," they say. "How was this Book given to your prophet?" "It came down on him in his sleep," they reply. "So the sneering jest has been fulfilled . . . for receiving it in sleep he would not be aware of what happened." (The jest is not reported. Commentators have suggested, "Sleeping, he dreams!" or "Tell me your dreams!") "Your prophet told you not to do anything without witnesses" (2:282), say the Christians. "Why did you not demand of him witnesses about this giving of a Book, and prophecies in support of it?" Ashamed, they have nothing to say. "No transaction whatever is legal for you without witnesses, yet you have accepted without a witness a faith and a Book, a Book received in sleep! There is no verification of any sort."

As to the charge of polytheism, the reply is made to the Muslims that, if the Christians are in error, the responsibility rests on the Hebrew prophets, for the Christians simply repeat what the prophets said, and the Muslims insist stoutly that they accept the prophets (2:136/130). To meet this reply Muslims know enough about the Scriptural passages in question to propose answers. One is that the Christians allegorize, reading into the passages the meanings which they claim to find there about Christ. The other allows that the interpretations made by the Christians are legitimate, but says that the passages were interpolated by the Jews to deceive the Christians, and work their ruin.

A second line of reply to the charge of polytheism makes use of the terms which the Muslims themselves apply to Christ. He is "Word" and "Spirit" of God (4:171/169). In view of this usage, Christians make the apparently axiomatic statement that God's Word and God's Spirit are inseparable from God Himself. Either conclusion from this premise is against the Muslims. If they allow the premise to be true, they must accept that Christ is God; if they deny its truth, they declare God to be "without-Word" and "without-Spirit," and so "mutilate" Him, which is worse than to "associate."

As to the charge of idolatry, "What about the stone in your *Kabatha* (i.e., *Ka'ba*) that you kiss and embrace?" Some Muslims reply that it was used as a bed by Abraham and Hagar; others that Abraham tied his camel to it, when he went to sacrifice Isaac *(sic)*. To this second explanation Christians retort that, according to the Scriptures, the mountain of Abraham's sacrifice was wooded, and not like Mecca; that there was wood there to burn that Abraham split, and in Mecca there is little fire-wood; that Abraham left behind asses, not camels, and that asses do not come as far south as Mecca (*cf.* Genesis 22:13, 3, 5). The Muslims are ashamed; yet they insist that the stone is the Stone of Abraham.

Turning then to the first explanation, the Muslims are ridiculed. And they are told, "Are you not ashamed, in either case, to kiss the stone for such reasons? Yet you blame Christians for worshipping the Cross, through which the power of demons and the deceit of the Devil have been destroyed."

In this account of Christian-Muslim discussions we are introduced to a situation in Syria in which three points of divergence in religious matters have become clearly defined, one maintained by Christians regarding Muslims and two by Muslims regarding Christians. We see in the discussions reflections of the characteristic mentalities of the two groups. The Muslims have their tradition about the giving of the Qur'ān, their solution for unanswerable questions in "the will of God," their professed acceptance of all the prophets, their requirement of witnesses for all transactions, their "Stone of Abraham" at Mecca and the stories told about it. The Christians appear as skilled disputants. They demand evidence for asserted statements of fact, from eye-witnesses or from Scripture. They rely on the Old Testament, and argue from the prophets. The Muslims know enough about Christian belief and practice to strike at what Christians say of Jesus, and at their reverence for the Cross; enough also about the Old Testament prophecies urged by the Christians to venture explanations of this phase of Christian apologetic, though in these they are not agreed. The Christians know enough about the Qur'ān to cite statements made there about Jesus, and a law requiring witnesses. They know that Mecca is treeless and fire-wood scarce, and that asses are not used. They know of the Ka'ba, of a Stone that is reverenced there, and of customs in veneration of the Stone. Making use of the Quranic designations for Jesus which they know, they apply a very simple logic which balks the Muslims completely.

One is impressed by the reported inability of the Muslims to make replies to the Christian charges, whereas they certainly could have done so, if they had known certain passages in the Qur'ān. For example, in sura 6 alone we find that the preaching of Muhammad was not accepted without protest (verse 37), that there were demands for proof (109), that there were charges of falsehood (66), that proofs were cited (104), that there were Jews who accepted Muhammad (20). As it is, the Muslims are simply nonplussed and brow-beaten by the intelligence and astuteness of the Christians. On the other hand, the Christian replies are on the *tu quoque* order. The Christians speak as though putting to rout ignorant people, on a lower level of culture. There is no serious religious discussion, no attempt to present Christian faith, no thoughtful consideration of Islam. Let it not pass unnoticed, also, that the Christians are as unaware as the Muslims of the Quranic passages which the Muslims might have brought forward.

John of Damascus goes on to inform us about the Book of the Muslims. It consists of chapters, each with a title. He makes reference to four.

The chapter "Concerning the Women" (sura 4) legalizes polygamy: four wives, and female slaves in addition (4:3). Divorce is authorized at will, and then further marriages (2:229). The story is recited of Zaid, who had a beautiful wife, of how the prophet made him divorce her and then married her himself, asserting a command of God as the reason. If a man after divorcing his wife wants to take her back, she must be married first to another man; it may be to the man's own brother, if he is willing. In the Book he tells, "Till the ground which God has given to you, and beautify it" (*cf.* 2:223), "not to say as he does things altogether shameful."

The chapter "Concerning the Camel of God" tells of a camel from God that drank up a whole river, and then could not pass between two mountains for lack of room. The camel and the people of the place were to have drunk the water of the river on alternate days. However, after the camel had drunk up the water, the camel fed the people with milk instead. Some evil men killed the camel. Now the camel had a foal, and when the mother was killed, the little camel cried to God, and God took her up to Himself. About this story the Christians say to the Muslims, "Where did that foal come from?" "From God," they reply. "Was there not a sire?" They say, "No." "Then how was it born?" "We see your foal without sire, mother, or pedigree; also after the foal was born the mother-camel was killed, but nothing appears about someone who had mated her; and the foal was taken up! You say God spoke to your prophet. Why did not your prophet find out about the foal—who fed it, milked it, took the milk? Was it, too, killed by evil men, or did it enter Paradise as your forerunner? Is the river of milk that you foolishly talk about from this foal? For you tell of three rivers in Paradise—of water, of wine, and of milk. If the foal is outside Paradise, it must have died, or else someone now has its milk. And if the foal is in Paradise, it will drink up the water there, and you will have none. Then, if you would drink wine instead, there will be no water to mix with the wine, and drinking unmixed wine you will become drunken and go to sleep, and so you will miss the pleasures of Paradise! How is it that your prophet did not think of these matters, or that you did not ask him to tell you about the three rivers? John of Damascus ends with further ridicule of the story, and bitter reviling of those who believe such stories, "brutish as you are."

The chapter "Concerning the Table" (sura 5) says that Christ asked a "Table" from God, and it was granted to him, God saying, "I have given you and yours an incorruptible table" (*cf.* 5:112-115). As for the quotation, it is quite incomplete, and the reference should be consulted. The passage concerns the Eucharist. It is not at once clear whether the intention here is a simple statement of fact, or whether attention is being drawn to another example of absurd notions in the Book, as though a meal of imperishable foods were sent down from heaven!

In the chapter "Concerning a Heifer" (sura 2) "he says many other things, foolish and ridiculous, but they may be omitted, they are so many," says the author.

The Tractate closes with mention of some Muslim regulations. Men and women are to be circumcised; Muslims are not to keep the Sabbath; they are not to be baptized; some things forbidden by the Mosaic Law are to be eaten by them, and others not (2:172/167, 173/168); no wine is to be drunk (5:90/92). With or without Quranic documentation, these would be customs well known to the Christians from Muslim practice. Circumcision and prohibition of baptism cannot be documented from the Qur'ān. Prohibition of observance of the Sabbath is inferential only (*cf.* 16:124/125; 62:9). One cannot but note the tendency in this description of the Qur'ān to discredit everything Muslim. It is as though the author had formed an unfavorable opinion in advance, and now brought exhibits in proof.

As to this material many things must be said. Matters that can be documented from the Qur'ān have been indicated already.

Of the items enumerated under "Concerning the Woman" (sura 4) only the first, concerning polygamy, is from that sura. "Ye may divorce your wives twice" is the law about divorce, and it is found in sura 2:229. An intervening marriage to another man (to make it repugnant?) is prescribed after a thrice-repeated divorce statement only (2:230). The law regarding remarriage after a first or second divorce is found in 58:3, 4. A man must free a captive, and men are warned to conform. If a man cannot find a captive to release, he must fast two months in succession, before the two can come together. If unable to do this, he must feed sixty poor men. Of these things our author could not have been aware.

The matter of Zaid is referred to in 33:37 only, and without mention of a personal name. He is spoken of, however, as an adopted son. If the author had known of this relationship, would he not have used it to give added force to what he says? The law promulgated in view of this incident is given in 33:37, but it is not about divorce. Evidently this, too, was not understood.

Regarding "Concerning the Camel of God," there is no such chapter in the Qur'ān. The Quranic versions of this story are found in 91:13; 26:155-157; 54:27, 28; 17:61/59; 11:64-66/67, 68; 7:73/71. The she-camel, "the Camel of God" (96:13), was a sign, given to test the people of Thamūd (Petra). She and the people were to drink from the river on alternate days. The people were to let the camel feed, and not harm her, lest punishment fall on them. Certain men maltreated her, and hamstrung her, and destruction followed. Other features of the story as given by our author are oral tradition. Also, instead of three rivers in Paradise there are four—of water, wine, milk, and honey (47:15/16, 17), and that men should become drunken from drinking unmixed wine in Paradise is impossible, for the wine of Paradise does not intoxicate (37:47/46).

Having reviewed in detail the description of this "heresy," let us consult the preliminary orientation with which the Tractate begins. The "heresy" is said to have arisen among the Ishmaelites, or Hagarenes, names indicating descent from Abraham through his son Ishmael, and from Ishmael's mother, Hagar. It is said that these Ishmaelites, however, call themselves "Saracens," and that they explain the name as signifying that they are descended from Hagar, "whom *Sara* sent away empty (in Greek, *kenē*)." So far as the etymology is concerned, Christians of widely different backgrounds, e.g., Jerome (*cir.* 400), Sozomen (*cir.* 440), and much later Bar-Salibi (*d.* 1171), upheld derivation from the name of Sara. To imagine Arabs who could give to themselves such a name of Greek derivation, we must think of Arabs long under Roman rule, Christianized, Hellenized, acquainted with the Old Testament stories in Greek, who might fabricate such an explanation. This could be true only of Arabs living in Syria or Mesopotamia. However, identification of the name "Saracen" with a Nabataean locality to the east of the Dead Sea, from which the appellation spread, would confirm the statement of the author that the Ishmaelites apply the name "Saracen" to themselves. This name is not found in the Qur'ān. Instead the appellation used is "Arabs" *(al-arab);* compare 9:90/91, and repeatedly in this sura, and elsewhere. Why did not John of Damascus use this name, or even mention it? Incidentally, the question arises whether John of Damascus did not think of the Arabs of the Hijaz as a southern branch of the Arabs of the north. If so, what was true of the latter might be supposed to be true of the former.

It is said that till the time of Heraclius (610-41) these people "served idols openly," and "worshipped the morning star and Aphrodite." Paganism was outlawed by Theodosius I (390). People who still practised pagan rites openly must have lived outside the empire, as indeed the Arabs south of the border did. That these Arabs worshipped idols is correct, as is the worship of the morning star, i.e., of al-Uzza (53:19, 20). But in this Quranic passage al-Lat and Manat are mentioned also; Djibt and Thagout are spoken of in 4:51/54, and Thagout repeatedly (2:257/258; 5:60/65; 4:60/63; 4:76/78). One wonders at the mention of "the morning star *and* Aphrodite." The morning star was Venus-Aphrodite. In another place our author says that the Stone of Abraham at Mecca bears a likeness of Aphrodite. There was once at al-Hirah in Iraq an image of gold of Venus, which was worshipped by the Arabs, and was destroyed when their king accepted Christianity. Many Arab tribesmen who worshipped Venus were converted to Christianity under the preaching of St. Simeon Stylites, whose pillar was not far from Antioch. Does the author have in mind a star-worship, and also a goddess-worship once prevalent among the Arabs of Syria?

Aphrodite is called *khabar* "in their own tongue," we are told, "which signifies 'great.'" This is, of course, the Arabic adjective. Whether merely adjectival use or use as a proper name is to be understood is not clear.

This brief historical introduction is followed by a paragraph about the founder of the "heresy." Again, it will be convenient to itemize the statement.

1. Since the days of Heraclius until now

2. a pseudo-prophet, named Mamed, has sprung up for them.

3. Happening upon the Old and New Testaments,

4. in likelihood perhaps conversing afterwards with an Arian,

5. he set up a heresy of his own.

6. As a pretense, having adopted toward the people the appearance of being religious,

7. he gives out that a writing has descended on him from heaven.

8. Inscribing in the book with him some things worthy of laughter,

9. he presents to them the revered object.

We note that the time element is correct. "Mamed" (item 2) may represent colloquial non-Muslim pronunciation. It is not a transcript of the written Arabic name, for the four consonants *m-h-m-d* would be unmistakable. "Happening on the Old and New Testaments" ignores the circumstances involved, the questions of language, and MS. copies, and ability to read. Or should the custom of targuming from Greek or Syriac be understood implicitly, and considered a sufficient explanation? He may have had a Christian friend (item 4); indeed the Qur'ān reports charges that he had a teacher (44:14), a foreigner (16:103). The Nestorian tradition is definite that a Nestorian monk named Sergius was his teacher. Had John of Damascus, a Greek Orthodox adherent in Syria, heard of this tradition current among the Nestorian "heretics" in Iraq, but was not able to make a positive statement? Why an Arian? Was it more than the author's inference from his view of Islam as a Christological heresy, with teachings resembling those of the Arians? "Set up a heresy (or a sect?) of his own." One would gladly have details. Why brand the religious practices of Muhammad as pretense (item 6)?

As the items of this statements are studied, one is struck by the absence of clear-cut, definite, circumstantial detail. In particular, what about the history of long opposition to Muhammad at Mecca, the migration to Yathrib, the establishment of the Islamic community, its defense against the Meccans, its growth to political supremacy over Arabia, the acceptance by the Meccans and the Arabs in general of Islam? There is no hint that the Book as a unified whole did not come into being till after Muhammad's death, or that the text had to be standardized twice because reciters differed. The Nestorian al-Kindi, an Arab from the Banu Kinda of Central Arabia, who wrote at Baghdad a century later, gives such information. Can John of Damascus have thought these matters unessential to his purpose? Or may it be that he was ignorant of them? Evidently, among the Arab Christians in Iraq there were traditions about Muhammad and the rise of Islam. Should we conclude that no comparable tradition existed among the Christians in Syria?

Finally, let us look once more at the Tractate as a whole.

In several connections it has been noted that the information of John of Damascus must have been limited. In the summary of Muslim belief it is said of Jesus, "He did not die" (item 16), and this is documented from the Qur'ān. But the author can hardly have been aware of the existence of two contrary statements: "the day I shall die" (19:33/34), and "I will cause thee to die" (3:55/48). Unawareness of this statement in sura 19 must call in question any documentation from that sura (cf. items 8, 10, 11, involving 19:27/28-28/29, 30/31). In the case of several other suras we have seen reason for questioning whether their contents were known: 33 (Zaid), 58 (first and second divorce), 47 (rivers in Paradise), 37 (wine in Paradise), 53 (objects adored by the Arabs). Nor can there have been knowledge, as has been noted, of the passages which the Muslims themselves failed to adduce in rebuttal, e.g., those in sura 6 already indicated; and passages which tell of methods of revelation (42:51, 52/50-52), of prophecy (7:157/156; 61:6), of Muhammad's visions (53:1-18; 81:15-23), of the Qur'ān as a confirmation of the earlier Scriptures (12:111; 46:12/11; 46:30/29; 6:92; 10:37/38; 3:3/2; 2:41/38, 89/83, 91/85, 97/91, 101/95), of Jewish approval (26:196, 197; 46:10/9).

How explain the idea that the story of the Camel is a sura in the Qur'ān, and the giving to it of a formal name? The story and its discussion occupy one-fifth of the entire Tractate, more space than is devoted to the introductory information about the Ishmaelites, the information about Muhammad, and the outline of Islamic belief, all together.

As we review the statements which we have found it possible to document from the Qur'ān, we come upon a further matter of surprise. Documentation has been made practically entirely through verses from the second, third, fourth, and fifth suras. Exceptions might be 112:3, which is textually inexact; 19:27,28,30/28,29,31, on knowledge of which doubt is cast by the author's ignorance of 19:33/34; references for not keeping the Sabbath, of inferential bearing only at best. That is, acquaintance with these four suras alone would have been sufficient to account for the statements that are made.

Confining attention, then, to these four suras, detailed study brings to light in them a whole series of passages that would have changed the statements and the argumentation of John of Damascus, had he known them. These passages tell of pre-Islamic worships, of protests against Muhammad and his message, of proofs, of prophecy, of Gabriel and the impartation of the Qur'ān, of the Qur'ān as confirming the previous Scriptures, of Jewish testimony. (Compare 2:41/38,89/83, 91/85, 97/91, 99/93, 101/95, 118/112, 121/115, 146/141; 3:4/3, 13/11, 70/63, 79/73, 81/75, 86/80, 183/179; 4:47/50, 51/54, 60/63, 76/78, 153/152, 174; 5:48/52, 60/65.) No other conclusion seems possible but that our author was not acquainted with even these four suras of the Qur'ān in detail.

Notes

[1] *De Haeresibus,* by John of Damascus. See Migne, *Patrologia Graeca,* vol. 94, 1864, cols. 763-73. An English translation by the Reverend John W. Voorhis appeared in *The Moslem World* for October, 1934, pp. 392-98.

[2] *The Christian Approach to the Moslem,* by James Thayer Addison, p. 26f.

John Meyendorff (lecture date 1963)

SOURCE: "Byzantine Views of Islam," in *Dumbarton Oaks Papers,* No. 18, 1964, pp. 113-32.

[In the following essay, originally delivered as a lecture in 1963, Meyendorff contends that although there was some sophisticated understanding on each side of the Christian-Moslem confrontation, the two realms generally "remained impenetrable" in terms of real influence. The critic also discusses the superficiality of the interpretations of Islam that were instituted largely by John of Damascus.]

No knowledge of the Islamic teachings is evident in Byzantine literature before the beginning of the eighth century. We know that the spiritual and intellectual encounter of Muhammad and the first generations of his followers with Christianity involved not the imperial Orthodox Church, but the Monophysite and Nestorian communities which made up the majority of the Christian population in Arabia, Egypt, Syria, and Mesopotamia. Until the end of the Umayyad period, these Syrian or Coptic Christians were the chief, and practically the only, spokesmen for the Christian faith in the Caliphate. And it was through the intermediary of these communities—and often by means of a double translation, from Greek into Syriac, and from Syriac into Arabic—that the Arabs first became acquainted with the works of Aristotle, Plato, Galien, Hippocrates, and Plotinus.[1] Among the Monophysites and Nestorians, the Arabs found many civil servants, diplomats, and businessmen who were willing to help in the building of their Empire, and who often preferred, at least in the beginning, to accomodate themselves to the Moslem yoke, rather than suffer oppression which in the Orthodox Chalcedonian Empire of Byzantium was the fate of all religious dissidents.

The first encounter of Islam with Orthodox Christianity took place on the battlefield, in the wars which since the seventh century have opposed the Arabs to the Greek emperors. Both civilizations thus confronted were, to a large extent, shaped by their respective religious ideologies, and each side interpreted the attitudes and actions of the other as motivated by religion. If the Qurran appealed to a holy war against "those who ascribe partners to God"—i.e., Christians who believe in the Trinity[2]—the Byzantine retaliated, after the example of St. John of Damascus, by considering Islam as a "forerunner of Antichrist" ([*prodromos tou Antichristou*]).[3] But, however abrupt were these statements of mutual intolerance, however fanatical the appeals to a holy war, a better mutual appreciation was gradually brought about by the requirements of diplomacy, the necessity of coexistence in the occupied areas, and the cool reflection of informed minds.

My purpose here is to examine the encounter between Byzantium and Islam in the sphere of religion. Limitations of space do not permit me to do more than offer a few selected examples illustrating various attitudes of the Byzantines towards the Moslem faith. These examples will be drawn from four categories of documents:

1. Polemical literature

2. Canonical and liturgical texts

3. Official letters sent by Byzantine dignitaries to their Moslem counterparts

4. Hagiographical materials.

I

The name of John of Damascus usually heads every list of Christian anti-Moslem polemicists.[4]

According to traditional accounts, John belonged to the wealthy Damascene family of Sergius Mansur, an official of the Byzantine financial administration of Damascus, who negotiated the surrender of the city to the Arabs in 635, preserved his civil functions under the new regime, and transmitted his office to his descendants. John, according to this tradition, was his grandson. After exercising his duties for a while, he retired to the monastery of Saint-Sabbas in Palestine and became one of the most famous theologians and hymnographers of the Greek Church.

If we are to believe this traditional account, the information that John was in the Arab administration of Damascus under the Umayyads and had, therefore, a first-hand knowledge of the Arab Moslem civilization, would, of course, be very valuable. Unfortunately, the story is mainly based upon an eleventh-century Arabic life, which in other respects is full of incredible legends. Earlier sources are much more reserved. Theophanes tells us that John's *father* was a [*genikos logothetēs*] under the Caliph Abdul-Melek (685-705),[5] which probably means that he was in charge of collecting taxes from the Christian community. Such a post would not necessarily imply deep acquaintance with the Arab civilization. The *Acts* of the Seventh Council seem to suggest that John inherited his father's post, for they compare his retirement to Saint-Sabbas to the conversion of the Apostle Matthew, who, before he became a follower of Christ, was a "publican" i.e., a "tax-collector."[6]

Since the information available to us on John's life is very meager, it is only from his writings that we can form an accurate idea of his thoughts and his views on Islam. Unfortunately, a close examination of his work reveals very few writings connected with Islam.

Johannes M. Hoeck, in his critical analysis of the Damascene's manuscript tradition,[7] mentions four works connected with John's name which deal with Islam:

1. A chapter of the ***De haeresibus,***[8] a catalogue of heresies, which is part of John of Damascus' main work, the ***Source of Knowledge*** ([*pēgē gnōseōs*]) and is based on a similar compilation drafted in the fifth century by St. Epiphanius of Cyprus. Islam, rather surprisingly, is treated as a Christian heresy and bears the number 101 in the printed edition. It follows a description of the sect of the [*Autoproskoptai*] (a peculiar deviation of Christian monasticism) and precedes the paragraph on the Iconoclasts. In some manuscripts Islam figures under No. 100 and follows immediately after the Monothelites (No. 99).

2. ***A Dialogue between a Saracen and a Christian,*** a combination of two *opuscula,* both of which are to be found also under the name of Theodore Abu-Qurra, an author who will be mentioned later in this paper. The ***Dialogue*** has been published twice under the name of John of Damascus, once by Lequien and once by Gallandus, both editions being reprinted in Migne.[9] In each of these editions, the two original *opuscula* are in reverse order, which underlines the inconsistency of the Damascene's manuscript tradition on this point and strongly suggests that the ***Dialogue*** is a compilation of Abu-Qurra's writings, attributed to John of Damascus by later scribes.[10]

3. Another dialogue, formally ascribed to Abu-Qurra in the title, which, however, specifies that Theodore had written [*dia phōnēs Iōannou Damaskēnou*]. The expression [*dia phōnēs*], an equivalent of [*apo phōnēs*], is a technical expression, recently and convincingly studied by M. Richard[11]: it means "according to the oral teaching" of John of Damascus. The real author here is obviously Abu-Qurra, and, as a matter of fact, the ***Dialogue*** is also found in some manuscripts under his name, without any mention of John of Damascus.[12]

4. The fourth anti-Islamic writing ascribed to John is an unpublished Arabic ***Refutation*** which has never been studied.

Out of all these texts, the chapter on Islam in the ***De haeresibus*** appears, therefore, to be the only reliable one. But even in this instance, doubts have been expressed concerning its authenticity and the quotations from the Qurran are considered by some scholars to be a later interpolation.[13]

Therefore, whatever the result of further critical investigation of the anti-Islamic writings attributed to John of Damascus, it appears that his contribution to the history of Byzantine polemics against Islam is slight. If one admits the authenticity of these writings even in part, it will be seen below that chronologically they were not the earliest to have been written on the subject by a Byzantine author. Theologically, they do not add much to the unquestionable glory of John of Damascus, defender of the veneration of icons, author of the first systematic ***Exposition of the Orthodox faith,*** and one of the most talented hymnographers of Eastern Christianity. The study of the liturgical texts ascribed to John of Damascus strongly confirms the impression first gained from reading the chapter on Islam in the ***De haeresibus***—that of John living in a Christian ghetto which preserves intact the Byzantine political and historical outlook. In his hymns he prays for "the victory of the Emperor over his enemies";[14] he hopes that through the intercession of the Theotokos, the *basileus* "will trample under his feet the barbarian nations."[15] He never fails to mention the "cross-bearing Sovereign ([*staurophoros Anax*])" as the shield protecting Christ's inheritance from the "blasphemous enemies."[16] And there is no ambiguity concerning the identity of these enemies: they are "the people of the Ishmaelites, who are fighting against us" and whom the Theotokos is asked to put under the feet of the piety-loving Emperor ([*Ismaēlitēn laon kathupotattōn ton polemounta hēmas phileusebounti basilei*]).[17]

In mind and in heart John still lives in Byzantium. The fact that the Byzantine Emperor—whose victorious return to the Middle East he is hopefully expecting—has actually fallen into the iconoclastic heresy is, for him, a matter of greater concern than are the beliefs of the Arab conquerors. And he is certainly much better informed about the events in Constantinople than about Islam.

Even if it is eventually proved that the last part of chapter 101 of the ***De haeresibus,*** which contains quotations from the Qurran, is not a later interpolation, this would not provide clear evidence that John had, in fact, *read* the Qurran.[18] Any knowledge of Islam, direct or indirect, which is betrayed by John, relates to four suras only—the second, the third, the fourth, and the fifth—and to the oral Islamic traditions, especially those connected with the veneration of the *Ka'aba* in Mecca, which give John a pretext to deride the Islamic legends about Abraham's camel having been attached to the sacred stone. The knowledge of oral Arab traditions, sometimes more ancient than Islam, displayed by John and by other Byzantine polemicists is perhaps one of the most interesting aspects of the type of literature which we are studying; yet, at the same time, it illustrates the casual and superficial character of their acquaintance with Islam. Legendary commonplaces about the origins of Islam are repeated by different authors in different ways. I shall mention but one example, one which shows that John is neither original nor better informed than other Greeks in this matter. John refers to a pre-Islamic Meccan cult of Aphrodite, named [*Chaber*] or [*Chabar*] by the Arabs, which survived in the form of the veneration of a sacred stone, the *Ka'aba.*[19] The same account is also mentioned by Constantine Porphyrogenitus in the *De administrando imperio.* This is what Constantine writes: "They pray also to the star of Aphrodite which they call [*Koubar*], and in their supplication cry out [*Alla oua Koubar*], that is, God and Aphrodite. For they call God [*Alla*]; and [*oua*] they use for the conjunction *and* and they call the star [*Koubar*]. And so they say [*Alla oua Koubar*]."[20]

It is for the Arabists to inform us how much of this imperial excursion into the field of etymology, which is obviously parallel to, though independent of, the Damascene's text, is of any value. The traditional Islamic invocation *Allahu akbar*—"God is very great"—which is obviously referred to here, puzzled the Byzantine authors from the eighth century onwards. About 725, that is before the time of John of Damascus, Germanus of Constantinople also mentions that "the Saracens, in the desert, address themselves to an inanimate stone and make an invocation to the so-called [*Chobar*] ([*tēn te legomenou Chobar epiklēsin*])."[21] John of Damascus identifies [*Chabar*] or [*Chaber*] (he uses the two forms) with both Aphrodite herself, and with the *Ka'aba,* which according to him represents the head of the pagan goddess.[22] In the ninth century, Nicetas also speaks of the "idol of [*Choubar*]" ([*proskunei tōi Choubar eidōlōi*]) said to represent Aphrodite.[23] That some cult of the Morning Star existed among the Arabs before the rise of Islam seems certain, and this was known to the Byzantines, who attempted, of course, to find traces of paganism in Islam itself. However, the example of the passage on Aphrodite proves that John of Damascus did not add anything substantial to the information on Islam already available to the Byzantines of his time,[24] and that he merely made use of an accepted argument which conveniently confirmed the Byzantine belief that the Arabs "were devoted to lechery."[25]

We have already noted, on the other hand, that John lists Islam among the Christian heresies. This attitude toward Islam was based on the fact that the Qurran admits the revealed character of both Judaism and Christianity. John and his contemporaries tended, therefore, to apply to Islam the criteria of Christian Orthodoxy and to assimilate Islam with a Christian heresy *already* condemned. Thus Muhammad was an Arian, because he denied the Divinity of the Logos and of the Holy Spirit; hence, probably, the legend of Muhammad being instructed in the Christian religion by an *Arian* monk.[26] In fact, the contact of early Islam with Christianity involved the Monophysite and the Nestorian communities, certainly not the Arians, and the appellation ascribed by John to the Moslems—[*koptai tou theou*] ("cutters of God")[27]—because they cut away from God the Logos and the Spirit, is but a reply to the Moslem accusation directed against Christians that they are [*hetairiastai*]—"those who admit partners of God."[28]

Together with these polemical arguments dealing with the opposition between the absolute monotheism of Islam and the Christian doctrine of the Trinity, John touches upon another acute point of disagreement—the question of free will and of predestination—and his whole argument is supported by the most violent epithets which he applies to Muhammad, the "pseudo-prophet," the "hyprocrite," the "liar," and the "adulterer." All this was, of course, later taken up at length by other polemicists.

Two names deserve quite special mention in the history of early Byzantine polemics against Islam. One is that of an Arabic-speaking Bishop, Theodore Abu-Qurra who lived in Moslem occupied territory, mainly in Syria, in the second half of the eighth century. The other is that of Nicetas Byzantios, a scholar from the entourage of Photius. Although they wrote in very different styles and were involved in different situations, both Theodore and Nicetas were much better acquainted with Islam than was John of Damascus; Theodore, because he lived side by side with the Moslems and engaged them in dialogue, and Nicetas, because he had studied the entire text of the Qurran.

Abu-Qurra wrote in both Greek and Arabic. Of his fifty-two short Greek treatises, most were composed in the form of dialogues with various heretics encountered by the author (Nestorians, Monophysites, Origenists) and seventeen are directed against Islam. It is from these short *Opuscula*[29] that one can sense the true nature of the relations which existed between Moslems and Christians in the eighth century. The dialogues of Theodore maintain, it is true, a strictly negative attitude towards the faith of Islam and towards the person of Muhammad, an Arianizing false prophet (1560 A), possessed by an evil spirit (1545 B-1548 A). But the arguments used are conceived in such a way as to be understood by the opponents; they correspond to an attempt at real conversation. Here are some examples: the Arabs refuse to believe in the Trinitarian doctrine, because it brings division of God?—But the Qurran is one, even if many copies can be made of it; in the same way, God is One and Three (1528 C D). A short dialogue is entirely devoted to the Christian doctrine of the Eucharist, which, of course, was difficult for Moslems to understand; here Theodore relies on medical images familiar to both sides: the descent of the Holy Spirit on bread and wine which are thereby changed into the Body and Blood of Christ is similar to the action of the liver which assimilates food through the emission of heat (1552 D-1553 C). In a question which was unavoidable in any conversation between a Moslem and a Christian, that of polygamy, Theodore adopts a pragmatic attitude, which he knows will be better understood by his opponent than any reference to high morality or to the sacrament of marriage. "A woman," Theodore writes, "marries a man for the sake of pleasure and childbirth." But can one imagine a greater human pleasure than that which Adam and Eve enjoyed in Paradise, where, however, they were under a regime of monogamy? And when the Moslem still maintains that he prefers polygamy because it secures quicker multiplication of the human race, Theodore answers that since God did not care for a quick multiplication of men when man was *alone* on earth, he certainly does not desire too great a proliferation today. . . . And he concludes the argument by reminding the Moslem of the unavoidable quarrels and scenes of jealousy which occur in a harem (1556 A-1558 D).

The pragmatic character of some of Abu-Qurra's dialogues does not preclude the use of more technical theological arguments. Theodore is a trained Aristotelian, and he is well aware of all of the refinements of Byzantine Trinitarian doctrine and Christology. When the Moslem objects to the doctrine of the death of Christ—the person of Christ is made up of a body and a soul, their separation would mean the disappearance of Christ as a person—Theodore answers by referring to the Orthodox doctrine of the hypostatic union which is based upon the unity of Christ's *divine* hypostasis which is and remains, even in death, the unifying factor of all the elements composing the God-man. This is why the body of Christ remained uncorrupted in the grave (1583-1584).

The discussion very often touches on the doctrine of predestination, which was promoted in orthodox Islam and was often discussed in the Moslem world. It is, of course, refuted by Theodore in a series of arguments which reflect actual conversations on a popular level: if Christ had to die voluntarily, says the Moslem, then the Christians must thank the Jews for having contributed to the realization of God's will, since *everything* which happens is in accordance with His will. Theodore replies: since you say that all those who die in the holy war against the infidels go to heaven, you must thank the Romans for killing so many of your brethren (1529 A). But the discussion on predestination runs also on a more philosophical and theological level: Theodore explains the Christian doctrine of the divine creative act, which was completed in the first six days and which, since then, has given to human free will the opportunity to act, to create, and to chose; if any predestination toward good exists, it is derived from baptism, which is a new birth and which should be freely accepted and followed by good works (1587 A-1592 C).[30]

Many of the theological points touched upon by Theodore are also discussed in the lengthy treatise written by Nicetas Byzantinos and dedicated to the Emperor Michael III.[31] Nicetas writes in Constantinople and has probably never spoken to a Moslem, but he has a complete text of the Qurran and gives a systematic criticism of it, with exact quotations of various suras under their titles and numbers. (The latter do not always correspond to those used in the modern editions of the Qurran.) Nicetas' book is in two parts:

1. An apologetical exposition of the Christian faith, concentrated mainly on the doctrine of the Trinity (673-701).

2. A systematic refutation of the Qurran in thirty chapters (701-805). Nicetas' refutation is purely academical and scholarly in character; it is an intellectual exercise of the kind one may expect from the learned circle of scholars gathered around Photius and financed by the Caesar Bardas and the court of Michael III. Basically it reflects the impression produced by the Qurran on a Byzantine intellectual of the ninth century who has been given the assignment of refuting the new faith. He performs his task carefully, but without any real concern for an eventual Moslem auditor or reader.

Comparing the Qurran with Christian Scripture, he speaks of the "most pitiful and the most inept little book of the Arab Muhammad ([*to oiktiston kai alogiston tou Arabos Mōamet biblidion*]), full of blasphemies against the Most High, with all its ugly and vulgar filth," which does not have even the appearance of any of the biblical *genres* and is neither prophetical, nor historical, nor juridical, nor theological, but all confused. How can this, he asks, be sent from heaven? Nicetas does not know Arabic himself and uses several different translations of the Qurran. This is apparent, for example, in his treatment of the famous sura CXII, directed against the Christian trinitarian doctrine, which is thenceforth an inevitable subject in every discussion of faith between Christians and Moslems:

> "Say, 'He is God alone!
> God the Eternal!
> He begets not and is not begotten!
> Nor is there like unto Him any one!'"
>
> (*Palmer's translation*)

The Arab word *šamad* which means "solid," "massive," "permanent"—rendered here by the English *eternal*—is at first, at the beginning of Nicetas' book, translated by the Greek [*holosphairos*], i.e., "all-spherical," which gives Nicetas an opportunity of ridiculing such a material conception of the Divinity (708 A). Later, he corrects his translation and renders *šamad* by [*holosphyros*], which evokes a solid metallic mass, beaten by a hammer, and which is closer to the concrete image of God given by the Coranic text (776 B).

Another example of a misunderstanding due to a faulty translation: Nicetas accuses the Qurran of teaching that man comes "from a leech" ([*ek bdellēs*]—708 A). In fact, the Arabic text (sura XCVI, 2) speaks of a particle of congealed blood.

I have chosen these examples, among many others in the Nicetas text, because they are repeated by many other Byzantine authors and occupy a central place in later polemics. They illustrate the permanent misunderstanding between the two cultures and the two religious mentalities, but also show the positive knowledge of Coranic texts on the part of some Byzantines. Nicetas Byzantios, for example, had obviously studied the Qurran, even if in faulty translations, which was probably unavoidable at this early stage of Byzantine-Arab relations. On the other hand, it can be asked whether, in some instances, such Byzantine interpretations of Islam doctrine as the alleged belief in the spherical shape of God or the leech as the origin of man, did not, in fact, come from some forms of popular Arab religion—distinct, of course, from orthodox Islam—which were known to the Byzantines.

A complete survey of the Byzantine literature directed against Islam should, of course, include the study of many Byzantine documents belonging chronologically to later periods which are outside the scope of our paper. It will be sufficient to mention here that, from the eleventh to the fifteenth century, the knowledge of Islam gradually increases in Byzantium. A thirteenth-century writer, Bartholomew of Edessa[32] already shows some knowledge of the role of Othman and Abu-Bakr after the death of Muhammad. In the fourteenth century, the retired Emperor John Cantacuzenus gathers an even richer documentation. He composes four *Apologies* of Christianity directed against the Moslems, and four treatises ([*logoi*]) refuting the Qurran.[33] In addition to earlier Byzantine sources, he uses the Latin *Refutation of Islam* by a Florentine Dominican monk, Ricaldus de Monte-Croce († 1309), translated by Demetrius Kydones.[34] Cantacuzenus seems to have regarded the publication of his anti-Islamic writings as a major event in his life: in the well-known, beautiful copy of his theological works, ordered for his private library by Cantacuzenus himself and which is now in Paris (*Paris. gr.* 1242), the ex-Emperor had himself represented holding a scroll with an inscription [*megas ho Theos tōn Christianōn*] which is the *Incipit* of his work against Islam. Although his general method of refutation remains rather academic and abstract, there is no doubt that Cantacuzenus is better aware than many of his predecessors of the new situation in which he lives. He faces the Islamic challenge realistically and shows readiness to seek information and arguments in any source, even in the work of a Latin monk (He quotes his source: "a monk of the order of the preachers—[*tēs taxeōs tōn Predikatorōn, ētoi tōn kērykōn*]—of the name of Ricaldos, went to Babylon . . . and, having worked much, learned the dialect of the Arabs."[35]). And his prayers are not only for the destruction, but also for the conversion of the Moslems:[36] all this proves that he took Islam much more seriously than did the authors of the eighth and the ninth centuries. It is perhaps worth recalling here that a friend of Cantacuzenus, the famous hesychast theologian and Archbishop of Thessalonica, Gregory Palamas, describes in 1354 his journey to Turkish-occupied Asia Minor in a rather optimistic tone, hoping, like Cantacuzenus, for a subsequent conversion of Moslems and implying the acceptance, for the time being, of a friendly coexistence.[37]

II

Byzantine polemical literature has largely determined the official canonical attitude of the Church towards Islam, an attitude which is reflected in the rites of the reception of Moslem converts to Christianity. One such very ancient rite contains a series of twenty-two anathemas against Moslem beliefs.[38] The convert is required to anathematize Muhammad, all the relatives of the Prophet (each by name) and all the caliphs until Yezid (680-683). The fact that no later caliph is mentioned has led Fr. Cumont to conclude that the rite dates from the early eighth century. However, since the list lacks any chronological order (the name of Yezid is followed by that of Othman, the third Caliph), the argument does not seem altogether conclusive.

Other anathemas are directed against the Qurran: the Moslem conception of paradise, where all sorts of sins will take place "since God cannot be ashamed"; polygamy; the doctrine of predestination, which leads to the idea that God Himself is the origin of evil; the Moslem interpretation of the Gospel stories and the Qurran's treatment of the Old Testament. The anathemas repeat many of the arguments used by polemicists: the Arab worship of Aphrodite, called [*Chabar*], and the theory that has man issuing from a leech are mentioned, and the convert to Christianity is required to renounce them formally.

The author of the rite obviously knew more about Islam than did John of Damascus. He probably made use of Nicetas' treatise and also of other contemporary sources. It seems reasonable, therefore, to place the composition of the rite in the ninth century, at a time when similar rituals for the admission of Jews and Paulicians were composed. At any rate, this particular rite was still in use in the twelfth century because Nicetas Choniates gives a detailed account of a conflict which opposed the Emperor Manuel I to the Patriarchal Synod and in which Eustathios, metropolitan of Thessalonica, played a leading role.[39] In 1178, Manuel published two decrees, ordering the deletion of the last anathema from the rite, starting with the copy in use at the Great Church of St. Sophia. The anathema, quoted from sura CXII, reads as follows: "I anathematize the God of Muhammad about whom he says: 'He is God alone, God the Eternal [the Greek text reads [*holosphyros*]—of "hammer-beaten metal"], He begets not and is not begotten, nor is there like unto Him any one.'"

The reason for this measure was that the Emperor was afraid to scandalize the converts by obliging them to anathematize not only the beliefs of Muhammad, but also "the God of Muhammad," for this seemed to imply that Christians and Moslems did not, in fact, believe in one and the same God. The imperial measure provoked strong opposition on the part of the Patriarch and the Synod. Eustathius of Thessalonica, who acted as the Church's spokesman in this matter, proclaimed that a God believed to be "of hammer-beaten metal" is not the true God, but a material idol, which should be anathematized as such. After some argument between the palace and the patriarchate, a compromise solution was found. The Emperor withdrew his original decree; the twenty-second anathema was retained in the ritual, but now it read simply: "Anathema to Muhammad, to all his teaching and all his inheritance." This text was preserved in the later editions of the *Euchologion.*

The episode is significant inasmuch as it clearly illustrates the existence in Byzantium of two views on Islam: the extreme and "closed" one, which adopted an absolutely negative attitude towards Muhammadanism and considered it a form of paganism, and another, the more moderate one, which tried to avoid burning all bridges and to preserve a measure of common reference, in particular, the recognition of a common allegiance to monotheism.

Manuel I belonged to this second group, and in this respect he followed the tradition which seems always to have been predominant in official governmental circles of Byzantium. One can see this from the next category of documents which we shall examine—the letters addressed by the Byzantine emperors and officials to their Arab colleagues.

III

First, and historically most important, is a letter of Leo III to the Caliph Omar II. Omar II reigned for only three years (717-720), and the letter can, therefore, be dated with relative precision. I cannot discuss here in detail the problem of its authenticity. The fact that there was some correspondence on questions of faith between Leo and Omar is explicitly attested by Theophanes,[40] but the original Greek text of Leo's letter (or letters) is lost. A short Latin version has been published by Champerius, who quite wrongly attributes the letter to Leo VI.[41] This attribution is accepted without question by Krumbacher and Eichner. A much longer Armenian version has been preserved by the Historian Ghevond. It reproduces the original text, possibly with some minor additions.[42]

The document is interesting in more than one respect: 1. It emanates from the first Iconoclastic emperor, but precedes the Iconoclastic controversy itself and thus provides valuable evidence on Leo's views about icon veneration at this early period; this evidence is confirmed, as we shall see later, in other contemporary sources. 2. It is the first known Byzantine text which refutes Islam, and it shows a knowledge of the subject much wider than that of other contemporary polemicists.

Leo's letter is a reply to a solemn appeal by Omar to send him an exposition of the Christian faith. In fact, it was customary for the early Caliphs, at their enthronment, to send such requests to infidel princes, denouncing their beliefs and calling upon them to join Islam. Omar asks Leo to furnish him with the arguments that make Leo prefer Christianity to any other faith, and puts several questions to him: "Why have the Christian peoples, since the death of the disciples of Jesus, split into seventy-two races? . . . Why do they profess three gods? . . . Why do they adore the bones of apostles and prophets, and also pictures and the cross? . . ."[43]

Leo's answers are all based on sound exegesis of both the Bible and the Qurran. For him there is no question of relying on popular legends or misrepresentations. He does not feel the need of condemning the alleged cult of Aphrodite in Islam or of having Omar renounce the doctrine which claims that man's origin was the leech. He does not doubt that he and his correspondent believe in the same God, that the latter accepts the Old Testament as revealed truth. Is Omar looking for arguments in support of the true religion? But there are numerous prophets and apostles who affirmed the divinity of Jesus, while Muhammad stands alone. . . . And how can one say that the Qurran is above all criticism? "We know," Leo writes "that it was 'Umar, Abu Turab and Solman the Persian, who composed [the Qurran], even though the rumour has got round among you that God sent it down from the heavens. . . . " And we know also that "a certain Hajjaj, named by you Governor of Persia, replaced ancient books by others, composed by himself, according to his taste. . . . "[44] And is not Islam, the younger of the two religions, torn apart by schisms, even more serious than those which beset the comparatively ancient Christianity? These divisions occurred in Islam, Leo continues, although it arose among only one people, the Arabs, all of whom spoke the same tongue, while Christianity from the beginning was adopted by Greeks, Latins, Jews, Chaldeans, Syrians, Ethiopians, Indians, Saracens, Persians, Armenians, Georgians, and Albanians: some disputes among them were inevitable![45]

A large part of Leo's letter is devoted to the problems of cult and worship, in reply to Omar's attack on the Christian doctrine of the sacraments. The Byzantine Emperor's criticism of the *Ka'aba* cult has nothing of the mythical exaggeration of the other polemicists. He writes: "The region to which the prophets turned when they made their prayers is not known. It is you alone who are carried away to venerate the pagan altar of sacrifice that you call the House of Abraham. Holy Scripture tells us nothing about Abraham having gone to the place. . . . "[46] And here is an interesting passage concerning the veneration of the Cross and the icons: "We honour the Cross because of the sufferings of that Word of God incarnate. . . . As for pictures, we do not give them a like respect, not having received in Holy Scripture any commandment whatsoever in this regard. Nevertheless, finding in the Old Testament that divine command which authorized Moses to have executed in the Tabernacle the figures of the Cherubim, and, animated by a sincere attachment for the disciples of the Lord who burned with love for the Saviour Himself, we have always felt a desire to conserve their images, which have come down to us from their times as their living representations. Their presence charms us, and we glorify God who has saved us by the intermediary of His Only-Begotten Son, who appeared in the world in a similar figure, and we glorify the saints. But as for the wood and the colors, we do not give them any reverence."[47]

This text clearly reflects a state of mind which was predominant at the court of Constantinople in the years which preceded the Iconoclastic decree of 726. The images are still a part of the official imperial orthodoxy, but Leo does not attach to them anything more than an educational and sentimental significance; the veneration of the Cross is more pronounced, and we know that it was preserved even by the Iconoclasts themselves. The use of images is justified explicitly by Old Testament texts, but no reverence is due to the "wood and colors." An attitude similar to that of Leo can be found in contemporary letters of Patriarch Germanus,[48] who, around 720, still represented the official point of view on images. The fact that it is expressed in the text of the letter, as preserved by Ghevond, is a clear indication of its authenticity, for neither the Iconoclasts, nor the Orthodox were capable, at a later date, of adopting towards the images so detached an attitude. The Orthodox, while still condemning the veneration of "wood and colors" in themselves, were to invoke the doctrine of the Incarnation in support of a sacramental—and not purely educational—approach to images, while the Iconoclasts were to condemn any image representing Christ and the saints.

Leo's text represents, therefore, an interesting example of Christian apologetics, based upon minimizing the role of images, and one can clearly see the importance of this apologetical attitude towards Islam in the early development of Iconoclasm. The Iconoclastic edict of 726 was merely the next and decisive stage of this development. As André Grabar has pungently remarked,[49] a "cold war" of propaganda and blackmail was carried on, side by side with the armed conflict which permanently opposed Byzantium to the caliphate, throughout the second part of the seventh century and the beginning of the eighth. Sacred images played an important role in this cold war, sometimes as a symbol of Christianity against the Infidel, sometimes as a proof of the Christians' idolatry. And, as in the cold war of today, the opponents often tended to use each other's methods. The correspondence between Leo III and Omar is an interesting phenomenon in the gradual emergence of the issues at stake.

The other extant letters of Byzantine officials relevant to our subject belong to the ninth and tenth century and are less important historically. About 850, the Emperor Michael III received a letter [*ek tōn Agarēnōn*], "from the Arabs," and asked Nicetas Byzantios, the polemicist whose major work we have already examined, to answer them in his name. It is justifiable to suppose that the epistle that Michael III had received from the Caliph was similar to the one that Omar had sent to Leo III; in this case the Caliph would have been Al-Mutawakkil (847-861). The two answers written by Nicetas are concerned entirely with an exposition of the Christian doctrine of the Trinity which, the writer asserts, does not essentially contradict monotheism.[50] In his first refutation Nicetas repeats part of his polemical treatise dedicated to a positive *exposé* of Christian faith, but omits the direct polemics and criticism of the Qurran. We do not know whether Nicetas' writings were actually communicated to the Emperor's correspondent, but one can see at this point that, already in the ninth century, a significant difference existed between the internal use made of polemics and the requirements of diplomatic courtesy.

There is no doubt that the latter was observed in the correspondence between Photius and the Caliph, the existence of which is mentioned by his nephew, the Patriarch Nicholas Mystikos.[51] Nicholas himself corresponded with the Caliph on political matters and three of his letters have been preserved. From them we learn that a good deal of mutual tolerance did, in fact, exist between Moslems and Christians, especially when the opponents were able to exercise retaliation in case of abuse. Since, according to the Patriarch's letter, the Arab prisoners could pray in a mosque in Constantinople without anyone obliging them to embrace Christianity, the Caliph should also cease to persecute Christians.[52] And Nicholas refers to those laws of Muhammad himself that favor religious tolerance.[53] In another letter, he expresses in strong terms the belief in a single God which is shared by both Christians and Moslems: all authority comes from God and it is "from this unique God that we all received the power of government," and "the two powers over all powers on earth, i.e., that of the Arabs and that of the Romans, have preeminence [over all] and shine as the two big lights of the firmament. And this in itself is a sufficient reason for them to live in fraternal fellowship."[54]

One wonders whether, side by side with these official diplomatic letters, one may not justifiably mention here an infamous and tasteless pamphlet composed about 905-906 in Constantinople and wrongly ascribed to Arethas, bishop of Caesarea, a famous scholar and a disciple of Photius. The pamphlet consists essentially of a number of jokes in poor taste about the Moslem conception of Paradise. As Professor R. J. H. Jenkins has recently shown, the real author of the pamphlet is a certain Leo Choirosphactes,[55] whom Arethas ridicules in a dialogue entitled [*Choirosphaktēs ē Misogoēs*].[56] For us, interest in this document resides in the fact that it shows that Byzantine anti-Islamic polemics could be pursued simultaneously at very different levels, and that diplomatic courtesy and intellectual understanding at the Government level did not prevent slander and caricaturization at others.

IV

In the early eighth century, John of Damascus describes with horror the heresy which appeared "in the time of Heraclius": "the deceptive error of the Ishmaelites, a forerunner of Antichrist." And six centuries later, John Cantacuzenus, in almost the same terms, refers to the same cataclysm "which appeared under Heraclius." There was an abyss between the two religions which no amount of polemics, no dialectical argument, no effort at diplomacy, was able to bridge. Insurmountable on the spiritual and the theological level, this opposition from the very beginning also took the shape of a gigantic struggle for world supremacy, because both religions claimed to have a universal mission, and both empires world supremacy. By the very conception of its religion, Islam was unable to draw a distinction between the "political" and "spiritual," but neither did Byzantium ever want to distinguish between the universality of the Gospel and the imperial universality of Christian Rome. This made mutual understanding difficult and led both sides to consider that holy war was, after all, the normal state of relations between the two Empires.

One may, nevertheless, be permitted to ask what the situation was on the popular level. What was the attitude of the average Christian towards the Moslem in their everyday relations both in the occupied lands and inside the limits of the Empire where Arab merchants, diplomats, and prisoners were numerous? Hagiography seems to be the best source for a possible answer to this question. My cursory observations in this area have shown, however, that here, too, the solution cannot be a simple one. On the one hand, we have a great number of the Lives of martyrs with the description of massacres perpetrated by Moslems—that of the monks of Saint Sabbas,[57] that of sixty Greek pilgrims to Jerusalem in 724, whose death marked the end of a seven-year truce between Leo III and the Caliphate,[58] that of the forty-two martyrs of Amorium captured during the reign of Theophilus,[59] that of numerous Christians who, having succumbed to pressure, adopted Islam, but later repented and went back to the Church, as did for example, two eighth-century saints—Bacchus the Young and Elias the New.[60] No wonder then that in popular imagination the Moslem, any Moslem, was a horrible and an odious being: in the life of St. Andrew the *Salos* (the "fool for Christ's sake") Satan himself appears in the guise of an Arab merchant.[61] Furthermore, Arabs who played a role in the Byzantine imperial administration had an extremely bad reputation among the people; such was the case with the "Saracens" who, according to the life of St. Theodore and St. Theophanes the *Graptoi,* were at the service of Emperor Theophilus,[62] or with Samonas, the *parakeimomenos* of Leo VI. In occupied areas Christians often lived in closed *ghettos,* avoiding any intercourse with the Moslem masters of the land: when St. Stephen, who was a monk at Saint-Sabbas and a man of great prestige among both Christians and Moslems, learned that Elias, Patriarch of Jerusalem, had been arrested, he refused to go and intercede for him, because he knew that it would be of no avail.[63]

Occasionally, the Lives of saints reproduce discussions which took place between Christians and Moslems, and in such cases they make use of the polemical literature examined above: in Euodius' account of the martyrdom of the forty-two martyrs of Amorium, the problem of predestination is mentioned as a major issue between the two religions.[64] Among documents of this kind, the richest in content and the most original is an account of a discussion which took place about 850, in which Constantine, imperial ambassador to Samarra and future apostle of the Slavs, was involved.

It is recorded in the Slavonic *Vita Constantini.* The attitude of the "Philosopher" Constantine is altogether apologetical: he defends the Christians against the accusation . . . of being "cutters of God,"[65] he quotes the Qurran (sura XIX, 17) in support of the Christian doctrine of the Virgin birth, and, as did Abu-Qurra, refutes the Moslem contention that the division of Christianity into various heresies and sects is proof of its inconsistency.[66] He counterattacks with the accusation of moral laxity among the Moslems—the standard Christian objection to the Islamic pretense of being a God-revealed religion—and, finally, expresses the classical Byzantine claim that "the Empire of the Romans" is the only one blessed by God. He finds even a Biblical basis for this claim: in giving to his disciples the commandment to pay tribute to the emperor and in paying that tax for Himself and for others (Matthew 17:24-27; 22: 19-21), Jesus had in mind the Roman Empire only, not just *any* state; there is, therefore, no obligation for Christians to accept the Caliph's rule. The Arabs have nothing to be proud of, even in the fields of arts or sciences, for they are only the pupils of the Romans. "All arts came from us" (*ot' nas' sout' v'sa khoudozh'stvia ish'la*), Constantine concludes.[67] Fr. Dvornik is certainly right when he sees in this attitude of Constantine a typical Byzantine approach to all "barbarians," Latin or Arab, as expressed in several ninth-century documents issued by Michael III, Basil I, or the Patriarch Photius himself.[68] A cultural and national pride of this kind did not, of course, contribute much to mutual understanding between Christians and Moslems.

However, here and there, in the hagiographical writings, a more positive note is struck. In another passage of the *Life* of St. Stephen we are told that the Saint "received with sympathy and respected everyone, Moslems as well as Christians."[69] The holiness, the hospitality of some Christian saints are said to have favorably impressed the Saracens, who are then described in more generous terms in the Lives. This occurs, for example, in the early tenth century, when the Arabs invading the Peloponnesus are impressed by the holiness of St. Peter of Argos, and at once accept baptism.[70] At approximately the same time a Cypriot bishop, Demetrianos, travelling to Bagdad, is received by the Caliph and obtains the return to Cyprus of a number of Greek prisoners.[71] Another significant story recounts that, under Michael II, after an attack on Nicopolis in Epirus, an Arab of the retreating Moslem army remains in the mountains and lives there for several years in complete isolation, afraid to mingle with the population. During these years, however, he manages to be baptized. One day a hunter kills him by mistake. He then is entered into the local *martyrologium* under the name of St. Barbaros, for even his name was not known. Again, Constantine Akropolis, starting his thirteenth-century account of St. Barbaros' life, begins with a quotation from St. Paul: "there is no Barbarian, nor Greek, but Christ is all in all."[72]

On the other hand, one cannot deny the existence, especially in the later period under discussion, of some communication between Islam and Christianity on the level of spiritual practice and piety. It has been pointed out that a startling similarity exists between the Moslem *dhikr*—the invocation of the name of God connected with breathing—and the practices of the Byzantine hesychasts[73]. Byzantine monasticism continued to flourish in Palestine and on Mount Sinai, while pilgrims continually visited the Holy Land. All this implies the existence of contacts that were other than polemical.

Yet, as we look at the over-all picture of the relations between the two religious worlds, we see that essentially they remained impenetrable by each other. Among all the historical consequences of the Arab conquest of the Middle East, one seems to me to be the *most important:* for *ages* Byzantine Christianity was kept on the defensive. Islam not only obliged the Christians to live in a tiny enclosed world which concentrated on the liturgical cult, it also made them feel that such an existence was a normal one. The old Byzantine instinct for conservatism, which is both the main force and the principal weakness of Eastern Christianity, became the last refuge which could ensure its survival in the face of Islam.

Notes

[1] Cf. L. Gardet, "Théologie musulmane et pensée, patristique," in *Revue Thomiste,* 47 (1947), pp. 51-53.

[2] Sura, IX, V, 5.

[3] *De haeresibus,* PG, 94, col. 764 A.

[4] On the Byzantine anti-Islamic polemics, see C. Güterbock, *Der Islam im Lichte der Byzantinischen Polemik* (Berlin, 1912); W. Eichner, "Die Nachrichten über den Islam bei den Byzantinern," *Der Islam,* 23 (1936), pp. 133-162, 197-244; and H. G. Beck, "Vorsehung und Vorherbestimmung in der Theologischen Literature der Byzantiner," *Orientalia Christiana Analecta,* 114 (1937), pp. 32-65. None of these studies goes further than to give a list of authors and to present a selection of their major arguments.

[5] *Chronographia,* Bonn, ed. I, p. 559.

[6] Mansi, *Concilia,* XIII, col. 357 B; cf. Matt. 9:9.

[7] "Stand und Aufgaben der Damaskenos-Forschung," in *Orientalia Christiana Periodica,* 17 (1951), pp. 18, 23-24.

[8] PG, 94, cols. 764-773.

[9] *Ibid.,* cols. 1585-1596 (Lequien); 96, cols. 1335-1348 (Gallandus). The text corresponds almost verbatim to the *Opuscula,* 35 (*ibid.,* cols. 1587 A-1592 C) and 36 (97, cols. 1592 CD) of Abu-Qurra.

[10] H. G. Beck, while still tending to accept John's authorship, mentions a manuscript where the *theologische Literatur im byzantinischen Reich* [Munich, 1959], p. 478).

[11] [Apo phōnēs], in *Byzantion,* 20 (1950), pp. 191-222.

[12] Cf. PG, 97, col. 1543.

[13] A. Abel, in *Byzantion,* 24 (1954), p. 353, note 2.

[14] *Octoechos,* Sunday Matins, Tone 1, canon 1, ode 9, *Theotokion.*

[15] *Ibid.,* Tone 3, canon 1, ode 9, *Theotokion.*

[16] *Ibid.,* Tone 4, canon 2, ode 9, *Theotokion.*

[17] *Ibid.,* Tone 8, canon 2, ode 9, *Theotokion.*

[18] J. R. Merrill, "On the Tractate of John of Damascus on Islam," *Muslim World,* 41 (1951), p. 97; cf. also P. Khoury, "Jean Damascène et l'Islam," *Proche Orient chrétien,* 7 (1957), pp. 44-63; 8 (1958), pp. 313-339.

[19] PG, 94, cols. 764 B, 769 B.

[20] Constantine Porphyrogenitus, *De administrando imperio,* I, 14, ed. by Moravcsik, trans. by R. J. H. Jenkins (Budapest, 1949), pp. 78-79.

[21] *Letter to Thomas of Claudiopolis,* PG, 98, col. 168 CD.

[22] *De haeresibus, ed. cit.,* 764 B, 769 B.

[23] *Refutatio Mohamedis,* PG, 105, col. 793 B.

[24] It should be noted, however, that the Damascene gives a *translation* of the word [*Chabar*], and interprets it as meaning "great" in the feminine form ([*hoper sēmainei megalē*]—col. 764 B). This has led G. Sablukov to see the origin of the form used by Nicetas and Constantine ([*Koubar or Choubar*]) in the *feminine form* of *akbar-koubra,* and to infer that the Byzantines knew of a pre-Islamic Arab invocation of Aphrodite—*Allata koubra* ("Zametki po voprosu o vizantiiskoi protivomusul'manskoi literature" in *Pravoslavnyi Sobesednik,* 2 [1878], pp. 303-327; cf. also a similar etymological argument put forward by Georgius Hamartolus, ed. by de Boor, II, p. 706).

[25] B. Lewis, in *Constantine Porphyrogenitus, De administrando,* II, *Commentary* (London, 1962), p. 72.

[26] PG, 94, 765, A.

[27] *Ibid.,* 768 D.

[28] *Ibid.,* 760 B.

[29] The Greek treatises of Abu-Qurra are published in PG, 97, cols. 1461-1609.

[30] This passage on predestination is reproduced verbatim in the *Dialogue* attributed to John of Damascus (PG, 96, cols. 1336-1340).

[31] PG, 105, cols. 669 A-805.

[32] [*Elenchos Agarēnou*], PG, 104, cols. 1384-1448; for the date, see Eichner, *op. cit.,* pp. 137-138.

[33] PG, 154, cols. 373-692.

[34] Translation published in PG, 154, cols. 1035-1152.

[35] PG, 154, col. 601.

[36] *Ibid.,* col. 584.

[37] On this episode, see J. Meyendorff, *Introduction à l'étude de Grégoire Palamas* (Paris, 1959), pp. 157-162.

[38] This rite has been published by F. Sylburg (Heidelberg, 1595). Sylburg's edition has been reprinted as a part of the *Thesaurus Orthodoxae fidei* of Nicetas Choniates in PG, 140, cols. 123-138. A new edition of the rite has been issued by F. Montet, "Le rituel d'abjuration des Musulmans dans l'Eglise grecque," in the *Revue de l'histoire des religions,* 53 (1906), pp. 145-163, with a French translation of the Anathemas. This new edition does not replace Sylburg's, which is more complete. Cf. observations on Montet's edition in S. Ebersolt, "Un nouveau manuscrit sur le rituel d'abjuration des Musulmans dans l'Eglise grecque" in the same *Revue de l'histoire des religions,* 54 (1906), pp. 231-232; Cf. Clermont-Ganneau, "Ancien rituel grec pour l'abjuration des Musulmans," *Recueil d'archéologie orientale,* 7 (Paris, 1906), pp. 254-257; Fr. Cumont, "L'origine de la formule grecque d'abjuration imposée aux Musulmans," in *Revue de l'histoire des religions,* 64 (1911), pp. 143-150.

[39] Nicetas Choniates, *Historia,* Bonn ed., pp. 278-286; on the whole episode, see C. G. Bonis "ὁ Θεσσαλονίκης Εὐστάθιος καὶ οἱ δύο «τόμοι» τοῦ αὐτοκράτορος

Μανουὴλ Α' Κομνηνοῦ (1143/80) ὑπὲρ τῶν εἰς τὴν χριστιανικὴν ὀρθοδοξίαν μετισταμένων Μωαμεθανῶν [*Ho Thessalonikēs Eusthios kai hoi duo «tomoi» tou autokratoros Manouēl A' Komnēnou* (1143/80) *hyper tōn eis tēn christianikēn orthodoxian metistamenōn Moamethanōn*]," in Ἐπετηρὶς Ἑταιρείας Βυζαντινῶν Σπουδῶν, 19 (1949), pp. 162-169.

[40] *Chronographia,* Bonn ed., II, p. 399.

[41] This version is reproduced in PG, 107, cols. 315-24.

[42] English translation, commentary, and bibliography in A. Jeffery, "Ghevond's Text of the Correspondence between Umar II and Leo III," in the *Harvard Theological Review,* 37 (1944), pp. 269-332. Jeffrey offers a convincing amount of internal and external evidence in favor of the letter's authenticity, in opposition to H. Beck, *Vorsehung und Vorherbestimmung,* pp. 43-46, who thinks that the letter could not be earlier than the late ninth century. Cf. also A. Abel's recent suggestion that Leo the Mathematician is possibly the author (*Byzantion,* 24 [1954], p. 348, note 1). Among earlier believers in the authenticity of the letter, see B. Berthold, "Khalif Omar II i protivorechivyia izvestiia o ego lichnosti," in *Khristianskii Vostok,* VI, 3 (1922), p. 219.

[43] A. Jeffrey, *op. cit.,* pp. 277-278.

[44] *Ibid.,* p. 292.

[45] Cf. *ibid.,* p. 297.

[46] *Ibid.,* p. 310.

[47] *Ibid.,* p. 322.

[48] Cf., for example, his letter to Thomas of Claudiopolis, PG, 98, col. 173 D.

[49] *L'iconoclasme byzantin; dossier archéologique* (Paris, 1957), p. 47.

[50] PG, 105, cols. 807-821, 821-841.

[51] PG, 111, cols. 36 D-37 A.

[52] *Ibid.,* cols. 309 C-316 C.

[53] *Ibid.,* col. 317 A.

[54] *Ibid.,* col. 28 B; on the true nature of this letter, addressed not to an "emir of Crete," as the present superscription states, but to the Caliph himself, see R. J. H. Jenkins, "The Mission of St. Demetrianus of Cyprus to Bagdad," *Annuaire de l'Institut de Phil. et d'Hist. Orient. et Slaves,* 9 (1949), pp. 267-275.

[55] The "letter to Arethas" has been published by J. Compernass, *Denkmäler der griechischen Volkssprache,* 1 (Bonn, 1911), pp. 1-9; French trans. by A. Abel, "La lettre polémique 'd'Aréthas' à l'émir de Damas," *Byzantion,* 24 (1954), pp. 343-370; another edition by P. Karlin-Hayter in *Byzantion,* 29-30 (1959-1960), pp. 281-302; for the definitive word, see R. J. H. Jenkins, "Leo Choerosphactes and the Saracen Vizier," *Vizant. Institut, Zbornik radova* (Belgrade, 1963), pp. 167-175.

[56] Ed. by J. Compernass, in *Didaskaleion,* 1, fasc. 3 (1912), pp. 295-318.

[57] Ed. by A. Papadopoulos-Kerameus, in *Pravoslavnyi Palestinskii Sbornik* (1907), pp. 1-41.

[58] The two versions of this *Life* were published by A. Papadopoulos-Kerameus, in *Pravoslavnyi Palest. Sbornik* (1892), pp. 1-7 and in *ibid.* (1907), pp. 136-163.

[59] Several versions of their Martyrium in Greek and in Slavonic were published by V. Vasil'evski and P. Nikitin in *Akademiia Nauk, Istoriko-filologicheskoe otdelenie, Zapiski,* 8th ser., VII, 2 (St. Petersburg, 1905).

[60] Chr. Loparev, "Vizantiiskiia Zhitiia Sviatykh," in *Vizant. Vremmenik,* 19 (1912), pp. 33-35.

[61] PG, 111, col. 688.

[62] PG, 116, cols. 673 C, 676 C.

[63] *Acta Sanctorum, Jul.* III, col. 511.

[64] *Ed. cit.,* pp. 73-74; cf. Abu-Qurra, *Opuscula,* 35, PG, 97, col. 1588 AB; Nicetas Byzantios, *Refutatio Mohammedis,* 30, PG, 105, col. 709; Bartholomew of Edessa, *Confutatio Agareni,* PG, 104, col. 1393 B.

[65] *Vita,* VI, 26, ed. by F. Grivec and F. Tomšič, in *Staroslovenski Institut, Radovi,* 5 (Zagreb, 1960), p. 104.

[66] *Ibid.,* VI, 16, p. 104.

[67] *Ibid.,* VI, 53, p. 105.

[68] *Les légendes de Constantin et de Méthode vues de Byzance* (Prague, 1933), pp. 110-111.

[69] *Acta Sanctorum, Jul.* III, col. 511.

[70] Mai, *Nova Patrum Bibliotheca,* IX, 3, 1-17.

[71] *Life* of St. Demetrianos, ed. by H. Grégoire in BZ, 16 (1907), pp. 232-233.

[72] Ed. by A. Papadopoulos-Kerameus, in Ἀναλέκτα Ἱεροσολυμιτικῆς Σταχυολογίας [*Analekta Ierosolymitikēs Stachyologias*], 1, pp. 405-420.

[73] Cf., for example, L. Gardet, "Un problème de mystique comparée," in *Revue Thomiste* (1956), I, pp. 197-200.

Daniel J. Sahas (essay date 1972)

SOURCE: "The Text and Its Content," in *John of Damascus on Islam: The 'Heresy of the Ishmaelites,'* E. J. Brill, 1972, pp. 67-95.

[*In the following essay, Sahas examines John of Damascus's criticisms of Islam as an idolatrous and superstitious heresy, and contends that he had an extensive knowledge of early Islamic theology.*]

It is important to study closely what John of Damascus had to report and remark on Islam. It is only then that one can draw a picture of his knowledge and his evaluation of Islam.[1]

> 1. "There is also the deceptive superstition of the Ishmaelites, prevailing until now . . ." (764A)

This opening sentence indicates clearly that other heresies have preceeded ("there is also . . ."), and it suggests, perhaps, that this chapter concludes a list of heresies[2] which, by this section, has been brought up to date ("which prevails until now . . .").

> 2. Islam is introduced as a "deceptive superstition of the Ishmaelites" and "forerunner of the Antichrist" (Cf., 764A)

a. The Greek text in Lequien's and Migne's editions reads [*skeia*], which the Latin has translated as *superstitio.*[3] This word, however, cannot be identified in Greek. Voorhis has suggested that the word was taken as [*skia*][4] which means, figuratively, "spiritual darkness" or "error" as in Matt. 4:16; Lk. 1:79; Jn. 1:5, and 8:12; I Jn. 1:5, and 2:8-11.[5] The adjective [*laoplanos*] (= leading men astray; deceptive) seems to favor this suggestion. This interpretation seems to find support from the text itself when, a few lines below, John of Damascus states explicitly that Muhammad "having conversed, *supposedly,* with an Arian monk, devised *his own* heresy".[6]

It is difficult to conclude from these statements that John of Damascus did not consider Islam as *another* religion, but as a "deceptive superstition" and a "heresy". There is much to be learned, first, about the meaning and the use of the terms, *religion, heresy* and *superstition.* The terminology, however, used by John of Damascus to describe Islam and especially the fact that he included it in his ***De Haeresibus,*** allows a wide range of consideration.

b. "Forerunner of the Antichrist": In the same year that the ***Fount of Knowledge*** was written (743) Peter, bishop of Maiuma, was sentenced to death because he condemned Islam publicly and he called Muhammad a "false prophet" and the "forerunner of the Antichrist".[7] This expression, however, was not employed for the first time against only Islam and Muhammad. It had been used for Emperor Leo III,[8] his son Constantine V,[9] the Patriarch of Constantinople John VII Grammaticos (836-842)[10] and possibly for some other prominent political and religious leaders. This grave accusation was directed against those who were believed to lead men astray from the Orthodox faith, by "deceiving" the believers. Thus, in a special chapter "On the Antichrist" in the ***De Fide Orthodoxa*** John of Damascus considers as Antichrist not only Satan, but also any man "who does not confess that the Son of God came in flesh, is perfect God and He became perfect man while at the same time He was God".[11] In accord with his definition John of Damascus applied this name to Nestorius, whom he called "Antichrist" as well as "son of Satan", for ascribing to Mary the name "Christotokos" instead of "Theotokos".[12] It is obvious, therefore, that the epithet "forerunner of the Antichrist" was a condemnation of those who perverted the basic doctrines of the Church especially with regard to the divinity of Christ, and as such it was used against Islam.[13]

> 3. Chapter 101 gives three names to the Muslims: Ishmaelites, Hagarenes, and Saracenes. (Cf., 764A).

All three names are inter-related within themselves and with the Muslim heritage. The religion of Islam is, from the Muslim point of view, "the religion of Abraham and Ishmael"[14] the forefathers of the Muslims.[15] According to Ibn al-Kalbi, who conveys also the belief of his predecessors, Ishmael settled in Mecca where he became the father of many children who supplanted the Amalekites of Mecca; to him is ascribed the origin of the Arabs.[16] The Qur'ān states that Abraham and Ishmael "raised the foundations of the House"[17] and established a "proper worship".[18] The rites of the pilgrimage, the circumambulation, the visitation of the lesser pilgrimage, the vigil of 'Arafāt, the sacrifice of the she-camels and the acclamation of the name of the deity "came down from the time of Abraham and Ishmael",[19] according to Ibn al-Kalbi, and they constitute a part of the religion. Therefore, when John of Damascus calls Islam "the 'religion' of the Ishmaelites", he uses a name fully acceptable to the Muslims.

Chapter 101 calls also the Muslims *Hagarenes,* a name derived from Hagar, the mother of Ishmael. The expression "the sons of Hagar" referring to the Muslims is widely used by the later Byzantine authors.[20]

For the etymology of the name "Saracen" Chapter 101 refers to the incident of Genesis 16:8, and in particular to the dialogue of Hagar with the angel: "I am fleeing from my mistress Sar'ai", which in a restatement reads "Sara has sent me away, empty".[21] John of Damascus, being perhaps aware of the arbitrariness of this explanation, states that this name is not his own invention, but that the Muslims "are called so".

> 4. They (the Ishmaelites) became idol worshippers—they worshipped the morning star, and Aphrodite, whom they called *Habar* (or *Haber*) in their language, which means great—and they remained as such until the time of Heraclius, when Muhammad appeared. (Cf., 764B)

John of Damascus speaks of a change in the religion of the Ishmaelites, from the religion of Ishmael to idolatry, which is in accord with the testimony of the Qur'ān and Muslim writers. The pure religion of Abraham and Ishmael deteriorated with the introduction of images and alien practices in the worship.[22] Those who "departed from the religion of Ishmael" made idols, which they worshipped on different occasions.[23] Ibn al-Kalbi states emphatically that "the Arabs were passionately fond of worshipping idols".[24] The veneration of the star and of Aphrodite to which John of Damascus refers is an aspect of this period of idolatry. In the statement "they worshipped the morning star *and* Aphrodite" we should, perhaps, see an allusion to the veneration of 'Athar, the principal stellar divinity of South Arabia in the pre-Islamic times, in its morning and evening position.[25]

John of Damascus' awareness of the idolatrous character of the pre-Islamic religion in Arabia leads him to a positive recognition of Muhammad as the person who brought his people back to monotheism. The author is, certainly, aware of the painful task that Muhammad had undertaken, as well as of the opposition to his mission, before he gained the favor of his people.[26]

> 5. Muhammad, the founder of Islam, is a false prophet who, by chance, came across the Old and New Testament and who, also, pretended that he encountered an Arian monk and thus he devised him own heresy. (Cf., 765A)

Another codex gives a more explicit account of the sources of influence upon Muhammad: Jews, Christians, Arians and Nestorians.[27] From each one of these Muhammad acquired a particular teaching and thus he formed his own heresy: from the Jews absolute monotheism ("monarchy"), from the Arians, the affirmation that the Word and the Spirit are creatures and from the Nestorians anthropolatry,[28] obviously because of their teaching that Christ was simply a human being.

With the reference to the "Arian monk", John of Damascus alludes to a *hadith* about a Syrian monk, Bahīrā, who had predicted the prophetic career of Muhammad.[29] This tradition was, later, utilized by the Muslims as an answer to the challenge of the Christians that Muhammad was an "un-announced" and, thus, a false prophet.[30] John of Damascus does not seem to know about this use of the tradition; he simply refers to this monk in order to identify the source and explain Muhammad's theology.[31] The fact that John of Damascus preferred to identify the monk as an Arian[32] reflects the initial impression that Islam made upon him, and it explains the content and the character of his refutation.

If the version which speaks more extensively of the sources that influenced Muhammad is the authentic one—an issue which cannot be decided until we have a critical edition of the text—it reveals that John of Damascus had a thorough knowledge of the Theology and the Christology of the Qur'ān. The belief that the Word and the Spirit of God are created, that Jesus was only a human being and, in all of this, an emphasis on an absolute "monarchy" are, indeed, the issues at stake in Islam which constitute what a Muslim and a Christian would consider as the most essential theological differences between the two.

> 6. Muhammad claims that a book was sent down to him from heaven. (Cf., 765A)

John of Damascus employs constantly the word [*graphē*] (scripture, book) in referring to the Qur'ān.[33] The Qur'ān itself uses the word *Kit b* (Book) as a self-designation,[34] as well as a name for all the revealed Scriptures.[35] "Sending down" of the scripture to Muhammad is also an expression found in the Qur'ān.[36] In contrast to John of Damascus, in the later Byzantine polemics we find the claim that Muhammad was an epileptic and that under this condition he thought that he received revelations from God; or that it was Khadīja who, in her effort to conceal and counter-act the misfortune of her marriage with Muhammad, as well as the illiteracy and the poor health of her husband, declared that he was a prophet of God.[37]

> 7. He says that there is one God, creator of all, who is neither begotten, nor has begotten. (765A)

This statement is the precise content of S. CXII, *al-Tawhīd,* the proclamation of the unity of God, which is "the essence of the Qur'ān".[38] The fact that John of Damascus starts his discussion of the Qur'ānic doctrine with this point seems to indicate that he had, indeed, detected the core of the Qur'ānic message. The notion of the unity of God is emphasized in the Qur'ān positively as the basis of Muslim faith and, at the same time, as a challenge to the polytheists and to those who "ascribe partners" to God, that is, the Christians.[39]

In John of Damascus' own theology the doctrine of the oneness and uniqueness of God plays an important role and it is stressed throughout the ***De Fide Orthodoxa.***[40] He speaks there about God in similar terms as the Qur'ān, and with the same emphasis:

> We believe in one God, one principle, without beginning, uncreated, *unbegotten,* indestructible and immortal, eternal, unlimited, uncircumscribed, unbounded, infinite in power, simple, uncompound, incorporeal, unchanging, unaffected, inalterate, invisible, source of goodness and justice, light intellectual and inaccessible . . . maker of all things visible and invisible . . . [41]

It is very interesting to notice that John of Damascus offers this list of attributes of God in a chapter under the title . . . "On the Holy Trinity"![42] That the unity of God is stressed in the context of a discussion on the Trinity must have been seen as a paradox by the Muslims. It is as if John of Damascus were convinced that Christian Theology has not placed the crucial question of "the Word of God" in the right perspective. For John of Damascus the issue at stake is not whether God is one or many; he simply assumes the former as *sine qua non;* the issue at stake is how God can be known. The question of Trinity, therefore, is for John of Damascus an answer to the question of the knowledge of God, who is:

> The very source of being for all things that are. Knowing all things before they begin to be; one substance, one Godhead, one virtue, one will, one operation, one principality, one power, one domination, one kingdom; *known* in three perfect persons . . . united without confusion, and distinct without separation, which is beyond understanding.[43]

And, although John of Damascus speaks in terms of *Father, Son* and Spirit, he explains that:

> We know one God, and Him in the properties of fatherhood, and sonship, and procession only. We perceive the difference in terms of cause and effect and perfection of subsistence, that is, in the manner of existence.[44]

The expression "nor has begotten" of the Qur'ān is, therefore, equally acceptable to John of Damascus, who speaks of fatherhood as a manner of existence of the same one substance, rather than in a physical sense.[45]

As for the notion of God as "creator of all", John of Damascus conveys rightly the Qur'ānic teaching.[46] The emphasis at this point is upon the idea of God as the omnipotent creator of the world and of man, without an explicit or implicit reference to the question of predestination. It seems that John of Damascus is aware of these two notions ("creator of all" and "agent of all things") and of their implications, but at this point he does not refer to the latter issue.

A last point, to which attention should be drawn, is the way in which John of Damascus on the one hand, and the later Byzantine polemicists on the other, convey the idea of Surah CXII, 2. The latter read the crucial word *Samad* as [*holosphairos*] (= all spherical) or [*holosphyros*] (= round hammered compact).[47] Modern translations read "Allah le Seul",[48] or "God the Eternal",[49] or "Allah the eternally besought of all",[50] or "Allah is He on whom all depend".[51] John of Damascus translates,[52] "God, the Creator of all". The misunderstanding of Nicetas is not simply an oversight of one word, but actually the result of a biased attitude and a wrong interpretation of the Qur'ānic proclamation of Allah. Later Byzantines continued the tradition of Nicetas, from whom they borrowed the distorted translation of *samad.*[53]

8. The account of the Muslim understanding of Christ,[54] as it has been recorded by John of Damascus, is very interesting and, as such it shall be reproduced here:

> He says that Christ is the Word of [from] God[55] and His Spirit,[56] created,[57] and a servant,[58] born from Mary,[59] the sister of Moses and Aaron[60] without seed[61] [i.e., without human father], because the Word of God entered Mary[62] and she gave birth to Jesus, a prophet[63] and a servant of God, and that the Jews, violating the law wanted to crucify him[64] and they seized him, but they crucified his shadow,[65] and Christ himself was not crucified, they say, nor did he die;[66] God took him up to heaven unto Himself[67] because He loved him. And he says that when he ascended into heaven God asked him, "Jesus, did you say that 'I am Son of God, and God'?" And Jesus answered "Be merciful to me, O Lord; you know that I did not say so, neither shall I boast that I am your servant, but men who have gone astray wrote that I said this thing, and they spoke lies against me, and they are in error".[68] And God answered to him: "I know that you would not say this thing". (765A-C)

This passage is one of the most convincing evidences of the accuracy of John of Damascus' knowledge of the teaching and the wording of the Qur'ān! The references to the Qur'ān which we have given show that each of these points which John mentions has a Qur'ānic origin and that he transmits to the Christians a most accurate account of the Muslim point of view with regard, especially, to the most delicate topic in a Muslim-Christian dialogue.

9. At the beginning of the Chapter John of Damascus had called Muhammad a "false prophet" (764B). After the discussion on Christ the next major issue under consideration is the authenticity of the prophethood of Muhammad. This discussion reveals that the author is reproducing here some of the most important points which emerged in actual conversations between himself, or other Christians, and Muslims. The subject of the prophethood of Muhammad is introduced by two questions. From the answers to these questions the author expects, obviously, to justify the thesis that Muhammad is a false prophet:

> Who is the one who gives witness that God gave him a book? Who of the prophets foretold that such a prophet would arise? (765C)

In connection with the first question the author mentions the example of Moses, who received the Law while his people were looking at the smoking mountain.[69] The answers that he receives are, first, that "God does whatever He wills"[70] and then a more specific one, that "while he [Muhammad] was asleep the scripture came down on him".[71] Perhaps this last answer, as it is recorded by John of Damascus, refers implicitly to Surah XCVII (*lāilat al-qadr* = the night of power). This Surah—one of the earliest in the Qur'ān—speaks of that night of Ramadan during which "The angels and the Spirit (Gabriel) descend therein, by the permission of their Lord, with all decrees".[72] This Surah, however, does not convey any information that Muhammad received the Qur'ān while he was asleep. The answer that the Muslim gives is, rather, a reference to a tradition which Ibn Ishāq recorded later in the *Sīrat:* " . . . Gabriel brought him the command of God. 'He came to me' said the Apostle of God, 'while I was asleep, with a coverlet of brocade, whereon was some writing, and said: "Read"! . . ."[73] The Christian challenges further the Muslim for having accepted a scripture without witnesses who could testify as to where this came from and how; while, according to the Christian of the conversation, his opponent's scripture does not permit one either to get married, or to buy, or take anything without witnesses. Indeed, the Qur'ān prescribes witnesses for different cases, as for debt, marriage, proof of the infidelity of one's wife, death of someone who leaves heirs, and for receiving back one's wife.[74]

In connection with the second question John of Damascus refers to Moses and the prophets after him, who foretold the advent of Christ. This argument caused an immediate reaction on the part of the Muslims, who during the following generations tried to meet this challenge by presenting long lists of Old and New Testament passages as prophecies of the coming of Muhammad.[75]

It seems that John of Damascus does not know yet of such a reaction on the part of the Muslims. When he asks the Muslim directly "And who of the prophets foretold that such a prophet would arise?" he has to offer him some examples of what he means by this (i.e., by previous witnesses from the prophets), because "they were wondering what he was talking about".[76] This is another indication that Chapter 101 belongs to an earlier period than the ninth century, the time when Muslims started to use biblical texts in defense of the prophethood of Muhammad. It is shortly after John of Damascus' direct provocation, expressed in the second question mentioned above, that such an effort begins and that such lists were compiled with an emphasis on texts from the Prophets of the Old Testament.[77]

> 10. The Muslims accuse the Christians of being "Associators", for ascribing a partner to God, by calling Christ "Son of God" and "God". The Christians, in turn, accuse the Muslims of being "Mutilators", by having disassociated God from His Word and Spirit. (Cf., 768B-D)

The accusation of the Muslims is based upon the affirmation of the Qur'ān that God has no son.[78] The expression "to ascribe partners unto Allah" (Pickthall, Blachère), or "to associate [others] with Allah" ('Ali) occurs frequently in the Qur'ān[79] and it refers not only to the "pagan" polytheists and the Jews,[80] but also to the Christians who call Christ "Son of God". John of Damascus has a correct knowledge of this Qur'ānic notion and he is well aware of the meaning that the Muslims ascribe to this issue.[81]

John of Damascus replies by calling the attention of the Muslims to the testimony of the prophets whom, as he knows, the Muslims also accept. Indeed the Qur'ān calls to belief in all prophets.[82] John of Damascus' representation of the Muslim position, at this point, is accurate. He shows also that he is aware of the Muslim criticism that the Christians have altered the books of the prophets, while the Jews have misled the Christians by concealing such prophecies (768C). These are, precisely, criticisms from the Qur'ān against the Christians.[83]

John of Damascus turns the accusation "associators" into a counter attack and he rebukes the Muslims for being "Mutilators" ([*Koptai*]), for having alienated God from His Word and His Spirit.[84] This, he claims, is untenable for:

> The Word and the Spirit are inseparable from that in which [or, in whom] they have been by nature. Therefore, if His Word is in God, it is obvious that He is God. But if He is outside of God then, according to you [Muslims], God is without reason and without Spirit . . . and you treat Him like wood, or a stone, or some irrational thing. (768C-D)

One may see in this dialectic accusation and counter accusation reflections of a fervent dialogue which was taking place in the eighth century between the Muslims and the Christians on the nature of God and His attributes.[85] From John of Damascus' criticism it is obvious that he is responding to the orthodox Muslim theology, which later would be criticized by other Muslims as setting God's names and qualities apart from His essence, as components of Deity. John of Damascus' theology seems to anticipate the Mu'tazilite position, according to which the attributes of God are not entities in themselves but are of the nature of God and constitute His essence.[86] John of Damascus, without stripping God of names and qualities, stresses that these are of His essence, although they do not describe His essence.[87] With his apophatic theology he avoided anthropomorphism (*tashbīh*) into which Orthodox Islam was eventually led,[88] while he preserved the attributes of God along with His unity, avoiding agnosticism (*ta'tīl*), into which the Mu'tazilites fell.[89]

Chapter 101 shows clearly that John of Damascus is well aware of the theological schools arising among the Muslims and that he, perhaps, became involved in those early discussions and stimulated them with his theology.[90]

> 11. The Muslims accuse the Christians also of idolatry, because they venerate the cross; and the Christians return the accusation to the Muslims, because they venerate the Ka'ba. (Cf., 768D-769B)

There is no reference in the Qur'ān in which the Christians are accused of being idolaters because of their respect for, and veneration of, the cross.[91] This Christian symbol is, however, indirectly rejected by the Qur'ān and despised by the Muslims. The Qur'ān denies that Jesus was crucified on the cross,[92] an idea related to the notion that, in spite of persecution, the Apostles of God ultimately triumph.[93] The Jews crucified only the "resemblance" or "similitude" of Jesus; they thought that they nailed him to the cross, but they did not. In the Hadīth literature it is even stated that Jesus himself will appear as *hakam* or *imām* and will destroy the cross.[94] Thus, that which the Christians venerate as the symbol "through which the power of the demons and the deceit of the devil has been demolished" (769B) is, actually, considered by the Muslims as a gross insult against God and disbelief in God's messengers.[95] When, therefore, John of Damascus says that the Muslims "despise the cross" he conveys exactly their feelings and ideas. Not only the veneration of the cross, but also that of any representation or image was despised by the Muslims.[96] As we have already discussed earlier, the policy of Yazīd II (720-724) may have had an impact upon the development of the Christian iconoclasm, which erupted only a few years later (726 or 730).[97] Yazīd's predecessor, 'Umar II (717-720) had questioned Leo III regarding the validity of the Christian veneration of the cross and of the icons,[98] which shows that the Muslims had early objections to it. It was, rather, the tolerance of some caliphs (e.g., 'Abd al-Malik, for his friend Akhtal) that permitted a few Arab Christians to appear in public with a silver cross hanging around their necks, than the tolerance of the public itself.[99]

Because the Muslims accuse the Christians of idolatry for venerating the cross John of Damascus challenges, in turn, their veneration of the Ka'ba. In this context John of Damascus wants to inform his reader about the religious practices of the Muslims connected with the Ka'ba. Chapter 101 contains the following information on this point:[100]

> a. There is a stone which the Muslims embrace and kiss in their [*Chabathan*][101] (*Habathan* or *Chabathan*).
>
> b. This—which they call "stone"—is a head of Aphrodite, whom they used to venerate, and whom they used to call [address] [*Chaber*] (*Haber*, or *Chaber*).[102]
>
> c. Upon this stone, even to this day, traces of an engraved image are visible, for those who know about it.

We have to refer here once more to the remark of Chapter 101 which we have discussed already:

> d. They venerated the morning star and Aphrodite, whom (Aphrodite) they called in their language [*Chabar*] (Habar, or Chabar), which means "great". (764B)

From this discussion it becomes obvious that John of Damascus is referring to two different, but related, subjects: the description of the sanctuary, and the description of the ritual.

From an earlier description, which speaks explicitly of an address and a supplication to the stone[103] and from the statement of John of Damascus that *Habar* "means *great* in their language" we must assume that under the expression *Habar* may be a reference to the exclamation *Allahu akbar* (= *The God is the most great*).[104] Germanus' description might leave some doubt as to whether this author confused *Hobar* with the stone itself, although the two phrases "address to the lifeless stone" and "invocation of the so-called Hobar" do not allow a justification of this interpretation.[105] In John of Damascus' account, however, there is no ambiguity whatsoever. In the first passage quoted above John of Damascus makes a clear distinction between *Habathan* and a "stone", referring with the former to the sanctuary of the Ka'ba. In the second point (b) he states the name [*lithos*] (= "Stone"—most likely the Black Stone) that was given to the stone, the head of Aphrodite, on which traces of an engraved image can be seen.

This information of John of Damascus confirms the theory that the pre-Islamic cult of Ka'ba was syncretistic, and that it had embraced elements of heathen worship and of astral symbolism.[106] Even more specifically, traces of the Semitic Venus (Gr. Aphrodite) could be identified during the time of Muhammad's life.[107]

The very faint traces of an image on the stone which John of Damascus mentions point out, perhaps, to the consecutive destructions and demolitions which the Ka'ba as a whole and the Black Stone itself had suffered in the past, as well as the wearing smooth of the stone by rubbing and kissing[108] which, as John of Damascus describes it, was extremely passionate.[109]

On the basis of what has been said so far we think that, the conclusion that "John of Damascus identifies [*Chabar*] or [*Chaber*] with both Aphrodite herself and with the Ka'ba which according to him represents the head of the pagan goddess",[110] is inaccurate. Furthermore, it seems to us unjustifiable to state that,

> The example of the passage on Aphrodite proves that John of Damascus did not add anything substantial to the information on Islam already available to the Byzantines of his time, and that he merely made use of an accepted argument which conveniently confirmed the Byzantine belief that the Arabs were devoted to lechery.[111]

This passage on the Ka'ba proves, rather, the opposite: that John of Damascus is more accurate and explicit than his predecessors and that he has a remarkable knowledge of its cult; and, most important, that this passage stresses that the Arabs before Muhammad were idolaters, rather than it accuses the Muslims of being devoted to lechery. What is called here "lechery" is, actually, a reference to Abraham with two clearly discernible subjects: the history of the pre-Islamic Ka'ba cult and the Muslim attitude toward the sanctuary. When John of Damascus questions the Muslims as to why they venerate the Ka'ba, he says that some of them reply that it is "because Abraham had sexual intercourse with Hagar on it" and others "because Abraham tied there his camel when he was about to sacrifice Isaac". (769A)[112]

There is no Qur'ānic reference which can support these interpretations. By referring to Abraham both explanations tend rather to stress that the origin of Islam goes back to Abraham and to relate the foundation of the Ka'ba to him, affirmations which are clearly Qur'ānic.[113] John of Damascus uses the two Muslim interpretations not in order to underline any scandal or lechery, but to criticize the Muslims for their inconsistency when they accuse the Christians of idolatry:

> Let us assume that it (the stone) is of Abraham, as you foolishly maintain. Then, just because he had intercourse with a woman on it, or he tied a camel to it, you are not ashamed to kiss it, *yet you blame us* because we venerate the cross . . . ? (769A-B)

12. John of Damascus refers to the Qur'ān in two places. In the first one, at the beginning of the Chapter, he spoke of "some doctrines" (lit. constitutions) which Muhammad inscribed in his book, and which "he entrusted to his followers to adhere to".[114] At this point he is dealing more extensively with some of the Surahs of the Qur'ān, which he describes as "preposterous" or "ridiculous" and "foolish".[115]

Regarding the Surahs—or as he calls them, "scriptures"—he gives the information that each bears a [*prosēgoria*] (title). No agreement has been reached on the question when the 114 Surahs in the Qur'ān received the names under which they are known.[116] John of Damascus' text shows that in the first half of the eighth century some Surahs were, already, referred to by specific names.[117] He gives the names of the four Surahs which he selected for discussion and with which we will deal briefly in the following pages.

(I) Surah IV: *The Women* (*al-Nis*)

Surah IV, which contains 177 verses (*ayat*), is discussed by John of Damascus in 25 lines, and the discussion is concentrated on one subject only, the legislation concerning marriage and divorce. The points that John of Damascus mentions here are the following:

(a) Marriage:

> He, (Muhammad) permits by law that one may, openly, take four wives and concubines, if he can, one thousand, that is as many as his hand can maintain, besides the four wives. (Cf., 769C)

This, obviously, is S. IV, 3, which reads:

> And if ye fear that ye will not deal fairly by the orphans ('Alī = that you cannot do justice to orphans), marry of the women, who seem good to you, two or three or four; and if ye fear that ye cannot do justice, then [marry] one of [the captives] that your right hand possesses. Thus it is more likely that ye will not do injustice.[118]

It is apparent that although these two texts show a striking similarity in their content, they differ considerably in their emphasis and intentions. John of Damascus' text seems to ignore the original emphasis and purpose of this legislation—namely to secure protection and justice for the orphans of the battle of Uhud (23rd. of March, 625)[119]—and to underline one-sidedly polygamy, which the author is interested in condemning as a general, now, practice among the Muslims.

(b) Divorce:

> One may divorce whom he desires and may take another. One should not reunite with his wife after he has divorced her, unless she shall have been married by another. And if a brother divorced his wife, another brother can marry her. (cf. 769B-D)

The Qur'ānic legislation on divorce is contained primarily in two Surahs: S. II, 226-241 and S. IV, 35, 128. Other statements about specific conditions, financial arrangements and rights of divorce, occur in a number of Surahs.[120] John of Damascus does not enter into all these complicated cases, but he gives only the basic Islamic laws on divorce in line with the Qur'ān.

(c) Muhammad's marriage to the wife of Zaid (769C):

This incident, which is recorded in the Qur'ān,[121] became a favorite subject for polemics. John of Damascus connects the incident with the discussion on divorce and he states it as the reason for the institution of the practice of *muhallil* or repudiation.[122] This incident, which John of Damascus viewed as a premeditated act by Muhammad, later Christian polemicists made a central theme in recriminating Muhammad as a Prophet.[123]

The closing sentence of this section characterizes one of the well known Qur'ānic passages on marriage as "obscene" or "shameful":

> Your women are a tilth for you [to cultivate], so go to your tilth as ye will, and send [good deeds] before you for your souls; and fear Allah, and know that ye will meet Him. Give glad tidings to believers.[124]

(2) *The "she-camel of God".*

There is no Surah in the Qur'ān under this title. The expression "she-camel of God" is known, however, from the frequently mentioned story of Sālih, the prophet and warner to the people of Thamūd.[125] The she-camel became the sign of the truth of Sālih's message and a trial for the people of Thamūd. The leaders of the tribe killed or mutilated the camel (XCI, 14; VII, 77) to test Sālih's warning as to its validity. God then caused them to die, buried under the ruins of their houses, obviously after an earthquake.[126] It may be for this reason that the Qur'ān refers to them as dwellers of the rock.[127]

The version of John of Damascus contains many of the same points, to which some traditional variations have been added. It comes closest to the story as recorded in S. XXVI, 141-159, where the camel and the people are presented as drinking water from the river in turns. Sālih's name is not mentioned, although there are clear indications about his involvement in this story.[128]

A discussion on Paradise is connected with this story and it is loosely related to it. The author is aware of the Qur'ānic teaching of Paradise as a garden underneath which flow rivers and where delight and pleasures prevail.[129] The description of Paradise, however, does not seem to have been the purpose of this paragraph. It is rather used as indicative of the inconsistencies that the story of the "she-camel of God" contains, and it turns as a criticism against the prophet[130] and a condemnation of those who believe in him (772C-D).

(3) Surah V: *"The Table Spread"* (*al-Mā'idah*)

This is the proper title of the Surah taken from verse 114. John of Damascus gives the following account of this Surah:

> Another writing which Muhammad calls *The Table.* He says that Christ asked from God a table, and this was given to him. And God said to him: "I have given to you and to your people a table which is incorruptible". (772D)

The corresponding verses in the Qur'ān are as follows:

> 114. Jesus, son of Mary, said: O Allah, Lord of us! Send down for us a table spread with food from heaven, that this may be a feast for us, . . . and a sign from Thee. Give us sustenance, for Thou art the Best of Sustainers.
>
> 115. Allah said: Lo! I send it down for you. And whoso disbelieveth of you afterward, him surely will I punish with a punishment wherewith I have not punished any of [my] creatures.[131]

Many scholars have seen in the verses 114-115 an allusion to the Last Supper.[132] Perhaps this is the reason why John of Damascus has mentioned this Surah, in order to show the "heretical" aspect of Islam in contrast to the Christian understanding of the sacrament.

(4) In addition to S. IV the "she-camel" and S. V, there is one more reference to the Qur'ān with S. II, the *"Heifer"* (*al-Baqarah*). John of Damascus gives only the name of this Surah which is taken from the verses 67-71 (Cf., 772D).

We believe that John of Damascus had read, or had heard of, more than the four Surahs which he mentions by their titles. This conclusion is based not only upon the references which have, already, been discussed in this chapter but, also, upon his own affirmation. At the beginning of his discussion on the Muslim scriptures he wrote: "This Muhammad, ... after he *wrote many* preposterous things (writings, i.e., Surahs) he set on each of them a title, such as . . ." (769B).[133]

And at the end of the discussion on these four Surahs he concluded in the following manner: "Again the writing of *Heifer, and other* preposterous things, worthy of ridicule, which because of their great number I think *I ought to pass over.*" (772D-773A).

These two sentences show that John of Damascus was only selecting a few Surahs which would suffice to demonstrate that the Muslim scriptures are preposterous and unworthy of serious consideration. We find, therefore, the suggestion that John of Damascus "was not acquainted with even the four suras of the Qur'ān in detail" unfounded.[134]

13. In the last part of Chapter 101 some aspects of Muslim practices are mentioned:

> He [Muhammad] made a law that men and women be circumcised and he gave orders not to observe the Sabbath, neither to be baptized; and to eat some foods which are forbidden by the Law, and to abstain from others; and he forbade entirely the drinking of wine. (773A)

Circumcision is not mentioned in the Qur'ān, but is found in Islam as a part of the whole idea of ablution and cleanliness[135] and as a practice from the "religion of Abraham" of which Islam, according to the Muslims, is a continuation.[136]

The renunciation of the Sabbath, as well as of baptism, are obviously reactions of the Muslim community and an expression of a sense of its independence from Judaism and Christianity.[137]

The prohibition of some foods and the approval of others is often discussed in the Qur'ān,[138] as is the prohibition of strong drinks as well.[139]

As a conclusion to this chapter we wish to defend the thesis that Chapter 101 of the ***De Haeresibus*** is an early systematic introduction to Islam written by a Christian writer. Its purpose was to inform the Christians of the newly-appeared "heresy" and to provide some preliminary answers to its "heretical" elements. The following tentative outline can clearly show the unity and coherence of the Chapter:

I. *Historical introduction.*

A. Name of the heresy and its derivation

B. Its historical background

C. Its founder

II. *Systematic Theology.*

A. Theology

B. Christology

C. Revelation

III. *Apologetics.*

A. Theology of the attributes of God

B. Devotional life and symbolism

IV. *Introduction to the Islamic Scriptures.*

Surah IV

Surah VII

Surah V

Reference to Surah II

V. *Legislation and Practices*

It has to be said, however, that this essay was written by a Christian writer for Christian readers who, although geared to contrast what is "heretical" to what is "Orthodox", are with the author ultimately interested in an instruction on the Christian orthodox theology. Chapter 100/101 can not be seen otherwise, than as a part of the ***De Haeresibus,*** and not as an independent polemic piece of literature. The author is not defending Christian Orthodoxy through this essay on Islam, neither does he consider this discussion as the final goal of his writing. This is not the final word that he reserves for each heresy and for Islam, and, perhaps, that is why he is not absorbed in making it, also, a "fatal" one. He presents the facts about Islam in an orderly and systematic way, although not at all complimentary; he demonstrates an accurate knowledge of the religion, perhaps higher than the one that an average Muslim could possess; he is aware of the cardinal doctrines and concepts in Islam, especially those which are of an immediate interest to a Christian; he knows well his sources and he is at home with the Muslim mentality. Chapter 100/101 is not inflammatory of hatred, neither grandiloquent and full of self-triumph; it is an essay on Islam, in a book of Christian heresies. In this simple fact lies its significance and its weakness!

Notes

[1] For an English translation see John W. Voorhis, "John of Damascus on the Moslem heresy", [*The Muslim World (MW)*], XXIV (1934), 391-398; and Chase, [Frederic H.,] *Saint John* [*of Damascus. Writings.* vol XXXVII of *The Fathers of the Church* (New York: Fathers of the Church, Inc. 1958)], pp. 153-160. A few inaccuracies have passed on into both these translations, most likely due to the fact that they relied heavily

upon the latin translation, instead of on the original Greek version. Cf. Appendix I, pp. 132-143 for the Greek text and a translation into English.

An excellent contribution to this discussion is Paul Khoury's work "Jean Damascène et l'Islam", [*Proche Orient Chrétien (POC)*] VII (1957), 44-63; VIII (1958), 313-339; although there is, at the end of this installment the indication "(à suivre)", the article has not been completed, to the best of our knowledge. In the first installment the author summarizes in sixteen groups the points with which Chapter 101 deals:

"1. Origines; 2. Ancienne religion; 3. Mahomet; 4. Le Coran, livre revelé; 5. Description du Coran; 6. Dieu; 7. Le mal et le libre arbitre; 8. Le Christ; 9. Prophètes et personnages bibliques; 10. Paradis; 11. Mariage; 12. Témoins; 13. Autres prescriptions; 14. Culte; 15. Ce que les musulmans pensent des juifs et des chrétiens; 16. Comportement des musulmanes dans une discussion".

Afterwards he gives for each of these units corresponding references from the Qur'ān, sometimes with very short comments. In a third section he states his conclusions from this study. We think that the above-mentioned grouping is inadequate. Section 7, e.g., is not an issue in Chapter 101. At this point "God does whatever He wants" is not used with the connotation of God being the source of good and evil neither of man's free will, but it is used in the framework of a discussion regarding the testimonies of the prophethood of Muhammad. Neither is group 9 a unit in itself, but an argument in the same discussion of the authenticity of Muhammad's prophethood. Khoury's arrangement does not show the emphasis upon the discussion of the person and of the prophetic mission of Muhammad, which, along with the discussion on Christ, is the major theme of Chapter 101.

In our discussion we will attempt to make a short analysis of each unit of the text as well as a critical discussion of the information that the text offers, in order to be able to assess the accuracy of John of Damascus' knowledge of Islam, his sources, emphases and his attitude toward this religion. In a way this remains a preliminary work, since the critical edition is not yet available. This new edition will provide the possibility to investigate the dependence upon the previous sources, the possible interpolations, variations of editions, their implications, etc. For a short discussion of Chapter 101, cf. J. Windrow Sweetman, *Islam and Christian Theology, A Study of the Interpretation of Theological Ideas in the two Religions.* Part I, vol. 1 (London: Lutterworth Press, 1945), pp. 65f.

[2] Cf. above, p. 59, n. 5.

[3] The version of Chapter 101 in Book XX of Acominatus' *Thesaurus* has completed the word from [*skei*] to [*threskeia*] (= religion). The Latin translation of the text has translated [*threskeia*] in one place as *superstitio* (cf. *De superstitio Agarenorum,* [*Patrologiae Cursus Completus.* Series Graeca Prior, ed. Jacques Paul Migne (Paris: J. P. Migne, 1857-1866) (*MPG*)], CXL, 105) and in another as *religio* (cf. *religio Agarenorum, Ibid.,* 106). The *Doctrina Patrum* has, also, [*threskeia*]. Cf. Diekamp [, Franz] *Doctrina* [*Patrum, de Incarnatione Verbi. Ein Griechisches Florilegium aus der wende des siebenten und achten Jarhunderts* (Münster: Aschendorffsche Verlagsbuchhandlung, 1907)], p. 270.

[4] The Greek word is [*skia*].

[5] Voorhis, *MW,* XXIV (1934), 392, n. 1.

[6] "[*homoiōs dēthen Areianōi prosomilēsas monachōi idian synestēsato hairesin*]" 765A; cf. also below, p. 73, n. 3.

[7] Theophanes, *Chronographia* [, Ex recensione Ioannis Classeni. Vol. XXXIX, *Corpus Scriptorum Historiae Byzantinae* (Bonnae: Ed. Weber, 1839)]. 734, p. 642. Cf. below, p. 75.

[8] *Ibid., ann.* 721, p. 627.

[9] *Ibid., ann.* 711, pp. 414f; Cedrenus, [Georgius,] *Compendium* [*Historiarum*], *MPG,* CXXX, 868.

[10] Symeon Magister, *Annales, MPG,* CIV, 668. All three cases stated above are related to Iconoclasm, and these three persons were leading Iconoclasts. It could be that the epithet "forerunner of the Antichrist" was extensively used by the iconolaters against their religious antagonists during the Iconoclastic Controversy. It must be noted here that Peter of Maiuma and John of Damascus were both iconolaters, and lived during this century.

[11] *MPG,* XCIV, 1216A.

[12] *Ibid.,* 1032A. Cf. also Athanasius (295-373) calling Emperor Constantius "forerunner of the Antichrist" for supporting the Arians; *MPG,* XXV, 773, 777ff; also in the *Vita St. Antonii,* the great anchorite is reported calling the Arians "forerunners of the Antichrist"; *MPG,* XXVI, 941. It is very interesting that the term "Antichrist" (*al-Dajjal*) is found also in the early Muslim literature, apparently taken from Christian writers! The Antichrist is depicted with horrifying features, as being an unbeliever and not among the "submitted ones to God", i.e., a Muslim. Cf. Hishām Ibn al-Kalbi (d. A.D. 821), *Kitāb al-Asnām*(*The Book of Idols*), tr. by Nabih Amin Faris, (Princeton University Press, 1952), pp. 50-51.

[13] John of Damascus, unlike Peter of Maiuma, did not call Muhammad personally the "forerunner of the Antichrist", but applied it to the "religion" of the

Ishmaelites, (764A). Nicetas of Byzantium called the Qur'ān "antitheos" and "Antichrist", *MPG,* CV, 717A. Cf. also, below, p. 77. The epithet "forerunner of the Antichrist" played a role in the formation of the Christian attitude toward Islam. John Meyendorff remarks that the relations between the Arab Muslims and the Greek Emperors "were shaped by their respective religious ideologies, and each side interpreted the attitudes and actions of the other as motivated by religion. If the Qur'ān appealed to a holy war against 'those who ascribe partners to God'—i.e., Christians who believe in the Trinity—the Byzantine retaliated after the example of St. John of Damascus, by considering Islam as a 'forerunner of Antichrist'" [, "Byzantine Views of Islam." *Dumbarton Oaks Papers (DOP)*] XVIII (1964), 115. Although this could be said as a generalization for the Byzantine Christians, one could not say that it was John of Damascus who gave this tone to the Christian attitude toward Islam. John of Damascus, on the contrary, preserved his dialogue with Islam within a theological framework, so that, to the Muslim accusation that the Christians are polytheists because they "ascribe partners to God", he retaliated with a theological, not emotional, counter-accusation that the Muslims are "mutilators" because "they disassociate God from His Word". Cf. below, pp. 82f.

[14] Ibn al-Kalbi, *Idols,* pp. 4ff. Cf. also, S. II, 135: "Nay, but (we follow) the religion of Abraham, the upright, and he was not of the idolaters".

[15] S. II, 133; al-Tabarī, *Chronique,* II, 356. Michael the Syrian calls Islam "la religion du sud" and the Muslims "les fils d'Ismael". *Chronique,* II, 413.

[16] Ibn al-Kalbi, *Idols,* p. 4. al-Tabarī, *Chronique,* I, 161f.

[17] S. II, 127.

[18] S. XIV, 40; al-Tabarī, [Abū Dja'far Muhammed b. Djarir,] *Chronique,* [tr. Herman Zotenberg (Paris: Imprimiere Nationale, 1867-1874. 4 vols.),] I, 188f.

[19] Ibn al-Kalbi, *Idols,* pp. 4f.

[20] Cf. e.g., the author of the *Vita* of John of Damascus *MPG,* XCIV, 436; Zonaras, [Ioannes,] *Annales, MPG,* CXXXIV, 1332; Constantine Acropolite, *Sermo, MPG,* CXL, 817. One cannot refrain from making the comment that, although these names are, possibly, cherished by the Muslims as indicative of their origin and of their adherence to the earliest monotheism, they were adopted by the Christian polemicists—not without a concealed sarcasm—in order to demonstrate that the Muslims are only Abraham's illegitimate children and false monotheists. The use of all these three names together is indicative of such a purpose in mind. The names *Ishmaelites* and *Saracens* are already mentioned by Epiphanius (d. 403) as referring to one and the same religious group, which practiced circumcision. Cf. *Panarion, MPG,* XLI, 469A.

[21] ". . . [*dia to eirēsthai hypo tēs Agar tōi angelōi' Sarra kenēn me apelysen*]", *MPG,* XCIV, 764A. Louis Cheikho, "L'origine du mot 'Sarasin'", *al-Machriq,* VII, 340, stated in *Table Décennales des articles parus dans la revue al-Machriq* 1898-1907. ([Beirut]: Imprimerie Catholique, 1910), p. 25. We were unable to locate this article. The name *Muslim* does not appear at all in Chapter 101; perhaps the other names were preferred not only because they were commonly known among the Christians, but also because they emphasize the links of this "heresy" with the Judeo-Christian tradition.

[22] Ibn al-Kalbi, *Idols,* p. 6.

[23] *Ibid.,* p. 6. Here is an account that shows the process of this religious deterioration: "The reason which led them to the worship of images and stones was the following: no one left Mecca without carrying away with him a stone from the stones of the Sacred House (*al-Harram*) as a token of reverence to it, and as a sign of affection to Mecca. Wherever he settled he would circumambulate it in the same manner he used to circumambulate Ka'abah [before he departed from Mecca] . . . In time this led to the worship of whatever took their fancy, and caused them to forget their former worship". *Ibid.,* p. 4.

[24] *Ibid.,* p. 28. For the religion in pre-Islamic Arabia, cf. A. Jamme, "La religion Arabe pré-islamique" in Maurice Brillant et René Aigrain, *Histoire des Religions,* IV (Paris: Bloud et Gay, 1953), pp. 239-307; Hamilton A. R. Gibb, "Pre-Islamic Monotheism in Arabia", [*Harverd Theological Reviews (HThR)*], LV (1962), 269-280; W. E. N. Kensdale, *The Religious Beliefs and Practices of the Ancient South Arabians.* (Ibadan: Ibadan University Press, 1955).

[25] This star was called with three epithets corresponding to its three stellar aspects: "morning" star (*shrqn*), "evening" star (*ghrbn*)—these two mark the two opposite aspects of Venus, which John of Damascus calls with its Greek name Aphrodite—and "dominating" or "elevated" star, which characterizes the star in its zenith. Jamme, in Brillant's *Histoire,* IV, 265; Khoury sees in the Qur'ān (S. LXXXVI, 1-3 and LIII, 1) an allusion to this morning and evening star. *POC,* VII (1957), 53.

[26] He implies this situation, when he states—even though in a negative way: "[*Kai prophasei to dokein theosebeias to ethnos eispoiēsamenos . . . diathryllei*]" ("And when he had infused the favor of the people, he declared . . ."), 764A. This is how an early *hadīth* describes the attitude of the Muslims toward Muhammad's mission, in an address of Ja'far b. Abū

Tālib to the Christian king of Abyssinia: "O King, we were an uncivilized people, worshipping idols, eating corpses, committing abominations, breaking natural ties, treating guests badly, and our strong devoured our weak. Thus we were until God sent us an apostle whose lineage, truth, trustworthiness, and clemency we know. He summoned us to acknowledge God's unity and to worship him and to renounce the stones and images which we and our fathers formerly worshipped. He commanded us to speak the truth, . . ." Alfred Guillaume, *The Life of Muhammad.* A translation of Ishāq's *Sīrat Rasūl Allāh,* Karachi, Pakistan: Oxford University Press, 1968, p. 151. Muhammad b. Ishāq lived between A.H. 85-151.

In the words of Ibn al-Kalbi: "When God sent His Prophet, who came preaching the Unity of God, and calling for His worship alone, without any associate, (the Arabs) said: 'Maketh he the god to be but one god? A strange thing forsooth is this'. They had in mind the idols". *Idols,* pp. 28f. Cf. also, S. XXXVIII, 6ff; LXIX, 33ff; and Régis Blachère, *Le Problème de Mahomet.* (Paris: Presses Universitaires de France, 1952), pp. 52ff; W. Montgomery Watt, *Muhammad, Prophet and Statesman.* (London: Oxford University Press, 1961), pp. 56ff; and Watt, *Muhammad at Mecca.* (Oxford: at the Clarendon Press, 1960), pp. 100ff.

[27] Codex R. 2508, "[*hos peritychōn Ebraiois kai Christianois dēthen, kai Areianois, kai Nestorianois, pantachothen hen arusamenos, ex Ioudaiōn men monarchian· ex Areianōn de Logon kai Pneuma ktista· apo de Nestorianōn anthrōpolatreian, kai heautōi thrēskeian peripoieitai . . .*]", *MPG,* XCIV, 765, (y); cf. also, *Contra Muhammad, Ibid.,* CIV, 1449A; and Acominatus, *Ibid.,* CXL, 105B; Cedrenus, [Georgius.] *Compendium [Historiarum], Ibid.,* CXXI, 809C.

[28] This expression is used to indicate the Nestorian teaching. Nestorius is called by some writers "anthropolater". Cf. e.g., Michael the Syrian, *Chronique* [*Universelle,* ed. and tr. J. B. Chabot (Paris: Ernest Leroux, 1901)] II, 406.

[29] Tor Andrae, *Mohammed, the man and his faith,* tr. by Theophil Menzel (New York: Harper and Row, 1960), pp. 37f; Armand Abel, "Bahīrā", [*Encyclopedia of Islam* New Edition. ed Hamilton A. R. Gibbs, et al. (Leiden: E. J. Brill, 1960) (*EIs*)], pp. 922f. Cf. above, p. 68, n. 5.

[30] Cf. below, p. 79. This tradition secures the testimony of an advocate, "chosen at the heart of the most important scriptural religion", which *Bahīrā* (Aram. = *the elect*) supposedly, represented. Abel, *EIs* (New Ed.) I, 1960, p. 922. Abel's reference to Djahiz's *Risālat fīl-Radd 'ala'l-Nasara* (A.D. 851) is very important at this point, to show that "the Christians, of whom the passage in the Kur an (V, 82) speaks with benevolence, are not members of the Byzantine Church, either Jacobite or Melchite, but, merely, those of the type of Bahīrā . . .", *Ibid.,* p. 922.

[31] The Muslim argument of Bahīrā, being a product of the eighth century (*Ibid.,* p. 922), presupposes a Christian challenge. The earliest account of the tradition seems to be the one given by Muhammad b. Ishāq in the *Sīrat,* pp. 79-81. Since John of Damascus seems unaware of the fact that the Muslims use this tradition as an answer to a Christian question, but he refers to it for a different purpose, it appears that we have here another internal indication of the earliest phase of Christian-Muslim dialogue, which chapter 100/101 represents. Abel's thesis, that the Chapter 101 is a text later than the time of John of Damascus, is once more questioned. Cf. [Abel, Armand. "Le chaptire CI du *Livre de Hérésies* de Jean Damascène: son inauthenticité" *studia Islamica* XIX (1963), 5-25.].

[32] 'Abd al-Māsih b. Ishāq al-Kind uses the name Sergius, and identifies him as a Nestorian. The Anonymous text in *MPG,* CIV, 1446, as Jacobite; Euthymius Zygabenus ([*Adversus Saracenos,*] *MPG,* CXXX, 1333) as Arian; Theophanes, *Chronographia ann.* 621, p. 513) and Cedrenus (*MPG,* CXXI, 809) do not identify him. Cf. Abel. *EIs* (New Ed.), 1960, 923. Cf. above, p. 26, n. 2.

[33] 765A; 768A. Once he speaks of [*syngraphē*] (scripture) 765C. The word [*graphē*] is used also by him when referring to a Surah.

[34] Cf. e.g., S. XIX, 16, 41, 51, 54; II, 2, etc. Other meanings of the word *Kitāb* are letter, document, or testimonial (XXVII, 28); book of decrees (XXXV, 11); the decree or decision of God (XXX, 56); the Record (XXXV, 11); the Heavenly Book, or Archetype (XIII, 39).

[35] Richard Bell, *Introduction to the Qur'ān.* (Edinburgh: at the University Press, 1963), pp. 151f.

[36] The phrase "to send down" is used frequently in the Qur'ān in connection with a revelation, e.g., more than 18 times in S. II, 4 (twice), 23, 41, 90 (twice), 97, 99, 159, 170, 174, 176, 185, 213, 231, 285. Cf. also, S. III, 23; IV, 105; V, 48; XVI; 64; XXVII, 6; LXXVI, 23; and Khoury, *POC,* VII (1957), 55.

[37] Theophanes, *Chronographia ann.* 621, pp. 512ff; Abū Qurra, [Theodore, *Opuscula,*] *MPG,* XCVII, 1548A; Bartholomeus [of Edessa,] [*Elenchus et*] *Confutatio Agareni, MPG,* CIV, 1388B-C; *Contra Muhammed, MPG,* CIV, 1449A-D; Cedrenus, *Compendium, MPG,* CXXI, 809A-B; Zygabenus, *Panoplia Dogmatica MPG,* CXXX, 1333B-C; Euthymius Monachus, *Disputatio de Fide, MPG,* CXXXI, 33D-36A; Zonaras, *Annales, MPG,* CXXXIV, 1285C. It is interesting that while the later

Byzantine authors adopted the idea that Muhammad was epileptic, Acominatus—if we accept the first part of Book XX of the *Thesaurus* as authentic—is the only one who does not mention such a point. This makes it difficult for one to accept that Acominatus' text is authentic and that he remained uninfluenced in this matter by previous authors to whom, otherwise, he is very much indebted. Cf. above, pp. 28ff.

[38] Pickthall, [Mohammed Marmaduke. *The Meaning of the Glorious Koran* (New York: Mentor Books, 1963)], p. 454; Cf. also, Blachère, [Régis.] *Le Coran* [(Paris: G. P. Maissonneuve & Larosc, 1966)], pp. 670 f.

[39] Cf. S. II, 133, 163; III, 18; XXXVII, 4; XXXVIII, 66; IX, 31; Cf. also, below, p. 81f.

[40] Cf. lib. I, cap. V; "A demonstration that God is one and not many" *MPG,* XCIV, 800C-801C; references to the unity of the Godhead are scattered throughout the *De Fide Orthodoxa,* and especially in the first Book.

[41] *MPG,* XCIV, 808B-C; Cf. Chase, *Saint John,* p. 176.

[42] *MPG,* XCIV, 808B-833A.

[43] *Ibid.,* 809A. The italicising is ours.

[44] *Ibid.,* 829D. Cf. also, *Libellus Orthodoxiae,* in Gordillo, [Mauritius. "Damascenica, I. Vita Marciana, II. Libellus Orthodoxiae". *Orientalia Christiane (OC),*], VIII (1926), 86f.

[45] *Ibid.,* 812B.

[46] For Qur'ānic data on God as creator—particularly as creator of man—cf. Dirk Bakker, *Man in the Qur'ān* (Amsterdam, Drukkerij Holland N.V., 1965), pp. 1-28. Cf. also, e.g., S. LIX, 24; V, 17; II, 117; VI, 101, 102; III, 6; VII, 11; XIII, 16; LXIV, 3; Cf. Khoury, *POC,* VII (1957), 56f.

[47] The idea, perhaps came from Abū Qurra (c. 750-825) who knew Arabic and translated the word figuratively as '[*sphyropēktos*]' = "firmly hammered in", or "solid". *MPG,* XCVII, 1545C. About Abū Qurra, cf. below, p. 99, n. 4. Nicetas of Byzantium (842-912), either because of lack of original knowledge of the Arabic Qur'ān, or for polemic purposes, translated the same word *samad* as "all spherical" (*MPG,* CV, 705D-708A) and in another place as "hammered all around" (*Ibid.,* 784C-788B). Nicetas elaborated, also, that the Muslims understand God as a solid body, otherwise they would not give Him a spherical shape. God being, therefore, a material sphere, is unable to hear, or to see, or to comprehend, nct even to act without the help of someone else. Cf. *Ibid.,* 708A. Nicetas of Byzantium, the Philosopher, wrote a *Refutation of the Book forged by Muhammad the Arab,* acting on the orders of the Byzantine Emperor Michael III, "The Drunk" (842-867). He called the Qur'ān "a rustic booklet" and "forged mythography" and Islam "a barbaric religion" *MPG,* CV, 709C. The *Refutation* is primarily a tool for the Emperor and for the Byzantine Christians to take political action against the Muslims. Cf. *Ibid.,* 672A. About Nicetas, cf. Khoury, [Adel-Théodore.] [*Les Théologiens Byzantins et l'Islam, I. Textes et auteurs (VIIIe-XIIIe S.).* 2nd tirage. Éditions Nauwelaerts (Paris: Louvain/Beatrice-Nauwelaerts, 1969)], pp. 110-162.

[48] Blachère, *Coran,* p. 671.

[49] Edward Henry Palmer, *The Qur'ān.* vols. VI and IX of *The Sacred Books of the East,* ed. by Max Müller (Oxford: at the Clarendon Press, 1900), II, p. 344.

[50] Pickthall, *Koran,* p. 454.

[51] Maulānā Muhammad 'Alī, *The Holy Qur'ān.* Arabic text, translation and commentary (Lahore: Ahmadiyyah Anjuman Ishā'at Islām, 1951), p. 1219.

[52] We believe that John of Damascus in 765A translates, indeed, and not simply interprets, or distorts the verse.

[53] Cf. Zygabenus, *MPG,* CXXX, 1348B; Kantakuzenos, *Ibid.,* CLIV, 692; the *Ritual of Abjuration* in Edouard Montet, "Un rituel d'abjuration des Musulmans dans l'Église Grecque", [*Revue de l'Histoire des Religions (RHR)*], LIII (1906), 155; (about the "Formula", cf. below, pp. 124); Wolfgang Eichner, "Die Nachrichten über den Islam bei den Byzantinern", [*Der Islam (DIs)*], XXIII (1936), 158f; Sweetman, *Islam,* pt. I, 2, 17f.

[54] For Qur'ānic data on Christ, cf. Henri Michaud, *Jésus selon le Coran* (Neuchatel: Éditions Delachaux et Niestlé, [1960]; Geoffrey Parrinder, *Jesus in the Qur'ān.* (New York: Barnes and Noble, 1965); James Robson, *Christ in Islam.* (London: J. Murray, 1929); Samuel M. Zwemer. *The Moslem Christ. An Essay of the life, character, and teaching of Jesus Christ according to the Koran.* (Edinburgh: Oliphant, Anderson and Ferris, 1912).

[55] S. (III, 39); III, 45; IV, 171; (II, 87) Cf. also, Thomas O'Shaughnessy, *The Koranic Concept of the Word of God* (Roma: Pontificio Instituto Biblico, 1948). Acominatus, in the section referred to, has "Son of God", instead of "Word of God" (*MPG,* CXL, 105). This is a serious misunderstanding and an indication-if this reading is correct—that Acominatus did not have any real knowledge

of the Qur'ān. The Qur'ān could never claim that Christ is the "Son of God". Acominatus' version repeats a Christian and not a Qur'ānic doctrine as John of Damascus wants to present.

[56] S. IV, 171. Cf. Thomas O'Shaughnessy, *The Development of the Meaning of Spirit in the Koran* (Roma: Pontificio Instituto Orientalium Studiorum, 1953).

[57] S. III, 59.

[58] S. IV, 172; XIX, 30, (93); XLIII, 59.

[59] S. II, 87, 253; III, 45; IV, 157, 171; V, 46, 75, 110, 112, 114, 116; XIX, 34; XXXIII, 7; LVII, 27; LXI, 6, 14.

[60] S. XIX, 28.

[61] S. III, 47; XIX, 19-22; XXI, 91.

[62] S. IV, 171, XIX, 17; XXI, 91; LXVI, 12.

[63] S. III, 39, 79; IV, 171; V, 75; XIX, 30; XXXIII, 7.

[64] S. III, 54.

[65] S. IV, 157 and II, 73. A literal translation of the Greek would be: "and after they seized his shadow, they crucified this".

[66] S. IV, 157.

[67] S. III, 55; IV, 158.

[68] S. V, 116; III, 55f; V, 17, 72; IV, 171; IX, 30, 31; XIX, 35, 90-93; XXXIX, 4; CXII, 3.

[69] Ex. 19, 9, 16-19; cf. also, above, pp. 73f. .

[70] 765D. This statement became a major issue in the discussion on predestination to which we shall refer below, pp. 102ff.

[71] 768A.

[72] S. XCVII, 4; Pickthall, *Koran,* p. 446; Bell, *Introduction,* p. 37.

[73] Ibn Ishāq, [Abū 'Abd Allah Muhammed. *Sīrat Rasūl Allāh (The Life of Muhammed).* tr. Alfred Guillaume, Second impression (Karachi, Pakistan: Oxford University Press, 1968)], p. 106.

[74] S. II, 282f; IV, 6, 15, 41; V, 106f; XXIV, 4ff, 13; LXV, 2.

[75] Cf. al-Tabarī, *The Book of Religion and Empire,* tr. by Alphonse Mingana (Manchester: at the University Press, 1922). Al-Tabarī (839-923) takes a favorable position toward the Christian Scriptures. He accepts them as authentic and reliable, and finds evidences in them of the coming of Muhammad. Ibn Hazm (994-1064) rejected totally the Christian Scriptures as having been entirely corrupted and falsified by the Christians. Therefore, for him such an effort is vain and meaningless. He mentions only three passages which he understands as prophecies to the advent of Muhammad (Deut. 18:18; 33:2; and Daniel 2:29). Cf. Myrta Rivera, "Ibn Hazm on Christianity: the polemics of an eleventh century European Muslim". M. A. Thesis, Hartford Seminary Foundation, 1968, pp. 77ff, and Appendices I, IV, V, VI. (About Ibn Hazm, cf. Erdman Fritsch, *Islam und Christentum im Mittelalter, Beiträge zur Geschichte der muslimischen Polemik gegen das Christentum in arabischer Sprache.* Breslau: Verlag Müller & Seiffert, 1930, pp. 15ff.). Ibn Taimiyya (d. 1328)—as in a third stage—took a more moderate position, and, although he considered the Bible as corrupted, not deliberately however, he found valid prophecies of Muhammad in it. (About Ibn Taimiyya, cf. *Ibid.,* pp. 25-33). On the same subject, cf. also the following studies: Karl Brockelmann, "Muhammedanische Weissagungen im Alten Testament" [*Zeitschrift für attestamentliche wissenschaft (ZAW)*], XV (1895), 135-142; M. Schreiner, "Zur Geschichte der Polemik zwischen Juden und Muhammedanern", [*Zeitschrift der deutschen morgenländischen Gesellschaft (ZDMG)*], XLII (1888), 600-601, 626-628; Ignaz Goldziher, "Über Muhammedanische Polemik gegen Ahl al-Kitāb", *ZDMG* XXXII (1878), 372-379; cf. also, G. D. Pearson, *Index Islamicus,* 1905-1955. (Cambridge: W. Heffer & Son, Ltd., 1958) nos. 1673, 1678, 1683, 1698.

[76] 765C. "[*Kai tis tōn prophētōn proeipen hoti toioutos anistatai prophētēs; kai diaporountōn autōn, hōs ho Mōysēs tou theou . . .*]". Voorhis and Chase have both translated this phrase more emphatically, although not accurately, as: "they are quite at a loss" [Voorhis, *MW,* XXIV (1934), 393] or "they are at a loss" (Chase, *Saint John,* p. 154).

[77] Already in the dialogue between the Nestorian Patriarch Timothy (780-823) and Caliph al-Mahdī (775-785), the Caliph claims that both the Old and the New Testament bear witness to Muhammad. For the Syriac text of this dialogue, with an English translation, cf. Alphonse Mingana, "The Apology of Timothy, the Patriarch, before the Caliph Mahdī" [*Bulletin of the John Rylands Library (BJRL)*], XII (1928), 137-298; cf. also, L. E. Browne, "The Patriarch Timothy and the Caliph al-Mahdī". *MW,* XXI (1931), 38-45. In Appendix VI of Rivera's thesis appears a list of texts from the Old and the New Testament, used by al-Tabarī as prophecies of the coming of Muhammad. This list has been compiled by Professor Willem A. Bijlefeld. It presents the following interesting statistics: of the sixty one references listed, 54 are from the Old Testament, and only 7 from the New Testament. Of those 54 from

the Old Testament, 40 are from the Prophets (Isaiah 26, Hosea 1, Micah 1, Hab. 1, Zeph. 1, Zach. 1, Jer. 4, Ezek. 1, Daniel 4) and only 14 from: Genesis (5), Deut. (3), and Psalms (6). Cf. S. III, 81, and LXI, 6 which are used by Muslims as Qur'ānic testimonies of the coming of Muhammad. The latter reference is to Jesus himself "bringing good tidings of a messenger who cometh after him (me), whose name is the Praised One" (*Ahmad*). The verse might remind the Christians of John, 14:16 but the name Ahmad is an undisputed identification of the name of Muhammad, for the Muslims! Cf. Blachère, *Le Coran,* pp. 593f.

[78] S. XIX, 88-93; XVIII, 103; cf. also, II, 116; XIX, 35; XXXIX, 3-4; CXII, 3; and above, p. 78, n. 15.

[79] S. IV, 48, 116; V, 72; XXVIII, 68; XXX, 35. The verb employed in the Arabic text is . . . (= to be a partner, to associate with) from which the words . . . (polytheism) and . . . (polytheist) derive.

[80] S. IX, 30.

[81] Abel's argument that the name *Mushrikuna* was not employed to indicate the Christians, before the ninth century, cannot be considered as valid because this is not a term invented by the Muslims at a later time, but is found in the Qur'ān itself (e.g., S. V, 72); Abel, *SIs,* XIX (1963), 11f.

[82] S. IV, 150-1; cf. also, IV, 164; VI, 90; XII, 110; XIII, 7; XVI, 36, 43, 44; XXII, 75; XXXV, 24; XL, 51, 78; LXXII, 27, 28. Throughout the Meccan period there is an affirmation of the validity of the teaching of the earlier scriptures, as well as of the idea that the scriptures of the Jews and Christians have derived from the same archetype—the Heavenly Book. Therefore, the Qurān confirms what was revealed previously; S. III, 81; VI, 92; XXXV, 31; XLVI, 30. A period of criticism of these scriptures, however, starts with the Medinan Surahs. Cf. F. Buhl, "al-Kur'ān", [*Shortes Encyclopedia of Islam.* ed Hamilton A. R. Gibb and J. H. Kramers (Ithaca: Cornell University Press, 1965) (*SEIs*)], pp. 275f.

[83] S. XIX, 58-9; also II, 146; III, 71. These criticisms refer to the notion of *tahrīf* (corruption) of the scriptures of the Christians and it is found especially in the Medinan Surahs. In the Qur'ān it is expressed in different terms to indicate the kind of corruption implied, as, e.g., malicious corruption (II, 75; III, 78; IV, 46; V, 13, 41), falsification (II, 79), exchange of words (II, 59; VII, 17), alteration (III, 78); concealing or suppressing the content (II, 146, 159, 174; III, 71; VI, 92), etc. F. Buhl, "Tahrīf", *SEIs,* pp. 560f. Cf. also above, p. 80, n. 3.

[84] Cf. above, p. 78, n. 2, 3, 4.

[85] Cf. Duncan Black Macdonald, *Development of Muslim Theology, Jurisprudence, and Constitutional Theory.* (Lahore: The Premier Book House, repr. 1964), p. 132.

[86] The Mu'tazilite theology, with its emphasis upon the absolute unity of God (*tawhīd*) could not tolerate other entities being eternal, apart from the divine essence itself. Therefore, it "deprived" God of His attributes in the sense that it understood them to be His essence itself. Cf. Henri Corbin, *Histoire de la philosophie islamique.* (Paris: Éditions Gallimard, 1964), pp. 166f. According to the Mu'tazilites, God is knowing, rather than He has knowledge; or: God knows not by His knowledge, but by His essence. In a more definite Mu'tazilite form of the Basra school, the attributes are not *in* God's essence but they *are* His essence. (Abū-'l Hudhayl Muhammad al-Allaf, d. ca. 841). Cf. Macdonald, *Theology,* p. 136. Cf. also, Arthur Stanley Tritton, *Muslim Theology.* (Bristol: Luzac and Co., 1947), pp. 56f, 79. Al-Ash'arī took, actually, a middle position and, while he accepted that God has attributes which as such are a positive reality, he stressed that they have neither existence nor reality apart from God's essence. Corbin, *Philosophie,* p. 166. Cf. also Michel Allard, *Le problème des attributs divins dans la doctrine d'al-Asarī et de ses premiers grands disciples.* (Beyrouth: Éditions de l'Imprimerie Catholique, [1965]); A. H. Wolfson, "The Muslim attributes and the Christian Trinity", *HThR,* XLIX (1956), 1-18.

[87] Cf. e.g., "The uncreated, the unoriginated, the immortal, the boundless, the eternal, the immaterial, the good, the creative, the just . . . all these and the like are possessed by His nature . . . it is His nature that communicates all good to His own creatures. *MPG,* XCIV, 860A-B. "The Godhead is simple and uncompounded . . . therefore one schould not think that any of these qualities ascribed to God is indicative of what He is in essence, but they show either what He is not, or some relation to something that is contrasted with Him, or something that is consequential to His nature or action." *Ibid.,* 833-836A. Cf. also, above, p. 75.

[88] Corbin, *Philosophie,* p. 166.

[89] *Ibid.,* p. 166. For John of Damascus "One who would like to define the essence of something must say what it is, and not what it is not. However, with regard to God, it is impossible to say what He is in His essence, but it is more proper to make reference (to Him) by abstraction from all things whatsoever, because He is not any of those that exist; not that He does not exist, but because He transcends all beings, and He is even beyond being itself". *MPG,* XCIV, 800B-C.

[90] Abel uses this passage under discussion (10) as an indication of an author who *was* influenced by the

Mu'tazilite theology, which developed after John of Damascus. Therefore, he insists, Chapter 101 is of a later author. *SIs,* XIX (1963), 12. It has just been shown, however, that John of Damascus had "his own" theology, which he has expressed explicitly in the *De Fide Orthodoxa.* Perhaps the opposite could be said, that the challenge of John of Damascus raised a stronger interest among the Mu'tazilites, offered them additional arguments and had an influence upon their theology, rather than the opposite.

[91] The Christians are accused as people "who ascribe partners to God" (*mushrikūn*), i.e., as polytheists (Cf. above, p. 181, n. 3, p. 182, n. I) and, possibly, once or twice as "unbelievers" (*kāfirūn*). Cf. Josef Horovitz, *Koranische Untersuchungen* (Berlin and Leipzig; Walter de Gruyter & Co., 1926), pp. 59ff. Mostly the Christians are distinguished from the unbelievers—along with the Jews—as the "people of the Book" (*ahl al-kitāb*). S. II, 105, 111f, 121, 145; III, 23, 64ff, 98f, 110f, 186f, 199; IV, 44f, 123, 153ff, 171; V, 5, 15, 19ff, 59, 65, 68, 77; XXIX, 46; XXXII, 26f; LVII, 29; XCVIII, 1ff.

[92] Cf. above, p. 78, n. 11, 12, 13, 14.

[93] S. XIV, 13-20; XL, 51. Cf. Willem Abraham Bijlefeld, "A Prophet and more than a Prophet? Some observations on the Qur'anic use of the words 'prophet' and 'apostle'", *MW,* LIX (1969), 22f, especially, n. 97.

[94] For references to al-Bukhārī, Muslim and Ahmad b. Hanbal, on this tradition, cf. Arent Jan Wensinck, *A Handbook of Early Muhammadan tradition, alphabetically arranged,* (Leiden: E. J. Brill, 1927), p. 113.

[95] S. IV, 154.

[96] Cf. Vasiliev, *DOP,* IX-X (1955-1956), 25, for reference to the Muslim attitude towards the icons: Ibn al-Kalbi attributes to the introduction of the images the deterioration of the early pure religion of the Arabs, "the religion of Abraham and Ishmael". (*Idols,* p. 6; cf. above, p. 71, n. 3); this must have been a general feeling among the Muslims. Reuben Levy, *The Social Structure of Islam* (Cambridge: at the University Press, 1965), pp. 252f.

[97] Cf. above, pp. 9. Before Yazīd II, Theophanes records, under the year 635, an incident with 'Umar I: When 'Umar was building the temple in Jerusalem the building could not stand, but kept falling. When 'Umar inquired as to the reason the Jews told him that unless he would take away the cross from the hill of the olive trees, this building would not stay erected. Theophanes adds that, indeed, the cross was taken away, and after that "those who hate Christ" pulled down many crosses. Theophanes, *Chronographia ann.* 635, p. 524. It is not clear from this text whether the words "those who hate Christ" refer to the Jews or to the Muslims. What is clear is that 'Umar ordered the taking away of, at least, the cross to which the Jews drew his attention. The temple that this story refers to is, obviously, the Dome of the Rock, often erroneously called the "Mosque of 'Umar", which was erected by Abd al-Malik in 691. Nevertheless, 'Umar had already started in 638 building a temple during his visit to Jerusalem. (Michael the Syrian, *Chronique,* II, p. 425). Cf. Hitti, [Philip Khūri. *History of the Arabs* (London: MacMillan, 1937)], pp. 220, 264. Michael the Syrian mentions that 'Abd al-Malik also, in the year 695, ordered that the crosses be pulled down and the swine be slaughtered. *Chronique,* II, 475. Theophanes refers only to the slaughtering of the swine. *Chronographia ann,* 686, p. 561.

[98] Arthur Jeffery, "Ghevond's Text of the Correspondence between 'Omar II and Leo III", *HThR,* XXXVII (1944), 322.

[99] Cf. Lammens, [Henri. *Études sur le Siécle des Omayyades* (Beyrosth: Imprimiere Catholique, 1930)], p. 212, and above, p. 25.

[100] We have to relate these data in more detail because some modern scholars have based their critical conclusions as to John of Damascus' knowledge of Islam on this description.

[101] " . . . [*hymeis lithōi prostribesthe kata tēn Chabathan hymōn kai phileite ton lithon aspazomenoi*]" 769A. Chase's translation of [*prostribesthe*] as "you rub yourselves against . . ." is too literal. The meaning of this statement is that "in your *Chabathan,* you embrace the stone, and you kiss it fervently". It is interesting that the version in Acominatus' text omits the word [*aspazomenoi*] and, instead, it has [*asmenoi*] (= with joy, or with passion, or pleasure). Lequien and Migne indicate that there are also two other forms for [*Chabathan*] in other codices, [*Bachthan*] and [*Chabothan*] (Lequien, [Michael. *Sancti Patris Nostri Joannis Damasceni Monachi et Presbyteri Hierosolymitani, Opera Omnia Quae extant* (Parissis: Apud Johannen Baptistan Delessine, 1712) 2 vols,] I, 113; *MPG,* XCIV, 769) which, along with that in the version of Acominatus. . . , are evidently closely related.

[102] "[*houtos de, hon phasi lithon, kephalē tēs Aphroditēs estin hēn prosekynoun, hēn Chaber prosēgoreuon*]". Voorhis' translation changes the past tense of the verbs into the present, and this change of tenses causes misunderstanding. John of Damascus refers here to the pre-Islamic religion of the Ishmaelites, and not to the Muslim practice. Cf. above, pp. 70ff.

[103] Germanus of Constantinople (715-730) in his letter (724) to Thomas of Claudiopolis, an iconoclast bishop in Asia Minor (cf. above, p. 10, n. 6a.), points out that the iconoclasts imitate the Jews and

the Muslims in their campaign against the icons, and he condemns the religious practices and symbols which they both use. Speaking about the Muslims he relates that even to this day they address themselves to a "lifeless stone" and they practice the so called invocation of *Hobar* ("[*tēn mechri tou nyn en tēi erēmōi teloumenēn par' autōn lithōi apsychōi prosphōnēsin tēn te tou legomenou Chobar epiklēsin*]"). The letter has been preserved in the Acts of the Seventh Ecumenical Council; Mansi, [Giovanni Domenico. Sacrorum Conciliorum Nova et amplissima Collectio (Florentiae, expensis Antonii Zatta Veneti, 1759-1798)], XIII, 109E.

[104] Ibn al-Kalbi informs us that circumambulation of the "House" and also "raising the voice in the acclamation of the name of the deity (*tahlīl*)" existed as practices in the pre-Islamic worship. *Idols,* p. 4f. We do not know whether the pre-Islamic acclamation was, indeed, *"Allahu akbar"*. John of Damascus seems to connect here the pre-Islamic practice with the, certainly, Islamic acclamation.

[105] In the sentence "[*tēn te tou legomenou Chobar epiklēsin*]" the masculine passive participle [*tou legomenou*]—unless it is mis-copied—can imply either the word stone, or, perhaps, the word Allah. If it implies the stone, the sentence says that the stone was called Hobar. It is possible for one—especially for an outsider—to identify the content of an invocation with the object to which it is addressed, i.e., to think that what the invocation contains is the name of the object of the cult. It is possible, also, that under the participle [*tou legomenou*] (masculine) the name of God may be implied, and in this case, the sentence of Germanus says that Allah was called *Hobar* (great).

[106] Arent Jan Wensinck, "Ka'ba" *SEIs,* p. 198.

[107] Wensinck states that "The dove of aloes wood which Muhammad found in the Ka'ba may have been devoted to the Semitic Venus". *Ibid.* p. 198. Cf. also, this tradition in Ibn Mādja, Wensinck, *Handbook,* p. 120.

[108] Wensinck, *SEIs.* p. 192.

[109] "[*Pōs oun hymeis lithōi prostribesthe . . . kai phileite ton lithon aspazomenoi*]", 769A.

[110] Meyendorff, *DOP,* XVIII (1964), 119. Vasiliev also states that "John of Damascus . . . refers to the Kaaba as [*Chabathō*] or Khaber". *DOP,* IX-X (1955-1956), 27.

[111] Meyendorff, *DOP,* XVII (1964), 119.

[112] John of Damascus challenges this last explanation on the ground of the Biblical information, (Genesis, 22:1-14) that there were trees on the hill of sacrifice and, on the other hand, that the ass remained with the two young men accompanying Abraham. (Cf. 769A).

[113] S. II, 127; XIV, 40; cf. above, pp. 69f.
[114] 765A; cf. above, pp. 74f.

[115] "[*Houtos ho Mamed pollas . . . lerōidias syntaxas*] . . ." 769B.

[116] The word *Surah* is used in the Qur'ān with a variety of meanings, such as "row", "chapter", "piece", "section", "writing", "discourses", "text of scripture", "scripture", "revelation"; Buhl, "Sūra", *SEIs,* pp. 553, and 281. Cf. also Bell, *Introduction,* p. 52.

[117] Buhl, "al-Kur'ān", *SEIs,* p. 282; Bell, *Introduction,* pp. 52ff.

[118] Pickthall, *Koran,* p. 79.

[119] W. Montgomery Watt. *Muhammad at Medina.* (Oxford: at the Clarendon Press, 1956), pp. 21-29.

[120] S. IV, 20, 23, 25, 130; XXXIII, 4, 49; LVIII, 2-4; LXV, 1f, 4, 6, 7.

[121] S. XXXIII, 37.

[122] S. II, 229.

[123] Khoury, *Théologiens,* II, 91ff.

[124] S. II, 223. John of Damascus has translated this passage almost verbatim: "[*Eirgasai tēn gēn, hēn ho Theos edōke soi, kai philokalēson autēn· [kai tode poiēson, kai toiōsde]*]" 769D.

[125] S. VII, 73-79; XI, 61-68; XIV, 9; XV, 80-84; XXV, 38; XXVI, 141-159; XXVII, 45-53; XXIX, 38; XLI, 13, 14, 17, 18; LI, 43-45; LIV, 23-31; LXIX, 4, 5; LXXXV, 18; LXXXIX, 9; XCI, 11-14. Cf. the same story in al-Tabarī, *Tafsīr. Jāmi' al-Bayān 'an Ta'wīl al-Qur'ān.* ed. by Mahmud Muhammad Shakir (Cairo: Dar-Mu arif, 1957), vol. XII, pp. 526. Sālih proclaimed the unity of God to the tribe of Thamūd, and he called his people to worship Allah alone. The people of Thamūd rejected the message of Sālih, who urged them to abandon the worship of their fathers. (XI, 61-62). Sālih "is usually depicted as a sign and a warning in the style of Muhammad". F. Buhl, "Sālih" *SEIs,* p. 499.

[126] The story seems to have some historical foundation, inasmuch as Thamud has been identified as an ancient Arab tribe. *Ibid.,* p. 500.

[127] S. XV, 80.

[128] "[*Ho oun prophētēs hymōn, hoi kathōs legete, elalēsen ho Theos, dia ti peri tēs kamēlou, ouk emathe, pou brisketai* . . .]" ("Your prophet, therefore, to whom as you say, God spoke, why did he not learn about the she-camel, where she grazed . . .") 772B; cf. also, 772C. From the version of Chapter 101 it is not clear whether the author implies Muhammad or any other prophet.

[129] S. II, 25; VII, 40ff; XIII, 23; XV, 45ff; XVIII, 32, 108; XXII, 23; XXXVI, 54ff; XXXVII, 42ff, XXXVIII, 51ff; XLIII, 70ff; XLVII, 15; LII, 17ff. Chapter 101 refers to three rivers, of water, wine, and milk, while it by-passes that of honey, which S. XLVII, 15 mentions.

[130] Cf. above, n. 3.

[131] Pickthall, *Koran,* p. 107.

[132] *Ibid.,* p. 95. According to Tor Andrae, Muhammad understood the Lord's Supper celebrated in the Church as an actual meal. *Mohammed,* pp. 38ff.

[133] The italicising is ours.

[134] Merrill, [J.R. "of The Tractate of John of Damascus on Islam"] *MW,* XLI (1951), 97. Cf. also below, p. 127, n. 4.

[135] Maulana Muhammad 'Alī, *The Religion of Islam.* (Lahore: The Ahmadiyyah Anjuman Ishā'at Islām. 1950), p. 397, n. 1.

[136] Cf. Levy, [Reuben. *The Social Structure of Islam* (Cambridge: University Press, 1965)], p. 252. During the Jahilīyya, circumcision was practiced, even on women, and it was adopted by Muhammad. The different schools differed as far as the indispensability of the practice was concerned, with those who objected to it doing so on the ground that the Qur'ān is silent on the subject. The statement made by the Caliph 'Umar II (717-729) "Allah sent Muhammad to summon men [to Islam] and not to circumcise" is significant. Quoted by Levy, *Structure,* p. 251, from al-Tabarī, *Annales,* arabic text, ed. by M. J. de Goeje, II, 1354.

[137] Watt, *Muhammad,* pp. 93ff. The Qur'ān refers to those "who violate the Sabbath" (S. II, 65; IV, 47; VII, 163) as a criticism against the religious inconsistencies of the Jews; it is not an implication on the Muslims who abolish the observance of the Sabbath.

[138] S. II, 172f; V, 1, 3ff, 96; VI, 119f, 146f; XVI, 114ff; XXII, 34, 36.

[139] S. II, 219; IV, 43; V, 90f. Wine, however, is promised to be one of the pleasant drinks in Paradise, along with water, milk, and honey. Cf. S. XLVII, 15.

David Anderson (essay date 1979)

SOURCE: Introduction to *On the Divine Images: Three Apologies against Those Who Attack the Divine Images,* by St. John of Damascus, translated by David Anderson, St. Vladimir's Seminary Press, 1980, pp. 7-12.

[*In the introduction that follows, written in 1979, Anderson argues that* On the Divine Images, *in which St. John of Damascus defended the veneration of images, retains its significance even today, especially with regard to tensions within present-day Christianity.*]

The iconoclastic controversy begun in the eighth century by the Byzantine emperor Leo III (717-741) and continued by his successor Constantine V (741-775) cannot be considered in isolation from the Christological controversies of the preceding centuries.[1] Just as earlier ecumenical councils had insisted that the incarnation of Jesus Christ united the second person of the Holy Trinity with human nature, thus making salvation possible by breaking down the wall of separation between God and man, so also the seventh council (787) upheld the doctrine of the veneration of images as an inevitable result of the incarnation. To say that God the Word assumed a human body and soul (and for Him to do so was the only means by which the reign of death and sin in the universe might be destroyed) is to say that the infinite consented to become circumscribed. Therefore, the material flesh of Jesus Christ became part of His divine person, the invisible was made visible, and henceforth it is a good and praiseworthy thing to depict Him as He is: God become man; God become matter. The three treatises of St. John of Damascus all are intended to defend the use and veneration of images as an extension of this most essential of Christian teachings.

St. John of Damascus lived in political isolation from Constantinople. Writing during the reign of Leo III from his monastery of St. Sabbas in a Palestine ruled by the Moslem caliph, he was unhindered by the persecution raging within the Empire against those who defended the images. His treatises provide the Orthodox response to the iconoclastic theologians, who based their opposition to the images on the severe condemnation of idolatry in the Old Testament, as well as an understanding of images as being always one in essence with their prototypes. Such an understanding makes every image pretend to be God; therefore every image is an idol. Furthermore, and most important, the iconoclasts seemed to be little concerned with the historical Jesus whom the apostles had seen and touched both before and after His resurrection; instead, they spoke of a divinity whose assumed humanity was in fact devoid of all uniquely human characteristics. In this way the iconoclasts dangerously approached the heresy of Eutyches, who spoke of the humanity of Christ as a mere drop in the ocean of His divinity, or of Origen, who taught that Christians ought to contemplate God in the purity of their hearts and not use images from a past that is now over.[2] John of Damascus, Nicephorus of Constantinople, Theodore the Studite, and the rest of the defenders of the images saw in these arguments an incomplete understanding of the incarnation, for by becoming a man, God had entered history, and would remain part of history until the end of time, and fully human beyond the end of time.

The crucial argument in the treatises is St. John's continual insistence that in the incarnation a decisive and eternal change took place in the relationship between God and material creation. He says in the first oration, "In former times, God, being without form or body, could in no way be represented. But today, since God has appeared in the flesh and lived among men, I can represent what is visible in God. I do not worship matter, but I worship the creator of matter who became matter for my sake . . . ; and who, through matter accomplished my salvation. Never will I cease to honor the matter which brought about my salvation!" He accuses those who insist that the Old Testament condemnations of idolatry include all images of quoting Scripture out of context, and then cites passage after passage showing how the same God who forbade the making of idols commanded the use of material objects and images in divine worship and whose temple was adorned with the likenesses of plants and animals which were not worshipped as idols. Each treatise concludes with an extensive selection of patristic passages and historical evidence showing how the use of images had existed in the tradition of the Church for centuries. It is also from Scripture that the treatises derive the indispensable distinction between absolute worship, or adoration . . . and relative worship, or veneration . . . , literally, bowing down before), for the Bible records a great number of incidents where the patriarchs and prophets worship, venerate, and bow before people or places or things to whom such honor is due, but never with the adoration which is given to God alone. He demonstrates that it is wrong to identify every image with its prototype, as the iconoclasts did; rather, the only case when this is so is the Son's relation to the Father as the natural image of the Father; all other images, whether material, symbolical, or allegorical, are essentially different from their prototypes. Thus, the *proskinesis* given by a Christian to an image of Christ is ontologically the same as the reverence he ought to give his fellow Christians, who are also images of Christ, but ontologically different from the *latreia* that is due God alone. In this way St. John warns the iconoclasts that their teaching in effect denies the doctrine of the communion of saints, because if *proskinesis* is forbidden to painted images of God incarnate it must be denied to all other images of Christ as well: the Mother of God, the apostles, and all the saints, who because they have been revealed as faithful members of Christ's body command the reverence of all believers. Thus St. John proves that the position of the iconoclasts begins with an incomplete understanding of God becoming fully man and ends with a religion so "purified" and "reformed" that it has become disincarnate, a Manichaeism in which the flesh is not worth saving and the corporate body of the Church is replaced by the individual's immaterial contemplation of a God who is no longer Jesus Christ, the Word who became flesh, who was born of the Virgin, died on the cross, rose from the tomb, and whose risen Body and Blood is the nourishment of the faithful in the Eucharistic offering. Iconoclasm, when carried to its extreme, results in Docetism, where God merely appears to use a body of flesh and then casts it away as so much dross. Such Docetic iconoclasm is much more than a problem of the past, for the "popular" or "civil" religion of our time, which most often is presented as Christianity, certainly does not revolve around the figure of God incarnate.[3]

A word of explanation is necessary here regarding how the English words "adoration," "worship," and "veneration" or "honor" are used in this text. As has already been noted, St. John of Damascus developed the use of the term *latreia* to indicate the absolute worship which only God is worthy by nature to receive, and describes the relative worship given to the Mother of God, the saints or sacred objects (books, relics, icons) by the word *proskinesis.* Although this distinction might appear to be very clear, there are two complications which might tend to confuse the reader or translator. First of all, anyone familiar with the Septuagint Old Testament (from which these treatises extract many passages) knows that no such distinction existed at the time when the Greek text of the Old Testament was written. *Latreia* was very seldom used and *proskinesis* was used to describe everything from the worship one gives to God to the respect one pays one's friend. Secondly, modern use of English tends to diminish the shades of meaning between words which although they share some similarity are certainly not synonyms. "Adoration," "worship," and "veneration" are regarded by many as synonyms. In order to be consistent with St. John's very exact use of the Greek terms I have in most cases translated *latreia* with "adoration" and *proskinesis* with "veneration" or "honor" or in some cases with the literal verbal rendering "to fall down before." I have not used the word "worship" in such a technical sense; rather it is a generic term of which "adoration" and "veneration" are forms.

It would be a very great mistake to treat the iconoclastic controversy as well as the treatises of St. John as anachronistic curiosities, of interest only to students of Church history. On the contrary, the treatises are written in simple and direct language meant to be easily understood. The errors which St. John fought by his writings are present in our times to an even more alarming extent than when they began. How often is "Christianity" presented solely as an individual's code of ethics, as a "pure" religion not needing the "crutches" of fallen matter; how often is the material placed in direct opposition to the spiritual? The logical result of a disincarnate "Christianity" is the modern "demythologizing" of doctrine which attacks the very core of the Gospel: the preaching of the resurrection of Jesus Christ and the future resurrection and eternal life of all those who believe in Him. St. John's defense of the veneration of images safeguards the witness of the Orthodox Church, that the Jesus of history and the Christ of faith are one and the same, and that division results in turning the Lord into an idea, rather than a person. "Every scribe who has been trained for the kingdom of heaven is like a householder who brings out of his treasure what is new and what is old." (Mt. 13:52) St. John's treatises, although old, are always new since they testify to the eternally new message of the Gospel, and it is to that end that this translation is dedicated. . . .

Notes

[1] For an historical and theological analysis of the iconoclastic controversy, the reader should refer to J. Meyendorff, *Christ in Eastern Christian Thought,* (St. Vladimir's Seminary Press, 1975), pp. 173-192.

[2] See Meyendorff, *op. cit.,* p. 135.

[3] For an edifying fictional portrayal of iconoclasm in the American religious consciousness, see Flannery O'Connor's story "Parker's Back," *The Complete Stories* (Farrar, Strauss, and Giroux, 1976).

Kenneth Parry (essay date 1996)

SOURCE: "Apophaticism and Deification," in *Depicting the Word: Byzantine Iconophile Thought of the Eighth and Ninth Centuries,* E. J. Brill, 1996, pp. 114-24.

[*In the following essay, Parry examines the paradoxical characterization of God by John of Damascus—in which he described God's humanity as well as His divinity—and discusses how this depiction affected the iconoclastic controversy.*]

The two doctrines of apophaticism . . . and deification . . . , are here treated together because they often complement one another in Byzantine theology. For example, Pseudo-Dionysius writes: 'Since the union of deified minds with that light which is beyond all deity occurs when all intellectual activity ceases, those deified and unified minds who imitate the angels, as far as they are capable, praise it most appropriately through the abstraction . . . of all things.'[1] In this passage the two doctrines we are dealing with are made the foundation of mystical theology.

Here our attention is drawn to the relationship that exists between them. On the one hand, the light of which Pseudo-Dionysius speaks beggars all description (apophaticism), while on the other, those who seek it find themselves participating in it (deification) to some extent. By the fourteenth century Gregory Palamas speaks of apophaticism with regard to the divine essence, and deification with regard to the divine energies.[2] Although the two doctrines may be considered the twin pillars of Byzantine mysticism they occur in fact in a variety of theological contexts, including iconophile *apologia.*

It is a matter of some interest that both doctrines attract the label of 'unwritten tradition' in Byzantine Christianity. They belong to a sphere of theologising that is not enshrined in scripture, canon law or the apostolic tradition. Gregory of Nazianzus says that some laughed at him when he spoke of the divine origin of human beings and their destiny in terms of *theosis.*[3] For Maximos the Confessor, the doctrine of *theosis* was a mystery of the Christian faith known through true worship. This 'theological mystagogy,' as he terms it, was something that went beyond the usual sources of authority.[4] The doctrine of salvation through deification was to be understood by way of liturgical experience.

Likewise, for Maximos, the only true statements about God are negative ones. The ultimate unknowability of God was to be grasped in that silence which comes from recognising the nature of true ignorance.[5] Similarly, Gregory of Nyssa considers human speech inadequate to express that reality which transcends all thought and every concept. The only option is silence when it comes to speaking of the divine essence, although God may be spoken of in terms of his works and operation.[6] The respective roots of the two doctrines of apophaticism and *theosis* may be traced to certain elements in the earlier Greek, and to a lesser extent, the Jewish approach to the divine.[7] We shall deal first with apophaticism.

At its most basic *apophasis* is an element of Greek grammar. The addition of the alpha privative is a common way of negating a word in Greek, as a cursory glance at Liddell and Scott will show. The theological significance of this grammatical point becomes apparent, however, when we look at the attributes of God. For example, in his ***First Oration,*** John of Damascus lists the divine attributes as follows: without beginning . . . , uncreated . . . , immortal . . . , unassailable . . . , eternal . . . , everlasting . . . , bodiless . . . , incomprehensible . . . , invisible . . . , uncircumscribed . . . , and formless . . . .[8]

. . . [Each] one of these attributes has as its prefix an alpha privative. John of Damascus discusses two ways in which negations may be used in speaking about God. They can either take the form of an affirmative proposition in which the predicate is prefixed by an alpha privative, as in 'God is incorruptible,' or they can be negative propositions such as 'God is not corruptible.'[9] The basic distinction he makes between 'privation' and 'negation' goes back to Aristotle, mediated through various commentators.[10] In contrast to these negative attributes, John mentions terms which are predicated of God affirmatively, such as 'being,' 'substance,' 'life,' 'power,' and the like. However, he suggests the best names are those which involve a combination of both negation and affirmation, such as 'superessential essence.'[11]

It is cataphaticism . . . that affirms what God is, and as both apophatic and cataphatic theology are of equal importance, the one should not be used in isolation from the other, although in the end knowledge of God may be beyond both apophatic and cataphatic thought.[12] But in general, as human language and thought is ultimately incapable of comprehending the divine nature, it is more appropriate to use negative expressions. In addition to preserving the divine transcendence, the doctrine of apophaticism also safeguards the doctrine of *theosis.* Without the counterweight of negative theology the doctrine of *theosis* is liable to be misunderstood.[13]

The relation between apophaticism and iconology, although not developed by iconophile writers, is, nevertheless, implicit in their discussions concerning the nature of Christ and what is or is not represented in his icon. If the divine nature is invisible, uncircumscribed, formless and bodiless, then what does the icon of Christ depict, for he is human as well as divine. It is this kind of question that is the main source of iconoclast attacks on the icon of Christ. To answer this question iconophile writers have recourse to the distinction between [*theologia*] and [*oikonomia*] and to the notion of the hypostatic union.[14]

It is worth turning aside for a moment to consider some other aspects of apophatic thought. Although we are primarily concerned with the application of apophaticism to theology, we should note that it is also found as a scientific method. We find it being used as such by the Middle Platonists in their speculations on the nature of matter. For example, in his work *On Matter,* Calcidius writes that when his teacher Numenius wanted to show an image of naked matter, he suggested that first all bodies should be taken away one by one.[15] This method allowed for the contemplation of pure matter, which was equated with the void, also referred to as the womb, left by the process of negation. Plotinus exploited this method when he developed his theory of the non-existence of matter, a theory that was to influence the thought of the Cappadocian fathers.[16]

Another aspect of apophaticism we should consider, is its application to prayer. We first encounter the method of 'imageless prayer' in the writings of the desert fathers of the fourth century. For example, Evagrius Ponticus writes: 'When you are praying, do not shape within yourself any image of the deity, and do not let your intellect be stamped with the impress of any form; but approach the immaterial in an immaterial manner.'[17] It is clear that stripping the intellect of images requires the monk to practice a mental discipline of negation. This type of imageless prayer became associated in Byzantium with the Jesus Prayer and the light-mysticism of the hesychast tradition. In order to achieve the pure state of imageless prayer it was recommended not to confront the thoughts and images that enter the mind, but rather to detach oneself from them through the invocation of the name of Jesus.[18] Perhaps this tradition of imageless prayer had some bearing on the iconoclast distaste for representations of the Word made flesh. Certainly the contemplative tradition of pure prayer would seem far removed from the icon cult. We may recall that Gregory Palamas himself was accused of iconoclasm because of his hesychast doctrine.[19]

There is a third aspect of apophaticism which we need to mention before moving on. It could be said that Byzantine iconoclasm itself is a form of apophaticism. If Meyendorff is correct in asserting that belief in the absolute transcendence and invisibility of God were part of Islamic anti-Christian polemic, and that the iconoclastic emperors decided to cleanse the church of idolatry in order to fight Islamic theology more effectively, then apophaticism may be said to have contributed to Byzantine iconoclasm.[20] However, as apophaticism was already an established part of Byzantine thought before the eighth century, the iconoclast emperors had no need to turn to Islamic theology to bolster their standing on that score. That they may have been ignorant of apophaticism in their own tradition is another matter. There is no doubt that the non-figural tradition in Islamic art does reflect a strong apophatic tendency. But the anti-image element in early Islam owes as much to the desire for socio-political hegemony as it does to the theology of transcendence.[21]

There is a sense, then, in which it is legitimate for the Christian to say 'God does not exist.' Or as John of Damascus puts it: 'As regards what God is, it is impossible to say what he is in his essence, so it is better to discuss him by abstraction . . . from all things. For he does not belong to the class of existing things, not because he does not exist, but because he transcends all existing things, even existence itself.'[22] Given that the nature of the deity is utterly incomprehensible to the human intellect, it may be better to say what he 'is' not. Yet the use of names to attribute positive qualities to him is not thought in any way to impose limits on his nature. 'That which is without limit is certainly not limited by name,' says Gregory of Nyssa.[23] While apophatic theology is concerned with such abstract attributes as infinity, invisibility, and uncircumscribability; cataphatic theology is concerned with what can be affirmed of God, namely that he is good, loving and merciful.

For Theodore the Studite it is clear to all that the Godhead . . . is incomprehensible, uncircumscribable, boundlesss, limitless, formless and whatever adjectives signify the abstraction . . . of what it is not. According to the doctrine of theology . . . , so far from inventing some kind of circumscription or comprehension, we do not even know that the Godhead exists at all, or what sort of thing it is, as it alone can refect upon itself (1.2).[24] Such is the nature of the Godhead that it remains beyond all predication. Because it is of an altogether different order from that which we know, we have recourse to negative descriptions. As far as God is concerned there is no designation, no likeness, no circumscription, no definition, nothing at all of what comes within the comprehension of the human mind (1.5).[25] Like John of Damascus Theodore operates with privations on the one hand and negations on the other.

Turning to the subject of *theosis,* we find that the Greek fathers base their teaching on both the Old Testament and the New. From the Old Testament they take 'I say, you are gods' of *Psalm* 82.6, and link it with the New Testament 'you shall become partakers of the divine nature' of 2 *Peter* 1.4. In general, however, *theosis* reflects biblical teaching rather than biblical texts.[26] This is apparent in the patristic dictum: 'God became man in order than man might become God.' *Theosis* through Christ is the means by which our original relationship with God is restored. According to Maximos the Confessor, as created beings we are not by nature able to attain deification, since we are not capable of grasping God. This can happen only by divine grace.[27] The Byzantine view of grace, and its relation to human salvation, is embodied in the idea of cooperation . . . . We have to work together with God because we cannot depend upon grace alone nor on our own efforts. Human beings are called to respond to divine grace, but they are free to accept it or to reject it. The process of *theosis* begins with baptism and continues through participation in the sacramental life of the church, especially the eucharist.[28]

That the concept of *theosis* is thought of as a process and not an event can be seen in the Cappadocian doctrine of extension . . . . For Gregory of Nyssa human participation in divine grace is unending, and although it may begin here and now, it cannot be fulfilled in time.[29] It is a present possibility and a future hope based on the restoration of the capacity for grace through the person of Jesus Christ. In the words of the fathers of Nicaea II: 'God re-created man for immortality, thus giving him a gift which cannot be revoked. This re-creation was more God-like and better that the first creation because it was an eternal gift.'[30]

Gregory of Nazianzus would appear to be the inspiration behind this.[31] Gregory's word for re-creation is [*anaplasis*] and he makes it clear that this re-creation is a more exalted creation that the first. John of Damascus makes a similar claim when he says that the new dispensation is better than the old because it is based on better promises (2.22).[32] This means that human salvation is not simply a recovery of the unfallen state, but rather a renewed capacity for growth and future progress in grace. For the Greek fathers, then, *theosis* is dynamic not static, progressive not retrogressive.

What Christ renews for us is the potential to move once more towards defication. He provides us with a focus of attention that our original ancestors lacked. According to Gregory of Nazianzus, it was due to the immaturity of Adam in contemplating God that the original paradise was lost.[33] We might infer from this that it was too much to expect Adam to contemplate God without the incarnation. In other words, from an iconophile point of view, Adam would have done better with an icon of Christ because he was not sufficiently mature to contemplate God in a spiritual way.[34] Put like this, it can be seen that the icon may form a rung on the ladder leading to the state of imageless prayer.

John of Damascus hints at this when he states that we use bodily sight . . . to attain spiritual contemplation . . . (3.12).[35] We find the patriarch Germanos speaks of the icon as a kind of guiding hand . . . for those who cannot attain spiritual contemplation.[36] We should note, however, that there are few references to the contemplation of icons as a form of prayer in the spiritual life. For this reason it is not always clear where the incarnation stands in this higher form of prayer. On this point it is of interest to find Origen stating that 'even at the very highest climax of contemplation we do not for a moment forget the incarnation.'[37] It seems ironic to quote Origen on this given the condemnation of so-called Origenist spirituality in Byzantium.[38]

It would appear that the icon belongs to liturgical spirituality rather than to hesychast spirituality.[39] But that being said, perhaps there is no hard and fast division between them, and it should not be thought that the tradition of imageless prayer is opposed to the veneration of icons. This was the mistake made by the opponents of Gregory Palamas in the fourteenth century, when they accused him of promoting an iconoclastic spirituality. Gregory is insistent that hesychasm does not invalidate other aspects of Orthodox practice.[40] Nevertheless, it should be pointed out that there are no references to icons in the liturgical commentaries of our period. However, from what Nikephoros says of the images displayed on the sanctuary barrier . . . ,[41] it is safe to assume that icons did play a role in the liturgy long before it was felt necessary to comment on their significance. Just as canon 82 of the Quinisext Council comes long after the painting of Christ's image, so lack of reference to images in the commentaries does not preclude their being censed and venerated during the liturgy.

John of Damascus refers to the serpent's temptation of Adam, who instilled in him the desire to become like God . . . , and as a result brought death into the world. Although humanity was created in God's image it was brought down to share the death of animals . . . (2.2).[42] It is clear from this that human beings cannot by their own efforts achieve *theosis.* John says of the saints that they are likenesses of God . . . , and are called gods not by nature but by adoption . . . (3.33).[43] It is common for our iconophiles to stipulate the phrase 'not by nature' in respect of deification.[44] The distinction between 'nature' and 'adoption' is strictly that between 'creator' and 'creature.' Only God is divine by nature. *Theosis* is to be understood above all in a relative sense, as signifying a relation between God and humanity. For John the saints become sons of God by adoption because they are not divine by nature, only through grace can they become partakers of the divine nature (3.26).[45] Nikephoros agrees in this by distinguishing our relation to God as one of adoption and grace . . . from that of the Son to the Father as one of nature and power . . . (3.31).[46]

According to John's christology salvation comes through the humanity of Christ participating in the divine nature. He did not depart from his divinity when he became man, nor was his human nature lost when it became part of the Godhead. He took on human nature in order to glorify us and make us partakers of the divine nature (1.4).[47] John follows the fathers in using the incarnation as an analogy for human deification. It is by means of the incarnation that Christ deifies our flesh and sanctifies us by surrendering his Godhead to our flesh without confusion (1.21).[48] John refers here to the negative definition at the heart of the hypostatic union as proclaimed at Chalcedon. He does so in order to show that the deification of the human nature in Christ is not an absorption into the Godhead. On the contrary, as our iconophiles stress, even after his ascension into heaven Christ retains his human nature.[49] The means by which Christians attain deification is through the sacraments of the church. It begins with the water of baptism and continues through the bloodless sacrifice of the eucharist (3.26).[50] If the doctrine of *theosis* is based upon a theological anthropology which recognises the value of the whole person, then the body must be included in the process as well. For John of Damascus Christ assumed both soul and body because human beings are made from both (3.12).[51] Or as the patriarch Nikephoros says, because human nature was in need of re-creation . . . , it was necessary for Christ to become the same in nature in all respects (1.26).[52] In Byzantine iconography the Transfiguration of Christ on the mountain is the supreme representation of the theology of deification.

This is the one occasion in the New Testament when the glorified body of the Lord is revealed to his disciples. In fact both *apophasis* and *theosis* meet in the iconography of the Transfiguration. For as Maximos the Confessor says: 'The light of the face of the Lord, which for the apostles surpassed human bliss, belongs to the mystical theology according to *apophasis.*'[53] This theological point is illustrated by the light symbolism of Christ's mandorla in depictions of the Transfiguration.

The sequence of blue bands in the mandorla is from dark at the centre to light at the edges, thus defying the natural diffusion of light from its source. This can be seen in the famous sixth-century mosaic of the Transfiguration in the church at St. Catherine's monastery at Mt Sinai.[54] For Gregory of Nyssa, the spiritual life is conceived as moving from light to darkness. He writes: 'Moses' vision of God began with light; afterwards God spoke to him in a cloud. But when Moses rose higher and became more perfect, he saw God in the darkness.'[55] Thus the divine darkness for Gregory becomes a symbol of the apophatic Godhead.

Futhermore, the blue in the mandorla is related to the state of spiritual prayer as described by Evagrius Ponticus. He writes: 'When the spirit has put off the old man to replace him with the new . . . he will see that his own state at the time of prayer resembles that of a sapphire; it is clear and bright as the very sky. The scriptures refer to this experience as the place of God which was seen by our ancestors, the elders, at Mount Sinai.'[56] These quotations from the fathers of the fourth century provide the theological background for the mosaic depiction of the sixth.

For Theodore the Studite there appear to be no restrictions on where divinity may be found. There is nowhere where divinity is not present, he says, in beings with or without reason . . . , with or without life . . . . However, it is present to a greater or lesser extent depending on the capacity of the nature which receives it. Therefore it would not be wrong to say that divinity is in the icon, but by the same token it is also in the representation of the cross, and in other sacred objects. Yet divinity is not present in them by a union of natures, for they are not the deified flesh, but by a relative participation . . . (1.12).[57] Theodore considers it heretical to think that in venerating the icon of Christ we are venerating Christ's divinity as if it were present naturally in the icon (1.20).[58] He again reminds us that in the debate about icons we should keep in the mind the distinction between [*theologia*] and [*oikonomia*]. For what is said about veneration in spirit and truth (*Jn.* 4.24) belongs to theology, but what is said about the veneration of Christ in the image belongs to economy (3.C15).[59]

In the thought of our iconophiles the apophaticism of the Godhead is balanced by the deifying grace of the economy. On the one hand it appears that 'God is not like a man' (*Num.* 23.19), while on the other, 'man is made in the image and likeness of God' (*Gen.* 1.26). We are presented with the paradox that God is not like us and yet we are like him. From the Christian point of view our relationship with God is at once distant and near. While our minds cannot grasp the divine transcendence we may at least experience something of his presence. As John of Damascus remarks, what makes both Christian salvation and Christian image-making possible, is the glorification of our nature (2.10).[60]

Notes

[1] *On the Divine Names,* 1.5, [*Patrologia Graeca* (PG)] 3, 593BC.

[2] *Gregory Palamas: The Triads,* ed. J. Meyendorff (London 1983) 93ff.

[3] *Oration* [(or.)] 2.7, PG 35, 416A. See Winslow, *The Dynamics of Salvation: a study in Gregory of Nazianzus,* (Cambridge, Mass. 1979) 181.

[4] J. Pelikan, '"Council or Father or Scripture": the concept of authority in the theology of Maximus Confessor,' in *The Heritage of the Early Church: essays in honor of Georges Florovsky,* ed. D. Neiman and M. Schatkin (Rome 1973) 277-88.

[5] *Centuries on Love,* 3.99, *The Philokalia,* vol. 2, 99.

[6] *Commentary on Ecclesiastes* 7, PG 44, 724D-732D.

[7] See Winslow above for *theosis,* and for apophaticism, R. Mortley, *From Word to Silence,* 2 vols. (Bonn 1986) esp. vol. 2, *'The way of negation, Christian and Greek.'*

[8] Or. 1.4, [Kotter (Kot.)] 3, 76; [*De Fide Orthodoxa* (DFO)] 1.4, Kot. 2, 12-13.
[9] DFO 1.9, Kot. 2, 32.

[10] Aristotle, *Metaphysica* IV, 2, 1004a, 10-16. See H. A. Wolfson, 'Negative Attributes in the Church Fathers and the Gnostic Basilides,' [*Harvard Theological Review (HTR)*] 50 (1957) 154.

[11] DFO 1.12, Kot. 2, 36.

[12] See the remarks to this effect by Gregory Palamas, *One Hundred and Fifty Chapters,* ed. R. E. Sinkewicz (Toronto 1988) 225-227.

[13] See, for example, the approach of B. Drewery, 'Deification,' in *Christian Spirituality: essays in honour of Gordon Rupp,* ed. P. Brooks (London 1975) 35-62.

[14] See Chapter 11.

[15] See J. G. M. van Winden, *Calcidius on Matter: his doctrine and sources,* (Leiden 1959) 119-20.

[16] A. H. Armstrong, 'The Theory of the Non-Existence of Matter in Plotinus and the Cappadocians,' [*Studia Patristica (SP)*] 8 (Berlin 1962) 427-429.

[17] *The Philokalia,* vol. 1, 63.

[18] See Diadochos of Photiki, *The Philokalia,* vol. 1, 270.

[19] See J. Meyendorff, *A Study of Gregory Palamas,* (Leighton Buzzard 1974) 95.

[20] *The Byzantine Legacy in the Orthodox Church,* (New York 1982) 23. For the view that Byzantine iconoclasm was a reaction against Islam, rather than an adoption of its tenets, see L. Barnard, *The Graeco-Roman and Oriental Background of the Iconoclastic Controversy,* (Leiden 1974) 13.

[21] See O. Grabar, *The Formation of Islamic Art,* (New Haven and London 1978) 96-103.

[22] DFO 1.4, Kot. 2, 13.

[23] *That there are not three gods,* PG 45, 115 36.

[24] PG 99, 329CD.

[25] PG 99, 333C.

[26] Winslow, *The Dynamics of Salvation,* 182.

[27] *Various Texts on Theology, The Philokalia,* vol. 2, 181-82.

[28] See Chapter 18.

[29] *From Glory to Glory: texts from Gregory of Nyssa's mystical writings,* intro. by J. Daniélou (New York 1979) 56-71.

[30] Mansi 13, 216A.

[31] *Oration* 40.7, PG 36, 365C. See Winslow, 191.

[32] Kot. 3, 121. Found also in his *Oration on the Transfiguration,* 4, Kot. 5, 441.

[33] See Winslow, above, 191.

[34] Cf. Irenacus, *Against Heresies,* 5.16.2, PG 7, 1167C 1168A.

[35] Kot. 3, 123 21. See further the remarks of Gouillard, *Synodicon,* 180.

[36] *Letter to Thomas of Claudiopolis,* PG 98, 173B.

[37] Quoted by H. Chadwick, *The Early Church,* (Harmondsworth 1967) 108.

[38] See J. Meyendorff, 'The Origenist Crisis of the Sixth Century,' in his *Christ in Eastern Christian Thought.*

[39] On the art historical evidence see, N. Patterson Ševčenko, 'Icons in the Liturgy,' [*Dumbarton Oaks Papers* (*DOP*)] 45 (1991) 45-57.

[40] Meyendorff, *A Study of Gregory Palamas,* 95.

[41] [*Antirrheticus* (Antir.)] 3, 45, PG 100, 465A. The *Horos* of 754 may make a similar reference, see Sahas, *Icon and Logos,* 103, n. 20. Euscbius of Caesarea is an early witness to a lattice-work barrier, *Ecclesiastical History,* 10.4.42. See most recently C. Walter, 'A New Look at the Bzyantine Sanctuary Barrier,' [*Revue des études byzantines* (*REB*)] 51 (1993) 203-28.

[42] Kot. 3, 69.

[43] Kot. 3, 137.

[44] See Chapter 19.

[45] Kot. 3, 134.

[46] PG 100, 421D 424A.

[47] Kot. 3, 77 78.

[48] Kot. 3, 109.

[49] See Chapter 11.

[50] Kot. 3, 134.

[51] Kot. 3, 124.

[52] PG 100, 273B.

[53] *Ambigua,* 10, PG 91, 1168A.

[54] See K. Weitzmann, *Studies in the Arts of Sinai,* (Princeton 1982) ch. 1.

[55] *From Glory to Glory,* above, 23.

[56] *Praktikos,* PG 40, 1244A. See *Evagrius Ponticus: the Praktikos and Chapters on Prayer,* tr. J. E. Bamberger (Kalamazoo 1981) xci.

[57] PG 99, 344C. See Chapter 6 and 17.

[58] PG 99, 349D.

[59] PG 99, 428B.

[60] Kot. 3, 101.

Works Cited

Primary sources

John of Damascus. *Conba imaginum calumnialores orationes tres,* ed. B. Kotter, *Schriflen des Johannes von Damaskos,* vol. 3 (Berlin 1975). Part English tr. D. Anderson, *St. John of Damascus On the Divine Images,* (New York 1980)

De Fide Orthodoxa, ed. B. Kotter, *Schriflen des Johannes von Damaskos,* vol. 2 (Berlin 1973). English tr. F. H. Chase, *St. John of Damascus: writings,* (Washington 1958)

Dialectica, ed. B. Kotter, *Schriflen des Johannes von Damaskos,* vol. 1 (Berlin 1969). English tr. F. H. Chase, *St. John of Damascus: writings,* (Washington 1958)

Mansi, J. D. *Sacrorum Conciliorum Nova et Amplissima Collectio,* vol. 13 Nicaca II (Florence 1767 repr. Graz 1960). English tr. of sixth session, D. Sahas, *Icon and Logos: sources in eighth century iconoclasm* (Toronto 1986)

Philokalia. The Philokalia: the complete text, tr. and ed. G. E. H. Palmer et al., vols. 1-2 (London 1979 81)

Secondary sources

Sahas, D. J. *John of Damascus on Islam: the heresy of the Ishmaelites* (Leiden 1972)

FURTHER READING

Addison, James Thayer. *The Christian Approach to the Moslem: A Historical Study.* New York: Columbia University Press, 1942, 365 p.

Discusses Christian missionary encounter with Islam beginning in the seventh century, with particular emphasis on the social and political atmosphere of these interactions.

Backus, Irena. "John of Damascus, *De Fide Orthodoxa:* Translations by Burgundio (1153/54), Grosseteste (1235/40) and Lefèvre d'Etaples (1507)." *Journal of the Warburg and Courtauld Institutes* 49 (1986): 211-17.

Compares three Latin translations of *De fide Orthodoxa,* the third part of the *Sources of Knowledge.*

Lieh Tzu

fl. c. 5th-7th century B.C.

(Also transliterated as Lieh-tze.) Chinese philosopher.

INTRODUCTION

One of the three major figures in Taoist philosophy, Lieh Tzu produced one of the most accessible texts of Taoism. The anecdotal and dramatic form of his only work, *The Treatise of the Transcendent Master of the Void,* more commonly known as the Book of Lieh Tzu, lends itself to elaborating the mystical and highly abstract beliefs that constitute philosophical Taoism. Although less well known in the west than Lao Tzu and Chuang Tzu, Lieh Tzu exhibits a unique literary style and theoretical world-view. His insightful and often ironic narrative enhances contemporary understanding of the diversity within the philosophical tradition of Taoism and provides a rich and entertaining representation of Taoist teachings.

Biographical Information

Very little is known of Lieh Tzu beyond his single work, and some early scholars challenged his very existence and claimed that the book was written by Chuang Tzu. However, ancient Chinese sources indicate that the term "master" (Tzu) was bestowed upon a historical figure by the name of Lieh Yü-K'ou. This thinker lived "in obscurity and poverty" but had disciples who probably produced the Book of Lieh Tzu by recording oral teachings, either during Lieh Tzu's lifetime or shortly thereafter. Most contemporary historians agree that Lieh Tzu lived between the seventh and fifth centuries B.C., during the late Chou dynasty. This was a time when Confucianism had been largely accepted as the dominant school of philosophy, despite challenges from Taoism. Chronologically, Lieh Tzu stands between the two great pillars of Taoist thought: Lao Tzu, the first well-known author to articulate Taoist beliefs (in the *Tao-Te-Ching*), and Chuang Tzu, who produced a relatively systematic treatment of Taoism. Chuang Tzu briefly mentions Lieh Tzu as someone who "travelled by riding the wind," which figuratively suggests Lieh Tzu's purity of spirit and ability to commune with the rhythms of nature. The Book of Lieh Tzu itself provides almost no information about its author.

Major Works

The Book of Lieh Tzu, divided into eight chapters, expresses a profoundly mystical world-view, contrary to the Confucian focus on the establishment of social institutions. In spite of this transcendental emphasis, its anecdotal teachings are accessible and often humorous, unlike the more obscure *Tao-Te-Ching.* Lieh Tzu is also distinguished as a Taoist thinker by his articulation of a cosmogony, according to D. T. Suzuki: the Book of Lieh Tzu provides a model of the universe that encompasses both determinate phenomena and an unnameable and indeterminate void, the ground of all phenomena. Taoism is the set of beliefs and practices that encourage the contemplation of this void, which leads to "heightened perceptiveness and responsiveness," rather than complete withdrawal from the ordinary world. The meditative practices associated with Taoism thus have no final goal or state of being, but are ways of comporting or orienting oneself in relation to the world. Lieh Tzu suggests that the two major tasks of Taoism are the abandonment of social and moral conventions and the comprehension of the natural order, so that one may bring oneself into harmony with that order. For Lieh Tzu, there is no natural or human freedom; instead, the universe operates through a predetermined, cyclical movement. Some scholars have associated Lieh Tzu with a strand of Taoism concerned primarily with physical immortality. Although his book does refer to immortality, this reference is probably allegorical, for other chapters explicitly condemn the search for eternal physiological life. The work has several inconsistencies, the most glaring appearing in the seventh chapter, which advocates an extreme form of hedonism that departs from the Taoist emphasis upon accordance with "the way."

Textual History

The Book of Lieh Tzu was in all likelihood compiled over a number of years (between 300 B.C. and 300 A.D.) by several disciples, and survives only in an edited and appended form. However, a core group of writings seem to have been recorded by Lieh Tzu's immediate disciples or their students. Some passages are taken directly from other sources; the anomalous seventh chapter (titled "Yang Chu," after the Chou dynasty philosopher) probably dates from the fourth or fifth century A.D.—later than the rest of the work.

Critical Reception

What has most impressed scholars about the work of

Lieh Tzu is the dramatic character of the anecdotes, which display "real insight into human nature," as Lionel Giles has suggested, as well as a frequently ironic or humorous tone. The vivid and fantastic stories are directly and simply narrated. As a collection of fables, the work has been judged highly accessible and even entertaining, but its allegorical meaning often remains obscure. Hence the Book of Lieh Tzu does not present an ordered and thorough articulation of Taoist beliefs, but rather an impressionistic complement to the more structured and scholarly works of Lao Tzu and Chuang Tzu. Lieh Tzu juxtaposes realistic characters in highly dramatic (and sometimes fantastic) situations to teach Taoist practices. Although Confucius himself appears in the work, critics have warned that this portrayal is not to be taken as historically accurate, but rather as a stylized rendering serving a particular role in a Taoist text responding to a dominant way of thinking. Many contemporary scholars consider Lieh Tzu's work to be less philosophically systematic than that of Chuang Tzu or Lao Tzu, but more colorful and richly narrated. In this regard, Lieh Tzu stands as an essential complement to more familiar works of Taoism.

PRINCIPAL WORKS

The Treatise of the Transcendent Master of the Void (Book of Lieh Tzu)

PRINCIPAL ENGLISH TRANSLATIONS

Taoist Teachings: From the Book of Lieh-Tzu [translated by Lionel Giles] 1925

The Book of Lieh-Tzu [translated by A. C. Graham] 1960

Ch'ung-Hu-Ch'En-Ching, or The Treatise of the Transcendent Master of the Void [translated by Leon Wieger] 1992

CRITICISM

Lionel Giles (essay date 1912)

SOURCE: Introduction to *Wisdom of the East, Taoist Teachings: From the Book of Lieh Tzu*, translated by Lionel Giles, John Murray, 1912, pp. 9-16.

[*In the essay that follows, Giles locates the book of Lieh Tzu in the more general context of Taoist philosophy, including the thought of Lao Tzu and Chuang Tzu.*]

The history of Taoist philosophy may be conveniently divided into three stages: the primitive stage, the stage of development, and the stage of degeneration. The first of these stages is only known to us through the medium of a single semi-historical figure, the philosopher Lao Tzŭ, whose birth is traditionally assigned to the year 604 B.C. Some would place the beginnings of Taoism much earlier than this, and consequently regard Lao Tzŭ rather as an expounder than as the actual founder of the system; just as Confucianism—that is, a moral code based on filial piety and buttressed by altruism and righteousness—may be said to have flourished long before Confucius. The two cases, however, are somewhat dissimilar. The teachings of Lao Tzŭ, as preserved in the *Tao Tê Ching,* are not such as one can easily imagine being handed down from generation among the people at large. The principle on which they are based is simple enough, but their application to everyday life is surrounded by difficulties. It is hazardous to assert that any great system of philosophy has sprung from the brain of one man; but the assertion is probably as true of Taoism as of any other body of speculation.

Condensed into a single phrase, the injunction of Lao Tzŭ to mankind is, "Follow Nature." This is a good practical equivalent for the Chinese expression, "Get hold of Tao," although "Tao" does not exactly correspond to the word Nature, as ordinarily used by us to denote the sum of phenomena in this ever-changing universe. It seems to me, however, that the conception of Tao must have been reached, originally, through this channel. Lao Tzŭ, interpreting the plain facts of Nature before his eyes, concludes that behind her manifold workings there exists an ultimate Reality which in its essence is unfathomable and unknowable, yet manifests itself in laws of unfailing regularity. To this Essential Principle, this Power underlying the sensible phenomena of Nature, he gives, tentatively and with hesitation, the name of Tao, "the Way," though fully realising the inadequacy of any name to express the idea of that which is beyond all power of comprehension.

A foreigner, imbued with Christian ideas, naturally feels inclined to substitute for Tao the term by which he is accustomed to denote the Supreme Being—God. But this is only admissible if he is prepared to use the term "God" in a much broader sense than we find in either the Old or the New Testament. That which chiefly impresses the Taoist in the operations of Nature is their absolute impersonality. The inexorable law of cause and effect seems to him equally removed from active goodness or benevolence on the one hand, and from active evil or malevolence on the other. This is a fact which will hardly be disputed by any intelligent observer. It is when he begins to draw inferences from it that the Taoist parts company from the average Christian. Believing, as he does, that the visible Universe is but a manifestation of the invisible Power behind it, he feels justified in arguing from the known to the unknown, and concluding that, whatever Tao may be in itself (which is unknowable), it is certainly not what we understand by a personal God—not a God endowed with the specific attributes of humanity, not even (and here we find a remarkable anticipation of Hegel) a *conscious* God. In other words, Tao transcends the illusory and unreal distinctions on which all human systems of morality depend, for in it all virtues and vices coalesce into One.

The Christian takes a different view altogether. he prefers to ignore the facts which Nature shows him, or else he reads them in an arbitrary and one-sided manner. His God, if no longer anthropomorphic, is undeniably anthropopathic. He is a personal Deity, now loving and merciful, now irascible and jealous, a Deity who is open to prayer and entreaty. With qualities such as these, it is difficult to see how he can be regarded as anything but a glorified Man. Which of these two views—the Taoist or the Christian—it is best for mankind to hold, may be a matter of dispute. There can be no doubt which is the more logical.

The weakness of Taoism lies in its application to the conduct of life. Lao Tzŭ was not content to be a metaphysician merely, he aspired to be a practical reformer as well. It was man's business, he thought, to model himself as closely as possible on the great Exemplar, Tao. It follows as a matter of course that his precepts are mostly of a negative order, and we are led straight to the doctrine of Passivity or Inaction, which was bound to be fatally misunderstood and perverted. Lao Tzŭ's teaching has reached us, if not in its original form, yet in much of its native purity, in the *Tao Tê Ching*. One of the most potent arguments for the high antiquity of this marvellous little treatise is that it shows no decided trace of the corruption which is discernible in the second of our periods, represented for us by the writings of Lieh Tzŭ and Chuang Tzŭ. I have called it the period of development because of the extraordinary quickening and blossoming of the buds of Lao Tzŭ's thought in the supple and imaginative minds of these two philosophers. The canker, alas! is already at the heart of the flower; but so rich and luxuriant is the feast of colour before us that we hardly notice it as yet.

Very little is known of our author beyond what he tells us himself. His full name was Lieh Yü-k'ou, and it appears that he was living in the Chêng State not long before the year 398 B.C., when the Prime Minister Tzŭ Yang was killed in a revolution. He figures prominently in the pages of Chuang Tzŭ, from whom we learn that he could "ride upon the wind." On the insufficient ground that he is not mentioned by the historian Ssŭ-ma Ch'ien, a certain critic of the Sung dynasty was led to declare that Lieh Tzŭ was only a fictitious personage invented by Chuang Tzŭ, and that the treatise which passes under his name was a forgery of later times. This theory is rejected by the compilers of the great Catalogue of Ch'ien Lung's Library, who represent the cream of Chinese scholarship in the eighteenth century. Although Lieh Tzŭ's work has evidently passed through the hands of many editors and gathered numerous accretions, there remains a considerable nucleus which in all probability was committed to writing by Lieh Tzŭ's immediate disciples, and is therefore older than the genuine parts of Chuang Tzŭ. There are some obvious analogies between the two authors, and indeed a certain amount of matter common to both; but on the whole Lieh Tzŭ's book bears an unmistakable impress of its own. The geniality of its tone contrasts with the somewhat hard brilliancy of Chuang Tzŭ, and a certain kindly sympathy with the aged, the poor and the humble of this life, not excluding the brute creation, makes itself felt throughout. The opposition between Taoism and Confucianism is not so sharp as we find it in Chuang Tzŭ, and Confucius, himself is treated with much greater respect. This alone is strong evidence in favour of the priority of Lieh Tzŭ's, for there is no doubt that the breach between the two systems widened as time went on. Lieh Tzŭ's, work is about half as long as Chuang Tzŭ's, and is now divided into eight books. The seventh of these deals exclusively with the doctrine of the egoistic philosopher Yang Chu, and has therefore been omitted altogether from the present selection.

Nearly all the Taoist writers are fond of parables and allegorical tales, but in none of them is this branch of literature brought to such perfection as in Lieh Tzŭ, who surpasses Chuang Tzŭ himself as a master of anecdote. His stories are almost invariably pithy and pointed. Many of them evince not only a keen sense of dramatic effect, but real insight into human nature. Others may appear fantastic and somewhat wildly imaginative. The story of the man who issued out of solid rock is a typical one of this class. It ends, however, with a streak of ironical humour which may lead us to doubt whether Lieh Tzŭ himself really believed in the possibility of transcending natural laws. His soberer judgment appears in other passages, like the following: "That which has life must by the law of its being come to an end; and the end can no more be avoided than the living creature can help having been born. So that he who hopes to perpetuate his life or to shut out death is deceived in his calculations." That leaves little doubt as to the light in which Lieh Tzŭ would have regarded the later Taoist speculations on the elixir of life. Perhaps the best solution of the problem is the theory I have already mentioned: that the "Lieh Tzŭ" which we possess now, while containing a solid and authentic core of the Master's own teaching, has been overlaid with much of the decadent Taoism of the age that followed.

Of this third period little need be said here. It is represented in literature by the lengthy treatise of Huainan Tzŭ, the spurious episodes in Lieh Tzŭ and Chuang Tzŭ, and a host of minor writers, some of whom tried to pass off their works as the genuine relics of ancient sages. Chang Chan, an officer of the Banqueting Court under the Eastern Chin dynasty (fourth century A.D.), is the author of the best commentary on Lieh Tzŭ; extracts from it, placed between inverted commas, will be found in the following pages. In the time of Chang Chan, although Taoism as a philosophical system had long run its course, its development into a national religion was only just beginning, and its subsequent influence on literature and art is hardly to be overestimated. It supplied the elements of mystery, romance and colour which were needed as a set-off against the uncompromising stiffness of the Confucianŭ ideal. For reviving and incorporating in itself the floating mass of folklore and mythology which had come down from the earliest ages, as well as for the many exquisite creations of its own fancy, it deserves the lasting gratitude of the Chinese people.

Daisetz Teitaro Suzuki (essay date 1914)

SOURCE: "Monism," in *A Brief History of Early Chinese Philosophy*, Probsthain & Co., 1914, pp. 25-33.

[*In the following excerpt, Suzuki characterizes Lieh Tzu as belonging to the mystical and monistic tradition of Taoism, which stood in opposition to the more practical Confucianism.*]

. . . There were not lacking, however, in the Ante-Ch'in period certain tendencies that counterbalanced the ultra-practical, positivistic train of thought as represented in Confucianism. Though these tendencies did not attain a full manifestation at any time in the history of Chinese thought, they showed a strong front at this incipient stage to their antagonistic systems. It was quite unfortunate that they were hampered in their development, and had from time to time to lose sight of their essential qualities. Probably this was in the nature of their system. They owe their origin mainly to the teachings of the *Tao Teh Ching*,[22] and may be characterized as monistic, mystic, transcendental, and sometimes pantheistic. Lao-tze, however, was not the first and sole expounder of these thoughts. He doubtless had many predecessors whose words and lives are scatteringly recorded by Confucius, Mencius, Chwang-tze, Lieh-tze, and others, including Lao-tze himself.[23] What was most significant in the author of the *Tao Teh Ching* was that he gave to these conceptions a literary form through which we are able to trace the history of the Chinese monistic movement to its sources.

When we pass from Confucius to Lao-tze, we experience almost complete change of scenery. Confucius, in whom the Chinese mind is most typically mirrored, rarely deviates from the plain, normal, prosaic, and practical path of human life, and his eyes are steadily kept upon our earthly moral relations. Lao-tze occasionally betrays his national traits, but he does not hesitate to climb the dizzy heights of speculation and imagination. The first passage of the *Tao Teh Ching* shows how different his mode of thought is from that of the Confucian school:

> The reason[24] (*tao*) that can be reasoned is not the eternal reason. The name that can be named is not the eternal name. The unnameable is the beginning of heaven and earth. The nameable is the mother of the ten thousand things. Therefore, in eternal non-being I wish to see the spirituality of things; and in eternal being I wish to see the limitation of things. These two things are the same in source, but different in name. Their sameness is called a mystery. Indeed, it is the mystery of mysteries. It is the door of all spirituality.

According to Lao-tze, there is only one thing which, though indefinable and beyond the comprehension of the human understanding, is the fountain-head of all beings, and the norm of all actions. Lao-tze calls this Tao. But the Tao is not only the formative principle of the universe; it also seems to be primordial matter. For he says in Chapter XXV of the *Tao Teh Ching*:[25]

> There is one thing, chaotic in its composition, which was born prior to heaven or earth. How noiseless! How formless! Standing in its solitude, it does not change. Universal in its activity, it does not relax; and thereby it is capable of becoming the mother of the world.

Again in Chapter XIV:

> We look at it, but cannot see it; it is colourless. We listen to it, but cannot hear it; it is called soundless. We grasp it, but cannot hold it; it is called bodiless. The limits of these three we cannot reach. Therefore, they are merged into one. Its top is not bright, its bottom is not murky; its eternity is indefinable; it again returns into nothingness. This I call the shapeless shape, the imageless form; this I call the obscure and vague. We proceed to meet it, but cannot see its beginning; we follow after it, but cannot see its end.

In what Lao-tze again seems to conceive his Tao, at once the formative principle of the universe and the primordial matter from which develops this phenomenal world.

> The nature of the Tao, how obscure, how vague! How vaguely obscure! and yet in its midst there is

> an image. How obscurely vague! and yet in its midst there is a character. How unfathomable, how indefinite! yet in its midst there is a reality, and the reality is truly pure; in it there is truthfulness. From of old till now, its name never departs, and thereby it reviews the beginning of all things (Chapter XXI).

The Tao, as the reason of the universe and as the principle of all activity, is something unnameable, and transcends the grasp of the intellect. The Tao, as primordial matter from which this world of particulars has been evolved, is a potentiality; it has a form which is formless; it has a shape which is shapeless; it is enveloped in obscurity and utter indeterminateness. According to what we learn from the *Tao Teh Ching,* Lao-tze seems to have comprehended two apparently distinct notions in the conception of Tao. He was evidently not conscious of this confusion. The physical conception, as we might call it, developed later into the evolution-idea of the T'ai Chi[26] by the early philosophers of the Sung dynasty, who endeavoured to reconcile the Yi philosophy with the Taoist cosmogony. The metaphysical side of Lao-tze's Tao conception not only was transformed by his early followers into pantheism and mysticism; it also served as an electric spark, as it were, to the explosion of the famous controversy of the Sung philosophers concerning Essence (*hsing*) and Reason (*li*). However this be, Lao-tze was the first monist in Chinese philosophy, as the *Yi Ching* was the first document that expounded dualism.

Lao-tze's philosophical successors in the Ante-Ch'in period, whose literary works have been fortunately preserved down to the present day, are Lieh-tze,[27] Chwang-tze, and perhaps Kwan-yin-tze. They all developed the monistic, mystical, idealistic thoughts broadly propounded in the *Tao Teh Ching.* Being ushered into the time when the first speculative activity of the Chinese mind had attained to its full vigour, the Taoist philosophers displayed a depth of intellectual power which has never been surpassed by later thinkers in brilliancy and freshness.

What most distinguishes Lieh-tze[28] in the galaxy of Taoists is his cosmogony. According to him, this nameable world of phenomena evolved from an unnameable absolute being. This being is called Tao, or Spirit of Valley (*ku shen*), or the Mysterious Mother (*hsuan p'in*), all these terms being used by his predecessor, Lao-tze.[29] The evolution did not take place through the direction of a personal will, that has a definite, conscious plan of its own in the creation or evolution of a universe. Lieh-tze says that the unnameable is the nameable, and the unknowable is the knowable; therefore, he did not see the need of creating a being or power that stands independent of this nameable and knowable world. It was in the very nature of the unnameable that it should evolve a world of names and particulars. It could not do otherwise. Its inherent nature necessitated it to unfold itself in the realm of the Yin and Yang.

To speak more definitely in the author's own words:

> There was in the beginning Chaos (*hun tun* or *hun lun*), an unorganized mass. It was a mingled potentiality of Form (*hsing*), Pneuma (*ch'i*), and Substance (*chih*). A Great Change (*tai yi*) took place in it, and there was a Great Starting (*tai chi*), which is the beginning of Form. The Great Starting evolved a Great Beginning (*tai shih*), which is the inception of Pneuma. The Great Beginning was followed by the Great Blank (*tai su*), which is the first formation of Substance. Substance, Pneuma, and Form being all evolved out of the primordial chaotic mass, this material world as it lies before us came into existence (Chapter I).

In these statements Lieh-tze appears to have understood by the so-called Chaos (*hun lun*) only a material potentiality. But, as we proceed, we notice that he did not ignore the reason by which the Chaos was at all possible to evolve. The reason is the Tao, or, as he calls it, the Solitary Indeterminate (*i tuh*), or the Going-and-Coming (*wang fuh*), or Non-activity (*wu wei*). The Solitary Indeterminate is that which creates and is not created, that which transforms and is not transformed. As it is not created, it is able to create everlastingly; as it is not transformed, it is able to transform eternally. The Going-and-Coming neither goes nor comes, for it is that which causes things to come and go. Those that come are doomed to go, and those that go are sure to come; but the Coming-and-Going itself remains for ever, and its limitations can never be known.

> What comes out of birth is death, but what creates life has no end. What makes a concrete object is substance, but what constitutes the reason of a concrete object has never come to exist. What makes a sound perceptible is the sense of hearing, but what constitutes the reason of sound has never manifested itself. What makes a colour perceptible is its visibility, but what constitutes the reason of colour has never been betrayed. What makes a taste tastable is the sense of taste, but what constitutes the reason of taste has never been tasted. For all this is the function of non-activity (*wu wei*)—that is, reason (Chapter I).

Will there be no end to this constant coming and going of things? Is the world running in an eternal cycle? Lieh-tze seems to think so, for he says:

> That which has life returns to that which is lifeless; that which has form returns to that which is formless. That which is lifeless does not eternally remain lifeless; that which is formless does not eternally remain formless. Things exist because they cannot be otherwise; things come to an end because they cannot do otherwise, just as those which are born because they cannot be unborn. They who aspire

> after an eternal life, or they who want to limit their life, are ignoring the law of necessity. The soul is heavenly and the bones are earthly. That which belongs to the heavens is clear, and dispenses itself; that which belongs to the earth is turbid, and agglomerates itself. The soul is separated from the body and returns (*kwei*) to its own essence. It is, therefore, called spirit (*kwei*). Spirit is returning—that is, it returns to its real abode (Chapter I).

Lieh-tze thus believes that the cycle of birth and death is an irrevocable ordeal of nature. This life is merely a temporary abode, and not the true one. Life means lodging, or sojourning, or tenanting, and death means coming back to its true abode. Life cannot necessarily be said to be better than death, or death than life. Life and death, existence and nonexistence, creation and annihilation, are the inherent law of nature, and the world must be said to be revolving on an eternal wheel. The wise man remains serene and unconcerned in the midst of this revolution; he lives as if not living. This is the characteristic attitude of all the Taoist philosophers; they begin with a monistic philosophy, and end with an ethical attitude of aloofness.

The following passage from Lieh-tze will illustrate what a transcendental attitude is assumed by the philosopher toward life and the universe, which is the psychological outcome of a philosophy of absolute identity:

> A man in the state of Ch'i was so grieved over the possible disintegration of heaven-and-earth, and the consequent destruction of his own existence, that he could neither sleep nor eat. A friend came to him and consolingly explained to him: "Heaven-and-earth is no more than an accumulated pneuma, and the sun, moon, stars, and constellations are pure luminary bodies in this accumulation of pneuma. Even when they may fall on the ground, they cannot strike anything. The earth is an accumulation of masses filling its four empty quarters. Treading on it will not cause it to sink." With this both were satisfied.
>
> Chang-tu-tze heard of it, and said: "The clouds and mists, the winds and rains are accumulated pneuma in the heavens; and the mountains and plains, the rivers and seas are accumulated forms on earth; and who can say that they will never disintegrate? Heaven-and-earth is merely a small atom in space, though the hugest among all concrete objects. It goes without saying that we cannot have its measurements and know its nature. He who grieves over its possible disintegration must be considered truly great, and he who thinks of it as indestructible is not quite right. Heaven-and-earth must suffer a disintegration. There must surely be the time when it falls to pieces. And could we be free from apprehension when it actually begins to fall?"
>
> When this was communicated to Lieh-tze, he laughed, saying: "It is as great a mistake to assert that heaven-and-earth is falling to pieces as to deny it. Whether it falls to pieces or not, we have no means to tell; be it this or that, it is all the same. Therefore, life does not know of death, nor does death know of life. Coming does not know of going, nor does going know of coming. To go to pieces or not to go to pieces—this does not at all concern me" (Chapter I). . . .

Notes

. . . [22] There exist several translations of this most widely known book of Taoism in the English as well as other European languages. It is a short work consisting of some five thousand Chinese characters. It is divided into eighty-one chapters as we have it now, but the division was not the author's own, and it sometimes distracts us from an intelligent reading of the book as a whole, which may best be considered a compilation of epigrams and aphorisms.

[23] That Lao-tze records many of his predecessors' views and sayings is seen from his frequent use of such expressions as: "Therefore says the sage," "This is what is anciently said," "So we have the early writers saying this."

[24] This is Dr. Carus's term for *tao*.

[25] It is difficult to determine the time when the book began to be divided into chapters; for, according to Sse Ma-ch'ien, the only division made by the author was into two parts. But later on commentators, each relying on his own judgment, divided the text into 55, 64, 68, 72, or 81, while some made no such attempts. The division here adopted is that of eighty-one, not because the present writer considers this the best way to understand the text, but merely because it is the most popular one.

[26] The term, *T'ai Chi,* first appears in one of the Confucian Appendices to the *Yi Ching.* "In the system of the Yi there is the Great Ultimate (or source or limit, *t'ai chi*). It produces the two regulators" . . . This passage has been quoted elsewhere. Here, however, the term *t'ai chi* does not seem to have a very weighty metaphysical sense. It only meant what it literally means, "great limit." The important philosophical signification it came to bear originated with a thinker of the Sung dynasty called Chou Tun-i (A.D. 1017-1073). According to him, "The Non-ultimate is the Great Ultimate. The Great Ultimate moved, and it produced Yang (male principle). At the consummation of the motion there was a rest in the Great Ultimate. While resting it produced Yin (female principle). At the consummation of rest it resumed motion. Now moving, now resting, each alternately became the root of the other. With this differentiation of the Yin and the Yang there have been permanently established the two principles."

[27] It may be explained here that the character *tze,* which is found in connection with most of the Chinese philosophers' names, has an honorary signification. It primarily means a child, then son, then any male, young, middle-aged, or old, and finally gentleman. It also means teacher, sage, philosopher. As a term of address it is equivalent to "sir."

[28] Lieh-tze, otherwise called Lieh Yu-kou, is generally known to have lived between the times of Lao-tze and Chwang-tze, that is, sometime in the fifth century before Christ. The work which goes under his name seems to have been compiled by his disciples. It consists of eight books or chapters, and was first edited in the fourth century A.D. by Chang Chen of the Tsin dynasty. My quotations here are mostly taken from Book I, in which his ontological views are comprehensively presented. A partial English translation of the Lieh-tze was published by Frederick Henry Balfour in his *"Leaves from My Chinese Scrapbook"* (pp. 85-135), under the heading, "A Philosopher who Never Lived" (London: Trübner and Co., 1887). There exists also a French translation, complete, by Ch. de Harlez in his *"Textes Taoistes,"* 1891, and a German translation by E. Faber, 1877.

[29] We find these terms used by Lao-tze (Chapter VI) without reference to an earlier authority; but Lieh-tze quotes them as from the *Book of the Yellow Emperor.* Is it possible that such an ancient literature was still in existence during the Chou dynasty? If such was the case, and the book really contained such passages as quoted by Lao-tze and Lieh-tze, we must seek the origin of the Taoistic thoughts in the earliest days of Chinese civilization. Indeed, the Yellow Emperor is frequently referred to as an ancient sage by all the writers, and we find the doctrine of "Huang Lao" (that is, the Yellow Emperor and Lao-tze) linked together, and usually put in contrast to that of Confucianism. . . .

H. G. Creel (essay date 1956)

SOURCE: "What Is Taoism?," in *Journal of the American Oriental Society*, Vol. 76, No. 3, July-September, 1956, pp. 139-43, 150-52.

[*In the following excerpt, Creel argues for a distinction between philosophical Taoism, exemplified by the ideas of Lieh Tzu, and Hsien Taoism, a doctrine oriented toward achieving physical immortality.*]

If anyone is apprehensive that I am going to give an answer to the question posed by the title of this paper, let me reassure him at once. I shall not be so foolish as to try to propound a single, sovereign definition of what Taoism is. In fact, the more one studies Taoism, the clearer it becomes that this term does not denote a school, but a whole congeries of doctrines. Nevertheless, if one is to discuss Taoism, he must at least have a reasonably clear conception of what it is. This is made extremely difficult by the nature of the Taoist texts. For every early Taoist book, including the *Chuang Tzŭ* and the *Lao Tzŭ,* is in fact an anthology of work by many writers. That the *Chuang Tzŭ* is a compilation has long been generally agreed,[1] but to deny that the *Lao Tzŭ* is homogeneous is still widely decried as heresy. Nevertheless a growing body of scholarship supports, with careful and impressive documentation, the statement of Fung Yu-lan that both the *Chuang Tzŭ* and the *Lao Tzŭ* "are really collections of Taoist writings and sayings, made by differing persons in differing times, rather than the single work of any one person."[2]

In such composite and sometimes contradictory materials,[3] commonly cryptic at best, it has been possible to find evidence for the most divergent views. This has been going on for a good two thousand years. If two passages in the *Chuang Tzŭ* support a particular view, it has not always been considered necessary to mention the fact that twenty passages may repudiate it, perhaps with derision.

In the kaleidoscopic firmament of Taoism there is one relatively fixed star: the term *tao.*[4] But if all that is Taoist has the term *tao,* not every Chinese philosophy that uses the term is Taoist, for in fact they all do. *Tao* at first meant "road" or "path." From this it developed the sense of a method, and of a course of conduct. As a philosophical term it appears first in the Confucian *Analects.* For the Confucians *tao* is the way, the method, of right conduct for the individual and for the state. And the Confucian *tao* was also an entity, since an individual or a state might "possess the *tao*" or "lack the *tao.*"[5] But this Confucian *tao* was still only a principle; it was never regarded as a substance, like the *tao* of the Taoists.

Like a number of other scholars I believe that the *Chuang Tzŭ* was written, in large part at least, not far from 300 B.C., and that it contains our finest exposition of Taoist thinking. As the *Chuang Tzŭ* describes the *tao* it is not merely a substance and a thing. It is the only substance and the only thing, for it is the totality of all things whatsoever. It includes, as a persistent questioner was told to his embarrassment, ordure and urine.[6] While it always seems to be in flux, the balance of its forces is forever the same, so that in a larger sense it is unchanging.[7] And it is absolutely indivisible.[8] Since it is indivisible, it follows that it cannot be described in words or even comprehended by thought. It also follows that apparent lesser objects, like you and me, exist only as inseparable parts of the great whole, and we are as old, and as young, as the heavens and the earth.[9] There is no point, then, in feverish attempts to move parts of the *tao* from one place to another. The enlightened man knows that all things are safe "in the one treasury"; he leaves his gold in the fastness of the mountains, his pearls in the depths of the sea.[10] Nor is there any cause for concern as to one's own fate. "In the universe," the *Chuang Tzŭ* tells us, "all things are one. For him who can but realize his indissoluble unity with the whole, the parts of his body mean no more than so much dust and dirt, and death and life, end and beginning, are no more to him than the succession of day and night. They are powerless to disturb his tranquillity."[11]

Sanskrit scholars will have been reminded of the famous statement of the Upanishads, *Tat tvam asi,* "That art Thou."[12] Such resemblances (they were by no means identities) were to play an important role when Buddhism entered China, around the beginning of the Christian Era.

In the *Chuang Tzŭ,* as for the Confucians, *tao* denoted method as well as entity. But a method of doing what? There is not, in this philosophy, a basis for any very positive action. The *tao* is unknowable, in its essence, and the most enlightened sage is ignorant.[13] Morally, Taoist philosophy is completely indifferent. All things are relative. "Right" and "wrong" are just words which we may apply to the same thing, depending upon which partial viewpoint we see it from. "For each individual there is a different 'true' and a different 'false'." From the transcendent standpoint of the *tao* all such things are irrelevant. To advocate such Confucian virtues as benevolence and righteousness is not merely foolish, but likely to do harm, for the advocate betrays an unwarranted and dangerous assurance.[14]

What, then, should one do? *Wu wei,* the *Chuang Tzŭ* says, "Do nothing, and everything will be done."[15] And it is very near to really meaning just that. "The small man sacrifices himself in the pursuit of gain, the superior man devotes his whole existence to the struggle for fame. Their reasons for relinquishing the normal feelings of men and warping their natures are quite different, but in that they abandon the proper human course and give over their whole lives to a strange and unnatural endeavor, they are exactly the same. Therefore it is said, 'Do not be a small man, thus to destroy the very essence of your being. And do not try to be a superior man, either. Follow the natural course. No matter whether crooked or straight, look at all things in the light of the great power of nature that resides within you. Look around you! Attune yourself to the rhythm of the seasons. What difference whether it is called "right" or "wrong"? Hold fast to the unfettered wholeness that is yours, carry out your own idea, bend only with the tao.'"[16]

But what, one may ask, does this come to in practice? Very little, it must be admitted. The *Chuang Tzŭ* says repeatedly that one should be selfless.[17] But a living being cannot be wholly selfless. At the least one must eat, and this means competition. The *Chuang Tzŭ* itself tells us that some critics said that only a dead man could be a good Taoist, in the sense we have been discussing.[18]

This is not the place to expatiate upon the merits of this particular aspect of Taoism. It may be noted, however, that while it is quite lacking in any practical program, it has provided a haven of inner strength, a refuge from vicissitude, for great numbers of Chinese from antiquity to the present day. Four years ago I read before this Society a paper in which I proposed calling this aspect of Taoism "contemplative Taoism."[19]

There is another aspect of philosophical Taoism, which I proposed to call "purposive." For reasons I suggested in the earlier paper, I believe that "contemplative" Taoism represents the philosophy in its original purity, while "purposive" Taoism was a secondary development. It is clear enough, for instance, that the poise and inner calm that may be derived from the attitude of contemplative Taoism elevates him who holds it above the struggling mass of harried men, and may even give a psychological advantage in dealing with them. Very well, says the "purposive" Taoist; cultivate this attitude as a means to power! Be without desire in order to gain the things that you desire.[20] It is by not venturing to put himself forward that one is able to gain the first place.[21] Thus a sage is able, by means of the *tao,* to become chief of all the ministers.[22] "He who wishes to be above the people must speak as though he were below them . . . It is just because he does not contend that no one in the world is able to contend with him."[23]

This tendency to treat the *tao* as a method of control, of acquiring power, occurs sporadically in the *Chuang Tzŭ,* but it is far more prominent in the text that is known both as the *Lao Tzŭ* and as the *Tao Tê Ching.*[24] Traditionally the *Lao Tzŭ* was held to have been written by an older contemporary of Confucius. Most critical scholars now believe that it was composed much later. And a considerable number, of whom I am one, believe that the *Lao Tzŭ* was probably put together somewhat later than the earliest parts of the *Chuang Tzŭ* were written.[25]

There was a great tendency, from at least the third century B.C. on, to attribute many sayings to the vague character known as *Lao Tzŭ,* "the Old Master." We even find good Confucian sayings that occur in the *Analects* repeated almost verbatim, prefaced by the words, "Lao Tzŭ said."[26] At some point someone brought together many of the best of these sayings, and may have collected and written other materials to go with them, and made the book called the *Lao Tzŭ.*[27] The fact that it is an anthology accounts for the large number of repetitions in the text.

The editing was excellent and gives, on the whole, a remarkable appearance of homogeneity. This is partly because the materials selected are always terse and aphoristic, commonly cryptic, and often rhymed. The *Lao Tzŭ* includes some of our finest expressions of Taoist philosophy, as well as some trivia. It has much of the "contemplative," but more of the "purposive" aspect. Thus whereas the *Chuang Tzŭ* is in the main politically in-different or even anarchistic, the *Lao Tzŭ* gives a great deal of advice to kings and feudal lords and ministers on how to get and hold power.[28] It is less concerned with the vision of the *tao* as the great whole, and more with the *tao* as a technique of control.[29]

The terse and cryptic nature of the sayings in the *Lao Tzŭ* had consequences not foressen by their authors. They could be, and were, interpreted in various and even opposite ways. The recently published translation by the late Professor J. J. L. Duyvendak aroused wide interest by its rendering of the first six characters of the *Lao Tzŭ,* which gave them a meaning quite opposed to the usual interpretation and new, in so far as I am aware, among translations.[30] Yet Duyvendak's interpretation is quite old in Chinese literature; it was evidently made by a wing of Taoist thought that leaned heavily toward Legalism.[31]

The convenient ambiguity of the *Lao Tzŭ* (which Granet said with some truth is impossible to translate)[32] was exploited to the full in what is sometimes called Neo-Taoism and sometimes called religious Taoism. This movement—one hesitates to call it a school—was in itself complex and various, including both ignorant religious fanatics and highly cultivated scholars. It appears to have arisen close to the beginning of the Christian Era, and taken form during the first several centuries A.D.

A distinctive name for this kind of Taoism is badly needed. Both "Neo-Taoism" and "religious Taoism" are somewhat ambiguous.[33] This kind of Taoism, in its varying manifestations, is marked by one constant aim: the achievement of immortality. The goal is to become a *hsien,* a Taoist immortal. In Chinese works written as early as the first century B.C. we find its practices called *hsien tao,* "the way of the *hsien.*"[34] I propose to call this doctrine "Hsien Taoism," to distinguish it from philosophical Taoism. . . .

A story in the philosophical Taoist work ***Lieh Tzŭ*** at once demonstrates the gulf between philosophic Taoism and Hsien Taoism, and the reasons why they could be confused. A magician of marvelous powers was entertained by the Chou king Mu with every luxury that royalty could command, and yet he seemed unsatisfied. The magician then invited the king to visit his home. Hand in hand they soared into the heavens, to an exquisite palace such as the world has never seen. After the king had enjoyed himself there for, it seemed to him, decades, they one day soared still higher, until the king became dizzy and asked to return. At once he found himself sitting on his throne, where, his courtiers told him, he had dozed for only a moment. When the king asked the magician for an explanation he was told, "We just made a mental journey. Why should our bodies have moved? And what difference could there be between those regions we visited and your own palace?"[114]

The ***Lieh Tzŭ,*** in which this incident occurs, is the only one of the major Taoist philosophical books that we have not yet considered. Its date has been hotly debated. While some Western scholars would assign it to a time as early as the third century B.C.,[115] the prevailing opinion of current Chinese scholarship, while granting that it incorporates early materials, considers the work to have reached its present form perhaps as late as the third century A.D.[116] Internal evidence seems clearly to indicate that this text, as we now have it, was produced early in the Christian Era, at a time when Buddhist philosophy and Taoist philosophy were influencing and enriching each other. The philosophy of the ***Lieh Tzŭ*** is very much like that of the *Chuang Tzŭ,* with a certain added scope similar to that of Buddhism and some admixture of Buddhist ideas and even Buddhist terminology.[117] But in the ***Lieh Tzŭ*** Confucius is almost always mentioned with great respect, as a figure of established and commanding prestige.[118] The struggle of Taoist ideas against Confucianism, a vital matter in the *Chuang Tzŭ,* has become almost a dead issue.

The struggle now is against the immortality cult, which is attacked with redoubled insistence.[119] This is quite natural if the ***Lieh Tzŭ*** as we have it was compiled in a period when the name of "Taoist" had been taken over by the immortality cult, so that Taoist philosophers felt obliged to dissociate themselves from the cult. The quest for immortality is now branded as not merely foolish and futile, but even immoral.[120] The practice of *yang shêng,* "preserving life," mentioned repeatedly in the *Chuang Tzŭ,* has been alleged to indicate that Taoist philosophy embraced the immortality cult. One passage in the ***Lieh Tzŭ*** is an outright refutation of this proposition. *Yang shêng,* it declares, should be understood to mean to give free rein to one's desires, regardless of whether this shortens one's life or not. But to submit to a repressive regimen, merely to prolong one's life, is not worth while even if it permits one to live "a thousand years, or ten thousand years!"[121]

Vigorous rebuttal, from the camp of the Hsien Taoists, was not lacking. Kê Hung, who flourished around 300 A.D., is perhaps the ablest theoretician of Hsien Taoism; he is quoted frequently by Maspero and others who write on the subject. He speaks slightingly of the *ch'ing t'an* or "pure conversation" in which his philosophical Taoist contemporaries engaged.[122] Kê Hung attacks the *Chuang Tzŭ* bitterly and repeatedly, declaring that it "says that life and death are just the same, brands the effort to preserve life as laborious servitude, and praises death as a rest; this doctrine is separated by millions of miles from that of *shên hsien* (spirits and immortals)."[123] Lao Tzŭ, as a patriarch of Hsien Taoism, is commonly though not always treated more respectfully. But the book attributed to Lao Tzŭ, the *Tao Tê Ching,* is entirely too vague and general, according to Kê Hung. He warns that anyone who hopes to learn from it the method of attaining immortality will be disappointed.[124]

The contrast between philosophic Taoism and Hsien Taoism may be seen in the two earliest commentaries on the *Lao Tzŭ* that have come down to us. One, of uncertain date,[125] is attributed to Hê Shang Kung, "the old man of the river bank," an unknown character who is alleged to have himself become a *hsien.*[126] In this commentary the *Lao Tzŭ* is found constantly to emphasize the cultivation of longevity, to state that immortality may be attained, to recommend breath control, and to speak of guardian spirits and spirits dwelling in the organs of the body.[127] All of these are characteristic of Hsien Taoism. Let us look now at the commentary of the philosophical scholar Wang Pi, who lived from 226 to 249. In the same text he finds none of these things, save for a single rather obscure reference to longevity.[128]

It would probably be possible to find representatives of these two kinds of Taoism at any subsequent period. In this connection it should not be forgotten that the philosophy of Ch'an (or Zen) Buddhism is remarkably similar to philosophic Taoism, and that at least some of its founders were quite familiar with the *Chuang Tzŭ.*[129]

What, then, is "Taoism"? Clearly, the term has been used to embrace the most diverse doctrines. They may be grouped, in the most general way, under two headings. On the one hand we have philosophic Taoism, a philosophy saying much that is still pertinent even in this day of great sophistication and scientific complexity. This philosophy has not always been studied with the seriousness it deserves, in part because it has often been regarded as a system of mystical incomprehensibilities. Another part of the reason is that it has sometimes been confused with the other kind of Taoism, which I suggest should be known as Hsien Taoism. The doctrines that fall under this heading, aiming at the achievement of immortality by a variety of means, have their roots in ancient Chinese magical practices and an immortality cult. Hsien Taoism also incorporates elements from Confucianism, Moism, and Buddhism. But there is one element that we might expect to find which is completely absent from Hsien Taoism. That is the central insight of philosophical Taoism.

Notes

[1] Opinions on this subject range from the view that the *Chuang Tzŭ* merely contains interpolations, to the conviction that no more than the first seven chapters (if those) can be ascribed to a single author. See: Fung Yu-lan, *A Short History of Chinese Philosophy* (New York, 1948; reprint of 1953), pp. 65, 104. Marcel Granet, *La Pensée Chinoise* (Paris, 1934), p. 503. James R. Hightower, *Topics in Chinese Literature* (Cambridge, Mass.; rev. ed. 1953), p. 8. Henri Maspero, *La Chine Antique* (Paris, 1928), pp. 489-492; and *Le Taoisme* (Paris, 1950), p. 230. Sun Tz'ŭ-tan, *Po Ku Shih Pien Ti Ssŭ Ts'ê Ping Lun Lao Tzŭ Chih Yu Wu* in Lo Kên-tsê, ed., *Ku Shih Pien* VI (Shanghai, 1938), 91. Takeuchi Yoshio *Rōshi Genshi,* translated in Chiang Chia-an, translator, *Hsien Ch'in Ching Chi K'ao* (Shanghai, 1933), II, 306. Arthur Waley, *The Way and Its Power* (1938; reprinted London, 1945), pp. 46, 51.

[2] Fung Yu-lan, *A Short History of Chinese Philosophy,* p. 65. The most voluminous collections of evidence on the composite nature of the *Lao Tzŭ,* known to me, are: Hsü Ti-shan, *Tao Chiao Shih,* I (Shanghai, 1934), 23-27. Ku Chieh-kang, *Ts'ung Lü Shih Ch'un Ch'iu T'ui Ts'ê Lao Tzŭ Chih Ch'êng Shu Nien Tai,* in Lo Kên-tsê, ed., *Ku Shih Pien,* IV (Peiping, 1933), 462-520. Takeuchi Yoshio, *Rōshi Genshi,* translated in Chiang Chia-an, *Hsien Ch'in Ching Chi K'ao,* II, 273-308.

[3] Contradictions in the *Chuang Tzŭ* are legion; the point of view of the final chapter, which is a survey of Taoist (and other) philosophies, seems to me quite at variance with the general tone of the work. Hightower (*Topics in Chinese Literature,* p. 8), comments that the *Chuang Tzŭ* "is not a consistent exposition of Taoist doctrine." Contradictions in the *Lao Tzŭ* are discussed in the works of Hsü Ti-shan and Takeuchi Yoshio, discussed in note 2 above.

[4] It seems impossible to find an appropriate rule for capitalizing *tao.* I therefore always write it lower case, which accords with Taoist simplicity.

[5] *Lun Yü,* 1.14, 3.24, 5.1, and passim.

[6] *Chuang Tzŭ* (*Ssŭ Pu Pei Yao* ed.), 7.26a. References to the *Chuang Tzŭ* will usually be given both to the text and to James Legge, translator, *The Writings of Kwange-zze,* "Sacred Books of the East" XXXIX, 125-392, and XL, 1-232 (1891; reprinted London, 1927); these works will be referred to as Legge, *Chuang Tzŭ,* I and II. This reference is Legge, *Chuang Tzŭ,* II, 66.

[7] *Chuang Tzŭ,* 1.15, 6.11a, 7.13b-14a, 7.18a, 7.29a; Legge, *Chuang Tzŭ,* I, 183, 382-383; II, 37, 47, 71-72. See also Maspero, *La Chine Antique,* p. 499.

[8] *Chuang Tzŭ,* 1.19a, 8.7a, 10.17. For translations, see: Fung Yu-lan, translator, *Chuang Tzŭ* (Shanghai, 1933), p. 57. Richard Wilhelm, translator, *Dschuang Dsi* (Jena, 1923), p. 177. Legge, *Chuang Tzŭ,* II, p. 224. See also Maspero, *La Chine Antique,* p. 504.

[9] *Chuang Tzŭ,* 1.18b-19a; Fung Yu-lan, *Chuang Tzŭ,* pp. 56-57.

[10] *Chuang Tzŭ,* 5.2a; Legge, *Chuang Tzŭ,* I, 309-310.

[11] *Chuang Tzŭ,* 7.18b; Wilhelm, *Dschuang Dsi,* p. 158.

[12] See Charles Eliot, *Hinduism and Buddhism* (1921; reprinted London, 1954), I, 81.

[13] *Chuang Tzŭ,* 1.16b, 7.22, 7.23b-24a; Legge, *Chuang Tzŭ,* I, 185; II, 57-58, 60-61.

[14] *Chuang Tzŭ,* 1.13b-15a, 3.13a-14a, 4.1b, 5.16; Legge, *Chuang Tzŭ,* I, 181-183, 255-257, 268, 338-340.

[15] *Chuang Tzŭ,* 7.22b; Legge, *Chuang Tzŭ,* II, 59. The expression *wu wei* is extremely common in the *Chuang Tzŭ.*

[16] *Chuang Tzŭ,* 9.23a. In my opinion this passage is not satisfactorily rendered either in Legge, *Chuang Tzŭ,* II, 179, or in Herbert A. Giles, translator, *Chuang Tzŭ* (revised ed., London, 1926), pp. 400-401. Certainly the passage is difficult. My own translation is based in part on Yüan Yü-sung, *Chuang Tzŭ Chi Chu* (revised ed., Shanghai, 1936), *hsia* 2.14b-15a.

[17] *Chuang Tzŭ,* 1.5a, 5.6a, 7.10b; Legge, *Chuang Tzŭ,* I, 169, 317-318, II, 31.

[18] *Chuang Tzŭ,* 10.18a; Legge, *Chuang Tzŭ,* II, 225. This *T'ien Hsia* chapter is itself critical of the point of view that has been described in this paper as typical of the *Chuang Tzŭ.* It was mentioned earlier that in my opinion the tone of the *T'ien Hsia* chapter is at variance with that of the rest of the work.

[19] At Boston on April 3, 1952. An expanded version, entitled "On Two Aspects in Early Taoism," was published in the *Silver Jubilee Volume of the Zinbun-Kagaku-Kenkyusyo, Kyoto University* (Kyoto, 1954), pp. 43-53.

[20] *Lao Tzŭ,* chap. 7.

[21] *Ibid.,* chap. 67.

[22] *Ibid.,* chap. 28. There is no doubt, I think, that *p'u* here is another name for the *tao.*

[23] *Ibid.,* chap. 66.

[24] For a somewhat similar opinion, see Fung Yu-lan, *A History of Chinese Philosophy,* translated by Derk Bodde (revised ed.; Princeton, 1952), I, 174-175, 334.

[25] See: Ch'ien Mu, *Kuan Yü Lao Tzŭ Ch'êng Shu Nien Tai Chih I Chung K'ao Ch'a,* in Lo Kên-tsê, ed., *Ku Shih Pien,* IV, 411. Fung Yu-lan, *A Short History of Chinese Philosophy,* pp. 83, 87, 93-94, 104, 172. Hightower, *Topics in Chinese Literature,* p. 8. Ku Chieh-kang, *Lun Shih Ching Ching Li Chi Lao Tzŭ Yü Tao Chia Shu,* in Ku Chieh-kang, ed., *Ku Shih Pien,* I (fourth ed.; Peking, 1927), 57. Sun Tz'ŭ-tan, *Po Ku Shih Pien Ti Ssŭ Ts'ê Ping Lun Lao Tzŭ Chih Yu Wu,* in Lo Kên-tsê, ed., *Ku Shih Pien,* VI, 91. Takeuchi Yoshio, *Rōshi Genshi,* in Chiang Chiaan, *Hsien Ch'in Ching Chi K'ao,* II, 304-306. Arthur Waley, *Three Ways of Thought in Ancient China* (1939; reprinted London, 1946), p. 11, and *The Way and Its Power,* p. 86.

[26] In the work known as *Wên Tzŭ,* virtually every paragraph is headed "Lao Tzŭ said." This, plus the fact that it contains many passages identical with material in other books and was said to have been written by "a disciple of Lao Tzŭ," has caused the *Wên Tzŭ* to be denounced as a late forgery. It is almost never quoted by writers on Taoism, although it contains material important for the history of Taoist thought. Liang Ch'i-ch'ao condemned the *Wên Tzŭ* on the basis, it seems to me, of inadequate evidence; see Liang Ch'i-ch'ao, *Han Shu I Wên Chih Chu Tzŭ Lüeh K'ao Shih,* p. 21, in *Yin Ping Shih Hê Chi,* Vol. 18 (Shanghai, 1936). A work by this name was listed in the *Han Shu I Wên Chih* and apparently in the *Ch'i Lüeh* of Liu Hsin. More than one hundred thirty passages in the *T'ai P'ing Yü Lan* are attributed to the *Wên Tzŭ;* I have checked a certain number of these with the current text and found them to correspond. Kê Hung, in his *Pao P'u Tzŭ* (*Ssŭ Pu Pei Yao* ed., 8.3b), refers to the *Wên Tzŭ* together with the *Lao Tzŭ* and the *Chuang Tzŭ;* this work dates from around 300 A.D. For these and other reasons I believe it is probable that at least a considerable portion of the present *Wên Tzŭ* dates from the Han period. For Confucian statements attributed to *Lao Tzŭ,* compare: *Wên Tzŭ* (*Ssŭ Pu Pei Yao* ed.), *hsia* 2a with *Lun Yü,* 12.22.1. *Wên Tzŭ, hsia* 27b with *Lun Yü,* 7.2.

[27] There is general agreement, even among scholars who do not consider the *Lao Tzŭ* to be an anthology, that it contains materials which also occur in other works; see: J. J. L. Duyvendak, translator, *Tao Tê Ching* (London, 1954), pp. 6-7. Waley, *The Way and Its Power,* pp. 128, 149 n. l.

[28] *Lao Tzŭ,* chapters 22, 25, 29, 30, 39, 57, 60, 65, 80.

[29] Cf. Duyvendak, *Tao Tê Ching,* p. 12; Fung Yu-lan, *A History of Chinese Philosophy,* I, 175; Waley, *The Way and Its Power,* p. 92.

[30] Duyvendak, *Tao Tê Ching,* p. 17.

[31] *Wên Tzŭ, hsia* 35b-36a. There is one other passage in the *Wên Tzŭ* (*shang* 3b-4a) which in its opening section espouses the interpretation favored by Duvendak, but then changes direction completely. This curious passage is in part based on one which appears both in the *Huai Nan Tzŭ* and in the *Han Fei Tzŭ,* adds statements found in the *Lao Tzŭ,* and confuses the whole almost hopelessly. A number of other passages in early literature seem to show that the interpretation made by Duyvendak was espoused only by distinctly minority opinion among early Taoists. I have written but not yet published a monograph on the meaning of the first twelve characters of the *Lao Tzŭ.*

[32] Granet, *La Pensée Chinoise,* pp. 502-503. See also Derk Bodde, "Two New Translations of Lao Tzu," in *JAOS,* LIV (1954), 216-217.

[33] Pelliot, like many others, used "Neo-Taoism" to denote the quest for immortality; Paul Pelliot, "Meoutseu ou les doutes levés," in *T'oung Pao,* XIX (Leyden, 1920), 414-415, n. 385. Fung Yu-lan, however, calls this "religious Taoism" while using "Neo-Taoism" to denote a "revived Taoist philosophy"; Fung Yu-lan, *A Short History of Chinese Philosophy,* p. 211.

[34] Takigawa Kametaro, *Shih Chi Hui Chu K'ao Chêng* (Tokyo, 1932-1934; referred to hereafter as *Shih Chi*), 117.79. . . . *Pao P'u Tzŭ, Nei* 8. 5a. *Wei Shu* (*T'ung Wên* ed., 1884), 114. 26a. . . .

[114] *Lieh Tzŭ* (*Ssŭ Pu Pei Yao* ed.), 3. 1a-3a; Lionel Giles, *Taoist Teachings from the Book of Lieh Tzŭ* (1912; reprinted London, 1947), pp. 58-61.

[115] Maspero, who is of his opinion, states that the argument of Ma Hsü-lun against assigning an early date to the *Lieh Tzŭ* "a été facilement réfuté par M. Takenouchi" (*La Chine Antique,* pp. 491-492). This is true, but it is also true that much of Ma's argument was of the most feeble character. Its refutation has little bearing upon the important, valid case that other scholars have made for placing the editing of our present text within the Christian Era.

[116] Fung Yu-lan, *A Short History of Chinese Philosophy,* p. 232. Chang Hsin-ch'êng, *Wei Shu T'ung K'ao,* pp. 699-712.

[117] A number of ideas in the *Lieh Tzŭ* are at least strongly suggestive of Buddhist influence. These include: the dissolution of the individual at death (cf. *skandhas*), the doctrine that heaven and earth will come to an end, the giving of alms to acquire merit, and the ceremonial release of living creatures to show benevolence; *Lieh Tzŭ,* 1.9b, 1.15a, 8.10a, 8.14b; Giles, *Taoist Teachings from the Book of Lieh Tzŭ,* pp. 24-25, 31, 118-119. The doctrine that all is illusion (*Lieh Tzŭ,* 3.4b-5a) sounds Indian, and the character used here, *huan,* is said to be used in Chinese Buddhist texts to translate the Sanskrit *māyā;* see W. E. Soothill and Lewis Hodous, *A Dictionary of Chinese Buddhist Terms* (London, 1937), p. 149, and Fung Yu-lan, *A History of Chinese Philosophy,* II, 257, 342. In fact, this passage in the *Lieh Tzŭ* seems to have some resemblance to one found in a Buddhist text; see Ting Fu-pao, *Fo Hsüeh Ta Tz'ŭ Tien* (3rd ed.; Shanghai, 1929), p. 741. For further data on Buddhist influence on the *Lieh Tzŭ,* see the discussion in Sung Lien, *Chu Tzŭ Pien,* in *Ku Shu Pien Wei Ssŭ Chung* (Shanghai, 1935), pp. 9-10.

[118] *Lieh Tzŭ,* 1.10a-12a, 2.14a, 2.23b-24b, 3.9b, 4.1a-6b, 6. 1a, 8.4b; Giles, *Taoist Teachings from the Book of Lieh Tzŭ,* pp. 26-27, 51, 55-57, 68, 73-75, 97-98, 111. In the *Chuang Tzŭ,* while Confucius is in some passages honored as a Taoist sage, in others he is sharply criticized.

[119] *Lieh Tzŭ,* 1.6a, 1.9b, 1.11a-13a, 2.2a, 6.1, 6.7a, 6.8a, 6.9a, 6.11a-12, 7.3a, 7.4a-5a, 7.7b-8a, 7.11b, 8.14; Giles, *Taoist Teachings from the Book of Lieh Tzŭ,* pp. 22-25, 27-28, 38, 97-99, 101-102. In two passages, in this composite and heterogeneous work, *hsien* are described as inhabiting distant and fanciful lands, but it is not suggested that men in general may become *hsien:* *Lieh Tzŭ,* 2.2b-3b, 5.4a-5b. One passage (*Lieh Tzŭ,* 8.14) discusses with Taoist impartiality the possibility that a man who claimed to know the technique of immortality, but died, might not have been a charlatan.

[120] *Lieh Tzŭ,* 1.12b-13a; Giles, *Taoist Teachings from the Book of Lieh Tzŭ,* p. 28.

[121] *Lieh Tzŭ,* 7.4.

[122] Kê Hung, *Pao P'u Tzŭ, Wai* 25.5a, 46.3a.

[123] *Ibid., Nei* 8.3b. See also *Wai* 4.3a, 14.3b-4a, 33.1b, 42.1, 43.2a, 48.1a. Kê Hung is not always of the same mind about Chuang Tzŭ; see also *ibid., Nei* 14.2a.

[124] *Ibid., Nei* 8.3.

[125] Traditionally dating from the second century B.C.; see *Lao Tzŭ Tao Tê Ching, Hê Shang Kung Chang Chü,* (*Ssŭ Pu Ts'ung K'an* ed.), preface. Eduard Erkes dates it at "about 200 A.D."; see Eduard Erkes, "Hoshang-kung's Commentary on Lao-tse," in *Artibus Asiae,* VIII (Basel, 1940), 124-127. It is evidently to this work that Waley refers (in *The Way and Its Power,* p. 129) when he says that "some time about the fourth century A.D. an unknown Taoist produced what purported to be an independent text, together with what pretended to be a lost Han commentary." Waley adds that it was "a commentary designed to bring the *Tao*

Tê Ching into line with contemporary Taoism, which was a very different thing from the Taoism of six hundred years before." Paul Pelliott assigned it to a time not later than the end of the sixth century; see Pelliot, "Meou-tseu ou les Doutes Levés," p. 334, n. 22. For the opinions of Chinese scholars, see Chang Hsin-ch'êng, *Wei Shu T'ung K'ao,* pp. 743-745.

[126] Kê Hung, *Shên Hsien Chuan,* 3.1a-2a.

[127] *Lao Tzŭ Tao Tê Ching, Hê Shang Kung Chang Chü, shang* la, 2b-3b, 4b-5b, 8, 14b, 17a-18a; *hsia* 7a, 8b, 11b, 17a.

[128] *Lao Tzŭ, shang* 19.

[129] Eliot, *Hinduism and Buddhism,* III, 305-306. Fung Yu-lan, *A Short History of Chinese Philosophy,* pp. 246-247, 257. Hu Shih, "Development of Zen Buddhism in China," in *The Chinese Social and Political Science Review,* XV (Peiping, 1931-1932), 475-505. Hu Shih "Ch'an (Zen) Buddhism in China," in *Philosophy East and West,* III (Honolulu, 1953), 3-24. Granet, *La Pensée Chinoise,* p. 581. Waley, *The Way and Its Power,* p. 120.

Holmes Welch (essay date 1957)

SOURCE: "The Taoist Movement," in *The Parting of the Way: Lao Tzu and the Taoist Movement*, Beacon Press, 1957, pp. 88-97.

[*In the essay that follows, Welch discusses the rise of philosophical Taoism, with particular consideration of its connections to medical and scientific beliefs.*]

Lists of the world's principal religions usually include "Taoism." We might therefore suppose that "Taoism" was a religion comparable to Christianity, Buddhism, or Islam. We might suppose that like them it could be traced back to a founding prophet—in its case, Lao Tzu—whose followers set up a church—the Taoist church; that various branches of Taoism developed as the church divided into sects; and that the church and its doctrines, originally pure, became corrupted with the passing of centuries until they ended up as the Taoist priests and sorcery of today.

This is almost wholly mistaken. Taoism cannot be traced back to Lao Tzu or any other single man. Its principal branches were not offshoots of the Taoist church. Those who set up the church were not followers of Lao Tzu (they turned their backs on almost every precept in his book). The doctrines of Taoism are no more "corrupt" today than they were when it began. And to call it a religion at all is misleading because, though it included a religion, its other elements were equally important.

These other elements were oddly assorted. There was, for example, the science of alchemy; maritime expeditions in search of the Isles of the Blest; an indigenous Chinese form of yoga; a cult of wine and poetry; collective sexual orgies; church armies defending a theocratic state; revolutionary secret societies; and the philosophy of Lao Tzu. Since all these things can properly be termed "Taoist," it is, as you can see, a very broad term indeed, which has proved confusing for students of the Far East and of the history of religion.

No less confusing has been the primary source on Taoism—the Taoist Canon or Tao Tsang. This is a bible in 1,120 *volumes*—not pages—compiled over a period of fifteen centuries. Many of the books that compose it use an esoteric vocabulary which only initiates were meant to understand, and in some cases the last initiate may have died a thousand years ago. It includes books of divine revelations received by the adept in trance, which are partly or wholly incoherent. Almost no book bears a date or the name of its author. We do not even know the order in which the Canon was written.

It would take decades and whole teams of scholars to make order out of this vast heap of textual material, and more decades to collate it with the related material, even larger in bulk, that may be found in the dynastic histories and collections. The task is so appalling that it is never likely to be undertaken. But until it is, all discussion of the history of Taoism must be tentative.

To find his way through the complexities ahead the reader may want to equip himself with a map. Let him think of Taoism, then, as a river which united four streams. None of the four was bigger than the others, so none can be singled out as the real headwaters. The river simply began where they met. Lower down in its course it was joined by other streams. Only a little lower, as it approached a long delta, it began to throw off branches. Many of these branches can be identified as the same streams that had flowed in higher up. It was indeed a strange sort of river, with currents flowing side by side, half mingling, half separate. Finally as it broadened towards the mouth at which we stand today, there developed a crisscrossing of water-courses, branching off not merely from our Taoist river, but from the rivers of Confucianism and Buddhism which share the same delta. A complicated picture! But it is no more complicated than the facts.

The four streams which were later to converge in the river of Taoism appear to rise into history about the middle of the fourth century before Christ. It was probably between 350 and 250 B.C. that the names of Lao Tzu, Chuang Tzu, and Lieh Tzu became associated with what we shall call "philosophical Taoism"; their books testified in turn to the existence of a "hygiene school," which cultivated longevity through breathing exercises and gymnastics; early in the same period the theory of the Five Elements was propounded by Tsou Yen, whose followers are thought to have started research on the elixir of life; and lastly, along the northeastern coasts of China, ships began to sail out in search of the Isles of the Blest, hoping to return with the mushroom that "prevented death." Notice that the pursuit of immortality is an element common to three of the four streams I have just mentioned. For the Chinese of that time immortality could only be physical. This was because they considered the personality a composite of several complementary souls that dispersed at death.[2]

Though in history as we have it the appearance of the four streams of Taoism is sudden, clearly each must have had a long period of development. In this development—in the watersheds, so to speak, of the streams—some contribution was probably made by the ancient Chinese shamans who danced and prophesied in trance; by the mediums who represented the dead at funerals; by the anarchistic hermits and agriculturalists mentioned in the Confucian *Analects;* by men like Yang Chu and Sung Tzu; and by experts in the *I Ching,* the oldest scripture we have on divination. But just what their contributions were, we can only conjecture.[3]

We have already discussed the first of the philosophical Taoists, Lao Tzu. What about his successors, Chuang Tzu and Lieh Tzu? They are figures almost as shadowy and controversial as he was. The *Chuang Tzu* was probably compiled during the early decades of the third century B.C. and the ***Lieh Tzu*** either shortly thereafter (in the opinion of Western scholars) or in the third century A.D. (according to Chinese scholars). The doctrines that both these books expound are essentially the same as those we have met in the *Tao Te Ching:* inaction, government by *te,* the relativity of opposites, the search for Tao through meditation, and so forth. There are differences, however, especially in emphasis. Lao Tzu emphasized humility while Chuang Tzu emphasized the danger of high position. From Chuang Tzu we learn more specifically than from Lao Tzu that the artist creates not by reason, but by intuition, not by the study of books and rules, but by losing himself in what he creates—a doctrine that was eventually to determine the course of Chinese art. Chuang Tzu attacks by name the sainted kings of antiquity and ridicules Confucius, who held them up as a model. Lieh Tzu, on the other hand, emphasizes determinism. He taught that cause and effect rather than fate are responsible for the vagaries of life. One chapter of his book is devoted to the doctrines of a certain Yang Chu, who shocked the Confucians by saying that a Sage would not sacrifice one hair from his body to save the whole world (on the principle that if everyone did this the world would be saved). Yang Chu's heroes were men who devoted themselves to the most stupefying debauchery. The stupefaction of debauchery was an analogue and possibly a precursor of the stupefaction of trance. Chuang Tzu and Lieh Tzu, unlike Lao Tzu, were the first Chinese thinkers to suggest that the physical world might be illusory. Each of the three, incidentally, has his own special flavour. While Lao Tzu is reserved, Chuang Tzu is exuberant and imaginative, and Lieh Tzu is ironically witty.[4]

I have not yet mentioned their most interesting difference. There are certain passages where Chuang Tzu and Lieh Tzu allude to magic islands and describe the apparently magic powers of the individual who has perfected himself in Tao. These passages, which have no parallel in Lao Tzu, have been misunderstood, and their misunderstanding has been partly responsible for the development of the Taoist movement. We must give them close attention.

Chuang Tzu tells us, for instance, that on the river island of Ku I there is a Spiritualized Man (*shen jen*) whose skin is white, who does not eat the five grains,[5] but inhales air and drinks dew. He can mount the clouds and drive flying dragons; he can save men from disease and assure a plentiful harvest. He is immune to flood and fire.

In many similar passages Chuang Tzu attributes these and other magic powers to his idealized individual, emphasizing particularly the purity of the latter's essence or breath (*ch'i*). He calls him *chen jen* (Realized Man), *chih jen* (Perfected Man), and *sheng jen* (Sage). There are parallel passages in Lieh Tzu. From Lieh Tzu we also hear for the first time about the Isles of the Blest. They lie in an archipelago far out to sea. The most famous is called P'eng-lai. On these islands the buildings are gold; all living creatures are white; "immortal sages" live there, who eat sweet flowers and never die. The word used for "immortal" is *hsien.*

We are faced here with a choice that will determine our picture of how the Taoist movement developed. Do Chuang Tzu and Lieh Tzu intend their descriptions of magic powers and island to be taken literally or allegorically? The argument for taking them literally is strong. A few centuries after Chuang Tzu the Immortals, or *hsien,* took over the center of the stage in Taoism. They became the celestial officials who governed the world from Heaven and, who, though born as men, had won magic powers and immortality through the practice of hygiene. By purifying their breath or essence they acquired immunity to fire and water, could ride the wind, and became immortal; if only the adept could win their favour, they would teach him how to follow in their footsteps.

These later *hsien* were no longer an incidental feature of the misty Isles of the Blessed. They were the saints and archangels of the Taoist pantheon. But it certainly sounds as though they had originated in the philosophical Taoists' descriptions of the Realized Man and the island of P'eng-lai. To a large degree this is true, but it was not, I think, the intent of the philosophical Taoists that it should happen. There are good reasons for supposing that the magical passages in Chuang Tzu and Lieh Tzu are really allegorical, and that it was a literalistic misinterpretation of these passages which was responsible for the later union between the "pure" stream of philosophical Taoism and the "impure" streams of the search for immortality. What are these reasons?

First of all, the *hsien* of later centuries acquired immortality, as I have said, through the practice of hygiene. If Chuang Tzu embraced the cult of *hsien,* we should be able to find people in his book who indulged in that cult's typical pursuits: searching the woods for herbs, living on famous mountains, preparing medicines, retaining and circulating their breath, and practicing gymnastics. And we can find such people. The trouble is that Chuang Tzu unequivocally condemns them. He ridicules those who dwell in solitary places, those who "pant, puff, hail, and sip," who practice "bear-hangings and bird-stretchings" in order to "nourish the body" (*yang hsing*) and live as long as P'eng Tsu, the Chinese Methuselah,[6] He contrasts them unfavourably with the true Sage, who attains old age without hygiene or anchoritism. In this respect, at least, the Sage is not a *hsien.*

The second respect in which he differs from the *hsien* is in his "lyrical acceptance of death," as Mr. Waley has so well described it. Chuang Tzu's idealized individual not only "offered no resistance to death," but he embraced it with joy. This doctrine, which is implicit in Lao Tzu, becomes explicit in Chuang Tzu and has the highest significance. It is a wholly original answer to the dread that has converted most of mankind to organized religion. Chuang Tzu says that life and death are one, for they are phases of the grand process of Nature in which death can no more be avoided than life and to which submission is the only wisdom. In death the spirit decomposes along with the body, but even physical decomposition is, in Chuang Tzu's view, something wonderful and moving, for new life arises from the materials of the old. Thus it is that the transformations both of living and of dying "afford occasion for joys incalculable. . . . Early death or old age, beginning or end, all are good."[7]

When Chuang Tzu himself was about to die, his disciples expressed a wish to give him a splendid funeral. He said: "With Heaven and Earth for my coffin and shell; with the sun, moon, and stars as my burial regalia; and with all creation to escort me to the grave—are not my funeral paraphernalia ready to hand?"

"We fear," argued the disciples, "lest the carrion kite should eat the body of our Master"; to which Chuang Tzu replied: "Above ground I shall be food for kites; below I shall be food for mole-crickets and ants. Why rob one to feed the other?"[8]

There is danger of a misunderstanding here. I do not mean that Chuang Tzu was lyrical in accepting *premature* death. Death was something that should only come in its time. Immortality in Chinese is *ch'ang sheng pu ssu,* "long life no death." Chuang Tzu does accept the ideal of "long life"; he does not accept the ideal of "no death." The Sage lives long because he models himself on nature, and because he models himself on nature, he has to die.

The third reason we may know the Sage is not a *hsien* is because at the end of some passages on magic powers Chuang Tzu and Lieh Tzu take us behind the scenes and either give us a rational explanation of what was apparently magical or say point blank that it was only an allegory. In *Chuang Tzu* XVII, 7, for instance, we find an example of the former. "He who knows the Tao . . . is sure to understand how to regulate his conduct in all varying circumstances. Having that understanding, he will not allow things to injure himself. Fire cannot burn him who is perfect in virtue, nor water drown him; neither cold nor heat can affect him injuriously; neither bird nor beast can hurt him. This does not mean he is indifferent to these things; it means that he discriminates between where he may safely rest and where he will be in peril; that he is tranquil equally in calamity and happiness; that he is careful what he avoids and approaches; so that nothing can injure him" (Legge translation).

Lieh Tzu gives a similarly rational explanation of immunity to wild animals, and as to the magic islands in his book, they evidently belong to the same allegorical category as the other magical regions he mentions. Such regions are beyond the reach of mortal foot. "Only the soul can travel so far."[9] Journeys of the soul are one of the themes of the philosophical Taoists.

Finally, I think that a literal interpretation of these magic powers and islands is simply against good literary instinct. Chuang Tzu was a poet, though he wrote in prose. He is reaching out for the infinite and wishes us, too, to reach for the infinite. To help us, he gives our imagination the shock treatment. He wants to knock the sense out of us, to make us realize that up is down, asleep is awake, and that we are gross and dull compared with those who have lost themselves in Tao. To take him literally is completely to miss the spirit in which he wrote. He no more intends us to believe that his Spiritualized Man actually rode the clouds or avoided cereals than that the *p'eng* bird was actually many thousand miles in breadth or that Tzu Yü's cheeks were actually level with his navel. Not that I think such fabulous beasts and saints were manufactured out of whole cloth. Probably they were based on folklore that was current at the time. The search for the Isles of the Blest had already begun along the northeastern coast when the *Chuang Tzu* and ***Lieh Tzu*** were written. To utilize them in allegory was altogether natural.

It is my own opinion,[10] therefore, that though the word *hsien,* or Immortal, is used by Chuang Tzu and Lieh Tzu, and though they attributed to their idealized individual the magic powers that were attributed to the *hsien* in later times, nonetheless the *hsien* ideal was something they did not believe in—either that it was possible or that it was good. The magic powers are allegories and hyperboles for the *natural* powers that come from identification with Tao. Spiritualized Man, P'eng-lai, and the rest are features of a *genre* which is meant to entertain, disturb, and exalt us, not to be taken as literal hagiography. Then and later, the philosophical Taoists were distinguished from all other schools of Taoism by their rejection of the pursuit of immortality. As we shall see, their books came to be adopted as scriptural authority by those who did practice magic and seek to become immortal. But it was their misunderstanding of philosophical Taoism that was the reason they adopted it.

I have given so much space to this question of magic versus allegory not only because the Western reader is in danger of going astray if he should turn to certain pages of Chuang Tzu or Lieh Tzu, but also to support the thesis that the four streams of Taoism—philosophy, P'eng-lai, alchemy, and hygiene—were *separate* when they flowed into history in the middle of the fourth century B.C. Expeditions were by then sailing out in search of the mushroom of immortality, but I do not think Chuang Tzu or Lieh Tzu would have advocated either joining the expeditions or eating the mushroom. In both of their books there is opposition to hygiene and in neither of them is there reference to alchemy. As for Lao Tzu, he does not allude to magic islands or to alchemy. Whether he alludes to breathing exercises is uncertain, but if he does, they are exercises undertaken as a part of meditation leading to union with Tao, not as hygiene leading to immortality. Lao Tzu does refer to immunity from wild beasts—a standard privilege of the later *hsien*—but the first reference is presented as hearsay and the second as a simile.[11] Immunity in the *Tao Te Ching* is of the same nature as immunity in Chuang Tzu and Lieh Tzu.

So much for the philosophical Taoists. So much for the hygiene school, there being little we can add to our knowledge of the school at this early period beyond what we have noted in Chuang Tzu.[12] There is still something to be said about the other two currents of early Taoism: alchemy and P'eng-lai.

The works of Tsou Yen, to whom the origin of alchemy is usually traced, have been lost. But from quotations and discussions of his works we know something of his theories. He believed that the physical processes of the universe were due to the interaction of the five elements of earth, wood, metal, fire, and water. In that order they destroyed one another, and dynasties, each governed by an element, succeeded one another. Tsou Yen was also one of the first geographers. He regarded China as only a small part of the world. In none of this is there anything specifically alchemistic.

Tsou Yen flourished about 325 B.C. A little before 200 B.C. magicians appeared along the northeastern coasts who "transmitted his arts without being able to understand them." Specifically, they "practised the Tao of recipes and immortality (*fang hsien tao*). Their bodies were released, dissolved, and transformed. They relied on serving ghosts (*kuei*) and spirits (*shen*)."[13] . . . They were known as *fang shih,* or "recipe gentlemen."

The magic they practiced is no evidence that Tsou Yen was an alchemist or, for that matter, that they were alchemists. Alchemy, in China, was the search for a chemical elixir of immortality. Their elixirs may have been herbal. Furthermore, we do not know whether they compounded them in spite of or because of their "misunderstanding" of Tsou Yen's arts.

By 100 A.D., however, Tsou Yen had come to be *regarded* as an alchemist. This is clear from a reference in the history of the Early Han dynasty, which was complied about that time. I think we can conclude that, although Tsou Yen gradually acquired alchemistical stature, he himself knew nothing of the art. It was probably developed by those of his followers who became interested in physical experimentation with the Five Elements. The first elixir they developed was cinnabar, or mercuric sulphide. Arthur Waley has pointed to the use of cinnabar as a pigment on early grave ornaments and suggested that it was thought to have "life-giving" properties. This might have been the germ of the theory that, when properly purified and eaten, it confers immortality. It is actually a poison.

We come finally to the magic island of P'eng-lai, not as a feature of allegory, but as the object of serious maritime expeditions. Ships were sent out as early as the reign of Duke Wei of Ch'i (357-320 B.C.). By the time of Ssu-ma Ch'ien, whose history alludes to these expeditions, the magic islands were no longer thought of as inaccessibly remote, but nearby in the Gulf of Chihli. They might just as well have been remote, however, for everyone who approached them was either blown away by headwinds or found the islands upside down in the water. Nonetheless, because P'eng-lai had "the drug that prevented death . . . there was not one of the feudal lords who would not like to have gotten there."

The origins of the P'eng-lai cult are as obscure as the origins of alchemy. But it may have begun like the legends of other maritime peoples. Traders and fishermen are blown out to sea, land on *terra incognita,* and, when they get home, spin a good yarn about it. Eventually it develops into the Isles of the Hesperides or Prospero's Bermuda. We have no right to scoff at a civilized people like the ancient Chinese for taking such things seriously. There is a parallel here and now in the cult of flying saucers. Other planets take the place of magic islands. Their inhabitants take the place of the Immortals. Already these "Masters" are making their presence known to the adepts of today. I suppose we shall soon have books of revelation, dictated to the adepts by our interstellar visitors in remote and secret places. That, at least, was the way it developed in China.

Notes

[2] This is further explained on p. 112.

[3] For a good discussion of the origins of philosophical Taoism, see the Introduction to Arthur Waley's *The Way and Its Power.*

[4] Complete English translations of Chuang Tzu have been made by James Legge and Herbert a. Giles. Fung Yu-lan has translated the first seven chapters. Extensive selections will be found in Lin Yutang's *The Wisdom of Lao Tzu* and in Arthur Waley's *Three Ways of Thought in Ancient China.* There is a nearly complete translation of *Lieh Tzu* in two volumes of the Wisdom of the East series: *Taoist Teachings* and *Yang Chu's Garden of Pleasure* by Lionel Giles and Anton Forke respectively. I recommend Chuang Tzu to the attention of readers who do not know him. From a literary point of view his book is superior to the *Tao Te Ching,* and perhaps to any other book in Chinese. Mr. Waley's translations are excellent.

[5] Rice, millet, wheat, barley, and beans. Lists vary. This passage is from *Chuang Tzu* I, 5.

[6] *Chuang Tzu,* XV, 1.

[7] *Chuang Tzu* VI, 6 (tr. Legge).

[8] *Chuang Tzu* XXXII, 14 (tr. H. A. Giles).

[9] *Lieh Tzu* II, A.

[10] In contrast to the opinion of Henri Maspero, the great French Sinologist, who took Chuang Tzu literally. See his *Le taoisme,* pp. 201-218. I have been encouraged to find that H. G. Creel agrees with me on this and other conclusions. Indeed there are such close parallels between his paper *What is Taoism?* and my nearly simultaneous paper *Syncretism in the Early Taoist Movement* that I take this opportunity to say that neither of us was aware of the work of the other. I cannot help feeling that similar conclusions independently arrived at are likely to be right.

[11] See pp. 74-75.

[12] See p. 92.

[13] *Shih Chi,* 28/10b.

Works Cited

Creel, H. G., *Chinese Thought* (Chicago, 1953).

Creel, H. G., *The Birth of China* (New York, 1937).

Creel, H. G., "What is Taoism?" *Journal of the American Oriental Society,* Vol. 76, No. 3, July-Sept., 1956.

Fung Yu-lan, *Short History of Chinese Philosophy* (New York, 1948).

Fung Yu-lan, *History of Chinese Philosophy* (Princeton, 1937, 1953).

Legge, James, *The Texts of Taoism* (London, 1891).

Maspero, Henri, *La Chine Antique* (Paris, 1927).

Maspero, Henri, "The mythology of modern China," in J. Hackin *et al., Asiatique Mythology* (London, 1932), 252-384.

Maspero, Henri, "James R. Ware, "The *Wei shu* and *Sui shu* on Taoism,'" *Journal Asiatique,* 226:313-317 (1935).

Maspero, Henri, "Les procédés de nourir le principe vital dans la religion Taoiste ancienne," *Journal Asiatique,* 229:177-252, 353-430 (1937).

Maspero, Henri, *Le taoisme* (Paris, 1950).

Waley, Arthur, *The Way and Its Power* (London, 1934).

A. C. Graham (essay date 1960)

SOURCE: *The Book of Lieh-Tzu,* translated by A. C. Graham, John Murray, 1960, pp. 1-17, 32-3, 58-61, 74-5, 92-4, 118-21, 135-37, 158.

[*In the following excerpt, Graham examines the teachings of Lieh Tzu in relation to other formulations of Taoism and provides an introduction to each chapter of the Book of Lieh Tzu.*]

Taoism is the greatest philosophical tradition of China after Confucianism. From its first maturity in the 3rd century B.C. we find references to a certain Lieh-tzŭ, who travelled by riding the wind. His historicity is doubtful, and it is not even clear when he is supposed to have lived; some indications point to 600, others to 400 B.C. The book which carries his name is a collection of stories, sayings and brief essays grouped in eight chapters, each loosely organised around a single theme. Among these the 'Yang Chu' chapter preaches a hedonism out of keeping with the rest of the book; but the remaining seven chapters make up the most important Taoist document after the *Tao-te-ching* and the *Chuang-tzŭ*. Some authorities still maintain that it belongs (like the latter two books) to the 3rd century B.C. It certainly contains material coming from this period; but the predominant opinion of scholars in China is now that it was written as late as A.D. 300, only a little earlier than the first extant commentary, that of Chang Chan (fl. 370). If so, it belongs to the second great creative period of Taoism, which is otherwise known mainly by works hardly suitable for translation, the commentaries of Wang Pi (226-249) on the *Tao-te-ching* and of Kuo Hsiang (died 312) on the *Chuang-tzŭ*. But apart from its value as a representative document of this period, the ***Lieh-tzŭ*** has the merit of being by far the most easily intelligible of the classics of Taoism. For a Westerner it is perhaps the best introduction to this strange and elusive philosophy of life; for however obscure some of it may look, it does not present the infinite possibilities of divergent interpretation and sheer misunderstanding offered by the *Tao-te-ching* itself.

The Tao or 'Way', the path along which all things move, is a concept shared by all the philosophical schools of China. Heaven, earth and the 'myriad things' between them all follow a regular course, an unvarying sequence of day and night, spring, summer, autumn and winter, growth and decay, birth and death. Man alone is uncertain of his true path. The sages of the remote past knew the right way to live and to rule the Empire. But in the degenerate present each school (Confucians, Mohists, Taoists, Legalists) has its own 'Way', which it presents as the doctrine of the ancient sages. For Chinese thinkers, who are never much interested in speculation for its own sake, the basic question is 'Where is the Way?'—that is, 'How shall I live? How should the Empire be governed?'

The Way of Confucianism is primarily a system of government and a moral code, mastered by study, thought and discipline. Man is the centre of the universe, 'making a trinity with heaven and earth'; heaven is a vaguely personal power, ruling as the Emperor, the 'Son of Heaven', rules men; destiny is the 'decree of heaven', the world order is a counterpart of the social order, and the myriad things follow a Way which is essentially moral, given life by the kindness of spring, executed by the justice of autumn. For Taoists, on the other hand, man occupies the humble position of the tiny figures in Sung landscape paintings, and lives rightly by bringing himself into accord with an inhuman Way which does not favour his ambitions, tastes and moral principles:

> Heaven and earth are ruthless;
> For them the myriad things are straw dogs.
> The sage is ruthless;
> For him the people are straw dogs.[1]

One characteristic of this accord with the Way is 'spontaneity' (*tzŭ-jan,* literally 'being so of itself')—a concept, prominent from the beginnings of Taoism, which assumes the central place in the thought of the ***Lieh-tzŭ*** and of philosophers of the same period such as Kuo Hsiang. Heaven and earth operate without thought or purpose, through processes which are *tzŭ-jan,* 'so of themselves'. Man follows the same course, through the process of growth and decay, without choosing either to be born or to die. Yet alone among the myriad things he tries to base his actions on thought and knowledge, to distinguish between benefit and harm, pose alternative courses of action, form moral and practical principles of conduct. If he wishes to return to the Way he must discard knowledge, cease to make distinctions, refuse to impose his will and his principles on nature, recover the spontaneity of the newborn child, allow his actions to be 'so of themselves' like physical processes. He must reflect things like a mirror, respond to them like an echo, without intermediate thought, perfectly concentrated and perfectly relaxed, like the angler or the charioteer whose hand reacts immediately to the give and pull of the line or the reins, or like the swimmer who can find his way through the whirlpool:

> I enter the vortex with the inflow and leave with the outflow, follow the Way of the water instead of imposing a course of my own. . . . I do it without knowing how I do it.[2]

This does not mean that we should act 'thoughtlessly' in the English sense, that is inattentively. The spontaneous reaction can be sound only if we are fully attentive to the external situation. But we must not analyse (*pien* 'discriminate'), must not split the changing but undifferentiated world to which, in spontaneous activity, we make a varying but unified response. In thought we distinguish alternatives, joy and sorrow, life and death, liking and dislike, and we mistake the principles which guide us to the preferred alternative for the Way itself. But the alternation of joy and sorrow, life and death, is itself the Way, and we run counter to it when we strive to perpetuate joy and life. If, on the other hand, we cease to make distinctions, we experience, beneath joy and sorrow, the underlying joy of according with the Way.

The Taoist must 'know nothing' and 'do nothing'—two claims which are deliberately paradoxical. He knows how to act, but this awareness is a knack which cannot be reduced to communicable information; he acts, but in the manner of natural processes, not of the unenlightened man who tries to force his will on events. Translators sometimes resort to special phrases such as 'non-action' for the second of these terms (*wu-wei*), in order to avoid the impression that Taoism recommends idleness; but it seems better to choose an equivalent which, like the Chinese phrase, is strong enough to be obviously paradoxical. *Wu-wei,* 'doing nothing', is one of the main themes of the *Tao-teching,* where it implies governing the state by following the line of least resistance, yielding until the moment when the opposing force reaches its limit and begins to decline—for it is the Way that, to use an English instead of a Chinese expression, 'Everything that goes up must come down.' *Wu-wei* is less prominent in the ***Lieh-tzŭ,*** which directly discusses the principle of conquering by yielding only in a single passage.[3] With the growing stress on spontaneity, 'knowing nothing' tends to usurp the place of 'doing nothing'.

Confucians can describe their Way; it consists of explicit rules of conduct, customs, institutions. But Taoists hold that fixed standards originated when men forgot the Way and, although designed to repair the damage, only made it worse. We must respond differently to different situations; action should depend, not on subjective standards, but on the objective situation, to which we should adjust ourselves with the immediacy of the shadow adjusting itself to the moving body. It is therefore impossible to define the Way in words, just as the swimmer cannot describe what he does to keep afloat. The ***Lieh-tzŭ*** opens with a denial that the Way can be taught in words, echoing the opening sentence of the *Tao-te-ching:* 'The Way that can be told is not the constant Way.'

How then can we discover the Way? By a spiritual training comparable to the physical training by which the angler, archer, swimmer or boatman learns his incommunicable skill. The Taoist classics give no details about the techniques of contemplation which lead us to the Way. Writers belonging to a branch of Taoism which aimed at physical immortality have recorded their methods in some detail—breathing exercises, sexual gymnastics, herbal drugs, alchemy; and breath control is mentioned in the ***Lieh-tzŭ.***[4] However, the cult of immortality is quite foreign to philosophical Taoism, which recommends acceptance of the Way, by which everything which is born must in due course die; indeed Pao-p'u-tzŭ (c. 300), the greatest of the Taoist alchemists, goes so far as to question the authority of *Chuang-tzŭ* and even of the *Tao-te-ching.*[5] All that philosophical Taoists tell us about their technique of meditation is its object—to return from motion to stillness, from existence to the Void, the Nothing out of which all things emerge and to which they go back in endlessly recurring cycles.

This conception of mystical contemplation as a withdrawal into the ground underlying the multiple and changing world is of course shared by many mystical schools, Western and Eastern. But Taoists think of this experience in terms peculiar to China. A Westerner tends to fit the mysticism of other civilisations into a Neo-Platonist frame, thinking of a primarily cognitive experience in which the seer rends the veil of illusion and discovers his oneness with the underlying Absolute, Reality, Being. For Chinese thinkers however the basic question is not 'What is the Truth?' but 'Where is the Way?' They conceive the ground to which they return in meditation, not as ultimate Reality, but as the Way for which they are searching. This explains an apparent contradiction in the concept of the Tao. As long as they are concerned with action, Taoists, like Confucians, conceive it as a metaphorical path to be followed. But when, as in the opening section of the ***Lieh-tzŭ,*** they eulogise the Tao revealed in contemplation, they use such metaphors as 'root', 'ancestor', 'mother', the 'Unborn' from which all things are born. They present it as the source from which the myriad things emerge, and even contradict the metaphor of a highway by calling it the 'gate' from which the highway starts.

It is therefore a mistake for the Western reader to connect the Way with his own concepts of Being and Reality. Indeed, in terms of the Chinese words (*yu/wu, shih/hsü*) which are closest to these words in function, it is material things which exist and are solid (real), the Tao which is Nothing and tenuous or void (unreal). 'Nothing' is conceived (as Hegel and other Westerners have also conceived it) as a positive complement of Something, not its mere absence. The Tao is like the hole in the wheel which takes the axle, the inside of a vessel, the doors and windows of a house; they are Nothing, but we draw advantage from the wheel, vessel or house only by using its empty spaces.[6]

One consequence of this difference of viewpoint is that for Taoists the absolute stilling of the mind in contemplation is only a means of discovering the Way to live; it cannot be (as it may be for those who conceive it as a revelation of absolute Truth, in comparison with which all normal experience seems trivial) a state supremely valuable in itself. Just as Nothing has no significance except as the complement of Something, so the withdrawal into Nothing has no significance except in relation to the ordinary life to which the mystic returns. Pure trance states in fact have a very modest place in the ***Lieh-tzŭ.*** We read of a certain Nan-kuo-tzŭ who sat like a clay image:

> Nan-kuo-tzŭ's face is full but his mind void; his ears hear nothing, his eyes see nothing, his

> mouth says nothing, his mind knows nothing, his body never alters.[7]

But the ideal in the ***Lieh-tzŭ*** is a state, not of withdrawal, but of heightened perceptiveness and responsiveness in an undifferentiated world:

> My body is in accord with my mind, my mind with my energies, my energies with my spirit, my spirit with Nothing. Whenever the minutest existing thing or the faintest sound affects me, whether it is far away beyond the eight borderlands, or close at hand between my eyebrows and eyelashes, I am bound to know it. However, I do not know whether I perceived it with the seven holes in my head and my four limbs, or knew it through my heart and belly and internal organs. It is simply self-knowledge.[8]

> Only then, when I had come to the end of everything inside me and outside me, my eyes became like my ears, my ears like my nose, my nose like my mouth; everything was the same. My mind concentrated and my body relaxed, bones and flesh fused completely, I did not notice what my body leaned against and my feet trod, I drifted with the wind East or West, like a leaf from a tree or a dry husk, and never knew whether it was the wind that rode me or I that rode the wind.[9]

> If nothing within you stays rigid,
> Outward things will disclose themselves.
> Moving, be like water.
> Still, be like a mirror.
> Respond like an echo.[10]

Lieh-tzŭ riding the wind is superior only in degree to a skilful charioteer, whose dexterity is described in very similar terms:

> If you respond with the bridle to what you feel in the bit, with the hand to what you feel in the bridle, with the mind to what you feel in the hand, then you will see without eyes and urge without a goad; relaxed in mind and straight in posture, holding six bridles without confusing them, you will place the twenty-four hooves exactly where you want them, and swing round, advance and withdraw with perfect precision. Only then will you be able to drive carving a rut no wider than the chariot's wheel, on a cliff which drops at the edge of the horse's hoof, never noticing that mountains and valleys are steep and plains and marshlands are flat, seeing them as all the same.[11]

Unlike many mystical schools (including Zen Buddhism, which continued its cult of spontaneity), Taoism does not seek an absolute, unique and final illumination different in kind from all other experiences. Its ideal state of enhanced sensitivity, nourished by withdrawal into absolute stillness, is the same in kind as more ordinary and limited sorts of spontaneous dexterity. The practical applications of Taoism interested other schools such as the Legalists, who present them in the same mystical-sounding language, so that we are often in doubt whether an author is really recommending a 'mystical' attitude to life at all. Even in the case of the *Tao-te-ching,* which teaches that 'reversion is the movement of the Way',[12] that strength and hardness always revert to weakness and softness, so that the sage conquers by yielding until the turning-point, we may well ask whether the author is advising the rulers of his time to seek mystical illumination or merely to cultivate a knack of ruling in the manner of *judō* wrestling. (*Judō,* as is well known, is an application of this Taoist principle, which was disseminated in Japan by Zen Buddhists.) But the question is probably an empty one. A Taoist would no doubt answer, on the one hand that the skilled wrestler is, within the limits of his art, in possession of the Way, on the other that only the fully illumined Taoist adept can entirely master the knack of responding immediately to the give and pull of political events.

Taoism represents everything which is spontaneous, imaginative, private, unconventional, in Chinese society, Confucianism everything which is controlled, prosaic, public, respectable; the division runs through the whole of Chinese civilisation. We might be inclined to call one tendency 'romantic', the other 'classical'. However, these terms imply a preconception, foreign to China, that order and spontaneity are mutually exclusive. The 'classicist', we tend to assume, forces order on to recalcitrant material by thought and effort; the 'romantic' freely expresses his emotions at the risk of disorder. But order, for the Chinese, does not depend on intellectual manipulation, and is the goal of Taoists as well as Confucians. The spontaneity of Taoism and its successor Zen is not a disruption of self-control, but an unthinking control won, like the skill of an angler or charioteer, by a long discipline. The tendency in Chinese and Japanese poetry and painting which shows the influence of Taoism and Zen is often called 'romantic', but it would be misleading to take this label too seriously. Out of seven qualities which Dr S. Hisamatsu[13] proposes as characteristic of the Zen tradition in the arts, spontaneity, distrust of symmetry, and the suggestion of a mystery which the artist refuses to define may seem 'romantic'; but simplicity, detachment, stillness, and the austerity which prefers the aged to the young and beautiful face and the withered branch to the flower, accord rather with our ideas of 'classicism'. Order and discipline are taken for granted; but the work assumes its proper order following the Way only if the artist refrains from imposing order on it.

Nearly all the early Chinese philosophies, Mohism and Legalism as well as Confucianism, are primarily theories of government. They prescribe the conduct of individuals within society, but first of all they address the ruler. The Taoism of the *Tao-te-ching* is no exception to this generalisation. Its political doctrine is sometimes described as 'anarchism', since its essence is that events accord with the Way only if the ruler refrains from interfering with their natural tendency. But the fact remains that the *Tao-te-ching* assumes that there is a ruler, addresses itself to him rather than to the private individual, and advises Doing Nothing as a means of ruling, not as an abdication of ruling. Its doctrine is a development of the ancient Chinese belief (also visible in the background of Confucianism and Legalism) that the true Emperor does not need to govern at all, because the pervading influence of his *mana,* nourished by proper observance of ritual, is enough to maintain social harmony, avert natural disasters, and ensure good harvests.

However, from the first Taoism was also, notably in the *Chuang-tzŭ,* a philosophy of life for the private individual. The only fit occupation for a gentleman in traditional Chinese society was a career in the civil service; Taoism appealed especially to those who rebelled against this convention, or who failed to realise their worldly ambitions. In the reign of Wu-ti (140-87 B.C.) Confucianism finally ousted its rivals as the official theory of government and the moral code of the ruling class. The philosophical Taoism which revived about A.D. 200, in an age of political disunion and social disruption, was a private mysticism appealing, against the growing competition of Buddhism (which arrived from India in the 1st century A.D.), to individuals more interested in personal than in public life. Some Taoists of the period, such as Yüan Chi (210-263) and Pao Ching-yen (c. 300), were 'anarchists' in a new and different sense; they completely rejected the political institutions of the Empire, and imagined a simpler society without ruler and subject.[14]

The ***Lieh-tzŭ*** itself reflects this tendency, although very cautiously. The hedonist chapter explicitly recommends a society in which each pursues his own pleasure without interfering with others, and 'the Way of ruler and subject is brought to an end'.[15] The Taoist chapters retain the old assumption that the power emanating from a true sage maintains the harmony of society without the need of government, but imply that he is not an Emperor; such sages have only existed either before or outside the Chinese Empire. The ideal society of which the Yellow Emperor dreams is that of Hua-hsü, mother of the first Emperor Fu-hsi, and he does not quite succeed in realising it.[16] Confucius is made to deny that any Emperor since the beginning of history has been a sage, although there may be a sage in the Western regions outside China.[17] In the earthly paradise in the far North 'no one is ruler or subject'.[18] Yao abdicates when he discovers that the Empire is in perfect order and no one is aware he is ruling.[19]

The Taoist, it will already be clear, cannot be a 'philosopher in the Western sense, establishing his case by rational argument; he can only guide us in the direction of the Way by aphorisms, poetry and parable. The talents which he needs are those of an artist and not of a thinker, and in fact the three classics of Taoism are all in their different ways remarkable purely as literature (in the original Chinese, I hasten to add). The strength of the ***Lieh-tzŭ*** is in its stories, vivid, lively, full of marvels, often humorous, to all outward appearances guilelessly simple. More abstract passages, such as the rhapsodies about the Way with which the book opens, tend to be vague and long-winded, lacking both the enigmatic terseness of the *Tao-te-ching* and the lyrical drive of the *Chuang-tzŭ.*

The ***Lieh-tzŭ*** contains many passages which are common to other books, and seem on internal evidence to be borrowed directly from them. Nearly half of ch. 2 comes from the *Chuang-tzŭ* (c. 300 B.C.), and more than half of ch. 8 from sources of the 3rd and 2nd centuries B.C. The *Chuang-tzŭ,* although heterogeneous in authorship, shows marked differences in style from the ***Lieh-tzŭ,*** some of them visible even in translation.[20] Stories from this source have a very simple narrative organisation, being little more than settings for dialogue; on the other hand, while the characteristic ***Lieh-tzŭ*** stories are straightforward prose, these are written with the metaphorical concentration of poetry, in a rhythmic prose which often changes into rhymed verse and back again.

No doubt the ***Lieh-tzŭ*** contains other passages taken from older works now lost. But when known parallels are excluded, its thought and style are fairly uniform. I incline to the opinion (which is however far from universally accepted) that most of it comes from one period (c. A.D. 300) and may even, except for the hedonist chapter, be the work of a single hand.

The Western reader of this book, struck first of all by its naïve delight in the irrational and marvellous, may well feel that no way of thought could be more alien to the climate of twentieth-century science. Looking more closely, he may be surprised to discover that Taoism coincides with the scientific world-view at just those points where the latter most disturbs Westerners rooted in the Christian tradition—the littleness of man in a vast universe; the inhuman Tao which all things follow, without purpose and indifferent to human needs; the transience of life, the impossibility of knowing what comes after death; unending change in which the possibility of progress is not even conceived; the relativity of values; a fatalism very close to determinism, even a suggestion that the human organism operates like a machine.[21] The Taoist lives in a world remarkably like ours, but by a shift of viewpoint it does not look so bleak to him as it looks to many of us. The answer to Shun's question, 'Can one succeed in possessing the

Way?', will sound to some ears like a confession that life is meaningless, that we might as well never have been born. Yet its tone is one of lyrical acceptance, of the universal order and of man's place in it:

> Your own body is not your possession. . . . It is the shape lent to you by heaven and earth. Your life is not your possession; it is harmony between your forces, granted for a time by heaven and earth. Your nature and destiny are not your possessions; they are the course laid down for you by heaven and earth. Your children and grandchildren are not your possessions; heaven and earth lend them to you to cast off from your body as an insect sheds its skin. Therefore you travel without knowing where you go, stay without knowing what you cling to, are fed without knowing how. You are the breath of heaven and earth which goes to and fro; how can you ever possess it?[22]

Heaven's Gifts

The theme of this chapter is reconciliation with death. It begins by stating its metaphysical premises; all things follow a course of growth and decline between birth and death; nothing can escape change except the Tao, from which they come and to which they return. A series of anecdotes follows, illustrating the theme that we should accept death with equanimity.

The cosmology of the ***Lieh-tzŭ,*** and of Chinese philosophy generally, assumes that *ch'i,* 'breath', 'air', is the basic material of the universe. The *ch'i* is constantly solidifying or dissolving; its substantiality is a matter of degree, one term of which is the absolute tenuity, the nothingness, of the Tao itself. The universe began with the condensation of the *ch'i* out of the void, the relatively light and pure *ch'i* rising to become heaven, the heavy and impure falling to become earth. Moving, opening out, expanding, the *ch'i* is called Yang; returning to stillness, closing, contracting, it is called Yin. Between heaven and earth the Yang and Yin alternate like breathing out and in ('Is not the space between heaven and earth like a bellows?'[23]) accounting for all pairs of opposites, movement and stillness, light and darkness, male and female, hardness and softness. Solid things are begotten by the active, rarefied, Yang breath of heaven, shaped by the passive, dense, Yin breath of earth, and in due course dissolve back into the nothingness from which they came. The human body is dense *ch'i* which has solidified and assumed shape, activated by the purer, free moving *ch'i* present inside it as breath and as the vital energies which circulate through the limbs. (In the present translation the words 'forces' and 'energies' as well as 'breath' are used for the *ch'i* inside the body.)

The chapter gives a number of separate reasons for reconciling ourselves to death, and even to the final destruction of heaven and earth:

(1) Opposites are complementary, and one is impossible without the other. We cannot have life without having death as well.

(2) Individual identity is an illusion, and the birth and death of an individual are merely episodes in the endless transformations of the *ch'i.* ('You were never born and will never die.' 'Will heaven and earth end? They will end together with me.' 'You are the breath of heaven and earth which goes to and fro.')

(3) The nothingness from which we came is our true home, from which we cannot stray for long.

(4) We cannot conceive what it is like to be dead, so there is no need to be afraid. Perhaps we shall enjoy death more than life (the theme of a famous passage from the *Chuang-tzŭ* which will be quoted later).[24] Perhaps we shall be reborn elsewhere. ('How do I know that when I die here I shall not be born somewhere else?' evidently refers to the Buddhist doctrine of transmigration, but only as a remote possibility.) This kind of speculation implies something less than a complete acceptance of death, and the ***Lieh-tzŭ*** presents it with reservations, through the mouth of Lin Lei, who had 'found it, but not found all of it'.

(5) Life is perpetual toil, and death is a well-earned rest. This point of view is confined to the dialogue between Confucius and Tzŭ-kung, a Confucian story which first appears in ch. 27 of the *Hsün-tzŭ* (3rd century B.C.).

All philosophical Taoists agree in admitting the inevitability of death. But there was a cult of physical immortality in China (using, among other means, an elixir distilled by alchemy), and by the 1st century A.D. at latest its practitioners were claiming the authority of the *Tao-te-ching* and calling themselves Taoists. The relation between this cult and philosophical Taoism remains something of a mystery. Alchemists, in China as in Europe, made genuine discoveries in the course of their search for the elixir; and Joseph Needham, in the second volume of his *Science and Civilization in China,* combining the experiments of the alchemists with certain theses of the philosophers which connect with Western scientific theories and principles of research,[25] presents even the philosophical Taoists as scientists not quite emancipated from the mystical ideas common in the primitive stage of a scientific tradition. His argument, ingenious as it is, prevents him from recognising just how far the philosophical Taoists go in their rejection of knowledge, of analytic thinking, of the whole basis of scientific method. However, for present purposes it is enough to say that in the 3rd and 4th centuries A.D. philosophers still kept aloof from the alchemists who had usurped the name of 'Taoist'.[26] With one dubious exception,[27] references in the ***Lieh-tzŭ*** to the cult of immortality are hostile.[28]

It may be noticed that the mythology of the ***Lieh-tzŭ,*** if taken literally, often seems to contradict its philosophy. Its stories mention immortals living in remote regions,[29] a supreme God (*Ti*),[30] even a personal Creator[31]—the last a pure metaphor for the process of transformation, without basis even in popular religion. The Yellow Emperor at death 'rose into the sky'[32]—a ritual phrase for the death of Emperors, but apparently meant literally, since elsewhere it is implied that King Mu of Chou did not rise into the sky.[33] It is not easy to decide how far the author believed in the historical truth of some of his stories; certainly many of them are *yü-yen,* 'parables', an acknowledged literary form among Taoists from the 3rd century B.C. Very likely he did not ask the question himself. A delight in the marvellous, a confidence that there are astonishing things beyond the reach of our knowledge, is an important part of the Taoist sensibility. One has the impression that stories of immortals, not here and now, but in remote times and places, are in a twilight between dream and reality, true enough to remind us of the limitations of ordinary knowledge, not quite true enough to suggest the possibility of becoming immortal ourselves. . . .

The Yellow Emperor

This chapter is concerned with the Taoist principle of action. Faced with an obstacle, the unenlightened man begins to think about possible benefit and injury, and ponder alternative courses of action. But this thinking does him harm instead of good. A gambler plays better for tiles than for money, because he does not bother to think; a good swimmer learns to handle a boat quickly, because he does not care if it turns over; a drunken man falling from a cart escapes with his life because, being unconscious, he does not stiffen himself before collision. It is especially dangerous to be conscious of oneself. A woman aware that she is beautiful ceases to be beautiful; teachers aware of their own merit soon degenerate.

Boatmen, swimmers and insect-catchers do not think what to do next and are not conscious of themselves; their minds are totally concentrated on the object, to which they react without intermediate thought. One whose mind is a pure mirror of his situation, unaware of himself and therefore making no distinction between advantage and danger, will act with absolute assurance, and nothing will stand in his way. 'The man who is in harmony is absolutely the same as other things, and no thing succeeds in wounding or obstructing him. To pass through metal and stone, and tread through water and fire, are all possible.' Not that such powers are his goal; even when he gets them, he may not want to put on such a vulgar performance. Confucius himself 'is one who, though able to do it, is able not to do it'.

Outside things can obstruct and injure us only if we are assertive instead of adaptable. To take a simile from the *Tao-te-ching,* we must be like water making its way through cracks. If we do not try to impose our will, but adjust ourselves to the object, we shall find the Way round or though it. The softer a substance is, the narrower the crack through which it can pass; the absolutely soft 'comes out of nothingness and finds its way where there is no crack'.[34] Wang Pi (226-249), commenting on this passage, writes:

'The air (*ch'i*) finds its way in everywhere, water passes through everything.'

'The tenuous, non-existent, soft and weak goes through everything; nothingness cannot be confined, the softest thing cannot be snapped.'

Possession of the Way is thus a capacity for dealing effortlessly with external things. Its theoretical limit is absolute power, or rather absolute liberty; for the whole point is that, instead of controlling things, the sage ceases to be obstructed by them. Lieh-tzŭ riding the winds is an image, not of mastery, but of free, unimpeded movement. . . .

King Mu of Chou

The doctrine that the world perceived by the senses is an illusion is familiar in mystical philosophies everywhere; we expect it to have the corollary that illumination is an awakening from illusion to the Reality behind it. It is impossible to draw this conclusion within the metaphysical framework of Taoism, which assumes, as we saw in the Introduction, that the visible world is more real than the Tao, the Nothing out of which it emerges. Nevertheless, the idea that life is a dream appears occasionally in early Taoism, not as a metaphysical thesis, but as a fancy exciting the imagination. In the first of these two passages from the *Chuang-tzŭ* it is connected with a Taoist argument for accepting death: we cannot know what it is like to be dead, and when the time comes we may find we prefer it to life:

> 'How do I know that the love of life is not a delusion? How do I know that we who hate death are not lost children who have forgotten their way home? The lady of Li was the daughter of the frontier commander of Ai. When the army of Chin first took her, the tears soaked her dress; only when she came to the royal palace, and shared the King's square couch, and ate the flesh of grain-fed beasts, did she begin to regret her tears. How do I know that the dead do not regret that they ever prayed for life? We drink wine in our dreams, and at dawn shed tears; we shed tears in our dreams, and at dawn

go hunting. While we dream we do not know we are dreaming, and in the middle of a dream interpret a dream within it; not until we wake do we know we were dreaming. Only at the ultimate awakening shall we know that this is the ultimate dream. Yet fools think they are awake; they know just what they are, princes, herdsmen, so obstinately sure of themselves! Confucius and you are both dreams; and I who call you a dream am also a dream.'

'Once Chuang-tzŭ dreamed that he was a butterfly. He was a butterfly gaily flapping its wings (Was it because he saw that this was just what he wanted to be?), and did not know he was Chuang-tzŭ. Suddenly he awoke, and all at once he was Chuang-tzŭ.

He does not know whether he is Chuang-tzŭ who dreamed he was a butterfly, or a butterfly dreaming he is Chuang-tzŭ.'

There is no suggestion here that meditation can penetrate illusion; life is a dream which lasts until death, the 'ultimate awakening'. Chuang-tzŭ's dream that he is a butterfly suggests to him, not that there is some deeper Reality, but simply that he may be a butterfly dreaming that he is a man.

In the ***Lieh-tzŭ*** this theme occupies a whole chapter. Although its new prominence may well be the result of Buddhist influence, the treatment of the theme remains purely Taoist; there is no implication that it is either possible or desirable for the living to awake from their dream. Indeed, except in the second episode (where Yin Wen says that 'the breath of all that lives, the appearance of all that has shape, is illusion'), perception and dreaming are given equal weight. If waking experience is no more real than dreams, then dreams are as real as waking experience. We perceive when a thing makes contact with the body, dream when it makes contact with the mind, and there is nothing to choose between one experience and another—a claim supported by a series of parables designed to abolish the division between illusion and reality. If a magician transformed your house into a fairy palace in the clouds, and turned it back again in a few minutes, you would think the cloud palace a hallucination—although all things are in constant transformation, and in this case the difference is only that the change is relatively short and abrupt. (In China the magician is conceived to transform rather than conjure out of nothing, just as the generation of things is conceived as a process of transformation, not an act of creation.) A people awake for only one day in fifty would trust in dreams and doubt its waking consciousness. A slave who dreamed every night that he was a rich man would lead the same life as a rich man who dreamed every night that he was a slave.

We generally assume that the comparison of life to a dream is inherently pessimistic, implying that no joy is real and no achievement lasting. This is indeed the aspect on which Buddhism and other Indian systems lay most stress. But it is only one implication of a simile which in poetry, Eastern and Western, is very complex; and it would certainly be more useful to explore the significance of the comparison in the ***Lieh-tzŭ*** by the techniques with which literary critics sort out the implications of 'We are such stuff as dreams are made on' in the *Tempest* than by philosophical analysis. Unlike the Indian philosophies, neither of the great Chinese philosophies, Confucianism and Taoism, can be called pessimistic; both assume, not that life is misery, but that joy and misery alternate like day and night, each having its proper place in the world order. If 'Life is a dream' implies that no achievement is lasting, it also implies that life can be charged with the wonder of dreams, that we drift spontaneously through events which follow a logic different from that of everyday intelligence, that fears and regrets are as unreal as hopes and desires. The first and longest story in this chapter compares the visible world to a magician's illusion; and the dominant feeling throughout is not that life is futile, but that it can assume the marvellous quality of magic and dreams.

The story of the Chou Emperor Mu (?1001-947 B.C.) at the head of this chapter seems designed to contrast with the story of the Yellow Emperor at the head of the preceding chapter. The Yellow Emperor, after trying and rejecting both hedonism and Confucian moralism, travels in a dream to the ideal country of Hua-hsü; on waking he applies what he has learned, almost achieves perfect government, and at death 'rises into the sky'. King Mu on the other hand is a lifelong hedonist; he travels to the magician's palace in the clouds, enjoys its pleasures, but is terrified when the magician tries to lead him to still higher regions. On waking he has learned nothing but a taste for travel. He sets out on a journey to the West, is disillusioned with pleasure, and dies without 'rising into the sky'. Is it a coincidence that Hua-hsü's country is West of Yen (the place where the sun goes down), while King Mu's journey ends at Yen after passing a palace of the Yellow Emperor? King Mu on his earthly journey unwittingly follows the tracks of the Yellow Emperor. . . .

Confucius

Early Taoist stories sometimes make fun of Confucius, sometimes claim him as an ally. The ***Lieh-tzŭ,*** written after Confucianism won official recognition, confines itself to the second course, and criticises the doctrine through the mouth of its founder. The theme of the present chapter is the futility of the Confucian faith in knowledge.

The most important Taoist critique of knowledge is the chapter *Treating Things as Equal* in the *Chuang-tzŭ*. Its target is the analytic method of the Dialecticians, the one Chinese school which studied logical problems for their own sake.[35] The earlier Dialecticians, such as Kung-sun Lung (c. 300 B.C.), were sophists who dazzled their audience with paradoxes. During the 3rd century B.C. the authors of the *Mohist Canons* advanced from this stage to the clarification of problems by exposing false analogies and establishing rules of reasoning. But the movement soon came to an end, defeated on one side by the Confucian suspicion of speculation without practical or moral relevance, on the other by Taoist irrationalism.

When interest in the paradoxes of the Dialecticians revived for a time in the 3rd century A.D., it was, curiously enough, in Taoist circles. By this period the major enemy of Taoist mysticism was not logical analysis, but the practical thinking of Confucians, who insisted on weighing benefit and harm, and distinguishing between right and wrong. Sophistries without practical application rather pleased the Taoist taste for marvels. One episode in the present chapter makes fun of Kung-sun Lung, and quotes a number of paradoxes ascribed to him, four of which are known to have been discussed by the original Dialecticians ('Pointing does not reach', 'The shadow of a flying bird never moves', 'A white horse is not a horse', 'An orphan colt has never had a mother'). The author of the ***Lieh-tzŭ*** is quite kind to him, as he is to all eccentrics, and enjoys his sophistries without taking them seriously. The same pleasure in ingenious argument, providing it is unsound, is visible at the end of the *Yellow Emperor* chapter, where he reproduces the story of Hui Ang, first found in ch. 15 of the *Lü-shih ch'un-ch'iu* (c. 240 B.C.), a philosophical encyclopaedia representing the opinions of several schools. He quotes the *Mohist Canons* three times in the course of the ***Lieh-tzŭ***[36] and at the beginning of the *Questions of T'ang* even makes serious use of the paradox of infinity. . . .

The Questions of Tang

The universe is infinite in space and time. Outside heaven and earth, who knows whether there may not be a greater heaven and earth? Beyond the narrow range of human perception there must be things too large or small for us to see; who knows whether there may not be insects so minute that they can settle in swarms on the eyelashes of mosquitoes? The *Questions of T'ang* is a prolonged assault against the unenlightened man's ignorance of the limitations of prosaic, everyday knowledge, beginning with a discussion of infinity (the only analytic reasoning in the ***Lieh-tzŭ*** which, against all the author's principles, is intended seriously), continuing with myths, folk tales and reports of monstrous animals and trees, proceeding to accounts of the strange customs of remote peoples, then to a tale which shows that even Confucius did not know everything, at last to a sequence of tall stories about anglers, surgeons, musicians, craftsmen, archers, charioteers and swordsmen. It concludes, as a final proof of the futility of common sense, with the case of the jade-cutting knife and the fireproof cloth (asbestos), two articles which reached China from Central Asia not long before the ***Lieh-tzŭ*** was written, confounding hard-headed people who had refused to believe ancient records of their existence.

It must not be supposed that the ***Lieh-tzŭ*** belongs to an age in which marvels were taken for granted. The whole range of Chinese sensibility associated with Confucianism is thoroughly sensible, sceptical, contemptuous of fantasy; the ascendency of Confucianism indeed obliterated most of the ancient mythology of China. The Taoist delight in the extraordinary is a protest against the imaginative poverty of Confucianism, a recovery of numinous wonder, a reversion to a primitive and child-like vision. Taoism cultivates naivety as it cultivates spontaneity. In particular its insistence that we can know only a minute fraction of an immeasurable universe serves as another weapon against the pretensions of ordinary common-sense knowledge. This is the point stressed by the commentator Chang Chan, who is well aware that the fantasies of this chapter will not appeal to everyone. 'How can anyone suppose,' he asks, apostrophising Lieh-tzŭ, 'that you engage in pointless extravagances simply from a love of marvels and esteem for the extraordinary? Alas, when even Lao-tzŭ and Chuang-tzŭ are ridiculed by critics of the age, how can you escape?'

A second theme, which falls out of sight early in the chapter, is the relativity of judgments. Everthing is bigger than some things and smaller than others, similar to other things if you take account of resemblances and unlike them if you take account of differences, good by some standards and bad by others. In some parts of the *Chuang-tzŭ* this is the basic argument against analytic thought—it is useless to conceive alternatives because neither of them will be right or wrong. *The Questions of T'ang* assumes, without developing it further, the relativism of such passages as this:

> From the point of view of the Tao, no thing is noble or base. From the point of view of things, each considers itself noble and others base. From the point of view of conventions, nobility and baseness do not depend on oneself. From the point of view of degree, if you judge them arguing from positions where they are big (judge in relation to smaller things), all things are big; if you argue from positions where they are small, all things are small. If you know that heaven and earth may be treated as a tiny grain, and the tip of a hair as a hill or a mountain, estimates of degree will be graded.

> From the point of view of their functions, if you judge them arguing from those which they have, all things have them; if you judge them arguing from those which they lack, all things lack them. If you know that East and West are opposites yet cannot do without each other, the allotment of functions will be decided.
>
> From the point of view of tastes, if you judge them arguing from positions where they are right (judge in relation to people who approve them), all things are right; if you argue from positions where they are wrong, all things are wrong. If you know that the sage Yao and the tyrant Chieh each considered himself right and the other wrong, standards of taste will be seen in proportion.[37] . . .

Endeavour and Destiny

The Chinese word for 'destiny' is *t'ien-ming,* 'the decree of heaven', often reduced to *ming* alone, 'the decree'. Behind it is the image of heaven ruling events as the Emperor, the 'son of heaven', rules men. But heaven is only vaguely personal even for Confucians, and quite impersonal for Taoists. In the ***Lieh-tzŭ*** the 'decree' is a pure metaphor; events either happen 'of themselves', spontaneously, or are the effects of human endeavour, and are 'decreed' if they belong to the former class.

Where to place the dividing line between 'heaven' and 'man', the 'decree of heaven' and 'human action', is one of the constant problems of Chinese thought. According to Confucianism, whether we act rightly or wrongly depends on ourselves, but whether our actions lead to wealth or poverty, long life or early death, is decreed by heaven.[38] The Mohist school rejected this limited fatalism, claiming that wealth and long life also depend on ourselves, since they are heaven's reward's for righteous conduct. Both these theories of destiny are designed to encourage moral endeavour. Mohism, like the great Western and West Asiatic religions, promises rewards for the good. Confucianism, recognising that good is not always rewarded in practice, argues from a different direction, claiming that it is a mistake to let selfish considerations distract us from acting morally, since wealth and long life are the gifts of destiny, and no endeavour can bring them nearer.

Taoists are less interested in the problem of destiny, and it is interesting to find in the ***Lieh-tzŭ*** a complete theory which can stand beside those of the other schools. Its central point is that all endeavour is powerless against destiny. It is useless to weigh benefit and harm, right and wrong; the result will be the same whatever you do. If you fall ill, don't bother to call a doctor; you will recover if you are destined to recover. This extreme fatalism is something quite unusual in Chinese philosophy, although the sceptic Wang Ch'ung (born A.D. 27), an independent thinker who criticised all the schools, held a very similar position. Lu Ch'ung-hsüan, who wrote a commentary on the ***Lieh-tzŭ*** for the Taoist Emperor. Ming-huang (713-755), found the fatalism of this chapter as detestable as the hedonism of the next.

At first sight such an extreme fatalism, like the Taoist principle of 'Doing Nothing', seems to be an invitation to complete inertia. On closer inspection we see that it is designed to encourage spontaneity in the same way that the Confucian and Mohist theories are designed to encourage moral endeavour. Fatalism disturbs us because it undermines our faith in the value of the moral choice. However, we do not mind hearing that actions are destined, if they are of a kind outside the range of conscious decision; the claim that a man may be destined to commit a murder no doubt alarms us, the suggestion that he may be fated to fall in love with a particular woman on the contrary has a romantic charm. But the ***Lieh-tzŭ*** directly repudiates conscious choice; it advises us to develop the capacity to respond without conceiving alternatives, and activities which are spontaneous in the sense of being unpremeditated are just those which we do not mind admitting are predictable. If we ought to train ourselves to allow our actions to be 'so of themselves', 'destined' instead of forced by conscious endeavour, then pure fatalism is healthy instead of baleful, precisely because it undermines our faith in the utility of conscious choice. Thus fatalism (like Calvinist predestination and Marxist determinism) paradoxically provides a motive for disciplining oneself for a certain kind of action.

Chinese theories of destiny seldom touch the problem of free will. They assume the capacity to choose; the question is whether the success or failure of the chosen course of action is due to heaven or to man. But the ***Lieh-tzŭ*** comes near to crossing the line which separates fatalism from predestination and determinism. This chapter ends with the pronouncement that aims as well as achievements are outside our control, since they depend on our situation; a man's situation makes him aim at profit if he is a merchant, at power if he is an official. A series of anecdotes illustrates the claim that certain famous men who are praised for making the right choice in fact had no choice. However, in the last resort the author does not deny that we can choose if we make the mistake of supposing that it will benefit us to do so. His point is rather that we ought not to choose. The true Taoist empties his mind of all subjective principles, attends to the external situation with perfect concentration, and responds to it without conceiving alternatives. It is usual to praise Duke Huan of Ch'i (685-643 B.C.) for his lack of prejudice when he made his enemy Kuan Chung chief minister. But he wanted to become master of the Empire, and only Kuan Chung could achieve this for him. No doubt he could have acted differently, if he had let subjective preferences distort his vision; but if his mind accurately mirrored the objective situation, what choice had he?

'The highest man at rest is as though dead, in movement is like a machine.' The comparison with a machine recalls the story of the robot which performed before King Mu, and Chang Chan's comment that some of his contemporaries believed that the human organism is a mechanism without a spirit inside it.[39] It is at first sight surprising to find such a conception in a mystical philosophy. In the West this is an idea forced on us by science, very offensive to moral, religious and aesthetic prejudices. Taoists, on the contrary, believe that there *ought* not to be any will preventing our actions from according with the Way like the movements of inanimate objects; the comparison with a mindless machine occurs naturally to them, even without the scientific basis which could give it plausibility. A Western example of a similar way of thinking is Kleist's essay *Über das Marionetten Theater,* which argues that a puppet is more spontaneous than a living actor, since its movements depend on the interaction of parts, not on the mind of an actor thinking outside his role. . . .

Yang Chu

The 'Yang Chu' chapter is so unlike the rest of the ***Lieh-tzŭ*** that it must be the work of another hand, although probably of the same period (3rd or 4th century A.D.). Its message is very simple: life is short, and the only good reasons for living are music, women, fine clothes and tasty food. Their full enjoyment is hindered by moral conventions which we obey from an idle desire to win a good reputation in the eyes of others and fame which will outlast our deaths. If there is any philosophy which is near enough to the rock bottom of human experience to be the same through all variations of culture, this is it; and the author presents it with uncompromising lucidity. The 'Yang Chu' chapter is the one part of the ***Lieh-tzŭ*** in which everything is familiar, and we follow effortlessly nearly every turn of the thought without ever sensing elusive differences of preconception which obscure the point.

The historical Yang Chu (c. 350 B.C.) was the first important Chinese thinker who developed a philosophy for the individual disinclined to join in the struggle for wealth and power. Little is known of his teaching, which was submerged in Taoism during the next century. He seems to have held that, since external possessions are replaceable while the body is not, we should never permit the least injury to the body, even the loss of a hair, for the sake of any external benefit, even the throne of the Empire. For moralists such as the Confucians and Mohists, to refuse a throne would not be a proof of high-minded indifference to personal gain, but a selfish rejection of the opportunity to benefit the people. They therefore derided Yang Chu as a man who would not sacrifice a hair even to benefit the whole world. On the other hand the Taoists of the 3rd century B.C. and later, also concerned with the cultivation of personal life, easily accepted Yang Chu as one of themselves. Outside this chapter the Yang Chu of the ***Lieh-tzŭ*** is a Taoist, although a group of sayings and stories in 'Explaining Conjunctions'[40] shows some traces of his original doctrine.

When the hedonist author puts his very different theories into the mouth of Yang Chu he is merely following a recognised literary convention of his time. He expressed the same opinions through a dialogue between Kuan Chung (died 645 B.C.) and Yen-tzŭ (died 493 B.C.), although he must have known that these famous ministers of the state of Ch'i were not even contemporaries. However, there is evidence that the editor of the ***Lieh-tzŭ*** has expanded the hedonist document with five additions alternating with its last five sections, and that the first three of these are from older sources and concern the historical Yang Chu. Consequently there is danger of confusion, and in the present translation these passages (as well as a minor interpolation) are printed in italics in order to distinguish them.

The first of them is a dialogue between Yang Chu and Ch'in Ku-li, the chief disciple of Mo-tz (c. 479-c. 381 B.C.). It is evidently from a Mohist source, among other reasons because the story is told from the side of Ch'in Ku-li. This passage, in which Yang Chu refuses to give a hair to benefit the world, gives the false impression, if we overlook its separate origin, that the author of the 'Yang Chu' chapter was an amoral egoist as well as a hedonist. But there is nothing else in the chapter which supports this conclusion. The hedonist author is a rebel against all moral conventions which hinder sensual enjoyment, and an enemy of the respectability, the obsession with face, which the Chinese and the English confuse with morality; but he wants pleasure for other men as well as for himself. In one story the voluptuary Tuan-mu Shu gives away all his possessions as soon as he is too old to enjoy them, and dies without the money for his own funeral; those whom he has helped then club together to restore the property to his children.

There is no sign of hedonism elsewhere in the ***Lieh-tzŭ,*** and the opening stories of the 'Yellow Emperor' and 'King Mu' chapters both reject it explicitly. The 'Yang Chu' chapter on the other hand is almost untouched by Taoist thought and language. The contrast is all the more striking since Chinese poets in their cups, exhorting us to enjoy life while it lasts, find it very easy to mix hedonism with mysticism. No other part of the book evokes a mood in the least like the sombre and passionate tone of this chapter. There is no question, for this writer, of seeking a stand-point from which to look with equanimity on life and death. The word 'Death' echoes through everything he writes, warning us to make merry while we can, and the only consolation which he admits is the thought that life, brief as it is, is long enough to weary us of its few pleasures. A Taoist, just as much as a Confucian, is a moderate, a compromiser who balances every consideration against its opposite, and avoids any excess which might shorten his natural span of life. This hedonist, on the contrary, is by temperament an extremist, who presents all issues with harsh clarity, and prefers the intense enjoyment of an hour to any consideration of health, safety or morality. A Taoist laughs at social conventions, and eludes or adapts himself to them; the hedonist abhors them as a prison from which he must escape at any cost. Any Taoist would understand part of what we mean by 'Liberty', but the author of this chapter is perhaps the only early Chinese thinker who would have appreciated the passion which this word excites in the West. . . .

Explaining Conjunctions

Explaining Conjunctions is the most heterogeneous of the eight chapters. More than half of it is taken from known sources of the 3rd and 2nd centuries B.C., not all Taoist, and it is likely that much of the rest is from sources no longer extant. Nevertheless, there is a single theme guiding the selection, the effect of chance conjunctions of events. The chance combinations which make each situation unique decide both whether an action is right and how others interpret its motives. The moral is that we should discard fixed standards, and follow the external situation as the shadow follows the body. 'Whether we should be active or passive depends on other things and not on ourselves.' . . .

Notes

[1] *Tao-te-ching,* ch. 5.

[2] p. 44 below (also in *Chuang-tzŭ,* ch. 19).

[3] pp. 52 ff.

[4] pp. 47 ff. (also in *Chuang-tzŭ* , ch. 7).

[5] Cf. Creel (*Short Reading List,* p. 182), p. 152.

[6] *Tao-te-ching,* ch. II.

[7] p. 80.

[8] pp. 77 ff.

[9] pp. 36 ff. and 90.

[10] (also in *Chuang-tzŭ,* ch. 33).

[11] p. 114.

[12] *Tao-te-ching,* ch. 40.

[13] There is an English summary of the argument of his *Zen to Bijutsu* in Sohaku Ogata, *Zen for the West* (London, 1959), pp. 24-26.

[14] Cf. Lin Mou-sheng, *Men and Ideas* (New York, 1942), pp. 150-8.

[15] p. 146.

[16] pp. 34 ff.

[17] p. 78.

[18] p. 102.

[19] p. 90.

[20] Sixteen complete episodes (and sections from others) are from the *Chuang-tzŭ:* Lieh-tzŭ and the skull (pp. 20-22), Shun's question (pp. 29 ff.), Lieh-tzŭ and Kuan-yin (pp. 37 ff.), Lieh-tzŭ's archery (pp. 38 ff.), Confucius and the boatman (pp. 43 ff.), Confucius and the swimmer (p. 44), Confucius and the catcher of cicadas (pp. 44 ff.), the seagulls (p. 45, mentioned as *Chuang-tzŭ* in early quotations), Lieh-tzŭ and the shaman (pp. 47-49), Lieh-tzŭ and Po-hun Wu-jen (pp. 49 ff.), Yang Chu and Lao-tzŭ (pp. 51 ff.), the innkeeper's concubines (p. 52), the fighting cocks (p. 56), Kuan-yin's saying (p. 90), Kuan Chung's dying advice (pp. 126 ff.), Lieh-tzŭ in poverty (p. 162).

[21] pp. 111, 120.

[22] pp. 29 ff. (also in *Chuang-tzŭ,* ch. 22).

[23] *Tao-te-ching,* ch. 5.

[24] pp. 58 ff.

[25] Cf. p. 13.

[26] Creel, op. cit., pp. 150-2.

[27] pp. 177 ff. This story, in order to make the point that some men can teach what they cannot practise, leaves open the possibility that there may be something in the arts for prolonging life.

[28] pp. 23, 129, 147.

[29] pp. 35, 97.

[30] pp. 97, 100, etc.

[31] pp. 65, 111.

[32] p. 35.

[33] p. 64, cf. p. 104.

[34] *Tao-te-ching,* ch. 43.

[35] Cf. Fung Yu-lan (Short Reading List, p. 183), vol. I, chs. 9 and 11.

[36] pp. 22, 89, 1

[37] *Chuang-tzŭ,* ch. 17.

[38] Cf. p. 76.

[39] p. III above.

[40] pp. 174-7.

Works Cited

Translations

Tao-te-ching:

J. J. L. Duyvendak, *Tao te ching,* Wisdom of the East, London, 1954. Arthur Waley, *The Way and its Power,* London, 1934.

Chuang-tzŭ:

H. A. Giles, *Chuang Tzŭ,* 2nd edition (revised), London, 1926.

———*Musings of a Chinese Mystic* (selective translation), Wisdom of the East, London, 1906.

Y. L. Fung, *Chuang Tzŭ* (English translation of ch. 1-7), Shanghai Commercial Press, 1931.

Lieh-tzŭ:

Lionel Giles, *Taoist Teachings from the Book of Lieh-Tzŭ* (selective translation), Wisdom of the East, London, 1912.

A. Forke, *Young Chu's Garden of Pleasure* (translation of ch. 7), Wisdom of the East, London, 1912.

General

H. Creel, *What is Taoism?* Journal of the American Oriental Society, vol. 76, No. 3 (July 1956), pp. 139-52.

Y. L. Fung, *History of Chinese Philosophy,* translated Derk Bodde, 2 vols., Princeton, 1952.

H. Maspéro, *Le Taoïsme* (*Mélanges posthumes sur les religions et l'histoire de la Chine,* vol. 2), Paris, 1950.

Arthur Waley, *Three Ways of Thought in Ancient China,* London, 1939. (Part 1, *Chuang Tzŭ*).

Derek Bryce (essay date 1992)

SOURCE: "Translator's Preface," in *Ch'ung-Hu-Ch'en-Ching or The Treatise of the Transcendent Master of the Void,* translated by Leon Wieger, Llanerch Publishers, 1992, pp. 7-9.

[*In the following excerpt, Bryce introduces the Book of Lieh Tzu by briefly recounting what is known of the author's life and teaching. He specifically warns against taking the characters presented in the work as realistic portrayals of historical figures.*]

Whereas the *Tao-te-ching* of Lao-tzu, the most famous of the Taoist (or Daoist) writings, is concise to the point of being difficult to understand, the book of Lieh-tzu proceeds at a more leisurely pace with many points explained by means of anecdotes.

Lieh-tzu, Master Lieh, from the name Lieh-yü-k'ou, lived some forty years in obscurity and poverty in the Principality of Cheng. He was driven away by famine in 398 B.C. At that time his disciples could have written down the substance of his teaching. This is according to the Taoist tradition; it has often been strongly attacked, but the critics of the bibliographic index, Ssu-k'u-ts'uan Shu, judged that the writing should be upheld. However the book as we now know it no doubt includes interpolations, some of which are non-Taoist, and it has suffered from the accident which muddled so many old Chinese writings, the breaking of the tie of a bundle of laths, and the mixing up of the latter. The present arrangement into chapters is the work of later collators who brought together parts which were more or less similar. None of the facts alleged by Lieh-tzu are of historical value. The men he names are no more real than the personified abstractions he puts on stage. They are oratory procedures, and nothing more. Above all one should guard oneself from taking the assertions of Confucius, which have been invented at will, as real. Likewise the paragons of Confucianism, the Yellow Emperor, Yü the Great, Yao, Shun, and others, are shown in three postures.—First, abhorred as authors or falsifiers of artificial civilization; these are authentic texts.—Second, praised for a particular point, common to Confucians and Taoists; these texts also are authentic.—Third, praised in general without restriction; these are Confucian interpolations. In 742 A.D., Emperor Huan-chung, of the T'ang dynasty, gave the treatise of Lieh-tzu the title of ***Ch'ung-hu-ch'en-ching,*** or ***Treatise of the Transcendent Master of the Void. . . .***

FURTHER READING

Fung Yu-Lan. "Materialism and Mechanism in the Lieh-tzu." In *A History of Chinese Philosophy: Vol. II, The Period of Classical Learning (From the Second Century B.C. to the Twentieth Century A.D.)*, translated by Derk Bodde, pp. 190-4. George Allen & Unwin, Ltd., 1953.

Examines the central tenets of abandonment and comprehension presented in the Book of Lieh Tzu.

Kaltenmark, Max. "Chuang Tzu." In *Lao Tzu and Taoism,* translated by Roger Greaves, pp. 70-106. Stanford: Stanford University Press, 1969.

Briefly describes the wanderings of the soul, presented in the Book of Lieh Tzu as a harmonious relation with the cosmos.

Wilhelm, Richard, transl. *The Secret of the Golden Flower: A Chinese Book of Life.* New York: Harcourt, Brace & World, 1962, 149 p.

A translation of an anonymous Taoist text on meditation and health. This work includes general introductions to the beliefs and history of Taoism by the translator and Carl Jung.

Longinus

fl. c. First Century

Roman critic. Also known as Dionysius Longinus, Cassius Longinus, and pseudo-Longinus.

INTRODUCTION

Despite its relative anonymity prior to its rediscovery in 1554, Longinus' treatise *Peri Hypsos* [*On the Sublime*] strongly influenced the English and European literary landscape from John Dryden onwards. It served as a touchstone for English Neoclassical critics, and its emphasis on the emotive element of poetry and on the author as the focus of poetical meaning resonated with such Romantic writers as Samuel Taylor Coleridge. *On the Sublime* is now considered one of the most important works of ancient literary theory.

Biographical Information

When *On the Sublime* was first published in its original Greek by Franciscus Robortello in 1554, the volume–previously unknown to modern scholars–was attributed to Dionysius Longinus, a prolific rhetorician and critic of the third century. Longinus served as prime minister to Zenobia, Queen of Palmyra, and was put to death after a failed insurrection against Aurelian. The attribution of the manuscript held until 1808, when a version of the treatise at the Vatican was shown to refer to the author as 'Dionysius *or* Longinus.' *On the Sublime* was later attributed to Cassius Longinus, a third-century critic; however, because the treatise was not listed among his accredited writings, and because the treatise differs fundamentally from his other writings with regard to style, terminology, and literary judgment, this attribution seems likewise without basis. Literary historians now believe that textual evidence–the lack of references to writers later than the early part of the first century, and the treatment of contemporary authors and schools that flourished during that time–supports the attribution of the text to a first-century Roman critic whose name cannot be determined. Most translators and commentators, then, have adhered to the convention of referring to the unknown author of *On the Sublime* simply as "Longinus."

Major Works

The only work attributed to Longinus is *On the Sublime,* a treatise designed as a pedagogical corrective to a (now lost) essay by Caecilius. Longinus confronts a pupil named Postumius with a treatment of the role of emotion, which, he claims, Caecilius had omitted from his study. Longinus thus focuses on the human condition generally rather than merely on literary genres and explores the worth of writing in terms of its elevating the soul of the audience–that is, its sublimity. According to Longinus, the sublime issues from five sources: grandeur of thought, inspired passion, effective use of stylistic figures, noble diction and phrasing, and elevated composition. For Longinus, rhetorical techniques become instruments for the author to convey his own sublimity, so that great writing results not only from honed skill but from a cultivated sublimity of the soul attending the innate ability to have elevated ideas and strong passions.

Textual History

Eleven manuscripts of *On the Sublime* are extant, all of which are imperfect tenth-, fifteenth-, and sixteenth-century copies that contain lacunae, or gaps, amounting to approximately one-third of the original text. The oldest and most complete manuscript, known as Paris MS 2036, has traditionally been considered the authoritative (though incomplete) version, and was used for the first modern publication of the Greek treatise by Robortello. Two other versions of the Greek text were published in Italy before Pagano published its first translation into Latin in 1572. A Latin edition also appeared at Oxford in 1636, marking the text's introduction in England, followed by its first English translation by John Hall in 1652. However, not until Nicolas Boileau's translation of *On the Sublime* into French in 1674, and the subsequent non-literal translation of his edition into English by John Pulteney (1680) and Leonard Welsted (1712), did Longinus gain widespread acceptance by the larger literary community.

Critical Reception

There is no mention of *On the Sublime* in any ancient text still extant, and it was largely unknown prior to its rediscovery during the Italian Renaissance. Following Boileau's popular translation of 1674, however, the treatise became a standard object of study for literary critics from Dryden onwards. During the seventeenth and eighteenth centuries, Neoclassical critics, primarily in England, frequently cited the text. Its influence is evident in such works as Edmund Burke's *Philosophical Inquiry into the Origin of Our Ideas of the*

Sublime and Beautiful, and extends to such critics as Gotthold Ephraim Lessing, Burke, Joseph Addison, Coleridge, and Alexander Pope. Despite its relative anonymity prior to the seventeenth and eighteenth centuries, modern critics have found *On the Sublime* to prefigure their own literary perspectives and to be as relevant and insightful as other standard ancient texts by Aristotle, Horace, and Quintilian.

PRINCIPAL WORKS

Peri Hypsos [*On the Sublime*] (criticism) first century A.D.

PRINCIPAL ENGLISH TRANSLATIONS

Dionysius Longinus on the Sublime [translated by William Smith] 1739

Longinus on the Sublime [translated by W. Rhys Roberts] 1899

Longinus on the Sublime [translated by A. O. Prickard] 1906

"Longinus" on Sublimity [translated by D. A. Russell] 1965

CRITICISM

George Saintsbury (essay date 1900)

SOURCE: "Dionysius of Halicarnassus, Plutarch, Lucian, Longinus," in *A History of Criticism and Literary Taste in Europe: From the Earliest Texts to the Present Day,* William Blackwood and Sons, 1900, pp. 152-72.

[*In the following excerpt, Saintsbury discusses elements of the sublime and comments on Longinus's literary and historico-critical importance.*]

. . . It does not fall within the plan of this work to examine at any length the recently much-debated question whether the treatise ***Peri Hypsos*** is, as after its first publication by Robortello in 1554 it was for nearly three centuries unquestioningly taken to be, the work of the rhetorician Longinus, who was Queen Zenobia's Prime Minister, and was put to death by Aurelian. It has been the mania of the nineteenth century to prove that everybody's work was written by somebody else, and it will not be the most useless task of the twentieth to betake itself to more profitable inquiries. References which will enable any one who cares to investigate the matter are given in a note.[1] Here it may be sufficient to say two things. The first is, that these questions appertain for settlement, less to the technical expert than to the intelligent *judex,* the half-juryman, half-judge, who is generally acquainted with the rules of logic and the laws of evidence. The second is, that the verdict of the majority of such *judices* on this particular question is, until some entirely new documents turn up, likely to be couched in something like the following form:—

1. The positive evidence for the authorship of Longinus is very weak, consisting in MS. attributions, the oldest of which[2] is irresolute in form, while it certainly does not date earlier than the tenth century.

2. There is absolutely no *evidence* against the authorship of Longinus, only a set of presumptions, most of which are sheer opinion, and carry no weight except as such. Moreover, no plausible competitor has even been hinted at. I hope it is not illiberal to say that the suggestion of Plutarch, which was made by Vaucher, and has met with some favour, carries with it irresistible evidence that the persons who make it know little about criticism. No two things could possibly be more different than the amiable ethical knack of the author of the *Moralia,* and the intense literary gift of the author of the ***Peri Hypsos.***

Another of the "Academic questions" connected with the book, however, is of more literary importance, and that is its proper designation in the modern languages. There has been a consensus of the best authorities of late years, even though they may not agree on other points, that "The Sublime" is a far from happy translation of *hypsos.* Not only has "Sublime" in the modern languages, and especially in English, a signification too much specialised, but the specialisation is partly in the wrong direction. No one, for instance, who uses English correctly, however great his enthusiasm for the magnificent Sapphic ode which Longinus has had the well-deserved good fortune to preserve to us, would call it exactly sublime,[3] there being, in the English connotation of that word, an element of calmness, or at any rate (for a storm may be sublime) of mastery, which is absent here. And so in other cases; "Sublime" being more especially unfortunate in bringing out (what no doubt remains to some extent in any case) the inadequateness and tautology of the attempts to define the *sources* of *hypsos.* Hall, the seventeenth-century translator, avoided these difficulties by a simple rendering, "the height of eloquence," which is more than literally exact, though it is neither elegant nor handy. Nor is there perhaps any single word that is not open to almost as many objections as Sublime itself. So that (and again this is the common conclusion) it is well to keep it, with a very careful preliminary explanation that the Longinian Sublime is not sublimity in its narrower sense, but all that quality, or combination of qualities, which creates *enthusiasm* in literature, all that gives *consummateness* to it, all that deserves the highest critical encomium either in prose or poetry.

Few persons, however, whom the gods have made critical will care to spend much time *in limine* over the authorship, the date,[4] the title, and the other beggarly elements in respect to this astonishing treatise. Incomplete as it is—and its incompleteness is as evident as that of the *Poetics,* and probably not much less substantial—difficult as are some of its terms, deprived as we are in some cases of the power of appreciating its citations fully, through our ignorance of their context, puzzled as we may even be now and then by that radical difference in taste and view-point, that "great gulf fixed," which sometimes, though only sometimes, does interpose itself between modern and ancient,—no student of criticism, hardly one would think any fairly educated and intelligent man, can read a dozen lines of the book without finding himself in a new world, as he compares it with even the best of his earlier critical masters. He is in the presence of a man who has accidentally far greater advantages of field than Aristotle, essentially far more powerful genius, and an intenser appreciation of literature, than Dionysius or Quintilian. And probably the first thought—not of the student, who will be prepared for it, but of the fairly educated man who knows something of Pope and Boileau and the rest of them—will be, "How on earth did this book come to be quoted as an authority by a school like that of the 'classical' critics of the seventeenth-eighteenth century, whose every principle almost, whose general opinions certainly, it seems to have been designedly written to crush, conclude, and quell?" Of this more hereafter. Let us begin, as in former important cases, by a short abstract of the actual contents of the book.

The author commences by addressing a young friend or pupil, a certain Postumius (Terentianus or Florentianus?), on the inefficiency of the Treatise on the Sublime by a certain Cæcilius[5] In endeavouring to provide something more satisfactory, especially as to the sources of Sublimity, he premises little more in the shape of definition than that it is "a certain consummateness and eminence" of words, completing this with the remark (the first epoch-making one of the treatise) that the effect of such things is "not persuasion but transport," not the result of skill, pains, and arrangement, but something which, "opportunely outflung," carries everything before it. But can it be taught? Is it not innate? The doubt implies a fallacy. Nature is necessary, but it must be guided and helped by art. Then comes a gap, a specially annoying one, since the farther shore lands us in the midst of an unfavourable criticism of a passage supposed to come from the lost *Orithyia* of Æschylus, which is succeeded by, or grouped with, other specimens of the false sublime, bombast, tumidity, and the *parenthurson.*[6] Next we pass to "frigidity," a term which Longinus uses with a slightly different connotation from Aristotle's, applying it chiefly to what he thinks undue flings and quips and conceits. These particular strictures are, in Chapter V., generalised off into a brief but admirable censure of the quest for mere novelty, of that "horror of the obvious" which bad taste at all times has taken for a virtue. To cure this and other faults, there is nothing for it but to make for the true Sublime, hard as it may be. For (again a memorable and epoch-making saying) "the judgment of words is the latest begotten fruit of many an attempt."[7]

The first canon of sublimity is not unlike the famous *Quod Semper,* &c. If a thing does not transport *at all,* it is certainly not Sublime. If its transporting power fails with repetition, with submission to different but still competent judges, it is not sublime. When men different in habits, lives, aims, ages, speech, agree about it, then no mistake is possible.

The sources of Sublimity are next defined as five in number: Command of strong and manly thought; Vehement and enthusiastic passion—these are congenital; Skilfulness with Figures; Nobility of phrase; Dignified and elevated *ordonnance.*[8] These, after a rebuke of some length to Cæcilius for omitting Passion, he proceeds to discuss seriatim. . . . [What] he now calls "great-naturedness," holds the first place in value as in order, and examples of it, and of the failure to reach it, are given from many writers, Homer and "the Legislator of the Jews" being specially praised. This laudation leads to one of the best known and most interesting passages of the whole book, a short criticism and comparison of the *Iliad* and the *Odyssey,* whereon, as on other things in this abstract, more hereafter. The interest certainly does not sink with the quotation from Sappho, whether we agree or not (again *vide post*) that the source of its charm is "the selection and composition of her details." Other typical passages are then cited and criticised.

We next come to Amplification,—almost the first evidence in the treatise, and not a fatal one, of the numbing power of "Figures." Longinus takes occasion by it for many illuminative animadversions, not merely on Homer, but on Plato, Herodotus, Demosthenes, and Thucydides, whom (it is very satisfactory to observe) he includes among those who have "sublimity." This handling of Figures, professedly eclectic, is fertile in such animadversions in regard to others besides Amplification—Hyperbata, Polyptota, Antimetathesis, and others still—with especial attention to Periphrasis, to his praise of which the eighteenth century perhaps attended without due attention to his cautions.

Then comes another of the flashes of light. Dismissing the figures, he turns to diction in itself, and has a wonderful passage on it, culminating in the dictum,

"For beautiful words are in deed and in fact the very light of the spirit,"—the Declaration of Independence and the "Let there be light" at once of Literary Criticism.

Here the Enemy seems to have thought that he was getting too good, for another and greater gap occurs, and when we are allowed to read again, we are back among the Figures and dealing with Metaphor—the criticism of examples, however, being still illuminative. It leads him, moreover, to another of his nugget-grounds, the discussion on "Faultlessness," which introduces some especially valuable parallels—Apollonius and Homer, Bacchylides and Pindar, Ion and Sophocles, Hyperides and Demosthenes, Lysias and Plato. Then we pass to the figure Hyperbole after a gap, and then to *ordonnance* and arrangement, with a passage, valuable but, like all similar passages in the ancient critics, difficult, on rhythm. After this a section on . . .—"littleness," "triviality"—leads abruptly to the close, which is not the close, and which, after some extremely interesting remarks on the ethical and other conditions of the time, ends with an unfulfilled promise of treating the subject of the Passions. The loss of this is perhaps more to be regretted than the loss of any other single tractate of the kind in antiquity. It might have been, and possibly was, only a freshening up of the usual rhetorical commonplaces about the "colours of good and evil," and the probable disposition of the hearer or reader. But it might also, and from Longinus's handling of the other stock subject of the Figures it is much more likely to, have been something mainly, if not wholly, new: in fact, something that to this day we have not got—an analysis of the direct appeals of literature to the primary emotions of the soul.

In considering this inestimable book, it is hardly possible to exaggerate the importance of these early words of it to which attention has been drawn above. The yoke of "persuasion" has at last been broken from the neck of the critic. He does not consider literature as something which will help a man to carry an assembly with him, to persuade a jury, to gain a declamation prize. He does indeed still mention the listener rather than the reader; but that is partly tradition, partly a consequence of the still existing prevalence of recitation or reading aloud. Further, it is sufficiently evident that the critic has come to regard literature as a whole, and is not distracted by supposed requirements of "invention" on the part of the poet, of "persuasion" on the part of the orator, and so forth. He looks at the true and only test of literary greatness—the "transport," the absorption of the reader. And he sees as no one, so far as we know, saw before him (except Dionysius for a moment and "in a glass darkly"), as Dante was the only man after him to see for a millennium and much more, that the beautiful words, the "mots rayonnants," are at least a main means whereby this effect is produced. Instead of style and its criticism being dismissed, or admitted at best with impatience as something *fortikon,* we have that gravest and truest judgment of the latter as the latest-born offspring of many a painful endeavour. Far is it indeed from him to stick to the word only: his remarks on novelty, his peroration (not intended as such, but so coming to us), and many other things, are proof of that. But in the main his criticism is of the pure æsthetic kind, and of the best of that kind. It will not delay us too much to examine it a little more in detail.

The opening passage as to Cæcilius, though it has tempted some into perilous hypothetic reconstructions of that critic's possible teaching, really comes to little more than this—that Longinus, like most of us, was not exactly satisfied with another man's handling of his favourite subject. And, curiously enough, the only specific fault that he here finds—namely, that his predecessor, while illustrating the nature of the Sublime amply, neglected to discuss the means of reaching it—rather recoils on himself. For there can be little doubt that the weakest part of the ***Peri Hypsos*** is its discussion of "sources." But the great phrase, already more than once referred to, as to transport or ecstasy, not persuasion, lifts us at once—itself transports us—into a region entirely different from that of all preceding Rhetorics, without at the same time giving any reason to fear loss of touch with the common ground and common-sense. For nothing can be saner than the handling, in the second chapter, of that *aporia* concerning nature and art, genius and painstaking, which has not infrequently been the cause of anything but sane writing.

After the gap, however, we come to one of the passages recently glanced at, and mentioned or to be mentioned so often elsewhere, which warn us as to difference of view. The passage, supposed to be, as we said, Æschylean and from the *Orithyia,* is no doubt at rather more than "concert-pitch." It is Marlowe rather than Shakespeare; yet Shakespeare himself has come near to it in *Lear* and elsewhere, and one line at least—

mian pareiras plektamen kheimarron—

is a really splendid piece of metre and phrase, worthy, high-pitched as it is, of the author of the *Oresteia* and the *Prometheus* at his very best. So, too, the much-enduring Gorgias would hardly have received very severe reprehension from any but the extremest precisians of modern criticism, at its most starched time, for calling vultures "living tombs." But the horror of the Greeks on the one hand for anything extravagant, bizarre, out of measure, on the other for the slightest approach in serious work to the unbecoming, the unpleasantly suggestive, makes Longinus here a very little prudish. And his general remarks are excellent, especially in reference to *to parenthurson,* which I have ventured to interpret, not quite in accordance with the general rendering, "the poking in of the thyrsus at the wrong time," the affectation of Bacchanalian fury where no fury need be.

But we still have the same warning in the chapter on Frigidity, coupled with another—that, perhaps, as sometimes happens, Longinus' sense of humour was not quite equal to his sense of sublimity, and yet another—that the historic sense, so late developed everywhere, was, perhaps, not very strong in him. We, at least, should give Timæus the benefit of a doubt, as to the presence of a certain not inexcusable irony in the comparison (in which, for instance, neither Swift nor Carlyle would have hesitated to indulge) of the times taken by Alexander to conquer Asia and by Isocrates to write the *Panegyric.* On the other hand, he seems to forget the date of Timæus when he finds . . . the paltrily funny, in the historian's connection of the Athenian Hermocopidæ and their punishment by Hermocrates, the son of Hermon. There is no reason why Timæus should not have been quite serious, though in the third century after Christ, and even in the first, the allusion might seem either a tasteless freethinking jest or a silly piece of superstition.

But by far the most interesting thing in this context is Longinus' irreconcilable objection to a fanciful metaphor which, as it happens most oddly, was, with a very slight variation, an equal pet of the Greeks of the great age and of our own Elizabethans. Every reader of the latter knows the phrase, "to look babies in the eyes" of the beloved—that is to say, to keep the face so close to hers that the little reflections of the gazer in the pupils of her eyes are discernible. The Greek term for these little images, and the pupils that mirrored them, was slightly different—it was . . . maidens. And as, from the famous quarrel scene in Homer downwards, the eyes were always, in Greek literature, the seat of modesty or of impudence, the combination suggested, not merely to Timæus but even to Xenophon, a play of words, "more modest than the maidens in their eyes," or conversely, as where Timæus, speaking of the lawless lust of Agathocles, says that he must have had "harlots" . . . , not "maidens" . . . , in his eyes. And Longinus is even more angry or sad with Xenophon than with Timæus, as expecting more propriety from him.

But whether we agree with him in detail or not, the inestimable passage, on the mere quest and craze for novelty, which follows, more than reconciles us, as well as the other great saying in cap. vi. as to the "late-born" character of the judgment of style, and that in the next as to the canon of Sublimity being the effect produced unaltered in altered circumstances and cases. When we read these things we feel that literary criticism is at last fully constituted,—that it wants nothing more save greater variety, quantity, and continuance of literary creation, upon which to exercise itself.

No nervous check or chill need be caused by the tolerably certain fact that more than one hole may be picked in the subsequent classification of the sources[9] of *hypsos.* These attempts at an over-methodical classification (it has been said before) are always full of snares and pitfalls to the critic. Especially do they tempt him to the sin of arguing in a circle. It cannot be denied that in every one of the five divisions (except, perhaps, the valuable vindication of the quality of Passion) there is some treacherous word or other, which is a mere synonym of "sublime." Thus in the first we have *hadrēpobolon,* mastery of the *hadron,* a curious word, the nearest equivalent of which in English is, perhaps, "stout" or "full-bodied," as we apply these terms to wine; in the fourth. . . , "noble," which is only "sublime" in disguise; and in the fifth *axiōma kai diarsis,* of which much the same may be said.

Any suggestion, however, of paralogism which might arise from this and be confirmed by the curious introduction in the third of the Figures, as if they were machines for automatic sublime-coining, must be dispelled by the remarks on Passion of the right kind as tending to sublimity, and by the special stress laid on the primary necessity of *megalophrosunē,* whereof *hypsos* itself is the mere *apēkhēma* or echo. Unfortunately here, as so often, the gap comes just in the most important place.

When the cloud lifts, however, we find ourselves in one of the most interesting passages of the whole, the selection of "sublime" passages from Homer. A little superfluous matter about Homer's "impiety" (the old, the respectable, Platonic mistake) occurs; but it matters not, especially in face of the two praises of the "Let there be light" of the Jewish legislator, "no chance comer," and of the great *en de phei kai olesson* of Ajax, the mere juxtaposition of which once more shows what a critic we have got in our hands.

Not quite such a great one perhaps have we—yet one in the circumstances equally fascinating—in the contrasted remarks on the *Odyssey.* Longinus is not himself impious; he is no Separatist (he is indeed far too good a critic to be that). But he will have the Romance of Ulysses to be "old age, though the old age of Homer." "When a great nature is a little gone under, philomythia is characteristic of its decline." Evidently, he thinks, the *Odyssey* was Homer's second subject, not his first. He is "a setting sun as mighty as ever, but less intense": he is more unequal: he takes to the fabulous and the incredible. The Wine of Circe, the foodless voyage of Ulysses, the killing of the suitors—nay, the very attention paid to Character and Manners—tell the tale of decadence.

He is wrong, undoubtedly wrong—we may swear it boldly by those who fell in Lyonnesse, and in the palace of Atli, and under the echoes of the horn of Roland.

The *Odyssey* is not less than the *Iliad;* it is different. But we can hardly quarrel with him for being wrong, because his error is so instructive, so interesting. We see in it first (even side by side with not a little innovation) that clinging to the great doctrines of old, to the skirts of Aristotle and of Plato, which is so often found in noble minds and so seldom in base ones. And we see, moreover, that far as he had advanced—near as he was to an actual peep over the verge of the old world and into the new—he was still a Greek himself at heart, with the foibles and limitations—no despicable foibles and limitations—of the race. Here is the instinctive unreasoning terror of the unknown Romance; the dislike of the vague and the fabulous; even that curious craze about Character being in some way inferior to Action, which we have seen before. By the time of Longinus—if he lived in the third century certainly, if he lived in the first probably—the romance did exist. But it was looked upon askance; it had no regular literary rank; and a sort of resentment was apparently felt at its daring to claim equality with the epic. Now the *Odyssey* is the first, and not far from the greatest, of romances. It has the Romantic Unity in the endurance and triumph of its hero. It has the Romantic Passion in the episodes of Circe and Calypso and others: above all, it has the great Romantic breadth, the free sweep of scene and subject, the variety, the contrast of fact and fancy, the sparkle and hurry and throb. But these things, to men trained in the admiration of the *other* Unity, the *other* Passion, the more formal, regulated, limited, measured detail and incident of the usual tragedy and the usual epic—were at best unfamiliar innovations, and at worst horrible and daring impieties. Longinus will not go this length: he cannot help seeing the beauty of the *Odyssey.* But he must reconcile his principles to his feelings by inventing a theory of decadence, for which, to speak frankly, there is no critical justification at all.

One may almost equally disagree with the *special* criticism which serves as setting to the great jewel among the quotations of the treatise, the so-called "Ode to Anactoria." The charm of this wonderful piece consists, according to Longinus, in the skill with which Sappho chooses the accompanying emotions of "erotic mania."[10] To which one may answer, "Hardly so," but in the skill with which she expresses those emotions which she selects, and in the wonderful adaptation of the metre to the expression, in the mastery of the picture of the most favoured lover, drawing close and closer to the beloved to catch the sweet speech,[11] and the laughter full of desire. In saying this we should have the support of the Longinus of other parts of the treatise against the Longinus of this. Yet here, too, he is illuminative; here, too, the "noble error" of the Aristotelian conception of poetry distinguishes and acquits him.

With the remarks on . . . "amplification," as it is traditionally but by no means satisfactorily rendered, another phase of the critical disease of antiquity (which is no doubt balanced by other diseases in the modern critical body) may be thought to appear. Both in the definition of this figure and in the description of its method we may, not too suspiciously, detect evidences of that excessive technicality which gave to Rhetoric itself the exclusive title of *techne. Auxesis,* it seems, comes in when the business, or the point at issue, admits at its various stages of divers fresh starts and rests, of one great phrase being wheeled upon the stage after another, continually introduced in regular ascent. This, it seems, can be done either by means of . . . handling of *topoi* or commonplaces," or by *deinōsis*, which may perhaps be best rendered *tour de force,* or by cunning successive disposition . . . of facts or feelings. For, says he, there are ten thousand kinds of *auxesis.*

The first description of the method will recall to all comparative students of literature the manner of Burke, though it is not exactly identical with that manner; but the instances of means, besides being admittedly inadequate, savour, with their technicalities of terminology, much too strongly of the cut-and-dried manual. The third article, on a reasonable interpretation of *epoikonomia*, really includes all that need be said. But one sees here, as later, that even Longinus had not quite outgrown the notion that the teacher of Rhetoric was bound to present his student with a sort of hand-list of "tips" and dodges—with the kind of Cabbala wherewith the old-fashioned crammer used to supply his pupils for inscription on wristband or finger-nail. Yet he hastens to give a sign of grace by avowing his dissatisfaction with the usual Rhetorical view, and by distinguishing *auxesis* and the Sublime itself, in a manner which brings the former still nearer to Burke's "winding into a subject like a serpent," and which might have been more edifying still if one of the usual gaps did not occur. Part, at least, of the lost matter must have been occupied with a contrast or comparison between the methods of Plato and Demosthenes, the end of which we have, and which passes into one between Demosthenes and Cicero. "If we Greeks may be allowed to have an opinion," says Longinus, with demure humility, "Demosthenes shall be compared to a flash of thunder and lightning, Cicero to an ordinary terrestrial conflagration," which is very handsome to Cicero.

Then he returns to Plato, and rightly insists that much of his splendour is derived from imitation, or at least from emulation, of that very Homer whom he so often attacks. The great writers of the past are to be constantly before us, and we are not to be deterred from "letting ourselves go" by any mistaken sense of inferiority, or any dread of posterity's verdict.

Then comes a digression of extreme importance on the subject of . . . "images." One of the points in which a history of the kind here attempted may prove to be of most service, lies in the opportunity it affords of keeping the changes of certain terms, commonly used in criticism, more clearly before the mind than has always been done. And of these, none requires more care than "Images" and "Imagination." At the first reading, the mere use of such a word as *phantasiai* may seem to make all over-scrupulousness unnecessary, though if we remember that even Fancy is not quite Imagination, the danger may be lessened. At any rate, it is nearly certain that no ancient writer, and no modern critic before a very recent period (Shakespeare uses it rightly, but then he was Shakespeare and not a critic), attached our full sense to the term. To Aristotle *phantasia* is merely . . . a "weakened sensation," a copy furnished by memory from sensation itself. Even animals have it. No idea of Invention seems to have mingled with it, or only of such invention as the artist's is when he faithfully represents natural objects. Of the Imagination, which is in our minds when we call Shelley an imaginative poet, and Pope not one, Sir Edward Burne Jones an imaginative painter, and any contemporary whom it may be least invidious to name not one, there does not seem to have been a trace even in the enthusiastic mind of Longinus, though he expressly includes Enthusiasm—nay, Passion—in his notion of it. You think you see what you say, and you make your hearers see it. Good; but Crabbe does that constantly, and one would hardly, save in the rarest cases, call Crabbe imaginative. In short, öáíôáóßáé here are vivid illustrations drawn from nature—Orestes' hallucination of the Eumenides, Euripides' picture of Phaethon, that in the *Seven* of the slaying of the bull over the black-bound shield, and many others. No doubt he glances at the fabulous and incredible, the actually "imagined"; but he seems, as in the case of the *Odyssey,* to be a little doubtful of these even in poetry, while in oratory he bars them altogether. You must at one and the same time reason and illustrate—again the very method of Burke.

In the rest of the illustrations of the use of Figures—for the central part of the treatise expressly disclaims being a formal discussion of these idols—the positive literary criticisms scattered in them—the actual "reviewing"—will give most of the interest. The great Oath of Demosthenes, "By those who fell at Marathon!" with its possible suggestion by a passage of Eupolis, supplies a whole chapter and part of another. And now we find the curious expression (showing how even Longinus was juggled by terms) that Figures "fight on the side of the Sublime, and in turn draw a wonderful reinforcement from it," wherein a mighty if vague reality like the Sublime, and mere shadows (though neatly cut-out shadows) like the Figures, are most quaintly yoked together.

Though still harassed by gaps, we find plenty of good pasture in the remarks, the handling of Periphrasis being especially attractive. For the eighteenth century—the time which honoured Longinus most in theory, and went against him most in practice—undoubtedly took part of his advice as to this figure. It had no doubt that Periphrasis contributed to the Sublime, was *hypsēlopoion*: unluckily it paid less attention to his subsequent caution, that it is a risky affair, and that it smells of triviality.[12] In fact, it is extremely noticeable that in the examples of Periphrasis which he praises we should hardly apply that name to it, but should call it "Allusion" or "Metaphor," while the examples that he condemns are actually of the character of Armstrong's "gelid cistern" and Delille's "game which Palamede invented."

At no time perhaps has the tricksy, if not (as one is almost driven to suspect) deliberately malignant, mutilator played such a trick as in abstracting four leaves from the MS. between caps. xxx. and xxxi. Here Longinus has begun to speak of diction generally; here he has made that admirable descant on "beautiful words" which, though almost all the book deserves to be written in letters of gold, would tempt one to indulge here in precious stones, so as to mimic, in jacinth and sapphire and chrysoprase, the effect which it celebrates. When we are permitted another glimpse we are back in particular criticism, interesting but less valuable save indirectly, and in criticisms, too, of Cæcilius, criticisms which we could do without. No great good can ever come of inquiries, at least general inquiries, into the permissible number and the permissible strength of Metaphors. Once more we may fall back on the Master, though perhaps rather in opposition to some of the Master's dicta in this very field. "As the intelligent man shall decide" is the decision here, and the intelligent man will never decide till the case is before him. One bad metaphor is too much: twenty good ones are not too many. Nor is "the multitudinous seas incarnadine" an "excess," though no doubt there have been bad critics who thought so.

Longinus himself, though he had not had the happiness to read *Macbeth,* was clearly not far out of agreement with the concluding sentiment of the last paragraph, and he makes this certain by the disquisition on Faultlessness which follows. As a general question this is probably, for the present time at any rate, past argument, not so much because the possibility of a "faultless" great poem is denied, as because under the leaden rule of the best modern criticism—leaden not from dulness but from adaptability—few things are recognised as "faults" *in se* and *per se.* A pun may be a gross fault in one place and a grace beyond the reach of art in another: an aposiopesis may be either a proof of clumsy inequality to the situation or a stroke of genius. But the declaration of Longinus that he is not on the side of Faultlessness is of infinitely greater importance than any such declaration from an equally great critic ("Where is he? Show him to me," as Rabelais would say) could possess to-day. The general Greek theory undoubtedly did make for excessive severity to faultfulness, just as our general theory makes perhaps for undue leniency to it. That Longinus could withstand this tendency—could point out the faults of the faultless—was a very great thing.

As always, too, his individual remarks frequently give us, not merely the satisfaction of agreement, but that of piquant difference or curiosity. We may agree with him about Bacchylides and Pindar—though, by the way, the man who had the taste and the courage to admire a girl . . . as possessing that yellow ivory tint of skin which lights so magnificently[13]—was certainly one to dare to challenge convention with what its lilies-and-roses standard must have thought a "fault." But we cannot help astonishment at being told that both Pindar and Sophocles "often have their light quenched without any obvious reason, and stumble in the most unfortunate manner." For those of us who are less, as well as those who are more, enthusiastic about Sophocles would probably agree in asking, "Where does he 'go out in snuff,' where does he 'fall prostrate' in this fashion?" Surely all the faults cannot be in the lost plays! We want a rather fuller text of Hyperides than we possess to enable us quite to appreciate the justice of the comparison of him with Demosthenes, but that justice is striking even on what we have. On the other hand, we are rather thrown out by the contrast of Plato and Lysias—it may be owing to the same cause. Even if the comparison were one of style only, we should think it odd to make one between Burke and Berkeley, though the *Sublime and Beautiful* would help us a little here.

But all this is a digression,[14] and the author seems to have returned to his Metaphors (in a gap where the demon has interfered with less malice than usual), and to Hyperboles, under the head of which we get a useful touch of contempt for Isocrates. We are in deeper and more living waters when we come to the handling, alas! too brief (though nothing seems here to be lost), of *ordonnance,* "composition," selection and arrangement of words. Here is yet another of those great law-making phrases which are the charter of a new criticism. "Harmony is to men not only physically connected with persuasion and pleasure, but a wonderful instrument of magniloquence and passion." It may be difficult for us, with our very slight knowledge (it would, perhaps, be wiser to say almost absolute ignorance) of Greek pronunciation, to appreciate his illustrations here in detail. But we can appreciate the principle of them exactly, and apply that principle, in any language of which we do know the pronunciation, with perfect ease and the completest success. The silly critics (they exist at the present day) who pooh-pooh, as niceties and fiddle-faddle, the order of words, the application of rhythmical tests to prose, and the like, are answered here beforehand with convincing force by a critic whom no one can possibly charge with preferring sound to sense.

This refers to prose, but the following chapter carries out the same principle as to poetry with equal acuteness. Longinus, great as his name is, probably is but little in the hands of those who object (sometimes almost with foam at the mouth) to the practice of analysing the mere harmonic effect of poetry. But it is pleasant to think of these passages when one reads the outcries, nor is the pleasantness rendered less pleasant by the subsequent cautions against that over-rhythmical fashion of writing which falls to the level of mere dance-music.

The caution against over-conciseness and over-prolixity is rather more of a matter of course, and the strictures on the *microtis,* occasionally to be found in Herodotus, like some in the earlier parts of the treatise, sometimes elude us, as is the case with similar verbal criticisms even in languages with which we are colloquially familiar.

And then there is the curious Conclusion which, as we have said, is no conclusion at all, as it would seem, and which yet has an unmistakable air of "peroration, with [much] circumstance," on the everlasting question, "Why is the Sublime so rare in our time?" In that day, as in this, we learn (the fact being, as in King Charles II.'s fish-experiment, taken for granted), divers explanations, chiefly political, were given for the fact. Democracy was a good nurse of greatness: aristocracy was not. But Longinus did not agree. It was money-getting and money-seeking, pleasure-loving and pleasure-hunting, he thought. Plain living and high thinking must be returned to if the Heights were to be once more scaled. A noble conclusion, if perhaps only a generous fallacy. Had Longinus had our illegitimate prerogative-*post*rogative of experience, he would have known that the blowing of the wind of the spirit admits of no such explanations as these. Ages of Liberty and Ages of Servitude, Ages of Luxury and Ages of Simplicity, Ages of Faith and Ages of Freethought—all give us the Sublime if the right man is there: none will give it us if he is not. But our critic had not the full premisses before him, and we could not expect the adequate conclusion.

Yet how great a book have we here! Of the partly otiose disputes about its date and origin and authorship one or two things are worth recalling, though for other purposes than those of the disputants. Let it be remembered that it is not quoted, or even referred to, by a single writer of antiquity.[15] There is absolutely no evidence for it, except its own internal character, before the date of its oldest manuscript, which is assigned to the tenth century. Even if, assuming it to be the work of Longinus, we suppose it to have been part of one of the works which *are* ascribed to him (a possible assumption, see note), there is still the absence of quotation, still the absence even of reference to views so clearly formulated, so eloquently enforced, and in some ways so remarkably different from those of the usual Greek and Roman rhetorician. That the book can be of very late date—much later, that is to say, than that of Longinus himself—is almost impossible. One of its features, the lack of any reference to even a single writer later than the first century, has indeed been relied upon to prove that it is not later itself than that date. This is inconclusive for that purpose. But it makes every succeeding century less and less probable, while the style, though in some respects peculiar, is not in the least Byzantine.

This detachment from any particular age—nay, more, this *vita fallens*, this unrecognised existence of a book so remarkable—stands in no merely fanciful relation to the characteristics of the book itself. It abides alone in thought as well as in history. That it is a genuine, if a late, production of the classical or semi-classical age we cannot reasonably doubt, for a multitude of reasons, small in themselves but strong in a bundle,—its style, its diction, its limitations of material, and even occasionally of literary view, its standards, all sorts of little touches like the remark about Cicero, and so forth. Yet it has, in the most important points, almost more difference from than resemblance to the views of classical critics generally. The much greater antiquity of Aristotle may be thought to make comparison with him infructuous, if not unfair. But we have seen already how far Longinus is from Dionysius, how much further from Plutarch; and we shall see in the next Book how far he is from Quintilian. Let us look where we will, to critics by profession or to critics by chance, to the Alexandrians as far as we know them, to the professional writers on Rhetoric, to Aristophanes earlier and Lucian later, always we see Longinus apart—among them by dispensation and time, but not of them by tone, by tendency, by temper.

For though he himself was almost certainly unconscious of it, and might even have denied the fact with some warmth if it had been put to him, Longinus has marked out grounds of criticism very far from those of the ancient period generally, further still from those which were occupied by any critic (except Dante) of the Middle Ages and the Classical revival, and close to, if not in all cases overlapping the territory of, the modern Romantic criticism itself. As we have seen, the ancient critic was wont either to neglect the effect of a work of art altogether, and to judge it by its supposed agreement with certain antecedent requirements, or else, if effects were considered at all, to consider them from the merely practical point of view, as in the supposed persuasive effect of Rhetoric, or from the ethical, as in the purging, the elevating, and so forth, assigned to Tragedy, and to Poetry generally. Longinus has changed all this. It is the enjoyment, the transport, the carrying away of the reader or auditor, that, whether expressedly or not, is always at bottom the chief consideration with him. He has not lowered the ethical standard one jot, but he has silently refused to give it precedence of the æsthetic; he is in no way for lawlessness, but he makes it clear, again and again, that mere compliance with law, mere fulfilment of the requirements of the stop-watch and the hundredth-of-an-inch rule, will not suffice. Aristotle had been forced, equally by his system and his sense, to admit that pleasure was an end—perhaps the end—of art; but he blenches and swerves from the consequences. Longinus faces them and follows them out.

In his attention to rhythm, especially of prose, Longinus is much less unique, for this point (as we have seen and shall see) was never neglected by the best ancient critics. But there is again something particularly distinguishing in his attempt to trace the sources of the literary pleasure in specimen passages. The ancient tendency is, though not universally, yet too generally, the other way, to select specimen passages merely as illustrations of general rules.

And this brings us to his greatest claim of all—that is to say, his attitude towards his subject as a whole. Although he nowhere says as much in so many words, no one can read his book with attention—above all, no one can read it again and again critically—without seeing that to him literature was not a schedule of forms, departments, kinds, with candidates presenting themselves for the critic to admit them to one or the other, on and during their good behaviour; but a body of matter to be examined according to its fruits, according to its provision of the literary pleasure. When it has been examined it is still for the critic to explain and justify (according to those unwritten laws which govern him) his decision that this was good, this not so good, this bad,—to point out the reasons of success and failure, to arrange the symptoms, classify the methods, and so forth. Where Longinus fell short it was almost always because ancient literature had not provided him with enough material of certain kinds, not because he ruled these kinds out *a priori.* Longinus was no Rymer. We could submit even Shakespeare to him with very little fear, and be perfectly certain that he would not, with Rapin, pronounce Dantes Aligerus wanting in fire.[16] Nay, with a sufficient body of material to set before him, we could trust him with very much more dangerous cases than Shakespeare and Dantes Aligerus.

Yet, as we have said, he stands alone. We must skip fifteen hundred years and come to Coleridge before we meet any critic entirely of his class, yet free from some of his limitations. The hand of the author of the ***Peri Hypsos*** is not subdued, but raised to what he deals in. And his work remains towering among all other work of the class, the work of a critic at once Promethean and Epimethean in his kind, learning by the mistakes of all that had gone before, and presaging, with instinctive genius, much that was not to come for centuries after.

Notes

[1] The most elaborate discussion of the whole matter still is that of Vaucher (Geneva, 1854). The editions I myself use are those of Toup (Oxford, 1778); Egger (Paris, 1837), a particularly handy little volume, *with the fragments;* and Prof. Rhys Roberts (Cambridge, 1899), with translation and full editorial apparatus. Those who do not read the Greek lose much: but they will find a good (though somewhat too free) translation, with an excellent introduction by Mr Andrew Lang, in the work of Mr H. L. Havell (London, 1890).

[2] *Dionysiou ē Longinous* of the Paris MS. 2036. (Others even have íùíýìïõ.) Robortello intentionally or unintentionally dropped the *ē* [or], thereby putting students off the scent.

[3] Blair saw this, but, with the ill-luck of his century, regarded the work as merely "elegant."

[4] Longinus (? 213-273) represents the middle of the *third* century. Nobody puts it later than this, and nobody earlier than the *first.*

[5] A Sicilian rhetor, probably of Calacte, said by Suidas to have been of Greek, or at any rate non-Roman, birth, and a Jew in religion. Dionysius knew him, and he lived in the time of Augustus. There was another (confused by Suidas) in that of Hadrain. This *may* be our C.

[6] A phrase of the rhetor Theodorus, meaning "the thyrsus poked in at the wrong time," "enthusiasm out of place."

[7] *Logon krisis pollēs esti peiras teleutaīon epigenēma.* Dionysius (*v. supra,* pp. 130, 131) had said as much in sense, but less magisterially in phrase. I have translated *logon* in its narrowest equivalent, instead of "style" or "literature," which it doubtless also means, in order to bring out the antithesis better. I have small doubt that Longinus meant, here as elsewhere, to fling back the old contempt of the opposition of "words" and "things."

[8] This word, which has the stamp of Dryden, is often preferable to "composition."

[9] It may, however, be plausibly argued that the circle is more apparent than real, resulting from a kind of ambiguity in the word *pēgai.* If Longinus had slightly altered his expression, so as to make it something of this kind, "There are five points [or ways, or aspects] in which *hypsos* may be attained, thought, feeling, 'figure,' diction, and composition," he would be much less vulnerable. And, after all, this is probably what he meant.

[10] Literal.

[11] Fond and foolish fancy as it may be, there seems to me something miraculous in the mere juxtaposition of *plēsion* and *adu*—the silent adoring lover, jealous, as it were, of the very air robbing him of a portion of the sweetness.

[12] . . . [This] means literally "perishable," "apt to go off," to get stale or flat.

[13] Simonides had used the word literally of the nightingale, and there are those who hold that Bacchylides merely meant to compliment the lady's *voice.* But let us think more nobly of him.

[14] I must be allowed to say that it contains one of the most ambitious and successful passages of Longinus as an original writer—the vindication of Nature's command to man to admire the magnificent—in cap. xxxv. It is a temptation to quote it.

[15] "John of Sicily" (Walz, vi. 225), who in the thirteenth century cites the lost *philologoi homiliai* almost as if he was citing the *Peri Hypsous,* is certainly no exception. The undated Byzantine (Cramer, *Aneed. Oxon.,* iii. 159, quoted by Professor Roberts after Usener), who couples *logginou kriseis* with those of Dionysius, may come nearer, as may the anonymous scholiast on Hermogenes (Walz, vii. 963), who cites the *druiliai* on *to stomphōdes,* "mouthing."

[16] Sir Thomas Pope Blount, *Characters and Censures of the most Considerable Poets.* London, 1694. P. 58. "Rapin tells us that Dantes Aligerus wants fire, and that he has not heat enough."

W. Rhys Roberts (essay date 1928)

SOURCE: "Longinus on the Sublime: Some Historical and Literary Problems," in *Philological Quarterly,* Vol. 7, No. 3, July, 1928, pp. 209-19.

[*In the following essay, Roberts uses linguistic evidence to argue that, contrary to the claims of many scholars,* De Sublimitate *was written in the first rather than the third century* A.D.]

As long ago as the year 1899 the Cambridge University Press published for me an edition of "Longinus."[1] At the moment I am correcting the proof-sheets of a small volume on Greek Rhetoric and Literary Criticism for an American Series. It would be a great help if you would allow me to confer with you on some of the many problems presented by the ***De Sublimitate.***

You will not disappoint me by failing (as too often happens) to join, young and old, in the discussion at the close. I still remember gratefully a valuable piece of information[2] I had, on a posteard in September 1901, from a boy, Donald S. Robertson, who was then (I believe) at Westminster School, where the ***Sublime*** was being read as a holiday task or treat. That postcard is here to-day as one of two exhibits, the other being the sumptuous Bodoni edition of "Longinus."

More than ever, I am convinced that the essay—this seems the nearest English equivalent for *hypomnēma*—belongs not to the third century of our era but to the first. Its Roman, Greek, and Jewish affinities appear to point that way. Suppose that the last chapter (chapter 44) alone was before us, as a newly discovered fragment, in modern print (with no palaeographical indication of date). Could we take that famous lament for perished liberty, eloquence, and genius to have been written so late as the third century? In the first century the topic of such degeneracy, and its causes, was a commonplace among Roman authors: we think of Tacitus (*Dialogus de Oratoribus*), the two Plinys, Quintilian (*Institutio Oratoria* and the lost *De Causis Corruptae Eloquentiae*), Petronius, and Seneca the philosopher. We notice that, in this chapter, "Longinus" (it is convenient so to call him; and I shall do so throughout) speaks of "the world's peace" . . . , and we recall the "Pax Romana," and a sentence close to the beginning of Tacitus' *Histories:* "postquam bellatum apud Actium atque omnem potentiam ad unum conferri pacis interfuit, magna illa ingenia cessere." What, by the way, is the nearest equivalent in any Roman author for *hetēs oikoumenos eirēne*, a greater phrase (and a greater idea) than "Pax Romana"?

The striking comparison, in the essay, between Demosthenes and Cicero unites with certain Latinisms to make it likely that the author, notwithstanding his modest disclaimer in chapter 12, had some direct knowledge of the Latin language and literature. Consequently the "philosopher" who starts the discussion in chapter 44 may conceivably be a Roman, and of the first century. Apropos of my edition, the late Professor Robinson Ellis in the *Classical Review* (xiii. 294) pointed out a double parallelism between the ***Sublime*** chapter 13, sections 3 and 4, and the *Astronomica* (book ii, lines 8-10 and 57, 58) of Manilius, who was probably writing between A.D. 9 and A.D. 14. Professor Ellis assumed that here either Manilius must be copying the ***Sublime*** or the ***Sublime*** Manilius. The latter alternative seems possible, but my own feeling, rather, is that both were drawing from some common source (Greek or Latin) now lost: the modern student is always in danger of forgetting the great losses there have surely been of Greek critical works belonging to the century before and the century after Christ. Still, I now incline, in this difficult problem of dating, to think (for reasons to be given in a moment) that the essay does belong to the earlier, rather than the later, half of the first century, and to somewhere about the year 40 A.D. But I want your help and criticism throughout.

Of the Greek affinities of the essay little need at this point be said: after all, it is written in Greek and shows a remarkable familiarity with the whole course of Greek literature. But, as bearing on its date, it is important to observe that, at its very start, a Greek author of the Augustan period is named and attacked: Caecilius of Calacte. The pugnacity, and pertinacity, with which "Longinus" assails Caecilius's book on *hypsos* ("sublimity") makes it seem probable that he was writing not much more than a generation after its appearance—not so long after as the time of Plutarch, who makes but passing references to Caecilius, and certainly not so long after as the third century.

To pass from the Roman and Greek to the Jewish side,—to the surpassingly sublime illustration drawn from the beginning of the *Book of Genesis.* The passage, in chapter 9, is: "Similarly, the legislator of the Jews, no ordinary man, having formed and expressed a worthy conception of the power of the Godhead, writes at the very beginning of his Laws, 'God said'—what? 'Let there be light, and there was light; let there be earth, and there was earth.'"

First of all, is this passage of "Longinus" genuine? In my edition I maintained that it is and gave my reasons. During the year 1915 the German scholar Konrat Ziegler, in an able and vigorous paper published in *Hermes,* attacked my views, singling me out no doubt because I had made the fullest recent statement of a case which has never lacked defenders. I did not see the article at the time; I was busy in other ways, *patriai tempore iniquo.* But a pleasant thing happened. The reply—to me a convincing one—came from Germany itself two years later,—in 1917 and in the same classical journal. Hermann Mutschmann,[3] a no less able and vigorous scholar than Ziegler and one better known for special work on "Longinus," dealt with the attack in a long article which still holds the field. To review fully the arguments on the two sides I have no space in half-an-hour's paper. I will select a small but interesting point of language passed over by Mutschmann, and then give my own present views on this issue of authenticity and on the general question of date.

Professor Ziegler will have it, indeed, that *exephēnen*, which I have translated by "expressed," here means "revealed" in that very special sense of "revealed" which you would expect from a Jewish or Christian interpolator. But surely Jew or Christian would have employed the (for him) most significant . . . "to draw the veil from sacred mysteries"; Ziegler himself uses the German word "offenbaren" . . . , but this only serves to remind us that "Offenbarung" is the accepted

German title of the New Testament book which we often call (as in the Greek) "the Apocalypse." *Alokalupim* occurs twenty-six times in the New Testament, *ekphaino* never. In the Septuagint *ekphaino* is found thirteen times, *alokalupim* over a hundred times. So that an argument on which Ziegler lays much stress seems rather to turn against himself. Further, the general diction of the section (short as it is) can be shown to tally with the rest of the essay: *Ekphaino* itself occurs in the first chapter, in the passive voice and in the somewhat colourless sense "appear from," "emerge from"; and the section contains also the characteristic expressions . . . ("similarly"), . . . ("extraordinary"), . . . ("at the very beginning"), and the still more characteristic rhetorical question,—"'God said'—what?",—which tells, assuredly, not of a devout Jewish or Christian believer but of an enthusiastic literary guide and teacher who is resolved to arrest attention even though some solemnity may be lost. The inexactitude of the citation, and a certain rhythmical and symmetrical turn which the great *fiat* has (perhaps unconsciously) received, leave the same impression on the mind, and also suggest a quotation made from memory.

It is with the relation of the whole passage to the difficult question of date that we are now specially concerned. My own view of the date (on which I want your criticism) is briefly this. Thirty years ago I maintained, on internal evidence (the *external* being, in my opinion, no better than Byzantine guesswork, since it describes the author either as "*Dionysius* (not *Cassius*) Longinus," or "Dionysius *or* Longinus," or "An *Anonymous* Writer"),—I maintained that the essay belongs to the first century, not to the third. Now I would go further and suggest that it was written in the earlier half, rather than the later half, of the first century, and probably during the twenty years from 30 A.D. to 50 A.D.,—say 40 A.D. I would bring it nearer in time to Philo than to Plutarch. I have no positive proof to offer; I shall only urge that, alike on the Jewish, Greek, and Roman sides, the period 30-50 A.D. seems highly probable. Let us seize on any known dates we can and make the most of them, especially if they are near the birth of Christ, slightly before or slightly after. The author is replying (as I think, within a generation or so) to Caecilius. Caecilius was a contemporary of Dionysius of Halicarnassus whom we know to have been living at Rome in the year 8 B.C. (the year of Horace's death) and who was probably still living there at and beyond the birth of Christ. With Dionysius, "Longinus" has in common an extensive critical terminology; with Caecilius, whom he opposes vehemently, he at any rate shares an interest in the Jewish race—we have it on the authority of Suidas that Caecilius was in religion a Jew. "Longinus" is connected with the East in yet another way. In chapter 3 we read: "A third, and closely allied, defect in outbursts of passion is that which Theodorus used to call *parenthyrsos*. By this is meant unseasonable and empty passion, where no passion is required; or immoderate, where moderation is needed." Modern scholars assume (in my opinion, rightly) that this Theodorus is the eminent rhetorician Theodorus of Gadara who taught in Rhodes and Rome. In my edition[4] I suggested that the imperfect *ekalei* ("used to call") implies that "Longinus" had been a pupil of Theodorus. This view is also taken by Ziegler and Mutschmann. It is important as providing another clue by which we may hope approximately to date the essay. Quintilian (iii. 1, 17) tells us that Tiberius Caesar, during his retirement in Rhodes, was a diligent hearer of Theodorus. This retirement of Tiberius lasted from B.C. 6 to A.D. 2. It seems to me also possible that Theodorus was not only a Syrian but a Jew (a Jew passing under a Gentile name, like many another Jew in ancient and modern times), and that "Longinus" had heard from him not only about the "dragging-in of the thyrsus" (a verbal coinage suggested no doubt to Theodorus by Euripides' *Bacchae,* so famous in the East and so well known to "Longinus," as his essay proves), but about the legislator of the Jews and his great written opening now reproduced from memory. It is true that Theodorus liked to be called a "Rhodian" rather than a "Gadarene"; but the man who dubbed the young Tiberius "a lump of clay kneaded with blood" had, surely, courage and independence enough to quote *Genesis* in his lectures if he knew it; and at Gadara, where Jewish as well as Greek influences had long been felt, he would be likely to know it, even if he were no more than a Syrian cousin of the Jews.

However, I do not in the least insist on this detail nor on the possibility that "Longinus" may owe his knowledge of the quotation not to Theodorus but to the book he criticizes,—that by the Judaizer Caecilius. Word about the greatest opening perhaps in all literature may have come from sources altogether unknown to us. Is it not the case that the Jews are surprisingly to the fore even in the scanty Greek literature which to-day survives from the age of Augustus or slightly later? Please recall the dates of Diodorus Siculus, Strabo, and Philo: these rather than Josephus, whose *floruit* comes somewhat later. Diodorus probably wrote his *History* soon after 8 B.C., and in it he speaks of Moses' claim that his Laws came to him from the God called "Jehovah." Strabo's life extended from (about) B.C. 54 to A.D. 24. In the 16th Book of his *Geography,* Strabo expresses, in set terms and at some length, his admiration for the work accomplished by Moses, and says of the theocracy which Moses had instituted that it was "no ordinary one," the same two Greek words which "Longinus" has applied to Moses himself.

Take, again, Philo and *his* date. Philo (who would be born about 20 B.C.) came from Alexandria to Rome, on his celebrated embassy to Caligula, in or near the year 40 A.D.: a date only slightly earlier than the newly-discovered *Letter* sent by Claudius to Alexandria. That

Letter, and Philo's embassy, are enough to show that Alexandria, and the Jews of Alexandria, were much in the mind of Rome (and "Longinus" is writing to a Roman) about this time; and not simply Alexandrian Jews, nor simply turbulent Jews. Some of the widely-dispersed Jews were beginning to hold important posts in the Roman imperial system as financiers, administrators, soldiers, secretaries, and teachers, showing no doubt the same intellectual gifts that they have so often shown in modern times and places; and as to the *width* of the dispersion, Josephus (*Ant. Iud.* xiv. 7, 2) reports Strabo to have said that "it is not easy to find a spot in the inhabited world which has not admitted this race and is not controlled by it." (Think of it: in New York to-day there are 1,750,000 Jews,—nearly one-third of the total population!)

Aloof as the Jews in some ways were and are, is it likely (apart altogether from what the word "proselyte" teaches us as to the active Jewish propaganda in the century before, and the earlier part of the century after, Christ's birth),—is it *in itself* likely that, when spread across the world, the Jews should not, as occasion offered, dwell on the great things of their faith to congenial souls, and that a Greek writer like "Longinus" (I take him, subject to your criticism, to have been a Greek, and not simply a Roman or Jew writing in Greek, like Marcus Aurelius, or Philo Judaeus) should record, incidentally, what he had somehow heard? For want of time, I must pass over the verbal coincidences between Philo and "Longinus," which seem to point to a growing contact in word and thought between Greek and Jewish authors; one of them so striking that it might almost have been written by "Longinus's" "philosopher" in chapter 44. But notice this. Philo, in his puritan sermons on Old Testament texts, occasionally quotes Homer: why should not a contemporary Greek author, once only in a short essay, refer to *Genesis* if the quotation were apposite? And it *is* apposite, supremely apposite. In the context, "Longinus" has condemned the human frailties of Homer's Olympian gods, and then turns with relief to a Homeric passage in which the divine nature is (he says) represented "as it really is—pure and great and undefiled." It is at this point that he mentions (with true literary and religious instinct) Moses' high conception of "the Godhead," using the same expression . . . as Strabo uses in his 16th book. The great idea and its simple setting have, alike, impressed him. The whole chapter deals with greatness of mind and soul, and near its beginning he has observed that a "bare idea" can be more sublime than words, instancing the silence of Ajax among the Shades.

Ziegler (whose doubts and difficulties I have kept in mind while stating my own position) seems to me to take altogether too narrow a view of this Greek "classical man" of (let us say) 40 A.D., when he supposes that he would have shrunk from quoting Moses side by side with Homer. That "Longinus" was a "classical man," we know; no one could have offered better tests of truly "classical" excellence than he has done in his seventh chapter. But the special virtue of these tests is that they are as applicable to one great literature as to another. We must not conceive of "Longinus" as a Greek *rhetorician* in any narrow and invidious sense; he refers to Isocrates, the idol of the rhetoricians, with some disdain. He is a philosopher and a man of letters; he is a great literary critic (do we, by the way, find in any Greek writer a nearer equivalent for the words "literary criticism" than in the sixth chapter of our essay, where we are told that "literary criticism . . . is the last and crowning fruit of long experience"?); and (more than all this) he is a man of his own day who has also the good fortune to be endowed with a true historical sense. In thinking of him, we simply must not speak as if Alexander and Alexandria, and Stoicism (half religion, half philosophy, with Greek, Roman, and Semitic elements; Zeno was a Semite), and the later Platonism had never been. We must not forget, either, that the Greek Septuagint version of the Old Testament had existed, in its earlier part at least, for two or three centuries, and that the interactions between it and Alexandrian Greek literature may have been more far-reaching than we know; did not so sober a scholar as the late Dr. Leaf[5] go so far as to suggest that, through some channel or other, Callimachus knew Isaiah's paean over the fall of Babylon, "How art thou fallen from heaven, O Lucifer, son of the morning!"?

And if we turn to Rome, why should not the Roman Terentianus (the addressee of the book; I wish you could identify him from some inscription new or old) have hailed, in a Greek essay, the great words of Moses with even more surprise and admiration than he would greet the comparison between Demosthenes and Cicero, a comparison which Ziegler describes, in error, as a "favourite theme." It was not so among the *Greek* literary critics; "Longinus," in this as in other ways, is exceptional. On the evidence of the essay itself, Terentianus would seem to have been an apt and high-minded pupil (past or present) of the author's, at whose somewhat mannered style he may sometimes have smiled, remembering that "Longinus" had (he mentions it in his book) written more than once on the subject of word-arrangement and was much given to that verbal heightening and recasting which belongs to his conception of *hypsos,* but not forgetting either that he loved, and could make his pupils love, the greater aspects of literature,—the noble thought, character, and feeling enshrined in it. When this literary letter (this classical essay in criticism) was written to him, Terentianus was clearly a man of some standing; the adjective *hratistos* by which he is once addressed suggests that he was of official rank. In the *Acts of the Apostles* we remember that the two Roman procurators Felix and Festus are addressed as *kratiste Phēlix* and *kratiste Phēste*—"your Excellency" almost. When, from (about 61 A.D. to 63 A.D., St. Paul "dwelt two whole years" in a hired lodging of his own at Rome, those that "came in unto him" would come mainly from the poorer quarters of the city. But, in the course of the first century, there faces us also what has recently been called "that most obscure problem regarding the penetration of Christianity during the first century among the aristocracy of Rome";[6] and I would ask whether that penetration had not been made less difficult because, here and there, men like Terentianus had previously been led to welcome truth even when presented in the Old Testament of the Jews? Be this as it may: if, looking alike to the period and to the man as he is seen in his book, we decide to place "Longinus" about 40 A.D., that will bring him into the earliest years of St. Paul's great career as a convert to Christianity. St. Paul's native town of Tarsus had been a seat of Stoic teaching at least as early as 130 B.C.; and I have lately (in the Loeb Series) offered some reasons for thinking that Plutarch's Demetrius of Tarsus may have written the extant tract on *Style,* and that, not more than twenty years after St. Paul's death at Rome, this Demetrius was (as a member of Agricola's personal staff) teaching Greek at York, the years about 80 A.D. being thus the birth-years of Classical Education in Great Britain: to be followed later by the great things we owe, through the influence of Christianity and of men like Dean Colet, to such foundations as St. Paul's Schools for Boys and Girls.[7] All this is, of course, highly problematical; but, for "Longinus," can anyone think of a more likely period than round about 40 A.D.? And can anyone, further, throw fresh light on the date from such details as (1) the *nanoi* in chapter 44; (2) the *hēmartēmenas kolossos* in chapter 36; (3) or the reference to Mt. Etna in chapter 35? As to the last point: it is sometimes thought that, if "Longinus" had been writing later than the great eruption of Vesuvius in 79 A.D., he would have mentioned that volcano rather than Etna. But did not Etna remain (even in its more tranquil days) the typical volcano, in the Christian era as well as in the earlier centuries, and in Latin literature as well as in Greek? Still, if the essay should be discovered among the charred remains at Herculaneum, we shall have no manner of doubt that its date is not later than 79 A.D.

By way of conclusion, I will propose (without developing) two problems suggested by the main theme of the essay itself. "Longinus" loses no time in defining "the Sublime" as "a certain distinction and excellence of style"; and in chapter nine he describes it, in two resounding words, as . . . "the reverberation of magnanimity," "the far-heard echo of a great soul." Throughout he connects it with greatness, ringing the changes on *megas, megathos, megathopoiein̄, megathunein, megalēgoria, megalothuia, megalopsukhia*; greatness and beauty (rather than littleness and baseness) he seeks for everywhere, alike in the world of nature and of man. The style itself we might well describe as "the great style"; avoiding "grand," with its suggestion of "grandiose." But the question I wish to ask is: how much farther back than Caecilius and "Longinus" can anyone trace, in Greek or Latin, the history of the terms *hypsos* and *hypsēlos*? A difficult question, when so much Greek critical literature has been lost between Aristotle and Dionysius,[8] and when "sublimis" and "sublimitas" do not come into Cicero's prose vocabulary. And, leaping from Cicero right onward to Chaucer, can you tell me whether the "heigh style," in the Prologe of the Clerkes Tale of Oxenford harks back in some way to øçëüò, and how? Here I think I see a clue.

My final problem may seem a bathos, but it stands in close relation to *hypsos,* and it possesses much literary and lexicographical interest, in Greek and English. What *is* the meaning of *e bathous* at the beginning of the second chapter, where we read, "First of all, we must raise the question whether there is *hypsous tis e bathous tekhnē*? Is *bathos* the opposite of *hypos,* or is it an alternative expression ((profundity")? The revised Liddell and Scott renders here by the English word "bathos"; but it quotes no Greek parallel, from the essay or elsewhere. Do you know of any? I know of none, and I believe that Mr. George Loane (now, or formerly, a Master at St. Paul's School, and also a member, I see, of this Association) may be right when, in his excellent *Handbook of Literary Terms,* he writes, "*Bathos.*—This is a sudden descent from the sublime, in description . . . The term was first used by Pope, as the antithesis of the Greek *hypsos,*[9] height, sublimity; bathos means depth, but was never used by the Greeks in this literary sense." The reference here is of course to the satire attributed to the joint efforts of Pope, Swift, and Arbuthnot, *Martinus Scriblerus peri bathous*: Or, *of the Art of Sinking in Poetry,* a title suggested by the ***De Sublimitate.*** The literary insight of Pope (whose six lines on "Longinus," in the *Essay on Criticism,* are still the best appreciation of him that has ever been penned), and the fact that the "sinkings" of style are much in "Longinus's" mind and mouth, keep me from speaking quite as positively as Mr. Loane. But I should much like to be fortified by a Greek parallel. *Anticlimax* we must, I fear, give up as an ancient Greek word: must we also surrender to Alexander Pope *bathos* in the sense of "bathos"?

In the discussion,[10] I shall hope to have the benefit of my fellow-members' opinions on the various points of language I have raised, and on the broader questions of the date of the essay and of the genuineness of its citation from *Genesis.* In my present view of his date, "Longinus" (the earliest of comparative, or international, Greek critics) belongs to a period of marked fusion in the world's intellectual and spiritual history, and has in him something that is characteristic of each of three great races: the Greek, the Roman, the Jewish. This it is that makes and will always make him (unidentified though he may remain) a unique and outstanding figure in the domain of literature.

Notes

[1] A paper read to the Classical Association at its Annual General Meeting held in London, January 9th-11th, 1928.

[2] As to the mention of the . . . [term] in Conrad Gesner's *Bibliotheca Universalis,* published in 1545, nine years before Robortello's *editio princeps.*

[3] The writer of the paper has since heard that in July, 1918, Professor Hermann Mutschmann fell, fighting *pro patria.*

[4] Roberts' edition of *Longinus on the Sublime,* p. 9, where the suggestion was more tentative, in 1899, than it would be in 1928.

[5] Walter Leaf, *Little Poems from the Greek,* pp. 92-94.

[6] Cf. W. M. Ramsay, *Journal of Roman Studies* XVI (1926), 210.

[7] The Classical Association met, this year, in St. Paul's School for Girls.

[8] Here Poseidonius might help us greatly, but there are risks in what we may call . . . "the dragging-in of Poseidonius."

[9] Or *hupsos,* as Dean Swift transliterates it.

[10] Part was taken in the discussion by Dr. J. W. Mackail (Chairman), Canon G. C. Richards, Professor J. Wight Duff, Professor R. S. Conway (President of the Association), Mr. A. O. Prickard, and Professor Wilhelm Kroll of Breslau. The last-named supported Professor Roberts's views, as against those of Professor Ziegler.

J. W. H. Atkins (essay date 1934)

SOURCE: "The New Critical Outlook and Methods: 'Longinus'," in *Literary Criticism in Antiquity: A Sketch of Its Development,* Peter Smith, 1961, pp. 210-53.

[*In the essay that follows, originally written in 1934, Atkins considers the question of the authorship of* On the Sublime *and its immediate instructive purpose, evaluating its achievement in terms of its "definite and practical effort to grapple with those excesses of style which were notoriously prevalent among first-century orators and writers."*]

With the revived interest in critical matters which had become evident during the latter half of the first century A.D., yet another and an important work must also be associated, namely, the Greek treatise of "Longinus", best known perhaps under the title of ***On the Sublime*** . . . though it may at once be said that the work in all probability was not due to Longinus, nor does it deal with what we understand by "the sublime".[1] As with the works of Tacitus and Demetrius, here also there are difficulties of date and authorship to be faced before linking up the treatise with this stage of the critical development; and puzzling as are many of the questions relating to the genesis of literary works, there are few that are more complicated than those bound up with the present treatise. To the solution of those questions antiquity has little or nothing to offer. There is no mention of the work by any ancient writer; and when in 1554 Robortello first presented the work to modern readers it was as a volume previously unknown, which he attributed to a rhetorician named Dionysius Longinus. From the date of that first edition to the beginning of the nineteenth century this ascription was generally accepted. The tradition arose that the work was a production of Longinus (A.D. 213-72), that famous minister of Zenobia, Queen of Palmyra, who had been put to death by Aurelian on account of insurrection; and in regarding this picturesque figure as the author of the work all the scholars of the seventeenth and eighteenth centuries, both in England and France, were in agreement. In assuming this position, however, they had either tacitly ignored or glossed over the fact that the Longinus in question had been named not Dionysius but Cassius Longinus; and it was left for the closer scrutiny of the extant MSS. in the nineteenth century to challenge the assumption and to present fresh considerations bearing on the question of authorship.

Of the MSS.[2] (eleven in number) the oldest and incomparably the best is the Paris MS. 2036. It belongs to the tenth century, whereas the rest all date from the fifteenth or sixteenth century; and since in all probability it is the original from which the other MSS. were copied, its value in general is of the first importance. On the question of authorship, however, its evidence is curiously perplexing. In the table of contents of the MS. the treatise is ascribed to Dionysius *or* Longinus; whereas in the superscription of the treatise itself the two names are given as one, with a considerable space between them. So that the choice may be said to lie between Dionysius or Longinus or Dionysius Longinus. And in the later Paris MS. 985 these statements are merely repeated in identical form. Nor is further information forthcoming from the other MSS. In the Vatican MS. 285, for instance, the inscription once again runs "Dionysius or Longinus", while in the Florence MS. the work is simply ascribed to an anonymous writer. This much therefore becomes clear: that from the point of view of evidence the earliest MS. is the only one that counts, the others merely copying or commenting on statements previously made. As for the significance of the statements contained in the original Paris MS. all that can be said is that their conflicting character wholly discounts their value and suggests that they are almost certainly conjectures on the part of the copyist. Faced with the task of copying an anonymous work he ventured to suggest alternatively what seemed to be likely authors. And to him the name of Dionysius of Halicarnassus would naturally suggest itself in view of the author's claim to have written on "the arrangement of words";[3] whereas Longinus was also doubtless familiar as an interesting historical figure who had won some reputation in the field of rhetoric. Neither, however, for reasons to be stated later, can have been the author; while the third name to appear, that of Dionysius Longinus, may well have been the result of the scribal omission of "or" . . . unless indeed it stand for some otherwise unknown writer, in which case the conflicting testimony of the table of contents has to be taken into account. Altogether then it must be confessed that the evidence of the MSS. does not take us far; it is most probably conjectural, and confused conjecture at that.

For safer ground on which to discuss the genesis of the treatise we must turn to the work itself; though it may at once be said that no further positive information as to the authorship will be forthcoming. At the same time some idea of the approximate date may reasonably be formed; and in the first place the evidence all points, consistently and fairly conclusively, to a date of writing prior to the traditional date, which was that of the third century A.D. It is not without its significance, to begin with, that while the treatise has references to all sorts of writers from Homer down to rhetoricians of the Augustan age, there is no mention whatsoever of any writer later than the early part of the first century A.D. The presence of these Augustan references, it is true, gives positive assurance as to the late appearance of the work in Greek literary history. It cannot have been earlier than the first century A.D.; and with this the evidence of its style and vocabulary, in some ways akin to those of Plutarch in his early work, is in general accord. But what is one to say about the absence of references later than the first century A.D.? In connexion with a writer of the third century it could only be described as, to say the least, surprising. But when the writer in question is one, as the author undoubtedly is, whose range in literature is otherwise catholic and whose immediate interests are betrayed by the fire and urgency of his writing, then the omission seems capable of no rational explanation, and we are forced to question seriously the hypothesis of a third-century author. There is here at least a case for accepting the traditional date with some amount of reserve. Nor are we reassured when we refer to what is known of rhetorical activities in the third century. There is of course the outstanding figure of Cassius Longinus,[4] in whose work, the *Philological Discourses,* some coincidences of doctrine with the present treatise have latterly been traced. But apart from this there is nothing to show that Longinus was the author, while there is much to suggest a negative conclusion. Thus the absence of the work from the accredited list of Longinus's writings; the absence, too, from the same list, of works definitely claimed by the author of the treatise;[5] or again, the marked differences in style, terminology, and literary judgments between the known work of Longinus and the present treatise; all these are serious obstacles to the acceptance of Longinian authorship. The truth indeed would seem to be that the surprise affected by the historian Gibbon was only too well founded, when in reflecting on the age in which Longinus lived, "an age which produced scarce any other writer worthy of the attention of posterity, when real learning was almost extinct, (and) Philosophy sunk down to the quibbles of Grammarians and the tricks of mountebanks", he proceeded to express his amazement that "at such a period, in the heart of Syria, and at the court of an Eastern monarch, Longinus should (have) produced a work worthy of the best and freest days at Athens".[6] But this antecedent improbability applies with equal force to other rhetoricians of the period, when sophistry was engaging the attention of all, and when the study of rhetoric had fallen somewhat from its former high estate. It is in short upon the hypothesis of Longinian authorship that the ascription of the work to the third century mainly rests; and in the absence of more substantial evidence in favour of Longinus there is little to be said for regarding the work as a third-century production.

Results of a more positive kind are obtained when we assume, and assume naturally enough, that the limitation of references in the body of the work to first-century and earlier authors was simply due to the fact that the work was written in the course of that century. That this is no idle assumption is suggested in the first place by the purpose and nature of the work. It was a treatise written confessedly[7] to correct the errors of an essay on the same subject by Caecilius, the friend of Dionysius of Halicarnassus; and from the vital and forceful character of the treatment we are led to infer that it represents more probably a first-century polemic than a detached and academic utterance of some later writer to whom Caecilius was merely an influence of the distant past. And in this view we are encouraged by the reference in the text to Theodorus of Gadara,[8] couched as it is in terms suggesting discipleship on the part of the writer; and further, by the attitude adopted by our author, in which it is not altogether fanciful to see the hostility of a follower of Theodorus for one who belonged to the rival school of Apollodorus. The quarrel between the two schools lasted throughout the first century A.D. and was representative of two distinct tendencies in rhetorical work. And since our author confessedly aims at a freer, less doctrinaire treatment, as opposed to the more rigid system of classifications and rules, it is difficult not to see here the workings of first-century influences and the adoption by the writer of the Theodoran point of view. But however this may be, and at least it is not improbable, there can be little doubt as to the nature of the interests reflected in the work; and that they are characteristic of the first century A.D. and no other is seen from a comparison of the matters treated with the questions raised by the main body of critics belonging to that century. Thus, to begin with, there are two definite references in the text to contemporary oratory, one alluding in withering terms to those "fine fellows",[9] the orators of the day, the other declaring that the pursuit of novelty in expression was the prevailing craze of the author's own age.[10] The inevitable result of such a fashion, so the author explained, was to give rise to improprieties of style such as bombast, puerility, misplaced emotion and the like;[11] and from what he says of the high-flown manner, the learned trifling, the unseasonable and empty passion, it is difficult to avoid the conclusion that what he had in mind were the excesses of the Asiatics and the Atticists, more especially as Hegesias, the first of the Asiatics, is mentioned in connexion with one of these faults. But these are precisely the abuses censured by most of the first-century critics, by Dionysius and Caecilius, the elder Seneca, Persius and Tacitus, each in his own way. And if, unlike most of the other critics, our author does not draw his illustrations from contemporary performers, that was because he was concerned primarily with Greek and Greek authors and thus ignored with one exception all Latin writers. Still more convincing in its implications is the inquiry made at the end of the treatise[12] into the causes of the decline of eloquence; for here undoubtedly is a question that was agitating the minds of all first-century critics alike. Similar speculations have already been traced in the writings of the two Senecas, Petronius, Tacitus, and Velleius Paterculus; and to these discussions later contributions were to be made by Quintilian and the younger Pliny. The matter was thus obviously a burning question of the time; it excited no curiosity after the close of the first century A.D., if we may judge from later writings. So that this much seems certain, that the environment amidst which our treatise was written was that of Rome in the first century A.D., and that the author wrote with contemporary interests and problems in mind. Nor is this all, for his treatment of this question has much in common with that of Tacitus in his *Dialogue.* Like Tacitus, for instance, our author takes into account political factors; and in reply to the theory that great oratory had vanished with the loss of democratic freedom, he enlarges, as Tacitus had done, on the advantages enjoyed by those who lived under a beneficent Imperial government.[13] In both cases, it would seem, the argument was inspired by the prosperity and peace which returned under Imperial rule, probably under Vespasian and Titus; while in the discussion itself it is not unlikely that we have an echo of a controversy of the time. In the reign of Vespasian, for instance, the praise of Republican institutions had become fashionable among a certain group of philosophers who claimed to see in the decay of oratory a confirmation of their theories; and this is the position that both Tacitus and our author assailed. Their conclusions differed somewhat, but they had one object in common; and in this connexion it is not without its significance that the case for the opposition in our treatise is put into the mouth of a philosopher. Altogether, then, it must be conceded that the evidence for a first-century authorship is strong. There is nothing in the work to confute the theory, while further details might be quoted in its support. Indeed most scholars nowadays agree in accepting this position; and if a more exact date is to be hazarded, the work might reasonably be regarded as contemporaneous with Tacitus's *Dialogue,* and thus assigned to some such date as *c.* A.D. 80. Who the author was, on the other hand, must remain uncertain; though many conjectures have in the past been made, including among others the names of Dionysius of Halicarnassus and Plutarch. But Dionysius is ruled out by considerations of date and by the attack on Caecilius; while with all his merits as a critic his work lacks the unique qualities of the present treatise. And as for Plutarch, the evidence is so weak and unconvincing that the theory of his authorship is no longer seriously maintained.[14] Hence the work is best described as the production of an anonymous writer of the latter half of the first century A.D., probably one of those Greeks who migrated to Rome under Augustus or one of his successors. And if nowadays the traditional authorship with some difference is usually retained and the work assigned to one "Longinus", this at least is convenient owing to the long association of the name of Longinus with the work; while in addition there is this to be said, that the name "Longinus" will do as well as any other to stand for the unknown.

With this then as our conception of the genesis of the work ***On the Sublime,*** we turn now to consider the nature of its achievement and its value as a contribution to the critical literature of antiquity. Of the original treatise it must first be said that only an imperfect copy has come down. Frequent and sometimes extensive gaps occur in the MSS. amounting, it has been calculated, to more than one-third of the whole; so that what we have is a part only of the actual work, and that in a mutilated form that in places lacks coherence. At the same time sufficient has been preserved to make plain the broad outline and the intention of the author; and while much that was valuable has undoubtedly perished, there is still an abundance of good things in the treatise as it stands, enough to warrant its inclusion among the choicest pieces of criticism that have reached posterity. Concerning the immediate occasion of the work something has already been said. "Longinus", we gather, had embarked on the task in view of what he regarded as the inadequacy of Caecilius's essay on the same theme. The earlier teacher, he complained, had failed to deal with the essential aspects of his subject, and at the same time had not been sufficiently practical in his treatment.[15] He had for instance omitted to treat of emotion, one of the primary causes of "the sublime";[16] and while incidentally he had dealt with such details as the number of metaphors permitted in a given passage,[17] he had also betrayed a preference for the faultless Lysias, as compared with the less correct but more gifted Plato.[18] But while the defects of an earlier text-book apparently supplied the immediate occasion for "Longinus's" treatise, it is also quite possible that the real inspiration may have been due to another and a more general cause. Written at a time when efforts were being made to attain distinction of style at all costs, efforts which resulted in all kinds of improprieties, the grandiose, the discordant, and the bizarre, the work of "Longinus" can scarcely have been independent of such conditions, a treatise written as it were *in vacuo.* And indeed, if we may judge from the nature of the work itself, this was precisely the situation he was endeavouring to meet. That his subject . . . is not "the sublime" in the narrow modern sense of the term is a truth that becomes evident from the most cursory reading. In his survey, for instance, are included not only the "sublime" Pindar and Aeschylus but also Herodotus and Thucydides, in connexion with whom the term would be simply unmeaning. The fact therefore is that "sublimity" in its modern sense is not wide enough to cover his treatment. What he has in mind is rather "elevation", all that raises style above the ordinary and gives to it distinction in its widest and truest sense;[19] and sound ideas on this subject were what the age most needed, as was shown by the efforts of Tacitus directed to the same end. Hence the work has all the appearance of a treatise written to meet a pressing need of the time; and a proper apprehension of this fact gives to the reading of the text a fuller and deeper meaning.

As regards its structure and general treatment the work may be said to have much to commend it in spite of what seems at first sight its somewhat formless arrangement. Like so many of the critical writings that appeared at the time, the treatise in the first place is addressed to one who was certainly a friend, and possibly a pupil, one Terentianus, in all probability a cultured Roman, of whose identity however nothing is definitely known. Apart from this conventional detail, however, the structure is mainly determined by the object in view, and in spite of omissions it must be described as well planned and adequate. First comes an introduction (cc. 1-6) leading up to the central theme by a discussion of those vices of style which constituted in contemporary oratory a false "sublime"; a topic to which the author reverts later in cc. 41-3. This is followed by a section (cc. 7-40) representing the main substance of the treatise, in which are specified the five sources whence springs true distinction of style, as well as the details of the treatment necessary for its attainment. The five sources are said to be: (1) grandeur of conception, treated in cc. 8-15; (2) intensity of emotion, the consideration of which is reserved for a separate work; and both of these, as the author points out, are largely the fruit of natural genius. Then follows some account of the remaining sources due primarily to art: (3) the appropriate use of Figures, dealt with in cc. 16-29; (4) nobility of diction, in cc. 30-8; (5) dignity and elevation of word-order, in cc. 39-40. And the work is brought to a close by a discussion of the causes of the decay of eloquence (c. 44), a return to the opening theme which rounds off the treatment and suggests the motive that has been animating the author throughout. The general plan is therefore obvious. The central theme is treated on comprehensive lines, embodying an approach to the subject from both the psychological and the technical points of view; while something of the usual rhetorical procedure is also adopted in treating first of subject-matter (*inventio*) and its arrangement (*dispositio*) under the head of "grandeur of conception", and then of the choice and arrangement of words (*elocutio, compositio*) in subsequent sections. At the same time the treatment is never rigidly systematic; though the author, in his care to avoid the mistake of Caecilius, never fails to indicate how the qualities he advocates may in practice be attained. Throughout the work, moreover, an easy conversational tone is maintained, rising at times to an appropriate eloquence. And by means of an abundance of illustrative quotations, by his shrewd and convincing analysis of literary qualities, the author succeeds in calling attention to some of the fundamental principles underlying all good writing, while commending them to his readers by the freshness and charm of his style.

In attempting now to form some estimate of the teaching of "Longinus", it is as well to recall once again what we conceive to be the purpose of the work; that it was no abstract or detached inquiry into a rare yet valuable literary quality, but rather a definite and practical effort to grapple with those excesses of style which were notoriously prevalent among first-century orators and writers, and which formed the staple of discussion among the critics of the age. That the author achieves more than this will be readily conceded. In pointing out a better way in matters of style he directs attention to not a few of the great simple truths of literature, and at the same time throws new light on critical standards and methods. These things, it must be confessed, form the glory of the work; they are what has given it its value in the eyes of posterity. But nevertheless, viewed historically, the treatise is first and foremost an attempt at solving a contemporary problem; and since it is only when it is regarded as such that its meaning becomes fully intelligible, some consideration must first be given to that aspect of the author's achievement.

In the first place there can be little doubt as to the nature of the indictment he brings against the orators and men of letters of his time. Without being laboured it is fairly comprehensive, embracing most of the characteristic vices; and if the evils are alluded to somewhat lightly rather than dealt with in detail, that is because Terentianus, to whom he was writing, would be familiar with the condition of things. Thus he recalls the bombastic manner of the Asiatics, high-flown and turgid,[20] the "puerility" of the Atticists, which "beginning in learned trifling ends in frigidity";[21] or again, the impassioned style used out of season,[22] the indulgence in strange and absurd conceits,[23] the over-rhythmical style suggestive of dance music,[24] undue conciseness and undue prolixity,[25] as well as the use of sordid or vulgar words lacking in dignity[26]—all of which were characteristic of first-century innovators and were the features of style decried by all contemporary critics. By way of comment on these improprieties "Longinus" is content with but few though pertinent remarks. Like Horace he is conscious of that human weakness which urges men in avoiding one fault to fall into the opposite extreme.[27] And the prevailing bombast he ascribes in part to that particular cause: to the effort on the part of writers to escape the charge of being trite or colourless. Then, too, he explains that all such excesses really arose out of the quest for novelty, then a popular craze, but in itself no bad thing.[28] "Our merits and our defects", he adds, "spring from much the same sources"; and in this sympathetic attitude, this unwillingness to condemn outright the lawless innovations of the time, may be found a suggestive parallel with the position taken up by Tacitus on this same question.

Upon this negative side of his subject, however, "Longinus" does not linger unduly. His aim is constructive and positive; what he sets out to do is to represent in its true light that excellence in expression for which so many of his contemporaries were blindly and unsuccessfully groping. And he describes forthwith his conception of the real object of their mistaken quest as a certain distinction or elevation [*hypos*] of style present in all the earlier masterpieces, whether in prose or verse, that quality which indeed gave to them their supreme and lasting value.[29] Thus at the outset does "Longinus" establish himself firmly on the standards of the classical Greeks, and this position he maintains throughout the work. In the meantime, however, he has a word or two to add concerning the special excellence he has in mind. And in the first place he explains that the effect of this quality is not mere persuasion or pleasure, but transport . . . ; that is to say, it works like a charm carrying irresistibly away all hearers (or readers).[30] And further, he adds, its effect is as immediate as it is subtle; it does not come as the result of a painful observance of the rhetorician's rules.[31] This brings him then to the question as to how this charm or "distinction" of style was in general to be come by; whether for instance it was acquired by the light of nature or whether it was the result of following the precepts of art. In reply he reiterates what Horace and others had said, namely, that both Nature and Art were equally necessary;[32] but from the trouble he takes to establish his point it is clear that here he is indulging in no idle pronouncement. Thus he quotes the opinion of some that such skill was inborn, and came not by teaching; that indeed genius itself shrivelled up at the touch of the rules.[33] And here it cannot be doubted that he is quoting those of his contemporaries who justified their excesses by the workings of that "divine frenzy" (*plena deo*) of which Gallio was wont to prate;[34] those, in short, who wrote "without the guidance of knowledge . . . and at the whim of mere impulse and ignorant audacity".[35] Hence to such he replies that while Nature works freely in matters of expression, she does not work haphazard or wholly without system; but that she herself creates the system which Art merely brings to light.[36] To Art, therefore, "Longinus" attaches a two-fold function. In the first place it provides a safeguard against undue licence, and in the second, it makes plain to men Nature's methods of expression. "Fine writing", says "Longinus",[37] "needs the curb as well as the spur"; and in this saying is happily summed up his conception of the importance of Art.

These preliminaries completed, "Longinus" now comes to grips with what is his real subject; and he proceeds with many a digression to suggest how this "distinction" of style may be in general attained. In the first place he insists on the need for grandeur of conception . . . ; since thoughts that are lofty and awe-inspiring find their natural expression in exalted phrase. Such loftiness of thought, he grants, is normally a gift of nature rather than a quality acquired; and he quotes in this connexion an earlier dictum of his own, that "great utterance is the echo of greatness of soul" . . . [38]—one of those pronouncements of which we could wish for more. At the same time he maintains that this nobility of soul may in some measure also be cultivated by nourishing the mind on thoughts that are elevating, and impregnating them, as it were, with lofty inspiration. In any case loftiness of utterance, he adds, can never be inspired by mean or ignoble thoughts; and he proceeds to illustrate his point by examples taken from Homer and elsewhere. But while this elevation of style is primarily inspired by exalted thought, whether innate or cultivated, "Longinus" further intimates that such grandeur of conception and the consequent largeness of utterance might also be attained by submitting to the spell of the great masters . . . , and capturing from them something of their greatness;[39] a doctrine, it might be added, that has been subject to misrepresentation in the past. That "Longinus" has here in mind a process of the spirit, rather than a mere formal imitation or emulation of their methods, is made plain by the context. For there he explains that men catch fire from the spirit of others, just as the Pythian priestess was moved to deliver her oracles by virtue of the divine vapour which arose out of the rocky floor of her chamber at Delphi. And so, adds "Longinus", it is with men; they are inspired by the effluences . . . that flow from such masters as Homer, and thus uplifted, they share in the afflatus of genius.[40] Nor is the process, he declares, one of mere plagiarism; for the effect is like that produced by impressions made of beautiful forms of statuary which fire men to emulation. And here he would seem to have in mind that enthusiastic form of imitation which Dionysius of Halicarnassus had previously described as "an activity of the soul inspired by the spectacle of the seemingly beautiful".[41] In any event the "imitation" he here advocates is worlds apart from the formal copying usually associated with that term; it is different, too, from Horace's rather loftier conception which stood for an assimilation of ancient methods with a view to producing something new. To "Longinus" the operation is one that aimed at capturing something of the ancient spirit, something of that vital creative force which had gone to the making of the earlier masterpieces; and its effect he describes as that of illumination, guiding the mind in some mysterious way to the lofty standards of the ideal.[42] Here then is something new in the critical outlook; a recognition of that imaginative stimulus derived from great creative genius, as well as an interpretation of "imitation" that raised it to a higher plane. And it is such theorising as this that constitutes the greatness of "Longinus". Of the remaining methods of attaining grandeur of conception and through it distinction of style, as mentioned by "Longinus", there is rather less to say, though they are by no means unimportant. They relate for the most part to the treatment of material, and are concerned with the ways of rendering subject-matter effective. Thus the desired effect, it is stated, may be obtained by the choice and combination of significant details so as to present an organic whole;[43] a process which is illustrated from Sappho and Homer. It may also result from "amplification",[44] that is, from an accumulation of all the different aspects of a given subject, which by their very profusion suggest overwhelming strength and magnitude; a feature seen in the work of Demosthenes and Cicero. And lastly there is the use of vivid and compelling images which infuse vehemence and passion into the spoken or written word;[45] an effect that is illustrated from Homer, Euripides, and others.

Such then is "Longinus's" analysis of the part played by grandeur of conception in giving distinction to style: and in view of the penetration displayed in that analysis it is all the more to be regretted that his ideas on what he regards as another prime factor, namely, vehement and inspired passion, have unfortunately been lost. Beyond asserting that nothing conduces more to loftiness of tone than genuine emotion in writing, "Longinus" does not deal with the topic. And whereas at the end of the present work he states his intention of devoting a separate treatise to the subject, of the outcome of this intention nothing is known. In proceeding then with his exposition of the methods of attaining the desired excellence of style, "Longinus" now turns to a consideration of those artistic devices which contribute to that end; and in the first place he deals with the use of Figures, selecting for treatment those which more especially were adapted for his purpose. Here at first sight he seems to be reverting to the usual rhetorical routine which comprised instruction in the choice and arrangement of words, and then in what was known as stylistic ornament, including the Figures. But while in his treatment there is much that is conventional, there are also signs of independent thinking, and of discrimination in the handling of his various details. It is not without its significance, for instance, that he reverses the usual order of treatment and devotes his attention primarily to a consideration of the Figures. This may possibly be accounted for by the fact that he,[46] as well as Dionysius, had already written on "the arrangement of words", so that a further detailed treatment of the subject was unnecessary; though other reasons may also have weighed with him, reasons to which reference will be made later.[47] What at any rate is certain is that he devotes nearly one-third of the work as it stands (cc. 16-29) to a consideration of the Figures; and it is therefore not strange to find that to them he attaches considerable value as a means of giving "distinction" to style.

From the first he makes it plain that to him Figures are no arbitrary devices invented by rhetoricians for mechanical application; but rather a natural means of giving to style an element of fine surprise, something rooted in genuine emotion, responsive to the artistic sense of man, and thus capable of explanation in terms of human nature. This idea, by the way, is implicit throughout his teaching; and he begins by showing how natural and intimate are the relations between Figures and "distinction" of style, the one assisting and being in turn assisted by the other.[48] Thus he explains that while Figures are instrumental in giving excellence to style, there is nothing on the other hand that renders Figures more effective than a style that is already in some degree "elevated". In the use of Figures, he points out, there is normally a suggestion of artifice which excites mistrust in the minds of the hearers (or readers), often rendering them hostile to the effects intended. And in countering this suspicion there is no surer antidote than elevation of style, which by its very qualities casts a veil over artifice, just as dim lights are extinguished in the radiance of the sun. As he acutely adds, "a Figure is most effective when the fact that it is a Figure is happily concealed";[49] and this function, he maintains, is best performed by a setting that is the result of splendour or "distinction" of style.

When he turns to consider more particularly the effects of Figures, it will be noticed that he makes no attempt to deal with the Figures as a whole. As has been already said, he discusses only those that give elevation to style; and he is content to illustrate the general principles of their workings together with some of their effects, selecting for that purpose examples taken from Demosthenes, Thucydides, Homer and the rest. Among the more familiar of the Figures treated are the rhetorical question, Asyndeton or the omission of conjunctions, Hyperbaton or inversion, and Periphrasis; and his main contention throughout is that Figures properly treated are a valuable means of giving emotional quality to style, thus supplementing by devices of art the animation or ardour which normally results from the genuine emotion of the speaker (or writer). In the first place, for instance, he illustrates from a passage of Demosthenes his effective use of question and answer; and then goes on to explain how by the rapid play of question and answer, anticipating as it were the questions of his hearers, Demosthenes has simulated a natural outburst of passion and given to his statement a vigour and a fire which would have been lacking in a plain straightforward assertion.[50] And similar effects are said to result from the use of Asyndeton, when words are poured forth without connecting links, as for example in the passage taken from Xenophon: "Locking their shields, they thrust, fought, slew, fell".[51] Here, it is explained, the broken but rapid expression suggests an agitation of spirit which checks the utterance and yet at the same time drives it on; an effect, it is noted, of which Homer made use. But this device, it is added, may also be combined with others such as Anaphora (or repetition of words), when the effect is heightened, as in the phrase: "by his manner, his looks, his voice, *etc.*".[52] The essence of such breaks and repetitions is said to be the suggestion of an impassioned disorder and emphasis that strike the minds of the hearers (or readers) as with a swift succession of blows, while betokening a disturbance of soul on the part of the speaker. And for the better appreciation of these effects "Longinus" advises that such passages be turned into the style characteristic of Isocrates and his school, that is, with all the connectives restored and the repetitions removed. It would then be seen that, with order and smoothness attained, all the force and impetuosity of the passages had vanished. For, added "Longinus" in his illuminating fashion, just as runners were impeded by bands that cramped their movement, so impassioned utterance was fettered by such things as connectives which deprived it of its freedom and rapidity of expression.[53]

Much the same in their effects were said to be the Figures known as Hyperbata (or inversions), which consisted of departures from the normal order in both expression and idea; a sure and certain sign of utterance made under stress of great emotion. For, as "Longinus" proceeds to point out,[54] men moved by passion are wont to express themselves in disjointed fashion, skipping from subject to subject, indulging in irrelevancies, rapidly turning now this way now that, thus setting at defiance by their unexpected movements the recognised laws of normal and logical speech. Of this he gives an example from Herodotus; while to Thucydides he attributes the greatest skill and boldness in the use of such transitions. Demosthenes, too, he describes as abounding most of all writers in the use of this Figure, even though he employs it in a less daring manner than did Thucydides. And then in his comment on the effects of this Figure in composition "Longinus" supplies a practical and striking illustration of the very qualities with which he is dealing. Thus Demosthenes, he states, "will often leave in suspense the thought which he has begun to express, and meanwhile he will heap, into a position seemingly alien and unnatural, one thing upon another parenthetically and from any external source whatsoever, throwing his hearer into alarm lest the whole structure of his words should fall to pieces, and compelling him in anxious sympathy to share the peril of the speaker; and then unexpectedly, after a long interval, he adds the long-awaited conclusion at the right place, namely the end, and produces a far greater effect by this very use, so bold and hazardous, of Hyperbaton".[55] Here, then, may be detected something of the breathless vehemence, the studied disorder, and the air of unpremeditation characteristic of impassioned utterance, but largely due in this instance to the employment of one of the Figures. It is in short an example of artistic expression reproducing the effects of natural expression; a principle emphasised by "Longinus" in his statement that "art is perfect when it seems to be nature, and nature hits the mark when she contains art hidden within her".[56]

Among the other Figures treated by "Longinus" are the Apostrophe or adjuration, the Figures embodying changes of syntax, and lastly Periphrasis; all of which are said to be instrumental in heightening the expression. The use of the Apostrophe in the first place he illustrates from the work of Demosthenes. He explains how that orator, in defending his policy which had brought disaster at Chaeronea, reverts to past history, and in recalling the policy which had prevailed at Marathon, swears by those earlier champions as though they were gods; thus raising the argument to the emotional plane and carrying away his hearers by the very force of his passion.[57] Then, too, he points out the enlivening effects of variations of syntax; the use of the plural for the singular, or the singular for the plural, or again, the representation of things past as though they were present. The first he illustrates by the sentence, "a countless host . . . were clamouring"; and here he suggests that the plural verb . . . , besides being more sonorous, also conveys more effectively the sense of multitude contained in the word "host".[58] The second he illustrates by Demosthenes's phrase, "all Peloponnesus was at variance"; and here he maintains that the excellence arises from the effective way in which the sense of oneness is brought out by the singular verb.[59] And again, the representation of things past as present he commends as giving vividness to a narrative; "your story", he explains,[60] "is then no longer a narration but an actuality". Of greater interest, however, are his remarks on Periphrasis with which he concludes his treatment of Figures. That Periphrasis has a heightening effect on expression he states as a generally recognised fact.[61] By its very magniloquence, provided it is free from bombastic or discordant elements, it adds to expression a richer note and more tuneful rhythms, thus affording assistance to one who is endeavouring to set forth some lofty thought. And "Longinus" likens its effects to those musical accompaniments which help to bring out the charm of a melody. On the other hand he adds that its use is attended with considerable risk and needs much care; for otherwise it falls flat and is apt to degenerate into a trivial and cumbrous form of expression[62]—a truth that was subsequently to be borne out by certain aspects of English poetry in the eighteenth century.

From what has now been said of the nature and scope of "Longinus's" treatment of the Figures it becomes clear that unlike most of the contemporary rhetoricians he attempts no mere enumeration of their different varieties, but aims rather at establishing the general idea of their function and at illustrating his teaching by some selected examples. Moreover, by way of inculcating a more intelligent use of such devices, he explains where possible the psychological basis on which they rested; while more than once he lays stress on the need for their proper handling. Nor does he confine himself to caveats of merely a general kind. His exposition throughout is characterised by warnings of which the injunction as to Periphrasis is but one example. Thus he insists that Figures are not to be used indiscriminately. "The place, the manner, the circumstances, and the motive",[63] he explains, must all be taken into account; and in particular, the device of Repetition or accumulation must only be used where the occasion or subject invites inflation, redundance, exaggeration or passion.[64] Then, too, he points out that in employing a Figure the orator (or writer) should exercise sobriety and judgment; "in the midst of the riot of the imagination", as he puts it, "restraint is necessary".[65] Again, he adds that the exhibition of passion is most effective when it seems to be unstudied on the part of the speaker and to arise naturally out of the occasion itself.[66] Such remarks as these are not without their significance in a treatise of the first century A.D. That they are designed to combat the prevailing faults of contemporary orators and writers would perhaps be generally conceded; but they also seem to do more than this. They seem also to account in part for the prominence given by "Longinus" to the discussion of Figures in his work. It is, in short, as if in his opinion it was the perverted ingenuity bound up with the abuse of Figures that lay at the root of the stylistic improprieties of the time, and that therefore called most urgently for serious consideration.

However this may be, at the same time it is clear that questions relating to the Figures do not occupy the whole attention of our author. And in developing further his main thesis he proceeds to discuss yet another factor that contributes to "distinction" of style, namely, words themselves. Of this discussion on diction, unfortunately, only a mutilated section has come down, no less than four leaves of the MS. having been lost; though what remains is characterised by the same discerning treatment as before. In the first place he is content to remind his readers of the importance of a suitable choice of both ordinary and striking words in the formation of an impressive style. He does not labour the point unnecessarily; but by means of a brief comment on what after all was a commonplace to his generation he presents the ancient doctrine in a new and memorable light. Dionysius of Halicarnassus, for one, had previously remarked on the innate beauty of words; he had discussed them mainly in terms of form and sound-quality, apart from their meaning. "Longinus", however, now insists on their magic as a means of expression, a beauty intimately bound up with the thought itself. And he declares that what gives to literature its enduring charm, whether it be the quality of grandeur, or beauty, or mellowness, or force, is in the last resort this verbal magic, which "invests dead things with a sort of living voice". "Beautiful words", he adds,[67] "are in truth the very light (or illumination) of thought" . . . ; and it may safely be said that nowhere in the work does "Longinus" approach more nearly to the mysteries of art than in this suggestive and striking pronouncement of his.

Of the rest of his fragmentary remarks on diction there is this to be said, that while scarcely maintaining the high level of his opening comment they invariably touch on points of importance to his contemporaries, and this, rather than an exhaustive treatment, is his aim throughout. Thus he issues a warning against the indiscriminate use of stately words; to employ magnificent diction, he states, in connexion with trivial matters would be about as effective as to put on a child a man's tragic mask.[68] On the other hand he has a word of approval for homely and racy expressions in the proper place; and he quotes by way of illustration a sentence from Theopompus to the effect that "Philip had a way of stomaching things" . . . —a somewhat daring expression which Caecilius had previously condemned.[69] To "Longinus", however, the term "stomaching" seemed preferable to a more elegant word, and this on account of its familiarity and force. Such words, he conceded, were dangerously near vulgarity; but from that they were saved by their very expressiveness. Passing then to another aspect of diction, presumably a topic of current debate, he next deals with the use of metaphor; and here again he gives evidence of a singular breadth of outlook and of a penetrating insight into the elements of art, none too common in any age. That metaphors were a valuable factor in giving "distinction" to style he takes more or less for granted; and he proceeds as before to confute a doctrine which Caecilius had seemingly countenanced, to the effect that the number of metaphors permissible in any given passage should be limited to two or at the most three.[70] Behind this rule, he is aware, lay the authority of Aristotle and Theophrastus, who had advocated the use of not more than two at a time, and had further advised the employment of such saving clauses as "as it were" or "if one may venture the expression". Such disparaging phrases, he conceded, often moderated the audacity of risky metaphors, thus rendering them acceptable; though this device he regards as not the most effective, while to the mechanical limitation of their number he takes strong exception. With the insight of genius he brushes aside all rules, and, declaring that in this matter Demosthenes was the guide, he boldly asserts that the passion which gives rise to metaphors will not only determine their number but will also provide the necessary palliatives as well. Thus impassioned utterance, he explains, demands the use of these striking turns, often in a sustained series; so that there can be no fixed limit to the number used. Then, too, a reader stirred does not stop to count or weigh up metaphors; carried away by emotion he needs no other palliative. And in this way, it is implied, does passion help metaphor and metaphor passion; the relation between the two being of a natural and fundamental kind. And lastly concerning hyperboles he has also a word to say, though for the most part his remarks merely reiterate principles already laid down. That hyperboles should spring naturally from great emotion which renders plausible and acceptable the most daring use, that moreover they are most effective when their art is concealed, and that a hyperbole overdone results in bathos, all these are ideas that are implied in his earlier discussion; and the true working of the device he illustrates by examples taken from Thucydides and Herodotus.[71]

This brings him then to his last source of "distinction" in style, namely, the arrangement of words; and this section, for reasons already given, he treats in summary fashion. Hence, for the most part, he is content to generalise on the effects of a harmonious setting of words. He points out, for instance, that the resultant harmony is a natural instrument not only of persuasion and pleasure but of lofty emotion as well; and he further describes it as something that appeals to the soul of man, awakening in him a host of sensations, and enabling him to share in the emotion of the speaker (or writer).[72] Foremost among the rhythms that make for grandeur of utterance is said to be the dactylic, upon which, as "Longinus" reminds his readers, that most beautiful of metres, the hexameter, is built. On the other hand, weak and broken rhythms made up of pyrrhics, trochees, and the like, are instrumental solely in lowering the dignity of a passage.[73] But so, adds "Longinus", does also writing in which the rhythm is too pronounced; for there it is the quality of the rhythm rather than the meaning of the words that engages the attention, and the effect is said to be not unlike that of dance-music to which hearers were wont to keep time with their feet.[74] That "Longinus" has here in mind those degrading tricks of contemporary orators mentioned by Tacitus[75] can scarcely be doubted. And in his further warning against undue conciseness of expression[76] may be found another topical allusion. Extreme conciseness, as he points out, cramps and cripples the thought; whereas brevity in the true sense is effective because of its economy and directness.

With the conclusion of this analysis "Longinus" may be said to have completed his task, that of pointing out to his generation the foundations of a noble style. And the speculations that follow on the causes that had led to the decline of literary excellence in his day are of the nature of an appendix; an expression of views on a subject arising naturally out of his main theme. For this purpose he adopts the dialogue form, ascribing to a contemporary philosopher some of the current arguments, to which he in turn replies. The main argument advanced by the philosopher, somewhat tentatively it is true, is the orthodox political one, namely, that democracy was the foster-mother of genius, and that literature had accordingly flourished under the earlier democratic régime and had declined with the passing of those conditions.[77] In support of this view it was urged that the freedom of the individual under a democracy was what really counted. It gave scope to the imagination, filled men with high hopes, inspired them to public activities and to competition for the many prizes open under popular government; all of which was claimed to have fostered literary achievement. On the other hand it was the loss of freedom under Imperial rule that was said to account for the subsequent decline. Nurtured on doctrines of servitude and forbidden all liberty of speech, men were described as no better than slaves, with faculties stunted like those of the Pygmies; and such servitude, it was added, even though of the most benevolent kind . . . , was undoubtedly fatal to all forms of literary activity.[78] Here then was Cicero's theory, with some modification it is true, and with also the saving clause as to the beneficence of Imperial rule. To this "Longinus" replies by approaching the problem from another angle. To him the causes of the decline were ethical rather than political; a conviction quite in keeping with his former pronouncement that "great utterance" was but the counterpart of "greatness of soul". And he proceeds to enlarge on the moral evils of his day; the love of money and pleasure with its degrading effects, the insolence and shamelessness that followed in its train, the loss of all sense of the ideal and spiritual, and the consequent atrophy of man's immortal soul.[79] These in his opinion were the causes of the decay of literature; and he can suggest no remedy, save an enlightened autocracy which should exercise over men the control they lacked.

Such then in broad outline is the scheme of the treatise ***On the Sublime;*** and before passing on to a consideration of other aspects of the work some estimate may now be formed of the success with which the author has achieved his main purpose, that of pointing out to a distracted age the principles underlying true charm and "distinction" of style. That he has shed new light on the much-vexed question becomes evident from a comparison with the efforts made by Dionysius, Tacitus, and Demetrius in much the same field. Not that their efforts were wanting in merit; on the contrary, as has been shown, they betrayed keen insight into certain aspects of the problem, and were helpful and suggestive in a high degree. Compared however with the teachings of "Longinus" those efforts seem incomplete, tentative, and to some extent conventional; whereas "Longinus" as if by some stroke of genius has contrived to grasp the problem in its entirety, and has gone unerringly to the heart of the matter. Thus greatness of utterance, he points out, is rooted in personality. It is a fruit of the spirit, of the whole nature of man; and as such, it requires above all the play of the imagination as well as the exercise of genuine emotion, both of which are to be communicated to the hearer (or reader). "What comes from the heart goes to the heart"; this in reality is the basis on which he builds, and it represents perhaps the most valuable part of his teaching on style. In addition to this he considers the need for a knowledge of art to enable the speaker (or writer) to make a conscious and rational use of his powers. And here while retaining the old rhetorical terminology he breathes into the system a new life-giving spirit. Thus he deals with principles rather than with rules; and interpreting technique in terms of emotion he makes plain the "why" and the "wherefore" of each rhetorical device. The Figures, for instance, are to him no mechanical tricks but a natural means of appealing to human emotions; and as such, they require for their use a sense of fitness and psychological tact. This is the principle that runs through his teaching; and in this demand, together with the importance he attaches to the imaginative and emotional aspects of style, lay the substance of his message for his generation. That the instruction was what the age most needed can scarcely be doubted; and equally certain is it that its fundamental doctrines are those which no age can safely ignore.

So far then we have been considering the primary object of the work, and the skill shown by the author in handling his main theme. And this much may at once with confidence be said, that, were there nothing more to add concerning his achievement, our author's claim to eminence as a critic would still rank very high, on account of the originality and penetration shown in his analysis of the contemporary problem. As it is, however, there is much besides that commands attention.

Digressions, explanations, illustrations, and the like, incidentally supply further relevant passages in which fresh light is thrown on such matters as critical standards, critical methods and judgments. And as a consequence another aspect of the treatment may be said to emerge. The treatise, ostensibly on style, widens considerably in scope and becomes one on literary criticism in the larger sense of the term. Nothing, for instance, is of more lasting value than the remarks of our author on the standards for forming judgment in literature. It is a subject on which he has not a little to say; and such judgment he describes as an arduous business, indeed, "the crowning fruit of ripe experience". . . . [80] To some extent it would be true to say that his standard of taste is implied in what has already been said concerning "distinction" in style; so that for him the qualities of great utterance are likewise the qualities of great literature. Hence, as his first criterion of excellence in literature, he demands the presence of an imaginative and emotional appeal; the power, that is, of uplifting the soul of the reader and of filling him with joy and pride, by arousing in him noble thoughts and suggesting more than the words actually convey.[81] And here, it will be noticed, the test is no longer that of mere pleasure or persuasion; nor is the appeal made to the emotions or the intellect alone. The effects are such as concern the whole nature of man; and they are essentially of a bracing and tonic quality. Along with this test however he combines another of equal importance, that requiring in great literature a permanence of appeal. "In general", he states,[82] "you should regard that greatness in art to be noble and genuine which appeals to all men in all ages" . . . ; an anticipation of the later statement due to St Vincent (d. 304)[83] that the test of great literature was *quod semper, quod ubique, quod ab omnibus.* To this general statement of his, it is true, "Longinus" makes one qualification. By "all men" he means "men of sense, well acquainted with literature"; so that the tribunal he has in mind is neither the connoisseur nor the masses, but educated mankind in all the ages. For the rest, however, he insists on this test of time in positive fashion; and also gives reasons for the faith that is in him. When men, he argues, differing in all possible respects, in their interests, their ways of life, their tastes, ages and languages, all agree notwithstanding in the views they hold on any particular subject, then the unanimity of a tribunal otherwise so discordant is surely undeniable proof of the justice of their verdict and of the value to be attached to works thus commended.[84] And with the justice of this reasoning modern readers would readily agree; for to them the best practical test of what is literature and what is not is still this power of reading and re-reading a book with undiminished delight. The fact is that "Longinus" has here called attention to one of the basic truths of literature and literary criticism, namely, the inexhaustible vitality of all great art, and its power of communicating life right down through the ages. In all great literature there are latent correspondences with human nature which time alone can reveal; and it is by virtue of this fact that the test of time, this permanence of appeal, is on the whole the soundest criterion of what constitutes greatness in literature.

With the enunciation of these principles "Longinus" may be said in some measure to have broken new ground; and in what he has further to say on the formation of literary judgment there is also much that is of interest to modern readers. More than once, it is true, he reiterates his conception of posterity as the final arbiter in literary matters;[85] a tribunal, he adds, "whose judgments no jealousy can dispute".[86] But he has also something new to suggest when in his practical way he commends as touchstones the works of the great masters, and advises his readers in forming their judgments to consider how Homer or Plato or Demosthenes would have handled the theme.[87] For such an application in concrete form of the qualities of great literature there is much to be said. It is judgment by classical standards at its simplest and best; and the method has since been familiarised by Matthew Arnold, who in a well-known passage recommended for adoption much the same procedure.[88] Of greater importance, however, is our author's pronouncement on the value to be attached to "correctness" in estimating literary work, and the relative merits of a flawless mediocrity on the one hand, and of genuine greatness allied with some defects on the other. The question is one to which he devotes considerable attention; and the full significance of the discussion can only be appreciated in the light of contemporary conditions. That he was here debating an urgent question of the day seems highly probable, if we may judge from Caecilius's disparagement of Plato as compared with the faultless Lysias,[89] Dionysius's reply in one of his *Letters* to the remonstrances of Gnaeus Pompeius on the same subject,[90] or again the remarks subsequently made on the evils resulting from the craze for "correctness". By Quintilian,[91] the younger Pliny,[92] and others, references are made to this particular matter; and more especially to the crippling effects of over-niceness, the loss of sincerity, the dryness and tenuity produced by the excessive use of the file. And among the factors which contributed to the persistence of the doctrine there were the Atticists, preoccupied mainly with the avoidance of faults, and again, the coteries, engaged for the most part in the meticulous correction of the compositions of their friends.[93] So that there would seem to have been in existence throughout the first century a marked tendency to give the primacy in literature to the quality of "correctness". And although Horace had declared for a more indulgent attitude to faults where excellence was also present,[94] "Longinus" himself describes the matter as one that urgently called for a decision. . . . [95] In any case to this question he addresses himself with enthusiasm and zest, declaring without hesitation in favour of the work of genius, even though it be not flawless, as compared with work which, correct in all its details, never succeeds in rising to the loftiest heights. For one thing, he explains,[96] great flights of necessity involve great risks from which on the other hand pedestrian natures are free; so that soaring genius is often found to lose her way while moderate talent travels safely. Thus Homer, he points out, is occasionally found tripping; but is he for that reason inferior to Apollonius? Or is the neatness of Eratosthenes to be preferred to the inspiration of Archilochus, the lyric utterance of Bacchylides to that of Pindar, or the tragedies of Ion to those of Sophocles? In this impassioned way, with the help of rhetorical questions, does he excuse the lapses of genius. But he also does more than this when he advances definite reasons for his preference, explaining for instance that one touch of genius can redeem a multitude of faults, that unfailing accuracy savours somewhat of pettiness, that it is the fruit not of genius but of an observance of art, and that while such "correctness" is successful in escaping censure, it is greatness alone that compels admiration.[97] The real gist of his argument, however, consists in the claim he makes that grandeur in literature appeals irresistibly to man, in a way that mere "correctness" can never do. Thus in man, he explains,[98] there has been implanted a love for all that is great and more divine than himself. Even the universe itself cannot limit his thoughts which tend to range freely beyond the bounds of space. And this is why mankind is drawn to what is vast or great or beautiful in Nature, to the great waters of the Nile, the Danube or the Rhine, to the lightning flash of heaven or the fierce fires of Etna; even though in smaller streams and in flames of man's own kindling there is much that is good and of service to the race. Such objects however are wont to be regarded as commonplace, admiration being reserved for the greater phenomena of Nature. And so, argues "Longinus", it is with literature. It is loftiness and grandeur that carry men away, and supply (to use Bacon's phrase)[99] that "more ample greatness" which affords satisfaction to something that lies deep in their nature. "Correctness" in a writer may indeed be described as a human virtue; but grandeur alone, adds "Longinus", can give to him something of the magnanimity of God. . . . [100]

Possessed of such views regarding the standards of literary judgments, it is not strange to find that "Longinus" in practice has also some illuminating comments to make on literature in the concrete; comments interesting, moreover, on account of the methods employed as well as for the light they throw on the writers concerned. His range in these matters is that of Greek literature, from Homer to the Alexandrians; and while he includes in his survey Greek poets and dramatists, orators and historians, he has also something to say on Cicero and Hebrew literature. What he has to offer in this kind, it is true, has certain obvious limitations. From the nature of his work his critical judgments are nearly all incidental in character, illustrative directly or indirectly of "distinction" in style; and they are therefore for the most part casual appreciations of certain aspects of the writers in question, not considered estimates of their performances as wholes. Yet within these limits his critical judgments are of outstanding quality. There had been nothing like them hitherto in the work of antiquity; and by their insight and penetration they succeed in bringing to light not a few of the finer literary qualities.

Nothing in the first place is more remarkable than the way in which he makes use of aesthetic tests in forming his judgments; as when for instance he brings to light the imaginative qualities of Homer, Sappho, and others. Of the workings of the poetic imagination—for this in modern parlance is what is implied in "grandeur of conception", the term used by "Longinus"—he gives numerous examples. Thus he quotes freely from Homer, supplying illustrations of the immensity of his ideas, his power of creating extra-natural worlds, or strange and exalted types of being, and of giving to these imaginary creations the force of reality. Typical Homeric passages to which he calls attention are those relating to the world-embracing stride of the steeds of Hera,[101] the cosmic nature of the upheaval occasioned by the battle of the gods,[102] the transcendent image of Poseidon under whose footsteps mountains and forests tremble,[103] or again the divine heroism of Ajax praying for light, not safety, in the darkness of defeat.[104] And as if these were not sufficient to make his point clear, he adds yet one other example, this time from the book of *Genesis;* the tremendous utterance of the Creator at the beginning of things: "Let there be light, and there was light".[105] In each case it is the overwhelming imaginative appeal to which he calls the attention: while at the same time he does not fail to suggest the exhilarating emotional effects of such passages, which are said to be awe-inspiring in their grandeur, their beauty or terror. But similar imaginative effects are also said to result from the poet's treatment of the phenomena of life, when he selects only the most significant details, and by combining them into an organic whole, contrives to suggest a new and comprehensive vision of things. Here again the creative imagination is at work as the "realising" faculty, modifying, transforming, and producing awe-inspiring effects; and this is illustrated by "Longinus" first from Homer, and then from Sappho. In the first instance he quotes Homer's description of a storm, pointing out that a selection had been made of the most terrifying circumstances: the swift onrush of the waves lifted high and swollen by the tempest, the black overhanging clouds, the mad seas breaking and shrouding the ship in foam, the winds howling in the sails, and the sailors terror-stricken, conscious of the near approach of death.[106] And in the second place he gives Sappho's *Ode to Anactoria,*[107] possibly though not certainly in full, at the same time commenting on the choice of the most striking symptoms of the love passion, vehement, contradictory, and realistic, as "she glows, she chills, she raves, she reasons, now she is in tumult, now she is dying away". By way of further comment "Longinus" explains that in all things there exist by nature certain elements which constitute the essence of their being; and that it is by a happy organic combination of those elements that power and grandeur in literature are attained. To neither of these processes, it is true, does "Longinus" anywhere apply the term "imaginative"; though imagination [*fantasia*] in general he describes as concepts of the mind, significantly adding that in his day it was usually applied to vivid and realistic representations of things, resulting from strong emotion or passion.[108] Yet no one can mistake his realisation of the workings of those "shaping fantasies" which, apprehending more than comes within the scope of cold reason, are yet able to give to "airy nothings" a seeming substance of reality; or again the effects of that synthesis of significant elements abstracted from life itself. Terminology and definition it was left for a modern age to elaborate; but the creative imagination was already active in Homer, Sappho, and the rest, and "Longinus" is the first to grasp the importance of that fact.

Less striking, though by no means devoid of interest, are his observations on the *Odyssey* which he discusses in its relation to the *Iliad,* to the disadvantage of the former. That he takes for granted the Homeric authorship of both poems is in itself significant; he at any rate is no separatist, whatever may have been the prevailing notion at the time. Between the two poems however he finds certain marked differences.[109] Whereas the *Iliad* is said to be full of dramatic action and conflict, treated with energy and a never-failing greatness, and in a style impassioned, supple, and packed with images drawn from actual life, the *Odyssey* on the other hand is described as lacking in most of these qualities, consisting in the main of narrative from which much of the intensity had vanished, with numerous character sketches, and a host of foolish fables of the most trifling kind. Some of these broad differences had already been noted by Aristotle; as was also the suggestion that the *Odyssey,* as distinct from the *Iliad,* had elements in its composition that were akin to comedy. But in commenting on these differences "Longinus" has now a new theory to offer; namely, that the *Odyssey* was of later composition than the *Iliad* and that it was a product of Homer's genius when his powers were in decline. In support of this theory he reminds his readers that in the *Odyssey* the poet is concerned with episodes that were, so to speak, fragments left over from his treatment of the Trojan war in the *Iliad;* and that, moreover, in the *Odyssey* the poet seems to be completing his earlier story by a moving tribute to heroes previously celebrated. At the same time, the arguments on which he relies are mainly aesthetic in kind. They are, the loss of the earlier fire, the increase of characterisation, and the growing fondness for story-telling even of the most incredible kind. And all alike he regards as evidence of advancing years; though he is careful to add that in speaking of old age it is the old age of Homer that he is considering. With the majority of these inferences, however, readers of to-day would find some difficulty in agreeing. It might indeed be conceded that the less vigorous and intense manner of the *Odyssey* in some measure lends colour to the theory; but that character-drawing or the indulgence in fabling was a sign of waning powers would be, and indeed has been, stoutly denied. It is true that Aristotle had held characterisation to be of but secondary importance; and since character-drawing had figured in the New Comedy as a comparatively late development, these considerations may have led "Longinus" to regard this feature as a mark of decline, and, by a false analogy, a decline associated with the later stages of a poet's development. And similarly with the view he takes of the marvellous tales, that they were trifles, not concerned with the serious business of life, and therefore a sign of decadence; this also might be described as a representative view of antiquity. Yet in the light of later experience neither of these points can be seriously maintained. And indeed "Longinus" himself, in spite of his cavils, betrays his sense of the essential greatness of the *Odyssey;* its grandeur is said to be that of the setting sun, the fanciful fables are dreams, but the dreams of Zeus. The truth would therefore seem to be either that "Longinus" is here not greatly in advance of his age, or that he is indulging in a piece of special pleading. In any case his contention is not established, at least on the grounds adduced; though the discussion has incidentally this further interest of its own. As an attempt to view poetry in relation to its author it may be said to mark an advance in critical method; while it also affords an early if imperfect instance of that historical criticism which by means of an imaginative sympathy with the literature of the past was to yield valuable results in later ages.

More characteristic of "Longinus's" treatment and more successful in its results, however, was his use of the comparative method of criticism; of which indeed the foregoing discussion was in a sense an illustration. It was a method in which he had been anticipated by Cicero, Dionysius of Halicarnassus, and others; but by no one was it turned to better account or employed with a fuller sense of its various possibilities. Of his reference to Hebrew literature something has already been said. It was an attempt to reinforce his argument by means of a wider outlook suggesting the universal nature of the phenomenon he was discussing; and the passage which takes cognisance of a literature outside the Graeco-Roman tradition, has since been hailed as the beginning of the comparative study of literature. More commonly, however, his purpose in employing the method is to bring out by means of contrast the salient characteristics of this or that writer; though in some instances he aims also at deciding their respective values, owing possibly to the controversies which persisted concerning the merits of such writers as Demosthenes and Plato. At any rate there can be no doubt about the efficacy of the method in his hands, whether he is dealing with orators of different countries, orators belonging to one and the same age, or with poets of the classical and post-classical eras. In each case he contrives to throw into relief some particular quality or qualities with a clearness and a force that no unaided comment could have done. And this is seen for instance in his comparison of Demosthenes and Cicero. By this time Demosthenes's grandeur of utterance had become to some extent a commonplace of criticism; but "Longinus" refines on that estimate by calling attention to the different effects of the eloquence of Cicero and Demosthenes. Both writers are described as "consuming fires"; but whereas Cicero succeeds by the profusion, the sustained and cumulative character of his efforts, Demosthenes on the other hand is said to excel in vehemence, swiftness, and intensity. The one is likened to an ever-windening conflagration devouring everything in its path and growing by what it feeds on; the other to a thunderbolt or lightning flash, sudden and irresistible.[110] "One could sooner face with unflinching eyes a descending thunderbolt", adds "Longinus" elsewhere, "than meet with steady gaze his bursts of passion in their swift succession."[111] Then, too, there is the comparison drawn between Demosthenes and Hyperides which is instrumental in bringing out other aspects of Demosthenes's genius, more particularly his limitations.[112] Thus Hyperides is said to be endowed with all the graces; he is capable of simplicity, elegance, and wit, he has variety and charm, and he touches all the stops save those of the highest emotional quality. In comparison, Demosthenes is held to be wanting in most of these qualities; his tone never varies, he is always on the heights; he lacks ease and charm, while his attempts at a lighter vein are apt to result in the ludicrous. Yet in the highest reaches he is said to be unapproachable; and by virtue of this quality, as opposed to mere versatility, he is declared to be the supreme orator. Or again, there is the comparative estimate formed of classical Greek and Alexandrian poets,[113] which brings to light unmistakably the essential points of difference between the two schools. Thus the flawless elegance of such Alexandrian poets as Apollonius and Eratosthenes is contrasted with the more exalted but less "correct" utterances of Homer and Sophocles. And the point is emphasised elsewhere when in a comparison of parallel passages, both descriptions of a storm, taken from Homer and Aratus, Homer's naturalness is contrasted with the artificiality of Aratus, who, according to "Longinus", succeeds in being neat and trivial instead of impressive.[114]

These then were some of the judgments passed by "Longinus" on earlier literature; and among them was included much that was memorable in his achievement in this field. At the same time there were in his work other pronouncements on many of the great writers; and of these his remarks on Plato are not the least interesting, being doubtless an echo of that controversy already mentioned, in which Caecilius, Dionysius, and Gnaeus Pompeius had each played a part. Hence the unusual vigour of "Longinus's" reply to Caecilius whom he charges with gross prejudice and critical blindness, adding that Caecilius was animated with a hatred for Plato even greater than his love for Lysias.[115] And in the same downright fashion he submits his own view that Plato was altogether superior to Lysias, whether merits or faults were the criterion. That he indulged in cheap effects occasionally, that he sometimes fell into excess in figurative writing, making use of harsh metaphors and an inflated style;[116] these things are conceded by "Longinus". But for the rest, he stoutly maintains the overwhelming distinction of Plato's style, the stately dignity of his movement, less fiery and vehement than that of Demosthenes, yet with the noiseless grandeur of a vast sea,[117] his Homeric reminiscences,[118] the tuneful harmonics of his periphrases;[119] in short, he is one of the great masters recommended by "Longinus" as touchstones for forming judgments as to literary value. In addition, scattered throughout his work are comments on writers such as Herodotus, Xenophon, Timaeus, and Theopompus, most of whom are quoted to illustrate some lapse of taste. And more significant still are the appreciations of Greek dramatists, which while probably representing the established judgments of antiquity, are valuable also as indicating "Longinus's" own preferences and tastes. Thus Aeschylus is praised for his magnificence, but is censured for occasional bombast and turgidity.[120] Sophocles is ranked among the greatest by virtue of his *Oedipus Rex;*[121] though the extant plays do not support the censure of faultiness implied by "Longinus" when he compares him with Ion.[122] And again, Euripides is commended for his artistry rather than his ideas; his use of compelling images, the tragic nature of his vivid descriptions, and his supreme skill in scenes of madness and love, are all duly noted.[123]

From what has now been said of "Longinus's" literary judgments something may be gathered of his work as a judicial critic, his standards, his methods, the range and quality of his pronouncements. That he approached his task unhampered by rules and with a mind disinterested and free from prejudice, this much at least will be readily conceded. Nor can it be denied that his estimates are singularly just. They coincide in a great measure with the considered verdicts of posterity; and where necessary he is not sparing in his censures, the weakness as well as the strength of the greatest being brought to light. Everywhere, in short, he shows a keen eye for essentials; he discriminates clearly between fine shades and effects; and his verdicts are always free from dogmatism and pedantry. Yet more important than all this are those judgments that aim not at assessing, but at interpreting, literary values; those appreciations of his that enlighten and stimulate, and enable us to read with quickened intelligence. Of these the illuminating commentary on Homer provides perhaps the best example. It is the chapter (c. IX) described by Gibbon as "one of the finest monuments of antiquity"; and in it "Longinus" not only lays bare his own spiritual experiences, the appeal made by Homer to his imagination and emotions, but he does so in such a way and with such enthusiasm that he succeeds in communicating his feelings to his readers. This is none other than criticism of the highest kind; "the praise, the infectious praise, of the greatest literature", according to the modern formula. From mere impressionism it differs in that it is based on sound psychological grounds; it is the fruit of conscious analysis and a delicate imaginative sympathy with this or that piece of art. And in this form of criticism "Longinus" was something of a pioneer; for although Dionysius before him had entered the same field his efforts were mainly confined to technical points. There are, in short, many respects in which "Longinus" stands high as a judicial critic; and not least is the fact that he takes account of three separate literatures. Yet more significant still is his anticipation of modern criticism, in those interpretations of his which lead to a more intimate understanding of ancient art, and reveal in the clearest light his appreciation of the essence of literature.

Such then in their main details are the contents of this work ***On the Sublime***—the dissertation on style, and the literary appreciations with which the essay is illuminated—and it now remains to attempt some estimate of the contribution as a whole, as well as of the place it occupies in the critical development. Of "Longinus's" indebtedness to his predecessors in the first place there can be no question. Many of his remarks are of the nature of commonplaces familiar to his contemporaries; while other suggestions or ideas are occasionally drawn from earlier writers. Thus the conception of literary criticism as "the crowning fruit of ripe experience" was already present in the *Grammar* of Dionysius Thrax, where it figures as the final and noblest function of the grammatical discipline; and the notion almost certainly was common property at the time. The *quod semper* principle, again, the danger in avoiding one fault of falling into another, the limitations of mere "correctness", and the fact that Homer occasionally nodded: all these were ideas familiar to Horace and probably to others, and in one form or another were utilised by "Longinus". Then, too, the secrets of verbal felicity had to some extent been explored by Horace and Dionysius of Halicarnassus; from Caecilius it is not improbable that he drew his reference to *Genesis,* as well as the idea of his comparison between Demosthenes and Cicero; while to Tacitus, or to Tacitus's sources, he may also have been indebted for some of his views as to the causes of the decline of contemporary style. All this and more may freely be granted; and yet nothing emerges more clearly than the originality of his treatment, the new outlook he affords on literary questions, and the permanent and universal value of many of his utterances.

In some measure these facts have already been suggested: in his new sense of literary values, the fresh life he breathes into rhetorical discussions, the importance he attaches to such things as the imagination, the emotions, the beauty of words, and not least, the aesthetic appreciation of literature. But over and above all these are other suggestions on literature in general, which not only represented something new at the time but are also full of meaning for later ages. Highly significant for one thing is his attitude to style, and the nature of the remedy he proposes for the contemporary chaos and licence. Faced with the same problem, Quintilian, as we shall see, was recommending a return to a sort of modified classicism; whereas Tacitus, alive to new influences at work, which possibly demanded some modification of earlier standards, was for developing the latent possibilities of the prevailing discord in style, while discarding its obvious abuses. With neither of these prescriptions, however, is "Longinus" wholly satisfied. The orthodox Ciceronianism he possibly regarded as limited and mechanical; while Tacitus's tentative proposals for the recognition of new methods may have seemed to him vague and even dangerous. At all events what he advocates is a return to the standards, and above all the spirit, of the classical Greeks; his governing doctrine being that despite all changes in political and social life there exist certain unchanging principles of all good writing, principles that are best revealed by an interpretation of the spirit of the ancient masterpieces. To his contemporaries this teaching should have come as a reminder of the true essence of classicism, a doctrine that was positive, well founded, and of universal application. And since his principles are firmly rooted in human nature, they are not without their significance for later ages.

Equally original and suggestive, however, are his views regarding literature in the wider sense of the term; for here again he stands alone in the keenness of his vision, his penetrating insight into the nature and function of the literary art. That he conceived it to be no mere craft but a thing of the spirit is shown throughout by the character of his treatment. Thus to him a poet was great, not by reason of his technique, but in virtue of his imagination, his gift of feeling, and his power of conveying those qualities to others. And this conception, which is essentially modern, had not hitherto been formulated by any critic. Then, too, from the same standpoint he asserts that the ultimate causes of decline in literature are of a spiritual kind; the loss of the sense of the ideal and visionary, and the consequent deadening of man's immortal part. Others before him had referred to the growing materialism of the age; but "Longinus's" statement is couched in more specific terms and in accordance with his animating theory. Great literature and little minds, he seems to say, go ill together. And in many other ways does he foster the same outlook in literature, by directing attention from the technical to the more elusive side of art. Thus he hints in more than one place that formal rules may be disregarded at the bidding of a higher law: an important aesthetic truth which was to be rediscovered by modern critics. Elsewhere he points out the inevitable and organic relation existing between thought and expression;[124] or again, the atmosphere of infinite suggestion bound up with all great literature;[125] while he also establishes once for all the survival value attached to great art. Nor is he less suggestive in his remarks on the function of literature. Of the earlier didactic conception he gives not a hint; and what is perhaps more surprising, he disregards entirely the stock theories of "pleasure" and "persuasion". What he sees in literature is a great aesthetic force, appealing irresistibly to the whole nature of man, uplifting, bracing, and stimulating, while nourishing something that lies deep in his nature. With Aristotle he perceives that literature works mainly through the emotions, and that its process in effect is one of a cathartic kind—though he nowhere alludes to that theory. But in addition he also brings to light something not covered by Aristotelian theory; the wider view attained by means of the imagination, the more comprehensive and more stimulating catharsis which embraced the whole of the higher nature of man. And in this larger conception of the aesthetic function he approaches more nearly to modern ideas than did any of his predecessors.

It therefore becomes clear that in "Longinus" we have a great original critic, one who, propounding the truths of art as he sees them, succeeds in opening men's eyes to new aspects of literature. Nor is his manner any less original than his matter; for in his subjectivity, his enthusiasm, his lively and personal style, may be noted features which for the most part were wanting in earlier critical work. It is not too much to say, paradoxical as it may sound, that from no other of the ancient critical writings does the author emerge more clearly than from this work, the authorship of which is unknown. And this is partly the result of the sincerity and ardour of the thought, the generosity of the judgments, and the modesty with which the author puts forward his opinions. Of his acute sensibilities and his catholic taste something has already been said; but along with these there went also a certain directness of vision and an instinct for seeking first principles in his various discussions. That he is not altogether exempt from laboured refinements may be conceded; while in one place he seems to give countenance to the allegorical interpretation of Homer.[126] Nevertheless in the work as a whole there is surprisingly little dead matter; on the other hand much that is vital, expressed in memorable fashion. Nor is his style an unworthy medium of his thought, lacking though it may be in Attic purity of speech. Reminiscent in some ways of Plato's manner, and rich with metaphors, compounds, and poetical expressions, it has at the same time a peculiar intensity of its own; and this was due partly to striking epigrams and picturesque similes, partly also to long periods brought in each instance to a triumphant close.

As for the place he occupies in the critical development this much at least is obvious, that in an age of confused standards he advocated in unique fashion a return to the ideals of Greek classical art. The doctrine as such was no new thing: it had been put forward by Cicero, Horace, Dionysius and others. But whereas their teaching had been partial, with technical and formal tendencies, a classicism in short which was to become still narrower in later ages, "Longinus" alone succeeded in recapturing the spirit of the ancient art, and in laying bare by his analysis the unchanging principles of that art. This, when all is said, must be regarded as his great achievement, that with a clearer perception of the influence of changing conditions than his predecessors had possessed, he still maintained the permanent validity of those principles where literature was concerned. It is therefore as an exponent of the genuine classical spirit that he is perhaps best described; and not, as he has been called, the first romantic critic.[127] Throughout his discussion, it has been noted, he is concerned mainly with ancient Greek models, while his theory is solely based on the conception of art as the product of principles deduced from the practice of the past. Nor is this reverence for tradition the only classical element in his constitution. He is classical also in the balance he maintains between genius and unimpassioned hard work, in his sense of the need for fitness, selection, and a fine adjustment of means to ends; while in addition, a "romantic" critic would not have been blind to the "romance" in the *Odyssey.* So that it is as one of the last of classical critics that he figures primarily in ancient critical history. But while this is true, it is true also that he anticipates much that is modern in critical work. And this is shown by his concern with the essence rather than with the form of literature, his understanding of the part played by the imagination and the feelings in creative work, his efforts at literary interpretation and appreciation, his widening outlook and the variety of his judicial methods; features which were to reappear only after the lapse of centuries. The fact is that in him were combined faculties that were characteristic of the greatest of his predecessors. Like Aristotle, for instance, he based his theories on existing Greek literature; he likewise aimed at a rational explanation of literary phenomena; and his methods of theorising are analytic, inductive, psychological, and historical. On the other hand, he is spiritually the antithesis of Aristotle; for nothing could be farther removed from the cold intellectualism of Aristotle than the impassioned and suggestive teaching of "Longinus". And in this respect he is reminiscent of Plato, for whom he betrays everywhere the warmest admiration. Platonic affinities, in short, are seen in his use of the imaginative reason as well as in his idealism and enthusiasms; and these are among the things that make the work what it is, one of the great masterpieces. Hence his claim to rank with the greatest of ancient critics, whose work he may be said to have supplemented to a marked degree. In one respect indeed he may be fairly regarded as unique; in the quality of his criticism both theoretical and applied. And for the rest he must be numbered among the seminal minds of all time. Conspicuous for his suggestiveness and for the number of aesthetic truths he revealed or made familiar, he stands as a reminder of some of the essentials of literature, and as a lasting and stimulating force in the field of literary taste.

Of the subsequent history of the work there is this to be said, that its influence, despite its value, was comparatively slight. Rediscovered at the Renascence, it remained for a century or more a close preserve of scholars,[128] until Boileau's popular translation of 1674 introduced it to a wider sphere and led to its recognition as a work of the first importance, worthy of being ranked in the contemporary estimate with the works of Aristotle, Horace, and Quintilian. After this the treatise was edited and translated with increasing frequency throughout the eighteenth century; and both in England and abroad it became familiar to men of letters. Yet even so, its true significance was far from being realised; owing partly to the looseness of Boileau's translation, partly also to its unfamiliar style and the many difficulties of interpretation presented by the text. Some acquaintance with the work was shown by most English critics from Dryden onwards; Dennis, derisively dubbed "Sir Longinus", being regarded as its chief exponent. But its influence was nevertheless limited to minor, if not negligible, points. It gave for instance a new impetus to the attack on those "ultra-Crepidarians", who deemed criticism to consist in the mere detection of faults; and in this way it strengthened the hands of those who held that the true critic was concerned with beauties rather than with defects. It also led to fresh emphasis being laid on emotion as the basis of poetry, and on the aesthetic values of charm and power as opposed to regularity and "correctness". These things, along with the new critical terms "bathos" and "the sublime", were practically the sole results of acquaintance with the ancient masterpiece; and it is not without its significance that both additions to critical terminology were based on misunderstandings. Whatever "Longinus" may have meant by the terms he originally employed it was certainly not the meanings read into them by Pope, Burke, and others. With him the word [*bathos*],[129] for instance, did not stand for a ludicrous descent from the sublime to the commonplace; nor did [*hypos*] carry with it the suggestion of obscurity and infinity. Such then was the limited appreciation accorded to "Longinus" at the height of his popularity in the eighteenth century; and it is only within the last generation or so that his real merits have received anything like due recognition. Nowadays the supreme qualities of the work are no longer in question. Ranking in antiquity with the greatest critical achievements, it "remains towering among all other works of its class"; and for sheer originality and power it has not been surpassed. The story of its fortunes, it must be confessed, is one of the most curious; there are but few instances in literary history of merit being so long and so persistently ignored. And this has been facilitated perhaps by the tendency to view the treatise in isolation; a work, as it has been described, "abiding alone in thought and history". Yet its true meaning would seem to emerge only when viewed against its historical background; and in that same setting its manifold excellences are also most clearly seen. There are things in its pages that can never grow old; while its freshness and light will continue to charm all ages. All beautiful things, it has been said, belong to the same age; and the work of "Longinus" is in a sense contemporaneous with that of Plato and Aristotle and Coleridge.

Notes

[1] *Text and Translation: Longinus, On the Sublime,* by W. Rhys Roberts, Cambridge, 1899; by W. Hamilton Fyfe (Loeb Cl. Lib.), 1927.

Translation: by H. L. Havell, London, 1890; extracts in Saintsbury, *Loci Critici,* pp. 41-53, London, 1903; also in J. D. Denniston, *Greek Literary Criticism,* pp. 165-95, London, 1924.

[2] For a full discussion of the MSS, and authorship see W. Rhys Roberts, *Longinus, On the Sublime,* Intro. pp. 3ff.

[3] c. 39, *ad init.*

[4] See W. Rhys Roberts, *op. cit.* pp. 245-6.

[5] c. 39, 1.

[6] E. Gibbon, *Journal* (Sept. 11, 1762).

[7] c. 1, 1.

[8] c. 3, 5.

[9] c. 15, 8.

[10] c. 5, 1.

[11] cc. 3-4.

[12] c. 44.

[13] c. 44, 10, *passim.* See also pp. 183, 193 *supra.*

[14] See W. Rhys Roberts, *op. cit.* p. 17.

[15] c. 1, 1.

[16] c. 8, 1.

[17] c. 32, 1.

[18] c. 32, 8.

[19] It is not without its interest to note that both Wordsworth and De Quincey were clear as to the true significance of the treatise. Thus Wordsworth is surprised that its theme should ever have been mistaken. . .

[20] c. 3, 1-3.

[21] c. 3, 4.

[22] c. 3, 5.

[23] c. 4.

[24] c. 41.

[25] c. 42.

[26] c. 43.

[27] c. 3, 3.

[28] c. 5, 1.

[29] c. 1, 3.

[30] c. 1, 4.

[31] *Ibid.*

[32] c. 2.

[33] c. 2, 1.

[34] Seneca, *Suas.* 111, 7.

[35] c. 2, 2.

[36] See p. 263 *infra.*

[37] c. 2, 2.

[38] c. 9, 2.

[39] c. 13, 2.

[40] c. 13, 2.

[41] See p. 112 *supra.*

[42] c. 13, 1. Dryden interpreted this passage correctly in his *Preface to Troilus and Cressida* when he stated that "those great men whom we propose to ourselves as patterns of our imitation, serve us as a torch, which is lifted up before us, to enlighten our passage and often elevate our thoughts as high as the conception we have of our author's genius" (Ker, *Essays of Dryden,* 1, 206).

[43] c. 10.

[44] cc. 11-12.

[45] c. 15.

[46] c. 39, *ad init.*

[47] See p. 229 *infra.*

[48] c. 17.

[49] c. 17, 1.

[50] c. 18.

[51] c. 19, 1.

[52] c. 20, 1.

[53] c. 21, 2.

[54] c. 22, 1.

[55] c. 22, 4 (tr. W. R. R.).

[56] c. 22, 1.

[57] c. 16.

[58] c. 23, 2.

[59] c. 24, 1.

[60] c. 25.

[61] c. 28.

[62] c. 29.

[63] c. 16, 3.

[64] c. 23, 4.

[65] c. 16, 4.

[66] c. 18, 2.

[67] c. 30, 1.

[68] c. 30, 2.

[69] c. 31, 1.

[70] c. 32, 1.

[71] c. 38.

[72] c. 39, 1 ff.

[73] c. 41.

[74] *Ibid.*

[75] See p. 188 *supra.*

[76] c. 42.

[77] c. 44, 2.

[78] c. 44, 5.

[79] c. 44, 6-8.

[80] c. 6.

[81] c. 7, 2-3.

[82] c. 7, 4.

[83] See Sikes, *Greek View of Poetry,* p. 237.

[84] c. 7, 4.

[85] c. 14, 3.

[86] c. 36, 2.

[87] c. 14, 1.

[88] *Essays in Criticism* (Second Series), p. 16.

[89] c. 32, 8.

[90] See pp. 110, 124 *supra.*

[91] *Inst. Orat.* VIII, Pr. 23 ff.

[92] *Letters, passim.*

[93] See A. Guillemin, "Sociétés de gens de lettres all temps de Pline" (*Rev. d'Études latines,* 1927, vol. V, pp. 261-92).

[94] See p. 90 *supra.*

[95] c. 33, 1.

[96] c. 33.

[97] cc. 33, 35, *passim.*

[98] c. 35.

[99] *Advancement of Learning,* ed. W. Aldis Wright, p. 101.

[100] c. 36, 1.

[101] c. 9, 5.

[102] c. 9, 6.

[103] c. 9, 8.

[104] c. 9, 10.

[105] c. 9, 9.

[106] c. 10, 5.

[107] c. 10, 2.

[108] c. 15, 1.

[109] c. 9, 11 ff.

[110] c. 12, 4-5.

[111] c. 34, 4 (tr. W. R. R.).

[112] c. 34.

[113] c. 33, 4-5.

[114] c. 10, 6.

[115] c. 32, 8.

[116] c. 32, 7.

[117] c. 12, 3.

[118] c. 13, 3.

[119] c. 28, 1.

[120] c. 3, 1.

[121] c. 33, 5.

[122] Cf. Demetrius, *On Style,* [sect.] 114, where a Sophoclean line is quoted to illustrate "frigidity" and magniloquence; also Plutarch's *How to study Poetry* (*de aud. poet.*), 45, II, where Sophocles is charged with unevenness. . . . Such censures were commonplaces of Graeco-Roman criticism and were possibly due to occasional lapses from his usual dignity arising out of his attempts at parodying Aeschylus (see W. Rhys Roberts, *Class. Rev.* vol. XL, p. 115).

[123] cc. 15, 40.

[124] c. 30, 1.

[125] c. 7, 3.

[126] c. 9, 7.

[127] See R. A. Scott-James, *The Making of Literature,* c. VIII.

[128] See W. Rhys Roberts, *Longinus on the Sublime,* pp. 247 ff., and A. Rosenberg, *Longinus in England bis zum Ende des* 18 *Jahrhunderts,* Berl. Diss. 1917.

[129] c. 2, 1; see E. D. T. Jenkins, *Class. Rev.* XLV (1930), p. 174 for a discussion of this term.

Samuel H. Monk (essay date 1935)

SOURCE: "Longinus and the Longinian Tradition in England," in *The Sublime: A Study of Critical Theories in XVIII-Century England,* The University of Michigan Press, 1960, pp. 10-28.

[*In this essay, originally written in 1935, Monk discusses the rhetorical style and aesthetic claims of* On the Sublime *and briefly discusses its influence on the writings of eighteenth-century English authors.*]

Any historical discussion of the sublime must take into account the fountain-head of all ideas on that subject—the pseudo-Longinian treatise, ***Peri Hupsous,*** known for over two centuries as Longinus, ***On the Sublime.*** In a sense, the study of the eighteenth-century sublime is the study of the Longinian tradition in England, although, as may be supposed, the student will be led far away from the Greek critic's views. Only by stretching the meaning of the term out of all conscience can Longinus's treatise be considered an essay on æsthetic, but it is none the less true that it was in ***On the Sublime*** that the eighteenth century found ideas that motivated many of its children, important and unimportant, to attempt an analysis of the sources and the effects of sublimity, and it was out of the interest in this analysis that there began to emerge, early in the century, a concept that was truly, if rudimentarily, æsthetic. Therefore, it becomes of some importance to look again at the treatise, and if possible to see it as the eighteenth century habitually saw it. We shall never entirely escape its influence as we progress through the century, for certain ideas implicit in it become fundamental in eighteenth-century theories and criticism, and the tendency of the writer of the period to seek support from the ancients will keep the name of Longinus alive until well after 1800.

Since this is true, a summary, however brief, of ***Peri Hupsous*** becomes necessary. The best edition and translation is that of Mr. W. Rhys Roberts, but to become familiar with the Longinian vocabulary of our period, it seems best to quote from the translation of William Smith, which appeared in 1739 and reached its fifth edition in 1800.[1] This was the standard translation during the period in which Longinus attained his greatest fame and influence.

Of course Longinus did not invent the rhetorical conception of the sublime style; it is older than his essay.[2] Although Aristotle did not draw a very clear distinction between the styles, his conception of language as pragmatic and dialectical or emotional implied styles suitable to each function. The idea that rhetoric is an instrument of emotional transport was dominant among the ancients, and the grand style, the purpose of which was to move, was an integral part of their rhetoric.

The three styles, familiar in the treatises on rhetoric of the sixteenth, seventeenth, and eighteenth centuries, did not make their appearance until Roman times. They arose out of the threefold definition of the function of oratory—*docere, conciliare, movere*—set forth in Cicero's *De Oratore* and *Orator*. Once Cicero had made this division, a style which was the *tertium quid* between the plain and the grand (the pragmatic and the emotional) inevitably came into being. The Ciceronian categories are *gravis* (*grandis, vehemens*), *medius*, and *subtilis* (*tenuis*), the great, the middle, and the plain. The important fact for us is that from its inception the grand style had as its purpose the awakening of emotion in the audience, for, as we shall see, this is the point of departure for the earliest eighteenth-century discussions of sublimity.

Other ancients wrote on the various styles. Demetrius finds that there are four sorts of style—the plain, the elevated, the elegant, and the forcible. The elevated is ornate, and is therefore diametrically opposed to the plain, with which it can never be united. Three ingredients, thought, diction, and appropriate composition, go to make up elevation.[3] Dionysius of Halicarnassus uses the more customary tripartite division into the austere, the smooth (or florid), and the harmoniously blended. Of the austere, which corresponds to the great style, he says that it is rugged, and even frequently harsh. It uses stately rhythms and long words in order to effect its end, which is "to suggest nature rather than art, and to stir emotion rather than to reflect character."[4] These ideas might have been developed to interesting conclusions, but Dionyslus is intent on discussing the best order of words, and therefore rests content with a brief treatment of the grand style. Quintilian, in the third chapter of his eighth book, while discussing ornament (the principal element in the grand style) definitely connects the idea of sublimity with the ornate and the pathetic.[5]

It is evident that Longinus is well within the tradition of ancient rhetoric when he treats the sublime style as emotive in purpose and as capable of being expressed both in ornamental and in simple language. The subject that he wrote on was an old question in rhetoric, and he might easily have repeated the old formulæ and illustrated the old figures that were conventionally regarded as being conductive to sublimity; he might have done this and no more. But he was at the same time rhetorician and critic, and as a critic he saw more deeply into the nature of art than did most of his fellows. His critical intuitions found their way into his treatise, where they lay dormant until they became in a later age and among a modern race, an influence in criticism and æsthetic theory.

Nevertheless, his treatment of the subject is primarily rhetorical; the essay is a discussion of style, and only incidentally does Longinus allow his deeper perceptions to find expression. He states that his intention is to show how the sublime in writing and in discourse (i.e., in literature and in oratory) may be attained, and in so doing it is natural and proper that he should devote much space to an analysis of the various figures of speech which were so important in ancient rhetoric. Fortunately, much of what he says on this subject need not delay us, for, however interested the eighteenth century may have been in rhetoric, it had nothing new to offer on the subject. The numerous treatises on oratory and rhetoric are almost without exception no more than summaries of Cicero, with Longinus and Quintilian thrown in, the whole perhaps plagiarized from the work of some Frenchman. With this static rhetoric we are in no way concerned. The abiding interest of Longinus for the eighteenth century, and consequently for us, lay in his conception of the sublime that underlies sublimity of style and that is an expression of a quality of mind and of experience. To write on the sublime style is to write on rhetoric; to write on sublimity is to write on æsthetic. The sublime style is a means to an end; sublimity is an end in itself. It is the latent æsthetic aspect of ***Peri Hupsous*** that was Longinus's contribution to eighteenth-century thought, and it is with that aspect that this chapter deals.

The author begins by stating that "the *Sublime* is a certain eminence or perfection of language,"[6] but he hastens to described the effect of the sublime, which "not only persuades, but even throws an audience into transport. . . . In most cases it is wholly in our power, either to resist or yield to persuasion. But the *Sublime,* endued with strength irresistible, strikes home, and triumphs over every hearer."[7] The test of the sublime is in its effect. "For the mind is naturally elevated by the true *Sublime* and so sensibly affected with its lively strokes, that it swells in transport and an inward pride, as if what was only heard had been the product of its own invention."[8] This idea is important because it emphasizes the relation between the sublime and emotion; it transcends the realm of rhetoric and begins that analysis of the effect of sublime objects on the mind which is to lead later to an æsthetic concept of sublimity.

Energy enters into the Longinian sublime. "*That* . . . is grand and lofty,[9] which the more we consider, the greater ideas we conceive of it; *whose* force we cannot possibly withstand; *which* immediately sinks deep, and makes such impressions on the mind as cannot be easily worn out or effaced." There follows a statement which must have been welcome to the neo-classicists, for it brought the sublime into close relationship with their own theory of art: "In a word, you may pronounce *that* sublime, beautiful and genuine, which always pleases, and takes equally with all sorts of men."[10] Here is the *quod ubique, quod semper* of classical and neo-classical art.

Assuming that a natural ability to speak well must be a source of all sublime writing and discourse, Longinus enumerates five qualities that go to the creation of the sublime.

> The *first* and most excellent of these is a boldness and grandeur in the *Thoughts*. . . . The *second* is call'd the *Pathetic*, or the power of raising the passions to a violent and even enthusiastic degree; and these two being genuine constituents of the *Sublime*, are the gifts of nature, whereas the other sorts depend in some measure upon art.[11]

These are the gift of nature, and cannot be attained through the technique of rhetoric. And it was on these two sources that the eighteenth century was to fix its attention. The emphasis on great thought led Longinus and his followers into a consideration of the mind that creates a work of art; the emphasis on emotion, in the hands of English critics, developed into a study of the effect of a work on the perceiving mind.

The three remaining sources—"*Figures* of sentiment and language,"—"a noble and graceful manner of *Expression*," and "The *Structure* or composition of all the periods, in all possible dignity and grandeur"[12]—are rhetorical, and as such are of minor interest historically, although, as we shall see, the tradition of a sublime style survived for many centuries, and even long after sublimity came to be a matter of major importance. But once the sublime was isolated as a quality of art, having its source in the mind of the artist and arousing an intense emotion in the mind of the reader or spectator, emphasis naturally tended to center on the first two sources, which were considered to be independent of and even to transcend artistic skill.

The question of the pathetic receives little attention, since Longinus had devoted to it a separate essay, now lost. Although he admits that the grand and the pathetic do not include each other, since many passions are "vastly different from grandeur, and are in themselves of a low degree; as lamentation, sorrow, fear," and although he declares that many grand and lofty objects and ideas raise no passion whatever, he none the less avers that "nothing so much raises discourse, as a fine *Pathos* seasonably applied. It animates a whole performance with uncommon life and spirit, and gives mere words the force (as it were) of inspiration."[13]

These hints form the nucleus of much that was written and thought in the eighteenth century as to the relation of the sublime to the pathetic. Although Longinus does not consider emotion as absolutely necessary to sublimity, he nevertheless habitually associates the two, since the orator's task was to persuade by affecting the emotions of his audience as well as by convincing their reason. The presence of emotion in art is the point of departure for the eighteenth-century sublime, and indeed the study of art as the evoker of emotion is perhaps even more characteristic of the æsthetic thought of the period than the study of the rules. The importance of Longinus's purely conventional and rhetorical ideas on the relation between the sublime and the pathetic becomes increasingly evident as the quantity of æsthetic speculation increases. The traditional view of the sublime as the strongly emotive quality of art, the sanction of a great Greek's authority for such a view, and the generally heterodox tastes of the British public and critics easily served to stretch the boundaries of the sublime far beyond the point which strictly neo-classic theory permitted. Longinus was to become the patron saint of much that is unclassical and unneoclassical, and eventually of much that is romantic, in eighteenth-century England.

A very few more of Longinus's remarks need be quoted, but these are of importance. *A propos* of elevation of thought, he declares: "the *Sublime* is an image reflected from the inward greatness of the soul. Hence it comes to pass, that a naked thought without words challenges admiration, and strikes by its grandeur."[14] The silence of Ajax in the eleventh book of the *Odyssey* is given as an example of this kind of sublimity, an example that is repeated *ad nauseum* in the eighteenth century. Once again we notice the emphasis on the creative mind and its thoughts rather than on technique and style; this idea was to help Boileau formulate his theory of the difference between *le sublime* and *le style sublime*.[15] It is in this connection that Longinus points out the sublimity of the Mosaic account of the creation.

In speaking of amplification—one of the rhetorical devices of the sublime style—Longinus expresses again, and very clearly, his conviction that sublimity in the last analysis is to be found in content rather than in the mode of expression.

> But the orator must never forget this maxim, that in things however *amplified* there cannot be perfection, without a sentiment which is truly *sublime*, unless

> when we are to move compassion, or to make things appear vile and contemptible. But in all other methods of *Amplification,* if you take away the *sublime* meaning, you separate as it were the soul from the body. . . . *Sublimity* consists in loftiness, and *Amplification* in number; whence the *former* is often visible in one single thought; the *other* cannot be discerned, but in a series and chain of thoughts rising one upon another.[16]

The implication here is that there is a real distinction to be drawn between content and style, "the soul and body" of art. We shall see how this conception fares at the hands of Boileau.

Two utterances extremely important for the eighteenth-century were the praise of an erring and irregular genius as opposed to a mediocrity that attains correctness by merely following rules, and the recognition of sublimity in nature. Of the first, Longinus says:

> I readily allow, that writers of a lofty and tow'ring genius are by no means pure and correct, since whatever is neat and accurate throughout, must be exceedingly liable to flatness. In the *Sublime,* as in great affluence of fortune, some minuter articles will unavoidably escape observation. . . . And for this reason I give it as my real opinion, that the great and noble flights, tho' they cannot every where boast an equality of perfection, yet they ought to carry off the prize, by the sole merit of their own intrinsic grandeur.[17]

These statements helped to support the method of criticism that weighed beauties against faults.[18] Horace had expressed the same idea less vividly in *Ars Poetica,* ll. 347-365, and the combined influence of the two critics was sufficient to inculcate the idea that great beauties can atone for small faults. Thus the emphasis of all the better critics of the eighteenth century falls on the discovery of beauties rather than the condemning of irregularities, and in England at any rate criticism by rules early began to fall into disrepute, and criticism by taste to come into vogue, for had not Longinus himself shown that true genius transcends the rules?

> Great Wits sometimes may gloriously offend,
> And rise to faults true critics dare not mend;
> From vulgar bounds with brave disorder part
> And snatch a grace beyond the reach of art,
> Which, without passing thro' the judgment, gains
> The heart, and all its ends at once attains.[19]

Addison, for example, obviously represents this method of criticism. His critique of *Paradise Lost,* despite the strong Aristotelian influence, is written throughout in the beauties-and-faults manner. Almost with the exactness of an accountant, he records Milton's beauties and his faults, credit and debit, and finally strikes a balance that leaves the poet rich in reputation. In *Spectator* 291, he speaks with displeasure of those critics who judge by "a few general rules extracted out of the French authors," and proceeds:

> A true Critick ought to dwell rather upon Excellencies than Imperfections, to discover the concealed Beauties of a writer, and communicate to the world such things as are worth their Observation. . . .

And that Longinus is not far from his mind when he makes this statement is shown by his subsequent apology for the fact that he must point out some of Milton's faults:

> I must also observe with *Longinus,* that the Productions of a great Genius, with many Lapses and Inadvertencies, are infinitely preferable to the works of an inferior kind of Author, which are scrupulously exact and conformable to all the rules of correct writing.[20]

It was this idea of Longinus that was to become the basis of so much liberal critical thought in eighteenth-century England. The theory of original genius as developed by Young and Duff, the decline in the power of the rules and the rise of a realization of the validity of the individual impression, and the association of the sublime with these ideas—all of this is attributable in some degree to Longinus.

The other important idea is the discussion of sublimity in external nature, and the deduction, from man's ability to enjoy and to be moved by natural grandeur, of an innate greatness in human nature that instinctively responds to greatness in the external world. We shall see in a later chapter that at the time when Longinus was introduced into England by Boileau, there was little enthusiasm for natural sublimities, and there can be little doubt that ***Peri Hupsous*** played a small part in increasing the chorus of praise that the eighteenth century came to sing in honor of the wilder aspects of the external world. The passage in question is much too long to be quoted in full, but a summary will doubtless suffice to recall it to mind.

> Man, says Longinus, was not created to be "a grov'ling and ungenerous animal," but was placed in this world to pursue glory. For this purpose nature planted in his soul an invincible love of grandeur, and a desire to emulate whatever seems to approach nearer to divinity than himself. "Hence it is, that the whole universe is not sufficient, for the extensive reach and piercing speculation of the human understanding. It passes the bounds of the material world, and launches forth at pleasure into endless space." Nature impels us to admire not a small river "that ministers to our necessities," but the Nile, the Ister, and the Rhine; likewise the sun and the stars "surprise" us, and Aetna in eruption commands our wonder.[21]

This summary has intentionally emphasized certain thoughts out of proportion to the amount of space that they occupy in ***Peri Hupsous.*** The greater part of the essay is concerned with style and the tricks of rhetoric. But from our point of view the ideas here quoted have importance. They form the starting point for the development of the eighteenth-century sublime. Much was read into them—doubtless much more than Longinus meant—and much was taken from them, and some of them were to survive throughout our period.

The story of Longinus in England, his neglect in the seventeenth century, and his sudden rise to fame in the eighteenth, is known in a general way to most students of the criticism of that period. Rosenberg has demonstrated the enormous popularity of the Greek critic in the eighteenth century, and has taken a backward glance at the criticism of the seventeenth century;[22] but he has not made it his business to consider the history of the word *sublimity* before Boileau's translation in 1674 started the sublime on its long career as an æsthetic concept. We shall do so briefly, since the results are almost purely negative.

The first edition of Longinus appeared in 1554 at Basle. Franciscus Robertello was the editor. This was followed in the next year by the edition of Paulus Manutius, published at Venice. The third and last edition of the sixteenth century was that of Franciscus Portus, published at Geneva in 1569. In 1572 there appeared the first translation from the Greek—the Latin version of Pagano, published at Venice.[23] One would expect to find in England during the last half of the sixteenth century some traces of the interest that was being manifested in Longinus by Continental humanists, but one looks for them in vain.

Of course the three styles of Latin thetoric had been known and practiced throughout the middle ages. This is no occasion for a disquisition on medieval rhetoric, and we need not multiply illustrations. A poet so learned as Chaucer certainly knew his rhetoric. It will be recalled that he wrote of the "heigh style."[24] The use of the word *high* in this metaphorical sense might seem to suggest the Greek *hupsos,* but there can hardly be any connection with Longinus. There is no doubt that Chaucer means no more than the ornate, rhetorical style, "your termes, your colours, and your figures," the *genus grande* of the Romans.[25] Spenser uses *sublime* only once and then in the sense of "proud."[26] He too knew the "lofty style,"[27] but there is no hint that he or his circle had any interest in the conception of the sublime as Longinus discusses it.

The earliest example of the use of *sublime* in connection with style listed in the *N.E.D.* is from A. Day's *English Secretorie,* 1586. He says:

> We do find three sorts [sc, of the style of epistles] . . . to have bene generally commended. Sublime, the highest and stateliest maner, and loftiest deliverance of any thing that may be, expressing the heroical and mighty actions of Kings.

This shows clearly enough the use of the Latin term *sublimitas* to express the same idea that lies behind Chaucer's "heigh style" and Spenser's "lofty style." A new term has been applied to an old idea, but a conception of the sublime is as yet unborn. Apparently Longinus was of no importance to the sixteenth-century critics and poets. Mr. Gregory Smith is able to dismiss his influence in one short sentence: "From Longinus little or nothing has been borrowed."[28] There is no mention of his name in this period, or indeed for many years to come.

In 1612, appeared the second Latin translation of ***Peri Hupsos,*** by Gabriel de Petra. Rosenberg regards this version as the first real advance in the growth of Longinus's reputation. But it was not until 1636 that Gerard Langbaine translated the treatise into Latin and brought out at Oxford the first version made by an Englishman and printed at an English press. Although we have no evidence of the growth of interest in Longinus in the years preceding 1636, it is not unreasonable to conclude that Langbaine's translation was evoked by some sort of demand for a new Latin rendering of the treatise; but the critical writings of this period are still devoid of Longinian influence. Clark declares: "None of the Elizabethan or Jacobean critics (not even Ben Jonson) mention his [Longinus's] name or show any trace of his influence."[29] My own investigations have given me no reason to modify this statement.

In 1652 there appeared the first translation of Longinus into English; it was made by John Hall, and was entitled, ***Peri Hupsons, or Dionysius Longinus of the Height of Eloquence rendred out of the originall by J. H. Esq.*** Hall is the earliest of the moderns to show that he understood Longinus's purpose. In the dedication, he formulates for the first time in English the idea of the sublime.

> It must therefore have somewhat I cannot tell how divine in it, for it depends not of the single amassing or embroidery of words, there must be in it, excellent knowledge of Man, deep and studied acquaintance with the passions, a man must not onely know very perfectly the agitation of his own mind, but be sure and conversant in those of others. . . . And yet all this, without somewhat which I cannot expresse, is but the smallest part that goes to the building up of such a prodigy, there must be somewhat *Ethereal,* somewhat above man, much of a soul *separate,* that must animate all this, and breath [*sic*] into it a fire to make it both warm and shine.[30]

Hall is decidedly on the way to stating a conception of the sublime similar to that formulated later by Boileau, but he does not get beyond this fumbling and groping definition, and his words seem not to have provoked speculation on the subject.

One might reasonably hope to find a noticeable increase in reference to Longinus from this time. Ninety-eight years had passed since the *editio princeps* had been printed; in the meantime several editions had appeared, and both a Latin and an English translation were in existence. But the time had not yet come for Longinus to gain the ear of the critical world, and we find his name mentioned seldom.[31] Milton himself, with all of his interest in the ancients, seems not to have felt Longinus's charm. In his essay "Of Education," he mentions Longinus as one of the teachers of "a graceful and ornate rhetoric," but that is all.[32] It is a strange paradox that the most sublime of English poets should not have caught from Longinus the suggestion of the sublime as the expression of ultimate values in art, beyond the reach of rhetoric and her handmaidens, the rules, He did not; and it was left to the propounders of an adolescent æsthetic in the next century to find in John Milton's poems, not a "graceful and ornate rhetoric," but the supreme illustration of whatever particular type of the sublime they advocated.

This seems to have been the state of Longinus and the sublime in England until after 1674. He was known, but was not often quoted, and he had not yet become an authority.[33] *Sublime* was known and used as an adjective, signifying physical or metaphorical height, and the lofty or sublime style continued purely in the realm of rhetoric. The substantive *sublime* in its æsthetic connotation had not yet come into use. Our own investigations bear out Rosenberg's statement that between 1612 and 1674 Longinus and all that Longinus was later to stand for meant little enough.[34]

In his *Dictionary* (1755), Johnson defines the substantive *sublime* as "the grand or lofty style," and adds, "*The sublime* is a Gallicism, but now naturalized." In this sentence he epitomizes the history of that phase of criticism which we are discussing. The sublime came to England from France in Boileau's translation of Longinus (1674)—came with a certain accretion of æsthetic concepts that it had gathered from Boileau's *Préface.* It will be recalled that John Hall had translated ***Peri Hupsous*** as "the Height of Eloquence"; likewise Pulteney, the second translator of the treatise into English, adopted the title, ***A Treatise of the Loftiness or Elegancy of Speech,*** even though he translated not from the Greek but from Boileau's version. It was an anonymous translator who, in 1698, first translated *hupsos* by the Latin and Romance derivative, *sublime,*[35] although, as we shall see, the word was by that time established in critical usage.[36]

Boileau's translation was the turning point of Longinus's reputation in England and France. By the end of the century the two English translations referred to above had appeared, and as the next chapter will show, the sublime had become a subject of speculation. There is no reason to labor the proof of Longinus's subsequent popularity in England. Rosenberg has treated the subject at length, but it needs no dissertation come from Germany to convince even a casual reader of the criticism of the period that Longinus was a presence not to be put by.

The bibliographical evidence of his vogue is interesting. Two editions of the Greek text were brought out during the eighteenth century, and were many times reprinted. The one was by J. Hudson, published at Oxford in 1710, the other was that of Z. Pearce (London, 1724). Rosenberg gives the following list of the years in which editions of ***Peri Hupsous*** were printed: 1710, 1718, 1724, 1730, 1732, 1733, 1743, 1751, 1752, 1762, 1763, 1773, 1778, 1789.[37] This is an extraordinary number especially when we remember that Welsted's and Smith's translations appeared in 1712 and 1739, respectively; the first was reprinted with the translator's complete works in 1789, and the second reached its fourth edition in 1770.[38] Moreover, Boileau's version went through eighteen editions in France, copies of which surely reached England, and there were three translations of Boileau's translation in the editions of his complete works which were englished in 1711-13, 1736, and 1752.[39] It should not be overlooked that most of this interest in Longinus is concentrated in the first half of the century.[40] Only five of the fourteen printings mentioned by Rosenberg appeared after 1752; the third edition of Smith's version is dated 1752, along with the last complete edition of the translation of Boileau's works. In France, after 1747, Boileau's translation had only two editions.

This remarkable interest in Longinus is symbolic of the power that he exercised over the minds of eighteenth-century Englishmen. Pope's eulogy in the *Essay on Criticism,* 1711, in which Longinus is praised as being "himself the great Sublime he draws" (a *cliché* echoed from Boileau),[41] is an expression of contemporary as well as personal opinion. Rosenberg's dissertation mentions fifty-nine authors who show a knowledge of Longinus, and the list is far from being complete. Early in the century the author of ***Peri Hupsous*** had become the delight of the critics, as well as of the wits and would-be critics. As early as 1679, for that matter, in *A True Widow,* Shadwell had satirized the sublime as a cant phrase. Young Maggot, the conventional "Inns-of-Court Man who neglects his law and runs mad after wit," says of a play:

> I saw it Scene by Scene . . . it breaks well, the *Protasis* good, the *Catastasis* excellent; there's no

> *Episode*, but the *Catastrophe* is admirable; I lent him [the author] that, and the Love Parts, and the Songs. There are a great many Sublimes, that are very Poetical.[42]

Young Maggot reminds us of that member of the Club which is described in the second *Spectator,* who belonged to the Inner Temple, and knew more of Aristotle and Longinus than of Littleton and Coke.

In 1712, Steele could refer to the distinction between the true and the false sublime quite as if Boileau's ideas were then general property;[43] and in the same year Welsted published his translation, and in the Remarks which accompanied it, linked the names of Shakespeare and Milton to the increasingly popular word *sublime,* an early example of how Longinus served to supply reasons to justify tastes that were natural to Englishmen.[44]

Keen satire on the critical terms popular with the wits is found in James Ralph's *The Touchstone,* 1728. He says:

> These Gentlemen [criticasters], at the Expense of much Labour and Birch, are whipp'd at School into bad Translations, false *Latin* and dull Themes; from thence they run the Gantlope through all the pedantick Forms of an University-Education; There they grow familiar with the Title-Pages of Antient and modern Authors, and will talk of *Aristotle, Longinus, Horace, Scaliger, Rapin, Bossu, Dacier,* as freely, as if bosom Acquaintance. Their Mouths are fill'd with the Fable, the Moral, Catastrophe, Unity, Probability, Poetick Justice, true Sublime, Bombast, Simplicity, Magnificance, and all the critical Jargon, which is learn'd in a quarter of an Hour, and serves to talk of one's whole Life after.[45]

The sublime was evidently frequently mentioned at the coffee houses, since Pope felt safe in using ***Peri Hupsous*** as the medium for his attack on the dunces preparatory to the publication of the *Dunciad.* The delicious parody of Longinus, *Peri Bathous, or the Art of Sinking in Poetry,* 1728, presupposes a familiarity with the treatise on the part of the town, and bears out other pieces of evidence that indicate that Longinus had come into his own.[46]

Swift had his fling at the sham critics in his *On Poetry: a Rhapsody,* 1733. He advises the youth who is bent on becoming a man of letters despite his native dullness to take up criticism, not poetry. The passage is too long to quote in full, but "our modern critic's jargon" is set forth in detail. The Dean concludes:

> A forward Critick often dupes us
> With sham Quotations ***Peri Hupsous:***
> And if we have not read *Longinus,*
> Will magisterially out-shine us.
> Then lest with *Greek* he over-run ye,
> Procure the Book for Love or Money,
> Translated from *Boileau's* Translation,
> And quote Quotation on Quotation.[47]

Longinus had evidently become the victim of a cult, and as the object of a constant lip-service he must have become a bore to the serious men of letters. Charles Lamotte was able to speak of him, in 1730, as one "whose Authority will be thought unexceptionable,"[48] and when any critic attains such fame he is a legitimate object of satire.

Though Longinus probably reached the height of his fame at about 1738, he nevertheless had to face no sudden decline in popularity and prominence. The interest in sublimity which emanated from his treatise kept his name alive, even after the sublime had grown into a concept far different from that found in ***Peri Hupsous.*** Rosenberg has given an incomplete, but a competent, account of Longinus's reputation. Longinus's name was on every one's tongue, and his influence in unexpected places. For example, Turnbull called in Longinus when he wrote on the theory of painting in 1740; Hurd in 1751, considered Longinus, together with Bouhours and Addison, "the most eminent, at least the most popular" of critics, and he found Longinus the "most instructive" of the three.[49] Longinus's voice was heard in the liberal criticism of Young and Duff, in whose discussions of original genius the Greek becomes a true enemy of the rules, and an ardent advocate of the licenses that inspired and untutored genius takes.[50] Smith's translation and Pearce's edition were used as school books in 1766;[51] young and earnest Mr. Gibbon read through ***Peri Hupsous*** in the autumn of 1762, and found it "valuable," "worthy of the best and freest days of Athens," pleasing, and astonishing.[52] As late as 1774 Mrs. Elizabeth Carter read Longinus because she "thought one must read Longinus," but gained little pleasure from following the fashion.[53] John Lanson thought that he could take a knowledge of Longinus for granted when he delivered his lectures to the students of Trinity College, Dublin, and a few years later the general interest in Longinus justified the publication of Greene's dull commentary on ***Peri Hupsous.***[54] John Ogilvie declared in 1774 that Longinus has preoccupied the province of the sublime, and that he is universally read and admired by readers of even the smallest classical knowledge.[55]

Such general and widespread fame, however, did not keep æsthetic speculation subservient to Longinus. It was rather as a critic than as a guide to æsthetic that Longinus was powerful. Speculation soon outgrew ***Peri Hupsous,*** which indeed is the point of departure rather than the guiding influence of theories of the sublime, especially after the middle of the century. Silvain had early complained that the Greek critic did not give a clear idea of the sublime,[56] and a similar dissatisfaction was felt by all the more important theorizers. Burke simply did not discuss Longinus; Blair and Beattie complained of the dominatingly rhetorical character of ***Peri Hupsous;***[57] and these are typical cases. Occasionally, as in the case of Stack,[58] Longinus found his defenders. As late as the first decade of the nineteenth century, so advanced a thinker as Richard Payne Knight could quote Longinus against Burke, as though he considered the Greek a weightier authority.[59] But despite the popularity of Longinus, and despite the reputation of ***Peri Hupsous*** among critics, speculation grew more and more purely æsthetic, and, so far as the sublime is concerned, Longinus's influence decreased as the century drew to a close. In 1829 it was possible for James Mill to speak with contempt of a work that had been one of the chief influences on the critical thought of the eighteenth century, and that was the source of the sort of speculation in which Mill himself was indulging when he condemned Longinus.[60]

It is not difficult to explain the fact that Longinus rose to so lofty a position in the eighteenth century, after his neglect during the preceding age. Hans Hecht, reviewing Rosenberg's dissertation, offers as a reason the ease with which ***Peri Hupsous*** could be employed in the interest of either side in the controversy of the Ancients and the Moderns, and the fact that Longinus offered a reputable authority for a love of such irregular writers as Shakespeare, Milton, and Spenser.[61]

Longinus did ride into fame on the crest of the controversary between the Ancients and the Moderns, as we shall see in the next chapter. He became an ally of either party, used now to defend the ancients, now to champion original and untutored genius. He is moderate, urbane, and eloquent, and his moderation discouraged dogmatism, his eloquence stirred enthusiasm, and he was sufficiently liberal in his opinions to appeal to eighteenth-century modernism. His high seriousness, his moral point of view, his insistance that the great poet is the good man, would be understood and valued in an age whose æsthetic had not yet divorced itself from the ethical point of view. In the last section of his treatise, Longinus accounts for the decline of genius in his age on the grounds that liberty no longer existed, and that only in a state of freedom can great art be produced—an opinion that would naturally commend itself to the English in an age when they complacently contrasted their own constitutional monarchy with the despotism that prevailed on the Continent, and when they prided themselves on the prevalence of individual liberty in the body politic. Moreover, Longinus's essay must have seemed a complement to the more analytical criticism of Aristotle and Horace, and must have been welcome, as Gibbon suggested, because of its impressioniatic and interpretive quality.

Finally, it may be said that Longinus was not needed in the seventeenth century, and that he had a very definite function to fulfil in the early years of the eighteenth century. An age that produced poets so different as Ben Jonson and Donne, Herrick and Crashaw, Carew and Herbert, Milton and Cowley, surely had no need for a theoretical defence of individualism in art. But when, shortly after the Restoration, the reaction against the decadent Donne tradition set in, and when, England after her experiment in political liberty, settled down to enjoy a comfortable and urbane enlightenment under a constitutional monarchy, the tendency was to regiment taste and the art of poetry under the rules which sought to control in the interest of neo-classicism.

But the English genius was never comfortable in the borrowed garments cut to the pattern of the rules. Despite the stand made by various poets and critics in their defence, clarity and correctness were exotic growths on English soil. There was an instinctive and uneasy feeling that the true destiny of English letters lay with Shakespeare and not with Horace and Boileau, and even when, say from 1660 to 1740, the ideas of neo-classicism were dominant, it is dangerous for the student to generalize as to the tastes and theories of the age. Of course no age is unanimous in its tastes, and romanticism and classicism of one variety or another always exist side by side. The study of eighteenth-century criticism is in fact the study of the increasingly rapid disintegration of the neo-classical standards, and the re-emerging of a freer, more individualistic, and consequently more native theory of art. Longinus is not the cause of this disintegration, but it is none the less true that during the century ***Peri Hupsous*** was a sort of *locus classicus* for that type of critical thought which sought to combat and destroy the rules.

The case of Samuel Cobb is indicative of the process which united Longinus with those spirits who wished to justify the conception that the greatest art can be produced only by native genius expressing itself after its own manner, rather than in the tradition of Horace and Boileau. His was not a voice crying in the wilderness; he was no lone romanticist foretelling the advent of a Byron, but he was representative of the protest against the overemphasis of the rules, a protest that became vocal very early indeed, that, in fact, was never silent. And his use of Longinus is typical of the practice of those modifiers of the neo-classical tradition who contributed to its transformation as the century drew to a close. His language and ideas are very closely akin to those of Young more than fifty years later.

To study to be correct, he says in his A Discourse on Criticism, and the Liberty of Writing, 1707, "enervates the Vigour of the Mind, slackens the Spirits, and cramps the Genius of a *Free Writer*. He who creeps by the Shore, may shelter himself from a Storm, but is likely to make few Discoveries: . . ." The rules are "leading strings" to be laid aside by a mature genius in the interest of the expression of "a free generous, and manly Spirit." He concludes: "Let a Man follow the Talent that Nature has furnish'd him with, and his own Observation has improv'd, we may hope to see Inventions in all Arts, which may dispute Superiority with the best of the *Athenian* and *Roman* Excellencies."[62]

These statements are made on the authority of Longinus, and in protest against "a slavish Bigotry to the Ancients." In principle there is little here that Pope and Addison would not have agreed with; their own statements on the subject differ only in degree of emphasis. The importance of Cobb's Discourse for us is that it offers concrete evidence as to the promptness with which the ideas of Longinus were assimilated, and the ease with which they joined in the protest of the liberal criticism against a type of literature in essence foreign to the national tradition. Longinus came into favor because he could fill a need; he alone of the ancients could be used to support the idea of "the liberty of writing."

But the Longinus who is of value for this study is really the creation of Boileau, who called ***Peri Hupsous*** to the attention of his contemporaries, and who initiated speculation on the nature of the sublime in his *Préface* and in his *Réflexions*. The sublime that came into existence in 1674 was the offspring of two minds so startlingly unlike as those of the Greek critic and the author of *L'Art Poétique*. To that sublime we turn in the following chapter.

Notes

[1] *Dionysius Longinus on the Sublime,* translated from the Greek, by William Smith, D.D. The Fourth Edition Corrected and Improved. London, 1770.

[2] See G. L. Hendrickson, "The Origin and Meaning of the Ancient Characters of Style," *American Journal of Philology,* XXVI (1905), 249-290, to which I am indebted, as well as to the introduction to W. Rhys Roberts' edition of Demetrius, *On Style* (London, 1927). For a brief discussion of the whole matter see C. S. Baldwin's *Ancient Rhetoric and Poetic* (New York, 1924), pp. 56-58.

[3] *On Style,* pp. 323-325.

[4] Dionysius of Halicarnassus, *On Literary Composition,* ed. W. Rhys Roberts (London, 1910), pp. 211-213.

[5] Quintilian, *Institutio Oratoria,* tr. H. E. Butler (London and New York, 1922), Loeb Classical Library, 111, 211, 213, and 215.

[6] *On the Sublime,* p. 3.

[7] *Ibid.,* pp. 3, 4.

[8] *Ibid.,* p. 21.

[9] Observe the synonyms that Smith uses for *sublime.*

[10] *On the Sublime,* pp. 21, 22.

[11] *Ibid.,* pp. 23, 24.—Perhaps it is necessary to call attention to the fact that in all eighteenth-century critical writings the term *pathetic* is used in its generic sense of "producing an effect upon the emotions," not necessarily the tender emotions. In his *Cyclopedia,* 1727, Ephraim Chambers defines the word as "something that relates to the passions; and particularly that is proper to awake, or excite them." Bailey's *Dictionarium Britannicum,* 1721, gives a similar definition, and adds that "pathetick Musick" is "very moving, expressive, passionate, capable of exciting pity, compassion, anger, or the like passions." This definition shows the broad application of the term. Parnell, in his *Essay on the Different Stiles of Poetry* (London, 1713), p. 21, distinguishes two sorts of pathetic:

> Here all the *Passions,* for their greater sway,
> In all the Pow'r of Words themselves array;
> And hence the soft *Pathetick* gently charms,
> And hence the Bolder fills the Breast with
> Arms.

Johnson does not record the modern specialized meaning of the term, but shortly after the publication of the *Dictionary* Owen Ruffhead defines it as "a term usually confined to such ideas, as raise in us an emotion of pity." *Life of Pope* (London, 1769), p. 339.

[12] *Ibid.,* pp. 24, 25.

[13] *Ibid.,* 25-27.

[14] *Ibid.,* pp. 28, 29.

[15] See Chapter II.

[16] *On the Sublime,* pp. 62 and 63.

[17] *Ibid.,* pp. 136, 137; and 138.

[18] For helpful discussions of Longinus as a liberalizing factor in eighteenth-century critical thought see A. F. Clark, *Boileau and the French Classical Critics in England* (Paris, 1925), pp. 391-393; and

H. G. Paul, *John Dennis: His Life and Criticism* (New York, 1911), pp. 124, 125.

[19] A. Pope, "An Essay on Criticism," I, 152-157. *Works,* II, 43. For the relation of Pope to Longinus, see Austen Warren, *Pope as a Critic and Humanist* (1929), pp. 11-13.

[20] *The Spectator,* ed. H. Morley (London, 1891), II, 298 and 299. See also Number 592.

[21] *On the Sublime,* pp. 145-147.—

Mighty rivers, the heavenly bodies, and volcanoes played a part in eighteenth-century sublimities. They awakened admiration and wonder in the breasts of man and woman before the century ended. In view of this fact it is worth noticing that when the sublime was given to England it was already associated with the external world, as well as with literature and with rhetoric. Especially interesting, in the light of Kant's theory, is the idea that the human understanding seeks to transcend the material world and to grasp infinity, and that the appreciation of sublimity is a token of the spiritual greatness of man. Is it not this idea which Kant expresses in his more technical language and which is, of course modified by his own philosophical system? At any rate the sublime at its very inception points inward to the mind and soul of man, and the eighteenth century will modify after its own fashion this rhetorical passage in which deep is said to cry unto deep.

[22] A. Rosenberg, *Longinus in England bis zur Ende des 18. Jahrhunderts* (Weimar and Berlin, 1917).

[23] For information as to the early editions of Longinus, I am indebted to Rosenberg's dissertation, pp. 1-19, and to Roberts' *Longinus on the Sublime* (Cambridge, 1899), App. D, pp. 247-261.

[24] *Canterbury Tales,* E, 18, 41, 1148.

[25] For an excellent description and discussion of the three styles of discourse inherited by the middle ages from ancient rhetoric, see C. S. Baldwin's *Medieval Rhetoric and Poetic* (New York, 1928), pp. 67-72. "The third, or great style," says Mr. Baldwin, "whether it be elegant or not, has for its distinguishing quality the force of emotional appeal" (p. 70). Thus in preaching and in oratory, the ancient sublime style survived. In poetic it became more concerned with questions of ornate form. For rhetoric in Chaucer's poetry, see Baldwin, pp. 284-301, and J. M. Manly's *Chaucer and the Rhetoricians,* Warton Lecture on Poetry, XVII (London, 1926), *passim.*

[26] *Faerie Queene,* V, VIII, 30, 4.

[27] *Ruines of Rome,* XXV, 13, 14.

[28] Gregory Smith, *Elizabethan Critical Essays* (Oxford, 1904), I, lxxiv. See also D. L. Clark, *Rhetoric and Poetry in the Renaissance* (New York, 1922), pp. 62 and 67, where the same conclusion is reached.

[29] *Boileau and the French Classical Critics in England,* p. 368.

[30] See the Dedication to the Lord Commissioner Whitelock.

[31] Thomas Blount quotes from Hall's version, and refers to Longinus occasionally. See *The Academy of Eloquence* (London, 1653), pp. 47 and 65. But his own *Glossographia* (1656), and Phillips's *A New World of English Words* (1658), define *sublime* simply as "height."

[32] *The Prose Works of John Milton,* ed. J. A. St. John (London, 1848), III, 473, 474.

[33] Rosenberg (p. 7) points out Davenant's borrowing from Longinus the statement that Homer's gods are like men (*Preface to Gondibert,* 1650, Spingarn, II, 2), but it is a matter of no importance here.

[34] *Longinus in England,* p. 7.

[35] The translations in question are: *A Treatise of the Loftiness or Elegancy of Speech. Written originally in Greek by Longinus; and now translated out of the French by Mr. J. P.* London, 1680; and *An Essay on Sublime: Translated from the Greek of Dionysius Longinus Cassius the Rhetorician. Compared with the French of Sieur Despréaux Boileau.* Oxford, 1698.

[36] For the history of *hupsos* see Roberts, pp. 209, 210. The word has a variety of meanings, even in Longinus's essay. Roberts gives "elevation," "dignity," "grandeur," "eloquence" as the most important variations. The Latin words used to translate *Peri Hupsous* have been *de grandi sive sublimi orationis genere, de sublimi genere dicendi, de sublimitate.* The French naturally adopted the Latin word, which in turn, through Boileau's influence, drove out the native English *loftiness* or *height.*

[37] Rosenberg, p. 9.

[38] W. T. Lowndes, *The Bibliographer's Manual of English Literature* (London, 1865), III, I, 1395.

[39] *Boileau and the French Classical Critics in England,* p. 370.

[40] Two other translations are lost to us. One was by Edmund Smith, whose life Dr. Johnson wrote; the other was by the Rev. Mr. McCarthy of Dublin. For a discussion of these versions, see Rosenberg, pp. 12-15.

THE
WORKS
OF
DIONYSIUS LONGINUS,
On the Sublime:
OR, A
TREATISE
Concerning the
Sovereign Perfection of Writing.
Tranſlated from the *Greek.*
WITH
Some REMARKS on the
Engliſh POETS.

By Mr. *WELSTED.*

Deſcriptas ſervare vices operumque colores,
Cur ego, ſi nequo ignoroque Poeta ſalutor?
Cur neſcire, pudens pravé, quam diſcere malo?
Hor. Ars. Poet.

London, Printed for SAM. BRISCOE, and Sold by *John Graves* next *Whites-Chocolate-houſe* in *St. James's-ſtreet*, and *Owen Lloyd* near the Church in the *Temple*. 1712.

Title Page of a 1712 edition of On the Sublime.

[41] Boileau, (*Euvres Complètes,* ed. A. Ch. Gidel (Paris, 1873), III, 437.

[42] *Works of Thomas Shadwell* (London, 1720), III, 122. The passage is quoted in the *N.E.D.*

[43] *Spectator,* 350, April 11, 1712.

[44] *The Works of Dionysius Longinus on the Sublime,* etc., tr. Leonard Welsted (London, 1712), pp. 145; 146; 147; 151; 154; 156; 160.

[45] [James Ralph], *The Touchstone,* etc. (London, 1728), p. 161.

[46] In his unpublished dissertation, *Alexander Pope's Art of Sinking in Poetry* (Princeton, 1932) Dr. Archibald Hart has made a thorough study of Pope's satire. He points out the close relation of *Peri Bathous* to Boileau's translation of Longinus.

[47] [Jonathan Swift], *On Poetry: A Rhapsody* (London, 1733), p. 16.—Satire on the use of the sublime as a cant term of the pseudo-critic continued at least into the 1750's. The word is a favorite with Dick Minim, the honest dullard of Johnson's creation, who established his fame as a critic by becoming an echo of coffee-house critiques. "Sometimes he is sunk in despair, and perceives false delicacy gaining ground, and sometimes brightens his countenance with a gleam of hope and predicts the revival of the true sublime." *Idler,* 61, *Works* (Oxford, 1825), IV, 330.

[48] Charles Lamotte, *An Essay upon Poetry and Painting* (London, 1730), p. 7.

[49] George Turnbull, *A Treatise on Ancient Painting* (London, 1740), pp. 76; 83; 84:etc.—Q. Horatii Flacci, *Epistola ad Augustum,* ed. Richard Hurd (London, 1751), pp. 99 and 101.

[50] [Edward Young], *Conjectures on Original Composition* (London, 1759). [W. Duff], *An Essay on Original Genius* (London, 1769).

[51] "A Catalogue of the School Books Now in General Use," *A Complete Catalogue of Modern Books* (London, 1766), pp. 91 and 92.

[52] Edward Gibbon, *Journal,* ed. D. M. Low (London, 1929), pp. 138, 139; 142. Gibbon has indicated clearly one reason for Longinus's success with the eighteenth-century mind. He says that hitherto he had known but two methods of criticizing a book—to analyze its beauties and to exclaim. "Longinus," he says, "has shown me a third. He tells me his own feelings upon reading it; and tells them with such energy, that he communicates them" (p. 155).

[53] Elizabeth Carter, *Letters to Mrs. Montagu,* ed. Rev. Montagu Pennington (London, 1817), II, 273.

[54] John Lanson, *Lectures Concerning Oratory,* Second Edition (Dublin, 1759), p. 59. [Richard Burnaby Greene], *Critical Essays* (London, 1770). Greene did not express a new or a singular idea when he said that Longinus was "the best of the ancients" (p. ii).

[55] John Ogilvie, *Philosophical and Critical Observations on the Nature, Character, and Various Specimens of Composition* (London, 1774), II, 161.

[56] Silvain, *Traité du Sublime* (Paris, 1732), p. 2.

[57] Hugh Blair, *Lectures on Rhetoric and Belles Lettres* (London, 1783), I, 59.—James Beattie, "Illustrations on Sublimity," *Dissertations Moral and Critical* (London, 1783), p. 605.

[58] Richard Stack, "An Essay on Sublimity of Writing," *Transactions of the Royal Irish Academy* (Dublin, 1787), I, 19-26.

[59] Richard Payne Knight, *An Analytical Inquiry into the Principles of Taste,* The Second Edition (London, 1805), p. 376.

[60] James Mill, *Analysis of the Phenomena of the Human Mind* (London, 1829), II, 192.

[61] *Beiblatt zur Anglia,* XXXI (1920), 163.

[62] Samuel Cobb, *Poems on Several Occasions* (London, 1710), The Third Edition. The pages of the Discourse are not numbered.

Elder Olson (essay date 1942)

SOURCE: "The Argument of Longinus on the Sublime," in *Modern Philology,* Vol. XXXIX, No. 3, February, 1942, pp. 225-58.

[*In this essay, Olson analyzes the structures of the various arguments that lead up to* On the Sublime*'s conclusions and, from this, concludes that Longinus intended sublimity to be bound up with the communication of spiritual nobility rather than with mere stylistic manipulation.*]

The brief and fragmentary treatise [***Peri Hypsous***] presents the spectacle, not too uncommon in literature, of a major critical document which has gained assent—in this case almost universal assent—to its statements while the arguments which developed and guaranteed those statements have gone nearly unexamined.[1] Since its publication at Basel by Robortello in 1554, and more particularly since Boileau's translation a hundred and twenty years later, the treatise has been frequently edited and translated, admired and eulogized, cited and discussed; but the quality of sensibility for which it has been chiefly esteemed, and which has won for it innumerable and illustrious admirers, seems unfortunately to have discouraged logical analysis. Twentieth-century commentators on the work, from Churton Collins[2] to Mr. J. W. H. Atkins,[3] seem to have written with Gibbon's famous remark in mind and consequently to have been occupied chiefly with the insight, the enthusiasm, and the originality displayed in the treatise; and while these preoccupations have in their turn produced eloquence and insight, as well as some excellent outlines and précis, they have as often led to the neglect and, in Saintsbury's case at least, even to the deprecation of the dialectical apparatus which underlies the work.[4]

Yet Longinus, if, indeed, he was the author of this treatise, exhibits on every page a concern with problems which could scarcely have arisen in a random discussion wherein literary enthusiasm was the solitary guiding principle of the critic; and even to grant, as numerous commentators have done, that the work presents clearly marked divisions, amid the ruins of which some fragments of an argument may still be discerned, is to offer insufficient explanation of the portions of the manuscript which are still extant. The eleven manuscripts of the work have been the object of much learned scrutiny from a philological point of view, but even in the collect they scarcely present, by the methods of consideration possible to grammarians, anything like an adequate representation of the whole treatise. As a consequence two courses, the pursuit of both of which has been sufficiently exemplified, have been open to the scholar operating on purely grammatical principles: either the lacunae might be made the subject of learned lamentation, in the absence of further manuscripts, or the text as we have it might be called in question on the basis of philological arguments of varying direction and cogency. To the literary historian yet another course is open: the topics with which Longinus is concerned may be treated as the conventional topics of Greek and Roman writers on rhetorical theory, and questions of their order and even of the manner of their discussion may be answered in terms of the practice of earlier, and not infrequently even of later, rhetoricians.[5] The objection to both the grammatical and the historical solutions is properly, not that either approach is inferior or that distinguished efforts have been wanting in either, but that, in terms of what Longinus himself says, as I have suggested, many questions of importance remain unanswerable. The first page of the treatise, for example, presents to us an author who is pre-eminently concerned with method, for the criticism of Caecilius rests upon methodological grounds and the major preoccupation evinced by the introductory remarks is with the precepts according to which a technical treatise must be constructed. Again, the discussion of whether an art of sublimity is possible[6] becomes transformed, if we regard it as a matter of convention, into a servile and meaningless imitation of other and more philosophic inquiries; and, in like manner, topics of discussion throughout the treatise become unimportant and ineffectual, sometimes indeed wholly unintelligible, efforts to conform to a literary tradition. To such a place of unimportance, thus, we should have to consign the criticism of the *Odyssey,* the discussion of faultlessness versus faulty grandeur, the chapters on pettiness, and the discussion of literary decadence which closes the portion of the work which we have; and, similarly, numerous minor passages would become intrusions into a work which, in the judgment of many critics and scholars, would have been better without them. In the general disregard, then, of the logical schematism of the work, the ***Peri Hypsous*** has become an aggregation of fragments, important chiefly for the extraordinary "insights" which they contain; and those passages wherein the power of insight seems to have failed, or wherein the author does not make his judgments intelligible, may be dismissed—by the author's own canon as expressed in sections xxxiii-xxxv—as faults which cannot dim the grandeur of the whole.

In opposition to these methods of consideration and as a possibly convenient auxiliary to them in the problems which they pose, a third approach might be suggested. While the treatise is doubtless of striking philological and historical interest, it is, nonetheless, as Longinus himself points out, a treatise on a certain kind of literary art, that is, it is a practical treatise expounding certain means as conducive to a certain end; as a consequence, unless the citation of means is to be regarded as purely arbitrary and dogmatic, the treatise might be exhibited as a reasoned structure, that is, as an argument, and considered wholly in that light.

The treatment of the work purely as a reasoned structure would turn, it goes without saying, on questions at most only equivocally connected with those ordering other methods. Indeed, it would be proper to lay down at once a series of postulates governing the procedure. In the first place, we may assume that any argument whatsoever—provided, of course, that it is strictly argument—comes about through the necessity of resolving some question and that the argument proper terminates, as having achieved its end, when that question is really or apparently resolved. Second, since the resolution of a question is the end of argument, it is clear that the question must be expounded solely from the text as from the only proper clue to the meaning and that the argument itself must be regarded at all times as the means by which, previous knowledge mediating, the end is achieved. In the third place, since in any extended inquiry a problem contains a series of subproblems, the argument must be divided according to these in its primary divisions, and into further subdivisions if these have subsidiaries. In the fourth place, we may assume that every device—distinction, definition, example, analogy, quotation, etc.—is used deliberately and that the use of every such device is to be explained in terms of the necessity of the end and to be noted as a sign of what the author considers to be demonstration. Finally, the order of the text as a whole is to be explained in terms of demonstration as the author conceives it, that is, in terms of his method. It may be objected to such a proposal that the resultant analysis would depend wholly on the assumption that Longinus had indeed constructed the treatise with this particular end in view. The objection must, of course, be accepted; but the grounds of its acceptance would make it clear that it is acceptable not as an objection but as a general comment concerning any mode of consideration and interpretation of a work whatsoever. Any mode of grammatical analysis must depend on the assumption that the work in question was composed according to grammatical principles; any mode of historical consideration must rest, likewise, either on the assumption that the writer was to an extent shaped by his times and his admirations, consciously or unconsciously, or on the assumption that some relation, however tenuous, is traceable between the writer as a historical entity and certain other historical entities. Similarly, it is true, the philosophical analysis of the work must be based on some assumption appropriate to the mode of consideration, since no method proceeds *ex nihilo;* but it must be added that it can scarcely be dangerous or groundless to assume that philosophic works would be ordered to a philosophic end or that this treatise in particular is composed upon principles which alone—if we except sheer accident—could have given it the character which it is universally conceded to possess.

The treatise ***On the sublime*** is an inquiry into the methods by which a certain quality of literary composition may be achieved. The question which it seeks primarily to answer, thus, is a question which neither Plato nor Aristotle nor the "scholastic" rhetoricians of Greece and Rome would have indicated as a principal question even in the study of literature. For Plato, rhetoric and poetics are arts which are occupied with the construction of semblances of the truth; and since the semblance is most perfect when its maker is one who knows what the truth is, the ultimate questions of poetic and rhetoric transcend the limitations of these arts and fall under dialectic, for they must involve knowledge—a problem which is properly to be treated by the dialectician alone. Thus in the *Ion* the true poet, and in the *Phaedrus* the true rhetorician, is ultimately he who knows, i.e., the dialectician; and those who are rhetoricians and poets merely, like Lysias and Ion, are men in possession merely of the elements of their arts and, in sharper statement, indeed possess no art whatsoever. The question posed by Longinus is, therefore, for Plato, at best an elementary one; for Aristotle, on the other hand, it would have been an impossible one, since Aristotle's method entails a distinction between rhetoric and poetics and involves, even within these, a specialized treatment dependent upon a distinction into kinds. In such a method the question which Longinus poses as the primary question of his art consequently would not have been answerable as a generality; even in specific treatment, on the other hand, it would not have served as the subject matter even of an opusculum and in its reduction to the Aristotelian method would have been relegated, perhaps, only to the discussion of appropriate and impressive stylistic in the third book of the *Rhetoric.* Lastly, for the "scholastic" rhetoricians of Greece and Rome, the question of sublimity is posed never as an end but as a question relevant to the various means—more specifically, to the different kinds of styles—of rhetoric; and, while for these rhetoricians the question would have been one of greater importance than for Plato or Aristotle, it would have been, nonetheless, specifically a rhetorical problem, and its solution would have consisted in the enumeration of stylistic devices—chiefly the "figures" of rhetoric—which are constitutive of the elevated style. Whereas Plato draws a distinction between literary kinds and transcends it, whereas Aristotle discriminates among kinds of works and uses this discrimination as a principle of his treatment of them, and whereas the scholastic rhetoricians find their primary distinctions among rhetorical ends rather than among kinds of means, Longinus obliterates ultimately all such distinctions of kinds and end and makes the focal point of his inquiry a certain quality discriminated from among other qualities of composition. A treatise so ordered is distinct in method from these other treatments; and the statements which are employed in the prosecution of that method cannot be compared directly, without a precarious shift of meanings, to the statements which arise out of such variously opposed treatments as those of Plato, Aristotle, and, let us say, the author of the *Ad Herennium.*

The criticism of Caecilius with which the treatise opens is significant of Longinus' awareness of the problems which a literary treatise, as a practical work, would involve. The criticism turns on two main issues: first, the earlier treatise had been too low and had failed especially in the omission of vital points; second, it had failed to give readers sufficient assistance in accordance with the proper first aim of every writer. While the generality of the statement of these censures allows a certain latitude of interpretation, the exemplification of Caecilius' errors, together with the positive precepts immediately laid down for a technical treatise—a treatise stating the various means to a practical end—perhaps makes the import of the criticism sufficiently clear. There are two main rules, Longinus tells us, for a practical treatise, the first dealing with the end aimed at, the second with the means toward that end: first, the end must be made evident, and, second, specific means to its achievement must be indicated;

and it is a mark of Longinus' concern with the practical that the first question, which is a theoretical one, should be adjudged less important in the present treatise than the second, which is a practical one. By both these precepts, Caecilius has utterly failed: with respect to the first, he has sought to define the sublime by the mere collection of instances of sublimity; this is useless, either for a theoretical or for a practical inquiry, inasmuch as in the first consideration it does not provide a definition of sublimity and so affords no knowledge, and, in the second consideration, it does not afford such knowledge of the end as will permit the enumeration of the various means directed toward it. Sublimity is known instantially to all men of education and taste; and to write after the manner of Caecilius, thus, "as though we did not know," is to fail to construct an art of the sublime. With respect to the second precept, Caecilius, we are told, "unaccountably passed over" the indication of the means. Hence the earlier treatise has neither theoretical nor practical value.

Even from these earliest remarks, the ordering of the treatise, i.e., the principal division of its problems, can be seen clearly. Any art approached in this fashion must have three primary problems: clarification of the end aimed at, enumeration of the means to this end, and demonstration that the means are actually conducive to the proposed end. Since art involves purpose, the end must be known in some manner to the artist, or else his operations will be only vaguely purposive, if purposive at all; since any art affords instruments to its end and since not all instruments are appropriate to a given end, the appropriate means must be designated; and, since the efficacy of the art depends upon whether the instruments are actually efficient of the end, the connection of means and end must be demonstrated. The consideration of the end is clearly prior in a practical inquiry, since the means are determined by it; and we know the means when we know the causes of the end, so that what in a theoretical inquiry would be the causes would become in a practical inquiry the means; and to know the means as causes, third, of a given end is to know that the means are indeed efficacious of that end. The main body of Longinus' discussion, therefore, turns on these three problems: from the end of section ii to section vii he treats of the end of the practical inquiry, i.e., of sublimity and its opposites, together with the causes of all these; from section viii to the lacuna occurring in section ix, he deals with the demonstration of the means as conducive to sublimity; and the remainder of the work is given over to a discussion of the means and the divers problems which they entail.

Before these questions can be asked or answered, however, certain preliminary problems must be solved. Longinus has already treated, in his first paragraph, of the rules by which a technical treatise must be regulated; he must now ask, also, whether an art of the subject matter he proposes is in fact possible. To ask whether an art is possible is to pose two fundamental problems: it is, first, to ask whether the object produced by the art has existence (and Longinus is concerned with this question from sec. i. 3 to sec. ii) and, second, to ask whether there are modes of artificial production of that object (and this question occupies the extant whole of sec. ii). The object to be produced must first of all be something which can exist, for there could obviously be no production of what cannot exist; and in this proof of the existence of the object Longinus finds it necessary only to select from among admittedly existent psychological phenomena. These phenomena have as their immediate cause literary works; but it will be necessary to distinguish these from the phenomena caused by rhetoric, or the art of the sublime will not itself be distinct from rhetoric and, indeed, would be subsumed by it as a part under a whole, thereby precipitating the inquiry into an enumeration of the usual rhetorical devices. Consequently, to avert this danger, Longinus distinguishes his proposed art from rhetoric,[7] with which it might be so easily confused, and in his distinction he introduces the triad of terms—author, work, and audience—which constitute the fundamental framework of his argument. With respect to the author, sublimity is that which has constituted the greatest poets and prose writers in their high place and given them their fame; with respect to the audience, the effect of sublimity is transport . . . and not persuasion . . . ; and the former differs from the latter in that it is stronger than persuasion or the incidental pleasure attendant on persuasion, for the audience is powerless to resist [transport], although [persuasion] may be resisted; and, finally, with respect to the work, the excellences of rhetoric are contextual, that is, they emerge from the whole and are temporal, whereas the virtue of sublimity is that it emerges from the part and is instantaneous. Since there are psychological phenomena answering to this description, as, according to Longinus, all men of education and taste are aware, since there are productions of the kind described, and since there are men who are designated as the greatest writers, it is evident that sublimity has been proved to exist.

Next it is necessary to show that modes of artificial production exist by which sublimity may be generated, inasmuch as not every existent object is the product of art. Since Longinus assumes that man can produce literary works which have the quality of sublimity and that hence the quality exists, the argument[8] reduces to two questions which form the center of a dispute as to whether sublimity is produced, since produced it clearly is, by nature or by art and to a third question as to whether in any case its modes of acquisition are teachable. The import of these problems is clear: the first objection, that genius is innate, i.e., natural, and that the natural is spoiled by art, is countered by the statement that nature itself is systematic; were this not so, the present art would be impossible, since art must be an improvement upon nature; there are no arts of doing badly what nature can do well. The second objection, that nature is sufficient, elicits Longinus' response that even in genius it is insufficient, since genius falls into faults, exemplified fully in the later discussion, if left to itself without the controls of science; were this not so, again there would be no possibility of an art of the sublime, since there would be only a natural basis of sublimity and since there are no arts for doing what nature does adequately and infallibly. But, says Longinus, nature is to art as good fortune is to good counsel; and as good fortune is annulled where good counsel is wanting, so is genius annulled by lack of art. The third objection, that production of the sublime is unteachable, is removed by an argument which turns on the very possibility of making the judgments which led to the first two objections: if those who argue against the possibility of an art of the sublime can make such objections, then, since these statements concerning sublimity themselves fall under art and not under nature, they serve to substantiate the existence of the art, and, since they are preceptual, the production of sublimity is teachable. Hence, by all considerations, there is possible an art of the sublime.

Since an art of sublimity is possible, Longinus now takes up the problems of the art itself; and the fundamental triad of terms signifying author, work, and audience makes possible an argument of considerable clarity and power. In the order of composition the genius (author) composes a work which has a certain literary quality of sublimity (work) and which effects [transport] in hearers or readers (audience); the order of inquiry into the technique of composition, however, is the reverse of this; for we begin with a sensation in ourselves, as audience, which we recognize to be [transport]. Inquiring into the cause of this sensation, we find it to be a certain quality of sublimity in the work; but, while this is perhaps explicative of our sensation, we can at this stage say nothing concerning the manner in which a work must be composed. Consequently, we must inquire beyond the work into the faculties of the author which permitted its composition; and when we have achieved a statement of these, we have only to ask how these may be acquired or cultivated to answer the question of how the sublimity of a work may be achieved or the ecstasy of an audience effected. The manner in which the terms of the triad may be employed is clear: the dialectic moves in the one direction or in the other across the triad, using a reaction of the audience to define a fault or virtue of a work, a quality of the work to illustrate a faculty of the author; and what warrants this motion, primarily, is that our sensibility distinguishes [transport] from any other effect of discourse upon us and that we know ourselves to be moved to ecstasy by a literary work produced by a human agent. To argue in this manner, Longinus is well aware, is ultimately to analogize author, work, and reader; but the legitimacy of the procedure can hardly be called in doubt, particularly when we recall that the statements in the work which have gained most general assent—such statements as "the effect of sublimity is not persuasion but transport"[9] and "sublimity is the ring of a great soul"[10]—constitute the very foundations of the argument. So analogizing, however, Longinus has made it impossible to discuss separately the various literary kinds; there can be here no theory of tragedy, of comedy, epic, or comic-epic and no theory of rhetoric, since sublimity may be found in all these and in philosophic and historical literature as well and since it results from the nature of neither one nor another of these kinds of literary production but from the faculties of the agent who produced these. So analogizing, too, it is impossible to escape the consequence that the foundations of the art must be stated in psychological terms; this, however, scarcely affords a foothold for objection, since it means merely that Longinus, in answering the question of how the sublime is produced, has chosen to answer it in terms of human character and faculties rather than in terms of the characteristics of a literary work or of the literary devices which must be employed. We may deny the analogy constituted by the triad, we may demand an answer in other terms; but the argument of the treatise itself could be called in question only if we insist on affixing other significances to the terms which Longinus employs or on asserting that the study of literature involves totally different questions.

The text resumes, after a lacuna amounting to two pages of the Paris MS 2036, in the midst of a discussion of the faults into which unassisted genius may fall. Fragmentary as the whole treatise is, however, one perhaps need not despair of the intelligibility of the work; a careful consideration of the direction and method of argument and of the assumptions involved in the critical judgments affords excellent ground for some restoration of the lacunae, at least to the extent of reconstructing the argument. In the case of this—the first—lacuna, the missing argument can be reconstructed by an analysis of the most immediate problems of Longinus, and the reconstruction is supported by the resumption of the text itself. The argument has begun, let us remember, with an inquiry into [transport], a term falling under the audience-term of the triad; and the term itself has been defined, since a mere selection was intended, only by reference to a term in some way its opposite, persuasion, this term being taken also in the sense of an affection of the audience. This treatment by opposites is characteristic of the method of the entire treatise; sublimity itself is defined, at one stage, by contrast with opposite qualities of style, and the causes of sublimity are contrasted with the causes of these opposites; truth is held up against fiction, impeccability against sublimity, and the treatise closes, in fact, with an analysis of the mean style which parallels the analysis of the sublime and with an inquiry into the degeneration of contemporary writers. It is clear, therefore, that Longinus must have argued, from effects upon an audience contrary to that of [transport], toward qualities of style contrary to that of sublimity, since, indeed, we find him discussing, after the lacuna, exactly such qualities of style; and since the warrant for the existence of sublimity depended upon the audience's sensibility of a certain kind of passion, viz., [transport], it is clear that, if the treatise is consistent, the existence of the opposite qualities must have rested upon the same basis. For there are no topical terms (i.e., terms central to the discussion) which do not fall under one or another term of the triad of author, audience, and work; and since explication of qualities of style in terms of the author would be impossible, inasmuch as the argument has not yet reached that stage of development, and since explication of qualities in terms of kinds of works would likewise be impossible, inasmuch as no discrimination of kinds has been made—for, as we remarked, sublimity is a term predicable of any kind of work—therefore explication must have been made in terms of diverse effects upon the audience. And this is shown, furthermore, by the fact that the discussion, when it resumes, presupposes such discrimination of effects. On the grounds of these four arguments, then, such discrimination must have been made.

If this is so, we may attempt to reconstruct the discrimination; and this may be done either by considering the procedure of the previous argument or by asking what the resumption of argument presupposes. First, in the former manner, we may note that since the discrimination is of effects upon the audience and since one known effect is that of [transport], which is defined as an irresistible moving of the souls of the audience, and since the other effects are the opposites of these, the opposites must therefore have in common the general characteristic of nonmovement in that special respect; and since [transport] is literally a being-put-out-of-place so that, as Longinus later remarks, the audience is as one with the speaker, it follows that the opposite effects will differ specifically in that they are different kinds of movement away from that unity with the speaker. How they differ specifically may be discerned from examination of the text when it resumes.[11] Longinus is discussing three vices of style, two of which arise from certain relations of the passion of the speaker to the subject matter of the work, one of which arises from a lack of relation of his passion to the subject matter. Given a subject matter which lends itself to sublimity, the passion of the speaker may exceed the subject, and so the style will be turgid; or fall below it, and so the style will be frigid; or be unrelated to it, i.e., inappropriate to it, and so *parenthyrsus* results. If the classification of vices of style is on this principle, it is exhaustive; and there seems, consequently, no reason to suppose that parts of the classification are missing. The different opposites of [transport], therefore, would be effects upon an audience corresponding to each of these stylistic vices. In one sense, then, they are various kinds of indifference to the speaker; but they will be diversely attended, as special kinds of boredom, by risibility, mere contempt, and the confusion resulting from a display of unintelligible emotion.

It must be noted that Longinus has now moved in his discussion to a treatment of stylistic qualities; yet, from the resumption of the text at section iii, his discussion of them is still in terms of sensibilities of the audience, and properly so: at this stage qualities of style can be discussed only through their effects, that is, either by naming the effect as contempt, risibility, etc., or by providing examples of stylistic viciousness which indicate the intended effect by actually inducing it in the cultivated and sensible reader. The author enters into the discussion not as one possessed or not possessed of the sources of sublimity but as one who aimed at sublimity and in some way missed in each case; and his introduction depends upon the necessity for illustrating his failure—a failure in art, in the strictest sense, since the intention of sublimity is actually present—to achieve that unification of author and audience which is [transport]. The audience must feel what he feels—hence the statement of stylistic vices, in terms of passion as related to subject, becomes at this stage the only possible statement. When the vices of style are made clear in this manner, their cause can be stated, although not as yet with respect to the causes of sublimity, since sublimity itself has not yet been defined; and so Longinus remarks, in section v, that the general cause of these vices is a craving for intellectual novelties. The reason why no other vices of style have been treated becomes clear when we recognize that this is an exhaustive division, *given a sublime subject;* other vices would fall outside an art of the sublime, as not resulting from an intention of sublimity; but these may be confused with sublimity itself because, as he remarks, they are "thus intimately mingled with it," since sublimity is aimed at.[12]

Longinus has treated the opposites of sublimity in order to exhibit what constitutes failure in the art and what is to be avoided; and he has treated these vices before he has dealt with sublimity itself because sublimity is more readily located, as a kind of mean between these various extremes which are more easily apparent to sensibility—the latter being still his chief point of reference—than would be sublimity. Now, following his precedent treatment he turns in section vi to a discussion of sublimity itself. For him sublimity permits neither of definition by example (as his criticism of the "instances of the sublime" provided by Caecilius would indicate) nor, on the other hand, of a purely theoretical statement; this is a practical problem, and hence discourse will not serve as a substitute for experience, for "judgment of style is the last and ripest fruit of much experience."[13] Now, if mere experience, on the one hand, or mere theoretical discussion, on the other, cannot provide knowledge of the sublime, there is a third way by which such knowledge may be achieved; and that is by means of an amalgamation of the two into touchstones for the sublime. Hence Longinus enumerates the signs or notes by which we may know whether or not a given work has true sublimity; drawing an analogy between true and false greatness in general, Longinus is enabled, first of all, to state his criteria in terms of proper and improper admiration and, proceeding thence, to adumbrate the sublime in terms of the character of admiration which it excites. The soul is elevated by sublimity to joy and exultation;[14] the reader feels an identification with the author, for the soul feels "as though itself had produced what it hears";[15] hence what does not elevate at all would not even be false sublimity, and that which elevates only temporarily and has a diminishing force forever after is false sublimity, while that which has a permanent force and which provides a perpetual nourishment for the soul is the sublime itself. Hence it is that transport which is impossible to resist and which establishes itself firmly in the memory and which always leaves material for fresh reflection. Since the sublime would have these characteristics, the most certain attestation of sublimity would be the discovery of its universal appreciation; thus the *consensus gentium* constitutes, for Longinus, an unquestionable test, since it abstracts from any possibility of individual error.[16]

The provision of these touchstones makes possible the recognition of individual works as instances of the sublime, on the one hand, and a knowledge of the nature of the sublime, on the other. Hence, since we now know what the sublime is, in something other than a merely instantial mode, we may know what its causes or sources are, and so state its nature causally. Thus Longinus, in section viii, passes to a consideration of the sources of sublimity, to their enumeration and demonstration as exhaustive and discrete; and in so doing he completes his fundamental triad of terms by now stating sublimity in terms of characteristics of the author—that is, in terms of what the author must *be* in order to produce sublimity. That this is the case is clear; for Longinus is careful to use predicates which are strictly predicable only of a human subject: "having power of expression,"[17] "empowered with great (full-bodied) conception,"[18] "having passion,"[19] etc.; and his treatment of them, moreover, is precisely as human characteristics, for his preliminary classification of them is according to whether they are innate or acquired.[20]

The manner of derivation of the five sources is not explicit in the treatise; consequently, the enumeration of the sources has not infrequently been called in question, and sometimes, even, their importance for the treatise has been minimized. Saintsbury remarks:

> No nervous check or chill need be caused by the tolerably certain fact that more than one hole may be picked in the subsequent classification of the sources of [*hypos*]. These attempts at an overmethodical classification (it has been said before) are always full of snares and pitfalls to the critic. Especially do they tempt him to the sin of arguing in a circle. It cannot be denied that in every one of the five divisions (except, perhaps, the valuable vindication of the quality of Passion) there is some treacherous word or other, which is a mere synonym of "sublime." Thus in the first we have . . . mastery of the *hadron,* a curious word, the nearest equivalent of which in English is, perhaps, "stout" or "full-bodied," as we apply these terms to wine; in the fourth *gennaia,* "noble," which is only "sublime" in disguise; and in the fifth *axioma kai diarsis,* of which much the same may be said.[21]

If we may overlook in this statement what is merely dogmatic—as, for example, the curious carping that an art or method of achieving sublimity is somehow at fault for being methodical—we may concentrate on the principal issue of the objection, i.e., whether there is any circularity of argument. Longinus has been asking the causes of sublimity here, as in section v he discussed the causes of failures in sublimity. Since the fundamental triad of terms must be in alignment with a term signifying the subject matter which is sublime, the basis for an enumeration of five sources, and of only five, is fairly obvious. Sublimity of subject matter is not achieved by art, or there would be a fundamental tetrad rather than triad; since, given a sublime subject, an author must first conceive it, secondly feel concerning it if it is excitative of passion, and thirdly express it, it is clear immediately that the sources would, at first sight, involve conception, passion, and expression. But the third factor is complex: since expression deals with words, words can be considered either as signs, simple or combined, or merely as sounds. If we consider words as signs in combination, we can regard them nonsyntactically, as constitutive of such modes of discourse as question, prayer, oath, etc. (in which case we have *figures of thought,* since such modes are prior to and independent of any syntactical consideration), or we may regard them syntactically, as constituted of certain grammatical elements (in which case we have *figures of language,* such as asyndeton, hyperbaton, polyptota, etc.); and Longinus groups these two under the head of Figures, as his third source of the sublime. On the other hand, words may be regarded as simple, and here again there are two possibilities; all grammatical distinctions being dropped out, the problem is reduced to the imposition of signs for things and their qualities; and the imposition may be strict, i.e., literally stand for the thing, when the problem reduces to a choice of synonyms, or it may involve a comparison when the matter is one of a choice of tropes and metaphors. These problems are problems strictly of diction for Longinus, and their solution establishes the fourth source of the sublime. Finally, words may be regarded as sounds constitutive of rhythms and harmony; and he so treats of them under the head of *sunthesis*.

If, indeed, there is a circularity here, the whole argument collapses; but Saintsbury's charge of paralogism falls a little oddly on our ears. It is difficult to see how an argument from effect to cause could involve a circularity, even though apparently synonymous adjectives be applied to both cause and effect; for example, there is nothing wrong with the statement that it takes a human being as cause to produce a human being as effect. In an alternative statement, we might simply say that Longinus' derivation of the sources depends upon the possibility of identifying the human faculties which make a literary work of a certain quality possible; and though for Longinus the soul of the great writer reflects the sublime subject and the work reflects the soul and the mind of the audience ultimately reflects the work, the similarities which the analogical argument discloses, and upon which, indeed, it depends, are not to be confused with such circularity as would vitiate syllogistic procedure.

The insistence of Longinus, in section viii, that Caecilius is in error in his enumeration of the . . . sources of sublimity, suggests, since the attack has a rational basis, that he regarded his own statement of them as defensible; and the nature of its defense may be reconstructed, perhaps, despite the length of the lacuna in section ix, without exceeding the evidences of that defense which the extant portions provide. The latter portion of viii, for example, indicates through the objections posed to Caecilius the general character of the dialectic which would be used to establish any one of the five sources as actually distinct means conducive to sublimity. If Caecilius has omitted passion, Longinus argues, it is either because he has identified passion with sublimity or because he has not thought it conducive to sublimity. In the first case, he is in error because, if passion is inseparable from sublimity, then what is passionate must also always be sublime, and conversely; but both this consequence and its converse can be seen to be false, as well from an examination of works as from an examination of the faculties of orators.[22] In the second case, Caccilius is in error because "nothing attains the heights of eloquence so certainly as genuine passion in the right place."[23] The argument establishing the existence of any one source, thus, would turn on whether the "source" in question was distinct from any other and whether in fact it was a source at all. It is probable, therefore, that, since such questions have been raised, they will be answered; and undoubtedly the missing section in ix must have been devoted, in great part at least, to the settling of just these questions with respect to the remaining sources. The extant portion of section ix before the lacuna bears out this hypothesis: for Longinus proceeds to argue in it, first, that great conception is distinct from any of the linguistic sources, since "without any utterance a notion, unclothed and unsupported, often moves our wonder, because the very thought is great"[24]—the example of Ajax' silence entering in as proof of this proposition—and, second, that greatness of conception is actually conducive to sublimity because "great words issue, and it cannot be otherwise, from those whose thoughts are weighty",[25] and the text is interrupted as Longinus is apparently proving this proposition also by example, in all likelihood the speech of Alexander to Parmenio which is reported in Arrian.[26] The third question which would be pertinent to each source—whether it permits of acquisition, since otherwise it could not fall under art—has likewise its answer in this section: even though, as Longinus has already remarked, great conception and passion are primarily natural, means for their development and cultivation may be indicated.[27]

In a similar manner, the missing portion must have treated of the remaining sources; and the character of the argument may be outlined. Once great conception and passion have been shown to be sources, Longinus has completed his treatment of those topics which would be common to all arts; the remaining discussion enters as resulting from the means. Since the treatise is concerned only with literary sublimity—although, as Longinus frequently remarks,[28] the *hypsos,* in a wider sense, may be found in any of the other arts, painting, sculpture, architecture, music, etc.—and since conception and passion are independent of words,[29] it is necessary to consider how sublimity is achieved through the use of words, peculiarly; and, as we have seen, Longinus accomplishes this by considering words in connection with thought, the figures of thought resulting; next, by dropping out thought and considering words in relation to one another, the figures of language so resulting; next, by considering isolated words in their application to things, so that the problems of word choice emerge for solution; and, finally, by considering the word as a collocation of syllables, thus opening the questions of rhythm, and as an aggregation of letters, thus raising the problem of harmony, both rhythm and harmony being parts of the problem of *synthesis* or *compositio.* The power of expression, Longinus says, must be presupposed;[30] it is natural and does not fall under art; the latter three sources are not a substitute for it but grow out of it as special determinations of the exercise of that power. This presupposition made, however, it is impossible to attack Longinus' treatment of the verbal sources; since they arise from a consideration of the ways in which words may be employed, there must be a separate verbal faculty for each such employment; in the case of Figures, mere use of figures does not constitute sublimity,[31] although a proper use of them is conducive to that end, so that a consideration of figures falls clearly within the art, but as a means; hence it falls among the sources, but it is a source distinct—on the one hand—

from great conception and passion because these are primarily natural, whereas skill with figures is acquired, and because these are independent of words, whereas skill with figures is not, and—on the other hand—from diction and synthesis, although both of these involve words and are acquired faculties, because, as we have seen, different aspects of words are the object of each; and Longinus defends these distinctions by pointing out again and again[32] that works fall short of the sublime or achieve it by failures or successes in one of these respects or another and that authors who are skilful or inept in certain respects are not necessarily so in all. These matters are ascertainable by sensibility alone: "it is mere folly to raise problems over things which are so fully admitted, for experience is proof sufficient," but he does not therefore refrain from argument.[33]

The resumption of the text[34] reveals Longinus in the midst of a development of the means by which greatness of conception, as the first source of the sublime, may be achieved; and the first means, from various indications of the context, is by the direction of the author's mind toward great objects, so that, if true greatness be truly and completely ascertained, a commensurate greatness of conception must needs follow. The various indications of which I speak may be briefly stated. First, that this section falls within the means would be arguable, even if the problems of the treatise and their manner of treatment were less evident than they are, from Longinus' statement (x. 1) that we may pass on to consider any "further means"; and, second, that all this is relevant to greatness of conception may be seen from the close of xv, in which he remarks that that topic may now be considered as closed. If this section is relative to *megalophues* (or *hadrepābolon*) then, the quotations here must be taken, not as striking instances of hyperbole or other verbal devices, but as examples of noetic magnificence; it is the *conception*, here, which interests the critic and not the words. His first treatment of conception is in terms of the gods as its object; his second in terms of heroes; and conception is evidently subjected to two criteria: the first, truth; the second, completeness. Thus Homer is praised for his conceptions of Strife, of the horses of the gods, of theomachies, of Poseidon, and of Ares, in so far as he realizes the loftiness of deity, i.e., the truth about the gods; he is blamed, however, when the gods are conceived as in any way less than they actually are, as, for example, when "he presents to us woundings of the gods, their factions, revenges, tears, bonds, sufferings. . . . "; for then "he has made the gods men."[35] On similar grounds Hesiod is condemned and Moses is praised;[36] and the assignment of the *Odyssey* to a lower place than that of the *Iliad* depends precisely on these considerations as well; and what we have here is no "instinctive, unreasoning terror" of the Greek at the "unknown Romance," as Saintsbury phrases it,[37] for the objection is not that these are myths but that they are myths which could not possibly be true of their subjects. The criticism which appears in this section has been frequently censured; but the censure is hardly justifiable on logical grounds. Longinus is saying that if you wish to nature your soul to great conceptions you must contemplate great objects—gods, heroes, the majesty of nature, etc.—and that your conception will not be great if you fail to conceive the greatness of your object, i.e., if you fail to form a true and complete conception; for a true and complete conception of a great subject would necessarily be great. Thus the "dreams of Zeus" which occur in the *Odyssey*—"the stories of the wine-skin, of the companions turned by Circe into swine," and the many marvelous episodes of a similar nature—might well be the fantasies of the gods, they are certainly excellent literature; but they are hardly true and complete conceptions either of gods or of heroes, and they are therefore hardly sublime. Both the *Iliad* and the *Odyssey* are by Homer and are marks of his transcendent genius; but the former is "a throng of images all drawn from the truth," while the latter is "a wandering among the shallows of the fabulous and incredible."[38]

Next, according to Longinus (sec. x), "since with all things are associated certain elements, constituents which are essentially inherent in the substance of each," the writer who would gain greatness of conception must select and integrate these essentials. The meaning of this statement becomes clear if we consider the context. Greatness of conception is cultivated by the true apprehension of great objects, as we have seen; but, given a sublime subject matter of which the author has conceived, not all of its aspects are equally responsible for its sublimity, and hence it is the business of the writer to select those aspects which are most responsible and to integrate them in such fashion as that in which they are integrated in the object itself. Thus, for example, a storm is terrible, and hence sublime, inspiring fear and awe; however, not all its characteristics inspire these feelings, but only such as relate to its power and danger; hence the writer must choose those most relative and unite them in such manner, in his mind, that they are not scattered conceptions but "the form and features of that peril."[39] The integration must be present because it is the integration of the characteristics in the object itself which inspired such feelings as were peculiar to it; without such unification, the various conceptions would not induce a feeling comparable to that caused by the object. The *Ode to Anactoria* is praised for such selection and collocation; considering still the conception as opposed to the diction, Longinus remarks that the subject matter—"love-madness"—has been well treated, since Sappho has chosen to speak of those effects, physical as well as intellectual, which are the essential symptoms of love frenzy.[40] On the other hand, Aristeas of Proconnesus is blamed for the evident and just reason that the details of seafaring which he enumerates are hardly those by virtue of which the sea itself is sublime—seasickness, which forms the climax of his description, scarcely gives the impression of sublimity; and though Aristeas has talked around that painful subject by saying that the sailors' "inward parts, even, are tossed terribly to and fro," the trick is purely a verbal one, and so the description is more embroidery than sublimity.[41] Similarly, Aratus, in saying that "only a tiny plank keeps off bitter destruction," is not sublime[42] because he is merely verbalizing also; in all cases of sailing, a few planks keep off death, but there is no terror here because those planks are generally sufficient; the sea itself is not a source of terror at all times, but only when it rages; and so the device of Aratus constitutes an attempt to rhetoricize, to falsify a quite normal situation. One must understand Longinus as still speaking of *conception;* on that ground, the passage is bad; on a purely verbal ground he might have considered it excellent.

Again, the writer may achieve sublimity by the accumulation of vast detail, with the assurance that this multiplicity of detail will tend to give any subject importance and also to bring out whatever effects would be caused by that subject itself. The second mode—the mode of selection and integration—is conducive to sublimity in that the writer seeks those aspects upon which the effect of the subject depends; in this, the third mode, the effect depends, in so far as it is mere amplification, strictly upon number; as Longinus remarks, amplification always implies quantity and abundance. We may adumbrate a subject either by stating its essential characteristics or by enumerating at large its characteristics both essential and accidental; for in fact the thing itself so presents itself to us, as a mixture of the essential and accidental. It matters not how we effect this quantitative expansion, Longinus tells us; there are numberless varieties of amplification; we may either work through the topics or commonplaces or exaggerate (in the sense of forming a conception which exceeds the thing or fact or event) or emphasize, or do any one of ten thousand things; in any case, the writer must dwell upon the subject with accumulation and insistence, building always toward sublimity. If the subject contemplated is in truth a great subject, sublimity will be reached in this manner; if not, a merely rhetorical amplification will result; and Longinus is careful here, as throughout the treatise, to discriminate between a device in its merely rhetorical use and the same device as a means of achieving sublimity; he finds it necessary, indeed, to redefine amplification, lest it be thought synonymous with the sublime itself and lest, consequently, the art of the sublime be collapsed into an art of rhetorical amplification. Like other modes of achieving sublimity, amplification is only conducive to sublimity, not identical with it; nor is Longinus so incautious as to omit a demonstration of this point. The comparatively brief lacuna which occurs at this place in the text interrupts both the demonstration and the exposition of its significance; but here, for once, the main lines of the discussion are not destroyed. When the text resumes,[43] Longinus is discussing, clearly enough, the proprieties of diffuseness (which would be achieved by amplification) and intensity.

So far, in his treatment of *megalophues,* Longinus has considered the author as contemplating the great subject in order to formulate great conceptions; and, as we have seen, he has shown that the author may attempt either to formulate a conception commensurate with the sublime subject or to select and integrate those characteristics upon which its sublimity depends or to enumerate at large until the multiplicity of conceived detail approximates the real fulness of the thing. Following section xii, however, he suggests two other modes by which greatness of conception may be achieved. First, if the sublime authors, e.g., Homer, Plato, Demosthenes, etc., have attained sublimity by greatness of conception, so that their thoughts were commensurate with great subjects, it follows that, if an author can make his thoughts commensurate with their thoughts, he likewise will achieve greatness of conception; thus, greatness of thought can be attained by the imitation of great authors.[44] Longinus is not speaking of the reproduction exclusively of tricks of style; he says explicitly, "Therefore even we, when we are working out a theme which requires lofty speech and greatness of thought" must call to mind the performances of great authors;[45] and the analogy of this sort of literary inspiration to the Pythian vapors makes his meaning completely clear; if we are not able to achieve greatness of thought by contemplating the thing itself, we may contemplate instead those authors whose thoughts were stretched to its stature, as "even those not too highly susceptible to the god are possessed by the greatness which was in others."[46] And he gives the author touchstones again, formulating them in terms of the fundamental triad of author, work, and audience: in composing, the author is to consider Homer and the great ones as composing in his place, knowing them as he does through the medium of their works; in judging his work, he must regard them as his audience, and, further, he must ask how the ages to come will esteem his composition.[47]

Second, if we neither contemplate the object directly nor contemplate it through the contemplations of others, we may invent, we may imagine;[48] where our knowledge is partial and incomplete, we may piece out what is missing by imagination, and the examples which Longinus uses seem intended to illustrate invention out of whole cloth, as in the case of the sane Euripides imagining madness,[49] or of detail only, as in the ride of Phaethon in *Iphigenia in Tauris.*[50] According to Longinus, there is a difference between the application of imagination in poetry and in rhetoric, the latter being limited by what is known to be true and what is thought to be probable. This much done, Longinus remarks that his treatment of the "sublime effects which belong to great thoughts, and which are produced by the greatness of man's soul, and secondarily by imitation or by imagination" has been adequate.

Longinus now[51] passes on to a discussion of the Figures, postponing his treatment of passion for reasons which will be indicated later in this essay. As he remarks, there are infinite kinds of Figures; dividing them into Figures of Thought and Figures of Language, he mentions in the former class adjuration (or apostrophe or oath), questions and interrogations, in the latter class, asyndeton, hyperbaton, polyptota (including all departures from the normal usage of case, tense, gender, person, and number), and periphrasis. Figures by themselves, Longinus tells us repeatedly, do not constitute sublimity; thus any merely rhetorical definitions of the Figures are insufficient to indicate their use toward effecting sublimity, since such definitions are only recipes for the construction of the Figures themselves, without consideration of the context of their use; consequently, in his treatment of the Figures, Longinus is careful always to include some statement of the literary circumstances in which they would effect sublimity and of those in which they would not. Adjuration or apostrophe, for example, is an oath, discourse involving a solemn appeal to something sacred to witness that a statement is true or that a contract is binding; the rhetoricians tell us merely to swear by those names which are most sacred; "but," says Longinus, "it is not the mere swearing by a name which is great; place, manner, occasion, purpose are all essential";[52] and the rhetoricians have failed in their prescriptions because they have treated these variables of place, manner, occasion, and purpose as constants. Thus, though both Demosthenes and Eupolis swore by Marathon, so that in a sense their oath is the same, the apostrophe of the latter is merely that, whereas the apostrophe of the former is at once an assurance resting upon oaths, a demonstration, an example, a eulogy, and an exhortation.[53] His point, of course, is extremely well taken; indeed, any other statement would have been irrelevant or insufficient, since the sources stand related to sublimity as means to end.

While a formula of the constitution of a Figure is necessary therefore, so that the orator may know what it is and hence be able to construct it at will, he must also know what effect it produces; consequently, throughout his treatment of the Figures, Longinus states the effect of each Figure, so that we may know whether it is conducive to the proper end. Questions and interrogations, thus, "reproduce the spontaneity of passion" and give intensity and vehemence and conviction to the discourse, "drawing the hearer off until he thinks that each point in the inquiry has been raised and put into words without preparation, and so it imposes upon him."[54] Asyndeton, wherein "the words drop unconnected and are, so to speak, poured forth almost too fast for the speaker himself," gives "the impression of a struggle, where the meaning is at once checked and hurried on."[55] Similarly, hyperbaton "is the surest impress of vehement passion"; the hearer fears that a failure of both syntax and logic is imminent, and, since this is a sign of vehement passion, he is persuaded that the discourse is an instance of vehement passion.[56] And thus Longinus treats also of the other Figures. The principal determinant throughout is the tendency of the audience to reason from the consequent; and, although Longinus never makes such explicit reference to the tendency as Aristotle (*Poetics* xxiv), all the instances which he mentions are plainly arguments from signs.

Concerning the choice of words, next, Longinus clearly lays a basis for selection. Certain words are noble and beautiful, while others are inferior;[57] a similar distinction, as he remarks particularly in xxxv, may be made among things and also among thoughts. Thus the primary determinant in the choice of words is the necessity of maintaining a correspondence between these hierarchies; and, while the choice of grand words is necessary for noble composition, the words must be accurate as well; and, like Quintilian, he likens the choice of a grand word for a thing of lesser stature to the fastening of a large tragic mask upon a little child.[58] An unfortunate lacuna occurs at this place, apparently just as Longinus was about to say that in poetry, however, which like fiction is less bound by probability than rhetoric or history, these restrictions do not always apply. Doubtless he proceeded to treat of the various possible permutations of the central terms of his discussion here; if we take only two elements—words and things—then two principles emerge; since the hierarchies, verbal and real, must correspond and since the effect is to be one of greatness, one must use the grand word as well as the right word, and the choice of diction thus becomes merely a choice of objects of discourse. But this solution of the problem of word choice—one common enough in the history of rhetoric—is too simple for Longinus; it will do as a preliminary consideration, but one must also take into account the element of thought; and since it is possible that a low conception may be entertained of a great thing and conversely, several consequences emerge; in tragedy, for instance, Longinus would have been likely to argue, since the effect is to be one of grandeur, the characters are lofty, and their thoughts must consequently be lofty, even where the object of thought is common or mean; hence, too, their discourse must be lofty—even bombast is admissible in tragedy, he has said earlier, provided it does not degenerate into tasteless rant. On the other hand, vulgar words, as he is remarking when the text resumes,[59] may be preferable to ornamental language, may be used with an effect which is not vulgar when sheer accuracy and credibility are concerned.

Longinus' treatment of metaphor, trope, and simile under word choice, unconventional as it is, is consequent upon his careful separation of the sources. Since all grammatical collocations would fall under the Figures, word choice deals with the selection of names for things, thought being an intermediary term: now words either stand for things strictly and literally or they do not, in which case they are either metaphors, paraboles, similes, or hyperboles. The differences obtaining between these (although they are in a sense akin) may be seen by an examination of the schematism which has developed them. On the one hand, Longinus clearly ranks words and things; on the other, within this hierarchy, words must either stand for what they strictly mean, and hence for what is like or different, or not. Hyperbole, thus, results, as he says,[60] when words exaggerate the thing in terms either of excess or of defect by likening it to what is more than it or less than it; the other tropes result when, although a comparison is involved, inasmuch as something is likened to what it is not, it is strict, i.e., is not of a greater to a less or of a less to a greater; and the distinctions between these are apparently that metaphor is absolute comparison, inasmuch as the name of the thing is actually substituted, whereas *parabolai* and *eikoēs* are not, these differing in turn from each other in that the former is in terms of difference, the latter in terms of likeness. Were the differences stated in grammatical terms—that is, in terms of the grammatical particles employed in the case of simile, for example—simile, parabole, and hyperbole would have fallen under the Figures and would have been statable merely as formulas in consequence of this; but to state the problem as one of signification, as here, is to permit the choice of words to depend on the imposition of names and to introduce again the variable factors of place, manner, occasion, and purpose—which again would appear as constants in a merely rhetorical formulation—as determinatives of the choice of diction. And in the problem of word selection, as elsewhere, Longinus is insistent that metaphor, simile, parabole, and hyperbole are always means, never ends; the device must be dependent upon the use, never the use upon the device; to provide mere recipes for the formulation of rhetorical devices, without clear indication of the variable literary circumstances in which they would be appropriate, is, in effect, to constitute them as ends not means, so that the work becomes not a final unity but an aggregation of ends; and since, for Longinus, the use is always statable in terms of the audience—a certain effect of [transport] in the hearers—the unity of a work is properly stated not in terms of the work itself or of exclusively literary formulations but in terms of the unity of effect upon those reading or hearing. Consequently, Longinus remarks that there are no literary regulations as such governing the use of such devices as metaphor;[61] the proper determinant is the passion of the author, since whatever numbers and kinds of metaphors would appear appropriate to him in his passion would also appear appropriate to an audience to which that passion has been communicated; and Longinus is scornful, consequently, of the apparent decision of Caecilius that the number of metaphors to be applied to a single object should not exceed two or three.[62]

The treatment of synthesis,[63] finally, offers but little difficulty. In his first mention of this source of sublimity,[64] Longinus had remarked that synthesis included all the others; however, in his actual treatment of the source, it appears solely as a topic dealing with the arrangement of words into harmony and rhythm. While at first sight there seems to be a contradiction here, the contradiction is readily resolved from an examination of the contexts of the discussions. Snythesis—the arrangement of words—presupposes thought, passion, the Figures, and the choice of words, and in a mere enumeration of the sources would be stated, therefore, as the consummation of all of them, as inclusive of all of them in the sense that any literary work may be ultimately regarded as a certain arrangement of words. If, on the other hand, one deals with the sources as means, expounding what is proper to each source, then synthesis appears only as the arrangement, rhythmic and harmonic, of words which have already been selected as a consequence of all the other artistic operations.

Longinus' argument concerning the importance of synthesis is a simple analogy; words considered merely as sound and incorporated into harmony and rhythm are to musical tones similarly incorporated as the effect of the former to the effect of the latter; then, if we recall what is superadded to words by their significance and recall also how tremendous is the effect of music, we may gauge adequately the effect of the arrangement of words. Hence, section xl points out that synthesis is the ultimate collocation, in which all the sources meet.

The remainder of the extant treatise is given over, first, to a consideration of how literary works fall short of sublimity[65] and, second, to a consideration of the causes of the lack of sublimity among the authors of Longinus' time.[66] The first topic need scarcely be discussed; as Longinus remarks, "there is no present need to enumerate by their kinds the means of producing pettiness; when we have once shown what things make writings noble and sublime, it is clear that in most cases their opposites will make them low and uncouth"; and Longinus proceeds to treat them in reverse order to that of the sources of sublimity, going no further, however, than the choice of words. The second consideration enters into the topic importantly; if the times constrain the artist to the point where he cannot operate, then rhetorical tuition is useless; hence the artist must be demonstrated to be a free and independent agent. And, as he shows, in any failure of art it is the artist and not his time which is at fault, so that art remains a permanent possibility. At this point the extant treatise concludes, with a broken transition to the topic of the passions.

Unfortunate as the loss of the remaining discussion is, it cannot and need not be accepted as a permanent mutilation of the text. Since, as this essay has doubtless made clear, passion is one of the important determinants as well as a source in itself of literary operation, it follows that there must be some specification of the conception of passion if the ***Peri Hypsous*** is to appear as an intelligible technical treatise. And further, although we have no part of the promised treatise on the passions, we have in the text ample reference and comment on the subject of the passions from which Longinus' treatment of passion might be reconstructed, in sufficient part to render the technique of ***Peri Hypsous*** operable at least, although perhaps not sufficiently to permit a reconstruction of his entire theory of psychology.

Happily we have in section xx a definition of passion; it is a rush and commotion of the soul,[67] its contrary, calm, is a rest, a stasis of the soul,[68] and, although Longinus explicitly says that "passions are many, nay countless, past the power of man to reckon,"[69] so that an attempt to achieve their complete enumeration would clearly be useless, the text nevertheless furnishes us not only with many examples of the passions but with some indication of their causation and determination, their course, their symptoms, and their ordering. Pity, joy, fear, grief, pride, wonder, awe, hate, disgust, love, reverence, inspiration, madness, persuasion, ecstasy, suspicion, anger, indignation, jealousy, patience, shame, laughter, weeping, and envy constitute a partial list, and one more than adequate for our purposes; and Longinus' comments concerning those which are directly mentioned by him make it evident that, first of all, every passion has a cause—a cause which is its object. Since passion is a motion of the soul, then either the soul itself is the cause of motion or something external to the soul; but it is clear from Longinus' statements that something external to the soul is the cause, as peril of fear, safety of confidence, the gods of awe and reverence, the mean and vicious of disgust, etc. And it is clear, further, that passion admits of degree, since Longinus speaks frequently of vehement passion and since such statements constitute an admission of the possibility of degree. Further, it is clear that not every passion has the same object, since Longinus remarks that certain things excite terror, certain things disgust, and that not every object excites passion in the same degree, since he says also that one thing may be more terrible than another. It follows, therefore, that the object is by nature determinative both of the kind and of the degree of the passion which it excites. Hence, as he says, passions are infinite in number, since the objects are causative of unique effects. His remark concerning laughter, that "it is a passion, a passion which has its root in pleasure,"[70] provides the determination of the degree of passion; for, if pleasure is a root of passion, then pain must be a root also; and it follows from what has been discovered so far that every object is capable of inducing passion in so far as it is capable of inducing a motion of the soul attended either by pleasure or by pain and that the degree of passion which it induces would be proportional to the amount of attendant pain or pleasure. It would not be difficult, once this much is known, to construct definitions of at least the more familiar emotions, since the extant text provides ample illustration of Longinus' method of framing definitions; but perhaps this will be unnecessary if we remark that each such definition would state that the passion in question is an agitation of the soul, accompanied by pleasure or pain, and slight or great in proportion to that pleasure or pain, attended by such and such symptoms, the moving cause being something which in such and such a fashion is capable of inflicting pain or inducing pleasure.

Further, Longinus clearly ranks objects as high, common, or low; now, since it is possible that any object is capable of inducing passion and since passion is determined in kind and degree by the object, it follows that passions themselves must be capable of similar classification to that of objects; hence as high, common, or low; and this is borne out by his statement in section viii that wretchedness, annoyance, and fear are passions of a mean order. They are such because they cannot properly be caused by the highest objects; what is itself good in the highest degree must naturally cause, in the highest degree, those passions which are highest; for example, love, reverence, and awe are passions which are properly excited in us to the highest degree by the gods; but disgust, pity, or annoyance they could not properly cause.

It is clear, furthermore, that for Longinus the soul has both an active and a passive principle, since the soul is capable of thought and since thought cannot here be passion, for if it were passion, it could not be reckoned as a distinct source of sublimity. And this is clear also from his statement that men have the power to be good and to think elevated thoughts;[71] for this would be impossible if the soul were passive only, and, indeed, it would be impossible for the soul to initiate any action whatsoever; hence, on the same grounds, an active principle of the soul is implied by the very possibility of an art of anything. If, then, there is this active principle, then either it governs the passive, or the passive governs it, or they govern reciprocally, or both are ruled together by some other thing. But this last is impossible; for if the active is governed by something further, there is no active principle; but we have seen that there is. Now passion can be known to be unseasonable or excessive or defective, while thought can be known to be false; and in whatever principle the criterion rests there must also be governance; but passion cannot know anything. It follows, then, that the active principle must be the ruling principle. Hence reason must rule appetite and passion, and, when it so rules with all propriety, virtue results. But in such cases as those in which passion and appetite gain the upper hand and either become dislocated from their proper objects or become excessive or defective, in these vice or madness must result.

The gods are passionless;[72] heroes are distinguished from common men in that they suffer a passion different either in kind or in degree from that which common men undergo, for the heroic passions have higher objects; thus the anger of Ajax arises from no common cause and exhibits itself in no common fashion, and similarly the fear of an Ajax is not of death but of a death which is unheroic.[73] Sublimity of passion, then, must be of this heroic order; but its evocation is ultimately dependent upon thought, noble passion resulting where thought itself is noble, and ignoble passion where thought is mean. The noble mind, if not passionless like the divine, is at least free of the meaner passions because it is averted from the objects which call these forth.

So much for the reconstruction of Longinus' theory of the passions; it remains to observe the consequences of such a theory for the Longinian art of the sublime. The method would now appear to be perfect and complete. Certain things are by nature sublime; by nature man is capable of recognizing them as sublime and of loving them with an eternal and invincible love, for nature determined man to be no low and ignoble animal; admitted into the universe in part as spectator, in part as participant, and driven by his love into rivalry and competition with the supremacy of the marvelous, the great, and the beautiful, he fulfils the function which these in a manner appoint him; and, although human understanding is limited and wonder results when marvels surpass human thought, in a sense also the mind grows beyond its ordinary bounds, so that "for the speculation and thought which are within the scope of human endeavor, not all the universe is sufficient."[74] The nobility of man's thought, then, finds its warrant in these sublimities, and thought itself is the warrant of all else; for it determines passion, and thought and passion together, in literary endeavor, determine the use of all literary devices and guarantee their success.

Consequently, the artist must himself be sublime in soul if he is to reflect the sublime; if he is led by the love of pleasure or the love of money, he becomes little and ignoble. Like a corrupted judge he mistakes his own interest for what is good and noble, he admires his mortal parts and neglects to improve the immortal, and he becomes eventually the prisoner of his passions.[75] And the ignoble man, the slave, cannot produce what is admirable; "the true Orator must have no low ungenerous spirit, for it is not possible that those who think small thoughts fit for slaves, and practise them in all their daily life, should put out anything to deserve wonder and immortality."[76] But "great words issue, and it cannot be otherwise, from those whose thoughts are weighty";[77] and literary greatness is to be estimated not by mere freedom from fault but by the greatness of the spirit reflected in the words as in a mirror. Art thus in a sense is a double discipline, being both moral and aesthetic; but its literary function is ultimately only to provide some suitable medium which the spirit of the writer transcends and illuminates. So the spirit of the writer be sublime and the mirror of words present an adequate image, hearers who are properly prepared cannot fail to be stirred, for words carry "the passion which is present to the speaker into the souls of the bystanders, bringing them into partnership with himself";[78] and the admiration of men for what is truly great is "as it were, a law of nature," failing only when men have sunk beneath their natural state or have not reached their proper development.[79]

The topic of the passions is not treated with the other sources because the passions are not, like them, open to voluntary acquisition; they are per se passive movements of the soul, hence cannot be initiated by the soul itself; but in the properly controlled spirit they are mastered by reason; and it is only then that, moving among higher objects which contemplation has discovered and provided, they form an important factor in sublimity. Passion alone, Longinus tells us, is not enough to effect sublimity, for not all passion is sublime; indeed, the soul wherein passion reigns deteriorates from its nobility. But, although reason must master passion for sublimity to obtain, the acquisition of that mastery is not an aesthetic, but an ethical, problem; there is no skill of the passions; and in so far as there are quasi-literary means for their control, the means must be found in elevated thought.

It should appear from this discussion that the term "sublimity" can scarcely be taken as referring to a mere elevation of diction, for to take it in this sense is to regard a literary work as a mere arrangement of words and to collapse all the sources of sublimity into those which are merely verbal, and perhaps all of these, even, into synthesis alone. The treatise of Longinus affords every evidence that he sought to avoid such a reduction and that hence the word should not be taken in its merely stylistic sense but should receive its definition in terms of that communication of nobility which is made possible by the perfection of the human soul and of art, and which receives its answer in the wonder and admiration of all men.

Notes

[1] [It is intended to print from time to time in *Modern philology* a series of papers dealing, from fresh points of view, with the history of the basic disciplines which have influenced literary study in modern times. The present paper is in some sense a sequel to the essay on "Literary criticism and the concept of imitation in antiquity," by Richard McKeon, which appeared in August, 1936 (XXXIV, 1-35); it will be followed, in an early number, by a similar reappraisal of Scaliger.—EDITOR.]

[2] *Studies in poetry and criticism* (London, 1905).

[3] *Literary criticism in antiquity* (Cambridge, 1934), II, 210 ff.

[4] George Saintsbury, *A history of criticism and literary taste in Europe* (New York, 1902), I, 159, 161-62.

[5] Mr. Atkins' explication seems to me to be chiefly of this sort.

[6] Sec. ii. For this essay I have chiefly used the text and Latin translation of Benjamin Weiske (Leipzig, 1809) and the text and English translation of W. Rhys Roberts (Cambridge, 1899). Most of the translated phrases which occur in the essay have been taken, however, from the translation of A. O. Prickard (Oxford, 1926). Since this essay does not depend upon genetic questions, such as that of the authorship of the treatise. I have chosen to refer to the author simply as "Longinus," whatever his actual name may have been.

[7] i. 3-4.

[8] ii.

[9] ii. 4.

[10] ix. 2.

[11] iii.

[12] v.

[13] vi.

[14] vii. 2.

[15] *Ibid.*

[16] vii. 4.

[17] viii. 1.

[18] *Ibid.*

[19] *Ibid.*

[20] *Ibid.*

[21] *History of criticism,* I, 161-62.

[22] viii. 2-3.

[23] viii. 4.

[24] ix. 2.

[25] ix. 3.

[26] *Exp. Alex.* ii. 25. 2.

[27] ix. 1.

[28] E.g., xvii. 3; xxxix. 3.

[29] viii-ix.

[30] viii. 1.

[31] xvii. 1.

[32] See, e.g., x. 4, 5, 6; xvi. 2-3.

[33] xxxix. 3.

[34] ix. 4-5.

[35] ix. 7.

[36] ix. 5, 9.

[37] *History of criticism,* I, 163.

[38] ix. 13.

[39] x. 6.

[40] x. 1-3.

[41] x. 4.

[42] x. 5.

[43] xii. 3.

[44] xiii. 2.

[45] xiv. 1.

[46] xiii. 2.

[47] xiv.

[48] xv.

49 xv. 2-3.

50 xv. 4.

51 xvi.

52 xvi. 3.

53 *Ibid.*

54 xviii

55 xix.

56 xxii.

57 xxx.

58 Cf. Quintilian vi. i. 36.

59 xxxi.

60 xxxviii. 6.

61 xxxii. 4.

62 xxxii. 8.

63 xxxix.

64 viii.

65 xli-xliii.

66 xliv.

67 xx. 2.

68 *Ibid.*

69 *Ibid.*

70 xxxviii. 6.

71 xliv.

72 ix. 8.

73 ix. 10.

74 xxxv. 3.

75 xliv. 5.

76 ix. 3.

77 *Ibid.*

78 xxxix. 3.

79 xxxv.

Paul H. Fry (essay date 1983)

SOURCE: "Longinus at Colonus: The Grounding of Sublimity," in *The Reach of Criticism: Method and Perception in Literary Theory,* Yale University Press, 1983, pp. 47-80.

[*Below, Fry uses Sophocles's Oedipus as a touchstone to compare Longinus and Aristotle. He concludes that the former discards fundamental distinctions—e.g., language and spirit—that are fundamental and problematic in the* Poetics *of the latter.*]

> *The capacity to be able to act theoretically is defined for us by the fact that in attending to something it is possible to forget one's own purposes. . . . Theoria is a true sharing, not something active, but something passive (pathos), namely being totally involved in and carried away by what one sees* [Hans-Georg Gadamer, *Truth and Method]*

In undertaking to show the relevance of Longinus to the concerns of criticism at the present time, it may be useful to begin by considering opinions of his treatise that are recorded by two modern theorists of criticism. W. K. Wimsatt thinks that ***On the Sublime*** is incoherent in every way, that Longinus is incapable of distinguishing clearly among author, text, and audience and incapable likewise of distinguishing between such pairs of terms as nature and art or thought and language. The result of these confusions is, according to Wimsatt, that Longinus cannot sufficiently distinguish even between his own five "causes" of the sublime, the two that are inborn (the power of forming great thoughts and the ability to feel passion) and the three that can be learned (use of figures, use of diction, and word order). It is imprecision of this sort that augurs poorly, in Wimsatt and Brooks's *Short History,* for the future of author-oriented criticism.[1] As far as Longinus is concerned, according to Wimsatt, a verbal work is only an accidental spark of contact between two souls, like a piece of loose wiring.

Elder Olson agrees with this last view, in effect, but he feels that the spark is a happy occasion. As he puts it, the Longinian sublime is "the communication of nobility."[2] Apart from this point, Olson's view of Longinus is almost entirely in disagreement with Wimsatt's. He tries to make Longinus a kind of Aristotle, with the result that in his hands ***On the Sublime*** becomes so coherent that even the contents of the massive lacunae can be inferred.[3] Olson neatly determines that the "great thoughts" are the province of the author, the strong passions belong to the audience, and the three rhetorical categories refer the work to its own composition, to the author's choice of words, and to the affective quality of the words as sounds, respectively.

I think it inadvisable to attempt the rehabilitation of an obviously intuitive writer by stressing the well-ordered complexity of his ideas. Olson saw something he liked in Longinus but had to distort his author's way of proceeding enormously in order to bring it out. Wimsatt saw nothing he liked, but he saw the way Longinus's mind worked very clearly. He saw that Longinus is always talking about the same thing no matter how various the headings he devises may seem. I should like to make use of Olson's sympathy and Wimsatt's insight in order to show that the tendency of Longinus to slide from category to category and to leave large areas of overlap between his terms is in fact a highly desirable approach to theory, and one that is preferable to the formalism of Aristotle.

As theorists, both Olson and Wimsatt are primarily concerned, in their different ways, with structure: Olson to establish generic structures within which works can be identified, Wimsatt to define structure as an intrinsic quality of the works themselves.[4] This common concern brings both of them, but especially Olson, closer to Aristotle than to Longinus. Longinus takes a Chicagoan view of the accidental or intermediary function of language, but he takes a decidedly anti-Chicagoan, agnostic view of the conceptual structures, if there are any, that exist apart from words. As Wimsatt points out unsympathetically, text and soul seem to be analogous in Longinus;[5] neither has any definite shape or identity because each tends so easily to merge with other texts and other souls. Here too Longinus can be shown, however, to have taken a wise course. For him the question that has plagued Aristotle and his descendants never arises, the question as to whether structures are extrinsic or intrinsic to embodied works. The main question for Longinus is whether the knowledge that passes through discourse is finally to be understood in structural terms at all.

I do not wish to speculate, here or later, about the degree to which the argument of Longinus as I will interpret it is self-conscious, or cognizant of the implications that I will find in it. The ***Peri Hupsous*** is a series of fragments written by an unknown author; I will not deny that I take advantage of the vagueness that both characterizes and surrounds this work in order to build a poetics out of its hints and obliquities that can preside over the rest of this book. I will say, though, that I have paid more attention to the continuity of detail in the text than any commentator before me, and that I have not ignored or deliberately slanted any of it. To summarize what follows, then: I will concentrate on Wimsatt's observation that the difference between text and soul is very slight in Longinus. His *hupsos,* which means "height," or, in context, "elevated language," must be understood both as elevation *and* as language, difficult as it is to do so. His thinking can be viewed in two different but closely related ways. Either it is a theory of the interaction of consciousness with a phenomental world that is perceived almost as another consciousness, or else it is a theory of the fluidity with which utterances can move from one consciousness to another. The quality that gets transmitted can be understood either as language or as spirit but it cannot be divided into language *and* spirit, language and thought, or language and reference. Once these distinctions are set aside, it will become apparent that it is much the same, though never wholly the same, whether one speaks of nature or art, author or audience; or whether one speaks—to return to the distinction that emerged at the end of the last chapter—of unconsciously or consciously imposed form.[6] Thus I will show Longinus to have accommodated, without by any means cathartically "resolving," the difficulty concerning the place and function of form that disturbs the argument of the *Poetics.*

I

In comparing Longinus and Aristotle it would be most appropriate, perhaps, to align the rhetoric handbook called ***Peri Hupsous*** with Aristotle's *Rhetoric,* especially because in the *Rhetoric* Aristotle allows more vividness and energy to the oratorical performer (1413b-14a) than he allows to the players in the *Poetics.* Speechmaking in the *Rhetoric* requires pathos and spectacle before all things, whereas dramatic imitation uses these aids as sparingly as possible. However, although in some ways the *Rhetoric* resembles the treatise of Longinus more closely than the *Poetics* does, the ***Peri Hupsous*** itself can be as readily considered a poetics as a rhetoric. Longinus maintains no distinction between modes of utterance, at least not in a systematic way. At the outset he speaks of his topic as a special quality that belongs to "the very greatest poets and prose writers."[7] On two occasions later he does discriminate between poetry and prose (15.8, 30.2), but at these moments of greater specificity he has evidently remembered suddenly that he is supposed to be a *rhetor*—which would imply, of course, that oratory must be a special discipline.[8] If it be granted, though, that the ***Peri Hupsous*** is both a rhetoric *and* a poetics, in this respect being yet another reflection of Longinus's failure, or unwillingness, to make distinctions, then the *Poetics* will not appear to be an inappropriate text for comparison after all.

Longinus intermittently discusses tragedy. He twice mentions *Oedipus the King,* once apparently to concur with Aristotle that it is supreme among tragedies (33.5) and once again to quote it, to quote as an instance of the sublime a central passage of the sort that Aristotle never considers:

Weddings, weddings,
You bred me and again released my seed,
Made fathers, brothers, children, blood of kin,
Brides, wives, mothers—all
The deeds most horrid ever seen in men.

[23.3; trans. Russell]

Longinus cites this passage as an example of troping singular objects with plural endings. That is what it is; it stresses the multiplicity of horrors that befall Oedipus as if to remind Aristotle that misfortunes rarely come singly: they are not "one." There is nothing in Longinus about tragic structure,[9] but still, on the strength of this passage alone, he inspires confidence in his ability to get at what is tragic in general, irrespective of what may be tragic in genre. In Aristotle, art, which is a movement external to the thing moved, traces a curve of order; in Longinus, as his plunge into the midst of the *Oedipus* would signify, "disorder goes with emotion, which is a disturbance and movement of the mind" (20.2; *ataxia de to pathos, epei phora psuches kai sunkinesis estin*). If the mind moves at all, if it transports or is transported, its movement is disordered and traces a disorder.

Longinus is not quite the rhapsodist that his cooler readers have made him out to be but he certainly lacks the Peripatetic neutrality of voice. His own consciousness of this difference is plain in his one citation of Aristotle, whom he makes to say, with Theophrastus, "that there are ways of softening bold metaphors—namely by saying 'as if, . . . Apology, they say, is a remedy for audacity." "I accept this doctrine," Longinus continues, "but . . ." (32.3).[10] No one can either be or give the impression of being inspired who thus says "as if." *Si vis me flere:* he who expresses emotion must not just move but be, if not always witlessly possessed, at least greatly moved in his turn. Thus in moments of emotion the writer has "no chance to delay," as the onrush of what he says will have "outstripped its creator" (27.2, 1). Although Longinus is capable of sarcasm concerning the affectation of madness (see 15.8), this is not because madness or a state like it is extravagant but rather because its affectation in the wrong place is *not* extravagant. It is one form, "the pseudo-bacchanalian" form, of the false sublime (3.5). To be transported we must first have our feet on the ground; we cannot be duly and unflaggingly inspired, after the perfunctory suggestion of Aristotle, "by a strain of madness" (ch. 17).

Although he willingly turns to the tragic literature of the Attic period for his examples of the sublime, Longinus appears to have little use for "the trappings of the stage" (7.1).[11] His distaste for the excitements of performance seems even more extreme than Aristotle's and may at first confirm one's fear that the "sublime" (as Boileau translated *hupsos,* following Latin translations) will prove to be nothing but a fancy word for sublimation. Here, ostensibly, is the closest agreement between Longinus and the *Poetics,* to the effect, namely, that characterization, or the mere portrayal of "manners" (*ethe*), is inferior to, is indeed inessential to, the highest kind of expression. Narratives of manners, says Longinus, are the pastimes of old age: In the *Odyssey* the dotard Homer returns to the mere imitation of character which, as Aristotle had said, is also natural to childhood. (Whatever one may think of this judgment of the *Odyssey,* one should notice that at least it safeguards Longinus from emulating Aristotle's attempt to isolate a single course of action in that poem.)

For Longinus, as for Plato, greatness is steadfast, perhaps even inflexible; it eludes the many-talented Hyperides, for example, and appears instead in Demosthenes, who "has no sense of character" (34.3). Character in Longinus cannot be as freely varied as it is even in Aristotle. Slaves and women are permitted to speak by Aristotle as long as they speak in character, whereas in Longinus the drunkards of Herodotus (one who could arguably be released, as a historian, from the precept of poetic heightening) are censured for having spoken at all, even though, or rather because, they spoke in character (4.6-7). Longinus evidently feels, with Plato, that an ignoble taste for ventriloquism estranges the soul from the singleness of purpose it should cultivate. Even though Longinus easily violates this viewpoint in both taste and practice, it remains the most rigid, least thoughtfully integrated, and, I would say, least original feature of his thinking. That this view of character is what unfortunately leads to the facile indictment of his contemporaries in the last chapter is a disquieting aspect of Longinus's approach to art. It authorizes the Superman at certain moments; but in general, as I will try to show later, the sublime threatens more than it consoles autocracy of all kinds.

Not only is Longinus uninterested in the symmetries of dialogue and conflict that are made available by the imitation of character, but he also disdains, again in company with Plato, the group of emotions that carries drama forward. "Emotions, such as pity, grief, and fear" (8.2), he says, are "divorced from sublimity and [have] a low effect." These are just the emotions that determine the tragic structure in Aristotle. Again, though, this judgment is probably connected with Longinus's dislike of the ventriloquistic part of dramatic composition. His "fear" (*phobos,* as in Aristotle) refers only to cowardice, for example the cowardice, one may conjecture, of the suppliant Lykaon in the *Iliad,* which draws forth the famous response of Achilles: "Come friend, face your death, you too" (book 21; trans. Fitzgerald). But the fear involved in this exchange is not only dramatic; it is not only Lykaon's fear. There is fear for *any* listener in the reply of Achilles, and fear even for Achilles himself, perhaps, in having come to fathom the apathy of his own clearsightedness.[12] In a nondramatic setting, where emotions like fear can become ontologically charged rather than merely pragmatic, they could probably be restored, with the approval of Longinus, to the circle of emotions "without number" (22.1) that do readily supplement the sublime. But in rejecting pity and fear Longinus still does tellingly reverse the judgment of Aristotle. "In ordinary life," writes Longinus, "nothing is truly great which it is great to despise: wealth, honour, reputation, absolute power" (7.1). These are the "trappings" of status upon which the interest of the drama, considered as a representation of society, must solely depend. For a king who is not allowed to have developed a real personality, these possessions make up the whole of what is lost in the moment of tragic reversal.

As Longinus almost certainly did not know the *Poetics,* it is remarkable how precisely he inverted Aristotle's values.[13] But to what end? Would it not seem again that Longinus, even more than Aristotle, is bent on doing away with the last contingencies of human life in criticism? I would say decidedly not. It is most important to qualify and delimit his distaste for the material things that have enslaved his sottish contemporaries and that the dramatization of despotism relies upon. Longinus describes the domestic atmosphere of the *Odyssey,* to take up a case in point, as a "realistic" one (9.15); that is, it is made up of *biologoumena,* the stuff of daily life that every theory of criticism until 1800 or thereabouts may be said to have banished from the precincts of all but the lowest genres. Now, this stuff cannot be what is missing in Longinus's earlier complaint that in the *Odyssey* "the mythical element [*muthikon*] predominates over the realistic [*praktikon*]" (9.14). Admittedly, it is not the details of reality but the Aristotelian "probable" that is in question here, a factor that I took to be purely intellectual in the last chapter. But in the case of Longinus there is, in the *praktikos,* a bias toward actual experience.

It is difficult to agree with Longinus that myth outweighs reality in the *Odyssey.* Instead we would want to say that the poem quite amazingly holds the mythical and the realistic in balance. The all-too-human gullibility of Polyphemus and the fireside knitting of Calypso are "natural" (for that is perhaps a better word than "realistic") whereas the massacre of the female domestics, on the other hand, is savage on a scale that is plausible only in myth. Perhaps, though, for Longinus, this interdependence of the real and the fantastic is just the problem. Homer's realism, he may feel, is not in good faith because it is not made interesting for itself or its determination of the action but only for its meretricious connection with the mood of folktale. If this is what Longinus means, it will not redeem his judgment of the *Odyssey,* but it will provide us with some reassurance that, for him, reality is indeed the basis of the sublime. And this basis is crucial, as I shall argue everywhere in the present book; without it the sublime is merely the quaint remnant from the rhetoric of ahistorical aestheticism that its critics suppose it to be. Longinus does not care for moonshine; he dislikes the fabulous in Homer because one cannot discover it either in "real life" (3.2) or in any religion that truly inspires awe, like that of "the lawgiver of the Jews"—"no ordinary man" (9.9), says Longinus, but certainly, he must suppose, a real one.

II

The sublime is "grounded," then. There is a necessary connection between sublimity and the earth, or more necessary in any case than the connection between art and nature in Aristotle. The Longinian sublime is also more closely connected with the earth than the Kantian sublime, which is the opposite of the beautiful precisely in not being given but only implied as an absence by the natural world. What makes this connection possible in Longinus is the absence of radical dualism from his thinking. The effect of his penchant for sliding categories is to promote mergers.[14] There are mergers between genres, as we have seen, and there is also the merger of gods and men. This occurs in a passage that is mildly critical of Homer for having promoted the merger himself, but I think that too much has been made of Longinus's Platonic piety in this instance.[15] Homer exalts even while he demeans: In the *Iliad* he has made "the men of the Trojan war gods, and the gods men" (6.7). It is quite a different matter to have blended superstition and folkways in the *Odyssey;* in the *Iliad* the stakes of existence, and its conditions, are fought for at the height of human potential, which is figured forth in the attacks of Diomedes and Achilles on the gods and in the appearance of the unarmed Achilles, under the aegis of Athena, that fells twelve Trojans with heart failure. This height (*hupsos*) of human strength merges in turn with the voice of the poet, whose *Iliad* was composed "at the height of his powers" and at a "consistent level of elevation" (9.13).

It is this last sort of fusion, in which the person inspired takes on the qualities of what inspired him, that is most often noted both by sympathetic and by hostile readers of Longinus. The commentator in turn is inspired. The sublime, understood as the "echo of a noble mind" (9.2), is transmitted from the text to the voice of its author to the voice of the commentator, who can stand, as a result, in the place of the author: "Filled with joy and pride, we come to believe we have created what we have only heard" (7.2). As it is effected rhetorically by Longinus, this identification may remind one of the fallacy of imitative form, with the important proviso that it is *not formal.* Thanks to the looseness of his categories, Longinus can subordinate the structure even of his own insights to the continuousness of experience. He does not deliberately constitute himself, or so he would imply, as one who is inspired—as the great sublime he draws. We are conscious of his rhetoric not as the imposition of a pattern but as a movement;[16] first there is the interjection into his own text of some fragment, which is often broken up still further by misquotation; then Longinus reminds us of the force of heroism—or divinity—that is mirrored in authorship; and finally there comes an onrush of commentary, tumbling out, confused, in every way the record of experience, not of reflection (see 9.6-7, 10.3). The sublime in the theory and practice of Longinus is not infinite, though it may intimate boundlessness; it is always an experience in time, and thus restores to reading what formalization, which is necessarily spatial, has removed.

I have made no proper distinction, so far, between intention and accomplishment. I have spoken of "false" madness as though sincere madness were easy—and desirable—to single out, and then again I have spoken of sublimity and "rhetoric" in the style of Longinus as though there were no difference between them, or as though the difference did not matter. It does matter, but perhaps only when it is considered as success or failure in the representation of perceptiveness. All the least futile discussions of sincerity, from Johnson on *Lycidas* to Richards on *The Chinese Classics* to Lionel Trilling on Jane Austen, have touched only lightly on the question of hypocrisy and stressed, instead, a correlation that can be demonstrated, at least in part, between the occasion of an utterance and its manner. Thus in Longinus insincere madness is "untimely . . . emotion where none is in place" (3.5). If madness is appropriate to an occasion, however, one is then free to affect it in all sanity. If the real Erinyes should attack an orator where he stands as though he were Orestes, then even if he is calm at heart he may resort hypocritically to the figure called *phantasia,* or "visualization," which is said to betoken madness.

There is no necessary connection, therefore, between sincerity—considered as spontaneity—and the sublime. Even the noble Demosthenes could scarcely stand trial for sincerity in Longinus's reading of his rhetorical questions: "Emotion carries us away more easily when it seems to be generated by the occasion rather than deliberately assumed by the speaker. . . . The figure of question and answer arrests the hearer and cheats him into believing that all the points made were raised and are being put into words on the spur of the moment" (18.2). On the other hand, however—and this is a crucial distinction—at the affective end of the sublime experience sincerity is essential. For the reader or commentator it is not enough even to be persuaded, "for persuasion on the whole is something we can control" (1.4). If we are free to disregard the sublime, it is not the sublime. With respect not to one's reading but to one's reader, however, as the chain adds links, one is again freed, having taken the place of the author, to dissemble enthusiasm if need be.[17]

The very complexity of this issue, which is scarcely allowed to arise in the *Poetics,* must show that in Longinus there is no easy way to subsume art in nature or nature in art. There remains evidence in his own text, instead, of the conflict between the two which is just the conflict between design and compulsion that I discussed earlier. One reason why no clear relation can be established between art and nature is that for Longinus they are not easy to distinguish. He vacillates in his treatment of them but his vacillation is rigorous, I think, rather than weak-minded. For him the issue is at bottom a moral one, touching as it does on the question whether "we can develop our nature to some degree of greatness" (1.1)—the question, in other words, whether we can improve our nature by art. As a teacher justifying his own existence, he must part company with the widespread opinion, dating from Pindar, that greatness is solely "a natural product" (2.1), but he plainly feels that he must also stop short of the Sophists' notion that there are rules for all things given that all things are unknowable and must therefore be devised by artifice as need arises. The former view is typically that of the poets and the latter that of the rhetors, and Longinus, as usual, takes his stand between them.

Although his eventual assignment of two natural and three artificial causes to the sublime suggests that nature and art are fully separable, the discussion that leads up to this list is more complicated and—apparently—more confused. Of the "three points" (2.2) he makes to refute the contention that genius is artless, the second anticipates the later headings and the third is mostly cliché, but the first is significant: "Though nature is on the whole a law unto herself in matters of emotion and elevation, she is not a random force and does not work altogether without method." If this is so, nature is partly art and can receive from art, in that case, only a supplement of itself. The last sentence of the next paragraph (2.3) again undermines the standard contrast, this time not by merger but by dialectic: "The very fact that some things in literature depend on nature alone can itself be learned only from art." Whether by "art" here is meant criticism, or the reflective judgment, or the recognition of having failed to achieve nature by artificial means, is not wholly clear. What is clear, though, is that the sentence is reversible: "Art" and "nature" could change places, with "nature" now meaning "experience."[18] This possible reversal would point to an exactly complementary moment in the learning process, and would suggest, in its very exactness, that nature and art are not casual aids to each other but two facets of an indivisible dynamic. The exemplary Demosthenes later illustrates this dyad more than once, showing, for example, that "sobriety is needed even under the influence of inspiration" (16.4).

A more interesting later outgrowth of this interaction of categories occurs near the end of Longinus's by and large conventional contrast between genius and mediocrity: "We may say that accuracy is admired in art and grandeur in nature, and it is by *nature* that man is endowed with the power of speech" (36.3). Thus, language belongs to man's natural course of development and is not an art implanted in man by fiat. The notion that man differs from the animals in possessing inborn art, the chief sign of which is his conversion of random sounds into the articulate sounds of speech, was perhaps the most crucial presupposition of Aristotle's formalism in the *Poetics.* Longinus's view is neither that art complements nature nor that it is nature but simply that it comes to us along with the rest of our inheritance. If this is so, art cannot be an activity we perform but must be instead an activity that takes place in us—like nature. Longinus cannot quite say, then, with the formalist tradition from Aristotle to the present, that art, "in cooperation with the conscious will" (Coleridge), defends the fortress of the self against the siege of nature. He appears to suggest, rather, that both art and nature come as strangers to hold their combat in a remote corner of what at first we may not even recognize as the self: "Do you not admire the way in which [Sappho] brings everything together—mind and body, hearing and tongue, eyes and skin? She seems to have lost them all, and to be looking for them as though they were external to her" (10.3). This difficult response to the so-called "Ode to Anactoria" is drawn forth in particular from Sappho's "My tongue is broken, a subtle fire runs under my skin."[19]

III

The "broken tongue" of Sappho could be an emblem of the Longinian sublime. Her alienation from herself resembles the sudden switch to apostrophe whereby Demosthenes "divides a single thought between two persons in his passion" (27.3) and thus parodies the course of the sublime from transmitter to receiver: "this shameless monster, who—you vile wretch!" Longinus says that Demosthenes is touched by genius because, unlike Hyperides, he "lacks fluency" (34.3). But it is not only this loose application of Sappho's trope that merits attention. There is also the more precise metaphor in which the broken tongue represents the lapse into incoherence, the disarticulation of syntax or "semiotic discontinuity," as Thomas Weiskel has called it, that is caused by certain figures of speech.[20] *Polyptoton,* the term that designates all repetitions of a word in different inflections, is also the general term that includes Demosthenes' change of person, and it is one of the figures that Longinus stresses most.

The sublime figures and tropes, which I shall now survey, are not quite sublime in themselves any more than art is quite nature, although, as we have seen, neither of these paired sets of terms constitutes a clear dichotomy. Just as Sappho's broken tongue is not itself her speech—neither her allegedly inarticulate stammerings nor the well-formed "sapphics" that record them—so in turn speech itself is not the sublime.[21] If the sublime were indeed a property of words themselves, it could be quantified with respect to their combinations. It might prove, for example, to be some "principle of equivalence" like that of Jakobson and would in any case certainly appear as a function of structure. In other words it would be part of the matrix of continuous, orderly composition by which, according to Longinus, the orator effects "persuasion." But "persuasion" in Longinus is just the opposite of "transport," which is caused by the sublime (1.4). Persuasion is an affect that we are free to resist. It arises from the "ability to order and arrange material" and takes its effect, such as it is, "when we see the whole context" (1.4). The sublime, on the other hand, is what we cannot resist. It is not surprising that we can stand aloof from persuasion. It is more surprising that we can be persuaded at all, except by the most translucent of styles, because carefully organized discourse forms a latticework that seems to resist *us;* it proclaims its autonomy far more than its authority. In recognition of these characteristics, the New Criticism affirms the autonomy of the work of art. The sublime, on the other hand, as Longinus's descriptive terms for it will show, is that which forces its way through an opening it has widened in the latticework of persuasion. It has no other way of appearing; as Kant also showed, its occasion is natural, but it cannot appear in or through nature without a prior appeal to a formulation of the mind—an inner discourse—that arises in response to nature. Thus it is not a quality of words, but it does depend on their close proximity.

Just so in criticism, I would venture to add, the sublime will not appear in formal discussion as such, but it cannot appear without the context of a formal discussion. The sublime is "what is left to the imagination"; it is not the words in the text or a paraphrase of them but it is still prompted by them. Where the text has left words out or transposed or delayed them, the imagination must supply them. I shall try to demonstrate that this familiar exercise of multiple choice has all the attributes that Longinus and his successors call sublime. Far from cloaking itself in a nimbus of ineffability, the sublime is closely related to interpretation itself. "It is only through inevitable omissions," writes Wolfgang Iser, "that a story gains its dynamism."[22] These omissions are the reader's share. The sublime (to continue to call it that for the time being) is potential in any interpretation that does not suppose that it can either leave a text as it found it or else exhaust it by assigning it a form. The sublime that is closest to interpretation responds to a text by augmenting it. What Longinus calls *auxesis,* or "amplification," is not the sublime, he says, because, like persuasion, it is determined finally by quantity; but it is still close to the sublime, close enough to call for a fine discrimination.

"Sublimity depends on elevation, whereas amplification involves extension; sublimity exists often in a single thought, amplification cannot exist without a certain . . . superfluity" (12.1).

Amplification, about which there will be more to say in another place, is not a "broken" figure. One of the few exceptions to the criterion of fragmentation in Longinus's survey of figures, it remains close to the sublime because it overloads "persuasive" composition as much as the sublime disrupts it. A more typical figure that generates the sublime is asyndeton, which presents words or phrases "without connection" (19.1). There is nothing deliberative or slow, nothing spondaic, as it were, in the wide spacing of this figure; rather it rushes by in order to get beyond an impasse which is passed along, in the process, to the reader's effort of reconstruction: "Disconnected and yet hurried phrases convey the impression of an agitation which obstructs the reader and drives him on. Such is the effect of Homer's asyndeta" (ibid.). The passage Longinus has quoted just before this observation marks a crisis of speech in the *Odyssey* which is also a crisis for the status of speech as a means of persuasion. The breathless Eurylochus returns to tell Odysseus that Circe has turned their comrades into "squealing," inarticulate swine, "though [their] minds were still unchanged" (book 10; trans. Fitzgerald). Panic-stricken as he is, Eurylochus is unable to imitate in his asyndetic speech the well-knit construction of what he saw: "We went as you told us, noble Odysseus, up the woods, / We saw a beautiful palace built in the glades" (ibid.; trans. Russell, 19.2). As befits its ambiguity for men, Circe's palace is both persuasive *and* sublime, a contexture in a "glade" or gap; but in its outward structure it is like the figure that constrasts with asyndeton in Longinus, polysyndeton, which creates "smoothness by conjunctions" between phrases (21.2) and thus undermines the "harsh character of the emotion" (21.1) one would find in the same phrases written without conjunctions.

Another figure conducive to the sublime is hyperbaton, which is an arrangement of words that differs from the "normal sequence" (22.1). This figure creates gaps not in syntax but in expectation, whether by delay or by prematurity. From the standpoint of the author, however, hyperbaton is fully unified, not in the arrangement of its parts but with respect to the ground of thought or feeling from which it arises. More than any other figure, hyperbaton implies spontaneity and brings the problematic terms *art* and *nature* into their closest possible conjunction: "Hyperbaton is the means by which . . . imitation approaches the effect of nature" (22.1). Again, *ars est celare artem.* Yet, working under this concealment, the art of hyperbaton actually disrupts the nature it pretends to resemble: Thucydides and Demosthenes "show ingenuity in separating by transpositions even things which are by nature completely unified and indivisible" (22.3). Thus it is not the figure of speech itself that the sublime thunderbolt gaps (as one gaps a sparkplug) but rather the natural ground of the figure. Hyperbaton opens abysses, vacancies. If we recall the full play of the word *arthra* in Aristotle, which according to usage means both the presence and the absence of jointure, we may also grasp the significance for Longinus not only of Sappho's broken tongue but also of the antifeminist trope, quoted from Plato's *Timaeus,* that labels "the seat of the desires 'the woman's quarters'" (32.5). The sublime thus can be further understood as a condition of desire, an intimation of presence transmitted not only through a figural rift but also through a "cleft in the ground" (13.2; the phrase appears in an important passage that will occupy us below).

The topics of Longinus's quotations nearly always reflect, in some way, the rhetorical devices they are chosen to illustrate.[23] This is to some extent a consequence of the "representative" form that Pope was inspired—partly by Longinus—to illustrate in his *Essay on Criticism.* But in the case of Longinus the pattern of representative form is so continuous that it seems, irrespective of purpose, to be a necessity of expression. Evidently Longinus is drawn as much to a certain view of nature as to a certain group of tropes and figures. As hyperbaton reveals, nature itself is noble, impassioned, and broken. We noticed before that Longinus, unlike Aristotle, stresses the plurality of Oedipus's misfortunes; he assumes that the heart of tragic experience is the moment of dismemberment, not resolution, and he expects that that moment will be represented in language that risks inarticulateness. The language that prepares for tragedy's bloody sowing will likewise be scattered abroad; hyperbaton, asyndeton, and polyptoton are all present in the passage about careening flight that Longinus quotes from Euripides' lost *Phaethon:*

> "Steer towards the seven Pleiads."
> The boy listened so far, then seized the reins,
> Whipped up the winged team, and let them go.
> To heaven's expanse they flew.
> His father rode behind on Sirius,
> Giving the boy advice: "That's your way, there:
> Turn here, turn there."

Equally characteristic are the passages that describe in nature the wound they illustrate in syntax. Under the heading of "ordinary words" and how to use them, Longinus indulges in an outburst of rapid-fire quotation: "'Cleomenes in his madness cut his own flesh into little pieces with a knife till he sliced himself to death.' 'Pythes continued fighting on the ship until he was cut into joints [i.e., steaks]'" (31.2). The effect of slicing is just the same in hyperbaton as Demosthenes uses it: "Now, for our affairs are on the razor's edge, men of Ionia . . ." (22.1).

Nothing could have a more overtly rhetorical effect than the violence in these "ordinary words." At present among critics there is a tendency to discredit the discipline of "rhetoric" as it has been traditionally practiced because it is so difficult to imagine a "pure" employment of language that would not be rhetorical.[24] If to some degree nature is revealed as art by the ubiquity of rhetoric, it is equally true, however, that in the absence of a zero-degree or full transparency in language, art disappears back into nature simply for the reason that the province of art has no discernible boundaries. One wonders whether Longinus, whose technical categories so readily dissolve, might not agree with this recent view. Is there an Ordinary Language (*idiotismos;* 31.1) whose idioms are not cut to pieces by use? What is the "normal sequence" that the artifice of hyperbaton disrupts?

IV

Although for the most part Longinus's observations about the need of art to conceal art are commonplace, there is one moment at which he seems to become fully attentive to Horace's maxim. In preparing to assert, inter alia, that hyperbaton approaches nature most nearly of all the figures, Longinus declares that "figures are natural allies of sublimity" (17.1). "Allies," here, is a precise metaphor. Longinus is about to describe with surprising, almost digressive, amplitude the adversary relation between the orator and the prince or judge who listens to him. What the orator must avoid, says Longinus, is the danger of making the figural gaps, or "fallacies," of his oration look like subterfuges; he must not "raise the suspicion of a trap, a deep design." For Longinus, again, the irregularity of figures reflects the violence in nature, and now he seems to perceive that with a provenance thus shocking figuration itself will appear to be an evil that must be concealed. And certainly, for all his complaisance, the orator is indeed an aggressor.[25] Except in epideictic oratory, which Longinus does not discuss, the orator is always trying to prevail over opposition while frequently pretending not to be hostile. If his eloquence fails, the violence of nature, of his nature, and of the nature of his speech, will have a colorful outlet indeed: "Such a person [as "tyrants, kings, governors . . ."] immediately becomes angry if he is led astray like a foolish child by some orator's figures. He takes the fallacy as indicating contempt for himself. He becomes *like a wild animal*" (italics mine).

Here a complication arises. Although there is violence in all figures, evidently it is not the studied figures but the ones that are most wildly irregular that will seem the most natural and hence irritate the hearer as little as possible. The inkhorn techniques, on the other hand, the ones that are conducive to the unity of composition and are therefore not sublime, bring on a violent reaction—the reaction, say, of Wordsworth to "poetic diction" or of Whitman to "the *beauty disease*" ("Poetry To-day in America"). The force of figures that are themselves broken by violence goes unnoticed but does so only because it has overwhelmed and disarmed opposition without the knowledge of the opponent. "Amazement and wonder exert invincible power and force and get the better of every hearer" (1.4). The sublime stuns the hearer, spends its aggression in so doing and becomes, once it has entered the hearer, the appreciative condition known as "transport" (*ecstasis*). This process is parallel to, and I think more generally useful in criticism than, the process of catharsis in Aristotle.

The Longinian catharsis is a conversion of power into light, and in this Longinus differs from later theorists of the sublime. The difference between hupsos and the sublime of Edmund Burke is not so great as it is sometimes said to be,[26] but there is, in tendency at least, one important distinction to be stressed. Burke's sublime wears many guises but in general it inclines toward mist and obscurity, whereas the sublime of Longinus begins in darkness but then bursts forth into clarity and illumination: "'God said'—now what?— 'Let there be light,' and there was light" (9.9). The illustration that comes next makes the pattern clear while showing what the triumph of light in the sublime is like. The "sheer brilliance" (17.2) of the sublime speaker may be a cruel light but it is also honest; without sublimation it shows even death for what it is: "Darkness falls suddenly. Thickest night blinds the Greek army. Ajax is bewildered. 'O Father Zeus,' he cries,"

> 'Deliver the sons of the Achacans out of the
>   mist,
> Make the sky clear, and let us see;
> In the light—kill us.'

It is as if, through the premature expiation of having asked to be killed by his "Father," Ajax is hoping that in coming to light prior to its manifestation as force, the oedipal situation need never develop.[27] The wished-for moment will be violent, certainly, but at least the suppliant will have deferred to authority, just as the orator must defer to the ruler who will become "a wild animal" if he suspects that he is being mocked by the evasions of figure. In each of these three instances the coming-to-light is a purification of aggression: of divine omnipotence heretofore without an outlet, of blind rage in battle, and of rhetorical guile, respectively. It is a blazing forth that is apt to be followed by a general diffusion of force once pressure has been released by the cleft in the ground. Power becomes light in an allegory of acculturation.

Longinus's famous list of natural analogies for the sublime includes the brilliant light that issues from "the craters of Etna, whose eruptions bring up rocks and whole hills out of the depths, and sometimes pour forth rivers of earth-born, spontaneous fire" (35.4). It also includes the force of the ocean, which elsewhere has the might of a god, as when Poseidon causes Hades to quake in the underworld "for fear the earth-shaker . . . might break through the ground" (9.6). In every analogy Longinus can think of, some force breaks through a natural barrier, just as the sublime breaks through the contexture of figures. But what Poseidon threatens in this last instance is in fact such a powerful rupture that even Longinus wishes to channel it. The threat of "the whole universe overthrown and broken up" makes Homer's battle of the gods "blasphemous and indecent unless it is interpreted allegorically" (9.7). "Much better," says Longinus in the next paragraph, are the passages in which the gods, like the orator or like his judge bemused in a state of transport, are no longer hostile. Even then, in an episode Longinus prefers to the battle of the gods, the image of the gap appears once more, this time constructively, with the coming of Poseidon: "The sea parted in joy, and the horses flew onward" (9.8). The effect of these two passages about Poseidon when they are read in sequence exactly parallels the progress of the sublime from the broken ground of chaos toward the benign channeling of its force. Longinus's next two examples, to confirm the pattern, are the one given from Moses, in which "now what?" makes a gap in the quotation, and the one from Homer's speech of Ajax, who longs for the incisiveness—"kill us"—of the light that pierces darkness.

In keeping with this same pattern, the effect of Demosthenes' oratory is at first violent and then less so. Longinus quotes the passage beginning "The aggressor would do many things" (20.1), and then shows how Demosthenes responds in kind: "The orator is doing here exactly what the bully does—hitting the jury in the mind with blow after blow" (20.2). By the end of the paragraph, which concerns the mixture of a regular, recurrent figure, anaphora, with an irregular one, asyndeton, Demosthenes has somewhat diffused his force: "His order becomes disorderly, and his disorder in turn acquires a certain order" (20.3). Demosthenes, who has "divine gifts, it is almost blasphemous to call them human" (34.4), always subjects the hearer to an "abrupt sublimity" (12.4) which has the effect of being "catapulted out" (21.2) from the gap or opening we have been keeping in view. The effect he has on his audience is twice compared with thunder and lightning (12.4, 34.4). This simile as Longinus uses it is not at all novel in ancient literature, even with reference to Demosthenes, but in Longinus it becomes a motif and recalls the crucial preliminary definition of the sublime: "Sublimity . . . tears everything up [*panta diaphorese*] like a whirlwind [1.4; Prickard: "lightning flash"; Roberts: "scatters everything before it like a thunderbolt"]." When Aristotle expresses his fear that if one part of a tragedy is moved from its place "the whole will be disjointed," he uses the word *diapheresthai*. Once again, then, Longinus can be seen to have planted his unstable compound in the very midst of the Aristotelian order.

V

It is not clear whether Longinus's "good friend" the philospher in the final chapter is an opponent putting a wrongheaded argument or simply Longinus himself varying his delivery, good orator that he is, by putting one of two equally valid arguments in another voice. I incline to the second possibility, in part because to suppose that the two speakers are one will bring into consideration a special effect of the Longinian sublime, namely, the identification of the listener with the speaker, which I shall now discuss from various standpoints. Whatever the diagnostic merits of the friend's case (which will be found in Tacitus and many others), the rhetoric of his closing comment provides the essential background for the sublime: "I understand that the cages in which dwarfs or Pygmies are kept not only prevent the growth of the prisoners but cripple them. . . . One might describe all slavery, even the most justified, as a cage for the soul, a universal prison" (44.5).

Although this speaker does retain a conception of "justified" slavery (meaning only justified imprisonment, perhaps), we can still infer from his remarks a state of culture in which, despite the overthrow of democracy by despotism, the institution of slavery could be subject to criticism as it never really was in the thought of Plato or Aristotle. For them, each person, even if he is not officially a slave, must understand his station in the social and moral order to be fixed within justifiable restraints. Especially in Plato, this narrowness (adherence to one vocation, for example) is good for the soul and best suits its natural, uncorrupted wish for conformance with the Good. Hence Plato cannot share the rather complex opinion without which the idea of the sublime cannot be entertained, the opinion of Longinus that the soul by nature craves freedom whether its constraint is justified or not. Supposing that there is merit in this opinion, either man is an entity divided against itself or else his soul is a visitant from without, longing for escape from an oppressive host. Either of these views makes a sublime object of man himself: no longer a whole or a unity, man is divided by a fault through which what is sensed as alien and senses him as alien comes and goes.

There is unquestionably an element of the uncanny in the sublime, a quality which has been convincingly evoked by Freud as the sudden appearance of oneself as another.[28] It is by his sense of the uncanny, arguably, that Longinus's ascription of sublimity to speeches favoring the oppression of aliens is dictated. In light of these remarks, here is a long passage in which it is hard to decide, as one reads, who is the slave, who the governor, and who the liberator, or to decide which of these is the host, at the present moment, of the sublime in transit:

> It is when it [visualization] is closely involved with factual arguments that it enslaves the hearer as well as persuading him. "Suppose you heard a shout this very moment outside the court, and someone said that the prison had been broken open and the prisoners had escaped—no one, young or old, would be so casual as not to give what help he could. And if someone then came forward and said 'This is the man who let them out,' our friend would never get a hearing; it would be the end of him." There is a similar instance in Hyperides' defense of himself when he was on trial for the proposal to liberate the slaves which he put forward after the defeat. "It was not the proposer," he said, "who drew up this decree: it was the battle of Chaeronea." (15.9-10)

The first emphasis falls upon fact—ironically, perhaps, because the facts will be very difficult to pin down. It is visualization" *(phantasia)* that "enslaves" the hearer, that much is clear, but we do not know whether this device works for or against the facts. Neither do we know, as yet, why the sublime is said to be an enslavement of the hearer that cooperates with rational persuasion, when hitherto in the ***Peri Hupsous*** transport and persuasion have been treated as alternatives that are practically synonymous with rebellion and conformity, respectively.

All these questions are answered, but in a very surprising way, in a later passage: "We are diverted from the demonstration [of fact] to the astonishment caused by the visualization which by its very brilliance conceals the factual aspect. This is a natural reaction: when two things are joined together, the stronger attracts to itself the force of the weaker." In short, might makes right, but *only* when might is subversive. Whatever the opinion of Demosthenes concerning slavery and whatever sympathy his idolator Longinus may have for it, the force of the sublime as Longinus records it covertly transfers power from the oppressor to the oppressed. The "enslaved" hearer, in the first place, is the citizen who has custody of the prisoners; or, if he is a first-century reader of Demosthenes, he is a slave by virtue of the despotism he lives under. (Longinus's interlocutor Terentianus was possibly a Roman senator in prospect,[29] but he would nonetheless merely have been one of the emperor's "flatterers in the grand manner" [44.3].) Furthermore, in the first quotation, a voice from "outside the court" penetrates it with tidings of escaping prisoners, and the prison in turn is said to have been "broken open." Liberator, prisoners, messenger: these in turn burst through some barrier and thereby prove themselves, and not the possessors of temporal power, to have carried out the movement of the sublime exactly.

The situation of Hyperides, who is not elsewhere considered to be sublime (see 34.1-4), is equally complex. He was once a liberator and is now on trial for his temerity, an outcome which in the previous citation Demosthenes declares to be impossible (so great is his respect for lawless force). Thus enslaved, Hyperides would appear to have transmitted his power to the slaves he released, and yet he is now speaking with sublime effect on his own behalf because the power of yet another has been transmitted to *him:* It was not me, he says, but the disruption caused by the battle which did this thing.

All the confusion in this long passage arises, then, from the unexpected discovery on the part of each speaker in turn, including Longinus, of the self in the other. If perhaps in some cases it is the other way around, if it is the self that seems to have been invaded, that is because the sense of demoniacal possession Freud speaks of in this context is sure to appear where there are political passions. It is the rule of "transport" in the sublime, as this passage also shows repeatedly, that to have power one must be enslaved, possessed by another. As an instance of this intimation of Hegel's master-slave dialectic in operation, one may cite the subversion of Edmund Burke's politics by his aesthetics. In his *Reflections on the Revolution in France,* the established throne and all the other "fixed forms" of government, especially the pitiable queen, exactly conform with Burke's condescending notion of the Beautiful in the *Enquiry,* whereas the mob in full cry on 6 October is much closer to his notion of the awesome Sublime. Cattle are nothing much, he says in the *Enquiry,* but the wild ass in *Job* who knows no master is sublime.[30] What then, in the *Reflections,* of the "thousands of great cattle reposed beneath the shadow of the British oak," who commendably "chew the cud and are silent"?[31]

By "visualization," Longinus means that in phantasy, as hearers, we subvert our own identities. We conjure up presences that usurp our places. The hearer neither sees Demosthenes nor remains conscious of his own freedom but sees instead the hitherto unknown liberator of the slaves and becomes himself a slave to what he sees. He discovers himself to be Oedipus as surely as the Aristotelian audience does not. But in this discovery there is strength. If the sublime is a possession that is distinguished by a coming-to-light, and thus casts out the uncanny almost in the instant of evoking it, its effect may be "amazement" (12.5) and clarity all at once, an epiphanic moment of presence that quickly becomes self-presence. When what is absent stands before one, even takes possession of one's consciousness, first there is a recoil, as from an invader, and then there is a surge of empathy, as in the "momentary checking of the vital powers and . . . consequent stronger outflow of them" that accompanies the sublime in Kant's *Critique of Judgment.*[32]

Common and nowadays somewhat ineffective rhetorical devices for this making present in Longinus are the sudden switch from past to present tense in narrative (25) and the sudden apostrophe to the hearer (26.1-2). We can still be affected, though, by the skillful use of a third device, conjuration. Demosthenes' oath, "By those who risked their lives at Marathon" (16.2), is remarkably glossed by Longinus: "He was suddenly inspired to give voice to the oath by the heroes of Greece." Demosthenes does not call up the past, then; past voices call through him, thus enacting the course of the sublime from speaker to speaker. The finest event of this kind in Longinus is "the appearance of Achilles to the departing fleet over his tomb" (15.7). The heroic past, which is in a sense the whole text of the *Iliad* and the other cyclic poems, stands above a gap in the ground whence it has come, still alive with, or revived by, the charge for posterity it carries. The past in the person of Achilles haunts the puny survivors whose victory has been won and who are now launched, a "departing fleet," upon the historic decline Longinus laments in his final chapter. "Greatness of mind wanes," he says there (44.8)—unless it should return to possess the living.

VI

The sublime is chthonic, "earth-born" like the volcano, yet it is also divine—or else it is the human euhemeristically exalted. It appears at the horizons of perceptual experience that are left out of the *Poetics.* Hence Longinus's touchstones frequently bring extreme conceptions of matter and spirit together. He quotes, for example, the Homeric account of the rebellious giants, who themselves are heavy and dull and make heavy work of their climb into the sky: "Ossa on Olympus they sought to heap; and on Ossa / Pelion with its shaking forest"—shaking like the beard of a giant—"to make a path to heaven—" (8.2). In their lumpishness these giants must use the arithmetical *auxesis* rather than the true *hupsos* or *megethos* (greatness) to serve their purpose. At the same time, however, their instinct cannot be taken lightly if it enables them to forge a "path" toward their goal: "And they would have finished their work. . . . " This coincidence of the animal and the divine is repeated, not so much in the next Homeric passage itself—"So long is the stride of the gods' thundering horses,"—as in Longinus's response to it: "If the horses of the gods took two more strides like that, they would find there was not enough room in the world" (9.5).

The oxymoron of measureless substance is exemplified for Longinus by the ocean. He himself takes its measure, thinking perhaps of a strait or bay that becomes a lake at low tide, in the course of assigning an inferior place to the *Odyssey:* "We see greatness on the ebb," he says, glancing forward again to the waning of greatness in his last chapter: "It is as though the Ocean were withdrawing into itself and flowing quietly in its own bed" (9.13). When a vast, possibly boundless expanse becomes a self-contained structure, it stops flowing out of itself. It no longer *influences* in the way the ghost of Achilles, representing Homer, can influence, not to say inundate, a departing fleet. There is no "outpouring" (ibid.) from the *Odyssey* that can affect us. In a passage that wholly anticipates Kant, Longinus identifies the sublime as something illimitable in the mind, something that must overflow and appear in contrast with the finite objects in nature: "The universe therefore is not wide enough for the range of human speculation and intellect. Our thoughts often travel beyond the boundaries of our surroundings. If anyone wants to know what we were born for, let him look . . . above all [at] the Ocean" (35.3-4). Just as boundlessness and measure are closely interdependent, so also, it will be recalled, art and nature, words and thought, are nonidentical word pairs that are nonetheless inseparable. Freedom, to repeat the essential homily concerning the sublime, needs its obverse in confinement. We could not identify the "abundant, uncontrolled flood" of Archilochus if it were not a "bursting forth of the divine spirit" from "under the rule of law" (33.5).

The sublime, again, is neither a great mind, precisely, nor the words of a great mind but rather "the echo of a noble mind" (9.2).[33] If we are to take this turn of phrase seriously, the sublime must then be the reverberation, or resonance, of words. That characterization may bring it a shade too close to language, however, too close to uttered language, that is, and for this reason Longinus's ensuing sentences seem to counteract the sense of the word *echo:* "This is why a mere idea, without verbal expression, is sometimes admired for its nobility—just as Ajax's silence in the Vision of the Dead is grand and indeed more sublime than any words could have been."[34]

The distinction between silence and the echo in this passage is as crucial as it is subtle. Again Longinus has turned to a crisis of communication in the *Odyssey.* An attempt to open a path between heroic ghosts and present needs, the crisis begins when Odysseus invites the sublime by making a wound in the earth. "With my drawn blade / I spaded up the votive pit," he recalls, all for the purpose of speaking with Tiresias, "the prince of those with gift of speech" (book 11). All the women and men who are allowed to approach after Tiresias has spoken his fill are echoes of the seer, reverse echoes, as it were, which confirm the authenticity of his prophecies with the accuracy of their recollections. The eloquent silence of Ajax, which is balanced as a motif by the vagueness of Tiresias's forecast beyond the moment of planting the oar, is made possible by the eloquence of Tiresias on all prior topics, without the exhaustion of which Ajax could not have approached the pit.[35] Furthermore, the silence of

Ajax is itself pregnant with speech, as even the snubbed Odysseus realizes: "Who knows if in that darkness he might still / have spoken, and I answered?" The silence of Ajax, in short, is wholly dependent on words—on Odysseus's present narrative, on the speech Odysseus made to Ajax rehearsing the old grievance, and on our own feeling that even in that moment of growing darkness, which recalls Ajax's darkling petition for death quoted earlier by Longinus, the suicide could have said much.[36]

The sublime echo thus wavers between the aftersound of words and their negation. It is as difficult to locate precisely as the ghost of Ajax disappearing into Erebus. The "voice of the dead" in such moments is not really a voice; rather it is the speaker's memory short-circuited so that it seems as though the dead were now saying what the speaker has always known them to have said when alive. Even if the "dead" should in fact be living persons, the effect of astonishment brought about in the speaker by means of visualization, brokenness of figure, and his accession to "divine gifts" makes the speaker seem merely a mouthpiece for what is remote from his ordinary sphere. "'The dead writers are remote from us,'" wrote Eliot, "'because we *know* so much more than they did.' Precisely, and they are that which we know."[37] In the experience of the sublime they are not remote, however, but so vividly present that they take possession of consciousness.

The controversy that surrounds the theory of influence today has in part to do with the question of whether influence occurs in the form of words or thought, echo or silence. The early Humanists thought that it is the words of the past that either intimidate or educate us. Edward Young thought that the *spirit* of the past can liberate our own genius if we disregard the words. Harold Bloom imagines a powerful presence from the past, at once word and spirit, which will dominate the new speaker unless he contrives to sap its strength. Longinus can be helpful in ascertaining how far the idea of influence can be carried beyond the discussion of buried allusion, but more importantly he can show how far beyond this point it *needs* to be carried. If nonverbal thought is necessarily at least "colored" by reading, that coloring is not washable. It must be seen as a dye: "The choice of correct and magnificant words . . . makes . . . a kind of lustre bloom upon our words as upon beautiful statues . . . it is indeed true that beautiful words are the light that illuminates thought" (30.1-2). Allusion, then, which can be defined as words taken from their place in history, colors the whole mind. This is a far subtler view than the notion of words as the "dress" of thought, but it is also more troublesome when it comes to assessing originality. When it is difficult to discriminate between words and thought, it becomes more difficult to know how great a portion of what is spoken belongs properly to the speaker.

In that case more than ever, the speaker must fight for his share of credit as an originator or "author."[38] This is the point at which he ceases to be the "hearer" and assumes, in his turn, the role of orator. Whatever it is that reaches the hearer, and perhaps *echo* will have proved as good a word as any for it, he is at first stunned but then he reacts, and in so doing he passes into the speaker's role.[39] The aggression of the original speaker is met with counteraggression on the part of the listener. One such listener is Longinus, who cannot praise his literary ancestor Plato without some word of qualification. There is a measure of tension in his reverence for Plato from which his reverence for Demosthenes, for example, is wholly free. On several occasions Longinus taxes Plato with abuses of style. The "otherwise divine Plato" (4.6) too often exhibits the vice of frigidity, and he is also given to such needless and dull embellishments as periphrasis (29.1) and surplus metaphors (32.2). In these belittling gestures, which have the effect of pointing to something petty in Plato's nature, the reader will recognize one reflex of the anxiety of influence in the theory of Harold Bloom. It is hard not to conclude that Demosthenes is praised more unreservedly than Plato is because he is less important. Demosthenes commanded only one register of the sublime, and his style does not exert any direct influence on the sinuous and chameleonic style of Longinus himself. By far the more powerful influence upon Longinus is Plato, whose style and whose thinking—his concept of nobility, his dislike of the theater—figure with great prominence in the ***Peri Hupsous.***

There is an additional charge to be whispered against Plato. With Xenophon, says Longinus, Plato was "trained in Socrates' school" (4.4); or again, late in the passage toward which the present analysis is tending, Plato "diverted to himself countless rills from the Homeric spring" (13.3). In short, Plato can be charged with unoriginality as well as pettiness. Longinus is aware that his readiness to find fault is a fault—"I myself cited not a few mistakes in Homer and other great writers" (33.4)—but he goes on to argue, notoriously from the standpoint of his detractors, that the faults he finds in others are sure proofs of their genius; and in that case his own fault would prove that he himself is at least not insipid. Even in this gesture of restitution toward genius, however, there is a trace of malice. Take Caecilius, he continues, author of the treatise on the sublime against which he has pitched his present essay: consider what Caecilius says against Plato. Apparently Longinus is about to defend Plato. But then, with a devious stratagem common both in oratory and in neoclassical wit, Longinus faithfully repeats the indictment made by Caecilius: "Loving Lysias more deeply than he loves himself"—possibly the talk of *philia* here is meant to recall the *Phaedrus*—"[Caecilius] yet hates Plato with an even greater intensity. . . . In preferring Lysias to Plato he thinks he is preferring a faultless and pure writer to one who makes many mistakes" (32.8). Plato is ever so faintly damned, then, both by contrast with Lysias—for Longinus will not glorify mistakes until the next chapter—and also by comparison with him. In repeating the invidious comparison of Caecilius, Longinus himself causes Plato to appear merely as a competitor, and an unsuccessful one at that, for superiority in phrasemaking.

Longinus's attitude toward Plato is not in itself terribly significant. I have lingered over it to show further that captiousness of some kind belongs properly to the dynamics of the sublime (a point to which I shall return), and to suggest that this inevitably critical moment does raise an epistemological question: Is the sublime firmly enough situated in the nature of things to survive criticism? It is the first premise of Longinus that the sublime is objectively verifiable. What he says to establish this point has a Johnsonian ring: "Reckon those things which please everybody all the time as genuinely and finely sublime" (7.4). Here Longinus differs from Kant, whom he anticipates in so many other respects, and rejoins the eighteenth-century "empiricist" writers, from Addison to Burke and Kames, who found the sublime indisputably to be present in certain works of art and natural objects.

At least, this is partly so. Coleridge, a Kantian whose *Biographia* attacks the premises of empiricism, still struggles whenever possible, more clearly so in other writings, to establish an objective ground of judgment,[40] and Longinus, no matter what he says, must undertake the same struggle. Although, again, nature plays a vital role in the production of the sublime for Longinus, it is not clear that nature, which "is not a random force and does not work altogether without method," can be very safely distinguished from art. It is not easy to decide whether the sublime passes from object to subject as a volcanic echo or from subject to subject as an oratorical echo. Coleridge, in the well-known anecdote of the lady he heard calling a waterfall "pretty," himself knew, absolutely, that it was "sublime." But the anecdote at least partly bears witness against itself because Coleridge's knowledge, absolute or otherwise, would not have been possible without information given by reading and by the oral tradition of the educated.[41]

The Longinian sublime cannot be located in words or things with confidence for similar reasons. His conviction that the sublime pleases all at all times must be undermined, furthermore, by the prevalence of the instinct he notices in himself and his predecessors, like Caecilius, for faultfinding. If the sublime is the most exalting experience one can have that is not purely religious, and if it must therefore be spontaneously desired by the soul (we can reasonably expect that Longinus would want to take a Platonic view of the question), then why do we act so aggressively toward it? Why do we decry its pretenders and even express doubts about the illustrations of it that we bring forward ourselves? It may be replied that vigilance is needed to protect the fane of the sublime from false priests who go about "poking the thyrsus in at the wrong place" (3.5; my adaptation of the term *parenthyrsus*). Yet it is troubling that such vigilance leaves so little intact. The *Odyssey,* the battle of the gods in the *Iliad,* Plato—all but the safely peripheral Demosthenes, peripheral both in style and in politics, are quite badly mauled. As Longinus himself would say, they are "dissected": "We have to ask ourselves whether any particular example does not give a show of grandeur which, for all its accidental trappings, will, when dissected, prove vain and hollow" (7.1).

It appears from this metaphor that the aggression of the hearer is an imitative aggression, corresponding as it does to the tearing apart that marks the appearance of the sublime itself. Although it takes place in a different mood, perhaps, the rending of the sublime still anticipates interpretation, the dissection that Wordsworth called murder. The listener's response to the sublime resists its assault. At first the listener is possessed, and then he bestirs himself to expel the alien voice, which ceases to possess him in the process and becomes his property instead: "It is our nature to be elevated and exalted by true sublimity, Filled with joy and pride, we come to believe we have created what we only heard" (7.2).[42]

After these last observations have been made, the dramatization of mimesis that follows will almost interpret itself:

> Many are possessed by a spirit not their own. It is like what we are told of the Pythia at Delphi: she is in contact with the tripod near the cleft in the ground which (they say) exhales a divine vapour, and she is thereupon made pregnant by the supernatural power and prophesies as one inspired. Similarly, the genius of the ancients acts as a kind of oracular cavern, and effluences flow from it into the minds of their imitators. . . . Plato could not have put such a brilliant finish on his philosophical doctrines or so often risen to poetical subjects and poetical language, if he had not tried, and tried wholeheartedly, to compete for the prize against Homer. . . . As Hesiod says, "this strife is good for men[.]" Truly it is a noble contest and prize of honour, and one well worth winning, in which to be defeated by one's elders is itself no disgrace.
>
> We can apply this to ourselves.
>
> (13.2-14.1)

Possession, which is divine, comes from a cleft in the ground that represents the natural origin of the sublime. The priestess is then the "author" of the sublime, and we who receive her prophecies are hearers-turned-authors or hearers-turned-interpreters. After the Delphic comparison Longinus changes the subject a little, revealing from that point forward the aggression in the relationship between speaker and listener.

VII

Nearly all commentators suppose that there is a drastic narrowing of the Aristotelian *mimesis* in Longinus and other late Greek and Latin writers. Verbal imitation has replaced ideal representation, symptomizing the overthrow of true philosophy by the "Alexandrian" logomachy. But in the case of Longinus this judgment is unduly harsh.[43] In his treatise the spirit is not suppressed, leaving only the gaunt body of philosophy in view; rather spirit and letter are nearly interchangeable, and each very adequately embraces the *mimesis* of Aristotle. The common distinction we make between *mimesis,* alluding to Plato and Aristotle, and *imitatio,* alluding chiefly to Quintilian, Longinus, and the rise of Humanism, is a good deal more radical than it should be. Pope's lines on Virgil are perhaps closest to the equipoise of Longinus: "When t'examine every part he came, / Nature and Homer were, he found, the same" (Essay on Criticism, I, 134-35). The "nature" that Pope has in mind is the *phusis,* or "rules," of Aristotle, but the "nature" of Longinus, had he written this couplet, would have been more dynamic.

One way in which Longinus does maintain a slight functional separation between nature and art is in speaking, as he routinely does, of "mere" words. These are what the false sublime is made of: it looks sublime, but in the long run, for "the man of sense and literary experience . . . , it fails to dispose his mind to greatness or to leave him with more to reflect upon than was contained in the mere words" (7.3). Only the implications of the word *more* can save Longinus from saying, here, that the sublime itself is merely a matter of words. It is not solely because this conclusion would trivialize the sublime that Longinus is fortunate to have evaded it; he also escapes having to admit that as a "text-book" (1.1) his treatise must be a failure. And indeed it is a failure in that genre. Because by his own demonstration there is no trope or figure that is not subject to abuse, then truly, though Longinus has argued to the contrary (2.1), the sublime cannot be taught as a rhetoric. This he does later admit in an unguarded moment: "Evils often come from the same source as blessings; and so, since beauty of style, sublimity, and charm all conduce to successful writing, they are also causes and principles not only of success but of failure" (5).

If the sublime is not a rhetoric, and I think Longinus knows it is not, it cannot be identified with any structure. This article of belief must be kept in mind in turning to a number of passages that seem to undermine it by identifying the sublime with order and resolution. The first of these describes the *Iliad* during Longinus's contrast of that poem with the *Odyssey.* The *Iliad,* he says, has a "consistent level of elevation which never admit[s] of any falling off" (9.13). What is perplexing about this statement is that elsewhere Longinus has insisted that the sublime appears in disruptive fragments of less brilliant surrounding compositions. If "persuasion" is achieved by observing the Horatian decorum (see 1.4), the "transport" of the sublime must be a breach of decorum. There are several ways of resolving this anomaly. First, it could be said that a whole text, seamless in itself, would become sublime if it disrupted other texts. The reader of the *Iliad,* especially if he or she is a poet, might find that as a whole it overwhelms his or her own inspiration. It could also be said that for the *Iliad* to have unified the story of Troy is a feat that surpasses ordinary powers of composition. Thus the composition of the *Iliad* is an extreme instance of making the plural singular, which will always result, as Longinus says elsewhere, in "surprise" (24.2).

A third rationale for Longinus's suddenly holistic phrasing, briefly stated, might be this: When he speaks of sustained elevation he is not actually touching upon questions of structure or even of unity. He is speaking, rather, of a device that more closely resembles the blows of Demosthenes' bully, the device, namely, of repetition. This is the most satisfactory explanation for Longinus's praise of the *Iliad* because it can also be applied to his other totalizing figures. This I shall do in a moment, having first resisted the temptation to gloss over the anomalous passages prematurely. For they *are* anomalous. Recalling Aristotle, for example, Longinus claims that periodic structure in a sentence can be sublime: "The beauty of the body depends on the way the limbs are joined together, each one when severed from the others having nothing remarkable about it, but the whole forming a perfect unity" (40.1). He pursues this train of thought pertinaciously: "Similarly, great thoughts which lack connexion are themselves wasted and waste the total sublime effect" (*sundiaphorei kai to hupsos*). Because it is not evident how more than one great thought can appear in, or even be discussed with respect to, the structure of a single sentence, Longinus's notion of the "total sublime effect" continues, in this context, to be unintelligible. Perhaps he is affirming what is crucial, again, in any theory of the sublime that has subtlety: the principle that sublime moments need a formal context of some sort and cannot take their course in a vacuum.

If this is so, it remains only to characterize the interstices of the "great thoughts." It is not clear from this passage alone whether sublimities should come at us in a steady stream, creating, e.g., the *Iliad*'s "consistent level of elevation," or whether they should be indirectly but no less surely connected by decent intervals of decorum. Longinus himself begins to resolve this question, and to show how the sublime can indeed appear in formal composition, a few sentences later in this same discussion of periodicity. Having quoted a passage from a lost play of Euripides about Dirce being haled up and down by a bull, a passage that is as agitated as its subject ("it writhed and twisted round"), Longinus remarks that "the word-harmony is not hurried and does not run smoothly" (40.4). He means that clusters like *perix helixas* and *petran drun* slow one down in pronouncing them. For this reason "the words are propped up by one another and rest on the intervals between them; set wide apart like that, they give the impression of solid strength." Like Antony bestriding the world, they are colossal. It is in this manner, then, that Longinus can praise unifying effects in style without contradicting himself. Apparently neither sustained elevation nor periodicity is to be considered smooth or even fluent. The sublime elements of composition are like the stone slabs of an entryway before the invention of the keystone; up to a point, the strength of the arch is proportionate to the width of its base. Thus even in passages in which a sustained effect is aimed for, the composition should be, as Longinus puts it in the next section, "rough at the joins" (41.3; *skleroteta episundedemena*).

Longinus more than once resorts to architectural metaphors—rather surprisingly, it has been pointed out, considering that the Greeks did not rank architecture among the fine arts.[44] Having in general insisted on the need for a "cleft" through which the sublime can pass, Longinus at one point seems to change his mind. In a discussion of gathering details for a sublime effect, he says that good writers "have taken only the very best pieces [i.e., stones], polished them up and fitted them together. They have inserted nothing inflated, undignified or pedantic. Such things ruin the whole effect, because they produce, as it were, gaps and crevices" (10.7). But again there is really no contradiction. An architecture in which wedges of foreign matter (wood, perhaps, or roughcast) leave actual "chinks and crannies" in a wall would be much cruder than the rough architecture of the sublime needs to be or can be.[45] It would be ludicrous architecture, like the wall with its chink that separates Pyramus and Thisby in *A Midsummer Night's Dream.* The opening of the sublime must be well-knit to a certain degree in order to resist what will tear through it.[46]

After this review it can be asserted with some confidence that Longinus's fifth "source" of sublimity, which is "dignified and elevated word-arrangement" (8.1; *sunthesis*), is not out of keeping with the other four, at least three of which stress division and passion rather than composition and composure. But the exact nature of the linguistic "joins" under this fifth heading remains difficult to determine. Much depends, in any theory of form, on whether connecting links are thought to be interstices, like the cushion of air that keeps colliding bodies from touching in the physical world, or joints, like helical or chain structures. Whichever of these models may seem more accurate, there can be no question of a third, of the blending or ooze that is implied in the Goethean concept of "organic form." There is nothing liquid or even porous about those linguistic signs which are not themselves the sublime but remain necessarily its vehicle. A sign cannot merge with its neighbors without losing the syntagmatic features—the differences—that make it intelligible. This observation may be an instance of what the German hermeneuticians condemn as *Modernisierung,* but it still provides a convenient way of loosening the strong grip that the word *sunthesis* appears to exert upon the disruptive potential of the sublime. Even the evidence of the ***Peri Hupsous*** itself makes it clear, in any case, that *sunthesis* is not synthesis. Longinus's *sunthesis* is actually a somewhat limited technical term meaning the order in which words are written down; it is quite closely equivalent, that is, to the modern word *syntagmatics.*

Although the semantic possibilities of imitative form are not to be overlooked in studying word arrangement (one thinks of the poetic line in Virgil), the primary concern of Longinus in this regard is with rhythm.[47] This being so, the word *composition* that is used in most translations of the section on *sunthesis* is especially misleading. Rhythm may be syncopated but it cannot form an are or return on itself. It is essentially repetitious, "the ticking of a watch made softer," as Yeats put it,[48] and thus has very little to do with the *techne* of the classical formalists. Longinus himself tips the balance between variation and repetition clearly toward the latter by devoting a section (20) to the sublime effects of asyndeton combined with anaphora. He stresses the need for variety "to save the sentence from monotony and a stationary effect" (20.2), but much more significantly he recommends that anaphora be used with asyndeton, which is percussive in effect, rather than, e.g., with hyperbaton, which would involve an unexpected deviance from norms of recurrence. At this point, furthermore, he expatiates on the bullying of Demosthenes, "hitting the jury in the mind with blow after blow" (20.3). It may be observed in addition concerning this point that Longinus later contrasts the "wonderful spell of harmony" cast by the "varied sounds of the lyre"—the mild spell of "persuasion," that is, or of the beautiful—with the Phrygian pulsation of the flute, which inspires one mood, though by no means the only one, of the sublime (39.2-3).

In short, repetition is more important than variety if one's purpose is to stun the auditor. Again we come to an aspect of the sublime that we may prefer to wish away. Mesmerism, demagoguery, Madison Avenue, ecstatic dancing, and the "meditation" on a name or a sacred mantra—all undertake to "enslave" the hearer, to bring about the identification of an audience with some transcendently authoritative voice by means of repetition.[49] But Longinus is able to show that repetition has more acceptable uses. A mature taste in the discrimination of sublimities, for example, comes from experiences that take place "many times over" (7.3). From this standpoint taste can be defined, very plausibly, as a superior force of habit, an informed, at least partly voluntary self-hypnosis. Repetition also provides a way, finally, of revealing what the sublime is and what it is not. Partly owing to the element of sameness in repetition, the sublime is *one*—and largely indivisible—but no version of the sublime is ever *unified,* anywhere in the ***Peri Hupsous,*** as an increment of structure or of harmony.

VIII

Some difference remains, however, between the repetitious sublime and the sublimity that takes effect with a single blow. Verbal composition is mainly a process of accretion, "building up" (39.3), a process that is equivalent to what Longinus describes, on the figural level of composition, as *auxesis,* or amplification. There are enough passages assigning repetition rather than singleness to the sublime to warrant the suggestion that Longinus anticipates Kant's distinction between the "dynamic" and the "mathematical" sublime,[50] which latter heading denotes the effect of being staggered by the sheer volume of something: too much information, too many anxieties, mountains too high, and so on. The addition of this category completes my discussion of the rhetoric, the conditions, and the modes of the Longinian sublime. Using the mathematical sublime as a point of departure, I shall now discuss some of the implications of the sublime, with an eye toward showing why I think it is preferable to the identification of form as an end in view for contemporary criticism.

The mathematical sublime has been analyzed by Thomas Weiskel, and more recently by Neil Hertz, as a frustrating buildup or sedimentation that finally causes the sensation of "blockage," the "checking of vital powers" noted by Kant. Hertz admires Weiskel's thesis but argues that Weiskel identifies the blocking agent in Kant—the Reason (*Vernunft*), which implicitly rebukes the Imagination (*Einbildungskraft*) for failing to reduce the overload to proportion—too hastily and arbitrarily with the Father in the "family romance" of Freud.[51] Weiskel cuts his way through the blockage of his own knotty problem, in other words, simply in order to have got through it. Passed on from commentator to commentator, each time with a new qualification, the mathematical sublime renews itself according to the pattern described earlier: possession, resistance, response. Hertz's solution—not to cut through the blockage but to learn to live with it until its familiar presence ceases to frustrate—is designed to put an end to the game, but that may not be possible. It is too likely that one's orientation in the chain of audition along which the sublime is passed is, as Weiskel says, irreducibly oedipal. Any forfeit of that orientation would then simply become a promise that one will not mind being overwhelmed.

There is another topic in Freud, however, that brings one closer to the way it feels to cope with the mathematical sublime from day to day. This topic is the "mastery of repetition" that Freud supposes to be a constructive displacement of the death instinct.[52] At least one phase of the sublime, the initial phase that all the eighteenth-century theorists agreed in calling awe-struck or frightened, is loaded with intimations of mortality. Freud described the favorite topics of the obsessional neurotic as those "upon which all mankind are uncertain,"[53] including the afterlife and the reliability of memory. The neurotic's repeated efforts to break through to conclusions about these topics, efforts which transfer to waking life the unpleasant doing and undoing that everyone performs during a feverish doze, are futile attempts at *auxesis.* Replete with its "great thoughts," on the other hand, the sublime can become a working through that makes the neurotic compulsion purposeful. The sublime reveals its power of sublimation even in what it does to the signals of repetition itself: a dripping faucet becomes the sound of waves, a metronome softens into meter, and the dullest monotony becomes "The murmurous haunt of flies on summer eves."

The issue of repetition dominates even Longinus's passing remarks about metaphor. A structurally oriented poetics is likely to make metaphor, whether Aristotle's "transference of an alien name" or Jakobson's "poetic function," the microcosm of its largest concerns. Both in the *Poetics* and in the *Rhetoric* Aristotle showed how metaphor is the most important trope in the repertory of the artist because the "eye for resemblances" that it requires is what is also needed to connect the beginning with the end of a composition. On the other hand, Longinus, whose poetics is disruptive, evinces no interest in the structural properties of metaphor.[54] What does interest him is the traditional question among the rhetors concerning the relation between metaphor and repetition:[55] How often should the trope be repeated in elaborating a single topos? The answer Longinus gives is that there should be no limit as long as the result of any repetition is the pathos, or mesmerism, that erases one's memory of repetition and "never allow[s] the hearer to count the metaphors because he too shares the speaker's enthusiasm" (32.4). It is not metaphors themselves, then, but their repetition that achieves the sense of identity—empathetic rather than semantic identity—that can be managed only by the "transference of alien names" from the standpoint of structural analysis. Because the temporality of tropes and figures is unrelieved in Longinus, the vertical structure even of metaphor collapses into sequence.[56] He says nothing about the synonymy and identity that are enforced by radical metaphor in formalist thinking.

Repetition in the mathematical sublime can function as a homeopathic cure and thus resembles one widely sanctioned interpretation of catharsis in Aristotle. Like the frenzied music mentioned as a *katharsis* in the *Politics* (1341b-42a) and as a form of repetition by Longinus in his section on rhythm, repetition in excess precipitates the hearer toward a state of calm. Such is the outcome, Longinus thinks, of the onslaught of metaphors describing the "bodily tabernacle" in the *Timaeus:* "Finally," writes Longinus, at once quoting the passage and describing the effect of it on the reader, "when the end is at hand, the soul's 'ship's cables' are 'loosed,' and she herself 'set free.'" This extended metaphor seems to invite death, and in that respect it can be compared with both homeopathic medicine (more poison) and homeopathic catharsis (more suffering). But the therapy of repetition does not depend on the suspension of life that is required by the unified structure of catharsis. Rather it comes about in keeping with the ordinary footfall of time, which is metric, rhythmic, and anaphoric. The dynamic sublime, a single thunderbolt, has somewhat different purposes, but in the mathematical sublime there is reassurance in knowing that "Hectors and Sarpedons came forth" and kept on doing so (23.3), and there is likewise a sense of being "renewed" by the Ciceronian discourse that is "repeatedly fed with fresh fuel" (12.5).

IX

I have tried to show in my analysis of the *Poetics* that the crisis—the "recognition scene"—of a unified structure exposes the function of the double, or projected self, at the crossroads of choice; sexual or otherwise, this choice is always equivalent to the "ambiguity" of the New Critics. The crisis that comes with the sublime, on the other hand, exposes the function of the double in the prefiguration of death; confronting the uncanny, the listener tries to wrest authority from what seems to be a former self. Just as Addison and Burke associate the Beautiful, which is soft, smooth, round, and well-formed with sex, generation, and the plenitude of earthly existence, so they and most other theorists incline to associate the sublime with darkness, solitude, the unknown, and the "checking of vital powers." The sublime seems always to have been viewed as a trial confrontation with death. Whereas the theme of the Beautiful is the destiny of others as it appears manifest in their forms (their shapeliness in life, their roles in drama), the theme of the sublime is the destiny of ourselves, which we confront in the act of trying to win an authentic self from the forms that stand in our way. When the contrast between these old rivals for aesthetic attention is put thus provocatively, awarding all sanity, vital health, and humanity to the Beautiful—which is the flesh of formalism—then anyone who is not merely morbid and still prefers the sublime as an objective for interpretation has a lot of explaining to do. The worst that can be said about the sublime is now said: In bringing the death instinct rather than the pleasure principle close to the surface of aesthetic experience, it is necessary for the sublime to risk the irresponsible and exhibitionistic courtship of danger. To this effect Longinus praises a Homeric passage about mariners in a storm: "He has in effect stamped the special character of the danger on the diction: 'they are being carried away from under death'" (10.7). However, the immediate danger attendant upon the sublime is not death, but ridicule. With the slightest overemphasis the sublime becomes the ridiculous: hamhanded, humorless, and provincial. This risk may be unavoidable unless the sublime is transformed into another, quieter quality, one that I think Longinus himself has anticipated.

The false sublime gets puffed up and loses control. The danger of visionary speech (the dynamic sublime) is Icarean, the risk of a great fall, as when "the writer's soul . . . shares the danger" with Phaethon (15.4) or when the listener must share "the speaker's peril" during the suspension of meaning in hyperbaton (22.4). The danger of interpretive speech (the mathematical sublime) is Daedalian, the temptation "to go too far" in the proliferation of tropes (32.7), to lose the sublime in confusion rather than achieving it by sustained attention. The mathematical sublime must turn out to have been pregnant and not dropsical (3.3). All its amplifications may be nothing but "puffy and false tumours" (3.4). These dangers, which once more show the close proximity of words and nature, have to do in general with bodily malfunction and monstrosity.[57] Expressions may be "incomplete and abortive" (14.3), constipated, as when the "bowels" of the too-literary mariners of Aristeas "heave in pain" (10.4), or dwarfed, hardened beneath the surface like chancres, by the pettiness of conception that dwarfs reality: vultures that are tombs for men (3.2), a book that compresses the conquest of Asia (4.2), and the forced synecdoche crossed with homonymity (in the word *kore*) that traps a maiden in an eyeball (4.4). The failure of the mathematical sublime, then, which is the failure of interpretation, results in monsters, grotesqueries, and misbirths of the study.[58]

Dangers of visionary speech, however, are not so easily dispelled, nor are they quite so clearly deserving as targets for satire. A transitional instance between the two kinds of sublimity, an instance of euphemism, runs a more complex risk: "The goddess struck the Scythians who plundered the temple with a feminine disease" (28.4), by which is meant, presumably, impotence.[59] We could classify this misfortune as a bodily disorder that is related merely to the collapse of the mathematical sublime, for there are certainly as many Scythians as Hectors and Sarpedons. There is a key difference, however: for a prior offense, a rape, the Scythians are now cast as victims of authority instead of hapless authors. The danger now becomes ethical, in other words, and returns us to the issue of enslavement. Originary power endangers audiences just insofar as it realizes itself. If Icarus falls, no one notices; that, I take it, is what Brueghel meant and Auden emphasized:

> the ploughman may
> Have heard the splash, the forsaken cry,
> But for him it was not an important failure.

But if Phaethon, having risen against the order of things and having succeeded in driving the sun, should survive, or transmit his blinding success as a legacy, we would then find ourselves at the mercy of a petulant and spoiled youth. "Persuasion" is a democratic, tolerant discourse that leaves the hearer free to choose whether to be persuaded. It may be a novel, a book of self-help, a primer in economics, a discourse on Method; in the marketplace the ploughman listens attentively and casts his vote. "Transport," on the other hand, as we have seen, whether it drives the hearer across the sky or drives him mad, casts him into slavery, robbing him even of his proper self.

It is "natural," as Longinus says, that '"when two things are joined together, the stronger attracts to itself the force of the weaker" (15.11). The sublime seems too readily to belong in Plato's utopia; the integrity of the unenslaved individual counts for very little in either case. We cannot pretend that the concluding remarks of the ***Peri Hupsous*** as we have it are not in the main the sort of diatribe against the herd instinct that betrays a longing for tyranny. Longinus offers himself the chance to blame the disappearance of the sublime on the defeat of democracy but he refuses the offer—and is right, by his own lights, to do so. Always excepting Demosthenes, the oratory of "persuasion" that best suits the forum of democracy is not in any sense sublime. It is not certain, in fact, whether even persuasion is dependent on one political climate more than another: "In our age there are minds which are strikingly persuasive and practical, shrewd, versatile, and well endowed with the ability to write agreeably" (44.1). The more insidious enemy of the sublime, materialism, likewise flourishes regardless of most political changes; "most," that is, however, because the possibility of founding an austere tyranny, a reign of philosopher-kings or perhaps a theocracy, is the greatest temptation of those who are capable of "great thoughts."[60] Hence, again, there appears to be a bond of sympathy between tyranny and the sublime.

I think, however, that this sympathy exists in appearance only. In the course of its attack on materialism the argument of Longinus is almost undermined by a reversal of the values attached to certain metaphors. This reversal is inevitable and ultimately robs the austere tyrant of his authority, leading to the democratization of the sublime that I wish to propose. In Longinus's last chapter the tropes associated with materialism gradually begin to imply that materialism is an epidemic so far-flung that it must itself be accounted sublime. The grosser passions fight an "unlimited war," wealth and the lust for it are "measureless and uncontrolled," and we are "slaves" to the love of pleasure (44.6-7). The rout of the sublime being sublime, then, Longinus is almost prepared to acquiesce in things as they are, to let the inundation come in whatever form: "Perhaps people like us are better as subjects than given our freedom. Greed would flood the world in woe, if it were really released and let out of its cage, to prey on its neighbors" (44.10). The Longinian sublime is certainly a tyrant but it is not always, as we might have supposed, a celestial dictator, a sky-god or Platonic Houyhnhnm; it is not surprising, when one considers the intimacy between mind and nature that is revealed elsewhere in the text, that the tyrant is sometimes our own instinctual life. A Yahoo tyrant, at least nominally the oppressed rather than the oppressor, it is demagogic, revolting, universally in charge, so much so that it must be softened and coaxed into epicurean channels, sublimated like our "private parts," which nature "concealed as well as she could": "and as Xenophon says, [she] made the channels of those organs as remote as possible, so as not to spoil the beauty of the creature as a whole" (43.5). The term *beauty*—*kallos*—is no doubt a vague one here but it may serve to remind us that if the "creature" in question were sublime, or conducive to the sublime, all its gaps might be visible. It should be clear, in any case, that the sublime extends the lower as well as the upper reaches of the *Poetics.*

X

The bridge between the sublime, thus revealed in its role as a negative force, and the beautiful, a tender-hearted experience that could not in itself entail the possibility of being *critical,* is the mathematical sublime, or sublime of interpretation. The most elementary temptation of any antiformalist interpreter is to identify with all the darkest visionaries and to find dark values exclusively, with Melville in *The Encantadas,* on the only side of the tortoise he or she can see. But the interpretive sublime is on neither side. It exists as an alternative to alternation and reveals the lack of opposition in false dichotomies. The discovery of hidden meanings is no more adequate as an exclusive end of criticism than the summary of overt ones.[61] Derivative myth-criticism, "Freudian interpretation," and most of the merely rancorous modes of demystification oversimplify in this way. At the end of the last chapter I suggested that any criticism necessarily goes astray in some measure because it can never estimate the distance between the architectonic purpose and the instinctual purposiveness of its object—or of its own subjectivity. The "effect" of literature, the sublime or uncanny effect which sets it apart (but not categorically apart) from the relatively featureless discourse of practical exchange, does not appear squarely within either form or the negation of form but in the signs of estrangement, the gaps, between formal design and the form of its attempted negation. Neither of these forms completely occludes or represses the other; each harbors an unsubdued strength that deforms the other in ways that cannot be scientifically reduced any more than psychology can fully discriminate or arbitrate between will and instinct in the mind.

So the sublime is *not* identical with the unconscious, and its appearance is not properly to be described as sublimation, although that plays its role. Undoubtedly we have grown too familiar with our fictions about the fictions of the unconscious, with all their pathos and economy—so familiar, indeed, that the whole psychoanalytic romance may turn out to have sublimated whatever it is that is *still* wholly unconscious. The sufficiency of the oedipal explanation is undergoing attack from every direction—humanist, feminist, Marxist, deconstructionist—because too obviously it cuts the Gordian knot of interpretation. As Hertz argues, the oedipal explanation breaks through the mathematical sublime arbitrarily. I am not quite sure; in my view the oedipal explanation seems arbitrary because it overdetermines the language of desire, desire which is not for one thing, arguably, but for the sheer sensation of presence. But the oedipal explanation is still, if I may so put it, a valid allegory. Roughly the same objection can be made, followed by a roughly comparable defense, concerning the closely related explanations called "bourgeois ideology," *langue,* and the "precursor"—concerning any explanation, in short, that seems unequivocally to insist that poets are written, not writers.

Antithetical factors are not interpretive ends in themselves any more than the factors conducive to formal unity were before them. Systematically approached, antithetical factors will soon constitute an antithetical formalism. There is undoubted value in a science of this sort, which will certainly find ways of making whole dimensions of art visible for the first time, but I do not see how this or any other quickly exhausted way of processing literature—for that is what it is—can be heralded as the future task of criticism and recommended specifically as an antidote to interpretation.[62] It is under the banner of science, and not as a hindrance to science, that the interpretation industry has come to monopolize criticism in the last forty years. Interpretation has supplanted both judgment and taxonomy in scholarship; this triumph has been a recent one, not because interpretation had never been done before but because for the most part until this century it had seemed a simple job that could be done silently. It may be noted that the interpretation industry has always dominated theology, and always will dominate it, because where it really matters interpretation has never seemed easy. Interpretation is inevitable; it is thought itself, and it will seem exhaustible, not when it is supplanted by science, but only when it is itself mistaken for science.

The New Critics used to ask the philological historians how they could confidently classify ideas, terms, and texts without reading them attentively, without a due concern for nuance and irony. It seemed a good and fair question, and the answer came as too much interpretation—to the point of "blockage"—with that sort of concern. But ridicule and self-exhaustion alike have now done their work, and very few more new books with titles like "Ordered Flux" are likely to appear. The new blockage is more likely to consist of general rhetorics, revisionary histories, and narratologies, entitling us to ask, in behalf of interpretation, the same old question: How can the new anatomies proceed with confidence if they do not read attentively, openly, and to some extent unsystematically? The science of the greatest modern anatomist, Northrop Frye, has passed inevitably into eclipse, but rival sciences alone are churlish enough to scorn the grace of his interpretations.

The function of the sublime is to keep interpretation from closure. It persists between forms, as close to one as to another; it should be remarked in this regard that the most sophisticated operative terms of formalism, from Aristotle's "recognition"—duly interpreted—to Skhlovsky's "defamiliarization" and Sigurd Burckhardt's "disturbing element,"[63] point clearly toward what I mean by the sublime. A valuable instance of the necessary interaction between forms and the sublime appears in Longinus's reading of Sappho's "ode" to Anactoria. Self-convicted of fragmentation, her tongue "broken" by passion, Sappho "brings everything together," as Longinus says (10.3) with commanding metrical skill. If this were all, the topic of interpretation would still be "ordered flux," but Longinus has merely set interpretation in motion by suggesting an equipoise of motive. One would have to continue—to point out, for example, the consecrating excitement of love-anguish in contrast with an encroaching ennui that is intimated in the very composure and elegance of these sapphics, thus questioning the presupposition we have as readers that form is comfort. One would have to show, always inconclusively, how passion and control infect and finally disfigure each other in the course of their endless give-and-take of values.

The effect of a well-conducted interpretation along these lines, drawn out more and more finely in a dialectic that never quite repeats itself, is the effect of the mathematical sublime. But we still have not faced the imputation of tyranny in our victimage by the victim Sappho. Rumors of tyranny have followed the concept of the sublime ever since they were first prompted by the typical metaphors of Longinus himself. Perhaps it can be shown at least that they have been greatly exaggerated. Tyranny exists without legitimate authority but it still requires that some authority, however specious, be invoked for it. The sublime by contrast is unauthorized, as we have seen, a phantom of possession that is always in retreat from one site to another. Although the sublime never falsifies its nature (*quod semper, quod ubique, quod ab omnibus*) and thus evades the charge of fickleness leveled by Plato against both poets and democracies, yet at the same time it never regiments response; it always surprises and elevates, as Longinus says. Its tonic effect is not subject to conventionalization and it also lacks the monotonous insistence of obsession. Not at all necessarily suggestive of spectacular gloom but of the happy absence, rather, of inhibition, it is best seen, on reflection, as a grace beyond the reach of art.

In an article called "'A Grace Beyond the Reach of Art,'" which is meant to supplement his book on the sublime, Samuel Holt Monk demonstrates that Pope's phrase is less directly indebted to Longinus than to a flourishing and longstanding concept of "grace" per se.[64] *Charis, venustas, gratia, je ne sais quoi, sprezzatura:*—roughly synonymous with all these terms, *grace* was very nearly equivalent in seventeenth-century poetics to *sublimity* in the century succeeding Boileau's translation of Longinus (1674).[65] (Hazlitt's *gusto* may offer itself as a nineteenth-century equivalent, while *indeterminacy* and *free-play* are somewhat unsatisfactory candidates for our own.) The very real difference between the two terms was that *grace* in the aesthetic milieu of the Restoration suggested nothing gothic, ponderous, or frightening. It encompassed the baroque fillip, the shining of a countenance, the unexpected twist of a period, or the simplicity of an epigram. Its effect, says Monk, was "sudden and surprising," like that of the sublime, and in its time it was, like the sublime, "a repository for the irregular and irrational elements in art,"[66] but apart from these parallels it was a very different quality, a carelessness in elegance (like Pyrrha's hair in Horace) rather than a breach of decorum.

Monk says ("Grace Beyond the Reach of Art," p. 134) that Lysias was the stock example of grace in literature, an example taken by seventeenth-century writers from Longinus's probable contemporary Demetrius (see *On Style,* 3, 128). When one considers what Longinus says about Lysias, one comes to suspect that he may be extending the terms *hupsos* and *megethos* to incorporate the *charis* discussed at length by Demetrius (127-42) and also in passing by Dionysius of Halicarnassus. It is important not only that Longinus compares Plato with Lysias while pretending not to, showing thereby that grace, whatever Plato may lack, is certainly what Demosthenes lacks. What is more telling is the fact that the concept of grace would rationalize the presence in Longinus's canon of Sappho's ode, a poem that many scholars, most notably Saintsbury, have refused to call sublime.[67] When Demetrius affirms that "one cannot sufficiently admire [the charm: *epicharitos*] in the divine Sappho,"[68] Longinus would certainly applaud the precision of his sentiment. All things considered, he would not demur unduly, I think, if one were to introduce grace into the domain of the sublime.

A modern essay that is splendidly Longinian, provided that one is willing to extend the meaning of *hupsos* in this manner, is "Language as Gesture" by R. P. Blackmur, whose examples, especially those taken from the plastic arts, have a quality resembling "grace." Blackmur reminds one of Longinus both in his virtuoso, paronomasiac style and also in his way of choosing and then sympathetically fusing his commentary with his examples. He concludes "Language as Gesture" with a tribute to Shakespearean gesture that could be a translation of Longinus: the power of implication in Shakespeare "must overwhelm us even though we realize as we consent to it, that we have made it ourselves."[69]

XI

I suggested [elsewhere] that the tradition deriving from Aristotle has tended to constitute itself as the only tradition. In recommending a different perspective I have tried (a victim, perhaps, of some obscure law of recoil) to recover nearly the whole field for Longinus, including much to which he never explicitly laid claim: a theory of representation, a rigorous understanding of the interplay among nature, feeling, and language, and a grasp of aesthetic qualities beyond the so-called sublime—the Burkean trombone—extending even to amplification, charm, and delicacy. For the moment I have not pressed these conclusions into a theory of interpretation, but in rough terms the orientation of such a theory will be obvious. Even though the theory itself should remain as evasive as the sublime, in practice it amounts to this: whenever possible, the interpreter should delay the semantic closure that is urged upon him by his or her own will to form and that of the text. The enterprise of interpretation is best honored by those who do *not* agree to go no further, to get no closer, to honor tenuous symmetries. Having arrived at a liminal understanding of form (both as the determination of consciousness and as unconscious determination[70]) by feeling along its edges like someone who is blind, the interpreter begins, at that point of exhaustion, to interpret.

The Sophoclean Oedipus disregarded by Aristotle but nonetheless present in the *Poetics* realizes that, as Longinus says, his misfortunes are plural. Because of his resolution to become a scapegoat he sacrifices the "external trappings" of his governorship—as helmsman and *tyrannos*—to the interior form of his family romance, scattering the symbols of his far-seeing guardianship on the ground in order to make the character beneath his role visible for the first time. In Longinus all of this seems a preliminary matter; it is a model for the structure of disruption that tells us very little in itself, "catharsis" notwithstanding, about the way the experience reaches the spectator. A fuller and subtler moment in the Oedipus story is commemorated by Longinus, just before he cites the apparition of Achilles over his tomb, as "Sophocles' account of Oedipus dying and giving himself burial to the accompaniment of a sign from heaven" (15.7).

In the messenger's speech recording this event, there are "clefts" in the sky, in the earth, and in knowledge, all of which regions at this moment, especially as Oedipus views them, are nearly indistinguishable. Although each region is sundered, there is still no point of division between them:

> Then very quickly we saw him do reverence
> To earth and to the powers of air,
> With one address to both.
> But in what manner
> Oedipus perished, no one of mortal men
> Could tell but Theseus. It was not lightning,
> Bearing its fire from God, that took him off;
> No hurricane was blowing.
> But some attendant from the train of Heaven
> Came for him; or else the underworld
> Opened in love the unlit door of earth.[71]

Longinus recognizes his affinity with a seer who can bring mind and nature so close together that one sudden obeisance will do for both. A sweep as unconfined as this cannot be imagined without some loss of categorical nicety. Theseus, like Horatio and so many others to come, survives to interpret the experience, reconstructing in his own person the monarchical form of Oedipus while passing on the family form to Hippolytus. Like Longinus, Theseus will aspire to the mathematical sublime; he will be concerned with the quality of life in society after the dynamic sublime has been buried. Leaving the sacred ground, he carries the vision of Oedipus into a community that is preserved, in all its necessary forms, by taking that vision to heart in order not to relive it. The power of Oedipus is now explanatory, descriptive, and perhaps lacking in magnificance, but in being recalled by the voice of Theseus it is made to return from its antisocial isolation. To follow and confirm that return is the whole art, or nature, of interpretation.

Notes

[1] For these arguments, see William K. Wimsatt and Cleanth Brooks, *Literary Criticism: A Short History,* 2 vols. (Chicago: Univ. of Chicago Press, 1978), I, 97-111.

[2] Olson, "The Argument of Longinus' *On the Sublime,*" in *Critics and Criticism: Ancient and Modern,* ed. R. S. Crane (Chicago: Univ. of Chicago Press, 1954), p. 259.

[3] See "ibid.," p. 233. Should there be any doubt of Aristotle's influence on Olson's allegedly "pluralistic" interpretation, Olson's assertion that the sublime "is a kind of mean" between vices of style ("ibid.," p. 242) will indicate what I mean.

[4] For the differences between these views as assessed by the participants, see R. S. Crane, "The Critical Monism of Cleanth Brooks," in *Critics and Criticism,* ed. Crane, pp. 83-107; Wimsatt, "The Chicago Critics: The Fallacy of Neoclassic Species," in *The Verbal Icon: Studies in the Meaning of Poetry* (Lexington: Univ. of Kentucky Press, 1967), pp. 41-65; Elder Olson, "The Dialectical Foundations of Critical Pluralism," *TQ* 9 (1966), 202-30. Under the tutelage of Richard McKeon, the Chicagoans tended to read Aristotle as though the distinction between language and concept, or referent, were the keystone of his system. See especially McKeon, "Aristotle's Conception of Language and the Arts of Language," *Critics and Criticism,* pp. 173-231.

[5] *Literary Criticism,* I, 101.

[6] Thomas Weiskel points to "the confusion of nature and art, author and work, which will become the trademark of the Longinian or affective sublime" *(The Romantic Sublime: Studies in the Structure and Psychology of Transcendence* [Baltimore: Johns Hopkins Univ. Press, 1976], p. 12).

[7] *"Longinus" on Sublimity,* trans. D. A. Russell (Oxford: Clarendon Press, 1965), to be cited by section number and marginal number, 1.3. For translations I have also consulted *Longinus on the Sublime,* trans. A. O. Prickard (Oxford: Clarendon Press, 1906), and *On the Sublime,* trans. W. Rhys Roberts (Cambridge: Cambridge Univ. Press, 1899). I have used the Greek edition and commentary of D. A. Russell, *"Longinus" on the Sublime* (Oxford: Clarendon Press, 1964). Although the identity of the author is unknown, I follow the nearly universal convention of calling him "Longinus." It is interesting to note that a leading Longinus scholar, G. M. A. Grube, has returned to the belief, or at least leans toward it, that our author was indeed the third-century Cassius Longinus celebrated by Boileau and Gibbon *(The Greek and Roman Critics* [London: Methuen, 1965], p. 341).

[8] The most extreme instance of debunking based on this error is Walter Allen, Jr., "The Terentianus of the *Peri Hupsous,*" *American Journal of Philology* 62 (1941), 51-64.

[9] Neil Hertz describes the "oedipal moment" itself, insofar as Oedipus's recognition can be identified with

resolution, as the "sublime of conflict and structure" ("The Notion of Blockage in the Literature of the Sublime," in *Psychoanalysis and the Question of the Text,* ed. Geoffrey H. Hartman [Baltimore: Johns Hopkins Univ. Press, 1978], p. 76).

[10] The fact that Longinus almost certainly found this remark in Quintilian (*Institutio Oratoria,* 8, 3, 37) makes his assignment of it to the Peripatetics yet more significant.

[11] So Roberts. Russell settles for "external trappings" even though the word is *prostragodoumenon.*

[12] Grube has also argued (*Greek and Roman Critics,* p. 344) that Longinus must have in mind the emotions of characters, not audiences. Aristotle himself says, however (*Rhetoric* 1408a), that pity, grief, and fear are "low emotions" in oratory. On this point see also Allen Tate, "Longinus and the 'New Criticism,'" in *The Man of Letters in the Modern World* (New York: Meridian, 1955), p. 188.

[13] I mean only the structural values of the *Poetics.* In the *Nicomachean Ethics* (1124a) there is a portrait of the "magnanimous man" which closely anticipates the sublime individual in Longinus.

[14] I do not think that Longinus's distinctions are completely empty. I would agree, for instance, with Russell's excellent summary (*"Longinus" on the Sublime,* p. 126) of the difference between figures *(schemata)* and *tropoi,* which is, to put it negatively, that if a figure fails the result is a solecism whereas if a trope fails the result is a barbarism. Deconstruction is not the only current school of thought, in any case, which professes a disregard for generic and other such distinctions. See the persuasive article by John Bayley, "Against a New Formalism," *Crit Q* 10 (1968), 60-71.

[15] See, e.g., Russell, *"Longinus" on the Sublime,* p. 91, and G. M. A. Grube, "Notes on the *Peri Hupsous,*" *American Journal of Philology* 78 (1957), pp. 365-66.

[16] Olson's "Argument" notwithstanding, I would agree with Neil Hertz that one cannot keep a fixed pattern or structure of the text clearly in mind ("Lecture de Longin," *Poétique* 4 [1973], p. 292).

[17] Readers familiar with Jacques Lacan's "Seminar on 'The Purloined Letter'" (*YES* 48 [1972], 38-72) will recognize in this chain of dissimulation and enthrallment, which is so much more complex than the Horation *Si vis me flere,* the ring of pursuit as Lacan understands it in Poe's story—and in the psychoanalytic transference.

[18] On this point see Tate, "Longinus and the 'New Criticism,'" p. 183.

[19] Hertz's reading of Longinus's response to Sappho differs from mine in stressing compositional qualities; I do not agree with his assertion that "La doctrine de l'unité organique a rarement été presentée avec autant de ferveur" ("Lecture de Longin," p. 295).

[20] *Romantic Sublime,* p. 17. Weiskel feels on the whole, however, with Hertz, that Longinus is committed to "organic continuity" (ibid., p. 21). Wimsatt is nearly alone among the commentators in having remarked that Longinus's figures "tend to have to do with abnormalities of syntax and peculiarities of structure" (*Literary Criticism,* I, 103).

[21] Allen Tate is the most extreme proponent of the notion that the sublime is a quality of words ("Longinus and the 'New Criticism,'" p. 177). See also Elizabeth Nitchie, "Longinus and the Theory of Poetic Imitation in the Seventeenth and Eighteenth Centuries," *SP* 23 (1935), p. 586. Boileau in the "Préface" to his 1674 translation of Longinus insisted persuasively that the sublime is *not* wholly a question of style (*The Continental Model: Selected French Critical Essays of the Seventeenth Century,* ed. Scott Elledge and Donald Schier [Ithaca: Cornell Univ. Press, 1970], p. 272).

[22] Iser, *The Implied Reader* (Baltimore: Johns Hopkins Univ. Press, 1974), p. 280.

[23] See Hertz, "Lecture de Longin," p. 292.

[24] See Geoffrey Hartman on the impossible ideal of "purity" in language in *Criticism in the Wilderness: The Study of Literature Today* (New Haven: Yale Univ. Press, 1980), esp. pp. 115-57.

[25] As Weiskel says (*Romantic Sublime,* p. 5), the sublime "is always cloaked in metaphors of aggression."

[26] D. A. Russell is especially concerned to deny the similarities between Burke and Longinus. See, e.g., the introduction to his translation, *"Longinus" on Sublimity,* p. xvi.

[27] Hertz ("Lecture de Longin," p. 299) discusses the oedipal situation that appears in this and many more of Longinus's quotations, including the passage on Phaethon's flight cited above.

[28] Freud, "The 'Uncanny,'" in *On Creativity and the Unconscious,* ed. Benjamin Nelson (New York: Harper Torchbooks, 1958), p. 156n. I return to this issue in chapter 5 (p. 175).

[29] Allen, "Terentianus of the *Peri Hupsous,*" pp. 52-53.

[30] Burke, *A Philosophical Enquiry into the Origin of our Ideas of the Sublime and the Beautiful,* ed. James T. Boulton (London: Routledge & Kegan Paul, 1958), p. 66.

[31] Burke, *Reflections on the Revolution in France* (London: J. M. Dent, 1960), p. 82.

[32] Kant, *Critique of Judgment,* trans. J. H. Bernard (New York: Hafner, 1972), p. 83.

[33] Perhaps the only commentator who approaches this distinction carefully is George Saintsbury in his eccentric but interesting essay on Longinus in *A History of Criticism and Literary Taste,* 3 vols. (Edinburgh: William Blackwood and Sons, 1900), I, 162.

[34] Russell cautions us that grammatically the silence of Ajax is only an analogy and not an example (*"Longinus" on Sublimity,* p. 9n.), but I am not sure it matters which way we take it.

[35] On the elaborateness of the frame composition in Homer, which encodes information in specular pairs of the kind I have stressed in this passage, see Cedric Whitman, *Homer and the Heroic Tradition* (Cambridge, Mass.: Harvard Univ. Press, 1958), esp. p. 294-84.

[36] A. C. Bradley describes nocturnal silence as "a peace . . . that may make the face of death sublime" ("The Sublime," in *Oxford Lectures on Poetry* [London: Macmillan & Co., 1955], p. 49).

[37] Eliot, "Tradition and the Individual Talent," in *The Sacred Wood* (London: Methuen, 1964), p. 52.

[38] Not all hearers do so, clearly, but the response which does not in itself become an "influence" becomes, however idiosyncratic and interesting, a terminal mutation. Every significant reader is in some sense also a writer. See the text of Longinus at 7.4.

[39] Harold Bloom's theory of influence presides over these next few pages in roughly the form of development, lacking the tropes and defenses, that appeared in *The Anxiety of Influence* (London: Oxford Univ. Press, 1975). Also in this context Weiskel writes admirably as follows (*Romantic Sublime,* p. 32): "To consider the problem of originality is to find the two kinds of sublimation, poet's and reader's, compounded or superimposed."

[40] I refer especially to the second of three newspaper essays that are usually entitled "On Genial Criticism": see "On the Principles of Sound Criticism: Essay Second," in *Miscellanies Aesthetic and Literary,* ed. T. Ashe (London: George Bell, 1885), pp. 10-14.

[41] There are several versions of this anecdote. All of them are conveniently reviewed by C. D. Thorpe, "Coleridge on the Sublime," in *Wordsworth and Coleridge,* ed. E. L. Griggs (Princeton: Princeton Univ. Press, 1939), pp. 193-94. See also Bradley, "The Sublime," p. 37.

[42] Quintilian's well-known anticipation of this passage (*Institutio Oratoria,* 8, 2, 21) is a sarcastic joke at the expense of those who pride themselves on deciphering obscure passages. The relevance of this joke for anyone listening, say, to the priestess at Delphi, should be clear.

[43] As Grube writes (*Greek and Roman Critics,* p. 347), "Clearly Longinus uses mimesis in the broadest, not the restricted rhetorical sense."

[44] See Prickard, *Longinus on the Sublime,* p. xvi.

[45] On the complexities of this passage, see Russell, *"Longinus" on the Sublime,* p. 106. Some scholars have suggested emending *psugmata* (gaps) to *psegmata* (dust, chippings).

[46] Hertz argues ("Notion of Blockage," p. 70) that a theoretical concern with "blockage" arises only after the decline of Longinus's influence. I think that this concern is already present in Longinus and can be found in certain phrasings of Addison (especially *Spectator* 412) more apparently than in any author in the decades just preceding Kant.

[47] Wimsatt (*Literary Criticism,* I, 109) goes so far as to equate *sunthesis* with rhythm.

[48] Yeats, "The Symbolism of Poetry," in *Essays and Introductions* (New York: MacMillan, 1961), p. 159.

[49] As I understand it, the meaning of Kierkegaard's allegory, *Repetition: An Essay in Experimental Psychology,* is that repetition, for the reasons here outlined, is a means of finding grace. It is, in any case, as Valéry explained, an enemy of our rational wish to process art as information (see "The Idea of Art," in *Aesthetics,* ed. Harold Osborne [Oxford: Oxford Univ. Press, 1978], p. 28).

[50] Kant, *Critique of Judgment,* pp. 86-106. The mathematical sublime is what Thomas Weiskel calls the "hermeneutical sublime," anticipating what I have said earlier in the present essay about the sublime in interpretation (see *Romantic Sublime,* esp. p. 28).

[51] Hertz, "Notion of Blockage," p. 74. See also p. 76 and Hertz, "Lecture de Longin," p. 304. It seems to me that in order to project an adequate dynamic into the *structure* of the Kantian sublime, Weiskel has had to draw *imagination* and *reason* dangerously close to their English meanings, so that *imagination* swells into the glorious faculty of Wordsworth, significantly an "unfathered vapour from the abyss," and *reason* shrinks from the radiant proportions Kant awards it to the old patriarchal bogey that the Romantics attributed to the Augustans.

[52] Freud, *Beyond the Pleasure Principle,* trans. James Strachey (New York: Norton, 1961), pp. 8-13, 30.

[53] Freud, "Notes upon a Case of Obsessional Neurosis" ("The Rat Man"), in *Three Case Histories,* ed. Philip Rieff (New York: Collier Books, 1976), p. 88.

[54] It has been speculated that there is a lost section on metaphor; that may be, but I would prefer, of course, to think not. See T. R. Henn, *Longinus and English Criticism* (Cambridge: Cambridge Univ. Press, 1934), p. 65.

[55] Jakobson would see metaphor as a basis for repetition in that the "poetic function" is an imposition of equivalence on signs ("Linguistics and Poetics," in *The Structuralists from Marx to Lévi-Strauss,* ed. Richard DeGeorge and Fernande DeGeorge [Garden City, N.Y.: Doubleday Anchor, 1972], p. 95).

[56] The definitive discussion of the absence of simultaneity from the functioning of tropes is that of Paul de Man, "The Rhetoric of Temporality," in *Interpretation,* ed. Charles Singleton (Baltimore: Johns Hopkins Univ. Press, 1964), pp. 173-209.

[57] What all the faults have in common, says Grube, is "swellings" ("Notes on the *Peri Hupsous,*" p. 364).

[58] The use of the topoi of malformation in satire has been treated theoretically by Michael Seidel, *Satiric Inheritance, Rabelais to Sterne* (Princeton: Princeton Univ. Press, 1979), esp. pp. 3-59.

[59] I would not have guessed it, frankly, but see the conjecture of Russell, *"Longinus" on the Sublime,* p. 148.

[60] For a modern discussion of the politics of sublimity, see Iris Murdoch, "The Sublime and the Beautiful Revisited," *YR* 49 (1959-60), 247-71. For the fullest discussion of Longinus's closing remarks, see Charles P. Segal, "*Hupsos* and the Problem of Cultural Decline," *Harvard Studies in Classical Philology* 64 (1959), 121 ff.

[61] Errors of this sort are well discussed by Martin Price, "Form and Discontent," *NLH* 4 (1972-73), 383.

[62] See Jonathan Culler, "Beyond Interpretation: The Prospects of Contemporary Criticism," *CL* 28 (1976), 244-56.

[63] See Skhlovsky, "Art and Technique," in *Russian Formalist Criticism: Four Essays,* ed. Lee T. Lemon and Marion J. Reis (Lincoln: Univ. of Nebraska Press, 1965), pp. 3-57, and Burckhardt, *Shakespearean Meanings* (Princeton: Princeton Univ. Press, 1968), 285-313. Weiskel (*Romantic Sublime,* p. 19) speaks well in this context of Wordsworth's "great program of defamiliarization."

[64] Monk, "'A Grace Beyond the Reach of Art,'" *JHI* 5 (1944), 131-50.

[65] Or somewhat more than a century. Although Burke ignored Longinus and Hugh Blair abused him, his influence is still reflected, according to Monk, as late as 1787 (*The Sublime: A Study of Critical Theories in XVIII-Century England* [Ann Arbor: Univ. of Michigan Press, 1960], p. 25).

[66] Monk, "A Grace Beyond the Reach of Art," pp. 132, 150.

[67] Saintsbury, *History of Criticism,* I, 154.

[68] *Demetrius on Style,* ed. W. Rhys Roberts (Cambridge: Cambridge Univ. Press, 1902), p. 131.

[69] Blackmur, "Language as Gesture," in *Language as Gesture: Essays in Poetry* (Westport, Ct.: Greenwood Press, 1974), p. 24.

[70] I do not know of a fully developed argument that anticipates what I have been suggesting about the two "forms" and their relations; M. H. Abrams has written interestingly, however, in discussing John Keble, of a "conflict of motives" between composition and repression (*Mirror and the Lamp* [New York: Norton, 1958], p. 146).

[71] *Oedipus at Colonus,* trans. Robert Fitzgerald, *Sophocles I,* ed. David Grene (Chicago: Univ. of Chicago Press, 1970), p. 150.

FURTHER READING

Bibliography

Weinberg, Bernard. "Translations and Commentaries of Longinus, *On the Sublime,* to 1600: A Bibliography." *Modern Philology* 47, No. 3 (Feb. 1950): 145-51.

Chronological list (through 1600) of Latin commentaries and translations and Greek texts and vernacular translations.

Criticism

Abrams, M. H. "Longinus and the Longinians." In *The Mirror and the Lamp: Romantic Theory and the Critical Tradition,* pp. 72-78. New York: Oxford University Press, 1953.

Considers Longinus's *On the Sublime* as an influential precursor to nineteenth-century romantic theory.

Baldwin, Charles Sears. "The Literary Criticism of Rhetoric." In *Ancient Rhetoric and Poetic, Interpreted from Representative Works,* pp. 102-31. Gloucester, Mass.: Peter Smith, 1959.

Considers *De Compositione Verborum* of Dionysius of Halicarnassus and *De Sublimitate* of Longinus as complementary approaches to the classical conception of rhetoric.

Brody, Jules. "Longinus Rediscovered." In *Boileau and Longinus,* pp. 9-35. Genève: Librairie E. Droz, 1958.

Surveys the editions of Longinus published in Renaissance Italy and seventeenth-century France, and discusses the reception of *On the Sublime* by Nicolas Boileau.

Collins, John Churton. "Longinus and Greek Criticism." In *Studies in Poetry and Criticism,* pp. 204-62. London: George Bell and Sons, 1905.

Surveys the editions and translations of *On the Sublime* and critical approaches to the question of authorship in European scholarship.

Henn, T. R. *Longinus and English Criticism.* Cambridge: Cambridge at the University Press, 1934, 163p.

Assesses the aesthetic positions advanced by Longinus–particularly what later readers consider to be his literary "rules"–and his reception by later critics such as Hugh Blair, Edmund Burke, and Andrew Bradley.

Innes, Doreen C. "Longinus: Structure and Unity." In *Greek Literary Theory after Aristotle: A Collection of Papers in Honour of D. M. Schenkeveld,* edited by J. G. J. Abbenes, S. R. Slings, and I. Sluiter, pp. 111-24. Amsterdam: VU University Press, 1995.

Discusses the textbook structure (and its undermining) in *On the Sublime* and its patterns of imagery.

Kennedy, William J. "Voice as Frame: Longinus, Kant, Ong, and Deconstruction in Literary Studies." In *Media, Consciousness, and Culture: Explorations of Walter Ong's Thought,* edited by Bruce E. Gronbeck, Thomas J. Farrell, and Paul A. Soukup, pp. 77-89. Newbury Park: Sage Publications, 1991.

Contends that Ong's insight into the literary voice draws on work by Longinus and Immanuel Kant.

Wimsatt, William K., and Cleanth Brooks. "Roman Classicism: Longinus." In *Literary Criticism: A Short History,* Vol. 1, pp. 97-111. Chicago: University of Chicago, 1978.

Explores the historical context and critical legacy of *Peri Hupsous,* including its rhetorical strategies and its treatment of the sublime (*ekstasis*) and the sources of sublimity.

Additional coverage of Longinus's life and career is contained in the following source published by Gale Research: *Dictionary of Literary Biography, Vol. 176: Ancient Greek Authors.*

Socrates
469 B.C.- 399 B.C.

Greek philosopher.

INTRODUCTION

Socrates is revered for his shifting of Greek philosophical thought from the contemplation of the nature of the universe, which occupied the philosophers before him, to the examination of human life and its problems. He was the first to study ethics as a science—that is, to study morality in a systematic, consistent manner. Scholars have noted that the impact of Socrates on the development of Western culture and philosophy cannot be overstated, and some have suggested that his teachings influenced the development of Christianity. Yet the study of Socrates's philosophy is plagued by the "problem of Socrates": he wrote nothing. After his death, and perhaps before it, his followers began to record details of his life and thought, but these are arguably more interpretive in nature than they are biographical. Therefore, one of the greatest debates surrounding Socrates is that of the accuracy and validity of the Socratic sources, primarily the writings of Xenophon and Plato. Other critical issues include the interpretation of Socrates's ethical theses that virtue is knowledge, wrong-doing is involuntary, and that the care of the soul is the primary condition for living well; and of his controversial views regarding the treatment of enemies and retaliation.

Socrates was born in 469 B.C. in Athens to a stonemason (some sources state that Socrates's father was a sculptor) named Sophroniscus and his spouse, a midwife. He was a student of a physicist, Archelaus, and was perhaps interested in the philosophy of Anaxagoras. He is believed to have lived on a small inheritance and on investments made through a wealthy friend. Socrates served in the army, fought in the Peloponnesian War, and married a woman named Xanthippe, who bore two or three sons, sources say. When Socrates was 70 years old, he was accused of "irreligion," or impiety, and of corrupting the youth of Athens. In 399 B.C. he was tried, convicted, and condemned to die by drinking hemlock.

While Socrates did not leave any writings, his followers Xenophon and Plato both wrote extensively about Socrates's beliefs and experiences. Yet their respective accounts differ markedly. In addition to the records of Xenophon and Plato, Aristophanes ridiculed Socrates in one of his comedies, *Clouds* (423 B.C.), and Aristotle commented on the philosopher and Plato's representation of him. Some critics have relied on a combination of these sources as a means of accessing the historical Socrates, and others place more weight on either Xenophon's or Plato's version. Despite early preference for Xenophon, many twentieth-century scholars have argued that Plato's portrayal of Socrates presents the more accurate version, however flawed by idealism it may be. Xenophon has been criticized by scholars such as E. Zeller for the simple and unphilosophic manner in which Socrates is depicted. Others, such as J. T. Forbes, have suggested that Xenophon's presentation of Socrates as a moral censor and teacher of practical values, rather than as a philosophic revolutionary, may have been driven by Xenophon's intention of minimizing the "revolutionary aspects of the thought of Socrates." Forbes has also noted that Plato's account of Socrates is "largely ideal" and that Plato was more concerned with presenting abstract truth than with historical or chronological accuracy. A. K. Rogers has argued that preference for Xenophon stems from the distrust of Plato, who may have created his version of Socrates as a mouthpiece for his own philosophy. Yet

Rogers has gone on to caution that Xenophon is an apologist and should not be trusted more than Plato. Homer H. Dubs has supported the case for Plato and has suggested that Xenophon may have gotten some of his information about Socrates from Plato. Dubs has also argued that while Plato may have "put words in So-crates's mouth" it is precisely because of the fact that Plato was an accomplished artist that we should trust his portrayal of Socrates: Plato, Dubs stressed, would have only made Socrates utter what would have been "thoroughly appropriate" for Socrates to say. J. B. Bury has also stressed the value of Plato's version over that of Xenophon, stating that the Socrates who emerges from Plato's *Dialogues* is "a figure probably resembling the real Socrates." Yet others, such as R. Hackforth, have maintained that criticism of Xeno-phon is too harsh, and that while Xenophon may have not been sufficiently interested in philosophy to do justice to the portrayal of Socrates, Plato was too much involved in his subject matter to be objective. Critics such as Luis Navia have suggested ways in which these apparently contradictory accounts may be reconciled. Forbes has also argued for using a combination of testimonies, as well as a study of the development of Socrates's philosophy, in order to identify a consistent and faithful view of Socrates.

The concepts of knowledge, virtue, and goodness are intertwined in the philosophy of Socrates. He taught that "virtue is knowledge"; that the aim of a good man is to care for his soul; and that to care for the soul is to make oneself as wise as possible– that is, to attain knowledge, or virtue. Norman Gulley has examined the concept of "the good" by reviewing the role of goodness in the political and religious views of Socrates. Alfonso Gomez-Lobo has studied the types of things Socrates claims to have knowledge of and the types of knowledge he disavows in order to make sense of Socrates's admission of ignorance at his trial. W. K. C. Guthrie has discussed the various ways that the idea that virtue is knowledge was interpreted by Xenophon, Plato, and Aristotle. Related to such discussions of the nature of virtue, knowledge, goodness, and the soul, is the concept of wrongdoing. As A. E. Taylor has explained, Socrates taught that virtue is identical to knowledge and that vice is, in all cases, the result of ignorance, or intellectual error, so that wrongdoing is always involuntary. This idea has presented difficulties for many who study philosophy, from the time of Socrates through the twentieth century, and scholars have attempted to interpret Socrates's meaning in a variety of ways. Taylor has argued that Socrates's statement that wrongdoing is involuntary means that a person does evil in spite of the fact that it is evil, for the person falsely believes that he or she can gain some good (wealth, power, pleasure) by doing evil.

Another view that was regarded as controversial in the fifth century was Socrates's belief that injustice is never justified. It was commonly held during Socrates's time that injuring one's enemies was acceptable, particularly if one had been injured by those enemies. R. Nicol Cross and Gregory Vlastos both have examined Socrates's views on the treatment of enemies and retaliation. Cross has studied apparently contradictory statements made by Socrates on the injustice of injuring one's enemies and has concluded that Socrates held that under no circumstances is it just to injure anyone. Vlastos has identified five Socratic principles related to injustice and has discussed each one in detail. Vlastos also has noted that the Socratic view that one should never do injustice in return for injustice marks a significant break with established Greek views on morality, but the critic has also pointed out that Socrates does not treat the issue of injustices done to social inferiors (women, aliens, slaves) in the Greek world.

However Socrates's views are interpreted by scholars and students of philosophy, most agree that the philosopher dedicated his life to seeking individual wisdom and goodness for the betterment of himself and his society, and that he encouraged others by teaching and by example to do the same.

* REPRESENTATIVE WORKS

Aristophanes

Clouds (comedy) 423 B.C.

Aristotle

Metaphysics (philosophical treatise)

Rhetoric (philosophical treatise)

Plato

Protagoras (dialogue)

Meno (dialogue)

Apology (account of Socrates's trial)

Crito (dialogue)

Phaedo (dialogue)

Xenophon

Memorabilia (memoirs)

* As Socrates's philosophical thought is known only through sec-

ondary sources, these are listed here. While exact composition dates for most of the works are unknown, the chronological order of Plato's works has been determined by critics and therefore his works have been listed in chronological order.

PRINCIPAL ENGLISH TRANSLATIONS

The Works of Plato [translated by T. Taylor and F. Sydenham] 1804

The Works of Plato [translated by H. Clary, H. Davis, and G. Burges] 1848-52

The Complete Works of Xenophon [translated by Ashley, Spelman, Smith, Fielding, Welwood, et al.] 1877

The Dialogues of Plato [translated by B. Jowett, 3rd ed.] 1892

Socrates: A Source Book [compiled and in part translated by John Ferguson] 1970

CRITICISM

E. Zeller (essay date 1868)

SOURCE: "Sources and Characteristics of the Philosophy of Socrates," in *Socrates and The Socratic Schools*, translated by E. Zeller and Oswald J. Reichel, Longmans, Green and Co., 1868, pp. 82-149.

[*In the following essay, Zeller discusses the questions surrounding the validity of Xenophon and Plato as Socratic sources and identifies Socrates's quest for "true knowledge" as the heart of the philosopher's intellectual and moral theories.*]

There is considerable difficulty in arriving at an accurate view of the philosophy of Socrates, owing to the discrepancies in the accounts of the original authorities. Socrates himself committed nothing to writing,[1] and there are only the works of two of his pupils, Xenophon and Plato, preserved, in which he is made to speak in his own person.[2] But the accounts of these two writers are so little alike, that we gather from the one quite a different view of the teaching of Socrates to what the other gives us. It was the fashion among early historians of philosophy to construct a picture of the Athenian philosopher, without any principles of criticism to guide them, from the writings of Xenophon and Plato indiscriminately, as well as from later, and for the most part untrustworthy authorities. Since the time of Brucker, however, it became the custom to look to Xenophon as the only authority to be perfectly trusted on the philosophy of Socrates, and to allow to others, Plato included, at most only a supplementary value. Quite recently, however, Schleiermacher has lodged a protest against the preference shown for Xenophon.[3] Xenophon, he argues, not being a philosopher himself, was scarcely capable of understanding a philosopher like Socrates; the object, moreover, of the Memorabilia was only a limited one, to defend his teacher from definite charges; we are therefore justified in assuming à priori that there must have been more in Socrates than Xenophon allows, or else he could not have played so important a part in the history of philosophy, nor have exerted so marvellous a power of attraction on the most intellectual and cultivated men of his time. The character too which is given him by Plato, would have otherwise been a manifest contradiction of the picture presented by him to the mind of his reader. Besides, Xenophon's dialogues create the impression, that philosophic matter has been put into the unphilosophic language of every-day life, with detriment to its full and proper meaning; and there are gaps left in his account which we must look to Plato to fill up. We can hardly, however, adopt the view of Meiners,[4] that only those parts of the dialogues of Plato may be considered historical, which are either to be found in Xenophon, or immediately follow from what Xenophon says, or which are opposed to Plato's own views. This hypothesis would only give us the Socrates of Xenophon slightly modified, whilst the deeper spring of Socratic thought would still be wanting. The only safe course is adopted by Schleiermacher, who asks: What *may* Socrates have been, in addition to what Xenophon says he was, without denying the character and maxims which Xenophon distinctly assigns to him? and what *must* he have been to call for and to justify such a description as is given of him in the dialogues of Plato? Several other writers have since acquiesced in Schleiermacher's estimate of Xenophon,[5] and even before Schleiermacher, Dissen[6] had expressed his inability to see in the pages of Xenophon anything but a description of the outward appearance of Socrates. The same approval has been bestowed on Schleiermacher's canon for finding out the real Socrates, and only when it failed has an addition been made,[7] that the expressions of Aristotle may be used as a touchstone to discover the teaching of Socrates. On the other hand Xenophon's authority has been warmly supported by several critics.[8]

In deciding between these two views a difficulty, however, presents itself. The authority of the one or the other of our accounts can only be ascertained by a comparison with the true historical picture, and the true historical picture can only be known from these conflicting accounts. This difficulty would be insurmountable, if the two narratives had the same claim to be considered historical in points which they state varyingly; nor would Aristotle's scanty notices of the Socratic philosophy have been sufficient to settle the question. Fortunately one thing is clear, that Plato only claims to be true to facts in those points on which he agrees with Xenophon, as for instance, in the Apology and the Symposium. On other points no one could well assert that he wished all to be taken as historical which he puts into the mouth of Socrates. Of Xenophon, on the contrary, it may be asserted, that in the Memorabilia he intended to unfold a lifelike picture of the views and the conduct of his teacher, although he did not feel himself bound to reproduce his discourses verbatim, and may have thus expanded in his own way many a conversation, of which he only knew the general substance. The objections to his account are only based on an indirect argument, that the historical importance of Socrates can hardly be explained from the picture he gives, and that if it were true, it is impossible to conceive how Socrates could have said what Plato makes him say, without violating the strongest probabilities. And supposing this objection to be established, it would be necessary in order to gain an idea of his philosophy, to look to the very questionable picture of Plato, and to the few expressions of Aristotle. But before these can be received, an examination of them must be made in a more careful manner than the opponents of Xenophon have generally cared to do. The enquiry is closely bound up with an exposition of the teaching of Socrates, and can only be distinguished from it in theory. It will not, therefore, be separated from it here. Socrates must be drawn after the three accounts of Xenophon, Plato, and Aristotle. If the attempt to form a harmonious picture from them all succeeds, Xenophon will be justified. Should it not succeed, it will then be necessary to ask, which of the traditional accounts is the true one.

We will begin with enquiring into the general point of view and the fundamental conception of Socrates. But, on the very threshold of the enquiry, different lines seem to be taken by our main authorities. According to Plato, Socrates appears as a perfect thinker—at home in all branches of knowledge; whereas, in Xenophon he is represented far less as a philosopher than as an innocent and excellent man, full of piety and common sense. It is from Xenophon's account that the ordinary view of Socrates has arisen, that he was only a popular teacher holding aloof from speculative questions, and that he was far less a philosopher than a teacher of morality and instructor of youth.[9] It cannot, indeed, be denied, nor have we attempted to do so, that he *was* full of the most lively enthusiasm for morality, and made it the business of his life to exercise a moral influence upon others. But if he had only discharged this duty in the superficial way of a popular teacher, and had only imparted and inculcated the ordinary notions of duty and virtue, it would be a mystery how he could have exerted the influence he did, not only on weak-minded and thoughtless young men, but on the most talented and cultivated of his cotemporaries. It would be inexplicable what induced Plato to connect the deepest philosophical enquiries with his person, or what induced all later philosophers, from Aristotle down to the Stoics and Neoplatonists to regard him as having inaugurated a new epoch in philosophy, and to trace their own peculiar systems to the stimulus imparted by him.

There is also more than one feature in the personal habits of Socrates to refute the idea that he thought knowledge only of value in as far as it was instrumental for action. So far is this view even from being the true one, that we shall find that he considered actions to have a value only when they proceeded from correct knowledge, the conception of knowledge being the higher one to which he referred that of moral action or virtue, and perfection of knowledge being the measure for perfection of action. Again, the ordinary view represents him as aiming in his intercourse with others at moral training alone; but it would appear[10] from his own words, that love of knowledge was the original motive for his activity; and accordingly we observe him in his dialogues pursuing enquiries, which not only have no moral end,[11] but which, in their practical application, could only serve immoral purposes.[12] These traits are not met with exclusively in one or other of our authorities, but they appear equally through the accounts given by the three main sources. This fact would be wholly inexplicable if Socrates had been only the moralist for which he was formerly taken. The key which explains it will be found in the assumption that, in all his investigations, even when he appears specially as a moral teacher, a deeper philosophic interest was concealed below.

Our authorities do not leave us any room to doubt in what his purpose consisted. He sought for true knowledge in the service of the Delphic God. He busied himself unweariedly with his friends to gain a knowledge of the essence of things. He referred all the claims of morality to the claims of knowledge. In a word, the idea of knowledge forms the centre of the Socratic philosophy.[13] Now, as all philosophy aims at knowledge, a further determination must be added to this definition:—that the pursuit of true knowledge, which had been hitherto an immediate and instinctive activity, became with Socrates a conscious and methodical pursuit. He became conscious of the idea of knowledge as knowledge, and when once conscious of it, he raised it to be his leading idea.[14] This, again, requires further explanation. If the love of knowledge was in existence before, it may be asked why did it not develope into a conscious and critical pursuit? The answer can only be found in the fact, that the knowledge which earlier philosophers pursued, was, in itself, different from the knowledge which Socrates required, and therefore they were not led on as Socrates was by this idea of knowledge to direct their attention to the intellectual processes and conditions, by which it was truly to be acquired. Such a necessity was, however, imposed on Socrates by the theory which he held, according to the most trustworthy accounts, as the soul of all his teaching—that all true knowledge must be based on correct conceptions, and that nothing can be known, unless it can be referred to a general conception, and judged of by that.[15] With this fundamental theory, however simple it may appear, an entire change in the intellectual process was demanded. The ordinary view regards things as being what they appear to be to the senses; or if contradictory experiences forbid this, it clings to those appearances which make the strongest impression on the observer, declares these to constitute the essence, and thence draws further conclusions. This was exactly what philosophers had hitherto done. Even those who decried the senses as not to be depended upon had started from one-sided observations, without being conscious of the necessity of grounding every judgment on an exhaustive enquiry into the object. This dogmatism had been overthrown by the Sophists, and it was recognised that all impressions derived from the senses were relative and personal, that they do not represent things as they are, but as they appear; and, that, consequently, whatever assertion we may take, its opposite may be advanced with equal justice. For, if for one person at this moment *this* is true, for another person at another moment *that* is true.

Socrates expresses the same sentiment relative to the value of common opinions. He is aware that they cannot furnish us with knowledge, but only involve us in contradictions. But he does not draw the inference, which the Sophists did, that real knowledge is impossible, but only that it is impossible in that way. The majority of mankind have no true knowledge, because they confine themselves to suppositions, the accuracy of which they have never examined, and they only take into consideration one property or another, but not the essence. Amend this fault; consider every object in all its bearings, and endeavour from such many-sided observation to determine its essence; we shall then have conceptions instead of vague notions—a regular examination, instead of an unmethodical procedure without reflection—a true, instead of a supposed knowledge. By requiring knowledge to be made of conceptions, Socrates not only broke away from the current view, but, generally speaking, from all previous philosophy. A thorough observation from every side, a critical examination, a methodical enquiry conscious of its own basis, was demanded; all that had hitherto been regarded as knowledge was rejected, because it fell short of these conditions; and at the same time the conviction was expressed that, by observing these rules, real knowledge could be secured.

This theory had not only an intellectual, but more immediately a moral value for Socrates. It is in fact one of the most striking traits in his character that he was unable to divide the intellectual from the moral, and neither admitted knowledge without virtue, nor virtue without knowledge. In this respect he is the man of his age, and herein consists his greatness, that he made its needs and lawful desires felt with great penetration and keenness. When advancing civilisation had created the demand for a higher education amongst the Greeks, and the course of their intellectual development had diverted their attention from nature, and fixed it on mind, a closer connection became necessary between philosophy and life. Philosophy could only find its highest object in man, and man could only find in philosophy the help and support which he needed for life. The Sophists endeavoured to meet this want with great skill and vigour, and hence their extraordinary success. But the sophistic philosophy of life suffered too much from the want of a tenable ground. It had by universal doubting loosened its intellectual roots too effectually to save itself from degenerating with terrific speed, and serving to foster every wicked and selfish impulse. Instead of the moral life being raised by the influence of the Sophists, both life and philosophy were taking the same downward course.

The sad tendencies of the age were fully understood by Socrates, and while his contemporaries, struck blind with admiration, were either insensible to the dangers of the sophistic education, or else through fear and singular indifference to the wants of the times and the march of history, confined themselves, as did Aristophanes, to denouncing the innovators, he was able with penetrating look to discern, what was right and what was wrong in the spirit of his time. The unsatisfactory nature of the older culture, the untenableness of the ordinary virtue, the obscurity of the prevailing notions so full of contradictions, the necessity for intellectual education, were all recognised by him as much as by any other of the Sophists. But he held out other and higher ends to education. He sought not to destroy the belief in truth, but rather to show how truth might be acquired, by a new intellectual process. His aim was not to minister to the selfishness of the age, but rather to rescue the age from selfishness and apathy, by teaching it what was truly good and useful: not to undermine morality and piety, but to rear them up on a new foundation of knowledge. Thus Socrates was at once a moral and an intellectual reformer. His one great thought was to transform and restore moral conduct by means of knowledge, and these two elements were so intimately united by him, that he could find no other subject of knowledge but human conduct, and could discover no security for conduct but knowledge. The service which he rendered to both morality and science by his labours, and the standard which he set up for the intellectual condition of his people and of mankind generally, were felt in after times. If in the sequel, the distinction between moral and intellectual activity in addition to their unity, was fully brought out, yet the knot by which he connected them, has never been untied; and if in the last centuries of the old world, philosophy took the place of the waning religion, and gave a new ground to morality, purifying and exalting the inner moral life, this great and beneficial result was due to Socrates in as far as it can be assigned to any one individual.

The interest of philosophy was now turned away from the outer world, and directed to man and his moral nature. But, inasmuch as man can only regard a thing as true and connected when he has been convinced of its truth by personal research, great attention was bestowed by Socrates on the culture of his own personality. In this some modern writers have thought that they discerned the peculiar character of his philosophy.[16] But the life and personality of Socrates is a very different thing from the caprice of the Sophists, nor must it be confounded with the extreme individualism of the post-Aristotelian schools. Socrates was aware, that each individual must seek the grounds of his own conviction, that truth is not something given from without, but must be found by the exercise of a man's own thought. He required all assumptions to be examined anew, no matter how old or how current they were, and that dependence should only be placed on proof and not on authority. But he was far from making man, as Protagoras did, the measure of all things. He did not even as the Stoics and Epicureans did, declare personal conviction and practical need to be the ultimate standard of truth, nor yet as the Sceptics, resolve all truth into probability; but as knowledge was to him an end in itself, he was convinced that true knowledge could be obtained by a thoughtful consideration of things. Moreover he saw in man the proper object of philosophy, but instead of making personal caprice the law, as the Sophists did, he subordinated it to the general law residing in nature and in abstract moral relations.[17] Instead too of making, with later philosophers, the self-contentment of the wise man his highest end, he confined himself to the old Greek morality, which could not conceive of the individual independent of the state,[18] and which accordingly made the first duty of a citizen to consist in living for the state,[19] and regarded the law of the state as his natural rule of conduct.[20] Hence the political indifference or the universal patriotism of the Stoa and its contemporary rivals were entirely alien to Socrates. If it can be truly said 'that in him commences an unbounded reference to the person, to the freedom of the inner life,'[21] it must also be added that this statement by no means exhausts the theory of Socrates; and thus the disputes about the purely personal, or the really general character of the Socratic doctrine,[22] will have to be decided in such a way, that it is allowed that his theory exhibits an inward personal bent, in comparison with former systems, but is not by any means purely relative. Its object is to gain a knowledge which does more than serve a personal want, and which is true and desirable for more than the person who seeks it, but the ground on which it is sought is only the personal thought[23] of the individual.

It is true that this theory is not further expanded by Socrates. He has established the principle, that only the knowledge which has to do with conceptions is true knowledge; that true being only belongs to conceptions, and that therefore conceptions are alone true; but he never reached to a systematic exposition of what conceptions are true in themselves. Knowledge is here laid down as a postulate, and set as a problem for individuals to solve. Philosophy is rather philosophic impulse, and philosophic method, a seeking for truth, but not yet a possessing it; and this incompleteness has countenanced the view that the theory of Socrates was a theory of a personal and one-sided knowledge. It should, however, never be forgotten, that the aim of Socrates was always to find out and describe what was really true and good. Mankind is to be intellectually and morally framed, but the one only means for the purpose is the acquisition of knowledge.

As the great aim of Socrates was to train men to think, rather than to construct a system for them, it seemed to be his main business to determine the way which would lead them to truth, or in other words to find out the true method of philosophy. The substance of his teaching appears to have been confined on the one hand to questions having an immediate bearing on human conduct; and it does not, on the other hand, go beyond the general and theoretical demand, that all action should be determined by a knowledge of conceptions. There is no systematic tracing of the development of morality in the individual; no attempt to ground it upon other than external reasons.

Notes

[1] The unimportant poetical attempts of his last days (Plato, Phædo, 60, C.) could hardly be taken into account, even if they were extant. They appear, however, to have been very soon lost. See Diog. ii. 42. The genuineness of the Socratic letters need not occupy us for a moment, and that Socrates committed nothing to writing is clear from the silence of Xenophon, Plato, and all antiquity on the point, not to mention the positive testimony of Cie, de Orat. iii. 16, 60; Diog. i. 16; Plut. De Alex. Virt. i. 4.

[2] For instance, those of Eschines, Antisthenes, Phædo.

[3] On the philosophical merits of Socrates, Schleiermacher, Works, iii. 2, 293.

[4] Geschichte der Wissenschaften in Griechenland und Rom, ii. 420.

[5] Brandis, Ritter, Van Heusde.

[6] De philosophia morali.

[7] By Brandis.

[8] Hegel, Gesch. d. Phil. ii. 69; Rötscher, Herrman, &c.

[9] How common this view was in past times, needs not to be proved by authorities which abound from Cicero down to Wiggers and Reinhold. That it is not yet altogether exploded may be gathered not only from writers like Van Heusde, but even Marbach, a disciple of the Hegelian philosophy, asserts that Socrates 'regarded the speculative philosophy which aimed at general knowledge, as useless, vain, and foolish,' and that he 'took the field not only against the Sophists as pretenders to knowledge, but against all philosophy;' in short that 'he was no philosopher.'

[10] Plato, Apol. 21, where Socrates deduces his whole activity from the fact that he pursued a real knowledge.

[11] Examples are to be found in the conversation (Mem. iii. 10), in which Socrates conducts the painter Parrhasius, the sculptor Clito, and Pistias, the forger of armour, to the conceptions of their respective arts. It is true Xenophon introduces this conversation with the remark that Socrates knew how to make himself useful to artisans. But the desire to make himself useful can only have been a very subordinate one; he was no doubt really actuated by the motive mentioned in the Apology, a praiseworthy curiosity to learn from intercourse with all classes, whether they were clearly conscious of what their arts were for. Xenophon himself attests this, Mem. IV. 6, 1. . . . This pursuit of the conceptions of things, aiming not at the application of knowledge, but at knowledge itself, is quite enough to prove that Socrates was not only a preacher of virtue, but a philosopher. Even Xenophon found some difficulty in subordinating it to his practical view of things, as his words show: from which it may be seen that Socrates made his friends more critical. But criticism is the organ of knowledge.

[12] Mem. iii. 11 contains a paragraph adapted more than any other to refute the idea that Socrates was only a popular teacher. Socrates hears one of his companions commending the beauty of Theodota, and at once goes with his company to see her. He finds her acting as a painter's model, and he thereupon enters into a conversation with her, in which he endeavours to lead her to a conception of her trade, and shows her how she will best be able to win lovers. Now although such a step would not give that offence to the Greeks which it would to us, still there is not the least trace of a moral purpose in it.

[13] Schleiermacher, Works, iii. 2, 300: 'The awakening of the idea of knowledge, and its first utterances, must have been the substance of the philosophy of Socrates.' Ritter agrees with this, Gesch. d. Philosophie, ii. 50. Brandis only differs in unessential points. To him the origin of the doctrine of Socrates appears to be his desire to establish against the Sophists the absolute worth of moral determinations, and then he adds: to secure this purpose the first aim of Socrates was to gain a deeper insight into his inner life, in order to be able to distinguish false and true knowledge with certainty. Similarly Braniss.

[14] Schleiermacher. Brandis.

[15] Xenoph. Mem. iv. 6, 1. . . . As is explained by the context, he referred all doubtful points to the universal conceptions, in order to decide by them; iv. 5, 12. . . . Comp. i. 1-16, and the many instances in the Memorabilia. Aristotle (Met. xiii. 4, 1078, b, 17, 27). . . .

[16] Hegel, Gesch. d. Phil. ii. 40; Rötscher, Aristoph., p. 245.

[17] Proofs may be found Xen. Mem. ii. 2; ii. 6, 1-7; iii. 8, 1-3; iv, 4, 20.

[18] Compare the conversation with Aristippus, Xen. Mem. ii. 1, 13; and Plato's Crito, 53, A.

[19] See Xen. Mem. i. 6, 15; Plato, Apol. 30, A.

[20] Mem. iv. 4, 12, and 3, 15.

[21] Hegel.

[22] Compare the views of Rötscher and Brandis.

[23] Hegel says nothing very different, when in distinguishing (Gesch. d. Phil. ii. 40) Socrates from the Sophists he says: 'in Socrates the creation of thought is at once clad with an independent existence of its own,' and what is purely personal is 'externalised and made universal by him as the good.' Socrates is said to have substituted 'thinking man is the measure of all things,' in place of the Sophistic doctrine 'man is the measure of all things.' In a word, his leading thought is not the individual as he knows himself experimentally, but the universal element which is found running through all individuals.

Ralph Waldo Emerson (essay date 1882?)

SOURCE: "The Character of Socrates," in *Two Unpublished Essays*, Lamson, Wolffe & Co., 1895, pp. 1-39.

[*In the following excerpt, Emerson discusses the "uncommon and admirable" character of Socrates and acknowledges the debt owed by "modern improvement" to the wisdom of Socrates. Emerson explores the moral background of Socrates's age and discusses Socrates's moral philosophy, noting that the philosopher sought to reform the "abuses of morals and virtue which had become a national calamity." Because the date of composition of this essay is not known, Emerson's death date has been used to date the essay.*]

> Guide my way
> Through fair Lyceum's walk, the green
> retreats
> Of Academus, and the thymy vale
> Where, oft enchanted with Socratic sounds,
> Ilissus pure devolved his tuneful stream
> In gentler murmurs. From the blooming store
> Of these auspicious fields, may I unblamed
> Transplant some living blossoms to adorn
> My native clime.

The philosophy of the human mind has of late years commanded an unusual degree of attention from the curious and the learned. The increasing notice which it obtains is owing much to the genius of those men who have raised themselves with the science to general regard, but chiefly, as its patrons contend, to the uncontrolled progress of human improvement. The zeal of its advocates, however, in other respects commendable, has sinned in one particular,—they have laid a little too much self-complacent stress on the merit and success of their own unselfish exertions, and in their first contempt of the absurd and trifling speculations of former metaphysicians, appear to have confounded sophists and true philosophers, and to have been disdainful of some who have enlightened the world and marked out a path for future advancement.

Indeed, the giant strength of modern improvement is more indebted to the early wisdom of Thales and Socrates and Plato than is generally allowed, or perhaps than modern philosophers have been well aware.

This supposition is strongly confirmed by a consideration of the character of Socrates, which, in every view, is uncommon and admirable. To one who should read his life as recorded by Xenophon and Plato without previous knowledge of the man, the extraordinary character and circumstances of his biography would appear incredible. It would seem that antiquity had endeavored to fable forth a being clothed with all the perfection which the purest and brightest imagination could conceive or combine, bestowing upon the piece only so much of mortality as to make it tangible and imitable. Even in this imaginary view of the character, we have been inclined to wonder that men, without a revelation, by the light of reason only, should set forth a model of moral perfection which the wise of any age would do well to imitate. And, further, it might offer a subject of ingenious speculation, to mark the points of difference, should modern fancy, with all its superiority of philosophic and theological knowledge, endeavor to create a similar paragon. But this is foreign to our purpose.

It will be well, in reviewing the character of Socrates, to mark the age in which he lived, as the moral and political circumstances of the times would probably exert an important and immediate influence on his opinions and character. The dark ages of Greece, from the settlement of the colonies to the Trojan War, had long closed. The young republics had been growing in strength, population, and territory, digesting their constitutions and building up their name and importance. The Persian War, that hard but memorable controversy of rage and spite, conflicting with energetic and disciplined independence, had shed over their land an effulgence of glory which richly deserved all that applause which after ages have bestowed. It was a stern trial of human effort, and the Greeks might be pardoned if, in their intercourse with less glorious nations, they carried the record of their long triumph too far to conciliate national jealousies. The aggrandizement of Greece which followed this memorable war was the zenith of its powers and splendor, and ushered in the decay and fall of the political fabric.

The age of Pericles has caused Athens to be remembered in history. At no time during her existence were the arts so flourishing, popular taste and feeling so exalted and refined, or her political relations so extensive and respected. The Athenian people were happy at home, reverenced abroad,—and at the head of the Grecian confederacy. Their commerce was lucrative, and their wars few and honorable. In this mild period it was to be expected that literature and science would grow up vigorously under the fostering patronage of taste and power. The Olympian games awakened the emulation of genius and produced the dramatic efforts of Æschylus, Sophocles, Euripides, and Aristophanes, and philosophy came down from heaven to Anaxagoras, Archelaus, and Socrates.

Such was the external and obvious condition of Athens,—apparently prosperous, but a concealed evil began to display specific and disastrous consequences. The sophists had acquired the brightest popularity and influence, by the exhibition of those superficial accomplishments whose novelty captivated the minds of an ingenious people, among whom true learning was yet in its infancy. Learning was not yet loved for its own sake. It was prized as a saleable commodity. The sophists bargained their literature, such as it was, for a price; and this price, ever exorbitant, was yet regulated by the ability of the scholar.

That this singular order of men should possess so strong an influence over the Athenian public argues no strange or unnatural state of society, as has been sometimes represented; it is the proper and natural result of improvement in a money-making community. By the prosperity of their trading interests all the common wants of society were satisfied, and it was natural that the mind should next urge its claim to cultivation, and the surplus of property be expended for the gratification of the intellect. This has been found true in the growth of all nations,—that after successful trade, literature soon throve well,—provided the human mind was cramped by no disadvantages of climate or "skyey influences."

The Athenian sophists adapted their course of pursuits of knowledge, with admirable skill, to the taste of the people. They first approved themselves masters of athletic exercises, for the want of which no superiority of intellect, however consummate, would compensate in the Grecian republics. They then applied themselves to the cultivation of forensic eloquence, which enabled them to discourse volubly, if ignorantly, on any subject and on any occasion, however unexpected. To become perfect in this grand art, it was necessary to acquire, by habit and diligence, an imperturbable self-possession which could confront, unabashed, the rudest accident; and moreover, a flood of respondent and exclamatory phrases, skilfully constructed to meet the emergencies of a difficult conversation. After this laudable education had thus far accomplished its aim, the young sophist became partially conversant with the limited learning of the age in all its subjects. The poets, the historians, the sages, the writers on the useful arts, each and all occupied by turns his glancing observation. And when the motley composition of his mind was full, it only remained to stamp upon his character some few peculiarities,—to make him what the moderns have called a "mannerist,"—and his professional education was considered complete.

When the sophists made themselves known, they assumed a sanctity of manners, which awed familiarity and very conveniently cloaked their sinister designs. Pythagoras, after his persevering exertions for the attainment of knowledge, after his varied and laborious travels, had established a romantic school at Crotona with institutions resembling free masonry, which had planted in Greece prepossessions favorable to philosophy.

The sophists availed themselves of their prejudices, and amused the crowds who gathered at the rumor of novelty, with riddles and definitions, with gorgeous theories of existence,—splendid fables and presumptuous professions. They laid claim to all knowledge, and craftily continued to steal the respect of a credulous populace, and to enrich themselves by pretending to instruct the children of the opulent. When they had thus fatally secured their own emolument, they rapidly threw off the assumed rigidity of their morals, and, under covert of a sort of *perfumed* morality, indulged themselves and their followers in abominable excesses, degrading the mind and debauching virtue. Unhappily for Greece, the contaminating vices of Asiatic luxury, the sumptuous heritage of Persian War, had but too naturally seconded the growing depravity.

The youth of great men is seldom marked by any peculiarities which arrest observation. Their minds have secret workings; and, though they feel and enjoy the consciousness of genius, they seldom betray prognostics of greatness. Many who were cradled by misfortune and want have reproached the sun as he rose and went down, for amidst the baseness of circumstances their large minds were unsatisfied, unfed; many have bowed lowly to those whose names their own were destined to outlive; many have gone down to their graves in obscurity, for fortune withheld them from eminence, and to beg they were ashamed.

Of the son of the sculptor and midwife we only know that he became eminent as a sculptor, but displaying genius for higher pursuits, Crito, who afterward became his disciple, procured for him admission to the schools and to such education as the times furnished. But the rudiments of his character and his homely virtues were formed in the workshop, secluded from temptation; and those inward operations of his strong mind were begun which were afterwards mature in the ripeness of life.

We shall proceed to examine the character of the philosopher, after premising that we do not intend to give the detail of his life, but shall occasionally adduce facts of biography as illustrative of the opinions we have formed. With regard to the method pursued in the arrangement of our remarks, we must observe that sketches of the character of an individual can admit of little definiteness of plan, but we shall direct our attention to a consideration of the leading features of his mind, and to a few of his moral excellences which went to make up the great aggregate of his character.

The chief advantage which he owed to nature, the source of his philosophy and the foundation of his character, was a large share of plain good sense,—a shrewdness which would not suffer itself to be duped, and withal, concealed under a semblance of the frankest simplicity, which beguiled the objects of his pursuit into conversation and confidence which met his wishes. This was the faculty which enabled him to investigate his own character, to learn the natural tendency and bias of his own genius, and thus to perfectly control his mental energies.

There is a story of Socrates, related by Cicero, which militates somewhat with the opinion we have formed of his mind,—that when a physiognomist, after having examined his features, had pronounced him a man of bad passions and depraved character, Socrates reproved the indignation of his disciples by acknowledging the truth of the assertion so far as nature was concerned, saying that it had been the object of his life to eradicate these violent passions. This might have been merely a trick of art, and as such is consistent with his character. We cannot view it in any other light; for although it is very probable that natural malignity might have darkened his early life, yet no assertion of his own would convince us, in contradiction with his whole life and instruction, that he was ever subject to the fiercer passions. Such, too, was the order of his intellect. He was a man of strong and vivid conceptions, but utterly destitute of fancy. Still, he possessed originality and sometimes sublimity of thought. His powerful mind had surmounted the unavoidable errors of education, and had retained those acquirements which are found applicable to the uses of common life, whilst he had discarded whatever was absurd or unprofitable.

He studied the nature and explored the destinies of men with a chastised enthusiasm. Notwithstanding the sober, dispassionate turn of mind which we have mentioned, he is not unmoved at all times; when he enters into the discussion upon the immortality of the soul and the nature and attributes of Deity, he forgets his quibbles upon terms, and his celebrated irony, and sensibly warms and expands with his theme. This was aided by the constant activity of his mind, which endowed him with energy of thought and language, and its discipline never suffered him to obtrude an unguarded emotion.

In perfect accordance with this view of his mind is his conduct under circumstances related by Plato. In prison, whilst under condemnation, he was directed in vision to seek the favor of the Muses. This new discipline enjoined upon him was utterly incongruous with the temper and habits of feeling usual to the philosopher. His plain sense and logical mind, which would reduce everything, however impressive, to mathematical measurement, were little conversant, we may suppose, with poetical visions. In fact, we could not suppose a character more diametrically opposite to the soul of the poet, in all the gradations of cultivated mind, than the soul of Socrates.

The food and occupation of the former has to do with golden dreams,—airy nothings, bright personifications of glory and joy and evil,—and we imagine him sitting apart, like Brahma, moulding magnificent forms, clothing them with beauty and grandeur. The latter dwells on earth, dealing plainly and bluntly with men and men's actions, instructing them what to do and to forbear; and even when he desires to lift his tone, it is only to mingle with higher reality, but never forsaking safe, but tedious, paths of certainty.

All this we know, and the manner which Socrates selected to perform the task assigned him creates neither disappointment nor surprise; for perhaps in the biographical annals of his country there was no intellect whose leading feature more nearly resembled his own than Æsop, whose fables he undertook to versify.

It may well be supposed that a mind thus cast was eminently calculated to instruct, and his didactic disposition always rendered him rather the teacher than the companion of his friends. Add to all this an unrivalled keenness of penetration into the character of others, and hence arose his ruling motive in all his intercourse with men; it was not to impart literary knowledge or information in science or art, but to lay open to his own view the human mind, and all its unacknowledged propensities, its weak and fortified positions, and the springs of human action. All this was achieved by the power of his art, and it enabled him easily to grasp the mind, and mould it at will, and to unite and direct the wandering energies of the human soul.

His mind was cultivated, though his learning was little. He was acquainted with the works of the most eminent poets of his country, but as he seems never to have made literature his study, the limited erudition he possessed was probably gleaned from the declamations of the sophists, whose pride never scrupled to borrow abundantly from the superfluous light which departed genius afforded. His own acquisitions had been made in the workshops of the Athenian artisans, in the society of Aspasia and Theombrota, and by intelligent, experienced observation.

Though living in Athens, he acquired little taste for the elegance or pride of life; surrounded as he was by the living marbles which all succeeding ages have consented to admire, and then just breathing from the hand of the artist, he appeared utterly dead to their beauties, and used them only as casual illustrations of an argument. In the gratification of his desire to learn and know mankind, he visited the poor and the rich, the virtuous and the degraded, and set himself to explore all the varieties of circumstances occurring in a great city, that he might discover what were "the elements which furnish forth creation."

We may judge from the acquaintances of the philosopher what were the minds most congenial to his own. Of his great contemporaries,—Sophocles, Euripides, Aristophanes,—Euripides alone was his pupil and friend. He never attended the theatre only as his tragedies were to be performed. This warmth of feeling for the chaste and tender dramatist should defend his mind from the imputation of utter deafness to taste and beauty. The majestic and sublime genius of Sophocles was not so intimately allied to the every-day morals of Socrates; Euripides knew and taught more human nature in its common aspects. . . .

We have attempted to draw the outline of one of the most remarkable minds which human history has recorded, and which was rendered extraordinary by its wonderful adaptation to the times in which he lived. We must now hasten to our great task of developing the moral superiority of the philosopher.

A manly philosophy has named fortitude, temperance, and prudence its prime virtues. All belonged, in a high degree of perfection, to the son of Sophroniscus, but fortitude more particularly. Perhaps it was not a natural virtue, but the first-fruits of his philosophy. A mind whose constitution was built up like his—the will of the philosopher moulding the roughest materials into form and order—might create its own virtues, and set them in array to compose the aggregate of character. He was not like other men, the sport of circumstances, but by the persevering habits of forbearance and self-denial he had acquired that control over his whole being which enabled him to hold the same even, unchangeable temperament in all the extremes of his fortunes. This exemption from the influences of circumstances in the moral world is almost like exemption from the law of gravitation in the natural economy. The exemplifications of this fortitude are familiar. When all the judges of the senate, betraying an unworthy pusillanimity, gave way to an iniquitous demand of the populace, Socrates alone disdained to sacrifice justice to the fear of the people.

On another occasion, in the forefront of a broken battle, Alcibiades owed his life to the firmness of his master. Patriotic steadfastness in resistance to the oppression of the Thirty Tyrants is recorded to his honor. Although we are unwilling to multiply these familiar instances, we would not be supposed to undervalue that milder fortitude which Diogenes Laertius has lauded, and which clouded his domestic joys. The victory over human habits and passions which shall bring them into such subjection as to be subservient to the real advantage of the possessor is that necessary virtue which philosophers denominate temperance. We are led to speak of this particularly because its existence in the character of Socrates has been questioned.

The impurity of public morals and the prevalence of a debasing vice has left a festering reproach on the name of Athens, which deepens as the manners of civilized nations have altered and improved. Certain equivocal expressions and paragraphs in the Dialogues of Plato have formerly led many to fasten the stigma on Socrates. This abomination has likewise been laid to the charge of Virgil, and probably with as little justice. Socrates taught that every soul was an eternal, immutable form of beauty in the divine mind, and that the most beautiful mortals approached nearest to that celestial mould; that it was the honor and delight of human intellect to contemplate this *beau ideal,* and that this was better done through the medium of earthly perfection. For this reason this sober enthusiast associated with such companions as Alcibiades, Critias, and other beautiful Athenians.

A late article in the *Quarterly Review,* the better to vindicate the character of Aristophanes from the reproach attached to him as the author of "The Clouds," has taken some pains to attack the unfortunate butt of the comedian's buffoonery. It is unpleasant at this day to find facts misrepresented in order to conform to a system, and unwarranted insinuations wantonly thrown out to vilify the most pure philosopher of antiquity, for no other purpose than to add the interest of novelty to a transient publication. It is a strong, and one would think an unanswerable, argument against the allegation, that his unsparing calumniator, the bitter Aristophanes, should have utterly omitted this grand reproach, while he wearies his sarcasm on more insignificant follies. Nor did he pass it by because it was not accounted a crime, as if the fashion of the age justifies the enormity; for in this identical play he introduces his Just Orator, declaiming against this vice in particular and remembering with regret the better manners of better times, when lascivious gestures were unstudied and avoided and the cultivated strength of manhood was devoted to austere, laborious virtue. The whole character and public instructions of Socrates ought to have shielded him from this imputation, while they manifest its utter improbability. When the malignity of an early historian had given birth to the suspicion, the fathers, who often bore no good-will to Socrates (whose acquired greatness eclipsed their natural parts), often employed their pens to confirm and diffuse it, and it owes its old currency chiefly to their exertions.

We shall not speak particularly of the prudence of Socrates. He possessed it abundantly, in the philosophical signification of the term,—but none of that timorous caution which might interfere with the impulses of patriotism, duty, or courage.

It seems to have been a grand aim of his life to become a patriot,—a reformer of the abuses of morals and virtue which had become a national calamity. He saw his country embarrassed, and plunging without help in the abyss of moral degradation. Dissipation and excess made Athens their home and revelled with impunity. "Give us a song of Anacreon or Alcæus!" was the common cry. A frightful voluptuousness had entwined itself about the devoted city, and its ultimate baneful consequences had begun their work. In these circumstances, when all eyes appeared to be blinded to the jeopardy by the fatal incantations of vagrant vine clad Muses, this high-toned moralist saw the havoc that was in operation. He desired to restore his countrymen; he would not treacherously descend to flatter them.

To accomplish this, he selected a different course from the ordinary plans of young men. To an Athenian entering on life and aspiring after eminence, the inducements to virtue were weak and few, but to vice numberless and strong. Popularity was to be acquired among these degenerate republicans; not as formerly among their great ancestors, by toilsome struggles for pre-eminence in purity, by discipline and austere virtue, but by squandered wealth, profligacy, and flattery of the corrupt populace. What, then, had an obscure young man, poor and friendless, to expect, sternly binding himself to virtue, and attacking the prevalent vices and prejudices of a great nation? This was certainly no unworthy prototype of the circumstances of the founders of the Christian religion. He devoted himself entirely to the instruction of the young, astonishing them with a strange system of doctrines which inculcated the love of poverty, the forgiveness of injuries, with other virtues equally unknown and unpractised.

His philosophy was a source of good sense and of sublime and practical morality. He directs his disciples to know and practise the purest principles of virtue; to be upright, benevolent, and brave; to shun vice . . . the dreadful monster which was roaring through earth for his prey. The motives which he presented for their encouragement were as pure as the life they recommended. Such inducements were held up as advancement in the gradations of moral and intellectual perfection,—the proud delight of becoming more acceptable in the eyes of Divinity, and the promise to virtue of communications from other and higher spheres of existence. The notions of the nature of God which Socrates entertained were infinitely more correct and adequate than those of any other philosopher before him whose opinions have come down to us.

Additional praise is due to him, since he alone dared to express his sentiments on the subject and his infidelity to the popular religion. "What is God?" said the disciples to Plato. "It is hard," answered the philosopher, "to know, and impossible to divulge." Here is that reluctance which timorous believers were obliged to display. "What is God?" said they to Socrates, and he replied, "The great God himself, who has formed the universe and sustains the stupendous work whose every part is finished with the utmost goodness and harmony; he who preserves them perfect in immortal vigor and causes them to obey him with unfailing punctuality and a rapidity not to be followed by the imagination—this God makes himself sufficiently visible by the endless wonders of which he is the author, but continues always invisible in himself." This is explicit and noble. He continues, "Let us not, then, refuse to believe even what we do not behold, and let us supply the defect of our corporeal eyes by using those of the soul; but especially let us learn to render the just homage of respect and veneration to that Divinity whose will it seems to be that we should have no other perception of him but by his effects in our favor. Now this adoration, this homage, consists in pleasing him, and we can only please him by doing his will."

These are the exalted sentiments and motives which Socrates enforced upon men, not in insulated or extraordinary portions of his system but through the whole compass of his instructions. Convinced that the soul is endowed with energies and powers, by which, if well directed, she strives and climbs continually towards perfection, it was his object to stimulate and guide her; to quicken her aspirations with new motives, to discover and apply whatever might spur on conscientious endeavor or back its efforts with omnipotent strength. He wished the care and improvement of the soul to be of chief concern, that of the body comparatively trifling. The natural effect of his philosophy was to form an accomplished pagan,—so perfect a man as was compatible with the state of society; and this state should not be underrated. A nation of disciples of Socrates would suppose a state of human advancement which modern ambition and zeal, with all its superiority of knowledge and religion, might never hope to attain. And, could Athens have expelled her sophists and corruptors, and by exhibiting respect for his instructions have extended the influence of her most mighty mind until the chastity of her manners was restored and the infirmities of her dotage displaced by active virtues,—had her citizens then become the converts and advocates of Socratic sentiments,—she might have flourished and triumphed on till this day, a free and admirable commonwealth of philosophers, and looked with enviable unconcern on all the revolutions about her that have agitated and swallowed up nations; and Philip of Macedon and Mummius of Rome might have slept in obscurity. But this is digression, and we can offer no apology except the pleasure which such revision affords. We must now proceed to say something of his ambiguous genius.

The *daimōn* of Socrates partakes so much of the marvellous that there is no cause for wonder arising from the difference of opinion manifested in its discussion. Those who love to ascribe the most to inspiration in the prophets of God's revealed religion claim this mysterious personage as akin to the ministering spirits of the Hebrew faith. Those who, with Xenophon, know not of this similarity, or who do not find foundation for this belief, look upon the *daimōn* only as a personification of natural sagacity; some have charitably supposed that the philosopher himself was deluded into a false conviction that he enjoyed a peculiar communication with the gods by the intervention of a supernatural being,—learned their will and accomplished their ends. These supposed claims which Socrates laid to divine inspiration have induced many to carry their veneration to a more marvellous extent than we can safely follow.

We are willing to allow that they have plausible arguments who have considered the philosopher in the more imposing view, as an especial light of the world commissioned from heaven and as a distant forerunner of the Savior himself. Dr. Priestley, with a bolder hand, has instituted a comparison between Socrates and the Saviour himself. We are not disposed to enter upon these discussions, as they do not lead to truth and serve only to bewilder.

R. M. Wenley (essay date 1889)

SOURCE: "Socrates and Christ" in *Socrates and Christ: A Study in the Philosophy of Religion*, William Blackwood and Sons, 1889, pp. 236-64.

[*Here, Wenley contrasts Socrates with Christ, stating that while there exist "points of external contact" between the two men which "render comparison by no means unreasonable," they nevertheless had little in common in terms of "inner spirit."*]

The "great solicitude" sometimes "shown by popular Christianity to establish a radical difference between Jesus and a teacher like Socrates,"[1] is a misapplication of effort. The contrast stands in need of no further emphasis than that which history has so plainly given it. Antecedents, problems, contemporary influences, were different for both, not in degree alone, but also in essential nature. Neither special pleading, nor introduction of supernatural attributes, is necessary in face of authentic occurrences, which must after all be largely self-explanatory. Every leader of men exists, "not for what he can accomplish, but for what can be accomplished in him."[2] But the "in him" has reference to a living organism, and not to dead matter. What can be accomplished depends very largely upon the co-operation with which the man is able to aid circumstances. Opportunity is the world's work, but no amount of external pressure will cause two rational beings to interpret opportunity in precisely the same manner. Each reacts upon it in his own way, and so the results are invariably diverse. Much more is this true when not only the opportunities, but also the individuals, are entirely different, at the beginning of the process. Action and reaction are not equal and opposite in the spiritual world, for in every given case the rule receives a new application. Abstract from Socrates and Christ everything, except the attributes "Athenian" and "Nazarene," and the "radical difference," which so many sincerely desiderate, but place on a wrong basis, remains unimpaired.

But no such narrow distinction needs to be adopted. The natural course of history, without any *tendenz* interpretation, has set a great gulf between Socrates and Christ. It could be shown, for example, that even if Greek philosophy and Christianity were traceable to a common source, the latter possessed elements which the former had not.[3] The factors of a complete revelation, which the Greeks had failed to derive from their Aryan ancestors, reappeared, by some inexplicable process, in Palestine, and that at the time of Christ. These, and like considerations, are, however, foreign to the present task. It is sufficient now to take Socrates and Christ as we find them, and to note, that totally different circumstances influenced them, that alien civilisations produced them, that self-consciousness found distinctive expression in each. The sense of defect which swayed Socrates had reference wholly to man's knowledge of himself. The power of the Sophists was both founded on, and productive of, misbelief. Socrates saw nothing to prevent individual wellbeing, if only self-knowledge could be obtained. Nor had the time arrived at which to regard spiritual or mental research as hopeless. The external world, which the older Greek philosophers had studied so assiduously, seemed less important to Socrates than the inner sphere of mind. Of this view, and of the self-study which it implied, he was the Greek pioneer. The difficulties complicating such a search, and the possible illusoriness of the self-perfection in which it was to end, did not impress Socrates so much as the conviction, of which his *daimonion* was but an aspect, that there is a permanent principle in man. This, in his view, was far more worthy of attention than culture, than phenomena, material or political.

To one thus assured of the actual, the question of possible or impossible, probable or improbable, did not appeal with much force. Socrates had nothing to remove, he rather desired to arrive at something which certainly existed. He was thus able, as, for example, in 'Protagoras,' to deny the possibility of virtue through self-knowledge, and yet, by this very denial, to show that his negative is better than the Sophists' positive. Protagoras professed to teach virtue without a basis; Socrates was only seeking for it. Yet, his tentative efforts resulted in an assurance the bare possibility of which his contemporaries scouted. He set himself to discover a new realm of thought, but he was certain of its discoverableness ere he began to search. His it was to bring this reality home to the everyday life of the time, and to follow out his method of so doing, even though its conclusions were the prison and the poison-cup. He gave himself for the progress of rational inquiry at a crisis in its development, and on this account we enrol him with the greatest. Yet to mistake his work, in this matter, were certainly a poor way to do him reverence.

The circumstances into which Jesus was born were of a totally different character. Unacquainted with the learning of the Greeks, and in all probability quite unaware of that peculiar Judaism[4] which Philo represented, his work had little relation to the discovery of new intellectual spheres. Nay, it was brought about by causes which were in strange contrast to any operative in previous times. The answer to the cry of a world in pain, its inherent force proceeded in great part from its very simplicity, as compared with systems which the mental subtlety of a single people had previously produced. Christ found it necessary not only to enunciate, but also to prove the perfectibility of man. And at the time, such was the state of the nations, that the proposition was sufficiently improbable to be startling, the practice unprecedented enough to be convincing.

The condition of the Roman Empire need not be made subject of too complacent comparison. "It is a common remark, that very few lines need be altered in Juvenal's Satires, beyond what is purely local, to make them applicable to the London, or Paris, or Vienna of to-day."[5] But even thus, there is an irreducible difference. The spirit—to take but one instance—which was so greedy of blood, that the amusing slaughter of 20,000 men, slaves no doubt, could take place almost without comment, has disappeared. Superadd nigh inconceivable brutality, rampant cynicism, and barefaced lust, to all that is most devilish in our modern capitals; take away shame from vice, cancel the sneaking admiration for goodness which even the worst will to-day accord, and think of the absolute need, yet apparent folly, of a doctrine of perfectibility. In Palestine itself, where a larger remnant of moral effort still remained, goodness was mainly misdirected. For, when morality takes the form of special commands, it loses much of its cogency in transmission. Conventional rules serve but to dry up the springs of sympathy from which all that is most valuable in life—all that is not of mere prescription—flows. Christ gave Himself for the perfecting of humanity at a period when perfection either appeared an absurdity, or was fenced round with regulations that rendered its attainment impossible. To show Rome that there was a life of the spirit, to tell Judæa that her law was morally suicidal, this was His mission. Even Pilate felt that his conduct had finished the former work. As a cultivated Roman he might hopelessly inquire "What is truth?" but as a responsible man, he could declare, "I am innocent of the blood of this *just* person." Christ's statement of perfectibility was proved by His practice, but for the finality of the proof He died. "We have a law, and by our law He ought to die." The execution of this condemnation broke the law in pieces, and issued in the possibility of perfection for others everywhere.

But even here we cannot stop. Socrates and Christ are separated, once more, by racial diversity. No juggling with subjective presuppositions[6] can explain away the fact that Christianity grew out of Judaism. It did not come forth from a religious idea, but from a religion. No law of abstract logical categories was the cause of its birth. Had the stern intensity of the Hebrew spirit been absent, Christianity might have appeared, as did Philonism, in the guise of an intellectual system, it would never have been a religion. One might as well hope to Hebraise Socrates as to Hellenise Christ. Athens under Pericles brought forth men whose like has never been seen. Yet in a few short years others sprang up, in Greece and elsewhere, to inquire what might be the meaning and permanent value of all that had been achieved by their Periclean predecessors. Socrates was the first of such inquirers. A citizen of a unique city, he found it necessary to ask himself what were the presuppositions of his citizenship. Because he was a Greek, he had the means at his command to found the science which treats of man's relations with his fellows. Nevertheless, the subject-matter of his inquiry—a society based on rational principles—was known to the Israelites from early times. But they did not come together spontaneously like the Greeks, and thereafter proceed to reflect on the happy chance. They were members of an ordered community, whose relationships had been determined according to the dictates of a national conscience. Socrates could demand justice between Greek and Greek; Christ could require purity of all men. Race distinction rendered their respective interpretations of life's realities radically different.

In several of its aspects Socrates' work overlaps that commonly considered peculiar to the religious teacher. His conviction, that "the penalty of unrighteousness is swifter than death,"[7] might be taken as the motto of his career. While others had been content thoughtlessly to assume the inner life, he was determined to know it, and, in the light of this knowledge, to guide his action. Indeed, the formation of character on a new basis, rather than the systematic discussion of ethics, was his lifework. It was ethical in its aim, rational in its method, practical in its results. Without any dry body of doctrine to inculcate, Socrates was able, mainly by the force of example, and by the application of new standards to things wrongly held precious, to alter current conceptions concerning conduct. By no means a metaphysician, he yet made life subservient to ideas obtained and tested in dialectic dispute. For he had already laid hold on the principle that conduct consists in "the application of ideas to life." Not to change his fellow-citizens, but to show clearly the generally accepted yet half-apprehended principles, on a tacit understanding of which the state found basis, was Socrates' business. The just man has only to perceive the "general definitions" underlying society, to become straightway the good man. In wisdom he realises what is highest. Thus, however little he may have known what the good was, Socrates saw that social wellbeing is dependent upon individual morality. The Athenians had doubtless some vague notion of what "morality" meant for themselves. But, like Euthyphro's piety, it stood in need of definition. Socrates, by his conduct and conversation, indicated this need, if he did not absolutely supply it.

Hence his personality was possessed of a semi-religious influence, or rather, he exerted himself for the conscious moralising of his fellows. The manner in which the entire man Socrates pervades the work of his greatest disciple, and is traceable neither here nor there, neither with this limitation nor with that, but is a constant living presence, may be taken as typical. In such a view Socrates' mission so far overlaps that of the religious teacher. The jailer in 'Phædo' felt the magnetism of the martyr's character. It was not the subtlety of metaphysics that caused him, on the bare enunciation of his errand, to burst into tears and go out.[8] He needed no more than Socrates' presence to convince him that this was a just man, for whose death he could assign no adequate reason. The possession of self, which true self-knowledge alone bestows, was in the highest degree distinctive of Socrates. He cannot but have impressed himself upon others more by his personality than by his doctrines. He could not tell Plato what "the good" was, but Plato knew that Socrates was good. Conviction was written upon his conduct, and this, far rather than set phrases, must have helped his friends to clearer notions of the "ought-to-be."

It is exceedingly difficult, if not altogether impossible now, to determine to what extent Socrates' ethico-rational work received from his living presence the "touch of emotion" inseparable from religious principle. Enthusiasm for the man could not, in any case, remove the limitations under which he necessarily laboured. Zeal for a more clearly defined political morality, and supreme confidence in the mental capacity to discover principles of social action, cannot but have been quickened to fullest life by Socrates' personal example. Yet, in the modern sense of the term, religious influences were but little formative of his career. His petition for "inward purity and for a lot that shall best agree with a right disposition of the mind," is limited not only in its conception of deity, but also in its grasp of the possible relationships between divine and human. Concerned chiefly for self-knowledge,[9] he did not depart from this his way to overturn popular belief, and he was satisfied if he could see in the world a principle analogous to the self in individual life. Speculation, and nothing else, led him to entertain such doubts as he may have had respecting traditional polytheism. The unity of purpose, which characterised his whole career, was but the other, and the familiar side, of such well-grounded scepticism. Socrates was therefore a religious teacher in that he was true to what he understood. Strength to be himself was his, and, as a consequence, all the qualities of gentle manliness, which issued from conviction of personal superiority, linked, however, with hesitation in deep consciousness of ignorance, served to endow him with a sway sweeter as well as stronger from its artlessness.

Knowledge that the Athenian citizen lacked the inner sense which would have enabled him to act upon principle rather than from habit, and a presentiment that he could do something to fill this gap, stood to Socrates in place of the more spiritual religion only attainable by a later generation. Had he not been a "religious" man, after the manner in which it was then possible for him to be such, neither Xenophon nor Plato could have had such a testimony to bequeath. His religion consisted in his life, spent as it was in the exercise of his best social and intellectual powers for the discovery of a "good," which all Greeks might consciously pursue. He was "religious," because, realising the reason for his being, he used his life, regardless of consequences to self, in the true spirit of the moral artist.

Nevertheless, it remains true that Socrates was primarily a moralist. The genius of the Greeks produced a unique species of civilisation, which was mainly remarkable for the external presentation of an artistic ideal. Socrates applied this ideal to the life of the individual in the city state. He taught men, that by taking thought, they might put opportunity to better uses, or might be enabled, by the application of discoverable methods, to substitute dignity and beauty for the querulousness customary in common life. Laudable and indispensable as an aim of this sort is, one cannot but admit that it differs widely from the object of religion. Moral philosophy can furnish ideals, but it is unable to tell how far conduct, oppressed as it is by adverse conditions, may be brought into harmony with the universal "ought." "A man's religion is the chief fact with regard to him,"[10] not because he can put his signature below the Thirty-Nine Articles or the Westminster Confession, but rather because he has certain convictions with respect to the possibility of realising what is best, even in circumstances which might make the worse appear the more profitable act. Religion presents a concrete reality to man's consciousness, while morality witnesses to a mental ideal which is the *terminus ad quem* of an infinite being. The one is, the other may be. What Christianity has to tell is embodied in a life; the teaching of Greek philosophy is, that happiness must be sought in wisdom, but what that wisdom contains for the bettering of men it never definitely declares.

Moral life continually projects itself towards the best conceivable ideal. Formally, it may be entirely an extension of self for the sake of self-improvement. But the religious man cannot rest content with this. The mere growth of self is not sufficient. Nay, the direction which advancement takes, and the process in which it shapes itself, are both altered with him. Perception of goodness may assuredly be accompanied by a reaching forth to something like it. This is the highest form of the moral life. But religion implies, in addition, the possession of a goodness which, in the shape of a creative principle, transforms the entire man. It is so far easy to know and to discuss a speculative ideal, and it is well to conform to such an ideal, always granted that it is capable of partial realisation. Yet all this may be done, and thoroughly done, solely with reference to the self. In this sense personal morality is largely illusory, and so remains devoid of that ideal actuality which religion demands. It leaves something to be discovered, of which religion feels itself to be in possession. Morality testifies to the consciousness of a higher life, but it does not give man his kingdom *quâ* that life. Just as idolatry is a makeshift for the satisfaction of faith, so morality is a temporary salve to religious aspiration. It connects man with a supersensible sphere, through the inner conflict of his own nature, but it can affirm nothing with regard to the reality of that sphere. The truth is, that the ideal which morality sets forth mediately on rational principles, religion reveals immediately to the soul. The apparatus of proof that points to an unattainable "is" which "ought to be," finds substitute in a positive conviction of a real "is" which "has been." Self-sacrifice takes the place of mere self-projection towards the ideal, and this means, that the ideal is no longer beyond man, hid away perhaps in some impossible region, but is in him, and is attainable only through his willingness to actualise his own undoubted inner capacity for well-doing.

There are many who cannot see that morality finds any extension in religion, or who consider it derogatory to man's dignity, that reverence should be paid to a God—known or unknowable. But on the view just stated, religion is an advance upon morality, and its aim is not primarily the glory of God. "It is not for the benefit and honour of God, but for the benefit and ennobleiment of Man. . . . God has nothing to gain by our devotion, but men have very much to gain by other men's righteousness."[11] But righteousness is not the result of precept, it is consequent upon the building up of character. And character is fully formed only when, by its own inner force, it brings forth the best that *is,* and does not merely abase itself before an external "ought-to-be." Righteousness, in other words, is a religious product. The moral greatness of Socrates, of Plato, and of many Stoics of antiquity, has rarely found equal in the Christian ages. Yet, in these last, the types of holy living have added something to moral greatness. The ideal has been brought down from an abstract heaven to earth. It *is* in man's own heart. Not the assertion of self, with its proud humility, but the real sacrifice of the whole man to that which is known to be good character—this is the Christian conception. Because the ideal is in man, self-sacrifice must be recognised as the sole self-realisation. The beauty of holiness transfigures him in whom others first bear witness to its presence. Socrates gave direction to life, but Christ revealed in His own person the very principle without which there would be no life. The ancient world, in the work of Socrates and of the few who were like him, sought to reconstruct man's life on the basis of a reinterpretation of his nature; and this must always remain the work of morality. But with the appearance of Christianity, God and man were shown to be co-essential, and the task of morality was superseded, if not eliminated, by the affirmative declaration of religion. Finally, within its sphere, the Socratic teaching had not fathomed reality fully. It is in no sense unfair to say, that the Greek sage knew almost nothing of the inner force by which men, as indeed all things, "fulfil the law of their being."

But on the other hand, it would be merest childishness to deny the influence of Socrates as a forerunner of Christ. The revelation of the one was preparatory to that of the other, just as morality is frequently the seed of religion. In the development of the religious consciousness, for example, the progress towards monotheism, so conspicuous in Socrates and the other Greek philosophers, was but one of the many lines that ultimately converged towards Christianity. No doubt, such ideas were peculiar to thinkers who regarded superstition as spiritual food fit for the mob. Yet the confidence of Socrates in a supreme being was the foundation of Plato's affirmation, that man is like to God,[12] and this, in turn, is not very far removed from Christian doctrine. The Greeks had, in short, discovered a certain element in human nature, which demanded definite satisfaction. With this they were unable to supply it. God night be "single and one" for them, yet they could not conceive how, being such, he was able to enter into relationship with the many. They adumbrated one element in the religious conception, more than that they could not grasp. But Socrates, in that he tended to replace polytheism with a species of quietist monotheism, must not be denied his place as a forerunner of fuller religious development. Whatever may be said of the varied semi-religious conceptions of Greek philosophy, there can be no question that the light thrown back upon the past now enables one to estimate Socrates' value as a herald of Christianity. Here his true greatness must be sought, and that in well-authenticated facts. For "the ideal of Christian life is far more clearly distinguishable from the ideal of Greek and Roman, than the elements of opinion and belief which have come from a Christian source are from those which have come from a secular or heathen one."[13]

Now ethically, that is, in principles of rational action, Socrates and his followers were but one remove from Christianity. The investigation of self, begun by Socrates, although it ended for him in the identity of the knowledge of virtue with virtue itself, was the groundwork of the difference between goodness and counterfeit goodness, which Plato and Aristotle afterwards formulated. For these thinkers virtue is its own reward, and their praise is, that whatever be the form of man's religion, virtue must ever remain self-satisfying. This was the great principle which, by means of rational investigation, Socrates was the first to bring to light. The common measure of all the virtues is the desire of virtue, which is excited by the knowledge that virtue can be obtained. Thus, Socrates represents in practical life the preparation for Christianity, which the Hebrew prophets supplied on the more strictly religious side. He taught that to be good is good because it is good, and thereby furnished the form in which true Christian morality has always presented itself. In this respect Socrates was a real prophet, reaching forth to an end which he could not fully see. His life, no less than his teaching, pointed at once to an ideal, and to an acknowledged human need, which he could neither reach nor supply. When he thus gifted the Greeks with a perception of moral quality, he set the seal of insufficiency alike upon their exclusive citizenship,[14] and their polytheistic religion. But he could not tell what "the good" was, and his philosophy was powerless to stay the appetite which it had created. After him ancient thought occupied itself in the attempt to fathom human nature. Ethical need, infinite then as now, was man's to increase knowledge and sorrow. Religious aspiration was also his. But for the former no full satisfaction was obtainable, for the latter none at all. The Greek protomartyr merits, and surely none would grudge him, the homage due to his consistent life and glorious death. Yet he was separated from Christ both by attainment and by distance in time. He felt the yearning that Christ came to soothe. And whatever praise may be his, it must always be remembered that the end was not then. When, through what Socrates had *not* done, "philosophy had grown sad by thinking beyond its depth," there was necessity for a greater than he.

If the mission of Socrates had been mainly ethical, that of Christ was at once moral and religious. But the religion, of which he was the chief corner-stone, cannot be defined as "morality touched by emotion." Ethical and emotional elements it doubtless had, but these do not represent its entire content. So long as man is upon this earth his lot is to struggle with sin and misery. At no period in history did the issue of the conflict seem darker than when ancient philosophy, in the person of Seneca, became helpless to stay Nero's brutality.[15] Consciously or unconsciously, the Roman Empire was crying aloud for light upon the awful problem of evil. And the light burst forth in a life which, although moral and human, had itself a magnetic influence which all have agreed to recognise as unique. This is the point which, in the estimation of the properly equipped sceptic, even nineteenth-century blasphemy cannot blaspheme away. Christ taught man how to bear sorrow, and by the sacrifice of self, to eliminate sin from life. It was not possible that the cup of suffering should pass from Him, and as He drained it, He created righteousness, thereby proving that even for us the draught is not too terrible. Now the implication of this holy life is, that the moral philosophy of Socrates had been superseded. The ideal had been made actual, and that not as an abstraction, substantive or other, to which men could only progress. It had taken personal form—that is, it had been revealed as a principle organic to life. "If any man be in Christ, he is a new creature," not because something mysterious has been done for him, but because, by his own recognition of kinship with Christ, he is assured that he too can do what the Master did. Self-sacrifice is not only the character of Christ, it is also the one key to the movement of the entire spiritual universe.

> Stirb und werde!
> Denn so lang du das nicht hast,
> Bist du nur ein trüber Gast
> Auf der dunkeln Erde.

The deepest testimony to this truth is Jesus' growing conviction of it, which only found culmination on Calvary.

Nor is this self-sacrifice a mere piece of mechanism for the manufacture of happiness. It is rather a principle of moralisation which, in its long conflict with sin and selfishness, develops new faculties in the individual character. The width of the Christian conception, including as it does all men, imposes responsibilities upon us which the Greeks, even in their finest moods, could not have imagined. For it points to no small society cinctured with a holiness wrought out of the degradation of all beyond its own circle. It constitutes the pursuit of the good by self in sacrifice a means to the bettering of all men. Christ set forth, not the doctrine alone, but its application. He did not come unawares, but brought to an end the problem of evil, then ready for solution. Moreover, he proved the practical value of his solution as a working scheme. His self-sacrifice has nothing in common with asceticism. Renunciation of self is not sought for the mere sake of renunciation, but in order that, purified of all the self-seeking which shuts out true riches, man may become the instrument at once of his own and of his fellows' perfection. If any one apprehend perfectibility, as it stands revealed in Christ, he cannot but adopt Christian ethics. For only thus will he gain for himself a completeness, which is indissolubly bound up with an identical perfection in others. As Christ was the first to proclaim that God can only be served in man, so He was the first to tell that such service will never be absolutely worthy until wrought in humanity as a whole. In this, His true humanitarianism, Christ supersedes Socrates. He appeals to the whole man and to mankind, while the Greek sage speaks only to the free-born citizen, and to him rather as a thinker than as an essentially moral agent. For this reason, Christ's work is eternal, and whatever one may think of His nature, Christianity cannot be separated from His person.

Eliminate the *theory* of Christ which was diffused among the Jews prior to His advent;[16] admit that nothing is directly known of Him, save what is told in the discourses collected by Matthew, and in Peter's reminiscences edited by Mark—who had never seen the

Master;[17] allow that the "pedantic ingenuity of rationalism" is misdirected scarce at all,—and you do not detract one whit from the value of Christ's Christianity. His "application of ideas to life" still remains the one essential and commanding fact in His career. He not only promulgated but lived a principle, against which intellect cannot revolt, and for which conscience records its whole testimony. His religion is His, not because He formulated any creed concerning Himself, but because He alone trod the only road to man's natural perfection. Christianity is inseparable from His person in no dogmatic sense, but as a matter of everyday experience. We cannot look back across the ages and fortify our faltering faith with "a tremulous *quasi*-knowledge of a whole globe of dogmas."[18] Only if the Christ-life be reproducing itself here and now, can Christianity be regarded as in vital connection with the Person of its founder. That it is thus connected His veritable creation of righteousness proves. He did good for the sake of so doing, and this His revelation may, nay, must go on reproducing itself.

> So, each ray of thy will,
> Every flash of thy passion and prowess, long over, shall thrill
> Thy whole people, the countless, with ardour, till they too give forth
> A little cheer to their sons: who in turn, fill the South and the North
> With the radiance thy seed was the germ of.[19]

Reasonableness and naturalness are the chief characteristics of Christ's revelation. *Non mors sed voluntas sponte morientis.*[20] Only an unrivalled knowledge of the human heart in its origin and destiny could have effected the combination of material necessity and spiritual inevitableness by which it continues to sway the world. The complete humanity of Christ's life is the cause of the permanence of His religion.

"To say that a man has genius is to say that all he effects is truly and entirely the result of others' labours and done by their power; that he is merely a stimulus, and owes his influence solely to his relation to an organisation built up, and a functional power accumulated, wholly by others. . . . Genius does things without force *because it does not do them,* as the fall of an uplifted body needs no force."[21] Of all the great this is true. But in relation to Christ, it receives an application *sui generis.* Theirs is the result of others' labours, and for Him too the whole course of civilisation had been preparing. But what he effected was not brought about once for all by the co-operation of prior and contemporary influences. His genius is not a mere expression of what others thought and urgently desired; it is a living force which still remains, and reproduces its own qualities in the lives of men now. "Heroes" and "Representative Men" are the quintessence of epochs; He is the germ which fructifies at all times. In this respect He is without parallel, and so we cannot separate His *Person* from His work.[22]

Nor does the contrast between Christ and the other masters cease here. He superseded Socrates, and it might very well seem, that after so many centuries, and in view of the "service of man," His time to depart had now also come. Notwithstanding, Christ's work cannot but remain so long as human nature retains its present constitution. Expansion is not without conditions. "Because our present house is too small for us, it is not to be inferred that we shall live henceforth in the open air. As a general rule of life and conduct, we see as yet no reason to believe that *liberty,* if this be its meaning, is better than service."[23] Christ revealed the source of virtue in His life of lowly obedience. The "service of man," of which we now boast ourselves, is a bare possibility only through Christ's subservience and humiliation. It is easy to take humanity as we find it, and convenient to ignore this fact, but then it is also easy to accept light without a scrupulous recognition of the sun's agency. The peculiarity of Positivism is that, apart from its distinctive philosophical tenets, it is virtually a reproduction of one portion of Christ's principle.[24] Why go about with a candle to see the sun? Its altruism is His also, but without the integration which He deemed necessary to complete the character of an individual. His consciousness of God—which is but the more spiritualised expression of what has been rediscovered as "cosmic religion"—had its counterpart in His consciousness of mankind, which is to-day the *raison d'être* of that second faith so called, the "religion of humanity."

The supremacy of Christ is further enhanced by the strange circumstance that His revelation is not, like the work of Socrates, of Luther, or of Carlyle, representative only of a specific stage in the world's development. Like others, He came at a crisis which was for Him. It used to be supposed that in Him divine revelation culminated, and remained final thenceforward. After a sort it did, but progress has been continuous since. "God did not retire to rest after the well-known six days of creation; but, on the contrary, is constantly active as on the first. It would have been for Him a poor occupation to compose this heavy world out of simple elements, and to keep it rolling in the sunbeams from year to year, if He had not had the plan of founding a nursery for a world of spirits upon this material basis. So He is now constantly active in higher natures to attract the lower ones."[25] In this later advance the Christian revelation is continually renewing itself. Historically it appeared at the time which was prepared for it. But it is not only a stage like others, for it is perpetuated in a principle which is the motive force of human nature, and must remain operative, no matter how circumstances may change. In the other masters we see all that is, in Christ there was all that ought to be. Socrates was the forerunner of later ideals, Christ Himself was the exhibition of the ideal in history. Christianity, just on account of those elements which differentiate it from Greek philosophy, constantly stimulates the higher life, and that without laying any restrictions upon intellectual activity. For Christ's work is a spontaneous revelation of human nature—of a nature which has spiritual as well as mental and material needs. His kingdom is not of this world, and only in so far as this is true can it remain in the world. It makes little difference what dogmatic views recommend themselves to the individual mind. For there is religion without rites, and there may be churches without religion. But the power of a perfect life can never pass away. It is for humanity, because in man full expression was given to it.

The eternity of Christianity is based on human nature, the kaleidoscopic creeds are but accidental embodiments of the true reality. What boots it for practical life that Christianity is often no better to its professors than was Islam to Mrs Skewton.[26] Presented in such shape it is indeed useless, and the sooner that science completes its destruction the better. But the answer given in Christ's life to the timeless question of man's relation to sin and misery, continues among the eternal verities. And so long as man is

> Created half to rise and half to fall,

it must remain. Art may to-day revive Hellenism, in so far as that is possible, and baptise its find the "Religion of Beauty." Physical science may go back to the abstract monotheism of Palestine, and call its setting of God over against man "Agnosticism." But the interpretation of the great truths contained in each of these movements is already beforehand with them in Christianity. There Hellenism and Hebraism met, not under the form of a doctrinal system, but in a nature which at once realised God's transcendence, yet continual presence, in the beauty of the world and in the human spirit.

The inner life which Christ illustrated and actualised is the highest revelation to man of the universal moral order. But no seal is thus set upon the potentiality of things. Men are Christians, not because they accept a few dogmas which outrage both intellect and conscience, but because they perceive in the man Christ Jesus a *kind* of being which is the one permanent index of a universal human "capacity of using and modifying any existing state of things," for the furtherance of wellbeing, intellectual and social, no less than moral and religious. Man's chief athcism is sin, and if the consecrated life of Jesus be without message to those who would live sin down, then, so far as revelation has gone, atheist man is doomed to remain. But there is a message which, whether willing or unwilling, human nature cannot shut out. The modernness of Christianity lies in this—that for sin we must even now "*suffer* with Christ whether we *believe* in Him or not."[27]

While, then, there are points of external contact between Socrates and Christ, which render comparison by no means unreasonable, it must be remembered that in inner spirit they have little in common. Above all is it necessary to avoid the radical misconception of regarding Christianity as a species of sublimated Greek philosophy. The life of Christ could only have been lived when and where it was lived. No speculative system contemplating, like Greek philosophy, an explanation of being, could have produced that sense of sin which culminated in a life of grace. Socrates was able to consider his death an inevitable sacrifice, just as Christ did. Yet he died in the full assurance that punishment had already overtaken the evil men who composed the majority of the Dicastery. For this reason, were there none other, his fate does not appeal to us with the same power as Christ's. Both had strength given them to die in a just cause. But the occasions were not identical. The calmness of Socrates and the agony of Christ are separated by constituent elements which, if subtle, are none the less obvious. The Socratic philosophy represents the bringing to birth of what was highest in Greek thought. Its founder was able to die calmly, because he was persuaded that the world-order had universality. This universality he had tried to find in the life of each man. Yet even had he known the reign of law, and of liberty, as it is now understood, his revelation would still have been imperfect. Later thinkers, persuaded of this imperfection, sought to surmount it in various ways. But the conception of the moral governance of man was not to be completed from Greek civilisation. The wise man, so called, might think about it, and describe it, but unfortunately, the wise man himself never appeared, nor could he.

Only in the matrix of Judaism, surrounded by the consciousness of an ethical God, and determined by the idea of living to this deity, could the wise man appear. The Greek ideal of a mediator between the transcendent God and the world, the Græco-Roman conception of the sage's life, and the Jewish thought of a saviour, were all requisite to, as they were realised by, the Christ. He did not protest that He was such, but, by living as He did, He solved the universal problem. In a sense, He added nothing to the *knowledge* of Greek and Jewish thinkers,—Philo had all the elements,—but he brought thought about God and morality out of the theoretical region of discussion down to the practical sphere of the God-like and moralised life. And of this change the Jewish religion was the prime cause. Socrates and Christ are both revealers of principles, which they incarnated. For each the crisis of history called. The religious intensity of Jesus was impossible to Socrates, because utterly foreign to the entire mode of thought which he expressed. Yet without it, the lesson of the ages would have been proper only to the Greek man, not to humanity.

Socrates and Christ alike had faith in the ideal, but this was different for each. The artistically rounded life of the Greek citizen, set with nicest care into the united social fabric, could not, Socrates was persuaded, be produced on the Sophistic method. His work, therefore, was to find a new way to the ideal which his age contemplated. Like the other masters, he had to "fit to the finite his infinity." But the ideal, partial even as it was, still remained ideal, and no struggle of later thought availed, save as a process of development, to bring it nearer. Yet, although in Christ the moral possibilities of human nature found realisation, Christianity is no exceptionally supernatural phenomenon. It came in the fulness of time, when the passage of thought from the phenomenal to the real, as seen in Greek philosophy, had prepared a way for it. The spiritual discipline of the Jews was the determining factor in the life of Christ, but the problem, which He died to solve, was also set in the Gentile world. Judaism saw heaven from earth, Hellenism imagined earth heaven, and both at last felt that their conceptions were illusory. Christianity brought heaven to earth, and, by inculcating, as Christ lived, that this is the place of self-sacrifice for the moralisation of humanity and of the individual,

> Goes changing what was wrought,
> From falsehood like the truth, to truth itself.[28]

The comprehensiveness of Christianity is the evidence that it is no transfigured Hellenism. Christ breathed a new spirit into the world by living for the sake of righteousness. He put the existence of an ideal life beyond possibility of question. To-day His religion is not a mere recorded fact of intellectual history, but because His work is completed and human, Christianity goes on reproducing itself as a manner of life. In its essential eternity for man it depends ultimately, neither on historical occurrences, nor on theological dogmas, but on the constitution of human nature. Knowledge of Christ must be gleaned as is knowledge of Socrates. But, seeing that Socrates was a searcher after the ultimate in man and God, and Christ a verification of the divine in the human, knowledge of Him comes with power. The perfection which is possible for man He had. His life was the answer to every cry for deliverance from the burden of sin, because in it are to be seen certain spiritual experiences which, let knowledge be what it may, are continually repeating themselves in human nature as the sole means to moral perfection. What those experiences were, Socrates did not understand. But he was among the first to awaken that consciousness of defect, which went on deepening through the ancient world, until all spiritual functions were "smothered in surmise" of superstition. The appearance of Christ was eminently natural, and in the principle of His life all that the world desired was granted. His Personality, and the possibilities of human nature which it revealed, form His indestructible contribution to moral progress. As the great *Person,* who subdued the greatest crisis in man's history, He is, and, so long as the world is governed by Reason, must remain, the type, in assimilating themselves to which other persons may rise to further self-completeness.

"The true reality that is and ought to be, is not matter, and is still less Idea, but is the living personal Spirit of God and the world of personal spirits which He has created."[29] Before Christ the conception that self-conscious personality was common to God and man alike had been but dimly foreshadowed. The Christ-life elevated it into a certain fact. Here then is Christ's inalienable contribution to human progress. His religion cannot fail of endless application; for His perfect character is the sole guarantee that every man, though knowing the evil, can be true to himself only in being holy and in following after righteousness. But this righteousness is not an external thing upon which one can lay hold or towards which one can progress. In the self-conscious sphere the category of law, as usually conceived, has little or no application. Yet it must not be supposed, on this account, that personality develops aimlessly. True, present conditions are nought save as interpreted by it: but, wanting them, the interpretation could not be. Both are essential factors in a life which is constantly revealing and actualising an immanent cause—an inner principle. Socrates was the first to observe the importance of this *causa sui.* It was Christ's to realise the absolute value of personality as such, and to show how, by a full apprehension of all that self-mediation implies, each may, nay, cannot but escape the yoke of the law, by using it as a means to his own perfecting. And this perfecting is righteousness. The good man is truly free; for, by appreciation of the transforming power of character, he finds himself capable of subduing all circumstances to his own growth in moral stature—a growth inseparably bound up with a like advancement in his fellows. Christ's life and teaching embody in full that freedom which exists only amid limitation, and issues the more triumphant the more it is circumscribed—freedom which, for this very reason, can be attained, in some measure, by all who, as partakers of His humanity, are able to make weakness the perfection of strength.

Notes

[1] St Paul and Protestantism, Matthew Arnold, pp. 78, 79.

[2] Representative Men, Emerson, p. 393 (Bell's edition).

[3] La Science des Religions, Emil Burnouf, p. 220.

[4] Cf. Is God Knowable? Prof. J. Iverach, p. 186.

[5] Catholic Doctrine of the Atonement, Oxenham, p. 202.

[6] Cf. Hegel, Werke, xii. 166.

[7] Cf. Apology (Introduction), Jowett, vol. i. p. 326 (first edition).

[8] Cf. Phædo, 116.

[9] Cf. History of Greece, Thirlwall, vol. iv. p. 268 *sq.*

[10] Carlyle, On Heroes, p. 2.

[11] Christianity in its Cradle, F. W. Newman, p. 127. I have taken the liberty of using the customary orthography.

[12] Cf. Theætetus, 176.

[13] St Paul's Epistles, Jowett, vol. ii. p. 392.

[14] Cf. Prolegomena to Ethies, T. H. Green, pp. 264-308.

[15] Cf. Essays and Addresses, J. M. Wilson, p. 107.

[16] Cf. La Science des Religious, E. Burnouf, p. 242.

[17] Cf. Through Nature to Christ, E. A. Abbott, p. 346 *sq.;* 373 note.

[18] The Kernel and the Husk, p. 257.

[19] Saul, Robert Browning, Works, vol. vi. p. 122.

[20] St Bernard.

[21] Philosophy and Religion, James Hinton, pp. 113, 114.

[22] Lessing, in Die Religion Christi, and Herder in Ideen, like Goethe and others of the anti-eighteenth century school, seem to forget that the eternity of Christianity is not based, as they suppose, on a Person who is temporal, but on their own article of faith, that persons alone can transform a momentary act into an eternal principle.

[23] Prose Remains of A. H. Clough, p. 409.

[24] Cf. The Service of Man, J. C. Morison, p. 177 (head fifth).

[25] Conversations of Goethe, Eckermann, pp. 569, 570.

[26] "There is no What's-his-name but Thingummy, and What-you-may-call-it is his prophet."

[27] John Inglesant, J. H. Shorthouse, p. 259.

[28] A Death in the Desert, Robert Browning, Works, vol. vii. p. 145.

[29] Microcosmus, Lotze, vol. ii. p. 728.

J. T. Forbes (essay date 1905)

SOURCE: "The Teaching of Socrates: The Prosaic and Ideal Interpretations; The Criteria," in *Socrates*, T. & T. Clark, 1905, pp. 101-50.

[*In the following excerpt, Forbes studies the controversy over the Socratic sources, examining the versions of Socrates presented by Xenophon and Plato and identifying the possible biases of each author. Forbes concludes that through the use of Aristotle's comments on Socrates, "the artistic verisimilitude of the Xenophontic and Platonic portraits," and the analysis of the development of Socrates's philosophy, a consistent view of Socrates can be attained.*]

The question of authorities for the teaching of Socrates meets us at the outset of any attempt to deal with the subject. To two writers mainly, Plato and Xenophon, we are indebted for our knowledge; their testimonies being supplemented or corrected by what comes to us from Aristotle and others. Broadly speaking, outside the three named, allusions to Socrates are scanty, or of poor authority. The testimonies of Xenophon and Plato are very full, but differ much from each other. The references of Aristotle are brief, but of great value.

What, then, was the historic connection of our two chief witnesses with their subject? Xenophon is supposed to have become a follower of Socrates at an early age. The story of his life being saved by the philosopher in the retreat from Delium (424 B.C.) is not now accepted on account of its chronological inconsistency with the impression received from the *Anabasis* as to the author's age.[1] Another story, which relates his first contact with Socrates, tells how the philosopher met the youth in a narrow lane, and, barring the path with his stick, asked him where this and that kind of thing could be purchased. The lad answered him modestly, and was then asked "where men were made good and virtuous." And on his answering that he did not know, Socrates said, "Follow me, then, and learn."[2] This was the beginning of his discipleship.[3] From the same source we learn that he kept records of the informal discourse of his master. Out of these doubtless the *Memorabilia* grew. The number and variety of the incidents and teachings recorded imply a lengthy and close intercourse between the philosopher and his pupil. They include correction of personal faults in disciples, discourses on filial and fraternal duty, on public life and military command, on finance and statesmanship, and many other practical matters interesting to a practical mind. To the truth of some of the stories he relates, he testifies of his own knowledge. Many times he says he himself heard such and such teachings. As to counsel given to himself, for example, he relates[4] that, when invited by Proxenus to join the expedition of Cyrus, who had been the friend of the Lacedæmonians in the war, he had consulted Socrates as to his acceptance or refusal of the invitation, and had received the counsel to consult the Delphian oracle; but having, like many another, first decided on his course, he inquired of the oracle to which of the Gods he ought to pray in order to successfully accomplish his journey. After he had received the response, he returned and told Socrates the result of his visit, and was censured by him for not inquiring first of all whether the journey was one to be undertaken or not. After this determination his whole life-course was altered. His exile resulted from his connection with the enemy of his country. It is uncertain whether he ever returned to Athens. Socrates was sentenced to death in 399 B.C., and if Xenophon did return before then it can only have been for a brief period. But he had enjoyed years of close intercourse with the philosopher, and it was a labour of love to write a vindication of the faith and morality of that misjudged heretic.

Plato's connection with Socrates was perhaps scarcely so lengthened. It appears to have begun about 410 B.C. It is not marked by any very special incidents. But the enthusiasm of discipleship has glorified Socrates by making him the spokesman of the Platonic Philosophy, and by preserving pictures beyond price of the living as of the martyred teacher. In the closing years of the Peloponnesian War, and thence right on to the fatal year 399 B.C., Plato was in the closest intimacy with his master.

So far as opportunity is concerned, both men, Plato and Xenophon, were most favourably situated. Long and close connection with a teacher whose pupils were in each case personal friends, equalises circumstance, and leaves the accounting for differences in the presentation of the Socratic philosophy to the personal equation. Here there is the greatest possible difference. Xenophon, it has usually been held, was an essentially simple nature, a man neither inclined toward speculative thought nor fitted for it, but one who conceived philosophy as largely a process of moral training. He was a cavalry officer and a country gentleman, and at the same time a literary man, interested in history, politics, war, and sport; fully alive to the practical side of things, but apprehending less clearly the relation of all this to ideal principle. He disliked Athenian democracy and admired Spartan institutions; and soon after his return from the East ceased to be an Athenian citizen, and, making a virtue of his exile, became as much of a Spartan as he could.

His bent was practical. Philosophic discussion was not for the purpose of gaining intellectual satisfaction in the possession of a consistent scheme of things; it was a true training as opposed to the culture of the Sophists; an implanting of pious convictions and virtuous habits. The metaphysical basis of his master's theories could not be expected to attract such a mind. What he would give us, according to this view, we should expect to be a popular presentation of the easier and more external aspects of the Socratic teaching. His Socrates would be the moral censor of his time and the preacher of practical virtue, but hardly the leader of a philosophic revolution.

The case with Plato is altogether different. It is manifest that his presentation of Socrates is largely ideal. He chooses to put his own boldest speculations into the mouth of the teacher whose own thoughts, original and powerful as they were, clothed themselves in plain and homespun dress, and took a more modest range. The truth Plato is concerned about is ideal truth, not historical and chronological accuracy. It is his way of honouring the memory of his great master, to represent him setting forth cosmical and epistemological theories foreign to his actual thought. His own mind is the antithesis of Xenophon's. He breathes freely in the upper air of abstractions. His view of anything may be unusual, extraordinary, wrong; it is never likely to be commonplace. Hence the Socrates we expect to find in his pages, and do find, is an enlarged, idealised figure, in which it is not easy sometimes to discern the homely lineaments of the original.

Now, when it was held that the one drawback to Xenophon's testimony was, to put it bluntly, his somewhat prosaic mind, incapacitating him from seeing the deepest things in his subject, and that, so far as he saw, his testimony could be absolutely accepted, which was, till recently, the orthodox view, the problem was simpler. Plato could enter into the full mind of his master, and, while persuading himself that his presentation was but the full development of what was germinally present in the Socratic teaching, did, it was certain, sometimes expand and idealise that teaching beyond recognition. What was said, then, was this, "We must go to Xenophon for the plain facts of the case: and if he only gives a limited and prosaic view, we can fill this out by the generous Platonic interpretation in so far as the two views are not flatly in contradiction." Xenophon is thus the check on Plato, who is really the deeper and truer interpreter so far as he can be accepted, which is, when held to fact by the plodding record of the humbler writer.

But it becomes clear to any patient reading that the matter is less simple. Xenophon is no more a mere recorder or annalist than Plato. In his own way he writes history "with a thesis." If he has not a special philosophy to teach in the same full sense, he writes, in any case, in a particular apologetic interest. He is concerned to minimise the revolutionary aspects of the thought of Socrates. He wants to present a picture of the blameless teacher of virtue, the pious worshipper of the Gods; and he certainly succeeds in his aim. But we cannot but feel that it is at the expense of completeness. If Xenophon relates of his master nothing but what is true, he can hardly be cleared of sins of omission. The man he describes is too much clipped and shorn of his originality; not as daring or as radical as we feel the real Socrates must have been; too purely a moraliser, and even a proser. He could neither have inaugurated a new philosophy nor met a reformer's death. But this is not all. Xenophon has a constructive scheme in his mind. He writes not as a simple chronicler, but as a practised literary man. And his thesis is indeed constantly before him as he writes: He is not penning history in the modern sense. It is a eulogy that he gives us, not a biography, much less an estimate; and his view is limited by his apologetic and eulogistic aim as much as by his personal incapacity for pure speculation.

There was doubtless a temptation to each writer to simplify the complex personality of his subject by selection and omission. It was not easy to reduce to the simple moralist the man who could sit out the strongest at a drinking party, whose jests touched themes on which silence is deemed best to-day, and who could apply the principles of his philosophy to the arts of the courtesan. Nor, on the other hand, is it easy to recognise as a purely speculative thinker one who tells Aristippus that he knows nothing of any but relative good.

It is plain, indeed, that we do not attain to colourless history in either of the great witnesses. We cannot escape from an altered Socrates by the simple process of taking Xenophon as final. It is as serious an error to lessen and make commonplace what was great and original, as to idealise and magnify. Plato's view is that of the poet and the idealist, but there is little question that he saw the inner truth of Socrates more clearly than the practical Xenophon. It has been seen before that the *Memorabilia* partakes little of the nature of notes. Xenophon is not a Greek Boswell, keeping chronological records of his master's words and doings. What he gives is a defensive plea with a collection of sample teachings, and a description of the method of their impartation. The individual characters of the discussions recorded are but indifferently realised. The answers put into the mouths of those who converse with Socrates seem sometimes prepared so as to minister to the greater glory of the principal speaker. It may be no objection that the opinions of Socrates are the opinions of Xenophon, for he may have accepted his philosophy complete from his teacher; but whether an objection or not, it is true. There is, too, about the whole of the Xenophontic portraiture a flatness that contrasts with the dramatically sharp realisation of individual features in the Platonic dialogues. Some few passages, like the talk with poor Euthydemus, make an approach to vigour and vividness, but a good deal of the matter of the *Memorabilia* is a little dull and insipid. Now, the charm of the conversation of Socrates was, we may be certain, very great, to attract men as it did through so many years, and it is permissible to think that some of its fascination has been missed in the record, as well as some of its less facile elements, and much of the deep radical thought covered by its light play.

The most modern view of Xenophon's Socratic writings,[5] is that they are really composed in the spirit of "tendency." As Xenophon departs from history in his idealisation of Agesilaus, and makes Cyrus the central figure of a historical romance containing views of his own on education and government and many other matters, so in his Socratic writing he is not by any means a rigid historian, but an artist in literary portraiture, and the Socrates of the *Memorabilia* and the *Œconomicus* is to some extent an imaginative production. According to this view, we have to deal not with the plodding chronicler whose historic veracity is unquestionable if his vision is limited, but with a literary artist who presents a picture of his hero's life and teaching in accordance with a certain thesis of personal goodness in character and positive philosophic content in teaching. If he has read his master aright, a true picture may be given, but it is not got by historical exactitude. On its literary and quasi-historical side it will be a view analogous to his view of Agesilaus. Philosophically, other views representing the negative and hortatory sides of the Socratic work had been put forth with which Xenophon was dissatisfied, not because of incorrectness so much as of incompleteness. He was determined to show his master not as the perpetual questioner so much as the oracle of his friends, the teacher of positive truth, the guide in personal perplexity, the trainer of intellectual gifts for the public service. And religiously, too, he felt that he could give a more satisfactory representation of Socrates the pious man and the good citizen than could be gathered by those who had not personally known him, and whose impressions came to them from accounts that emphasized the perplexity in which, from their negative character, his discussions left men, modified by praises of his personal faith and piety.

Of the record thus given, the doctrine that virtue is knowledge and the dialectic of definitions are absolutely certain Socratic teachings. These things, indeed, are known as such through the testimony of Aristotle and the agreement of the Socratic schools. Teachings there are, it is thought, in the *Memorabilia* which find no analogies in the other writings of Xenophon; and, provided other more probable sources do not offer themselves, these may turn out to be truly Socratic. Other matter must be judged by its affinity with the ascertained teaching. The result is that we fall back inevitably on more or less subjective grounds of judgment. The references of Aristotle being accepted as of unquestionable accuracy, there remains the task of sifting Socratic teaching from the mass of Plato's dialogues and the Socratic works of Xenophon.

One or two principles tend to safeguard the truth of the matter. If Platonism is Socratic teaching idealised and developed in some directions almost beyond recognition, the artistic sense of Plato, as Fouillée[6] remarks, is too perfect for him to attribute to his characters doctrines of which they could not even have possessed the germ. The outgrowth is not monstrous but harmonious. And again in Xenophon the special appeal of his apology would have missed its aim had the real Socrates been to the ordinary Athenian a figure broadly irreconcilable with Xenophon's presentation. It is a view something like that of the unprejudiced man of average intelligence, although written by a man who is to the limit of his capacity a devoted disciple.

Taking whatever truth this view may hold into consideration, what we shall be led to will be careful judgment of all Xenophon's testimony, and the elimination of whatever can be shown to spring from his idiosyncrasies. In his Socratic writings it is evident, from criticism,[7] that there is much that is suspiciously like a personal contribution rather than a record,—the interest in strategy and cavalry generalship generally, in field sports and the management of a country estate, the fondness for Persian illustrations, the comparisons of Lacedæmon with Athens. We cannot build a true account of the Socratic philosophy merely by making an uncritical collection of quotations from all writings that mention the name of Socrates. There must be a "discerning of the spirits." But with the few but sure criteria given, the task, while difficult, is not impossible. It is not contended that much will not remain doubtful, nevertheless we may by taking pains reach a substantially correct view.

The difficulty, indeed, of this is not to be minimised. Take one point, supposed to be, above all, well established, the Socratic confession of ignorance, so beautifully dealt with in the *Apology,* as the basis of the oracular verdict awarding Socrates the crown of wisdom. Turn to Xenophon, and, as Benn has shown, nothing is more certain than that, if his testimony is to be accepted, Socrates was of all persons the least self-distrustful. He was accused sometimes of virtually saying, "Come unto me and I will give you restlessness";[8] but in the *Memorabilia* he appears as a person who has no doubt whatever as to his own competency to pronounce verdicts on matters the most difficult and the most diverse. He can instruct a field officer or a statesman, can pluck out the heart of the mystery of artist and artisan alike. As was said of Macaulay, many would be glad to be as sure of anything as he is of everything. Compare this somewhat self-complacent state of mind with the enquirer of the Socratic dialogues of Plato, and it will be seen immediately how great must be the allowance for the point of view. Can we simply, as Benn does, attribute Socrates' confession of ignorance to Plato, who had a rigorous conception of knowledge, and who here puts his own idea into the mouth of his master and draws "a discreet veil over the positive side" of his teaching (for which we must resort to Xenophon), or can we reach a point where these apparent contradictions are reconciled?

As to this particular point we have incidental but emphatic testimony from Aristotle, from whom words can be quoted that seem to deny positive teaching to Socrates, of whom he says that he asked questions but did not give replies, confessing that he had no knowledge.[9] But while such an utterance establishes the point against which Benn contends, by showing the characteristic attitude of Socrates, it cannot, of course, in view of other and ampler testimonies, be taken as more than a mere description of a method that was habitual.

The authority of Aristotle again enables us to say that of the mass of matter put forward in the name of Socrates, certain doctrines belong to the Platonic Socrates, not to the Socrates of history. He is "accredited" by Aristotle with two things, inductive arguments and definition by universal concepts;[10] and with being also the first to apply this procedure in the province of ethics.[11] But these concepts, upon which knowledge must rest, have not in the thought of Socrates become hypostatised into independent realities of a world above sense upon which the mind prepared by dialectic discipline alone can gaze.[12] This is Platonic doctrine. What with Socrates is as yet a product of abstraction, having reality in the mind only, is in the Platonic development an existence above and beyond individual objects, is indeed the only reality. Where this doctrine is taught, and where knowledge is traced to the mind's prenatal view of an eternal ideal world, recollection of which is awakened through the dialectical process, we have left the historic Socrates behind and are listening to Plato. In the identification of virtue and knowledge, too, Socrates and Plato agree; but there is, as Zeller points out,[13] a difference not negligible. Socrates knows but one virtue which, because it is science, is communicable. Plato does not consider conventional virtue altogether valueless;[14] it is a step to that which is based on knowledge.[15] Nor does his doctrine of the unity of virtue coincide with that of Socrates, for he admits the existence of particular virtues, such as temperance and bravery, fostered by music and gymnastic,[16] in the absence of the knowledge upon which alone, he yet holds, perfect virtue can be based.

By the use mainly of such criteria as the Aristotelian testimony, the artistic verisimilitude of the Xenophontic and Platonic portraits, and the study of the various developments of the Socratic philosophy, a view at once self-consistent and faithful to critically sifted testimony may be gained. It is by its success or failure in approximating to this that any attempt must be judged.

Notes

[1] Dakyns, *The Works of Xenophon,* vol. i. Note iii.

[2] Diog. Laërt. ii. 48.

[3] *Circa* (?) 415 B.C.

[4] *Anab.* III. i. 4-7.

[5] Dakyns, *Works of Xenophon,* iii. pp. xxi, xxii.

[6] *La Philosophic de Socrate, Méthode Generale,* i. ix.

[7] Cf. Dakyns, *loc. cit.*

[8] Drummond.

[9] Arist., *De Soph. Elench.* 183*b,* 7.

[10] *Meta.* 1078*b,* 27-30.

[11] *Ib.* 1078*b,* 17-23.

[12] *Ib.* 1078*b,* 30-32; 1085*a,* 37.

[13] *Plato and the older Academy,* p. 448 *sq.*

[14] *Meno,* 97 *sq.*

[15] *Repub.* 518 D, E.

[16] *Repub.* 410; Zeller, *Plato,* p. 451.

R. Nicol Cross (essay date 1914)

SOURCE: "His Teaching: Treatment of Enemies," in *Socrates: The Man and His Mission,* Books for Libraries Press, 1914, pp. 142-94.

[*In the following essay, Cross points out that Socrates was known for his teaching that "in no circumstances is it just to injure anyone," including one's enemies. This concept, states Cross, contrasted sharply with popular sentiment at the time. Below, Cross identifies an incident in which Socrates appears to be saying that injuring one's enemies is acceptable. After exploring the apparent contradiction, Cross concludes that "we may take it as certain that Socrates practised, and practically certain that before his death he taught, the doctrine . . . that 'neither injury, nor retaliation, nor warding off evil by evil is ever right'."*]

Reason and Reflection are radical forces, much more so than is sentiment; and just because more radical in their standards, they are more Catholic and universal in their judgments. Their function and tendency is to strip off the accidental and transient and penetrate to the essential. . . . Socrates, by appealing to the Reason within, was at once carried to a view which broke down the great conventional distinction between the class of the free who toiled not neither did they spin, and the class which had to toil and spin for them, a distinction which in any case was counting for less and less in the public life of Athens, as the Aristophanic drama shows.

The critical principle applied by Socrates not only cut at the root of the conventional opinion in regard to labour which set up a cleavage within the same society, but it was bound also to operate as a solvent for the unnatural divisions and relations between members of different societies.

If a man, *e.g.,* ought to love his neighbour as himself, the inference of Reason is that he ought also to love everybody else's neighbour as himself. The consideration as to whether a man lives in the same street and the same society or in another street and different society, makes no difference from the point of view of the Reason in the way in which you ought to treat him. Taking them simply as individuals, the colour of men's skin, or their position geographically on the surface of the globe, does not affect the fundamental rights and duties which the Moral Law imposes as between them and ourselves. This was one of the great principles of the Practical Reason in the thought of Kant, who expressed it in the imperative so to act as if the maxim on which you act were to become through your will a universal law of nature. That means that *ethically* every person must have equal value for us, and we must treat all in the same spirit, and it leads to what may be called a rational or ethical Humanitarianism in which all such divisions and antipathies and hatreds as have no justification in reason and morality are abolished.

The question is, did Socrates see all to which the principle committed him, and did the vision liberate him from the ordinary ethic of his time, which drew a sharp line between friends and enemies, and sanctioned opposite modes of conduct toward them? "It is commonly held to redound to a man's praise," he says in conversation with Chærecrates, "to have outstripped an enemy in mischief or a friend in kindness,"[1] a quotation of ordinary sentiment which it is worth observing occurs in a talk in which Socrates is pressing Chærecrates to take the initiative in healing the quarrel which has arisen between him and his brother. He advises him to go and frankly offer his hand to his brother in reconciliation. He will be sure to find his generosity reciprocated, but even if it should not be so, then "at the worst you will have shown yourself to be a good, honest, brotherly man, and he will appear as a sorry creature on whom kindness is wasted."[2]

But Socrates had a very high ideal of family relationships, and brotherhood was a natural tie which he believed God intended should bind members of the family together closer than hands and feet, or ears and eyes, in a community of mutual good;[3] and the "Recollections" don't represent Socrates as inculcating the same attitude in the case of mutual enemies in general. Take the following words addressed to Critobulus by Socrates, who assumes the rôle of an agent for promoting friendships:

"If you will authorise me to say that you are devoted to your friends; that nothing gives you so much joy as a good friend; that you pride yourself no less on the fine deeds of those you love than on your own; that you never weary of plotting and planning to procure them a rich harvest of the same; and lastly, that you have discovered a man's virtue is to *excel his friends in kindness and his foes in hostility*. If I am authorised thus to report of you, I think you will find me a serviceable fellow-hunter in the quest of friends, which is the conquest of the good."[4]

It would seem as though Socrates had failed of his own principles in this matter, and that the pressure of environing ideas was too strong for the fidelity of his own spirit to itself. We confess we find it difficult, in virtue of the impression which the whole character of the man makes upon us, and which we have tried to convey . . . to believe that Socrates could be satisfied with such an attitude of mind towards his enemies. It conflicts with all we know of him, in his bearing towards others. We are not convinced by Professor A. E. Taylor's "Varia Socratica" that Socrates was actually a member of a Pythagorean brotherhood, but he was intimate with Pythagoreans, and it is not credible to us that one whom they affectionately recognised to be greater than themselves should have fallen below the moral level of the teaching of their school, which was, according to Aristotle, that they were "never to injure anyone, but endure patiently wrongs, and injury, and, in a word, do all the good they could." This was the very doctrine that Socrates practised. It was he of whom his jailor at the last could say that he was unlike other prisoners, for he had never railed at him, but had spoken only kindly words, and showed nothing but courtesy and benevolence; of whom Demetrius, quoted by Diogenes Laertius, could relate that once when he was kicked by some cad in passing, he only laughed, and when his friends expressed astonishment at this meek and mild behaviour, asked whether when asses kicked him he was to have the law of them;[5] of whom Xenophon himself says that "he was never the cause of evil to the state, was free of offence in private as in public life, never hurt a single soul either by deprivation of good or infliction of evil, and never lay under the imputation of any such wrong-doing"; who, according to Plato's "Apology," found at heart no cause of anger against his accusers or those who condemned him to death,[6] and could say in the presence of his fellow-citizens that he had never intentionally wronged anyone;[7] who held that men do not commit wrong except because of ignorance, error, or illusion, not seeing the true character and consequence of their action. Could such an one believe in the doctrine of retaliation or of injuring enemies?

We confess we derive little consolation from Professor Joël's theory that Xenophon's account would be influenced by the Cynic doctrine that Justice consists in duct with his doctrine of ill-doing as ignorance, drives us to accept the unanimous testimony of the Platonic dialogues, which is to the effect that to return evil for evil on a man would only be to aggravate the evil.

In the "Apology," Socrates states his inmost conviction that "to be unjust and to disobey any one better than oneself, whether God or man, is contrary to duty and honour." The point, then, is as to whether or no it is unjust to render evil for evil, or under any circumstance to injure a fellow-creature. And to that we reply in the first place, that if doing evil is the result of ignorance, then to retaliate in like manner *is* unjust and wrong, and can only be the result of ignorance also, and we suggest that Socrates was not so dull and obtuse as to fail to recognise the obvious inference from his own principles.

Nor can we fall back on the idea that his conception of justice was, in itself, too confused and imperfect to exclude the maxim of retaliation. Socrates had got beyond the current position on this matter. "In questions of just and unjust, fair and foul," he says to Crito, "which are the subjects of our present consultation, ought we to follow the opinion of the many and to fear them; or the opinion of the one man who has understanding? Ought we not to fear and reverence him more than all the rest of the world; and if we desert him, shall we not destroy and injure that principle in us which may be assumed to be improved by justice and deteriorated by injustice?"[8]

> In spite of the opinion of the many, and in spite of consequences whether better or worse, shall we insist as before, that *injustice is always an evil and dishonour to him who acts unjustly?*
>
> CR. Yes.
>
> SOC. Then we must do no wrong?
>
> CR. Certainly not.

> SOC. *Nor when injured, injure in return, as the many imagine;* for *we must injure no one at all?*
>
> CR. Clearly not.
>
> SOC. Again, Crito, may we do evil?
>
> CR. Surely not, Socrates.
>
> SOC. And what of doing evil in return for evil, which is the morality of the many—is that just or not?
>
> CR. Not just.
>
> SOC. *Then we ought not to retaliate or render evil for evil to any one whatever evil we may have suffered from him.*[9]

The same conclusion is put into Socrates' mouth in the Republic:[10]

> SOC. If, then, someone says that it is just to render to each what is due to him, by that understanding that injury is due to enemies, and service to friends, such an one would not be wise in so expressing himself. He has not spoken the truth. For it has been seen that *in no circumstances is it just to injure anyone.*

Socrates' argument has turned on the point, to him self-evident, that nothing that is right and good can possibly do hurt or injury to anyone.

In the "Gorgias" Plato makes him declare that the worst evil that can ever befall a man is to do wrong,[11] and that if it were a choice between acting unjustly and suffering unjustly, between doing wrong and having wrong done to himself, he would choose the latter.[12]

In these dialogues, then, there is not a quaver of uncertainty about the conviction that the just and good man will never repay injury with injury but always with good, and it fits in beautifully with Socrates' character.

Are we to suppose, then, that Plato gives us the truth, and that Xenophon was mistaken and inconsistent in his reminiscences of the master's teaching on this theme? We should have no hesitation in taking that position, only there is one other dialogue ascribed to Plato—the fragmentary dialogue "Clitophon"—in which Socrates is taken to task for the obscurity and ambiguity of his opinions on certain matters, and this very question of the treatment of enemies is mentioned. Clitophon speaks thus to him: "Finally, Socrates, I applied directly to yourself, and *you told me that it was the principle of justice to injure enemies and do good to friends.* But *afterwards it came out that the just man never injures anyone, for he acts with a view to the good of everybody in everything.* And this was my experience not once or twice but for a long time, so I gave up my persistency, having come to the conclusion either that while you were without a rival in stirring up people to the concern of virtue, but could do no more . . . either you do not know really what justice is or you do not choose to communicate your knowledge."

This is a most interesting and significant passage, and the vacillation which it attributes to Socrates is not without commentary and witness in the Platonic literature at large. It has the note of authenticity about it, and on the strength of it we would suggest that while Socrates had long risen in spirit and sympathy above the ethics of contemporary orthodoxy, yet in the realm of theory it cost him a prolonged struggle to shake himself quite free of the views in which his upbringing had been steeped, and which were strongly entrenched in the social and even religious authorities around him. He experienced a protracted duel between the loftier and the lower conception of moral obligations, and in the end the loftier vanquished, so that he found it impossible to conceive that a just man would do any injury to any fellow mortal, even if injured by him. In his speculations and discussions he would start off from the generally accepted hypotheses on the subject; but would by the force of his own reasoning always be driven to the higher point of view. Perhaps, indeed, it would be on the whole the most fitting inference from the evidence before us to hold that, in accordance with his usual method, he only laid down the accepted opinion as a point of departure from which he could set out and carry others with him to the recognition of its untenability and the acceptance of his own real view, a method which was obviously liable to create misunderstanding in those who did not clearly grasp it. The contradiction alluded to by Clitophon would thus receive explanation as being due to the fact that he mistook for an admission what was only a concession for the purposes of an argument, whose issue was its overthrow.

Reviewing all the evidence, we may take it as certain that Socrates practised, and practically certain that before his death he taught, the doctrine of returning good for evil, that "neither injury, nor retaliation, nor warding off evil by evil is ever right."[13]

Emerson achieved an insight into moral law which led him to pronounce in his own oracular way that "the good man has absolute good, which like fire turns everything to his own nature, so that you cannot do him any harm."[14]

But 400 years before Christ Plato put the same deep spiritual truth on the lips of Socrates, who after his sentence of death calmly declares that *"no evil can happen to a good man in life or in death.*"[15] Virtue makes its possessor invulnerable; all things, even the rage of enemies, work together for good to those who love the good and are good. They are the protégés of Heaven; *"neither they nor theirs are neglected by the gods."*[16]

With such conviction as that it would indeed be a degradation of self, not to say a grave inconsistency, to entertain the idea of revenge. Let a man be true to the divine law and ideal within him, and he has already conquered his enemies and the world. He can afford to do only good to every man, whether friend or foe. It is the same idea as was later promulgated by the Cynics, that all things were theirs. Spiritually they appropriated the universe. "The Cynic hath begotten all mankind, he hath all men for his sons, all women for his daughters; so doth he visit all and care for all. Thinkest thou that he is a mere meddler and busybody in rebuking those whom he meets? As a father he doth it, as a brother, and as a servant of the Universal Father, which is God."

It is worthy of grateful recognition that the principle of overcoming evil with good, which is the very flower of Christian ethic, was thus the possession of the great thinkers of Greece some centuries before Jesus and Paul inculcated it. And yet we must recognise a certain difference. Its root was not the same in Greek philosophy and in Christian teaching. In the former it was rather the flower of reason, in the latter the blossom of love. Perhaps in the case of Socrates we may say it was the fruit of both, as in that of Jesus; it grew not only out of his beautiful love but also out of his sweet reasonableness. We should not be doing more than justice to the Athenian saint to say that it was the natural product alike of his mind and his heart as they lie open to us in these wonderful records. The keenness of his intellect, the geniality of his nature, and the largeness of his soul, all led him to it, and it is as high as morality can take us.

Let us remember that for him all evil and wrongdoing has its origin in ignorance, ignorance of the true Good. That good, if we could only see it clearly, would be recognised to be one and the same for all. In it or moving towards it we are all in harmony and at peace. We only become enemies as we lose sight of the Highest and turn our hearts to lower and relative goods, poor deluded fools, divided not only from others but divided within ourselves. With the Apostle, Socrates could devoutly say, "Avenge not yourselves, beloved. For it is written, Vengeance is mine; I will repay, saith the Lord."[17] Only that Socrates would have said that the man who does evil takes revenge on himself.

Notes

1 Xen., Mem., bk. ii. ch. 3, 14.

2 *Ibid.,* 17.

3 Xen., Mem., bk. ii. ch. 3, 18, 19.

4 Xen., Mem., bk. ii. ch. 6, 35.

5 Diogenes Laertius, bk. ii. ch. 6, 21.

6 Apol., 41 d.

7 Apol., 37 a.

8 Plato, Crito, 47. (Jowett's trans.)

9 Plato's Crito, 49. (Jowett's trans.)

10 Bk. i. 335 e.

11 Plato, Gorgias, 469 b.

12 *Ibid.,* 469 c.

13 Plato, Crito, p. 49 d.

14 Essay on "Compensation."

15 Apol., 41 d.

16 *Ibid.*

17 Romans, ch. 12, v. 19.

William Ellery Leonard (essay date 1915)

SOURCE: "The Thinker," in *Socrates: Master of Life,* The Open Court Publishing Co., 1915, pp. 62-118.

[*In this excerpt, Leonard explores the relationship between Socrates's philosophy and personal morality. The philosopher's goal, Leonard claims, was to reform human conduct.*]

I.

Every exposition of Greek thought, from the most pedantic to the most popular, has been divided into the two chapters, "Before Socrates," "After Socrates"; between which has stood a third, devoted to Socrates himself. Though he published no book in prose or verse, no philosophic hexameters on nature, no dialectic treatise on the Absolute, no criticism on ethics, politics, or the divinities that shape or refuse to shape the ends of man, his centrality to the development of speculation, as the mind which, while itself indifferent to the activities of its predecessors, brought to light other principles not only directive for thought in hitherto uncharted realms, but essential for any rational solution of those problems already broached, has been until very recently beyond all dispute, and will always in any case challenge disproof. And the importance of his practical wisdom for the unwritten history of conduct is presumably quite as great. Thus we are now face to face with one of the five or six most impressive and vital questions in the history of intelligence (as opposed to the history of human vanities and insanities—the rise and fall of dynasties and the interminable slaughters on land and sea): just what did this man stand for who lived so long ago under the hill temple-crowned, in the market-place girded by porticoes, within the walls against which even then the hostile armies were more than once encamped?

The question is difficult not alone because it is so much larger than every writer who would answer it; but because it is just here that our sources are so difficult and confusing. Biographical reports, when uncontaminated by miraculous elements or by suspicion of rhetorical purpose or partisanship, when squaring with the public customs and affairs of the times, and finally, when tending toward a consistent portrayal of character and conduct, we may trust, in default of any contrary evidence. Allowing for some possible ambiguities of imperfect expression, I suppose no scholar would seriously quarrel with the statements of the preceding chapter, as not being founded on serviceable authority. It called for no special gift to note and record the concrete events, whatever gifts were needed to record them beautifully. But to understand thought, thought new and deep, expressed symbolically, whimsically, mischievously, now to this one, now to that, now here, now there, now touching this matter, now that, did call for an alertness of attention, a keenness of perception, a steadiness of memory, and an objectivity of judgment not present at Athens, nor indeed commensurate with man's limited brains yet anywhere; while to set it all down as if verbatim was, as shown in a previous chapter, the attempt either of self-delusion or of literary fiction. We are shut up forever to reading between the lines and to estimating the cumulative evidence of innumerable hints, which, taken separately, we would have no means of testing, and no right to feel sure of. We can bring the difficulty home to ourselves, if we imagine posterity, without the *Essays,* dependent for its knowledge of Emerson's thought, on (hypothetical) miscellanies of conversation reported and edited by Alcott, Thoreau, Margaret Fuller, and other neighbors of the Concord apple-trees and pines.

The histories of philosophy, despite the imposing names on their title pages, mislead us (to borrow the language of Frau Academia) with the specious clarity of a rationalizing schematismus. Here just what Socrates repudiated and contributed is numbered and sectioned and paragraphed with that illuminating precision which facilitates preparation for the final examination. The studies of Grote and of Zeller, based upon a wide erudition and developed with a philosophic grasp it were pedantry to commend, convey also a misleading impression of certainty, which the contradictory results of the German scholarship of the last twenty years (of Doering with his Xenophontic Socrates, of Joël who clings to Aristotle, of Roeck who picks his data from portions of Xenophon and from much indirect and elusive testimony in the attitude of contemporaries or in the comment of tradition) tend to destroy, without, however, furnishing any constructive substitution in which we can feel full confidence. The new critics confuse while they help[1]; and the day has gone by when even a popular essayist can content himself with compiling from the old. Tentatively and modestly I will set down my own opinions, which, I suppose, will differ from those of better men in lacking the organization and definitiveness that, though much to be desired, it is impossible for me with intellectual honesty to reach.

II.

What thought had been busied with before Socrates is, from the point of view of its dynamic contributions, far more important in the case of Plato in whom unite elements of the Eleatic, the Heraclitic, and the Pythagorean speculation, than in the case of his master, who is notorious for his break with the past. From the point of view of a crisis in the human intellect, however, it is necessary to make some mention of that thought here. A few words, then, with the emphasis on antecedents rather than on influence.

During a generation or two preceding Socrates, in the sea-washed colonies to east and west had developed a number of theories of universal nature, as free and large and intangible as the starry heavens and salt winds about them. The search for the universal explanation of things which had begun in the naive materialistic monisms of the Milesians, Thales, Anaximander, and Anaximines, as deductions from the apparent omnipresence of water or the atmospheric indefinite, turned, with that sudden acceleration which characterized Greek progress everywhere in the fifth century, very shortly to rational analysis of concept and sense-impression of the phenomenal world: The Eleatics of Magna Graecia, holding the primacy of reason over sense, discovered the antinomies which forced them to deny reality to change and plurality; the first of metaphysicians, they proclaimed the absolute and pointed a way to scepticism. The great Ephesian, though positing like the physicists of Miletus, a material principle, fire, as the substratum of the multitudinous visible universe, is chiefly notable for paradoxes, as analytically derived as those of the Eleatics, which forced him to deny ultimate and permanent reality to anything but the Logos, the law of change itself, and to affirm relativity, the absolute instability of all things, as the inherent logical implication of being—pleasure conditioned by pain, life by death, thesis by anti-thesis. In the eternal flux there can be no certainty of truth, and Heraclitus, too, points a way to scepticism.

Pythagoreanism, coming after all pretty close to the intellectual basis of the world-ground in its doctrine of numbers, however fantastically applied and involved in that hocus-pocus which so often has accompanied primitive mathematics, is an esoteric cult of religious mystics with liturgy and rites.

Empedocles of Agrigentum, imagining a cosmogony almost as mythical and arbitrary as that of Hesiod, yet peopling creation with eternal substances (earth, air, fire, and water) and eternal principles of cosmic energy (attraction and repulsion), is, from our point of view to-day, physicist rather than philosopher.[2] So too chiefly Anaxagoras of Athens, as far as we can judge, who taught infinite atoms and a universal mind-stuff.

Contemporary with Socrates, off at Abdera in Thrace, Democritus was teaching in numerous books now lost a mechanism of nature—atoms, motion, and the void—which, with modifications and extensions and a more elaborate terminology, is the physics and chemistry of to-day—or at least of yesterday.

These courageous efforts to master experience were all primarily directed outward. The challenge came from the majesty and mystery of the external universe. But in meeting it thought soon became conscious of its own mystery, and man himself became part of the problem. In the irremediable flux of Heraclitus and the cold atomism of Democritus men's minds tend to vanish into mere sensations differing for each: truth is as multiple as humanity; there is no universal principle of knowledge or thinking or conduct; man is the measure of all things. So Protagoras, the sophist. Meantime the later Eleatic, the sophist Gorgias, perhaps in half-jest, has pushed the dialectic reasoning of the school to the negation of being itself.

The path is open to absolute scepticism. The exploration of reason is ending in unreason. Speculation has thus far approached man from without; and that way madness lies. It must make a new start,—with man himself, man in his humble activities and daily round, irrespective of atoms clashing in the void and theories clashing in the brain. The philosophic implications in the simple mental life of an Athenian cobbler or saddler or armorsmith may bring us back to some conviction of permanence and certainty in thought. Thereafter it will be time enough to look again at the cosmos. Socrates, beginning and ending with man, ultimately saves Greek philosophy from self-slaughter. It is not for nothing that he is an Athenian.

But it is easy to present the situation too academically. Scepticism is troubling a few speculative heads. Their notions are abroad in Athens, imported over seas in parchment-rolls, well boxed from the damp salt air, or stalking the streets on the lips of the traveling professors. They are affecting not only the intellects of the abstracted, but doubtless the moral conduct of some of the active young men; but that Socrates in his new direction was consciously phrasing a philosophic task, or by saving philosophy was saving mankind, are propositions which distort both the larger mission of the sage and the relatively secondary importance of technically philosophic systems for the public health. From Socrates, as must be noted later, most subsequent Greek schools seem directly or indirectly to derive. But he was not aiming to reform philosophy. Nor could his re-formation of philosophy be a revolution—except in philosophy, a fairly negligible phase of human progress, if we take into account the few in any age who mull over its puzzles. No, Socrates's interest was in men and his aim to reform men; and, though he doubtless checkmated philosophic nihilism in more than one aggressive young dupe, he awoke to a sense of their ignorance and their heritage in the laws of the spirit many more, less sicklied o'er with the pale cast of thought than ailing from moral lethargy.

It is easy in another matter to misrepresent the situation. It is not as if philosophy and morals came to a standstill, say about 440, to await help from Socrates. Historians distort the chronology. Gorgias, Protagoras, and Anaxagoras were teaching in Athens long after that date, and scepticism itself may not have been full blown when Socrates began his public work. Direct evidence is lacking, but there is plausibility in the conjecture that his first conversations antedated even the first appearance of the sophists. Gorgias, for example, came to Athens in 427, only five years before Socrates was lampooned in the *Clouds*.

In still a third matter the situation may be misrepresented. Socrates, during his long life, was not the only teacher at Athens who held that the proper study of mankind is man. Protagoras himself laid the stress there, as the logical result of his own scepticism, and the later sophists seem to have occupied themselves entirely with intellectual conduct and with moral conduct, like Socrates, independent, as to the former, of cosmic speculations and, as to the latter, of mere tradition. They certainly also used the cross-examining method, associated now with Socrates. As with Socrates, their business was the education of youth.

But Socrates is a greater sophist—not simply because he tarries in Athens, and they wander from city to city; not only because he teaches in the Agora and they in private homes; not altogether because he gives and they sell instruction, nor even because his wisdom is humble that it knows no more and their knowledge sometimes proud that it learned so much—greater because of greater moral earnestness. There were honest sophists, although contemporary writers and later anecdotists testify that some even then were the unprincipled jugglers with reason that have given the name its long current and unfortunate association. But none except Socrates made truth and righteousness the be-all and the end-all. A greater sophist, also, it need not be added, because a greater intellect and a greater personality.

And now, if with a little more imagination than poor Wagner, the student has begun

> "Sich in den Geist der Zeiten zu versetzen,"

let him attempt

> "Zu schauen, wie vor uns ein weiser Mann gedacht."

III.

The thought of Socrates is implicit in his method. He was not a formal lecturer, as other sophists doubtless were at times, and as Plato and Aristotle were later. He talked, as all Athens was talking; he asked questions, and applied the answers to the business of further questions, as men had done before and have done ever since. He utilized on occasion the keener procedure of the disciplined mind, the dialectic which, applied earlier by Zeno the Eleatic to abstract matter and motion, etc., it was now the sophists' service to apply to human conduct—a dialectic which, as developed in the law-courts, was used *against* the examinee to ferret out his crime, but by Socrates *for* the examinee to ferret out his intellectual error. He shared, I repeat, his cross-examining method of instruction with the sophists, just as Jesus shared his parabolic instruction with the rabbis. But like Jesus, by a powerful originality he made a common device so much his own that we now connect it only with him.

Aristophanes, as we have seen, represents him as formally teaching his method, but this appears to be a wilful or reckless identification of Socrates with his fellow sophists who we know imparted the art of clever reasoning as a practical instrument, whereas Socrates, according to all other traditions, used it to impart truths beyond itself, teaching method merely by showing it in operation.

"He conducted discussion by proceeding step by step from one point of general agreement to another" (*Memorabilia,* IV, 6), and "by shredding off all superficial qualities laid bare the kernel of the matter" (*Memorabilia,* III, 2). He begins with the point of view of his interlocutor or opponent and, with an irony kindly or irritating according to circumstances and with frequent use of homely illustrations, leads him on inductively to one admission after another, until that interlocutor or opponent sees the implication in his own thought, that is, until he is face to face with himself as the unwitting possessor of a particular truth. Each man has within him truth, though as yet foetal and powerless to be born; Socrates comes calling himself the midwife. This was presumably his interpretation of the Delphic adage, "know thyself"; and, far from proud of his midwifery, he was "eager to cultivate a spirit of independence in others" (*Memorabilia,* IV, 7). He bored deeper into the strata of thought than the other sophists, and knew better its hidden caverns and springs; and, more than they, tapped it for living waters. The *intellectus sibi permissus,* "the intellect left to itself,"—the phrase is Bacon's,—the spontaneous reason of haphazard man he strove to make conscious and self-directive. His aim implied confidence in universals of the truth of which each individual partook, as well as confidence in human nature capable of self-salvation.

All our sources indicate that Socrates was unweary in his inquiries for . . . the What, the essential meaning of a thing. In Xenophon he appears discriminating, defining. The Platonic figure is presumably dramatically true to his intellectual attitude. The nub of the satire of the *Clouds* is rationalizing fanaticism corrupting the youth. And Aristotle says in a famous passage (*Metaphysics,* I, 6, 3) that has caused a deal of trouble: "Socrates discovered inductive discourse and the definition of general terms," in contrast, as the modern critics point out, to the mere grammatical distinctions of the sophists. But our critics have certainly exaggerated what were for Socrates simply short formularies of the factors to be examined, not logic-proof concepts of abstract philosophy. Socrates was not a *Begriffsphilosoph* and would have enjoyed the practical joke of Diogenes (of the school of Antisthenes, a disciple of the midwife), who, hearing (as the story goes) of Plato's definition of *homo sapiens* as a featherless biped, plucked a rooster and carried it over to the Academy as an example of Plato's "man."

IV.

But these short formularies of the factors to be examined were of prime importance. Socrates emphasized the rational, the cognitive, aspect of virtue, as no other teacher: . . . "He made the virtues knowledges" (Aristotle, *Magna Moralia,* I, 1), and since our first historian of philosophy recurs to the theory at length a dozen times (in all three *Ethics*), to explain and refute it, with that modernity and subtilty that forever astonishes us in

> "Il maestro di color che sanno,"

we must accept it as true at least to one side of Socrates's thought. Virtue is knowledge. In a sense: "To be pious is to *know* what is due to the gods; to be just is to *know* what is due to men; to be courageous is to *know* what is to be feared and what is not; to be temperate is to *know* how to use what is good and avoid what is evil" (*Encycl. Brit.*).

Various comments difficult to organize crowd upon us for expression. What of this dynamic relation between right thinking and right conduct, between ignorance and evil? How did Socrates arrive at the idea? How far did he admit its modification by other factors in human nature? Has it an element of truth?

The idea, in the first place, were a witness to the character of Socrates, whom a noble serenity of reason dominated like an irrefragable god. It were, too, an idea typically Ionic, Athenian, sprung from that stock which stressed the [*logos*] of life, even as the ideal of the Doric (Sparta) was the [*enkrateia*], the [*erga*] (deeds).

Socrates saw the actual identity of knowing and being in the theoretical sciences: to know geometry is to be a geometer. He may not have appreciated the difference of aim in the practical arts. He may have said that to know medicine is to be a physician, and thus have construed conduct itself as the science-art of life, so that knowing virtue was the same as being virtuous, and he may not have sufficiently perceived that the aim of every theoretic science is included *within* that science, while the aim of every practical art is some good *beyond* that art itself.

However, I do not care to push the Aristotelian critique further, as my imagination is haunted by an all but inscrutable chuckle of Socrates that yet seems to say: "This great man's subtilty and system takes the old beggar too solemnly. And I didn't reckon in the irrational part of the soul . . . ? And the will being in my view subservient to thought, the result is determinism? And was the market-place, then, such a poorly equipped laboratory that my researches left me so ignorant of the twists and starts and explosions of human nature? And will he deny the larger implications for systematic thought (if he must make me a system) which may be read out of my dealings with men?"

Granted that Socrates in speech and practice proceeded from the proposition to know is to be, applied specifically to conduct; granted that like every new and great thought, like the Copernican astronomy, like Biblical criticism, it was at first formulated too absolutely; granted that Socrates was not a theoretic psychologist and that indeed the psychology of the will and the emotions was not very extensively developed even till long after Aristotle; granted that life is forever in advance of all speculation upon it and that the first serious speculations on morals may as such have been an inadequate or inconsistent phrasing of impulses, motives, and ethical stimulus obvious even in the veriest honey-smeared brat screaming under his mother's sandal in an Athenian alley-way: it is yet impossible to square the thought and service of Socrates entirely with Aristotle's report; it is yet impossible to identify Socrates entirely with the Socrates of the text-books.

The fear of the Lord is the beginning of wisdom, said the adoring Hebrew; to know the right, as implicit in thy nature, is the beginning of wisdom, doubtless said the quizzical Greek: each in his own tongue. Knowledge is the *sine qua non:* not following a Pythagorean ritual, not following the Attic sires, not in itself following the laws of the state, but ethical insight. Socrates preached the self-reliance of an individual moral vision which was yet founded in universal man.

After the insight, what? For a finely balanced soul, in a sense, nothing. Insight merges into conduct; the initial readjustments of knowledge become, if not considered too curiously by the analytic psychologist, the readjustments of action; there is no fight pending with the world, the flesh, or the devil; he sees and he forthwith is what he sees. This was, I think, Socrates's ideal man. Socrates made less than we do of character up-builded by struggle and of the glories of doing one's duty against the grain. He was a Greek; we are Teutons with a Hebraic education.

Note, however, the condition: "for a finely balanced soul." Self-control, balance, poise, is the cardinal Socratic virtue. When present, moral insight is moral conduct. But more than that, its presence is practically identical with moral insight as well. "Between wisdom and balance of soul he drew no distinction"— . . . (*Memorabilia,* III, 9)—is Xenophon's comment, and not too much stress is to be laid on the fact that his word is . . . (wisdom), not . . . (knowledge). And in a neighboring passage, "He said that justice, moreover, and all other virtue is wisdom."

Is, then, complete insight itself possible without this balance? If we take Xenophon absolutely, apparently not. Wrong conduct is either blindness or madness, i. e., either failure of insight or lack of soul balance; but these are practically two aspects of the same thing. Balance of soul, insight, right conduct, is the Socratic manhood, the not entirely mysterious three-in-one of this pagan anthropologist.

But what of the avowed situation of Ovid's *Medea,* and of so many others less damned to fame—

> "Video meliora, proboque:
> Deteriora sequor"?

Would Socrates have denied the major?—Presumably he would first have questioned it; but often enough he was face to face with gifted men, like Alcibiades, who knew right and did wrong, with intelligent but vicious humanity where the cure, if any, could not be alone merely more intellectuality. He believed in training soul and body to self-mastery, not only as right conduct in itself but as the prerequisite for right thinking and right conduct (cf. *Memorabilia,* IV, 5). This is patent to any one who reads between the lines of our sources, and has perceived that Socrates's identification of different factors, is, if anything more than an insistence on the primary importance of moral cognition, but an immortal hyperbole of an original mind, not busied with a formal system, and not bothered by its inconsistencies, as when perhaps he said "courageous men are those who have knowledge to cope with terrors and dangers well and nobly," the adverbs seeming to imply the recognition of traits of character antecedent to the knowledge.

He recognized, though he may never have formulated, lack of self-control, insight, and conduct, the facts of temperament and environment, without wavering in practice from his belief in the relative teachability of virtue analogous to the teaching of a trade or art. He does not, however, seem to have valued over-much teaching through the emotions. There are hints that he more than once stirred the emulous heart by noble examples cited, but the oft mentioned enthusiasm of his listeners was roused usually either by his sweet reasonableness or the unplanned and unmeditated effect of his own brave and kindly personality. Of the blazing passion, in plea or threat, of Mohammed and the Hebrew prophets, or of the austere yet plangent appeal of the loving Jesus there is not a trace. There are many different voices for the schooling of man.

The new pedagogy stands quite across the world from where Socrates stood. With its experiments on the ethical emotions of cats and dogs, its statistics of innocent nursery prayers and depravities, its questionnaires on the moral agitations at puberty, and its roll-calls of public pensioners in Sing Sing or Fort Leavenworth, it has all but demonstrated the negligibility of knowing as a factor in virtue. And the parlor-philosopher, calling Sunday afternoon, shakes his head and assures me there is no connection between education and morality. Sad. And true, possibly, if by knowing we mean knowing mathematics and by education education in linguistics or the new pedagogy; verbiage, if we mean knowing moral values. The intellectual is still fundamental, and great character is still impossible without just thought as a big block in the underpinning. Meantime the common sense of mankind is rather with Socrates at bottom than with the new pedagogy, unconsciously testifying something of its unshaken viewpoint in countless familiar turns of speech: "*Know* the right and do it;" "You ought to *know* better;" "Poor fellow, he didn't *know* how disgraceful his actions were;" "What could you expect from a man who never had a chance to *know* the ideals of good citizenship;" "You're wrong, can't you *see* it?" etc., etc., all of which adumbrate the cognitive (without psychologizing it away from the imagination) and neglect the emotional altogether, as dynamic for conduct.

Kant founded the moral life in the good will; Socrates in right thinking. Yet each implies the factor made paramount by the other: Kant says act so that the maxim of thy conduct is fit to become universal law and implies the rationalizing, generalizing, judging, knowing mind; Socrates says a man without self-control is little better than the beasts, and implies that energy of soul to which modern psychology gives the name will. A worthy moral life is impossible without both, but the romantic ethical tendencies of to-day need the propaedeutic of Socrates more than of Kant. The good will we have always with us, giving often enough, with ghastly best wishes, unwittingly a serpent for a fish and a stone for bread; but the intelligence to see the practical bearings of conduct and to discriminate between higher and lower ideals is too often lacking—to the dwarfing of the individual and to the confusion of society. The fool in Sill's poem (which goes deep) prayed not for the good will, but for wisdom; and therefore the less fool he.

Socrates associated . . . "virtue," with some further ideas more prominent in his thought than would be presumed from the brief mention that can here be made of them.

He was, I believe, an incorrigible utilitarian. The measure of any thing's worth was to him in its adaptation to use. But after all, the crux is in the content of use; and Socrates recognized only noble uses. Reason as we will, we cannot reason away his implicit idealism: such and such conduct is useful—for what—for making you useful to the state, a brave soldier? for making you worth while to yourself, self-respecting? "But what's the use?" We cannot go far without standing before the mystery of the approving or condemning moral consciousness itself. Socrates appears never to have thought the matter out; nor need we just here. In spite of his rationalistic bent, he accepted as instinctively as most men the obligation to the ideal.

He preached companionship; and boasted himself to be both lover and the pander too. "I am an adept in love's lore". . . . the disciples "will not suffer me day or night to leave them, forever studying to learn love-charms and incantations at my lips." These words are found not in Plato's *Symposium,* but in the prosaic narrative of Xenophon, whose placidity in assuring us in another passage that "all the while it was obvious the going forth of his soul was not toward excellence of body in the bloom of beauty, but rather toward faculties of the soul unfolding in virtue," is a good indication that we have here an element of the historic Socrates. But friendship was founded on character: "In whatsoever you desire to be esteemed good, endeavor to be good" (*Memorabilia,* II, 6); to be a good friend, you must be a good man. Love was also fellow-service: the good friend tried to make his friend better. On the other hand, it was useful to acquire friends—they were the best possessions. The politic utilitarian peeps out again. But useful for what?—for the cult of generous helpers, for the freemasons of the Good. We come round again and again to the center of the Socratic utilitarianism which measured finally the useful things in the moral realm by their usefulness for the ideal manhood. The term has here little in common with its force in modern philosophy, though modern utilitarians have been too ready to exclaim, "Lo, he has become as one of us."

Socrates would not have been a Greek if his ethics had not had a social and political reference. Ideal manhood and ideal citizenship would have been for practical teaching one thing to him. He would have been hugely impressed with the adroit patience and clever tinkering amid loneliness and deprivation of Robinson Crusoe; he would have admitted doubtless that the brooding, skinclad sailor was not without some insight and some self-control which is of virtue; but for Socrates he would have lacked both the main opportunities and the main ends of good conduct: a state of fellow men. Thus the Athenian stands in almost brutal contrast to those gentle hermits of the inner life who have in times past peopled the caves of Egypt and the crags of the Himalayas.

This is clear for instance in the emphasis he seems to have put upon the ideal of a leader, the man best equipped to manage something, whether the drilling of a chorus for the theater, or the marshalling of soldiers into battle, or the ruling of a commonwealth.

Some aspects of this ideal are, to be sure, extra-ethical. The Greek [*aretē*] means human excellence, *Tüchtigkeit,* efficiency, with or without what we would call an ethical connotation, and it illustrates that differing focus of thought, that differing idea-group, that differing line of cleavage that so often strikes the student of a foreign tongue. I have not hesitated, however, heretofore, to translate it "virtue," for it is its aspect of moral efficiency that is so prominent in Socrates, though its absolute sense of simple efficiency doubtless tended in his thinking to specious analogies. Our word "good" offers a modern parallel, both in its double sense and in its sometimes ambiguous and misleading use in thought.

Socrates would not have been a Greek if he had not emphasized the sanctity of the sovereign laws as a guiding principle of conduct. The Greeks often spoke as if the state were the end of man; that is, as if man received his justification only in so far as he contributed to its perfection. That a state is but the wise communal means to opportunity, variety, unfoldment, manhood, of the only earthly reality that counts, individual human beings, is scarcely the point of departure of Plato's *Republic* or even of Aristotle's *Politics,* but is the result of a long development in political science, fascinating, but irrelevant here. Just how far Socrates failed to see it as we do, we have no certain knowledge. It is, however, on several grounds, to be confidently presumed that he derived the sanction of the civil law from justice, and not as is often declared, justice from the law. In the corrupt and shifting politics of Athens there were laws which he condemned and deliberately disobeyed in the interests of higher laws. And he would have taken courageously by the arm the Sophoclean Antigone, as she determined to bury her brother Polyneices in spite of the state decree, and have said, "Thou art right, my child; indeed,

> "'The life of these laws is not of to-day,
> Or yesterday; but from all time, and, lo,
> Knoweth no man when first they were
> put forth.'"

V.

That Socrates conceived the laws of right thinking and doing as organic and not statutory, as not imposed from without but as implicated in the nature of the organism and as universal as man, seems clear from the general tendency and headway of his teachings. A ship may tack more than once in its course, but we measure the meaning and purpose of the voyage correctly only when we have checked up the casual deviations in a more comprehensive cartography. His conception of virtue has the transcendental implication; it roots in a beyond; conceptually, in the universality of the ideal; categorically, in his naive and unexamined assumption of man's sense of obligation to the ideal when discovered.

This is the thoroughfare from ethics to religion. When the soul, finally conscious of that transcendental implication (though it be named more simply, or named not at all), is awake with rejoicing or dismay to the realization that virtue streams ultimately from the shining foreheads of the gods, it seems inevitably to reach out with trust or prayer. Nor is the essential attitude altered if for his baffled spirit the Divine Singular or Plural merges into the Infinite Mystery that rebukes our petty vocabularies. There is no other highway. The philosophic reason that, examining the transcendental bearings of logic and nature, arrives at a world-ground, arrives only at the intellectual last, at the speculative satisfaction, which, though it may bulwark religion, can scarcely compel it. The feeling of physical helplessness or dependence or terror, the suggestion of spirit-things from dream or hallucination, or eery winds or nodding tree, may issue in beliefs with incantations and petitions and burnt offerings, reachings out to a Superior or a Host, but this is religion only in the

Lucretian sense, denying often enough even the majesty of man himself—

> "Tantum religio potuit suadere malorum."

A not ignoble morality is possible, uncompanioned by the reaching out which merges it with religion; but religion (apart from anthropological investigation) gives over not only its dignity and its beauty, but even its meaning if sundered from exalted morality.

If to Socrates was not revealed the transcendental implication of his life, if Socrates reached not out for the justification and sustenance of his ethic towards a Divine, then Socrates, though at the temple door, and though a servant there who worked righteousness and thus, according to bluff and honest Peter, also acceptable to Him, was still not a teacher of religion. His character, his service would remain, lofty memorial of humanity, lofty witness of a god unknown; but he were still not a religious mind. This *if* we have yet to consider.

It becomes more and more plausible that the fatal indictment is rooted in observed fact: "Socrates is guilty of not worshiping the gods whom the city worships." If he had been initiated into the Eleusinian mysteries at that time newly popular, his apologists would have risen forthwith against the dicasts. Plato's *Apology* practically dodged this charge of the indictment. Aristophanes, years before, had formulated it, and we cannot any longer throw Aristophanes peremptorily out of court as a mere irresponsible buffoon in an ugly temper. Satire makes no appeal unless it phrases a common belief: there would be nothing fetching about a satire on Roosevelt as an atheist, or on Emerson as a hunter and rough-rider, except as a cheaply comic inversion of well-known habits and traits, and Aristophanes was hardly perpetrating that sort of jest. His satire on the sordidness of the schoolhouse was founded on the fact of the poor and mean estate of Socrates's person; his satire on the Socratic speculations was founded in the fact of Socrates's perpetual rationalizing; his satire on the corruption of youth on the fact of Socrates's influencing young men to think new thoughts unprescribed by the elders; and his satire on Socrates's irreligion must likewise have been founded on fact—misunderstood fact, possibly, but fact misunderstood only as most of Athens may have misunderstood it. The Socrates of Plato, perhaps, helps us little; but it is to be observed that his remarks on dreams, oracles, and the gods have an elusive playfulness or poetry, pointing, if pointing at all beyond Plato, to a mind rather mischievously at ease in Zion, but not hostile to contemporary beliefs only because so far above them; and that his beautiful prayer to "Pan and ye other gods who frequent this spot" asks, quite contrary to popular petition, "in the first place to be good within"; and that the nearer Plato's Socrates seems to approach historic reality the more his religious allusions approach the indefinite "Divine," and the more eloquent is the expression of the moral law. The movement of thought with which Socrates was most nearly associated was away from the folk religion. Socrates was so much with Euripides, the infidel poet of the Enlightenment, that rumor accused him of dramatic collaboration. The chorus at the end of the *Frogs*—a satire on that poet—sings with meaning: "Hail to him who [unlike Euripides] neither keeps company nor gossips with Socrates." And, again, the keen intelligence of Socrates, as we have tried to analyze him, consorts awkwardly with the popular Olympians.

Against all this, we have the explicit testimony of the *Memorabilia:* Socrates was the most orthodox son of the state religion; the pillar and deacon of the church; the ambling odor of sanctity, now closeted with this priest, now with that, running about from altar to altar with incense and winecup or telling his beads to every saint in the calendar. We share Xenophon's own puzzlement that the state could have condemned to death such a simple-minded old gentleman for impiety.

But this was not the man they condemned. As suggested in the first chapter, it was almost a formula with Xenophon, when he admired a man (and he had in excess the goodly gift of admiration) to extol him for the piety and pious practices which played a dominant part in the eulogist's own life. That he deliberately grafted these domestic pieties upon Socrates is impossible; if he had conceived Socrates as the impious neglecter or defamer of the gods, he would have been the last to attach himself to the man or to rise in his defense. But that he absurdly misconstrued him seems patent. Socrates shared, as no other teacher, the life of his city; and the religious rites were so closely associated with folk-habits that he may well have attended them from time to time in the satisfaction of the social instinct of man. He may well not have sloughed off some deep-rooted ancestral prejudices: even Emerson raised his hands with the dismay of all his Puritan sires when he discovered the children in the house playing battledore and shuttlecock one Sabbath morn. He may well have used often enough the current coin of speech, in Greek, as in all languages, full of conventional religious phrases. But it was not alone in whatever unconscious relations Socrates may have maintained to the state religion that Xenophon misconstrued him. The profounder interests and ideas and temperament of Socrates he equally misread. Socrates visited everybody and studied everywhere: but he was not necessarily more a hierophant for visiting a seer than he was a shoemaker for visiting a cobbler. "When any one came seeking for help which no human wisdom could supply, he would counsel him to give heed to divination" (*Memorabilia,* IV, 7): the Socratic irony Xenophon presumably never half mastered. And, again, if Xenophon had asked him if he believed in Zeus and

Athene and Apollo, he would doubtless have said yes, without hypocrisy, but also without explaining the ethnic period which lay between Xenophon's meaning of belief and his own. I myself believe in those resplendent deities. The fact is that religious narrowness always naively interprets the religious life of another by its own, unless kept back by clubs and spears. Give it the salute of mere human recognition, and it claims you for its sect. I have heard of an old lady who was moved by the orthodoxy of "that devout man, Mr. Gibbon." Joseph Cook, after an impertinent pilgrimage to Concord, announced so blatantly his conversion of Emerson that the family finally caused a printed denial to be circulated. That evangelist's methods were sometimes disingenuous; but here he seems merely to have fallen victim to his fatuity. The apostle probably asked: "Mr. Emerson, do you believe in sin? in salvation? in the Saviour? in rewards and punishments? in the Scriptures?" And the patient heathen as probably nodded a winsome assent of infinite detachment. I used to see at Cambridge my revered teacher William James crossing over every morning at nine o'clock to the brief chapel exercises in the yard, and have heard him both condemned and ridiculed by students who equally misconceived the simplicity and depth of that analytic yet brooding mind.

But we are approaching a point of view. If Xenophon cannot be taken literally, he adumbrates a positive truth. If Socrates was not religious in the folk-sense, he was religious in a higher sense. He did recognize the transcendental implication. Even Xenophon now and then seems to have caught his larger phrase: "His formula of prayer was simple—Give me that which is best for me." And it is difficult to imagine Plato making an absolute atheist even the dramatic protagonist of an ethical philosophy in which the transcendental implication is consciously conceived as fundamental. But much further it seems impossible to go. Socrates recognized the divine foundation and sanction of the moral law, whether he ever uttered the argument from design so rhetorically developed by Xenophon or not. But the rest is silence. Whether he held to one divine being, as is not unlikely; and whether immortality was more than the high hope of the *Apology,* as seems doubtful—we cannot report. An early tradition tells of a Hindu conversing with Socrates (and it is not historically impossible that some soldier from the Indus, impressed into the Persian armies, remained in Greece, as exile or slave, after the defeat). And he said, "Tell me, Socrates, what is the substance of your teaching?" "Human affairs." "But you cannot know human affairs if you don't know first the divine." Socrates, though no Oriental, may have assented in his own fashion. Yet the tradition hints at the true situation. He proclaimed the nobility of man, rather than the decrees of a god. He found the divine written in the human heart and brain, not on tablets of stone in the mountains. He came with no avowed revelation; he burned with no wrath against the folk-religion; he inaugurated no specifically religious reform. He was a messenger, a ministrant, a saviour, whose ethical idealism in word and conduct had its conscious religious aspect; but he was not primarily a religious leader. Mohammed passed from Allah down to man; it was man who led Socrates on to Zeus.

Yet, the indictment went on to accuse him of introducing gods of his own. Of this there is no evidence in the sense apparently intended. Plato makes Meletus call Socrates during the trial "a complete atheist"; and, when Meletus hung up the indictment he was either wilfully lying or but stating an assumed corollary to what was possibly to him the sum of atheism—denial of the city's gods.[3] Or the historic kernel may be to seek in Socrates's modes of thinking and speaking about the Divine. What's in a name? Everything for popular thought. Emerson's "Brahma" is to many people either a meaningless or a blasphemous poem; change the name to "God" and they would paste it in their hymn-books. Describe with all science and beauty the life-habits and appearance of a flower, and then halt in a momentary slip of memory, and your amateur botanist supposes you an ignoramus because you can't name it. For most people a rose, if named *Symplocarpus foetidus,* would *not* smell as sweet. If the originality of Socrates ever invented new names for divine things, that would have been sufficient grounds for his enemies to suspect him of inventing new divinities; just as his use at other times of familiar names seems to have been a good ground for such friends as Xenophon to suppose him orthodox. For the rest, to me this specification in the indictment is but one more proof that the Socratic message of righteousness was often enough verbally associated with the transcendental implication. For, when we say that Socrates was not primarily a religious teacher, we do not forget that he was put to death partially on a charge of religious teaching; the inconsistency is merely formal.

Xenophon refers the charge to a misunderstanding of the *daimonion* which, according to common tradition, Socrates often mentioned as his warning voice or sign. Whether this explanation be in line with a hint in the preceding paragraph or not, may be left to the reader. We are forced, however, to examine the phenomenon in itself. What was the *daimonion* . . . ? The question is double: what was it to Socrates? what is it for us? Though Socrates seems to have treated it, or pretended to treat it, somewhat like a familiar spirit or good genius, the word has properly no personal or theological meaning. Euripides and Thucydides, both men of the Enlightenment, use it of that which, given by fate, man must adjust himself toward and to. It was not synonymous with "demon"; Cicero rightly translated it "divinum quiddam" (*De Divinatione,* I, 54, 122). To Socrates it may have been a literal voice, sounding in the inner ear. Not alone visionaries like Joan of Arc and Swedenborg have heard voices: Pascal and Luther heard them, though the former was the shrewdest intellect and the latter the soundest stomach of his age, and both men rooted in solid earth. If so, we turn the problem over to the psychologists—without, however, implying the neurotic decadence that becomes the business of the alienist. And they may name it a manifestation of the transcendental ego, or an instance of double personality, or an objectification of an unusually developed instinct of antipathy or of an abhorrent conscience, a non-rational residuum in the most rationalistic of men. Or to Socrates it may have been but a playful mode of referring to his disapproval of whatnots of conduct, ethical or otherwise, a disapproval reasoned out or immediately felt. The suggestion, tentative as it is, is still not an arbitrary assimilation of an ancient mind to modern rationalism. We know the ironic habit of Socrates, ironic not only toward others, but, with that deeper wisdom, ironic toward himself. We know he was given to playful exaggeration, especially to quizzical tropes. His pedagogic method he called midwifery; his faculty for friendship and for bringing friends together he referred to as incantations or pandering, using the most erotic expressions, which, in literal use, referred to things often even from the Greek point of view immoral; so too he seems to have spoken of his mantic, his oracular power, meaning simply foresight or premonition. The conception of the mind and temper of Socrates to which I have come inclines me to number the *daimonion* also among the tropes.

Again, if we take the *daimonion* literally, what of the Dog? The Platonic Socrates is found enforcing his asseverations by a blasphemous canine oath, which sounds like a historic reminiscence and may hint at another source of the charge of impiety and new divinities. "By the Dog they would" (*Phaedo*); "By the Dog, Gorgias, there will be a great deal of discussion before we get at the truth of all this" (*Gorgias*); "Not until, by the Dog, as I believe, he had simply learned by heart the entire discourse" (*Phaedrus*); and "By the Dog" he swears again in the *Charmides,* in the *Lysis,* and in the *Republic.* By what Dog? Molossian hound or Xanthippe's terrier? or some Egyptian deity that barks, not bellows? or Cerberus? More like. Strange and gruesome idolatry, which troubled some patristic admirers of the old pagan, as much as the cock his dying gasp bade sacrifice to Asclepius.

Notes

[1] And a year after this was written, A.E. Taylor published his *Varia Socratica,* Oxford, 1911.

[2] See *The Fragments of Empedocles,* by William Ellery Leonard, Open Court Publishing Co., Chicago.

[3] But cf. Taylor, *Varia Socratica,* Chapter I, "The Impiety of Socrates," and the footnote on page 54 of this essay.

Leonard Nelson (lecture date 1922)

SOURCE: "The Socratic Method," in *Socratic Method and Critical Philosophy: Selected Essays*, translated by Thomas K. Brown III, Yale University Press, 1949, pp. 1-40.

[*In the following essay, originally delivered as a lecture in 1922, Nelson discusses the Socratic method, defining it as "the art of teaching not philosophy but philosophizing, the art not of teaching about philosophers but of making philosophers of the students." Nelson goes on to offer examples of how the method works in practice and notes some difficulties of applying the Socratic method.*]

As a faithful disciple of Socrates and of his great successor Plato, I find it rather difficult to justify my acceptance of your invitation to talk to you about the Socratic method. You know the Socratic method as a method of teaching philosophy. But philosophy is different from other subjects of instruction; in Plato's own words: "It does not at all admit of verbal expression like other studies, but as a result of continued application to the subject itself and communion therewith, it is brought to birth in the soul on a sudden, as light that is kindled by a leaping spark, and thereafter it nourishes itself."[1]

I therefore find myself in a quandary, not unlike that of a violinist who, when asked how he goes about playing the violin, can of course demonstrate his art but cannot explain his technique in abstract terms.

The Socratic method, then, is the art of teaching not philosophy but philosophizing, the art not of teaching about philosophers but of making philosophers of the students. So, in order to give a true idea of the Socratic method, I should halt my discourse right here and, instead of lecturing to you, take up with you a philosophical problem and deal with it according to the Socratic method. But what did Plato say? Only "continued application to the subject itself and communion therewith" kindle the light of philosophical cognition.

Despite the short time at my disposal I shall nevertheless venture a description of the Socratic method and attempt through words to bring home to you its meaning and significance. I justify this compromise by limiting my task, the sole object of my exposition being to direct your attention to this method of teaching and thereby to promote an appreciation of it.

A person who knows no more about the Grand Inquisitor's speech in Dostoevsky's novel, *The Brothers Karamazov,* than that it is a most magnificent discussion of a fundamental ethical problem, knows little enough about it; yet that little will make him more disposed to read the speech attentively. Similarly, whoever looks at the memorial tablet here in the former Physics Institute [Göttingen] that tells of the first electric telegraph invented by Gauss and Wilhelm Weber and how it served to connect that institute with the astronomical observatory will at least feel inclined to follow up the history of this invention with greater reverence. And so I hope that in presenting my subject I, too, may arouse your interest in the significant and, for all its simplicity, profound method that bears the name of the Athenian sage to whom we owe its invention.

A stepchild of philosophy, slighted and rejected, the Socratic method has survived only in name beside its more popular older sister, the more insinuating and more easily manipulated dogmatic method.

You may perhaps suspect me of a personal inclination for the younger of the two sisters. And, indeed, I freely confess that the longer I enjoy her company, the more I am captivated by her charms; so that it has become a matter of chivalry with me to lead her back to life who has been forgotten and pronounced dead, and to win her here that place of honor hitherto reserved for the wanton sister who, though dead at heart, has time and again appeared all decked out.

Let me add, however—and this much I hope to demonstrate to you today—that it is not blind partiality that actuates me; it is the inner worth of her whose appearance is so plain that attracts me to her. But, you say, her sad fate—being disdained by the overwhelming majority of philosophers—could not have been undeserved and it is therefore idle to try to breathe new life into her by artificial means.

In reply I shall not resort to the general proposition that history shows no pre-established harmony between merit and success, for, indeed, the success or failure of a *method* as a means to an end is a very real test of its value.

However, a fair judgment requires consideration of a preliminary question, namely, whether a particular science is so far advanced that the solution of its problems is sought in a prescribed way; in other words, whether generally valid methods are recognized in it.

In mathematics and in the natural sciences based on it this question of method was long ago decided affirmatively. There is not a mathematician who is not familiar with and who does not employ the progressive method. All serious research in the natural sciences makes use of the inductive method. In fact, method enjoys in these sciences a recognition so unchallenged and matter of course that the students following its guidance are often hardly conscious of the assured course of their researches. All dispute about methods here turns exclusively on their reliability and fruitfulness. If, in this field, a method is dropped or retains merely a historic interest, the presumption is justified that it can offer nothing more to research.

It is quite otherwise, however, in a science where everyone still claims the right to make his own laws and rules, where methodological directives are evaluated *ab initio* as temporally or individually conditioned, subject only to historical appraisal. With luck one method may find favor and for a time determine the direction of future work. But in such a science errors, concomitants of every scientific achievement, do not inspire efforts in the already established direction to correct the defects; errors here are looked upon as faults of construction and must give way to entirely new structures, which in their turn all too soon meet the same fate.

What passes for philosophical science is still in this youthful stage of development. In this judgment I have the support of Windelband, the renowned historian of philosophy. He tells us that "even among the philosophers who claim a special method for their science"—and by no means all philosophers make such a claim—"there is not the least agreement concerning this 'philosophical method.'"[2]

This conclusion appears the more depressing in view of his previous admission that it is impossible to establish a constant criterion even for the very subject matter of philosophy.

In view of this, one wonders what such philosophers really think of their science. At any rate, in this anarchy the question is left open whether the disesteem into which a philosophical theory falls in itself proves that the theory is scientifically worthless. For how can we expect to judge the scientific value or lack of value of a philosophical achievement when generally valid criteria for passing judgment do not exist?

Now, it is not that the diversity of the *results* made it difficult for philosophers to set up a systematic guide to their science. On the contrary, the great philosophical truths have been from the beginning the common property of all the great thinkers. Here, then, a common starting point was provided. But the verification of these results according to unequivocal rules that preclude arbitrariness and even the mere formulation of the pertinent methodological task with definiteness and precision, both these tasks in the general interest of philosophy have thus far been given so little attention that we must not be surprised that the devoted efforts of a few men to satisfy this interest have proved in vain. True, the lifelong work of Socrates and of Kant in the service of this methodological task has earned immeasurable historical glory. But, as far as its revolutionary significance for the establishment of philosophy as a science is concerned, it has remained sterile and ineffectual.

Twice in its history there was some prospect of getting philosophy out of its groping stage and onto the certain path of science. The ancient world punished the first courageous attempt with death: Socrates was condemned as a corrupter of youth. The modern world disdains to execute the heretic. It has passed sentence by "going beyond" Kant—to let Windelband speak once more.[3]

But there is no need for labored interpretation to appreciate the significance of these two men. They themselves stressed the meaning of their endeavors, explicitly and unceasingly. As everyone knows, Socrates constructed no system. Time and again he admitted his not-knowing. He met every assertion with an invitation to seek the ground of its truth. As the *Apology* shows, he "questioned and examined and cross-examined"[4] his fellow citizens, not to convey a new truth to them in the manner of an instructor but only to point out the path along which it might be found.

His ethical doctrine, in so far as this designation is appropriate to his inquiries, is based on the proposition that virtue can be taught, or, to put it in more precise terms, that ethics is a science. He did not develop this science because the initial question, *How* do I gain knowledge about virtue? continued to absorb him. He held fast to this initial question. He accepted the absence of fruitful results with composure, without a trace of skepticism as to the soundness of his method, unshakable in the conviction that with his question he was, in spite of everything, on the only right road.

All subsequent philosophy, with the sole exception of Plato, stands helpless before that memorable fact. Plato took over and adhered to the method of Socrates, even after his own researches had carried him far beyond the results reached by his master. He adopted it with all its imperfections. He failed to eliminate its weaknesses and inflexibilities, surely not because of reverence for the memory of his teacher but because he could not overcome these defects. Like Socrates, he was guided by a feeling for truth. Having dealt so boldly with the content of the Socratic philosophy that philosophical philologists are still quarreling about what is Socratic in Plato's doctrine and what Platonic, he turned this boldness into homage by putting all his own discoveries into the mouth of his great teacher. But he paid Socrates even greater homage by clothing these discoveries in the uneven, often dragging, often digressive form of the Socratic dialogue, burdening his own teachings with his teacher's faults. In this manner, of course, he safeguarded the yet unmined treasure and thus gave posterity the opportunity of taking possession of it anew and of developing its riches.

But in vain. Today, after two thousand years, opinion on Socrates is more uncertain and more divided than ever. Over against the judgment of an expert like Joel, that Socrates was "the first and perhaps the last quite genuine, *quite pure* philosopher,"[5] there is Heinrich Maier's statement "that Socrates has been labeled as what he quite certainly was *not,* a philosopher."[6]

This difference of opinion has its roots in the inadequacy of the criticism, which still exercises its ingenuity on the conclusions of Socrates' philosophy. But as these conclusions were handed down only indirectly and perhaps were never even given definite form by Socrates, they remain exposed to the most contradictory interpretations. Where criticism touches on the method, it either praises trivialities or assigns the value of the Socratic method exclusively to the personality of Socrates, as shown in the opinion voiced by Wilamowitz in his *Plato:* "The Socratic method without Socrates is no more than a pedagogy that, aping how some inspired spiritual leader clears his throat and spits, bottles his alleged method and then imagines it is dispensing the water of life."[7]

If Socrates' philosophy, lively as it was and rooted in concrete problems, found no emulators, it is little wonder then that the truth content of Kant's far more abstract methodological investigations failed to be understood and adopted—except by those few who comprehended his doctrine and developed it further, but who in their turn were pushed completely into the background by the irresistible *Zeitgeist* and passed over by history. The preconditions were lacking for the realization that Kant's critical method was the resumption of Socratic-Platonic philosophizing, and for the acceptance of the *Critique of Pure Reason* as a "treatise on the method," which its author, according to his own words, intended it to be.[8]

In addition to this treatise on method, Kant produced a system. He enriched the broad domain of philosophy with an abundance of fruitful results. It was these results that became the subject of controversy; but the hope of a satisfactory settlement was bound to remain illusory as long as no attempt was made to retrace the creative path by which Kant had reached his conclusions. Dogmatism remained dominant, more triumphant than ever in the erection of arbitrary systems that vied with one another in bizarreness and estranged public interest altogether from the sober and critical philosophizing of the Kantian period. Such fragments of Kant's results as were transplanted to this alien soil could not thrive there and maintained only an artificial existence, thanks to a fancy for the history of philosophy that displaced philosophy itself.

Why is it, asked Kant, that nothing is being done to prevent the "scandal" which, "sooner or later, is sure to become obvious even to the masses, as the result of the disputes in which metaphysicians . . . without critique inevitably become involved."[9]

It is manifestly the aim of every science to verify its judgments by reducing them to more general propositions, which themselves must be made certain. We can then proceed from these principles to the erection of the scientific system through logical inference. However difficult this may be in its details, in its essence it is accomplished in all sciences by the same method, that of progressive reasoning. The methodological problems are encountered in every science where the regress from the particular to the general has to be accomplished, where the task is to secure the most fundamental propositions, the most general principles.

The brilliant development of the science of mathematics and its universally acknowledged advance are explained by the fact that its principles—ignoring for the moment the problems of axiomatics—are easily grasped by the consciousness. They are intuitively clear and thus completely evident, so evident that, as Hilbert recently remarked on this same platform, mathematical comprehension can be forced on everyone. The mathematician does not even have to perform the laborious regress to these principles. He is free to start from arbitrarily formed concepts and go on confidently to propositions; in short, he can immediately proceed systematically, and in this sense dogmatically. He can do so because the fact that his concepts lend themselves to construction is a criterion of their reality, a sure indication that his theory does not deal with mere fictions.

The natural sciences, on their part, do not enjoy this advantage. The laws underlying natural phenomena can be uncovered only by induction. But since induction proceeds from the observation of facts, from which accidental elements are eliminated by experimentation; since, moreover, all events in space and in time are susceptible of mathematical calculation; and, finally, since the theoretical generalizations obtained are, as empirical propositions, subject to check by confirmatory or contradictory experience, the natural sciences have, in close relation to mathematics, likewise achieved the ascent to the scientific level. Where this claim is still contested, as in biology, the metaphysical premises within the inductive science are involved. There, to be sure, we find at once the confusion that is encountered whenever we pass into the realm of philosophy.

Philosophy does not rest on principles that are self-evident truths. On the contrary, its principles are the focus of obscurity, uncertainty, and controversy. There is unanimity only with respect to the concrete application of these principles. But the moment we try to disregard the particular instance of application and to isolate the principles from experience, that is, if we try to formulate them in pure abstraction, then our search gets lost in metaphysical darkness unless we illuminate our way by the artificial light of a method.

Under these circumstances one would expect to find interest in the problem of method nowhere so great as among philosophers. It should be noted, however, that the consideration just put forward itself depends on a methodological point of view. It raises, in advance of any philosophical speculation proper, the question of the nature of philosophical cognition; and it is only through this preliminary question that light is shed on the real content of the problems besetting philosophy.

Let us pause here a moment and take a closer look at the concept of the method with which we are concerned. What, precisely, is meant by a method that subjects the thinking of philosophers to its rules? Obviously, it is something other than just the rules of logical thinking. Obedience to the laws of logic is an indispensable precondition of any science. The essential factor distinguishing a method of philosophy can therefore not be found in the fact that it avails itself of logic. That would too narrowly circumscribe the function devolving on it. On the other hand, the demands made on method must not go too far, nor should the impossible be expected of it, namely, the creative increase of philosophical knowledge.

The function to be performed by the philosophical method is nothing other than making secure the contemplated regress to principles, for without the guidance of method, such a regress would be merely a leap in the dark and would leave us where we were before—prey to the arbitrary.

But how to find the clarity requisite for discovering such a guide, since nothing is clear save only judgments relative to individual instances? For these judgments the concrete use of our intelligence, as applied in every empirical judgment in science and in daily life, suffices. Once we go beyond these judgments, how can we orient ourselves at all? The difficulty that seems to be present here is resolved upon critical examination of these empirical judgments. Each of them comprises, in addition to the particular data supplied by observation, a cognition hidden in the very form of the judgment. This cognition, however, is not separately perceived, but by virtue of it we already actually assume and apply the principle we seek.

To give a commonplace illustration: If we were here to discuss the meaning of the philosophical concept of substance, we should most probably become involved in a hopeless dispute, in which the skeptics would very likely soon get the best of it. But if, on the conclusion of our debate, one of the skeptics failed to find his overcoat beside the door where he had hung it, he would hardly reconcile himself to the unfortunate loss of his coat on the ground that it simply confirmed his philosophical doubt of the permanence of substance. Like anyone else hunting for a lost object, the skeptic assumes in the judgment that motivates his search the universal truth that no thing can become nothing, and thus, without being conscious of the inconsistency with his doctrine, he employs the metaphysical principle of the permanence of substance.

Or, suppose we discussed the universal validity of the idea of justice. Our discussion would have the same outcome and once more seem to favor the skeptic who denies the universal validity of ethical truths. When, however, this skeptic reads in his evening paper that farmers are still holding back grain deliveries to exploit a favorable market and that bread will therefore have to be rationed again, he will not readily be disposed to suppress his indignation on the ground that there is no common principle of right applicable to producer and consumer. Like everyone else he condemns profiteering and thereby demonstrates that in fact he acknowledges the metaphysical assumption of equal rights to the satisfaction of interests, regardless of the favorableness or unfavorableness of any individual's personal situation.

It is the same with all experiential judgments. If we inquire into the conditions of their possibility, we come upon more general propositions that constitute the basis of the particular judgments passed. By analyzing conceded judgments we go back to their presuppositions. We operate regressively from the consequences to the reason. In this regression we eliminate the accidental facts to which the particular judgment relates and by this separation bring into relief the originally obscure assumption that lies at the bottom of the judgment on the concrete instance. The regressive method of abstraction, which serves to disclose philosophical principles, produces no new knowledge either of facts or of laws. It merely utilizes reflection to transform into clear concepts what reposed in our reason as an original possession and made itself obscurely heard in every individual judgment.

It seems as though this discussion has carried us far from our real theme, the method of teaching philosophy. Let us then find the connection. We have discovered philosophy to be the sum total of those universal rational truths that become clear only through reflection. To philosophize, then, is simply to isolate these rational truths with our intellect and to express them in general judgments.

What implications does this hold for the teaching of philosophy? When expressed in words, these universal truths will be heard, but it does not necessarily follow that they will be comprehended. We can understand them only when, beginning with their application in our judgments, we then personally undertake the regress to the premises of these empirical judgments and recognize in them our own presuppositions.

It is accordingly impossible to communicate philosophy, the sum total of these philosophical principles, by instruction as we communicate historical facts or even geometrical theorems. The facts of history as such are not objects of insight; they can only be noted.

True, the principles of mathematics are comprehensible, but we gain insight into them without treading the circuitous path of our own creative thinking. They become immediately evident as soon as attention is directed to their content. The mathematics teacher who anticipates his pupil's independent investigation by presenting these principles in lectures does not thereby impair their clarity. In this case the pupil is able to follow even though he does not himself travel the exploratory path to them. To what extent such instruction makes sure that the pupil follows with real comprehension is of course another question.

But to present philosophy in this manner is to treat it as a science of facts that are to be accepted as such. The result is at best a mere history of philosophy. For what the instructor communicates is not philosophical truth itself but merely the fact that he or somebody else considers this or that to be a philosophical truth. In claiming that he is teaching philosophy, he deceives both himself and his students.

The teacher who seriously wishes to impart philosophical insight can aim only at teaching the art of philosophizing. He can do no more than show his students how to undertake, each for himself, the laborious regress that alone affords insight into basic principles. If there is such a thing at all as instruction in philosophy, it can only be instruction in doing one's own thinking; more precisely, in the independent practice of the art of abstraction. The meaning of my initial remark, that the Socratic method, as a method of instruction in philosophy, is the art not of teaching philosophy but of teaching philosophizing, will now become clear. But we have gone further than that. We also know now that, in order to succeed, this art must be guided by the rules of the regressive method.

We have still to examine the subsidiary question, whether this, the only appropriate method of teaching philosophy, is rightfully called the Socratic method. For my earlier references to the significance of Socrates bore only on the fact that his procedure pertained to method.

To begin with, it goes without saying that his way of teaching is full of faults. Every intelligent college freshman reading Plato's dialogues raises the objection that Socrates, at the most decisive points, engages in monologues and that his pupils are scarcely more than yes men—at times, as Fries remarks, one does not even quite see how they arrived at the "yes."[10] In addition to these didactic defects, there are grave philosophical errors, so that we often find ourselves concurring in the dissenting opinions of some of the participants.

In order to reach a conclusion concerning truth and error, the valuable and the valueless, let us take another glance at Plato's account. No one has appraised Socrates' manner of teaching and its effect on his pupils with greater objectivity or deeper knowledge of human nature. Whenever the reader is moved to protest against long-windedness or hair splitting in the conversations, against the monotony of the deductions, against the futility of the battle of words, a like protest arises at once from some participant in the dialogue. How openly Plato allows the pupils to voice their displeasure, their doubt, their boredom—just think of the railing of Callicles in the *Gorgias.*[11] He even has conversations breaking off because the patience of the participants is exhausted; and the reader's judgment is by no means always in favor of Socrates. But does this criticism reveal anything except the sovereign assurance with which Plato stands by the method of his teacher for all its shortcomings? Is there any better proof of confidence in the inherent value of a cause than to depict it with all its imperfections, certain that it will nevertheless prevail? Plato's attitude toward his teacher's work is like that displayed toward Socrates, the man, in the well-known oration by Alcibiades in the *Symposium.* There, by contrasting the uncouth physical appearance of Socrates with his inner nature, he makes his noble personality shine forth with greater radiance and compares him to a silenus who bears within him the mark of the gods.

What, then, is the positive element in the work of Socrates? Where do we find the beginnings of the art of teaching philosophy? Surely not in the mere transition from the rhetoric of the sophists to the dialogue with pupils, even though we ignore the fact that, as I have already indicated, the questions put by Socrates are for the most part leading questions eliciting no more than "Undoubtedly, Socrates!" "Truly, so it is, by Zeus! How could it be otherwise?"

But suppose Socrates' philosophical ardor and his awkwardness had allowed the pupils more self-expression. We should still have to inquire first into the deeper significance of the dialogue in philosophical instruction and into the lessons to be derived from Plato's use of it.

We find dialogue employed as an art form in fiction and drama and as a pedagogic form in instruction. Theoretically these forms are separable but actually we require of every conversation liveliness, clarity, and beauty of expression, as well as espousal of truth, decisiveness, and strength of conviction. Even though the emphasis varies, we like to recognize the teacher in the artist and the artist in the teacher.

We must furthermore distinguish between a conversation reduced to writing—even though it is a reproduction of actual speech—and a real conversation carried on between persons. Conversations that are written down lose their original liveliness, "like the flower in the botanist's case." If, in spite of this, we are to find them satisfactory, the atmosphere must be spiritualized and purified, standards must be raised; and then there may come forth some rare and admirable production as the conversation of the Grand Inquisitor, which is carried on with a silent opponent who by his silence defeats him.

Conversation as a pedagogic form, however, must sound like actual talk; otherwise it does not fulfill its task of being model and guide. To catch, in the mirror of a written reproduction, the fleeting form of such talk with its irregularities, to strike the mean between fidelity to the sense and fidelity to the word—this is a problem that can perhaps be solved didactically; but the solution, serving as it does a definite purpose, will rarely meet the demands of free art and therefore as a whole will nearly always produce a mixed impression. I know of only a few didactic conversations in literature from which this discord has been even partially eliminated. I have in mind, for instance, some passages in the three well-known dialogues by Solovyeff; then there is the Socratic dialogue with which the American socialist writer Bellamy opens his didactic novel, *Looking Backward;* and finally—by no means the least successful—the conversations in August Niemann's novel, *Bakchen und Thyrsosträger,* which is imbued with the true Socratic spirit.

To the difficulty just described one must add another, more basic objection, that to reduce the evolving didactic conversation to writing borders on the absurd. For by offering the solution along with the problem, the transcription violates, with respect to the reader, the rule of individual effort and honesty and thus, as Socrates puts it in the *Phaedrus,* imparts to the novice "the appearance of wisdom, not true wisdom."[12] Such writing has meaning only for those to whom it recalls their own intellectual efforts. On all others it acts as an obstacle to insight—it seduces them into the naive notion that, as Socrates says further on, "anything in writing will be clear and certain."[13] Thus Plato speaks of his own "perplexity and uncertainty"[14] in setting down his thoughts in writing.

> It does not at all admit of verbal expression. . . . But were I to undertake this task it would not, as I think, prove a good thing for men, save for some few who are able to discover the truth themselves with but little instruction; for as to the rest, some it would most unseasonably fill with mistaken

> contempt, and others with an overweening empty aspiration, as though they had learnt some sublime mysteries.[15]
>
> . . . Whenever one sees a man's written compositions—whether they be the laws of a legislator or anything else in any other form—these are not his most serious works, if so be that the writer himself is serious: rather those works abide in the fairest region he possesses. If, however, these really are his serious efforts, and put into writing, it is not "the gods" but mortal men who "then of a truth themselves have utterly ruined his senses."[16]

We must bear this discord in mind as we scrutinize the Platonic dialogue to discover how Socrates accomplished his pedagogic task.

One achievement is universally conceded to him: that by his questioning he leads his pupils to confess their ignorance and thus cuts through the roots of their dogmatism. This result, which indeed cannot be *forced* in any other way, discloses the significance of the dialogue as an instrument of instruction. The lecture, too, can stimulate spontaneous thinking, particularly in more mature students; but no matter what allure such stimulus may possess, it is not *irresistible.* Only persistent pressure to speak one's mind, to meet every counterquestion, and to state the reasons for every assertion transforms the power of that allure into an irresistible compulsion. This art of *forcing* minds *to freedom* constitutes the first secret of the Socratic method.

But only the first. For it does not take the pupil beyond the abandonment of his prejudices, the realization of his not-knowing, this negative determinant of all genuine and certain knowledge.

Socrates, after this higher level of ignorance is reached, far from directing the discussion toward the metaphysical problems, blocks every attempt of his pupils to push straight on to them with the injunction that they had better first learn about the life of the weavers, the blacksmiths, the carters. In this pattern of the discussion we recognize the philosophical instinct for the only correct method: first to derive the general premises from the observed facts of everyday life, and thus to proceed from judgments of which we are sure to those that are less sure.

It is astonishing how little understood this simple guiding idea of method is even in our own day. Take, for example, the assertion that his use of the affairs of the workaday world as a point of departure exhibits merely the practical interest Socrates took in the moral jolting of his fellow citizens. No, had Socrates been concerned with natural philosophy rather than with ethics, he would still have introduced his ideas in the same way. We arrive at no better understanding of the Socratic method when we consider the way it works back from particulars to universals as a method of regressive inference, thereby identifying it with the inductive method. Though Aristotle praised him for it, Socrates was not the inventor of the inductive method. Rather, he pursued the path of abstraction, which employs reflection to lift the knowledge we already possess into consciousness. Had Aristotle been correct in his interpretation, we should not be surprised at the failure of Socrates' endeavors. For ethical principles cannot be derived from observed facts.

The truth is that in the execution of his design Socrates does fail. His sense of truth guides him surely through the introduction of the abstraction; but further on so many erroneous methodological ideas intrude that the success of the conversation is almost always frustrated.

In this process of separation from the particulars of experience and in his search for the more universal truths, Socrates concentrates his attention wholly on the general characteristics of concepts as we grasp them and devotes himself to the task of making these concepts explicit by definition. Without concepts, of course, there is no definite comprehension of general rational truths; but the elucidation of concepts and the discussion of their interrelations do not suffice to gain the content of the synthetic truths that are the true object of his quest.

What holds Socrates on his futile course is a mistake that comes to light only in Plato and gives his doctrine of ideas its ambivalent, half-mystic, half-logicizing character. This doctrine assumes that concepts are images of the ideas that constitute ultimate reality. This is why the Socratic-Platonic dialogues see the summit of scientific knowledge in the elucidation of concepts.

It is not difficult for us to discern in retrospect the error that caused philosophy here to stray from the right path, and consequently hindered the elaboration of methods of abstraction requisite for scientific metaphysics. However, it would be beside the point to dwell on the shortcomings of a philosophy that made for the first time an attempt at critical self-analysis. Our present concern is not with its errors or with the incompleteness of its system but with its bold and sure beginnings that opened the road to philosophical truth.

Socrates was the first to combine with confidence in the ability of the human mind to recognize philosophical truth the conviction that this truth is not arrived at through occasional bright ideas or mechanical teaching but that only planned, unremitting, and consistent thinking leads us from darkness into its light. Therein lies Socrates' greatness as a philosopher. His greatness as a pedagogue is based on another innovation: he made his pupils do their own thinking and introduced the interchange of ideas as a safeguard against self-deception.

In the light of this evaluation, the Socratic method, for all its deficiencies, remains the only method for teaching philosophy. Conversely, all philosophical instruction is fruitless if it conflicts with Socrates' basic methodic requirements.

Of course, the development of philosophical knowledge had to free from its entanglement with Platonic mysticism the doctrine of reminiscence, the truth of which constitutes the real and most profound reason for the possibility of and necessity for the Socratic method. This liberation was achieved after two thousand years by the critical philosophies of Kant and Fries. They carried the regressive method of abstraction to completion. Beyond this, they firmly secured the results of abstraction—which as basic principles do not admit of proof but as propositions must nevertheless be verified—by the method of *deduction.*

In the idea of this deduction—with which only Fries really succeeded—the doctrine of reminiscence experienced its resurrection. It is not too much to say that the Socratic-Platonic concept was thus transmuted from the prophetic-symbolic form, in which it had been confined by the two Greek sages, into the solidly welded and unshakably established form of a science.

Deduction, this master achievement of philosophy, is not easy to explain. If I were to attempt to convey some idea of it, I could not indicate its nature more succinctly than by saying that it is quite literally the instrumentality for carrying out the Socratic design to instruct the ignorant by compelling them to realize that they actually know what they did not know they knew.

Kant and Fries did not pursue the problem of instruction in philosophy beyond some incidental pedagogic observations of a general character. But, thanks to critical philosophy, philosophical science has made such progress in surmounting its inherent methodological difficulties that now the most urgent task of critical philosophy is the revival and furtherance of the Socratic method, especially in its bearing on teaching. Must another two thousand years elapse before a kindred genius appears and rediscovers the ancient truth? Our science requires a continuous succession of trained philosophers, at once independent and well schooled, to avert the danger that critical philosophy may either fall a victim of incomprehension or, though continuing in name, it yet may become petrified into dogmatism.

In view of the importance of this task, we shall do well to pause once more and scrutinize the whole of the difficulty we must face. The exposition of our problem has disclosed the profound relation between critical philosophy and the Socratic method, on the basis of which we determine that the essence of the Socratic method consists in freeing instruction from dogmatism; in other words, in excluding all didactic judgments from instruction. Now we are confronted with the full gravity of the pedagogic problem we are to solve. Consider the question: How is any instruction and therefore any teaching at all possible when every instructive judgment is forbidden? Let us not attempt evasion by assuming that the requirement cannot possibly be meant to go to the extreme of prohibiting an occasional discrect helpful hint from teacher to student. No, there must be an honest choice: either dogmatism or following Socrates. The question then becomes all the more insistent: How is Socratic instruction possible?

Here we actually come up against the basic problem of education, which in its general form points to the question: How is education at all possible? If the end of education is rational self-determination, i.e., a condition in which the individual does not allow his behavior to be determined by outside influences but judges and acts according to his own insight, the question arises: How can we affect a person by outside influences so that he will not permit himself to be affected by outside influences? We must resolve this paradox or abandon the task of education.

The first thing to note is that in nature the human mind is always under external influences and, indeed, that the mind cannot develop without external stimulus. We then are confronted with the still broader question: Is self-determination compatible with the fact that in nature the mind is subject to external influence?

It will help us to clarify our thinking if we distinguish between the two senses in which the term "external influence" is used. It may mean external influence in general or an external determinant. Similarly, in teaching it may mean external stimulation of the mind or molding the mind to the acceptance of outside judgments.

Now, it is clearly no contradiction to hold both that the human mind finds within itself the cognitive source of philosophical truth and that insight into this truth is awakened in the mind by external stimuli. Indeed, the mind requires such external stimulation if the initial obscurity of philosophical truth is to grow into clear knowledge. Within the limits set by these conditions, instruction in philosophy is possible and even necessary if the development of the pupil is to be independent of mere chance.

Philosophical instruction fulfills its task when it systematically weakens the influences that obstruct the growth of philosophical comprehension and reinforces those that promote it. Without going into the question of other relevant influences, let us keep firmly in mind the one that must be excluded unconditionally: the influence that may emanate from the instructor's assertions. If this influence is not eliminated, all labor is vain. The instructor will have done everything possible to forestall the pupil's own judgment by offering him a ready-made judgment.

We are now arrived at a point from which we have a clear view both of the task of the Socratic method and of the possibility of fulfilling it. The rest must be left to the experiment and the degree of conviction it may carry.

But it would be underrating the difficulty presented not to consider what the experiment must call for if from its outcome we are to decide whether or not our goal is attainable. Although I have been taxing your patience for some time, I should render a poor service to our cause, and thus to you too, if I did not engage your attention a while longer to consider the *procedure* of such an experiment.

There is a danger inherent in the nature of an exacting enterprise, whose success has met with little recognition, and it is this: that the participants in it, once they become involved in its mounting difficulties and unexpected distractions, will repent of their good intentions or at least will begin to think of ways of modifying the method to make it easier. This tendency, springing from purely subjective discomfort, is likely to distort or completely frustrate the object of the undertaking. It is therefore advisable, lest expectations be disappointed, to envisage in advance as clearly as possible the manifold difficulties that will surely arise and, with due appreciation of these difficulties, to set down what will be required of teachers and students.

We must bear in mind that instruction in philosophy is not concerned with heaping solution on solution, nor indeed with establishing results, but solely with learning the method of reaching solutions. If we do this, we shall observe at once that the teacher's proper role cannot be that of a guide keeping his party from wrong paths and accidents. Nor yet is he a guide going in the lead while his party simply follow in the expectation that this will prepare them to find the same path later on by themselves. On the contrary, the essential thing is the skill with which the teacher puts the pupils on their own responsibility at the very beginning by teaching them to go by themselves—although they would not on that account go alone—and by so developing this independence that one day they may be able to venture forth alone, self-guidance having replaced the teacher's supervision.

As to the observations I am about to make, I must beg to be allowed to cull incidental examples from my own long experience as a teacher of philosophy, for unfortunately the experiences of others are not at my disposal.

Let me take up first the requirements imposed on the teacher and then go on to those placed on the pupil. Once a student of mine, endeavoring to reproduce a Socratically conducted exercise, presented a version in which he put the replies now into the teacher's mouth, now into the pupil's. Only my astonished question, "Have you ever heard me say 'yes' or 'no'?" stopped him short. Thrasymachus saw the point more clearly; in Plato's *Republic* he calls out to Socrates: "Ye gods! . . . I knew it . . . that you would refuse and do anything rather than answer."[17] The teacher who follows the Socratic model does not answer. Neither does he question. More precisely, he puts no philosophical questions, and when such questions are addressed to him, he under no circumstances gives the answer sought. Does he then remain silent? We shall see. During such a session we may often hear the despairing appeal to the teacher: "I don't know what it is you want!" Whereupon the teacher replies: "I? I want nothing at all." This certainly does not convey the desired information. What is it, then, that the teacher actually does? He sets the interplay of question and answer going between the students, perhaps by the introductory remark: "Has anyone a question?"

Now, everyone will realize that, as Kant said, "to know what questions may reasonably be asked is already a great and necessary proof of sagacity and insight."[18] What about foolish questions, or what if there are no questions at all? Suppose nobody answers?

You see, at the very beginning the difficulty presents itself of getting the students to the point of spontaneous activity, and with it arises the temptation for the teacher to pay out a clue like Ariadne's thread. But the teacher must be firm from the beginning, and especially at the beginning. If a student approaches philosophy without having a single question to put to it, what can we expect in the way of his capacity to persevere in exploring its complex and profound problems?

What should the teacher do if there are no questions? He should wait—until questions come. At most, he should request that in the future, in order to save time, questions be thought over in advance. But he should not, just to save time, save the students the effort of formulating their own questions. If he does, he may for the moment temper their impatience, but only at the cost of nipping in the bud the philosophical impatience we seek to awaken.

Once questions start coming—one by one, hesitantly, good ones and foolish ones—how does the teacher receive them, how does he handle them? He now seems to have easy going since the rule of the Socratic method forbids his answering them. He submits the questions to discussion.

All of them? The appropriate and the inappropriate?

By no means. He ignores all questions uttered in too low a voice. Likewise those that are phrased incoherently. How can difficult ideas be grasped when they are expressed in mutilated language?

Thanks to the extraordinary instruction in the mother tongue given in our schools, over half the questions are thus eliminated. [Nelson refers, of course, to German schools. The reader may judge to what degree this criticism also applies to schools in the United States and England.] As for the rest, many are confused or vague. Sometimes clarification comes with the counterquestion: "Just what do you mean by that?" But very often this will not work because the speaker does not know what he means himself. The work of the discussion group thus tends automatically either to take up the clear, simple questions or to clear up unclear, vague ones first.

We are not so fortunate in the problems of philosophy as we are in the problems of mathematics, which, as Hilbert says, fairly call to us: "Here I am, find the solution!" The philosophical problem is wrapped in obscurity. To be able to come to grips with it by framing clear-cut, searching questions demands many trials and much effort. It will therefore scarcely surprise you to learn that a semester's work in a seminar in ethics yielded nothing except agreement on the fact that the initial question was incongruous. The question was, "Is it not stupid to act morally?"

Of course, the instructor will not submit every incongruous question to such protracted examination. He will seek to advance the discussion through his own appraisal of the questions. But he will do no more than allow a certain question to come to the fore because it is instructive in itself or because threshing it out will bring to light typical errors. And he will do this by some such expedient as following the question up with the query: "Who understood what was said just now?" This contains no indication of the relevance or irrelevance of the question; it is merely an invitation to consider it, to extract its meaning by intensive cross-examination.

What is his policy as regards the answers? How are they handled? They are treated like the questions. Unintelligible answers are ignored in order to teach the students to meet the requirements of scientific speech. Answers, too, are probed through such questions as:

"What has this answer to do with our question?"

"Which word do you wish to emphasize?"

"Who has been following?"

"Do you still know what you said a few moments ago?"

"What question are we talking about?"

The simpler these questions, the more flustered the students become. Then, if some fellow student takes pity on his colleague's distress and comes to his aid with the explanation, "He surely wanted to say . . . ," this helpful gesture is unfeelingly cut short with the request to let the art of mind reading alone and cultivate instead the more modest art of saying what one actually wants to say.

By this time you will have gathered that the investigations run a far from even course. Questions and answers tumble over one another. Some of the students understand the development, some do not. The latter cut in with groping questions, trying to reestablish contact, but the others will not be stopped from going ahead. They disregard the interruptions. New questions crop up, wider of the mark. Here and there a debater falls silent; then whole groups. Meanwhile, the agitation continues, and questions become constantly more pointless. Even those who were originally sure of their ground become confused. They, too, lose the thread and do not know how to find it again. Finally, nobody knows where the discussion is headed.

The bewilderment famed in the Socratic circle closes in. Everyone is at his wit's end. What had been certain at the outset has become uncertain. The students, instead of clarifying their own conceptions, now feel as though they had been robbed of their capacity to make anything clear by thinking.

And does the teacher tolerate this too?

"I consider," says Meno to his teacher Socrates, in the dialogue bearing his name, "that both in appearance and in other respects you are extremely like the flat torpedo fish; for it benumbs anyone who approaches and touches it. . . . For in truth I feel my soul and my tongue quite benumbed and I am at a loss what answer to give you."[19]

When Socrates replies, "It is from being in more doubt than anyone else that I cause doubts in others," Meno counters with the celebrated question: "Why, on what lines will you look, Socrates, for a thing of whose nature you know nothing at all?" And this draws from Socrates the more celebrated answer: "Because the soul should be able to recollect all that she knew before."[20] We all know that these words are an echo of the Platonic doctrine of ideas, which the historic Socrates did

The prison of Socrates.

not teach. Yet there is in them the Socratic spirit, the stout spirit of reason's self-confidence, its reverence for its own self-sufficient strength. This strength gives Socrates the composure that permits him to let the seekers after truth go astray and stumble. More than that, it gives him the courage to send them astray in order to test their convictions, to separate knowledge simply taken over from the truth that slowly attains clarity in us through our own reflection. He is unafraid of the confession of not-knowing; indeed, he even induces it. In this he is guided by an attitude of thinking so far from skeptical that he regards this admission as the first step toward deeper knowledge. "He does not think he knows . . . and is he not better off in respect of the matter which he did not know?" he says of the slave to whom he gives instruction in mathematics. "For now he will push on in the search gladly, as lacking knowledge."[21]

To Socrates the test of whether a man loves wisdom is whether he welcomes his ignorance in order to attain to better knowledge. The slave in the *Meno* does this and goes on with the task. Many, however, slacken and tire of the effort when they find their knowledge belittled, when they find that their first few unaided steps do not get them far. The teacher of philosophy who lacks the courage to put his pupils to the test of perplexity and discouragement not only deprives them of the opportunity to develop the endurance needed for research but also deludes them concerning their capabilities and makes them dishonest with themselves.

Now we can discern one of the sources of error that provoke the familiar unjust criticisms of the Socratic method. This method is charged with a defect which it merely reveals and which it must reveal to prepare the ground on which alone the continuation of serious work is possible. It simply uncovers the harm that has been done to men's minds by dogmatic teaching.

Is it a fault of the Socratic method that it must take time for such elementary matters as ascertaining what question is being discussed or determining what the speaker intended to say about it? It is easy for dogmatic instruction to soar into higher regions. Indifferent to self-understanding, it purchases its illusory success at the cost of more and more deeply rooted dishonesty. It is not surprising, then, that the Socratic method is compelled to fight a desperate battle for integrity of thought and speech before it can turn to larger tasks. It must also suffer the additional reproach of being unphilosophical enough to orient itself by means of examples and facts.

The only way one can learn to recognize and avoid the pitfalls of reflection is to become acquainted with them in *application,* even at the risk of gaining wisdom only by sad experience. It is useless to preface philosophizing proper with an introductory course in logic in the hope of thus saving the novice from the risk of taking the wrong path. Knowledge of the principles of logic and the rules of the syllogism, even the ability to illustrate every fallacy by examples, remains after all an art *in abstracto.* An individual is far from learning to think logically even though he has learned to conclude by all the syllogistic rules that Caius is mortal. The test of one's own conclusions and their subjection to the rules of logic is the province of one's faculty of judgment, not at all the province of logic. The faculty of judgment, said Kant, being the power of rightly employing given rules, "must belong to the learner himself; and in the absence of such a natural gift no rule that may be prescribed to him for this purpose can ensure against misuse."[22] If, therefore, this natural gift is weak, it must be strengthened. But it can be strengthened only by exercise.

Thus, after our instructor breaks the spell of numbness by calling for a return to the original question, and the students trace their way back to the point from which they started, each must, by critical examination of every one of his steps, study the sources of error and work out for himself his own school of logic. Rules of logic derived from personal experience retain a living relation with the judgments they are to govern. Furthermore, the fact that dialectics, though indispensable, is introduced as an auxiliary only prevents attaching an exaggerated value to it in the manner of scholasticism, to which the most trivial metaphysical problem served for the exercise of logical ingenuity. Segregation of the philosophical disciplines with a view to reducing the difficulties of instruction by separate treatment would be worse than a waste of time. Other ways will have to be found to satisfy the pedagogic maxim that our requirements of the pupil should become progressively more stringent.

This question, if examined carefully, presents no further difficulties for us. If there is such a thing as a research method for philosophy, its essential element must consist of practical directives for the step-by-step solution of problems. It is therefore simply a question of letting the student himself follow the path of the regressive method. The first step, obviously, is to have him secure a firm footing in experience—which is harder to do than an outsider might think. For your adept in philosophy scorns nothing so much as using his intelligence concretely in forming judgments on real facts, an operation that obliges him to remember those lowly instruments of cognition, his five senses. Ask anyone at a philosophy seminar, "What do you see on the blackboard?" and depend on it, he will look at the floor. Upon your repeating, "What do you see *on the blackboard?*" he will finally wrench out a sentence that begins with "If" and demonstrates that for him the world of facts does not exist.

He shows the same disdain for reality when asked to give an example. Forthwith he goes off into a world of fantasy or, if forced to stay on this planet, he at least makes off to the sea or into the desert, so that one wonders whether being attacked by lions and saved from drowning are typical experiences among the acquaintances of a philosopher. The "if" sentences, the far-fetched examples, and the premature desire for definitions characterize not the ingenuous beginner but rather the philosophically indoctrinated dilettante. And it is always he, with his pseudowisdom, who disturbs the quiet and simple progress of an investigation.

I recall a seminar in logic, in which the desire to start from general definitions—under the impression that otherwise the concepts being discussed could not be employed—caused much fruitless trouble. Despite my warning, the group stuck to the opening question: "What is a concept?"

It was not long before a casual reference to the concept "lamp" as an example was followed by the appearance of the "lamp in general" provided with all the essential characteristics of all particular lamps. The students waxed warm in vehement dispute regarding the proof of the existence of this lamp furnished with all the essential features of all particular lamps. My diffident question, whether the lamp-in-general was fed with gas, electricity, or kerosene, went unanswered as unworthy of philosophical debate until, hours later, the resumption of this very question of the source of energy forced the negation of the existence of the lamp-in-general. That is to say, the disputants discovered that different illuminants for one and the same lamp, be it ever so general, were mutually exclusive. Thus, starting with practical application, they had unexpectedly found the law of contradiction by the regressive method. But to define the concept of a concept had proved a vain endeavor; just as in the Socratic circle the definitions nearly always miscarried.

Are we justified, however, in assuming that the cause of such failures always lies in conditions unconnected with the Socratic method itself? Does not this method perhaps suffer from an inherent limitation that makes the solution of deeper problems impossible?

Before coming to a final decision on this point, we must consider one more factor that creates difficulty in the employment of the Socratic method. Though intimately associated with the latter, it lies outside it, yet demands consideration before we can set the limits of the method itself.

The significance of the Socratic dialogue has been sought in the assumption that deliberating with others makes us more easily cognizant of truth than silent reflection. Obviously, there is much soundness in this view. Yet many a person may be moved to doubt this praise after he has listened to the hodgepodge of questions and answers at a philosophical debate and noted the absence, despite the outward discipline, of the tranquillity that belongs to reflection. It is inevitable that what is said by one participant may prove disturbing to another, whether he feels himself placed in a dependent position by intelligent remarks or is distracted by poor ones. It is inevitable that collaboration should progressively become a trial of nerves, made more difficult by increasing demands on personal tact and tolerance.

To a great extent these disturbances can be obviated by an instructor who, for instance, will ignore the innumerable senseless answers, cast doubt on the right ones with Socratic irony, or ease nervous unrest with some understanding word. But his power to restore harmony to the play of ideas is limited unless the others are willing to pursue the common task with determination.

It should be admitted that many disturbances are unavoidable because of the students' imperfect understanding; but the obstacles I have in mind do not lie in the intellectual sphere and for that reason even the most skillful teacher finds them an insurmountable barrier. He can enforce intellectual discipline only if the students are possessed of a disciplined will. This may sound strange but it is a fact that one becomes a philosopher, not by virtue of intellectual gifts but by the exercise of will.

True, philosophizing demands considerable power of intellect. But who will exercise it? Surely not the man who relies merely on his intellectual power. As he delves more deeply into his studies and his difficulties multiply, he will without fail weaken. Because of his intelligence he will recognize these difficulties, even see them very clearly. But the elasticity required to face a problem again and again, to stay with it until it is solved, and not to succumb to disintegrating doubt—this elasticity is achieved only through the power of an iron will, a power of which the entertaining ingenuity of the mere sophist knows nothing. In the end, his intellectual fireworks are as sterile for science as the intellectual dullness that shrinks back at the first obstacle. It is no accident that the investigators whom the history of philosophy records as having made the most decisive advances in dialectics were at the same time philosophers in the original meaning of the word. Only because they loved wisdom were they able to take upon themselves the "many preliminary subjects it entails and [so] much labor," as Plato says in a letter that continues:

> For on hearing this, if the pupil be truly philosophical, in sympathy with the subject and worthy of it, because divinely gifted, he believes that he has been shown a marvelous pathway and that he must brace himself at once to follow it, and that life will not be worth living if he does otherwise. . . .
>
> Those, on the other hand, who are in reality not philosophical, but superficially tinged with opinions—like men whose bodies are sunburnt on the surface—when they see how many studies are required and how great labor, and how the disciplined mode of daily life is that which benefits the subject, they deem it difficult or impossible for themselves.[23]

That is the clear and most definite characteristic of "those who are luxurious and incapable of enduring labor, since [the test] prevents any of them from ever casting the blame on his instructor instead of on himself and his own inability to pursue all the studies which are necessary to his subject."[23]

"In one word, neither receptivity nor memory will ever produce knowledge in him who has no affinity with the object, since it does not germinate to start with in alien states of mind."[24]

We, in common with Plato, require of the philosopher that he strengthen his will power, but it is impossible to achieve this as a by-product in the course of philosophical instruction. The student's will power must be the fruit of his prior education. It is the instructor's duty to make no concession in maintaining the rigorous and indispensable demands on the will; indeed, he must do so out of respect for the students themselves. If, for the want of requisite firmness, he allows himself to be persuaded to relax his stand, or if he does so of his own accord to hold his following, he will have betrayed his philosophical goal. He has no alternative: he must insist on his demands or give up the task. Everything else is abject compromise.

Of course, the student should know the details of the demands to be made on his will. They constitute the minimum required for examining ideas in a group. This means, first, the communication of thoughts, not of acquired fragments of knowledge, not even the knowledge of other people's thoughts. It means, further, the use of clear, unambiguous language. Only the compulsion to communicate provides a means of testing the definiteness and clarity of one's own conceptions. Here, protesting that one has the right feeling but cannot express it will not avail. Feeling is indeed the first and best guide on the path to truth, but it is just as often the protector of prejudice. In a scientific matter, therefore, feeling must be interpreted so that it may be evaluated in accordance with concepts and ordered logic. Moreover, our investigation demands the communication of ideas in distinctly audible and generally comprehensible speech, free from ambiguities. A technical terminology is not only unnecessary for philosophizing but is actually detrimental to its steady progress. It imparts to metaphysical matters, abstract and difficult in any case, the appearance of an esoteric science, which only superior minds are qualified to penetrate. It prevents us from considering the conclusions of unprejudiced judgment, which we have seen to be the starting point of meaningful philosophizing. Unprejudiced judgment, in its operation, relies on concepts that we have, not on artificial reflections, and it makes its conclusions understood by strict adherence to current linguistic usage.

In order to grasp those concepts clearly it is necessary, of course, to isolate them. By the process of abstraction it is possible to separate them from other ideas, to reduce them gradually to their elements, and through such analyses to advance to basic concepts. By holding fast to existing concepts, the philosopher guards himself against peopling his future system with the products of mere speculation and with fantastic brain children. For, if he does not consult unprejudiced judgment, he will allow himself to be lured into forming philosophical concepts by the arbitrary combination of specific characteristics, without any assurance that objects corresponding to his constructions actually exist. Only the use of the same vocabulary still connects him with the critical philosopher. He denotes his artificial concept by the same word the critical philosopher uses to denote his real concept, although, to be sure, he uses this word in a different sense. He says "I" and means "cosmic reason." He says "God" and means "peace of mind." He says "state" and means "power subject to no law." He says "marriage" and means "indissoluble communion of love." He says "space" and means "the labyrinth of the ear." His language is full of artificial meanings. Although it is not apparent, his is actually a technical language; and because this is so, the situation is far more dangerous than it would be if the philosopher indicated the special sense of his language by coining specific new terms. For the sameness of the words tricks the unwary into associating their own familiar concepts with them, and a misunderstanding results. What is more pernicious, this artificial language tempts its own creator to the covert use of the same words in different meanings, and by such a shift of concepts he produces sham proofs. In this abuse of purely verbal definitions we encounter one of the most prevalent and profound of dialectical errors, an error that is rendered more difficult to track down by the fact that the shift of concepts cannot be discovered simply by calling on intuition. However, it betrays itself through its consequences, through the curious phenomenon that with the help of the same verbal definition the pseudoproof presented can be confronted with a contrary proof that has the same air of validity.

The most celebrated and memorable instance of such antitheses is found in the antinomies that Kant discovered and solved. Kant said of these classic examples of contradiction that they were the most beneficent aberration in the history of reason because they furnished the incentive to investigate the cause of the illusion and to reconcile reason to itself. This remark is applicable to every instance of such dialectical conflict.

It will seem, perhaps, that in these last considerations we have strayed somewhat from our subject: the requirement that the student use distinctly audible and generally comprehensible language. But, as a matter of fact, we have secured a deeper understanding of the significance of that requirement.

After all that we have said, what is it that we gain with this demand on the pupil? Only those who, by using comprehensible language, adhere to the concepts we have and become practiced in discussing them will sharpen their critical sense for every arbitrary definition and for every sham proof adroitly derived from such verbal definition. If the requirement of simple and clear language is observed, it is possible, in Socratic teaching, merely by writing the theses of two mutually contradictory doctrines on the blackboard, to focus attention on the verbal definition underlying them, disclose its abuse, and thereby overthrow both doctrinal opinions. The success of such a dialectical performance is achieved—and this is its significant feature—not by flashes of inspiration but methodically, i.e., through a step-by-step search for the hidden premise at the bottom of the contradictory judgments. This method will succeed if the student, struck with suspicion at such a sophism, attends closely to the meaning of the words, for these words, when used in an in-artificial sense, put him on the track of the error.

Do not misunderstand me. I do not advocate the point of view that so-called common sense and its language can satisfy the demands of scientific philosophizing. Nor is it my purpose, in dwelling on simple elementary conditions seemingly easy to fulfill, to veil the fact that the pursuit of philosophizing requires rigorous training in the art of abstraction, one difficult to master. My point is this: We cannot with impunity skip the first steps in the development of this art. Abstraction must have something to abstract from. The immediate and tangible material of philosophy is language which presents concepts through words. In its wealth, supplied from many sources, reason dwells concealed. Reflection discloses this rational knowledge by separating it from intuitive notions.

Just as Socrates took pains to question locksmiths and blacksmiths and made their activities the first subject of discussion with his pupils, so every philosopher ought to start out with the vernacular and develop the language of his abstract science from its pure elements.

I am now done with the requirements that apply to the students. Their difficulty lies not in the fulfillment of details but in the observance of the whole. I said earlier that the working agreement with the students requires of them nothing but the communication of their ideas. You will understand if I now express the same demand in another form: It requires of the students submission to the method of philosophizing, for it is the sole aim of Socratic instruction to enable the students to judge for themselves their observance of the agreement.

Our examination of the Socratic method is nearing its conclusion. Now that we have discussed the difficulties of its application, there remains only one query: May not the reason for the unfavorable reception of the method lie, in part at least, within itself? Is there not perhaps some limitation inherent in it that restricts its usefulness?

One singular fact, more than any other, is calculated to make us consider this doubt seriously. Fries, the one man who actually completed critical philosophy and restored the Socratic-Platonic doctrine of reminiscence and the self-certainty of intelligence, Fries, the most genuine of all Socrateans, gave the Socratic method only qualified recognition because he considered it inadequate for achieving complete self-examination of the intellect. He acknowledged its capacity to guide the novice in the early stages; he even demanded emphatically that all instruction in philosophy follow the spirit of the Socratic method, the essence of which, he held, lay not in its use of dialogue but in its "starting from the common things of everyday life and only then going on from these to scientific views."[25] "But as soon as higher truths, further removed from intuition and everyday experience, are involved,"[26] Fries did not approve of letting the students find these truths by themselves. "Here the instructor must employ a language molded upon subtle abstractions, of which the student does not yet have complete command, and to which he must be educated by instruction."[27]

In Fries's own words, this lecture method of instruction "step by step invites cooperative thinking."[28] An illustration of it is given in his didactic novel, *Julius und Evagoras*. And indeed it is not a form of Socratic instruction.

I should not think of choosing a really successful dialogue of Plato's—were there such—as subject matter for a philosophy seminar as it would forestall the creative thinking of the students, but there is nothing in *Julius und Evagoras* to preclude its use for such a purpose. For the development of abstract ideas which it presents to the reader does indeed "invite" critical verification by the students, as Fries desires. However, though otherwise exemplary, it offers no assurance that the students will accept the invitation or, if made to stand on their own feet, that they will master such difficulties as they may encounter on their way. Have your students study the fine and instructive chapter on "The Sources of Certainty," and I stand ready to demonstrate in a Socratic discussion that those students will still lack everything that would enable them to defend what they have learned. The key to this riddle is to be found in Goethe's words: "One sees only what one already knows."

It is futile to lay a sound, clear, and well-grounded theory before the students; futile though they respond to the invitation to follow in their thinking. It is even useless to point out to them the difficulties they would have to overcome in order to work out such results independently. If they are to become independent masters of philosophical theory, it is imperative that they go beyond the mere learning of problems and their difficulties; they must wrestle with them in constant practical application so that, through day-by-day dealing with them, they may learn to overcome them with all their snares and pitfalls and diversities of form. However, the instructor's lecture that Fries would have delivered "in language molded upon subtle abstractions," just because of its definiteness and clearness, will obscure the difficulties that hamper the development of this very lucidity of thought and verbal precision. The outcome will be that in the end only those already expert in Socratic thinking will assimilate the philosophical substance and appreciate the solidness and originality of the exposition.

Fries underrated the Socratic method because, for one thing, he did not and could not find the Socratic method in the method of Socrates, and he considered this fact as confirming his opinion of the inadequacy of the Socratic method. Another reason—and the more profound, I think—lay in the particular character of Fries's genius. He combined with a sense of truth unparalleled in the history of philosophy a linguistic gift that produced with the assurance of a somnambulist the words that were most appropriate to a philosophical idea. A man with a mind so superior, rich, and free will always find it difficult to maintain close contact with the minds of less independent thinkers. He is prone to overlook the danger of dogmatism that threatens the more dependent mind even when the instructor's lecture has reached the highest degree of lucidity and exactitude of expression. A man of such superiority can become a leader of generations of men. But this is contingent on the appearance of teachers who will find the key to his language by resorting to the "maieutic" services [Maieutic: "The word means performing midwife's service (to thought or ideas); Socrates figured himself as a midwife (*maia*) bringing others' thoughts to birth with his questionings; . . ." (H. D. Fowler, *A Dictionary of Modern English Usage* [New York, 1944], p. 339.) . . .] of the Socratic method, instituting the laborious and protracted exercises that must not frighten away those who plan to dedicate themselves to philosophy.

I maintain that this art has no limitations. I have seen a Socratic seminar not only deal successfully with such an abstract subject as the philosophy of law but even proceed to the construction of its system.

This is claiming a good deal, you will say. Well, I have enough Socratic irony to acknowledge the awkwardness of my position, which, incidentally, I admitted in the opening sentence of my address. For when all is said and done, no one will be won over to the cause I am pleading here except by the evidence of the experiment, that is, through his own experience.

But let us look about us: Can we not find some sufficiently simple and well-known control experiment that permits a valid conclusion on the question at issue? What sort of experiment might that be? If non-Socratically conducted instruction could accomplish the designated end in philosophy, such a procedure should succeed all the more readily in a science that does not have to struggle with the particular difficulties of philosophical knowledge—a science in which, on the contrary, everything from first to last becomes absolutely and completely clear even when set forth in a dogmatic lecture.

If we inquire whether there is such a science and, if so, whether it has a place among the subjects of instruction in our schools and universities, we find that such a science actually does exist. Mathematics satisfies both conditions. "We are in possession," said a classic French mathematician. The relevant experiment is thus available, and we need only consider its outcome with an unprejudiced mind.

What does it teach? Just among ourselves and without glossing over anything or blaming anyone, we teachers might as well confess to what is a public secret: on the whole the result is negative. We all know from personal experience that diligent and even gifted students in our secondary schools and colleges, if seriously put to the test, are not sure of even the rudiments of mathematics and discover their own ignorance.

Our experiment therefore points to the conclusion I spoke of; as a matter of fact, there is no escaping it. Suppose someone were to say there is no such thing as understanding, regardless of the kind of instruction. That is arguable, but not for us as pedagogues. We start from the assumption that meaningful instruction is possible. And then we must come to the conclusion that, if there is any assurance that a subject can be understood, Socratic instruction offers such assurance. And with that we have found more than we sought, for this conclusion applies not only to philosophy but to every subject that involves comprehension.

An experiment conducted by history itself on a grand scale confirms the fact that the pedagogic inadequacy in the field of mathematics is not due merely to incompetent teachers but must have a more fundamental cause; or, to put it differently, that even the best mathematics instruction, if it follows the dogmatic method, cannot, despite all its clearness, bring about thorough understanding. This experiment deserves the attention of everyone interested in the teaching of mathematics.

The basic principles of calculus (nowadays included in the curricula of some of our high schools) became the secure and acknowledged possession of science only about the middle of the nineteenth century, when they were first established with clarity and exactitude. Although the most important results had been a matter of general knowledge ever since Newton and Leibniz, their foundations remained in dispute. Endlessly repeated attempts at elucidation only resulted in new obscurities and paradoxes. Considering the state of this branch of mathematics at that time, Berkeley was not unjustified when he undertook to prove that in the unintelligibility of its theories it was not one whit behind the dogmas and mysteries of theology.[29] We know today that those riddles were solvable, that, thanks to the work of Cauchy and Weierstrass, they have been solved, and that this branch of mathematics is susceptible of the same clarity and lucidity of structure as elementary geometry. Here, too, everything becomes evident as soon as attention is focused on the decisive point. But it is precisely this that is hard to achieve, an art each student must acquire by his own efforts.

To demonstrate how true this is, I shall mention two especially noteworthy facts. The first is this: Newton's treatise, widely known and celebrated since its appearance, not only expounds the decisive point of view established by Cauchy and Weierstrass but formulates it with a clarity, precision, and succinctness that would satisfy the most exacting requirements contemporary science could lay down. Moreover, it contains an explicit warning against that very misunderstanding which, as we now know, kept succeeding generations of mathematicians so completely in bondage that their minds remained closed to the emphatic "Cave!" of the classic passage in Newton's work,[30] familiar to all of them.

The second, the complement, as it were, of the first, is that, even after Weierstrass and after the argument had at long last been settled, it was possible to revive it not only among dilettanti, whom we shall always have with us, but even under the leadership of a man of research as distinguished for his work on the theory of functions as Paul du Bois-Reymond. In his own words, his "solution is that it remains and will remain a riddle."[31]

There is an impressive warning in this instance of the disparity between the objective lucidity and systematic completeness of a scientific theory, on the one hand, and any pedagogic assurance that it will be understood, on the other. It is precisely the man with a philosophical turn of mind who is unwilling, in mathematics as elsewhere, simply to accept a result; he philosophizes about it, i.e., he strives to understand its fundamentals and bring it into harmony with the rest of his knowledge. But it is just he who is sure to fail unless he is one of the few who find their way to clarity by their own efforts. We thus discover that even mathematics, instead of remaining the unassailable standard and model that might help philosophy, is drawn along by it into the whirlpool of confusion.

Herewith, I believe, I have also answered the weightiest comment I know on the value of the Socratic method in teaching mathematics. It comes from no less a man than Weierstrass. He devoted a special essay to the Socratic method,[32] an indication of the esteem and comprehension this profound mathematician and pedagogue had for our subject. His detailed argument is proof of this. He demonstrated the basic practicability of the Socratic method in philosophy and pure mathematics, in contradistinction to the empirical sciences. That he nevertheless rated it as of little value for use in the school was due, for one thing, to the fact that he considered insurmountable the external difficulties which undeniably exist, and which I have dwelt on extensively. For another, he was obviously partial to the coherent lecture with its large perspectives and architectonic beauty of structure, a partiality easily understandable in a scientist of his genius. Still, he admitted that such a lecture "presupposes students of rather more mature intelligence, if it is to be effective." Since, however, it was also his opinion that "the Socratic method, carried out in its true spirit, . . . is less suitable for boys than for more mature youths," one is impelled to ask (but in vain) how the maturity of mind can develop that will assure success to a non-Socratic mode of instruction.

What maturity of mind our students must have if they are to surpass Paul du Bois-Reymond, the pupil of Weierstrass, and Euler, the pupil of Newton, in depth of understanding!

Our findings might lead us to pessimism. But, if we view the matter rightly, we are not yet finished. What we have found actually indicates the way we can remove the cause of this lamentable state of affairs, which itself can hardly be regarded pessimistically enough.

The way lies in mathematics. It is within the power of the mathematicians to end the scandal that not only has completely undermined the authority of philosophy but also threatens mathematics itself with the loss of the prestige that, thanks to its powerful position in education, it has until now maintained in the intellectual life of mankind. In view of the deplorable situation in which the cause of the Socratic method finds itself, help can come only through a science that combines the several advantages I have discussed, advantages that only mathematics has and that assure it a head start which philosophy can never overcome by its own efforts.

The character and repute of mathematics as a science still stand quite firm. In the long run, the evidence of its results cannot be obscured by any teaching, however wretched, and it will always offer a means of orientation though all else be plunged into darkness and confusion. I therefore appeal to the mathematicians. May they become aware of the spiritual power they hold and of their consequent mission of leadership in the fields of science and education. Philosophy cannot now assume the role, originally hers, of guardian of the intellectual values whose fate is bound up with that of the Socratic method. Having disowned her stepchild and thus deprived herself of its vitalizing and rejuvenating influence, philosophy has become so infirm that she must now beg of her sister science asylum and aid for her cast-off daughter.

Though I said at the beginning that a sense of chivalry has made me champion of the disdained one, I am nevertheless far from blind to my powerlessness. I can fulfill this command of chivalry only by commending my protégée to the care of mathematics—confident that the outcast will be nurtured by it and grow vigorously until, her strength renewed, she returns to her own home and there establishes law and order, thus requiting with good the evil done her.

Notes

[1] Plato, *Epistles,* R. G. Bury, tr., in Loeb Classical Library (London, New York, 1929), VII, 531.

[2] Wilhelm Windelband, *Präludien* (Freiburg and Tübingen, 1884), p. 9.

[3] Windelband, *Präludien,* p. vi.

[4] Plato, *Apology,* H. N. Fowler, tr., in Loeb Classical Library (London, New York, 1913), I, 109.

[5] Karl Joel, *Geschichte der antiken Philosophie* (Tübingen, 1921), p. 770.

[6] Heinrich Maier, *Sokrates* (Tübingen, 1913), p. 157.

[7] Ulrich von Wilamowitz-Moellendorff, *Platon* (Berlin, 1919), I, 108.

[8] Immanuel Kant, *Critique of Pure Reason,* Norman Kemp Smith, tr. (London, New York, 1933), p. 25.

[9] Kant, *Critique of Pure Reason,* pp. 31-32. [Translation revised by T. K. B.]

[10] J. F. Fries, *Die Geschichte der Philosophie* (Halle, 1837), I, 253.

[11] Plato, *Gorgias,* W. R. M. Lamb, tr., in Loeb Classical Library (London, New York, 1926), V, 381-395.

[12] Plato, *Phaedrus,* H. N. Fowler, tr., in Loeb Classical Library (London, New York, 1913), I, 563.

[13] *Ibid.,* p. 565.

[14] Plato, *Epistles,* p. 537.

[15] *Ibid.,* pp. 531-533.

[16] Plato, *Epistles,* p. 541.

[17] Plato, *The Republic,* Paul Shorey, tr., in Loeb Classical Library (London, New York), p. 41.

[18] Kant, *Critique of Pure Reason,* p. 97.

[19] Plato, *Meno,* W. R. M. Lamb, tr., in Loeb Classical Library (London, New York, 1924), IV, 297.

[20] *Ibid.,* pp. 299 ff.

[21] Plato, *Meno,* p. 313.

[22] Kant, *Critique of Pure Reason,* p. 178.

[23] Plato, *Epistles,* pp. 527 ff.

[24] Plato, *Epistles,* p. 539.

[25] J. F. Fries, *System der Logik* (3d ed., reissued, Leipzig, 1914), p. 449.

[26] Fries, *Die Geschichte der Philosophie,* I, 253.

[27] Fries, *System der Logik,* p. 436.

[28] *Ibid.*

[29] George Berkeley, *The Analyst; or a Discourse Addressed to an Infidel Mathematician, Wherein It Is Examined Whether the Object, Principles, and Inferences of the Modern Analysis Are More Distinctly Conceived, or More Evidently Deduced, Than Religious Mysteries and Points of Faith.* Selected Pamphlets, Vol. XVI (London, 1734).

[30] Isaac Newton, *Philosophiae naturalis principia mathematica* (1687), Liber primus, scholium.

[31] Paul du Bois-Reymond, *Die allgemeine Funktionentheorie* (Tübingen, 1882), Pt. I, p. 2.

[32] Karl Weierstrass, *Mathematische Werke* (Berlin, 1903), III, Appendix, 315-329.

A. K. Rogers (essay date 1925)

SOURCE: "The Ethics of Socrates," in *The Philosophical Review,* Vol. XXXVI, No. 200, March, 1925, pp. 117-43.

[*After reviewing the arguments for and against Xenophon and Plato as accurate sources of Socratic philosophy, Rogers argues that Plato provides sufficient evidence that Socrates's teaching focused on the proposition that "virtue is knowledge." Rogers then examines the meaning and significance of this statement.*]

The beginnings of ethics as a branch of human science it has been customary to trace to Socrates; and while any point of departure is bound to be arbitrary to some extent, since written history does not record a time when men showed no tendency whatever to reflect on the problems of conduct, there are good reasons for the usual procedure. It is true, at least, that it was Socrates who inspired the first efforts to think systematically about the moral life in a form that had historical continuity and a pervading influence upon all subsequent speculation.

Unfortunately, however, when we come to settle accounts with the available evidence, the features of the historical Socrates and the character of the services which he performed to ethical thought are left exceedingly uncertain and obscure. There is an abundance of testimony such as it is; only the testimony does not hang together. Our two main authorities are Xenophon and Plato; and a colorless description may indeed be framed on which the two agree. It is safe to take for granted that Socrates was a man who exerted a large influence upon the life of his day through notable personal qualities; that he was conspicuously self-controlled and temperate in character, and fearless in his speech and conduct; that he devoted himself not to politics but to private conversation and debate, in which he showed a keen and powerful mind, and a moral insight, that attracted the younger men in particular; and that it was problems of conduct that interested him rather than the scientific speculations that hitherto had chiefly engaged Greek thinkers. But when any attempt is made to clothe with flesh and blood these very general and abstract statements, it becomes at once apparent that, as concrete personalities, the Socrates of Plato and the Socrates of Xenophon are very far apart. Most readers have, or think they have, a clear and fairly consistent picture of the man. But the picture comes from Plato, whose gifts as an artist have fixed what probably will always be in the popular mind the Socratic type; and if Plato has created what to any appreciable extent is a fancy portrait, a question at once arises about our right to accept any features of this portrait in particular. Accordingly it becomes quite necessary to start with an attempt to evaluate the main sources from which our knowledge of Socrates is derived.

No one would be inclined to dispute that, of the two, Plato is the more capable witness if only we can rely upon his good faith. He was better acquainted with Socrates personally and with Socrates' most intimate friends; and he was far and away the more competent philosophical mind. Nevertheless it has been Xenophon's testimony that the majority of modern scholars have preferred. Few of them, indeed, have been thoroughgoing in this preference; they have borrowed traits from Plato whenever it has suited their convenience, without any too great a regard for consistency at times. But so far at any rate as Socrates' peculiar contribution to ethics is concerned—if in this form it can still be called a contribution—Xenophon rather than Plato has been taken as the more reliable witness.

The reason for this preference in general—apart from a belief that it is borne out by the very scanty evidence that Aristotle supplies—is the fact that Plato is felt to be quite capable of creating the character of Socrates out of whole cloth; and, if we do thus take the Platonic Socrates as a figure so highly idealized as to become to all intents and purposes a character of fiction, the discrepancies will of course have found a solution. It is the easier to suppose this in that everybody admits that Plato's dialogues cannot by any chance be regarded as literal reports, but are, to some extent at least, artistic constructions; and in the later dialogues, at any rate, he unquestionably does attribute things to Socrates that go beyond all historical probability. And along with this goes the less legitimate reason that critics have plainly often been overimpressed by the matter-of-factness of Xenophon's account, and have assumed too readily that, as between commonplaceness and artistic distinction, the former is more likely to be closer to the facts.

There seems, however, no apparent reason why a spirit of caution should be abandoned when we pass from Plato to Xenophon. To begin with, if Plato is an artist, Xenophon is confessedly an apologist. It is not historical truth at which he is aiming first of all. He is an advocate, concerned to clear the name of Socrates of the charge of being an irreligious and immoral influence in the state; and, with a pious purpose such as this, a writer not only is not bound to be overscrupulous about strict accuracy, but is really under obligations to tidy up his material somewhat. And, as a matter of fact, it is difficult to see how one is to escape the conclusion that Xenophon, no more than Plato, can be trusted for bringing us into contact with the actual words that Socrates uttered. That he had reminiscences to draw upon is probable. But that he should have been able to report with anything like literalness the many long speeches which he retails is in the nature of things altogether unlikely, especially when we remember that it was a recognized convention for historical writers to put speeches into the mouths of their characters.

It is worth noting that there are two distinct methods which Xenophon adopts. On the one hand, there are brief sayings of Socrates, brief historical anecdotes, and brief statements by Xenophon himself that Socrates held such and such views. Here there is on the whole no sufficient ground for denying that Xenophon often had, or supposed he had, something like distinct recollections to go upon, especially since some of these more casual utterances have a pith and pungency that seem to bring us into contact with a real personage.

But, along with these, there are also numerous more elaborate conversations which every reasonable consideration goes to show were framed by Xenophon himself to illustrate or enforce the conception of Socrates and his teaching which he believed himself justified in holding. Not only are these conversations too long and detailed to be vouched for by memory, but they are almost invariably lacking in intellectual distinction; the reasoning is confused and sometimes puerile, and the conclusions for the most part painfully commonplace. It is possible in some cases that the conversation is based on fact. It may very well, for example, have been within Xenophon's knowledge that Socrates had composed a quarrel between two brothers; and a few anecdotes, like that of his advice to Aristarchus, have a rather convincing ring. But that the actual words attributed to him are anywhere more than a natural attempt to dramatize the incident is inherently unlikely. And in other cases this embroidering and dramatizing of the somewhat meagre details of Xenophon's knowledge probably extends to the entire conversation; indeed, Xenophon at times almost says as much when he passes from brief and summary statements to inferences from these, or to an attempt at their concrete illustration.[1] That the name of Euthydemus, in particular, represents a literary device rather than a source of genuine reminiscences, seems almost certain. This is plainly evident in the chapter where Socrates, in a most un-Socratic way, defines for his benefit a number of ethical terms;[2] and the manner in which the conversations with him—the longest one taking place with no witnesses present—form a crude sort of plot, wherein the young man's aloofness and self-conceit is converted into a spirit of humble discipleship suited to the further reception of Socratic teachings, is much more suggestive of fiction than of fact.

While it is not necessary to suppose, then, that Xenophon's account of Socrates is intentionally misleading, or that he has no first-hand knowledge on which to base his *apologia,* the habit of quoting uncritically as evidence any statement that he happens to ascribe to Socrates is a most unfortunate one; and we cannot safely use him as a standard by which to condemn Plato whenever Plato's testimony disagrees. On the whole, the *a priori* probability lies on the other side; the testimony of a close and competent disciple has naturally the right of way. Even the appeal to Plato's artistic interest really points in this direction rather than the other. The more we grant that Plato was artist enough to have created, had he chosen, a new and fictitious character under the historic name of Socrates, the less reason there is for thinking he would actually have done this; from a true artist in Plato's day it is a much more realistic treatment that we should naturally have looked for, and not one that has transformed its original almost beyond recognition. And, in this connection, there is another curious fact that deserves attention. There is in existence a third and independent portrait of Socrates in his earlier days—that drawn by Aristophanes in the *Clouds.* This third portrait, while it has significant points of contact with that of Plato, is totally irreconcilable with the Socrates of Xenophon. And if, accordingly, we insist on taking the latter as a standard, we must suppose that Aristophanes also, wishing to present a notable Athenian character on the stage, first altered the character so completely that little but the name was left to identify it to his audience. That two such consummate artists as Aristophanes and Plato should both have adopted so unusual a method in dealing with the same contemporary, is to strain the probabilities too far.

In turning now to a closer consideration of the facts at our disposal, we are fortunately in a position to be reasonably confident of a starting point. There is a consensus of evidence that Socrates' teaching centered about the fundamental proposition that *virtue is knowledge,* along with the related claim that the virtues are all in essence one, and that no man does wrong voluntarily, but only through ignorance. Just what interpretation these general statements are to bear, however, is another and more difficult matter. And any interpretation must be an arbitrary one until some background is provided in the shape of an estimate of Socrates' intellectual characteristics and interests.

There are certain features in the intellectual portrait of Socrates which, as a matter of fact, nearly everyone accepts as historical; though it is seldom clearly recognized how almost exclusively it is to Plato, rather than to Xenophon, that the picture is due. On the very lowest terms, this Platonic Socrates stands out as a man in whom, against a background of strong moral convictions, there plays a quick, ironical, penetrating, sceptical intellect, always on the alert for absurdities and ready to track them down wherever they may lead; and a man who, moreover, directs this same irony against himself as well, and, far from professing to be a source of wisdom, neglects no opportunity of insisting that he knows nothing whatever except his own lack of knowledge, and that his office is simply that of midwife in assisting at the birth of thoughts in other men.

If we take seriously the outstanding features here—and they appear not only in the discussions in which Socrates is depicted as engaging, but, what is more important, in the outright statements where there is most reason to suppose that Plato intends, if anywhere, to tell the truth—we are led to certain conclusions which are not always kept sufficiently in mind. In this light Socrates reveals himself not as first of all an ethical theorist aiming at a scientific definition of the moral concepts, but as a reformer of a peculiar sort. We are overlooking the essential point in Plato, if we fail to keep well in the foreground the explicit assertion that, following the incident of the oracle at Delphi, Socrates conceived of his life as devoted to a special task in the service of the God and of the state. This service was, to awaken the citizens of Athens to the need of a real examination of the ends and ideals they supposed themselves to be accepting, by convincing them that they were by no means the wise and superior persons they were accustomed to assume, and by securing thus a sound starting point for the growth of true wisdom. This particular moral purpose Socrates declares solemnly before his judges is the key for understanding his life.

There is perhaps no better way of conveying the point here than by an expressive modern phrase. Socrates was the first great expert in 'debunking.'[3] It was the absurdity of human pretensions that chiefly caught his eye in every class of society about him—statesman, artist, artisan—and he made it his lifework to puncture these pretensions, and force men to the uncongenial task of an honest self-analysis. It is to this that Plato makes Socrates himself ascribe the hostility that issued in his condemnation—a statement which, following the decision of the judges, can hardly be suspected of any levity or tendency to quibbling such as might perhaps be thought discoverable in the earlier part of his defence. It is no doubt true that more than personal pique lay back of the action of the judges—in particular, the feeling that Socrates was somehow really dangerous to the Athenian democracy. But there is no real contradiction here. One has only to look about him to realize that to turn the sceptical intelligence upon the solid conventional reputations and estimates of worth that impress the average man, and to encourage any tendency to think freely and for oneself, is to lay the ground for just the charges that assailed Socrates; one is an enemy of sound morality and of the Constitution, a danger to the immaturity of youth, and doubtless an atheist at heart. This spirit of ridicule directed toward pretences and unrealities represents a familiar human type; Socrates differs from the ordinary satirist only in having a more intense personal background of moral conviction. In attacking human futilities, it was not their intellectual absurdity alone that influenced him, but their inadequacy to his own strong sense of values; he was not only a satirist, that is, but a reformer. But he was a reformer, once more, who had no panacea of his own to exploit except the panacea of clear thinking; Socrates' professions of ignorance are an essential part of the picture, and such professions continue to the very end of his life.

It will not be disputed that what has just been pointed to enters into the account that Plato gives of Socrates; and so far it hangs together. Before trying to add to it, however, it will be desirable to turn back briefly to Xenophon. And if we were not in a position to bring this view of Socrates with us to Xenophon's pages, it is quite clear we never should have supposed ourselves to find it there. Xenophon's Socrates is a man with much moral earnestness, indeed; but he has an almost stodgy mind, for the most part without salt or humor. The tone of ironic self-depreciation is conspicuous by its absence. Verbally, it is true, Xenophon admits that Socrates did not set up as a teacher of virtue directly; but in point of fact he appears continually as a preacher and exhorter, who sermonizes even in his attempts at dialectic. Worst of all, he is a good deal of a prig, and his whole life is represented as an earnest attempt to transfer to his associates the seeds of moral excellence of which he is conscious in himself. The difference in the two accounts is shown instructively in the two versions of the famous reply of the oracle. In Plato the reply to Chærophon's question calls Socrates the wisest of men; and the narrative goes on to tell of Socrates' modest perplexity over this, and of how finally he found a clue to the God's meaning by deciding that it was only in the consciousness of his own ignorance that he excelled other men. But in Xenophon's obviously secondary account, Socrates is made preëminent in righteousness as well as in wisdom—probably Xenophon argues that this follows if knowledge and virtue are the same—and Socrates accepts the answer placidly as his due, and uses it to confound his judges. As a matter of fact, the Socratic ignorance has no place in Xenophon. There is extremely scant evidence of the sceptical caution which according to Plato characterized his intellect; Socrates has perfectly definite ideas about virtue and the good, ideas that in the main coincide with traditional morality and popular opinion. So, while Xenophon seems to be aware of the real nature of the Socratic method as it appears in Plato, he himself follows it only at a remote distance. The conversations are for the most part only in appearance heuristic. Socrates' intentions are obtrusively didactic; he starts with ready-made results in his mind to which he is all the time obviously leading up; it is only formally that his hearers do any thinking of their own, since thought is not necessary to answer 'yes' or 'no' to leading questions; and, in general, the show of logical rigor fails entirely to cover the poverty of thought.

It is difficult to see, then, up to this point, the slightest reason for preferring Xenophon to Plato, while at least one good reason exists for the opposite conclusion. Apart from the superior impression of reality which Plato's picture makes, it is necessary to account for the historical fact of the powerful influence which Socrates exerted over the young men of Athens, an influence continuing throughout a long lifetime, and affecting men of such very different types as Plato, Aristippus, Alcibiades, Euclid, Antisthenes. This influence is a mystery on the supposition that Socrates was the sort of person that Xenophon describes. And such a conclusion becomes still more insistent when consideration is given to a further aspect in which the two portraits differ.

A brief characterization of Socrates' temperament as Xenophon conceives of him, is attained with a fair degree of adequacy by classifying him as an empiricist in method, a utilitarian in theory, and, in general, a devotee of what is ordinarily called common sense. And it is perfectly true that there are elements not obviously inconsistent with this that find a place also in the dialogues of Plato. But especially in a group of dialogues from which comes a peculiarly vivid impression of Socrates as a human being—the *Meno,* the *Phædrus,* the *Phædo,* the *Symposium*—the distinctive feature of his natural temperament appears in an entirely different light. He reveals, in other words, the essential temper of the mystic. It is hardly possible to exaggerate the measure in which this mystical note dominates the picture which such dialogues present. It is not as a plodding empiricist, collecting instances and drawing inductive definitions, that Socrates here is shown to us, but as a passionate enthusiast for an ideal goodness and righteousness and beauty as they exist unchanging in a changeless world. Of such eternal verties this actual world contains only faint and imperfect copies; our knowledge of them comes, accordingly, not from sense particulars, which only help suggest them, but from a vision of the realities themselves which we have had in a former and better existence unincumbered by the body. To reattain this vision is the end of all philosophy; for philosophy is the one method of satisfying fully that love for the beautiful and the good which is the central fact of human nature, and the guiding motive of all genuine wisdom and attainment. And it is only the mystic who is the true philosopher.[4] Are we to regard this as simply a literary expression of a phase of Plato's own earlier development, or is it to be taken as a true portrait?

It is worth while to return here for a moment to the question of inherent probability. It does not seem likely that most of those who take the traditional view have ever stopped to realize clearly what they are attributing to Plato. If anything is certain, it is that Plato genuinely revered his master, and believed himself to have received from him the impetus to the philosophic life. But is it credible that a disciple should have chosen to present to the world a figure purporting to be that of Socrates, when he himself knew, and his readers knew, that this was very largely a mask covering his own features? It is understandable that he might have attributed opinions to Socrates that went somewhat beyond his actual teachings, within certain limits presently to be noted; and as a matter of fact he did do this pretty clearly. But that he should have made these quite inconsistent with what he was aware that Socrates had really taught, and should even have chosen the sacred moments that preceded his master's martyrdom for exploiting his own contrary views, is very difficult to believe; and especially so when we note again the fact that it involves altering, not Socrates' theoretical opinions merely, but his whole concrete character as well. Surely this is the only instance on record where a pupil has conceived that he is doing honor to a beloved teacher by deliberately representing him to the world as almost the opposite sort of man from what he really was. If Socrates was not a mystic, this is just what Plato has done; and if he was a mystic, it becomes totally impossible to accept Xenophon's portrait. On the other hand, there is no great trouble in accounting for the absence of this trait in Xenophon, since Xenophon is the sort of man who could not possibly have understood the mystic temperament.

And to this may be added once more the point already noticed—that the procedure attributed to Plato is bad art as well. In the *Symposium,* for example, there is a remarkable portrait of the man Socrates, with his unique mixture of homely realism and of mystical enthusiasm; and the *Symposium* is commonly regarded as ranking among the very best of Plato's dialogues as a work of art. Now no one has ever suggested that the other characters of the dialogue are not intended to hit off their prototypes; but on the traditional view we are forced to believe that in the midst of his artistic realism, Plato intentionally introduces a discordant note by making his central figure talk in a way entirely out of character. His artistic conscience must have forbidden this had there been no other reason against it.

And there are a number of more or less well established facts that corroborate this reasoning. To begin with, the unquestioned fact of Socrates' historical influence, which Xenophon fails wholly to explain, is no longer a mystery, even apart from any further and more strictly philosophical traits that may be added to the picture. The multiform nature of this influence points unmistakably to a unique personality, with something more to recommend it to the most brilliant representatives of one of the most brilliant of historic epochs than an impressive moral character, and a stout defence of customary morality against his fellow empiricists the Sophists. It is adequately accounted for by that rare combination, which Plato shows us, of logical acuteness and a detached intellect with a wide human interest and sympathy, of an effortless superiority to all the sensual passions with a freedom from ascetic harshness or moral snobbery, and, in particular, of a clear-eyed and ironic appraisal of human life and human nature, and a chronic incapacity for its common idealistic glorification,[5] with an unclouded conviction of the reality of those standards of which actual life falls so far short, and a mystical enthusiasm for their eternal beauty and perfection.

And the point of this is particularly apparent in the case of Plato himself. Between the empiricist and utilitarian, and the rationalist and idealist, there has always been a spiritual incompatibility which nothing seems to bridge. And accordingly we should have to explain the curious fact that the influence of one of the first of the empiricists shows itself, not among the empiricists themselves, but in connection with a man of an entirely different intellectual temperament, who is constantly showing his dislike and contempt for doctrines with which the teacher he continues to reverence is supposed to have been identified.

And there is other and more detailed evidence to aid in judging the probabilities here. We know that Plato was an artist fully capable of entering into very diverse types of mind, among them the mystical type. But we also know pretty clearly the sort of mind that Plato himself possessed, since we have a large group of later dialogues in which artistic creation has given place to a primary interest in philosophic speculation. And the more these dialogues are examined, the more evident it is that Plato was himself not in any proper sense a mystic, but a rationalist of a somewhat pronounced type. Of course it is possible to suppose that, when he passes from the *Symposium* and the *Phœdo* to his later writings, he is holding his deeper beliefs in abeyance; or that mysticism represents an earlier phase which later he outgrew. But either supposition will present serious difficulties to one who has followed in any detail the workings of Plato's mind in the dialogues that are most unquestionably self-revealing, as well as in the evidence supplied by the reports of his disciple Aristotle, and by the history of the early Academy. It is far easier to believe that in the earlier portrait of Socrates Plato is really doing what he pretends to be doing—depicting a mind which in essential ways is temperamentally different from what we know to have been his own.

Of Socrates, on the contrary, we have strong reason to accept as true the attribution of a natural leaning toward mysticism. His trances, the divine voice in which he placed implicit reliance, and to which no purely matter-of-fact explanation does anything like justice, his pious regard for the revelation of the God in dreams and oracles, all point to a temperament far removed from that of his eminent disciple. So too the interest he is represented as taking in the not altogether reputable Orphic mysteries, goes a good deal more naturally with Socrates' character than it does with that of the more fastidious and aristocratic Plato, who indeed elsewhere expresses an opinion of them by no means flattering. And also we have independent testimony here that is conclusive; for some of Aristophanes' best jokes would have been absolutely without point if Socrates' connection with the mysteries had not been notorious in Athens.

But before considering the bearing which this will have on the interpretation of Socrates' ethical teaching, it will first be necessary to turn to another matter of fundamental importance. For we are now in a position to say something about the much disputed question of the relation of Socrates to the 'theory of Ideas.' In attributing to him the mystical vision of an absolute beauty and goodness, we are already in contact with the essence of the Ideal theory as it appears in the earlier dialogues. There is very slight plausibility to the older view that a belief in Ideas originated in the first instance in a process of objectifying what started out as mere conceptual definitions. It is only by a misconception, to begin with, that Socrates' 'method' can be said to be inductive in the modern sense; and there is a shorter and much more direct way in which a belief in Ideas can be accounted for. In the presence of any universally valid truth or notion in which it has a tendency to believe, especially if this possesses an emotional appeal as well, realism is the normal and indeed almost the necessary attitude of the human mind. Accordingly Plato always assumes quite as a matter of course that every man of real intelligence must needs recognize that equality and beauty and justice are objective realities, infinitely more real indeed than the fleeting particulars in which they find expression. Nothing, so Simmias is made to say, is more certain than that the beautiful and the good have a most real existence. The theory that the 'form' is simply a formula created by the human mind, Plato barely mentions, only to dismiss it casually with an argument in which the self-evidence of the contrary view reappears as a basic assumption.

There are two cases in particular where this assumption is especially easy and natural. These are the concepts of mathematics on the one hand, and of ethics on the other; and it is just here that the earlier emphasis of the Ideal theory is placed. Even the thoroughgoing empiricist finds it difficult to convince himself that the truths of arithmetic and geometry are nothing more than subjective points of view; and the testimony of Aristophanes as well as of Plato goes to show that sometime in his career Socrates had been influenced by the number philosophy of the Pythagoreans. And in the field of ethics, in particular, the reasons for the ordinary man are even more compelling. No one with intense moral convictions can without a wrenching of his natural bias look upon moral concepts in any other than a realistic and objective way. Justice stands naturally to him not as a generalized notion merely, gathered from acts of a particular empirical sort; it is an eternal and absolute value, which is only partially exhausted in the multitude of actual deeds of justice with which experience is familiar, and which is adequately realized not even in the most perfect of them. And therewith the search for a true definition comes almost inevitably to be, to the realistic mind, the search for a perfect justice suggested in particular just acts but not contained in them; and it is thence only a step to the speculative conclusion that pure justice has some sort of absolute existence—or our ethical values are jeopardized—in a world that cannot be identified with the shifting world of everyday experience.

It may reasonably be assumed, then, that the starting point of what issued in the historic theory of Ideas is to be looked for, not in any process of promoting human concepts or definitions to a higher realm—concepts as such carry no emotional appeal to explain the Socratic fervor—but in an immediate feeling for the significance and objective validity of norms or standards; on the one hand the intellectual standards that govern rigorous and scientific thinking, and on the other standards of objective value. On the former alternative it would be hard to understand, for example, why Plato makes the youthful Socrates express hesitation about admitting the reality of such Ideas as that of man, though he is perfectly assured of the reality of goodness; for as a concept nothing could be more typical than man. But the attitude attributed to Socrates is easy to explain if one has started with the universality of value standards, and then finds himself logically driven to raise a question about the status of other universals as well. In this way we understand, too, how the ideal realm comes to be characterized almost indiscriminately as one of truth, of goodness, and of beauty. Intellectual and moral values, the two main sides of Socrates' interest, it is nearly always impossible for the real enthusiast to disentangle; while both alike, just because they are values, have to contemplation a further emotional significance which translates them into beauty.

But now there is one further question that needs an answer before we are at liberty to turn to the actual form of Socrates' ethical teaching. Even supposing Socrates to have been a mystic, and to have felt toward moral values in a way that theory might easily translate into a belief in the existence of ideal Forms, how are we to tell where Socrates leaves off and Plato begins, in view of the undoubted fact that there are some things at any rate in the dialogues that cannot easily be regarded as historical? It may be that this is an insurmountable difficulty, and that the dividing line is one which it is impossible to point out. Nevertheless there are certain principles here that possess some plausibility, and that seem to render possible a measure of assurance.

The first of these helps at least to set a lower limit. The argument that Plato is not likely to have lent himself to an essential misrepresentation of his predecessor in view of his own personal relations to him cannot, as has been said, mean that he has been anything like a literal historian of Socrates' views. He may have, and undoubtedly he has, put words in Socrates' mouth which Socrates could not have uttered. But the argument, if valid at all, carries one definite implication. If Plato is restrained by any sense of historical reality, then while it is conceivable that he might hold himself justified at times in attributing what actually were his own thoughts to Socrates, this would only be under certain conditions—in case, that is, he believed that they were immediately implied in things that Socrates really did teach. The line would be no hard and fast one. But nevertheless it would exist; and as the theoretical deductions got farther and farther from their starting point we should expect to find, as we do find, a growing hesitation in making Socrates explicitly responsible for them, until at last Socrates ceases to be the mouthpiece of the Platonic speculations, and is replaced by the hazy figure of Parmenides or an Athenian Stranger.

It follows, then, that while we can be tolerably assured that Socrates really held that mystical belief in an absolute good which in logical language readily translates itself into a realism of universals, we ought perhaps to hesitate a little before concluding that of necessity such an inference was actually drawn by him. There is no inherent improbability that it was so drawn. But also by itself the supposition is quite possible that Plato was the first to call attention to it; for there would be no impiety, and no failure in artistic truth, if he were merely uncovering assumptions he saw to be implicit in his master's teaching. Which alternative is to be preferred depends upon the presence or absence of further evidence.

In considering this evidence, we may revert first to a point which has been already mentioned, and which suggests a second and more positive principle. In a mere series of expanding logical deductions there is no compelling reason for stopping at one point rather than another. But a characteristic personality or temperamental point of view supplies a more promising standard. It is conceivable, perhaps, that Plato's was so complex a character as to combine both the mystic and the scientific rationalist, in different contemporaneous compartments or as different phases of development. But it is at least equally reasonable to work on the hypothesis that he is portraying in Socrates a personality more or less different from his own. And in that case, since the maturer Plato at any rate is pretty well known to us, it is not hopeless to expect that, by using the two concrete types as a touchstone, we may be in a position to reach conclusions about certain matters of detail, provided any difference of doctrine is to be detected in the dialogues at all comparable to these differences of character. And as a matter of fact such a difference can be readily pointed out.

It has not always been sufficiently emphasized that the doctrine of Ideas assumes two fairly distinct and characteristic forms. In what roughly may be classed as the earlier and less metaphysical of two main groups of Plato's dialogues—and not including the *Republic*—the attitude adopted toward the Forms is primarily an ethical one; and, furthermore, it represents an interest in terms not of speculative ethics, but of ethics as a discipline or way of life. Here, as has appeared already, Socrates is shown as one whose final quest is that mystical vision of the absolute truth which is also absolute goodness and absolute beauty. For this attitude the notion of holiness is inextricably intermingled with that of contemplative blessedness. Holiness is for the sake of that immortality which mortal nature craves,[6] which gets partial expression in the desire for fame or children,[7] but which is only fully realized as all the trivialities of this earthly life are cast aside, and the soul comes into the presence of what is really and eternally true. Philosophy is the preparation for this perfect vision. Through it the soul undergoes a process of purgation from sensual delights which estrange it from the Good. But complete attainment can only come when death has released it wholly from the body, and it has come pure and blameless to the heavenly regions after a life of devotion to the disinterested search for truth.

Unless it is assumed, then, that almost any combination of temperaments is possible in a man of genius, we are in possession of a standard, any large deviation from which will require explanation. Now the fact is that, beginning with the *Republic* in particular, we do find subtle but important changes in the intellectual portrait of Socrates. On the surface there is still very much in common; but underneath there has been a significant shift of emphasis.

The underlying character of this change may be expressed by saying that the goal of philosophy has ceased to be mystic vision, and has become instead rational understanding. Since the two may so readily be expressed in the same verbal terms, it is easy to overlook the difference; but the difference is real nevertheless. A comparison of the metaphor of the winged horses with the famous analogy of the Cave will help to bring out the divergence. In the earlier presentations, it is almost without exception the ethical interest that is uppermost in Plato's description of the soul and its relation to the body. It is the sensual, not the sensible, that clogs the soul and drags it downward; the life of sense cuts us off from the vision of the Good because our passions and pleasures engross the attention, and turn it away from eternal objects to the trivialities of this passing world. But from the *Republic* onward the emphasis has passed from ethics to metaphysics. The great problem now becomes how knowledge of these eternal verities is possible. And the source of our human imperfection changes accordingly from pleasure, to sense perception, and the metaphysically unreal character of perceptual objects.

The more it is examined, the more far-reaching will the influence of this shifting of interest from ethics to epistemology appear to be. The life of intellect ceases to be a mystical purification for another and higher world, and scientific knowledge becomes an end in itself. A more or less systematic realm of Ideas, in which logical and mathematical concepts grow increasingly prominent, displaces those simple ideas of goodness and beauty whose very lack of sharp definition has helped to suggest the supreme values of existence; reason turns aside from the goal of contemplative blessedness and becomes the professional thinker's instrument for resolving logical contradictions; and the purgation of the mysteries is rationalized into the removing of man's ignorance, or education.[8] A striking illustration of this change is furnished by a feature common to the two pictures—the exaltation of the philosophic life. In the earlier Socrates, this means a life freed from the fetters of the body, and attainable even here and now in the occasional moments of mystical experience, though only completely attainable in another form of existence when the body has been left behind. But in its later expressions the idea of the philosophic life assumes a quite different form; as it appeals to Plato himself, it is the life of pure scientific activity, released from the obligation to return to the Cave and take one's part in the work of the state.[9] But a life apart from the body is altogether different from a life apart from the world of politics and business; and it is impossible to think of Socrates the talker, with his divine mission to stir the sluggish minds of his fellow citizens, and his reluctance to get away from the busy life of men even for a country walk, as setting his heart upon the quiet and remoteness of the scholar's life.

And there are various other things that bear this out. For Plato the Ideas, since they stand for scientific and dialectic truth, naturally will be open only to the elect few; the rest of the world can never be expected to believe in anything absolute.[10] As Socrates views it, on the other hand, the recognition of Ideas is due not to metaphysical competence but to the vision of them in another existence; they may be uncovered by questioning in the most unpromising material; and in general they are the property of human nature rather than of a professional class of philosophers. This exaltation of the philosopher is throughout characteristic of the later treatment. With Socrates it is philosophy alone that counts—the purifying power of the vision of truth—and it is hardly credible that he would not have found in the notion of a professional class of dialectitians, if it had occurred to him, the same source of ironical amusement that he found in the professional scientists and the professional Sophists. It also is worth noticing that the attitude of the earlier Socrates toward non-intellectual processes is more what we should expect from a mystic than Plato's rather harsh and unsympathetic treatment. It is true that Socrates finds the poets, as well as the politicians and the artisans, unable to give a clear account of their meaning; but he does not single them out for condemnation, or adopt that hostility towards the poet's art to which Plato's logic led him in defiance of his instincts. True poetry is God conversing with us,[11] and is no more to be deprecated than are the oracles which also come by inspiration rather than by reason, but which on that very account are to be preferred to the human wisdom that has little or no value.[12] Inspiration naturally will play in the mystic's life a rôle that is absent in the rationalist's. And so we find Socrates glorifying a divine madness as the special gift of Heaven and the source of the chiefest blessings among men;[13] while in his own conduct dreams and divination have an importance which they obviously never had for Plato.

We are not without fairly strong reasons for supposing, then, that Plato himself supplies a test by which, if we do not attempt to go too much into detail, we may separate the real Socrates and his teachings from the additions which Plato was led to make as his own independent thinking revealed what seemed to him the necessary implications of Socrates' standpoint. Whenever the Socrates of the dialogues is standing for an ethical idealism in terms of the mystical pursuit of those vague but preëminently real values which the terms goodness and beauty suggest, we apparently have no sound reason for refusing to believe that Plato is intending to present to us the actual historical outlines of his master; when, on the other hand, the interest of the dialogues turns to a logical analysis of the way in which the ideal is known, and to the relation between sense perception and the higher truth, the strong probability is that we are listening to Plato rather than to Socrates. And to this the external testimony also points; for Aristotle not only leaves a strong impression that Socrates' intellectual interests stopped with ethics, but he states explicitly that the theory of sensible reality belongs to Plato.

This will not mean that Socrates had no theory at all about the way we know Ideas. As a matter of fact there is weighty evidence that he did hold such a theory.

The doctrine of knowledge as recollection is assigned to Socrates so unequivocally and emphatically by Plato, as one which he was notoriously fond of setting forth, that Plato's veracity would seem almost to be involved. But meanwhile the theory of recollection itself goes to enforce the distinction that has just been drawn. For this is a speculation on an entirely different level from that analysis of knowledge as scientific method in which the real Plato is interested; and indeed it drops out of sight as soon as this interest appears.[14] It is a mystical solution, based upon the Pythagorean notion of transmigration rather than on logical analysis; it still remains subsidiary, therefore, to the ethical significance which this doctrine has for Socrates; and sensible reality enters into the situation not as a problem to be solved, but simply as it performs the positive service of suggesting to our minds the ideal pattern which has lapsed from memory.

If we are justified, then, in adopting the conclusions just set forth, we are now ready to return to the main problem, and ask what light these throw, if any, upon the doctrine that virtue is knowledge, together with its various corollaries.

There is one simple meaning attaching to the claim that virtue is knowledge, which is relatively beyond dispute. Not only in Xenophon, but in Plato as well, Socrates is frequently made to argue that only intelligence insures true happiness, that the things men call good are in reality only good when in possession of the wise man rather than the fool, that the unexamined life which takes the ends of conduct for granted without understanding them is hardly worth the living[15]; and such proofs that virtue and happiness are impossible without knowledge are then not infrequently converted directly into the proposition that they *are* knowledge. That Socrates argued thus we have no reason to doubt; and if we stop here, therefore, we should have to say that his epoch-making doctrine consisted of nothing more than a set of rather obvious practical considerations plus a logical fallacy. The best we could do would be to credit to Socrates the general insistence that problems of conduct be examined in the light of reason; though as he was certainly not the first to realize this, it does not permit us to rank his originality very high.

But it is impossible to do justice to Socrates' influence without recognizing that two distinct strains run through his utterances, whose combination constitutes indeed his uniqueness as a teacher. As Alcibiades tells us in the *Symposium,* on the surface his words were apt to seem matter-of-fact and homely, even ridiculously so; it is only as one penetrates beneath that there flashes out, for one who has the eyes to see, a soul-stirring beauty which calls forth a response from all that is most divine in his hearers. It follows that we are not on safe ground if we take the easiest and most commonplace interpretation as most adequate to Socrates' full meaning. And even apart from the fact that the shrewd and homely traits of common sense in Socrates' nature may lead us to overlook the other and more distinctive side, it is clear from Plato, who certainly is the more adequate reporter here, that allowance has always to be made for the requirements of Socrates' method of interrogation. For, if it is the essence of this method to adopt as its starting point some proposition on which his interlocutor is prepared to agree, then in proportion to the interest he takes in showing up human ignorance will be the likelihood that the assumptions on which the discussion rests fall short of Socrates' own beliefs.

And there is to be found in Plato himself another interpretation of the Socratic dictum. In the *Phædo,* in particular, virtue is made definitely to stand for something higher than civic or moral excellence with its background of utilitarian caution.[16] It is not prudence or practical intelligence, but passion and insight—that vision of eternal goodness which constitutes the highest goal of human nature. Now such a clue will render the doctrine that virtue is knowledge not only more significant, but more intelligible as well. If goodness is not utility, but an absolute and emotion-stirring value, it is possible to see how without a logical fallacy knowledge should come to be regarded, not as a *means* to happiness or virtue, but as virtue itself. The essence of virtue is the response of human nature to the best and highest; it is the insight which is at once knowledge and emotional love.

And this explains the related doctrine that evil is always due to ignorance in a way much more convincing than does the utilitarian consideration—though this too was doubtless used by Socrates in arguing with the worldling—that no one will voluntarily do that which is to his own ultimate hurt. If the knowledge of the Good is to be identified with the mystic fervor of insight, it is easy to see how, for Socrates, it would appear incredible that conduct should not follow inevitably from the perception of that which stirs our immediate love and reverence; if virtuous conduct does not follow, it must be because this vision of the real beauty of righteousness is lacking. It explains, again, why the virtues are not many but one. The moral life is not made up of separate compartments, but is a unity of insight; and from such a vision of things as they truly are all the virtues alike will flow. And it supplies, finally, a clue to Socrates' interminable discussions about the teachability of virtue. If virtue is knowledge, it must in some sense be capable of being taught; but where are we to look to find its teachers? Plainly they do not exist; and yet since virtue itself undoubtedly exists, they ought to be discoverable if virtue is only brought about by teaching. And so long as we mean by teaching what the Sophists meant—professional instruction—Socrates indicates no way out of the dilemma.

But for himself the difficulty is not really there; if the true teacher is he who arouses the dormant insight which the mind already possesses—if to be taught, that is, is the same thing as to remember[17]—we can understand how virtue can still be knowledge, even though it cannot be produced by the imparting of information or by exhortation. It can be elicited, if not strictly taught; and it is Socrates' whole mission to elicit it.

And this leads to one further point that at first might seem to raise a difficulty. Socrates' chief merit has often been taken to be that he was the originator of a new scientific method in the field of ethics—the method of logical definition; and he is conceived as having spent his life in an endeavor to define the virtues and the nature of the good. And it is true that Aristotle, and even Plato at times, both tend to convey such an impression. But their own technical interest in scientific methodology is sufficient to account for this without its being necessary to assume anything more than that they thought themselves to have discovered, in Socrates' way of arguing, something which when made explicit could be utilized by the philosopher.

And, as a matter of fact, the internal evidence for the common view is singularly weak. Concretely, Socrates' dialectic appears as incidental to his professed ethical purpose; it is his divine mission as a gadfly of the state that justifies his interest in it, and not the technical and sophisticated concern of the scientist for method. And it is even doubtful whether he could really have cared very much for the results of method, in the form of accurate definitions. When one stops to think about it, it certainly must seem a little strange that, if Socrates had made it his main business to define the virtues, he should not have had some results to show at the close of a life extended beyond the usual period; certainly the rather pitiful results that Xenophon reports would not have been beyond him. But to the end he continues to insist on his own lack of knowledge, and to assign to dialectic a negative rather than a positive value. And this is far more understandable if the demand for definitions was primarily a tool for exposing ignorance, than if it was the quest for a scientific terminology.

It is quite true that a call for clear thinking is at the bottom of Socrates' whole activity. But it is to a clarification of the ends of conduct, and of men's confused ideas about what is really good and worthy, that his dialectic really tends, rather than to a technique of scientific concepts. Indeed this is just what gives Socrates a real claim to originality. The working method of the ethical life is not induction, in the sense that it gets at human ends by generalizing past facts and deeds. It is precisely a matter of determining what is genuinely worth while. And for this we have to presuppose, just as Socrates did, the existence in each man of standards of value which are ultimate, but which also at the start are vague and muddled, so that they have to be cleared up and verified by an analysis of their nature and their consequences. In any case it is only on this showing that we have a natural explanation of the apparent paucity of results in Socrates' positive teaching. If his aim was definition, then he was a failure, and a rather unaccountable failure. But if his real purpose was to get men to discover in their own experience the nature of their ultimate standards of worth, or, in the language of the mystic, to attain to the vision of absolute goodness and beauty, the failure to arrive at technical concepts is a matter of no consequence. An ostentatious proclamation of an inability to reach knowledge is not unnatural in the mystic, and does not at all touch the certainty of his immediate vision of the good; it is hardly in place in the professed scientist and logician.

Socrates' interest lies, then, in the soul and not in logic. But because the soul's destiny is a vision of the good, it is in knowledge that its virtue may be said to lie; while also knowledge of a lower grade is needed, in the form of clear logical analysis and of the utilitarian judgments of 'good horse sense,' to help restore the dim visions that we bring with us into the world, and that have been overlaid by unthinking custom and by an indulgence of the bodily passions. In so far as Xenophon misses this, he fails to give us a true picture. At the same time Xenophon's testimony does not need to be entirely discarded, and it is usually possible to pick out with some measure of confidence the modicum of truth which it contains.

The case that is most important for the history of ethical theory has to do with Socrates' attitude toward pleasure. Xenophon tells us in no uncertain terms that Socrates was, so far as theory goes, what nowadays would be called a hedonistic utilitarian; he taught that utility is what determines not only the goodness of an act, but even the beauty of an object. On the other hand this is an opinion obviously difficult to reconcile with a mystical idealism. And, furthermore, there is abundant evidence, some of it from Xenophon himself, of a personal attitude on the part of Socrates which suggests a quite different conclusion. Certainly he is always represented as himself totally indifferent to pleasure or to worldly success; and Plato even makes him argue explicitly against the prudential conception of the virtues as only an inverted self-indulgence.

It might at first seem easier to set aside Xenophon's testimony, as out of harmony with better established evidence. But there are reasons against quite so drastic a course. Not only does the Platonic Socrates also occasionally use language not very dissimilar to Xenophon's, but it is scarcely credible that a school of professed hedonism should have sprung from Socrates' teaching had Aristippus not found in his words some apparent support. This same consideration, however, it has to be noticed, applies equally of course to another and quite opposed type of ethical doctrine that also claimed the authority of Socrates—the Cynicism of Antisthenes, with its contempt for pleasure. Accordingly the problem is to discover how three distinct and opposed ethical philosophies should have had their source in one man's teaching.

One conclusion follows pretty directly from the existence of the problem; and it bears out the conclusions already drawn as to the relatively non-technical character of Socrates' interest in philosophy. There is no reason to suppose that Socrates himself ever directly raised the question, 'Is pleasure the good'? Not only would the striking difference of opinion among his followers in that case be hard to account for, but it is difficult to see Socrates, the mystic, finding such a question worthy of discussion. And this granted, there are two or three considerations that go a certain way toward dispelling the impression of inconsistency.

First, there should be noticed the very distinctive nature of the personal attitude that is attributed to Socrates. It is not that he feels an ascetic hostility towards pleasure, as if there were something essentially evil about it. Socrates recommends the pleasures of self-control and moderation, the life of few wants and ready satisfaction; and he protests against the tendency of pleasure to seduce man from his true interests. But the point in both cases is the same; the case against pleasure is not its evil and sinister importance, but its insignificance. It occupies us with trivialities when we might be engaged with a vision of the absolute; it entails unnecessary anxieties and disproportionate effort for what in the end is not worth the trouble. And consequently we are not to give it an evil eminence; it is enough that we should refuse to let it dominate us. And this, the logical corollary of his doctrine, is just the attitude we are told that Socrates personally adopted. He did not practice asceticism; and on occasion he could drink his companions under the table. But he drank, not for the pleasure it gave him, but as an incident in the day's work; and he was just as well satisfied to go without.

It is obviously this side of Socrates' teaching and example that, by an exaggeration of emphasis, developed into the Cynicism of Antisthenes. Much less significant, as an aspect of Socrates' own thought, is the hedonism of Aristippus, even though it seems backed by Xenophon's testimony. This would be scarcely understandable, once more, if Socrates had thought pleasure important enough to go out of his way to define its relation to the good. But just because pleasure to Socrates was so emphatically not the good, it is possible to understand how he might have allowed himself to say things from which, taken by themselves, an impression of theoretic hedonism and utilitarianism might have been derived. Two things in particular explain this possibility. In the first place there is not the slightest reason to suppose that Socrates, any more than Plato, would have refused to identify man's destiny with happiness of some sort—the vision of the good is plainly the best and highest happiness—and since it is practically impossible always to use language in a way that makes a sharp distinction between happiness and pleasure, he may very well have talked at times in a manner open to misunderstanding by a literal-minded hearer, without straining at all his personal convictions. And to this is to be added the further fact, already commented on, that the nature of his method makes it necessary constantly to accept and argue on the premises of his interlocutor. And if in a discussion with Protagoras, he takes for granted popular judgments which he is aware that Protagoras will not dispute, only a total disregard of what we know about Socrates' habits can justify an unqualified assumption that he must have been expressing his personal opinions. Even Plato, whose views about pleasure are sufficiently clear, can talk like an ordinary hedonist when he is framing the preamble to a legal statute, intended to convince, not the philosopher, but the average citizen.[18]

The other outstanding feature of Xenophon's account—the disposition of Socrates to identify virtue in practice with a respectable acquiescence in existing law and custom—it is also not difficult to account for without accepting the emphasis that Xenophon gives it. That Socrates felt a genuine piety toward the state, as the mother and guardian of her children, would need no further evidence than the *Crito,* where he justifies his refusal to escape from prison at the expense of bringing discredit upon the lawful forms of government; but it is a far cry from the recognition that a virtuous man will not wantonly disregard his country's laws, to the claim that virtue consists mainly in conventionality and conformism. In all likelihood the traditional opinion is right in supposing that Socrates was not in harmony with the Sophistic tendency toward loosening the bonds of the customary morality. But this it may be reasonably conjectured was due less to a belief in its final value, than to a feeling, common to the mystic temperament, that no reform of conventions, aiming mostly as it does at greater liberty of individual conduct in this present world, is much worth troubling about when the true realm of value lies elsewhere, as well as to a sceptical distrust of the power of human reason to work sure-footedly at such a task.

Notes

[1] *Memorabilia,* III, 8, 8; IV, 2, 1; 5, 1; 6. 1.

[2] IV, 6.

[3] Cf. Alcibiades' remark, *Symposium,* 216.

[4] *Phado,* 69.

[5] *Symposium,* 198.

[6] *Meno,* 81.

[7] *Symposium,* 206 ff.

[8] *Sophist,* 231.

[9] *Theætetus,* 173-5. Cf. the *Republic* (Bk. VII) as interpreted by the account that follows of the content of philosophic education.

[10] *Republic,* 493-4.

[11] *Ion,* 534.

[12] *Apology,* 23.

[13] *Phædrus,* 244.

[14] Cf. *Philebus,* 34, where reminiscence is defined psychologically in a way that reverses what it meant for Socrates.

[15] Cf. *Laches,* 194; *Euthydemus,* 281; *Meno,* 88; *Apology,* 38.

[16] *Phædo,* 82-4.

[17] *Meno,* 87.

[18] *Laws,* 733-4.

Homer H. Dubs (essay date 1927)

SOURCE: "The Socratic Problem," in *The Philosophical Review,* Vol. XXXVI, No. 214, July 1927, pp. 287-306.

[*In the following essay, Dubs argues that, contrary to "the view commonly held," Plato's account of the character and philosophy of Socrates is "substantially correct." He concludes that, at the very least, Plato did not deliberately distort the historical Socrates's character or opinions.*]

The purpose of this paper is to present some considerations in support of the thesis that Plato's account of the character and philosophic opinions of Socrates is substantially correct, as against the view commonly held.

The usual interpretation of Socrates is based on scepticism of Plato's trustworthiness. In 1741, Brucker, sceptical of the accuracy of ancient writers, first refused to accept the unanimous opinion of antiquity as to the genuineness of Plato's account, and reasoned that Plato was a creative thinker, and so would naturally put his own original thoughts into the mouth of his master, Socrates; whereas Xenophon, just because he did not have any philosophic originality, would be more likely to preserve the historic Socrates. Therefore our knowledge of Socrates must be founded on Xenophon's account. This opinion gained the assent of Hegel and the Hegelians, and through their influence became accepted by the philosophic world. Schleiermacher proposed to add to Xenophon's testimony those elements from Plato's account which would be necessary to justify the picture of Plato. Zeller accepted that canon, and so there grew up the received interpretation of Socrates—that he was interested chiefly in ethics and conceptual definition, and certainly did *not* propound the theory of ideas.

The two chief foundations of this interpretation are the almost universal lack of a historic sense by writers of the ancient world, and the fact that Plato was undoubtedly an original thinker. When Xenophon wished to express his own views upon household management, land improvement, and agriculture, he put them into the mouth of Socrates. The picture of the man who was so little interested in the country that he never went out of the city of Athens except when compelled to do so, Socrates, teaching agriculture, was a little too much even for Xenophon, so he put most of his material into the form of a conversation related by Socrates, a literary form which had been adopted in some dialogues of Plato; but the fact that a work could be published which portrayed the city-loving Socrates relating a conversation on estate management twenty books long, shows how little sense of historic accuracy was possessed by people of the time. Since the author of the subtle and highly philosophic dialogues of Plato could have been no other than a great philosopher, and consequently a creative philosopher, it was also thought that, like Xenophon, he put his own opinions into the mouth of his master. And so the educated world has pretty generally accepted the theory that most of what Plato attributed to Socrates, especially the deeper philosophic views, are really views of Plato, and not of the historic Socrates at all.

But an argument such as the foregoing, which is based on general considerations only, may fail when applied to a particular case. It *might* be that Plato is an exception to the almost universal rule, and he *might* nevertheless be giving us a trustworthy account. Great men are always exceptional, and so we should not close our minds to this possibility. Socrates is generally credited with being the founder of the school of philosophy which includes Plato and Aristotle—the most influential philosophic movement the world has ever known. There is no case known where the founder of a great and original movement was himself a second- or third-rate thinker, whose historic importance is largely due to the fact that he attracted men who were much more brilliant and original than himself, to elaborate and develop the foundations which he himself laid. Yet that is the conclusion to which the received interpretation of Socrates is driven—that he was greatly inferior in philosophic ability to Plato, merely a second- or third-rate thinker, who was interested only in the 'practical' problems of philosophy, especially ethics and definition, and left the theoretical problems of metaphysics severely alone. How much more probable that the man who discovered the concept and founded the classic Greek philosophy should have himself been a great philosopher!

So we find that there are general probabilities on both sides of the question. It is indeed a most complex problem, and can best be compared, in its difficulty, with the problem of the authorship of the Pentateuch, and must be solved by like methods—the detailed consideration of verses and words, and the fitting of all into a harmonious whole. It is indeed a scientific, rather than a philosophic, problem. Since the author of this paper cannot claim to be an authority on Greek literature and language or Greek philosophy, he can only present a few considerations which have come to him as he has studied the works of Plato and Xenophon, and the interpretations of Professors Burnet and Taylor.

The received theory of the historic Socrates makes Xenophon the primary source for our knowledge of the man, and takes Plato only as a secondary source, in accordance with the dicta of Brucker, Hegel, and Schleiermacher. But how much reliance can we put upon Xenophon? He was not a philosopher. He had no interest in the theoretical problems of philosophy. A bluff general, he is at his best in the campaigns of the *Anabasis;* but when he attempts to portray a banquet, he only succeeds in giving a very ordinary conversation, which, had it not been for the historic characters portrayed, would not be worth preserving or reading. The *Cyropædia* shows that he had a taste for writing philosophical romance. Even in the *Memorabilia* it is impossible to believe that all of the conversations recorded there are genuinely historical. Who could suppose that while Socrates lectured his son on his duty to his mother, or when he urged Chærecrates to make up his quarrel with his brother, Xenophon was standing by, silent, treasuring up all that good advice in his memory? Again and again we meet with passages that sound suspiciously like the voice of the author of the other works of Xenophon. The first seven chapters of the third book are devoted to subjects in which Xenophon, the general, with his regimental interest in efficiency, was particularly interested. Ten passages are repeated from the *Cyropædia.* We have many other such indications that Xenophon is far from a trustworthy historian. Indeed, when we hear him imputing to Socrates the teaching that geometry should only be studied sufficiently to gain a knowledge of the principles of land measurement, and astronomy, to be able to discern the directions at night or to set the night watches, we seem to hear the voice of the practical and efficient general, Xenophon, especially when in the same passage he admits twice that Socrates was versed in exactly the purely theoretical portions of mathematics and astronomy which he said were worthless, and had attended lectures upon them.[1] We begin to suspect that the 'practical' man, Socrates, whom we have been inferring from the *Memorabilia,* is really Xenophon himself masquerading in the figure of his master!

Just how much actual contact Xenophon had with Socrates, we do not know. It was three years before the death of Socrates that he saw that teacher for the last time, when he left on the expedition of the immortal Ten Thousand. Xenophon was under thirty at the time. We know that he took the literary form of his dialogues from Plato, who invented the philosophic dialogue; the subjects of Xenophon's dialogues, the *Apology,* and probably also the *Banquet,* were taken from similar dialogues of Plato. Indeed there are surprisingly few facts of Socrates' life (as distinct from reports of his opinions) recorded by Xenophon, which he could not have gotten from the published writings of Plato. If we compare the writings of Xenophon with those of Plato, we find that exclusive of those things which are plainly the result of the working of imagination, there are very few statements about Socrates' life in Xenophon's writings, except those given by Plato. In fact Aristotle never quotes Xenophon, although he must certainly have known his writings. Xenophon is at best an unreliable witness to the historic Socrates, and his evidence may be almost entirely secondary, a distortion of the Platonic account.

It would be out of place here to discuss at length the result of the researches into the development of Plato's style as dating the different dialogues. From the importance which stylistic and linguistic considerations have assumed in the discussion of the Pentateuch, it is easy to see that such stylistic conclusions may have an important bearing upon our interpretation of Plato. If, for instance, it could be shown, from purely stylistic considerations, and quite independently of any presuppositions as to the development of Plato's thought, that the *Phaedo* was an earlier work, and was not his "last testament to his school," we should be very much more inclined to consider the teaching of the *Phaedo* as genuinely Socratic. That such may well be the case can be seen even by those ignorant of Greek. It is a well-known fact that the literary style and dramatic quality of some great writers have declined considerably with the approach of age. This was notably true in the case of Robert Browning. There are few poems written by him after the *Ring and the Book* which equal in literary quality those written earlier, although there is a gain in philosophic content. Plato died at the age of eighty-one, and the character of his literary style in his later years can be seen from a reading of the *Philebus,* which entirely lacks the subtle humor and dramatic quality of the earlier dialogues. But the *Phaedo,* not only in the description of the death of Socrates, but also in other passages, such as the passage on the dying swan of Apollo, ranks with Plato's best literary work, and is therefore not likely to have been composed in the same period when he wrote the *Philebus* and the *Laws,* but in his younger days, when his powers were at their height.

A more striking piece of evidence of the historicity of the Platonic Socrates is to be drawn from the character of Socrates himself. The *Protagoras* is generally conceded to be a 'Socratic' dialogue. It is in that dialogue that Alcibiades declares that Socrates exceeds all men in the power of grasping and pursuing an argument. Indeed there could be no better picture, than the one in that dialogue, of what the Chinese call the power to hold one subject through a thousand twists and turnings. And at the inconclusive end we are left with the impression that the Socrates who so pertinaciously pursued the argument and who showed such eagerness to continue the discussion, will certainly carry it further in his own mind. This impression we get from each of the inconclusive dialogues, such as the *Euthyphro*—that Socrates was a logical thinker who would pursue a problem as far as reason would carry it, and not stop in the middle of an inquiry.

When we turn to a consideration of the philosophy which Plato puts into Socrates' mouth, we find the same characteristic of logical coherence. If Socrates made any philosophic discovery at all, he at least discovered the concept. That is conceded to him by almost everyone. But the inquiry into concepts leads logically to the Socratic search for definitions. A definition is nothing more than an explicit statement of the content of a concept. And the Socratic practice of seeking for definitions led directly to the practice of the maieutic art. Socrates' way of discovering the definition of a concept was to question his hearers and lead them to express their own implicit convictions, much as in the *Meno* he led an ignorant slave lad to recognize what was the side of a square of twice the area of the original square. That this practice of spiritual midwifery was genuinely Socratic is shown by a passage in Aristophanes' *Clouds,* where the disciple tells Strepsiades that his loud knocking has caused the "miscarriage of a thought." But the maieutic art logically involves the doctrine of reminiscence. Whence could it be that different persons had the same content for their innermost conceptions? Either because they had had the same experiences or because these ideas were implicit in their souls. But this common content could not come from experience, since often they had never before thought of such matters, any more than the slave lad in the *Meno* had ever before heard of the term, the 'diagonal' of a square. But Socrates showed his audience that nevertheless the slave lad recognized the meaning of that concept, although he did not know the name for it. If these concepts are inherent in men, and not from experience, how could they come into human nature except in a previous existence, from which time they were unconsciously remembered? Even though for Socrates this doctrine of reminiscence might have been only a myth, and not literally true, he must certainly have thought that something like it was true. The maieutic method of eliciting conceptual definitions from different persons implies at the very least that these concepts are in some sense independent of the individual and so exist independently. This doctrine logically involves the preëxistence of these ideas. To be remembered from a former existence, the ideas must have existed in that former existence independently of individual human beings. So we are led to the notion of a realm of ideas, which realm is independent of human knowledge of them, and to the doctrine of two worlds—the world of preëxistent ideas and the changing world of experience—and to the theory of ideas with the worlds of Being and Becoming, knowledge and opinion, etc., by a logical chain of reasoning, beginning with the admittedly Socratic concept. Where can the chain be broken? Certainly not until we reach some form of the ideal theory; and if we must attribute a theory of ideas to Socrates, why not the particular theory so plainly attributed to him by Plato? It is the difficulty of presenting one end of the chain without being led, by the sheer force of its logical concatenation, to the other end, which led the writer to feel that the theory of ideas is Socratic. Indeed it is difficult to think that the logical thinker, Socrates, if he pursued arguments as relentlessly and pertinaciously as he is pictured as doing in the *Protagoras,* should not have followed his conceptions to their logical conclusion in the doctrine of the two worlds and the fully developed theory of ideas. A second-rate man, a Xenophon, might have stopped half way; Xenophon never pursued any chain of reasoning very far: but then Xenophon could never have discovered the concept, nor would the purely 'practical' Socrates, whom he presents, have done so! The persistent reasoner who seems to be drawn from life in even the earliest Platonic dialogues would hardly have refrained from carrying his argument to its ultimate conclusion. In view of the coherence of this doctrine, it would seem that we must either take the whole of it as Socratic, or else deny that any of it is Socratic at all, even the logical concept. Either we must deny that we know anything at all about Socrates, and assert that the accounts of Plato, Xenophon, and Aristophanes are alike fiction, or if we assert that Socrates had any philosophic originality at all, we must assert that the whole of the teachings which Plato attributes to him are really Socratic.

There is an apparently sufficient answer to this position in the statement of Aristotle: "Two things may be fairly ascribed to Socrates—epagogic arguments and universal definition. . . . Socrates did not make the universals or the definitions exist apart."[2] But we have no right to expect in the lecture notes of the *Metaphysics,* such careful statements as we would get in a history of philosophy. To understand the passage we must consider the context. In the previous part of the chapter, Aristotle is considering the sources of the ideal theory. In one sentence he talks about "the supporters of the ideal theory," and in the next he talks about Socrates. From the close connection we might well gather that Socrates was one of the supporters of the ideal theory! Then he speaks of how Socrates was led to make his contributions to the ideal theory, the source of which he finds especially in these two things, epagogic reasoning and universal definition. We cannot fairly interpret this passage as asserting that Socrates' interests were confined to these two things—even the received interpretation asserts that Socrates was interested in ethics, which is not mentioned here. As to the other sentence, that "Socrates did not make the universals or the definitions exist apart," Aristotle unfortunately does not explain what he means by "exist apart" or by whom they were made to exist apart. The people who declare the ideas to "exist apart" might very well be, as Professor Burnet has suggested, the "friends of the ideas" of the *Sophist* (248A), who made a far sharper separation between ideas and things than did Plato, and who are attacked in that dialogue. So upon closer consideration, this passage in Aristotle not only is no contradiction to the interpretation of Socrates' philosophy which is here upheld, but even points in the same direction.

There is an additional piece of evidence for the genuineness of Plato's picture of Socrates to be derived from what we know of Plato's own character and artistic ability. He was a man of extraordinarily keen and exact dramatic sense of fitness. There is little or no indication that Plato wrote with an ideal of historic accuracy such as that demanded by modern historians. Such a conception did not yet exist, and what we know of contemporary writings, such as those of Xenophon, shows that the reading public did not require or expect historical verisimilitude. But Plato was a dramatist who has rarely been equalled in the dramatic characterization of his figures. He can best be compared with Shakespeare in the way in which he completely effaced his own personality in the characters whom he depicted. Plato was able to throw himself into the most various and unlike characters and depict them with marvellous fidelity. So true to life are the figures we meet, and so great Plato's self-effacement, that the personality of Plato does not appear at all in his dialogues, and when we have read them all we know little more about Plato as a person than about Shakespeare. Undoubtedly he put speeches into Socrates' mouth, but so keen was his dramatic sense that he put only those things into the mouth of Socrates which were thoroughly appropriate. We must remember that Plato was thoroughly acquainted with the persons who figure in his pages and the subjects on which he makes Socrates discourse. Socrates was a close friend of several members of Plato's family. An uncle, Charmides, had been a close associate of Socrates. An older brother, Glaucon, had been a disciple. A half-brother, Antiphon, studied the Socratic philosophy. Plato probably heard Socrates and his philosophy discussed by members of his family from the time that he was a child. In addition, during the last eight years of Socrates' life, Plato was associated with him. Plato's own philosophic ability is a guarantee that he understood the subjects discussed and appreciated fine philosophical distinctions. The speakers in the dialogues are almost all men who were well known in Athens and with whom Plato could have become well acquainted. It is admitted by those who hold to the usual interpretation of Socrates that the other figures in the *Protagoras* are depicted with entire fidelity to life. With such a keen dramatic sense and such a full understanding of the subject and of the persons whom he portrays, it is hard to think that Plato did not also depict his chief character, Socrates, with full fidelity. Not that the conversations are historic records, but they are *dramatically* true to life—Plato, with his nice dramatic sense, would not have portrayed Socrates as discussing any subject or uttering any sentiment which he could not well have uttered historically. That such is the fact is further shown by certain peculiarities of some of the dialogues, which will next be considered.

Plato began his career as a writer, with full acceptance of Socrates' philosophy and with an intention of perpetuating the memory and teachings of his master. It was not until he was more than forty years old, that he came to differ from his master. We find a similarly late development of philosophic doctrine in the case of Immanuel Kant. But in Plato's first period he devoted himself solely to proclaiming the teachings of Socrates and to perpetuating his memory. In that attempt he was so successful that today it is still the Platonic Socrates who lives in our minds; while the Socrates whom we have created in accordance with the dictates of the received interpretation and the accounts of Xenophon remains only a poor lay figure. But there came a time when Plato, as every great thinker, began to differ from his master, and when he wished to elaborate upon what his master had taught. He wanted to say things which Socrates would never have said, and yet which were direct outgrowths of Socrates' own teaching. Sometimes the literary necessities of the dialogue made him put these things into Socrates' mouth, but Plato's dramatic sense of fitness was outraged in so doing, so he satisfied it by putting into the text a warning to the reader not to take this saying as genuinely Socratic. We find such warnings in various places in the later dialogues. In the *Republic,* when Socrates is enumerating the sciences which should constitute the curriculum of the guardians, and hence the ideal for the youth of the day, he comes to solid geometry. Solid geometry did not exist in the time of Socrates, and so Socrates could not have spoken about it; yet it did exist in the time of Plato, and Plato could not leave it out. So Plato has Socrates include solid geometry in the curriculum, but satisfies his own literary conscience by making Socrates' companion reply (528B), "But that does not seem to have been discovered yet"! In the *Thaetetus,* in which Plato discusses different theories of knowledge, he is so disturbed by the parts of this dialogue which are not quite faithful to the historic Socrates that he prefaces the discussion with an account of the maieutic art, in which he emphasizes that Socrates is not wise and did not originate anything of himself.[3] This statement cannot be literally true and must be an exaggeration, for in the *Meno* (98B) Socrates says that he does know some things. This statement is sometimes used in defence of the received interpretation; but even that interpretation admits that Socrates did know some things, even such important generalizations as that virtue is knowledge. The whole dialogue, in which Socrates propounds one epistemological theory after another, contradicts the statement that Socrates knew nothing, which sounds quite out of place. This statement is an example of the Socratic irony. Plato evidently means that Socrates did not know the things which he speaks of in this dialogue, and so the statement is exaggerated to counteract the general impression of the dialogue, because in it Plato makes Socrates know so much and propound such novel ideas! The Protagorean sensualistic theory (152D ff.) is plainly indicated as not Socratic and not that of Protagoras; one reason for connecting it with Protagoras was probably to make it possible that the historic Socrates could have known it. When Socrates is made to use the term *doxa* in a new sense to mean 'judgment,' he prefaces it by saying (189E), "I am speaking of what I do not know"! Later when Socrates comes to state an idealistic theory of knowledge, he says that he learned it in a dream! So we see that where Plato is obviously not dramatically accurate, he recognizes and indicates that fact. Evidently Plato was very much bothered by the lack of historical accuracy of this dialogue, and so was compelled by his literary conscience to indicate in various ways its shortcomings in that respect.

In other dialogues Socrates is no longer the chief speaker, and his place is taken by the Eleatic Stranger, Parmenides, Timæus, or the Athenian Stranger. Socrates listens to others or is absent altogether. Evidently there were some things which Plato could not put into Socrates' mouth at all. But in his old age, long after he had ceased writing Socratic dialogues, Plato did write another, the *Philebus.* The subject of the dialogue is an attack upon pleasure as the highest good, and consequently was fairly appropriate to Socrates. But Plato's dramatic power had waned very greatly, and so he was not so careful as to just what he made Socrates say. He had long before published his own views wherein he differed from Socrates, and probably thought that his readers would understand which doctrines were his and which really Socratic; but even here, when Socrates enunciates the central doctrine of the dialogue, Plato apologizes for putting it into Socrates' mouth by making him say (16C) that it is a gift from the gods handed down by tradition!

Were Plato a pious fabricator who sought to gain authority for his own ideas by putting them into the mouth of his better-known master, he would certainly not have boggled at adding such a detail as solid geometry or these other teachings to what Socrates is made to say. If Plato did not hesitate to put his own theory of ideas into the mouth of Socrates, why should he have refused to make him utter the teaching of the *Sophist* or the *Statesman?* Why should he warn his readers at times not to take some teachings as genuinely Socratic? A fabricator would not have warned his readers at all. If Plato thus warns his readers at times, and refuses to attribute some dialogues to Socrates at all, have we not a right to infer that where there is no warning, the teaching is genuinely Socratic, or at least like what Socrates did actually teach? At least it must follow that Plato never *deliberately* falsified the character and opinions of the historic Socrates. That he may have unconsciously attributed views of his own to Socrates is possible, but only to a very limited extent. That such unconscious attribution could not go very far is shown by Plato's carefulness and the delicacy of his dramatic sense. A writer who could portray the characters of the *Protagoras* with such dramatic fidelity could not go very far astray. Especially when in the *Parmenides* he came consciously to criticize Socrates' views and to distinguish them from his own, he would become aware of the differences between his own philosophy and that of Socrates. But the philosophic doctrines there attributed to Socrates are exactly those of the *Phœdo* and *Republic,* the theory of ideas. Plato's nice sense of dramatic fitness has preserved the historic Socrates for us.

In the Socratic irony there is to be found a seemingly conclusive reply to these arguments. If Socrates knew so much, if he worked out the metaphysical system of the *Phœdo* and the *Republic,* how could he say that he did not know anything? This asseveration of his ignorance is found in many dialogues, but it is stressed most of all in the *Apology,* where Socrates states that he alone is wise because he knows that he does not know anything. This assertion of ignorance cannot be denied, since it is too closely connected with passages which are universally conceded to be those picturing the historic Socrates, yet it appears to be quite inconsistent with the man who discovered the two worlds of Being and Becoming, and formulated the ideal state of the *Republic.*

This is indeed an important consideration, and unless Socrates' irony can be shown to be harmonious with the character of the Platonic Socrates, we must give up that interpretation altogether. But we must remember that the Socrates of Plato's dialogues is not a figure who always puts his philosophic theories into exact language, nor is he a man who always addresses himself to a philosophic audience. Plato was so much of a dramatist that the dramatic necessities of the dialogue take precedence over the ideal of technically philosophic accuracy. The Socrates of the dialogues is addressing his interlocutor, not the reader of the dialogue. To an ignorant person, Socrates would naturally speak in terms which could be understood; he would not speak of his deeper philosophic theories to men who could not comprehend them. Socrates was too keen a judge of men to do that. Furthermore his sense of humor and his eagerness to get some persons to discuss with him sometimes led him to subtle sarcasm and even exaggeration. Sometimes he was like the great scientist who says, 'I cannot explain anything,' or the great biologist who says, 'I know nothing about life,' or who may even say, 'I really as yet know nothing.' But in the *Apology* he was quite sincere, and there is no reason for thinking that in that case his irony was in any sense a pose. He was on trial for his life, and was concerned only with telling the truth. If Socrates was a philosopher seeking truth, his plain declaration of ignorance given in the *Apology* must be a confession of failure.

In interpreting this assertion of ignorance, we must ask two questions: What does Socrates mean by 'knowledge'? If he has some special definition of knowledge in mind, our interpretation of the Socratic irony must hang upon the meaning of that word. Secondly, we must ask how he could be honest and yet say that he did not know anything, if he had created what we recognize as one of the most brilliant of philosophical constructions—the theory of ideas of the *Phædo* and the *Republic?*

It is the greatest scientists who are most humble. It is the man who has achieved most in the advancement of human knowledge who recognizes most keenly what is lacking and is most conscious of his ignorance. It is a mark of Socrates' greatness that he too recognized his own limitations, and that much as he had accomplished, he saw that he had not attained the goal which he had set up for himself. He too confessed his failure.

Socrates was a thinker whose ideals were so high that he was compelled, again and again, to take what was only second best. In the *Phædo* (98 f.) he tells of his ideal of philosophy—that it would give a completed teleological account of the universe—that it would show that the world and everything in it, is as it is, because in that way it contributes to one universal good purpose. But he also says that he failed utterly to discover such a principle, and so had to turn to a second-best method of inquiry. In the *Republic* (504D) he admits that he has not given a detailed description of the virtues, but only an outline, and when he comes to the highest idea of all, the idea of good, he says that we know very little of it (505A); and he can only describe it by analogy with the sun. Here are important gaps which might well justify Socrates in a statement that he is not wise.

But he goes further than that; he says he has failed: and the implication is that he has failed, not only in some important aspects of metaphysical theory, but even in gaining the practical knowledge he sought. The social and political situation in Athens during the latter part of the Peloponnesian war and afterwards must have emphasized in Socrates' mind the importance of ethical knowledge, and so we find that in almost all of the dialogues except those with special students of philosophy, Socrates discusses ethical questions. Furthermore it is noteworthy that Socrates' statement of his ignorance occurs almost always only when ethical problems are under consideration.

In the *Meno* we find the clue to the answer of this problem. Socrates is discussing whether virtue can be taught, and he asserts that he "literally does not know what virtue is," and that he has "never known of any one else who did" (71A, C). This statement is not to be pressed, for further on (98B) he says that he does know some things. The explanation of such an extreme statement is to be found in the meaning of 'knowledge.' A study of the Greek text of the *Meno* shows that the words *epistēme* and *phronēsis*, and the verbs *oida* and *epistomei* are used interchangeably.[4] Socrates gives an example of knowledge—a geometrical proposition which he dramatically demonstrates to an ignorant slave lad. It is plainly said to be *epistēme* (85D). Knowledge is that which can be demonstrated in the same way as a geometrical proposition, which, like it, is inherent in the soul, and which has the compelling power of a mathematical proposition. Socrates has the deductive, mathematical ideal of knowledge. Virtue, to be taught, must be knowledge, *i.e.,* it must be capable of being put into the form of a proposition which can be deductively demonstrated.

This was the ideal of Socrates' ethics—to get the concepts of virtue and the virtues stated in such a form that they could not only be demonstrated to be correct, but could also be applied to any particular concrete situation in the same way that a geometrical proposition is applied to a concrete case. Then virtue could be taught, and everyone would be compelled to accept the idea of virtue in the same way that he must accept the Pythagorean proposition. In that way Socrates' mission to teach his fellow-citizens to care for virtue and their souls, would be fulfilled. For that purpose he must search into himself and other men.

But how far did he achieve that ideal? Only to a very small degree. He did succeed in identifying virtue with knowledge and temperance and justice. But he failed to demonstrate them from the highest idea of all, the idea of the good. He was not even able to define the idea of good in itself. As for the particular virtues, he was unable to get an exact definition which would enable any one to recognize an act as just or unjust without equivocation. He had to confess that he was able merely to give an outline, and could not give the perfect representation which would alone satisfy.[5] No wonder Socrates felt that he had failed! He was unable to make ethics the deductive science of his ideal, and to apply his brilliant metaphysical system to the concrete problems of ethics. Aristotle likewise recognized this difficulty when he made the larger part of ethics a mere empirical study.

Socrates' confession of failure created just the sort of situation which would naturally bring about the scattering of his disciples and the development of a number of schools of philosophy. Each disciple would naturally attempt to solve the problem which Socrates had left, and each in his own way. Aristippus and Antisthenes concentrated on the ethical problem; Euclid and Phædo emphasized the metaphysical problems; Plato alone was sufficiently keen to see the full greatness of the problem which Socrates had left, and he alone had sufficient Socratic humility to keep him from asserting that he had solved the problem. Only in later years did he venture to criticize Socrates' formulation; to the end of his days he was never sufficiently satisfied with his own views on the central doctrine of all—the good—so he never published his lecture on that subject. Indeed failure was inevitable for Socrates—he had separated the realms of being and becoming; knowledge could only be of being: but practical problems are only to be found in this changing world of becoming of which there can be no knowledge. Hence ethics, in as far as it deals with practical problems, cannot be a science or knowledge, and Socrates could not get more than abstract conceptual formulæ. How far Socrates recognized this as an inevitable necessity of his own philosophical system we do not know; but in the *Republic* he admits that no actual state can embody the ideal which he describes (473A): and in the *Meno* the conclusion is that virtue certainly *is* not taught; instead, people are guided by right opinion or intuition. Socrates was such an original and great thinker that he recognized his own failure to attain to his ideal, and confessed it publicly in his irony when he said he was not wise and did not have knowledge.

These considerations drawn from the logical character of Socrates' thought, the dramatic faithfulness of Plato, and the Socratic irony, are among the reasons which have commended the historical accuracy of Plato to the writer. There are other reasons which are equally cogent, but which need no more than a mention, since they are expounded so well by Professors Burnet and Taylor. Most striking is the extremely destructive criticism in the *Parmenides* of one form of the theory of ideas. Philosophers have often changed their views; but if the theory of ideas as given in the *Phædo* and the *Republic* is Platonic and not Socratic, it is strange that Plato should have devoted one of his works to a destructive criticism of his former teachings. Philosophers have never done that. If Plato did it, it is the only case in the history of philosophy. When philosophers have changed, they have done it silently; sometimes they have asserted, as Schelling did, that they have not changed at all. But Plato would not have publicly criticized his own theory, for he was keen enough to realize that public destructive criticism was quite unnecessary to invalidate his own theory. The very fact that the author of a theory has discarded it, is quite sufficient to discredit it. Public criticism is only for the theories of other philosophers.

If we have any doubts that Socrates held the ideal theory in the form given in the *Phædo* and the *Republic,* and think that it was elaborated, in many respects at least, by Plato, such doubts would be dispelled by a careful study of the *Parmenides*. Here, if anywhere, when Plato is openly criticizing his master, we would get a statement of the philosophy which Socrates actually held. What we find attributed to him is the theory that there are abstract ideas in which all things participate, but that the ideas do not participate in each other (129A). This is exactly the doctrine of the *Phædo;* in that dialogue the immortality of the soul is ultimately proven as a deduction from the propositions that the soul participates, as its essence, in the idea of life, and that ideas do not participate in each other, but repel their contradictories, *i.e.,* the idea of life repels its contradictory, death, and so the soul is immortal.

There are, in addition, differences between the political philosophies of the *Republic* on the one hand and the *Statesman* and the *Laws* on the other—just those differences which we should expect between an idealistic and uncompromising theorist who refused to engage in practical politics but criticized the Athenian democracy and its leaders, and the more practical founder of the world's first university, whose family were engaged in politics and had been close friends of Pericles.

Aristotle was not hesitant in criticizing his master, but he said nothing about a change in Plato's opinions, or of the *Laws* as being "the product of senile weakness." He had been a member of the Academy for the last twenty years of Plato's life and would have known of Plato's change of philosophy, if there had been one, and would have spoken of it at one of the many times when he criticized the ideal theory. In only one place he professes to give a careful statement of Plato's philosophy, and to distinguish the teachings of Plato from other philosophies.[6] In that passage, after speaking of the theory of ideas, Aristotle attributes to Plato a number theory which is unlike anything we have in the dialogues, although we have Plato's complete works. It is only in a few of the later dialogues, the *Philebus,* the *Timæus,* and the *Laws* that there is anything which approaches this number theory. Had Plato been anxious to spread his philosophy by attributing it to Socrates, he would certainly not have left out such an important doctrine. Had it been a mere "senile aberration," Aristotle would have known that fact and would have spoken of it instead of spending so much time in combating the theory. On the contrary he tells us that Plato's central doctrine was given in his "Lecture on the Good" which Plato never published and even forbade others to publish. That sort of conduct is just what we might expect of a disciple of Socrates who was enthusiastic in publishing his master's teachings, but ready to allow his own central teaching to be perpetuated only in the thought of the school which he had founded and by the individuals whom he had influenced, especially as he was not too sure of it. Aristotle was a nobler monument to Plato than another philosophic work would have been.

The problem of discovering the historic Socrates resolves itself into an attempt to account for the differing statements of Aristophanes, Xenophon, and Plato, and to explain each account as derived from the one true account. By starting with the wholly 'practical' Socrates of Xenophon, we could never arrive at the figure portrayed either by Aristophanes or by Plato. But it can be shown that the Socrates of Aristophanes, the leader of a school interested in physical and mathematical investigations, which practiced dialectic, observed some kind of mildly ascetic regimen, and spoke strangely of the soul, is a legitimate distortion of the Platonic figure, and that Xenophon's account is likewise explicable as a distortion of the same Platonic Socrates, this time by an advocate of practical efficiency and military regimentation of life. In this way the other two accounts are shown to be derivable only from the Platonic account, and so the substantial accuracy of Plato's account is assured.

To sum up, we find that the chief reasons for accepting the Platonic Socrates as historical are: that Xenophon, on whose testimony the usual interpretation of Socrates is based, often plainly attributed his own views to Socrates, and is quite untrustworthy; that stylistic criteria seem to group some important members of what have been called the 'Platonic' dialogues with the 'Socratic' dialogues; that Socrates was undoubtedly a man who thought his problems through to the end, and the Socratic doctrine of the concept and practice of the maieutic art lead inevitably to a theory of ideas involving independent existence of the ideas, and quite naturally to the theory of the *Phædo* and the *Republic;* that Plato's extraordinarily nice sense of dramatic fitness and his carefulness in pointing out where he deviates from what would be appropriate to the historic Socrates guarantee his historical accuracy; that the Socratic irony can be shown to be a logical and necessary consequence of the theory of ideas of the *Phædo* and the *Republic* and the interpretation of 'knowledge' in the *Meno* and the *Republic;* that the *Parmenides* can only be adequately interpreted on the supposition that in it Plato is criticizing the theory of another philosopher; that the differences of political theory in the *Republic* on the one hand and the *Statesman* and the *Laws* on the other can best be explained as due to the different character and family traditions of Socrates and Plato; and that Aristotle's explicit account of Plato's central philosophy is wholly different from that given by the usual interpretation of the Socratic problem, and can only be adequately accounted for by accepting this newer interpretation of Socrates and Plato.

As a result of this criticism, Socrates is restored to us as one of the greatest figures in the history of philosophy, and by his side we find Plato, equally great in philosophic ability, now recognized as not a mere poet, fabricating dramatic fictions, a person whom the author of the *Laws* would despise, but as one of the greatest dramatists the world has known, who succeeded in making the historic persons of Athens into the eternally living figures of his dialogues, a man who possessed the spirit of scientific accuracy in an age when it was almost unknown, who was at the same time the keenest critic of his master's philosophy and the person who developed it most powerfully.

Notes

[1] *Memorabilia,* IV, vii. 3-5.

[2] *Melaphysics,* XII, iv, 1078b.

[3] *Theætetus,* 150C; repeated in 157D and 161B.

[4] *Cf.* especially *Meno* 85, 89.

[5] *Republic* 504D.

[6] *Metaphysics* I, vi.

John A. Scott (lecture date 1928)

SOURCE: "Socrates and Christ," in *Socrates and Christ: A Lecture Given at Northwestern University,* Northwestern University, 1928, pp. 5-52.

[*In the following essay, originally delivered as a lecture, Scott reviews Socrates's life and philosophic thought in order to demonstrate the influence of Socrates on Christianity. He argues that Socrates rejected the Olympic gods and thus left his followers searching for "a god of purity and a god of justice"; and he suggests that Christianity was successfully established in Greece due to this legacy.*]

During September of 480 B.C. in the waters between the Island of Salamis and the harbor of Athens the great fleet of the Persians was defeated, and Xerxes returned to Asia leaving his foremost general with a huge army to subdue the small and divided forces of Greece, but the next summer this huge army was utterly destroyed,—so utterly that assurance was given to Athens of freedom from barbarian invasion, and permission to develop her own civilization.

Never has there been such an enthusiastic delight in the joys of the mind and in the reproduction of beauty in various and enduring forms. Never have so many outstanding men of genius of the highest creative order been found in one century or in one city as then moved within the streets of Athens.

Socrates was born in 469, or just ten years after the repulse of the Persians. His country still thrilled with pride in that unbelievable victory and was entering hopefully upon the great Age of Pericles. His life thus covered the morning, the noonday, and the evening of that mighty epoch.

His father was a sculptor, and it meant something to be a sculptor in an age and among a people that fashioned the Parthenon and carved its frieze and its pediments. The son followed the craft of his father and is said to have created a group of the Graces of such beauty that it was honored with a place on the Acropolis, where it was still to be seen after the lapse of several centuries.

Greek thought and Greek morals at that time were wholly materialistic. Thinking men tried to explain all things by laws of rest or of motion, by assumptious of infinite division or of all-embracing unity. There was no need of a Creator, since matter and motion explained everything. There was no such thing as a moral conscience or a moral law, and one of the greatest thinkers, Protagoras, proclaimed the axiom, "Man is himself the measure of all things," meaning that there is no such thing as absolute right or wrong, but only individual opinion and that all opinions were of equal value and all worthless,—thus introducing the germ of moral anarchy and the rejection of all authority. Gorgias followed by extending to science the agnosticism already existing in morals, and by declaring that knowledge of any sort is impossible, that nothing really exists, that if it did exist, it could not be known, and even if it existed and were known, this knowledge could not be imparted to others.

Teachers flocked to Athens eager to instruct the wealthier youth, for high fees, on how to succeed in nearly everything but in character, especially how to win without labor or merit and how to violate the laws without danger of punishment.

The young sculptor heard these men, asked them many questions, reasoned much, and became convinced that they were false prophets, also that there is a just ruler of the universe, that there is a law of the spirit and a moral law, and that these laws are as universal and unerring as the laws of matter. He put down his mallet and his chisel and spent the rest of his long and vigorous life in searching for this spiritual law.

In his searchings he met men of many sorts. He questioned them, reasoned with them in shops, markets, gymnasia, wherever he could find them. For almost forty years he must have been the most familiar figure in his own city. A list of the famous people who listened to him and to whom he listened would include at least one-half of the super-great of Greece. It may be doubted if any man ever knew intimately so many persons of the very highest order as did Socrates. He soon became conspicuous even in that great company and his society was sought not only by the élite of Athens but also by the great from all parts of Greece. Once when war had closed the frontier between Attica and Megara, the most distinguished citizen of Megara is said to have slipped into Athens disguised as a woman, just to enjoy the conversation of Socrates. The Oracle at Delphi proclaimed him as the wisest of men, and the rising young poet, Aristophanes, wrote a comedy, *The Clouds,* with Socrates at the center of the merriment. Aristophanes used Socrates at different times and other comic poets, as well as he, tried to win prizes and glory by making this familiar figure the butt of their humor.

However, the great event in two great lives was the meeting of Socrates and Plato, for this meeting meant a new birth for Plato, and through Plato the life and teachings of Socrates found a fitting immortality. Plato was then a poet of growing and assured distinction, about twenty years of age, while Socrates was a little more than sixty.

Plato lived more than fifty years after the death of his master and he wrote many books. We have from him the greatest bulk of any writer of classical Greece, yet in all these books except the very last, the work of extreme old age, his writings are essentially confined to the things he assumed he had heard from Socrates. Paul said, "For me to live is Christ." Plato with equal justice could have said, "For me to live is Socrates." The convincing proof of the greatness of Socrates is the lasting influence he had with such a competent judge as Plato.

The fixed principle of Socrates' life was that knowledge is the one thing needful, that sin is due to an error in thinking, that men who know the right will in the end do the right. A favorite theory of his was that a man who errs ignorantly is more dangerous than one who errs wilfully. Since the man who errs wilfully needs only to be convinced that his interests and aims are best served by following the better course, he will therefore follow that course. However, there is no need to convince the ignorant man, since he, not knowing the better course, cannot follow it and will blunder just the same. For example, a pilot who runs a ship on a reef wilfully can be shown that it is to his advantage to steer a safe course, but the ignorant pilot will continue to run on reefs, simply because he does not know how to do anything else. Such a statement would shock many a person who could not answer it. These people began to fear him.

He constantly argued that it took experts for everything but for politics, that no one would trust cloth to a tailor, leather to a cobbler, ships to a captain, unless he knew the people engaged had learned the trade and were able to show when and where they had learned it. In ruling the state, which he claimed was the most difficult, important and dangerous of all occupations, men were chosen who had no training, no experience, and no character. Hence the politicians hated him.

He put all the facts or the stories of religion and mythology to the test of reason and asked many hard questions that could not be answered by those in religious authority. Hence all the pious conservatives tried to silence him.

Athens had seen terrible days in the last five years of the fifth century. She had lost her colonies, had watched a hostile fleet ride in her harbor, with her own fleet scattered and destroyed; had been obliged to tear down the walls that protected her citizens and had seen this destruction carried on to the accompaniment of music and dancing, and then had seen her liberties taken from her and thirty brutal tyrants put in control. At last brutality went too far, a conquered people arose and recovered its liberties and started again upon the career of independent freedom. Under these conditions the people did not look ahead but back; they longed for the good old days of peace and power, when all the citizens had faith and when the gods visited the land with favoring prosperity. All the reactionaries shouted, "Faith of our Fathers, triumphant Faith!" And they were militant, too. The politicians joined them, also those who had been silenced by the reasoning of Socrates,—silenced but not convinced. He was just the man who carried in his own person all the forces which seemed to typify the new age when compared with the old, the old age of their imagination. He was tried for disbelief in the gods, and thus corrupting the youth; convicted, and he died by taking the hemlock in 399 B.C., when he was a little more than seventy.

To illustrate what I wish to say about Socrates I shall select four scenes: the conversation he had with Euthyphro just before the trial; the trial itself; a scene in the prison, also his last hours and death.

When it became known that he was to be tried on a capital charge, his friends urged him to prepare a defense, but he replied that somehow he could not get up any interest in the matter, and to their dismay he continued utterly indifferent to the trial and the outcome. On the way to the place where his trial was to be held he meets a young orthodox conservative, Euthyphro, and he finds to his delight that this man is an authority on all moral and religious matters, just the man to give him the needed instruction before the trial, for he is certain that if he can master the things Euthyphro knows and can tell the judges what he has learned, they will be convinced and everything will be settled. Socrates asked this expert if he could define holiness and unholiness. Instantly he replied, "Whatever pleases the gods is holy, whatever does not please them is unholy." "Fine!" replied Socrates. "Do you believe the tales that tell how the gods fought with each other, how Cronus mutilated his own father, and was in turn driven from power and from heaven by Zeus, his own son?" "I certainly do, and I can tell more startling tales than these," was the confident reply. Then Socrates continued, "If you and I do not agree regarding number we settle the matter by counting. If we differ regarding the size of anything we simply weigh or measure that thing and the dispute is ended. The only thing for which we would quarrel and which we cannot so easily settle is the question of right and of wrong, and the only thing that can produce quarrels and wars is the failure to agree on what is right and what is wrong. Hence, if the gods quarrel, as you affirm, it can only be because they disagree on moral issues. Therefore they cannot themselves be the criterion of holiness and unholiness, since some of the quarreling gods must think that identical thing is right which the opposing gods think is wrong."

When this little statement got repeated and its meaning understood there could no longer be any real faith in the gods of Greek mythology. He next asked the young man to define worship, and he replied: "Service of the gods." Socrates then asked him, if it is not the purpose of service to improve the thing served and if the only aim of service is not the betterment of the object of service. Thus, a server of dogs improves dogs, of horses improves horses, and a physician or server of health improves the health of the person served; hence service of the gods must improve the gods. "Oh, no!" exclaimed Euthyphro, "men cannot improve the gods and make them better!" "I thought not," replied Socrates, "but if worship does not improve the gods, just what does it do?" Euthyphro, not a whit abashed, answered that he knew, but that he was in a hurry and would answer later. Socrates expressed great disappointment that the man who knew it all was so thrifty of his knowledge and would not clear up these difficulties for him. These two questions,—how can the quarreling divinities of Greek mythology be the source of righteousness, and, if the gods are perfect, how can they be served by sacrifices which they neither need nor enjoy?—these questions could not be answered, and the fact that they were asked cleared the field for a new religion that could and did answer them.

The Greeks never arrived at the conception of a holy god, or looked upon worship as anything else than the purchase at a small price of great favors from unwilling and jealous deities. We cannot conceive of religion apart from morality, but they looked upon religion simply as the performance of ceremonies; it did not touch the life or conscience of the worshiper. There is no occasion in Greek history where the priests and religious leaders called the people to a higher moral life; these men thought only of ritual, and the enrichment of the temple or the sanctuary. The gods of their belief were cruel, jealous, and unscrupulous. The words of Jesus, "Be ye therefore perfect, even as your Heavenly Father is perfect," could have had little meaning for Greek ears.

In the course of the trial, after the accusers had made their charges, Socrates arose and spoke not in his own defense but on the necessity of searching for truth. He told of his great astonishment when assured that the Oracle at Delphi had declared him the wisest of men, since he was conscious of no knowledge at all. In his perplexity he went to different men of great reputation, hoping to find that these men were exceedingly wise. Then, when he found them wise, he would ask the god what he meant when he called Socrates the wisest, since these men were plainly much wiser. These different men were all alike, they did know some one thing better than Socrates, and this knowledge regarding one subject gave them conceit on all subjects, so that they were ready to give authoritative opinions regarding everything. When Socrates tried to show them their ignorance on all matters but their specialty, they became angry. Then after each fruitless encounter he would say to himself: "I am at least wiser than this man, because he thinks he knows many things which he does not, while I do *not* know and do not *think* I know." After long searchings and constant disappointments he reached this conclusion: "The oracle must have meant: 'Human wisdom is naught, and that person is wisest who like Socrates knows that he knows nothing.'" He then did not wholly despair, but he said: "I continued to search everywhere for wisdom, questioning whatever citizen or stranger seemed to be wise, but when I found he was not wise, I tried to point out his mistake and to remove his false impression of knowledge. This searching has taken all my time and I have been unable to enter politics, or to look after my own private affairs, and I have spent my life in unlimited poverty while seeking for wisdom.

"Perhaps someone might say, 'How foolish to pursue a course which has brought poverty and is sure to lead to danger and possibly to death.' I reply, 'Sir, you reason not well, if you think that any man who deserves the name of man, counts the cost of life or death, but does not fix his eye on this alone, whether he does what is just or unjust, deeds worthy of a noble man or of a coward. To say that a man must shun danger is to bring dishonor on all those heroes who have dared to die in defense of their country, when by flight they might have been saved. Thus matters stand. O men of Athens, wherever one takes his stand, whether from his own choice, or by higher orders, there he should remain, refusing to count any cost, even life itself, at the price of faithful obedience. God has appointed me to search for truth, I cannot now desert my post. I have no fear of death, since I do not know that death is an evil, for it may be the highest good; but I do know that to desert one's call to duty is an evil, and therefore I shall never seek to avoid a possible good by choosing that which I know is an evil, for, after all, fear of death is only a form of self-conceit, the conceit that one knows what he does not know. If you should now offer to acquit me on the sole condition that I should remain quiet and cease from this search, I would reply, 'Men of Athens, I love you and admire you, but I must obey God rather than you, and so long as I live I shall never cease searching and urging you to strive for the nobler life, for I am convinced that the greatest good I can do to my city is to urge my fellow citizens to search for wisdom and to exhort them not to care for their lives, nor for their possessions, but to care for righteousness since it is from righteousness that real success comes to both city and citizens. Therefore, men of Athens, acquit me or convict me, as you choose, but be assured of this: I will not change my course even to avoid many deaths.' My accusers cannot harm me, since a good man cannot be injured by a bad. True, they can deprive me of my property, drive me into exile, or even put me to death, but I do not count these as injuries, since they do not affect my moral nature." He then turned to the jury and told the jurors that they need not expect from him the thing they anticipate from other defendants; that he would not bring his children to beg for him, nor would he beg for himself; and that a judge does not sit to dispense justice as a favor, but to decide according to the laws; and in this spirit, he concluded: "I yield to you and to God to decide as it may prove best for me and also for you."

Since many of the jurors were already prejudiced, since many could not comprehend, and since many thought that they had been defied, such a speech could have but one result. The ballot showed 220 votes for acquittal and 281 for conviction, a vote so close that it is certain it would have been changed to an acquittal, if Socrates had been more courteous and less defiant in his tone. It must be said to the credit of Athens that 220 jurors voted his acquittal in the face of an extremely unyielding and almost taunting address.

Even the conviction meant little, as a second vote had yet to be taken to determine the punishment, and a very light one would have been accepted. All that he needed to have done, at the worst, was to have moved to Megara to the home of a famous pupil ready to welcome him. Or he could have gone to Thebes, where there was almost a colony of his admirers. If he moved to Megara or to Thebes, the distance was about thirty miles to one city and forty to the other. It is also said that he was invited to share the palace of the King of Macedon,—an invitation accepted but a few years before by the poet, Euripides. Socrates did not choose to withdraw to any friendly city, but determined to abide by the decision yet to be made by the jury. There was no superior court to reverse or change the decision. He knew that the punishment awarded would be final, and presumably immediate.

The prosecutor demanded that death be the penalty. Socrates must present an alternative punishment, and the jury was obliged to select from these two. There could be no compromise and no other punishment. It must be either the death demanded, or some other penalty deemed sufficient by a jury which had already found him guilty. It was certainly a tragic moment when Socrates arose with seeming indifference and expressed his great surprise that so many had voted his acquittal, as he had felt the vote would be almost solid against him, and then he continued: "My accuser fixes the punishment at death. What counter punishment should I offer? What should an old man suffer fittingly in return for the fact that during all his life he has neglected wealth, comfort, position, in order to search for wisdom and to encourage others to neglect everything else and to seek for righteousness? What is a just punishment for such a man? I can think of no more proper penalty than making him a guest of the city and dining him in that state building where the official guests of Athens are entertained. I am convinced that I never deliberately wronged a single person and I do not now propose to wrong myself by suggesting any sort of punishment. Some one of you might ask, 'Could you not at least agree to keep still?' Now that is just the thing you cannot comprehend, since I believe that the greatest good that can come to a man is for him each day to test his own life and the lives of others, for the untested life is no life at all for man. These things I cannot make you understand in the brief time allotted to me, but I have never accustomed myself to think that a life spent wholly in search for truth deserves any punishment."

Certainly such a proposal could have but one result as the jurors who had already voted him guilty could not then have voted him the guest of the state. His friends in the audience or in the jury, evidently in terror and despair, urged him to offer something which the jurors could accept. He then said at their request: "Plato, Crito, Critoboulus, and Apollodorus urge me to fix as the penalty a fine to be paid in money. All right; I am entirely indifferent about money, as money means nothing to me. I will set a money fine at 30 Minae [about $500], a fine which these men will guarantee, and these men are certainly good for that sum."

A bare majority was all that was needed in an Athenian court. There was always an odd number of jurors; therefore a single ballot settled the matter. The jury of course could not go back on itself; hence it accepted the penalty suggested by the prosecutor. Socrates was condemned to death. There were no possible technicalities, no reviews. The matter was at an end.

An Athenian audience was rarely in a hurry, so that while the clerk was making out the papers for commitment and execution, the jurors and spectators lingered. Then Socrates arose once more and discussed the meaning of death, summing the matter up with these words: "We ought then to be of good cheer in the face of death and to hold firmly that this one thing, at least, is true: no evil can come to a righteous man either in life or in death, and his interests are not neglected by the gods." Ordinarily a condemned criminal was executed at once, either on the day of the trial or the following; but a religious ceremony had just begun and it continued until a sacred ship had been prepared, sent to Delos, and returned to Athens. During this period the state could execute no prisoners. At this particular time the sacred festival lasted for thirty days, during which period Socrates was visited in his prison by friends with whom he discussed the problems of human understanding, the laws of logic, and the issues of life and death.

On the day of the expected return of the sacred ship his wealthy friend, Crito, came before dawn. He was at once admitted by the friendly jailer, and he was surprised to find Socrates in peaceful slumber. He sat long beside him, not wishing to disturb the rest of the friend who was to die so soon. When Socrates perceived that Crito was at his side, he asked "Why so early?" Crito replied that the ship had been sighted the day before, just off the entrance to the Athenian waters, that now everything was at stake, and there was no time to be lost. Another day would be too late. Socrates said: "I trust that that ship will have a safe and happy entrance into her hoped-for harbor, but what is the cause of all your excitement?" Crito then with tearful earnestness told Socrates that a home was ready for him in a near and friendly city, outside the jurisdiction of Athens; that his trial had been a farce; that he had been unjustly condemned, as he well knew; that his friends were in disgrace, because they did not come to his aid at the trial, as they would have done if he had allowed them; that he had three small children who needed his help and guidance; that for the sake of his friends and his family, if not for his own, he should walk out of the opened jail and follow eager friends to safety.

Socrates, deeply touched by the affection and earnestness of this faithful friend, answered: "Your zeal is great and I thank you much, but is the cause just? For if it is not, the greater the zeal the worse is the result. Let us forget that I am about to die, but let us, as reasonable men, calmly consider the facts. All my life I have never followed any course except that course which on mature deliberation seemed to me the wisest." That is, he had never allowed interest or passion to influence his acts or his judgment.

I wonder if any other man has ever been able to say that thing? Paul certainly could not, for he exclaimed: "That which I do I allow not: for what I would, that do I not; but what I hate, that do I."

Then Socrates continued: "*Life* is not the thing of supreme importance, but a *good* life. A good life must be the life of one who treats every person justly, whatever injustice he may have received. If I now leave the jail as you desire, I shall have flouted and injured the laws of my native city, and shall be a law-breaker the rest of this life and all of the life to come. Having lived seventy years as a law-abiding citizen, I propose to die that way."

He refused to follow his friends and chose to die rather than to break the laws, and in this choice he willingly met a punishment which he knew was unjust. The little book of Plato's which tells this story, the *Crito,* is certainly a trumpet call to the obedience of law by all who would care to be known as good citizens.

On the day set for his death the little prison was thronged by admirers who came not so much to comfort him as to receive comfort. The story is told by one disciple to another disciple who could not be present, and that story is in turn preserved by Plato, for poor Plato on that day was sick, he could not bear the strain. During the day Socrates talked almost constantly, discussing great moral problems, the relations of this world with the world to come, the moral aspects of suicide. Once when he was interrupted with word from the executioner that if he did not remain quiet it might be necessary for him to drink twice or three times as much of the poison, "All right," Socrates replied, "let there be prepared three times as much," and went right on with the discussion. He reasoned that the mind or the soul alone can grasp truth; that the body hinders the pursuit of that truth; that the senses could grasp only the temporal, the fleeting; that the mind catches hold of the permanent and unseen realities, or as is said by Paul: "For we look not at the things which are seen, but at the things which are not seen; for the things which are seen are temporal, but the things which are not seen are eternal."

Socrates argued that we can attain to wisdom only when the mind is freed from the restraints and imperfections of the body, hence it would be foolish to fear death. He then discussed a multitude of subjects with his companions, such as the powers of reasoning and the need of trusting in pure logic; the relations of numbers and why it is that two odd numbers make an even, as well as two even numbers make an even; what it is that makes people and things differ in size; then the shape of the earth, reaching the conclusion that the earth is a sphere unsupported in space. Next he advanced a series of arguments for his belief in the immortality of the soul, concluding with these words: "My friends, since the soul is to live forever we must care for it, not only for this time we call life but for all eternity, for if we neglect it the danger is terrible. If death meant the end of all it would be a boon for the wicked, since by their dying they could get rid of their wickedness, but inasmuch as the soul is immortal there is no escape except by striving after wisdom and righteousness, for the soul takes nothing with it but the moral nature it has acquired." These are not the words of a loose-reasoning fanatic, but the reasonings of one of the most logical thinkers mankind has known. He concludes: "This, then, is the reason why a man should be of good cheer in the face of death, a man who has adorned his soul with its own peculiar ornaments, such ornaments as temperance, justice, courage, freedom and truth."

When the moment came to take the hemlock, Crito asked: "How shall we bury you?" Socrates with a smile replied: "Any way you please, if you can only catch me," and then, laughing, he turned to his companions, saying: "I cannot persuade Crito that the Socrates who talks and reasons is the real Socrates, since he thinks that I am the one whom he will soon see as a corpse, and asks how he shall bury me? I shall not be here but shall already have gone to share in the joys of the blessed. Do not say at the funeral that you are burying Socrates, but only the body of Socrates." He prefaced this last sentence with a most characteristic Socratic remark: "For you know well, my good Crito, that careless and slipshod definition is not only an error in the thing itself, but produces a sort of moral deterioration in the soul." When the executioner came in, that officer was weeping, and he told Socrates how much he had come to love him, how hard his task was, and asked him not to make the task any harder by being angry at the thing his office made him do. With words of thanks and comfort, Socrates cheered the poor fellow, took the cup into his own hands and drank it without a sign of any regret or emotion. When his friends saw him drink they could not restrain their tears or hide their anguish. He turned to them and begged them to restrain themselves, since he had heard that one should die free from the sound of words of ill omen.

The friend who tells of his death, ends with these words: "Such was the death of our companion, the best, the wisest, and most just of all the men whom we have known."

Socrates left no writings, founded no school, and never called himself a teacher, since he was always a searcher, an unsuccessful searcher, as he thought, for wisdom and for truth. The example of his unselfish life and fearless death for an ideal was his great contribution to the betterment of the world. But a life that bases virtue solely on knowledge, that takes no account of human frailties, and the life of a man who could truthfully say that, so long as he had lived, he had never done a single thing contrary to the course which his deliberate reason had selected as the best,—such a life and such an example could appeal only to the few, to the elect; it offered little to the weak and the erring. Socrates must have had great influence on the thinking and the self-reliant, but the common mass could not have followed him.

We are dependent on two men for almost all of our knowledge of Socrates: Xenophon and Plato, each a writer of fame, and they only vaguely agree. Xenophon wrote many books describing other famous men and these men are distressingly like his portrait of Socrates. One of his heroes was Cyrus the Great of Persia, and this Cyrus was only his Socrates removed to Persia and put on the throne. I am inclined to think that his Cyrus and his Socrates are both ideal pictures of what Xenophon would have done in their position.

This throws us on Plato alone, but Plato is regarded as the world's greatest artist in prose, with the reasoning powers of a philosopher and with the imagination of the most daring poet. Therefore we are never sure, when Socrates speaks, that we are not reading the ideas as well as the words of Plato. It is certain that the spell of Socrates followed him all his life, that it was his ideal he sought to achieve, and that a man with the noble ambitions of Plato could not have been inspired by one whom he did not regard as his superior. The estimate of Socrates given by Plato cannot be far wrong.

We have two prayers by Socrates: "Thou beloved god, Pan, grant to me that I be made beautiful within and that the outward man be in harmony with that inward beauty. May I esteem as rich the man who is wise, and may I have only such wealth as a self-reliant man can support with safety." It seems absurd to address a prayer for beauty and purity to that ugly and licentious god, Pan. And the other prayer is: "O king Zeus, grant to us what is good, whether we ask for it or not, and turn away from us the evil, even if we pray for it."

No Greek ever had high or pure thoughts because of his theology, but in spite of it. Greek men were better than their gods. When the noble ideas of Socrates had once been uttered the world could not let them wholly die. Hence his followers continued his search for ideals worthy of sacrifice. But they soon became divided. One part thought happiness was the goal of life and that pleasure was the end of all well-being. These men were called Epicureans. Another group thought that the best life consisted in indifference alike to pain and to pleasure. They argued that if the ledger of life is balanced, one will find that the sorrows are more than the joys; hence the only way to keep the account from showing a deficit is neither to laugh nor to weep, but to accept with stern indifference both mirth and sorrow. These men were called Stoics. Still another group believed that true happiness consisted in removing one's self from all the comforts and associations of life and in despising the conventions of society. These were called Cynics. However these groups varied in method, they all agreed in this: they did not return to a belief in the gods as those gods had been worshipped before Socrates.

They wearied in the search for something worthy of faith and worship and ended for the most part in flat despair. Even the proofs of immortality brought them no comfort, but only fear and torments. One of the chief poets of Italy, Lucretius, wrote one of the great poems of all time with the noble purpose of freeing men from a belief in their own immortality, and in an eternity which they could only dread. He argued that there was no plan in the universe, that everything was the result of material forces, unguided by intelligence, that man was only matter, and that he need have no dread of a future in which he was not to have a share. This absolute negation of God, Providence, and immortality, led to a contempt not only for the future life but for the life that is, so that even this great poet is said to have put an end to his own career. Philosophers of that period, that is, just before and just after the beginning of the Christian era, had no hope and could find no source of comfort, so that a long list of the great thinkers of that age will show that they gave up the effort in despair and ended their despondency in suicide. The illustrious Cato, patriot, moralist, and philosopher, after having reread the story of the death of Socrates, is assumed to have said:

> It must be so, Plato, thou reasonest well,
> Else why this pleasing hope, this fond desire,
> This longing after immortality,

and then took his disillusioned and hopeless life.

At that time Socrates seemed not only to have lived in vain but to have inspired a search for the impossible and to have given birth to a dread of a hopeless immortality. He had forever shaken the beliefs in the old Olympian divinities and had sent men seeking for what they had not found: a god of purity and a god of justice. By the time of the Caesars his followers, for the most part, had no message and the best they could offer was contempt for the world and for life itself. Hence the indifference with which they contemplated and carried out suicide.

"Hope deferred maketh the heart sick," but high hope abandoned leaves nothing with which to face the future. Yet under these conditions the Athenians multiplied the number of their divinities and even erected a statue or shrine to the "unknown god." A highly significant thing about that remarkable chapter which contains Paul's address on Mars Hill, are the words which follow that marvelous address: "Howbeit certain clave unto him and believed, among the which was Dionysius the Areopagite." This man was not only a member of the supreme court of Athens but was presumably also a philosopher. Dionysius would not have accepted this strange faith at once if it had not been a thing long in his heart, for the Jesus preached by Paul seemed the fulfillment of the vision dimly seen by Socrates, and it was just because of that vision that Christianity so soon took root in Greece. The chapter which tells of Dionysius the Areopagite, contains these significant words: "and there believed of the devout Greeks a great multitude." Also "Therefore many of them believed; also of honorable women which were Greeks, and of men, not a few." The first disciples who gathered around Jesus were like him, Hebrews—and so was Paul—but the leaders of the next generation, as well as the author of the book of Acts, were Greeks. Most of the early Christian fathers and the martyrs, after the first disciples, have Greek names. Their writings show that they accepted Jesus as the realization of the hopes inspired by the teachings of Socrates.

The structure of the Church is Greek, as is shown by the vocabulary, since *bishop, priest, presbyter, deacon, episcopal, martyr, angel, esslesiastic, catholic, cathedral, choir, chorus, hymn, psalm, tune, clergy, laity, prophet, patriarch, evangel, apostle,* even the words *church* and *Bible,* are all Greek. Without the work done by Socrates in destroying belief in the gods of paganism and in creating a longing for some such God as that revealed by Jesus, it cannot be doubted that Christianity would have found as barren a soil in Greece as it found among the Pharisees,—and even worse, for the Pharisees looked for a Messiah as the fulfillment of prophecy, while there was no such expectancy among the Greeks.

It was no accident, then, that Christianity soon outgrew Judæa and Jewish leaders and found among the Greeks those thinkers which gave it the structure, the content, and the vocabulary which it has ever since maintained,—thus fulfilling the words of Jesus: "I say unto you, The kingdom of God shall be taken from you and given to a nation bringing forth the fruits thereof." This great religious conversion, the most striking and important that ever took place among a people already civilized and cultured, was largely due to that simple sculptor who gave up ease, fortune, position, even life itself in the search for truth and for spiritual riches.

Everything that has been said about the setting for the life and career of Socrates must be reversed when speaking of Jesus, for Athens was the center of greatness and Socrates moved among the greatest of the great, while Nazareth was so humble, even in the humble region of Galilee, that a young man from an inconspicuous neighboring village said with a sneer: "Can any good thing come out of Nazareth?" The companions of Jesus were of the lowliest sort, so lowly that they were noticeable "unlearned and ignorant men." Jesus never seems to have associated with a single person of outstanding education or position. Even Nicodemus, who came to him by night, would have had no high rank in Athens or in Rome.

We owe our knowledge of Socrates to two men, Xenophon and Plato, both men of such unusual literary ability and imagination that we never know how much of what they tell us about Socrates is pure invention and how much is fact. The men who tell us about Christ were simple men, men of no reputation apart from what they derive from telling us of him,—men without literary imagination, just fitted for the simple narration of unadorned facts. A thing which pleases me much in Boswell's *Life of Johnson* is the way Boswell makes clever side remarks when quoting Johnson. But the writers of the Gospels never had that much self-reliance or assumption; they made no clever side remarks.

No other character until well on in the age of printing has been described by so many different persons who knew him well as was Jesus. Of very few people who lived in antiquity have we any account written by those who knew them. We are obliged to rely for all that we know of even such outstanding men as Solon, Hannibal, or Scipio, on the writings of men who lived several generations later. Certainly the most prominent men of the time of Christ were Augustus, the Roman Emperor under whom he was born, and Tiberius, under whom he was crucified. Yet for most of our knowledge of these two emperiors we are forced to rely on Tacitus and Suetonius, neither of whom lived during the lives of either of these rulers.

We have letters written by James, Peter, John, and Jude, each an intimate companion of Jesus. We have many letters by Paul, an exact contemporary who knew, if not Jesus himself, many men who did. And we have four Gospels written by four men, two of them disciples; one other belonging to a family intimate with Jesus; one other written by a competent historian who lived at that time and moved through that land, a writer who says that he had full knowledge of all these matters from the very beginning. Here are eight writers, each thoroughly familiar with the facts, who vouch for the life of Jesus. The chance that the Church later gathered these writings into one book and labeled that book the New Testament does not reduce the number of first-hand authorities.

We have the unqualified statement of the best Roman historian, Tacitus, that Nero after the burning of Rome tried to escape the blame by punishing the Christians, who, says Tacitus, were the followers of Christ who had been put to death during the reign of Tiberius by Pontius Pilate, a Roman official. Here is positive proof that shortly after 60 A.D. there were already in Rome sufficient numbers of Christians to attract the attention of Nero. We have a long letter from Pliny, a governor in Asia Minor, a letter that was written to the Emperor Trajan asking him what to do with the large number of Christians who would not worship the old gods of the Romans, especially refusing to join in the cult of the Emperor.

We have a reference in Epictetus, a writer of that period, to the Christians, and we have a paragraph from Josephus who was present at Jerusalem when that city was destroyed by Titus in 70 A.D., besides a flood of references from writers who lived within a century of the time of the Apostles. Take it all in all, we have more evidence for the life of Christ outside of the New Testament than for the existence of any except very few of ancient times. But since we have the Gospels this outside evidence is needless. Here we have four contemporary documents, each written in a consistent style, and each in a style different from that of the others. Thus, the Gospel of Luke is written in long periodic sentences, evidently by a trained writer, while John is written in short sentences, evidently by a man whose education was delayed and who never dared to trust himself to the sweeping sentences so dear to the rhetorician. The style shows that we have four authors, and these four authors made no attempt to make their accounts coincide. They are telling the same story, but in different ways. Thus Matthew says that there was written on the cross: "This is Jesus, the King of the Jews." Mark says that on the cross was written: "The King of the Jews," leaving out the name of Jesus entirely. Luke says that the inscription was in Greek, Latin, and Hebrew: "This is the King of the Jews." He inserts the words "This is" to the words of Mark, but he adds that the inscription was in three languages. While John does not name the language, he gives the inscription as "Jesus of Nazareth, the King of the Jews." John is the only one to insert the word Nazareth, while both Luke and Mark omit even the name Jesus. Certainly, if a group of men had concocted the Gospels they would all have written in the same way so important a matter as the inscription on the cross. The reason is plain: the disciples at the cross were greatly excited and in great grief; some things they saw and remembered with clearness, others they did not. At that time no one of them expected ever to write this story; they did not take notes, but years later, each remembered the fact of the inscription and that Jesus was mocked by being called "King of the Jews." They all agree to that, but the rest was either vague or else forgotten.

All the Gospels tell the story of the trial, the crucifixion, and the resurrection in essentially the same way. These were facts that they could not misunderstand or forget. Except for these mighty truths, the four have little in common. Even so important a matter as the birth of Jesus is passed over in silence by Mark, who wrote the oldest Gospel, and by John, who wrote the latest. Matthew says that "Jesus taught many things in parables, and without a parable spake he not to them." Yet John who was closest to Jesus wrote an entire Gospel without quoting a single parable. Evidently there was no collusion between the authors of these two gospels.

It is the consensus of scholars that Mark is the oldest of the Gospels, and it is an axiom of criticism that writers who depend on any given document for what they write, may dilute, expand, or condense their source, but they never add anything of value to that original document. If the writers of the Gospel depended entirely on this oldest Gospel they could not hide that dependence.

We know that Matthew was a Jew, evidently in bitter trouble, so bitter that he took a job, the most despised in the world: he became a tax gatherer for a hated usurping foreign power, and wrung taxes from his poor countrymen to be sent to their masters. No wonder that when he saw a chance, not for something better but for any escape from what he was doing, he accepted it, and followed Jesus. Matthew tells the story of the birth of Jesus; he gives the account of five miracles, and he tells fourteen parables which are not in Mark. He is the only writer to give the *Beatitudes* and their larger setting in the *Sermon on the Mount;* also all the contents of that wonderful twenty-fifth chapter are found only in his story. That chapter gives the parable of the *Wise and Foolish Virgins,* the parable of the *Ten Talents,* and the words ending in the great conclusion: "Inasmuch as ye did it not to one of the least of these, my brethren, ye did it not to me." If Matthew, or the one whom Matthew is quoting, conceived and wrote the *Sermon on the Mount* and this twenty-fifth chapter, he is one of the greatest thinkers and literary artists that ever lived; but we have the best possible proof that he was nothing of the sort. He and Luke both tell of the attempt of the lawyer to tangle Jesus with hard questions. The lawyer begins by asking: "Good Master, what shall I do to inherit eternal life?" The answer ends with the famous verse: "Thou shalt love thy neighbor as thyself." Matthew stops right there; but Luke, the Greek, the literary Greek, continues the narrative by saying that the lawyer then asked Jesus: "And who is my neighbor?" And Jesus answered and said: "A certain man went down from Jerusalem to Jericho, and fell among thieves." Then follows the great story of the good Samaritan, one of the finest stories known. Yet Matthew who heard it thought nothing of it. A man so lacking in literary appreciation was not likely to make up the *Sermon on the Mount,* or the great chapter which I have quoted.

If Luke depended on these two we should expect to see a restatement in other words of what he had found in Matthew and Mark, but here again we find a similar though different story. Luke alone tells us that Jesus was born in a manager. You would never suspect that from the account in Matthew. Luke alone repeats the song of the angels: "Glory to God in the highest, and on earth peace, good will towards men." He alone tells the story of the Good Samatitan, and he alone tells the only story I know that can claim a place beside it, the story of the Prodigal Son. He is the only one who tells us that Jesus said on the cross: "Father, forgive them for they know not what they do," or his words to the thief: "This day shalt thou be with me in Paradise;" and the only one who repeats those other words: "Father, into thy hands I commend my spirit." It seems to me that these few passages which I have quoted from Luke and which are in Luke alone, would place him among the very greatest writers of all time, if they were all his own. But if they are his own, he is a fraud, robbing himself of the glory he deserves, and he is using these noble ideas to fortify the imposture of another. Why should the Greek physician bestow all these treasures on the son of a Hebrew carpenter?

The last Gospel is by John. Most of that Gospel is a new story and shows other sides of the Savior. John alone repeats the words: "God so loved the world that he gave his only begotten Son, that whosoever believeth in him should not perish, but have everlasting life." It is hard for us to put ourselves back into the period before these words were uttered and to feel their force and novelty. Homer said: "The gods have decreed that poor mortals shall live in grief, while they themselves are free from sorrow." Herodotus, whom I love more than any other writer of Greece, said: "The gods allow no one to have high aspirations but themselves." Aristotle argued that there could be no affection between a superior and one vastly his inferior; that therefore love between God and man is impossible; that God cannot be interested in finite affairs, but must spend all his time in contemplating himself. This sentence in John, thrown off like a commonplace, with no arguing and no doubt of its truth, if it originated with John would make him one of the greatest thinkers of all times. But it is not the only great sentence, for soon there appears "God is a spirit, and they that worship Him must worship Him in spirit and in truth"; shortly to be followed by: "Ye shall know the truth and the truth shall make you free." This sentence, in whole or in part, is the favorite motto of our universities. When Johns Hopkins University was founded a little over fifty years ago they tried to get a motto that would cover what this new university hoped to accomplish. At last they took this old and much used sentence, for nothing else seemed to express so well the real purpose of a university. It seems incredible that a man who was writing to support an impostor should have had the desire or the ability to give this mighty tribute to truth. Somehow this sentence was uttered and some one must have been the first to speak it. If Jesus did not utter it, who did?

Further, it is contrary to human nature that John could have made up and falsely put into the mouth of Jesus the words spoken just before his betrayal: "Peace I leave with you, my peace I give unto you," or those other words: "Be of good cheer, I have overcome the world." The words and their setting are in such terrible contrast. If John himself conceived these great ideas he deserves a place among the greatest thinkers of all time. But then he would be one of the greatest impostors,—an impostor who glorified righteousness and truth, two things in which an impostor never believes, and two things which he cannot comprehend.

Here we have four different writers, all showing by their language that they belong to the same century, all of them men of no outside renown, all presenting ideas unequaled by Socrates or by Plato, all giving the glory to another, and all making that other one the same person, Jesus Christ.

The things which they all tell in common and the things which but one tells, all unite in the one figure of Jesus, and they all agree in proving to me, at least, that they present a true picture of a real character. The very essence of greatness is that it should be honest. That one dishonest man should have pictured Jesus is thinkable, but that four dishonest men should agree in unity as well as in variety in imagining such a being is beyond the uttermost limits of reason.

There is a certain similarity between Socrates and Christ. Socrates realized that there is a moral law in the universe, that we are not helpless children of blind chance, that there is a soul in man and that the soul is of limitless worth, that above all and ruling over all there is a just power that rules in righteousness,—but it was all so hidden in darkness that despite his hope he constantly faltered. Even in those arguments just after his condemnation with which he consoled himself and his friends by reasonings for immortality, he used these sad words: "if indeed these things told us are true." Think of pillowing one's head in martyrdom on nothing more than an if!

Socrates felt that his sole superiority lay in the fact that he knew nothing and was aware of that ignorance; also that in spite of disappointment he continued the search for knowledge. Jesus never sought for knowledge or wisdom from anyone. He never used the words "I do not understand," or "I do not know." His very strongest authority was himself and his most emphatic utterance was "But I say unto you," and he even went so far as to claim that he was the very truth itself.

Socrates knew that he was but a simple and a mortal man, while Jesus never questioned or allowed others to question his own belief that he was divine. No one of the followers of Socrates ever claimed that he returned to them from the dead, while the disciples of Jesus who on that bitter Friday evening after Calvary abandoned all hope, lost faith in their Master, and started back to their old tasks, soon became the most enthusiastic of men, willing to go to prison or to death in the conviction that they had seen the risen Lord. The fact of this enthusiastic devotion and of their martyrdom is unquestioned; something made them change from despair to unflinching optimism, and no adequate reason for that change has ever been given except the reason which they themselves gave.

It takes less credulity to believe that Jesus was what he claimed to be than that he was not. It takes less blind faith to believe that the writers of the Gospels owed their greatness to Him rather than that He owed His greatness to them.

There are many parallels between the high and noble sentences uttered by Socrates and those of Jesus. Socrates believed that the first step in the pursuit of knowledge is the recognition of one's own ignorance and that humility is a sign of greatness. Jesus said "Blessed are the meek, for they shall inherit the earth," and "Whosoever therefore shall humble himself as this little child, the same is greatest in the kingdom of Heaven."

Socrates said that "Whatever a man might gain at the cost of his own moral nature is only loss." Jesus said: "For what shall it profit a man to gain the whole world and lose his own soul?"

Socrates said that truth is the great possession, not for any exterior advantage, but simply for its own sake. Jesus said, "The truth will make you free." Socrates argued that the soul is immortal and that a righteous soul will be rewarded with eternal blessedness. Jesus said, "Come, ye blessed of my Father, inherit the kingdom prepared for you from the foundation of the world." "And the righteous shall go into everlasting life."

Socrates said that in his zeal for truth he had sought no advantages for himself and had spent his life in poverty. Jesus said, "The foxes have holes and the birds of the air have nests, but the Son of man hath not where to lay his head."

Socrates said that he had never parted from that moral course which his reason had selected as the best. Jesus said: "Which of you convinceth me of sin?"

Socrates said: "We should injure no one however much that person has injured us." Jesus said: "Love your enemies, bless them that curse you, do good to them that hate you, and pray for them which despitefully use you and persecute you."

Socrates said that he had no fear of those who injured the body but could not injure the moral nature." Jesus said: "Fear not them which kill the body, but are not able to kill the soul."

Socrates said to those who had accused him and to those who had condemned him that he cherished no ill-will against them. Jesus said: "Father, forgive them, for they know not what they do."

In these matters and thus far they agree, but Socrates has nothing to place beside any of the following, since they belong to another world: "Son, thy sins be forgiven thee, but that ye may know that the Son of man hath power to forgive sin, I say unto thee, arise, and take up thy bed and go into thine own house."

"All things are delivered unto me of my Father, and no man knoweth the Son but the Father, neither knoweth any man the Father, save the Son, and he to whomsoever the Son shall reveal him. Come unto me all ye that labor and are heavy-laden, and I will give you rest."

"When the Son of man shall come in his glory and all the holy angels with him, then shall he sit on the throne of his glory."

"Inasmuch as ye have done it to one of the least of these my brethren, ye have done it unto me." This last verse is remarkable not only because of its assurance, but more than that, it is the first positive statement that God is best served by kindness to his creatures, even the humblest. This at last is the answer to the question asked by Socrates of the young man Euthyphro: "If service of the gods does not benefit the gods, just what is its purpose?"

There is nothing in Socrates like the following: "Your father Abraham rejoiced to see my day: and he saw it and was glad. Then said the Jews unto him, Thou art not yet fifty years old, and hast thou seen Abraham? Jesus said unto them, Verily, verily, I say unto you, before Abraham was, I am."

"All power is given unto me in heaven and in earth, and lo, I am with you always, even unto the end of the world."

"One of the crucified thieves said unto Jesus, 'Lord, remember me when thou comest into thy kingdom.'

"Jesus said unto him, 'Verily I say unto thee, today shalt thou be with me in Paradise.'"

Three crosses stood side by side suspending three wretches, all alike condemned as felons to a disgraceful and inhuman death. One of these writhing figures answered the jeers of the mob with curses, one began to pray, and one assumed to throw open the gates of Paradise. What a contrast!

And, again, there is no parallel in Socrates to the following: "For God so loved the world that he gave his only begotten Son that whosoever believeth in Him should not perish but have everlasting life."

The woman said unto him, "I know that Messias cometh, which is called the Christ; when he is come, he will tell us all things."

Jesus saith unto her, "I that speak unto thee am he."

Then Martha said unto Jesus, "Lord if thou hadst been here, my brother had not died."

Jesus said unto her, "Thy brother shall rise again."

Martha said unto him, "I know that he shall rise again in the resurrection at the last day."

Jesus said unto her, "I am the resurrection and the life: he that believeth on me, though he were dead, yet shall he live."

No wonder that the officers answered and said, "Never man spake like this man." No wonder that Peter answered, "Thou are the Christ, the Son of the living God," and no wonder that those who had known him best endured persecution "rejoicing that they were counted worthy to suffer shame for his name."

My great teacher, Professor Gildersleeve, said that "Socrates reached an arm's length toward Christ,—it was only an arm's length, but it was toward Christ." It is just this fact, that the greatest man of the most intellectual city and at its most exalted period saw but dimly and partially that which Jesus saw so clearly and so completely and with such assurance, which has strengthened my faith that the carpenter of Nazareth and the companion of simple men of lowly Galilee must have been something more than a man.

J. B. Bury (essay date 1935)

SOURCE: "The Life and Death of Socrates," in *The Cambridge Ancient History,* edited by J. B. Bury, S. A. Cook, and F. E. Adcock, Cambridge University Press, 1935, pp. 386-97.

[*Below, Bury briefly surveys the life of Socrates as presented in the dialogues and* Apology *of Plato, highlighting some of the philosopher's most significant philosophical views in the process.*]

. . . The book of Xenophon on the life and teaching of Socrates, known as the *Memorabilia,* would, if it stood alone, give us little idea of what Socrates was like, and no idea of the secret of his greatness. Xenophon belonged (probably for a very short time) to the Socratic circle, but he had no notion of what philosophy really means and but a slight first-hand knowledge of the master. He produced a portrait such as a journalist with a commonplace mind might contribute to a gallery of 'good men,' and in his endeavour to show that Socrates was a good man he succeeds in concealing the fact that he was a great man. Most of the anecdotes he tells are uninstructive or insignificant, and some, as edifying stories are apt to be, simply tedious, like the remonstrances of Socrates with his son Lamprocles who could not put up with the rough side of his mother Xanthippe's tongue. Discerning as Xenophon was in many practical things he displays conspicuous want of discernment here: and for appreciating the personality of Socrates his book is almost negligible, while for most of the bare external incidents of his life that are interesting and which a biographer ought to supply, we go to him in vain[1]. He was not present at the trial of Socrates.

It is in the *Dialogues* of his companion Plato that a figure probably resembling the real Socrates appears. There we find his *animae figura,* his mind and methods, and the features of his personality, and also many details of his life. At all events, it is very difficult to resist the impression that the Platonic Socrates is a genuine life-like portrait of the original man, however unsocratically Platonic may be the argument and ideas of which he is made the spokesman.

Socrates was born about 470 B.C., and since he served as a hoplite he must have inherited some property from his father, Sophroniscus. He is said to have possessed a house and a capital sum of 70 minae which was invested for him by his friend Crito, who belonged to the same deme (Alopece). He witnessed the development of the Athenian democracy under Pericles and lived through the Peloponnesian War, serving in some of the earlier campaigns. He was a man of strong physical constitution, and of eccentric appearance and habits. His features are well known from portrait busts which are probably faithful enough to reality. With his flat nose and prominent eyes he was compared by his contemporaries to a satyr. He was subject to trances of meditation; when rapt in thought he would stand for hours, unconscious of what was going on around him. He said that from his childhood he used to hear from time to time the monition of an inner voice; its monitions were always negative, never prompting him to an action, but always restraining him from doing things.

What we know of the external events of his life is not a great deal but it is interesting. In his youth he was a pupil of Archelaus, who was a disciple of Anaxagoras, and accompanied him to Samos in 440 B.C. when the Athenians were blockading it. In 437-6 B.C. he may have served as hoplite at Amphipolis,[2] and in 432 B.C. he served at Potidaea; again in 424 B.C. at Delium where he exhibited remarkable presence of mind in the retreat. On these military occasions he showed extraordinary powers of endurance in sustaining cold, hunger, and fatigue; barefooted in a severe frost he could outmarch the other soldiers who were shod.

Perhaps[3] it was not till he was an elderly man that he was called upon to perform any public duty, beyond serving in the army. In 406 B.C. he was a member of the Council of Five Hundred, being one of the fifty representatives of his tribe (Antiochis). It was the year of Arginusae, and when the unhappy Generals were tried, Socrates was the only member who stood out in refusing to agree with the illegal resolution that all should be tried together. Under the Thirty he risked his life by refusing to carry out an order which was illegal. In all the public affairs in which he happened to be concerned he displayed moral and physical courage and respect for the laws of his city. Thus remarkable for courage and justice, Socrates was no less distinguished for his sobriety and temperance, but he was not an ascetic nor a spoilsport. He would take part in potations, but his head was strong, and he was never the worse for them.

Athenians had taken no part in the scientific speculations which had been so vigorously pursued by men of Ionia and in far western Greece. Archelaus, the instructor of Socrates, was the earliest, and not a very eminent exception. The sharp intellectual curiosity of Socrates was accompanied by a sane spirit of scepticism which was confirmed by the influence of Zeno. He cannot have been much over twenty when he came under that influence which was powerful in determining the direction of his thought. Parmenides, with his young friend Zeno, may have visited Athens not long after 450 B.C. and, if so, every Athenian of inquiring mind was interested in their visit. In any case, Zeno seems to have resided at Athens for several years; he was the inventor of dialectic and Socrates learned his method.

In the course of time a small circle of friends gathered around Socrates, drawn to him by the stimulus of his conversation. Knowledge he consistently professed himself unable to impart, and these friends were associated with him not as disciples but as fellow-inquirers. Their inquiries appear to have been chiefly concerned with mathematical and physical questions, the doctrines of Anaxagoras and Archelaus and Diogenes of Apollonia and of Pythagoras. In fact during the first half of his life the studies of Socrates were devoted chiefly to physical science; it was in his later years that he turned to the logical and ethical problems with which we chiefly associate his name.

Socrates and his circle became notorious in Athens as the Thinkers . . . , and comic poets seized on them as an obvious and legitimate subject for ridicule. In 423 B.C. Ameipsias produced his *Connus*, in which the chorus consisted of Thinkers and Socrates was derided, and in the same year was acted the *Clouds* of Aristophanes in which the scene was laid in the Thinking-shop . . . of Socrates and his fellow-workers.

The most devoted in this group of students was a certain Chaerephon who adored Socrates so sincerely that he went to Delphi and put to the oracle the amazing question 'Is any man wiser than Socrates?' More amazing still was the categorical answer of the oracle, without any reservations, 'No one is wiser.' Socrates said that he was greatly puzzled by this reply, being acutely conscious how little he knew. If the oracle were true, it must mean that others were not so wise as they seemed, or imagined themselves to be; and in order to test its truth, he states that he went about questioning and cross-examining persons who were eminent as proficients in their special subjects—politicians, poets, handicraftsmen. None of them stood the test; they were all convinced that they were wise, but none possessed more wisdom than Socrates himself, but he was superior in that he was fully aware of his own ignorance. In this way the oracle was justified. We do not know at what time it was given, but in the later portion of his life Socrates seems to have spent much of his time, not only in his accustomed haunts, the gymnasia of the Academy and the Lyceum, but also in the market-place and the workshops of artisans, cross-examining people and exposing their erroneous convictions that they were wise, thus fulfilling, as he put it, a duty imposed upon him by the god. Defending himself at his trial he said 'People suppose that I am wise myself in those things in which I convict another of ignorance. They are mistaken. The god alone is wise, and his oracle declares that human wisdom is worth little or nothing, using the name of Socrates as an example. That man is wisest who like Socrates knows that he is worthless so far as wisdom is concerned. The disgraceful ignorance is to think you know that you do not know.' Sceptical as Socrates was and always careful to appeal to reason, we cannot fail to see, in some parts of his defence, that there was a side of his nature which was moved by reasons that reason does not know.

In all ages of active progress, the warfare between the ideas and fashions of a young critical generation, and the old strongly entrenched opinions and customs which the innovators mock and assail, always presents amusing and humorous pictures which can furnish material for comedy. Comic poets can laugh impartially at the extravagances and the prejudices of both the combatants. If Aristophanes held up to ridicule the scientific Thinkers and the modern critics of society, he did not spare the praisers of the past, the old fogies whose ideas are out of date . . . who bore you with faded memories of the veterans of Marathon, and descant on bygone virtues and modern degeneracy.

We are told nothing of personal relations between Socrates and Pericles, but it is difficult to think that they were not acquainted. Socrates, though he belonged to a different class of society, had such a high repute as a thinker and talker that he could hardly have failed to arouse the curiosity and interest of Pericles, and they had many common friends. On the other hand, we hear of an intimacy between Socrates and Aspasia,[4] who, it was even supposed, gave him instruction in the art of rhetoric.

Though Socrates consistently disclaimed the possession of knowledge and therefore of the power of imparting it, he was a master of dialectic, for which he had a natural gift, and he was really teaching all the time, disguising the instruction and the ideas which he communicated under the form of question and answer. Many young men attached themselves to him and were his constant companions, and among them were the men, both Athenians and foreigners, who in the next generation were to be the great thinkers of Greece, the founders of philosophical schools, each emphasizing according to his own temperament a different side of the master's teaching. Plato, son of Ariston, the greatest of them all; Antisthenes, a poor man, who founded the school of the Cynics, which was the parent of Stoicism; Aristippus of Cyrene, whose Cyrenaic school was to be the parent of Epicureanism; Eucleides of Megara; Phaedo of Eretria; Aeschines, generally called 'the Socratic,' to distinguish him from Aeschines the orator. Thus Socrates was in some sense the ancestor of all the later philosophies of Greece. Outside this circle of companions, who were virtually disciples, his society was sought by men who were not interested much in philosophical questions but who were interested in listening to him cross-examining people and perhaps hoped to learn the secret of his skill. Two of the most distinguished were the versatile man of letters, Critias, and Alcibiades, of whom the second was an ardent admirer and an intimate friend of the philosopher. It was natural that Socrates should, in the popular mind, have to bear some ill fame for associating with these enemies of the democracy and be held responsible for their mischievous conduct. Although he was always loyal to existing authorities he never concealed his unfavourable opinion of democracy, which must have seemed to him an irrational form of government; Alcibiades called it bluntly 'acknowledged folly[5].'

Throughout the Peloponnesian War Socrates had with perfect impunity pursued his unpopular mission. But under the restored democracy it seemed to some of the democratic leaders that he was a dangerous and insidious anti-democratic influence and that it was desirable to silence him. The fact that he had remained at Athens unharmed during the government of the Thirty could not be made a charge against him on account of the amnesty. As a matter of fact he had barely escaped with his life from the despotism of the Thirty. Two of these oligarchs had been his friends, Critias the leader, and Charmides the uncle of Plato, and knowing that he was no admirer of the democracy they thought they were sure of his adhesion. They did not realize the unshakable strength of his respect for law and his love of justice. But they would not tolerate free speech and Critias thought it well to warn the philosopher that his discussions with the young men who sought his society must cease, and the government then made an effort to associate him with their unjust and tyrannous acts. The tyrants ordered him and four others to go to Salamis and arrest there a certain Leon whom they had resolved to put to death. Socrates said nothing and simply went home. He would have been executed for his disobedience to the government, if it had not fallen. This notorious incident however did not convince the people in power that Socrates stood quite outside party sympathies, and cared only for justice and right. They considered him disloyal to democracy, and that his criticisms were more to be feared than the plots of an oligarchical conspirator. It was therefore deemed highly desirable to rid Athens of a citizen whose influence and fearless tongue were felt to be a danger, though he took no part in politics and was the least likely of men to do anything contrary to the law. Anytus, an honest and moderate democrat and at this moment perhaps the most important Athenian statesman next to Thrasybulus, was the prime mover in preparing a prosecution intended to silence the embarrassing philosopher. No one was more determined than Anytus to observe honestly and to interpret strictly the terms of the amnesty; so that he was concerned carefully to keep out of sight the political motive for the action. He decided that the best ground of attacking Socrates successfully would be irreligion; it was common knowledge that the philosopher was far from orthodox. Accordingly an arrangement was made with a minor poet named Meletus, who was a fanatical champion of religion,[6] that he should bring against Socrates a public suit for irreligion . . . and that Anytus should support it by acting as an advocate for the prosecution. . . . Anytus associated with himself a second advocate, a rhetorician named Lycon of whom otherwise we know nothing.

Legal actions having to do with religion came into the court of the King archon. The charge which Meletus lodged against Socrates was formulated thus: 'Socrates is guilty of not worshipping the gods whom the city worships, and of introducing religious novelties. He is guilty also of corrupting the young men.' This accusation seems to prove that neglect of the worship of the gods was an indictable offence under the laws of Solon; for no one could now be indicted under the decree of Diopeithes which had been passed to meet the case of Anaxagoras, inasmuch as the effect of the settlement of 403 B.C. was that no prosecution could be based solely on one decree passed before that date. . . .

Meletus, in the writ of indictment, named death as the penalty which he demanded, for irreligion was one of the offences for which there was no punishment fixed by the code; the court itself determined the penalty on each occasion. But the court was limited to a choice between two penalties, that which was demanded by the prosecutor and one which it was the right of the prisoner himself to propose in case he were found guilty. It was the prisoner's interest to name a substantial penalty milder than that named in the indictment, yet not so light that it could not be entertained by the jury. A result of this curious judicial method was that the prosecutor generally assessed a penalty greater than he expected or wished to inflict. This is emphatically a case in point. There is no reason to suppose that Anytus wished Socrates to be put to death. It was doubtless expected that if he were convicted he would, as he had a right to do, propose exile as an alternative penalty and the court would assuredly be satisfied with that. To have him out of Athens was the object.

Our knowledge of this famous trial is derived from one of the most memorable and impressive books in the literature of the world, Plato's *Apology of Socrates*. The view that it was Plato's own composition used generally to be held although it was never doubted that it was based on the facts of the trial, but some critics now believe that it is the actual speech of Socrates, edited by Plato for publication, and as near to what was said as, say, a speech of Demosthenes or Cicero in its published form to the speech the orator actually delivered. The truth probably lies between these two views. We cannot suppose that the prisoner was allowed to make an address to the court after the sentence was passed. The epilogue is an addition imagined by Plato, an artistic and moving conclusion. If this is admitted, it must also be allowed that Plato may have taken other liberties with the Defence; he may have left out parts of it and considerably expanded other parts. The most grave and perilous of the charges brought against Socrates was that of being a corrupter of youth. That would count for much with the judges because they knew that leading politicians who were enemies of the democracy had cultivated his society—Critias, Alcibiades, Charmides. But this was just the proof of the accusation which Meletus and his two advocates were prohibited from touching on. The amnesty forbade them to pronounce these names. They must however have made an attempt to show in what ways the conversation of Socrates misled and injured the young men. Of this there are no indications in the Defence according to Plato, nor can we discover from that defence how Meletus explained what were the strange religious practices which he alleged that Socrates introduced, as he assuredly must have done, producing some proof of his statements. It seems to follow that the *Apology* does not supply a full account of the trial.[7]

Socrates was found guilty by a majority of 60 votes, for he mentions in his Defence that he would have been acquitted if 30 of the votes recorded against him had been for acquittal. It is probable, though not certain, that the number of Athenians in the jury appointed by the king to try the case was 501. If that was so, 225 must have voted in his favour, and it is quite likely that he would have been acquitted if he had assumed a different attitude and had really been concerned to secure a verdict of 'not guilty.' But he adopted throughout a very high tone, which was far from calculated to conciliate the court though he expressed himself with his usual urbanity and politeness. He had not condescended to make the conventional appeal to pity by bringing into court his wife and children to excite the compassion of the judges by family tears, as was almost invariably done by prisoners tried on a grave issue, and the omission of which many of the judges might consider an affront to themselves.

When the verdict of his guilt was pronounced, it was for Socrates to submit a punishment less drastic than death, and there can be no question that he could have saved his life if he had proposed banishment. But Socrates was not as other men. His tone now became higher than ever and to the ears of his judges more offensive. 'Meletus,' he said, 'assesses the penalty at death. What fair counter-assessment then shall I make, Athenians? What do I deserve to suffer, or what fine to pay, because during my life I would not keep quiet, but neglecting the things that most people care for—making money, managing their property, public offices and political clubs—I considered myself really too good for such things, and instead of entering upon these ways of life in which I should have been no good either to you or to myself I set myself on the way of benefaction, to confer the greatest of all benefactions as I assert, by attempting to persuade each of you individually not to care for any of his own belongings before he cares for himself—for his being as good and as wise as possible, nor for any of the city's belongings before he cares for the city, and on the same principle in all other matters. What then do I deserve for this? Something good surely, Athenians, and a good that would be suitable to me personally, suitable to a poor man who is a benefactor and requires leisure. There is nothing so suitable than that such a man should have free commons in the Prytaneum, far more than for one of you who has won a victory at Olympia in a horse-race or a chariot-race; because while he makes you appear happy, I make you be happy, and he does not need public support while I do. Accordingly, if I am to propose what I deserve, I propose that my sentence be free board in the Prytaneum.' This was not calculated to conciliate the judges; it was an undisguised 'contempt of court' and was quite unnecessary; it seemed as if the prisoner was determined to make it certain that he should be condemned to death. Having by this digression done what he could to dispose the judges against him he returned to business and considered possible penalties which the court might accept. He knew quite well that banishment would probably be considered adequate. 'Perhaps,' he said, 'banishment is what you think I deserve. Yet I should be fond indeed of life, Athenians, if I were so poor a reckoner as to calculate that if you who are my fellow citizens could not put up with my lectures and discourses, and if they have become so onerous and offensive, that you are now wishing to rid yourselves of them, other people will readily tolerate them. Nay, a fine life I should have, leaving my own city at my age and moving from one city to another and continually being driven out. I know that wheresoever I came the young men would listen to my talk as they do here. If I repulse them they will persuade the older men to expel me, and if I do not, their fathers and relatives will do so for their sakes.

'But it will be said: But, Socrates, when you leave Athens, why not keep quiet and hold your tongue? This is just what is so difficult to make you understand. To do that would be to disobey the god, and therefore it is impossible to keep quiet. When I say this, you will not believe me, you will take it as irony. And again if I say that a man's greatest good is to debate every day concerning virtue and the other things you hear me discussing and cross-examining myself and others about, and that the life which is not tested and proved by such examination is not worth living—when I say this, still less do you believe me to be in earnest. If I had money I should be ready to offer all I have as a fine; paying it would do me no harm. I could pay a mina. Plato, however, and Crito and two other friends bid me name 30 minae and will stand as sureties for the payment. They are solvent. So I propose this fine.'

The majority voted for death and this majority was greater than the previous one. We can understand that the tone which Socrates had adopted caused resentment among some of those who had originally voted for acquittal. One knows the type of persons who would be reasonable and fair enough to see that the accuser had failed to prove his case and would vote accordingly, yet would feel it an outrage that any prisoner should value his life so little as to neglect all the customary and obvious methods of trying to save it and take no trouble to conciliate the judges. Such an attitude was indecent and dangerous. If prisoners were not afraid of death, what could any one do? Socrates, it almost seemed, was so impertinent as to reverse the rôles of judge and accused; he had treated them as if it was they who were on trial, and had gone too far in his insolent assumption that he was a great and good man.

A month intervened between the sentence and the execution, because it happened to be the feast of the Delian Apollo when every year Athens sent a ship to Delos, and the law was that from the time the ship set sail till it returned to the Piraeus the city should not be polluted by any death inflicted by the authority of the State. The ship had been adorned with the official garlands on the day before the trial of Socrates, and, as it turned out, a month elapsed before it returned, a month which he had to spend in the public prison in chains. He seems to have been treated there with much consideration; the overseer of the prison was a humane man and did what he could to make the confinement as little irksome as possible. His friends came daily to visit him and his last days were passed in philosophical discussion. Some of his companions, particularly Crito, urged him to escape; a plan was prepared, and there is little doubt that it could easily have been managed; even the authorities might not have been very unwilling to connive; but Socrates refused to consent. It had always been his principle to obey the laws and had he not been legally condemned? And to flee from prison and death would have been glaringly inconsistent with his own attitude at the trial and rendered it obviously absurd. If to live was such an important consideration as to prompt escape, which meant abiding in exile, he ought clearly to have proposed exile as the alternative penalty.

The last hours and death of Socrates have been described by Plato in his *Phaedo.* His friends were with him to the end, and he was killed by the painless method of a draught of hemlock poison which produced a gradual paralysis. It is the one famous execution, recorded in history, of which the circumstances are quite ideal; the end of Socrates is marred, for our memory, by no violence or shedding of blood; and modern critics have often praised the Athenians for their humane methods of punishment. But it would be an error to suppose that the ways of brutal evil-doers at Athens were made so easy for them, or that robbers and assassins were treated like Socrates. It is not long ago since excavations near Phalerum revealed[8] evidence that the Athenians used to inflict punishments which in agony rivalled crucifixion and hardly fell short of Assyrian atrocity. We do not know on what principle or in what cases execution by hemlock was adopted.

Among the companions of Socrates his memory was piously cherished, while they were stirred by a deep resentment against the democracy of Athens for the crime of his death. Seen through their eyes, the trial of Socrates by a jury of average practical citizens at the prosecution of an honest politician seems as absurd an event as, to use Plato's comparison, the trial of a physician in a court of little boys at the instance of a confectioner. The great memorial of Socrates is the body of Plato's works; no other man has had a more wonderful monument. Having described the last moments of his master, Plato wrote, 'Such was the end of our friend, whom I may truly call the wisest, the justest and the best of all the men I have ever known.' In the study of his imagination the revered master grew into the ideal figure of a perfect philosopher and as such has passed into history. The tragedy changed the course of Plato's own life. He had always meant to enter political life. The behaviour of the oligarchs during their short tenure of power, in which his relatives Critias and Charmides had been conspicuous, disgusted him so deeply that he was probably inclined to support the democracy, but the crowning injustice of the condemnation of Socrates decided him to abandon the idea of a political career. More than forty years later, in a letter addressed to 'the friends and associates' of Dion of Syracuse, he recalled his experience at this time, and his decision to embrace a life of philosophy. This is what he says[9]: 'Socrates an elderly friend of mine who, I should not be ashamed to say, was the justest man among the men of the time, was sent with others by the Thirty to arrest one of the citizens, to be executed, in order that he (Socrates) might himself share in their actions whether he wished it or not; he refused and ran the extreme risk, rather than become a participant in their wicked deeds. Seeing all these things, and other similar things which were not trifling, I was disgusted and withdrew and stood aloof from the crimes of that Government. Not long afterwards the Thirty fell and the existing constitution was changed. I felt myself again drawn though slowly towards public life. The new Government had merits, though it had also defects, but it so happened that this companion of ours, Socrates, was brought into court by certain men who were in power. They preferred against him a most wicked charge and one which was least applicable to Socrates of all men in the world. They accused him of impiety, and he was condemned and put to death, the man who had refused to take part in the wicked arrest of one of their friends who was trying to flee at the time when they were themselves unfortunate.'

He goes on to explain how this experience of the new democracy finally decided him to give up the idea of a political career.

How great Socrates was as an original thinker, whether he can be set beside Pythagoras, for instance, is a question that is open to dispute, and depends much on the view that is taken of the Platonic Dialogues. . . . But there can be only one opinion as to the greatness and the unique quality of his personality, and his unrivalled power as a stimulator of thought. The Athenians, with the exception of his personal friends, were quite unconscious of his greatness. Posterity looks back at him as the most remarkable figure of the Illumination; the contemporary man in the market-place of Athens probably remembered him merely as an eccentric Sophist. One can imagine what he would have said: 'Socrates—yes, an incessant talker, who fancied himself as a good-mixer. He was really an expert bore preaching for ever about virtue and other wearisome things. He got at last what he probably had richly deserved.'

Notes

[1] This has been shown by A. E. Taylor, *Plato's Biography of Socrates,* pp. 35 *sqq.*

[2] See Burnet's note on Plato's *Apology,* 28 E, p. 120.

[3] Perhaps; for it is possible that he served on the Council before 406, at some unknown date; see Burnet in his edition of Plato's *Apology,* p. 133.

[4] Aeschines wrote a Socratic dialogue *Aspasia.* See also the *Menexenus* which U. von Wilamowitz-Moellendorff has ingeniously defended as Platonic (*Platon,* 11, pp. 126 *sqq.*).

[5] Thucydides VI, 89, in the speech at Sparta, probably a genuine phrase of Alcibiades.

[6] There is a difference of opinion on the identity of this Meletus with the man who later in the same year, 399 B.C., prosecuted Andocides for impiety and part of whose speech is preserved among the works of Lysias (*Or.* VI). That two men of this name should have brought actions for impiety—such actions were not very frequent nor was the name very common—in the same year seems unlikely. It is interesting to observe that in this trial also Anytus was concerned, not however on the side of Meletus, but as a witness for Andocides, and his evidence seems to have secured an acquittal.

[7] Cp. Bury, *Trial of Socrates,* in *Rationalist Press Annual,* 1925, where it is argued that one or two points in the speech of defence may be got from Xenophon's *Apology,* that the speech of Anytus followed the speech of Meletus and dealt with the charge of corruption of the young men, while Meletus mainly confined himself to the charges of irreligion, and it is suggested that some of the points which Anytus made may possibly be gathered from the declamation (*Apologia Socratis*) in which Libanius replied to the attack on Socrates by the sophist Polycrates.

[8] Compare A. D. Keramopoullos. . . .

[9] Plato, *Ep.* VII, 324 E-325 c.

A. E. Taylor (essay date 1951)

SOURCE: "The Thought of Socrates," in *Socrates,* The Beacon Press, 1951, pp. 138-83.

[*In the following essay, Taylor asserts that Socrates significantly influenced the development of European thought by creating the concept of the soul "which has ever since dominated European thinking." Taylor differentiates between the "psyche" as described by Homer and the Orphic and Pythagorean traditions before Socrates, and goes on to examine the Socratic mission of caring for the soul in order to perfect it. Taylor then surveys and interprets Socrates's moral teachings, his theory of knowledge, and his scientific method.*]

What is the real significance of Socrates in the history of European thought? We may at once dismiss two views which have sometimes been held on this question as incapable of explaining the facts which need to be accounted for. Socrates was not a mere preacher of a commonplace morality of acting like an *homme de bien* for the utilitarian reason that bad ways 'do not pay'—a view of him suggested by undue attention to certain parts of Xenophon's *Memorabilia.* Such a man would hardly have been put to death as a public danger; he would not have won the devotion of Plato, nor the general admiration of all the outstanding men of his age, or been caricatured as he was actually caricatured by Aristophanes. You may say Anytus misunderstood his man, Plato 'idealized' him, Aristophanes distorted his features. But there must have been something to prompt the misunderstanding, the idealization, the distortion. The subject of them must have been in some way an extraordinary, in fact a *singular* character, an 'original,' and we have to discover in what his singularity consisted. Nor can Socrates have been what he has sometimes been taken to be by superficial readers of Plato, a mere sceptic, quick at disturbing the convictions of others by ingenious questions, but without convictions, and intense convictions, of his own. Mere clever scepticism is as ephemeral in its results as it is temporarily dazzling; Socrates created the intellectual and moral tradition by which Europe has ever since lived. *How* this could be is what has to be explained.

At bottom the answer seems to be a very simple one, and it may best be given in the elementary way in which it has been stated by Burnet.[1] It was Socrates who, so far as can be seen, created the conception of the *soul* which has ever since dominated European thinking. For more than two thousand years it has been the standing assumption of the civilized European man that he has a *soul,* something which is the seat of his normal waking intelligence and moral character, and that, since this *soul* is either identical with himself or at any rate the most important thing about him, his supreme business in life is to make the most of it and do the best for it. There are, of course, a minority of persons who reject this theory of life, and some of them even deny the existence of a soul, but they are a small minority; to the vast mass of Europeans, to this day, the existence and the importance of the soul is a doctrine so familiar that it seems self-evident. The direct influence, indeed, which has done most to make the doctrine so familiar to ourselves is that of Christianity—but when Christianity came to the Graeco-Roman world it found the general conception of the soul which it needed already prepared for it by philosophy. Now the remarkable thing is that we find this conception of the soul as the seat of normal intelligence and character current in the literature of the generation immediately subsequent to the death of Socrates; it is common ground to Isocrates, Plato, and Xenophon, and thus cannot be the discovery of any one of them. But it is wholly, or all but wholly, absent from the literature of earlier times. It must thus have originated with some contemporary of Socrates, and we know of no contemporary thinker to whom it can be attributed other than Socrates himself, who is consistently made to teach it in the pages of both Plato and Xenophon.

Of course, we hear frequently enough in Greek literature, from Homer onward, of a thing which is called the *psyche.* But the important point is that there is perhaps no single passage in the earlier literature in which *pysche* means what *soul* has meant to us for so many centuries, the conscious personality which may be wise or foolish, virtuous or vicious, according to the 'tendance' and discipline it gets. In the earlier literature *psyche* regularly means one of two things, neither identical with what we have been taught to call the *soul,* according as the word is being used with associations derived from Homer or from Orphic religion.

In Homer the *psyche* means quite literally the *ghost.* It is something which is present in a man so long as he lives, and leaves him at death. It is, in fact, the 'ghost' which the dying man 'gives up.' But it is not the *self;* for Homer the 'hero himself,' as distinguished from his *psyche,* is his *body.* Though a man cannot live when his *psyche* has left him, the *psyche* is never thought of as having anything to do with the 'mental life,' as we now call it; that is carried on, in Homer's language, by the *kear,* heart, or the *phrenes,* midriff, both bodily organs. And the *psyche* which has left the body has no consciousness whatsoever, any more than a man's shadow or his reflection in a pool; all that the departed *psyche* can do is to be seen from time to time in the dreams of the living. It is thus, at bottom, no more than the 'breath' which a man draws while he is alive and exhales finally when he 'expires.' Ionic science, in its account of the *psyche,* starts from these conceptions and carries the de-individualization of *psyche* still further. Its reigning view is that my *psyche* is simply that part of the ambient 'air' which I inhale. 'Air' is itself a 'god,' and so is conscious, and that is why I am conscious just so long as I can continue to replenish my system with fresh portions of 'the god.' When I 'breathe my last,' the divine air in me simply goes back again to mingle with the common stock of the 'air' in the world at large; there is no real and permanent individual bearer of my 'personality.' (In the philosophy of Heraclitus, indeed, we can see that the 'soul'—which he supposed to be not 'air' but 'fire'—was very important, but it is a standing contradiction in his thinking that it at once has got to possess some sort of permanent individuality, in order to pass through the vicissitudes of birth, death, and re-birth, and yet is only a temporarily detached portion of the cosmic 'fire.')

In the Orphic religion, on the other hand, as in the kindred religion of the early Pythagoreans, the *psyche* is a more important thing. It has a permanent individuality, and is consequently immortal, and, in fact, a temporarily 'fallen' and exiled divinity. The great concern of the devotee is to practise rules of life, partly moral, partly ceremonial, which will lead to the final deliverance of the *psyche* from the 'wheel of birth,' and its restoration to its place among the gods. But it is not the *soul,* if by the *soul* we mean 'that within us'—to use the words of Socrates in Plato—'in virtue of which we are pronounced wise or foolish, good or bad.' It is supposed by the Orphics to manifest its activity just when what we should call the 'normal' waking self is in abeyance—in dreams, visions, trances. As Pindar puts it, '[the psyche] sleeps while the members are active, but in men's sleep it bodes forth in many a dream the impending issues of weal and woe.'[2] *My* intelligence and *my* character thus do not belong to the *psyche* in me, and its immortality, important as it is held by the Orphic to be, is not, properly speaking, *my* immortality. Where the *psyche* is spoken of, exceptionally, in earlier literature as the source of any actions in the everyday waking life, it is commonly mentioned in connection with the freakish appetites of which sober sense disapproves.[3] It seems certain that at Athens in the fifth century the word *psyche* suggested to the ordinary man no more than 'ghost' does to us, and this is why Aristophanes in the *Clouds* talks about Socrates and his companions as *sophai psukhai*—he means to suggest that the life of these 'thinkers' is no better than that of so many 'ghosts.' So *philopsukhia,* concern for one's *psyche,* meant the cowardly hanging on to 'dear life' which leads a man to 'funk' in the field.

Clearly, what is needed for the development of a 'spiritual' morality and religion is that the Orphic insistence on the supreme importance of 'concern for the interests of the *psyche*' shall be combined with the identification of this supremely precious *psyche* with the seat of normal personal intelligence and character. This is just the step which is taken in the doctrine of the soul taught by Socrates in both Plato and Xenophon, and it is by this breach with the Orphic tradition as much as by giving the conduct of life the central place which earlier thinkers had given to astronomy or biology that Socrates, in the hackneyed Ciceronian phrase, 'brought philosophy down from heaven to earth.' In other words, what he did was definitely to create philosophy as something distinct at once from natural science and from theosophy, or any amalgam of the two, and to effect this result once for all. The soul, as he conceives of it, has all the importance and the permanent individuality of the Orphic *psyche.* For reasons already given, it seems plain to me that we must believe Plato's representations about his Master's firm conviction of the soul's immortality, and in the mouth of a Greek this means its essential *divinity.* This is the real justification of a mission to preach to all men, in season and out of season, the single duty of 'tending the soul,' and 'making it as good as possible,' whatever the cost to one's fortunes or one's body. But the identification of the soul which it is our first duty to 'tend' with the normal self means, of course, that the 'tendance' will not consist in the practice of ritual abstentions and purifications, but in the cultivation of rational thinking and rational conduct. A man's duty will be to be able to 'give account' of, to have a rational justification for, what he believes and what he does. It is precisely by asserting and doing that for which we can give no rational justification that we display our indifference to the duty of 'tending' our souls. This is why when Socrates came to discharge his mission his first task was to convict the unenlightened of 'ignorance,' to show them how little intelligent justification they have for what they do or believe.

This Socratic doctrine of the soul, we must note, is neither psychology, in our sense of the word, nor psycho-physics. It tells us nothing on the question what the soul *is,* except that it is 'that in us, whatever it is, in virtue of which we are denominated wise and foolish, good and evil,' and that it cannot be seen or apprehended by any of the senses. It is no doctrine of the 'faculties' of the soul, any more than of its 'substance.' The thought is that the 'work' or 'function' of this divine constituent in man is just to *know,* to apprehend things as they really are, and consequently, in particular, to *know* good and evil, and to *direct* or *govern* a man's acts so that they lead to a life in which evil is avoided and good achieved. What Socrates is concerned with is thus neither speculative nor empirical psychology,[4] but a common principle of epistemology and ethics. To 'make the soul as good as possible' would be on the one side to attain the knowledge of existence as it really is, on the other to base one's moral conduct on a true knowledge of 'moral values.' In both spheres the one thing to be overcome is the putting of 'opinion,' 'fancy' (*doxa*), assumptions which cannot be justified as true, in the place of knowledge. As science is ruined by the confusion of fancy with fact, so practical life is spoiled by a false estimate of good. We have now to see how this conception of knowledge of the truth as the one supreme business of the soul, and therefore of man, works out into the beginnings of a theory both of science and of moral conduct. We night be confident, even without the plain indications of Plato to guide us, that Socrates' interest in the scientific problem belongs more particularly to the earlier part of his life, and that the ethical side of his thinking must have been almost exclusively dominant in the later years devoted to his mission to mankind. But we shall take the two things in the reverse order, in view of the much more general consensus of scholars on the characteristic features of the Socratic ethic.

1. *Ethics.*—When Aristotle has occasion to speak of the distinctive moral teaching of Socrates, he ascribes to him three special tenets, all at first sight paradoxical: (*a*) virtue, *moral* excellence, is identical with knowledge, and for that reason, *all* the commonly discriminated virtues are one thing; (*b*) vice, bad moral conduct, is therefore in all cases ignorance, intellectual error; (*c*) wrong-doing is therefore always involuntary, and there is really no such state of soul as that which Aristotle himself calls 'moral weakness' (*acrasia*), 'knowing the good and yet doing the evil.' Aristotle pretty clearly took these statements directly from his reading of one particular great dialogue of Plato, the *Protagoras,* where they are all to be found, but they fairly describe the substance of what Socrates has to say about morality in the dialogues of Plato's earlier period, and they all reappear in a more commonplace form in the *Memorabilia* of Xenophon. We shall have the key to them if we can discover the point of view from which they cease to be paradoxes and begin to appear obvious.

We may most conveniently start with what appears to be the most violent paradox of all, the assertion that all wrong-doing is involuntary. 'Moral weakness,' the fact that men do what they themselves confess to be wrong, and that they do so without any forcing, is one of the most familiar facts of experience, and we are not to suppose that Socrates means to deny this. He means to say that the popular phrase we have just used gives an inadequate analysis of the fact. A man often enough does evil *in spite of* the fact that it is evil; no man ever does evil simply *because* he sees it to be evil, as a man may do good simply because he sees it to be good. A man has temporarily to sophisticate himself into regarding evil as good before he will choose to do it. As it is put in the *Gorgias,* there is one fundamental desire which is ineradicable in all of us: the desire for *good* or *happiness.* It is possible, in the case of all other objects, to prefer the appearance to the reality, the outward show, *e.g.* of power, or wealth, to the thing itself, but no one can wish for the show of good or happiness rather than the reality: this is the one case where the shadow cannot possibly be esteemed above the substance. To say that vice is involuntary means, therefore, that it never brings the vicious man that on which his heart, whether he knows it or not, like the heart of every one else, is really set. The typical Greek 'monster of wickedness,' the 'tyrant' who has raised himself above all the laws, may spend his whole life 'doing as he pleases' with the persons and property of all men, but just because he *always* does 'just as he pleases,' he never gets what he really wishes for. He wishes for felicity, and gets the extreme of infelicity, a hopelessly diseased *soul.* It would be better to be a criminal under sentence of death, because death may be just the sharp 'surgery' needed to cure the malady of the criminal's soul. Thus, if a man really knew as assured and certain truth, of which he can no more doubt than he can doubt of his own existence, that the so-called 'goods' of body and 'estate' are as nothing in comparison with the good of the soul, and knew what the good of the soul is, nothing would ever tempt him to do evil. Evil-doing always rests upon a false estimate of goods. A man does the evil deed because he falsely expects to gain good by it, to get wealth, or power, or enjoyment, and does not reckon with the fact that the guilt of soul contracted immeasurably outweighs these supposed gains. Socrates thus agrees on one point with Hedonism, that wrong-doing is due to miscalculation; but the miscalculation is not one of 'amounts of pleasure,' but of values of good.[5]

We see now what is meant by saying that all the virtues are one thing, and that thing knowledge. The current view of mankind, in Socrates' day as in ours, was that the moral virtues are a plurality; each is quite unlike the others, and you can have one in the highest degree without having any vestige of another—can, for example, be the *brave des braves* and yet as profligate as brave, or the most continent of men and yet the most grasping and unfair. Now Socrates admits that this is true, if by the virtues you mean what he calls in Plato 'vulgar virtue,' the sort of outward respect paid to an accepted code of conduct by men who have no personal conviction of the supreme importance of the soul, and the identity of true happiness with its 'health,' and merely conduct themselves decently because the habits of their society require it of them, and they expect to be made uncomfortable if they behave otherwise. But this 'vulgar' virtue is a mere illusory counterfeit of the true. True virtue is an affair of intense conviction, personal *knowledge* of the true moral 'values.' There is thus one single principle behind all its various manifestations in the varied situations of life. A man who has grasped this principle with the assured insight of knowledge cannot, then, apply it in some situations and not in others. Real knowledge of what is good for the soul will display itself in a right attitude to all the situations of life, and thus in the 'philosopher's' life the apparent dividing lines between one type of moral excellence and another will vanish. The whole of his conduct will be the exhibition of one excellence, steady and assured certainty of the true 'scale of good.' This explains the curious fact that more than one of the Platonic dialogues ends in a singular, apparently negative result. We are invited to consider what is the true character of some currently recognized virtue (*temperance* in the *Charmides, courage* in the *Laches*). Reflection seems to be leading us up to the conclusion that the quality under discussion is really *knowledge* of good, when we are brought to a pause by the observation that this appears to be the definition not of the particular virtue ostensibly under discussion, but of all virtue as a single whole. Formally this is treated as a proof that we are still as ignorant of the answer to the question propounded to us as we were at the outset. In fact, we are to understand, the attempt to define one virtue ends in something which is no more a definition of that virtue than of another, for the reason that in principle *all* virtue is one.

Of course, the *knowledge* with which Socrates thus identifies virtue is not anything and everything to which the name knowledge can be given; it is definitely knowledge of what is nowadays called 'moral value,' knowing what is my *good.* Now this leads to a real difficulty: how is such knowledge to be come by? On the one hand, if virtue is *knowledge,* the having or not having it is no matter of simple congenital endowment; men no more come into the world born good than they come into the world already born in possession of any other kind of knowledge; they have to *win* their knowledge. Yet the popularly current view that we automatically pick up 'goodness,' as we pick up the use of our mother-tongue, under the influence of good parents and a good social environment cannot be true. It is notorious that Pericles and the other outstanding men whom the Athenian public regards as eminently its 'best men' have been quite unable to impart their own excellences to their sons; the sons have commonly been quite inferior persons. On the other hand, the eminent 'sophists' profess to be able to 'teach goodness,' as they might teach some technical accomplishment, by a course of instruction. Now, if goodness is knowledge and nothing but knowledge, it certainly must be capable of being taught somehow; the man who has this knowledge must be able to direct another to the acquisition of it. And yet the sophistic profession of being able to teach it by a course of lectures must be hollow. The point which Socrates is represented by Plato as urging repeatedly against the sophists and their admirets is a simple one. What the sophist can teach is at best a professional speciality of some kind, how to do something which men in general cannot do. But virtue, or goodness, is no speciality with its restricted domain; its sphere is the whole domain of human conduct. And a specialism is, again, something which may be put to a good use or to an ill one, just as medical knowledge may be used to cure, but may equally be used to kill.[6] At best the sophist can impart the specialist knowledge; what he cannot impart is the 'knowledge of good' which will ensure that the use made of it shall be good and not evil.

How, then, does a man learn the one kind of knowledge which it steads him most to have, knowledge of good? It is not clear that Socrates had ever reached a final solution of the problem. But we can perhaps discover the general character of the answer he would have given. According to Plato,[7] he had been struck by the Orphic doctrine that there are means by which the soul can be restored to remembrance of her forgotten divine origin, and from this hint he had developed the conviction that the acquisition of knowledge generally is in reality a process of 'recollection' or 'recognition' (*anamnesis*) in which particular sensible facts prompt or suggest the assertion of a universal principle which transcends the facts themselves. By drawing a diagram and asking a series of pertinent questions, the mathematician leads a pupil to recognize a universal proposition. He need impart no information; if the right diagram is drawn, and the mind of the pupil set at work on it by the right questions, it will produce the right conclusion from within, by its own action, as though from a store of truth which it already possesses unconsciously. The truth so 'learned' is reached by a personal 'discovery,' to which the 'learner' has simply been stimulated by his 'teacher,' and yet is also 'recognized' as already implied in what the 'learner' had all along known. In the same way, the acute interrogations of a Socrates who compels us to 'give account' of our conduct of our lives, prompt the mind of the interrogated to 'recognition' of the implications of the moral standards by which we estimate our own conduct and our neighbour's. This is the starting-point from which Plato was to develop his own theory of 'philosophy' as created by the friction of minds employed in the joint pursuit after truth.

The Greek mind rightly made no distinction between the principles of private and those of public conduct, morals and 'politics'; and Socrates consistently applied his conviction of the identity of 'goodness' with a right estimate of 'values' to the morality of the State and its statesmen. The worth of a State, and of its public men, depended, in his eyes, wholly on the degree to which the national life was based on a true scale of good. It was out of the question that, with all his practical loyalty to the constitution, he should approve of the principle of democracy, the sovereignty of the multitude who have no knowledge of the good, and have never even dreamed that such knowledge is the necessary qualification for the direction of their affairs. The judgments on the Athenian democracy of the fifth century put into his mouth in Plato's *Gorgias* and *Republic* are much harder than anything Plato has to say of democratic government on his own account in such later dialogues as the *Politicus* and the *Laws,* and it seems to me probable that the severity of these verdicts comes from Socrates rather than from Plato.[8] The very principle of democracy, if it can be called a principle, according to the *Republic,* is the refusal to require any superiority of intellect or character as a qualification for leadership; in the democratic community, as Nietzsche puts it, there is 'one flock and no shepherd,' and this is why its normal fate is to fall into the hands of an able and unscrupulous 'dictator' (or, as the Greeks called him, 'tyrant'). Equally severe is the condemnation pronounced by the *Gorgias* on all the famous leaders of the Athenian democracy, from Themistocles to Pericles, with the one exception, in part, of the 'just' Aristides. None of them all had the knowledge of good which is the one thing needful in life, as we see from two considerations. None of them—not even Aristides—could impart any goodness he possessed to his own son, and none, except perhaps Aristides, made the public 'soul' better by his tendance of it. Themistocles and Pericles and the others made Athens powerful and wealthy, but they did nothing for the *moral* of the people; they 'filled the city with ships and docks, not with righteousness'; gave it worldly prosperity, but no true moral ideals. Hence we are told in the *Gorgias* that though they may have been efficient 'body-servants' of the public, they have no claim to be, as true statesmen must be, its 'physicians.' It is clear that Socrates really habitually used the kind of arguments Plato ascribes to him about the incapacity of the Athenian public men to impart 'goodness' to their sons as a proof that their own apparent 'goodness' was not the genuine thing. In the *Meno* Anytus is introduced expressly to warn him that this depreciation of the national heroes is a dangerous sport—a plain indication of Plato's belief that it had much to do with provoking the attack which ended in his prosecution.

From the Socratic point of view, the proper organization of society would be one in which every man's social status and function, as statesman, soldier, or producer, is determined by the nature of the work his aptitudes, understanding, and character fit him to discharge. This is precisely the ideal which is embodied in outline in the account of the ideal city which fills the earlier books of Plato's *Republic.* So far, the scheme may truly be said to be directly of Socratic inspiration. How far any of its details are actually of Socratic origin is another question, though it is suggestive that this seems to be so with one of its most original features, the proposal to admit women on the same terms as men to public employment, military and civil, and the education which qualifies for it. That Socrates actually entertained an ideal of this kind seems to be shown by the fact that Aeschines also in his dialogue *Aspasia* dwelt on the political capacity of Aspasia herself and others, and the military ability believed to have been shown by the real or legendary Persian princess Rhodogyne. Xenophon also incidentally puts into the mouth of his Socrates the thesis that, with the necessary training, a woman is capable of the same things as a man.[9]

2. *Theory of Knowledge and Scientific Method.*—Aristotle remarks in the *Metaphysics* that 'two things must in justice be ascribed to Socrates, inductive arguments and universal definition.'[10] This does not take us very far; Aristotle is clearly intending less to give us a complete characterization of Socrates than to specify certain constituents of his own philosophy as derived from him, and he seems to be basing his statement simply on his reading of Plato's dialogues, which illustrate the point abundantly. Xenophon's apologetic interest in the soundness of his old teacher's moral lessons leaves him little inclination to talk about anything else. Our chances of being able to discover something more about Socrates as a thinker on other than strictly ethical topics stand or fall with the historical truth of the autobiographical narrative put into his mouth in Plato's *Phaedo.*[11] Now it seems to me, as I have already said, that we are bound to take this narrative as being substantially what Plato regarded as historical fact. The alternative is to suppose that an account of what Socrates said of himself on the last day of his life, in the presence of a number of intimate friends who were all living when that account was published, and certain to read it, is a fiction which all these readers would immediately detect. No one is really courageous enough to be thorough with such a theory. Everybody, for instance, accepts as fact the story of the introduction of Socrates to the book of Anaxagoras, and his disappointment with it, though we have no evidence for the fact beyond the statement of the *Phaedo.* But that statement in the *Phaedo* is merely the beginning of a coherent narrative, and it is therefore incumbent on us in consistency either to accept the rest of the narrative as substantially accurate, or to treat the initial statement with the same scepticism as all that follows it. I have little doubt for myself which is the more reasonable course. No sane man, of course, would deny that Plato, like every great artist, mixed his own mind with his object. It is quite another matter to assert that he consciously presents us with his own features in a pretended portrait of Socrates.[12]

According to the *Phaedo,* then, the immediate effect on Socrates of his discovery that Anaxagoras dogmatized about Nature in the same arbitrary fashion as his precursors was to lead him to strike out a new *method* in the search for truth. If we cannot discover the truth about things by direct inspection of the things themselves, we may attempt to reach it by examining the *statements*, or *theories* (*logoi*), which we make about them. The apparent indirectness of the procedure is Socrates' reason for humorously proceeding to depreciate it as the 'make-shift of an amateur.' Really, of course, he holds that it affords us our one and only chance of getting any genuine knowledge. The procedure he is describing is precisely that which, as we see from Xenophon,[13] as well as from Plato, he called *dialectic*, a name which properly means the method of 'conversation.' The thought which explains the use of the name is that truth has to be reached by dint of dialogue, or debate, which may be carried on between two inquirers, or also within the heart of a single inquirer, as his 'soul' questions itself and answers its own questions. The truth, which is not to be discovered by any direct inspection of 'facts,' may be beaten out in the critical confrontation of rival interpretations of them. It comes, when it comes, as the conclusion to a debate.

It is this method of confrontation of rival 'arguments' or 'theories' which Aristophanes wittily and wickedly burlesques in the *Clouds*. Protagoras also had said, in a very different sense, that 'there are two arguments about everything,' two sides to every case, and that the art of effective advocacy which he taught aims at making the 'weaker case'—that which unskilfully presented would have got the worse with the audience—the 'stronger.' Aristophanes puts on this harmless dictum the sense that the object of advocacy is to make the morally worse case appear the better, and then transfers the procedure to Socrates, with the result that the rival 'arguments' are brought on the stage as Virtue and Vice, and Vice, of course, drives Virtue out of the field. This is pure burlesque, but it presupposes as its foundation the fact that, in the infancy of Plato, Socrates was already known as specially interested in the confrontation of 'arguments' of some kind.

The *Phaedo* gives us a fairly full account of the nature of the procedure. The method is that Socrates starts from some proposition which, on any grounds, commends itself to him as presumably true. This he calls his initial *hypothesis*, and he proceeds to ask himself 'what must follow if this is admitted,' that is, to deduce its consequences. The truth of the initial *hypothesis* being at present unquestioned, whatever follows from it is also set down as true, and whatever conflicts with it as false. Thus the assumption of the method is simply that truth is a coherent system, and that nothing which conflicts with a true principle can be true. We must note, of course, that the assumed principle which Socrates calls his *hypothesis* is not taken to be hypothetical in the sense of being a 'pure supposal.' Socrates takes it as the starting-point of an argument because he presumes it to be true, or because it is common ground to himself and the other party to the discussion. On the other hand, there is no question of asserting it as a self-evident and final truth. It may be called in question, and in that case requires to be defended by being deduced as a consequence from some more ultimate and less disputable *hypothesis*. The important rule of method is that the question what consequences follow from the *hypothesis*, and the question whether the *hypothesis* itself is true, must be kept distinct. So long as we are still concerned with the former question, that of the consequences, the *hypothesis* itself must be left unquestioned.

So far, the method ascribed to Socrates in the *Phaedo* is clearly in principle that which has proved itself the one path to truth in scientific theory down to our own time. The contrast drawn between the direct procedure of the Ionian physicists, which had led nowhere, and the method of studying things in the 'statements' we make about them is precisely that also drawn by De Morgan between the erroneous method of Bacon, who assumes that facts are there to *draw a theory from*, and the sound method of Newton, who treats the facts as there *to test theory by*.[14] The one notable difference is that Socrates makes no special reference to the *verification* of theory by the confrontation of theoretical consequences with observational fact. Verification, however, finds its proper place in the elaboration of the Socratic thought by Plato and his Academy, whose technical name for a scientific theory which clearly accounts for all the relevant observed facts was an *hypothesis* which 'saves appearances.' (The 'appearances' are the facts as observed; to 'save' them is to account for them all in a coherent way.) Of course, neither Socrates nor Plato could have contemplated the modern extension of verification by experiments devised expressly for the purpose.

So far there is some independent evidence that the statements of the *Phaedo* about the method of Socrates are historical. Xenophon was aware that his practice, when one of his theses was disputed, was to 'bring the whole discussion back to the *hypothesis*,' that is, the initial position which was common ground to himself and his opponent,[15] though this, of course, may only mean that Xenophon had read the *Phaedo* and seen no reason to distrust its statements. It is more significant to my mind that Plato himself apparently makes Protagoras refer, without any further explanation, to the method of taking some proposition as an *hypothesis* which is not to be questioned so long as we are concerned with discovering its consequences, as something distinctively characteristic of Socrates, in a dialogue feigned to have been held before Plato's own birth.[16] We can see, moreover, from what quarter Socrates is likely to have derived the suggestion of the method. Rigorous deduction of the consequences of an *hypothesis* was the peculiar method of the famous Zeno of Elea, though it was the *hypotheses* of his opponents which he treated in this way, and his object was to discredit them by showing that they led to impossible consequences, as he is made to explain himself to the youthful Socrates in Plato's *Parmenides.*[17]

As far as this many, if not most, careful students of the evidence would probably be willing to follow us. Most of them may decline to take the further step of accepting as fundamentally true to fact what the narrative of the *Phaedo* goes on to say about the nature of the particular *hypothesis* adopted by Socrates himself as the basis of his thinking. This, it is said, is nothing but the famous 'Theory of Ideas,' and it is commonly assumed without proof, or with no proof but a few ambiguous expressions in Aristotle, that this doctrine was discovered by Plato for the first time after the death of Socrates. For my own part, I feel with Burnet that it is inconceivable that any thinker should introduce an eminently original discovery of his own to the world by representing it as something which had long been familiar to a number of living contemporaries who were certain to read his work and detect any misrepresentation. I hold, therefore, that we must accept the statements of the *Phaedo* as substantially true to fact, and have to explain the evidence of Aristotle, if we accept it at all for more than his own private conjecture, in a way which will not conflict with Plato. We must remember, of course, that Plato has mixed his own personality with his object in the very act of depicting it, but we must take this to be done inevitably and without conscious distortion of truth.

The problem which had perplexed Socrates was that of the 'cause of coming-to-be and ceasing-to-be.' Why does a thing make its appearance in the world or disappear from it? Why does a thing come to exhibit a quality which it had not before, or to lose one which it had? The physicists had their answer to this question; they found the causes of these changes in physical agents, which they assigned variously and arbitrarily. Reflection on the implications of the thesis of Anaxagoras about *Mind* as the source of the order in the world suggested to Socrates that these physical agents, whatever they may be, are at best only *concomitant* causes, or indispensable conditions, of an event; the real cause is, in every case, that it is *best* that things should be as they are, and in a mind-ordered world everything will be disposed as it is *best* that it should be. In this way, Socrates introduced into philosophy that 'teleological' or 'finalist' conception of the order of the universe as realizing an end of absolute value which was to be fully worked out and transmitted to later times as the chief heritage of Greek philosophical thought by Plato, Aristotle, and Plotinus.

The abandonment of the old *naïf* method of trying to discover truth by a simple inspection of 'facts' meant, of course, that Socrates could not dream of learning by direct inspection what the particular details of the world-order are, and why it is *best* that they should be as they are. But his conviction that there is an intelligible order in everything, and that it is a wise order, gave him a characteristic point of view from which to approach the question why a thing comes to be or ceases to be, acquires or loses a character. He speaks of this attitude in the *Phaedo* as nothing novel to his auditors, but one of which they have repeatedly heard from him. If a thing becomes what it was not before, if, for example, it becomes beautiful, this is always for one and the same reason, that Beauty has 'become present to' the thing; if it ceases to be beautiful, Beauty has 'withdrawn' from it. Or, in an alternative phrase, a thing which is beautiful is so just because, and so long as, it 'partakes' of Beauty; a figure is triangular just so long as, and because it 'partakes of' *the* triangle; and so forth. Beauty, or, as the Greek language expresses it, '*the* Beautiful,' '*the* triangle,' and the like, are what in this doctrine are called Forms or Patterns (*eidē, ideai*),[18] and a thing is what it is, has the characters it has, because it 'partakes' of the Forms of which it does 'partake.' And there are the following important points to be noted about these Forms. (1) The 'things which partake of a Form' are all perishable; they begin to be and cease to be, but the Form, Beauty, *the* Triangle, etc., neither begins to be, nor ceases to be; it is strictly what Dr. Whitehead calls an '*eternal* object.' (2) The things which we perceive by our senses only 'partake of,' or 'resemble,' the Forms imperfectly. We never see a stick which is flawlessly straight, or a patch which is exactly and perfectly triangular, and we never perhaps meet with an act of perfect justice; we only see approximately straight sticks and approximately triangular patches, and come across acts of approximate justice. But 'the straight line' or 'the triangle' about which the geometer tells us is perfectly straight or triangular, and the justice of which the moralist talks as a duty is perfect justice. (3) The things which 'partake of the Form' may be indefinitely many; the Form itself is strictly one. Even in geometry, where we talk of many triangles which are all assumed to be perfectly triangular, what the geometer is interested in proving is not the properties of this triangle or that triangle, but those of 'the' triangle.[19] And it is always the Form, never this or that thing which 'partakes of' a Form, which is the object of which we are talking in science. I *know* as a scientific truth that any two sides of the triangle must be greater together than the third side; I do not *know* that two sides of this patch before me must be greater than the third, since I do not *know* that this visible patch really is triangular.

We should like, of course, if we could, to know something more of these Forms. Of what things are there Forms (and, consequently, of what things can we have scientific knowledge)? And, again, do the Forms constitute a system of any kind? We can see from the polemical allusions of Aristotle that at a later date Plato's Academy had answers, not always concordant

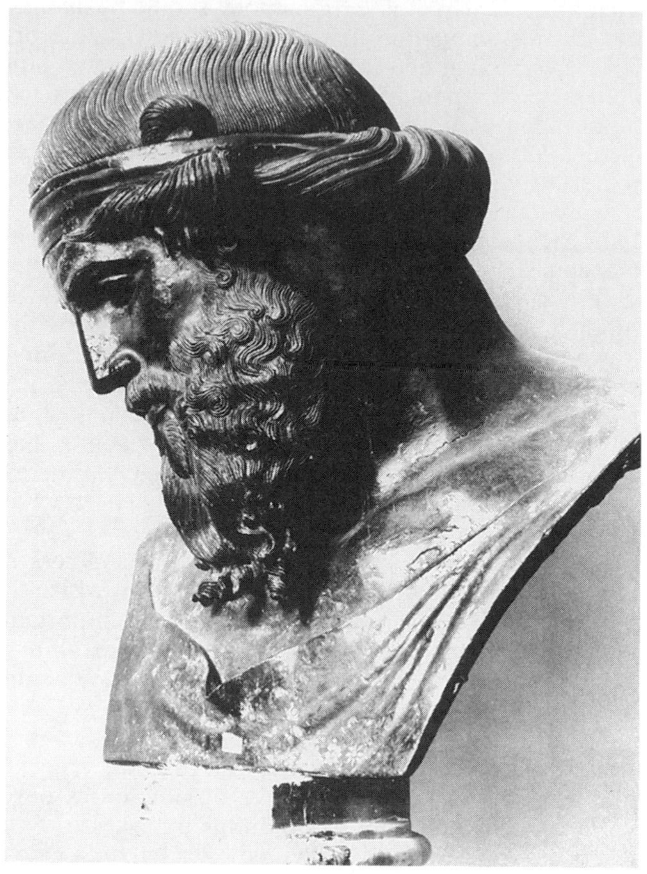

Plato

answers, to these questions, and that Aristotle found all these answers unsatisfactory. But we are not entitled to read back into the *Phaedo* developments which belong to Plato's old age, and we may even doubt whether in the *Republic* Plato may not be unconsciously 'colouring' his picture of Socrates more than he knows as his argument advances. From the examples given in the *Phaedo* itself it would seem that what Socrates was chiefly thinking of is, on the one side, the objects of which the mathematician can give us perfect and absolute definitions in geometry and arithmetic, and on the other the ideal standards and norms of the moralist (*the* number 3, *the* triangle, *the* Just, and the like). And this impression is borne out for us by a dialogue written by Plato at a late period in his career, the *Parmenides,* in which Socrates is expounding his theory to the great Eleatic philosophers Parmenides and Zeno, and defending it, not very satisfactorily, against their criticism. He is made there to say[20] that he feels quite sure that there are Forms of such things as Like and Unlike, Unity, Multitude, Just, Good, but very doubtful whether there are Forms of Man, Fire, Water, and still more doubtful about Hair, Mud, Dirt. In fact, he is sure of his ground in Mathematics and Morals, but very unsure of it everywhere else. We may infer that the first impulse to the formation of the theory came from reflection on mathematical and moral truth. This is what we should expect if the doctrine originated with Socrates, and if Socrates were the man Plato depicts. The very terminology used seems to come in the first instance from Pythagorean mathematics. There is clear evidence that the word *eidos* was the old Pythagorean name for 'figure,' a sense of the word which persists in some stereotyped phrases in Euclid and other third-century geometers, though their common word for *figure* is a different one (*schema*).[21] And Plato frequently represents Socrates as deeply impressed by the need for moral standards by which controversies about right and wrong may be determined, as disputes about area or volume are settled by an appeal to geometry, or disagreements about weight by resort to the balance.

We see that the doctrine is a first attempt to do justice to the *a priori* factor in knowledge, the *universality* and *necessity* of scientific truths most conspicuously evident in the propositions of pure mathematics and pure ethics, and that those disciplines are taken as the model of what all science should be. We understand thus why the Forms have been identified by later philosophers with 'universals,' 'concepts,' 'class-notions.' But to speak of them so involves a really unhistorical transposition of a simpler thought. It is to make Socrates talk like Aristotle, or Kant, and this cannot be done without risk of misunderstanding, though his doctrine is the ultimate source of theirs. If we would avoid all such misunderstandings, it is best to say simply that the Form is that—whatever it may be—which we mean to denote whenever we use a significant 'common name' as the subject of a strictly and absolutely true proposition, the object about which such a proposition makes a true assertion. Such objects, not the sensible things disclosed in bodily perception, are, according to Socrates, the most real things there are, and the only things which are fully real. The soul, as we saw, has one single fundamental activity, that of *knowing* realities as they really are, and it is only in knowing the Forms that this activity is successfully discharged. Where the mind is not face to face with a Form, we have only *opinion* or *belief,* a *belief* which may, of course, in many cases be quite sufficient for the needs of everyday life, but we have not *knowledge;* the element of '*necessary* connection' is missing.

Do the Forms, which are the proper objects of genuine knowledge, form an organized whole or system? They should do so, no doubt, since, according to the *Phaedo,* the whole doctrine of them as the explanation of 'coming-into-being and ceasing-to-be' is inspired by the still more ultimate conviction that in a mind-permeated world all things are ordered as it is best they should be, and the Good—itself a Form—is therefore the cause of the whole order. This is strictly in accord with a famous passage of the *Republic,*[22] where Socrates speaks of the Good, or Form of good, as holding the same supreme and central position in the realm of Forms apprehended by the intellect which its 'offspring' the Sun holds in the visible world. As the sun in the visible world is the source at once of the life of the things we see and the light by which they are seen, so the good in the world disclosed to thought is the source at once of the reality of the Forms we apprehend and of the knowledge by which they are apprehended. And as the sun, though the source of light and growth, is not the same thing as either, so the good is neither 'being' nor 'knowledge,' but something which is the transcendent source of both. But Socrates is made to confess that as it is the supreme feat of corporeal vision to be able to look on the sun, so it is the supreme and most difficult achievement of the mind to know the Good. He himself, in this passage, confesses his own inability to speak of it in any language but that of parable and metaphor. Plato has been commonly thought in this passage to be talking of a personal speculation of his own of which the Master whose voice he is borrowing had never dreamed. In view of the intimate connection made in the 'autobiographical' pages of the *Phaedo* between the *hypothesis* of Forms and the conviction that the Good is the universal cause, I find it difficult to subscribe to this opinion. I should rather judge that the language and imagery of this splendid passage are those of Plato in his 'golden prime,' but the thought is one directly necessitated by the meditations born of the first falling-in with the book of Anaxagoras.

It is clear that the doctrine of Forms, in the shape in which, as I hold, we must be prepared to ascribe it to Socrates, creates difficulties as well as removes them. In particular, it leaves wholly unexplained the relation of the Form to sensible fact which it calls its 'presence,' or its being 'participated in.' Is what we call a sensible thing merely a temporary assemblage of Forms, or 'universals,' and if it is more, what else is it? No one has pointed out these difficulties more incisively than Plato himself in his dialogue *Parmenides,* and it seems at least plain that the final form of Plato's own teaching, which we have to reconstruct imperfectly from the puzzling hints of Aristotle, was an attempt to find an answer to the problem. Aristotle himself was so perplexed by the results that he comes to treat the whole doctrine of Forms itself as a mistaken attempt to separate the 'universal characters' of individual sensible things from the things themselves, and then to set up these 'abstractions' as a second set of super-sensible things which somehow produce the things we see and handle. It is, he says, as though a man who had to count a number of articles were to fancy that he must begin by doubling it. He believed himself to have got rid once for all of an unreal and insoluble problem by his own formula that the 'form' only exists *in* the individual sensible thing, and is just its 'essential character.' Yet the problem is still with us, in spite of Aristotle, as a very real *crux* in the latest attempts to furnish a philosophy of the sciences. We still find ourselves asking what is the 'status' of 'scientific objects.' Just what *are* the things of which the mathematician and the physicist discourse? Or again, what is a moral 'ideal'? And what is the relation of the 'scientific object' to the things we touch or see, and how, again, are 'value' and 'fact' related? Natural and moral philosophy are still far from having answered these questions with finality, and even further from having escaped the necessity of asking them. The unique greatness of Socrates lies in the fact that he was the first man in the world to raise them with the clear understanding of what he was doing.

. . . . .

Several of the companions of Socrates were active after his death as heads of philosophical schools, and one, Antisthenes, was a voluminous writer. It has been common to speak of these men and their followers as 'minor Socratics.' It is, to my mind, very doubtful how far this language, which reflects the artificial schematism of Alexandrian biography, is justified. The Megarian opponents of Aristotle in the fourth century, their contemporaries, Diogenes and the other eccentrics popularly nicknamed Cynics, the Hedonist moralists of Cyrene in the third, were affiliated to Socrates through Euclides, Antisthenes, and Aristippus respectively. But there is no evidence of the existence of any Cyrenaic school before the days of the successors of Alexander; the Megarics, who showed themselves pugnacious opponents of Aristotle, clearly held views not to be reconciled with the strict Monism ascribed by all our authorities to Euclides; though Diogenes and his imitators professed a great reverence for Antisthenes, it is not clear that they regarded themselves as in any way related to him as a 'founder.' And Euclides, Aristippus, Antisthenes, were all rather admiring friends than 'disciples' of Socrates. The doctrines of Euclides were a direct inheritance from the Eleatics; Aristippus is expressly recorded to have had no doctrines at all; the paradoxical views for which Antisthenes is chiefly remembered, his denial of the possibility of contradiction, and the like, come not from Socrates, but from the 'sophists.' For all purposes of importance, Socrates had just one 'successor'—Plato.

Notes

[1] See, in particular, Burnet's essay, 'The Socratic Conception of the Soul' (*Proceedings of the British Academy,* viii. 235-260), and his article, 'Socrates,' in Hastings' *Encyclopaedia of Religion and Ethics,* xi.

[2] Fr. 131, Bergk.

[3] As when the Cyclops in Euripides says he will for once 'do his *psyche* a good turn' by a cannibal debauch (*Cycl.,* 340). So the Romans said *genio indulgere*

in the same sense, and *anima causa agere,* 'to act on one's whim.'

[4] Empirical psychology, founded by Alcmaeon of Crotona, is represented, in the age of Socrates, by those scientific Pythagoreans who taught that the soul is the 'attunement of' the melody given out by the body, a doctrine, as is shown in the *Phaedo,* quite inconsistent with the *religion* of both Pythagoras and Socrates.

[5] This is the real point of the argument in Plato's *Protagoras,* where Socrates appears at first sight to be talking Hedonism. He wants to prove to the 'many' that, *even on their own theory* that good and pleasure are the same thing, it is not a paradox to identify the courage of the virtuous man with knowledge, since they will admit that the coward who runs away from danger is making a false computation of the 'balance of pleasures and pains.'

[6] It is notorious that the clever poisoner in our criminal annals is commonly a medical man.

[7] See particularly *Meno,* 81 *a*-85 *e,* where the theory is elaborately illustrated by a 'lesson' in geometry given by Socrates to a slave-boy ignorant of the science, and *Phaedo,* 72 *e* ff., where there is a similar reference to the acquisition of geometrical knowledge. In both places the doctrine is brought into connection with the immortality of the soul, but it is made clear that, as a theory of what the discovery of a truth is, it is independent of this religious tenet. (It reappears, in fact, at the end of Aristotle's *Posterior Analytics,* ii, without any religious associations, as Aristotle's own account of the way in which first principles are suggested by 'induction.') In the *Phaedo* (*loc. cit.*) the doctrine that 'learning is just recognition' is expressly said by Simmias, speaking to Socrates, to be 'the doctrine *you* are so constantly repeating.' Unless we are willing to regard the *Phaedo* as a gigantic and unpardonable mystification, this seems to me proof that the theory really belongs to Socrates. For a brief statement of Plato's own allied convictions see *Ep.,* vii. 341 *c,* and the comments of Burnet on the passage (*Greek Philosophy,* Pt. 1, pp. 221-222).

[8] When the language of the earlier dialogues is taken as expressing Plato's personal opinions, the more favourable judgments of the later dialogues are explained as due to the mellowing influence of time on a mind lacerated by the fate of Socrates. It may be so, but there is also always the psychological possibility that the harsher verdicts are those of Socrates himself. His disillusionment as the temper of the Athenian democracy grew narrower and harder in the course of the great war would be all the bitterer that he had grown up in the great 'fifty years' before the war, and presumably had hoped and expected very different things. In a very late dialogue, the *Timaeus,* Plato makes Socrates confess to being something of a *doctrinaire* in politics, owing to his lack of personal experience of public life (*Tim.,* 19 *d*). We learn from Xenophon (*Mem.,* 1. ii. 9) that sarcasms about the democratic practice of filling magistracies by sortition was one count in the case against Socrates to which he is replying.

[9] See the fragments of the *Aspasia* in the editions of Krauss and Dittmar. Xenophon's testimony to Socrates' belief that 'a woman is no worse endowed by nature than a man, though not his equal in judgment or physical strength,' will be found at *Symp.,* ii. 9. For evidence from Xenophon to the demand of *knowledge* as the one qualification for sovereignty, see *Mem.,* III. ix. 10, and compare the whole of III. vi. where Socrates dissuades Glaucon from a premature entrance on public life by exposing his ignorance of military and financial statistics. That Xenophon speaks only of such ignorance of facts, not of the graver ignorance of 'moral values,' strikes me as characteristic of the man.

[10] *Met. M.,* 1078 *b* 27. Some good recent German students make a point of denying that Socrates was really interested in 'definition.' This is true in the sense that his concern was not with theoretical labels for their own sake, but with a practical rule of conduct. What justifies Aristotle's way of expressing himself is that he is thinking of the formal structure of such works as *Charmides, Laches, Protagoras, Meno, Republic* IV.

[11] *Phaedo,* 96 *a*-100 *c.* The whole passage should be studied carefully with the annotations to it in Burnet's edition of the dialogue (Oxford, 1911).

[12] A great portrait-painter always puts his own personality into his portraits. If he were an inferior artist, the portrait would be different. But he does not give his sitters his own nose or eyebrows.

[13] A chapter of some length in the *Memorabilia* (IV. vi.) is devoted to illustrations of the way in which Socrates made those who associated with him 'more dialectical.' He did this, according to Xenophon, by urging them to think precisely and to express their thought intelligibly.

[14] A. De Morgan, *A Budget of Paradoxes* (ed. 2), i. 88.

[15] *Mem.,* IV. vi. 13.

[16] *Prot.,* 351 *e.* The name *hypothesis* is not used here, but Protagoras proposes to Socrates to discuss the thesis that the good is pleasure 'in your regular way,' by working out its consequences.

[17] *Parm.,* 128 *c-e.*

[18] But it is misleading to call them, as they have so

long been called, *Ideas.* That suggests to us that they are some one's *thoughts,* 'ideas in some one's head,' precisely what the theory does *not* mean.

[19] We see this in an interesting way from the language, *e.g.,* of Analytical Geometry about '*the* equation to the circle,' or of Arithmetic about '*the* number six.'

[20] *Parm.,* 129-130.

[21] The same sense of 'patterns' accounts for our language about figures of speech, and figures of the syllogism.

[22] *Rep., 506 d-509 b.*

Norman Gulley (essay date 1968)

SOURCE: "The Good," in *The Philosophy of Socrates,* Macmillan, 1968, pp. 165-204.

[*In the following essay, Gulley explains that Socrates's teachings emphasize that "knowledge of the good is a necessary and sufficient condition of being good and of doing what is good," but that they do not explicitly state what "the good" is. Gulley examines the Socratic works of Plato, and Xenophon, as well as some references in Aristotle, in order to deduce a consistent understanding of "the good."*]

A. *Introduction*

. . . Socrates' method of analysis assumes that it is possible to determine with certainty what the good is. His moral paradoxes, with their intellectualist conception of moral knowledge, make the same assumption. But the analysis which yields the moral paradoxes does not yield a specification of the good. For the moral paradoxes themselves are in this respect non-informative. They tell us that knowledge of the good is a necessary and sufficient condition of being good and of doing what is good. They do not tell us what the good is.

There are two places in Xenophon's *Memorabilia* where Socrates talks about the *meaning* of good. In a conversation with Aristippus (III viii) he emphasises its instrumental sense of 'good for a particular purpose'. In this sense, he argues, it can be equated with 'fine' or 'beautiful' (*kalon*); 'things which men use are considered to be fine and good in relation to that for which they are serviceable'. Similarly, in a conversation with Euthydemus (IV vi 8), he defines 'good' in terms of 'beneficial' (*ōphelimon*). The emphasis again is on the sense of 'good for a particular purpose'. What is beneficial to one person, he says, may be harmful to another. But a thing cannot be called good which is not beneficial to someone in relation to a certain purpose. So 'what is beneficial is good for him to whom it is beneficial'.

This emphasis on the instrumental sense of 'good' is in keeping with those features of the Greeks' moral language . . . which give to all Greek moral thought its broadly utilitarian character. It illustrates how readily the Greeks used 'good' synonymously with 'useful' or 'beneficial'. And, remembering that in moral behaviour doing what is 'useful' or 'beneficial' means for a Greek doing what is conducive to happiness (*eudaimonia*), we can see that what Socrates says in Xenophon about the meaning of good is a basic part of what he is saying when he asserts that no one does wrong willingly. This becomes clear when we look at Xenophon's formulation of that paradox. At *Memorabilia* (III ix 4) Socrates says that everyone chooses from possible courses of action what he considers to be 'most profitable' (*sumphorōtata*) for him, and does this. And in Plato's *Protagoras,* in presenting the same thesis (358b-d), he links together 'fine' (*kalon*), 'good' (*agathon*) and 'beneficial' (*ōphelimon*) (358b; cf. 333d), just as he does in Xenophon in commenting on the meaning of good.

Now Socrates is not propounding a moral doctrine about what the good is when he talks about the instrumental sense of good, any more than he is propounding such a doctrine when he asserts that no one does wrong willingly. For to propound such a doctrine would be to give a descriptive specification of 'the good', considered as the end of human action, and distinguishable in this substantival use from its instrumental use as 'beneficial', 'profitable', or 'useful' (Plato, *Hippias Major* 296e-297d, 303e). Socrates' remarks are about this instrumental use, and are not concerned to specify a moral ideal.

It follows that those scholars have been mistaken who have tried to construct a moral ideal out of these remarks or out of the paradox that no one does wrong willingly. For there is nothing here which implies that Socrates was a relativist or subjectivist in his moral theory, or that he equated 'the good' with the useful or the advantageous.[1] Henry Jackson argued[2] that Socrates' answer to the question 'what is the good?' was that 'it is the useful, the advantageous. Utility, the immediate utility of the individual, thus becomes the measure of conduct and the foundation of all moral rule and legal enactment. Accordingly, each precept of which Socrates delivers himself is recommended on the ground that obedience to it will promote the pleasure, the comfort, the advancement, the well-being of the individual; and Prodicus's apologue of the Choice of Heracles, with its commonplace offers of worldly reward, is accepted as an adequate statement of the motives of virtuous action.'

The reference to Prodicus's Choice of Heracles is a reference to what Socrates is represented as narrating from Prodicus, with apparent approval of its sentiments, in conversation with Aristippus in Xenophon's *Memorabilia* (II i). The piece is in fact a recommendation of a life conscientiously devoted to the attainment of what is 'fine and good', and a condemnation of a life of maximum ease and pleasure. Neither here nor anywhere else in Xenophon's portrait is there evidence for thinking that Socrates was a hedonist. . . . He does indeed assume, in several of the conversations in Xenophon, that the good life is the most pleasant life. But this . . . is an assumption readily made by the Greeks in view of the natural 'eudaimonism' of their moral outlook. Both Plato and Aristotle assume it. It does not make them hedonists.

As for the other marks which Jackson ascribed to Socrates' conception of 'the good', such marks as the 'utility', the 'advancement', the 'well-being' of the individual, these are marks of the utilitarianism of the Greeks' moral language, not peculiar marks of Socrates' conception of 'the good'. The references to 'immediate' utility and 'the commonplace offers of wordly reward' are just misguided exaggerations, prompted to some extent, perhaps, by Xenophon's own severely practical outlook. So let us not look in this direction for Socrates' answer to 'what is the good?'. And let us not criticise him, as Jackson did, from this standpoint, as having 'no conception of the graver difficulties of ethical theory' or as a person to whom morality has so become 'a second nature' that 'the scrutiny of its credentials from an external standpoint has ceased to be possible'.[3]

What answer, then, did Socrates give to 'what is the good?'. The good is for him, as for any Greek, 'happiness' (*eudaimonia*). And we saw, in discussing his paradox that all the virtues are one, that a basis for this paradox is the notion that 'the good' or 'happiness' is a single unifying end of human action. It follows that any specification of it must maintain the unity of all morally good behaviour by specifying a single kind of activity or a single state of character as constituting happiness. Such a specification would be a descriptive specification of 'the good', the same in kind as, e.g., Aristotle's specification of happiness or human goodness as 'activity of the soul in accordance with philosophic wisdom (*sophia*)'. So our concern in the present chapter is to consider what particular specification of this kind was given by Socrates in answering the question 'what is the good?'.

An immediate difficulty is that in this respect Aristotle has virtually nothing to tell us. Nor is there in Plato's early dialogues, or in Xenophon's *Memorabilia,* any full and systematic discussion of the question we are considering. We do find in these sources, however, some portrayal of Socrates' views in politics, in theology, and in what it is not too pretentious to call philosophy of mind. We must see therefore whether, within these various views, it is possible to discern a consistent conception of the good.

B. *Political Views*

Socrates was not a practising politician. But in both Xenophon and Plato he expresses political views. He makes constitutional criticisms. He states his position with regard to matters of political concern such as 'conscientious objection', and a citizen's obligation to adhere to the laws. Finally, he indicates what he considers to be the relevance and value to the well-being of the state of his own activity as an educator of his fellow-citizens. These views are some guide to his political principles. And these principles, in so far as they reflect his moral ideals, are some guide to his conception of the good.

According to Xenophon (*Mem.* I ii 9) those who accused Socrates of corrupting the young men of Athens based their charge partly on the argument that he caused those who conversed with him to despise the established laws. Socrates is said to have maintained that it was foolish to elect the magistrates of a state by beans (i.e. by ballot), since no one would be willing to employ a pilot elected in that way, or an architect or a flute-player, or a person in any other such profession, where in fact errors caused far less harm than errors in the administration of a state. There are good grounds for thinking that this is a genuinely Socratic argument. Aristotle mentions it (*Rhetoric* 1393b) . . . as an illustration of a typically Socratic argument.

The implication of the argument is, of course, that expert knowledge is a necessary qualification for the statesman. One of Socrates' favourite analogies, the analogy between moral behaviour and the practice of professional skills, is here extended to political practice. The appeal to expert knowledge is made explicit in another part of the *Memorabilia* (III ix 10-11) where Socrates, arguing again from the practice of professional skills, asserts that true kings and commanders are 'not those who hold sceptres, not those chosen by the common crowd or elected by lot, not those who rely on violence or deceit, but those who know how to rule.'

Similarly (*Mem.* IV ii 6-7), he advocates the need for expert instruction in the art of government, an art which he subsequently characterises as the greatest art, 'the kingly art' (IV ii 11). And it is natural to associate with what Socrates says here his remarks on 'the kingly art' in Plato's *Euthydemus.* He describes this art (at 291b-292e) as a master-art which uses the results of the practice of all other arts or professional skills in the state in order to promote happiness. In developing this point Plato is possibly going beyond what Socrates himself had argued. But Xenophon's remarks are some confirmation that the notion is basically Socratic. There is no explicit specification here of what 'the good' is which the expert statesman is assumed to know and to be able to realise in the state. The *Euthydemus* (292a-e) admits this. But some definite standard of values for political practice is implicit in what Socrates says. In looking at the rest of his political views we must try to discover what these values are.

At the outset we should beware of construing Socrates' political views in terms of Plato's ideals in the *Republic*. It is easy enough to look at the thought of the *Republic* as a direct and consistent development of the political ideas which we find ascribed to Socrates by Xenophon. But closer examination will show that Socrates' notions of political reform and of the relations between the state and the individual are far different from Plato's. Professor Popper has remarked that 'the Platonic "Socrates" of the *Republic* is the embodiment of an unmitigated authoritarianism'.[4] He rightly dissociates Socrates from the Platonic Socrates in this respect. Socrates' apparent advocacy of government by experts is not intended to be the advocacy of an alternative form of government to democracy. Nor is it the advocacy of 'an unmitigated authoritarianism'.

Let us look first at Socrates' notion of political reform. The striking thing here is that, critical though Socrates is of methods of electing magistrates in a democracy, he emphatically asserts his loyalty to the laws of the state. 'He obeyed the magistrates', says Xenophon (*Mem.* IV iv 1), 'in all that the laws enjoined.' Xenophon represents him further as defining justice in terms of obedience to the laws (IV iv 18). As an example of Socrates' practice in this respect he mentions his behaviour in the public assembly when he stood alone in opposing a proposal which was contrary to recognised law. The occasion was the trial of the generals after the battle of Arginusae in 406 B.C. The generals were tried and sentenced to death in a body, though the recognised law was that they should have been tried separately (I i 18; IV iv 2; see also Plato *Apol.* 32b-c). This was under a democratic government.

Socrates' passionate respect for the law is further shown in his opposition to the government of the Thirty Tyrants when they tried to implicate him in their crimes. Xenophon says that 'when the Thirty ordered him to do anything contrary to the laws, he refused to obey them. For both when they forbade him to converse with the young, and when they ordered him, and some others of the citizens, to lead a certain person away to death, he stood alone in refusing to obey them, because the order was given contrary to the laws' (IV iv 3; Plato *Apol.* 32c-d).

In both these cases Socrates showed considerable personal courage and a high devotion to principle. But it was in his refusal to escape from prison when awaiting execution that he declared most strikingly his conviction that the laws must be obeyed.

Plato's *Crito* is devoted to explaining this refusal to escape. Socrates there defends his loyalty to the laws of the state by arguing that the foundation of law is an agreement or contract between the state and the individual, and that willingness on the part of an individual to live in a society governed by laws implies acceptance of that contract and hence willingness to obey the laws. To disobey the laws is to dishonour one's agreement. The right thing to do (*to dikaion*) is to obey them.

It seems to me that the complete consistency of everything that Xenophon and Plato tell us about Socrates' loyalty to the laws makes it very difficult to believe that they are not giving us a true picture. It is possible to argue that, in their desire to show that Socrates was unjustifiably condemned by a democratic government, both Xenophon and Plato would naturally be inclined to argue that he was always loyally obedient to the laws of the state, whether this was strictly true or not. But to argue in this way is to misconstrue Socrates' loyalty to the laws in one important respect.

For Socrates' loyalty is a loyalty not only to the laws of a democratic state, but to those of non-democratic states as well. Socrates, unlike Plato, does not appear to have been very interested in constitutional problems. He is not concerned to champion the case for, say, monarchy as against democracy, or vice-versa. And his opposition to any illegality is equally vehement whether it is a democracy or a tyranny which acts illegally. The examples of his opposition given by Plato and Xenophon make this clear. And since they make clear at the same time that Socrates' championing of the principle of loyalty to the laws is not necessarily a championing of democracy, it is unlikely that Plato and Xenophon are falsely insisting on Socrates' loyalty to the laws because they wish to make him out to be a loyal democrat.

It would be wrong, however, to infer from all this that Socrates approved of *all* forms of government and that he was concerned only to advocate loyalty to the laws under *any* government. In Xenophon he makes quite clear his disapproval of tyranny. And it follows from his definition of tyranny (*Mem.* IV vi 12) that his principle of loyalty to the laws has no application in the case of tyranny. Xenophon there says that Socrates considered tyranny a government which ruled men against their will and which was *not controlled by law* but only by the whim of the ruler. He considered that all other forms of government—including monarchy, aristocracy, and democracy—followed the rule of law and enjoyed the consent of those living under them.

The association made here between consent and the rule of law is in conformity with Socrates' views in the *Crito* about the implicit contract between state and individual in a society governed by laws that the individual should be obedient to those laws. Socrates, it is clear, was more broadly tolerant of different forms of government than a modern liberal democrat. He saw no incompatibility between monarchy and consent, and did not concern himself with the question of whether an aristocracy could be fully representative of the will of the majority of the citizens. The main distinction which he seems to make is between government by law and consent and government without law and consent. Under the former type of government he thinks that it is right to be loyal to the laws.

Socrates' distinction corresponds fairly closely to the distinction between 'democracy' and 'tyranny' made by Popper in discussing Plato's theory of sovereignty.[5] 'Democracy' is a type of government 'of which we can get rid without bloodshed', i.e., where 'the social institutions provide means by which the rulers may be dismissed by the ruled'. 'Tyranny' is a government 'which the ruled cannot get rid of except by way of successful revolution—that is to say, in most cases, not at all.'

Socrates was, I think rather more naïve than Popper in his attitude to tyranny. For he seems to have thought that the arbitrary rule of a tyrant is invariably suicidal. In Xenophon (*Mem.* III ix 12) he expresses the view that the tyrant always suffers for his indifference to the advice of others, and brings immediate destruction on himself if he puts to death wise counsellors whose policy differs from his own. But what Popper says about 'democracy' expresses admirably Socrates' attitude to non-tyrannical forms of government. He says that, in making possible the reform of institutions without using violence, 'democracy' thereby makes possible 'the use of reason in the designing of new institutions and the adjusting of old ones'.[6]

This is much more explicit, of course, than anything which we can ascribe to Socrates himself. But it is undoubtedly implicit in Socrates' attitude to government. And Popper is undoubtedly right in associating with Socrates the 'personalism' of what he calls 'democracy' in its attitudes to the education of its citizens and to political reform. The personalist attitude treats the question of 'the intellectual and moral standard of its citizens' as 'to a large degree a personal problem'. Moreover, it assumes that the problem of improving 'democratic' institutions 'is always a problem for *persons* rather than for institutions'.[7]

It is in Plato's *Apology* that Socrates expresses with the most passionate conviction his sense of the importance of his mission to serve the community, not by any direct participation in politics, but by a personal approach to individual citizens. It is God's bidding, he says (30-1), that he should serve the state by questioning and examining his fellow-citizens, stirring them from their apathy and intellectual self-satisfaction. In everything he says on this score he emphasises repeatedly the individual nature of his approach (30e, 31b, 36c). I turned aside, he says, from political offices, thinking that I would best benefit the state if I went around privately to each individual and did him what I consider to be the greatest of all services—trying to persuade him not to care for what he had but for the excellence of his moral and intellectual self, nor to care for what the state had, but for 'the state itself' (36b-c).[8] There are similar sentiments in Xenophon, and a similar emphasis on the value to the state of educating the individual in 'knowing himself' through self-criticism.[9]

We see from this the kind of political significance which Socrates ascribes to his educational activities. One reason he gives for preferring to serve the state in this way rather than through public participation in politics is the severely prudential reason that it is personally safer. 'You may be sure', he says at his trial, 'that if I had attempted to enter public life, I would have perished long ago, without any good to you or to myself. No man will ever be safe who genuinely stands up against you or against any other democracy, and tries to prevent a host of injustices and illegalities being committed in the state. The man who is to fight for justice must work in private rather than in public, if he is to keep his life even for a short time' (Plato *Apol.* 31e-32a).

This is not, of course, a mere concern for his own skin. It is a concern for the well-being of the state. Indeed, Socrates' deep conviction of the importance for this purpose of his educational mission makes him ready to lose his life rather than give up his activity. Nor should we try to interpret his loyalty to the laws as an expedient for his own safety. This loyalty again belongs to his conviction that it is not by flouting the laws of the state and not by any resort to revolution that the good of the state is advanced. His respect for government by law and consent is a genuine respect. *Within* such a government, improvement must come through personal education of the citizens.

As a political programme this Socratic ideal no doubt appears unduly sanguine, as well as unduly acquiescent in its attitude of loyalty to the laws. Its expectations are, however, more readily understandable when placed within the context of the small, close-knit community of a city-state. And Socrates is confident that there will be many more besides himself ready and able to further his ideal.[10] Moreover, his loyalty to the laws does not assume that the laws are necessarily the best laws for ensuring the happiness of the citizens. In defending his loyalty to the laws in the *Crito* he makes clear that the laws are open to 'persuasion' as to what is right and just (51b-e).

Besides claiming the right to 'persuade' the laws Socrates also claims the right of 'conscientious objection' to what the laws prescribe. He states at his trial that, if he were to be acquitted on condition that he put a stop to his philosophical activities, then he would refuse to give such an assurance. As long as life leaves him the ability to do so, he says, he will never give up his philosophical activities. He will continue to try to persuade each of the citizens to care for the excellence of his moral and intellectual self (Plato, *Apol.* 29c-e). He is ready, however, to accept whatever legal penalty is imposed as a punishment for his activities. His claim for the right of defiance is not also a claim for the right to escape the punishment of the law.

This is yet a further indication of Socrates' deep personal conviction of the rightness and the political value of his mission in life as an educator. And it helps us to appreciate more clearly his ideal that the wisest should rule. He does not think this ideal incompatible in any way with his ideal of government by law and consent, or with his claims for the rights of the individual's conscience and for the individual's right to happiness. He obviously thinks of the rule of the wisest as a type of government which ensures perfect harmony between the citizen's respect for the laws and his individual right to perfect his own good. There is, however, little of the political *theorist* about Socrates. As Popper has said, 'with his emphasis upon the human side of the political problem, he could not take much interest in institutional reform'. It was 'the immediate, the personal aspect' in which he was interested.[11] The ideal that the wisest should rule is, for Socrates, not so much one particular institutional form of government. Rather, it is the end result of an educational mission which aims to bring wisdom not only to those who will rule but to those also who will elect the rulers and themselves be ruled.

From what we have now seen of Socrates' political views it is clear how radically Socrates differs from Plato in his approach to politics. Plato . . . rejects the individualism of Socrates' ethics. He rejects, in the end, Socrates' belief in the supreme efficacy of individual reason in ensuring rightness of moral behaviour. And he rejects Socrates' belief that education is a personal affair, of individual by individual, and that education of this kind is the only proper education to promote the well-being of society. He turns instead to schemes of state control of education. And coupling with his view that only the wise should rule the view that only the few are wise, he gives to the wise supreme authority to determine the rights of the rest. In this respect the charge that Plato 'betrayed' Socrates is entirely justified.[12]

This contrast between Socrates and Plato in their political attitudes serves to emphasise what is distinctive in Socrates' attitude. What is distinctive about it is, in the first place, its individualism. This is in keeping with the spirit of Socrates' method and of his ethics. Socrates assumes the self-sufficiency of his method as a means of attaining moral knowledge. He further assumes the sufficiency of that knowledge for attaining virtue. And, finally, he assumes 'the moral self-sufficiency of the virtuous man'.[13] No evil, he says, can come to a good man, whether in life or death (Plato *Apol.* 41d).[14]

These are all marks of the individualism of Socratic ethics. It is this individualism which leads him to oppose[15] the traditional political virtue of doing good to friends and harm to enemies. For it follows from the good man's moral self-sufficiency that the only harm that can come to him is of his own making, i.e. by committing wrong himself. And if to do harm to others is to do wrong, then to do harm to those who have done wrong to oneself is to do wrong. Hence it is to impair one's own moral good. Moreover, one's moral self-sufficiency is proof against wrong done to one by others. So that it is 'better' to be wronged by others than to do wrong to others.

A corollary of this individualism is the liberalism of Socrates' attitude to politics. He considers the moral worth of the individual to be of paramount value. Hence he considers that the individual must be free to realise his own good. That is why he insists at his trial on the right of the individual to defy the state if it prescribes what he considers to be incompatible with realising that good. For it is clear from the assumptions of his own educational mission that the right he claims for himself is a right which he claims for *any* individual. Perhaps in some respects Socrates' attitude of acquiescence towards the laws of the state may appear to be unduly tolerant. Certainly his conviction of the individual's moral self-sufficiency predisposes him to think that the individual is able to realise his moral ends under most forms and conditions of government. But he always insists on the individual's right to be free to realise his own good. And he is confident that the vigorous exercise of this right will help to create the best political conditions for realising that good.

These political views of Socrates are clearly relevant to our inquiry into Socrates' conception of the good life. For they are a reflection of what Socrates holds to be valuable in human life. In the first place Socrates values the individual as an end in himself, and hence claims the right of the individual to pursue his own good. Hence he claims further for the individual the political freedom to do this. In the second place, he believes in the efficacy of reason as a means available to the individual of determining his good; he believes, moreover, in the possibility of persuading all citizens of any particular state to realise the value of applying their reason systematically, through self-criticism, to the realisation of that end.

This yields a conception of the good life as a life of free and independent criticism and inquiry, considered as the 'best' activity for the individual's self-development. Its general tendency is, of course, to emphasise the intrinsic value of the activity of impartially searching for the truth rather than its means-to-an-end value in establishing what the good is as an ultimate value. In this respect it might seem that there is some incompatibility between, on the one hand, the liberalism and individualism of Socrates' view that each person should be free to determine and to follow his own good, and, on the other hand, his conviction that there is only one proper method to determine what the good is, and that this method will yield certainty as to what it is.

The former view, emphasising the value of free and independent criticism and inquiry, seems more in keeping with the liberal ideal of morality as an individual and, indeed, private sphere of behaviour, immune from the interference of law and state; the concern here is not to evaluate the particular moral principles which the individual has determined to be the right ones for him; it is to champion the value of the individual's right to be free and independent in determining them. The latter view, in so far as it assumes that reason can establish certain principles of moral behaviour as indubitably true, seems to be more in keeping with the view that there is a rationally sanctioned code of morality which should be accepted by everybody and which law and state should uphold.[16] This is the view systematically developed by Plato. It excludes 'private morality'.

It is very unlikely that Socrates was aware of this apparent incompatibility between his individualistic views and the authoritarianism implicit in his conviction that certainty was possible in ethics and that those who had attained it should be rulers. Certainly there is much of the philosophical liberal about Socrates. This is reflected in almost all of his political views. And it is reflected also in his conception of the good in so far as this puts a high value on the activity of free and independent criticism and inquiry. But does he consider it a sufficient specification of the good to define it in terms of this activity? Or does he rather value this activity as a means to the end of establishing what the good is? Let us now look at his views in fields outside politics, to see what indications are given there about his conception of the good which might help to resolve this problem.

C. *Religious Views*

In a familiar passage in Plato's *Phaedo* Socrates tells how dissatisfied he was as a young man with the theories of the natural scientists of his time. They were wrong, he thought, in explaining everything in terms of mechanical causation; they should have adopted a teleological kind of explanation.

Here is his account of his reaction to the theory of Anaxagoras (*Phaedo* 97b ff.):[17]

> One day I heard someone reading an extract from what he said was a book by Anaxagoras, to the effect that it is Mind that arranges all things in order and causes all things; now there was a cause that delighted me, for I felt that in a way it was good that Mind should be the cause of everything; and I decided that if this were true Mind must do all its ordering and arranging in the fashion that is best for each individual thing. Hence if one wanted to discover the cause for anything coming into being or perishing or existing, the question to ask was how it was best for that thing to exist or to act or be acted upon. On this principle then the only thing that a man had to think about, whether in regard to himself or anything else, was what is best, what is the highest good; though of course he would also have to know what is bad, since knowledge of good involves knowledge of bad.
>
> With these reflexions I was delighted to think I had found in Anaxagoras an instructor about the cause of things after my own heart. . . . I imagined that in assigning the cause of particular things and of things in general he would proceed to explain what was the individual best and the general good; and I wouldn't have sold my hopes for a fortune.
>
> And then . . . I found the man making no use of Mind, not crediting it with any causality for setting things in order, but finding causes in things like air and aether and water and a host of other absurdities. It seemed to me that his position was like that of a man who said that all the actions of Socrates are due to his mind, and then attempted to give the cause of my several actions by saying that the reason why I am sitting here is that my body is composed of bones and sinews . . . so that when the bones move about in their sockets, the sinews, by lessening or increasing the tension, make it possible for me at this moment to bend my limbs, and that is the cause of my sitting here in this bent position.
>
> No: to call things like that causes is quite absurd; it would be true to say that if I did not possess things like that—bones and sinews and so on—I shouldn't be able to do what I had resolved upon; but to say that I do what I do because of them—and that too when I am acting with my mind—and not because of my choice of what is best, would be to use extremely careless language. Fancy not being able to distinguish between the cause of a thing and that without which the cause would not be a cause!

This is a clear and straightforward advocacy of the superiority of teleological explanations to mechanical ones. It emphasises the need to take account of the end or purpose to be realised in all natural processes, and characterises this end as 'the highest good'. It also emphasises the directive force of Mind (*nous*) in ordering these processes and realising 'the highest good'. Thus the principle that man has a realisable good is seen as part of the comprehensive principle that everything in the world is directed in its activity to the realising of a final good end.

The first thing to consider about this account in the *Phaedo* is, of course, whether it is truly Socratic. One ground for suspicion that it is not is that, after its rejection of the notion of mechanical causation, it goes on to explain its new conception of causation in terms of the metaphysical theory of Forms (100a ff.), a theory which we have Aristotle's authority for attributing to Plato, and not to Socrates. On the other hand, it is fairly certain that Socrates was acquainted with the theories of Anaxagoras. For there is a well attested tradition that Archelaus, a pupil of Anaxagoras, was the teacher of Socrates.[18] So we may reasonably ask whether it is likely that Socrates' reaction to the theories of Anaxagoras was such as the *Phaedo* describes. The fact that the later part of the *Phaedo's* discussion of causation is non-Socratic does not make it unreasonable to ask this. For that fact does not entail that the earlier part is non-Socratic.

Aristotle does not help us here. He says (*Met.* 987b1-6) that, at the time when Socrates influenced Plato, Socrates' interests were exclusively ethical and not directed at all to the world of nature as a whole. This is quite compatible, of course, with what Aristophanes' *Clouds,* Xenophon's *Memorabilia* (IV vii 4-7) and Plato's *Phaedo* all suggest—that Socrates was well acquainted with the theories of the fifth-century physical scientists and had reflected on the value of such studies. But Aristotle does not, unfortunately, make any comment about Socrates' later lack of interest in this field.

Xenophon, however, has a good deal to say. According to Xenophon, Socrates criticised the scientists on several counts—for the futility of their assumption that it was possible to achieve definite knowledge, for the lack of practical value in their studies, and for their presumption, amounting virtually to impiety, in seeking to explain the order of the universe (*Mem.* I i 11-15; IV vii 4-6). Admittedly, Xenophon has an axe to grind. He wishes to dissociate Socrates from any interests smacking of impiety, and hence from Aristophanes' caricature of him in the *Clouds* as an impious speculator in physical science. He also wishes to emphasise the practical benefits of Socrates' teaching. However, what he attributes to Socrates here is quite in keeping with what Plato's *Apology* represents him as arguing at his trial—that Aristophanes' portrayal of him is false and that it is wrong to associate him with the kind of theory he is there associated with (*Apol.* 18b-19d; 23d-e). Taken together, these passages from Xenophon and Plato give a consistent picture of Socrates' attitude to the theories of the fifth-century scientists.

Moreover, there are passages in Xenophon in which Socrates criticises these theories, just as he criticises them in Plato's *Phaedo,* on the ground of their materialism and their mechanistic explanations. These passages also attribute to Socrates a positive preference for teleological explanations of all the phenomena hitherto explained in terms of mechanical causation. Now it is easy enough to say that all that Xenophon is doing here is borrowing from the *Phaedo.* But the fact is that Xenophon goes well beyond the *Phaedo* in describing Socrates' teleological views. Some of these views have no parallel at all in the *Phaedo.* They are interesting and important.

In the first place, Xenophon (*Mem.* I iv 4 ff.) attributes to Socrates a teleological proof of the existence of a divine architect (*dēmiourgos*) of the order of the world. Socrates' argument from design appeals especially to the intricate and consistent adaptation of means to ends in the human body and personality. The major premiss of his argument here is that whatever is adapted to serve a useful purpose is the product of intelligence, not of chance (4). If then, he argues, we look at the human body, we see that the delicate structure of the different senses is adapted to man's needs and well-being. Similarly man's upright posture, his ability to speak, his intelligence are all adapted to benefit him, since they enable him to maintain himself in all sorts of conditions and to increase his happiness (5-17). Thus man is a most striking example of intelligent design. But he is only one example. Throughout the natural world an order is maintained which is evidence of a directing intelligence (8).

Thus the structure of the whole world is the product of intelligence and not of chance. A directing intelligence (*nous, phronēsis*) is manifested everywhere (17). And all this points to the existence of a divine architect (*dē miourgos,* 7), one who orders and holds together the whole cosmos (IV iii 13), exercising in the world a form of intelligent control which is conceived as analogous to the control of the human mind over the body (I iv 17).

Within this general teleological argument for the existence of a divine architect, Socrates introduces further the thesis that the pattern of adaptation of means to ends throughout the world is of a kind which shows that it is for the sake of man that the world is designed as it is. He develops this thesis at *Mem.* IV iii 3 ff. As evidence of man's privileged position in the order of the world he mentions his enjoyment of the 'gifts' of air, food, fire, of beneficial regulation of the seasons, of the use of other animals, of finely adjusted senses and intelligence, of speech, and of foreknowledge through divination of what is to his advantage. And on the basis of this evidence for man's privileged position within the cosmic pattern of means and ends, it is argued that God has a providential care for mankind and has designed the world to serve man's well-being.

If we compare the passage quoted from the *Phaedo* with these two chapters from the *Memorabilia,* we see that the arguments of the *Memorabilia* go beyond the arguments in the *Phaedo* in two main respects. The *Phaedo* argues that the order of the physical world as a whole and the purposive behaviour of human beings in particular are more plausibly explained in terms, not of a mechanical theory of causation, but of a teleological theory which recognises the directive force of mind (*nous*) in realising a good end. From this teleological viewpoint Socrates in the *Memorabilia* develops, first, a detailed argument for theism (the now familiar argument from design), and, second, a detailed argument to show that God in his providential care for man, has designed the world to serve man's well-being.

These arguments in the *Memorabilia* have a form which is closely parallel to the form of Stoic arguments to support the notion of divine providence. Indeed, in form and detail they immediately recall the arguments used by Balbus in his exposition of Stoic theology in the second book of Cicero's *De Natura Deorum,* especially those in the latter half of the book (133 ff.). The same examples are used in each case, the same conclusions are drawn. The parallel is close enough to make it likely that the Stoics made use of the arguments of the *Memorabilia* when formulating their own theological arguments. Sextus Empiricus, in his discussion of Stoic theology (*Adv. Math.* IX 92 ff.), certainly assumes this (see especially IX 101). And he gives a good deal of attention to the question of the proper interpretation of one highly important part of the argument in the *Memorabilia* (I iv 8).

In view of this, and in view also of the absence in earlier extant literature of any clear and explicit formulation of the *Memorabilia's* theistic arguments, the further likelihood is suggested that Socrates' arguments in Xenophon are in the main original arguments, and that Socrates is therefore a thinker of some importance in the development of a philosophy of theism. For there is no doubt that the two chapters of the *Memorabilia* we are considering present a theory which appears in many ways to be an 'advanced' theory for its time. The vocabulary of its account is not the least of the marks of its advanced nature. In this respect too the affinities are with later Stoic thought rather than with earlier or contemporary thought.[19] Nor, for most of the arguments of the *Memorabilia,* is it possible to find in the pre-Stoic period, whether in the Platonic theology of the *Timaeus* and the *Laws,* or in Aristotle, arguments for theism which are at all closely parallel in general form and in detail to those of the *Memorabilia.*

It has been argued, indeed, that these arguments are so advanced for their time that their place in the *Memorabilia* can plausibly be explained only by the assumption that they are late interpolations. For example, Lincke argued that the Stoic Zeno put them where they are.[20] But as alternatives to this speculative hypothesis, let us consider the probabilities of the views *either* that the arguments can be traced, in their essentials at least, to pre-Socratic thought *or* that they can be attributed, whether wholly or in part, to Socrates.

As we have already seen, it is acknowledged in Plato's *Phaedo* that Anaxagoras' introduction into his cosmogony of the element of Mind (*nous*) as that which 'arranges all things in order and causes all things'[21] suggests at once a teleological mode of explanation. But in both Plato and Aristotle the criticism is made that Anaxagoras, after introducing Mind to start the cosmic revolution, falls back on mechanical explanations in the rest of his cosmogony and makes no further use of Mind as that which 'arranges all things in order'.[22] Clearly the criticism was prompted by the lack of any use of the notion of end (*telos*) or purpose in Anaxagoras' detailed explanations.

But in the work of Diogenes of Apollonia a genuinely teleological outlook appears for the first time. Diogenes, described by Theophrastus as 'almost the youngest' of the cosmologists of the fifth century B.C., was no doubt influenced in his views by Anaxagoras' notion of Mind. Unlike Anaxagoras, however, Diogenes emphasises the conscious purpose and design to be found in nature. He assumes that this purpose is directed to the realisation of what is 'best'; this is the kind of end which Socrates, in the *Phaedo,* says that he looked for in vain in Anaxagoras' theory of causation. Finally, Diogenes thinks that the whole material world, in as much as it is infused by such purposive intelligence, is to be considered divine.

Let us see how he expresses all this. Without intelligence, he says, it would not be possible for the basic substance of the world to be distributed in such a way that it has a measure of everything—of winter and summer and night and day and rains and winds and periods of fine weather; other things too, if one cares to study them, will be found to be disposed in the best possible way.[23] Hence he describes the basic substance of the world as 'that which has intelligence'. He identifies it with air. All men, he says, are steered by this, and it has power over everything; for this itself seems to me to be God and to reach everywhere and to dispose all things and to be in everything.[24]

We can see more clearly what Diogenes means when he says that 'all men are steered by this' if we look at his account of human sensation and thought. He explains sensation in terms of interaction between external and 'internal' air. And what is especially interesting in his account is his statement that in perception it is 'the air within' which perceives, 'being a small portion of the God'; that this is so is indicated, he argues, 'by the fact that often, when we have our mind (*nous*) on other things we neither see nor hear'.[25]

What he means by this is that the divine *nous* which is operative in the whole cosmos is operative also in the act of human perception. For this act is not explicable simply in terms of interaction between external stimuli and sense-organs; for when the *nous* is directed elsewhere perception does not occur, even though physical interaction between external stimuli and sense-organs occurs. Hence 'the small portion of the God' which perceives is intelligence (*nous*). Cicero drew this conclusion from the passage when he said that it could readily be understood from it that it is the mind (*animus*) which sees and hears, not those parts which are as it were windows of the mind.[26] It affords one example of the ways in which man is 'steered' by 'that which has intelligence'.

There are obvious affinities between Diogenes' arguments and Socrates' arguments in the *Memorabilia.* In both cases there is agreement that all things are disposed 'for the best' (*kallista:* Diogenes in DK.64 B 3, Socrates in *Mem.* I iv 13), that this is a divine disposition, and that it is exemplified in the regulation of the seasons, of night and day, and of the weather, and in the human senses and intellect (Diogenes in DK.64 A 19, B 3-5, Socrates in *Mem.* I iv 8, 13, 17; IV iii 4-9, 11).

There is some agreement also in the use of the analogy between the intelligent behaviour of the human person and the orderly processes of the cosmos. Diogenes thinks of human intelligence (*nous*) as 'a small portion of the God'. And in identifying 'that which has intelligence' with air as a cosmic principle, he was certainly influenced by the connexion between air and breathing in men and animals, the further connexion between breathing and life, and, finally, the connexion between life, sensation and thought (DK.64 B 4, B 5). This kind of connexion between air and intelligence in the human personality no doubt played its part in prompting him to adopt the theory that air, possessing 'intelligence' to order all things 'for the best', is the basic substance of the cosmos.

The analogy between human and cosmic intelligence is much more explicit in Socrates' arguments. He says (*Mem.* I iv 17) that, just as the human mind (*nous*) directs the body, so the intelligence that pervades everything directs all things. He argues also that the physical constituents of a man are the same, though infinitely smaller in amount, as those of the cosmos, and that it is therefore arrogant to assume that, while intelligence exists in man, the order of the world is maintained without it (I iv 8). The argument is found also in a late dialogue of Plato, the *Philebus* (28c-30b).[27]

It is highly probable that Socrates was familiar with Diogenes' work. And in view of the affinities between Diogenes' arguments and Socrates' it is reasonable to assume that *in these respects* Diogenes' arguments had some influence on Socrates. Yet there is a good deal more in Socrates' teleological thesis than in Diogenes'. It is possible to argue, of course, that if we had all Diogenes' work, we would find a fuller and more detailed exposition of his teleological views and in all probability find there an anticipation of all Socrates' arguments. For example, it might be argued that Diogenes' serious interests in physiology[28] are likely to have led him to view the structure of the human body from the standpoint of a teleological thesis about the structure of the cosmos as a whole. And it might be argued from this that Socrates' detailed arguments (*Mem.* I iv 5-12)—to show that there is evidence of intelligent design in the purposive adaptation of means to ends in the structure of the human body—are in all probability taken from Diogenes.

But these speculative arguments carry little conviction. If Diogenes had indeed anticipated Socrates in the full range and direction of his teleological arguments, then it becomes quite incomprehensible that Diogenes should not be mentioned along with Anaxagoras in the account of the *Phaedo* as a teleological type of thinker. For what is said in the *Phaedo* about Anaxagoras as a possible pioneer in teleological thinking seems eminently fair in its assessment and criticisms; Aristotle has much the same criticism to make, and the extant fragments generally confirm the rightness of that criticism. So is it at all likely that Plato would at the same time be so singularly unfair as to suppress all reference to Diogenes' teleological views if Diogenes had in fact been the sort of teleologist that Socrates is in the *Memorabilia?*

It seems clear, then, from Plato's lack of reference to Diogenes[29] in the account of the *Phaedo,* that Plato cannot have thought of Diogenes as at all important as a teleological thinker. The probability is that he ranked Diogenes with Anaxagoras as a natural scientist who did recognise the mark of intelligent design in the structure of the world but who was content to rely in his detailed explanations on a mechanical notion of causation. The reason for selecting Anaxagoras rather than Diogenes for special mention as a possible pioneer in teleological thinking is presumably that Anaxagoras, unlike Diogenes, introduced into his system a dualism of mind and matter[30] which seemed to be a much more promising basis for a teleological theory than Diogenes' monism.

And if Plato was so unimpressed by Diogenes as a teleological thinker, it is likely that Socrates was similarly unimpressed and that he relied much less on Diogenes for his own teleological views than some scholars would maintain. For what is really distinctive about Socrates' arguments in the *Memorabilia* is the humanistic and moral orientation belonging to them. There is nothing of this either in Anaxagoras or in Diogenes. Diogenes does indeed speak of the direction of all things 'in the best possible way'. But there is no kind of moral connotation in this. It simply means a disposition in the most orderly or regular way, with the implication that this is in itself more admirable than a state of chaos. And there is nothing in the detail of Diogenes' cosmology or his physiological theory to suggest any sort of moral interest, or indeed to suggest anything beyond the interests of a natural scientist concerned with the mechanical explanation of natural processes.

Thus, if we look for anticipations of Socrates' arguments in the work of the fifth-century natural philosophers, we find some very general anticipation of a teleological approach, but comparatively little anticipation of either the range or the direction of Socrates' arguments. Is there anything, then, in the non-philosophical literature of the fifth century that provides any sort of parallel to Socrates' arguments?

It is clear from the tragedians that there was general recognition of a range of distinctively human abilities, skills, and advantages, which allowed man to lead a civilised life superior to that of all other animals. Sometimes these were looked on as gifts from the gods, sometimes as the results of man's own persistent endeavours in adapting himself to his environment. But there is a wide measure of agreement as to the specification of them. They are, with very little variation, the 'gifts' which Socrates appeals to (*Mem.* IV iii) in arguing for God's providential care of mankind. In Aeschylus, Sophocles, and Euripides we are given much the same list—fire, water, food and shelter, the beneficial regularity of the season, the use of other animals, sailing in ships, speech, thought and the power of divination (Aeschylus *P.V.* 442-506; Sophocles *Antigone* 332-75; Euripides *Supplices* 201-15). The closest parallel to Socrates' argument (*Mem.* IV iii) is the argument of Theseus in the *Supplices* passage. In arguing for the view that there is a preponderance of good over evil in the world Theseus mentions as examples of the way in which God 'orders' man's life his bestowal of just those 'gifts' which Socrates mentions (IV iii 5-6, 8, 11-12).[31]

There can be little doubt that it is on these popular examples of man's distinctive advantages that Socrates draws when he formulates his argument for God's providential care of mankind. There is, moreover, an obviously moral significance in the use made of these examples by the tragedians. Man's enjoyment of these advantages makes his life 'better' than that of other animals. And the higher the development of his advantages, the happier he is. No doubt this moral significance recommended the examples to Socrates as the basis of one of his main teleological arguments.

Having now reviewed the possible sources in fifth-century philosophical and non-philosophical literature of Socrates' teleological views, what remains in those views which is distinctively original? In the first place he puts forward, *as a theological argument,* the teleological argument from design for the existence of God as an architect (*dēmiourgos*) of the order of the world. This God is both omniscient and omnibenevolent (*Mem.* I iv 18). In the second place he puts forward, *as a moral argument,* the argument for God's providential care of mankind. For he considers that this divine providence entails an obligation (IV iii 14, 17) on the part of man to 'respect what is divine' in the order of the world and to refrain from what is impious, unjust, or disgraceful (I iv 19; IV iii 14).

In this way he dissociates from the context of theories in natural science any pointers to a teleological mode of interpretation that he finds in such theories. The dualism of mind and matter which he finds in the essentially mechanical theory of Anaxagoras is given a moral and theological interpretation. And the teleological arguments within Diogenes' monistic system become part of a theology which views the order of the world in terms of a dualism. The importance of this for Socrates is that, with his exclusively moral interests, he is able to make his teleological arguments for the existence of God a basis for justifying a moral ideal. So that his originality lies essentially in the formulation of a theology which not only introduces novel arguments for the existence of God but gives a new moral significance to such arguments of a teleological kind as he takes from others.

It seems to me plausible to claim this degree of originality for Socrates. From what we know of Xenophon it is hardly conceivable that Xenophon invented any of the arguments himself. And though the terminology of the arguments still strikes me as being in some respects rather sophisticated for the time when Xenophon was writing and rather reminiscent of Stoic terminology, I am inclined to think that this is not fatal to the acceptance of the view that Xenophon, in these parts of the *Memorabilia,* is presenting genuinely Socratic views.[32] Moreover, these views are in keeping with the convictions which are the basis of Socrates' defence of his ideals at his trial. They are in keeping with his conviction that his educational mission is a divinely appointed mission, with his conviction that man's moral aim should be to care for his soul rather than his body, and, finally, with his conviction that the good man's interests are not neglected by the gods (Plato, *Apology* 28d-31c, 41d). And if we add to Socrates' religious temperament his fondness for analogical arguments, we can see how readily inclined he would be to make use of the kind of analogy he finds between the practice of professional skills and moral behaviour, and to make it the basis of his argument for the existence of a divine architect of the order of the world.

So far we have tried to establish that in his teleological arguments for the existence of God the end or purpose which Socrates constantly has in view is the end of man's behaviour as a moral being, i.e. his goodness. But what sort of moral ideal is implied by Socrates' theology? It tells us that God 'knows best what things are good' (*Mem.* I iii 2) and that in his wisdom and benevolence he has given man the abilities and advantages which will enable him to achieve happiness. But in specifying these abilities and advantages Socrates is specifying in the main what he considers to be the principal conditions for the attainment of happiness. He is not specifying the *summum bonum* itself. His theology does, however, give some positive indications of what he considers to be the peculiar excellence of man.

We have seen that Socrates' view is that the providence of God entails an obligation on the part of man to 'respect what is divine' in the order of the world. The chief defining characteristic of God is reason or intelligence (*nous, phronēsis*). And the dualism of the ordering intelligence of God and the material world he orders is conceived by Socrates on the analogy of the dualism of the human mind and body. The moral significance of this for Socrates is that man's general obligation to 'respect what is divine' entails that he should place a far greater value on the activities of mind than on those of body within the dualism of his own personality. For the relation between human and divine intelligence is such that it entails that the human mind or *psychē* (soul) is the greatest, the most excellent element in the human personality (*Mem.* I iv 13). For man's *psyche* is that in him which 'partakes of the divine' (*Mem.* IV iii 14). In his *Philebus* Plato was later to argue, on basically the same grounds, that *nous* and *phronē sis* must be reckoned essential ingredients of the good life (28c-30b, 64b-66b).

All this clearly adds a new dimension to our inquiry into Socrates' conception of the good. We see that Socrates views the question of moral goodness within the context of a dualism of soul and body, and justifies on theological grounds his view (i) that goodness belongs to soul rather than to body, and (ii) that it is in virtue of the *nous* or *phronēsis* belonging to the human soul that the highest value can be placed on its activities. In order to give more precise definition to this moral ideal we must examine in more detail Socrates' notion of *psyche*.

D. *The Soul*

Much has been written about the development which took place in the Greek concept of soul in the two centuries before Socrates,[33] and the story of these developments is, in its broad outlines, a now familiar one. But something must be said briefly about it if we are to appreciate Socrates' distinctive contributions to the meaning of the concept.

Furley has remarked that 'it is typical of the development of *psychē* that it comes to replace other words in more and more contexts'.[34] In Homer it is a simple notion. It is the life which distinguishes the living person from the dead person. But in post-Homeric literature it is not long before the notion of soul is associated with various experiences and activities naturally associated with the living person.

In non-philosophical literature it is associated, from the early lyric poets onwards, with certain feelings and emotions—courage, grief, love, anger, etc.[35] In philosophical literature there are several ways in which its use is extended. Within the materialistic theories of the natural scientists its primary sense of life is retained in most cases without attempts to extend its meaning. There are, however, a few exceptional cases in which soul is associated with intellectual activities. Heraclitus is one such case.[36] But the most interesting and most explicit case is the Sophist Gorgias, in a work which is essentially a rhetorical exercise but which has some philosophical interest. The *Encomium on Helen* refers to both the emotional and the intellectual effect of persuasive argument on the soul. It says that wisdom (*sophia*) is the glory of the soul. Thus it assumes that the soul is the seat of intellectual activity as well as emotion.

Assuming that the *Encomium* is a genuine work of Gorgias, there still remains the difficulty of dating it. It probably belongs to the last quarter of the fifth century B.C., and thus suggests that the notion of associating the soul with intellectual activity was by then at least sufficiently acceptable in use to allow it to figure prominently in a rhetorical exercise.[37]

Diogenes of Apollonia appears to reflect in his work this new tendency to associate soul with intellect. We noted earlier his association of air with intelligence. And though he refers to soul (*psychē*) and intelligence (*noē sis*) separately, and is clearly not *identifying* soul with mind, yet the link he makes between air and intelligence is the more easily forged because he finds it possible to use *psychē* as his middle term. Moreover, it is clear that in his view the material substance of *psychē* is air, which is 'that which has intelligence' (DK.64 B 5). So the activity of *noē sis* can be included within the activities of soul.

Diogenes' work illustrates one further extension of the application of *psychē* in pre-Socratic thought. It is the connecting of the notion of *psychē* as life and breath in the human being with the life and motion belonging to all the processes of the physical world. This cosmic significance attached to soul is already apparent in Anaximenes.[38] When it appears later in Diogenes there is added to its cosmic significance as a principle of life and motion the notion of intelligence. This marks the culmination of developments in the notion of soul within the materialistic tradition of pre-Socratic thinking.[39]

Outside this tradition there is one important development to be noted. It concerns the nature of the *psychē* which survives the death of a man. In Homer the soul survives merely as a ghost-like shade. Any thought of survival after death was naturally associated with soul, since it was the soul, as the breath of life, which deserted the body at death. But a deeper significance was given to the notion of the soul's survival by the Orphics and Pythagoreans.

This new significance is already apparent in Pythagoras' doctrine of the transmigration of souls. In a well known fragment preserved by Diogenes Laertius (VIII 36), Xenophanes tells how Pythagoras, passing by when a puppy was being beaten, took pity on it and ordered the beating to be stopped, since 'this is really the soul of a man who was my friend; I recognised it as I heard it cry out'. What is implied by this is the survival of the *personal* soul. And this idea of the retention of personality from one life to another is associated with the idea of 'punishment in the body' and with the further idea of 'purifying' the soul in the hope of escaping further incarnation. The Orphics spoke of the body as the prison or as the tomb of the soul. Plato refers to their belief that the incarnate soul is suffering the punishment of sin, and that the body is a prison in which the soul is incarcerated (*Crat.* 400c; cf. *Men.* 81a-e, *Rep.* 364e-365a).

In this way a moral significance is attached to the behaviour of the soul. But there is little reliable evidence to show that the idea of 'purifying' one's soul was associated with anything other than ritualistic procedures. It seems fairly clear that the Pythagoreans associated purification with music and poetry.[40] But whether they associated it further with scientific or philosophic studies it is impossible to say. We do know that they broadened the basis of mathematics to give it the form of a 'liberal education'.[41] But this in itself does not imply any link between mathematical studies and purification.

What is remarkable about these religious ideas of the soul and its immortality is that they stand right outside the naturalistic theories which represent the main tradition of pre-Socratic thought. When the Pythagoreans speculated about the nature of the soul within the context of their scientific and cosmological theory they advanced theories about it quite incompatible with their religious views of its nature.[42] Empedocles, who was much influenced by these religious ideas, seems to have held some naturalistic view of the nature of soul within his general physical theory.[43] But when he expresses his religious views in the *Purifications* he speaks of that which survives bodily death as the *daimōn.*[44]

Thus the position in the latter half of the fifth century B.C. was that the concept of *psychē*, while it had been examined and developed within the materialistic cos-mologies of the pre-Socratics, had attracted no serious philosophical attention as a non-naturalistic concept. As such it remained a rather vague notion within a body of religious ideas which linked it with the notions of personal survival and of purification but which did not attempt any kind of theoretical justification for any of its views.

Socrates was no doubt familiar with these developments. His religious views suggest that he was familiar with the work of Diogenes, and hence that he was familiar with the notions of giving to soul a cosmic significance and of associating it with intelligence and reason. And the dualism in his religious views also makes it highly probable that he was not only familiar with, but attracted by Orphic and Pythagorean notions of the soul. It is interesting to note in this connexion that, in his caricature of Socrates' activities in the *Clouds,* Aristophanes describes Socrates' school as a 'reflectory (*phrontisterion*) of wise souls' (94). The unusual use here of 'soul' for 'person' is a possible reflection of Pythagorean ideas about the *personal* survival of the soul.

It would be wrong, however, to look for any extensive influence of Pythagorean religious views on the thought of Socrates. There is nothing at all in the ancient tradition about Socrates which links him with the Pythagoreans, though much is said about the link between Plato and the Pythagoreans. And I agree with Ross that 'this must in all probability come in the long run from a tradition in the early Academy that it was not Socrates that formed the link between Plato and the Pythagoreans; and I see no reason to doubt that Plato's interest in these doctrines was largely due to his association with the Pythagoreans of Magna Graecia several years after Socrates' death.'[45]

All that we can plausibly grant, then, in respect of Pythagorean influence on Socrates, is influence of a very general kind in turning Socrates' thought to the idea of associating moral behaviour with the soul and also of associating the personality of a man with his soul. And in view of the intellectualism of his ethics Socrates would naturally be inclined further to associate intellectual activities with the soul and would therefore be attracted by the new tendency to extend the range of meaning of soul in that direction.

We must now consider, in relation to these influences, how much originality there is in the Socratic concept of soul. We must look in particular for any developments in the analysis of it as a non-naturalistic entity, for hitherto, as we have noted, very little attention had been given to such analysis.

We have already seen that in Xenophon's *Memorabilia* Socrates says that the soul is the most excellent part of a man, and that it is that in him which 'partakes of the divine'. Elsewhere in the *Memorabilia* he emphasises the dualism of soul and body in a way which implies that for him the soul is incorporeal. Unlike the body, the soul is invisible (I iv 9; IV iii 14). It directs the body (I iv 9, 13-14). And it is because it is the seat of reason and intelligence (*nous, phronēsis*) that it is able to do this; for it is in the soul alone that intelligence resides (I ii 53; I iv 17). Moreover, a person's *moral* behaviour is the behaviour of his soul, not of his body. The 'performances that belong properly to the soul' are 'doing that which we ought to do' and 'refraining from that from which we ought to refrain' (I iv 19). In Plato's *Crito* (47e-48a) it is to the soul that Socrates implicitly refers when he distinguishes from the body 'that thing in us, whatever it is, which has to do with right or wrong.'

This dualism of soul and body is specially associated by Socrates in the *Memorabilia* with the notion of self-control or self-discipline (*sōphrosunē, enkrateia*). Self-control is, indeed, the key moral concept for Socrates in the *Memorabilia.* And he thinks of it essentially as a control of the soul over the body, just as he thinks of the lack of it as the result of a successful assault on the soul by the persuasive influences of *bodily* pleasures. Thus he says that 'pleasures that have been generated in the same body with the soul persuade the soul to abandon self-control and to gratify the pleasures and the body as soon as possible' (I ii 23). He speaks also of 'being a slave' to pleasures (I v 5), and says that every man ought to consider self-control to be the foundation of all virtue, and to establish it in his soul above all else (I v 4; cf. II i 20). It is in these terms that Xenophon claims that Socrates was superior to 'the pleasures of the body' (I v 6).

It is clear that this *moral* interpretation of the dualism of soul and body is for Socrates an additional ground for thinking that the soul, already characterised as invisible and divine, is a distinct part of a man, an entity different in kind from the body. What he says about self-control in terms of relations between body and soul constitutes in fact a new psychological argument in support of his dualistic views. And he bases on it a moral ideal, which prescribes 'care of the soul' (I ii 4) rather than of the body as the aim of the good man.

In Plato's *Apology* the ideal of 'care of the soul' mentioned by Xenophon is given an important place by Socrates in the defence of his activities at his trial. A measure of the importance which he gives to it is already indicated in Xenophon. For there it becomes apparent that Socrates uses the phrase 'the care of the soul' as equivalent both to 'the care of goodness' and to 'the care of oneself' (I ii 2 with I ii 4 and I ii 8). The same is true of what he says in Plato's *Apology* (29d-30b with 31b, 36c and 41e). He is saying that in caring for the good of one's soul one is caring for one's true self.

This identification of soul with self is the conclusion of an argument in *Alcibiades* I, a dialogue which cannot with any confidence be attributed to Plato but which presents a Socrates whose views can be matched in virtually all respects with the views of the Socrates of Xenophon and of Plato's early dialogues. One cannot confidently claim that the formal shape of its argument for the identification of soul with self is genuinely Socratic. But I think it fairly represents the sort of considerations which are at the back of what is a genuinely Socratic conclusion.

Here is the argument. If we ask what 'caring for one's self' means (127e), we must first ask what the self is (128e). It is clear that the user of anything is in all cases different from the thing used. The person who uses his hands, eyes, and so on is therefore different from the hands and eyes he uses. More generally, a man is different from the body as a whole which he *uses.* It is his soul which uses his body. And since man must be soul or body or both together, and since, as *user* of his body, he cannot be body or body and soul together, it follows that 'either man is nothing at all, or, if he is something, he turns out to be nothing else than soul'. The soul, then, is man (129b-130c).

This is just the view that Plato represents Socrates as taking at the end of the *Phaedo* (115c-d). Crito asks Socrates in what way he and his friends should bury him. 'In whatever way you like', says Socrates, 'if you can catch me'. The real Socrates, he points out, is the one at present taking part in discussion with them and marshalling the various arguments, not the one soon to be seen as a corpse. And he associates this view with the confident hope that this self will survive the death of the body.

Are we able to accept as Socratic this belief in personal immortality attributed to him by Plato in the *Phaedo?* It is certainly a belief in keeping with the conception of soul as a divine, invisible, and non-bodily entity which constitutes the true self. For to think of the soul in that way is to think of it as something which is not subject to the physical laws which govern the 'coming to be' and 'passing away' of the material body; at the same time the 'true self' is dissociated from what is subject to those laws. Hence it is possible to think of one's self as not subject to death in the sense in which the body is subject to death.

Socrates seems to have been content to hope, on the basis of these convictions, that his soul would in fact survive the death of his body, without pretending to have any certainty that this would be the case. This is the impression given by Plato's account in the *Apology* of his concluding remarks at his trial. 'Death', says Socrates, 'must be one of two things—either to have no consciousness at all of anything whatever, or else, as some say, to be a kind of change and migration of the soul from this world to another' (40c). And he adds that he would be ready 'to die many deaths' if the latter alternative was true (41a).

It is essentially the Socratic concept of soul which Plato attempts to justify in the *Phaedo,* on much more elaborate theoretical grounds than Socrates appears to have done. Plato himself soon abandoned the *Phaedo's* severely intellectual conception of the soul. For, once he had committed himself to the identification of the self with the substantial soul, Plato increasingly felt it necessary to widen his conception of soul beyond its intellectual activities. For there were non-intellectual activities which he found it impossible to dissociate from his notion of a person. Yet the *Phaedo,* while it allows us to see the difficulty of giving a satisfactory theoretical justification of Socrates' concept of soul, is at the same time the finest of tributes to its philosophical influence and importance.[46]

One thing which the *Phaedo* emphasises, and which Socrates himself emphasises, is the practical *moral* importance of understanding the nature of the soul and its relation to the body. His ideal of 'caring for the soul' is a moral ideal. It is essentially the same ideal which we found to be implied by his religious views. But what Socrates says in moral contexts about the distinction between soul and body gives to this ideal a little further specification.

For one thing, it gives practical significance to Socrates' view of the self-sufficiency of the morally good man who 'cares for his soul'. Like Socrates himself, such a man will be content with small material means and will have iron self-control in respect of all bodily pleasures (Xen. *Mem.* I ii 4-5, 14, 19-23). For to become a slave to bodily pleasures is to 'corrupt' the soul (*Mem.* IV 3-5). With regard to food, drink, dress, or sexual pleasures, Socrates' view is that these are things of the body and that only a very small regard for them is compatible with the moral self-sufficiency which belongs to the soul (*Mem.* II i).

This is, of course, the attitude of the *Phaedo.* It is also the attitude of the Socrates of Plato's *Apology.* Do not care, he says there, for one's body or for money and fame and reputation, but for truth and wisdom and making one's soul as good as it can be (29d-30b). And Socrates himself practised what he preached. He took no money for his instruction, and lived in poverty (19d-e, 23b-c, 31b-c).

This dualism of soul and body in Socrates' thought provides, then, a further context within which to appreciate his conception of the good life. It is from this viewpoint that many of the personal habits of Socrates caricatured by Aristophanes in the *Clouds* can best be appreciated. Negatively, the good life is a life of frugality and abstinence as far as material possessions and the indulgence of desires classed as bodily are concerned. Positively, it is a life devoted to making oneself 'as wise as possible'. For to 'care for one's soul' is to care for making oneself 'as wise as possible' (Xen. *Mem.* I ii 55). And self-control, the key moral notion of the *Memorabilia,* is equated by Socrates, in conformity with his thesis that virtue is knowledge, with 'wisdom' (*sophia*) (*Mem.* III ix 4).

E. *Conclusion*

Although we are now able to form a fairly definite picture of the Socratic good, a major problem still remains. Reason and intelligence (*nous, phronēsis*), says Socrates, belong essentially and exclusively to the soul. So to 'care for one's soul' is to care above all else for the full exercise and development of one's reason and intelligence. And his own example of a life devoted to free and independent criticism and inquiry in ethics seems to be intended by Socrates to be an example of what he means by exercising one's reason and intelligence to the full. But is it a sufficient definition of the good, in Socrates' view? For it still seems legitimate to ask what we asked at the end of our examination of his political views, i.e. whether the life of unremitting and unfettered criticism and analysis, as practised by Socrates, sufficiently specifies the good life, or whether Socrates values such activity as a means of establishing what is the good.

In favour of the latter alternative it can be argued that Socrates' search for general definitions in ethics is presented by Xenophon, Plato and Aristotle as at once an example of independent criticism and analysis and a method of discovering what is the good. In favour of the former alternative much more can, I think, be said. When we looked at Socrates' political views as a guide to his moral ideals we saw that those views placed a special value on the life of free and independent criticism and inquiry. This moral estimate is entirely consistent with Socrates' speculative views in theology and psychology. For both his theology and his psychology are designed to justify the claim that supreme moral value belongs to the intellectual activities of the human soul.

Moreover, if we accept the account in Plato's *Apology* as the clearest and most direct statement of Socrates' moral convictions, we find him saying there that the post which God has assigned to him is that of 'living a life of philosophy, examining himself and others' (28e). 'The greatest of all human goods', he says later, 'is to discuss virtue and the other things you hear me arguing about in my examination of myself and others. An unexamined life is not worth living' (38a). And in his concluding remarks he expresses the hope, not only that his soul will survive the death of his body, but also that in the after-life his soul will continue its activity of critical examination. For he is convinced that even then the 'greatest thing of all' for the soul will be 'to go on examining and questioning the men of that world in the same way as the men of this, to see who is wise among them, and who thinks he is, but is not. To converse with men there and associate with them and examine them would be happiness unspeakable' (41b-c).

Thus the life dedicated to philosophy is, for Socrates, the good life. And by this he means a life dedicated to the critical analysis which he himself has practised for the best part of his life. Clearly, in the *Apology,* he thinks of this activity as constituting in itself the good, and not as a means to attaining goodness by establishing what the good is.

In the light of this, Socrates' thesis that virtue is knowledge gains an additional significance. In this thesis knowledge means knowledge of what is the good. And the thesis means, as we have seen, that this knowledge is both a necessary and a sufficient condition of being good and thus of doing what is good. We have now examined Socrates' own conception of what is the good, and we have concluded that it was Socrates' conviction that the good is sufficiently defined in terms of the philosophical activity of 'examining oneself and others' by the method of critical analysis which he himself practised. Moreover, his educational mission assumes that this specification of the good is one which is possible for others to realise for themselves to be true. Thus it is, for Socrates, an objective specification which is valid as a standard of goodness for all men.

The thesis that virtue is knowledge becomes, therefore, the thesis that knowing that the good is specifiable in the above terms is a necessary and sufficient condition of practising what is thus specified as good. For I can see no good reason for not assuming that Socrates' convictions as regards the specification of the good were considered by him to amount to knowledge of the good, and, further, that he saw his educational mission as one which aimed to realise this knowledge in others.

The thesis that all the virtues are one also takes on a new descriptive significance when it is considered in the light of Socrates' specification of the good. This specification expresses the deep moral convictions which are reflected, as we saw, in Socrates' views about the soul and in his political and religious views. Against the background of these views it is easy to appreciate that the Socratic moral ideal of wholehearted dedication to the life of philosophy embraces and unifies all the accepted Greek virtues. It is a pious life, for to practise philosophy is to care for that element in man which 'partakes of the divine'. It is a courageous life, for it is a life which in all circumstances confidently and unswervingly follows the path of goodness, even at the risk of death. It is a life of self-control, for the conviction of its goodness is always strong enough to ensure that the care of the soul takes precedence over the care of the body. And it is a just life. For it is a life which respects the right of the individual to pursue his good and shrinks from doing any wrong to others, even if others have done wrong to oneself.

It remains true, of course, that Socrates' definition of what is the good is not a formal conclusion reached by his method of analysis. It is the expression of a moral conviction which the practice of his method of analysis itself helped to create. Socrates himself did not, it is clear, analyse as fully as he might have done the grounds of his conviction that his definition of the good was certainly true. Since all his speculative thinking in ethics led him to what seemed a certain conclusion about the good, he was perhaps able to persuade himself not only that the life of philosophy was the good life but also that the practise of it served to substantiate the truth of that view.

Aristotle saw clearly enough the limitations of Socrates' analysis. He is ready to accept Socrates' moral paradoxes except for their complete denial that there are cases of weakness of will. But he realises the need to analyse more fully the notion of moral knowledge, and is severely critical of Socrates' intellectualism in so far as it seemed to him to assume that the use of the intellect was sufficient to establish what is the good and thereby to ensure that the good is done. His criticism is valuable for the proper understanding of Socratic ethics. For quite apart from its contribution to the problem of weakness of will, its analysis of the nature of moral knowledge reveals just those features of moral knowledge which belong to Socrates' own convictions as to what the good is but which Socrates himself seems not to have recognised.

In this chapter we have examined Socrates' conception of the good, and we have argued that Socrates' moral paradoxes gain a new significance from their association with his conception of what is the good. Socrates does not think of them merely as the results of an analysis of the Greeks' moral language, nor does he consider them to be true only in an analytic sense. He considers them to be true also as practical principles of moral behaviour. For he considers that any person who is brought to share his own conviction as to what is the good will invariably practise that good. That he is able to think of his moral paradoxes as practical truths in this way is a measure of the intensity of his conviction that the good life is the life of philosophy.

This Socratic moral ideal had a considerable influence on all subsequent Greek ethics, the more so because of Socrates' remarkable personal example in remaining faithful to it in practice, even though he had to die for it. Both Plato and Aristotle were inspired by Socrates to find in the life of philosophy their ideal of human goodness. Yet his influence on their thought was much more than an influence in shaping their particular moral ideals. He determined in large part the direction of their philosophical inquiries. And in his method they found a pattern for fruitful philosophical analysis.

Notes

[1] Zeller, *Die Philosophie der Griechen,* ii I (5th ed., 1922), p. 152, suggests, on the basis of this evidence, that Socrates appears to hold that there is no absolute, but only a relative good, no standard for good and bad except advantage and disadvantage.

[2] *Encyclopaedia Britannica,* 11th ed., vol. 25, p. 36.

[3] Ibid.

[4] *The Open Society and its Enemies,* vol. i (4th ed., 1962), p. 131.

[5] Ibid. pp. 124-5.

[6] Ibid. p. 126.

[7] Ibid. p. 127. Popper's italics.

[8] The distinction between 'what the state has' and 'the state itself' is meant to distinguish material prosperity and military power from the moral well-being of the state. Compare Plato's remarks at *Gorgias* 519a, where he complains of fifth-century statesmen that 'they have filled the state with harbours and docks and walls and revenues and trash of that kind, to the neglect of moderation and justice'.

[9] See *Mem.* III vi-vii; IV i-ii.

[10] Plato *Apol.* 39c-d.

[11] Op. cit. p. 191.

[12] Popper, op. cit. p. 194. 'Plato, his most gifted disciple, was soon to prove the least faithful. He betrayed Socrates, just as his uncles had done. . . . Plato tried to implicate Socrates in his grandiose attempt to construct the theory of the arrested society; and he had no difficulty in succeeding, for Socrates was dead.'

[13] Popper, op. cit. p. 301.

[14] Cf. Plato *Republic* 387d-e.

[15] Plato *Crito* 49a-e. There are places in Xenophon's *Memorabilia* where Socrates appears to approve of the traditional virtue of benefiting friends and harming enemies (II iii 14; II vi 35). But I do not think, in view of their contexts, that they can be pressed as expressions of Socrates' serious views. See Burnet's note on *Crito* 49b10 (*Plato's Euthyphro, Apology of Socrates, and Crito* (Oxford, 1924), pp. 198-9).

[16] Cf. Professor H. L. A. Hart's remarks ('Immorality and Treason', *The Listener,* 30 July 1959) in criticism of the view that the function of human law should be not merely to provide men with the opportunity for leading a good life, but to see that they actually *do* lead it.

[17] Hackforth's translation (*Plato's Phaedo* (1955), pp. 124-6).

[18] See DK.60 A 1-3, A 5, A 7.

[19] I am thinking of the use, in the context of an argument for theism, of such words and phrases as *sophou tinos dēmiourgou kai philozou technēmati* (I iv 7), *pronoia* and *pronoē tikos* (I iv 6 and IV iii 7), *ho ton holon kosmon syntattōn* and *noēmatos anamartētōs hypēretounta* (IV iii 13). Compare with this sort of language the Latin of Cicero's account of Stoic theology at *D.N.D.* II 113 ff., and the Greek of Diogenes' summary of Zeno's views (Diogenes Laertius VII, 147-8).

[20] K. Lincke, *Neue Jahrbücher für Klassische Altertum,* xvii (1906), pp. 673-91.

[21] *Phaedo* 97c. For Anaxagoras' own statement on this see DK.59 B 12: 'And whatever things were going to be, and whatever things existed that are not now, and all things that now exist and whatever shall exist—Mind arranged them all, including the revolution now followed by the stars, the sun and moon, and the air and the aether which are being separated off.'

[22] DK.59 A 47.

[23] DK.64 B 3.

[24] DK.64 B 5.

[25] Theophrastus, *De sensu,* 42.

[26] Cic. *Tusc. Disp.* 120, 46; noted by W. K. C. Guthrie in *A History of Greek Philosophy,* vol. ii (1962), p. 374, n. 2.

[27] W. Jaeger, in *The Theology of the Early Greek Philosophers* (Oxford, 1947), p. 246, n. 91, argued that the *Philebus* passage 'proved' that at *Mem.* I iv 8 Xenophon is 'making his Socrates pronounce doctrines of pre-Socratic origin', since 'in the *Philebus* Socrates expressly names some earlier philosophers of nature as his source for this argument to which he subscribes'. Socrates does not in fact name any one when he refers at 28d, e to 'earlier philosophers'. And all he ascribes to them is the general thesis that mind (*nous*) is ruler over everything. When he says at 30d that the argument from human to cosmic intelligence gives support to that general thesis he implies that 'earlier philosophers' who subscribed to the general thesis did not have this particular argument. No doubt he is thinking of Anaxagoras, and possibly also of Diogenes, as the philosophers who maintained that mind is ruler over everything.

[28] See DK.64 B 6.

[29] A possible implicit reference is at *Phaedo* 96b, where Socrates mentions the theory that it is air that we think with as a theory he encountered in his early inquiries in natural science. The context of the reference shows that it is not considered to be a theory with any teleological implications.

[30] See especially DK.59 A 41, with the remarks of G. S. Kirk and J. E. Raven, *The Presocratic Philosophers* (Cambridge, 1957), p. 375.

[31] The most probable date for the *Supplices* is about 420 B.C. Possibly Euripides is adapting to his own purposes at 201-15 what he had heard from Socrates.

[32] For the terminology see note 19 above. Cf. Jaeger's comments (op. cit. pp. 244-5, n. 76) on the use by Xenophon's Socrates at *Mem.* I iv 7 of the term *dē miourgos.* Jaeger thinks that 'it is perfectly believable that this term had been used by previous philosophers who, like Diogenes, interpreted nature in this teleological way'.

[33] See especially D. J. Furley, *The Early History of the Concept of Soul* (University of London, Institute of Classical Studies, Bulletin no. 3 (1956), pp. 1-18), with references there to the most important recent literature on the subject.

[34] Ibid. p. 6.

[35] E.g., Pindar, *Pythian* 147; *Nemean* 9, 32: Aeschylus, *Persae* 840: Sophocles, *O.C.* 498; *Phil.* 1013; fr. 101: Euripides, *Hippolytus* 504, 526, 1006; Herodotus III 14, V 124; Thucydides II 40 3.

[36] DK.22 B 45, 107, 117, 118.

[37] See also Euripides, *Orestes* 1180, and Antiphon, *De Caede Herodis* 93.

[38] DK.13 A 2.

[39] In most important respects it is, of course, the theory of the Greek atomists which marks the culmination of this tradition of thought, and their views on the soul are perhaps, for that reason, worth mentioning here. Democritus associated the soul with life and also with sensation. As Aristotle says (*De An.* 403b25-8), sensation is one of the two chief characteristics in which that which has soul is thought to differ from that which has not. Democritus' view was that the soul is concerned with what is perceptible, whereas the mind (*nous*) is concerned with 'truth'. A condition of correctness of thought was, however, that the mixture of atoms constituting the soul should be a 'harmonious' one (DK.68 A 113, A 135, sec. 58). Democritus follows the general practice of pre-Socratic scientists in not allotting to the soul itself intellectual activities. Even at the end of the fifth century the idea of allotting intellectual activity to the soul was an unconventional one.

[40] DK.58 D I. The authorities for this are Aristoxenus and Iamblichus.

[41] DK.14, 6a.

[42] Aristotle *De An.* 404a, 407b with Plato *Phaedo* 86b-d.

[43] Aristotle *De An.* 408a.

[44] DK.31 B 115.

[45] *Proceedings of the Classical Association,* vol. xxx (1933), p. 22.

[46] In my account of Socrates' conception of the soul, as well as of his religious views, I have leaned rather heavily on Xenophon's *Memorabilia.* It might be argued that Xenophon is taking the essential parts of his own account of these matters from Plato, and especially from the *Phaedo,* and that his testimony therefore has no independent worth. But we have seen that in his account of Socrates' religious views Xenophon goes well beyond what he could have got from the *Phaedo.* And his remarks about the soul and the notion of 'caring for the soul' are made in contexts which distinguish his account quite clearly from any account which is simply a literal borrowing from the *Phaedo.* Even in the very fragmentary remains of the Socratic dialogues of Aeschines of Sphettus we find some reflection of Socrates' notion of 'caring for oneself' and of his religious views (*Aeschinis Socratici Reliquiae,* ed. Krauss: *Alcibiades,* fr. I, lines 49-64).

W. K. C. Guthrie (essay date 1969)

SOURCE: "Philosophical Significance," in *A History of Greek Philosophy,* Cambridge University Press, 1969, pp. 417-88.

[*In the following excerpt, Guthrie assesses the contribution of Socrates to the field of philosophy, arguing that Socrates's work marked a shift in philosophic thought from contemplation of the nature of the universe to contemplation of the problems of human life.*]

'Philosophia de Caelo Devocata'

For the Greeks themselves the name of Socrates formed a watershed in the history of their philosophy. The reason they give for this is that he turned men's eyes from the speculations about the nature of the physical world which had been characteristic of the Presocratic period, and concentrated attention on the problems of human life. In the most general terms, his message was that to investigate the origin and ultimate matter of the universe, the composition and motions of the heavenly bodies, the shape of the earth or the causes of natural growth and decay was of far less importance than to understand what it meant to be a human being and for what purpose one was in the world. This estimate of Socrates as a turning-point can be traced to Aristotle, though he does not perhaps give it such incontrovertible support as later writers supposed, and the exaggeratedly schematic view of Greek philosophy which it suggests was the work of the Hellenistic and Graeco-Roman periods. The chief testimonies in Aristotle are these:

(i) In the first chapter of *De partibus animalium* he is asserting the importance of recognizing the formal-final cause as well as the necessary or material. This had not been clear to earlier thinkers because they had no adequate conception of essence ('what it is to be' so-and-so) nor of how to define the real being of anything. Democritus had an inkling of it,[1] 'and in Socrates's time an advance was made as to the method, but the study of nature was given up . . . , and philosophers turned their attention to practical goodness and political science' (642a 28).

(ii) *Metaph.* 987b 1ff. (and 1078b 17 which repeats it in slightly different words) assigns the change more definitely to Socrates. Aristotle is explaining Plato's theory of transcendent forms as having arisen out of the problem of how knowledge could be possible in a world which, as the Heracliteans seemed to have demonstrated, was in a perpetual state of flux. This theory he had encountered in his young days.

> But when Socrates was busying himself with ethical questions to the complete neglect of nature as a whole, and was seeking in them for the universal and directing the mind for the first time to definitions, Plato, accepting his teaching, came to the conclusion that it applied to something other than the sensible world: the common definition, he reasoned, could not apply to any of the sensibles, since they were always changing.

It will be seen that in both these passages the switch from natural to ethical philosophy comes in by the way. The subject of both is what Aristotle consistently regarded as Socrates's chief contribution to scientific thought, namely his demand for definitions. The first does not even ascribe the switch to Socrates but to philosophers in his time, which is obviously correct. The second does not say that Socrates had never been interested in the study of external nature, but only that he had abandoned it by the time that Plato came into contact with him. Given that Plato was not only old enough to be interested in philosophy but had already been impressed by the difficulties of Heraclitean doctrine, this can hardly have been before his sixty-second year.

The tradition of Socrates as the philosopher who 'brought philosophy down from the skies' became widespread in the Hellenistic period, perhaps under the influence of the Stoic Panaetius,[2] and is familiar to us from Cicero. Its popularity has made it, whatever its historical basis, an important element in the history of thought. After speaking of Pythagoras Cicero says (*Tusc.* 5.4.10):

> Ancient philosophy up to Socrates, who was taught by Archelaus the pupil of Anaxagoras, dealt with number and movement, and the source from which all things arise and to which they return; and these early thinkers inquired zealously into the magnitude, intervals and courses of the stars, and all celestial matters. But Socrates first called philosophy down from the sky, set it in the cities and even introduced it into homes, and compelled it to consider life and morals, good and evil.

And in the *Academica* (1.4.15):

> Socrates I think—indeed it is universally agreed—was the first to divert philosophy from matters which nature herself has wrapped in obscurity, with which all philosophers before him had been concerned, and apply it to ordinary life, directing its inquiries to virtues and vices, and in general to good and evil. Celestial phenomena he regarded as beyond our comprehension, or at any rate, however well we might understand them, as irrelevant to the good life.

One may well wonder where the Sophists come in in all this. In the *Brutus* (8.30-1) Cicero acknowledges that they existed and that Socrates was acting in opposition to them. He introduces them mainly as rhetorical teachers (rhetoric being the subject of the *Brutus*), but sees the moral import of their teaching. As the power of expert oratory came to be recognized, he says, there arose a class of instructors in the art. This was the time when Gorgias, Protagoras, Prodicus, Hippias and many others rose to fame by claiming, arrogantly enough, to teach how speech could make the weaker cause the stronger.

> Socrates opposed them [he goes on] and used to refute their instruction by his own subtle brand of argument. His fertile talk gave rise to a succession of accomplished thinkers, and it is claimed that then for the first time philosophy was discovered—not the philosophy of nature, which was older, but this which we are speaking of, whose subject is good and evil, and the life and manners of men.

If Socrates alone brought about the revolution which redirected men's thoughts from nature to human affairs, the whole first part of this volume has been written in vain. It is one of those clichés or over-simplifications of which written history is full. No doubt the assumption was that the Sophists did not deserve the name of philosophers. The great tradition running from Socrates through Plato to Aristotle already had the upper hand, and with the notable exception of the Epicureans, most schools, however diverse, liked to think of themselves as the heirs of Socratic thought. On the complex causes of the switch of interest from natural science to human affairs enough has already been said. More interesting now is the much disputed question whether it took place not only in the fifth century at large but in the mind of Socrates himself. Cicero does not deny it any more than Aristotle; indeed by linking Socrates with Archelaus and Anaxagoras he strongly suggests it, and there is much contemporary evidence in its support.

Much of what Cicero says could have been taken from Xenophon, whose contention is, briefly, that on the one hand Socrates was entirely guiltless of the charge of teaching 'what goes on in the heavens and beneath the earth', with all that that implied of atheism and impiety; but on the other hand this was not for want of knowledge: he was himself well versed in such sciences, but disparaged them as being of no practical use. In the first chapter of the *Memorabilia* (11 ff.) we are told that he 'never discussed' nature in general—the origin of the cosmos, or the laws governing celestial phenomena—as most philosophers did. Xenophon gives four reasons why he dismissed all this as folly:[3] (*a*) It is wrong to neglect the study of human affairs, which concern us much more nearly, so long as knowledge of them is so incomplete;[4] (*b*) no two scientists agree[5] even on fundamental questions such as whether the sum of things is one or infinitely many, whether everything moves or nothing moves, whether everything comes into existence and decays or nothing does; (*c*) natural science is of no practical use: studying the laws governing winds, waters and seasons does not give one power over these things; (*d*) not only are the secrets of the universe unfathomable, but to pry into them is displeasing to the gods.[6]

Xenophon lays great emphasis on the primarily utilitarian character of Socrates's arguments. In general this was right. Socrates was an intensely practical person, and his equation of the good with what was useful or beneficial comes out as clearly in some of Plato's dialogues.[7] One may suspect, however, that having learned this, Xenophon sometimes made his own choice of examples according to his more commonplace ideas of what was truly beneficial, and that Socrates had other things in mind. Socrates, he says, advised studying geometry so far as it was necessary for measuring a plot of land to be bought or sold, or calculating the profit it would yield. Similarly astronomy should be learned in order to tell the time, the month and the year, in planning a journey, setting a watch and so on. Enough could be picked up from people like night hunters and pilots. 'But he strongly deprecated going so far as to study bodies revolving in different courses, planets and comets, or wearing oneself out in calculating their distances from the earth, their periods and the causes of them. He could see no use in it.' It is in this chapter too (*Mem.* 4.7.1-5) that he insists that Socrates knew what he was talking about. In the higher mathematics he was 'not inexperienced', and in the 'useless' parts of astronomy 'not uninstructed'.

All this accords sufficiently with the 'autobiographical' passage in Plato's *Phaedo* (96a ff.) to give good grounds for crediting the latter with some historical truth.[8] Socrates is there made to say that 'when he was young' he developed a passion for natural philosophy in the hope that it would explain the 'why' of things—why they are here, why they ever came into being, why they perish again. He studied the current theories of the origin of life, of physiology, psychology, astronomy and cosmology, but found them all unsatisfying and concluded that he had no aptitude for such subjects. His hopes were again raised by hearing that Anaxagoras had named 'mind' as the first cause, but dashed once more when he found that in its details Anaxagoras's system was just another set of physical theories like the rest. The distinctive character of mind as cause was simply ignored, and the explanations alleged were as material and mechanical as if intelligence had no part in them. Since Socrates remained convinced that a thing could only be explained in terms of its function, he gave up natural science after this and turned to entirely different methods of inquiry.

Plato uses this narrative for his own purposes, but it would be strange indeed if it had no basis in fact. To the inherent improbability may be added the congruence of the account with information from Xenophon, and with the equally reasonable supposition that the representation of Socrates in the *Clouds* is a farcical exaggeration of certain known trends of his thought rather than based on nothing at all. At the time of the *Clouds* Plato was a little boy, and may have slipped in the word 'young' about the Socrates of those days, so long before he knew him, even though he was a man of forty-six. Much more probably Aristophanes knew quite well that Socrates's enthusiasm for science had been on the wane for a long time: if he had ever embraced it, that was quite a sufficient handle for comedy,[9] once Aristophanes had decided to make Socrates the collective repository of most of his *bêtes noires.* The statement of Aristotle that the investigation of nature 'ceased' . . . in the time of Socrates is an exaggeration. One has only to think of Diogenes of Apollonia, Archelaus (whose association with Socrates is probably historical . . . and some of the Sophists themselves—Gorgias the pupil of Empedocles, and interested in his theory of pores and effluences, Alcidamas the author of a *Physicus,* Antiphon in the *Truth,* perhaps also Critias.[10] Democritus too was active until after the death of Socrates, though it is a moot point how much his work was known at Athens.

There is thus impressive evidence for a period in the life of Socrates when he was intensely interested in natural science. It would take a lot to shake it, but some have seen it all overthrown—Aristophanes, Xenophon, and Plato himself in the *Phaedo*—by some pleas of Socrates in the *Apology,* a work which all sides in the dispute accept as historical. At 18b he denies that he is 'a wise man who theorizes about the heavens and has investigated everything beneath the earth, and makes the weaker argument the stronger', and at 23 d he says these are the stock charges hurled at any philosopher whose accusers are at a loss for material. At 19 c he adds,

> You have seen it yourselves in the comedy of Aristophanes, someone called Socrates swinging around, declaring that he is treading the air and pouring out a great deal more nonsense about things of which I haven't the slightest understanding. I don't mean to disparage such knowledge . . . but the fact is that I take no interest in it. Moreover I can call most of you as witnesses to this, and I beg all who have ever listened to me talking (and there are a great many such) to inform each other by saying whether any of you have ever heard me discourse either much or little on these topics.

There is, then, the evidence that we have previously considered and there is this. It all happened some 2,400 years ago and our information is far from adequate. We cannot hope to know all that lies behind it. But it is reasonable to claim that these words of Socrates cannot annihilate all the rest. Assuming that they were actually used by him in his defence, we need not accuse him of 'lying for the sake of saving his skin'.[11] His study of the natural world may have ended forty years before, and was in any case an inquiry undertaken to satisfy himself. He never taught it publicly nor promulgated any theories of his own,[12] though no doubt he would eagerly debate the current theories with a few chosen friends. When he took to going round Athens accosting worthy citizens and questioning them, or talking to any bright young men whom he saw in the palaestra, it was because he had already recognized the futility of the scientists' speculations and the urgent need to know oneself, to find out 'what is pious, what impious; what fine, what ugly; what is just, what is unjust; what is prudence, madness, courage or cowardice; what is a state and what a statesman; what is meant by governing men, and what is a governor'.[13] If these were the questions that he had been pressing on the attention of all and sundry for the last thirty or forty years, can anyone say that his claim of indifference to natural science, made when he was on trial for his life, was falsified by an earlier period of study in it? In any case he had never taken it up for its own sake, or with the same questions in mind as the physical theorists themselves. His question was 'Why?' Why should there be a world like this, and why should we be in it? At first he thought this was what the scientists were asking too, and plunged into their discussions, until he discovered that they were only interested in the question *how* it all came about. Diogenes of Apollonia may have been an exception,[14] and it is noteworthy that in characterizing Socrates as a scientist it is first and foremost the air-theories of Diogenes which Aristophanes puts into his mouth. But Socrates may have already broken with natural science when Diogenes wrote, and while acknowledging his teleological tendency was not likely to be attracted back by a materialistic theory which embodied the directing power in one of the physical elements. Nevertheless, when he became unpopular with those in power, his earlier interest in the subject could be brought up against him like the youthful left-wing escapades of some respected American senator or philosopher today.

Socrates gave up science for ethics, the study of nature for the pursuit of practical principles. But, perhaps because of his early scientific studies, he insisted that ethics itself was a field of exact knowledge calling for the application of rigorous scientific method. For this method Aristotle believed that science would be for ever in his debt, while he deplored its exercise in a sphere to which he considered it inappropriate. In Aristotle's eyes (as Gigon has pointed out) Socrates plays a double role in the history of philosophy: he produced a method and a principle indispensable for the proper study and classification of natural phenomena, while at the same time his name marks the end of the scientific and the beginning of the ethical epoch in philosophy.[15] If the word *philosophy* is taken in its strict sense, as the search for knowledge, the old tradition was justified that he and he alone brought philosophy into human life. That is, he sought to make ethics and politics the subject of a scientific inquiry which should reveal universal laws or truths, in opposition to the scepticism and relativism that had turned all things into matters of opinion and left men's minds at the mercy of the persuader with the smoothest tongue. Even a Protagoras could not escape from this; a Gorgias or a Polus gloried in it. . . .

. . . . .

Virtue Is Knowledge

Three fundamental theses of Socrates are so closely related as to form scarcely separable parts of a single whole. They are: virtue is knowledge; its converse, that wrongdoing can only be due to ignorance and must therefore be considered involuntary; and 'care of the soul' as the primary condition of living well. As far as possible, something will be said about each in turn.

The Socratic paradox (as it is usually called) that virtue is knowledge bears directly on the characteristically fifth-century controversy over the method of acquiring it, whether by teaching or otherwise; and for this reason it has been necessary to say something about it already.[16] It puts Socrates squarely among his contemporaries, the great Sophists with whom he was crossing swords when Plato was unborn or an infant. We have also noted the wide sense of *areté* in earlier and current use (e.g. 'the *areté* of carpentry or any other craft', . . . , which must have made the 'paradox' less paradoxical in his own time, and also makes it essential to remember that, if we use the English word 'virtue', it is only as a counter to stand for the Greek expression.[17]

Once again let us start from Aristotle, about whose general value as a source enough has been said already. In this case much of what he says can be traced back to the Platonic dialogues, but he has not on this account confused Socrates with Plato. That is plain from the undoubtedly genuine references, and is stated explicitly if we may take the following passage from the *Magna Moralia* (as we surely may) to represent Aristotle's opinion. In a brief historical survey the writer mentions first Pythagoras, then Socrates, then Plato, distinguishing the last two thus:[18]

> The effect of his [*sc.* Socrates's] making the virtues into branches of knowledge was to eliminate the irrational part of the soul, and with it emotion and moral character. So his treatment of virtue was in this respect mistaken. After him Plato, rightly enough, divided the soul into the rational and irrational parts and explained the appropriate virtues of each.

This is valuable information, comparable to what Aristotle tells us about the difference between the Socratic and Platonic treatment of universals, and justifies a belief that what he has taken from Plato as Socratic is genuinely so. It excludes the 'Socrates' of the *Republic* and many other dialogues, and is supported, as we shall see, by Xenophon. At the same time, in his concise and more advanced terminology Aristotle presents us with the 'virtue-is-knowledge' doctrine in its most uncompromising form, in order to point out its shortcomings and contrast it with his own. We may look at it in this form first, and afterwards consider whether its intellectual severity needs any mitigation if we are to get at the mind of Socrates himself.

Aristotle repeats several times that Socrates said or thought that 'the virtues are sciences' or a single virtue (courage) 'is a science'.[19] This he interpreted as an unqualified intellectualism, reached by analogy with pure science and with the practical arts. So *EE* 1216b 2ff.:

> Socrates believed that knowledge of virtue was the final aim, and he inquired what justice is, and what courage and every other kind of virtue. This was reasonable in view of his conviction that all the virtues were sciences, so that to know justice was at the same time to be just; for as soon as we have learned geometry and architecture we are architects and geometricians. For this reason he inquired what virtue is, but not how or from what it is acquired.

Aristotle comments that this is true of the theoretical sciences but not of the productive, in which knowledge is only a means to a further end, e.g. health in medicine, law and order in political science. Therefore to know what virtue is matters less than to know what conditions will produce it, 'for we do not want to know what courage or justice is, but to *be* brave or just, just as we wish to be healthy rather than to know what health is'. This antithesis is one to make Socrates turn in his grave; 'for', he would protest, 'how can I know how virtue is acquired when I don't even know what it is?'[20] Aristotle on the other hand lays it down as his general policy for an ethical treatise (*EN* 1103b 26): 'The present study does not aim at theoretical knowledge as others do, for the object of our inquiry is not to know what goodness is but to become good.' Even if one were to agree with Socrates that knowledge of the nature of courage or justice is a necessary precondition of becoming brave or just,[21] it would be difficult to concede that it is a sufficient one. Elsewhere (1144b 18) Aristotle himself admits that Socrates was partly right: right in saying that reason was a *sine qua non* of virtue, but wrong in identifying the two.

In Plato's *Protagoras,* as part of an argument for the unity of virtue, Socrates tries to maintain that courage, like any other virtue, is knowledge, because in any dangerous enterprise—diving in a confined space, cavalry engagements, light-armed combat—the trained expert will show more courage than the ignorant. Thus courage is knowledge of what is and what is not to be feared.[22] In an obvious reference to this passage, Aristotle asserted that its claim is the opposite of the truth.[23] Some may be cowards but face what appear to others to be dangers because they know them not to be dangers at all, e.g. in war there are many false alarms which the trained and experienced soldier can recognize as such; but in general those who face dangers owing to experience are not really brave. Those who are skilled at climbing masts, he says, are confident not because they know what is to be feared but because they know what aids are available to them in dangers. The example is similar to Socrates's of the divers, and he would hardly have considered it to invalidate his point. In fact however he was arguing at a different level, as he shows at a later stage (354a-b). Courage is not to be considered in isolation, because all virtue is one, to be summed up as the knowledge of what is ultimately good or evil. At this level death itself may not be an evil to be feared, if one knows that it may result in a greater amount of good, for instance the freedom of one's country. The paradoxical nature of the doctrine appears in a comparison with the superficially similar words of Pericles in the funeral oration (Thuc. 2.40.3): some are made bold by ignorance, he says, but the bravest are those who recognize most clearly what things are fearful and what enjoyable, and are not by this knowledge deterred from dangers. By this high but orthodox standard, men face physical dangers although they know them to be fearful; according to Socrates, they face them in the knowledge that what may happen to them is not an evil at all, if it is more beneficial than cowardice to the real self, the *psyche.*

Aristotle's chief objection to the doctrine is that which would occur to most people, namely that it makes no allowance for weakness of will, lack of self-control, 'incontinence', the effect of appetite or passion.[24] In book 7 of the *Ethics* (*EN* 1145 b 25) he makes it the starting-point of his own discussion of the right use of these terms, and once again begins with a reference to the *Protagoras,* where the question was raised (at 352 b-c) whether knowledge, when it is present, can be 'hauled around like a slave by the passions'. 'Socrates', he continues, 'was totally opposed to this idea, on the ground that there is no such thing as incontinence: when a man acts contrary to what is best, he does not judge it to be so, but acts in ignorance.' So put, says Aristotle bluntly, the doctrine is in plain contradiction to experience; and most of us have to agree with Medea (as Euripides and Ovid depict her) that it is possible to see and approve the better course but follow the worse. Aristotle's own solution, cast in a form to deal most gently with the paradox, is reached through his more advanced technique of analysis. A crude dichotomy between knowledge and ignorance is not enough. Knowledge can be actual or potential (i.e. acquired but not consciously present, as in sleep or drunkenness), universal or particular. After considerable discussion (not relevant here), he concludes that the wrongdoer may know the universal rule, but this is not the efficient cause of a particular action, which is motivated by particular knowledge (i.e. that this present action, in my individual circumstances, is or is not contrary to the rule and therefore wrong). It is this kind of knowledge which is overcome (banished from consciousness, rendered merely potential) by the temptation of pleasure, fear, etc.; but such immediate awareness of particulars is a matter of sense-perception only, and ought not, according to Aristotle's epistemology, to be called knowledge.[25] Thus by the application of Aristotelian distinctions of which Socrates never dreamed, something of his paradox can be saved: 'Because the last term (i.e. the particular) is not a universal nor equally an object of knowledge with the universal, even what Socrates sought to establish seems to come about; for there is no incontinence when knowledge in the full sense is present, nor is it *that* knowledge which is "hauled about" by passion, but perceptual knowledge.' (1147b 14.)

Plato contains many passages which support the interpretation of Socrates's dictum as over-intellectual and neglectful of moral weakness. When Aristotle says that in his view to understand the nature of justice was at the same time to be just, he was simply echoing the *Gorgias,* where this conclusion is drawn from an analogy with the practical arts: to 'learn justice' is to be just and will inevitably lead to just action (460b). In the *Laches* Socrates leads the search for a definition of courage, first to knowledge of what is or is not to be feared, and then to include the knowledge of all good and all evil things. This however would make courage identical with virtue as a whole, and Socrates ostensibly writes off the argument as a failure because they had begun by agreeing that it was only a part of it. In fact it has led to precisely what he believed to be the truth and endeavoured to demonstrate in the *Protagoras.* In the *Meno* (87c ff.) he argues that virtue is knowledge on the ground that it must be held to be something good, i.e. always beneficial, never harmful, and all other so-called good things in life (health, wealth, and even a so-called virtue like courage if it is a thoughtless boldness, divorced from knowledge) may bring harm as well as good unless they are wisely and prudently used. Here again the argument is artfully contrived to stimulate thought by being led to ostensible breakdown. If virtue is knowledge, it can be taught, but a search for possible teachers (including the Sophists, who are somewhat lightly dismissed as a doubtful case) reveals none, so the deductive argument is wrecked on the shores of experience. A final suggestion is made, that 'right opinion', which comes to a man not by teaching but in some mysterious manner comparable to the gift of prophecy, may be as good a guide to action as knowledge, so long as it is present; its only fault is its fickleness. Once again the conclusion is that they do not yet know 'what virtue is in and by itself', and are therefore in no position to say how it is acquired.

Xenophon too bears out the intellectualism of Socratic ethics: 'Socrates said that justice and all the rest of virtue was knowledge' (*Mem.* 3.9.5),[26] and the same point is somewhat crudely developed in dialogue form at 4.6.6: no one who knows what he ought to do can think he ought not to do it, and no one acts otherwise than as he thinks he ought to act. In other places, however, Xenophon gives high praise not only to the continence of Socrates's own life but to his continual commendation, in his teaching, of the virtue of self-control—*enkrateia,* the opposite of that *akrasia,* or incontinence, which according to Aristotle was on his assumptions an impossibility.[27] This brings up the question whether the 'paradox' in fact represents such a one-sided view of morality as Aristotle made out. To Joël the solution was simple (*E. u. X. S.* 237): Aristotle, Plato's *Protagoras,* and Xenophon when he says Socrates believed virtue to be knowledge, are giving the genuine Socratic view; Xenophon when he makes Socrates preach self-control and condemn incontinence is giving his own. But it was scarcely as simple as that.

To start with Xenophon, his Socrates claims indeed that complete understanding of what is good will inevitably be reflected in action, but deplores *akrasia,* a yielding to the temptations of sensuality, greed or ambition, as the greatest obstacle to such understanding: 'Don't you agree that *akrasia* keeps men from wisdom (*sophia*) and drives them to its opposite? It prevents them from paying attention to, and properly learning, the things that are profitable by drawing them away to pleasures, and often so stuns their perception of good and evil[28] that they choose the worse instead of the better' (*Mem.* 4.5.6). This leads, later in the same conversation (4.5.11), to the assertion that the man of uncontrolled passions is as ignorant and stupid as a beast, because only the self-controlled are in a position 'to investigate the most important things, and classifying them according to their kinds, both in discussion and in action to choose the good and reject the bad'. Here the notions of moral self-control and the acquisition of knowledge are brought together in a way which involves no contradiction.[29] A teacher of mathematics would hardly be inconsistent in warning a weak-willed pupil that a life of drunkenness and debauchery is not conducive to success even in a purely intellectual pursuit. Some degree of moral discipline is a necessary prerequisite of all knowledge,[30] but most of all when what is sought is an understanding of relative values, in which a mind dulled and confused by unthinking indulgence in sensual pleasure will be especially at sea. It must also be remembered that Socrates's constant analogy for virtue was not theoretical science but art or craft (*techné*), mastery of which calls for both knowledge and practice. At *Mem.* 3.9. 1-3 Xenophon claims to give his answer to the question whether courage is natural or can be learned. It remains on the level of Xenophon's comprehension—there is no progress towards the unification of virtue in a single knowledge of good and evil—but so far as it goes it agrees with *Protagoras* 350a (pp. 452f. above). Nature, says Socrates, plays a part, 'but courage is increased in every man's nature by learning and practice'. Soldiers will fight more bravely if they are using weapons and tactics in which they have been thoroughly trained rather than those with which they are unfamiliar. So too on a higher level in the *Gorgias* (509d ff.), no one wishes to do wrong, but unwillingness is not enough; one needs a certain power, an art, and only by learning and practising this *techné* will he avoid wrongdoing. In the acquisition of *areté* Socrates did not deny a place to any of the three factors commonly recognized in the fifth century: natural gifts, learning, and practice.[31] Yet his view of the case was still original. Knowledge, in and by itself, of the nature of virtue was sufficient to make a man virtuous; but there was little chance of his learning the truth of it if he had not subjected his body to the negative discipline of resisting sensual indulgence and his mind to the practice of dialectic, the art of discriminating and defining.

Socrates's constant representation of *areté,* the art of good living, as the supreme art or craft, does then detract somewhat from Aristotle's criticism of him for treating it as if it were a theoretical science in which knowledge is the sole and final objective.[32] Although in the productive and practical arts the purpose is fulfilled in the product and not solely in the knowledge or skill itself, there is something in the argument that a skilled carpenter or weaver will inevitably turn out good work; to reduce his handiwork deliberately to the faulty level of a beginner's would be impossible for him. At the same time, no one would claim that a simple analogy between this and moral action provides a complete, mature ethical theory. Socrates was the initiator of a revolution, and the first step in a philosophic revolution has two characteristics: it is so rooted in the traditions of its time that its full effects are only gradually realized,[33] and it is presented in a simple and absolute form, leaving to future thinkers the job of providing the necessary qualifications and provisos. The tradition in which Socrates was caught up was that of the Sophists, and his teaching would have been impossible without theirs, much of which he accepted. They based their lives on the conviction that *areté* could be taught, and he concluded that therefore it must be knowledge. Like them he upheld, as we shall see, the principle of utility and was impressed by what they said about the relativity of the good. Antiphon emphasized the need to be master of one's passions as a precondition of choosing the better and avoiding the worse, nor was his advocacy of 'enlightened self-interest' without its appeal for Socrates. Much of this has emerged in ch. x, and more will appear later.

As for the sublime simplicity of Socrates's dictum, that certainly owed much to his own remarkable character. As Joël epigrammatically expressed it, 'in the strength of his character lay the weakness of his philosophy'.[34] But it also reflects the pioneer character of his thought. His was the first attempt to apply philosophical method to ethics, and Aristotle showed perspicacity in giving generous recognition to the value of his achievement for the advance of logic, while deprecating its immediate and universal application to moral theory and practice. Socrates, it may be said, with his 'Virtue is knowledge', did for ethics what Parmenides did for ontology with the assertion that 'what is, is'. Both turned philosophy in an entirely new direction, and both left to their successors the task of refining a simple statement by examining and analysing the concepts underlying its terms, the use of which as single terms had hitherto concealed from consciousness a variety of meanings. Both stated as an absolute and universal truth something which needed to be said, which the advance of philosophy would never refute, but to which it would assign its due place as part of a larger whole.[35] That is why it seemed worth mentioning Aristotle's refinements . . . , as an example of this process at work. 'Virtue is knowledge.' But what sort of knowledge? Actual, potential, universal, particular? And is knowledge the whole of virtue, or an essential integrating element in it?

If Socrates held virtue to be knowledge, whether or not he believed that either he or any man had acquired it, he must have had some conception of the object of that knowledge. Though a single object, it had two aspects. In one aspect it was knowledge of the end and aim of human life, which embraced and transcended all partial ends and individual arts such as those aiming at health, physical safety, wealth, political power and so on. These may or may not make for the best and happiest life, for they are all instrumental to further ends, and it depends how they are used. Secondly, the knowledge required is self-knowledge. We have seen that Socrates's conception of a definition is teleological . . . : to know the nature of anything is to know its function. If we could understand our own nature, therefore, we should know what is the right and natural goal of our life, and this is the knowledge which would give us the *areté* that we are seeking.

All Wrongdoing Is Involuntary: Socrates a Determinist?

If virtue is knowledge, and to know the good is to do it, wickedness is due to ignorance and therefore, strictly speaking, involuntary. This corollary made a deep impression on Plato, and in spite of his more advanced psychology he retained it as his own up to the end. If in his earlier works he attributes it to Socrates, he repeats it later in dialogues where Socrates is not even nominally the speaker. In the *Timaeus* the statement that 'no one is voluntarily wicked' is connected with a remarkable theory that all vices have their origin in somatic disorders, and in the *Laws* it is repeated on the more Socratic ground that no man will deliberately harm his most precious possession, which is his soul. In the *Protagoras* Socrates himself says: 'My own opinion is more or less this: no wise man believes that anyone sins willingly or willingly perpetrates any base or evil act; they know very well that every base or evil action is committed involuntarily.' In the *Meno,* an argument making a wickedly sophistical use of ambiguity is used to demonstrate that 'no one wishes evil', on the ground that 'to desire and obtain evil things' is a recipe for unhappiness, so that anyone who ostensibly wishes evil must be presumed to be ignorant that it is evil. The *Republic* asserts that, whether one considers pleasure, reputation or profit, the man who commends justice speaks the truth, while the man who disparages it (does not lie, but) speaks in ignorance. He must therefore be gently persuaded, for his error is not voluntary.[36]

Plato, then, maintained the paradox at all periods,[37] but Aristotle opposed it on the grounds that it makes men no longer masters of their own actions. 'It is irrational to suppose that a man who acts unjustly does not wish to be unjust or a man who acts dissolutely to be dissolute.' 'Wickedness *is* voluntary, or else we shall have to quarrel with what we have just said and deny that a man is the author and begetter of his actions.'[38] This criticism of the doctrine as deterministic is put most clearly in the *Magna Moralia,* and has been repeated in modern times. *M M* 1187a7 expresses it thus:

> Socrates claimed that it is not in our power to be worthy or worthless men. If, he said, you were to ask anyone whether he would like to be just or unjust, no one would choose injustice, and it is the same with courage and cowardice and the other virtues. Evidently any who are vicious will not be vicious voluntarily. Neither, in conse-quence, will they be voluntarily virtuous.

Karl Joël was one who took this as a complete description of Socratic ethics, which he therefore regarded as primitively deterministic.

> All wrong action is involuntary. Whether we are good or bad does not depend on ourselves. No one wills unrighteousness, cowardice etc., but only righteousness etc. (*M M* 1187a). On this basis it would be nonsensical to exhort to virtue. The will

as such cannot be improved, because it is entirely unfree, in bondage to the reason. (*E. u. X. S.* 266.)

That the beginning of psychology should be as primitive as the beginning of physical science (*ibid.* 227) is, as he says, natural enough; but what he is doing is to force this nascent psychology into the categories appropriate to a maturer stage. To say that if no one is voluntarily bad then no one is voluntarily good may seem an obvious inference, but it is nevertheless an inference drawn by Aristotle or his follower, not by Socrates.[39] Not for him the searching analysis, which we find in Aristotle, of the interrelated concepts of desire, wish, deliberation, choice, voluntary and involuntary, nor of the status of an act committed involuntarily but arising out of a condition brought on by voluntary action in the past. What Socrates did, as Aristotle frankly acknowledges, was to initiate the whole discussion out of which such analysis sprang. To Socrates the matter appeared thus. No man with full knowledge of his own and his fellows' nature, and of the consequences of his acts, would make a wrong choice of action. But what man has such knowledge? Neither himself nor anyone known to him. His awareness of this laid on him the obligation to make it clear to others, and having convinced them both of their ignorance and of the paramount need of knowledge, to persuade them to shun those ways of life which were an impediment to discovery and accept the help of his maieutic powers. As Joël himself goes on to say, he did not seek to prove (better, to discover) that virtue is good—that was a truism—but what virtue is. And he urged others to do the same. This *was* an exhortation to acquire virtue, in the only way in which Socrates thought it could be acquired.

NOTE. One of the best short expositions of the essence of Socraticism is Ritter's on pp. 54-7 of his *Sokrates,* where he states and answers four objections to the doctrine that virtue is knowledge. The fourth is that such intellectual determinism destroys the point of moral precept and the recognition of any strict or absolute duty. The gist of his answer is worth repeating to supplement the one above. True, he says, a man in possession of full knowledge would have no duty in the sense of a command laid on him by a higher authority which he must recognize, and it would be superfluous to demand moral action from him. Where there is natural necessity there is no duty. But in Socrates's (and Plato's) belief, imperfect and limited humanity is incapable of such complete insight. *Sophia* is for God, only *philosophia* for men.[40] Their search for wisdom is above all a search for self-knowledge. This cannot be taken for granted, but remains a duty, because the necessity of seeking knowledge is not always recognized, being in conflict with the urge towards pleasure and honour. It can only be maintained, in the face of many temptations, by an optimistic belief in its overriding value. Nevertheless the duty of self-examination may be felt so deeply that it sums up all duties in itself, and in content and importance does not fall below any of the fundamental moral demands that have ever been made or could be made.

The Good and the Useful

In *Republic* I (336c-d) Thrasymachus opens his attack by challenging Socrates to say what he means by justice or right conduct: 'And don't tell me that it is the necessary or the beneficial or the helpful or the profitable or the advantageous, but speak plainly and precisely, for if you give me such nonsensical answers I won't stand it.' Socrates was famous for this utilitarian approach to goodness and virtue.[41] At 339b he agrees that he believes justice to be something advantageous. In the *Hippias Major* he says: 'Let us postulate that whatever is useful is beautiful (or fine, *kalon*).'[42] In the *Gorgias* (474d) all things fine—bodies, colours, shapes, sounds, habits or pursuits—are so called either in view of their usefulness for some specific purpose or because they give pleasure. In the *Meno* (87d-e) he argues that, if *areté* is what makes us good, it must be something advantageous or useful, since all good things are useful. Many things normally considered such—health,[43] strength, wealth—may in certain circumstances lead to harm. What we have to find is something always, unfailingly advantageous. Sometimes goodness is coupled with pleasure as well as usefulness, as in the *Protagoras* (358b): 'All actions aimed at this end, namely a pleasant and painless life, must be fine actions, that is, good and beneficial. If then the pleasant is the good . . . ' The knowledge and wisdom necessary for a good life consist in acquiring an 'art of measurement' which will reveal the real, as opposed to the apparent, magnitude of pleasures. As with physical objects, they may deceive by appearing larger when close at hand, smaller when distant. If we are able to judge their actual measurements, we shall ensure not only a momentary, fleeting pleasure which may be followed by unhappiness, but the maximum of pleasure and minimum of pain throughout our lives. In the metric art, or hedonic calculus, lies salvation, since it 'cancels the effect of the immediate impression and by revealing the true state of affairs causes the soul to have peace and to abide in the truth, thus saving our life' (*Prot.* 356d-e).

The utilitarian conception of good is certainly Socratic. Xenophon makes him say, just before his identification of justice and the rest of virtue with knowledge (*Mem.* 3.9.4): 'All men, I believe, choose from the various courses open to them the one which they think will be most advantageous to them, and follow that.' An important consequence is that goodness is relative to a desired end. This is especially emphasized by Xenophon in two conversations, with Aristippus and Euthydemus.[44] Aristippus was a hedonist in the vulgar sense of indulging excessively in food, drink and sex, and had already been rebuked by Socrates for his unwisdom. He hopes to get his own back by asking Socrates if he knows of anything good, and then, when Socrates gives any of the usual answers and names some one thing commonly thought to be good, showing that in certain circumstances it can be bad. Socrates however counters by asking whether he is to name something good for a fever, or for ophthalmia, or for hunger or what, 'because if you are asking me whether I know of something good which is not the good *of* anything, I neither know nor want to know'. Similarly with what is beautiful (*kalon*), Socrates knows plenty of beautiful things, all unlike one another. 'How can what is beautiful be unlike what is beautiful?' In the way that a beautiful (fine) wrestler is unlike a beautiful runner, a shield, beautiful for protection, differs from a javelin which is beautiful for its swift and powerful motion. The answer is the same for good and beautiful because what is good in relation to anything is beautiful in relation to the same thing. *Areté* is expressly mentioned as an example. The question whether in that case a dung-basket is beautiful leaves Socrates unperturbed. 'Of course, and a golden shield is ugly if the one is well made for its special work and the other badly.' Since everything has its own limited province of usefulness, everything may be said to be both good and bad, beautiful and ugly: what is good for hunger is often bad for fever, a build that is beautiful for wrestling is often ugly for running, 'for all things are good and beautiful in relation to the purposes for which they are well adapted'.

The conversation with Euthydemus follows the same lines. The good is nothing but the useful, and what is useful to one man may be hurtful to another. Beauty is similarly related to function. What is useful is beautiful in relation to that for which it is useful, and it is impossible to mention anything—body, utensil or whatever—which is beautiful for *all* purposes.

In these conversations Socrates is making exactly the same point that Protagoras makes in Plato's dialogue, that nothing is good or bad, beneficial or harmful, *in abstracto*, but only in relation to a particular object. . . . Similarly in the *Phaedrus* (p. 187, n. 3) he asks how anyone can call himself a doctor because he knows the effect of certain drugs and treatments, if he has no idea which of them is appropriate to a particular patient with a particular illness, at what stage they should be applied or for how long. Socrates did not scorn empiricism in the ordinary exigencies of life, he was as alive as any Sophist to the folly of imposing rigid rules indiscriminately, and one of the most indisputably Socratic tenets is that the goodness of anything lies in its fitness to perform its proper function. But once the importance of calculation is admitted, and hence the need for knowledge if pleasures are to be chosen with discrimination (and even a Callicles is forced to admit in the end that there are bad pleasures as well as good, because some are beneficial and others harmful, *Gorg.* 499b-d), Socrates is able to proceed, by apparently common-sense arguments, to stand common sense on its head. According to Xenophon (*Mem.* 4.8.6), when on trial for his life he could claim that no one had lived a better, or a pleasanter, more enjoyable life than he; for they live best who make the best effort to become as good as possible, and most pleasantly they who are most conscious that they are improving. Good (= useful or needful) things can obviously be arranged in a hierarchy: the right arms and equipment give soldiers the means to fight well; over and above this, the right strategy and tactics are needed if their fighting is to be effective; if this has brought victory, that only leaves further aims, and the means to them, undecided, for which a yet higher wisdom and knowledge are required. How is the former enemy to be treated, and how is the country to be so ordered that the fruits of victory are a peaceful, prosperous and happy life?[45] Every art—strategy, medicine, politics and the rest—has its own particular aim, to which particular means are relative. This is 'the good' for it—victory, or health, or power over one's fellows. But at the end of each there is always a further aim. Victory may turn sour on the victors, restored health may mean only the continuation of an unhappy life, political power may be frustrating. 'Men think of the practically useful as that helping them to get what they want, but it is more useful to know what is worth wanting.'[46] Thrasymachus and Clitophon were right to be annoyed when they asked in what consisted human excellence, righteousness or good conduct, and were put off with the answer that it was 'the useful'; for this was an answer without content. *What* is useful, *what* will further the ends of human life? The doctor as such, the general as such, know what they want to achieve—in the one case health, in the other victory—and this guides them in their choice of implements and means. But when it comes to the aim of human existence, the good life which the *areté* that we are seeking is to ensure, one cannot name any single, material thing. Any that could be mentioned might be misused, and (as Versényi has pointed out, *Socr. Hum.* 76f.) would in any case be a particular instance incapable of universality. What is wanted is 'that quality, characteristic mark, or formal structure that all good things, no matter how relative, particular and materially different, must share if they are to be good at all'.

Socrates agreed with the Sophists that different specific, or subordinate, activities had their different ends or 'goods', calling for different means to acquire them. On the other hand he deplored the extreme, individualistic relativism which said that whatever any man thought right was right for him. The ends, and so the means, were objectively determined, and the expert would attain them while the ignorant would not. Hence his insistence on 'leading the discussion back to the definition'. To decide who is the better citizen, one must inquire what is the function of a good citizen.[47] First he is considered in separate aspects: who is the good citizen in economic matters, in war, in debate and so forth? From these instances (as dozens of examples show) must be extracted the *eidos* common to them all, which would turn out to be knowledge—in this case knowledge of what a *polis* is and for what end it was constituted. Where Socrates went beyond the Sophists was in seeing the need for this formal definition. Yet he could never have satisfied a Thrasymachus, for seeing the need did not mean that he could fulfil it easily or quickly. Indeed he was only too well aware that the search was long and difficult, if not endless. It might take a lifetime, but it would be a lifetime well spent, for 'the unexamined life is not the life for a human being' (*Apol.* 38a). He laid no claim to the knowledge which was virtue, but only a certain insight into the right way to look for it. The clue lay in the close connexion between essence and function, between what a thing is and what it is *for.* One cannot know what a shuttle is without understanding the work of the weaver and what he is trying to make. To know what a cook or a doctor or a general is is to know his job, and leads to a knowledge of the particular *areté* which will enable him to perform it. If therefore we want to learn what is *areté* as such, the supreme or universal excellence which will enable us all, whatever our craft, profession or standing, to live the span of human life in the best possible way, we must first know ourselves, for with that self-knowledge will come the knowledge of our chief end. Pursued to this extreme, the doctrine which started out as utilitarian and even selfish may end in such an apparently unpractical conclusion as that it is better to suffer wrong than to inflict it, and having done a wrong, better to be punished for it than to escape. For the real self, which is to be 'benefited', turns out to be the *psyche,* and this is only harmed by the commission of wrongful acts, and improved by chastisement.[48]

Self-Knowledge and 'Care of the Soul'

One of Socrates's most insistent exhortations to his fellow-citizens was that they should look after—care for, tend—their souls. . . . In the *Apology* he says (29d):

> I will not cease from philosophy and from exhorting you, and declaring the truth to every one of you I meet, saying in the words I am accustomed to use: 'My good friend . . . are you not ashamed of caring for money and how to get as much of it as you can, and for honour and reputation, and not caring or taking thought for wisdom and truth and for your *psyche,* and how to make it as good as possible?'

And at 30a:

> I go about doing nothing else but urging you, young and old alike, not to care for your bodies or for money sooner than, or as much as, for your *psyche,* and how to make it as good as you can.

The original word *psyche* avoids the overtones which the English translation 'soul' has acquired through centuries of use in a Christian context. As Socrates understood it, the effort that he demanded of his fellows was philosophic and intellectual rather than religious, though the *psyche* did not lack religious associations in and before his time. Burnet went so far as to say that 'not only had the word *psyche* never been used in this way, but the existence of what Socrates called by that name had never been realized'.[49] To make good this statement called for an inquiry into the history of the word which he proceeded to make, as others have also done. By the fifth century it had certainly acquired remarkably complex associations. There was still the Homeric conception of it as the breath-soul which was a worthless thing without the body and had no connexion with thought or emotion. There was the primitive ghost-*psyche* which could be summoned back to prophesy and to help or take vengeance on the living. There was the *psyche* of the mystery-religions, akin to the divine and capable of a blessed life after death if the necessary rites or practices had been observed, with the addition, among the Pythagoreans, of the pursuit of *philosophia. Psyche* could mean courage, and 'of a good *psyche*' . . . brave, or it could mean bare life, so that 'to love one's *psyche*' was to cling to life in a cowardly way,[50] and swooning was a temporary loss of *psyche.* . . . Both in the Orphic and in the Ionian-scientific tradition this life-substance was a portion of the surrounding air or *aither* enclosed in a body, and would fly off to rejoin it at death. This, though material, was the divine element and seems to have been associated with the power of thought, as the *psyche* also is in Sophocles when Creon says that only power reveals the *psyche,* thought and mind of a man (*Ant.* 175-7). Here it verges on character, and it is used in moral contexts also. Pindar speaks of 'keeping one's *psyche* from unrighteousness',[51] and Sophocles of 'a well-disposed *psyche* with righteous thoughts'.[52] The law of homicide demanded forfeiture of 'the *psyche* which did or planned the deed', combining the senses of life and the power of thought and deliberation.[53] When Aristophanes calls the school of Socrates 'a home of clever *psychai*', this may of course be a satirical allusion to his own use of the word (*Clouds,* 94).

These examples, many of them taken from Burnet's own collection, may make us hesitate to go the whole way with him in his belief that no one before Socrates had ever said 'that there is something in us which is capable of attaining wisdom, that this same thing is capable of attaining goodness and righteousness, and that it was called "soul". . . . More to the point is his observation (p. 158) that we do not dispose of Socrates's claim to originality by observing that his conception of the soul was reached by combining certain features of existing beliefs: 'the power of transfusing the apparently disparate is exactly what is meant by originality'. Nor does Burnet even mention what is perhaps the most distinctive feature of the Socratic doctrine, namely the description of the relationship of soul to body in terms of the craftsman analogy: soul is to body as the user to the used, the workman to his tool.

In brief, what Socrates thought about the human *psyche* was that it was the true self. The living man *is* the *psyche,* and the body (which for the Homeric heroes and those still brought up on Homer took such decided preference over it) is only the set of tools or instruments of which he makes use in order to live. A craftsman can only do good work if he is in command of his tools and can guide them as he wishes, an accomplishment which demands knowledge and practice. Similarly life can only be lived well if the *psyche* is in command of . . . the body.[54] It meant purely and simply the intelligence,[55] which in a properly ordered life is in complete control of the senses and emotions. Its proper virtue is wisdom . . . and thought . . . , and to improve the *psyche* is to take thought for wisdom . . . and truth (*Apol.* 29d . . .). This identification of the *psyche* with the self and the self with the reason might be said to have roots both in Ionian scientific thought and in Pythagoreanism, yet there was certainly novelty in Socrates's development of it,[56] apart from the fact that the ordinary Athenian, whom he particularly wished to persuade, was not in the habit of letting his life be ruled by either of these influences. The arguments leading to this conception of the soul have the familiar Socratic ring, and make clear its intimate connexion with his other fundamental conception, that of knowledge, and in particular self-knowledge, as the prerequisite of the good life. They are best set forth in the *First Alcibiades,* a dialogue which, whether or not Plato wrote it, was aptly described by Burnet as 'designed as a sort of introduction to Socratic philosophy for beginners'.[57]

Alcibiades, still under twenty, has ambitions to be a leader of men, both in politics and war. He ought then to have some understanding of such concepts as right and wrong, expedient and inexpedient. Socrates first gets him to contradict himself on these subjects, thus proving that he did not know their meaning although he thought he did. He next points out that it is not ignorance that matters, but ignorance that you are ignorant. Alcibiades does not know how to fly any more than he knows how to govern justly or for the good of the Athenians, but since he is aware of his ignorance he will not try, and no harm will be done. Again (a favourite illustration), there is no harm in his knowing nothing of seamanship if he is content to be a passenger and leave the steering to the skilled helmsman, but there may be disaster if he thinks himself capable of taking over the helm.

Socrates next gets Alcibiades to agree that for success in life it is necessary to care for, or take pains over, oneself . . . , to improve and train oneself, and goes on to demonstrate that you cannot tend and improve a thing unless you know its nature. As always, he is trying to 'lead the discussion back to a definition'. . . . 'Knowing how' for Socrates must be preceded by 'knowing what', a lesson that the Sophists had failed to learn. First he draws a distinction between tending a thing itself and tending something that belongs to it. These are generally the subjects of different skills. To tend the foot is the job of the trainer (or doctor or chiropodist); to tend what belongs to the foot—i.e. shoes—belongs to the cobbler. Now such things as wealth and reputation are not ourselves but things belonging to us, and therefore to augment these externals—which many regard as a proper aim in life—is not to look after ourselves at all, and the art of tending ourselves is a different one. What is this art? Well, can anyone make a good shoe or mend one if he does not know what a shoe is and what it is intended to do? No. One must understand the nature and purpose of anything before one can make, mend or look after it properly. So in life, we cannot acquire an art of self-improvement unless we first understand what we ourselves are. Our first duty, therefore, is to obey the Delphic command, 'Know thyself', 'for once we know ourselves, we may learn how to care for ourselves, but otherwise we never shall'.[58]

How do we come by this knowledge of our real selves? It is reached by means of a further distinction, between the user of anything and what he uses. Alcibiades is first made to admit that the two are always distinct: he and Socrates are people, conversing by means of *logoi,* and the *logoi* they use are different from themselves. A shoemaker is distinct from his knife and awl, a musician from his instrument. But we can go further. A shoemaker, we say, or any other craftsman, uses not only his tools but also his hands and eyes. We may generalize this and say that the body as a whole is something which a man uses to carry out his purposes, his legs to take him where he wants to go, and so on. And if we agree that such a statement is meaningful, we must agree that in speaking of a man we mean something different from his body—that, in fact, which makes use of the body as its instrument. There is nothing that this can be except the *psyche,* which uses and controls . . . the body.[59] Therefore he who said 'know thyself' was in fact bidding us know our *psyche* (130e). Going back to the earlier distinction, to know the body is to know something that belongs to oneself, as a shoe to a foot, but not one's real self; and likewise to look after the body is not to look after one's real self. To know oneself is at once an intellectual and a moral insight, for it is to know that the *psyche,* not the body, is intended by nature or God (cf. 124c) to be the ruling element: to know oneself is to be self-controlled (*sophron,* 131b, and 133c). This may throw some further light on our earlier discussions of Socratic intellectualism. . . . It is at this point, too, that Socrates makes use of the argument to oppose the prevailing sexual standards: he himself may be correctly described as a lover of Alcibiades, because he loves his *psyche;* those who love his body love not Alcibiades, but only something belonging to him. . . .

All of this is familiar Socratic doctrine, the elements of which can be found repeated many times in the Socratic writings, but are so presented here as to bring out their interrelations in a single continuous argument. We are not surprised therefore when, after establishing that to know ourselves is to know the *psyche* and not the body, he goes on to say that if we want to know what the *psyche* is, we must look 'particularly at that part of it in which its virtue resides', and adds at once that this virtue of the *psyche* is wisdom (*sophia*). To know what something is is to know what it is *for,* and we have already discovered that this *ergon* or function of the soul is to rule, govern or control. That virtue is knowledge is true right through the scale of human occupations. The virtue of a shoemaker is knowledge, of what shoes are for and how to make them; the virtue of a doctor is knowledge, of the body and how to tend it. And the virtue of a complete man both as an individual and as a social being is knowledge of the moral and statesmanlike virtues—justice, courage and the rest—which all ambitious Athenian politicians carelessly claimed to understand, but of the nature of which it was Socrates's painful duty to point out that they (and himself no less) were so far ignorant.[60] Here we have the whole train of thought that lay behind the exhortation in the *Apology* to care for the *psyche* and for wisdom and truth, rather than for money or reputation, which it would have been inappropriate, or rather impossible, to unfold in a speech before the judges at his trial.

Religious Beliefs of Socrates: Is the Soul Immortal?

The next point made in the *Alcibiades* comes rather unexpectedly to a modern reader, but is introduced by Socrates without preamble: 'Can we mention', he asks (133c), 'anything more divine about the soul than what is concerned with knowledge and thought? Then this aspect of it[61] resembles God, and it is by looking toward that and understanding all that is divine—God and wisdom—that a man will most fully know himself.' God, he goes on, reflects the nature of *psyche* more clearly and brightly than anything in our own souls, and we may therefore use him as a mirror for human nature too, if what we are looking for is the *areté* of the soul, and this is the best way to see and understand ourselves.[62] With this passage in mind, Jowett's editors (1. 601 n. 1) say that in the *Alcibiades* 'the religious spirit is more positive than in Plato's earlier dialogues', and give this as a reason for supposing it a later and possibly spurious work. But the religious references in the *Apology* are equally positive, and the conception of a divine mind as a universal and purer counterpart of our own was common in the fifth century and is attributed to Socrates by Xenophon. In Plato's *Apology* Socrates says that it would be wrong to disobey God's commands through fear of death (28e), and that, fond as he is of the Athenians, he will obey God rather than them (29d), that God has sent him to the city for its good (30d-e), and that the fortunes of the good are not neglected by the gods (41d). He claims that it is 'not permitted . . . ' for a better man to be harmed by a worse (30d), and the forbidding agent is clearly not human but divine. Both *Apology* and *Euthyphro* mention his serious acceptance of the 'divine sign', which he regarded as a voice from God. How far one is justified in translating *ho theos* simply as 'God' is a difficult question. At 29d Socrates presumably has chiefly in mind Apollo and his oracle, and at 41d he speaks of 'the gods' in the plural. Yet in some cases he seems to have advanced beyond the popular theology to the notion of a single divine power, for which 'God' is the least misleading modern equivalent. In any case it cannot be said that the religious language of the *Apology* is less 'positive' than that of the *Alcibiades,* and we certainly have no right to say that it is used in a different spirit.

Closest to the thought of the *Alcibiades* about God and the soul is the passage in Xenophon (*Mem.* 1.4.17) where Socrates says to Aristodemus: 'Just consider that your own mind within you controls your body as it will. So you must believe that the wisdom in the whole universe disposes all things according to its pleasure.' This supreme being appears at 4.3.13, in contrast to 'the other gods', as 'he who coordinates and holds together the whole cosmos', and a little further on in the same chapter the *psyche* of man is described as that which 'more than anything else that is human partakes of the divine'. The resemblance of the language here to that reported of Anaximenes, who compared the universal breath or air to the human soul, which is also air, and holds us together (vol. 1, 131), reminds us how old is this connexion between human and universal soul. The intellectual character of the universal soul as divine *mind,* and its creative role, were emphasized in Socrates's own lifetime by Anaxagoras and Diogenes of Apollonia, and considering its possibilities for spititualization it is not surprising that he should have taken over the belief and adapted it to his own teaching. At 1.4.8 he claims it is absurd that wisdom should 'by some lucky chance' reside in the tiny portions of matter which form our bodies, and yet 'all the huge and infinitely numerous bodies' in the universe should have achieved the regularity and order which they display without any thought at all.[63] His criticism of Anaxagoras was not that he made Mind the moving force behind the whole universe, but that having done so, he ignored it, and explained the cosmic phenomena by mechanical causes which seemed to have no relation whatsoever to intelligence.

The mentions of a god who is the supreme wisdom in the world, as our minds are in us, are associated with an insistence on his loving care for mankind. At 1.4.5 this being is 'he who created man from the beginning', and Socrates points out in detail how our own parts are designed to serve our ends, and at 4.3.10 how the lower animals too exist for the sake of man. God cares for men (as also in Plato's *Apology,* 41d), takes thought for them, loves them, assists them, as well as being their creator.[64] All this excludes the supposition that Socrates merely shared the vague pantheism of contemporary intellectuals. He uses 'God' or 'the gods' indifferently, but with a bias towards the former, and we have seen mention of a supreme governor of the universe contrasted with lesser gods. In so far as he genuinely believed in the gods of popular polytheism (and Xenophon was emphatic in defending him against charges of neglecting their cult), he probably thought of them as different manifestations of the one supreme spirit. This was the position of many thinking men, and an apparently indifferent use of 'the god', 'the gods' and 'the divine' (neuter) is characteristic of the age. 'If you make trial of the gods by serving them', says Xenophon's Socrates (*Mem.* 1.4.18), 'and see whether they will give you counsel in the things which are hidden from men, you will discover that the divine is such, and so great, that at one and the same time it sees and hears everything and is everywhere and takes care of everything.' The words 'in the things hidden from men' are a reminder that Socrates deprecated resort to oracles as a substitute for thought. In matters where the gods have given men the power to judge for themselves, they emphatically ought to take the trouble to learn what is necessary and make up their own minds: to trouble the gods about such things is contrary to true religion. . . . To sum up, Socrates believed in a god who was the supreme Mind, responsible for the ordering of the universe and at the same time the creator of men. Men moreover had a special relation with him in that their own minds, which controlled their bodies as God controlled the physical movements of the universe, were, though less perfect than the mind of God, of the same nature, and worked on the same principles. In fact, if one looked only to the *areté* of the human soul and disregarded its shortcomings, the two were identical. Whether or not because of this relationship, God had a special regard for man, and had designed both man's own body and the rest of nature for his benefit.

These religious views are amply attested for Socrates, and they create a presumption that he believed the soul to persist after death in a manner more satisfying than the shadowy and witless existence of the Homeric dead; but in deference to many scholars who have thought him to be agnostic on this point, it must be looked at further. To call the soul, or mind, the divine part of man does not by itself imply personal, individual survival. The hope of the mystic was to lose his individuality by being caught up into the one all-pervading spirit, and this absorption was probably the expectation of all, mystics or natural philosophers, who believed in the airy (and ultimately aetherial) nature of the *psyche* and in the *aither* as a living and 'governing' element in the universe. For believers in transmigration like the Orphics and Pythagoreans, individual survival, carrying with it rewards and punishments for the kind of life lived on earth, was the fate only of those who were still caught in the wheel and destined for reincarnation. The final goal was again reabsorption.[65] In one form or another—through the mysteries, the philosophers, and superstitions of a primitive antiquity—this belief would be fairly widespread in the fifth century, and is probably behind Euripides's lines about the mind of the dead 'plunging immortal into the immortal *aither*' (*Hel.* 1014ff.).

That is one reason for caution in using the reference in the *Alcibiades* to the soul as divine as evidence that Socrates believed in personal immortality. Another is the doubt expressed by some scholars concerning the date of the dialogue. Even if intended as 'an introduction to Socratic philosophy' it might, if not written before the middle of the fourth century, include in all innocence something that was not Socratic. For the closest parallel to its statement of the divinity of the human reason, put briefly and soberly with none of the language about initiation, rebirth and so on which Plato adopted from the mystery-religions, we have to look to Aristotle. In the tenth book of the *Ethics* he argues that the best and highest form of human life would consist in the uninterrupted exercise of the reason; 'but', he goes on (1177b27), 'it is not by virtue of our humanity that we can live this life, but in so far as there is something of the divine in us'. A little later on, in exact agreement with the *Alcibiades,* he says that nevertheless this divine faculty of reason is above all others a man's true self (1778a7). If the *Alcibiades* was written, as some think, about the time of Plato's death and Aristotle's maturity, the addition might be very natural. It might indeed be supposed (as Plato did suppose) that the soul's independence of the body, and hence its immortality, were the natural consequence of the sharp dualism of soul and body that is maintained in the main part of the dialogue, the thoroughly Socratic argument that the body is not the real man but only an instrument of which the man (that is, the *psyche*) makes use. But we cannot yet say for certain that Socrates drew that conclusion.

It is safer to turn first to the *Apology,* the most certainly Socratic of all Plato's works.[66] There Socrates says in several places what he thinks about death. On no other subject is it truer to say that everyone has his own Socrates. Some read into these passages agnosticism, others religious faith in a future life. First of all the text must speak for itself. At 28e he says it would be shameful if, after facing death in battle at the command of the state, he should now through fear of death disobey the god's command to philosophize by examining himself and others.

> To fear death is only an instance of thinking oneself wise when one is not; for it is to think one knows what one does not know. No one in fact knows whether death may not even be the greatest of all good things for man, yet men fear it as if they knew well that it was the greatest evil . . . This perhaps is the point in which I am different from the rest of men, and if I could make any claim to be wiser than another, it is in this, that just as I have no full knowledge about the things in Hades, so also I am aware of my ignorance. This however I do know, that it is both evil and base to do wrong and disobey a better, be he god or man. Therefore I shall never fear nor run away from something which for all I know may be good, but rather from evils which I know to be evils.

After the death-sentence Socrates addresses a few words to those who had voted for his acquittal. First he tells them of the silence of his divine sign or voice (p. 403 above), which means that 'what has happened to me must be something good, and those of us who think death is an evil cannot be right'. He continues (40c):

> Looking at it another way we may also feel a strong hope that it is good. Death is one of two things. Either the dead man is as if he no longer exists, and has no sensations at all; or else as men say it is a change and migration of the soul from here to another place. If we have no sensation, but death is like a sleep in which the sleeper has not even a dream, then it must be a wonderful boon; for if a man had to pick out the night in which he slept so soundly that he did not even dream, and setting beside it the other nights and days of his life, to compare them with that night and say how many better and pleasanter days and nights he had spent, I truly believe that not only an ordinary man but even the Great King himself would find them easy to count. If then that is death, I count it a gain, for in this way the whole of time will seem no more than a single night.
>
> If on the other hand death is a sort of migration to another place, and the common tales are true that all the dead are there, what finer thing could there be than this? Would it not be a good journey that takes one to Hades, away from these self-styled judges here, to find the true judges who are said to dispense justice there—Minos, Rhadamanthys, Aeacus, Triptolemus and other demigods who were just in their own lives? Or what would not one of you give to meet Orpheus and Musaeus and Hesiod and Homer? I myself would have a wonderful time there, with Palamedes and Ajax son of Telamon and any other of the ancients who had met his death as the result of an unjust verdict, comparing my experiences with theirs. There would be some pleasure in that. Best of all, I could examine and interrogate the inhabitants of Hades as I do the people here, to find out which of them is wise, and which thinks he is though he is not. What would not a man give to question the leader of the great army at Troy, or Odysseus or Sisyphus or thousands more whom one might mention, both men and women? It would be an infinite happiness to consort and converse with them and examine them—and at any rate they don't put people to death for it there! For among the advantages which those in Hades have over us is the fact that they are immortal for the rest of time, if what we are told is true.
>
> And you too, my friends, must face death with good hope, convinced of the truth of this one thing, that no evil can happen to a good man either in life or in death, nor are his fortunes neglected by the gods.

Then there is the final sentence of the whole *Apology:*

> Now the time is up and we must go, I to death and you to life; but which of us is going to the better fate is known to none, except it be to God.

It is only by reading such passages as this at length that one can catch something of the flavour of the man, which was at least as much of an influence on his friends and posterity as any positive doctrine that he had to teach. Indeed, as these same passages show, with such a naturally undogmatic person it is not always easy to say what he did teach, and the majority who like and admire him tend to see in his language whatever they themselves believe. The agnostic greets him as a kindred spirit because he has said that to claim knowledge of what happens after death is to claim to know what one does not know: he states possible alternatives and leaves them open. The religious-minded is impressed by the fact that whenever he mentions death it is to say that it is something good. In this speech, it is true, he entertains the possibility that it may be either a new life, in which one will meet the great men of the past, or a dreamless sleep, and professes to see good in both. But one would not expect him to assert his innermost convictions in a public speech, in which indeed he treats the matter with a certain amount of humour, as when he imagines himself carrying on in the next world the inquisitorial activities which had made him so unpopular in this. One may feel with Taylor that 'it requires a singularly dull and tasteless reader not to see that his own sympathies are with the hope of a blessed immortality' (*VS,* 31). Hints of his own belief appear rather in statements like 'the fortunes of a good man are not neglected by the gods'. The man who believed that the souls of the righteous are in the hand of God, it may be said, is unlikely to have believed that death means utter extinction. The nature of death, he concludes, is unknown *except it be to God;* and that exception, one might argue, makes all the difference.

My own reading of the *Apology* inclines me to this second interpretation, but there is too much to be said on both sides for the question to be resolved on the basis of these passages alone. They must be taken with other considerations. It would be unusual, to put it no higher, for anyone with Socrates's views both about man as the supreme object of the care and solicitude of God, for whose sake the rest of creation exists . . . , and about the nature and importance of the human soul, to hold at the same time that physical death was the end and the soul perished with the body. A belief in the independence of the soul, and its indifference to the fate of the body, goes naturally with that sharp distinction between them which we find drawn not only in the *Alcibiades* but in the *Apology* and elsewhere in the more indubitably Socratic parts of Plato. Always for Socrates they were two different things, with the *psyche* (that is, the rational faculty) superior and the body only its sometimes refractory instrument. Hence the supreme importance of 'tendance of the *psyche*' (i.e. the training of the mind), and although Socrates saw this as issuing primarily in the living of a practically good life on earth, he most probably thought that just as it was of an altogether superior nature to the body, so also it outlived it.

Of course if one took the *Phaedo* as a mere continuation of the *Apology,* relating what Socrates said to his intimate friends on the day of his death with as much fidelity as the *Apology* employs in telling what he said before the five hundred judges at his trial, there would be no question about it; for there Socrates does maintain that the *psyche* not only is distinct from, and superior to, the body, but differs from it as the eternal from the temporal. It would, however, be here too a 'dull and tasteless reader' who did not sense the entirely different character of the two works, the intellectual modesty of the one and the human simplicity of its alternatives—either a dreamless sleep or a new life much like this one—and the elaborate combination in the other of mystical language about reincarnation with metaphysical argument about the soul's relation to the eternal Forms. As to this, I have already expressed the view . . . that if Socrates had not felt confident of personal immortality, it would have been impossible for Plato to have written an account of his last conversation and death, however imaginative in its details, of which the whole purpose was to instil such confidence. In marked contrast to the *Apology,* he tells us that he himself was not present, and he has felt free to support the simple, unproved faith of his friend with the kind of arguments that appealed to his more speculative nature. Even so, there are many touches of the well-remembered Socrates, not only in the perfect calm and steadfastness with which he goes to meet his death. Surely Socratic is the 'quiet laugh' with which he replies to Crito's request as to how they should bury him: 'Any way you please, provided you can catch me', with the explanation that the dead body which they will shortly see is something quite different from Socrates, the person now talking to them. The *Apology,* though innocent of any theories of reincarnation, speaks of death as a 'change of abode for the soul from here to another place' and 'like going to another country', and this language is exactly paralleled in the *Phaedo.*[67] In the *Phaedo* also Socrates repeats his hope of meeting among the dead with better men than those now living (63b). Even the Socratic profession of ignorance and posing of alternatives is not forgotten there (91b): 'If what I say is true, it is indeed well to believe it; but if there is nothing for a man when he has died, at least I shall be less troublesome to the company than if I were bemoaning my fate.' That however was before the final arguments, after which the Platonic Socrates takes over, and when he has described a possible course of events for the soul both in and out of the body, claims that even if one cannot be positive on such a matter, yet something like it must be true 'because the soul has been clearly shown to be . . . immortal' (114d). Plato thinks he has proved what Socrates only believed, the fact of the soul's immortality, but when it comes to the details of its fate he remembers again how the undogmatic Socrates, the knower of his own ignorance, used to speak. Something like his *mythos* must be true, 'for it is fitting, and it is worth taking a chance on believing that it is so—the risk is a good one—and one should repeat such things to oneself like a charm, which is why I have spun out the story at such length'. The reason, as always with Socrates, is practical: belief in the scheme of transmigration which he has outlined, with promotion to better lives for the good and *vice versa,* will encourage a man to think little of bodily pleasures, to pursue knowledge and 'deck the *psyche* with her proper adornments, self-control, justice, courage, freedom and truth' (114d-e).

The *Phaedo* is a dialogue inspired by Socrates, but in certain important ways going beyond him. To claim to separate the Socratic from the Platonic will seem to many presumptuous, but one can only follow one's own best judgment and leave the verdict to others. I have already given a character sketch of Socrates based on what seemed the most trustworthy evidence, and it is to this impression of his personality as a whole that we must turn for the answer to a question like this,[68] He seems to have been a man who, as Aristotle said, applied the whole of his remarkable intellectual powers to the solution of questions of practical conduct. In higher matters I would suggest that he was guided by a simple religious faith. Certain problems were in principle soluble by human effort. To trouble the gods with these was lazy and stupid. But there would always be truths beyond the scope of human explanation, and for these one must trust the word of the gods, whether given by oracles or through other channels.[69] There was no irony in the way he talked of his divine sign: he put himself unreservedly in the hands of what he sincerely believed to be an inspiration from heaven. He possessed the religious virtue of humility (which in others also has sometimes been taken for arrogance), and with it, despite his ceaseless questioning of everything in the human sphere, of unquestioning belief. There is nothing impossible or unprecedented in the union of a keen and penetrating insight in human affairs, and an unerring eye for humbug, with a simple religious piety. He cannot have laid such emphasis on the 'care' of the *psyche* as the real man, without believing that as it was both truly human and had some share in the divine nature, so also it was the lasting part of us, and that the treatment accorded it in this life would affect its nature and fortunes in the next (*Phaedo,* 63c). The difference between him and Plato is that whereas he was content to believe in immortality as the humbler and less theologically minded Christian does, as an article of simple faith, Plato felt the need to support it with arguments which might at least strengthen the fearful, if not convert the unbelieving. He sought to promote the immortality of the soul from religious belief to philosophical doctrine.

This however involves in the end an essential change of attitude. Once focus attention on the *psyche* to the extent necessary for a proof of its immortality, and one is inevitably, if insensibly, led to the attitude which Plato adopts in the *Phaedo,* of contempt for this life and a fixation on the other. Life becomes something that the philosopher will long to escape from, and while it lasts, he will regard it as practice, or training, for death; that is to say, as death is the release of soul from body, so he will hold the body in contempt . . . , and keep the soul as pure from the taint of its senses and desires as is possible in this life.[70] One becomes immersed in Orphic and Pythagorean notions of the body as a tomb or prison for the soul, and this life as a kind of purgatory, from which the philosopher's eyes should be averted to gaze on the bliss of the world beyond. This attitude of Plato's I would venture to call essentially un-Socratic. One remark in Burnet's essay on the Socratic doctrine of the soul is profoundly true, but difficult to reconcile with his fixed idea that the *Phaedo* contains nothing but pure Socratic doctrine. 'It does not seem, then', he wrote, 'that this [belief in immortality] formed the ordinary theme of his discourse. What he did preach as the one thing needful for the soul was that it should strive after wisdom and goodness' (p. 159). These twin goals must be brought back to their Greek originals: *sophia,* the knowledge and skill essential for all good craftsmanship, from shoemaking to moral and political science; and *areté,* the excellence which meant being good *at* something, in this case living to the utmost of one's powers. Socrates saw his proper place not 'practising for death' in philosophic retirement (however Callicles might sneer), but thrashing out practical questions with the political and rhetorical teachers of Athens in her heyday, as well as instilling a proper sense of values into his younger friends in gymnasium or palaestra.

The Legacy of Socrates

Even systematic philosophers, whose ideas are perpetuated in voluminous writings, have been differently understood by their followers. This was even more certain to happen with Socrates, who taught by word of mouth and insisted that his only advantage over others was the knowledge of his own ignorance. His service to philosophy was the same as that which he claimed to have performed for the Athenian people, namely to be a gadfly which provoked and stung them into fresh activity. Much of his influence was due not to anything that he said at all, but to the magnetic effect of his personality and the example of his life and death, to the consistency and integrity with which he followed his own conscience rather than adopting any belief or legal enactment simply because it was accepted or enjoined, while unquestioningly admitting the right of the state, to which he owed parents, education, and lifelong protection, to deal with him as it thought fit if he could not persuade it otherwise. Inevitably, therefore, in the years following his death, the most diverse philosophers and schools could claim to be following in his footsteps though some at least of them may appear to us to be highly un-Socratic in their conclusions. Here was an inspiring talker, of outstanding intellect and, for his time at least, a unique power of logical discrimination, who was prepared to devote all his time to an examination of human conduct, in the conviction that life was not a meaningless chaos or the heartless jest of an unfeeling higher power but had a definite direction and purpose. Nothing therefore was more important for himself or for others than to ask themselves continually what was the good for man and what the peculiarly human *areté* or excellence which would enable him to attain that good. But it is essential to remember that, as we have seen already, Socrates himself never claimed to have the answer to these questions. He wished to counter those Sophists and others who saw the best life as one of self-indulgence or tyrannical power, those whom Plato's Callicles represents when he identifies the good with pleasure. It must be true, for instance, to say that the orator who pleases the demos may do them much harm, and that the one who aims at their good may have to say some very unpalatable things; and though pleasure in itself may be *a* good thing, such statements as these would be impossible if pleasure and good were identical. How was he to show that such Sophists were wrong?

To a large extent he tried to do it by meeting them on their own ground. Granted that self-interest is paramount, and our object is to maximize our own enjoyment, success demands that it be enlightened self-interest. Unreflecting pursuit of the pleasure of the moment may lead to future misery. This is the thin end of the Socratic wedge. Everyone admitted it, but it follows that actions pleasant in themselves may lead to great harm, even if the meaning of harm is still restricted to what is painful. Hence pleasure cannot be itself the end of life. If we want a word to be the equivalent of 'good' . . . and explain it, we must try another. Socrates himself suggested 'useful' or 'beneficial'. The good must be something which always benefits, never harms. Acts which in themselves give pleasure may now be referred to this as a higher standard. We may ask, still maintaining our attitude of pure self-interest, 'Will it be for my ultimate benefit to act thus?' Having got as far as this, it was easy for him to show that we cannot live the best life without knowledge or wisdom. We have seen how this is necessary to acquire the 'art of measurement' whereby we can calculate the course of action which will in the long term give us the maximum of pleasure and the minimum of pain. In the *Protagoras,* where to the dismay of some of his admirers he apparently champions the cause of pleasure as the good, he gets Protagoras first to agree that the pleasure on which we base our calculations must be in the future as well as the present, and finally to include under 'pleasure' everything that in other dialogues (e.g. *Meno*) he describes as 'beneficial'. All this is carefully excluded when in the *Gorgias* he argues *against* the equivalence of pleasure with the good. 'Pleasures' in the *Protagoras* include most of what in modern speech comes under the heading of 'values', with at least as much emphasis on spiritual values as on any others.

So it turned out that on a nominally hard-headed and even individualistically utilitarian basis one can, with Socrates for a guide, achieve at least as high and altruistic a code of morals as most people are ever likely to aspire to. It was not, as we know, the sum total of his teaching, which included the belief that the real self is the rational and moral *psyche,* and that therefore the true meaning of 'benefiting oneself' was benefiting one's *psyche,* which could only be harmed by a life of unpunished wrongdoing. I would add myself that in calculating the future benefit or harm likely to accrue from a course of action, he would include the treatment of the soul by the divine power in a future life. All this was an inspiration to his followers, but not a sufficient answer to moral sceptics, because it left open the question of what was in fact the ultimate end and purpose of human life. Advocacy of 'the beneficial' as the criterion of action leaves undecided the nature of the benefit which the doer hopes to receive. Socrates, the reverse of a hedonist by nature, had used the hedonistic argument, pressed to a logical conclusion, to turn the tables on the hedonists themselves, but this expedient had its limitations. It left open the question: 'Beneficial for what?' A man might still take even physical pleasure as his ultimate aim, provided he proceeded with just enough caution to ensure that the pleasures of the day did not interfere with those of the morrow. Or he might choose power. The attainment of this may well necessitate; as the biography of some dictators shows, a curtailment of pleasures in the ordinary sense, even a life of strict personal asceticism. The hedonic calculus provides no answer to this, and if Socrates says, 'But you are ignoring the effect on your *psyche* and what will happen to it after death', communication breaks down, as Plato showed in the *Gorgias;* for what he relies on is simply not believed by the adversary, nor is there any means of convincing him of what is to some extent an act of faith. (Cf. *Theaet.* 177 a.)

In one way, then, the aim of Socrates's immediate followers and their schools was to give content to the 'good' which he had set them to seek but himself left undetermined. On the side of method, he bequeathed to them the negative virtues of elenchus or refutation, the dispeller of false pretensions to knowledge, and a sense of the supreme importance of agreeing upon the meaning of words, working towards definitions by means of dialectic or discussion. His insistence on definitions was noted by such widely different characters as Plato and Xenophon, and could lead, according to temperament, to a form of linguistic philosophy on the one hand and, on the other, to philosophic realism when Plato hypostatized the objects of definition and gave them independent existence.[71] Similarly his dialectical and elenctic skill could either be used constructively or lose itself in a somewhat barren eristic. In the eyes of Grote, Socrates himself was the supreme eristic,[72] and certainly his arguments, as they appear in Plato, were sometimes of a rather dubious nature; but at least his aim was not personal victory in a Sophistic contest, but the elucidation of the truth. Otherwise his life would have taken a different course, and he might have died a natural death.

As for the various answers which his pupils gave to the unanswered question of the good for man, one or two of these may be made the subject of a short concluding section before we turn, in the next volume, to the one who, whatever we may think of his faithfulness to their master's teaching, was one of the most universal thinkers of all time. The others, so far as our knowledge goes, seem to have seized on one aspect of Socrates and developed it at the expense of the rest. Plato, however much he may have built on to Socraticism in the way of positive doctrine, shows himself aware of its true spirit when his Socrates says that education does not mean handing over knowledge ready made, nor conferring on the mind a capacity that it did not have before, as sight might be given to a blind eye. The eye of the mind is not blind, but in most people it is looking the wrong way. To educate is to convert or turn it round so that it looks in the right direction (*Rep.* 518b-d). . . .

Notes

[1] For Aristotle on definition before Socrates see vol. II, 483f. (Democritus and the Pythagoreans: for the latter add *Metaph.* A 987a 20.)

[2] So Pohlenz thought (*Die Stoa* I. 194f., 2.10). Panaetius lived *c.* 185-109 B.C.

[3] (*a*)-(*c*) are in 1.1.12-15 (with (*c*) repeated at 4.7.5) and (*d*) in 4.7.6.

[4] Xenophon and Plato agree on Socrates's point of view here. Cf. *Phaedr.* 229e: 'I cannot yet, in the words of the Delphic precept, "know myself", and it seems to me ridiculous to be studying alien matters when still ignorant of this.'

[5] This of course was not original. Cf. Gorgias, p. 51 above.

[6] It was probably from Cicero rather than Xenophon that Milton took the Socratic sentiments which Adam utters in *P.L.* book 8, when he agrees with Raphael

> That not to know at large of things remote
> From use, obscure and subtle, but to know
> That which before us lies in daily life
> Is the prime wisdom; what is more is fume,
> Or emptiness, or fond impertinence,
> And renders us in things that most concern
> Unpractis'd, unprepared, and still to seek.

[7] See pp. 462ff. below.

[8] It does not however accord with some of the more metaphysical parts of the *Republic,* where Socrates is made to express contempt for the application of mathematics and astronomy to practical ends, and to advocate using them as a means of directing the mind away from the physical world to that of the eternal Forms. See for instance the remarks about geometry at 526d-e, and their context. On a comprehensive view of all the evidence about Socrates, the only reasonable conclusion is that Plato is there reaching out beyond anything that the historical Socrates ever said. Kierkegaard drew attention to the contrast between Xenophon and Plato in this respect (*Irony,* 61 with n.).

[9] This chronological point unnecessarily troubled Zeller, who is one of those who have seen not a shred of truth in the autobiographical passage of the *Phaedo.* E. Edelstein (*X. u. P. Bild,* 69-73) thought the historicity of the *Phaedo* guaranteed by its agreement with Xenophon.

[10] For Gorgias see Plato, *Meno* 76c; for Alcidamas, D.L. 8.56; for Antiphon, his frr. 23-32, DK; for Critias, Ar. *De an.* 405b 5 (Empedoclean identification of the *psukhe* with blood). Diels made this point in *SB Berlin* (1894), but he was probably wrong to build up Polus as a student of physics on the basis of Socrates's ironical *ou gar toutÐn empeiros* at *Gorg.* 465d (p. 357). Some of these, like Gorgias (who laughed at the physical theorists) and Critias, were no doubt mere dabblers; but the theories were certainly continuing to attract interest.

[11] The phrase about 'lying to save his skin' occurs in almost identical words in Hackforth (*CPA,* 148) and Popper (*OS,* 308). Popper finds that *Apol.* and *Phaedo* flatly contract each other and that only *Apol.* is to be believed. Hackforth also accepts *Apol.* as historical, and goes so far as to say (p. 147): 'It is not the least use to say that Socrates had dropped these pursuits when he found science unsatisfying . . . for the language which he uses rules out . . . the possibility that at any age whatever he engaged in scientific speculation or research.' Yet rather puzzlingly he can still suppose it 'quite likely that he started with the eager enthusiasm which Plato attributes to him in the famous autobiographical passage of the *Phaedo*' (pp. 152f.).

[12] The 'intellectual autobiography' of the *Phaedo* is a cento of current theories which even now can be assigned to their authors without difficulty. (See Burnet's notes *ad loc.*) There is no hint that Socrates made any original contribution.

[13] Xen. *Mem.* 1.1.16. So also Aristotle, e.g. *EE* 1216b 4: Socrates used to investigate what is justice, what courage, and so with all the other parts of virtue, because he equated the virtues with knowledge.

[14] See vol. II, p. 362, n. I.

[15] See Gigon in *Mus. Helv.* 1959, 192. Compare also the interesting remarks of Deman, *Témoignage,* 78f.: 'Socrate s'est consacré à la recherche morale, mals il a apporté à cette recherche une préoccupation strictement scientifique', etc. . . .

[16] Pp. 257f., and for the question in general ch. x as a whole. Cf. also 25.

[17] The Greek habit of using 'knowledge' . . . to denote practical skill or trained ability, and of 'explaining character or behaviour in terms of knowledge', has often been remarked on. See Dodds, *Gks. & Irrat.* 16f., and cf. his *Gorgias,* 218; Snell, *Ausdrücke,* and *Philol.* 1948, 132. Adam on *Rep.* 382a . . . remarks that 'the identification of ignorance and vice is in harmony with popular Greek psychology'.

[18] 1182a 20. In general I have been sparing of quota-

tion from the *MM,* owing to the widespread view that it is a product of the Peripatos after Aristotle's death.

[19] *EN* 1144b 28 . . . (also *EE* 1230a7). . . . For the former, see O'Brien, *Socr. Parad.* 79, n. 58, and for the latter p. 452, n. 3, below. Cf. also p. 501, n. 3.

[20] *Meno* 71a, *Prot.* 360e-361a, *Laches* 190b.

[21] It is curious that Aristotle, in his irritation against Socrates, should go so far as to speak of knowing what goodness or health is and being good or healthy as alternatives, instead of saying only that Socrates's demand does not go far enough. In his own philosophy any practitioner must first have complete in his mind the *eidos* of what he wishes to produce—health if he is a doctor, a house if he is an architect or builder. Only then does he start to produce it. Thus the formal cause pre-exists in art as well as nature. See *Metaph.* 1032a 32-1032b 14. . . .

[22] 349e-350a, 360d.

[23] *EE* 1230a6, and cf. *EN* 1116b4.

[24] *Akraola,* usually translated 'incontinence', but more literally 'lack of mastery' over one's passions or lower nature; and *nasos,* emotion, passion.

[25] Knowledge . . . must be demonstrable, and can only be of the universal. See *EN* 1139b 18ff., 1140b 30ff. . . . and for a full account of its acquisition *An. Post.* 2, ch. 19. . . .

[26] Or 'skill acquired by learning', . . . (pp. 27f. above). For its equation with knowledge cf. also *Mem.* 4.6.7 . . . , and Plato, *Prot.* 350d.

[27] See e.g. *Mem.* 1.5, 2.1, 4.5.

[28] So Marchant (Loeb ed.) renders *aisthanomenous ekplexasa,* on the analogy of *pauein,* with participle. This gives a sense more obviously in keeping with the 'virtue is knowledge' doctrine, but I doubt if it can be paralleled. Simeterre (*Vertu-science,* 53, n. 72) more plausibly assumes it means that, *although* they perceive good and bad, yet, 'comme frappés d'égarement', they choose the bad, and he cites it as one of the rare passages that appear to contradict the 'virtue is knowledge' doctrine. . . .

[29] On the 'inner connexion between *diarein* and *proairisthoi* cf. the remarks of Stenzel in his *RE* article, 863f.

[30] As Aristotle agreed: intemperance distorts one's medical or grammatical knowledge (*EE* 1246b 27).

[31] For other examples in Xenophon see O'Brien, *Socr. Parad.* 146 n., and compare his whole note 27, from p. 144. On pp. 136-8 (n. 21) he discusses the qualifications to be made to the purely intellectualist interpretation of the definition of virtue as knowledge. When he speaks of Plato's doctrine that 'virtue is *not knowledge alone, but* knowledge (or right opinion) built on natural endowment and long training', one might well ask whether Plato believed that there was any other kind of knowledge. The selection and education of the guardians in the *Republic* suggest that he did not. Pp. 147f. state rather differently the way in which the virtues are 'not knowledge alone', bringing out more clearly one of the Platonic modifications of Socratic doctrine.

[32] Simeterre puts it well (*Vertu-science,* 71): 'Dans les techniques, et quelles qu'elles soient, on ne devient ma tre qu'après un long apprentissage, un sévère entra nement. On ne s'en dispense pas dans l'art difficile de la vertu.'

[33] See the quotation from T. S. Kuhn on p. 352 above.

[34] *E. u. X. S.* 1.256: 'Die Stärke des Charakters wird zur Schwäche der Philosophie.' See p. 258 above.

[35] Joël is good on this, e.g. on p. 222 where he speaks of 'the general historical law that every new truth is at first accepted absolutely before its individuality and relativity are recognized'; and p. 249: 'Every beginning is one-sided, and Socrates marks the beginning of *Geistesphilosophie.*' One may however, while admitting the rationalistic bias of Socrates, differ from him over the extent to which Xenophon has distorted it. Simeterre's conclusion on this is sound (*Vertu-science,* 54): with his practical inclinations, he may have exaggerated the role of *asknais* . . . but if he has not maintained his master's thesis at every point, he has not failed to give us the essentials.

[36] *Tim.* 86d, *Laws* 731c and 860d, *Prot.* 345 d, *Meno* 78a, *Rep.* 589c. Related are *Soph.* 228c, *Phileb.* 22b.

[37] Joël, as we have seen, rejected Xenophon's account on the grounds that it allowed for *eulein* which on the Socratic paradox is impossible. But if we wish to pick on every apparent inconsistency, we can say equally that Plato himself denied that according to Socrates it is impossible to do wrong willingly. . . .

[38] *EN* 1114a11, 1113b16.

[39] I think it is plain that the author of the *M M* has heard no more attributed to Socrates than that no one would choose to be unjust. . . .

[40] Cf. *Apol.* 23a-b: Apollo revealed to Socrates the inadequacy of human wisdom and laid on him the task of bringing it home to others; Xen. *Mem.* 1.3.2: he

prayed for no specific thing, because the gods know best what things are good.

[41] . . . With the *Rep.* passage cf. *Clitophon* 409c.

[42] P. 388 above. The beauty competition in Xenophon's *Symp.* (described just before) is fought on the same arguments. . . .

[43] In Xenophon (*Mem.* 4.2.32) Socrates gives an example of circumstances in which the sick may have an advantage over the healthy.

[44] *Mem.* 3.8.1-7, 4.6.8-9.

[45] This particular example is invented, not taken from a Socratic conversation; but it is essentially Socratic.

[46] Gouldner, *Enter Plato,* 182, which I quote to draw attention to his sensible remarks on this and the following page.

[47] This is Xenophon's example at *Mem.* 4.6.13 ff., quoted on pp. 433 f. above.

[48] Plato, *Gorg.* 469b, 509c, 477a. Such doctrine was not to be produced on every occasion, nor in answer to every kind of question. In judging conversations like that with Aristippus, it is important not to forget what Grote pointed out (*Plato,* III, 538): 'The real Socrates, since he talked incessantly and with everyone, must have known how to diversify his conversation and adapt it to each listener.'

[49] 'Socratic Doctrine of the Soul', *Ess. & Add.* 140. The above translations from the *Apology* are his.

[50] In the very speech in which he exhorts the Athenians to 'care for their *psyche*' in an entirely different sense, Socrates can also use *philopsukhia* in this sense of a clinging to mere life (*Apol.* 37c). . . .

[51] *Ol.*2.70. This might be said to be in an Orphic setting, since the passage deals with transmigration and the blessedness awaiting those who have lived three righteous lives in succession.

[52] Fr. 97 N. Since this is a little inconvenient for Burnet's argument, he can only say that it 'goes rather beyond its [the *psyche*'s] ordinary range' (p. 154), and he is similarly impelled to play down the significance of Soph. *Phil.* 55 and 1013 (p. 156). It must be said, however, that *psyche* is sometimes used as a synonym for a person, even redundantly or periphrastically. . . . Perhaps it has little more weight at *Ph.* 55, where 'to deceive the *psyche* of Philoctetes' means simply to deceive Philoctetes, though it is arguable that the periphrasis would hardly have been possible here if it had not been natural to associate the *psyche* with the mind.

[53] . . . Antiphon Tetr. Ã. á. 7. This is quoted by Burnet (154f.), who passes somewhat lightly over the evident power of the *psyche* to initiate and plan an action.

[54] . . . Thus the later, Stoic epithet for the intelligence, perpetuates the genuine Socratic idea. . . .

[55] Socrates's language is not completely consistent on this point. . . . This language is construed by Jowett's editors (I, 601 n. I) as expressing 'the view of reason as an innermost self *within* the human soul', a view which they call 'characteristic of the last phase of Plato's thought (*Philebus, Timaeus*)'. . . .

[56] It may be that in some respects Democritus came close to the Socratic position, in spite of the inclusion of soul in his all-embracing materialism. Vlastos has claimed that he 'would advise men, exactly as did Socrates, to care for their souls' (*Philos. Rev.* 1945, 578ff.) Yet there are legitimate doubts about the genuineness of his ethical fragments, as well as about the relative dates of his writings and Socrates's dialectical activity, and I can add nothing to what I have said in vol. II, 489 ff. On the constitution of the soul in Democritus, see the index *s.v.* 'atomists: soul'.

[57] *Ess. & Add.* 139. Cf. D. Tarrant in *CQ*, 1938, 167: . . . The personality of Socrates is . . . again drawn on familiar lines.' In antiquity the dialogue was universally accepted as Plato's, but its authorship has been doubted in modern times, especially by German critics, against whom it was stoutly defended by its Budé editor Croiset in 1920. More recently its authenticity has been upheld by A. Motte in *L'Ant. Class.* (1961). See also the appraisal by R. Weil in *L'Inf. Litt.* (1964), and the references given by the revisers of Jowett's *Dialogues of Plato,* vol. I, 601 n. I.

[58] 128b-129a, 124a. Commendation of the Delphic precept occurs again in Plato at *Phaedrus,* 229e, and in Xenophon at *Mem.* 4.2.24 and 3.9.6, where not knowing oneself is equated with not knowing one's own ignorance, a folly which in the *Alcibiades* has already been exposed. Plut. *Adv. Col.* 1118c quotes Aristotle as saying that it was the starting-point of Socrates's inquiries into the nature of man. . . .

[59] It is difficult to understand what was in Jaeger's mind when he wrote (*Paideia,* 11, 43) that 'in his [Socrates's] thought, there is no opposition between psychical and physical man'. The body is as extraneous to the man himself, his *psyche,* as the saw is to the carpenter.

[60] In describing the first serious attempt in history to define the meaning of the word 'good', I have not thought it helpful or fair to compare it directly with the ideas of the twentieth century A.D., as set forth in a book like R. M. Hare's *Language of Morals.* But one

outstanding difference between the two may be noted. On p. 100 of that book Professor Hare speaks of certain words which he calls 'functional words', and the example he gives is a Socratic one: 'We do not know what a carpenter is until we know what a carpenter is supposed to do.' But the extrapolation from this kind of case to man in general is no longer allowed: ' "man" in "good man" is not normally a functional word, and never so when moral commendation is being given' (p. 145). The point is elaborated in his essay reprinted in the Foot collection, pp. 78-82.

[61] . . . As often, one envies the elusiveness which the omission of the noun makes possible for a Greek. It is by no means certain that 'part' is the best word to supply. . . .

[62] The sentences about using God as a mirror are omitted from our manuscripts of the dialogue, but were read by Eusebius and other ancient authors. They are restored by Burnet in the Oxford text and in Jowett's translation, and are obviously necessary to complete the rather elaborate analogy with mirrors and the eye which Plato is drawing. Croiset's objection (Budé ed. 110 n. 1) that they only repeat what has gone before is misleading, nor is his claim convincing that their content has a Neoplatonic tinge.

[63] A similar argument is used in Plato's *Philebus* (29b-30b), a late dialogue which nevertheless has Socrates as its chief speaker. The idea behind it certainly goes back to the fifth century.

[64] See the phrases collected by Zeller, *Ph. d. Gr.* 178 n. 3.

[65] See vol. 1, especially 480f. and 466 with n. 2.

[66] Concerning the historicity of the *Apol.* every shade of opinion has been held (see Ehnmark in *Eranos,* 1946, 106ff. for this, especially in its bearing on the question of immortality), but few have been found to deny its essential faithfulness to the Socratic philosophy. Admittedly a special case has been made of the third speech (38cff.), delivered after sentence has been passed, but even a sceptic like Wilamowitz agreed that in composing it 'Plato must have carefully avoided saying anything that Socrates himself could not have said' (Ehnmark, *loc. cit.* 108). There is really no good reason to separate this speech from the rest, and about the whole the most reasonable supposition is that Plato (who makes a point of mentioning his own presence at the trial: 34a, 38b), while doubtless polishing up and reducing to better order what Socrates actually said, has not falsified the facts or the spirit of his remarks. At the very most, he will have gone no further than Thucydides in reporting speeches in his history, some of which he had only heard at second hand. See p. 85 above. In Plato's case we must take into account that he was present himself and that the occasion was the final crisis in the life of the man whom he admired most in all the world. It is sufficient guarantee that he has given the substance of what Socrates said, and that, if anything has been added by way of vindicating Socrates's memory, it will be in keeping with his real character and views.

If it is still denied that we can know for certain whether Socrates himself used the opportunity of his trial to make such a complete *apologia pro vita sua,* we can only reply that it would have been an entirely reasonable thing for him to do, and that in any case the account of his life and beliefs which Plato gives us is true to the real man.

[67] Cf. *Apol.* 40c, . . . *Phaedo,* 117c, . . . and 40e, . . . with 61 e. . . . On the relations between the *Apol.* and *Phaedo* see also Ehnmark in *Eranos,* 1946.

[68] It is obviously theoretically possible that parallels between *Apol.* and *Phaedo* are due to the Platonic character of the former rather than to Socratic elements in the latter. Only this feeling of personal acquaintance with an integral character, Socrates, enables one to reject such an—as I see it—incredible hypothesis.

[69] Xen. *Mem.* 1.1.6-9, especially 9: . . . . Hackforth put it well (*CPA,* 96): 'He was, I think, content and wisely content not to attempt an explicit reconciliation of reason with faith; not out of indifference, nor in a spirit of complacent, condescending toleration of traditional belief, but rather because he possessed that rare wisdom which knows that, while no bounds may properly be set to the activity of human reason. . . . '

[70] See especially in the *Phaedo,* 61b-c, 64a, 67c-e.

[71] Perhaps the man who came nearest to the aims of Socrates in his search for the meanings of words was not a Greek at all, but a contemporary in a distant land who knew nothing of him. It was said of Confucius (*Analects,* 13.3) that when asked what he would do first if he were given charge of the administration of a country, he replied: 'It would certainly be to correct language' (World's Classics translation). His hearers were surprised, so he explained that if language is not correct, then what is said is not what is meant; if what is said is not what is meant, what ought to be done remains undone; if this remains undone, morals and arts deteriorate, justice goes astray, and the people stand about in helpless confusion. With this may be compared the words given to Socrates by Plato, *Phaedo,* 115e: 'You may be sure, my dear Cebes, that inaccurate language is not only in itself a mistake: it implants evil in men's souls' (trans. Bluck).

[72] See especially his *Plato,* III, 479, where he says that although the Megarians acquired the name of eristics,

they 'cannot possibly have surpassed Socrates, and probably did not equal him, in the refutative elenchus . . . No one of these Megarics probably ever enunciated so sweeping a negative a negative programme, or declared so emphatically his own inability to communicate positive instruction, as Socrates in the Platonic Apology. A person more thoroughly eristic than Socrates never lived.'

A. D. Woozley (essay date 1971)

SOURCE: "Socrates on Disobeying the Law," in *The Philosophy of Socrates: A Collection of Critical Essays,* University of Notre Dame Press, 1971, pp. 299-318.

[*Here, Woozley studies the apparent discrepancy between (1) Socrates's statement at his trial that if he were discharged on the condition that he give up philosophy, he would disobey the order, and (2) Socrates's insistence after the trial, when prompted by a follower to escape, that he must obey the law.*]

I

Socrates is commonly characterised, and indeed on occasion characterised himself (or is so represented by Plato), as a negative thinker: one who provoked a member of his circle to propose a confident opinion on, say, the nature of virtue, or of one of the virtues, and who then proceeded, by unrelenting use of the *elenchus* method, to destroy first the opinion offered, and then the successive amendments and substitutions advanced to meet his earlier objections. The result of a philosophical conversation would be that half a dozen or so suggestions had been eliminated, but not even a tentative positive conclusion reached; the *Euthyphro* is a typical example. Although the method was liable to exasperate his victims, Socrates insisted that it was not eristic, but reflected his own genuine perplexity on the subject under discussion (cf. *Men.* 80C). His unremitting scrutiny of received opinions, deflating them but confessing himself ignorant of what the true answer was, must have done much to create the establishment's antipathy to him, resulting in his trial and conviction on a charge of corrupting youth.

A noteworthy feature of Socrates' discussion of a man's duty or obligation to obey the law is that it does not follow the usual would-be eliminative method. In the *Crito* he does not play the part of the interrogator, asking Crito whether and why we should obey the law, and wearing him down with counterquestions; he comes out forthrightly himself with his own answers and with his reasons for them. And the *Apology,* which also raises the question of obedience to the law, is not a dialogue at all; throughout, Socrates is represented as speaking in his own person, first defending himself at his trial, then, after his conviction, proposing a suitable sentence, and finally, after sentence of death had been passed by the court, making his final address.

While the detailed ordering and dating of Plato's dialogues are likely to remain beyond any definitive settlement, there is nowadays little disagreement among scholars about the general sequence. While both the *Apology* and the *Crito* cannot have been composed before Socrates' trial in 399 B.C., they were almost certainly written shortly afterwards and belong to the early group of dialogues in which the character "Socrates" may be taken fairly to represent the views of the actual Socrates. Furthermore, whatever use Plato later made of "Socrates" to expound and discuss Plato's own philosophical views, it is impossible to believe that, when writing about something on which he felt so strongly as the McCarthyite trial and execution of his revered teacher, he would have done anything other than present the beliefs and arguments of the historical Socrates as accurately as he could; both works are by way of being obituary memoirs. We can, therefore, confidently rely on them as a source of Socrates' views on one's duty to obey the law.

That in itself generates a problem, for there appears to be a flat contradiction between the two works. In the *Apology* Socrates says (29D) that if the court were to discharge him conditionally on his giving up engaging in philosophical enquiry and debate, he would unhesitatingly disobey the order. In the *Crito* he suggests (50B) that a city cannot survive if its court's verdicts and orders do not prevail; furthermore, if it is his general principle that any law must be obeyed, that, taken together with the statement (50C) that there is a law of Athens laying down that the judgement of a court is legally binding, entails the conclusion that one must not try to evade the court's judgement, including the prescribed sentence. The *Crito* proceeds to develop arguments, not merely for obeying the laws in general, but also for abiding by court decisions in particular, even if, in a particular case, the decision was unjust or wrongly given (50C). The underlying thesis here is that a court's judgement or order is verdictive (in this respect analogous to the ruling of an umpire or referee in a game), and that, even if the legal system provides for appeals, a series of appeals has to be finite, and where it stops it stops; if an error in justice persists right to the end, then, even so, the sentence must be carried out; and where the sentence is, as in the case of Socrates, execution by suicide, the sentenced man owes it to the laws to carry it out himself.

How are we to relate the views in the *Apology* with those in the *Crito*? In terms of Socrates' biography, the end of the trial and the conversation in his prison cell are separated by little, if any, more than four weeks. In terms of composition, the two works were probably more widely separated, by how much we cannot tell; but, for reasons already given, we can hardly doubt that they are substantially accurate in their report of Socrates at that time; that rules out misrepresentation by Plato.

One writer indeed has taken the step of supposing that the inconsistency was deliberate, and is to be attributed to Plato, not to Socrates. Grote (*Plato,* Vol. 1) maintains that in composing the *Crito* Plato quite deliberately presented Socrates as an out-and-out defender of the law, complete with highly emotional appeals to patriotism, in order to counteract the bad impression which he had made at his trial (correctly reported in the *Apology*) of being an intellectually arrogant person, who regarded himself as being a privileged exception who was above the law. One of the accusations levelled against him at his trial, according to Xenophon, was that of "inducing his associates to disregard the established laws . . ."; if he had such a reputation, his performance at his trial would have done nothing but confirm it. And people who claim for themselves the right to break the law with impunity do madden their fellows, both by their arrogance, and by the fact of their not being amenable to rational consideration of the possibility of their being wrong. It is not difficult to believe that, whether deservedly or not, Socrates had that reputation, and that for it he was widely hated. Plato then, according to Grote, deliberately set out in the *Crito* to do whatever he could to correct the unfortunate public impression which Socrates had made, and to restore his reputation; the dialogue, in consequence, is meant not as a serious philosophical discussion, but as a rhetorical performance designed solely to change people's attitude to Socrates; and that is why Plato has Socrates rest all the emphasis on two themes: first, the paramount necessity of obeying the law and a legal decision, however unjust it may be; and second, his own personal devotion to his native city of Athens.

The trouble with this interpretation of the *Crito* is that the only thing tolerably certain about it is the public reputation of Socrates from which it starts. The rest is pure conjecture; we have no evidence, external or internal, that the *Crito* was not a genuinely Socratic dialogue. If we could independently establish that it was not, then we could use that to explain the difference in Socrates' attitude towards disobedience to the law in it and in the *Apology* respectively. But, as we cannot independently establish that it was not a genuinely Socratic dialogue, we cannot just *say* that it was not, and then *conclude* that that accounts for the difference; this is simply to beg the question at issue. We have no positive reason to read the *Crito* as a job of rhetorical whitewashing by Plato. And, in view of Plato's known opinion of rhetoric, as expounded in the *Gorgias,* we should in any case only be patching up one inconsistency at the price of disclosing another.

In default of other evidence we have, then, to take it that, as presented by Plato, Socrates was speaking sincerely both in the *Apology* and in the *Crito;* which rules out *knowing* inconsistency. Similarly, we can rule out a change of mind within the last month of his life, for in the *Crito* he insists that there has been none; he cannot abandon his old principles unless confronted by arguments better than anything so far produced (46B-C). We are left, then, with two alternatives: (a) that there was an inconsistency, but he was unaware of it; (b) that there is an interpretation of the passages involved which does not render them incompatible. (a) is so implausible that it is very hard to accept. How could a man with any pretensions to being reasonable and high principled, let alone a Socrates, declare at his trial that he would not obey a particular court order, and then less than a month later refuse to disobey a court order because such orders must always be obeyed—and *not* notice the contradiction? Such an inconsistency cannot be rationally explained; it will have just to be accepted, but only if no alternative under (b) can be found.

Various possibilities offer themselves. (1) Is the court at *Apology* 29C being imagined to be offering Socrates a conditional discharge, the condition being that he will no longer spend his time in philosophical enquiry and discussion? Socrates, in his reply that he must obey God rather than them, and that he would not change his way of life, even if he had to die many deaths (30C), would be rejecting the offer. This would not be inconsistent with his line in the *Crito,* for he would be saying that he could not accept an offer, the terms of which were such that he could neither abide by them (this would be to disobey his God), nor violate them (this would be to disobey the law). But this interpretation will not do, because it depends on the notions of an offer and its acceptance or rejection; and they are not there in the text. We must not blur the distinction between a court offering an accused man a conditional discharge on the one hand, and a court discharging an accused man conditionally on the other. In the first case, the discharge is not made, unless and until the conditional offer is accepted; in the second case the discharge is made, but it holds good for only as long as the man meets the condition. It is like the difference between binding a man over in his own recognisances to keep the peace, and releasing him on probation, subject to his keeping the peace. There is no doubt that what we have in the *Apology* is the notion of the court discharging Socrates conditionally, not its offering him a conditional discharge. The court says (as imagined by Socrates): "This time we shall not be persuaded by Anytus; instead, we are discharging you—however, subject to this condition, that you no longer spend your time in this pursuit or in doing philosophy; and, if you are caught still doing it, you will die" (29C). And Socrates' reply begins: "If you were to discharge me on these terms . . ." (29D). There is nothing about offering to discharge, only about discharging.

(2) Could Socrates be making use of the distinction between a law, which must (as a matter of logic) be legally correct, and a legal decision of a court, which might not be? He would be announcing that he would not meet the condition laid down by the court, because it was itself in some way illegal; it might be unconstitutional, or the court might be acting *ultra vires—that* court might not have the authority to impose *that* condition. This situation is real enough. Leaving aside cases in which there is a problem of legal interpretation, it does happen from time to time that a trial court gets the law wrong or exceeds its jurisdiction; and one of the prime reasons for the existence of appeal courts is to provide an opportunity for reversing such errors. So Socrates would be maintaining throughout that we must obey the law, and consistently with that claiming the right, or even the duty, to ignore a court's judgement if it was illegal.

Nevertheless, this interpretation of Socrates' attitude in the *Apology* cannot be accepted either, and for two reasons. First, he nowhere does suggest that such a decision by the court would be illegal, let alone that its illegality would be his reason for refusing to comply with the condition which it imposed. The nearest he comes to giving his reason is in his references to God: "I will obey God rather than you" (29D); "for know well, this is what God commands, and I think no greater good has yet befallen you in the city than my service to God" (30A). Second, this interpretation would repair one inconsistency between the *Apology* and the *Crito,* but only by opening another; for, as previously mentioned, Socrates in the latter insists that requirement to obey the law carries with it requirement to abide by the judgement of a court, however unjust it may be (50B). It cannot be said that such a judgement is illegal, for there is a law on the books specifically excluding that. And if, for reasons yet to be considered, we are morally obligated to do whatever we are legally required to do, we cannot justify disobedience to a court along the lines of the present interpretation.

(3) Can Socrates in the *Apology* passage be advancing a doctrine of natural law—that no putative law or legal requirement which is not in accordance with the commands of God is legally valid? Socrates clearly is in a position in which he finds a conflict between a supposedly valid requirement of law and the commands of God, and he clearly is saying that the commands of God are to be preferred to the commands of man. But he cannot be saying that putative legal requirements are not actually legal requirements if they are in conflict with the commands of God; for, if he were, he would be involving himself in the same inconsistency as under the previous interpretation, allowing in the *Apology* and disallowing in the *Crito* that a court order could fail to be legally valid. Socrates may have been a natural law theorist of *a* sort, but he was not one of *that* sort. We have to distinguish between appealing to the will of God in justification of disobedience to a law or legal order, and appealing to the will of God in justification of a denial that they are a law or legal order. Correspondingly, while few of us were distressed by the fate of men like Goering or Eichmann, some had misgivings about the legality of the trials.

(4) It is certain that Socrates *is* appealing to the will of God in justification of his preparedness to disobey the court, if it puts a ban on his philosophical activities. In declaring that he will undergo anything, even death, rather than submit to what is morally wrong (32A), he is adhering to the principle of the conscientious objector. What is wrong and what is illegal may coincide; and they did in the case of the decision to try *collectively* the ten admirals after the battle of Arginusae, which Socrates was the only member of the executive of the time to oppose. But they may not coincide; Socrates does not suggest that the Thirty, in instructing him to go with others to arrest Leon of Salamis, were giving an order that was illegal. But, because he was not prepared to be terrified by a powerful government into doing anything that was either *adikon* or *anhosion* (i.e., either wrong in relation to men or wrong in relation to God), he disobeyed the order (32D). This is in line with one theme in the *Crito,* viz. that, regardless of what popular opinion may say, there are no circumstances in which one should willingly do wrong; if that is so, a man should not willingly do wrong, even when he receives an order from his government to do something which in fact is wrong (49A). It perhaps does not appear to be in line with another theme in the *Crito,* viz. that a man must either do whatever his city orders him to do or must persuade her where the rightness of the matter lies (51C); and he specifically mentions a law court as an instance where this rule must hold. It is true that Socrates distinguishes between a state and the politicians who act in its name, so that he was able with a clear conscience to disobey the wicked orders of the Thirty; and again he distinguishes between the laws and the men who supposedly implement them (54C). A convicted man may (if he is able to) console himself that it was human error or evil in the application of law that brought about his conviction; the law itself was not at fault. But this does not help us, because of Socrates' insistence that it is not for a private citizen to render a court's judgement ineffective; the rule that the judgement of a court is to be effective is itself a rule of law (50B).

(5) Nevertheless, the permitted alternative to obedience, viz. persuading the laws that their order is wrong, suggests a solution to the difficulty. What in the *Apology* Socrates is prepared to do against the court is not the same as what in the *Crito* he is not prepared to do against the court. Generically, it is in both cases a

question of obedience or disobedience, but at the specific level there is a difference. In the *Apology* Socrates is not taking the line which he had the reputation of taking, namely that being divinely directed he was altogether above the law, and consequently would ignore the court's judgement, no matter what it was. It is only one possible judgement that he is prepared to disobey, namely one banning him from further philosophizing in Athens. And his disobedience will take the single form of *openly* continuing to practise philosophy the way he always has; there is no suggestion of concealment, of trying to evade the law by holding clandestine philosophical meetings. He will conduct himself exactly as he always has, pursuing the truth with anybody he meets, foreigners or citizens of Athens alike (30A). On the other hand, the disobedience to a lawful command which he is not prepared to countenance in the *Crito* is of the kind which would do violence and injury to the law, and which would be exemplified by the course of action which Crito is urging on him, viz. escape. And all disobedience to lawful commands *is* of this kind, with the single exception of attempting to *convince* the state that it is wrong in the law or command concerned. But this permitted exception to the rule of obedience is precisely what he had proposed to follow in the *Apology*. There, while insisting that he must obey God rather than the court, he made it clear that obedience to God not merely coincided with trying to convince Athens that he was right, it actually consisted in that: "I shall obey God rather than you, and, as long as I breathe and have the ability, I shall never give up philosophizing, and both exhorting you and demonstrating the truth to you" (29D).

This is civil disobedience indeed, but of the kind that stays and attempts to change minds by reason, and does not try to escape the legal consequences of doing it; not of the kind that uses violence, or tries to dodge the law by escaping. Socrates' kind of civil disobedience may be quixotic; that will depend on how ineffective in the particular circumstances the lone voice of the protester is. But such obedience is not dishonourable: as long as the protester stays within the reach of the law, no harm is done to it, and it does not suffer any disrepute—as might be the case, if a successful escape were to show its ineffectiveness. The one course other than obedience to the law and its commands which Socrates' argument in the *Crito* (51-52) permits is the one course which he had said in the *Apology* (29-30) he would, if banned from philosophy, take. Once we see that it is not the doctrine of the *Crito* that a man must always, and no matter what, obey the laws of his state, the supposed conflict between that dialogue and the *Apology* disappears.

II

Socrates' arguments in the *Crito* why he should not make a last minute escape fall into two parts: first a negative section (44B-48D) in which he convinces Crito of the inadequacy, indeed the irrelevance (48C), of the reasons which he had given why Socrates should allow his friends to organize an escape; and then a positive section (49B-54D) in which he himself gives the reasons why he should not. The two points to notice about the first section are the nature of Crito's plea, and the unsatisfactoriness of Socrates' reply to it. Although it has not always been appreciated, the reasons which Crito advances are moral ones, reasons why Socrates *ought* to agree to the escape; appeals to Socrates' sense of prudence or personal advantage would, no doubt, have been useless, and Crito sensibly makes none. (It has to be acknowledged, however, that here, as in the *Republic,* Socrates does in the end rest the case for doing what is right on its being the best policy, i.e., to the advantage of the agent [54B-C].) Crito claims (1) that Socrates owes it to his friends to escape, (a) because, if he does not, he will be depriving them of his irreplaceable friendship (44B); (b) because, if he does not, they will thereby acquire a poor public reputation: it will be generally (although incorrectly) believed that, when they could have saved him, they failed either through meanness or from fear of the risk to themselves (44C-E). (That a man should, at such a time, be concerned with his own reputation may not be morally creditable. But that does not have the consequence that the claim that a second man should consider the effect of his conduct on the first man's reputation is not a moral claim.)

(2) Crito claims that it would not be right for Socrates to throw his life away when rescue is possible, (c) because he will be allowing his enemies to achieve the very result they wanted (45C); (d) because he will be betraying his children: either people should not have children at all, or they should discharge their responsibility of bringing them up and educating them. Socrates professes to have cared for goodness all his life, yet, when given a chance to play the part of a good and courageous man, he is just taking the easiest way out (45D-E).

Of those four arguments, Socrates makes no reference at all to (a) and (c), summarily dismisses (d) as irrelevant (48C), and concentrates only on (b), his reply to which is, in fact, not a refutation of Crito's claim, but at crosspurposes with it. Summarily, his line is not to disagree with the factual element of Crito's argument, viz. that Crito and Socrates' other friends, who could have helped him escape but did not, would be condemned by popular opinion for meanness or cowardice, but to maintain that on such difficult questions as those of right and wrong one should attend not to all opinions, but only to some, namely the sound opinions of those who really know about right and wrong (46D-48A). This does not answer Crito's point, which had been that one has to pay regard to public opinion, just because of the harm it can do, regardless of whether the opinion is correct or incorrect. If the question had been, not whether a certain popular opinion was held, but whether it was either correctly or justifiably held, Socrates' objection would have been to the point. The only assertion that he makes directly counter to Crito's claim is that public opinion is so fickle that it is incapable of doing either great harm or great good (44D). This, if it were true, would be a serious objection to Cri-to, but Socrates does not pursue it. Instead he switches to his theme that one cannot expect to get a well-informed or intelligent opinion from the man in the street. But, as any politician knows who takes seriously his public responsibility, there can be circumstances in which it is more important that a certain opinion is held than that it is incorrect. That such a recognition can easily degenerate into the most sycophantic form of demagoguery is a good reason for being cautious how much weight should be given to it in a particular situation, but is not a good reason for denying it. Erroneous public opinion has to be lived with, until it can be corrected. If living with it can take the form of ignoring it, so much the better; but, as the effect of public opinion is a function, not only of what the opinion is, but also of the strength with which it is held, it cannot be right to say, with Socrates, that the *only* question is that about the correctness or justifiability of the opinion concerned. If there is a reason why public opinion ought to be ignored in the particular situation of Socrates and his friends who wish to rescue him, it must be a reason more specific to the situation, or type of situation, than that which Socrates produces himself. Injury to Crito's reputation may not be a good, let alone a good enough, reason for Socrates to agree that he *ought* to escape, but it is not totally irrelevant to it.

In the only place where Socrates even mentions Crito's argument (d), he does so to lump it together with (b) as irrelevant to the question of whether or not it would be right to make an escape (48C). Why he should have been so casual in his attitude towards parental responsibility we cannot tell. He cannot have been reflecting a general attitude of the day: there is plenty of evidence in literature to the contrary, and Crito himself had just expressed the orthodox view. One would all the more like to know what Socrates really believed here, because of the great emphasis which he was shortly going to place on the responsibility of children to their parents: a generalised form of that was one of the two grounds on which he rested the proposition that we ought to obey the law.

He has two positive arguments about why we should obey the law, both stemming from the general principle that it can never be right to do what is wrong, even in requital for wrong treatment that one has suffered (49B); and, as there is no difference between ill treatment and doing wrong, one should not give ill treatment in return for ill treatment which he has suffered (49B-C).

It appears that in talking of giving ill treatment in return for ill treatment one has received, Socrates is thinking in terms of revenge or retaliation, of the injured party getting his own back. Whether he would have thought it was also wrong in the case of retribution, or of institutionalised punishment in general, we have no means of telling. But they do need distinguishing, for it does not follow from the fact that a certain action would be wrong if performed in retaliation that an otherwise identical action would be wrong if performed in retribution. Further, conduct which would be wrong, if it were not the execution of punishment, might not be wrong, if it were. One cannot answer the question whether to deprive a man of freedom by shutting him up in a cell is wrong, without a further description of the situation, in particular of the reasons for and the purpose of shutting him up, together with the rules, if any, which applied to the situation. Descriptions can be correct or incorrect; but, because even when correct they cannot be complete, i.e., such that it would be logically impossible for anything further to be added, selection of the specific description to be used determines the moral assessment to be given. The principle that it is always wrong to give out ill treatment, even in return for ill treatment received, needs more refinement before it can be accepted as the truth which Socrates took it to be.

In order to demonstrate that one should not disobey the law, Socrates develops two arguments showing how disobedience is wrong. Neither of them is the familiar straightforward utilitarian argument that the regulation of conduct by laws provides social benefits not otherwise (as readily, at least) obtainable; but underlying both is the utilitarian consideration of the social harm produced by disobedience, that disobedience destroys laws and state (50B): the appeal is an appeal to the *consequences* of disobedience. (Producing a utilitarian justification for having a system of laws at all is not necessary to a utilitarian justification, given that we have a system of laws, of the need for obedience to them.)

In view of the fact that concepts like duty and obligation do not fit happily into the framework of Socratic or Platonic thought, it may sound paradoxical to say that Socrates' two arguments foreshadow a distinction between duty and obligation, but nevertheless it seems to be true. The first argument is that a man ought to obey the laws of his country because he owes them the kind of regard he owes to his parents (50D); the second is that he ought to obey the laws because he has undertaken to do so (51E). (Although Socrates actually formulates the arguments in the singular form, as giving the reasons why *he,* Socrates, ought to obey the laws of *Athens,* he would have to allow that, being reasons, they must be general in their application.)

Given the personification of the laws which Socrates imagines for the purposes of the discussion, the representation of them as oversized parents is not too far-fetched to be illuminating. By making it possible for people to marry, and to secure the means of rearing and educating their children, the state (which, for these purposes, is not to be distinguished from its laws) has the same kind of rights, only more so, against an individual as his human parents have. The idea that is being foreshadowed here is of something being what we ought to do because it is a duty, where duties are things a man can find himself having without having incurred them. "Duty" is characteristically a role-word, "duty as a . . . ," e.g., duty as a citizen, subject, visitor, parent, child, etc.; and more widely, when used in the plural, it refers to the tasks or jobs that go with the role. The reason why a child ought to obey and respect those who gave him life and saw him through the insecure period before he could fend for himself can have nothing to do with his having taken on a role, for it is not true that he did; they took on theirs, but he did not take on his. A citizen has the role in his native state, although he did not take it on, and with the role go certain duties. In the end, the reason why a man has certain duties towards his parents, or ought to treat them in a certain way, has to come down to some form of gratitude or return for what they have done for him. Provided that the parents/laws have performed their function satisfactorily, they have rights, Socrates thinks, over the children/subjects which the latter do not have over them (51A). Socrates' parent-laws analogy is not perfect. Although the morality of some societies may require a man to obey his parents even after he has reached adulthood and maybe become a parent himself, this is neither common nor reasonable. And he will have other duties towards them besides; indeed the duty to obey is the first, and perhaps the only one, to lapse. In the case of the law, the only duty is to obey, and it does not lapse. Nevertheless, the analogy goes far enough. By being a citizen of a country which through its laws provides him with certain advantages of security and stability a man has duties which he has in no way undertaken. And his having them does not depend on his being free to leave; he may not be, and the duties do not vanish if he is not; this is indeed part of the reason why duty and obligation need to be distinguished.

Socrates' second argument is the argument later employed in the Social Contract theory of political obligation, that a man ought to obey the law to the extent that he has given an undertaking that he will. A man ought to do whatever he has undertaken to do, provided that what he has undertaken to do is right (49E), and that the undertaking has been freely given, i.e., not extracted by either duress or fraud (52E). Undertakings can be given by actions, as well as by formal written or spoken promises (52D). A man continuing to live in a state when he is free to leave it, as Athenians were (51D), thereby gives an undertaking to obey the law, which is nonetheless a real undertaking for being silent. Here again the basis of Socrates' argument is perfectly sound. However much the notion of tacit agreement or consent may have been overworked and overstretched by later political theorists, and by politicians trying to put rebellious youth in its place, the natural citizen of a state does not fail to have, or avoid having, the obligations which the naturalized citizen of it has, merely because it is false of the former, although true of the latter, that there was a time *t* at which he formally undertook the obligations, and that he undertook them by declaring that he did. It is tempting to add that Socrates, in juxtaposing but not treating as synonyms *syntheke* and *homologia* (52D-E), was recognising the difference between mutual promises (those for which a consideration is received) and gratuitous promises (those without consideration). Some legal systems (e.g., England) recognize only the first as promises and as eligible for legal enforcement, other systems (e.g., Scotland) recognize both; in morality we recognize both. Unfortunately, so little indication is given in the *Crito* of the difference supposed between *syntheke* and *homologia,* and Plato was always, as an author, so far from being a precise technician in his choice of words, that we run the risk of ascribing to Socrates a distinction which he had never thought of.

While Socrates in effect maintained that a man ought always to perform his duty as a citizen, and always to fulfil his obligation as a contracting party, to obey the law (subject to the qualification, previously discussed, of his right to attempt to convince the law that it was in some area and in some respect wrong), that was not, for him, the end of the line. While it appears that he would have regarded the propositions that a man ought to perform his duties, and that he ought to fulfil his obligations, as necessary (thereby excluding exceptions) and as nontautologous, he did not think that no reason could be given in support of them. What he would be doing, if he allowed the escape plan to go on and render the court's verdict and sentence ineffective, would be for his part to destroy the laws and the whole city (50B). A man ought to obey the law: he has both a duty and an obligation to do so; and a challenge to either is to be met by pointing out the socially destructive consequences of disobedience.

It may be questioned whether either of Socrates' theses is tenable: (1) that a man should always obey the law; (2) that he should always obey *because* the consequences of disobedience are, or would be, socially destructive. The weakness in (2) has to be shown first, because, although, even if (2) is false, (1) might still be true, the possibility of (1) being false is thereby opened up. As long as it is accepted as true that the consequences of any disobedience to law are socially destructive, it provides a strong inducement to retain (1).

First, it should be noticed that Socrates is using a "What would happen if . . . ?" argument. And we have to distinguish more clearly than he appears to do the question what would happen if he, as a single private individual, flouted the court's decision in his particular case, from the question what would happen if court decisions were always flouted by private individuals. We can allow that universal flouting of court decisions would sooner or later destroy the whole legal system; this is to justify the requirement of wholesale obedience by appeal to the socially destructive consequences of wholesale disobedience. But the harmful consequences of a single act of disobedience by a single individual would, unless his example triggered off wider disobedience, be negligible. So, the answer to the question "What would happen if . . . ?", more specifically "What would happen by way of harm to the state and its laws if . . . ?", asked of a single act of disobedience, as asked of a single broken promise, would almost always be "Nothing." For the "What would happen if . . . ?" question to have the effect of showing that conduct, which would be wrong in the wholesale case (because it would be socially destructive), would be wrong in the single case (although it would not be socially destructive), it has to be combined with a principle of fairness or justice; if a practice of everyone behaving in a certain way is justified by the social need for it, then it is not fair to the rest for anyone to gain an advantage for himself by making an exception of himself when his doing so will not imperil the practice. Disutility is the argument against destroying the practice, or against exceptions to it which will imperil it; the argument against exceptions which will not imperil the practice has to be the unfairness of exempting oneself from a practice which is socially useful or even indispensable.

If the only argument against general disobedience were of the kind produced by Socrates, namely that it has socially destructive effects, we have to ask how far it is true that it does. There are six possibilities of some or all people disobeying some or all of the laws:

i. Some people disobey some laws.
ii. All people disobey some laws.
iii. Some laws are disobeyed by all people.
iv. All laws are disobeyed by some people.
v. Some people disobey all laws.
vi. All people disobey all laws.

(The other mathematically possible cases are, in fact, identical with i. and vi. respectively.) i. almost certainly is true of every society, and probably ii. (there is nobody of whom it is true that there is no law which he ever disobeys) is also, but neither by itself has been enough to ruin any society. In the case of iii. (there are some laws of which it is true that nobody obeys them), if the laws in question are bad ones, the consequences of universal disobedience could be, although they are not necessarily, good; the same consideration, in a weaker form, applies to i. and ii. Similarly with iv.: although it may not be a good thing if it is the case that there is no law which is not disobeyed by someone, it is not in itself disastrous. v. could be true without its being much more than a nuisance, if the number of consistent violators were small enough for the officers of the law to be able to cope with them easily. Indeed, over all the cases i.-v., whether the disobedience imperilled the law and the state would depend on the extensiveness of the "some." This is not to say that in all these cases disobedience is right, or even all right, but it is to say that in plenty of instances falling under them it could not be maintained that disobedience was wrong for Socrates' reason, viz., that such disobedience threatened the survival of the state. And it is not cynical to say that, even if it were never right for anyone to disobey any of the laws to which he was subject, it might nevertheless be a good thing if somebody occasionally did, so that the example of his conviction and sentence might discourage other potential lawbreakers.

In fact, the only case to which the argument of social disaster clearly applies is vi. Some would regard even that as questionable, asking us to imagine a through-and-through evil legal system, the destruction of which we ought to hasten as fast as we can by systematic disobedience. But against that it can be objected that a 100 per cent pernicious legal system could not exist, for it could not meet one of the necessary conditions of being a legal system, viz., that of actually regulating men's conduct. Individual laws, even wide areas of a body of law, can be pernicious, but a whole system could not be.

It might be suggested that in 50B Socrates is using a quite different line of argument from the one here criticised, and be maintaining that a state cannot survive in which anyone is free to take the law into his own hands, i.e., to decide for himself when to obey or to disobey a law, and to decide with impunity. It is far from clear that that is what he does mean; but, even if it is, it is again incomplete without the fairness principle. Granted that it is true that a state could hardly survive the practice of everybody pleasing himself when to disobey the law, this has no bearing on the individual case (given that there is no risk of its generating the practice) except through the principle of fairness.

When Socrates' thesis (1), that a man should always obey the law, is separated from thesis (2), which gave the final reason for it, and which has been shown to be untenable, it itself appears less plausible. There are, of course, reasons both of utility and of fairness both why a man should obey the law, and why he should obey a particular law. But it follows from that that it cannot be true that a man should always, and in whatever circumstances, obey the law, or a particular law. If the case for obedience rests on fairness and utility, it must be conceivable that fairness and utility would, in certain circumstances be served by disobedience. Not only is it conceivable, it is actual: the American Revolution against English colonial rule will do as an example. And, if fairness and utility can lie at all on the side of disobedience, it is conceivable that they should outweigh the claims of obedience. We may be thankful to live in a society in which duty to disobey the law appears very rarely and in very extreme circumstances, but we should remember that we live in a society which owes its origin precisely to some men seeing that as their duty and following it.

James Haden (essay date 1979)

SOURCE: "On Socrates, with Reference to Gregory Vlastos," in *The Review of Metaphysics*, Vol. XXXIII, No. 2, December, 1979, pp. 371-89.

[*Below, Haden refers to an essay by Gregory Vlastos in which Vlastos maintains that Plato's Socrates is highly reflective of the historical Socrates. Haden argues that as Plato's Socrates has "exercised the decisive influence down through the centuries," it is valuable, whether or not one agrees with Vlastos, to examine Vlastos's conclusions and test them for their "adequacy." Haden goes on to fault Vlastos for measuring Socrates "by a New Testament model."*]

I

In his essay "The Paradox of Socrates,"[1] Gregory Vlastos paints a vivid and moving portrait of Socrates, or, as he puts it: "the Platonic Socrates, or, to be more precise, the Socrates of Plato's early dialogues."[2] That the man who emerges from these early dialogues is something very like the actual Socrates is Vlastos's opinion. He argues, with great plausibility, that the Xenophontic Socrates is not a man who, on the one hand, could have provoked the Athenians into indicting him and convicting him for subversion of Athenian faith and morals, and on the other could have aroused the devotion of an Alcibiades. The question of the "authentic" Socrates is the kind of question which simply does not admit of any ultimate solution, so there will always be divergent opinions, but regardless of whether or not Plato does portray the real Socrates as he knew him, it is certainly the Platonic Socrates who has exercised the decisive influence down through the centuries. Therefore irrespective of whether one accepts Vlastos's argument (and I for one do), it is worthwhile examining what Vlastos distills from the dialogues as his "recreation of the thought and character of the man,"[3] and testing it for its adequacy.

The Socrates of the dialogues has from the beginning fascinated, both attracting and repelling. He fascinates because we can feel that Plato has given us a *man,* not just a doctrine; it is the moral force of this Socrates which will not leave us alone. Vlastos acts rightly, then, in trying to probe to the heart of this singular character. What he believes he finds there is a living paradox. "Other philosophers have talked *about* paradox," he says. "Socrates did not. The paradox in Socrates is Socrates."[4] Perhaps this is true; certainly the Platonic Socrates is enigmatic, but is he a paradox?

What is the paradox which Vlastos believes he sees? It is the puzzle of a Socrates who says, with total sincerity, that "the care of the soul is the most important thing in the world, and that his mission in life is to get others to see this," and at the same time a Socrates who, in his mission and his labor, is not shown as

> saying anything about the improvement of the soul, nor acting as though he cared a straw for the improvement of his interlocutor's soul, but . . . simply arguing with him, forcing him into one corner after another, until it [becomes] plain to all the bystanders, if not the man himself, that his initial claim to know this or that was ridiculously false.[5]

That is to say, here is a man whose deepest concern is the care of the soul, who acts every minute out of that concern, and yet one whose actions are at best futile and at worst destructive. How an "evangelist" for the inner worth of each individual can knowingly and deliberately destroy those whom he evangelizes is the problem which troubles Vlastos.

Certainly Vlastos is pointing inexorably to an aspect or interpretation of Socrates which is enormously widespread. The normal initial reaction of the tyro in philosophy on reading his first Socratic dialogue is a revulsion from the pitiless inquisition that Plato shows us. As Vlastos confesses, the passages in which Socrates says that in these inquisitions he is really searching himself just as pitilessly[6] were originally and for a long time taken by him as simply ironic, so unprepared was he for such candid self-revelation. Socrates deflating the ego-balloons of his interlocutors with the rapier of his intelligence at the same time pinks our own egos, and we are all too likely to react defensively by attributing to him not humility, but an egotism equal to or greater than our own.

But Vlastos reveals his own considerable stature in coming to accept that Socrates really did have this aspect of humility, and thereby he arrives at a solution of the paradox which satisfies him. It is that for Socrates "knowledge" is taken in so strong a sense that one can only claim to *know* when "any further investigation . . . would be superfluous."[7] Like Parmenides, Socrates must have believed that the conclusion of a rational deductive argument should have the "same certainty as that which the devotees of mystic cults would attach to the poems of Orpheus or of some other divinely inspired cult."[8] Since Socrates is only human, and realizes that fact, no conclusion of his can be ultimate: not only does one need to keep "reexamining previously reached conclusions, it is not less a matter of hoping for new insights which may crop up right in this next argument and give the answer to some hitherto unanswered problem."[9]

Holding fast to this view of Socrates as eternal seeker, we can see that in his role of preacher he wants others to discover for themselves; in his role of teacher he offers a method of reaching conclusions and constantly testing and revising them; as critic he demonstrates his method by using it; as agnostic his "'I don't know' is a conscientious objection to the notion that the conclusions of any discussion are secure against further testing by further discussion."[10] And thus, Vlastos concludes, it is Socrates the searcher who unifies all the other roles.

This result seems harmless enough, and indeed quite conventional, but is seems to me that Vlastos has not really solved his paradox. If indeed Socrates is thinking along Parmenidean lines, and if his model of knowledge is deduction leading to absolute certainty as powerful as mystical intuition, then it is hard to see just how and why Socrates would regard the conclusions he reaches as forever open to revision; Parmenides surely did not. We might say that Vlastos's mention of the hope of stumbling on new insights points to the corrective deductive arrogance, but what Vlastos gives with one hand, he takes away with the other. For he says later:

> The knowledge which he sought, and with such marked success, is that which consists in arranging, whatever information one has in a luminous, perspicuous pattern, so one can see at a glance where run the bright lines of implication and where the dark ones of contradiction. But of the other way of knowing, the empirical way, Socrates had little understanding, and he paid for his ignorance by conceit of knowledge, failing to understand the limitations of his knowledge of fact generally, and of the fact of knowledge in particular.[11]

This seems a strange assertion, in the face of what has been said before. Instead of being a truly honest seeker, Socrates is now marked by "conceit of knowledge"; instead of hoping for fresh insights, he is now ignorant of empirical knowledge. The solution of the original paradox appears to have generated a new one. Vlastos's description does fit Parmenides, but does it fit Socrates except by cutting him to fit a Parmenidean, if not a Procrustean, bed?

We might make one last try at accepting Vlastos's interpretation by saying that the secret of Socrates is his simultaneous submission to the lofty, uncompromising ideal of logical cognitive certainty and to his recognition of his fallible humanity which forever prevents him from achieving absolute knowledge. But this leads us into an estimate of Socrates' character and his particular human qualities and constitution. That is a very difficult and obscure region, and it will be necessary to deal with it at considerable length, which is done in part 2 below.

How are we to account for this apparent inconsistency in the thought of someone as acute as Vlastos? There are two parts to the answer to this problem, I think. The second, and more profound part will be considered later, but the first and simpler part is Vlastos's easy and unqualified acceptance of the orthodox modern dichotomy between logical and empirical knowledge, exemplified in the quotation above. Even if we were to add in a third mode of knowledge, the mystical mode, which is at least suggested in Vlastos's earlier mention of the "devotees of mystical cults," we have not got enough to work with. Socrates is clearly not a mystic, though he does have reverence for something which may lie beyond reason itself; to a careless eye this reverence might look like mysticism. His clarity of intellect tempers that tendency, just as the latter in turn tempers his logicality so that he is not merely a logician. But does he or does he not recognize the claims of empiricism? Here a great deal depends on what class or classes of empirical facts Vlastos might be thinking of. Simply to speak of "empirical fact" suggests knowledge of the external world, where empiricism has its strongest claim and where its success lends authority to that method.

But in point of fact, Vlastos is talking about Socrates as a moralist, and hence we are not speaking of the external world and of nature, but about qualities like courage, self-control, piety, and so on. Therefore we are not at all in the realm of natural science, and "empirical fact" may have a radically different sense.

The evidence Vlastos brings forward for Socrates' ignorance of empiricism in the moral realm is, curiously enough, scanty. He says: "the bravest man I ever met would surely have flunked the Socratic examination on courage . . . a man may have great courage, yet make a fool of himself when he opens his mouth to explain what it is that he has."[12] And further:

> Aunt Rosie is afraid of mice, but she knows quite well that a mouse can do her no great harm. . . . This is absurd, but it happens; and her knowing that it is absurd does not prevent it from happening either, but only adds shame and guilt to fear. This is not evidence of a high order; it is just a *fact* that does not square with Socrates' theory.[13]

It is almost embarrassing to see these arguments, for surely Vlastos cannot seriously have supposed that

Socrates was unaware of these "facts." In the *Laches,* there is no reason to suppose that Socrates is ignorant that both Laches and Nicias are far from cowardly men in battle, though they wither under his cross-examination. Vlastos would seem to be suggesting that Socrates' claim is that *unless* one can clearly and thoroughly explain oneself verbally, one cannot be courageous in any sense at all, which is a proposition Socrates would surely have repudiated flatly.

The two propositions: (1) "If one cannot give a clear, precise verbal account of courage then one is not courageous" and (2) "If one is courageous then one can give a clear, precise account of courage" are in an abstract way logical equivalents, but perhaps here we are not dealing with abstractions, but instead with the complexities of how people really are. Both (1) and (2) are logically different from (3): "If one can give a clear, precise account of courage then one is courageous," and it almost seems as if Vlastos is thinking of (3) in the Aunt Rosie case, as refuting Socrates. She knows in a way that mice are harmless, but still acts as though they are not; she could give an account of what it would be like to act fearlessly in the presence of mice, yet in her actual behavior she is not courageous.

But Vlastos seems to believe that the empirical cases of Aunt Rosie and the tongue-tied man of courage refute Socrates, though he is oblivious to that since he ignores or does not appreciate facts. Although Aunt Rosie does not appear to figure in the dialogues (the early ones, at least, for Leontius the son of Aglaion in *Republic* 4, 439E-440A may be her nephew), at the common-sense level it is hard to hold seriously that no Greek, man or woman, sister, cousin, or aunt ever found himself or herself in Aunt Rosie's condition. And if there were in ancient Athens sufferers from fears which run counter to intellectual recognition, then it is very nearly certain that Socrates had known some of them or at least about them. He would not have to be reborn in our own day to discover this "fact."

So we can reasonably assume it *was* known to him that there are people who hold one proposition, such as "mice are terrifying," with their gut, so to speak, and a contradictory one, "mice are not terrifying," with their head. Yet in the face of this, Socrates still held fast to the doctrine that virtue is knowledge, and that he who knows cannot do otherwise than act consistently with that knowledge. Similarly, he knew experimentally that there are people who can honestly be called "courageous" who can readily be tied in verbal knots when asked to explain what courage is. The courage is in their gut, and they act from that; in contrast, there are highly verbal people who speak brilliantly about courage, but turn tail in the face of real danger.[14]

It looks, then, as though Vlastos is on very shaky ground in locating the basis of Socrate's supposed error in his blindness or indifference to empirical fact. "What Socrates called 'knowledge' he thought both necessary and sufficient for moral goodness," Vlastos says. "I think it neither."[15] The courageous man shows it not to be necessary, and Aunt Rosie tells us it is not sufficient. But what if the solution to the problem of how so perceptive and intelligent a man as Socrates could be so stupid lies rather in Vlastos's own mistake about what knowledge might be? Let us examine this for a little while.

Vlastos recognizes but two kinds of cognition: logical deduction and empirical observation, and for him these are radically distinct. It is clear that he is speaking as a man of his own time, for this dichotomy is nothing more nor less than Hume's distinction between relations of ideas and matters of fact. But despite the contemporary orthodoxy of that dichotomy, is it impossible to ask whether it must be taken as exhaustive and as definitive of knowledge itself? To be confident that we have arrived at a view which is absolute and final is always perilous, and especially perilous when our acceptance of it has become habitual and virtually subliminal. Therefore I suggest that we take a provisional attitude toward this dichotomy, not rejecting it but rather being open to the possibility of modifying it or supplementing it by attention to insights of major thinkers. Certainly for Kant the bare Humean analytic-synthetic division was inadequate, and there is no a priori reason why Plato may not have had insights denied to Hume's Enlightenment mentality.

In the area of morals, in particular, we must tread softly, because it is far less plain and clear than that of natural science. What works well for the latter may be inappropriate for the former, because too crude. It is not easy to say what a moral "fact" might be, in comparison with a sensory fact. If the moral facts are feelings, then they are private and inaccessible to objective observation, not to mention their indefiniteness. If moral facts are moral principles, then they are surely not objectively necessary in anything like the sense that a natural law is, nor are they pragmatically verifiable in the way that, say, the principle of conservation of energy is. And it does not seem to be the case that Vlastos would rest content with the claim that moral principles are no more than subjective and relative.

Aunt Rosie's overt behavior regarding mice is publicly observable, but the inner struggles she experiences are not nor are the guilt and shame brought on her by her fears. The true grounds of a man's courage are also inward; no amount of public observation of his courageous actions will reveal them. What the foundation of his courage in fact is, is for him alone to try to detect internally.

Knowledge is also something ultimately internal; it would be very odd to say that a computer "knows" something in a sense truly comparable to human cognition. There is no way, for instance, to talk of a computer having or lacking a sense of certainty about any of the information stored in it. It is the case that if one accepts the dichotomy that Vlastos does, then he slips over toward the assimilation of mind to computer, and is inclined to reject such things as a "sense of certainty" as a dispensable subjective adjunct to knowledge. Yet the analogy does start with our personal awareness of mind, and the sense of certainty is one guide to what knowledge is. In any case, the delicacy of the workings of the mind is extreme, and to date no one has definitively solved the problem of the true relation between mind and overt behavior.

Yet this last is precisely the dark area which Socrates and Plato are exploring. Whether or not one might conclude that they are right in their approach and results, it is advisable to regard what Plato put into the dialogues with respect and restraint, in the expectation that at the very least he and Socrates, being the exceptional thinkers they were, may well have something to say which is important, even if it runs counter to modern epistemological orthodoxy.

This is not the place to offer a full analysis and interpretation of the Socratic-Platonic theory of knowledge, which would of necessity be lengthy. The point that does need to be made, however, it this: the modern view assumes that the mind is a self-contained instrument of cognition, distinct from the rest of the psyche. In empirical knowledge, it is assumed that the mind comes to be inscribed with information from outside which it previously lacked. This schema works nicely with sensory information, at least to a first approximation, but in the case of morality it immediately becomes highly problematical and obscure. Is there a sort of moral "perception" exactly parallel to sensory perception? If morality is a matter of observable fact, are we observing others or ourselves? Self-scrutiny introduces complications beyond those of neutral observation of others.

But suppose that we bracket the assumption that the mind, in its rationally moral operations, is something self-contained and apart. We might then speak of moral knowledge as more a certain state of one's *whole* being or self, instead of as a particular kind of operation on the part of one portion of the self, the intellect. This is naturally an enormously difficult insight to put clearly and simply into words, and we should not expect to see it laid out neatly in the early dialogues. It can be argued that it does begin to emerge in the middle and late dialogues, which are more Platonic than Socratic, but a case can be made for finding it in a crude and archaic form in Parmenides. In fact, it may be this aspect of Parmenides, not the one Vlastos points to, which links Socrates to him.

If something like this is plausible, then the precise relation and function of logical clarity in the achievement of such a state of being must be explored, and perhaps this is exactly what Socrates is engaged in. For the modern philosopher, logic is just a tool and not anything charged with moral significance, a trend already setting in with Aristotle. But if logical lucidity is something which pervades or can pervade the entire self, then it must be connected with the desired state of being which is cognition in a peculiarly intimate way. To clarify this, we must briefly examine Socratic elenchus.

Vlastos's attitude toward elenchus is ambivalent. I have already quoted above his description of Socrates' rough and merciless treatment of his interlocutors in the agora (or anywhere else), and he adopts Nietzsche's characterization of Socrates as "this despotic logician" with approval. Yet on the other hand, he praises the Socratic method as "among the greatest achievements of humanity,"[16] and correctly points out that it "calls not only for the highest degree of mental alertness of which anyone is capable, but also for moral qualities of a high order: sincerity, humility, courage,"[17] which surely is not how one would characterize proving theorems in modern symbolic logic. Although in the essay he does not analyze the process of elenchus in detail, he does as editor reprint two chapters on elenchus from Richard Robinson's book, *Plato's Earlier Dialectic,*[18] and the reasonable assumption is that he concurs in general with what Robinson says.

Robinson quite explicitly treats Socrates simply as logician, as even a quick scrutiny of his book will show. He is, he believes, discussing dialectic in general and elenchus in particular as a chapter in the evolution of logic as such.[19] Placing himself firmly at the logician's vantage point, he rapidly finds himself led into moral judgments similar to those of Vlastos about Socrates at work. Socrates' claim that it is the logos that is doing the refuting, not he, and that he is simply following the argument, not guiding it toward a concealed, predetermined end, are to Robinson flatly "insincere," and this constitutes "what is known as the Socratic slyness or irony." In fact, "Socrates seems prepared to employ any kind of deception in order to get people into this elenchus."[20]

Further, elenchus as practiced by Socrates has vicious effects: it bewilders the respondent; it makes its victims "angry with Socrates and ill disposed towards him"; it can make "old friends quarrel"; and it amuses young men so that they "treat it as a game and imitate it in and out of season."[21] "Destructive and insincere [it] involved persistent hypocrisy; it showed a negative and destructive spirit; it caused pain to its victims; it thereby made them enemies of Socrates; it thereby brought him to trial . . . ; and so it brought him to his death." In the face of which, unaccountably, Socrates persevered in it.

Why did he? Robinson asks. According to the *Apology,* it is "to make men better men, to give them more of the highest virtue of a man." Yet in the opinion of many, this technique "would seem a most unsuitable instrument for moral education. They would argue that such logic-chopping cannot be followed by most persons, does not command respect, and at best improves only the agility of the mind while leaving the character untouched."[23]

Not only that, as logic it is seriously defective. "By addressing itself always to this person here and now, elenchus takes on particularity and accidentalness, which are defects. In this respect it is inferior to the impersonal and universal and rational march of a science axiomatized according to Aristotle's prescription."[24] Even Plato eventually came to realize as much, Robinson thinks, for in the middle dialogues "elenchus changes into dialectic, the negative into the positive, pedagogy into discovery, morality into science."[25] All of which is for the better, he seems to believe.

These last judgments of Robinson's give us a good guide to what needs to be said about elenchus. In the first place, its particularity is a defect *only* if we see knowledge as totally impersonal, a metallic instrument brought into play at will, which Robinson, in agreement with modern epistemology, does believe. If, however, we regard knowledge as a moral act of some important kind, then this particularity is instead a merit. For there can be no such thing as an impersonal morality, which is not to say that there is no such thing as a general morality. Personal morality is not subjective relativism, but rather a way in which the individual looks at himself as individual from the perspective of all mankind. This scrutiny must be thoroughly internalized; it is fatal to any genuine morality to see its universality as imposed from outside, through divine or social regulations, for example. Therefore the individual must within himself be able to fuse the personal and particular with the universal into a perfect union. The enormous difficulty of this is testified to by the age-long failure of all save a very few of us to accomplish that fusion.

In knowledge, as Socrates and Plato saw it, precisely the same requirement must be met, and equal difficulties are to be encountered. When Socrates discovered his mission of convincing others that they did not know what they thought they knew, what he discovered was that in most or all people there is a split between the self or ego and what the ego thinks it possesses in the way of knowledge. That is, the ego takes its knowledge to be something it *has,* not something it *is.* Knowledge on this view, which is the modern one, is like money: one has it or one doesn't. When one has it, one can either retain it or spend it, but in either case it is something in itself, residing loosely in a pocket and not integral with the person.

The effect of this is to allow the ego to bloat in proportion to the amount of coin possessed. Those who think they know in this fashion, regarding themselves as essentially separate from the knowledge they own, have no check on this bloating of the ego; cognitive wealth is used as a screen against the shock of any assault on the swollen ego. The result is a kind of immorality of cognition, akin to the pharisaical pride of those who take themselves to be spiritually and morally worthier than their fellows. This application of moral terms to cognition undoubtedly rings peculiarly in modern ears, but that is not the question: the issue is whether it would have sounded odd to Socrates.

If we can accept, then, that for Socrates there is a morality of cognition, it seems at least plausible that there is also a cognition of morality. That is not, as it may appear, a mere play on words; if knowledge is indeed something which at its highest and best must and does engage the whole soul, the same is true of morality. Therefore at its peak each becomes the other: the true is identical with the good. We seem, therefore, to have come in sight of what Socrates and Plato were trying to say in identifying knowledge and virtue, and it appears that Vlastos himself generated his paradox by an inadequate understanding of Socratic elenchus.

II

Thus far we have been talking about one aspect of what Vlastos regards as Socrates' "failure"; it is the intellectual side. Vlastos believes that Socrates was wrong about knowledge being necessary and sufficient for moral goodness, because, in Vlastos's eyes, he is wrong about knowledge. But the argument has been that it is Vlastos who is wrong about knowledge, not Socrates, and wrong because his view is too limited. Since it is, Vlastos says that Socrates owed his courage in the face of death to something "more akin to religious faith."[26] The argument here has not had to resort to faith, but now we will show in what sense Vlastos's appeal to religion may be indicative.

He has an even graver charge than failure of knowledge to lay at Socrates' door. Behind this "failure of knowledge," according to Vlastos, "lay a failure of love."[27] Even though Socrates does honestly care for the souls of others,

> the care is limited and conditional. If men's souls are to be saved, they must be saved his way. And when he sees they cannot, he watches them go down the road to perdition with regret but without anguish.

> Jesus wept for Jerusalem. Socrates warns Athens, scolds, exhorts it, condemns it. But he has no tears for it. . . . One feels there is a last zone of frigidity in the soul of the great erotic; had he loved his fellows more, he could hardly have laid on them the burdens of his "despotic logic," impossible to be borne.[28]

The pure logician may not see this as a particularly overwhelming charge; the technical faults he attributes to Socrates' reasoning may loom much larger. But Vlastos is more than a logician, and it is clear that he himself is agonizingly torn between his love for Socrates and this terrible judgment on him. We should attend to what Vlastos is saying.

But is he right? Indeed, Socrates does constantly warn, scold, exhort, and condemn Athens, but is his heart frigid? Does he feel no anguish, because he weeps no tears? Can we take that as definitive evidence that he felt nothing which in others would have taken the form of tears? Here we are necessarily in the uncertain realms of interpretation, where the kind of lantern one carries makes a great deal of difference to what one sees. Therefore we must examine Vlastos's perspective as best we can.

One thing should be clear from the first part of this paper: because Vlastos has difficulty construing the Socratic idea of knowledge as a function of one's whole soul, he in fact is tending, like the general public of Athens, to assimilate him to the sophists. They were men for whom the intellect and its activities were everything, and the rest, including love for one's native land and fellow men, nothing. But Socrates was not, like them, rootless; his intelligence was deeply and fruitfully rooted in the rich soil of feeling.

That may seem an extravagant statement to make, since when one reads the dialogues, one is blinded by Socrates' verbal and intellectual brilliance. Like the man who has escaped from the cave, in the *Republic,* one is at first unable to percieve the reality of this other side of Socrates. And if one becomes firmly persuaded that Socrates is first and foremost a logician, then one is unlikely ever to notice an apparently casual remark such as the one Socrates drops passingly into his comments to Phaedrus about the interpretation of myths and legends. He says:

> Consequently I don't bother about such things, but accept the current beliefs about them and direct my inquiries, as I have just said, rather to myself, to discover whether I really am a more complex creature and more puffed up with pride than Typhon, or a simpler, gentler being whom heaven has blessed with a quiet, un-Typhonic nature. By the way, isn't this the tree we were making for?[29]

If we read this passage unwarily and insensitively, we are easily misled by the cool, even bantering tone of what precedes it and the offhandedness of the final sentence. Socrates' concern with self-knowledge seems a distant, abstract relation to himself, as though he were some kind of impersonal zoologist of the soul. But this is precisely the way someone who felt very deeply but who had no interest in wearing his heart on his sleeve *would* express himself—making a confession and then diverting attention from it. Vlastos has admitted that for a long while he took Socrates' claims to be truly inquiring and to be himself at the mercy of the dialectic as mere artful irony, but has come to see them as genuine self-revelation. Similarly here. What Socrates is revealing is a genuine anguish over comprehending himself rightly, an anguish which is likely to be even more terrible than anguish over others felt by someone who sees himself as morally righteous and the other headed for perdition.

This self-anguish is in fact of a piece with true anguish over others; when one feels this way about himself, then one's relations with others are radically altered by that feeling. Through it, one is most intimately connected with the confusions and the conscious or unconscious sufferings of others. Kierkegaard warned, scolded, and condemned Copenhagen as Socrates did Athens; surely no one would accuse him of coldness toward others, and it is just this self-anguish, revealed on in his private journals, which provides his link to other people and also bound Kierkegaard to Socrates.

Vlastos seems almost to be attributing to Socrates something resembling the twentieth-century attitude expressed by Ernst Jünger, in his essay *Über den Schmerz.*[30] Jünger held that in our time (he was writing in the 1920s) man has moved into what he called "a second and coldest consciousness," forced to do so for self-preservation in the face of a disintegrating world and the loss of values.

> Instead of using his personal judgment as derived from his own experiences, wisdom, and values, instead of trying to resolve his situation independently in his unique fashion . . . and in some way acknowledging the legitimacy of his suffering and unhappiness, he will analyze himself by means of pre-established psychological and sociological categories—he will manipulate himself as a psycho- or socio-clinical case. Thus he makes himself into an object visualized by an alien transpersonal eye.[31]

This is the contemporary logico-scientific way, but it is not the Socratic way, even though Socrates too lived in an age of disintegration.

True, Socrates did hide behind a mask; so did Kierkegaard. Behind that mask there is no frozen zone, no "coldest consciousness." But was there love? It is very difficult to deal with Vlastos's charge since he makes no effort to tell us what he apprehends love, as he uses that term, to be. It might seem self-contradictory to accuse the "great erotic" of lacking love, but Vlastos does make one revelatory statement: "The best insight in this essay—that Socrates' ultimate failure is a failure in love—grew out of what [he] learned about love" from his wife.[32] The statement is tantalizing, and it would be wrong to wring it mercilessly for it is enormously touching. But it may be significant that Vlastos says his knowledge of love grew out of a conjugal situation. Certainly that is highly un-Greek; the whole of ancient Greek culture, as Vlastos knows, went against the idealization of that sort of relationship, though love in marriage was not unknown. Achilles and Patroclus are more germane models.

But there are special factors in love between man and woman which are normally absent from other forms of love: not the sexual aspect, for in Athens that could be satisfied between males, but rather a special kind of tenderness which flowers between male and female. If one were to look for that kind of tenderness, then, in Socrates going about his daily activities, one surely would not find it. Such tenderness is the precious gift of woman, and it is not a significant factor in a masculine culture such as that of ancient Greece. But I wish to argue that there is another kind of tenderness, and it is one which Socrates does possess. It is a tenderness for others simply as human beings, laboring in their human condition. If Socrates does lay on them a "despotic logic," he lays it also on himself, and it is not impossible to be borne, for he bears it.

Some further clues as to Vlastos's conception of love can be found in an essay postdating "The Paradox of Socrates" by over ten years.[33] Here Vlastos cites with approval Aristotle's definition of *philia,* which in its strongest sense can be translated "love," as "wishing for someone what you believe to be good things—wishing this not for your own sake but for his—and acting so far as you can to bring them about," which is on its face an essentially altruistic view of *philia.* When Vlastos applies this definition to the *Lysis,* which has *philia* as its subject, he concludes that Socratic love is at its heart egoistic. That perspective, he says,

> becomes unmistakable when Socrates, generalizing, argues that "if one were in want of nothing, one would feel no affect, . . . and he who felt no affection would not love." The lover Socrates has in view seems positively incapable of loving others for their own sake,[34]

which, for Vlastos, is the central characteristic of love truly conceived.[35]

Leaving aside the question frequently raised as to the egoism of Aristotle's own view of *philia* if we examine it whole, since he says that friendship and love for others derives from friendship and love for oneself, are we entitled to dismiss the Socratic position so offhandedly? In the first place, we cannot take Socrates' words which Vlastos quotes as necessarily expressing what Socrates and/or Plato did hold with regard to friendship; Vlastos does not appear to understand the *Lysis* very well. But further, one thing Plato (and undoubtedly Socrates also) knew and knew well: whenever one is dealing with one's feelings, there is immense latitude for error. Professed altruism is all too often a socially acceptable mask for unconscious egotism. He who proclaims his concern for others may be either sentimentalizing—as in the case of the "altruist" who finds it far easier to love mankind as an abstraction than to love the sweaty, cantankerous, ignorant, concrete individuals who compose it—and sentimentality is a kind of caressing one's own emotions; or else he may be projecting onto the others some unadmitted internal anxieties and problems of his own, too afraid to search and cleanse his own soul but too guilty not to attack the problems in some impersonal guise.

The antidote to this sort of error lies in what Iris Murdoch says (drawing on some suggestions by Simone Weil):

> The love which brings the right answer [to moral problems] is an exercise of justice and realism and really *looking.* The difficulty is to keep the attention fixed upon the real situation and to prevent it returning surreptitiously to the self with consolations of self-pity, resentment, fantasy, and despair. . . . Of course virtue is good habit and dutiful action. But the background condition of such good habit and such action, in human beings, is a just mode of vision and a good quality of consciousness. It is a *task* to come to see the world as it is.[36]

In other words, sentimentality or objectified self-concern can blind us; only a tough-minded clarity of vision of what is, *as* it is—and that must needs include ourselves—can serve us rightly in sound moral action as based on love. To attain that clarity is the task set us by Socrates, who first set it to himself.

But would not genuine love for others require that we not always lay on them what we ourselves bear, since they may be unable to follow us? Vlastos cites the example of Jesus weeping for Jerusalem, but Jesus also said, "This is my commandment, that ye love one another, as I have loved you." The evidence of the ages might seem to tell us that this also is something many, perhaps most, human beings have in fact found it impossible to bear, yet I doubt that Vlastos would therefore say that it did not show love. To command others to love appears a paradox, since love cannot be commanded. The Socratic way is not command; his whole method, as Vlastos himself admits, rests on a "vision of man as a mature, responsible being, claiming to the fullest extent his freedom to make his own choice between right and wrong, not only in action, but in judgment."[37] That is well and truly spoken, and it characterizes Socrates himself; it is not a logic that he confronts others with, to their discomfiture: it is a *man* who embodies these qualities, not a mere vision, in the hope that they can summon the strength to be likewise. When they fail, he sees them fail with regret, of course, but also with anguish at their failure to be free.

Love, if it is to be love, must always leave the other free or potentially free, whatever the power and the intimacy of the bond, and the Socratic way does this, preserving the vitality and the personality of freedom, whatever the seductions of the cold, "impersonal and universal and rational march of a science axiomatized according to Aristotle's prescription," which is indeed logical despotism.

The concrete human personality is always somehow greater than abstract logic, and therefore must not lose itself therein; this is the lesson of Socratic elenchus. Euthyphro commending himself for being so elevated in his thinking that he can pursue justice even though it requires that he prosecute his father (*Euthyphro* 3E-4B), and the clownish sophists of the *Euthydemus* illustrate two ways in which excessive regard for logic can dehumanize. But personality revenges itself inexorably, because such logicizing of oneself turns out to be the tool of ego, hiding behind the mask of logical impersonality.

The paradox is that reason as suprahuman must be reverenced if we are to be truly human; the *Euthyphro* tells us that too. But the reverence must not be for something construed as seated in a far-off empyrean realm, like the gods whom Euthyphro worships, but rather for reason which is integral to all of us as human; a one-story universe must replace the two-story one and the divine be secularized within man himself. So man is both man in the sense of an individual personality, and something more than man: the locus of reason. In reverencing reason, man reverences himself also, and this reverence is true humility, Socratic humility.

So Socrates could honestly say that he was following where the argument led and that *logos* was doing the refuting. At the same time his reverence for reason allowed full scope to his own personality in all its aspects, because its chastening presence prevented domination by an inflated ego. The mystery of how one's personality can reach its fullest flower only when one accepts something greater than self as an integral part of that self is not one soluble by Humean methods.

Such a person is a remarkable one, and a sign of this is the love which Plato himself bore for Socrates. He felt the full power and complexity of Socrates' personality, and loved him. But no one can be truly loved who cannot love; it is impossible to believe that Plato would not have sensed the ice in Socrates' heart, if Vlastos were right, and perhaps admired him but refrained from loving him. It is entirely trivial and beside the point that Socrates never wept, so far as we know, though this strikes Vlastos as exemplary evidence of Socrates' defect. That is merely a matter of an individual style, and Plato has shown us Socrates'. It is flatly false that tears are the only mark of genuine affection; Socrates did in fact lay down his life not only for himself but also for others, and there is no greater love.

Nor is his educational technique evidence of lack of love. This passage, though it was written with no reference to Socrates whatsoever, still sums up the quality of the Socratic teaching style beautifully:

> After all, we exist in love and anger, so let us admit it; only let the love be proper to the occasion, a sending out of tenderness from an inviolable soul, not a yearning for a completion *out* of the other; and let the anger be a "sharp, fierce reaction: sharp discipline, rigour; fierce, fierce severity" to rouse the child and bring him to his soul's pride.[38]

There is love at the heart of Socrates, much love, but it is just this marriage of tenderness with ferocity and rigor; it is love without softness. It is a mistake to measure him by a New Testament model, as Vlastos evidently does. Closer and truer models are Homer's virile Achilles and wily Odysseus, both of whom loved in characteristically Greek ways, but still Socrates is always uniquely himself.

Nor is it just to refract him through the prisms of any academic categories, be they Humean or Parmenidean. That is learned idiocy. The special glory of Plato's portrait is that it gives us a human being, and categories are made for human beings, not human beings for categories. We must approach that human being as we should any other, and as Socrates himself encountered his contemporaries: unsparingly active and searching, but still with a tempering reverence for what it is to be a human being, in our own person or in that of any other. The greatest *hubris* of all is to try to reduce his stature to our own: Socrates will always be the test of us, not we of him.

Notes

[1] Gregory Vlastos, ed., *The Philosophy of Socrates: A Collection of Critical Essays* (Garden City, N.Y.: Doubleday & Co., 1971), pp. 1-21.

[2] Ibid., p. 1.

[3] Ibid., p. 3.

[4] Ibid., p. 4.

[5] Ibid., p. 9.

[6] He cites *Protagoras* 348C and *Charmides* 166C-D and 165B.

[7] Vlastos, p. 10.

[8] Ibid.

[9] Ibid., p. 11.

[10] Ibid., p. 12.

[11] Ibid., p. 16.

[12] Ibid., p. 15.

[13] Ibid., pp. 15-16.

[14] Though the case was not available to Plato, one might think of Aristotle abandoning Athens after Alexander's death, having written in the *Nicomachean Ethics* that the greatest and noblest form of courage is to endure in the face of death, justifying his flight as depriving Athens of an opportunity to "sin twice against philosophy."

[15] Vlastos, p. 15.

[16] Ibid., p. 20.

[17] Ibid.

[18] 2d ed. (Oxford: At the Clarendon Press, 1953).

[19] See, for example, p. vi in *Plato's Earlier Dialectic,* which is not reprinted by Vlastos. Hereafter, page references will be both to the chapters as reprinted and to the entire second edition as cited in the preceding note; references to the former will be placed in parentheses following the references to the latter.

[20] Ibid., pp. 8-9 (79-81).

[21] Ibid., pp. 9-10 (81-82).

[22] Ibid.

[23] Ibid., p. 14 (86-87).

[24] Ibid., p. 16 (89).

[25] Ibid., p. 19 (93).

[26] Vlastos, p. 16.

[27] Ibid.

[28] Ibid., pp. 16-17.

[29] *Phaedrus* 230A; R. Hackforth trans.

[30] A brilliant concise account of Jünger's analysis can be found in Erich Kahler, *The Tower and the Abyss: An Inquiry Into the Transformation of the Individual* (New York: George Braziller, Inc., 1957), pp. 85-93.

[31] Ibid., pp. 91-92.

[32] Vlastos, preface, n.p.

[33] *"The Individual as Object of Love in Plato,"* in Gregory Vlastos, *Platonic Studies* (Princeton: Princeton University Press, 1973), which he notes began as an address in 1957.

[34] *Platonic Studies,* pp. 8-9.

[35] Some additional light may be shed by Vlastos's contribution to a volume which he coedited with R. B. Y. Scott in 1936, entitled *Towards the Christian Revolution* (Chicago and New York: Willet, Clark & Co). All the contributors apparently felt that in the social turmoil of the 1930s the time was ripe for the actualization of Christianity in society; Vlastos's essay concludes: "The Kingdom of God is at hand. Repent ye, and believe the gospel," a note sounded by various other contributors.

It is the ethic of Christian love which Vlastos says needs to be instituted, which he interprets as the ethic of the cooperative community. Plato's presumed disdain for and dismissal of the lower classes is contrasted with the Biblical insistence on their superior worth. Scorning a merely sentimental notion of love, he says: "The sense of love is genuine when it refers to that cooperative community in which my labor is necessary to your interest and your labor to mine. The fact of love is not the consciousness of love, any more than the fact of life is the consciousness of life. If love exists at all, it exists as a material activity: the material interaction of separate beings recognizing each other's interests and seeking common fulfillment." (p. 59.) He is using "material" in the sense of "economic," as Marx did, but perhaps it is ironic that if we substitute "educational" we have a not inaccurate description of Socratic inquiry.

[36] *The Sovereignty of Good* (London: Routledge & Kegan Paul, 1970), p. 91. "Good habits and dutiful actions" are, of course, what Aristotle recommends and takes as basic; it is Plato, however, who sees the true "background condition."

[37] Vlastos, *Philosophy of Socrates,* p.21.

[38] G. H. Bantock, *Freedom and Authority in Education: A Criticism of Modern Cultural and Educational Assumptions* (London: Faber and Faber, 1970), p. 177. The inner quotation is from D. H. Lawrence.

Gregory Vlastos (lecture date 1986)

SOURCE: "Socrates's Rejection of Retaliation," in *Socrates: Ironist and Moral Philosopher,* Cornell University Press, 1991, pp. 179-99.

[*In the following excerpt from a lecture originally delivered in 1986, Vlastos describes the aspects of ancient Greek morality related to retaliation and the concept that harming one's enemy or social inferior is acceptable. He traces Greek attitudes toward enemies through ancient mythology and literature in order to demonstrate the significance of Socrates's view that we should never do an injustice, specifically in retaliation for an injustice done to us. Vlastos goes on to delineate and discuss the five Socratic principles related to injustice.*]

> If therefore the light that is in thee be darkness, how great is that darkness.
>
> (Matt. 6:23)

In the last and most famous of his *Theses on Feuerbach* Marx observes: "The philosophers have done no more than interpret the world. The point, however, is to change it." Substitute "morality" for "world" and the observation would be true of almost all the leading philosophers of the West. Moralists as powerfully innovative as are Aristotle, Hume, and Kant take the morality into which they are born for granted. The task they set themselves is only to excogitate its rationale. It does not occur to them to subject its content to critical scrutiny, prepared to question norms ensconced in it which do not measure up to their rational standards. But there have been exceptions, unnoticed by Marx, and of these Socrates is the greatest. Proceeding entirely from within the morality of his own time and place, he nevertheless finds reason to stigmatize as unjust one of its most venerable, best established, rules of justice.

By the morality of a society I understand those norms of right and wrong, rules of conduct or excellences of character, publicly acknowledged within it, whose function it is to foster human well-being. The sense of justice centers in the concern that those norms be applied impartially. So if in a given society we were to find them habitually observed in a discriminatory way—applied strictly for the benefit of some and loosely, if at all, for that of others—we would know that to this extent the morality of the society is defective. When we scrutinize the morality of ancient Greece with this in mind two large areas of such deficiency come into view. (1) The application of its moral norms is grossly discriminatory in conduct towards personal enemies. (2) It is no less so, though for different reasons and in different ways, in the conduct of citizens towards their social inferiors—women, aliens, slaves. Coming to Scorates' practical moral teaching with this in mind we can see in good perspective the most strikingly new thing about it: its root-and-branch rejection of that first form of discrimination. And we can also see the limits of its innovative thrust: it has nothing to say against the second. Revolutionary on the first, it is conformist on the second.

To assess justly Socrates' contribution to the Greek sense of justice we must treat *it* impartially, recognizing its achievement without disguising its failure. Accordingly, though in this book I speak only of the former, I shall not lend it a false grandeur by concealing the latter. There is no evidence that Socrates' moral vision was exempt from that blindspot in the Athenian civic conscience which made it possible for Demosthenes, addressing a lot-selected court, to put compassion at the forefront of his city's ethos,[2] yet no less possible for his contemporary, Lycurgus, addressing a similar court, to declare that it is "most just and democratic . . ." to make it mandatory that court evidence by slaves should be given under torture.[3] To subject citizens to such treatment would be unthinkable in the Athenian judicial system.[4] Nowhere in our sources is there the slightest indication that this and other forms of grossly discriminatory conduct towards slaves, sanctioned by the prevailing moral code, drew any protest from Socrates. His critique of the code leaves institutional morality untouched. It is directed solely to that area of conduct which falls entirely within the limits of the habitual expectations sustained by the institutional framework.

I

Harming one's enemy to the full extent permitted by public law is not only tolerated, but glorified, in Greek moralizing. The sentiment is ubiquitous.[5] Solon (fr. 1 Diehl), aspiring to "good repute among all men," prays that that he may be "sweet to friends, bitter to enemies." Medea, scorning the role of feminine weakling, determined to be as strong as any male, vows that she will be "harsh to foes, gracious to friends, for such are they whose life is most glorious."[6] In Plato's *Meno* Socrates' interlocutor builds it into the formula meant to capture the essence of manly excellence:

> T1 Plato, *M.* 71E: "Socrates, if you want to know what manly virtue is, it is this: to be able to conduct the city's affairs doing good to friends and evil to enemies, while taking care not to be harmed oneself,"

Isocrates, mouthing traditional commonplaces, counsels Demonicus:

T2 Isocrates, *To Dem.* 26: Consider it as disgraceful to be outdone by enemies in inflicting harm, as by friends in conferring benefits.

If one is nurtured in this norm, what constraints on harming a foe would one accept? The authorities which recommend it lay down none. Consider Pindar, golden voice of conventional wisdom:

T3 Pindar, *2 Pyth.* 83-5: Let me love him who loves me, / But on a foe as foe I will descend, wolf-like, / In ever varying ways by crooked paths.[7]

The image—wolflike, stealthy, crooked attack—conveys the thought that underhanded malice, normally contemptible, would be in order here. If you were to deceive your enemy, corrupt his slave, seduce his wife, ruin his reputation by slander, you would not be ashamed of it, you could be proud of it. Are there then no limits to be observed in deviating from decent conduct at your foe's expense? So long as you keep the public law, traditional morality lays down none,[8] except those set by the *lex talionis,* the ancient doctrine of retaliation.

The metaphor through which this notion grips the moral imagination of the Greeks is the repayment of a debt: verbs for "paying" . . . and "paying back" . . . are the ones regularly used to express it. The idea is that if you do someone a wrong or a harm, you have thereby incurred a debt and must discharge it by suffering the same sort of evil yourself—a wrong or harm "such as" (*tale,* hence *talio*[9]) to repay what you did to him. At first blush this extension of the money-debt resists generalization. If you had stolen one of your neighbor's sheep, and he were then to steal it back, his action could be plausibly pictured as making you repay a surreptitious loan you had previously extracted from him. But what if you had killed one of his sheep, and he were now to retaliate by spitefully killing one of yours? What semblance of reason would there be in thinking that he thereby secures *repayment?* Does he get back his sheep by killing one of yours, leaving its carcass on the hillside to be picked off by jackals? But this is not to say that he gets nothing from the retaliatory act: he may get something he prizes much more than a sheep.[10] The passionate desire for revenge—i.e. to harm another person for no reason other than that he or she harmed one in the first place—is as blind to calculations of utility as to every other rational consideration. One may get all the greater satisfaction from an act of pure revenge, freed completely from concern for restitution. And this, precisely, is the *raison d'être* of the *lex talionis.* it aims to put a lid on the extravagance of passion by stipulating that for any given harm no greater may be inflicted in return.

T4 Exodus 21:24-5: . . . eye for eye, tooth for tooth, hand for hand, foot for foot, burning for burning, wound for wound, stripe for stripe.

If someone has knocked out one of your eyes you might well feel like knocking out both of his—or more, if he had more.[11] The rule says: Only one.

This constraint on revenge by a limit of equivalences so commends the *talio* to the moral sense of the Greeks that when their first philosophers come to think of the natural universe as an ordered world, a cosmos,[12] they project on it their idea of justice by picturing the grand periodicities of nature as enacting cycles of retaliatory retribution. In Anaximander's famous fragment (T5), the hot and the dry, encroaching upon the cold and wet in the summer, must "pay" for their "injustice" by suffering in return the like fate in the winter, when the cold and wet make converse aggression upon the erstwhile aggressors, completing one retaliatory cycle, to start another in endless succession:

T5 Anaximander, fr. 1 (Diels-Kranz): For they render justice and repayment to one another in accordance with the ordering of time.

So too the first recorded definition of "justice" identifies it with *to antipeponthos,* whose literal force, "to suffer in return," is lost in the unavoidably lame translation, "reciprocity":

T6 Aristotle, *Nic. Eth.* 1132b21-7: Some believe that reciprocity . . . simply *is* justice. So the Pythagoreans thought. For they defined "justice" as "reciprocity."

Ascribing this archaic formula to Pythagorean philosophers, Aristotle does not accept it as an adequate definition of "justice." But he concurs with its sentiment,[13] citing Hesiod in its support:

T7 Hesiod, fr. 174 Rzach: For if one suffered what one did, straight justice would be done. . . .

From the many testimonies to the currency of this notion I pick one from the *Oresteia:*

T8 Aeschylus, *Choephoroi* 309-14: "'For hostile word let hostile word / Be fulfilled . . . ,' Justice cries aloud / As she collects the debt. . . . / 'Let homicidal blow the homicidal / Blow repay. . . . Let him who did suffer in return . . . ,' / The thrice-venerable tale declares."

Aeschylus reaffirms the hallowed tradition of his people that to satisfy justice the wrongdoer must be made to suffer in return the evil he or she has done another. But as the action moves on, it becomes apparent that the maxim leaves the poet gravely troubled. As Orestes drags his mother offstage to kill her the poet makes him say:

> T9 Aeschylus, *Choephoroi* 930: "Since you killed whom you ought not, now suffer what you ought not. . . . "[14]

Why so? If the *talio* is quintessentially just, why should not Orestes be saying instead, "Since you killed whom you ought not, now suffer what *you ought?*" Orestes is in a bind. Instructed by Apollo that Clytemnestra should be made to pay with her own blood for the family blood she had spilled, he is still unable to shake off the horror of matricide.

In the *Electra* of Euripides we see him in the same bind. He remonstrates with Electra: "How shall I kill her who bore me and brought me up?" When she retorts, "Just as she killed your father and mine," he goes along but without conviction, railing against the "folly" of Apollo, "who prophesied that I should kill a mother, whom I ought not to kill."[15]

For further evidence that the rule of just repayment elicits less than full conviction from the conscience of those who invoke it, consider Euripides' Medea. Though her object is to extract from Jason "just repayment with God's help," she nonetheless reflects that "she has dared a most impious deed." The modern reader cannot but wonder how she could have brought herself to believe that the grisly crimes by which she retaliates against Jason are "just repayment" for his infidelity. By what stretch of the imagination could the murder of their two children along with that of his new bride qualify as wrongs "such as" his wrong to her? Yet neither the Chorus nor any of the principals—Medea herself, or Jason, or Creon—take the least notice of the grotesque disproportion of what she does to what she suffered. To anyone who protested the mismatch she would doubtless say that the pain Jason had caused her was as great as the one she is bent on causing him. Euripides makes us see that when revenge is accepted as just in principle the limit of just equivalences turns out in practice to be an all-too-flexible fiction.

We see more of the same when we turn from myth in the tragedians to tragic history in Thucydides. The people who filled the theatre to see the *Medea* in 431 B.C. reassemble on the Pnyx four years later to debate a more infamous proposal than any ever previously moved in the Athenian Assembly:[19] that rebellious Mytilene, now subdued, should be exterminated, all its adult males executed without trial, and all its women and children sold into slavery. In the speech for the proposal Cleon invokes justice on its behalf[20] and, as we might expect, it is the justice of the *talio:*

> T10 Thucydides 3.40.7: "Coming as close as possible[21] in thought to what you felt when they made you suffer, when you would have given anything to crush them, now pay them back. . . . "[22]

To justice so debased Diodotus, the spokesman for decency, makes no appeal. He lets Cleon have it all to

Xenophon

himself, turning to cool expediency instead. Conceding that the Athenians have been wronged, Diodotus wastes no words haggling over what would or would not be an equivalent return.[23] He asks them to reflect instead that they have more to lose than gain by an action which would bear down as harshly on the Mytilenean *dēmos* as on its oligarchic masters, prime movers of the revolt. He argues that such indiscriminate terror will lose Athens her best asset in the war—the sympathy of the democrats in each of her subject cities. He does come around to justice near the end of his address, warning the Athenians that if they were to destroy the *dē mos* who had forced the city's surrender when arms were put into its hands, "they would wrong their benefactors" (3.47.3). *But this is not the justice of the talio.* As to that, he implies, the Athenians would be better off as its victims than as its executors:

> T11 Thucydides 3.47.5: "I think it more conducive to the maintenance of our empire to allow ourselves to suffer wrong . . . rather than destroy, however justly . . . , those whom we ought not to destroy."[24]

The flaw in the justice of the *talio* shows up with startling clarity in the lightning flash of a crisis in which sane moral counsel is most desperately needed.

The sense of justice—which should have been the best resource of decent Athenians in their resistance to the promptings of blind, unreasoning, hatred—here strengthens the very force they seek to contain. Instead of giving Diodotus the backing he needs, the justice of the *talio* is a bludgeon in Cleon's hand.[25]

How was it then that the *lalio* had won and kept so long its commanding place in the moral code? Because it had been confused with one or more of three closely related, though entirely distinct, concepts: restitution, self-defense, punishment. The most widespread and, superficially, the most plausible of the three confusions is the one with restitution. If retaliation *were* restitution in principle, it *would* be paradigmatically just: what could be more just than the repayment of a debt? As for self-defense, at first blush it looks like a far cry from retaliation, but it will not if we notice that *amuein, antamunein,* "to ward off from oneself," "to defend oneself" were *also* used to *mean* "to retaliate," and reflect that when retaliation is the expected response to unjust aggression, failure to retaliate will be construed as weakness, inviting further assaults. By easy extension the preemptive strike becomes acceptable as righteous self-defense: those who see themselves as likely objects of attack feel justified in cracking down before the anticipated aggression has occurred.

In the case of punishment the linguistic bond is still more potent. It is positively tyrannical throughout the archaic period. Down to the last third of the fifth century, *timōria,* whose original and always primary sense is "vengeance," is *the* word for "punishment." The specialized word for the latter, . . . ("chastening," "disciplining"—with no collateral use for "taking vengeance"), does not acquire currency until we reach the prose of Thucydides and Antiphon. Earlier, as for example in Herodotus,[27] language traps one into using "vengeance" . . . , even when "punishment" is exactly what one means.[28] What is the difference? Rightly understood punishment is the application of a penalty . . . , that is to say, of a norm-mandated sanction of norms. As such, it differs from revenge in three closely connected ways.[29]

1. While inflicting a harm on the wrongdoer is common to punishment and revenge, doing him a wrong is not: to punish a wrongdoer is not to wrong him. To the return of wrong for wrong, which is normal in revenge, punishment gives absolutely no quarter: those who apply the penalty are not licensed wrongdoers, but instruments of norm-enforcement, agents of justice.

2. To give relief to the resentful feelings of victims is not, as in revenge, the dominant motivation of punishment, whose principal aim is not to do evil to the evildoer but to implement the community's concern that its norms should be observed and hence that norm-violators should be called to account by being made to suffer the lawful penalty.

3. Hatred for the wrongdoer, the core-sentiment in revenge, need not be present in punishment; those who apply the penalty to him should be impelled not by malice, but by a sense of duty in loyalty to the norms which he has breached and by fellow-feeling for the victims of wrongful harm. This motivation is entirely consistent with fellow-feeling for the wrongdoer himself: since he has alienated himself from his fellows by violating the common norms, it is for his own good, no less than that of others, that he be reunited with the community by submitting to the pain the community mandates for norm-violators.

The distinction of punishment from revenge must be regarded as one of the most momentous of the conceptual discoveries ever made by humanity in the course of its slow, tortuous, precarious, emergence from barbaric tribalism. With characteristic impartiality Plato assigns the discovery not to his personal hero, but to Protagoras, Socrates' arch-rival. We see it in the Great Speech Plato gives the sophist in the debate with Socrates in the *Protagoras.*[30] In support of his thesis that virtue is teachable, Protagoras in that speech propounds a comprehensive theory of the origins of culture which views all cultural institutions, including morality, as inventions through which men win the struggle for existence against wild beasts. He constructs a consequentionalist argument for the universal distribution of the "political art": all men must have been endowed with sensitiveness to moral norms ("share in shame and justice") else humanity would have lost that struggle: it would not have survived. Viewing punishment in this light, he explains it as a device designed to promote deterrence from wrongdoing:

> T12 Plato, *Pr.* 324A-B: "No one punishes . . . [32] wrongdoers putting his mind on what they did and for the sake of this-that they did wrong—not unless he is taking mindless vengeance . . . , like a savage brute. One who undertakes to punish rationally does not do so for the sake of the wrongdoing, which is now in the past—for what has been done cannot be undone—but for the sake of the future, that the wrongdoing shall not be repeated, either by him or by the others who see him punished. . . . One punishes . . . for the sake of deterrence. . . . "

Assuming[34] that this is a fair, if harshly abbreviated, statement of the Protagorean view, we must admit that the theory on which it predicates its analysis of the rationale of punishment is indefensibly lopsided. It invokes only deterrence to justify the practice. And this is clearly wrong. For while the reference of a penalty is indeed strongly prospective—to discourage recurrence of the offense—it must be also no less strongly retrospective, if it is to be just: it must apply to the offender the harm which he deserves to suffer under the norms because of *what he did.* We punish a man justly for a given breach of the rules only if we have reason to believe that *he* is guilty of it—that it is he, and no one else, who did commit just that offense. To visit that punishment on a surrogate who could serve as well its exemplary purpose would be the height of injustice, though the deterrent effect could be as great if the false accusation were well concealed. So *pace* Protagoras we do, and should, punish a wrongdoer "for the sake of what he did": our theory must recognize the retributive nature of the practice which we accept for the sake of its deterrent effect. Hence Protagoras' theory of the social function of punishment is unacceptable. It cites, correctly enough, deterrence as the *raison d'être* of the institution, but fails to see that the institution itself is unavoidably retributive.

But even so, though working with a defective theory, Protagoras succeeds brilliantly in sorting out punishment from revenge—he distinguishes perfectly the rational application of a penalty, designed to reinforce compliance with norms aiming at the common benefit, from the indulgence of anarchic vengeful passion. He disentangles what had been hopelessly jumbled for millennia in the past and was to remain entangled in popular thought for millennia to come. A leading Victorian jurist, James FitzJames Stephen, was still declaring, in 1883, that criminal justice is legally sanctioned revenge: "the criminal law," he claimed, "stands to the passion of revenge in much the same relation as marriage to the sexual instinct."[35] This articulates what many people believed at the time, and still believe today. That punishment is institutionalized revenge is still a popular view, voiced even by some philosophers,[36] and not without support from the dictionary: for "revenge" the *O.E.D.* gives "inflict punishment or exact retribution."

But after giving Protagoras full credit for having been two and a half millennia ahead of his time, we must still observe that neither does he undertake to give revenge its long overdue come-uppance. It is one thing to distinguish it clearly from punishment, quite another to discern that when thus distinguished revenge is morally repugnant. The first step by no means assures the second, as we can see in Aristotle. He draws the distinction in a way which leaves the moral acceptability of revenge untouched.[37] He still puts harming enemies morally on a par with helping friends:

> T13 Arist. *Top.* 113a2-3: Doing good to friends and evil to enemies are not contraries: for both are choiceworthy and belong to the same disposition. . . .

He still exalts retaliation as "just and noble":

> T14 Arist. *Rhet.* 1367a19-20: It is noble . . . to avenge oneself on one's enemies and not to come to terms with them: for retaliation . . . is just . . . , and the just is noble, and not to put up with defeat is courage.

Worse yet, Aristotle takes the desire for revenge to be a constant in human nature, as deep-seated and ineradicable in the psyche as is the emotion of anger. Defining "anger" as "desire to inflict retaliatory pain,"[38] he identifies the emotion of anger with vengeful impulse, strangely overlooking the absurd consequences of the supposed identity: what sense would it make to hold that when one is angry at oneself (a common enough occurrence) one desires to be revenged on oneself and that when one is angry at one's child (also common) one desires to be revenged on it?

Admittedly T13 and T14 do not come from Aristotle's ethical writings and do not express original moral insights of his own. But they do show that his creative moral thought does not transcend the traditional sentiment in which the justice of the *lalio* is enshrined. Great moralist though he is, Aristotle has not yet got it through his head that *if someone has done a nasty thing to me this does not give me the slightest moral justification for doing the same nasty thing, or any nasty thing, to him.* So far as we know, the first Greek to grasp in full generality this simple and absolutely fundamental moral truth is Socrates.

II

Innovations in history don't come out of the blue. Somewhere or other in earlier or contemporary Greek literature we might expect anticipations of Socrates' rejection of the *talio* or at least approximations to it. Let me put before you some of the best approximations I could find and you can judge for yourself if Socrates' originality suffers by comparison.

In the *Oresteia* Aeschylus confronts the futility and horror of the intrafamilial blood-feud and makes the trilogy culminate in a celebration of the supersession of private vengeance by the majesty of civic law. But he never recants on the principle that "each must suffer the thing he did" enunciated by the chorus as "ordained" in the *Agamemnon* (1564) and as the "thrice-venerable tale" in the *Choephoroi* (T8 above). In *Seven Against Thebes* Antigone invokes it (1049-50) to justify her brother's retaliatory assault against Thebes and does not question the validity of the principle: she only rebuts its application in the present case.

Nor does Herodotus succeed where Aeschylus falters. His Pausanias (9.78-9) rejects indignantly the proposal that he avenge Leonidas by doing to Mardonius' corpse what he and Xerxes had done to that of the Spartan hero. But what are his reasons for rejecting the proposal? (a) That to desecrate the dead "befits barbarians rather than Greeks," and (b) Leonidas has been already avenged in the huge casualties suffered by the Persians. The propriety of revenge is not denied in (a), and is assumed in (b). Herodotus' Xerxes (7.136), declining to retaliate against Sperthias and Bulis for what Sparta had done to his ambassadors, explains that "what he had blamed in the Spartans he would not do himself." This remarkable statement[39] *could* be used to derive Socrates' Principles II and IV below. But it is not. There is no hint of the insight that since one may not do oneself what one condemns in another, *therefore* one should not return wrong for wrong or harm for harm.

A third candidate comes from Thucydides in the speech of the Spartan envoys at Athens in 425 B.C. Their force at Sphacteria, now cut off, is in desperate straits. A truce has been patched up. Negotiations are afoot. The spokesmen for Sparta plead:

> T15 Thuc. 4.19.2-3: "We believe that great enmities are not best brought to secure resolution when the party that got the best of the war, bent on retaliation . . . ,[40] forces on the other a settlement on unequal terms, but rather when, though the victor has the chance to do just that, yet, aiming at decency . . . , he rises higher in virtue . . . to offer unexpectedly moderate terms. For if what the other now owes is not retaliation for what was forced on him . . . , but a return of virtue . . . , a sense of shame will make him readier to stand by the agreement."

The Spartans plead: Don't go by the *talio* this time or, better still, work it in reverse: leave us generosity, not injury, to repay. Defeat on these terms we could live with. Your moderation would evoke our best, not our worst, and you would have that further surety that the peace will endure.

Clear in this passage is the perception of a better way to settle a long-standing dispute. Morally better, certainly—perhaps even prudentially, since the victor might have more to gain from enhanced security that the agreement will be kept than from any immediate advantage he could extort. But is there so much as even a hint that the Spartans, and Thucydides himself who credits their spokesmen with this fine sentiment in this passage, perceive that the *talio* itself is unjust? None that I can see. To say that, if you did not drive the hardest bargain your present advantage puts within your grasp, your restraint will be admirable and will also pay off, is not to say that if you did prefer the other course you would be acting unjustly.[41]

My last candidate is the character of Odysseus in Sophocles' *Ajax.* The mad protagonist of this tragedy, imbued with mortal hatred for Odysseus, had planned to put him to a slow, tortured, death. He had announced the plan to Athena in Odysseus' hearing and reaffirmed the determination to carry it out despite her plea that he refrain. Knowing this, Odysseus takes no joy in the calamities which now afflict his enemy. When burial is denied to Ajax, Odysseus pleads with Agamemnon to rescind the edict.

> T16 Sophocles, *Ajax* 1332ff.: "Listen, For the gods' sake, do not dare / So callously to leave this man without a grave. / Do not let violence get the better of you / So as to hate this man so much that you trample justice./To me too he was bitterest enemy . . . / But nonetheless, though he was all of that, / I would not so dishonour him in return . . . as to deny / He was the best of us who went to Troy,/Save for Achilles . . . /It is not just to injure a good man/ After his death, even if you hate him.

From the standpoint of our own Christianized morality Odysseus' reaction to his enemy's downfall, however admirable, is not extraordinary. In his own time and place it is so far above anything that could be expected of a decent man that it takes Athena by surprise. She had offered Odysseus to parade before him Ajax in his disordered state, thinking it would please her favorite to see his rival, once so mighty, now laid low. She asks Odysseus,

> T16 *Ibid.* 79: "When is laughter sweeter than when we laugh at our foes?"[42]

When he declines the offer we are moved to agree with Albin Lesky that here "the man is greater than the goddess."[43]

Can we then say that what we see here is a man who has come to understand that retaliation itself is unjust? We cannot. What we see is a man of exceptional moral stature realizing that this particular application of the principle—in denial of burial (contrary to divine law) to this man (next to Achilles the best of the Achaeans)—would be unjust.[44] What we do not see is a man who would scruple to apply it in any circumstances against any man. Elsewhere in the play his Odysseus accepts the justice of retaliation as a moral commonplace. He remarks in another connection,

> T18 *Ibid.* 1322-3: "If he gave insult for insult I pardon him."

Odysseus has not come to see that the *talio* as such is wrong, a precept not of justice but of injustice. Neither has the poet for whom he speaks.

If we go back to to an earlier scene, near the start of the play, when Agamemnon's decree had not yet fouled the waters, and ask ourselves how Sophocles accounts for the pure nobility of Odysseus' rancorless response to his stricken enemy's state, we can tell, I believe, that the poet wants us to see it rooted in the sense not of justice but of compassion. He evokes what we all may feel for a fellow-creature when touched by the sense of our common frailty, our common defencelessness against implacable fate:

> T19 *Ibid.* 119-26: Athena: "Here was a man supreme in judgment, unsurpassed in action, matched to the hour. Did you ever see a better?"[45] Odysseus: Not one. And that is why, foe though he is, I pity his wretchedness, now yoked to a terrible fate. I have in view no more his plight than mine, I see the true condition of us all. We live, yet are no more than phantoms, weightless shades."

This is the mood of the eighth *Pythian:*

> T20 Pindar, *Pyth.* 8.1-2: Day-creatures. What is it to be or not to be? Man is a shadow in a dream.

It is the mood of Herodotus' Solon when he remarks, "Man is all accident." It is as old as the *Odyssey.* We hear it in book 18 in Odysseus' sombre musings (vv. 130-7) on the theme "Earth breeds no creature feebler than man." The moral import of the sentiment we see after the massacre of the suitors in book 22. When Eurycleia lets out a whoop of vengeful joy at the sight of the gore spattered about the banquet hall, Odysseus rebukes her sternly,

> T21 *Od.* 22.411-12: "Keep your gloating to yourself, old woman. Shut, up. Don't yell. It isn't pious to exult over corpses."[48]

More successfully than Pindar or Homer Sophocles distills moral therapy from the sense of man's brittleness. He reveals how it can purge the heart from the toxins of spite and hatred. But when he has done this, we still want to know: Has he seen that the *talio* is a fraud, its justice a delusion? To this we must reply that he has not even faced the question. So we return to Socrates, who did, and reasoned out an answer.

III

The reasoning which leads him to it is laid out in that short section of the *Crito* (48B-C)[49] which starts the deliberation by which Socrates justifies the decision to remain in jail and await execution. He calls this the *arche* of the deliberation, its "starting-point" or, as we would say, reading the metaphor differently, its foundation. This comprises five principles laid out in rapid-fire succession:

> T22 *Cr.* 48B4-C9:
>
> I. "We should never do injustice. . . . "
>
> II. "Therefore, we should never return an injustice. . . . "
>
> III. "We should never do evil . . . [to anyone]."[50]
>
> IV. "Therefore, we should never return evil for evil [to anyone]. . . . "
>
> V. "To do evil to a human being is no different from acting unjustly to him. . . . "

Of these five principles the one that would hit Plato's readers hardest are II and IV. Here Greeks would see a fellow-Greek cutting out of their morality part of its living tissue. Socrates is well aware of this. For after laying out all five principles he proceeds to zero in on just these two:

> T23 *Cr.* 49C10-D5:[51] "Therefore, we should never return a wrong [Principle II] or do evil to a single human being . . . no matter what we may have suffered at his hands [Principle IV]. And watch out, Crito, lest in agreeing with this you do so contrary to your real opinion. . . . For few are those who believe or will believe this. And between those who do and those who don't there can be no common counsel. . . . Of necessity they must feel contempt for one another when viewing each other's deliberations."[52]

What Socrates says here he never asserts about any other view he ever voices in Plato: with people who do not agree with him on these two principles which enunciate the interdict on retaliation he would be unable to take "common counsel" about anything. Is he saying that this disagreement would cause a total breakdown of communication? No. Socrates is not saying that he cannot *argue* with anyone who rejects Principles II and IV. Obviously he can: he does so, copiously, with Polus, Callicles, Thrasymachus, and who knows how many others. But what he *is* saying is serious enough: if agreement cannot be reached on these two principles there can be no common *deliberation:* the gulf created by this disagreement will be unbridgeable when it comes to deciding what is to be done. The political consequences of his remark I shall be unable to pursue in this book.[53] Here I must concentrate on Principles II and IV as norms of personal action within the limits fixed for the individual by public law.[54]

While they mark Socrates' break with the established morality they do not account for the break by themselves. Each is derived from one or more other principles in the set. Principle II is derived directly and exclusively from Principle I.

I. We should never do injustice. *Ergo:*

II. We should never do injustice in return for an injustice.

From the proposition that we should refrain from doing injustice in any circumstances whatever ("never" do it), Socrates infers by simple deduction that we should refrain from doing it in the special circumstances in which *we* have been victims of injustice ourselves. To derive IV he uses I again, this time in conjunction with V:

V. Doing any evil to a human being is the same as doing injustice to that person.

And since

I. We should never do injustice,

it follows from this in conjunction with Principle V, that

III. We should never do any evil to a human being. *Ergo*

IV. We should never return evil for evil.

From the proposition that we should refrain from doing evil to anyone in any circumstances whatever ("never" do it), he infers as before that we should not do it when evil has been done to us.

The commanding importance of Principle I in this reasoning should be evident: it is the sole premise for the derivation of Principle II, and it is used again for the derivation of Principle IV in conjunction with the further premise, Principle V. How would Socrates justify the latter? What reason would he give us to agree that to do any evil[55] to anyone is no different from doing that person an injustice? There is no fully satisfactory answer to this question anywhere in Plato's Socratic dialogues. The nearest Socrates comes to confronting the question is in that passage of *Republic* I where he refutes the conventional notion that justice consists of doing good to friends *and* evil to enemies (335A8-10). To rebut the second term in that conjunction Socrates picks what he believes to be the worst evil that could be done to a human being—to impair that person's justice—and argues that this would be *impossible:* justice in one person could not produce injustice in another—no more than heat in one thing could produce cold in another or drought in one thing produce moisture in another (335B-D). The force of these analogies is problematic.[56] And even if the validity of the reasoning were granted in this case, where the retaliatory evil would impair the enemy's justice, how it would be extended beyond it is not made clear: if the just man cannot impair another man's justice, how would it follow that neither could he harm another in any of innumerable ways in which one could do evil to an enemy *without* impairing the enemy's justice? The one thing that is made clear in this passage—and this is what we must settle for—is Socrates' intuition that true moral goodness is incapable of doing intentional injury to others, for it is inherently beneficent, radiant in its operation, spontaneously communicating goodness to those who come in contact with it, always producing benefit instead of injury, so that the idea of a just man injuring anyone, friend or foe, is unthinkable. This version of undeviatingly beneficent goodness guides Socrates' thought at so deep a level that he applies it even to the deity; it leads him to project a new concept of god as a being that can cause only good, never evil.[57] Let us then accept it as such, as a powerful intuition whose argumentative backing remains unclear in Plato's presentation of Socrates' thought.[58]

So the full weight of the justification of Socrates' rejection of retaliation must fall on Principle I. From this alone, without appeal to any further consideration whatsoever, Socrates derives the interdiction of returning wrong for wrong for wrong in Principle II and therewith the surgical excision of that malignancy in the traditional morality which surfaces in actions like the genocide Athens had all but inflicted on Mytilene and then, as the war dragged on, did inflict on Scione, Torone, and Melos.[59] Plato's awareness of the importance of Principle I shows up in the way he leads up to it in the text of the *Crito* which immediately precedes T22 above.[60] He takes the whole of that paragraph to introduce it, stating and restating it no less than three times,[61] reminding Crito that they had often agreed to it in the past and that he cannot go back on it now just because to stick to it would be to die.

How then should we read the modal language Socrates uses in the first two of those three statements of Principle I in that paragraph?

> T24 *Cr.* 49A4-B6: "Do we say that in no way *should we* intentionally do a wrong . . . ? Or that *we may* do wrong in some ways but not in others . . . ? Or that to do a wrong is never good or noble . . . , as has been often agreed between us in the past?"

In the preamble to a moral deliberation it would be natural to read the modal operators as signifying the "should" or "ought" of moral obligation, the "may" of moral acceptability. We must resist that reading: it would be too narrow: it would give us only part of what Socrates means. For he is not saying that if an action does a wrong then it is morally forbidden no matter what might be the circumstances. That would itself be a strong thing to say. But Socrates must mean much more than that. For he proceeds to ask, rephrasing the question with which he began, "Or that to do a wrong is never either *good* or noble. . . " Of these two adjectives, . . . the latter is the one normally used to express what is morally right as such. The use of the former is much broader-fully as broad as that of "good" in English, ranging over the whole spectrum of values: not only moral ones, but also hedonic, economic, political, psychological, physiological, or whatever.

Now it is all too obvious that there are circumstances in which by doing a wrong to someone we may reap a rich harvest of non-moral goods: win a huge sum of money, realize a long-cherished dream, gratify the dearest wishes of a much-loved friend; in the present case it would make the difference between life and death.[63] In saying that it is never *good* to do a wrong, and making this the foundational reason for breaking with the accepted morality, Socrates must be using the word in its most inclusive sense. He must be saying: "If an act of yours will wrong another, then it is bad for you, the agent, so bad that no other good it offers could compensate you for its evil for you. If everything else you value—pleasure, comfort, security, the good opinion of your fellows, the affection of those for whom you care, your own self-preservation—required you to do an unjust action, the mere fact that it is wrong would give you a final, insuperable, reason to refrain. Were there a world to win by wronging other persons, you must refrain. Life itself would not be good if you could keep it only by wronging someone else."

Compare Thoreau: "If I have wrested a plank from a drowning man, I must restore it to him though I drown myself." Here too the force of the modality must be the same. Were we to take Thoreau's "must restore" to mean no more than "I am morally required to restore" we would flatten out his dictum, we would squash it into a platitude. For then the consequent would follow with dreary obviousness from the antecedent. Who would galnsay that I am morally obligated to undo an Immoral act which is about to cost another man his life? But Thoreau is not asking us to endorse a moral commonplace. He wants us to declare for the most difficult choice anyone could ever be asked to make. Socrates is asking us to do the same—to acknowledge not only the validity of the claim of Principle I on us, but its sovereignty over all other claims. How Thoreau would justify that hard "must" in his dictum is not our affair: his transcendentalism would be a far cry from Socrates' eudaemonism, which is all that matters for us here; Principle I is an immediate consequence of Socrates' commitment to the Sovereignty of Virtue and therewith of his construction of eudaemonism. . . .

Notes

[2] *Against Timocrates,* 170.

[3] *Against Leocrates,* 29. Some scholars have claimed that this was rarely applied. Their claim is more of a wishful projection of humanitarian sentiment than a sober conclusion from evidence: see Marie-Paule Carrière-Hergavault, 1973: 45-79; also MacDowell, 1978: 245-7.

[4] It was forbidden by law: MacDowell, 1978: 247 and n. 563.

[5] For a rich documentation of this pervasive feature of Greek morality and for extensive references to comment on it in the scholarly literature, see especially Blundell, 1989: ch. 2.

[6] Euripides, *Med.* 807-10: "Let no one think me a low and feeble thing, / A quiet one, but of that other sort, / Harsh to foes, gracious to friends, / For such are they whose life is most glorious."

[7] I was reminded by the late Friedrich Solmsen that Schadewaldt (diss, Halle, 1928: 326, n. 1) had objected that Pindar could not have associated his own person with "crooked" action, and had amended the text accordingly . . . to make "crooked" refer to the adversary. But the received text is palaeographically impeccable, and no reason has been offered for assuming that Pindar would balk at "crooked paths" *against an enemy.*

[8] In Euripides' *Ion* (1046-7) the elderly slave remarks as he goes forth to carry out Creusa's errand (to poison the youth), "When one wants to do evil to enemies, no rule . . . bars the way." Here [rule] does not refer to statute law (else the sentiment would make no sense), but to the moral code.

[9] Blundell (ef. n. 5 above) notices that this is the Latin legal term for "repayment in kind."

[10] At this point I am indebted to Terry Irwin for criticism of an earlier version of this paper.

[11] Blundell cites (1989: 30) Hesiod, *Op.* 709-11 ("If he starts it, saying or doing some unpleasant thing, be sure to pay him back twice as much") among other expressions of the sentiment. As she notes, though Hesiod favors "twice as much," he does not say this would be just: cf. T7 below.

[12] Cf. Vlastos, 1975: chapter 1 ("The Greeks discover the cosmos").

[13] More to the same effect from Aristotle below: T13, T14.

[14] Translated by G. Thomson (1938) as "Wrong shall be done to you for the wrong you did."

[15] Euripides, *Electra* 969-73: Orestes: "How shall I kill her who bore me and brought me up?" Electra: "Just as she killed your father and mine." Orestes: "O Phoebus, you prophesied a great folly." Electra: "Where Apollo errs, who could be wise?" Orestes: "He prophesied that I should kill a mother whom I ought not to kill." . . .

[19] The obliteration of Histiaea in 447/446 (Thuc. 1.14.3) had also been brutal in the extreme and would even be bracketed with that of Melos, Scione, and Torone in retrospect (Xen. *Hell.* 2.2.3). But so far as we know

the action was not taken after formal debate in the Assembly but through summary decision in the field by military command; and the city was wiped out by expulsion of its people and parceling out of their land among Athenian cleruchs rather than by wholesale executions and enslavement.

[20] Emphasis on the violation of justice by the Mytileneans (3.38.1; 3.39.1 and 6) comes early on in his speech, and it culminates in the appeal that both justice and interest require the proposed action (3.40.4-7).

[21] He had argued earlier (3.38.1) that retaliatory action should be as prompt as possible because "the response upon the heels of what one suffered exacts a vengeance that most nearly matches the offense."

[22] Throughout the ages retaliation has been the standard justification for genocidal acts and policies. Pogroms in medieval Europe and then in Poland and the Ukraine in modern times were ostensibly carried out in retaliation against "Christ-killers." Massacres of Armenians in Anatolia were perpetrated in retaliation for an incendiary assault against the Bank of Turkey in Istanbul by Armenian terrorists. The Nuremberg outrages against the Jews which paved the way for the Holocaust gained a measure of mass support from the belief that Jewish bankers had conspired to "bring Germany to her knees."

[23] "If we are sensible we shall not make the issue turn on their injustice . . . , but on what is the wise course for us to follow . . . We are not involved in a lawsuit with them, so as to be concerned about the justice of their case; we are deliberating about them to determine how our treatment of them may best serve our interest" (3.44.2-4).

[24] Failure to notice that at 3.47.3 Diodotus has momentarily shifted to a different conception of justice, not tied to the *talio,* to which he returns at 3.47.4-5, may result in a misunderstanding of the position allowed him by Thucydides: it may lead one either to ignore the previous remark, thereby making Diodotus rest his whole case on imperial expediency (so Andrews takes him to "present his own case entirely in terms of expediency" [1962: 72]) or else to dismiss as "hollow" the remark in T11 that the Athenians should let themselves "suffer wrong" (so Macleod, 1978: 77, who doesn't see that by the justice of the *talio* they *would be* letting themselves be wronged if, in pursuit of self-interest, they were to forgo retaliation).

[25] In her essay on the Melian Dialogue, Jacqueline de Romilly (1963: part III, ch. 2) connects that Athenian atrocity (identical with the one they were to inflict, later in the war, on Scione and Torone) with Thrasymachean immoralism (*R.* 1, 338aff.) and Calli-clean antimoralism (*G.* 483Aff.). She might have reflected that the Athenians would not need to go so far as that to justify genocide against a powerless enemy: wherever they could see themselves as returning wrong for wrong (as at Mytilene, Scione, and Torone): the ultra-respectable *talio* could supply the hard-liners with a righteous fig-leaf. . . .

[27] In his prose *nouthetein*, which may also be used for "punishing" in the classical period, is never used for this purpose, but only in its literal sense of "admonishing."

[28] Even Socrates, who rejects revenge, is allowed by Plato occasional use of *timōrein*, when "punishing" is what he means (so e.g. at *G.* 472D-E, 525B-E), ...

[29] For a more complete analysis of the differences between revenge and deserved punishment ("retribution") see especially Nozick, 1981:366-8. He clears up well what remains most unclear in the common use of "revenge": cf. the definition of the word in the *O.E.D.* to which I refer in the text below.

[30] Were it not for its occurrence in this text we would not have known that Protagoras was the discoverer: there is no record of it in any of our other, all-too-meager, sources for his thought. So powerful an innovation could only have come from a daring and original thinker. When Plato (who has no motive for favoritism to the sophist) assigns it to him we have good reason to accept the assignment, as is done by the majority of scholars (for some references see Guthrie, 1969:64, n.1). . . .

[32] Plato makes Protogoras use this word for "punishment" throughout the passage in clear distinction from vengeance, reserving XXXX for the latter. . . .

[34] We have no positive reason for thinking otherwise.

[35] The quotation (which I owe to Allen, 1980a:137) is from Stephen's *History of the Criminal Law* (1883:83) where he argues that "it is highly desirable that criminals should be hated, that the punishment should be so contrived as to give expression to that hatred . . . , gratifying an healthy natural sentiment." It did not occur to Stephens that, while punishment does indeed have an "expressive" function (see Feinberg, 1970:95ff.), the sentiment it should express in a humane society is concern for the enforcement of justice and for the welfare of the community, which criminal legislation is designed to protect in solicitude for *all* members of the community (the law-breaker himself not excepted; see Vlastos, 1962:55: "The pain inflicted on him for his offence against the moral law has not put him outside the law . . . does not close out the reserve of goodwill on the part of others which is his birthright as a human being").

[36] See e.g. Oldenquist (1985:464-79), who calls penal justice "sanitized revenge." By the same token marriage would be sanitized fornication.

[37] Arist. *Rhet.* 1369b12-14: Revenge and punishment . . . differ: for punishment is for the sake of the person punished, revenge for that of the one who does the punishing, to satisfy [his feelings]. . . . " (At this point I am indebted to oral and written comments from John Procopé.)

[38] *De Anima* 403a29ff: explaining the difference between the natural and the dialectieal understanding of a psychological phenomenon, he says that in the case of anger . . . "the *dialektikos* would say that it is desire to cause retaliatory pain . . . or something of the kind, the *fisikōs* would say that it is boiling of the blood and the hot element about the heart." In the *Rhetoric* (1378a31 ff.) he gives a fuller definition of anger, whose core is "pained desire for conspicuous revenge". . . .

[39] The principle that it would be unseemly for you to do *x* if you are indignant when *x* is done by someone else (a special form of the "Universalization Principle" in ethics) is not without acknowledgement in Greek moral reflection. It is anticipated in the *Iliad* (6.329-30 and 23.492-4) and the *Odyssey* 6.285-6).

[40] Good example here and in the next occurrence of the word in this text of the traditional conflation of the concepts of retaliation with self-defense. . . . In both occurrences it is clear that only retaliation is meant: the victor is no longer in the position of having to defend himself against his defeated enemy; the only question is whether he should retaliate for the real or fancied wrong he has suffered.

[41] As MacDowell (1963: 127ff.) observes, the virtue the Spartan envoys are recommending to Athens is not justice ("there are no laws or rules that a foreign state defeated in war must be treated mercifully") but generosity ("giving one's opponent more than he could reasonably expect").

[42] Cf. Stanford (*loc. cit.*): "Athena here expresses . . . the normal heroic attitude, that nothing is more pleasant than to be able to exult and gloat over the misfortunes of one's enemies."

[43] 1967: 100.

[44] The grounds on which Odysseus protests Agamemnon's decree show very clearly that his objection has nothing to do with the moral impropriety of revenge. To leave the corpse of Ajax unburied would "trample justice" (a) because it would violate the divine interdict on denying burial to anyone in any circumstances whatsoever and would breach "the divine laws", 1343, to which Sophocles refers as "the unwritten unshakeable laws of the gods (*Antigone* 454-5) which constrain Antigone's obedience at frightful cost to herself, and also (b) because the high and well deserved esteem in which Ajax had been held entitles him to posthumous respect (1340-1; 1345).

[45] My translation here follows E. F. Watling's rendering of these lines in *Sophocles, Electra and Other Plays* (Baltimore, 1953). . . .

[48] Stanford (1963:67) remarks that Odysseus is the first character in Greek literature to proclaim that it is impious to exult over a fallen foe.

[49] A fuller encounter with this crucial text must await chapter 8, section III *sub fin.* Here I take a first look at its language and reasoning.

[50] For the justification of the expansion I have added in square brackets here and again in IV note how Socrates himself rephrases IV when he refers to it in T23.

[51] Will be quoted again in chapter 8 (there as T13).

[52] So far from allowing Socrates the same position on this fundamental point, Xenophon gives him its opposite, making him endorse repeatedly the traditional help-friends-hurt-enemies ethos: the good man "toils to win good friends and to worst his enemies" (*Mem.* 2.1.19); "it is thought worthy of the highest praise to anticipate enemies in causing them evil and friends in causing them good" (*ibid.* 2.3.14); "you have come to know that a man's virtue consists in outdoing friends in conferring benefits and enemies in inflicting harm" (*Mem.* 2.6.35; cf. TI above). On why Plato's testimony should be preferred to Xenophon's on this point see additional note 7.I.

[53] If Socrates cannot join in a common deliberation with people who disagree with him on Principles II and IV he excludes himself from the decision-making processes of Athens' participatory democracy: the "multitude" that staffs those processes would indeed disagree with him on his rejection of the *talio,* as he himself emphasizes in T23.

[54] Cf. what was said in the third paragraph of this chapter above.

[55] I.e. any *morally avoidable* evil—any evil which is not purely incidental to the execution of a non-malicious intent, as in the case of self-defensc (where harm is inflicted on an aggressor solely to prevent him from causing wrongful harm) or that of punishment (where infliction of the evil of the penalty Socrates takes to be moral therapy for the wrongdoer [*G.* 480A-D, 525B] and/or retribution and deterrence [*G.* 525A-527A]).

[56] Cf. the discussion of this argument in Annas, 1981: 31-4.

[57] Cf. chapter 6 (discussion of the text quoted there as T7).

[58] Plato's recreation of Socratic thought may limp at this point, possibly because he had not been fully in sympathy with this particular aspect of Socrates' teaching. The ethic expounded in the middle books of the *Republic* lacks the unqualified universalism of Principle III, "We should never do evil *to any human being.*" In *R.* V, 470A Socrates does not demur when Glaucon declares that the atrocities Greeks now commit against one another when fighting fellow-Greeks (devastation of the land, desecration of corpses, enslavement of prisoners) should be forbidden to "our citizens" when they are fighting fellow-Greeks, but "towards barbarians they should behave as Greeks now behave to one another."

[59] An apologist for Athens, like Isocrates, belittles the enormity of such actions, explaining them away as "severe discipline" of states which had made war on Athens, and alleges that the Spartans had done much worse (*Paneg,* 100, defending the Athenian action against Melos and Scione; and *Panath.* 70, excusing what Athens had done to unnamed "islets"). His apologia would have been hollow if it had not presupposed the justice of the *lex talionis* to which, as we heard from Cleon in the debate on Mytilene (T10 above), advocates of such actions would have appealed.

[60] *Cr.* 49A4-B6. I shall be returning to the discussion of this passage in chapter 8. Now I am rounding out my discussion of the passage which starts with the text quoted as T15 in chapter 8 and culminates in the text quoted as T13 in that chapter.

[61] A4-5; A5-7; 49B4-7. . . .

[63] Socrates is satisfied that if he were to save his skin by availing himself of the opportunity to escape, his action would be destructive of his city's laws, which command that one should submit to the authority of the verdicts of the courts (even if they are wrong in one's own opinion) (*Cr.* 50B8), and would thus flout the interdict on returning evil for evil (*Cr.* 54C2-4).

Nickolas Pappas (essay date 1989)

SOURCE: "Socrates's Charitable Treatment of Poetry," in *Philosophy and Literature*, Vol. 13, No. 2, October, 1989, pp. 248-61.

[*In the following essay, Pappas examines Socrates's interpretation of poetry and its relation to his philosophical positions.*]

Of course this title seems wrong. If anything is certain about Socrates' treatment of poetry in Plato's dialogues, it is that he never gives a poem a chance to explain itself. He dismisses poems altogether on the basis of their suspect moral content (*Republic* II and III), or their representational form (*Republic* X), or their dramatic structure (*Laws* 719); he calls poets ignorant (*Apology, Ion*) and—not obviously as a compliment—mad (*Ion, Phaedrus*); and when he wants to use a poem to support his own position, he unhesitatingly distorts its apparent meaning (*Protagoras, Lysis*).

I will not argue that, in spite of this behavior, Socrates occasionally gives poetry its due, nor that even as he dismisses it he is willing to preserve some portion of it. When I refer to Socrates' charitable interpretations of poetry, I mean a way of reading a poem that motivates and grounds the mistreatments I have catalogued. Socrates is, at all times, prone to read a poem charitably; and that is part of his hostility toward poetry.

To make this point I will discuss the last mistreatment of poetry I named: Socrates uses a poem in his defense by forcing it to say what its author plainly did not intend. We see the workings of his interpretive method in an extended analysis of Simonides in the *Protagoras,* and perhaps also in a use of Homer and Empedocles in the *Lysis.* I will argue that what looks at first simply odd in those passages may be shown to follow a principle of interpretation which in some extreme form resembles the principle of interpretive charity. Thus it is Socrates' excessive charity toward poetry that stands behind his abuse of it.

That charity points to a new attitude toward poets, perhaps the first theoretically motivated rejection of the author. I think that this fate of the author in Socrates' interpretation will illuminate both his hostility toward poetry and his examination of his live interlocutors. More generally, Socrates' example will show how the search for truth in an interpretation is one way to deny appeals to the author.

I

Although Socrates' interpretation of Simonides in the *Protagoras* has been discussed many times, its purport or explanation is usually left unexamined.[1] What is uncontroversial is that in *Protagoras* 338e-348a, Plato's most extensive depiction of Socrates saying what a poem means, we find Socrates systematically misreading Simonides. He plucks individual lines out of a poem, combines them with his own highly specific ethical beliefs, and from this conjunction deduces a point which he then attributes to the poet. We must decide whether this is all some sort of joke, or whether on the contrary, as I believe, the interpretation reveals a coherent and deliberate method.

The text examined is a nearly continuous piece of Simonides' writing, roughly twenty-five lines from a much longer poem. It is Protagoras who goads Socrates into interpreting the poem, as part of the intellectual battle between them that continues through the dialogue. Protagoras sets an interpretive problem for Socrates to solve: two bits of Simonides' poem seem to contradict one another, for the first bit says it is hard to become good, and the second denies that it is hard to be noble (339). Socrates begins with the more modest aim of resolving that contradiction, but goes on through the poem to hang a sophisticated moral point on Simonides.

At first Socrates tries to resolve the contradiction by saying that Simonides thinks it hard to *become* good or noble, but easy to remain in that state (to *be* noble) once it has been achieved (340d). Protagoras ridicules this explanation, and Socrates quickly drops it in the face of objections (341e); but already the tone of Socratic interpretation has been set. In a broad sense, this paradoxical notion of moral improvement is a Socratic notion: the steps toward clarity of understanding are slow and taken only reluctantly, but the state of enlightenment can be maintained, Socrates usually seems to think, without effort (see, e.g., *Symposium* 211d ff.). Socrates, in other words, has made Simonides' thought consistent by identifying it with his own.

But that is still too broadly put. We need to find specific interpretive decisions that bear out this general description. I claim that the rest of Socrates' interpretation does indeed retain the same spirit. His method emerges in the pages that follow, as he seeks to extract philosophical content from Simonides' poem. I want to look at four specific cases, all occurring within two pages, in which Socrates reinterprets or emends individual lines of poetry.

(a) Socrates restates a line he has begun with, "To become a truly good man is hard," as "To become a good man is truly hard" (343d-e). He moves the "truly" (*alētheōs*) to go with a later clause in the same line. (In Greek this requires a shift in phrasing, but no change in word order. Like Socrates' restatement of the poem in (d) below, this is a hyperbaton, a transposition of a word out of its normal place in the sentence.) Socrates explains his emendation thus: "He does not mean the 'truly' with ['good'], as if some men were truly good and others good but not truly so. That would seem silly and not the work of Simonides" (343e). Socrates is arguing (i) that it is nonsensical to speak of someone as good but not truly so, and (ii) that therefore Simonides cannot have meant his words that way.

But (i) is patently false. Anyone who thinks virtue can be partly achieved will unhesitatingly call some people truly good and others only somewhat good. What then can Socrates mean by (i)? I understand him to be assuming a position he argued for earlier in the *Protagoras*—that the virtues are (in some sense) identical (329ff). Later he will also claim all the virtues to be manifestations of some sort of knowledge (357). This knowledge guarantees perfectly virtuous behavior as soon as one begins to apply it. Now from *that* point of view it would indeed be silly to speak of someone as good but not truly so: once virtue has been reached it is possessed all at once, and with regard to every aspect of moral life. Socrates' real interpretive argument, then, is that *he* finds this reading of Simonides nonsensical, and that Simonides must therefore have meant something else. But this second step now looks less clearly warranted.

(b) At this point Socrates' reading becomes more explicitly paradoxical. He announces again that he will explain the "outline" (*typos*) and "purpose" (*boulēsis*) of this poem (344b), and starts with the pair of lines: "That man cannot help being bad / Whom extraordinary misfortune has cast down" (344c). To reconstruct the argument implicit in these lines, Socrates explains that to be cast down and left resourceless one must first be resourceful; then he implicitly glosses "resourceful" by "noble" (344d). Thus he can claim the lines to mean that disaster makes good people bad.

Here, although the conclusion attributed to Simonides is not shocking, the requisite gloss on "resourceful" is: to be *mēchanos* is not at all to be *agathos*. Socrates gets that translation of the term, I take it, from his earlier argument with Protagoras, in which he claimed that virtue is grounded in wisdom (e.g., 333b). Here he simply inserts that claim to get Simonides' meaning, by sliding unremarkably from "resourceful" to "wise" and then leaping to that word's equivalent (for him), "good."[2]

(c) The next lines Socrates looks at say, "For when doing well every man is good / But when doing badly evil" (344e). This platitude would seem to need (or admit of) no further explanation. But Socrates now wants to make the poem say that a good man cannot remain continuously good (345b-c). As a reading of the lines there is nothing strange about that; what is strange is the path Socrates takes from poem to implication. He begins with a typical craft example: "Now what is doing well in letters, and what makes a man good at them? Clearly it is the learning of them" (345a). Socrates understands "good" in terms of the capacity to perform a given craft; as in the previous example, he assumes that doing good involves knowledge. Then the danger, he says, lies in one's loss of knowledge, for that is the only way to do badly (345b). Therefore Simonides is saying that the good man cannot be continuously good. We may schematize Socrates' argument as follows:

(i) When he does well every man is good. (Simonides)

(ii) Doing well means possessing knowledge. (Socrates)

(iii) Knowledge may be lost.

(iv) Therefore, (Simonides says that) no one is continuously good.

Again, the conclusion attributed to Simonides is generated by a premise from Socrates' own supply.

(d) But the clearest case of Socrates' use of his own principles in an interpretation comes in his reading of "I praise and love everyone / Who does nothing shameful voluntarily"; he emends this to read, "I voluntarily praise and love everyone who does nothing shameful" (345d-e). This is another hyperbaton; *hekōn,* the word for "voluntarily," is moved from its place to the next line in the poem. In Greek the new word order is natural, but plainly not, in this context, the ordinary reading of those lines. Socrates' argument for such a radical change in meaning goes as follows: "Simonides was not so uneducated as to say that he praised all who did nothing bad voluntarily, as if there were some people who voluntarily act badly. For I think that no wise man believes any human being voluntarily sins, or does anything bad or shameful" (345d-e).

This last sentence is preposterous. Socrates, quite famously, was the only person to think wrongdoing was involuntary. He puts that position forward twice in this very dialogue (352d, 358e); here he attributes it casually to Simonides, allegedly in the interest of telling us what the poet thinks. As in the first example, Socrates changes the text to make the poet agree with him.

We have, in other words, two related interpretive procedures at work. In examples (a) and (d), Socrates straightforwardly emends the text to make Simonides agree with him. In (b) and (c), he derives the implication of Simonides' statements by assuming the poet to hold certain beliefs that Socrates (and nearly no one else) holds. In both cases, crucially, he assumes Simonides to know everything that he knows himself.

II

The latter interpretive method also appears in the *Lysis,* which contains several appeals to poets for philosophical ideas on the subject of friendship. In particular, after the failure of one proposed definition Socrates explicitly turns to poets for inspiration: they are, he says, "fathers of wisdom, and guides" (214a). He then quotes Homer (*Odyssey* 17.218) and, implicitly, Empedocles, to the effect that like is attracted to like. This is the new proposal about friendship which Socra-tes and his interlocutors will examine next.

Of course, Socrates adds right away, the premise cannot be accepted just as it stands, since that would imply the friendship of wicked men with one another. And "as it appears to us" (*dokei hē min*), he says, that is not the case: the wicked quickly turn on one another (214b-c). Therefore that implication of the poets' claim must be rejected right away. Socrates concludes, remarkably: "Therefore those who call like friendly with like are obscurely hinting that the good man is a friend only to the good man, but that the bad man never enters into true friendship either with a good man or with a bad" (214d). Homer and Empedocles are thus assumed, as Simonides had been, not to mean a statement that would deny things as they seem to Socrates.

The readings are astonishing. In Empedocles' vocabulary there is simply no room for the elaboration Socrates suggests. His explanation for natural forces could not work if attraction were restricted to the good.

Homer's case is more problematic. The line in the *Odyssey* about like being led to like is spoken by the goatherd Melanthius as an insult to the disguised Odysseus and his swineherd Eumaios. Melanthius says, "Now here's one worthless man leading another one," and concludes in the next line, "The god always brings like together with like that way." On the surface, then, the line Socrates quotes says precisely that bad men do become friends.

What might complicate this point is that Socrates could nevertheless be right in his interpretation; for Eumaios and Odysseus really are like each other, and they—being both good—enjoy a truer friendship than Melanthius is capable of with Penelope's suitors. In his own obscure way Homer may indeed be hinting that the good man is a friend only to the good man.[3] Still, as in examples (b) and (c) above, Socrates has reached his plausible reading by means of an unprecedented and implausible method. What strikes me about his interpretation here, as in the *Protagoras,* is that he arrives at it by casting out readings he considers false.

III

We must now ask what this puzzling behavior means. So far we can only say that Socrates has set out to misinterpret poetry, and that he has done so by arguing fallaciously about what the poets may be assumed to believe. Or, to catalogue his misdeeds as Rudolph Weingartner has, Socrates "puts words together that clearly do not belong together. . . . He ignores bits of text that would be difficult to harmonize with his thesis. . . . He puts in words that are not part of the poem" (p. 100). These "sins of interpretation" lead Weingartner to say, "This section is rich with humor and gives us a rest from the fatiguing duty of following complex arguments" (p. 101). Most other commentators have likewise set this passage aside as ironic or humorous, when they have not ignored it altogether.[4] (Indeed, it is striking how little is ever said about the *Protagoras* in any discussion of Plato's view of poetry.)

Certainly Socrates is ironical; nor is there any doubt that this particular passage is ironic. But unless we understand irony in the most simplistic sense—that Socrates simply doesn't mean what he says—an ironic tone by itself cannot license us to ignore the passage. Compare: When Socrates complains of his ignorance, he is usually ironic about it, and sometimes his interlocutors even point that out (*Symposium* 175e, *Republic* 337a). But for all the irony he nevertheless does believe himself to be ignorant. Therefore his irony is not a sufficient reason for us to call Socrates' professions of ignorance insincere. In the case at hand, too, Socrates' evident irony need not mean that he does not endorse his own interpretive method.

There are at least three reasons not to dismiss this passage, or even to call it a burlesque of poetic interpretation.[5] First, Socrates himself agrees with the claims he attributes to Simonides. He cannot be questioning poets' authority, in the sense of believing them mistaken, when he finds Simonides to equate virtue with knowledge, and deny the existence of voluntary wrongdoing. This is hardly the way to show the silliness of a procedure. So even if Socrates' interpretation is ironic, we have to explain why it is used to justify Socratic principles: this poses, rather than settles our problem.

We also need an explanation of what Socrates is doing here because it fits into the larger context of his behavior. To my ear, for instance, Socrates' treatment of Simonides resembles strikingly his treatment of his live interlocutors. His leading, even tendentious questions subject his interlocutors' statements to inquiry they were never prepared to address, and he reaches conclusions which the interlocutors would not have taken themselves to believe—indeed, which they typically deny. The questions, the unexpected inquiry, and the unintended conclusions are all here too, together with Socrates' insistence that this conclusion is what the other person really believes. If this is a parody of interpretation, then Socrates' whole interrogative method is a parody.

Finally, Socrates' attitude toward poetry in this passage is consistent with his positions in other dialogues. The *Lysis,* for one, at least suggests that Socrates' strategy toward Simonides reveals more about him than his ability to make an isolated joke. And I hope to show below how the attitude toward the author implicit in this interpretive method might fit together with the recurring attacks on poetry in Plato's dialogues.

That is all by way of saying that we need some explanation for Socrates' performance; the explanation of it as only ironic will not do. I find a clue to understanding Socrates in his own concluding comments to this section. Those comments are often put forward as the strongest reason to ignore the whole section, since Socrates urges his friends to leave poetry out of their discussion. But to use the conclusion in that way it must be understood as straightforward, empty of the ironies that commentators find in the philosophical digression itself; whereas, to my mind, the conclusion is the most problematic part of the passage.

Socrates suggests that the group carry on in direct philosophical conversation, without poetry or songs (347c). Like musical entertainment, he says, the appeal to poets brings "an outside [other, foreign, strange, extraneous] voice" (*allotria phōnē*) into the discussion (347e): "It is not possible to ask poets about what they are saying, and when they are introduced into discussions some claim them to think one thing and some another, and no one can argue decisively on the matter. But the best people leave such gatherings alone, and converse among themselves, exchanging their own words with one another to test what they have to say" (347e-348a). In other words, discourse about the poet's meaning cannot meet standards of philosophical discourse. Better to have only Socratic criticism.

This comment might be taken to rule out Socrates' own interpretation along with every other one. But Socrates' criticism of textual exegesis, that it wanders too far from the discussion at hand, is entirely opposite to the criticisms which have been made of *his* exegesis—namely, that it does not wander far enough. If Socrates has ascribed his own beliefs to Simonides, then his criticisms do not apply to his own reading. For to the extent that Socrates, in putting his ideas into Simonides' mouth, has blatantly ignored the question of what the poet actually believes, he is immune to the charge of having listened to an outside voice. He says it is wrong to search out the poet's particular beliefs; but since he never looked for them himself, there is no reason for him to set his own reading aside.

I see Socrates' advice about poetry rather as a warning to *other* readers, who will not be able to attack a poem as he has himself. None of them will be able to argue decisively about what the poet thinks, because for them that question will entail entering into the poet's private thoughts. In other readers' hands, then, the poet will draw us away from the independent search for the truth. We will have to understand the poet first and so never get to our original question. But since Socrates clearly has stayed with his original question, it follows that for him the poet has ceased to be an outside voice. His abandonment of the poet here is continuous with *Apology* 22b, in which he comments that authors themselves are usually the least capable interpreters of their own works; by Socratic standards, authorship can be no assurance of one's ability to generate true interpretations.

Thus, when Socrates does claim to aim at Simonides' thoughts, he must mean something quite different from the usual sense of that phrase. I have two passages in mind here: when exbarking on his most substantive discussion of Simonides, Socrates says, "Now I want to tell position on intentions, as I have construed it, is that intentions cannot be known—but not, as in some recent accounts, because they cannot be reached. Socrates does not suggest that Simonides' own thoughts on his poem cannot *in principle* be reached; indeed, he implies that if the poet were there the rest of them could ask him what he meant (347e). For a modern theory of the impossibility of intentions this is clearly fruitless and beside the point (Wimsatt and Beardsley, p. 18). From Socrates' point of view, though, it does not help to say that intentions can be reached, because reaching them does not count as knowledge. As Socrates sees them, intentions are idiosyncratic; inquiring about them is akin to familiarizing oneself with the peculiarities of one blade of grass, what sets that blade apart from the others. That is some sort of information, but it does not lie on the path to general knowledge about grass. So, too, learning Simonides' thoughts—what is peculiar to him—is possible, but stands in the way of learning about his subject matter. Thus nothing is gained from excavating the poets' thoughts, when more true statements may be attained by ignoring them.

(This is the clearest way in which Socrates' treatment of Simonides reflects anti-poetic views he expresses elsewhere. In the *Ion,* it is not poets' or critics' ignorance that Socrates wants to fault so much as the inevitable allure that the poet's person had for the reader: it is by trying to see the author's point of view, and not aiming separately at the facts of the matter, that the reader is always doomed to ignorance.[9] I further suspect, though I cannot argue for this point here, that the emphasis on mimesis of character in *Republic* X—on which Socrates there blames the ill effects of poetry—is of a piece with this avoidance of the author's person. In both lines of argument there seems to be something about the individual speaker as such that Socrates most wants to escape. Only when poetry is freed from its ties to individuals can it impart verifiable knowledge.)

At this point I expect an objection: Haven't I misunderstood the role of intentions? How can the principle of charity work against intentions when its goal is to attribute certain claims to the author? Why isn't this done precisely in *service* to intentions?

The ethical analogy may provide the best answer. If I give you a present because it is something I like myself, and I never wonder whether you will like or need it, then something has gone wrong with the gift-giving. To protest that nothing is wrong, that I am still genuinely interested in you as another person—I did give you a present, didn't I?—is plainly disingenuous.

Similarly, my explanation of what you said has gone wrong if I could in theory get the same words out of any horse's mouth. The attribution of intention does not consist simply in hanging the author's name on a sentence. Or to put it the other way around: the feeling that a search for the author's intention has somehow been violated does not arise only when the author's name is not mentioned; it arises also when the author's name *is* mentioned, but inappropriately.

The real joke for Socrates is that he does not care what Simonides may actually have believed. From this implicit disregard for authorial intention, it is a short step to Socrates' overt disregard for poets in other discussions, such as his bowdlerization of Homer in *Republic* II and III. Socrates feels justified in emending Homer for the young guardians' education because the unity of the poems, or Homer's greater purpose in writing them, is irrelevant to him. Ethical standards (here not so much what is true about the gods or about death, as what ought to be believed about those subjects) govern Socrates' decision about what is to be said in the ideal state.

The kind of intention lost in Socratic interpretation is intention understood as that which is fundamentally other, or outside. It begins with the sense that there is another person speaking here—the awareness that I am not the poet. An intention, unlike a meaning, must be someone's and must come from someone. The fact that someone said these words is why they are thought to be worth hearing. Thus, "Why did Simonides say that?" is really a way of asking, "Who is he?" We have all the reasons for wanting to know the author's intention (and all the reasons for avoiding it) that we have for wanting to understand another person. The problem of the author is the problem of the other.

Notes

[1] See Hermann Sauppe's commentary on *Protagoras,* trans. with additions by James A. Towle (Boston: Ginn and Company, 1889); E. G. Sihler's edition (New York: Harper & Brothers, 1881); Leon Woodbury, "Simonides on *Arete,*" *Transactions and Proceedings of the American Philological Association,* 84 (1953), pp. 135-63; W. K. C. Guthrie, *A History of Greek Philosophy* (Cambridge: Cambridge University Press, 1975), vol. 4, pp. 213-35; I. M. Crombie, *An Examination of Plato's Doctrines* (London: Routledge & Kegan Paul, 1962), vol. 1, pp. 232-45; Rudolph Weingartner, *The Unity of the Platonic Dialogue* (Indianapolis: Bobbs-Merrill, 1973). The general descriptive point I will stress concerning this passage—that Socrates imports his own philosophical doctrines into this reading of the poem—has been made by all these readers. They have also pointed out the particular instances of Socratic misinterpretation, though with varying degrees of specificity as to exactly what doctrines Socrates is importing.

[2] Sauppe says of this passage, "Here *sophon* [wise] is inserted as the characteristic mark of true excellence."

He adds that "in this whole exegesis Socrates keeps in mind his main argument" (p. 126n).

[3] This point was made to me by the anonymous reader for *Philosophy and Literature.*

[4] Thus Sauppe says at two points in the passage, "this is obviously ironical" (pp. 123n and 129n). Sihler says, "The entire point made in the philological episode, as we might call it, is a negative one" (p. 120); and Guthrie goes so far as to call the passage "splendid entertainment, but hardly philosophy" (p. 227).

[5] This phrase is Nicholas Smith's. I first heard this account of Socrates' behavior from Patrick Coby. See also Crombie, who finds in this passage the implication "that reliance on poetry as a means of education is misguided" (p. 234).

[6] Donald Davidson has systematically brought the principle of charity into discussions of radical interpretation. See esp., "On the Very Idea of a Conceptual Scheme," *Proceedings and Addresses of the American Philosophical Association* 47 (1973-74): 5-20; "Belief and the Basis of Meaning," *Synthese* 27 (1974): 309-23 (hereafter abbreviated "BBM"); "Mental Events," in Lawrence Foster and J. M. Swanson (eds.), *Experience and Theory* (Boston: University of Massachusetts Press, 1970), hereafter abbreviated "ME." For worries about the extent to which the principle of charity might be taken, see David Lewis, "Radical Interpretation," *Synthese* 27 (1974): 331-34; W. V. Quine, "Comment on Donald Davidson," *Synthese* 27 (1974): 325-29; Bruce Vermazen, "General Beliefs and the Principle of Charity," *Philosophical Studies* 42 (1982): 111-18.

[7] Even a review of the titles of works in that debate lies outside the scope of this paper. But I must at least mention W. K. Wimsatt and Monroe C. Beardsley, "The Intentional Fallacy," in Wimsatt, *The Verbal Icon* (Lexington: University of Kentucky Press, 1984), pp. 3-18. And although I need no position on the issue for my present purposes, my approach to intentions is indebted to Stanley Cavell, "A Matter of Meaning It," in *Must We Mean What We Say?* (Cambridge: Cambridge University Press, 1976), esp. pp. 225-37; see also "Music Discomposed" in the same volume, pp. 180-212. Specifically, I owe to Cavell the general point, implicit in those articles, that the problem of knowing the author is a recast (or miscast) version of the greater problem of other minds.

[8] That more recent proposal about intentions likewise does not enter into my discussion. But see Alexander Nehamas, "The Postulated Author: Critical Monism as a Regulative Ideal," *Critical Inquiry* 7 (1981): 133-49 and esp. 144-47; "What an Author Is," *Journal of Philosophy* 83 (1986): 685-91; Steven Knapp and Walter Benn Michaels, "Against Theory," *Critical Inquiry* 8 (1982): 723-42.

[9] As I have argued elsewhere; see my "Plato's *Ion:* The Problem of the Author," *Philosophy* 64 (1989): 1-9.

Luis E. Navia (essay date 1993)

SOURCE: "The Socratic Problem," in *The Socratic Presence,* Garland Publishing, Inc., 1993, pp. 1-19.

[*In the following essay, Navia offers an overview of the Socratic problem and suggests ways in which the apparent discrepancies between the various Socratic sources may be reconciled.*]

There are two facts about Socrates that can be affirmed without hesitation: that his influence on the development of Western culture in general and philosophy in particular has been extraordinary, and that his historical presence remains a baffling phenomenon. The first of these two facts does not need to be particularly emphasized, for it is widely acknowledged, even by those who are superficially acquainted with the history of ideas, that Socrates constitutes a major turning point in our civilization, and that he represents a new point of departure in the mind's quest for understanding and knowledge. With him, philosophy assumed a new direction, and all subsequent endeavors to come to grips with the mystery of existence have been compelled to take into account Socrates' own thoughts, convictions, and methodology. Without Socrates, one could venture to assert, culture would have probably followed a different route, or would have moved at a different pace, and this not only on account of Socrates' influence on Plato, but on account of the impact of his presence on all other philosophical schools of antiquity. If nothing else, one is certainly justified in saying that Socrates stands before our eyes as the embodiment of the philosophical spirit, and as a high plateau of intellectual and spiritual excellence to which few persons after him have been able to attain. To speak of Socrates is to speak of philosophy, especially because he was able to merge in one indivisible reality thought and action, theory and practice, which explains the undeniable circumstance that he was able to teach both through his words and through his deeds. For him, philosophy was not an inert academic discipline, but a living commitment to a set of principles that cannot be abandoned even in the presence of death.

The second fact, namely, Socrates' historical elusiveness, is something that must be reiterated from time to time. Its roots can be traced to various interrelated circumstances, chief among which is his refusal to confine his ideas to writing. For nothing written can be attributed to him, and about this, all the sources are in explicit or implicit agreement, the only exception being a passing reference by Arrian (*Discourses of Epictetus,* II,i,32) who wrote around the year A.D. 100.

Arrian speaks of the many writings of Socrates, but it is evident that what he had in mind was the copious Socratic literature that had become known as 'the discourses of Socrates' and which was the work of Socrates' disciples. This phrase appears already in Aristotle (*e.g.* in *Politics* 1265a), and refers to dialogues where Socrates is presented as the main interlocutor. Nowhere in the primary sources is there any reference to Socrates' writings, and the secondary sources (with the exception of Arrian) are in agreement with this. Plutarch (*Alex. fort.,* I,iv,328) states that Socrates, like Pythagoras, wrote nothing, and Dio-genes Laertius mentions no writings attributable to him. The poem and the fable alluded to by Diogenes (ii,42), no less than the poetical compositions which according to Plato (*Phaedo* 60d) were composed by Socrates at the end of his life, must have been, if genuine, probably compositions in the style of oral literature. Socrates spoke and conversed a great deal, and his mature life was literally spent talking to anyone who would care to discourse with him, as we learn from the *Euthyphro* (3d), but he felt disdain for the written word, as we are told in the *Phaedrus* (275c ff.): the written word, he said, is something inert and dead with which one cannot enter into meaningful discourse.

> Much has been said and written about Socrates' unwillingness to use the written word. The fact that for him the word is always something spoken and heard, not written and seen, has been viewed as a necessary consequence of his philosophical position, for if he claimed to know only that he knew little or nothing, how could he have chosen to express himself in a form which admits of no subsequent alterations? If he conceived of himself as a searcher after wisdom, not as someone who possessed wisdom, what better medium could he have opted for but the living and direct discourse with his contemporaries? Furthermore, it has been argued that Socrates belonged to a stage in the development of European culture during which orality remained the primary mode of expression, and that, his revolutionary spirit notwithstanding, he did not attempt to establish a bridge to a more elaborate stage in which first the written dialogue, and then the didactic prose, made their appearance.[1]

For us, however, Socrates' choice is one of the roots of his elusiveness, because on account of it, we are compelled to gather information about his person and philosophy from the testimonies of others who do not appear to convey to us one cohesive and unified picture. As one reviews the exceedingly rich Socratic literature, whether it be the primary or the secondary sources, one is often tempted to conclude that there must have been various persons by the name of Socrates, with different lives and diverse philosophical orientations, so that it is not always easy to avoid the conclusion, reached by a number of scholars, that the historical Socrates is a perfectly unknown entity, and that the literary Socrates is nothing more than a dramatic invention constructed by writers who used him as an eloquent mouthpiece for the expression of their ideas.[2] On this basis, accordingly, the search for the real Socrates is bound to end in disappointment, and Socrates emerges only as a focal point, or rather as a collection of focal points, around which various legends, myths, and ideologies have come into being: the historical reality behind such creations is a chimerical and insubstantial ghost that will always elude all endeavors to shed light upon it.

There is, however, another way of viewing the Socratic problem, and this entails the adherence to one of the primary sources and the downgrading of the others. From this point of view, then, we conclude that there must have been a 'true' Socrates, and that *one* of the sources must have succeeded in capturing his essence, both biographically and philosophically, while the others constitute either intentional deformations or self-serving trivializations of the truth. In general, and especially in our own times, this attitude has resulted in the tendency to regard the Platonic writings, particularly the early dialogues, as the most genuine Socratic testimony, while the other primary sources as mostly worthless pieces of fictional literature. It has been said, for instance, that if Plato's Socrates is the true one, the Socrates of Aristophanes and Xenophon must be false, and that since the former must be the true one, then the latter must be viewed as falsifications.[3] Occasionally, too, Xenophon's Socrates has been proclaimed as the true Socrates, and that of Plato as a philosophical fabrication which, its philosophical merit notwithstanding, does not do justice to the historical reality.[4] And even the comic character created by Aristophanes has been invested with an air of historical genuineness, which implies, of course, that what Plato and Xenophon wrote about Socrates can be viewed as mostly fiction.[5]

The hypothesis of one 'true' Socrates rests, it seems, on two complex assumptions which are not without enormous difficulties. First, there is the conviction that a person is something that can be described and analyzed from one singular perspective, as if it were a simple entity, and second, there is the belief that the portraits of Socrates which emerge from the primary sources are disparate representations that have little in common, and that stand in irremediable contradiction with one another. But reflection reveals that neither one of these assumptions has much value. A person is always a complex reality that exists and functions on a variety of levels which manifest themselves in different ways to the external world, and, accordingly, are perceived differently by different witnesses. In reality, the 'person' which is seen and heard by each witness is, as the etymology of the word reveals, a 'mask' behind which the self remains hidden.[6] Thus, every person is a collection of masks, and each one of them contains, as it were, an element of truth. As the person functions in the social world, its masks are perceived by different witnesses from various points of view, and each witness is able to understand and appreciate only those aspects of the person that are within his intellectual and emotional capacities. It is, therefore, futile to expect to obtain from the testimony of one single witness a complete or 'true' account of a person, regardless of the level of perceptiveness and understanding of that witness, for, in fact, all he may be able to provide for us is the rendering of one aspect or set of aspects of the person. And if this is the case in the instance of ordinary persons, it is much more so in that of someone as complex and paradoxical as Socrates.

The hypothesis of one 'true' Socrates generally leads us to conclude that it was Plato, and no one else, who can claim to be the real witness of the Socratic phenomenon. Given the enormity of Plato's mind and the extraordinary influence which his philosophy has exercised, this tendency is understandable, for we are naturally inclined to lend a more attentive ear to a witness of impressive credentials. The enthronement of Plato as the Socratic witness *par excellence* is laden, however, with problems which are not easy to resolve satisfactorily. For, to mention only one such problem, the figure of Socrates which emerges from the Platonic writings is not a monistic representation, but one that varies and undergoes transformations as Plato's own philosophical views change. The Socrates of the early dialogues, for instance in the *Euthyphro,* is in many respects different from the Socrates of the middle dialogues, as in the *Republic,* and this in turn is significantly distinct from the Socrates who speaks in the *Parmenides.* Which one of these Socratic characters is the 'true' one? It would be ill-advised to say, echoing the statement of Plato's second letter (*Epist.* 2.314c), that everything that Plato attributes to Socrates was actually spoken by Socrates, exactly as Socrates said it.[7] The fact is probably that there is much in the dialogues that belongs to the historical Socrates, and much, too, that does not; and that in reporting on the historical Socrates, Plato left for posterity those aspects of the Socratic phenomenon which he found significant and was best able to capture, and that in using the name of Socrates to advance some of his own views, Plato was convinced that, had the historical Socrates continued his own philosophical development, he would have espoused similar views. But there is a wide gap between saying this much and affirming that the Socrates of the Platonic writings is the 'true' one.

The same indeed can be said with respect to the testimonies of Aristophanes and Xenophon, and of the minor Socratics. In each case, what we find is a perceiver who captures an aspect, an element, of Socrates, precisely that aspect or element that fits comfortably within his idiosyncratic frame of reference, and serves the specific intentions of the witness. With Aristophanes, for instance, the frame of reference is the mentality of the uprooted Attic peasants who crow-ded the theater of Dionysus, because it was mostly for them (certainly not for the scholars of the twentieth century) that Aristophanes wrote his comedies; and his intention was to cause laughter among such peasants, and perhaps thereby to use the comic stage as an effective catalyst for social and political reforms.[8] Thus, his Socrates has to mould himself to the exigencies of the comic stage, and the end result is a curious mixture of biographical fact, and comic distortion and exaggeration. Aristophanes' Socrates stands related to the historical man as a pictorial lampoon to a portrait, or as a caricature to a photograph, and is therefore both true and false.

With Xenophon, on the other hand, things are not altogether different: his Socrates adjusts himself to the practical frame of mind of the reporter who saw in the philosopher a judicious and sensible citizen, and whose main intention was to vindicate him from the aura of eccentricity and abnormality which surrounded his memory. Behind Xenophon's Socrates, accordingly, we can discern the outlines of Xenophon himself, and still behind such outlines we can discover elements which in all probability reflect genuine historical circumstances. And if we had more ample testimonies from other Socratics, philosophers like Phaedo, Crito, and Antisthenes, we would surely find ourselves in a similar situation.

It is, therefore, unwise to opt for a pessimistic solution to the Socratic problem, and say that we will never know anything definite about Socrates, for information about him is plentiful—indeed as plentiful as that about any other major figure of antiquity. But it is equally unwise to attach undue weight to any one source of information, because no one witness could possibly give us the total picture of the historical phenomenon. The only meaningful approach is to tap all the sources of information, primary as well as secondary, in order to reconstruct from them a portrait as complete and cogent as possible of the historical Socrates, but in this endeavor, too, an element of subjective judgment is unavoidable, for the personality and philosophy of Socrates are so engaging and intense, that their examination always elicits the strongest personal reactions from us: as Guthrie has perceptively noted, "everyone who has written about him was also reacting to him in one way or another,"[9] which explains the curious circumstance that the Socrates of each person is always an idiosyncratic and personal image which is seldom in full agreement with those of others. After studying Socrates for many years, one is tempted to stand before the academic world and repeat those words of Alcibiades in Plato's *Symposium* (216c): "Let me tell you that none of you knows Socrates; but I shall reveal him to you." Such revelation, however, would be a combination of subjective and objective elements: in it, we would be revealing as much about ourselves as about Socrates.

The second assumption which apparently justifies the hypothesis of one 'true' Socrates, and which is also unwarranted, is the conviction that the various sources of information stand in irreconcilable disagreement with one another, and that it is not possible to sift through the differences in order to arrive at some sort of common basis. It is undeniable that the portraits of Socrates outlined by the primary sources are individually distinct: the Socrates of the *Clouds,* for instance, stands in sharp contrast with the Socrates of the *Memorabilia,* and this, in his turn, cannot be confused with the august and imposing philosopher of the Platonic dialogues. But, in reality, what we do have is the same person viewed from different perspectives and described with divergent aims in mind. Beneath the differences, it remains possible to discern a considerable number of common traits and features, so that a biographical and ideological picture of recognizable outlines can be eventually drawn. Surely, if we insist on emphasizing the divergent elements in the sources, without taking into account the character of the witnesses and their motivations in writing about Socrates, such a picture turns out quite blurry and confusing, but if we adopt the method suggested by Schleiermacher, that is, if we view the sources as complementary, and ask in each instance what else can each one add to the developing portrait of Socrates, then some progress in the resolution of the Socratic problem is possible.[10] In this way, by attempting to integrate eclectically, yet critically, the various sources, both primary and secondary, we may succeed at least in establishing a foundation from which we may proceed, and which may furnish us with a reasonably certain historical basis for the reconstruction of the actual Socrates.

Obviously, as in the instance of other major figures of antiquity, it will always remain impossible to arrive at a perfectly clear and unquestionable collection of statements concerning Socrates: by its very nature, historical description is not a science from which we can demand exactitude and finality, and dogmatism can have no place in it. Socrates has been dead for too many years, and we are already too removed from him in time in order for us to be able to capture all the aspects and details of his presence. Through the unavoidable process of bibliographical selectiveness, to which we shall return presently, innumerable primary and secondary sources are no longer extant, and there can be no hope of retrieving from the past the mountains of lost information which perished towards the end of Roman times. Thus, our existing sources, their significance notwithstanding, are limited and in many respects markedly prejudiced in one direction or another, and, accordingly, our knowledge of Socrates will always remain sketchy and incomplete.

And yet, there are many biographical and ideological details that can be accepted as reasonably certain—indeed as reasonably certain as our historical information of antiquity allows—and that are supported by their explicit affirmation in various sources and by the fact that they are not emphatically denied by any of them. These details constitute, so to speak, the bare 'facts' concerning Socrates' life and thought, and are generally viewed as genuine.

The date of his birth and death can be readily ascertained: he was born in the year 469 B.C. (fourth year of the 77th Olympiad), and died in 399 B.C. (first year of the 95th Olympiad)[11]: he was, therefore, seventy years of age at the time of his death. The allegation reported by Diogenes Laertius (ii,44), namely, that he died at the age of sixty, does not appear to hold any ground whatsoever. The coincidence of his birth and death with the Athenian festivity of Apollo and Artemis (Diogenes Laertius ii,44; Porphyry, *De vita Platonis,* ii,96) may have been the result of a pious legend created in Hellenistic times, although the testimony of Plato lends support to the belief that Socrates was executed at the conclusion of the Delian festival of Apollo, as we can read in the *Crito* and in the *Phaedo.* Both his birth and death took place in Athens. His father was a statuary or sculptor named Sophroniscus, and his mother was a midwife named Phaenarete, and both were Athenian by birth of the deme of Alopece.[12] Socrates was, therefore, born an Athenian citizen, and inherited all the rights and privileges of his father. His economic and social status at birth was probably that of what we might call 'middle class', that is, neither that of the wealthy oligarchs (like Alcibiades, Critias, and Plato) nor that of the indigent native population, and this is supported by the various testimonies that state that he served as a hoplite or infantry soldier in the Athenian army.[13] Wealthy citizens would normally serve in the cavalry, as in the case of Xenophon, whereas the poor would generally function as auxiliaries. In later years, it appears that Socrates' financial resources became significantly diminished, and that this was due to his choice of vocation: he devoted himself to intellectual pursuits and refused to receive payment for his instruction. The statement of Aristoxenus to the effect that Socrates made money by teaching (Diogenes Laertius, ii,20) is not supported either by Plato or by Xenophon, although in Aristophanes (*Clouds* 98) there is a reference to Socrates' practice of collecting fees. In Xenophon's *Oeconomicus* (ii,1-4), Socrates states that his possessions did not exceed more than 100 minae (the equivalent of approximately 1000 dollars), a circumstance by which he would have belonged to the fourth and lowest of social classes among the citizens as established by the constitution of Solon, and in the Platonic writings there are various references to his poverty (*Apology* 19d, 31c).

There is a report in Diogenes Laertius (ii,20) that in his youth Socrates worked as a statuary, and that he was 'rescued' from this occupation by Crito, a wealthy man himself; but there is no confirmation of this in Plato or Xenophon who do not speak of Socrates having ever actually worked for a living. In the *Crito* (45a), however, we learn that he was the beneficiary of his friends' generosity, and in Diogenes (ii,25) we are told about their willingness and ability to provide for his needs. In general, we can say that he enjoyed an extraordinary amount of leisure, but this was certainly nothing exceptional among the free Athenians of his time who looked upon the necessity of working for a living as something embarrassing and debasing.

He was married to a woman named Xanthippe who is mentioned by Plato and Xenophon (*Phaedo* 60a, 116a; Xenophon's *Symposium* ii,10). The report attributed by Diogenes (ii,26) to Aristotle, namely, that Socrates was also married at some time or another to a certain Myrto, a daughter of Aristides the statesman, is not found in the existing Aristotelian works, and is not confirmed by the primary sources. In Diogenes, Myrto is said to have been Socrates' second wife and the mother of his two youngest children, Sophroniscus and Menexenus, but in the *Phaedo* (60a) the sense is clear that it was Xanthippe who was his wife at the time of his death. The reference in the *Memorabilia* (II,ii,1-14) to the mother of Lamprocles (his oldest son) is inconclusive as to who she was, since her name is not given. In Aristophanes, on the other hand, there are no allusions to Socrates' family, but in reality there should not be anything surprising in this: the Athenians did not pay much public attention to the details and circumstances of a man's married life, and Aristophanes' silence on Xanthippe, therefore, has no special significance.

In the secondary sources, Xanthippe became a paradigm of bad temper and nagginess, as can be gathered from various anecdotes in Diogenes (ii,34-37), and there is some basis for this reputation in Xenophon (*Symposium* ii, 26), where Socrates says that he chose her as his wife in order to learn to cope with even the most difficult among strangers. From Plato, however, nothing definite can be deduced concerning her character or background, and one suspects that her uncomplimentary reputation is mostly the result of exaggeration and distortion, born out of bits of gossip in the secondary literature.

Little is known about Socrates' children, except for their names and approximate ages at the time of their father's death. Plato does not mention them by name, but states that the oldest (Lamprocles) was a boy already reaching manhood (*Apology* 34d), and that the youngest was small enough to be held in his mother's arms (*Phaedo* 60a), at the time of Socrates' execution. Xenophon gives us only the name of the oldest son, and says nothing about the other two (whose names appear in Diogenes, ii,26). Some bits of information about them can be gathered from the secondary sources: for instance, in Aristotle (*Rhetoric* 1390b) and in Plutarch (*Cato*, xx), they are said to have been rather stupid and vulgar, and to have amounted to little in life.[14]

Information regarding Socrates' education is unclear and difficult to sort out. We are told by Diogenes (ii,19) that he was a student of Anaxagoras, Damon, and Archelaus the natural philosopher, and in Ameipsias' comedy the *Connus* a certain man named Connus is introduced as Socrates' music teacher (cf. *Euthydemus* 272c, 295d).[15] Also, in the *Phaedo* (97c ff.), we learn of his having studied a work by Anaxagoras. But both in Plato and Xenophon there is the repeated assertion that he had no formal teachers, and that he regarded himself as the disciple of no one.

It is possible that we may be able to distinguish two different stages in his intellectual development—a first stage during which he actually studied under one or more teachers, and during which he was genuinely interested in questions and issues concerning the physical world, and a second stage during which he declared his independence from the ideas of others, and turned his attention almost exclusively inward, that is, towards his own self. The mature Socrates, accordingly, was a person that could rightfully regard himself as having no intellectual or philosophical mentors, and as a thinker completely indifferent towards the problems of natural philosophy or science. The point in time that separates these two stages constitutes undoubtedly one of the most enigmatic aspects of his life, and there is some justification in identifying that point with the famous Delphic pronouncement about him.

But be it as it may, one thing remains indisputable: the Socrates who speaks in the writings of Plato and Xenophon, and who inspired the numerous reports of the secondary sources, is a man thoroughly knowledgeable about the philosophical developments of his time, and a person of the most refined culture in a wide variety of fields, indeed someone who could have easily warranted the Pythia's statement about him, namely, that of all living men he was truly the wisest.

Of Socrates' social relations we are able to construct a reasonably accurate picture from the testimonies of Plato and Xenophon: in them, he appears to have been a gregarious man who was willing and able to enter into active discourse with various sorts of people. We find him conversing with statesmen and generals, with philosophers and sophists, with poets and musicians, with wealthy foreigners, with people of humble background, and even with slaves—in sum, with practically anyone who crossed his path, as if he were possessed by an irresistible passion to communicate his message. The Platonic and Xenophontean Socrates is indeed far removed in this respect from the representation given to us by Aristophanes, according to whom, he was an anti-social recluse who lived generally indoors, surrounded by a close entourage of stupefied disciples. The former Socrates, on the other hand, is an open and outgoing person, whose doctrines, as we read in Plato's *Apology* (33b), are never revealed in secret or by esoteric means: they are spoken in public and in a language that is accessible even to uneducated persons, and couched in metaphors related to the activities of shoemakers, horse-trainers, and other working folk. He functions well at ease among the mighty oligarchs as well as among the simple citizens, and is invariably a paradigm of politeness and civility. He is loved and admired by a small group of devoted friends, who, as in the case of Xenophon, regard him as a philosophical master whose words and memory are to be revered (*Memorabilia,* I,ii,61), or who, as in the instance of Plato, look upon him as the best, wisest, and most righteous of men (*Phaedo* 118a). Others, like Meno (*Meno* 80a-b), simply stand befuddled and perplexed in his presence, and, as if stung by a sting ray, are unable to speak or move. Still others, like the passionate and overwhelming Alcibiades, as we are told in Plato's *Symposium* (215 ff.), are literally in love with him and are unable to dispel the spell that he has cast upon their souls.

For his part, Socrates responds to his friends' love and admiration in a two-fold manner: he is modest and unassuming, and even makes protestations about his worthlessness, and he returns their love with an even greater love. For love, he says (*Theages* 128b),[16] is the only subject in the world in which he regards himself an unsurpassed master. In Xenophon's *Symposium* (viii,2), he makes the remarkable statement that he cannot remember a time of his life when he was not in love with someone: love appears to have been for him the fundamental force which animated and sustained all his endeavors.

But surely, the circle of Socrates' intimate friends must have been small, and in this respect the testimony of Aristophanes is in agreement with that of Plato and Xenophon: in the *Clouds,* the group of 'disciples' who remain close to the 'master' is insignificant in the context of the population at large. And in none of the primary or secondary sources does Socrates appear as a charismatic leader addressing the masses: unlike Jesus of Nazareth or Mahatma Gandhi, his message is not heard amid large gatherings of people, but is one that touches quietly only those few who have adequate ears for his words, for his style is not that accustomed in the courts or political assemblies (Plato's *Apology* 17d). We may assume that for most Athenians, Socrates was merely an eccentric and colorful figure in the Agora and public buildings, perhaps a clever Sophist and a restless philosopher, but in reality nothing else: they must have remained unconcerned about his activities and indifferent towards his philosophical preoccupations, although, as the testimony of the comedians show, they must not have missed the welcomed opportunity of laughing at his expense in the riotous performances at the theater of Dionysus. In Diogenes Laertius (ii,21), we read that often, as a result of his vehement questioning, people would set upon him with their fists and would tear his hair out, and both in Plato and Xenophon, he often succeeded in antagonizing his interlocutors with his frank comments or his persistent interrogations.

But this does not entail that Socrates earned for himself so dreadful a reputation as to be considered a public enemy, and certainly his trial does not appear to have had the trappings of a popular lynching, as was the case, for instance, with the trial of the generals of Arginusae.[17] In this regard, the comment attributed by Plutarch to Aristoxenus (*On the Malice of Herodotus* 856d), that even though Socrates was an uneducated and impudent fellow, there was no real harm in him,—this comment probably is an echo of the assessment of the Socratic presence on the part of the Athenian populace: for the average Athenian, Socrates was a mild and tolerable public nuisance.

If we assume this attitude on the part of the Athenians, we can then explain the otherwise perplexing impunity with which he was able to function in a city which despite its alleged democracy and openness was sometimes far from liberal and tolerant. In his seventh letter (*Epist.* 7.325b), Plato attributes Socrates' ability to remain unpunished for so long a time to an element of 'chance', and indeed this must have also been the case. But still, the climate of public indifference which probably surrounded the philosopher must also be taken into account. We have enough information to conclude, moreover, that the trial did not really have to take place, and that what the prosecutors actually wanted was for Socrates to leave the city permanently.

And yet, there is still another aspect of Socrates' life that should be considered, for side by side with his devoted friends, and against the background of the natural indifference of most people, there was the genuine hatred and dislike of a few who saw in him a formidable enemy of Athenian society—more formidable and dangerous than the Spartan infantry that during the Peloponnesian conflict would devastate yearly the Attic countryside. These enemies were few indeed but sufficiently influential to create for him a constant atmosphere of danger, of which he was obviously well aware (e.g. *Meno* 94e). They looked upon him as a dangerous man who would not hesitate to question and challenge the beliefs and practices of the State religion, who would pour contempt on long-established political practices and customs (such as the choosing of public officials by lot), who would persuade the youth to break away from parental authority, who through eristic trickery would baffle and corrupt the best among the citizens, and who would embarrass prominent political figures by public interrogations. Foremost in their minds, there must have been the indeed curious and historically ascertainable circumstance that many of Socrates' 'disciples' were men who at one time or another had gained notoriety for their unpatriotic leanings and Laconic tendencies[18]—men like Alcibiades, Critias, Charmides, Meno, Plato, Xenophon and others. The enemies of Socrates would allege that such people had been misguided and corrupted by his teachings, and had become, under his influence, the seeds of the destruction of the Athenian empire.

This destruction eventually took place in the year 404 B.C., when the Peloponnesians, under the command of Lysander, compelled the city to surrender. From this point on, the history of Athens was colored by decadence and confusion, and the last few years of Socrates' life witnessed the most unhappy period of its history: the reign of the Thirty, with whom Socrates had a relationship that could not have but appeared ambiguous to the democrats.[19] With the return of the democracy in 403 B.C., a sentiment of revenge surfaced in the political scene, and this, probably more than anything else, accelerated the vicissitudes that befell Socrates.[20] In 399 B.C., at last, he was indicted before the court of the King-Archon, on a charge of irreligiosity, and on the legal authority provided by a decree passed five decades earlier at the instance of a certain Diopeithes. The trial took place in the spring of that year, and Socrates was found guilty. One month later he was executed by poisoning.

Such are the bare 'facts' of Socrates' life. More extensive biographical information is not available, unless one is willing to lend an attentive ear to all sorts of reports that began to circulate after his death, reports which cannot be confirmed by reference to the primary sources, and which are probably the result of the imagination of later writers. The secondary sources provide innumerable anecdotal details and the most varied sort of doxographical comments, but, in general, it is difficult to assess their historical and philosophical value.

The sources of information concerning Socrates can be divided into two categories, namely, primary and secondary. The primary sources include exclusively the writings of Socrates' contemporaries which deal in one way or another with his life and ideas. Specifically, such sources are the writings of the poets of the Old Comedy who ridiculed Socrates on the stage, the testimonies of the minor Socratics, the indictment of Polycrates, the writings of Xenophon, and the Platonic dialogues.

If all these sources were extant, an enormous collection of documents would be available to us. Unfortunately, however, this is not the case. The circumstances and accidents of bibliographical history have brought about the irreparable loss of the bulk of the Socratic and related literature of the first one hundred years after Socrates' birth. For instance, of the fifty-four comedies attributed by Suidas to Aristophanes, only eleven have survived, and of the hundreds of comedies written by other poets of the Old Comedy none is extant except in the form of detached fragments. Accordingly, the references probably made to Socrates in many of those lost comic works cannot be retrieved. The many and lengthy writings of the Sophists also disappeared, again except for fragmentary quotations, and thus whatever light they might have shed on the Socratic presence can no longer be revived.

More important still is the loss of the works of the minor Socratics, to whom Diogenes Laertius attributes so many writings. Aristippus, for example, is said to have been the author of thirty-five philosophical volumes, and Aeschines of seven Socratic dialogues, Euclides of six, Stilpo of nine, Crito of seventeen, Simon of thirty-one, Glaucon of nine, Simmias of twenty-three, Antisthenes of sixty-two, and still others could be mentioned. It is difficult not to assume that in most of these writings, many of them written in the style of Xenophon's and Plato's dialogues (although not necessarily as imitations of them), the influence of Socrates must have been present in practically every line, for it was he who led such authors into the pursuit of philosophy.

One is, therefore, compelled to ask, what were the circumstances and accidents which were responsible for the preservation of some primary sources and for the destruction of others, but the answers to this question are inevitably many and quite hypothetical. We could mention, of course, the repeated burnings of the ancient libraries where, whether at Alexandria, Pergamum, or other major centers of learning, thousands of irreplaceable manuscripts perished at the hands of conquering armies or thoughtless religious zealots. And then there was the process of natural decay undergone by the original documents. Thus, either through the destructive hand of man or through the accidents of nature, the vast majority of documents of antiquity perished.

But more significant, however, is the process of bibliographical selectiveness which must be imputed to the scholiasts and librarians in whose hands the ancient documents were placed. They were the ultimate judges of what deserved to be preserved, and of what should be allowed to deteriorate, and thus what they saw fit to copy and annotate survived, and what they looked upon as less important or philosophically offensive eventually rotted away in the underground chambers of the libraries. Ancient scholars, so it seems, were not generally interested in preserving for posterity all the writings of their ancestors, but only those pieces which in their estimation had special value, and this explains, for instance, the far from accidental preservation of some of the tragedies of Sophocles and Euripides, and the destruction of others.

Surely, at a time when scholarship was dominated, particularly in Egypt, by adherents of Neoplatonism, it is to be expected that the writings of Plato (as opposed to those of the minor Socratics and even Aristotle) were to be carefully preserved and copied, and amply annotated. It is thus understandable that it is only Plato, among all the major philosophers and writers of ancient times, who has the privilege of having passed on to remote posterity the complete body of his writings. How in such an atmosphere the writings of Xenophon managed to survive, is, therefore, indeed a marvel, accountable only by reference to Xenophon's reputation as a historian and military strategist, for his value as a Socratic witness must not have impressed the Alexandrian scholars for whom Plato's testimony in that regard was of paramount importance.

Thus, by the fifteenth century, when the Medici and Venetian noblemen traveled to Constantinople in search of ancient documents, what they found available to them was indeed only a minuscule portion of what antiquity had produced, a portion that had been 'critically' preserved by the Hellenistic scholiasts. Undoubtedly, the documents rescued were the most impressive and instructive, but what was never rescued must have also been quite significant. If we had at our disposal, for instance, the Socratic documents available to Diogenes Laertius, it is difficult not to assume that our representation of Socrates would have been far more complete, albeit perhaps no less challenging and paradoxical.

With respect to the secondary sources, something similar can be said. Here, too, we are in the presence of only a few valuable pieces, the bulk of information having perished by the end of Roman times. By secondary sources we specifically mean the writings of those who were not Socrates' contemporaries, whose information was based either on direct oral traditions or on the reading of the primary sources, or on both, and who belong to Greek and Roman times. A review of Diogenes Laertius' *Life of Socrates* can give us a general idea of the enormous extent of the secondary sources available to him, but most of these sources remain for us only titles and occasional quotations.

The major secondary sources available to us are Aristotle's references to Socrates (approximately fifty in his extant works), various references in Cicero's works, a dialogue by Plutarch entitled *On the Sign of Socrates,* one of Lucian's *Dialogues of the Dead,* Apuleius' *On the God of Socrates,* Diogenes Laertius' *Life of Socrates,* and Libanius' reconstruction of the indictment of Socrates attributed to Polycrates. Aside from these sources, the rest of the secondary information is of limited historical value, since it ultimately repeats in brief comments what is revealed in them and in the primary sources.

The reconstruction of the Socratic presence, both in its biographical and philosophical dimensions, must take into account all the information furnished by the primary and secondary sources, endeavoring at every point to integrate into one harmonious representation their many apparently disparate and discordant statements. In the end, at least the general outlines of such a harmonious representation can be delineated, especially if we bear in mind at all times that the testimonies about Socrates vary so much from one another because the witnesses themselves approached one and the same subject from vastly different points of view. As a person, Socrates must have been a paradoxical and controversial individual who elicited from those who knew him very different responses, from the unconditional devotion and deep love of some of his friends, to the unforgiving hatred of some of his enemies. His ideas, often couched in the form of confusing questions, must have given rise to different reactions, from the fascination with which friends endeavored to follow the tortuous path of his inquiries, to the exasperation and impatience with which his adversaries dismissed his discourse as empty chatter. Thus, both his life and his philosophy were destined to be the ground on which innumerable interpretations and assessments would grow in time. . . .

Notes

[1] For a perceptive discussion of the role of the spoken word in Socrates, see E. A. Havelock, "The Orality of Socrates and the Literacy of Plato: With Some Reflections on the Historical Origins of Moral Philosophy in Europe," *New Essays on Socrates,* ed. Eugene Kelly (Lanham, Md.: University Press of America, 1984), pp. 67-93.

[2] Such are, for instance, A. H. Chroust's view with respect to much of Xenophon's testimony (*Socrates: Man and Myth; The Two Socratic Apologies of Xenophon,* University of Notre Dame Press, 1957), and K. Popper's view with respect to Socrates' political ideas as these are reported by Plato (*The Open Society and Its Enemies,* New York: Harper Torchbooks, 1967). The insoluble character of the Socratic problem is an idea expressed by H. Diels who referred to Socrates as "an unknown X" (quoted in A. E. Taylor, *Socrates,* Garden City, N. Y.: Doubl-eday, 1953, p. 18).

[3] According to G. Vlastos, for instance, the testimonies of Xenophon and Plato cannot be both right,

and his conclusion is that it is the latter's account that must be chiefly borne in mind. This attitude generally prevails in contemporary philosophical circles, and while its roots are readily understandable, it fails to do full justice to the Socratic problem. Undoubtedly, as Vlastos says, Plato's Socrates is a more interesting figure than Xenophon's, although this does not mean that the former is, to quote Vlastos, "the only Socrates worth talking about" ("The Paradox of Socrates," *The Philosophy of Socrates: A Collection of Critical Essays,* ed. Gregory Vlastos, University of Notre Dame Press, 1971, p. 2).

[4] The idea that the testimony of Xenophon should be given precedence over that of Plato with respect to the historical aspects of the Socratic presence was defended by Hegel. In his *Lectures on the History of Philosophy* (tran. E. S. Haldane, London: Routledge and Kegan Paul, 1963, Vol. I, p. 426), he states that

> . . . in regard to the content of Socrates' teaching and the point reached by him in the development of thought, we have in the main to look to Xenophon.

[5] Aristophanes' testimony will be discussed in Chapter 2.

[6] The word *persona* literally means a 'mask' such as those worn by actors in Greek and Roman drama.

[7] The statement from Plato's second letter (*Epist.* 2.314c) is as follows:

> Therefore I have never myself written a word on these matters [philosophy], and there is no written treatise of Plato—no, and neither has been nor shall ever be; what now bears the name of Plato belongs to Socrates, beautified and rejuvenated.

[8] Comments on Aristophanes' possible intention in ridiculing Socrates will be made in Chapter 2.

[9] W. K. C. Guthrie, *Socrates* (Cambridge University Press, 1971), p. 4.

[10] This suggestion was made by George Grote (*Plato and the Other Companions of Socrates,* New York: B. Franklin, 1974, Vol. I, p. 206), and is a reflection of the approach insisted on by Schleiermacher in his *Introductions to the Dialogues of Plato* (trans. William Dobson, New York: Arno Press, 1973).

[11] Although there are no explicit references to the dates of Socrates' birth and death either in Plato or in Xenophon, there can be hardly any reason for challenging the statement of Diogenes Laertius (ii,44) concerning such dates, specifically, the fourth year of the 77th Olympiad, during the archonship of Apsephion, and the first year of the 95th Olympiad, respectively.

[12] The name of Socrates' father is given by Plato in the *Euthydemus* (297e), in the *Hippias Major* (298b), and in the *Laches* (180d ff.). His mother is referred to by Plato in the *Theaetetus* (149a). They are both mentioned by Diogenes Laertius (ii,18), but in Xenophon's writings they do not appear anywhere.

[13] Socrates' participation in Athenian military engagements is mentioned, for instance, in Plato's *Apology* (28e), in the *Laches* (181b), and in the *Symposium* (221a ff.).

[14] A summary statement concerning our knowledge about Socrates' family can be found in E. Zeller's *Socrates and the Socratic Schools* (trans. Oswald J. Reichel, New York: Russell and Russell, 1962), pp. 62 ff.

[15] Further comments on Ameipsias' comedy will be made in Chapter 2.

[16] As will be indicated in Chapter 4, the *Theages* is not generally viewed as an authentic dialogue of Plato. Still, it remains undeniable that in it, as well as in other pseudo-Platonic writings, it is possible to find abundant bits of biographical and ideological information concerning Socrates which are extremely useful in the endeavor to reconstruct a fuller representation of him.

[17] Plato's *Apology* 32b.

[18] Laconism involved the tendency of extolling Sparta and its constitution, and in some cases the actual siding with the Spartan cause during the Peloponnesian conflict. It is unquestionable, although by no means something easy to explain, that many of Socrates' close acquaintances were at some time or another accused of this tendency, as can be seen in the examples of Alcibiades, Xenophon, Meno, Critias, Charmides, and perhaps Plato himself. That Socrates was also suspected of Laconism is clear from a line from Aristophanes' the *Birds* (1281) where the poet bitterly complains about the representatives of the new intelligentsia who had fallen into the habit of 'Socratizing'.

[19] Plato's *Apology* 32b.

[20] The apparent absence of any direct political references from the indictment drawn against Socrates (as this is reported by Xenophon and Plato) should not lead us to the conclusion that the charges against him were not also politically motivated. It must be remembered that after the re-establishment of the

democracy, on the overthrow of the Thirty by Thrasybulus, Anytus, and other democrats, the Athenians pledged under the most solemn oaths not to mention or even remember the tragic circumstances that had led to their defeat, as Xenophon reports in the *Hellenica* (II,iv,43). We may thus assume that references to political complicity involving Laconism and the support of the Thirty were seldom allowed as evidence in the courts.

Alfonso Gomez-Lobo (essay date 1994)

SOURCE: "Is There a Socratic Moral Philosophy?," in *The Foundations of Socratic Ethics,* Hackett Publishing Company, Inc., 1994, pp. 3-44.

[*Here, Gomez-Lobo contends that Socrates's own admission of ignorance does not undermine what has long been recognized as the philosopher's significant contribution to the field of ethics. Gomez-Lobo concludes that by disavowing moral knowledge, Socrates does not refer to a complete lack of knowledge, but rather asserts his willingness to constantly reexamine his beliefs.*]

Socrates, as he appears in the Platonic dialogues, is a living paradox. He has become impoverished, but he nevertheless interacts with rich aristocrats such as Critias and the relatives of Plato. He implicitly criticizes Athenian democracy and yet fulfills his basic civic and military duties faithfully. He opposes an illegal measure under the democratic regime; he also disobeys orders issued by the tyrannic government of the Thirty. He is physically ugly but his beauty of soul is highly praised. He does not long for political power and yet manages to attract some of the most ambitious politicians of the day. He extols his homoerotic inclinations but refuses to engage in homosexual sex.

These apparent contradictions also extend to his philosophizing. He seems to hold that knowledge of a virtue is a necessary and sufficient condition for virtuous behavior, while denying that he has that knowledge. When he looks for the definition of a virtue, he relies on instances of that virtue which, so it seems, could only be identified by someone who already knew the definition; Socrates claims he does not know it. Moreover, we attribute to him a decisive influence on the development of Greek thought, whereas he would perhaps be ready to deny it. In fact, many people who have heard about Socrates only remember his claim to know nothing.

Hence, the first difficulty we must confront is whether it makes sense to attribute a body of moral philosophy to someone who seems flatly to deny any claim to knowledge. Is this just another aspect of the Socratic paradox, or is it an outright misinterpretation?

The difference between a contradiction and a paradox, in the sense I shall be using these terms, is that a paradox admits of resolution whereas a contradiction does not. If there is a way of showing that there is no ultimate inconsistency between Socrates the ironist and Socrates the constructive moral philosopher, the paradox will stand explained.

In what follows, I shall attempt to show that Socrates' admission of ignorance does not preclude the possibility of a substantial Socratic contribution to the field of ethics.

Let us first examine the concept of irony and the textual evidence for Socrates' disavowal of knowledge.

Three Interpretations of Disavowals of Knowledge

In several early Platonic dialogues there is a search for the definition of moral excellence. Socrates questions an interlocutor who puts forward successive replies which Socrates then rejects by way of a procedure called the *elenchus,* or "elenctic refutation." This normally consists in getting the interlocutor to accept one or more propositions which logically entail the denial of a definition he has formulated.[11] Since Socrates applies the same destructive strategy to any fresh definition submitted, and does not offer a definition of his own, the conversation ends without any accepted definition.

Socrates' method must have caused exasperation and resentment. In Book I of the *Republic,* Plato presents Thrasymachus, one of Socrates' most vigorous antagonists, who reacts in the following manner:

> (S1) Having heard this he [*SC.* Thrasymachus] gave a big sardonic laugh and said: By Heracies, this is the usual dissembling [*eironeia*] of Socrates. I knew it and had warned these people that you would not be willing to reply but would dissemble [*eironeu-soio*] and would do anything rather than give an answer if someone asked you something.[12]

Thrasymachus believes that Socratic irony of the usual sort consists in the conjunction of two alleged facts: (a) that Socrates habitually refuses to give an answer and to state his own conviction with regard to the question he is putting to others, but (b) that Socrates does in fact have an answer and a conviction. Socrates is thus perceived as a dissembler, as someone who hides under a false pretense of ignorance and hence induces deceit. Irony here is the equivalent of dissimulation.

But the term "irony" . . . has also come to signify something rather different.[13] We say that our utterance is ironic if we use the words to mean the opposite of what they normally mean, but without intending to deceive. It would be ironic to say that the weather is fine if it is right now raining cats and dogs, or that J. S. Bach was an unimaginative composer while the Goldberg Variations are being performed. Given the appropriate context, and perhaps a certain tone of voice, no deception should occur, unless special conditions obtain.

Alcibiades alludes to this form of irony in a passage in Plato's *Symposium* where he gives an account of his past experience with Socrates:

> (S2) He listened to me, and then, most ironically [*eironikos*] and in his extremely typical and usual manner, he said: "My dear Alcibiades, I'm afraid you are not really a worthless fellow, if what you say about me happens to be true: that there is in me a power that could make you a better man. You must have seen within me an inconceivable beauty which is totally different from your good looks. If, having seen it, you are trying to strike a bargain and exchange beauty for beauty, you intend to get much more than your fair share out of me: you are trying to get true beauty in return for seeming beauty. You aim in fact to exchange 'gold for brass'."[14]

The irony that Alcibiades attributes to Socrates in this humorous passage appears at different levels. There is mocking irony in Socrates' praise of the young man ("not a worthless fellow," "not stupid," . . .), because it is reasonably clear that it would be an illusion to think that he can get away with the sort of bargain he is trying to strike. But there is also irony in Socrates' concession, made in jest, that there is an inconceivable beauty within himself. If the first sort of irony could deceive someone blinded by his own self-conceit, the second one clearly would not, given what Socrates is reported to have said immediately afterward:

> (S2) But, my fortunate friend, take a closer look lest it has escaped you that I am nothing.[15]

The implication, of course, is that Socrates is far from wanting to deceive Alcibiades into thinking that he was serious in mentioning a beauty of his own far superior to Alcibiades' physical bloom. He is warning Alcibiades, precisely, *not* to take his claim seriously.

This in turn generates a third level of irony. Socrates suggests that someone who looks twice into his soul may not find anything there, a comment almost certainly interpreted as ironic by Alcibiades, who openly claims to have already seen "the statues within" Socrates' soul, which appeared to be "divine and golden, most beautiful and admirable."[16] The inner beauty is there. Socrates disavows it, but his interlocutor is not deceived.

The exchange between Alcibiades and Socrates in the *Symposium,* then, leads to a second interpretation of Socratic irony. According to the first one, (A) Socrates has knowledge, denies it, and thereby deceives people. This was Thrasymachus' view. According to the second, (B) Socrates has knowledge, denies it, but does not intend deception. It is true that some of his interlocutors may be deceived, but others will not be misled. On the other hand, it is unclear what kind of knowledge is attributed to Socrates by those who do not assume that he is dissembling.

There is a third interpretation to consider. If (A) implies lack of sincerity and (B) implies a certain form of playfulness and oftentimes mockery, nothing prevents us from assuming that perhaps Socrates is being sincere. This third interpretation may be characterized as follows: (C) Socrates denies that he has knowledge, and this may be strictly true; he is simply being honest about it.

If we were to take these three possible interpretations of Socratic irony as mutually exclusive, we would be guilty of oversimplification. It could certainly be the case that for different forms of knowledge (or for the knowledge of different sorts of items), the Socratic confession of ignorance has a different import. The correct reply, then, to the question of whether Socrates is insincere, simply playful, or straightforwardly sincere is a function of the sort of knowledge Socrates happens to be disclaiming on a given occasion.

What kinds of knowledge does Socrates disavow?

Disavowal of Knowledge in the Apology

The attempt to answer this important question should begin with a careful examination of the *Apology.* If this work was intended to serve as a minimally effective defense of the memory of Socrates, we may reasonably expect it to reflect to some extent what Socrates actually said in front of the jury. Had Plato composed a speech that was radically different from the one delivered by Socrates during the actual proceedings, he would have severely weakened the case for Socrates, since many Athenians who were present at the trial would have been alive and active in politics at the time the *Apology* started to circulate.

There is a second reason to begin with the *Apology,* if indeed we can rely on its being a Platonic recreation of what went on during the trial. In it we get a picture of Socrates attempting to justify his life as a whole. Hence, his disavowal of knowledge is set in a broader context than in the early dialogues. He is trying to present his claim of ignorance as both central to his philosophical mission to Athens, and a clear indication that the accusations raised against him are false.

In fact, during the trial, Socrates had to face charges that were officially formulated in these terms:

> (S3) Socrates does wrong [. . . does something unjust, commits a crime] [a] by corrupting the young and [b] by not acknowledging the gods that the city acknowledges, [c] but rather other new divinities.[17]

According to Socrates, these charges reflect "the first accusations," the charges derived from the false image of Socrates created earlier by Athenian comedians, particularly by Aristophanes. These are given a fictitious official wording by Socrates:

> (S4) Socrates does wrong . . . and busies himself [d] searching things under the earth and in the sky, and [e] making the worse argument the stronger, and [f] teaching others these same things.[18]

The direct implication of charge [d]—which represents the background for charges [b] and [c] in the official accusations—is that Socrates is a "natural philosopher"; i.e., that he belongs to that group of philosophers which Aristotle later called "the physicists" (*physikoi*).

Natural philosophy attempts to explain events in the world by recourse to the unalterable and involuntary behavior of the ultimate constituents of things. It is the innermost nature of things and not external divine intervention that accounts for their properties and for certain occurrences.

To study "things below the earth and in the sky" (in a parallel passage the latter are called *ta meteora,* "things aloft")[19] should be understood as the attempt to give naturalistic explanations of geological phenomena such as earthquakes and volcanic eruptions, on the one hand, and of meteorological phenomena (broadly conceived) such as rain, thunder or eclipses on the other. This way of specifying the domain of natural philosophy is highly significant, because it covers precisely the phenomena which had been traditionally taken to reveal the will of the gods. Soothsayers and prophets who were expected to provide members of the community with religious interpretations of those events were thus likely to regard the new physics as a threat to their craft and, if adopted on a larger scale, as a threat to the religion of the state.[20] Socrates, as an alleged advocate of the novel approach to nature, would, on such a view, be guilty of atheism.

Associating Socrates with the Sophistic movement—[e], above—would have been particularly damaging to him given the negative sentiment toward teachers of rhetoric current at the time. The leaders of the democratic restoration in Athens viewed the sophists as the teachers of the young oligarchs who destroyed the democratic constitution in 411 B.C. and who went on to participate in the dictatorship of the Thirty after 404.[21]

Even someone like Socrates' younger friend Alcibiades, a radical democrat often suspected of aiming at tyranny, was probably perceived as a product of the education provided by the sophists.[22] Such utter disregard for the constitutional order is, of course, a form of corruption, and anyone suspected of having led the young in this direction could be labeled a corruptor of youth. We should therefore assume a close association between charge [e] and charges [a] and [f].[23]

It is important to observe that Socrates denies the charges and does so by appealing to the testimony of those present at the trial.[24] In doing so, he unmistakenly disavows knowledge within two domains:

(1) The science of nature,[25] and

(2) the art of rhetoric, and, in general, the field of education.[26]

Since many of those attending the proceedings could bear witness to the fact that they had never heard Socrates talking about natural philosophy, nor seen him become wealthy as a teacher of excellence, the accusers do not seem to have sufficient evidence to show the jury that Socrates was indeed a physicist and a sophist. But we do know that the accusers were politically able men who would not lightheartedly risk failure. What were they relying on when they brought forth legal action on those specific charges? What had Aristophanes had in mind many years earlier when he hoped the public would laugh if he put Socrates on stage as a representative of the new intellectuals?

We must assume, I think, that there was something about Socrates' public image that made both the caricature in the *Clouds* and the indictment effective.

According to Plato, Socrates saw the problem and faced it squarely by posing an imaginary objection:

> (S5) Perhaps one of you might retort: "But, Socrates, what is your own pursuit? Whence did these slanders arise? For surely if you had not been busying your-self with something out of the

> common, all this talk and gossip would not have arisen, unless you were doing something different from most people. Tell us what it is, so that we won't improvise in speaking about you." It seems to me that whoever says this is making a fair request, and I will try to show you what it is that has generated this reputation and slander.[27]

The main thrust of his reply to the hypothetical question is to connect his own pursuit with a divine source, viz. Apollo, the god of Delphi:

> (S6) Well, at one time he [= Chairephon, a friend of Socrates, now dead, who had fought for the restoration of democracy] went to Delphi and was bold enough to ask the oracle—as I said before, gentlemen, please remain silent—he asked in fact whether there was anyone wiser than I. The Pythia [= the priestess through which the god spoke and whose words were then interpreted by the priests of the sanctuary] replied that no one was wiser.[28]

Socrates' reaction to this pronouncement was marked by initial puzzlement, a natural reaction on the part of someone who is aware of his own ignorance:

> (S7) I am conscious of not being wise in anything great or small.[29]

Anyone seriously convinced of this would be naturally inclined to think that Apollo's pronouncement must be false. It is reasonable to expect that there will be someone wiser than a person who is not wise at all. But this, according to Socrates, is intolerable:

> (S8) For he [= the god] surely does not lie; it is not right . . . for him to do so.[30]

Hence, if the statement

> "Socrates is wise"

is known by Socrates himself to be false, but the god affirms something which implies that it is true (and his truthfulness cannot be doubted), then the only way out for Socrates is to suppose that the god is speaking in riddles, a not uncommon expectation on the part of those consulting the oracle.[31]

Accordingly, Socrates sets out to inquire into the *meaning* of the pronouncement, not into its *truth.*[32] And yet, at least formally, his inquiry seems to aim at refuting the oracle by showing that the claim that no one is wiser than Socrates is false. Socrates' inquiry takes on the task of trying to find someone who surpasses him in wisdom. Finding such an individual would amount to providing a decisive counterexample to the pronouncement of the oracle.

Socrates proceeds to question individuals classified as politicians, poets and craftsmen; i.e., individuals who are expected to be superior to him in their respective domains and who therefore would qualify as being wiser.

Among representatives of the first group, Socrates detects the appearance of wisdom (especially in their own eyes) but no true knowledge. Socrates infers that he is slightly wiser than they are because neither he nor they "know anything fine and good" . . . ; but he, at least, does not think he knows what he does not know.[33] The expression *ouden kalon kagathon,* used here without the article, does not stand for "the fine and the good";[34] i.e., for the primary object of moral knowledge. Rather it suggests that what politicians claim to have, and do not, is the general kind of evaluative knowledge needed to manage the affairs of the state on a day-to-day basis. Socrates is not disavowing moral knowledge.

The poets, in turn, say many fine things "by some inborn nature and from inspiration" and hence, strictly speaking, "do not understand anything they say."[35] This in itself is not to be regarded as a particularly negative trait of poetry. What seems intolerable to Socrates is that

> (S9) because of their poetry they thought they were the wisest of men in other subjects in which they were not [sc. wise].[36]

The poets, then, seem to make two different claims: to know how to compose poetry (but they actually do not *know* because they are driven by the nonrational force of inspiration) and to know about matters outside the domain of poetry (and again in this area they turn out to be ignorant).[37]

In the craftsmen, Socrates also detected a step beyond the boundaries of their fields of competence. Members of this group are here called . . . "handcrafters," i.e., "people who work with their hands." They include carpenters, shoemakers, builders, etc., and also those we would call sculptors, painters, architects, etc., and even physicians. Common to all of them is the fact that they generate a product or work. . . . This product may or may not be a tangible object. A musical performer is also a craftsman of a sort, as is a doctor, though health, the goal of the doctor, is not an object in the normal sense of the word. Socrates admits that

> (S10) . . . they knew things I did not know and in this respect they were wiser than I. And yet, Athe-nians, our good craftsmen also seemed to me to have exactly the same shortcoming as the poets: because of the fine exercise of his craft each of them claimed . . . to be very wise also in other most important matters, and this excess of theirs over-clouded the wisdom they had.[38]

The craftsmen, then, while knowledgeable . . . having *episteme* or "science") in their own craft (. . . *techne*), are also said to claim knowledge of "the greatest things" . . . an expression which the jurors doubtless understood as a reference to the domain of politics.[39] Within the context of the relatively small Greek city-state, the most important decisions were indeed the political ones. Frequently, not only the welfare but even the life of the citizens was a function of the wisdom of certain policies or of particular decrees. But the sharpest among the jurors must have also perceived a veiled criticism of democracy, a system that allows craftsmen to attend the meetings of the Assembly and make decisions about matters that lie beyond their field of competence. Hence, when he claims that he is "neither wise in their wisdom nor ignorant in their ignorance," Socrates is disavowing craft knowledge and political expertise.[40] He is not disavowing moral knowledge.

Note that Socrates takes craft-knowledge to be a genuine form of knowledge while denying that alleged forms of knowledge which cannot be construed as a peculiar craft or skill, such as the insight of the politician or the inspiration of the poet, have any value at all. The Socratic claim of ignorance has now been extended to three new areas:

(3) politics,

(4) poetry,

(5) craft-knowledge.

If we pause for a moment and ask how we should understand Socrates' disavowals in these areas, we will arrive at relatively unproblematic answers for items (1) natural philosophy, (4) poetry, and (5) the crafts.

In the *Phaedo* there is a well-known autobiographical passage where Socrates describes his initial interest in, and ultimate disappointment with, inquiries of the sort earlier philosophers engaged in.[41] Hence, we can readily explain the reference in the *Apology* to Anaxagoras and his doctrines,[42] but it is clear that Socrates is in no way committed to the truth of these or other explanations of natural phenomena. Socrates had long given up such pursuits, as those present could attest. Moreover, it is also reasonably clear that Socrates was neither a poet nor a craftsman.[43]

If we consider (3), i.e., Socrates' claim of ignorance in political matters, a contradiction seems to arise because of Socrates' claim in the *Gorgias* that he is "the only one among [his] contemporaries who engages in politics."[44] This startling piece of self-interpretation, however, appears in a dialogue written later which develops the view that the improvement of the citizens is not a peculiar duty of a philosopher functioning in a private capacity, but a primary duty of the state as such. Hence the qualification "the true political craft" included in the wording of this alleged Socratic claim. It is easy to see, of course, that we are here only one step away from the specifically Platonic thesis that philosophers should wield political power because they are the only ones who have adequate knowledge of the eternal and unchanging Forms.[45]

By contrast, Socrates' reluctance to participate in the deliberations of the Athenian Assembly or of the Council (though he is willing to do so when strictly required by law)—that is, his unwillingness to engage in the day-to-day managing of the state; i.e., in politics in the ordinary sense of that word[46]—is consistent with his having no special insight into the best way to conduct contingent public affairs. It is safe, therefore, to assume that Socrates is being sincere when he professes to be as ignorant as Athens' practicing politicians.

Finally, Socrates' avowal of ignorance with regard to (2), the teaching of rhetoric, leads him to deny that he attempts to educate young men. To be able to educate in the sense in which the sophists profess to educate, one would have to have knowledge of "political" excellence, i.e., of the excellence that makes for successful politicians.[47] There is, therefore, a close connection between disavowing knowledge in domain (2), the specific area of sophistic expertise, and in (3), the alleged area of competence of Athens' practicing politicians. We must emphasize once more that when Socrates disavows knowledge in areas in which sophists and politicians claim it, he is not claiming moral ignorance.

If these reflections are correct, Socrates' disavowal of knowledge in areas (1) through (5) can be interpreted as instances of (C): Socrates is simply being honest in admitting his lack of expertise in fields in which he genuinely has none.

Another, rather specific instance of the Socratic avowal of ignorance must be examined. Given the penalty assessed by his accusers, Socrates is confronted with the prospect of death. In reply to a new hypothetical objection that fear of death should have made him feel ashamed of his "occupation," he says:

> (S11) . . . to fear death, gentlemen, is nothing but to think that one is wise when one is not, for it is to think that one knows what one doesn't know. No one, in fact, knows death nor whether it happens to be the greatest of all goods for a man, and yet people are afraid of it as if they knew very well that it was the greatest of evils. And isn't this the most blameworthy ignorance, to

> think one knows what one doesn't know? By this much and in this respect too, gentlemen, I am perhaps different from most people; and if I were to say that I am wiser than someone in some respect, it would be in this: that having no ade-quate knowledge about things in Hades [= the underworld, the realm of the dead], I likewise do not think I have it.[48]

We must therefore add to our list of those things encompassed by the Socratic disavowal of knowledge the following:

(6) death.

What Socrates claims not to know about death is not so much what kind of event it is, but rather what its correct evaluation should be: whether it is the best thing that can happen to someone or the worst thing. In his denial of possessing this evaluative knowledge, Socrates is not being insincere or ironic. His disavowal is, again, of type (C): he denies knowing something which could only be accessible to someone who has experienced the state that follows death. Neither he nor anyone else, of course, knows what that state is like.[49]

If we look at the early dialogues which have at their center the search for the definition of a moral excellence, we find one more item to add to the list of things Socrates claims not to know:

(7) the excellences or virtues, virtue in general, and their respective definitions.

The inclusion of this class of objects among the things Socrates claims not to know generates a difficulty that did not arise with the previous items on our list. We here seem to be confronted with a specific disavowal of moral knowledge.

Before facing this new difficulty, it is important to call attention to the fact that there are numerous passages in which Socrates affirms that he *does* know something. Socratic irony is not equivalent to a form of radical skepticism.

Socratic Claims to Knowledge

Some Socratic claims to knowledge are based on everyday experience and commonsense reflection on it:

> (S12) And yet I know . . . well enough that these words make me unpopular, which also proves that I am telling the truth.[50]

> (S13) For I know very well . . . that wherever I go and speak, the young wili listen to me as they do here.[51]

We should also recall those passages in which the object of knowledge is immediately present to Socrates' consciousness:

> (S14) = (S7) I am conscious . . . of not being wise in anything great or small.[52]

> (S15) For I was conscious . . . of knowing nothing, so to speak.[53]

Of greater interest for the present inquiry are the lines that immediately follow (S15), the statement of uncertainty about the evaluation of death:

(S16) That to do what's unjust and to disobey one's superior, be he god or man, is bad . . . and shameful . . . , that I do know . . . the position of the verb is emphatic]. Hence, I shall never fear or flee from things of which I do not know whether they even happen to be good [in this case, death] instead of from bad things which I know to be bad [in this case, injustice and disobedience].[54]

In this passage, the only one of its kind in the early dialogues, Socrates declares that he possesses evaluative knowledge of two types of acts: acts of injustice and acts of disobedience. He claims to know (i) that each of them is shameful. The Greek predicate makes clear in this instance that the evaluation is moral. To say that what someone has done is *aischron* is to label it as ugly and dishonorable, as blameworthy from the moral point of view. But Socrates also claims to know (ii) that each of them is bad.

Since *kakon* in Greek (and "bad" in English) can be used in both a moral and a nonmoral sense, it is not clear how we should understand Socrates' second claim. An action such as lying to a friend can be said to be bad because it is blameworthy, but something can also be bad without moral implications, such as being mistaken. We are worse off if we make a mistake about a certain state of affairs than we would be if we had got it right, but being mistaken does not make us wicked.

The subsequent contrast, however, between things known to be bad, and death, which may turn out to be good, strongly suggests that the occurrence of "bad" here is an instance of the nonmoral use. The goodness or badness of death can only be the nonmoral quality of that mysterious event.[55] We shall return to this point shortly.

Setting aside disobedience as a particular case of injustice, wc can recapitulate Socrates' claim in (S16) as follows:

> (a) I know that injustice is shameful and bad.

We can readily assume that this statement implies a symmetrical statement:

(b) I know that justice is fine and good.[56]

An Avowal of Moral Ignorance

Let us note that Book I of the *Republic* ends with the following words:

(S17) For, so long as I do not know what the just [= justice] is, I will hardly know whether it happens to be an excellence or not, and whether he who possesses it is unhappy or happy.[57]

In this context, to say that something designated by the neuter adjective or the abstract noun is an excellence (*arete,* "virtue") implies that the corresponding predicate can be used to commend someone from the moral point of view. If justice is a virtue, then to say that someone is just is to morally praise him for that noble and praiseworthy attribute. On the other hand, "to be happy" is first and foremost a nonmoral attribute, since happiness (. . . flourishing) is understood as the possession of an abundance of those things which make us better off, and normally people take these to be the nonmoral goods.[58] Hence, *mutatis mutandis* it is fair to say that (S17) entails that Socrates is claiming:

(c) I do not know whether justice is fine and good.

It seems obvious that (b) and (c) are contradictory statements.

If we accepted (c) as a genuine Socratic belief and rejected (b), we would have to admit that there is no Socratic moral philosophy, since it is natural to assume that a system of philosophical ethics would include evaluations such as the one expressed by the subordinate clause of (c). Socrates, however, claims not to know whether it is true or false.

In order to show that the conjunction of (b) and (c) does not constitute a contradiction but rather a paradox, it is useful to ask how an Athenian would have reacted to someone's claim not to know whether justice is or is not an *arete,* i.e., a noble and praiseworthy quality.

The early dialogues provide us with an interesting clue. On two similar occasions, Socrates asks an interlocutor whether courage and self-control, respectively, are among the (very, . . .) fine (admirable, noble) things. In each case, not only does the person respond with great, positive assurance, but in one instance he even adds an emphatic comment on Socrates' conviction regarding such clear matters: "You really know well that it is one of the noblest."[59] Since, like "courageous" and "self-controlled," the predicate equivalent to "just" was used in ordinary Greek for moral commendation,[60] Socrates' claim not to know whether justice is an excellence can hardly have been taken seriously by his audience, because doubting such an obvious truth was an oddity. Its truth is pellucid because of the very meaning of the terms "justice" and "virtue." Hence, they probably understood him as expressing irony of type (B), i.e., possessing the knowledge he disclaimed, but playfully denying it.

Socrates' plea of ignorance as to whether or not justice produces happiness is not as simple to interpret. As I shall try to show in chapter III, it is a substantive moral question and not a self-evident truth readily available to members of the community by virtue of the language they speak.

At the end of *Republic* Book I the connections between happiness and justice are not clarified because no satisfactory definition of the latter is found. This failure is realized in the midst of an impassioned and at times tense conversation. Yet the discussion itself was a free and open-ended exchange, proceeding with no urgency to make any specific, practical decision. A practical notion is subject to scrutiny, but the dramatic setting makes it clear that the connection with actual choice and action is remote. Socrates has gone down to the Piraeus to attend a religious festival and is invited to the house of Cephalus. Upon hearing the host's reflections on the prospect of dying while still owing sacrifices to a good, or money to a man—i.e., having failed to redress instances of injustice—Socrates takes the occasion to ask, in general, what justice is. There is, however, no urgency to resolve any particular instance of injustice.

Strictly speaking, Socrates' final admission of ignorance in Book I of the *Republic,* whether or not it is good to fulfill the requirements of justice, would, if in earnest, cast him as someone who has drastically abandoned any sensible rule for morally correct action. "Just" can be taken in many contexts as a predicate that characterize all action that is morally right and praiseworthy. "Good," in turn, stands for an attribute that provides the ultimate reason for doing something. Hence, it is doubtful that Socrates' friends would have been led to think that he had adopted a radical moral agnosticism that would have left him without any rational justification to behave in a morally upright man-ner. It seems more likely that this part of his closing remarks should also be understood as ironic in sense (B), i.e., as implying the contrary of what he said, without thereby intending to deceive.

If these conjectures are correct, we must hold that Socrates does indeed know that justice is praiseworthy and worth having; i.e., that it is something fine and good, as stated in (b). But how are we to explain his denial in *Republic* I, and his affirmation in the *Apology,* of those very same convictions?

The trial, of course, is not by any means the appropriate setting for what I have called a "free and open-ended discussion." The way Socrates chooses to conduct his defense makes it even more removed from a free form of exchange. Socrates describes his predicament as his being forced to choose between obeying Apollo, even at the risk of his own life, and preserving his life at the cost of disobeying the divine injunction. In the face of such a dramatic choice, Socrates declares that choosing the second option follows from the belief that one knows that death is something bad, whereas choosing the first option is a consequence of believing that disobedience and injustice are bad. Socra-tes asserts that he does not know whether the former of these two beliefs is true or not, but he does claim to know that the latter is true. *The inescapable need to choose between life and death (and to justify his choice) leads Socrates openly and firmly to avow, at least once, that he knows something of considerable moral import.*

I have argued that Socrates' sincere disavowals of knowledge in politics, poetry, and the crafts do not imply sincere disavowals of moral knowledge. The domain, beyond their skills, to which the craftsmen extended their claims—and within which Socrates also declared himself incompetent—was the domain of contingent political matters, not the field of moral philosophy.

In contrast, as I mentioned above, Socrates does disavow moral knowledge in some of the early aporetic dialogues. However, those denials should not be understood either as sincere or as insincere and hence as misleading disavowals. But if Socrates is not being insincere, why does he not abandon the ironic stance and declare that he knows what the corresponding moral excellence is?

A brief examination of some aspects of the *Euthyphro* may be helpful at this point.

Euthyphro's Claim to Knowledge

During a conversation with Socrates at the Portico of the Archon-King in the Athenian *agora,* Euthyphro declares that he is prosecuting his father for murder in a rather obscure case involving the death of a laborer who had killed a slave and who was neglected while the father awaited official instructions as to what he should do with the man. Since the popular notion of piety involves respect for the gods and for one's parents, Euthyphro seems to be doing something which most men would hesitate to do. Most men would not seek punishment for their fathers because they would not know whether they were doing the right thing or not.[61] Hence Socrates' question:

> (S18) Soc.: By Zeus, Euthyphro, do you think your knowledge of divine matters, and of pious and impious things, is so accurate . . . that even if things happened as you say, you are not afraid of doing something impious yourself in prosecuting your father?
>
> Euth.: I would be worthless, Socrates, and Euthyphro would be no different from the com-mon run of men, if I did not know all such things accurately. . . . [62]

Here the emphasis clearly falls on the self-assurance with which Euthyphro claims to have strict knowledge (the opposite would be to know . . . "roughly," "in broad outline")[63] about things divine and the right and wrong ways to relate to them. Only someone who has such exact knowledge would run the moral risk Euthy-phro is assuming by taking his father to court. A very fine line separates Euthyphro's action, if it is indeed a requirement of piety to prosecute a wrongdoer even if it is your father,[64] from an impious undertaking.

As the dialogue proceeds, Socrates offers his assessment of the kind of precise knowledge that the circumstances require: one would have to know the character or trait (. . . "aspect," "form") that is common to all pious actions and in virtue of which they are pious.[65] Once that is identified, one should look upon it and use it as a model or standard (. . . "paradigm") to decide whether a particular event is or is not an instance of piety.[66] It is a further Socratic assumption that the definition of a moral term is expected to capture such a character or trait.

In the remainder of the dialogue, Socrates' strategy consists in an attempt to undermine Euthyphro's self-assurance by showing him that he does not know how to define piety. Every definition proposed or accepted by Euthyphro is rejected once it is subjected to a Socra-tic counterargument. The outcome is that Euthyphro is shown not to have a clear view of the standard that would allow him to judge with confidence whether or not he is doing the right thing.

If we reflect on the whole dialogue, we will feel compelled to say that any witness to the conversation (or a modern reader, for that matter) would walk away convinced that Socrates' requests to become Euthy-phro's pupil, because of the former's own ignorance in divine affairs, are made in jest.[67] The firm direction in which he guides the conversation suggests that Socrates is by no means in the dark with regard to the topic under scrutiny. It is Socrates who introduces the notion of establishing justice as the generic concept under which piety may be subsumed,[68] and it is also under his initiative that "service [or the art of serving, . . . to the gods" is substituted for the misleading expression "care . . . of the gods."[69] The latter suggests, inappropriately (like "therapy," the English term derived from it), that the object of our care may be improved. The former is an expression which Socrates can earnestly apply to his own obedience to the oracle: "I believe no greater good has come to you in the city than this service of mine to the god."[70] Finally, Socrates does not hesitate to indicate in the *Euthyphro* that he does have views about the gods: he finds stories about immoral behavior on their part hard to accept. In the *Apology,* we saw this conviction surface as one of the key assumptions in his interpretation of the oracle given to Chairephon: Apollo, the god of Delphi, cannot lie.

Euthyphro's initial claim can be accounted for as follows:

> *When an individual claims to know, (i) he states that he has true beliefs within a given domain, and (ii) he is confident that his beliefs are unshakably true and, hence, not open to revision.*

Ignorance on the part of an individual who claims to know will then obtain if his beliefs are false and therefore his confidence turns out to be unfounded.

Socratic Wisdom

In light of the proposed analysis of Euthyphro's claim, we can understand Socrates' disavowal of knowledge as a denial that he has true beliefs or as a denial that his beliefs are definitely settled.

As we have seen, Socrates does admit lack of true beliefs in certain domains: cases (1) through (6), i.e., in physics, rhetoric, politics, poetry, the crafts, and death.

With respect to his denial of knowledge of items in (7), viz. the moral virtues, it seems reasonable to assume that Socrates recognizes that he does not totally lack true opinions or convictions (otherwise, as we saw, he would be a man without a moral rudder, something hard to extract from our sources). In all likelihood he wishes to deny that he has firm and unshakable knowledge of the moral virtues, and thus that he remains open to a reexamination of his beliefs.

With regard to many of Socrates' convictions, such scrutiny has often taken place, but this does not lead him to give up, in principle, the possibility of further revision of his views, as is suggested by the wording of the following passage from the *Crito:*

> (S19) Soc.: But, my admirable friend, this argument . . . we have gone through still seems to me to be the same as it did before. Examine in turn the following one [to see] if it still holds good for us or not, namely that it is not to live that should be deemed most important, but to live well.
>
> Crito: It holds good.
>
> Soc.: And that to live well and finely and justly are the same, does this hold good or does it not hold good?
>
> Crito: It does hold good.[71]

The repeated expression "hold good" translates a Greek word . . . which conveys the idea of something remaining as it was, standing fast even though it could have changed or given way. This suggests that the two friends have agreed in the past on the truth of the statements, and that Socrates wants to know whether Crito still abides by these convictions or has had reason to change his mind about them. The possibility of reopening the discussion is not precluded in principle, but in this circumstance they move on.[72]

In the privacy of his cell, Socrates can remind Crito of past conversations and resulting agreements. He can gently inquire whether Crito wants to revise them or not. This he cannot do in the confrontation with his judges. Hence the dogmatic tone Socrates employs in (S16) where, without hesitation, he claims to know that something is true: that injustice and disobedience are bad and shameful. His confidence, we may suppose, is derived from the fact that he has often considered the point and found no reason to believe it false. It is conceivable that in a different setting Socrates might have been willing to reopen a discussion of even this fundamental piece of moral knowledge.

In the context of the *Apology* and the *Crito,* we find no indication of what would count as settled true belief, and therefore of what would constitute stable, definitive knowledge.[73] We are offered instead two passages that may confirm the suggestion that in those cases where Socratic irony seems to be insincere, it amounts, in fact, to Socrates' willingness to revise his own moral convictions:

> (S20) For I, gentlemen of Athens, have acquired this reputation from nothing but a certain wisdom. What sort of wisdom is this? The one which is perhaps human wisdom, for in fact it may be I

> am wise in this sense. Those men, the ones I just mentioned [= the sophists], are perhaps wise in a wisdom more than human. Otherwise I do not know what to call it, for I in fact do not possess it. Whoever says I do is lying and speaks to slander me.[74]

And further on:

> (S21) I'm afraid, gentlemen, that in fact the god [= Apollo] is wise and that by means of the oracle he is saying that human wisdom is worth little or nothing. He seems to mention this man Socrates, using my name and proposing me as an example, as if he said: "He is the wisest among you, who, like Socrates, recognizes that he is truly worth nothing with respect to wisdom."[75]

Socrates' suggestion in (S20) that there is a form of sophistic wisdom that is more than human is certainly ironic. We are not deceived. The distinction that these passages make is a distinction between the divine wisdom of Apollo and the human wisdom of Socrates. It is not a bold guess that the former fully satisfies the conditions that make the claim to knowledge definitive: divine wisdom embraces true beliefs and the unshakable conviction that they are indeed true. Socratic wisdom, on the other hand, is either a sincere admission of not possessing true beliefs about certain matters, or an openness to the reexamination of beliefs previously accepted as true.

If this is correct, we have failed to discover any instance of insincere Socratic disavowals of knowledge. To do so would require identifying matters which Socrates, in principle, refuses to submit to reexamination, and of which he also denies knowledge. Thrasy-machus' accusations, we can now affirm, amount to a deep misunderstanding of the fundamental Socratic attitude toward knowledge.
The alleged contradiction that arises when Apollo affirms, and Socrates denies, the assertion

> Socrates is wise

has now been resolved by reinterpreting the predicate.

At the outset, Socrates takes the word "wise" to mean "a person who knows and who is justifiably confident that he does indeed know." After his search for someone wiser than he, Socrates realizes that what Apollo meant was "a person who makes no claim to know with full confidence."

If this is correct, the path of inquiry into Socratic ethics has cleared a major obstacle. Socrates' disavowal of moral knowledge should not be taken to imply Socrates' strict lack of knowledge, but rather his consistent willingness to reexamine his convictions. This suggests that Socrates views his moral philosophy not as divine wisdom, i.e., as a definitive and unshakable system, but rather as a body of ideas he is willing to modify or even to abandon, should he be offered persuasive objections.

We may conclude, then, that there is no ultimate inconsistency between Socrates the ironist and Socrates the constructive moral philosopher.

Notes

[11] On the structure of the Socratic *elenchus,* cf. Vlastos (1983a) with comments by Kraut (1983). See also Stemmer (1992), esp. pp. 96-127.

[12] *Republic* I, 337a 3-7. At *Apology* 23a 3-5 Socrates admits that people consistently perceived him as "wise" in those subjects in which they saw him refuting someone. For all quotations from Plato I have used Burnet (1900-1907) as my main source. Translations are my own unless otherwise noted. In the renderings I have aimed almost exclusively at accuracy, even at the price of neglecting the elegance and flexibility of Plato's style. Readers are encouraged to consult the main sources in excellent translations by Grube (1981) and Zeyl (1987).

[13] Vlastos (1991), pp. 21-30, conjectures that the modern sense of the term "irony," which in Western rhetorical theory goes back to Cicero and Quintilian, is ultimately due to Socrates. Before him the meaning of *eroniea* and its cognates almost always implied an intention to deceive.

[14] *Symp.* 218d 6-219a 1. Cf. Vlastos (1991), p. 36.

[15] *Symp.* 219a 1-2.

[16] *Symp.* 216e 6-217a 1.

[17] *Apol.* 24b 8-c 1. I have added bracketed letters to make references more expedient. The evidence for this being virtually the official wording of the indictment is a statement in *Diogenes Laertius* (2. 40) which claims that Favorinus, a Roman rhetorician of the second century A.D., reported that it was still preserved in the sanctuary of the Mother of the Gods in Athens. On the meaning of the accusations, see Brickhouse and Smith (1989), pp. 30-37, and Reeve (1989), pp. 74-79.

[18] *Apol.* 19b 4-c 1.

[19] *Apol.* 18b 7. Cf. Burnet (1924), *ad loc.*

[20] Cf. Cornford (1952), pp. 127-142.

[21] Thuc. 8. 65. 2. Cf. *Meno* 89e-95a. For a lively

account of the general historical background (and of Alcibiades in particular), cf. Burn (1966), pp. 193-304.

[22] On the assumed influence of Gorgias of Leontini on Alcibiades, cf. Guthrie (1971b), p. 274.

[23] The label "corruptor of youth" has moral connotations both in Greek and in English. It singles out the person who leads the young from moral virtue to vice. Xenophon stresses this aspect of the accusations: Xen. *Apol.* 19 and *Mem.* 1. 2. 1-5. Cf. *Mem.* 1. 5. 1-6.

[24] *Apol.* 19d.

[25] *Apol.* 19c 4-8.

[26] *Apol.* 19d 8-20c 3.

[27] *Apol.* 20c 4-d 4.

[28] *Apol.* 21a 4-7.

[29] *Apol.* 21b 4-5.

[30] *Apol.* 21b 6-7. The claim that the god is subject to a superior moral order represented by *themis,* the divine order of the universe, is quite strong. Cf. Hirzel (1907) and Ehrenberg (1921).

[31] Cf. Heraclitus Frg. B93 (Diels-Kranz): "The Lord to whom the oracle that is in Delphi belongs neither speaks out plainly nor conceals, but gives hints." On some of the famous ambiguous replies given by the oracle, cf. Fontenrose (1978).

[32] *Apol.* 21b 3-4: "What is the god saying? What is his riddle?" Cf. 21e 6.

[33] *Apol.* 21c d.

[34] *Pace* Lesher (1987), p. 281. Cf. 22d 2 where the craftsmen are said to know many fine things (*kala*). The implication is surely that they possess not moral knowledge but the kind of knowledge required for the successful exercise of their crafts.

[35] *Apol.* 22a 8-c 3.

[36] *Apol.* 22c 5-6.

[37] On specific claims to knowledge extrapolated from poetic inspiration, cf. Plato's *Ion* and Flashar (1958).

[38] *Apol.* 22d 3-e 1.

[39] On this point I side with Burnet (1924), p. 96, and against Brickhouse and Smith (1989), p. 97, and Reeve (1989), p. 33. I find it hard to believe that Socrates is here implying that, e.g., good carpenters walk around the *agora* claiming to know the definition of a handful of moral virtues. The expression "the greatest things" should be understood here from the perspective of those who allegedly make the claim. The average Athenian citizen surely felt that political issues were the most important ones and that he was competent to deal with them.

[40] For the close linkage of the two, cf. *Apol.* 23d 5-24a 1.

[41] Cf. *Phaedo* 96a-102a. The correct historical interpretation of this "autobiography" is still one of the most vexing problems for Platonic scholars who raise the Socratic question.

[42] *Apol.* 26d 6-e 1. Socrates appears to be familiar with some doctrines of Anaxagoras, a philosopher from Asia Minor who was a friend of Pericles, but in the same passage he makes it known that such information was readily available to anyone, for Anaxagoras' book could be purchased for a modest price at the *agora.*

[43] Burnet (1924), pp. 50-51, argues against taking *Euthyphro* 11b as proof that Socrates (and/or his father) was a stonemason. The earliest reference to Socrates as a stonecutter goes back to Timon of Phlius, a skeptic philosopher who lived in the third century B.C.

[44] Cf. *Gorgias* 521d 6-8. Cf. Dodds's comment *ad loc.:* "One may doubt, however, whether the historical Socrates would have made any such claim."

[45] Cf. *Rep.* 473 c-d; 484b.

[46] "Politics" should be understood in this sense at *Gorgias* 473e 6 where Socrates *denies* being a politician. This claim and the opposite one made at 521d (quoted above) do not contradict each other.

[47] Cf. *Apol.* 20b 4-5. Cf. *Protagoras* 318e 5-319a 5; *Meno* 73c 6-9.

[48] *Apol.* 29a 6-b 6.

[49] At the end of the *Apology* (40c ff.), Socrates conjectures that there is hope (*elpis*) that death is something good, for it is either like a dreamless night or, if (religious) tales are true, like a migration to a better place. Expressing such hope is not tantamount to claiming knowledge.

[50] *Apol.* 24a 6-8.

[51] *Apol.* 37d 6-7.

[52] *Apol.* 21b 4-5.

[53] *Apol.* 22b 9-d 1. I owe this reference and the four preceding ones to Lesher (1987), p. 280.

[54] *Apol.* 29b 6-9.

[55] When the claim that wrongdoing is bad and shameful is repeated in the *Crito* (49b 4), the qualification "for the wrongdoer" is introduced immediately before the term "bad." This seems to count in favor of the interpretation defended above. Moral predicates are true or false without qualification. Nonmoral benefit usually requires specification: what is good for me may be bad for you (e.g., my getting a job for which both of us have applied). To hold that doing wrong is bad *for the one who does it,* is, of course, paradoxical.

[56] I am assuming that, with normal Greek usage, . . . ("fine," "admirable," "noble," "beautiful") is the opposite of *aiskron* and can be used to convey moral commendation.

[57] *Rep.* I. 354c 1-3. Some nineteenth-century scholars argued on the basis of stylistic evidence that Book I of the *Republic* was an independent dialogue written during Plato's earlier years that was later used as the opening section of a more mature work that includes Books II-X. Vlastos has argued that independently of the truth or falsehood of this thesis, the Socrates of Book I in fact shares most of his traits with the Socrates of the early dialogues. Cf. Vlastos (1991), chapter 2, *passim* and pp. 248-251. The separate composition of Book I has been vigorously contested by Kahn (1993).

[58] Cf. *Euthydemus* 279a 1-3; 280b 5-6; *Symp.* 204e 1-7.

[59] *Laches* 192c 5-7; *Charmides* 159c 1-2.

[60] At *Gorgias* 492a-c, Callicles, a strong opponent of Socrates, makes an effort to explain why in everyday life "the many" (*hoi polloi,* 492a 3) praise justice. This habit is due, in his opinion, to sheer cowardice. But the need of an explanation simply confirms the view that categorizing justice as a virtue was commonplace for fifth- and fourth-century Greeks.

[61] Cf. *Euth.* 4a 11-12.

[62] *Euth.* 4e 4-5a 2.

[63] Cf. Aristotle, *Nicomachean Ethics* 1. 2. 1104a 1-2.

[64] *Euth.* 5d 8-e 2.

[65] *Euth.* 5d 1-5; 6d 9-e 1.

[66] *Euth.* 6e 3-6.

[67] *Euth.* 5a 3-b 7; 5c 4-5; 15e 5-16a 4.

[68] *Euth.* 11e 4-12e 8.

[69] *Euth.* 12e 5-8; 13d 4.

[70] *Apol.* 30a 5-7 (trans. Vlastos). Cf. Vlastos (1991), p. 175.

[71] *Crito* 48b 3-10.

[72] Cf. *Crito* 46b 6-c 6.

[73] This silence probably reflects a lack of interest in strictly epistemological questions on the part of the historical Socrates. The first attempts to deal with this problem are found in *Gorgias* 454c ff. and in the transition dialogues. Cf. *Meno* 98a.

[74] *Apol.* 20d 6-e 3.

[75] *Apol.* 23a 5-b 4.

FURTHER READING

Benson, Hugh. *Essays on the Philosophy of Socrates.* New York: Oxford University Press, 1992, 361p.

Collection of essays analyzing various aspects of Socrates's philosophy and other related issues, including Socratic irony, the charges against Socrates, the theory of the unity of virtue, and the involuntary nature of wrongdoing.

Brickhouse, Thomas C. and Nicholas D. Smith. *Socrates on Trial.* Princeton, N.J.: Princeton University Press, 1989, 337p.

Offers an account of Socrates's trial based on Plato's *Apology,* including discussion of the accusations against Socrates, the defense put for-ward by Socrates, and his final speeches. Also includes extensive bibliography.

Burnet, John. "The Life of Sokrates," "The Philosophy of Sokrates," and "The Trial and Death of Sokrates." In *Greek Philosophy: Thales to Plato,* pp. 102-122, 123-145, and 146-156. London: Macmillan & Co., 1964.

Three chapters on Socrates providing a detailed account of what is known from various sources of his life, beliefs and teachings, condemnation, trial, and execution.

Capaldi, Nicholas; Eugene Kelley; and Luis E. Navia. "A Certain Man Named Socrates." In *An Invitation to Philosophy,* pp. 35-56. Buffalo, N.Y.: Prometheus Books, 1981.
Reviews the intellectual atmosphere of Greece at the time of the emergence of Socrates, and discusses his life and thought.

Chroust, Anton-Hermann. "The Political Aspects of the Socratic Problem." In *Socrates Man and Myth: The Two Socratic Apologies of Xenophon,* pp. 164-197. London: Routledge & Kegan Paul, 1957.
Questions the "paucity of reports on the political activities of Socrates," noting that while Socrates did advise most of his followers to avoid entering into politics, he himself did express political views, such as his disdain for Athenian democracy.

Ferguson, John. *Socrates: A Source Book,* compiled and in part translated by John Ferguson. London: Macmillan, 1970, 335p.
Provides English translations of the "main source material about Socrates." Includes translations of works by Plato, Xenophon, Aristophanes, and Aristotle, as well as the writings of Diogenes Laertius, several Athenian orators, and a number of later writers, including Christian commentators.

Gooch, Paul W. "Socrates: Devious or Divine?" *Greece & Rome* XXXII, No. 1 (April 1985): 32-41.
Examines the "ways in which Plato's Socrates has been represented and assessed," arguing that the Platonic Socrates has been characterized both as an ideal man, a "model for life and thought," and as a "devious devil whose major aim is to destroy other people's beliefs and arguments."

Hackforth, R. "Great Thinkers: Socrates." *Philosophy: The Journal of the British Institute of Philosophy,* VIII, No. 31 (July, 1933): 259-72.
Discusses the debate regarding the accuracy of Plato's and Xenophon's portrayals of Socrates.

Hegel, Georg Wilhelm Friedrich. "Greek Philosophy: First Period, Second Division." In *Hegel's Lectures on the History of Philosophy,* Volume One, translated by E. S. Haldane and Frances H. Simson, pp. 350-487. London: Routledge and Kegan Paul, 1892.
Section B (pp. 384-447) of this chapter is devoted to Socrates, the Socratic method, his principle of "the good," and his trial and death.

Jaspers, Karl. "Socrates." In *The Great Philosophers,* edited by Hannah Arendt, translated by Ralph Manheim, pp. 15-31. New York: Jarcourt, Brace & World, 1962.
A brief overview of Socrates's life, intellectual development, the form and substance of his philosophy, his trial, the "Platonic transfiguration" of Socrates, and an assessment of Socrates's influence and significance.

Montgomery, John D., ed. *The State versus Socrates: A Case Study in Civic Freedom.* Boston: The Beacon Press, 1954, 247p.
A collection of essays which discusses the background of the case against Socrates; arguments which highlight the State's opposition to Socrates; essays portraying Socrates as an innocent, pious victim, and as an advocate of political criticism; and four essays which assess Socrates, his beliefs, and his significance from a historical standpoint.

Montuori, Mario. "Socrates: Philosophy and Politics." In *Socrates: Physiology of a Myth,* pp. 177-200. Amsterdam: J. C. Gieben, 1981.
Argues that the concept of Socrates as a non-political figure is a false one, and that while the philosopher may not have been a politician, he was indeed a teacher of politics.

———. *The Socratic Problem: The History—The Solutions.* Amsterdam: J. C. Gieben, 1992, 475p.
A collection of extracts from fifty-four authors from the eighteenth century to the present focussing on the issue of the "Socratic problem," that is, the lack of writings by Socrates, and the question of the validity and accuracy of Socratic sources.

O'Brien, Michael J. "Socrates and the Fifth Century." In *The Socratic Paradoxes and the Greek Mind,* pp. 56-82. Chapel Hill, N.C.: University of North Carolina Press, 1967.
Places the teachings of Socrates within the context of fifth-century Greek thought.

Russell, Bertrand. "Socrates." In *A History of Western Philosophy,* pp. 82-93. New York: Simon and Schuster, 1945.
Reviews the problem of Socrates by discussing the two authors, Xenophon and Plato, who wrote about him. Discusses Plato's *Apology* as a generally historical account of Socrates's speech made in his own defense at the trial.

Sauvage, Micheline. "Socrates through the Ages." In *Socrates and the Conscience of Man,* pp. 137-67. London: Longman, Green & Co., 1960.
Examines some of the critical issues regarding Socrates and his legacy, including the question of the authenticity and reliability of Socratic sources and the influence of Socratic philisophy on such spiritual movements as Christianity.

Stone. I. F. "The Prejudices of Socrates." In *The Trial of Socrates,* pp. 90-129. New York: Little, Brown and Co., 1988.

Explores Socrates's denigration of the middle class (of which he was a member), of other philosophers, and of democracy in general.

Vlastos, Gregory. *Socratic Studies,* edited by Myles Burnyeat. Cambridge: Cambridge University Press, 1994, 152p.

Discusses several aspects of Socrates's philosophy including the Socratic method, his disavowal of knowledge, and the views of Socrates on Athenian democracy.

CLASSICAL AND MEDIEVAL LITERATURE CRITICISM

INDEXES

Literary Criticism Series
Cumulative Author Index

Literary Criticism Series
Cumulative Topic Index

CMLC Cumulative Nationality Index

CMLC Cumulative Title Index

CMLC Cumulative Critic Index

How to Use This Index

The main references

Calvino, Italo
1923-1985.....CLC 5, 8, 11, 22, 33, 39, 73; SSC 3

list all author entries in the following Gale Literary Criticism series:

BLC = *Black Literature Criticism*
CLC = *Contemporary Literary Criticism*
CLR = *Children's Literature Review*
CMLC = *Classical and Medieval Literature Criticism*
DA = *DISCovering Authors*
DAB = *DISCovering Authors: British*
DAC = *DISCovering Authors: Canadian*
DAM = *DISCovering Authors Modules*
DRAM: *Dramatists module*
MST: *Most-studied authors module*
MULT: *Multicultural authors module*
NOV: *Novelists module*
POET: *Poets module*
POP: *Popular/genre writers module*
DC = *Drama Criticism*
HLC = *Hispanic Literature Criticism*
LC = *Literature Criticism from 1400 to 1800*
NCLC = *Nineteenth-Century Literature Criticism*
PC = *Poetry Criticism*
SSC = *Short Story Criticism*
TCLC = *Twentieth-Century Literary Criticism*
WLC = *World Literature Criticism, 1500 to the Present*

The cross-references

See also CANR 23; CA 85-88;
obituary CA 116

list all author entries in the following Gale biographical and literary sources:

AAYA = *Authors & Artists for Young Adults*
AITN = *Authors in the News*
BEST = *Bestsellers*
BW = *Black Writers*
CA = *Contemporary Authors*
CAAS = *Contemporary Authors Autobiography Series*
CABS = *Contemporary Authors Bibliographical Series*
CANR = *Contemporary Authors New Revision Series*
CAP = *Contemporary Authors Permanent Series*
CDALB = *Concise Dictionary of American Literary Biography*
CDBLB = *Concise Dictionary of British Literary Biography*
DLB = *Dictionary of Literary Biography*
DLBD = *Dictionary of Literary Biography Documentary Series*
DLBY = *Dictionary of Literary Biography Yearbook*
HW = *Hispanic Writers*
JRDA = *Junior DISCovering Authors*
MAICYA = *Major Authors and Illustrators for Children and Young Adults*
MTCW = *Major 20th-Century Writers*
NNAL = *Native North American Literature*
SAAS = *Something about the Author Autobiography Series*
SATA = *Something about the Author*
YABC = *Yesterday's Authors of Books for Children*

CUMULATIVE INDEX TO AUTHORS

Abasiyanik, Sait Faik 1906-1954
See Sait Faik
See also CA 123

Abbey, Edward 1927-1989 .... **CLC 36, 59**
See also CA 45-48; 128; CANR 2, 41

Abbott, Lee K(ittredge) 1947- .... **CLC 48**
See also CA 124; CANR 51; DLB 130

Abe, Kobo 1924-1993 **CLC 8, 22, 53, 81; DAM NOV**
See also CA 65-68; 140; CANR 24, 60; DLB 182; MTCW

Abelard, Peter c. 1079-c. 1142 .... **CMLC 11**
See also DLB 115

Abell, Kjeld 1901-1961 .... **CLC 15**
See also CA 111

Abish, Walter 1931- .... **CLC 22**
See also CA 101; CANR 37; DLB 130

Abrahams, Peter (Henry) 1919- .... **CLC 4**
See also BW 1; CA 57-60; CANR 26; DLB 117; MTCW

Abrams, M(eyer) H(oward) 1912- .... **CLC 24**
See also CA 57-60; CANR 13, 33; DLB 67

Abse, Dannie 1923- **CLC 7, 29; DAB; DAM POET**
See also CA 53-56; CAAS 1; CANR 4, 46; DLB 27

Achebe, (Albert) Chinua(lumogu) 1930- **CLC 1, 3, 5, 7, 11, 26, 51, 75; BLC; DA; DAB; DAC; DAM MST, MULT, NOV; WLC**
See also AAYA 15; BW 2; CA 1-4R; CANR 6, 26, 47; CLR 20; DLB 117; MAICYA; MTCW; SATA 40; SATA-Brief 38

Acker, Kathy 1948-1997 .... **CLC 45**
See also CA 117; 122; 162; CANR 55

Ackroyd, Peter 1949- .... **CLC 34, 52**
See also CA 123; 127; CANR 51; DLB 155; INT 127

Acorn, Milton 1923- .... **CLC 15; DAC**
See also CA 103; DLB 53; INT 103

Adamov, Arthur 1908-1970 ..... **CLC 4, 25; DAM DRAM**
See also CA 17-18; 25-28R; CAP 2; MTCW

Adams, Alice (Boyd) 1926- **CLC 6, 13, 46; SSC 24**
See also CA 81-84; CANR 26, 53; DLBY 86; INT CANR-26; MTCW

Adams, Andy 1859-1935 .... **TCLC 56**
See also YABC 1

Adams, Brooks 1848-1927 .... **TCLC 80**
See also CA 123; DLB 47

Adams, Douglas (Noel) 1952- **CLC 27, 60; DAM POP**
See also AAYA 4; BEST 89:3; CA 106; CANR 34, 64; DLBY 83; JRDA

Adams, Francis 1862-1893 .... **NCLC 33**

Adams, Henry (Brooks) 1838-1918 **TCLC 4, 52; DA; DAB; DAC; DAM MST**
See also CA 104; 133; DLB 12, 47, 189

Adams, Richard (George) 1920- .. **CLC 4, 5, 18; DAM NOV**
See also AAYA 16; AITN 1, 2; CA 49-52; CANR 3, 35; CLR 20; JRDA; MAICYA; MTCW; SATA 7, 69

Adamson, Joy(-Friederike Victoria) 1910-1980 **CLC 17**
See also CA 69-72; 93-96; CANR 22; MTCW; SATA 11; SATA-Obit 22

Adcock, Fleur 1934- .... **CLC 41**
See also CA 25-28R; CAAS 23; CANR 11, 34; DLB 40

Addams, Charles (Samuel) 1912-1988 .. **CLC 30**
See also CA 61-64; 126; CANR 12

Addams, Jane 1860-1945 .... **TCLC 76**

Addison, Joseph 1672-1719 .... **LC 18**
See also CDBLB 1660-1789; DLB 101

Adler, Alfred (F.) 1870-1937 .... **TCLC 61**
See also CA 119; 159

Adler, C(arole) S(chwerdtfeger) 1932- . **CLC 35**
See also AAYA 4; CA 89-92; CANR 19, 40; JRDA; MAICYA; SAAS 15; SATA 26, 63

Adler, Renata 1938- .... **CLC 8, 31**
See also CA 49-52; CANR 5, 22, 52; MTCW

Ady, Endre 1877-1919 .... **TCLC 11**
See also CA 107

A.E. 1867-1935 .... **TCLC 3, 10**
See also Russell, George William

Aeschylus 525B.C.-456B.C. **CMLC 11; DA; DAB; DAC; DAM DRAM, MST; DC 8; WLCS**
See also DLB 176

Aesop 620(?)B.C.-564(?)B.C. .... **CMLC 24**
See also CLR 14; MAICYA; SATA 64

Africa, Ben
See Bosman, Herman Charles

Afton, Effie
See Harper, Frances Ellen Watkins

Agapida, Fray Antonio
See Irving, Washington

Agee, James (Rufus) 1909-1955 ..... **TCLC 1, 19; DAM NOV**
See also AITN 1; CA 108; 148; CDALB 1941-1968; DLB 2, 26, 152

Aghill, Gordon
See Silverberg, Robert

Agnon, S(hmuel) Y(osef Halevi) 1888-1970 **CLC 4, 8, 14; SSC 30**
See also CA 17-18; 25-28R; CANR 60; CAP 2; MTCW

Agrippa von Nettesheim, Henry Cornelius 1486-1535 .... **LC 27**

Aherne, Owen
See Cassill, R(onald) V(erlin)

Ai 1947- .... **CLC 4, 14, 69**
See also CA 85-88; CAAS 13; DLB 120

Aickman, Robert (Fordyce) 1914-1981 .. **CLC 57**
See also CA 5-8R; CANR 3

Aiken, Conrad (Potter) 1889-1973 **CLC 1, 3, 5, 10, 52; DAM NOV, POET; SSC 9**
See also CA 5-8R; 45-48; CANR 4, 60; CDALB 1929-1941; DLB 9, 45, 102; MTCW; SATA 3, 30

Aiken, Joan (Delano) 1924- .... **CLC 35**
See also AAYA 1, 25; CA 9-12R; CANR 4, 23, 34, 64; CLR 1, 19; DLB 161; JRDA; MAICYA; MTCW; SAAS 1; SATA 2, 30, 73

Ainsworth, William Harrison 1805-1882 **NCLC 13**
See also DLB 21; SATA 24

Aitmatov, Chingiz (Torekulovich) 1928- **CLC 71**
See also CA 103; CANR 38; MTCW; SATA 56

Akers, Floyd
See Baum, L(yman) Frank

Akhmadulina, Bella Akhatovna 1937- . **CLC 53; DAM POET**
See also CA 65-68

Akhmatova, Anna 1888-1966 **CLC 11, 25, 64; DAM POET; PC 2**
See also CA 19-20; 25-28R; CANR 35; CAP 1; MTCW

Aksakov, Sergei Timofeyvich 1791-1859 **NCLC 2**

Aksenov, Vassily
See Aksyonov, Vassily (Pavlovich)

Akst, Daniel 1956- .... **CLC 109**
See also CA 161

Aksyonov, Vassily (Pavlovich) 1932- **CLC 22, 37, 101**
See also CA 53-56; CANR 12, 48

Akutagawa, Ryunosuke 1892-1927 ..... **TCLC 16**
See also CA 117; 154

Alain 1868-1951 .... **TCLC 41**
See also CA 163

Alain-Fournier .... **TCLC 6**
See also Fournier, Henri Alban
See also DLB 65

Alarcon, Pedro Antonio de 1833-1891 .. **NCLC 1**

Alas (y Urena), Leopoldo (Enrique Garcia) 1852-1901 .... **TCLC 29**
See also CA 113; 131; HW

Albee, Edward (Franklin III) 1928-**CLC 1, 2, 3, 5, 9, 11, 13, 25, 53, 86; DA; DAB; DAC; DAM DRAM, MST; WLC**
See also AITN 1; CA 5-8R; CABS 3; CANR 8, 54; CDALB 1941-1968; DLB 7; INT CANR-8; MTCW

Alberti, Rafael 1902- .... **CLC 7**
See also CA 85-88; DLB 108

Albert the Great 1200(?)-1280 .... **CMLC 16**
See also DLB 115

Alcala-Galiano, Juan Valera y
See Valera y Alcala-Galiano, Juan

Alcott, Amos Bronson 1799-1888 .... **NCLC 1**
See also DLB 1

Alcott, Louisa May 1832-1888 **NCLC 6, 58; DA; DAB; DAC; DAM MST, NOV; SSC 27; WLC**
See also AAYA 20; CDALB 1865-1917; CLR 1, 38; DLB 1, 42, 79; DLBD 14; JRDA; MAICYA; YABC 1

Aldanov, M. A.
See Aldanov, Mark (Alexandrovich)

Aldanov, Mark (Alexandrovich) 1886(?)-1957 **TCLC 23**
See also CA 118

Aldington, Richard 1892-1962 .... **CLC 49**
See also CA 85-88; CANR 45; DLB 20, 36, 100, 149

Aldiss, Brian W(ilson) 1925-**CLC 5, 14, 40; DAM NOV**
See also CA 5-8R; CAAS 2; CANR 5, 28, 64; DLB 14; MTCW; SATA 34

Alegria, Claribel 1924- ... **CLC 75; DAM MULT**
See also CA 131; CAAS 15; CANR 66; DLB 145; HW

Alegria, Fernando 1918- .... **CLC 57**
See also CA 9-12R; CANR 5, 32; HW

Aleichem, Sholom .... **TCLC 1, 35**
See also Rabinovitch, Sholem

Aleixandre, Vicente 1898-1984 **CLC 9, 36; DAM POET; PC 15**
See also CA 85-88; 114; CANR 26; DLB 108; HW; MTCW

Alepoudelis, Odysseus
See Elytis, Odysseus

Aleshkovsky, Joseph 1929-
See Aleshkovsky, Yuz
See also CA 121; 128

Aleshkovsky, Yuz .... **CLC 44**
See also Aleshkovsky, Joseph

Alexander, Lloyd (Chudley) 1924- .... **CLC 35**
See also AAYA 1; CA 1-4R; CANR 1, 24, 38, 55; CLR 1, 5, 48; DLB 52; JRDA; MAICYA; MTCW; SAAS 19; SATA 3, 49, 81

Alexander, Samuel 1859-1938 .... **TCLC 77**

Alexie, Sherman (Joseph, Jr.) 1966- ... **CLC 96; DAM MULT**
See also CA 138; CANR 65; DLB 175; NNAL

Alfau, Felipe 1902- .... **CLC 66**
See also CA 137

Alger, Horatio, Jr. 1832-1899 .... **NCLC 8**
See also DLB 42; SATA 16

Algren, Nelson 1909-1981 .... **CLC 4, 10, 33**
See also CA 13-16R; 103; CANR 20, 61; CDALB 1941-1968; DLB 9; DLBY 81, 82; MTCW

Ali, Ahmed 1910- .... **CLC 69**
See also CA 25-28R; CANR 15, 34

Alighieri, Dante
See Dante

Allan, John B.
See Westlake, Donald E(dwin)

Allan, Sidney
See Hartmann, Sadakichi

Allan, Sydney
See Hartmann, Sadakichi

Allen, Edward 1948- .... **CLC 59**

Allen, Paula Gunn 1939- . **CLC 84; DAM MULT**
See also CA 112; 143; CANR 63; DLB 175; NNAL

Allen, Roland
See Ayckbourn, Alan

Allen, Sarah A.
See Hopkins, Pauline Elizabeth

Allen, Sidney H.
See Hartmann, Sadakichi

Allen, Woody 1935- ...... **CLC 16, 52; DAM POP**
See also AAYA 10; CA 33-36R; CANR 27, 38, 63; DLB 44; MTCW

Allende, Isabel 1942-**CLC 39, 57, 97; DAM MULT, NOV; HLC; WLCS**
See also AAYA 18; CA 125; 130; CANR 51; DLB 145; HW; INT 130; MTCW

Alleyn, Ellen
See Rossetti, Christina (Georgina)

Allingham, Margery (Louise) 1904-1966**CLC 19**
See also CA 5-8R; 25-28R; CANR 4, 58; DLB 77; MTCW

Allingham, William 1824-1889 .... **NCLC 25**
See also DLB 35

Allison, Dorothy E. 1949- .... **CLC 78**
See also CA 140; CANR 66

Allston, Washington 1779-1843 .... **NCLC 2**
See also DLB 1

Almedingen, E. M. .... **CLC 12**
See also Almedingen, Martha Edith von
See also SATA 3

Almedingen, Martha Edith von 1898-1971
See Almedingen, E. M.
See also CA 1-4R; CANR 1

Almqvist, Carl Jonas Love 1793-1866 **NCLC 42**

Alonso, Damaso 1898-1990 .... **CLC 14**
See also CA 110; 131; 130; DLB 108; HW

Alov
See Gogol, Nikolai (Vasilyevich)

Alta 1942- .... **CLC 19**
See also CA 57-60

Alter, Robert B(ernard) 1935- .... **CLC 34**
See also CA 49-52; CANR 1, 47

Alther, Lisa 1944- .... **CLC 7, 41**
See also CA 65-68; CANR 12, 30, 51; MTCW

Althusser, L.
See Althusser, Louis

Althusser, Louis 1918-1990 .... **CLC 106**
See also CA 131; 132

Altman, Robert 1925- .... **CLC 16**
See also CA 73-76; CANR 43

Alvarez, A(lfred) 1929- .... **CLC 5, 13**
See also CA 1-4R; CANR 3, 33, 63; DLB 14, 40

Alvarez, Alejandro Rodriguez 1903-1965
See Casona, Alejandro
See also CA 131; 93-96; HW

Alvarez, Julia 1950- .... **CLC 93**
See also AAYA 25; CA 147

Alvaro, Corrado 1896-1956 .... **TCLC 60**
See also CA 163

Amado, Jorge 1912- ..... **CLC 13, 40, 106; DAM MULT, NOV; HLC**
See also CA 77-80; CANR 35; DLB 113; MTCW

Ambler, Eric 1909- .... **CLC 4, 6, 9**
See also CA 9-12R; CANR 7, 38; DLB 77; MTCW

Amichai, Yehuda 1924- .... **CLC 9, 22, 57**
See also CA 85-88; CANR 46, 60; MTCW

Amichai, Yehudah
See Amichai, Yehuda

Amiel, Henri Frederic 1821-1881 .... **NCLC 4**

Amis, Kingsley (William) 1922-1995**CLC 1, 2, 3, 5, 8, 13, 40, 44; DA; DAB; DAC; DAM MST, NOV**
See also AITN 2; CA 9-12R; 150; CANR 8, 28, 54; CDBLB 1945-1960; DLB 15, 27, 100, 139; DLBY 96; INT CANR-8; MTCW

Amis, Martin (Louis) 1949-**CLC 4, 9, 38, 62, 101**
See also BEST 90:3; CA 65-68; CANR 8, 27, 54; DLB 14, 194; INT CANR-27

Ammons, A(rchie) R(andolph) 1926-**CLC 2, 3, 5, 8, 9, 25, 57, 108; DAM POET; PC 16**
See also AITN 1; CA 9-12R; CANR 6, 36, 51; DLB 5, 165; MTCW

Amo, Tauraatua i
See Adams, Henry (Brooks)

Anand, Mulk Raj 1905- **CLC 23, 93; DAM NOV**
See also CA 65-68; CANR 32, 64; MTCW

Anatol
See Schnitzler, Arthur

Anaximander c. 610B.C.-c. 546B.C. .... **CMLC 22**

Anaya, Rudolfo A(lfonso) 1937- . **CLC 23; DAM MULT, NOV; HLC**
See also AAYA 20; CA 45-48; CAAS 4; CANR 1, 32, 51; DLB 82; HW 1; MTCW

Andersen, Hans Christian 1805-1875 . **NCLC 7; DA; DAB; DAC; DAM MST, POP; SSC 6; WLC**
See also CLR 6; MAICYA; YABC 1

Anderson, C. Farley
See Mencken, H(enry) L(ouis); Nathan, George Jean

Anderson, Jessica (Margaret) Queale 1916-**CLC 37**
See also CA 9-12R; CANR 4, 62

Anderson, Jon (Victor) 1940-**CLC 9; DAM POET**
See also CA 25-28R; CANR 20

Anderson, Lindsay (Gordon) 1923-1994 **CLC 20**
See also CA 125; 128; 146

Anderson, Maxwell 1888-1959 ... **TCLC 2; DAM DRAM**
See also CA 105; 152; DLB 7

Anderson, Poul (William) 1926- .... **CLC 15**
See also AAYA 5; CA 1-4R; CAAS 2; CANR 2, 15, 34, 64; DLB 8; INT CANR-15; MTCW; SATA 90; SATA-Brief 39

Anderson, Robert (Woodruff) 1917- .... **CLC 23; DAM DRAM**
See also AITN 1; CA 21-24R; CANR 32; DLB 7

Anderson, Sherwood 1876-1941 **TCLC 1, 10, 24; DA; DAB; DAC; DAM MST, NOV; SSC 1; WLC**
See also CA 104; 121; CANR 61; CDALB 1917-1929; DLB 4, 9, 86; DLBD 1; MTCW

Andier, Pierre
See Desnos, Robert

Andouard
See Giraudoux, (Hippolyte) Jean

Andrade, Carlos Drummond de .... **CLC 18**
See also Drummond de Andrade, Carlos

Andrade, Mario de 1893-1945 .... **TCLC 43**

Andreae, Johann V(alentin) 1586-1654 .... **LC 32**
See also DLB 164

Andreas-Salome, Lou 1861-1937 .... **TCLC 56**
See also DLB 66

Andress, Lesley
See Sanders, Lawrence

Andrewes, Lancelot 1555-1626 .... **LC 5**
See also DLB 151, 172

Andrews, Cicily Fairfield
See West, Rebecca

Andrews, Elton V.
See Pohl, Frederik

Andreyev, Leonid (Nikolaevich) 1871-1919**TCLC 3**
See also CA 104

Andric, Ivo 1892-1975 .... **CLC 8**
See also CA 81-84; 57-60; CANR 43, 60; DLB 147; MTCW

Androvar
See Prado (Calvo), Pedro

Angelique, Pierre
See Bataille, Georges

Angell, Roger 1920- .... **CLC 26**
See also CA 57-60; CANR 13, 44; DLB 171, 185

Angelou, Maya 1928- **CLC 12, 35, 64, 77; BLC; DA; DAB; DAC; DAM MST, MULT, POET, POP; WLCS**
See also AAYA 7, 20; BW 2; CA 65-68; CANR 19, 42, 65; DLB 38; MTCW; SATA 49

Anna Comnena 1083-1153 .... **CMLC 25**

Annensky, Innokenty (Fyodorovich) 1856-1909 **TCLC 14**
See also CA 110; 155

Annunzio, Gabriele d'
See D'Annunzio, Gabriele

Anodos
See Coleridge, Mary E(lizabeth)

Anon, Charles Robert
See Pessoa, Fernando (Antonio Nogueira)

Anouilh, Jean (Marie Lucien Pierre) 1910-1987 **CLC 1, 3, 8, 13, 40, 50; DAM DRAM; DC 8**
See also CA 17-20R; 123; CANR 32; MTCW

Anthony, Florence
See Ai

Anthony, John
See Ciardi, John (Anthony)

Anthony, Peter
See Shaffer, Anthony (Joshua); Shaffer, Peter (Levin)

Anthony, Piers 1934- .... **CLC 35; DAM POP**
See also AAYA 11; CA 21-24R; CANR 28, 56; DLB 8; MTCW; SAAS 22; SATA 84

Antoine, Marc
See Proust, (Valentin-Louis-George-Eugene-) Marcel

Antoninus, Brother
See Everson, William (Oliver)

Antonioni, Michelangelo 1912- .... **CLC 20**
See also CA 73-76; CANR 45

Antschel, Paul 1920-1970
See Celan, Paul
See also CA 85-88; CANR 33, 61; MTCW

Anwar, Chairil 1922-1949 .... **TCLC 22**
See also CA 121

Apollinaire, Guillaume 1880-1918**TCLC 3, 8, 51; DAM POET; PC 7**
See also Kostrowitzki, Wilhelm Apollinaris de
See also CA 152

Appelfeld, Aharon 1932- .... **CLC 23, 47**
See also CA 112; 133

Apple, Max (Isaac) 1941- .... **CLC 9, 33**
See also CA 81-84; CANR 19, 54; DLB 130

Appleman, Philip (Dean) 1926- .... **CLC 51**
See also CA 13-16R; CAAS 18; CANR 6, 29, 56

Appleton, Lawrence
See Lovecraft, H(oward) P(hillips)

Apteryx
See Eliot, T(homas) S(tearns)

Apuleius, (Lucius Madaurensis) 125(?)-175(?) **CMLC 1**

Aquin, Hubert 1929-1977 .... **CLC 15**
See also CA 105; DLB 53

Aragon, Louis 1897-1982**CLC 3, 22; DAM NOV, POET**
See also CA 69-72; 108; CANR 28; DLB 72; MTCW

Arany, Janos 1817-1882 .... **NCLC 34**

Arbuthnot, John 1667-1735 .... **LC 1**
See also DLB 101

Archer, Herbert Winslow
See Mencken, H(enry) L(ouis)

Archer, Jeffrey (Howard) 1940- . **CLC 28; DAM POP**
See also AAYA 16; BEST 89:3; CA 77-80; CANR 22, 52; INT CANR-22

Archer, Jules 1915- .... **CLC 12**
See also CA 9-12R; CANR 6; SAAS 5; SATA 4, 85

Archer, Lee
See Ellison, Harlan (Jay)

Arden, John 1930- **CLC 6, 13, 15; DAM DRAM**
See also CA 13-16R; CAAS 4; CANR 31, 65, 67; DLB 13; MTCW

Arenas, Reinaldo 1943-1990**CLC 41; DAM MULT; HLC**
See also CA 124; 128; 133; DLB 145; HW

Arendt, Hannah 1906-1975 .... **CLC 66, 98**
See also CA 17-20R; 61-64; CANR 26, 60; MTCW

Aretino, Pietro 1492-1556 .... **LC 12**

Arghezi, Tudor .... **CLC 80**
See also Theodorescu, Ion N.

Arguedas, Jose Maria 1911-1969 ... **CLC 10, 18**
See also CA 89-92; DLB 113; HW

Argueta, Manlio 1936- .... **CLC 31**
See also CA 131; DLB 145; HW

Ariosto, Ludovico 1474-1533 .... **LC 6**

Aristides
See Epstein, Joseph

Aristophanes 450B.C.-385B.C. **CMLC 4; DA; DAB; DAC; DAM DRAM, MST; DC 2; WLCS**
See also DLB 176

Arlt, Roberto (Godofredo Christophersen) 1900-1942 .... **TCLC 29; DAM MULT; HLC**
See also CA 123; 131; CANR 67; HW

Armah, Ayi Kwei 1939- . **CLC 5, 33; BLC; DAM MULT, POET**
See also BW 1; CA 61-64; CANR 21, 64; DLB 117; MTCW

Armatrading, Joan 1950- .... **CLC 17**
See also CA 114

Arnette, Robert
See Silverberg, Robert

Arnim, Achim von (Ludwig Joachim von Arnim) 1781-1831 .... **NCLC 5; SSC 29**
See also DLB 90

Arnim, Bettina von 1785-1859 .... **NCLC 38**
See also DLB 90

Arnold, Matthew 1822-1888 .... **NCLC 6, 29; DA; DAB; DAC; DAM MST, POET; PC 5; WLC**
See also CDBLB 1832-1890; DLB 32, 57

Arnold, Thomas 1795-1842 .... **NCLC 18**
See also DLB 55

Arnow, Harriette (Louisa) Simpson 1908-1986 **CLC 2, 7, 18**
See also CA 9-12R; 118; CANR 14; DLB 6; MTCW; SATA 42; SATA-Obit 47

Arp, Hans
See Arp, Jean

Arp, Jean 1887-1966 .... **CLC 5**
See also CA 81-84; 25-28R; CANR 42

Arrabal
See Arrabal, Fernando

Arrabal, Fernando 1932- .... **CLC 2, 9, 18, 58**
See also CA 9-12R; CANR 15

Arrick, Fran .... **CLC 30**
See also Gaberman, Judie Angell

Artaud, Antonin (Marie Joseph) 1896-1948 **TCLC 3, 36; DAM DRAM**
See also CA 104; 149

Arthur, Ruth M(abel) 1905-1979 .... **CLC 12**
See also CA 9-12R; 85-88; CANR 4; SATA 7, 26

Artsybashev, Mikhail (Petrovich) 1878-1927 **TCLC 31**

Arundel, Honor (Morfydd) 1919-1973 ... **CLC 17**
See also CA 21-22; 41-44R; CAP 2; CLR 35; SATA 4; SATA-Obit 24

Arzner, Dorothy 1897-1979 .... **CLC 98**

Asch, Sholem 1880-1957 .... **TCLC 3**
See also CA 105

Ash, Shalom
See Asch, Sholem

Ashbery, John (Lawrence) 1927- **CLC 2, 3, 4, 6, 9, 13, 15, 25, 41, 77; DAM POET**
See also CA 5-8R; CANR 9, 37, 66; DLB 5, 165; DLBY 81; INT CANR-9; MTCW

Ashdown, Clifford
See Freeman, R(ichard) Austin

Ashe, Gordon
See Creasey, John

Ashton-Warner, Sylvia (Constance) 1908-1984 **CLC 19**
See also CA 69-72; 112; CANR 29; MTCW

Asimov, Isaac 1920-1992 **CLC 1, 3, 9, 19, 26, 76, 92; DAM POP**
See also AAYA 13; BEST 90:2; CA 1-4R; 137; CANR 2, 19, 36, 60; CLR 12; DLB 8; DLBY 92; INT CANR-19; JRDA; MAICYA; MTCW; SATA 1, 26, 74

Assis, Joaquim Maria Machado de
See Machado de Assis, Joaquim Maria

Astley, Thea (Beatrice May) 1925- .... **CLC 41**
See also CA 65-68; CANR 11, 43

Aston, James
See White, T(erence) H(anbury)

Asturias, Miguel Angel 1899-1974 **CLC 3, 8, 13; DAM MULT, NOV; HLC**
See also CA 25-28; 49-52; CANR 32; CAP 2; DLB 113; HW; MTCW

Atares, Carlos Saura
See Saura (Atares), Carlos

Atheling, William
See Pound, Ezra (Weston Loomis)

Atheling, William, Jr.
See Blish, James (Benjamin)

Atherton, Gertrude (Franklin Horn) 1857-1948 **TCLC 2**
See also CA 104; 155; DLB 9, 78, 186

Atherton, Lucius
See Masters, Edgar Lee

Atkins, Jack
See Harris, Mark

Atkinson, Kate .... **CLC 99**

Attaway, William (Alexander) 1911-1986 **CLC 92; BLC; DAM MULT**
See also BW 2; CA 143; DLB 76

Atticus
See Fleming, Ian (Lancaster)

Atwood, Margaret (Eleanor) 1939- **CLC 2, 3, 4, 8, 13, 15, 25, 44, 84; DA; DAB; DAC; DAM MST, NOV, POET; PC 8; SSC 2; WLC**
See also AAYA 12; BEST 89:2; CA 49-52; CANR 3, 24, 33, 59; DLB 53; INT CANR-24; MTCW; SATA 50

Aubigny, Pierre d'
See Mencken, H(enry) L(ouis)

Aubin, Penelope 1685-1731(?) .... **LC 9**
See also DLB 39

Auchincloss, Louis (Stanton) 1917- **CLC 4, 6, 9, 18, 45; DAM NOV; SSC 22**
See also CA 1-4R; CANR 6, 29, 55; DLB 2; DLBY 80; INT CANR-29; MTCW

Auden, W(ystan) H(ugh) 1907-1973 **CLC 1, 2, 3, 4, 6, 9, 11, 14, 43; DA; DAB; DAC; DAM DRAM, MST, POET; PC 1; WLC**
See also AAYA 18; CA 9-12R; 45-48; CANR 5, 61; CDBLB 1914-1945; DLB 10, 20; MTCW

Audiberti, Jacques 1900-1965 .... **CLC 38; DAM DRAM**
See also CA 25-28R

Audubon, John James 1785-1851 .... **NCLC 47**

Auel, Jean M(arie) 1936- **CLC 31, 107; DAM POP**
See also AAYA 7; BEST 90:4; CA 103; CANR 21, 64; INT CANR-21; SATA 91

Auerbach, Erich 1892-1957 .... **TCLC 43**
See also CA 118; 155

Augier, Emile 1820-1889 .... **NCLC 31**
See also DLB 192

August, John
See De Voto, Bernard (Augustine)

Augustine, St. 354-430 .... **CMLC 6; DAB**

Aurelius
See Bourne, Randolph S(illiman)

Aurobindo, Sri
See Aurobindo Ghose

Aurobindo Ghose 1872-1950 .... **TCLC 63**
See also CA 163

Austen, Jane 1775-1817 **NCLC 1, 13, 19, 33, 51; DA; DAB; DAC; DAM MST, NOV; WLC**
See also AAYA 19; CDBLB 1789-1832; DLB 116

Auster, Paul 1947- .... **CLC 47**
See also CA 69-72; CANR 23, 52

Austin, Frank
See Faust, Frederick (Schiller)

Austin, Mary (Hunter) 1868-1934 .... **TCLC 25**
See also CA 109; DLB 9, 78

Autran Dourado, Waldomiro
See Dourado, (Waldomiro Freitas) Autran

Averroes 1126-1198 .... **CMLC 7**
See also DLB 115

Avicenna 980-1037 .... **CMLC 16**
See also DLB 115

Avison, Margaret 1918- **CLC 2, 4, 97; DAC; DAM POET**
See also CA 17-20R; DLB 53; MTCW

Axton, David
See Koontz, Dean R(ay)

Ayckbourn, Alan 1939- **CLC 5, 8, 18, 33, 74; DAB; DAM DRAM**
See also CA 21-24R; CANR 31, 59; DLB 13; MTCW

Aydy, Catherine
See Tennant, Emma (Christina)

Ayme, Marcel (Andre) 1902-1967 .... **CLC 11**
See also CA 89-92; CANR 67; CLR 25; DLB 72; SATA 91

Ayrton, Michael 1921-1975 .... **CLC 7**
See also CA 5-8R; 61-64; CANR 9, 21

Azorin .... **CLC 11**
See also Martinez Ruiz, Jose

Azuela, Mariano 1873-1952**TCLC 3; DAM MULT; HLC**
See also CA 104; 131; HW; MTCW

Baastad, Babbis Friis
See Friis-Baastad, Babbis Ellinor

Bab
See Gilbert, W(illiam) S(chwenck)

Babbis, Eleanor
See Friis-Baastad, Babbis Ellinor

Babel, Isaac
See Babel, Isaak (Emmanuilovich)

Babel, Isaak (Emmanuilovich) 1894-1941(?) **TCLC 2, 13; SSC 16**
See also CA 104; 155

Babits, Mihaly 1883-1941 .... **TCLC 14**
See also CA 114

Babur 1483-1530 .... **LC 18**

Bacchelli, Riccardo 1891-1985 .... **CLC 19**
See also CA 29-32R; 117

Bach, Richard (David) 1936-**CLC 14; DAM NOV, POP**
See also AITN 1; BEST 89:2; CA 9-12R; CANR 18; MTCW; SATA 13

Bachman, Richard
See King, Stephen (Edwin)

Bachmann, Ingeborg 1926-1973 .... **CLC 69**
See also CA 93-96; 45-48; DLB 85

Bacon, Francis 1561-1626 .... **LC 18, 32**
See also CDBLB Before 1660; DLB 151

Bacon, Roger 1214(?)-1292 .... **CMLC 14**
See also DLB 115

Bacovia, George .... **TCLC 24**
See also Vasiliu, Gheorghe

Badanes, Jerome 1937- .... **CLC 59**

Bagehot, Walter 1826-1877 .... **NCLC 10**
See also DLB 55

Bagnold, Enid 1889-1981 **CLC 25; DAM DRAM**
See also CA 5-8R; 103; CANR 5, 40; DLB 13, 160, 191; MAICYA; SATA 1, 25

Bagritsky, Eduard 1895-1934 .... **TCLC 60**

Bagrjana, Elisaveta
See Belcheva, Elisaveta

Bagryana, Elisaveta .... **CLC 10**
See also Belcheva, Elisaveta
See also DLB 147

Bailey, Paul 1937- .... **CLC 45**
See also CA 21-24R; CANR 16, 62; DLB 14

Baillie, Joanna 1762-1851 .... **NCLC 2**
See also DLB 93

Bainbridge, Beryl (Margaret) 1933-**CLC 4, 5, 8, 10, 14, 18, 22, 62; DAM NOV**
See also CA 21-24R; CANR 24, 55; DLB 14; MTCW

Baker, Elliott 1922- .... **CLC 8**
See also CA 45-48; CANR 2, 63

Baker, Jean H. .... **TCLC 3, 10**
See also Russell, George William

Baker, Nicholson 1957- ..... **CLC 61; DAM POP**
See also CA 135; CANR 63

Baker, Ray Stannard 1870-1946 .... **TCLC 47**
See also CA 118

Baker, Russell (Wayne) 1925- .... **CLC 31**
See also BEST 89:4; CA 57-60; CANR 11, 41, 59; MTCW

Bakhtin, M.
See Bakhtin, Mikhail Mikhailovich

Bakhtin, M. M.
See Bakhtin, Mikhail Mikhailovich

Bakhtin, Mikhail
See Bakhtin, Mikhail Mikhailovich

Bakhtin, Mikhail Mikhailovich 1895-1975 **CLC 83**
See also CA 128; 113

Bakshi, Ralph 1938(?)- .... **CLC 26**
See also CA 112; 138

Bakunin, Mikhail (Alexandrovich) 1814-1876 **NCLC 25, 58**

Baldwin, James (Arthur) 1924-1987 **CLC 1, 2, 3, 4, 5, 8, 13, 15, 17, 42, 50, 67, 90; BLC; DA; DAB; DAC; DAM MST, MULT, NOV, POP; DC 1; SSC 10; WLC**
See also AAYA 4; BW 1; CA 1-4R; 124; CABS 1; CANR 3, 24; CDALB 1941-1968; DLB 2, 7, 33; DLBY 87; MTCW; SATA 9; SATA-Obit 54

Ballard, J(ames) G(raham) 1930- **CLC 3, 6, 14, 36; DAM NOV, POP; SSC 1**
See also AAYA 3; CA 5-8R; CANR 15, 39, 65; DLB 14; MTCW; SATA 93

Balmont, Konstantin (Dmitriyevich) 1867-1943 **TCLC 11**
See also CA 109; 155

Balzac, Honore de 1799-1850**NCLC 5, 35, 53; DA; DAB; DAC; DAM MST, NOV; SSC 5; WLC**
See also DLB 119

Bambara, Toni Cade 1939-1995**CLC 19, 88; BLC; DA; DAC; DAM MST, MULT; WLCS**
See also AAYA 5; BW 2; CA 29-32R; 150; CANR 24, 49; DLB 38; MTCW

Bamdad, A.
See Shamlu, Ahmad

Banat, D. R.
See Bradbury, Ray (Douglas)

Bancroft, Laura
See Baum, L(yman) Frank

Banim, John 1798-1842 .... **NCLC 13**
See also DLB 116, 158, 159

Banim, Michael 1796-1874 .... **NCLC 13**
See also DLB 158, 159

Banjo, The
See Paterson, A(ndrew) B(arton)

Banks, Iain
See Banks, Iain M(enzies)

Banks, Iain M(enzies) 1954- .... **CLC 34**
See also CA 123; 128; CANR 61; DLB 194; INT 128

Banks, Lynne Reid .... **CLC 23**
See also Reid Banks, Lynne
See also AAYA 6

Banks, Russell 1940- .... **CLC 37, 72**
See also CA 65-68; CAAS 15; CANR 19, 52; DLB 130

Banville, John 1945- .... **CLC 46**
See also CA 117; 128; DLB 14; INT 128

Banville, Theodore (Faullain) de 1832-1891**NCLC 9**

Baraka, Amiri 1934- **CLC 1, 2, 3, 5, 10, 14, 33; BLC; DA; DAC; DAM MST, MULT, POET, POP; DC 6; PC 4; WLCS**
See also Jones, LeRoi
See also BW 2; CA 21-24R; CABS 3; CANR 27, 38, 61; CDALB 1941-1968; DLB 5, 7, 16, 38; DLBD 8; MTCW

Barbauld, Anna Laetitia 1743-1825 .... **NCLC 50**
See also DLB 107, 109, 142, 158

Barbellion, W. N. P. .... **TCLC 24**
See also Cummings, Bruce F(rederick)

Barbera, Jack (Vincent) 1945- .... **CLC 44**
See also CA 110; CANR 45

Barbey d'Aurevilly, Jules Amedee 1808-1889 **NCLC 1; SSC 17**
See also DLB 119

Barbusse, Henri 1873-1935 .... **TCLC 5**
See also CA 105; 154; DLB 65

Barclay, Bill
See Moorcock, Michael (John)

Barclay, William Ewert
See Moorcock, Michael (John)

Barea, Arturo 1897-1957 .... **TCLC 14**
See also CA 111

Barfoot, Joan 1946- .... **CLC 18**
See also CA 105

Baring, Maurice 1874-1945 .... **TCLC 8**
See also CA 105; DLB 34

Barker, Clive 1952- .... **CLC 52; DAM POP**
See also AAYA 10; BEST 90:3; CA 121; 129; INT 129; MTCW

Barker, George Granville 1913-1991 **CLC 8, 48; DAM POET**
See also CA 9-12R; 135; CANR 7, 38; DLB 20; MTCW

Barker, Harley Granville
See Granville-Barker, Harley
See also DLB 10

Bede c. 673-735 .... **CMLC 20**
See also DLB 146

Bedford, Donald F.
See Fearing, Kenneth (Flexner)

Beecher, Catharine Esther 1800-1878 **NCLC 30**
See also DLB 1

Beecher, John 1904-1980 .... **CLC 6**
See also AITN 1; CA 5-8R; 105; CANR 8

Beer, Johann 1655-1700 .... **LC 5**
See also DLB 168

Beer, Patricia 1924- .... **CLC 58**
See also CA 61-64; CANR 13, 46; DLB 40

Beerbohm, Max
See Beerbohm, (Henry) Max(imilian)

Beerbohm, (Henry) Max(imilian) 1872-1956 **TCLC 1, 24**
See also CA 104; 154; DLB 34, 100

Beer-Hofmann, Richard 1866-1945 ..... **TCLC 60**
See also CA 160; DLB 81

Begiebing, Robert J(ohn) 1946- .... **CLC 70**
See also CA 122; CANR 40

Behan, Brendan 1923-1964 **CLC 1, 8, 11, 15, 79; DAM DRAM**
See also CA 73-76; CANR 33; CDBLB 1945-1960; DLB 13; MTCW

Behn, Aphra 1640(?)-1689 . **LC 1, 30; DA; DAB; DAC; DAM DRAM, MST, NOV, POET; DC 4; PC 13; WLC**
See also DLB 39, 80, 131

Behrman, S(amuel) N(athaniel) 1893-1973 **CLC 40**
See also CA 13-16; 45-48; CAP 1; DLB 7, 44

Belasco, David 1853-1931 .... **TCLC 3**
See also CA 104; DLB 7

Belcheva, Elisaveta 1893- .... **CLC 10**
See also Bagryana, Elisaveta

Beldone, Phil "Cheech"
See Ellison, Harlan (Jay)

Beleno
See Azuela, Mariano

Belinski, Vissarion Grigoryevich 1811-1848 **NCLC 5**

Belitt, Ben 1911- .... **CLC 22**
See also CA 13-16R; CAAS 4; CANR 7; DLB 5

Bell, Gertrude 1868-1926 .... **TCLC 67**
See also DLB 174

Bell, James Madison 1826-1902 **TCLC 43; BLC; DAM MULT**
See also BW 1; CA 122; 124; DLB 50

Bell, Madison Smartt 1957- .... **CLC 41, 102**
See also CA 111; CANR 28, 54

Bell, Marvin (Hartley) 1937- .. **CLC 8, 31; DAM POET**
See also CA 21-24R; CAAS 14; CANR 59; DLB 5; MTCW

Bell, W. L. D.
See Mencken, H(enry) L(ouis)

Bellamy, Atwood C.
See Mencken, H(enry) L(ouis)

Bellamy, Edward 1850-1898 .... **NCLC 4**
See also DLB 12

Bellin, Edward J.
See Kuttner, Henry

Belloc, (Joseph) Hilaire (Pierre Sebastien Rene Swanton) 1870-1953 **TCLC 7, 18; DAM POET**
See also CA 106; 152; DLB 19, 100, 141, 174; YABC 1

Belloc, Joseph Peter Rene Hilaire
See Belloc, (Joseph) Hilaire (Pierre Sebastien Rene Swanton)

Belloc, Joseph Pierre Hilaire
See Belloc, (Joseph) Hilaire (Pierre Sebastien Rene Swanton)

Belloc, M. A.
See Lowndes, Marie Adelaide (Belloc)

Bellow, Saul 1915- **CLC 1, 2, 3, 6, 8, 10, 13, 15, 25, 33, 34, 63, 79; DA; DAB; DAC; DAM MST, NOV, POP; SSC 14; WLC**
See also AITN 2; BEST 89:3; CA 5-8R; CABS 1; CANR 29, 53; CDALB 1941-1968; DLB 2, 28; DLBD 3; DLBY 82; MTCW

Belser, Reimond Karel Maria de 1929-
See Ruyslinck, Ward
See also CA 152

Bely, Andrey .... **TCLC 7; PC 11**
See also Bugayev, Boris Nikolayevich

Belyi, Andrei
See Bugayev, Boris Nikolayevich

Benary, Margot
See Benary-Isbert, Margot

Benary-Isbert, Margot 1889-1979 .... **CLC 12**
See also CA 5-8R; 89-92; CANR 4; CLR 12; MAICYA; SATA 2; SATA-Obit 21

Benavente (y Martinez), Jacinto 1866-1954 **TCLC 3; DAM DRAM, MULT**
See also CA 106; 131; HW; MTCW

Benchley, Peter (Bradford) 1940- **CLC 4, 8; DAM NOV, POP**
See also AAYA 14; AITN 2; CA 17-20R; CANR 12, 35, 66; MTCW; SATA 3, 89

Benchley, Robert (Charles) 1889-1945 **TCLC 1, 55**
See also CA 105; 153; DLB 11

Benda, Julien 1867-1956 .... **TCLC 60**
See also CA 120; 154

Benedict, Ruth (Fulton) 1887-1948 ..... **TCLC 60**
See also CA 158

Benedikt, Michael 1935- .... **CLC 4, 14**
See also CA 13-16R; CANR 7; DLB 5

Benet, Juan 1927- .... **CLC 28**
See also CA 143

Benet, Stephen Vincent 1898-1943 **TCLC 7; DAM POET; SSC 10**
See also CA 104; 152; DLB 4, 48, 102; DLBY 97; YABC 1

Benet, William Rose 1886-1950 **TCLC 28; DAM POET**
See also CA 118; 152; DLB 45

Benford, Gregory (Albert) 1941- .... **CLC 52**
See also CA 69-72; CAAS 27; CANR 12, 24, 49; DLBY 82

Bengtsson, Frans (Gunnar) 1894-1954 **TCLC 48**

Benjamin, David
See Slavitt, David R(ytman)

Benjamin, Lois
See Gould, Lois

Benjamin, Walter 1892-1940 .... **TCLC 39**
See also CA 164

Benn, Gottfried 1886-1956 .... **TCLC 3**
See also CA 106; 153; DLB 56

Bennett, Alan 1934- **CLC 45, 77; DAB; DAM MST**
See also CA 103; CANR 35, 55; MTCW

Bennett, (Enoch) Arnold 1867-1931 **TCLC 5, 20**
See also CA 106; 155; CDBLB 1890-1914; DLB 10, 34, 98, 135

Bennett, Elizabeth
See Mitchell, Margaret (Munnerlyn)

Bennett, George Harold 1930-
See Bennett, Hal
See also BW 1; CA 97-100

Bennett, Hal .... **CLC 5**
See also Bennett, George Harold
See also DLB 33

Bennett, Jay 1912- .... **CLC 35**
See also AAYA 10; CA 69-72; CANR 11, 42; JRDA; SAAS 4; SATA 41, 87; SATA-Brief 27

Bennett, Louise (Simone) 1919- **CLC 28; BLC; DAM MULT**
See also BW 2; CA 151; DLB 117

Benson, E(dward) F(rederic) 1867-1940 **TCLC 27**
See also CA 114; 157; DLB 135, 153

Benson, Jackson J. 1930- .... **CLC 34**
See also CA 25-28R; DLB 111

Benson, Sally 1900-1972 .... **CLC 17**
See also CA 19-20; 37-40R; CAP 1; SATA 1, 35; SATA-Obit 27

Benson, Stella 1892-1933 .... **TCLC 17**
See also CA 117; 155; DLB 36, 162

Bentham, Jeremy 1748-1832 .... **NCLC 38**
See also DLB 107, 158

Bentley, E(dmund) C(lerihew) 1875-1956 **TCLC 12**
See also CA 108; DLB 70

Bentley, Eric (Russell) 1916- .... **CLC 24**
See also CA 5-8R; CANR 6, 67; INT CANR-6

Bosschere, Jean de 1878(?)-1953 .... **TCLC 19**
See also CA 115

Boswell, James 1740-1795**LC 4; DA; DAB; DAC; DAM MST; WLC**
See also CDBLB 1660-1789; DLB 104, 142

Bottoms, David 1949- .... **CLC 53**
See also CA 105; CANR 22; DLB 120; DLBY 83

Boucicault, Dion 1820-1890 .... **NCLC 41**

Boucolon, Maryse 1937(?)-
See Conde, Maryse
See also CA 110; CANR 30, 53

Bourget, Paul (Charles Joseph) 1852-1935**TCLC 12**
See also CA 107; DLB 123

Bourjaily, Vance (Nye) 1922- .... **CLC 8, 62**
See also CA 1-4R; CAAS 1; CANR 2; DLB 2, 143

Bourne, Randolph S(illiman) 1886-1918**TCLC 16**
See also CA 117; 155; DLB 63

Bova, Ben(jamin William) 1932- .... **CLC 45**
See also AAYA 16; CA 5-8R; CAAS 18; CANR 11, 56; CLR 3; DLBY 81; INT CANR-11; MAICYA; MTCW; SATA 6, 68

Bowen, Elizabeth (Dorothea Cole) 1899-1973**CLC 1, 3, 6, 11, 15, 22; DAM NOV; SSC 3, 28**
See also CA 17-18; 41-44R; CANR 35; CAP 2; CDBLB 1945-1960; DLB 15, 162; MTCW

Bowering, George 1935- .... **CLC 15, 47**
See also CA 21-24R; CAAS 16; CANR 10; DLB 53

Bowering, Marilyn R(uthe) 1949- .... **CLC 32**
See also CA 101; CANR 49

Bowers, Edgar 1924- .... **CLC 9**
See also CA 5-8R; CANR 24; DLB 5

Bowie, David .... **CLC 17**
See also Jones, David Robert

Bowles, Jane (Sydney) 1917-1973 ..... **CLC 3, 68**
See also CA 19-20; 41-44R; CAP 2

Bowles, Paul (Frederick) 1910-1986**CLC 1, 2, 19, 53; SSC 3**
See also CA 1-4R; CAAS 1; CANR 1, 19, 50; DLB 5, 6; MTCW

Box, Edgar
See Vidal, Gore

Boyd, Nancy
See Millay, Edna St. Vincent

Boyd, William 1952- .... **CLC 28, 53, 70**
See also CA 114; 120; CANR 51

Boyle, Kay 1902-1992 .. **CLC 1, 5, 19, 58; SSC 5**
See also CA 13-16R; 140; CAAS 1; CANR 29, 61; DLB 4, 9, 48, 86; DLBY 93; MTCW

Boyle, Mark
See Kienzle, William X(avier)

Boyle, Patrick 1905-1982 .... **CLC 19**
See also CA 127

Boyle, T. C. 1948-
See Boyle, T(homas) Coraghessan

Boyle, T(homas) Coraghessan 1948-**CLC 36, 55, 90; DAM POP; SSC 16**
See also BEST 90:4; CA 120; CANR 44; DLBY 86

Boz
See Dickens, Charles (John Huffam)

Brackenridge, Hugh Henry 1748-1816 **NCLC 7**
See also DLB 11, 37

Bradbury, Edward P.
See Moorcock, Michael (John)

Bradbury, Malcolm (Stanley) 1932- **CLC 32, 61; DAM NOV**
See also CA 1-4R; CANR 1, 33; DLB 14; MTCW

Bradbury, Ray (Douglas) 1920-**CLC 1, 3, 10, 15, 42, 98; DA; DAB; DAC; DAM MST, NOV, POP; SSC 29; WLC**
See also AAYA 15; AITN 1, 2; CA 1-4R; CANR 2, 30; CDALB 1968-1988; DLB 2, 8; MTCW; SATA 11, 64

Bradford, Gamaliel 1863-1932 .... **TCLC 36**
See also CA 160; DLB 17

Bradley, David (Henry, Jr.) 1950- **CLC 23; BLC; DAM MULT**
See also BW 1; CA 104; CANR 26; DLB 33

Bradley, John Ed(mund, Jr.) 1958- .... **CLC 55**
See also CA 139

Bradley, Marion Zimmer 1930- . **CLC 30; DAM POP**
See also AAYA 9; CA 57-60; CAAS 10; CANR 7, 31, 51; DLB 8; MTCW; SATA 90

Bradstreet, Anne 1612(?)-1672 ... **LC 4, 30; DA; DAC; DAM MST, POET; PC 10**
See also CDALB 1640-1865; DLB 24

Brady, Joan 1939- .... **CLC 86**
See also CA 141

Bragg, Melvyn 1939- .... **CLC 10**
See also BEST 89:3; CA 57-60; CANR 10, 48; DLB 14

Braine, John (Gerard) 1922-1986 . **CLC 1, 3, 41**
See also CA 1-4R; 120; CANR 1, 33; CDBLB 1945-1960; DLB 15; DLBY 86; MTCW

Bramah, Ernest 1868-1942 .... **TCLC 72**
See also CA 156; DLB 70

Brammer, William 1930(?)-1978 .... **CLC 31**
See also CA 77-80

Brancati, Vitaliano 1907-1954 .... **TCLC 12**
See also CA 109

Brancato, Robin F(idler) 1936- .... **CLC 35**
See also AAYA 9; CA 69-72; CANR 11, 45; CLR 32; JRDA; SAAS 9; SATA 97

Brand, Max
See Faust, Frederick (Schiller)

Brand, Millen 1906-1980 .... **CLC 7**
See also CA 21-24R; 97-100

Branden, Barbara .... **CLC 44**
See also CA 148

Brandes, Georg (Morris Cohen) 1842-1927**TCLC 10**
See also CA 105

Brandys, Kazimierz 1916- .... **CLC 62**

Branley, Franklyn M(ansfield) 1915- ... **CLC 21**
See also CA 33-36R; CANR 14, 39; CLR 13; MAICYA; SAAS 16; SATA 4, 68

Brathwaite, Edward Kamau 1930- **CLC 11; DAM POET**
See also BW 2; CA 25-28R; CANR 11, 26, 47; DLB 125

Brautigan, Richard (Gary) 1935-1984**CLC 1, 3, 5, 9, 12, 34, 42; DAM NOV**
See also CA 53-56; 113; CANR 34; DLB 2, 5; DLBY 80, 84; MTCW; SATA 56

Brave Bird, Mary 1953-
See Crow Dog, Mary (Ellen)
See also NNAL

Braverman, Kate 1950- .... **CLC 67**
See also CA 89-92

Brecht, (Eugen) Bertolt (Friedrich) 1898-1956 **TCLC 1, 6, 13, 35; DA; DAB; DAC; DAM DRAM, MST; DC 3; WLC**
See also CA 104; 133; CANR 62; DLB 56, 124; MTCW

Brecht, Eugen Berthold Friedrich
See Brecht, (Eugen) Bertolt (Friedrich)

Bremer, Fredrika 1801-1865 .... **NCLC 11**

Brennan, Christopher John 1870-1932**TCLC 17**
See also CA 117

Brennan, Maeve 1917- .... **CLC 5**
See also CA 81-84

Brent, Linda
See Jacobs, Harriet

Brentano, Clemens (Maria) 1778-1842 **NCLC 1**
See also DLB 90

Brent of Bin Bin
See Franklin, (Stella Maria Sarah) Miles

Brenton, Howard 1942- .... **CLC 31**
See also CA 69-72; CANR 33, 67; DLB 13; MTCW

Breslin, James 1930-1996
See Breslin, Jimmy
See also CA 73-76; CANR 31; DAM NOV; MTCW

Breslin, Jimmy .... **CLC 4, 43**
See also Breslin, James
See also AITN 1; DLB 185

Bresson, Robert 1901- .... **CLC 16**
See also CA 110; CANR 49

Breton, Andre 1896-1966**CLC 2, 9, 15, 54; PC 15**
See also CA 19-20; 25-28R; CANR 40, 60; CAP 2; DLB 65; MTCW

Breytenbach, Breyten 1939(?)-**CLC 23, 37; DAM POET**
See also CA 113; 129; CANR 61

Bridgers, Sue Ellen 1942- .... **CLC 26**
See also AAYA 8; CA 65-68; CANR 11, 36; CLR 18; DLB 52; JRDA; MAICYA; SAAS 1; SATA 22, 90

Bridges, Robert (Seymour) 1844-1930 . **TCLC 1; DAM POET**
See also CA 104; 152; CDBLB 1890-1914; DLB 19, 98

Bridie, James .... **TCLC 3**
See also Mavor, Osborne Henry
See also DLB 10

Brin, David 1950- .... **CLC 34**
See also AAYA 21; CA 102; CANR 24; INT CANR-24; SATA 65

Brink, Andre (Philippus) 1935-**CLC 18, 36, 106**
See also CA 104; CANR 39, 62; INT 103; MTCW

Brinsmead, H(esba) F(ay) 1922- .... **CLC 21**
See also CA 21-24R; CANR 10; CLR 47; MAICYA; SAAS 5; SATA 18, 78

Brittain, Vera (Mary) 1893(?)-1970 ...... **CLC 23**
See also CA 13-16; 25-28R; CANR 58; CAP 1; DLB 191; MTCW

Broch, Hermann 1886-1951 .... **TCLC 20**
See also CA 117; DLB 85, 124

Brock, Rose
See Hansen, Joseph

Brodkey, Harold (Roy) 1930-1996 .... **CLC 56**
See also CA 111; 151; DLB 130

Brodsky, Iosif Alexandrovich 1940-1996
See Brodsky, Joseph
See also AITN 1; CA 41-44R; 151; CANR 37; DAM POET; MTCW

Brodsky, Joseph 1940-1996**CLC 4, 6, 13, 36, 100; PC 9**
See also Brodsky, Iosif Alexandrovich

Brodsky, Michael (Mark) 1948- .... **CLC 19**
See also CA 102; CANR 18, 41, 58

Bromell, Henry 1947- .... **CLC 5**
See also CA 53-56; CANR 9

Bromfield, Louis (Brucker) 1896-1956**TCLC 11**
See also CA 107; 155; DLB 4, 9, 86

Broner, E(sther) M(asserman) 1930- ... **CLC 19**
See also CA 17-20R; CANR 8, 25; DLB 28

Bronk, William 1918- .... **CLC 10**
See also CA 89-92; CANR 23; DLB 165

Bronstein, Lev Davidovich
See Trotsky, Leon

Bronte, Anne 1820-1849 .... **NCLC 4**
See also DLB 21

Bronte, Charlotte 1816-1855 **NCLC 3, 8, 33, 58; DA; DAB; DAC; DAM MST, NOV; WLC**
See also AAYA 17; CDBLB 1832-1890; DLB 21, 159

Bronte, Emily (Jane) 1818-1848**NCLC 16, 35; DA; DAB; DAC; DAM MST, NOV, POET; PC 8; WLC**
See also AAYA 17; CDBLB 1832-1890; DLB 21, 32

Brooke, Frances 1724-1789 .... **LC 6**
See also DLB 39, 99

Brooke, Henry 1703(?)-1783 .... **LC 1**
See also DLB 39

Brooke, Rupert (Chawner) 1887-1915**TCLC 2, 7; DA; DAB; DAC; DAM MST, POET; WLC**
See also CA 104; 132; CANR 61; CDBLB 1914-1945; DLB 19; MTCW

Brooke-Haven, P.
See Wodehouse, P(elham) G(renville)

Brooke-Rose, Christine 1926(?)- .... **CLC 40**
See also CA 13-16R; CANR 58; DLB 14

Brookner, Anita 1928- ... **CLC 32, 34, 51; DAB; DAM POP**
See also CA 114; 120; CANR 37, 56; DLB 194; DLBY 87; MTCW

Brooks, Cleanth 1906-1994 .... **CLC 24, 86**
See also CA 17-20R; 145; CANR 33, 35; DLB 63; DLBY 94; INT CANR-35; MTCW

Brooks, George
See Baum, L(yman) Frank

Brooks, Gwendolyn 1917-**CLC 1, 2, 4, 5, 15, 49; BLC; DA; DAC; DAM MST, MULT, POET; PC 7; WLC**
See also AAYA 20; AITN 1; BW 2; CA 1-4R; CANR 1, 27, 52; CDALB 1941-1968; CLR 27; DLB 5, 76, 165; MTCW; SATA 6

Brooks, Mel .... **CLC 12**
See also Kaminsky, Melvin
See also AAYA 13; DLB 26

Brooks, Peter 1938- .... **CLC 34**
See also CA 45-48; CANR 1

Brooks, Van Wyck 1886-1963 .... **CLC 29**
See also CA 1-4R; CANR 6; DLB 45, 63, 103

Brophy, Brigid (Antonia) 1929-1995 . **CLC 6, 11, 29, 105**
See also CA 5-8R; 149; CAAS 4; CANR 25, 53; DLB 14; MTCW

Brosman, Catharine Savage 1934- .... **CLC 9**
See also CA 61-64; CANR 21, 46

Brother Antoninus
See Everson, William (Oliver)

The Brothers Quay
See Quay, Stephen; Quay, Timothy

Broughton, T(homas) Alan 1936- .... **CLC 19**
See also CA 45-48; CANR 2, 23, 48

Broumas, Olga 1949- .... **CLC 10, 73**
See also CA 85-88; CANR 20

Brown, Alan 1951- .... **CLC 99**

Brown, Charles Brockden 1771-1810 **NCLC 22**
See also CDALB 1640-1865; DLB 37, 59, 73

Brown, Christy 1932-1981 .... **CLC 63**
See also CA 105; 104; DLB 14

Brown, Claude 1937-**CLC 30; BLC; DAM MULT**
See also AAYA 7; BW 1; CA 73-76

Brown, Dee (Alexander) 1908-**CLC 18, 47; DAM POP**
See also CA 13-16R; CAAS 6; CANR 11, 45, 60; DLBY 80; MTCW; SATA 5

Brown, George
See Wertmueller, Lina

Brown, George Douglas 1869-1902 ..... **TCLC 28**
See also CA 162

Brown, George Mackay 1921-1996**CLC 5, 48, 100**
See also CA 21-24R; 151; CAAS 6; CANR 12, 37, 67; DLB 14, 27, 139; MTCW; SATA 35

Brown, (William) Larry 1951- .... **CLC 73**
See also CA 130; 134; INT 133

Brown, Moses
See Barrett, William (Christopher)

Brown, Rita Mae 1944- .. **CLC 18, 43, 79; DAM NOV, POP**
See also CA 45-48; CANR 2, 11, 35, 62; INT CANR-11; MTCW

Brown, Roderick (Langmere) Haig-
See Haig-Brown, Roderick (Langmere)

Brown, Rosellen 1939- .... **CLC 32**
See also CA 77-80; CAAS 10; CANR 14, 44

Brown, Sterling Allen 1901-1989**CLC 1, 23, 59; BLC; DAM MULT, POET**
See also BW 1; CA 85-88; 127; CANR 26; DLB 48, 51, 63; MTCW

Brown, Will
See Ainsworth, William Harrison

Brown, William Wells 1813-1884**NCLC 2; BLC; DAM MULT; DC 1**
See also DLB 3, 50

Browne, (Clyde) Jackson 1948(?)- .... **CLC 21**
See also CA 120

Browning, Elizabeth Barrett 1806-1861**NCLC 1, 16, 61, 66; DA; DAB; DAC; DAM MST, POET; PC 6; WLC**
See also CDBLB 1832-1890; DLB 32

Browning, Robert 1812-1889**NCLC 19; DA; DAB; DAC; DAM MST, POET; PC 2; WLCS**
See also CDBLB 1832-1890; DLB 32, 163; YABC 1

Browning, Tod 1882-1962 .... **CLC 16**
See also CA 141; 117

Brownson, Orestes (Augustus) 1803-1876**NCLC 50**

Bruccoli, Matthew J(oseph) 1931- .... **CLC 34**
See also CA 9-12R; CANR 7; DLB 103

Bruce, Lenny .... **CLC 21**
See also Schneider, Leonard Alfred

Bruin, John
See Brutus, Dennis

Brulard, Henri
See Stendhal

Brulls, Christian
See Simenon, Georges (Jacques Christian)

Brunner, John (Kilian Houston) 1934-1995 **CLC 8, 10; DAM POP**
See also CA 1-4R; 149; CAAS 8; CANR 2, 37; MTCW

Bruno, Giordano 1548-1600 .... **LC 27**

Brutus, Dennis 1924-**CLC 43; BLC; DAM MULT, POET**
See also BW 2; CA 49-52; CAAS 14; CANR 2, 27, 42; DLB 117

Bryan, C(ourtlandt) D(ixon) B(arnes) 1936-**CLC 29**
See also CA 73-76; CANR 13, 68; DLB 185; INT CANR-13

Bryan, Michael
See Moore, Brian

Bryant, William Cullen 1794-1878 **NCLC 6, 46; DA; DAB; DAC; DAM MST, POET; PC 20**
See also CDALB 1640-1865; DLB 3, 43, 59, 189

Bryusov, Valery Yakovlevich 1873-1924**TCLC 10**
See also CA 107; 155

Buchan, John 1875-1940 **TCLC 41; DAB; DAM POP**
See also CA 108; 145; DLB 34, 70, 156; YABC 2

Buchanan, George 1506-1582 .... **LC 4**

Buchheim, Lothar-Guenther 1918- .... **CLC 6**
See also CA 85-88

Buchner, (Karl) Georg 1813-1837 ...... **NCLC 26**

Buchwald, Art(hur) 1925- .... **CLC 33**
See also AITN 1; CA 5-8R; CANR 21, 67; MTCW; SATA 10

Buck, Pearl S(ydenstricker) 1892-1973 **CLC 7, 11, 18; DA; DAB; DAC; DAM MST, NOV**
See also AITN 1; CA 1-4R; 41-44R; CANR 1, 34; DLB 9, 102; MTCW; SATA 1, 25

Buckler, Ernest 1908-1984 **CLC 13; DAC; DAM MST**
See also CA 11-12; 114; CAP 1; DLB 68; SATA 47

Buckley, Vincent (Thomas) 1925-1988 . **CLC 57**
See also CA 101

Buckley, William F(rank), Jr. 1925- **CLC 7, 18, 37; DAM POP**
See also AITN 1; CA 1-4R; CANR 1, 24, 53; DLB 137; DLBY 80; INT CANR-24; MTCW

Buechner, (Carl) Frederick 1926-**CLC 2, 4, 6, 9; DAM NOV**
See also CA 13-16R; CANR 11, 39, 64; DLBY 80; INT CANR-11; MTCW

Buell, John (Edward) 1927- .... **CLC 10**
See also CA 1-4R; DLB 53

Buero Vallejo, Antonio 1916- .... **CLC 15, 46**
See also CA 106; CANR 24, 49; HW; MTCW

Bufalino, Gesualdo 1920(?)- .... **CLC 74**
See also DLB 196

Bugayev, Boris Nikolayevich 1880-1934**TCLC 7; PC 11**
See also Bely, Andrey
See also CA 104; 165

Bukowski, Charles 1920-1994**CLC 2, 5, 9, 41, 82, 108; DAM NOV, POET; PC 18**
See also CA 17-20R; 144; CANR 40, 62; DLB 5, 130, 169; MTCW

Bulgakov, Mikhail (Afanas'evich) 1891-1940 **TCLC 2, 16; DAM DRAM, NOV; SSC 18**
See also CA 105; 152

Bulgya, Alexander Alexandrovich 1901-1956 **TCLC 53**
See also Fadeyev, Alexander
See also CA 117

Bullins, Ed 1935-**CLC 1, 5, 7; BLC; DAM DRAM, MULT; DC 6**
See also BW 2; CA 49-52; CAAS 16; CANR 24, 46; DLB 7, 38; MTCW

Bulwer-Lytton, Edward (George Earle Lytton) 1803-1873 .... **NCLC 1, 45**
See also DLB 21

Bunin, Ivan Alexeyevich 1870-1953**TCLC 6; SSC 5**
See also CA 104

Bunting, Basil 1900-1985 **CLC 10, 39, 47; DAM POET**
See also CA 53-56; 115; CANR 7; DLB 20

Bunuel, Luis 1900-1983**CLC 16, 80; DAM MULT; HLC**
See also CA 101; 110; CANR 32; HW

Bunyan, John 1628-1688 **LC 4; DA; DAB; DAC; DAM MST; WLC**
See also CDBLB 1660-1789; DLB 39

Burckhardt, Jacob (Christoph) 1818-1897**NCLC 49**

Burford, Eleanor
See Hibbert, Eleanor Alice Burford

Burgess, Anthony **CLC 1, 2, 4, 5, 8, 10, 13, 15, 22, 40, 62, 81, 94; DAB**
See also Wilson, John (Anthony) Burgess
See also AAYA 25; AITN 1; CDBLB 1960 to Present; DLB 14, 194

Burke, Edmund 1729(?)-1797**LC 7, 36; DA; DAB; DAC; DAM MST; WLC**
See also DLB 104

Burke, Kenneth (Duva) 1897-1993 .... **CLC 2, 24**
See also CA 5-8R; 143; CANR 39; DLB 45, 63; MTCW

Burke, Leda
See Garnett, David

Burke, Ralph
See Silverberg, Robert

Burke, Thomas 1886-1945 .... **TCLC 63**
See also CA 113; 155

Burney, Fanny 1752-1840 .... **NCLC 12, 54**
See also DLB 39

Burns, Robert 1759-1796 **PC 6**
See also CDBLB 1789-1832; DA; DAB; DAC; DAM MST, POET; DLB 109; WLC

Burns, Tex
See L'Amour, Louis (Dearborn)

Burnshaw, Stanley 1906- .... **CLC 3, 13, 44**
See also CA 9-12R; DLB 48; DLBY 97

Burr, Anne 1937- .... **CLC 6**
See also CA 25-28R

Burroughs, Edgar Rice 1875-1950 **TCLC 2, 32; DAM NOV**
See also AAYA 11; CA 104; 132; DLB 8; MTCW; SATA 41

Burroughs, William S(eward) 1914-1997**CLC 1, 2, 5, 15, 22, 42, 75, 109; DA; DAB; DAC; DAM MST, NOV, POP; WLC**
See also AITN 2; CA 9-12R; 160; CANR 20, 52; DLB 2, 8, 16, 152; DLBY 81, 97; MTCW

Burton, Richard F. 1821-1890 .... **NCLC 42**
See also DLB 55, 184

Busch, Frederick 1941- .... **CLC 7, 10, 18, 47**
See also CA 33-36R; CAAS 1; CANR 45; DLB 6

Bush, Ronald 1946- .... **CLC 34**
See also CA 136

Bustos, F(rancisco)
See Borges, Jorge Luis

Bustos Domecq, H(onorio)
See Bioy Casares, Adolfo; Borges, Jorge Luis

Butler, Octavia E(stelle) 1947- ... **CLC 38; DAM MULT, POP**
See also AAYA 18; BW 2; CA 73-76; CANR 12, 24, 38; DLB 33; MTCW; SATA 84

Butler, Robert Olen (Jr.) 1945- . **CLC 81; DAM POP**
See also CA 112; CANR 66; DLB 173; INT 112

Butler, Samuel 1612-1680 .... **LC 16**
See also DLB 101, 126

Butler, Samuel 1835-1902**TCLC 1, 33; DA; DAB; DAC; DAM MST, NOV; WLC**
See also CA 143; CDBLB 1890-1914; DLB 18, 57, 174

Butler, Walter C.
See Faust, Frederick (Schiller)

Butor, Michel (Marie Francois) 1926- **CLC 1, 3, 8, 11, 15**
See also CA 9-12R; CANR 33, 66; DLB 83; MTCW

Butts, Mary 1892(?)-1937 .... **TCLC 77**
See also CA 148

Buzo, Alexander (John) 1944- .... **CLC 61**
See also CA 97-100; CANR 17, 39

Buzzati, Dino 1906-1972 .... **CLC 36**
See also CA 160; 33-36R; DLB 177

Byars, Betsy (Cromer) 1928- .... **CLC 35**
See also AAYA 19; CA 33-36R; CANR 18, 36, 57; CLR 1, 16; DLB 52; INT CANR-18; JRDA; MAICYA; MTCW; SAAS 1; SATA 4, 46, 80

Byatt, A(ntonia) S(usan Drabble) 1936- **CLC 19, 65; DAM NOV, POP**
See also CA 13-16R; CANR 13, 33, 50; DLB 14, 194; MTCW

Carlisle, Henry (Coffin) 1926- .... **CLC 33**
See also CA 13-16R; CANR 15

Carlsen, Chris
See Holdstock, Robert P.

Carlson, Ron(ald F.) 1947- .... **CLC 54**
See also CA 105; CANR 27

Carlyle, Thomas 1795-1881 **NCLC 22; DA; DAB; DAC; DAM MST**
See also CDBLB 1789-1832; DLB 55; 144

Carman, (William) Bliss 1861-1929 **TCLC 7; DAC**
See also CA 104; 152; DLB 92

Carnegie, Dale 1888-1955 .... **TCLC 53**

Carossa, Hans 1878-1956 .... **TCLC 48**
See also DLB 66

Carpenter, Don(ald Richard) 1931-1995 **CLC 41**
See also CA 45-48; 149; CANR 1

Carpentier (y Valmont), Alejo 1904-1980 **CLC 8, 11, 38; DAM MULT; HLC**
See also CA 65-68; 97-100; CANR 11; DLB 113; HW

Carr, Caleb 1955(?)- .... **CLC 86**
See also CA 147

Carr, Emily 1871-1945 .... **TCLC 32**
See also CA 159; DLB 68

Carr, John Dickson 1906-1977 .... **CLC 3**
See also Fairbairn, Roger
See also CA 49-52; 69-72; CANR 3, 33, 60; MTCW

Carr, Philippa
See Hibbert, Eleanor Alice Burford

Carr, Virginia Spencer 1929- .... **CLC 34**
See also CA 61-64; DLB 111

Carrere, Emmanuel 1957- .... **CLC 89**

Carrier, Roch 1937- ... **CLC 13, 78; DAC; DAM MST**
See also CA 130; CANR 61; DLB 53

Carroll, James P. 1943(?)- .... **CLC 38**
See also CA 81-84

Carroll, Jim 1951- .... **CLC 35**
See also AAYA 17; CA 45-48; CANR 42

Carroll, Lewis .... **NCLC 2, 53; PC 18; WLC**
See also Dodgson, Charles Lutwidge
See also CDBLB 1832-1890; CLR 2, 18; DLB 18, 163, 178; JRDA

Carroll, Paul Vincent 1900-1968 .... **CLC 10**
See also CA 9-12R; 25-28R; DLB 10

Carruth, Hayden 1921- **CLC 4, 7, 10, 18, 84; PC 10**
See also CA 9-12R; CANR 4, 38, 59; DLB 5, 165; INT CANR-4; MTCW; SATA 47

Carson, Rachel Louise 1907-1964 **CLC 71; DAM POP**
See also CA 77-80; CANR 35; MTCW; SATA 23

Carter, Angela (Olive) 1940-1992 **CLC 5, 41, 76; SSC 13**
See also CA 53-56; 136; CANR 12, 36, 61; DLB 14; MTCW; SATA 66; SATA-Obit 70

Carter, Nick
See Smith, Martin Cruz

Carver, Raymond 1938-1988 **CLC 22, 36, 53, 55; DAM NOV; SSC 8**
See also CA 33-36R; 126; CANR 17, 34, 61; DLB 130; DLBY 84, 88; MTCW

Cary, Elizabeth, Lady Falkland 1585-1639 **LC 30**

Cary, (Arthur) Joyce (Lunel) 1888-1957 **TCLC 1, 29**
See also CA 104; 164; CDBLB 1914-1945; DLB 15, 100

Casanova de Seingalt, Giovanni Jacopo 1725-1798 **LC 13**

Casares, Adolfo Bioy
See Bioy Casares, Adolfo

Casely-Hayford, J(oseph) E(phraim) 1866-1930 **TCLC 24; BLC; DAM MULT**
See also BW 2; CA 123; 152

Casey, John (Dudley) 1939- .... **CLC 59**
See also BEST 90:2; CA 69-72; CANR 23

Casey, Michael 1947- .... **CLC 2**
See also CA 65-68; DLB 5

Casey, Patrick
See Thurman, Wallace (Henry)

Casey, Warren (Peter) 1935-1988 .... **CLC 12**
See also CA 101; 127; INT 101

Casona, Alejandro .... **CLC 49**
See also Alvarez, Alejandro Rodriguez

Cassavetes, John 1929-1989 .... **CLC 20**
See also CA 85-88; 127

Cassian, Nina 1924- .... **PC 17**

Cassill, R(onald) V(erlin) 1919- .... **CLC 4, 23**
See also CA 9-12R; CAAS 1; CANR 7, 45; DLB 6

Cassirer, Ernst 1874-1945 .... **TCLC 61**
See also CA 157

Cassity, (Allen) Turner 1929- .... **CLC 6, 42**
See also CA 17-20R; CAAS 8; CANR 11; DLB 105

Castaneda, Carlos 1931(?)- .... **CLC 12**
See also CA 25-28R; CANR 32, 66; HW; MTCW

Castedo, Elena 1937- **CLC 65**
See also CA 132

Castedo-Ellerman, Elena
See Castedo, Elena

Castellanos, Rosario 1925-1974 **CLC 66; DAM MULT; HLC**
See also CA 131; 53-56; CANR 58; DLB 113; HW

Castelvetro, Lodovico 1505-1571 .... **LC 12**

Castiglione, Baldassare 1478-1529 .... **LC 12**

Castle, Robert
See Hamilton, Edmond

Castro, Guillen de 1569-1631 .... **LC 19**

Castro, Rosalia de 1837-1885 ..... **NCLC 3; DAM MULT**

Cather, Willa
See Cather, Willa Sibert

Cather, Willa Sibert 1873-1947 **TCLC 1, 11, 31; DA; DAB; DAC; DAM MST, NOV; SSC 2; WLC**
See also AAYA 24; CA 104; 128; CDALB 1865-1917; DLB 9, 54, 78; DLBD 1; MTCW; SATA 30

Catherine, Saint 1347-1380 .... **CMLC 27**

Cato, Marcus Porcius 234B.C.-149B.C. **CMLC 21**

Catton, (Charles) Bruce 1899-1978 ...... **CLC 35**
See also AITN 1; CA 5-8R; 81-84; CANR 7; DLB 17; SATA 2; SATA-Obit 24

Catullus c. 84B.C.-c. 54B.C. .... **CMLC 18**

Cauldwell, Frank
See King, Francis (Henry)

Caunitz, William J. 1933-1996 .... **CLC 34**
See also BEST 89:3; CA 125; 130; 152; INT 130

Causley, Charles (Stanley) 1917- .... **CLC 7**
See also CA 9-12R; CANR 5, 35; CLR 30; DLB 27; MTCW; SATA 3, 66

Caute, (John) David 1936- . **CLC 29; DAM NOV**
See also CA 1-4R; CAAS 4; CANR 1, 33, 64; DLB 14

Cavafy, C(onstantine) P(eter) 1863-1933 **TCLC 2, 7; DAM POET**
See also Kavafis, Konstantinos Petrou
See also CA 148

Cavallo, Evelyn
See Spark, Muriel (Sarah)

Cavanna, Betty .... **CLC 12**
See also Harrison, Elizabeth Cavanna
See also JRDA; MAICYA; SAAS 4; SATA 1, 30

Cavendish, Margaret Lucas 1623-1673 .... **LC 30**
See also DLB 131

Caxton, William 1421(?)-1491(?) .... **LC 17**
See also DLB 170

Cayer, D. M.
See Duffy, Maureen

Cayrol, Jean 1911- **CLC 11**
See also CA 89-92; DLB 83

Cela, Camilo Jose 1916- **CLC 4, 13, 59; DAM MULT; HLC**
See also BEST 90:2; CA 21-24R; CAAS 10; CANR 21, 32; DLBY 89; HW; MTCW

Celan, Paul **CLC 10, 19, 53, 82; PC 10**
See also Antschel, Paul
See also DLB 69

Celine, Louis-Ferdinand CLC **1, 3, 4, 7, 9, 15, 47**
See also Destouches, Louis-Ferdinand
See also DLB 72

Cellini, Benvenuto 1500-1571 .... **LC 7**

Cendrars, Blaise 1887-1961 .... **CLC 18, 106**
See also Sauser-Hall, Frederic

Cernuda (y Bidon), Luis 1902-1963 **CLC 54; DAM POET**
See also CA 131; 89-92; DLB 134; HW

Cervantes (Saavedra), Miguel de 1547-1616 **LC 6, 23; DA; DAB; DAC; DAM MST, NOV; SSC 12; WLC**

Cesaire, Aime (Fernand) 1913- **CLC 19, 32; BLC; DAM MULT, POET**
See also BW 2; CA 65-68; CANR 24, 43; MTCW

Chabon, Michael 1963- .... **CLC 55**
See also CA 139; CANR 57

Chabrol, Claude 1930- .... **CLC 16**
See also CA 110

Challans, Mary 1905-1983
See Renault, Mary
See also CA 81-84; 111; SATA 23; SATA-Obit 36

Challis, George
See Faust, Frederick (Schiller)

Chambers, Aidan 1934- .... **CLC 35**
See also CA 25-28R; CANR 12, 31, 58; JRDA; MAICYA; SAAS 12; SATA 1, 69

Chambers, James 1948-
See Cliff, Jimmy
See also CA 124

Chambers, Jessie
See Lawrence, D(avid) H(erbert Richards)

Chambers, Robert W. 1865-1933 .... **TCLC 41**
See also CA 165

Chandler, Raymond (Thornton) 1888-1959 **TCLC 1, 7; SSC 23**
See also AAYA 25; CA 104; 129; CANR 60; CDALB 1929-1941; DLBD 6; MTCW

Chang, Eileen 1921- .... **SSC 28**

Chang, Jung 1952- .... **CLC 71**
See also CA 142

Channing, William Ellery 1780-1842 **NCLC 17**
See also DLB 1, 59

Chaplin, Charles Spencer 1889-1977 ... **CLC 16**
See also Chaplin, Charlie
See also CA 81-84; 73-76

Chaplin, Charlie
See Chaplin, Charles Spencer
See also DLB 44

Chapman, George 1559(?)-1634 .... **LC 22; DAM DRAM**
See also DLB 62, 121

Chapman, Graham 1941-1989 .... **CLC 21**
See also Monty Python
See also CA 116; 129; CANR 35

Chapman, John Jay 1862-1933 .... **TCLC 7**
See also CA 104

Chapman, Lee
See Bradley, Marion Zimmer

Chapman, Walker
See Silverberg, Robert

Chappell, Fred (Davis) 1936- .... **CLC 40, 78**
See also CA 5-8R; CAAS 4; CANR 8, 33, 67; DLB 6, 105

Char, Rene(-Emile) 1907-1988 **CLC 9, 11, 14, 55; DAM POET**
See also CA 13-16R; 124; CANR 32; MTCW

Charby, Jay
See Ellison, Harlan (Jay)

Chardin, Pierre Teilhard de
See Teilhard de Chardin, (Marie Joseph) Pierre

Charles I 1600-1649 .... **LC 13**

Charriere, Isabelle de 1740-1805 .... **NCLC 66**

Charyn, Jerome 1937- .... **CLC 5, 8, 18**
See also CA 5-8R; CAAS 1; CANR 7, 61; DLBY 83; MTCW

Chase, Mary (Coyle) 1907-1981 .... **DC 1**
See also CA 77-80; 105; SATA 17; SATA-Obit 29

Chase, Mary Ellen 1887-1973 .... **CLC 2**
See also CA 13-16; 41-44R; CAP 1; SATA 10

Chase, Nicholas
See Hyde, Anthony

Chateaubriand, Francois Rene de 1768-1848 **NCLC 3**
See also DLB 119

Chatterje, Sarat Chandra 1876-1936(?)
See Chatterji, Saratchandra
See also CA 109

Chatterji, Bankim Chandra 1838-1894 **NCLC 19**

Chatterji, Saratchandra .... **TCLC 13**
See also Chatterje, Sarat Chandra

Chatterton, Thomas 1752-1770 **LC 3; DAM POET**
See also DLB 109

Chatwin, (Charles) Bruce 1940-1989 **CLC 28, 57, 59; DAM POP**
See also AAYA 4; BEST 90:1; CA 85-88; 127; DLB 194

Chaucer, Daniel
See Ford, Ford Madox

Chaucer, Geoffrey 1340(?)-1400 **LC 17; DA; DAB; DAC; DAM MST, POET; PC 19; WLCS**
See also CDBLB Before 1660; DLB 146

Chaviaras, Strates 1935-
See Haviaras, Stratis
See also CA 105

Chayefsky, Paddy .... **CLC 23**
See also Chayefsky, Sidney
See also DLB 7, 44; DLBY 81

Chayefsky, Sidney 1923-1981
See Chayefsky, Paddy
See also CA 9-12R; 104; CANR 18; DAM DRAM

Chedid, Andree 1920- .... **CLC 47**
See also CA 145

Cheever, John 1912-1982 **CLC 3, 7, 8, 11, 15, 25, 64; DA; DAB; DAC; DAM MST, NOV, POP; SSC 1; WLC**
See also CA 5-8R; 106; CABS 1; CANR 5, 27; CDALB 1941-1968; DLB 2, 102; DLBY 80, 82; INT CANR-5; MTCW

Cheever, Susan 1943- .... **CLC 18, 48**
See also CA 103; CANR 27, 51; DLBY 82; INT CANR-27

Chekhonte, Antosha
See Chekhov, Anton (Pavlovich)

Chekhov, Anton (Pavlovich) 1860-1904 **TCLC 3, 10, 31, 55; DA; DAB; DAC; DAM DRAM, MST; SSC 2, 28; WLC**
See also CA 104; 124; SATA 90

Chernyshevsky, Nikolay Gavrilovich 1828-1889 **NCLC 1**

Cherry, Carolyn Janice 1942-
See Cherryh, C. J.
See also CA 65-68; CANR 10

Cherryh, C. J. .... **CLC 35**
See also Cherry, Carolyn Janice
See also AAYA 24; DLBY 80; SATA 93

Chesnutt, Charles W(addell) 1858-1932 **TCLC 5, 39; BLC; DAM MULT; SSC 7**
See also BW 1; CA 106; 125; DLB 12, 50, 78; MTCW

Chester, Alfred 1929(?)-1971 .... **CLC 49**
See also CA 33-36R; DLB 130

Chesterton, G(ilbert) K(eith) 1874-1936 **TCLC 1, 6, 64; DAM NOV, POET; SSC 1**
See also CA 104; 132; CDBLB 1914-1945; DLB 10, 19, 34, 70, 98, 149, 178; MTCW; SATA 27

Chiang Pin-chin 1904-1986
See Ding Ling
See also CA 118

Ch'ien Chung-shu 1910- .... **CLC 22**
See also CA 130; MTCW

Child, L. Maria
See Child, Lydia Maria

Child, Lydia Maria 1802-1880 .... **NCLC 6**
See also DLB 1, 74; SATA 67

Child, Mrs.
See Child, Lydia Maria

Child, Philip 1898-1978 .... **CLC 19, 68**
See also CA 13-14; CAP 1; SATA 47

Childers, (Robert) Erskine 1870-1922 **TCLC 65**
See also CA 113; 153; DLB 70

Childress, Alice 1920-1994 **CLC 12, 15, 86, 96; BLC; DAM DRAM, MULT, NOV; DC 4**
See also AAYA 8; BW 2; CA 45-48; 146; CANR 3, 27, 50; CLR 14; DLB 7, 38; JRDA; MAICYA; MTCW; SATA 7, 48, 81

Chin, Frank (Chew, Jr.) 1940- .... **DC 7**
See also CA 33-36R; DAM MULT

Chislett, (Margaret) Anne 1943- .... **CLC 34**
See also CA 151

Chitty, Thomas Willes 1926- .... **CLC 11**
See also Hinde, Thomas
See also CA 5-8R

Chivers, Thomas Holley 1809-1858 .... **NCLC 49**
See also DLB 3

Chomette, Rene Lucien 1898-1981
See Clair, Rene
See also CA 103

Chopin, Kate **TCLC 5, 14; DA; DAB; SSC 8; WLCS**
See also Chopin, Katherine
See also CDALB 1865-1917; DLB 12, 78

Chopin, Katherine 1851-1904
See Chopin, Kate
See also CA 104; 122; DAC; DAM MST, NOV

Chretien de Troyes c. 12th cent. - ...... **CMLC 10**

Christie
See Ichikawa, Kon

Christie, Agatha (Mary Clarissa) 1890-1976 **CLC 1, 6, 8, 12, 39, 48; DAB; DAC; DAM NOV**
See also AAYA 9; AITN 1, 2; CA 17-20R; 61-64; CANR 10, 37; CDBLB 1914-1945; DLB 13, 77; MTCW; SATA 36

Christie, (Ann) Philippa
See Pearce, Philippa
See also CA 5-8R; CANR 4

Christine de Pizan 1365(?)-1431(?) .... **LC 9**

Chubb, Elmer
See Masters, Edgar Lee

Chulkov, Mikhail Dmitrievich 1743-1792 .. **LC 2**
See also DLB 150

Churchill, Caryl 1938- .... **CLC 31, 55; DC 5**
See also CA 102; CANR 22, 46; DLB 13; MTCW

Churchill, Charles 1731-1764 .... **LC 3**
See also DLB 109

Chute, Carolyn 1947- .... **CLC 39**
See also CA 123

Ciardi, John (Anthony) 1916-1986 . **CLC 10, 40, 44; DAM POET**
See also CA 5-8R; 118; CAAS 2; CANR 5, 33; CLR 19; DLB 5; DLBY 86; INT CANR-5; MAICYA; MTCW; SAAS 26; SATA 1, 65; SATA-Obit 46

Cicero, Marcus Tullius 106B.C.-43B.C. **CMLC 3**

Cimino, Michael 1943- .... **CLC 16**
See also CA 105

Cioran, E(mil) M. 1911-1995 .... **CLC 64**
See also CA 25-28R; 149

Cisneros, Sandra 1954- . **CLC 69; DAM MULT; HLC**
See also AAYA 9; CA 131; CANR 64; DLB 122, 152; HW

Cixous, Helene 1937- .... **CLC 92**
See also CA 126; CANR 55; DLB 83; MTCW

Clair, Rene .... **CLC 20**
See also Chomette, Rene Lucien

Clampitt, Amy 1920-1994 .... **CLC 32; PC 19**
See also CA 110; 146; CANR 29; DLB 105

Clancy, Thomas L., Jr. 1947-
See Clancy, Tom
See also CA 125; 131; CANR 62; INT 131; MTCW

Clancy, Tom .... **CLC 45; DAM NOV, POP**
See also Clancy, Thomas L., Jr.
See also AAYA 9; BEST 89:1, 90:1

Clare, John 1793-1864 **NCLC 9; DAB; DAM POET**
See also DLB 55, 96

Clarin
See Alas (y Urena), Leopoldo (Enrique Garcia)

Clark, Al C.
See Goines, Donald

Clark, (Robert) Brian 1932- .... **CLC 29**
See also CA 41-44R; CANR 67

Clark, Curt
See Westlake, Donald E(dwin)

Clark, Eleanor 1913-1996 .... **CLC 5, 19**
See also CA 9-12R; 151; CANR 41; DLB 6

Clark, J. P.
See Clark, John Pepper
See also DLB 117

Clark, John Pepper 1935- **CLC 38; BLC; DAM DRAM, MULT; DC 5**
See also Clark, J. P.
See also BW 1; CA 65-68; CANR 16

Clark, M. R.
See Clark, Mavis Thorpe

Clark, Mavis Thorpe 1909- .... **CLC 12**
See also CA 57-60; CANR 8, 37; CLR 30; MAICYA; SAAS 5; SATA 8, 74

Clark, Walter Van Tilburg 1909-1971 .. **CLC 28**
See also CA 9-12R; 33-36R; CANR 63; DLB 9; SATA 8

Clarke, Arthur C(harles) 1917- **CLC 1, 4, 13, 18, 35; DAM POP; SSC 3**
See also AAYA 4; CA 1-4R; CANR 2, 28, 55; JRDA; MAICYA; MTCW; SATA 13, 70

Clarke, Austin 1896-1974 **CLC 6, 9; DAM POET**
See also CA 29-32; 49-52; CAP 2; DLB 10, 20

Clarke, Austin C(hesterfield) 1934- **CLC 8, 53; BLC; DAC; DAM MULT**
See also BW 1; CA 25-28R; CAAS 16; CANR 14, 32, 68; DLB 53, 125..........................

Clarke, Gillian 1937- **CLC 61**
See also CA 106; DLB 40

Clarke, Marcus (Andrew Hislop) 1846-1881 **NCLC 19**

Clarke, Shirley 1925- .... **CLC 16**

Clash, The
See Headon, (Nicky) Topper; Jones, Mick; Simonon, Paul; Strummer, Joe

Claudel, Paul (Louis Charles Marie) 1868-1955 **TCLC 2, 10**
See also CA 104; 165; DLB 192

Clavell, James (duMaresq) 1925-1994 **CLC 6, 25, 87; DAM NOV, POP**
See also CA 25-28R; 146; CANR 26, 48; MTCW

Cleaver, (Leroy) Eldridge 1935- . **CLC 30; BLC; DAM MULT**
See also BW 1; CA 21-24R; CANR 16

Cleese, John (Marwood) 1939- .... **CLC 21**
See also Monty Python
See also CA 112; 116; CANR 35; MTCW

Cleishbotham, Jebediah
See Scott, Walter

Cleland, John 1710-1789 .... **LC 2**
See also DLB 39

Clemens, Samuel Langhorne 1835-1910
See Twain, Mark
See also CA 104; 135; CDALB 1865-1917; DA; DAB; DAC; DAM MST, NOV; DLB 11, 12, 23, 64, 74, 186, 189; JRDA; MAICYA; YABC 2

Cleophil
See Congreve, William

Clerihew, E.
See Bentley, E(dmund) C(lerihew)

Clerk, N. W.
See Lewis, C(live) S(taples)

Cliff, Jimmy .... **CLC 21**
See also Chambers, James

Clifton, (Thelma) Lucille 1936- **CLC 19, 66; BLC; DAM MULT, POET; PC 17**
See also BW 2; CA 49-52; CANR 2, 24, 42; CLR 5; DLB 5, 41; MAICYA; MTCW; SATA 20, 69

Clinton, Dirk
See Silverberg, Robert

Clough, Arthur Hugh 1819-1861 .... **NCLC 27**
See also DLB 32

Clutha, Janet Paterson Frame 1924-
See Frame, Janet
See also CA 1-4R; CANR 2, 36; MTCW

Clyne, Terence
See Blatty, William Peter

Cobalt, Martin
See Mayne, William (James Carter)

Cobb, Irvin S. 1876-1944 .... **TCLC 77**
See also DLB 11, 25, 86

Cobbett, William 1763-1835 .... **NCLC 49**
See also DLB 43, 107, 158

Cooke, M. E.
See Creasey, John

Cooke, Margaret
See Creasey, John

Cook-Lynn, Elizabeth 1930-**CLC 93; DAM MULT**
See also CA 133; DLB 175; NNAL

Cooney, Ray .... **CLC 62**

Cooper, Douglas 1960- .... **CLC 86**

Cooper, Henry St. John
See Creasey, John

Cooper, J(oan) California **CLC 56; DAM MULT**
See also AAYA 12; BW 1; CA 125; CANR 55

Cooper, James Fenimore 1789-1851**NCLC 1, 27, 54**
See also AAYA 22; CDALB 1640-1865; DLB 3; SATA 19

Coover, Robert (Lowell) 1932- **CLC 3, 7, 15, 32, 46, 87; DAM NOV; SSC 15**
See also CA 45-48; CANR 3, 37, 58; DLB 2; DLBY 81; MTCW

Copeland, Stewart (Armstrong) 1952- .. **CLC 26**

Coppard, A(lfred) E(dgar) 1878-1957**TCLC 5; SSC 21**
See also CA 114; DLB 162; YABC 1

Coppee, Francois 1842-1908 .... **TCLC 25**

Coppola, Francis Ford 1939- .... **CLC 16**
See also CA 77-80; CANR 40; DLB 44

Corbiere, Tristan 1845-1875 .... **NCLC 43**

Corcoran, Barbara 1911- .... **CLC 17**
See also AAYA 14; CA 21-24R; CAAS 2; CANR 11, 28, 48; DLB 52; JRDA; SAAS 20; SATA 3, 77

Cordelier, Maurice
See Giraudoux, (Hippolyte) Jean

Corelli, Marie 1855-1924 .... **TCLC 51**
See also Mackay, Mary
See also DLB 34, 156

Corman, Cid 1924- .... **CLC 9**
See also Corman, Sidney
See also CAAS 2; DLB 5, 193

Corman, Sidney 1924-
See Corman, Cid
See also CA 85-88; CANR 44; DAM POET

Cormier, Robert (Edmund) 1925-**CLC 12, 30; DA; DAB; DAC; DAM MST, NOV**
See also AAYA 3, 19; CA 1-4R; CANR 5, 23; CDALB 1968-1988; CLR 12; DLB 52; INT CANR-23; JRDA; MAICYA; MTCW; SATA 10, 45, 83

Corn, Alfred (DeWitt III) 1943- .... **CLC 33**
See also CA 104; CAAS 25; CANR 44; DLB 120; DLBY 80

Corneille, Pierre 1606-1684 **LC 28; DAB; DAM MST**

Cornwell, David (John Moore) 1931- **CLC 9, 15; DAM POP**
See also le Carre, John
See also CA 5-8R; CANR 13, 33, 59; MTCW

Corso, (Nunzio) Gregory 1930- .... **CLC 1, 11**
See also CA 5-8R; CANR 41; DLB 5, 16; MTCW

Cortazar, Julio 1914-1984**CLC 2, 3, 5, 10, 13, 15, 33, 34, 92; DAM MULT, NOV; HLC; SSC 7**
See also CA 21-24R; CANR 12, 32; DLB 113; HW; MTCW

CORTES, HERNAN 1484-1547 .... **LC 31**

Corwin, Cecil
See Kornbluth, C(yril) M.

Cosic, Dobrica 1921- .... **CLC 14**
See also CA 122; 138; DLB 181

Costain, Thomas B(ertram) 1885-1965 . **CLC 30**
See also CA 5-8R; 25-28R; DLB 9

Costantini, Humberto 1924(?)-1987 ...... **CLC 49**
See also CA 131; 122; HW

Costello, Elvis 1955- .... **CLC 21**

Cotes, Cecil V.
See Duncan, Sara Jeannette

Cotter, Joseph Seamon Sr. 1861-1949 **TCLC 28; BLC; DAM MULT**
See also BW 1; CA 124; DLB 50

Couch, Arthur Thomas Quiller
See Quiller-Couch, SirArthur Thomas

Coulton, James
See Hansen, Joseph

Couperus, Louis (Marie Anne) 1863-1923 **TCLC 15**
See also CA 115

Coupland, Douglas 1961- . **CLC 85; DAC; DAM POP**
See also CA 142; CANR 57

Court, Wesli
See Turco, Lewis (Putnam)

Courtenay, Bryce 1933- .... **CLC 59**
See also CA 138

Courtney, Robert
See Ellison, Harlan (Jay)

Cousteau, Jacques-Yves 1910-1997 .... **CLC 30**
See also CA 65-68; 159; CANR 15, 67; MTCW; SATA 38, 98

Cowan, Peter (Walkinshaw) 1914- .... **SSC 28**
See also CA 21-24R; CANR 9, 25, 50

Coward, Noel (Peirce) 1899-1973**CLC 1, 9, 29, 51; DAM DRAM**
See also AITN 1; CA 17-18; 41-44R; CANR 35; CAP 2; CDBLB 1914-1945; DLB 10; MTCW

Cowley, Malcolm 1898-1989 **CLC 39**
See also CA 5-8R; 128; CANR 3, 55; DLB 4, 48; DLBY 81, 89; MTCW

Cowper, William 1731-1800**NCLC 8; DAM POET**
See also DLB 104, 109

Cox, William Trevor 1928- **CLC 9, 14, 71; DAM NOV**
See also Trevor, William
See also CA 9-12R; CANR 4, 37, 55; DLB 14; INT CANR-37; MTCW

Coyne, P. J.
See Masters, Hilary

Cozzens, James Gould 1903-1978**CLC 1, 4, 11, 92**
See also CA 9-12R; 81-84; CANR 19; CDALB 1941-1968; DLB 9; DLBD 2; DLBY 84, 97; MTCW

Crabbe, George 1754-1832 .... **NCLC 26**
See also DLB 93

Craddock, Charles Egbert
See Murfree, Mary Noailles

Craig, A. A.
See Anderson, Poul (William)

Craik, Dinah Maria (Mulock) 1826-1887 **NCLC 38**
See also DLB 35, 163; MAICYA; SATA 34

Cram, Ralph Adams 1863-1942 .... **TCLC 45**
See also CA 160

Crane, (Harold) Hart 1899-1932 . **TCLC 2, 5, 80; DA; DAB; DAC; DAM MST, POET; PC 3; WLC**
See also CA 104; 127; CDALB 1917-1929; DLB 4, 48; MTCW

Crane, R(onald) S(almon) 1886-1967 .... **CLC 27**
See also CA 85-88; DLB 63

Crane, Stephen (Townley) 1871-1900**TCLC 11, 17, 32; DA; DAB; DAC; DAM MST, NOV, POET; SSC 7; WLC**
See also AAYA 21; CA 109; 140; CDALB 1865-1917; DLB 12, 54, 78; YABC 2

Crase, Douglas 1944- .... **CLC 58**
See also CA 106

Crashaw, Richard 1612(?)-1649 .... **LC 24**
See also DLB 126

Craven, Margaret 1901-1980 .... **CLC 17; DAC**
See also CA 103

Crawford, F(rancis) Marion 1854-1909**TCLC 10**
See also CA 107; DLB 71

Crawford, Isabella Valancy 1850-1887 **NCLC 12**
See also DLB 92

Crayon, Geoffrey
See Irving, Washington

Creasey, John 1908-1973 .... **CLC 11**
See also CA 5-8R; 41-44R; CANR 8, 59; DLB 77; MTCW

Crebillon, Claude Prosper Jolyot de (fils) 1707-1777 .... **LC 28**

Credo
See Creasey, John

Credo, Alvaro J. de
See Prado (Calvo), Pedro

Author Index

del Castillo, Michel 1933- .... **CLC 38**
See also CA 109

Deledda, Grazia (Cosima) 1875(?)-1936 **TCLC 23**
See also CA 123

Delibes, Miguel .... **CLC 8, 18**
See also Delibes Setien, Miguel

Delibes Setien, Miguel 1920-
See Delibes, Miguel
See also CA 45-48; CANR 1, 32; HW; MTCW

DeLillo, Don 1936- **CLC 8, 10, 13, 27, 39, 54, 76; DAM NOV, POP**
See also BEST 89:1; CA 81-84; CANR 21; DLB 6, 173; MTCW

de Lisser, H. G.
See De Lisser, H(erbert) G(eorge)
See also DLB 117

De Lisser, H(erbert) G(eorge) 1878-1944 **TCLC 12**
See also de Lisser, H. G.
See also BW 2; CA 109; 152

Deloney, Thomas 1560-1600 .... **LC 41**

Deloria, Vine (Victor), Jr. 1933- **CLC 21; DAM MULT**
See also CA 53-56; CANR 5, 20, 48; DLB 175; MTCW; NNAL; SATA 21

Del Vecchio, John M(ichael) 1947- .... **CLC 29**
See also CA 110; DLBD 9

de Man, Paul (Adolph Michel) 1919-1983 **CLC 55**
See also CA 128; 111; CANR 61; DLB 67; MTCW

De Marinis, Rick 1934- .... **CLC 54**
See also CA 57-60; CAAS 24; CANR 9, 25, 50

Dembry, R. Emmet
See Murfree, Mary Noailles

Demby, William 1922- **CLC 53; BLC; DAM MULT**
See also BW 1; CA 81-84; DLB 33

de Menton, Francisco
See Chin, Frank (Chew, Jr.)

Demijohn, Thom
See Disch, Thomas M(ichael)

de Montherlant, Henry (Milon)
See Montherlant, Henry (Milon) de

Demosthenes 384B.C.-322B.C. .... **CMLC 13**
See also DLB 176

de Natale, Francine
See Malzberg, Barry N(athaniel)

Denby, Edwin (Orr) 1903-1983 .... **CLC 48**
See also CA 138; 110

Denis, Julio
See Cortazar, Julio

Denmark, Harrison
See Zelazny, Roger (Joseph)

Dennis, John 1658-1734 .... **LC 11**
See also DLB 101

Dennis, Nigel (Forbes) 1912-1989 .... **CLC 8**
See also CA 25-28R; 129; DLB 13, 15; MTCW

Dent, Lester 1904(?)-1959 .... **TCLC 72**
See also CA 112; 161

De Palma, Brian (Russell) 1940- .... **CLC 20**
See also CA 109

De Quincey, Thomas 1785-1859 .... **NCLC 4**
See also CDBLB 1789-1832; DLB 110; 144

Deren, Eleanora 1908(?)-1961
See Deren, Maya
See also CA 111

Deren, Maya 1917-1961 .... **CLC 16, 102**
See also Deren, Eleanora

Derleth, August (William) 1909-1971 .. **CLC 31**
See also CA 1-4R; 29-32R; CANR 4; DLB 9; SATA 5

Der Nister 1884-1950 .... **TCLC 56**

de Routisie, Albert
See Aragon, Louis

Derrida, Jacques 1930- .... **CLC 24, 87**
See also CA 124; 127

Derry Down Derry
See Lear, Edward

Dersonnes, Jacques
See Simenon, Georges (Jacques Christian)

Desai, Anita 1937- **CLC 19, 37, 97; DAB; DAM NOV**
See also CA 81-84; CANR 33, 53; MTCW; SATA 63

de Saint-Luc, Jean
See Glassco, John

de Saint Roman, Arnaud
See Aragon, Louis

Descartes, Rene 1596-1650 .... **LC 20, 35**

De Sica, Vittorio 1901(?)-1974 .... **CLC 20**
See also CA 117

Desnos, Robert 1900-1945 .... **TCLC 22**
See also CA 121; 151

Destouches, Louis-Ferdinand 1894-1961 **CLC 9, 15**
See also Celine, Louis-Ferdinand
See also CA 85-88; CANR 28; MTCW

de Tolignac, Gaston
See Griffith, D(avid Lewelyn) W(ark)

Deutsch, Babette 1895-1982 .... **CLC 18**
See also CA 1-4R; 108; CANR 4; DLB 45; SATA 1; SATA-Obit 33

Devenant, William 1606-1649 .... **LC 13**

Devkota, Laxmiprasad 1909-1959 .... **TCLC 23**
See also CA 123

De Voto, Bernard (Augustine) 1897-1955 **TCLC 29**
See also CA 113; 160; DLB 9

De Vries, Peter 1910-1993 **CLC 1, 2, 3, 7, 10, 28, 46; DAM NOV**
See also CA 17-20R; 142; CANR 41; DLB 6; DLBY 82; MTCW

Dexter, John
See Bradley, Marion Zimmer

Dexter, Martin
See Faust, Frederick (Schiller)

Dexter, Pete 1943- .... **CLC 34, 55; DAM POP**
See also BEST 89:2; CA 127; 131; INT 131; MTCW

Diamano, Silmang
See Senghor, Leopold Sedar

Diamond, Neil 1941- .... **CLC 30**
See also CA 108

Diaz del Castillo, Bernal 1496-1584 .... **LC 31**

di Bassetto, Corno
See Shaw, George Bernard

Dick, Philip K(indred) 1928-1982 **CLC 10, 30, 72; DAM NOV, POP**
See also AAYA 24; CA 49-52; 106; CANR 2, 16; DLB 8; MTCW

Dickens, Charles (John Huffam) 1812-1870 **NCLC 3, 8, 18, 26, 37, 50; DA; DAB; DAC; DAM MST, NOV; SSC 17; WLC**
See also AAYA 23; CDBLB 1832-1890; DLB 21, 55, 70, 159, 166; JRDA; MAICYA; SATA 15

Dickey, James (Lafayette) 1923-1997 **CLC 1, 2, 4, 7, 10, 15, 47, 109; DAM NOV, POET, POP**
See also AITN 1, 2; CA 9-12R; 156; CABS 2; CANR 10, 48, 61; CDALB 1968-1988; DLB 5, 193; DLBD 7; DLBY 82, 93, 96, 97; INT CANR-10; MTCW

Dickey, William 1928-1994 .... **CLC 3, 28**
See also CA 9-12R; 145; CANR 24; DLB 5

Dickinson, Charles 1951- .... **CLC 49**
See also CA 128

Dickinson, Emily (Elizabeth) 1830-1886 .. **NCLC 21; DA; DAB; DAC; DAM MST, POET; PC 1; WLC**
See also AAYA 22; CDALB 1865-1917; DLB 1; SATA 29

Dickinson, Peter (Malcolm) 1927- . **CLC 12, 35**
See also AAYA 9; CA 41-44R; CANR 31, 58; CLR 29; DLB 87, 161; JRDA; MAICYA; SATA 5, 62, 95

Dickson, Carr
See Carr, John Dickson

Dickson, Carter
See Carr, John Dickson

Diderot, Denis 1713-1784 .... **LC 26**

Didion, Joan 1934- **CLC 1, 3, 8, 14, 32; DAM NOV**
See also AITN 1; CA 5-8R; CANR 14, 52; CDALB 1968-1988; DLB 2, 173, 185; DLBY 81, 86; MTCW

Dietrich, Robert
See Hunt, E(verette) Howard, (Jr.)

Dillard, Annie 1945- **CLC 9, 60; DAM NOV**
See also AAYA 6; CA 49-52; CANR 3, 43, 62; DLBY 80; MTCW; SATA 10

Doyle, Sir Arthur Conan
See Doyle, Arthur Conan

Dr. A
See Asimov, Isaac; Silverstein, Alvin

Drabble, Margaret 1939- **CLC 2, 3, 5, 8, 10, 22, 53; DAB; DAC; DAM MST, NOV, POP**
See also CA 13-16R; CANR 18, 35, 63; CDBLB 1960 to Present; DLB 14, 155; MTCW; SATA 48

Drapier, M. B.
See Swift, Jonathan

Drayham, James
See Mencken, H(enry) L(ouis)

Drayton, Michael 1563-1631 .... **LC 8**

Dreadstone, Carl
See Campbell, (John) Ramsey

Dreiser, Theodore (Herman Albert) 1871-1945 **TCLC 10, 18, 35; DA; DAC; DAM MST, NOV; SSC 30; WLC**
See also CA 106; 132; CDALB 1865-1917; DLB 9, 12, 102, 137; DLBD 1; MTCW

Drexler, Rosalyn 1926- .... **CLC 2, 6**
See also CA 81-84; CANR 68

Dreyer, Carl Theodor 1889-1968 .... **CLC 16**
See also CA 116

Drieu la Rochelle, Pierre(-Eugene) 1893-1945 **TCLC 21**
See also CA 117; DLB 72

Drinkwater, John 1882-1937 .... **TCLC 57**
See also CA 109; 149; DLB 10, 19, 149

Drop Shot
See Cable, George Washington

Droste-Hulshoff, Annette Freiin von 1797-1848 **NCLC 3**
See also DLB 133

Drummond, Walter
See Silverberg, Robert

Drummond, William Henry 1854-1907 **TCLC 25**
See also CA 160; DLB 92

Drummond de Andrade, Carlos 1902-1987 **CLC 18**
See also Andrade, Carlos Drummond de
See also CA 132; 123

Drury, Allen (Stuart) 1918- .... **CLC 37**
See also CA 57-60; CANR 18, 52; INT CANR-18

Dryden, John 1631-1700 .... **LC 3, 21; DA; DAB; DAC; DAM DRAM, MST, POET; DC 3; WLC**
See also CDBLB 1660-1789; DLB 80, 101, 131

Duberman, Martin (Bauml) 1930- .... **CLC 8**
See also CA 1-4R; CANR 2, 63

Dubie, Norman (Evans) 1945- **CLC 36**
See also CA 69-72; CANR 12; DLB 120

Du Bois, W(illiam) E(dward) B(urghardt) 1868-1963 **CLC 1, 2, 13, 64, 96; BLC; DA; DAC; DAM MST, MULT, NOV; WLC**
See also BW 1; CA 85-88; CANR 34; CDALB 1865-1917; DLB 47, 50, 91; MTCW; SATA 42

Dubus, Andre 1936- ... **CLC 13, 36, 97; SSC 15**
See also CA 21-24R; CANR 17; DLB 130; INT CANR-17

Duca Minimo
See D'Annunzio, Gabriele

Ducharme, Rejean 1941- .... **CLC 74**
See also CA 165; DLB 60

Duclos, Charles Pinot 1704-1772 .... **LC 1**

Dudek, Louis 1918- .... **CLC 11, 19**
See also CA 45-48; CAAS 14; CANR 1; DLB 88

Duerrenmatt, Friedrich 1921-1990 . **CLC 1, 4, 8, 11, 15, 43, 102; DAM DRAM**
See also CA 17-20R; CANR 33; DLB 69, 124; MTCW

Duffy, Bruce (?)- .... **CLC 50**

Duffy, Maureen 1933- .... **CLC 37**
See also CA 25-28R; CANR 33, 68; DLB 14; MTCW

Dugan, Alan 1923- .... **CLC 2, 6**
See also CA 81-84; DLB 5

du Gard, Roger Martin
See Martin du Gard, Roger

Duhamel, Georges 1884-1966 .... **CLC 8**
See also CA 81-84; 25-28R; CANR 35; DLB 65; MTCW

Dujardin, Edouard (Emile Louis) 1861-1949 **TCLC 13**
See also CA 109; DLB 123

Dulles, John Foster 1888-1959 .... **TCLC 72**
See also CA 115; 149

Dumas, Alexandre (Davy de la Pailleterie) 1802-1870 **NCLC 11; DA; DAB; DAC; DAM MST, NOV; WLC**
See also DLB 119, 192; SATA 18

Dumas, Alexandre 1824-1895 ..... **NCLC 9; DC 1**
See also AAYA 22; DLB 192

Dumas, Claudine
See Malzberg, Barry N(athaniel)

Dumas, Henry L. 1934-1968 .... **CLC 6, 62**
See also BW 1; CA 85-88; DLB 41

du Maurier, Daphne 1907-1989 .. **CLC 6, 11, 59; DAB; DAC; DAM MST, POP; SSC 18**
See also CA 5-8R; 128; CANR 6, 55; DLB 191; MTCW; SATA 27; SATA-Obit 60

Dunbar, Paul Laurence 1872-1906 . **TCLC 2, 12; BLC; DA; DAC; DAM MST, MULT, POET; PC 5; SSC 8; WLC**
See also BW 1; CA 104; 124; CDALB 1865-1917; DLB 50, 54, 78; SATA 34

Dunbar, William 1460(?)-1530(?) .... **LC 20**
See also DLB 132, 146

Duncan, Dora Angela
See Duncan, Isadora

Duncan, Isadora 1877(?)-1927 .... **TCLC 68**
See also CA 118; 149

Duncan, Lois 1934- .... **CLC 26**
See also AAYA 4; CA 1-4R; CANR 2, 23, 36; CLR 29; JRDA; MAICYA; SAAS 2; SATA 1, 36, 75

Duncan, Robert (Edward) 1919-1988 **CLC 1, 2, 4, 7, 15, 41, 55; DAM POET; PC 2**
See also CA 9-12R; 124; CANR 28, 62; DLB 5, 16, 193; MTCW

Duncan, Sara Jeannette 1861-1922 ..... **TCLC 60**
See also CA 157; DLB 92

Dunlap, William 1766-1839 .... **NCLC 2**
See also DLB 30, 37, 59

Dunn, Douglas (Eaglesham) 1942- ... **CLC 6, 40**
See also CA 45-48; CANR 2, 33; DLB 40; MTCW

Dunn, Katherine (Karen) 1945- .... **CLC 71**
See also CA 33-36R

Dunn, Stephen 1939- .... **CLC 36**
See also CA 33-36R; CANR 12, 48, 53; DLB 105

Dunne, Finley Peter 1867-1936 .... **TCLC 28**
See also CA 108; DLB 11, 23

Dunne, John Gregory 1932- .... **CLC 28**
See also CA 25-28R; CANR 14, 50; DLBY 80

Dunsany, Edward John Moreton Drax Plunkett 1878-1957
See Dunsany, Lord
See also CA 104; 148; DLB 10

Dunsany, Lord .... **TCLC 2, 59**
See also Dunsany, Edward John Moreton Drax Plunkett
See also DLB 77, 153, 156

du Perry, Jean
See Simenon, Georges (Jacques Christian)

Durang, Christopher (Ferdinand) 1949- **CLC 27, 38**
See also CA 105; CANR 50

Duras, Marguerite 1914-1996 **CLC 3, 6, 11, 20, 34, 40, 68, 100**
See also CA 25-28R; 151; CANR 50; DLB 83; MTCW

Durban, (Rosa) Pam 1947- .... **CLC 39**
See also CA 123

Durcan, Paul 1944- .... **CLC 43, 70; DAM POET**
See also CA 134

Durkheim, Emile 1858-1917 .... **TCLC 55**

Durrell, Lawrence (George) 1912-1990 **CLC 1, 4, 6, 8, 13, 27, 41; DAM NOV**
See also CA 9-12R; 132; CANR 40; CDBLB 1945-1960; DLB 15, 27; DLBY 90; MTCW

Durrenmatt, Friedrich
See Duerrenmatt, Friedrich

Dutt, Toru 1856-1877 .... **NCLC 29**

Dwight, Timothy 1752-1817 .... **NCLC 13**
See also DLB 37

Dworkin, Andrea 1946- .... **CLC 43**
See also CA 77-80; CAAS 21; CANR 16, 39; INT CANR-16; MTCW

Dwyer, Deanna
See Koontz, Dean R(ay)

Dwyer, K. R.
See Koontz, Dean R(ay)

Dye, Richard
See De Voto, Bernard (Augustine)

Dylan, Bob 1941- .... **CLC 3, 4, 6, 12, 77**
See also CA 41-44R; DLB 16

Eagleton, Terence (Francis) 1943-
See Eagleton, Terry
See also CA 57-60; CANR 7, 23, 68; MTCW

Eagleton, Terry .... **CLC 63**
See also Eagleton, Terence (Francis)

Early, Jack
See Scoppettone, Sandra

East, Michael
See West, Morris L(anglo)

Eastaway, Edward
See Thomas, (Philip) Edward

Eastlake, William (Derry) 1917-1997 ..... **CLC 8**
See also CA 5-8R; 158; CAAS 1; CANR 5, 63; DLB 6; INT CANR-5

Eastman, Charles A(lexander) 1858-1939 **TCLC 55; DAM MULT**
See also DLB 175; NNAL; YABC 1

Eberhart, Richard (Ghormley) 1904- **CLC 3, 11, 19, 56; DAM POET**
See also CA 1-4R; CANR 2; CDALB 1941-1968; DLB 48; MTCW

Eberstadt, Fernanda 1960- .... **CLC 39**
See also CA 136

Echegaray (y Eizaguirre), Jose (Maria Waldo) 1832-1916 .... **TCLC 4**
See also CA 104; CANR 32; HW; MTCW

Echeverria, (Jose) Esteban (Antonino) 1805-1851 **NCLC 18**

Echo
See Proust, (Valentin-Louis-George-Eugene-) Marcel

Eckert, Allan W. 1931- .... **CLC 17**
See also AAYA 18; CA 13-16R; CANR 14, 45; INT CANR-14; SAAS 21; SATA 29, 91; SATA-Brief 27

Eckhart, Meister 1260(?)-1328(?) .... **CMLC 9**
See also DLB 115

Eckmar, F. R.
See de Hartog, Jan

Eco, Umberto 1932-**CLC 28, 60; DAM NOV, POP**
See also BEST 90:1; CA 77-80; CANR 12, 33, 55; DLB 196; MTCW

Eddison, E(ric) R(ucker) 1882-1945 .... **TCLC 15**
See also CA 109; 156

Eddy, Mary (Morse) Baker 1821-1910 **TCLC 71**
See also CA 113

Edel, (Joseph) Leon 1907-1997 .... **CLC 29, 34**
See also CA 1-4R; 161; CANR 1, 22; DLB 103; INT CANR-22

Eden, Emily 1797-1869 .... **NCLC 10**

Edgar, David 1948- .... **CLC 42; DAM DRAM**
See also CA 57-60; CANR 12, 61; DLB 13; MTCW

Edgerton, Clyde (Carlyle) 1944- .... **CLC 39**
See also AAYA 17; CA 118; 134; CANR 64; INT 134

Edgeworth, Maria 1768-1849 .... **NCLC 1, 51**
See also DLB 116, 159, 163; SATA 21

Edmonds, Paul
See Kuttner, Henry

Edmonds, Walter D(umaux) 1903- .... **CLC 35**
See also CA 5-8R; CANR 2; DLB 9; MAICYA; SAAS 4; SATA 1, 27

Edmondson, Wallace
See Ellison, Harlan (Jay)

Edson, Russell .... **CLC 13**
See also CA 33-36R

Edwards, Bronwen Elizabeth
See Rose, Wendy

Edwards, G(erald) B(asil) 1899-1976 ..... **CLC 25**
See also CA 110

Edwards, Gus 1939- .... **CLC 43**
See also CA 108; INT 108

Edwards, Jonathan 1703-1758 . **LC 7; DA; DAC; DAM MST**
See also DLB 24

Efron, Marina Ivanovna Tsvetaeva
See Tsvetaeva (Efron), Marina (Ivanovna)

Ehle, John (Marsden, Jr.) 1925- .... **CLC 27**
See also CA 9-12R

Ehrenbourg, Ilya (Grigoryevich)
See Ehrenburg, Ilya (Grigoryevich)

Ehrenburg, Ilya (Grigoryevich) 1891-1967 **CLC 18, 34, 62**
See also CA 102; 25-28R

Ehrenburg, Ilyo (Grigoryevich)
See Ehrenburg, Ilya (Grigoryevich)

Eich, Guenter 1907-1972 .... **CLC 15**
See also CA 111; 93-96; DLB 69, 124

Eichendorff, Joseph Freiherr von 1788-1857 **NCLC 8**
See also DLB 90

Eigner, Larry .... **CLC 9**
See also Eigner, Laurence (Joel)
See also CAAS 23; DLB 5

Eigner, Laurence (Joel) 1927-1996
See Eigner, Larry
See also CA 9-12R; 151; CANR 6; DLB 193

Einstein, Albert 1879-1955 .... **TCLC 65**
See also CA 121; 133; MTCW

Eiseley, Loren Corey 1907-1977 .... **CLC 7**
See also AAYA 5; CA 1-4R; 73-76; CANR 6

Eisenstadt, Jill 1963- .... **CLC 50**
See also CA 140

Eisenstein, Sergei (Mikhailovich) 1898-1948 **TCLC 57**
See also CA 114; 149

Eisner, Simon
See Kornbluth, C(yril) M.

Ekeloef, (Bengt) Gunnar 1907-1968 ..... **CLC 27; DAM POET**
See also CA 123; 25-28R

Ekelof, (Bengt) Gunnar
See Ekeloef, (Bengt) Gunnar

Ekelund, Vilhelm 1880-1949 .... **TCLC 75**

Ekwensi, C. O. D.
See Ekwensi, Cyprian (Odiatu Duaka)

Ekwensi, Cyprian (Odiatu Duaka) 1921- **CLC 4; BLC; DAM MULT**
See also BW 2; CA 29-32R; CANR 18, 42; DLB 117; MTCW; SATA 66

Elaine .... **TCLC 18**
See also Leverson, Ada

El Crummo
See Crumb, R(obert)

Elder, Lonne III 1931-1996 .... **DC 8**
See also BLC; BW 1; CA 81-84; 152; CANR 25; DAM MULT; DLB 7, 38, 44

Elia
See Lamb, Charles

Eliade, Mircea 1907-1986 .... **CLC 19**
See also CA 65-68; 119; CANR 30, 62; MTCW

Eliot, A. D.
See Jewett, (Theodora) Sarah Orne

Eliot, Alice
See Jewett, (Theodora) Sarah Orne

Eliot, Dan
See Silverberg, Robert

Eliot, George 1819-1880 **NCLC 4, 13, 23, 41, 49; DA; DAB; DAC; DAM MST, NOV; PC 20; WLC**
See also CDBLB 1832-1890; DLB 21, 35, 55

Eliot, John 1604-1690 .... **LC 5**
See also DLB 24

Eliot, T(homas) S(tearns) 1888-1965 **CLC 1, 2, 3, 6, 9, 10, 13, 15, 24, 34, 41, 55, 57; DA; DAB; DAC; DAM DRAM, MST, POET; PC 5; WLC 2**
See also CA 5-8R; 25-28R; CANR 41; CDALB 1929-1941; DLB 7, 10, 45, 63; DLBY 88; MTCW

Elizabeth 1866-1941 .... **TCLC 41**

Elkin, Stanley L(awrence) 1930-1995 **CLC 4, 6, 9, 14, 27, 51, 91; DAM NOV, POP; SSC 12**
See also CA 9-12R; 148; CANR 8, 46; DLB 2, 28; DLBY 80; INT CANR-8; MTCW

Elledge, Scott .... **CLC 34**

Elliot, Don
See Silverberg, Robert

Elliott, Don
See Silverberg, Robert

Elliott, George P(aul) 1918-1980 .... **CLC 2**
See also CA 1-4R; 97-100; CANR 2

Elliott, Janice 1931- .... **CLC 47**
See also CA 13-16R; CANR 8, 29; DLB 14

Elliott, Sumner Locke 1917-1991 .... **CLC 38**
See also CA 5-8R; 134; CANR 2, 21

Elliott, William
See Bradbury, Ray (Douglas)

Ellis, A. E. .... **CLC 7**

Ellis, Alice Thomas .... **CLC 40**
See also Haycraft, Anna
See also DLB 194

Ellis, Bret Easton 1964- **CLC 39, 71; DAM POP**
See also AAYA 2; CA 118; 123; CANR 51; INT 123

Ellis, (Henry) Havelock 1859-1939 ...... **TCLC 14**
See also CA 109; DLB 190

Ellis, Landon
See Ellison, Harlan (Jay)

Ellis, Trey 1962- .... **CLC 55**
See also CA 146

Ellison, Harlan (Jay) 1934- **CLC 1, 13, 42; DAM POP; SSC 14**
See also CA 5-8R; CANR 5, 46; DLB 8; INT CANR-5; MTCW

Ellison, Ralph (Waldo) 1914-1994 **CLC 1, 3, 11, 54, 86; BLC; DA; DAB; DAC; DAM MST, MULT, NOV; SSC 26; WLC**
See also AAYA 19; BW 1; CA 9-12R; 145; CANR 24, 53; CDALB 1941-1968; DLB 2, 76; DLBY 94; MTCW

Ellmann, Lucy (Elizabeth) 1956- .... **CLC 61**
See also CA 128

Ellmann, Richard (David) 1918-1987 ..... **CLC 50**
See also BEST 89:2; CA 1-4R; 122; CANR 2, 28, 61; DLB 103; DLBY 87; MTCW

Elman, Richard (Martin) 1934-1997 ...... **CLC 19**
See also CA 17-20R; 163; CAAS 3; CANR 47

Elron
See Hubbard, L(afayette) Ron(ald)

Eluard, Paul .... **TCLC 7, 41**
See also Grindel, Eugene

Elyot, Sir Thomas 1490(?)-1546 .... **LC 11**

Elytis, Odysseus 1911-1996 .... **CLC 15, 49, 100; DAM POET; PC 21**
See also CA 102; 151; MTCW

Emecheta, (Florence Onye) Buchi 1944- **CLC 14, 48; BLC; DAM MULT**
See also BW 2; CA 81-84; CANR 27; DLB 117; MTCW; SATA 66

Emerson, Mary Moody 1774-1863 ...... **NCLC 66**

Emerson, Ralph Waldo 1803-1882 . **NCLC 1, 38; DA; DAB; DAC; DAM MST, POET; PC 18; WLC**
See also CDALB 1640-1865; DLB 1, 59, 73

Eminescu, Mihail 1850-1889 .... **NCLC 33**

Empson, William 1906-1984 **CLC 3, 8, 19, 33, 34**
See also CA 17-20R; 112; CANR 31, 61; DLB 20; MTCW

Enchi Fumiko (Ueda) 1905-1986 .... **CLC 31**
See also CA 129; 121

Ende, Michael (Andreas Helmuth) 1929-1995 **CLC 31**
See also CA 118; 124; 149; CANR 36; CLR 14; DLB 75; MAICYA; SATA 61; SATA-Brief 42; SATA-Obit 86

Endo, Shusaku 1923-1996 **CLC 7, 14, 19, 54, 99; DAM NOV**
See also CA 29-32R; 153; CANR 21, 54; DLB 182; MTCW

Engel, Marian 1933-1985 .... **CLC 36**
See also CA 25-28R; CANR 12; DLB 53; INT CANR-12

Engelhardt, Frederick
See Hubbard, L(afayette) Ron(ald)

Enright, D(ennis) J(oseph) 1920- . **CLC 4, 8, 31**
See also CA 1-4R; CANR 1, 42; DLB 27; SATA 25

Enzensberger, Hans Magnus 1929- ...... **CLC 43**
See also CA 116; 119

Ephron, Nora 1941- .... **CLC 17, 31**
See also AITN 2; CA 65-68; CANR 12, 39

Epicurus 341B.C.-270B.C. .... **CMLC 21**
See also DLB 176

Epsilon
See Betjeman, John

Epstein, Daniel Mark 1948- .... **CLC 7**
See also CA 49-52; CANR 2, 53

Epstein, Jacob 1956- .... **CLC 19**
See also CA 114

Epstein, Joseph 1937- .... **CLC 39**
See also CA 112; 119; CANR 50, 65

Epstein, Leslie 1938- .... **CLC 27**
See also CA 73-76; CAAS 12; CANR 23

Equiano, Olaudah 1745(?)-1797 **LC 16; BLC; DAM MULT**
See also DLB 37, 50

ER .... **TCLC 33**
See also CA 160; DLB 85

Erasmus, Desiderius 1469(?)-1536 .... **LC 16**

Erdman, Paul E(mil) 1932- **CLC 25**
See also AITN 1; CA 61-64; CANR 13, 43

Erdrich, Louise 1954- **CLC 39, 54; DAM MULT, NOV, POP**
See also AAYA 10; BEST 89:1; CA 114; CANR 41, 62; DLB 152, 175; MTCW; NNAL; SATA 94

Erenburg, Ilya (Grigoryevich)
See Ehrenburg, Ilya (Grigoryevich)

Erickson, Stephen Michael 1950-
See Erickson, Steve
See also CA 129

Erickson, Steve 1950- .... **CLC 64**
See also Erickson, Stephen Michael
See also CANR 60, 68

Ericson, Walter
See Fast, Howard (Melvin)

Eriksson, Buntel
See Bergman, (Ernst) Ingmar

Ernaux, Annie 1940- .... **CLC 88**
See also CA 147

Eschenbach, Wolfram von
See Wolfram von Eschenbach

Eseki, Bruno
See Mphahlele, Ezekiel

Esenin, Sergei (Alexandrovich) 1895-1925 **TCLC 4**
See also CA 104

Eshleman, Clayton 1935- .... **CLC 7**
See also CA 33-36R; CAAS 6; DLB 5

Espriella, Don Manuel Alvarez
See Southey, Robert

Espriu, Salvador 1913-1985 .... **CLC 9**
See also CA 154; 115; DLB 134

Espronceda, Jose de 1808-1842 .... **NCLC 39**

Esse, James
See Stephens, James

Esterbrook, Tom
See Hubbard, L(afayette) Ron(ald)

Estleman, Loren D. 1952- .. **CLC 48; DAM NOV, POP**
See also CA 85-88; CANR 27; INT CANR-27; MTCW

Euclid 306B.C.-283B.C. .... **CMLC 25**

Eugenides, Jeffrey 1960(?)- .... **CLC 81**
See also CA 144

Euripides c. 485B.C.-406B.C. **CMLC 23; DA; DAB; DAC; DAM DRAM, MST; DC 4; WLCS**
See also DLB 176

Evan, Evin
See Faust, Frederick (Schiller)

Evans, Evan
See Faust, Frederick (Schiller)

Evans, Marian
See Eliot, George

Evans, Mary Ann
See Eliot, George

Evarts, Esther
See Benson, Sally

Author Index

Everett, Percival L. 1956- .... **CLC 57**
See also BW 2; CA 129

Everson, R(onald) G(ilmour) 1903- .... **CLC 27**
See also CA 17-20R; DLB 88

Everson, William (Oliver) 1912-1994**CLC 1, 5, 14**
See also CA 9-12R; 145; CANR 20; DLB 5, 16; MTCW

Evtushenko, Evgenii Aleksandrovich
See Yevtushenko, Yevgeny (Alexandrovich)

Ewart, Gavin (Buchanan) 1916-1995 **CLC 13, 46**
See also CA 89-92; 150; CANR 17, 46; DLB 40; MTCW

Ewers, Hanns Heinz 1871-1943 .... **TCLC 12**
See also CA 109; 149

Ewing, Frederick R.
See Sturgeon, Theodore (Hamilton)

Exley, Frederick (Earl) 1929-1992 ...... **CLC 6, 11**
See also AITN 2; CA 81-84; 138; DLB 143; DLBY 81

Eynhardt, Guillermo
See Quiroga, Horacio (Sylvestre)

Ezekiel, Nissim 1924- .... **CLC 61**
See also CA 61-64

Ezekiel, Tish O'Dowd 1943- .... **CLC 34**
See also CA 129

Fadeyev, A.
See Bulgya, Alexander Alexandrovich

Fadeyev, Alexander .... **TCLC 53**
See also Bulgya, Alexander Alexandrovich

Fagen, Donald 1948- .... **CLC 26**

Fainzilberg, Ilya Arnoldovich 1897-1937
See Ilf, Ilya
See also CA 120; 165

Fair, Ronald L. 1932- .... **CLC 18**
See also BW 1; CA 69-72; CANR 25; DLB 33

Fairbairn, Roger
See Carr, John Dickson

Fairbairns, Zoe (Ann) 1948- .... **CLC 32**
See also CA 103; CANR 21

Falco, Gian
See Papini, Giovanni

Falconer, James
See Kirkup, James

Falconer, Kenneth
See Kornbluth, C(yril) M.

Falkland, Samuel
See Heijermans, Herman

Fallaci, Oriana 1930- .... **CLC 11**
See also CA 77-80; CANR 15, 58; MTCW

Faludy, George 1913- .... **CLC 42**
See also CA 21-24R

Faludy, Gyoergy
See Faludy, George

Fanon, Frantz 1925-1961 .. **CLC 74; BLC; DAM MULT**
See also BW 1; CA 116; 89-92

Fanshawe, Ann 1625-1680 .... **LC 11**

Fante, John (Thomas) 1911-1983 .... **CLC 60**
See also CA 69-72; 109; CANR 23; DLB 130; DLBY 83

Farah, Nuruddin 1945- ..... **CLC 53; BLC; DAM MULT**
See also BW 2; CA 106; DLB 125

Fargue, Leon-Paul 1876(?)-1947 .... **TCLC 11**
See also CA 109

Farigoule, Louis
See Romains, Jules

Farina, Richard 1936(?)-1966 .... **CLC 9**
See also CA 81-84; 25-28R

Farley, Walter (Lorimer) 1915-1989 ..... **CLC 17**
See also CA 17-20R; CANR 8, 29; DLB 22; JRDA; MAICYA; SATA 2, 43

Farmer, Philip Jose 1918- .... **CLC 1, 19**
See also CA 1-4R; CANR 4, 35; DLB 8; MTCW; SATA 93

Farquhar, George 1677-1707**LC 21; DAM DRAM**
See also DLB 84

Farrell, J(ames) G(ordon) 1935-1979 ...... **CLC 6**
See also CA 73-76; 89-92; CANR 36; DLB 14; MTCW

Farrell, James T(homas) 1904-1979 **CLC 1, 4, 8, 11, 66; SSC 28**
See also CA 5-8R; 89-92; CANR 9, 61; DLB 4, 9, 86; DLBD 2; MTCW

Farren, Richard J.
See Betjeman, John

Farren, Richard M.
See Betjeman, John

Fassbinder, Rainer Werner 1946-1982 . **CLC 20**
See also CA 93-96; 106; CANR 31

Fast, Howard (Melvin) 1914-**CLC 23; DAM NOV**
See also AAYA 16; CA 1-4R; CAAS 18; CANR 1, 33, 54; DLB 9; INT CANR-33; SATA 7

Faulcon, Robert
See Holdstock, Robert P.

Faulkner, William (Cuthbert) 1897-1962**CLC 1, 3, 6, 8, 9, 11, 14, 18, 28, 52, 68; DA; DAB; DAC; DAM MST, NOV; SSC 1; WLC**
See also AAYA 7; CA 81-84; CANR 33; CDALB 1929-1941; DLB 9, 11, 44, 102; DLBD 2; DLBY 86, 97; MTCW

Fauset, Jessie Redmon 1884(?)-1961**CLC 19, 54; BLC; DAM MULT**
See also BW 1; CA 109; DLB 51

Faust, Frederick (Schiller) 1892-1944(?) **TCLC 49; DAM POP**
See also CA 108; 152

Faust, Irvin 1924- **CLC 8**
See also CA 33-36R; CANR 28, 67; DLB 2, 28; DLBY 80

Fawkes, Guy
See Benchley, Robert (Charles)

Fearing, Kenneth (Flexner) 1902-1961 . **CLC 51**
See also CA 93-96; CANR 59; DLB 9

Fecamps, Elise
See Creasey, John

Federman, Raymond 1928- .... **CLC 6, 47**
See also CA 17-20R; CAAS 8; CANR 10, 43; DLBY 80

Federspiel, J(uerg) F. 1931- .... **CLC 42**
See also CA 146

Feiffer, Jules (Ralph) 1929- **CLC 2, 8, 64; DAM DRAM**
See also AAYA 3; CA 17-20R; CANR 30, 59; DLB 7, 44; INT CANR-30; MTCW; SATA 8, 61

Feige, Hermann Albert Otto Maximilian
See Traven, B.

Feinberg, David B. 1956-1994 .... **CLC 59**
See also CA 135; 147

Feinstein, Elaine 1930- .... **CLC 36**
See also CA 69-72; CAAS 1; CANR 31, 68; DLB 14, 40; MTCW

Feldman, Irving (Mordecai) 1928- .... **CLC 7**
See also CA 1-4R; CANR 1; DLB 169

Felix-Tchicaya, Gerald
See Tchicaya, Gerald Felix

Fellini, Federico 1920-1993 .... **CLC 16, 85**
See also CA 65-68; 143; CANR 33

Felsen, Henry Gregor 1916- .... **CLC 17**
See also CA 1-4R; CANR 1; SAAS 2; SATA 1

Fenno, Jack
See Calisher, Hortense

Fenton, James Martin 1949- .... **CLC 32**
See also CA 102; DLB 40

Ferber, Edna 1887-1968 .... **CLC 18, 93**
See also AITN 1; CA 5-8R; 25-28R; CANR 68; DLB 9, 28, 86; MTCW; SATA 7

Ferguson, Helen
See Kavan, Anna

Ferguson, Samuel 1810-1886 .... **NCLC 33**
See also DLB 32

Fergusson, Robert 1750-1774 .... **LC 29**
See also DLB 109

Ferling, Lawrence
See Ferlinghetti, Lawrence (Monsanto)

Ferlinghetti, Lawrence (Monsanto) 1919(?)-**CLC 2, 6, 10, 27; DAM POET; PC 1**
See also CA 5-8R; CANR 3, 41; CDALB 1941-1968; DLB 5, 16; MTCW

Fernandez, Vicente Garcia Huidobro
See Huidobro Fernandez, Vicente Garcia

Ferrer, Gabriel (Francisco Victor) Miro
See Miro (Ferrer), Gabriel (Francisco Victor)

Ford, Richard .... **CLC 99**

Ford, Richard 1944- .... **CLC 46**
See also CA 69-72; CANR 11, 47

Ford, Webster
See Masters, Edgar Lee

Foreman, Richard 1937- .... **CLC 50**
See also CA 65-68; CANR 32, 63

Forester, C(ecil) S(cott) 1899-1966 .... **CLC 35**
See also CA 73-76; 25-28R; DLB 191; SATA 13

Forez
See Mauriac, Francois (Charles)

Forman, James Douglas 1932- .... **CLC 21**
See also AAYA 17; CA 9-12R; CANR 4, 19, 42; JRDA; MAICYA; SATA 8, 70

Fornes, Maria Irene 1930- .... **CLC 39, 61**
See also CA 25-28R; CANR 28; DLB 7; HW; INT CANR-28; MTCW

Forrest, Leon (Richard) 1937-1997 .... **CLC 4**
See also BW 2; CA 89-92; 162; CAAS 7; CANR 25, 52; DLB 33

Forster, E(dward) M(organ) 1879-1970 **CLC 1, 2, 3, 4, 9, 10, 13, 15, 22, 45, 77; DA; DAB; DAC; DAM MST, NOV; SSC 27; WLC**
See also AAYA 2; CA 13-14; 25-28R; CANR 45; CAP 1; CDBLB 1914-1945; DLB 34, 98, 162, 178, 195; DLBD 10; MTCW; SATA 57

Forster, John 1812-1876 .... **NCLC 11**
See also DLB 144, 184

Forsyth, Frederick 1938- .... **CLC 2, 5, 36; DAM NOV, POP**
See also BEST 89:4; CA 85-88; CANR 38, 62; DLB 87; MTCW

Forten, Charlotte L. .... **TCLC 16; BLC**
See also Grimke, Charlotte L(ottie) Forten
See also DLB 50

Foscolo, Ugo 1778-1827 .... **NCLC 8**

Fosse, Bob .... **CLC 20**
See also Fosse, Robert Louis

Fosse, Robert Louis 1927-1987
See Fosse, Bob
See also CA 110; 123

Foster, Stephen Collins 1826-1864 .... **NCLC 26**

Foucault, Michel 1926-1984 ...... **CLC 31, 34, 69**
See also CA 105; 113; CANR 34; MTCW

Fouque, Friedrich (Heinrich Karl) de la Motte 1777-1843 .... **NCLC 2**
See also DLB 90

Fourier, Charles 1772-1837 .... **NCLC 51**

Fournier, Henri Alban 1886-1914
See Alain-Fournier
See also CA 104

Fournier, Pierre 1916- .... **CLC 11**
See also Gascar, Pierre
See also CA 89-92; CANR 16, 40

Fowles, John 1926-**CLC 1, 2, 3, 4, 6, 9, 10, 15, 33, 87; DAB; DAC; DAM MST**
See also CA 5-8R; CANR 25; CDBLB 1960 to Present; DLB 14, 139; MTCW; SATA 22

Fox, Paula 1923- .... **CLC 2, 8**
See also AAYA 3; CA 73-76; CANR 20, 36, 62; CLR 1, 44; DLB 52; JRDA; MAICYA; MTCW; SATA 17, 60

Fox, William Price (Jr.) 1926- .... **CLC 22**
See also CA 17-20R; CAAS 19; CANR 11; DLB 2; DLBY 81

Foxe, John 1516(?)-1587 .... **LC 14**

Frame, Janet 1924-**CLC 2, 3, 6, 22, 66, 96; SSC 29**
See also Clutha, Janet Paterson Frame

France, Anatole .... **TCLC 9**
See also Thibault, Jacques Anatole Francois
See also DLB 123

Francis, Claude 19(?)- .... **CLC 50**

Francis, Dick 1920- . **CLC 2, 22, 42, 102; DAM POP**
See also AAYA 5, 21; BEST 89:3; CA 5-8R; CANR 9, 42, 68; CDBLB 1960 to Present; DLB 87; INT CANR-9; MTCW

Francis, Robert (Churchill) 1901-1987 **CLC 15**
See also CA 1-4R; 123; CANR 1

Frank, Anne(lies Marie) 1929-1945**TCLC 17; DA; DAB; DAC; DAM MST; WLC**
See also AAYA 12; CA 113; 133; CANR 68; MTCW; SATA 87; SATA-Brief 42

Frank, Elizabeth 1945- .... **CLC 39**
See also CA 121; 126; INT 126

Frankl, Viktor E(mil) 1905-1997 .... **CLC 93**
See also CA 65-68; 161

Franklin, Benjamin
See Hasek, Jaroslav (Matej Frantisek)

Franklin, Benjamin 1706-1790**LC 25; DA; DAB; DAC; DAM MST; WLCS**
See also CDALB 1640-1865; DLB 24, 43, 73

Franklin, (Stella Maria Sarah) Miles 1879-1954 **TCLC 7**
See also CA 104; 164

Fraser, (Lady) Antonia (Pakenham) 1932- **CLC 32, 107**
See also CA 85-88; CANR 44, 65; MTCW; SATA-Brief 32

Fraser, George MacDonald 1925- .... **CLC 7**
See also CA 45-48; CANR 2, 48

Fraser, Sylvia 1935- .... **CLC 64**
See also CA 45-48; CANR 1, 16, 60

Frayn, Michael 1933- ... **CLC 3, 7, 31, 47; DAM DRAM, NOV**
See also CA 5-8R; CANR 30; DLB 13, 14, 194; MTCW

Fraze, Candida (Merrill) 1945- .... **CLC 50**
See also CA 126

Frazer, J(ames) G(eorge) 1854-1941 ... **TCLC 32**
See also CA 118

Frazer, Robert Caine
See Creasey, John

Frazer, Sir James George
See Frazer, J(ames) G(eorge)

Frazier, Charles 1950- .... **CLC 109**
See also CA 161

Frazier, Ian 1951- .... **CLC 46**
See also CA 130; CANR 54

Frederic, Harold 1856-1898 .... **NCLC 10**
See also DLB 12, 23; DLBD 13

Frederick, John
See Faust, Frederick (Schiller)

Frederick the Great 1712-1786 .... **LC 14**

Fredro, Aleksander 1793-1876 .... **NCLC 8**

Freeling, Nicolas 1927- .... **CLC 38**
See also CA 49-52; CAAS 12; CANR 1, 17, 50; DLB 87

Freeman, Douglas Southall 1886-1953 **TCLC 11**
See also CA 109; DLB 17

Freeman, Judith 1946- .... **CLC 55**
See also CA 148

Freeman, Mary Eleanor Wilkins 1852-1930 **TCLC 9; SSC 1**
See also CA 106; DLB 12, 78

Freeman, R(ichard) Austin 1862-1943 **TCLC 21**
See also CA 113; DLB 70

French, Albert 1943- .... **CLC 86**

French, Marilyn 1929- ... **CLC 10, 18, 60; DAM DRAM, NOV, POP**
See also CA 69-72; CANR 3, 31; INT CANR-31; MTCW

French, Paul
See Asimov, Isaac

Freneau, Philip Morin 1752-1832 .... **NCLC 1**
See also DLB 37, 43

Freud, Sigmund 1856-1939 .... **TCLC 52**
See also CA 115; 133; MTCW

Friedan, Betty (Naomi) 1921- .... **CLC 74**
See also CA 65-68; CANR 18, 45; MTCW

Friedlander, Saul 1932- .... **CLC 90**
See also CA 117; 130

Friedman, B(ernard) H(arper) 1926- ...... **CLC 7**
See also CA 1-4R; CANR 3, 48

Friedman, Bruce Jay 1930- .... **CLC 3, 5, 56**
See also CA 9-12R; CANR 25, 52; DLB 2, 28; INT CANR-25

Friel, Brian 1929- .... **CLC 5, 42, 59; DC 8**
See also CA 21-24R; CANR 33; DLB 13; MTCW

Friis-Baastad, Babbis Ellinor 1921-1970**CLC 12**
See also CA 17-20R; 134; SATA 7

Frisch, Max (Rudolf) 1911-1991 **CLC 3, 9, 14, 18, 32, 44; DAM DRAM, NOV**
See also CA 85-88; 134; CANR 32; DLB 69, 124; MTCW

Fromentin, Eugene (Samuel Auguste) 1820-1876 **NCLC 10**
See also DLB 123

Frost, Frederick
See Faust, Frederick (Schiller)

Frost, Robert (Lee) 1874-1963 **CLC 1, 3, 4, 9, 10, 13, 15, 26, 34, 44; DA; DAB; DAC; DAM MST, POET; PC 1; WLC**
See also AAYA 21; CA 89-92; CANR 33; CDALB 1917-1929; DLB 54; DLBD 7; MTCW; SATA 14

Froude, James Anthony 1818-1894 .... **NCLC 43**
See also DLB 18, 57, 144

Froy, Herald
See Waterhouse, Keith (Spencer)

Fry, Christopher 1907- .... **CLC 2, 10, 14; DAM DRAM**
See also CA 17-20R; CAAS 23; CANR 9, 30; DLB 13; MTCW; SATA 66

Frye, (Herman) Northrop 1912-1991 **CLC 24, 70**
See also CA 5-8R; 133; CANR 8, 37; DLB 67, 68; MTCW

Fuchs, Daniel 1909-1993 .... **CLC 8, 22**
See also CA 81-84; 142; CAAS 5; CANR 40; DLB 9, 26, 28; DLBY 93

Fuchs, Daniel 1934- .... **CLC 34**
See also CA 37-40R; CANR 14, 48

Fuentes, Carlos 1928- **CLC 3, 8, 10, 13, 22, 41, 60; DA; DAB; DAC; DAM MST, MULT, NOV; HLC; SSC 24; WLC**
See also AAYA 4; AITN 2; CA 69-72; CANR 10, 32, 68; DLB 113; HW; MTCW

Fuentes, Gregorio Lopez y
See Lopez y Fuentes, Gregorio

Fugard, (Harold) Athol 1932- **CLC 5, 9, 14, 25, 40, 80; DAM DRAM; DC 3**
See also AAYA 17; CA 85-88; CANR 32, 54; MTCW

Fugard, Sheila 1932- .... **CLC 48**
See also CA 125

Fuller, Charles (H., Jr.) 1939- ... **CLC 25; BLC; DAM DRAM, MULT; DC 1**
See also BW 2; CA 108; 112; DLB 38; INT 112; MTCW

Fuller, John (Leopold) 1937- .... **CLC 62**
See also CA 21-24R; CANR 9, 44; DLB 40

Fuller, Margaret .... **NCLC 5, 50**
See also Ossoli, Sarah Margaret (Fuller marchesa d')

Fuller, Roy (Broadbent) 1912-1991 ... **CLC 4, 28**
See also CA 5-8R; 135; CAAS 10; CANR 53; DLB 15, 20; SATA 87

Fulton, Alice 1952- .... **CLC 52**
See also CA 116; CANR 57; DLB 193

Furphy, Joseph 1843-1912 .... **TCLC 25**
See also CA 163

Fussell, Paul 1924- .... **CLC 74**
See also BEST 90:1; CA 17-20R; CANR 8, 21, 35; INT CANR-21; MTCW

Futabatei, Shimei 1864-1909 .... **TCLC 44**
See also CA 162; DLB 180

Futrelle, Jacques 1875-1912 .... **TCLC 19**
See also CA 113; 155

Gaboriau, Emile 1835-1873 .... **NCLC 14**

Gadda, Carlo Emilio 1893-1973 .... **CLC 11**
See also CA 89-92; DLB 177

Gaddis, William 1922- **CLC 1, 3, 6, 8, 10, 19, 43, 86**
See also CA 17-20R; CANR 21, 48; DLB 2; MTCW

Gage, Walter
See Inge, William (Motter)

Gaines, Ernest J(ames) 1933- **CLC 3, 11, 18, 86; BLC; DAM MULT**
See also AAYA 18; AITN 1; BW 2; CA 9-12R; CANR 6, 24, 42; CDALB 1968-1988; DLB 2, 33, 152; DLBY 80; MTCW; SATA 86

Gaitskill, Mary 1954- .... **CLC 69**
See also CA 128; CANR 61

Galdos, Benito Perez
See Perez Galdos, Benito

Gale, Zona 1874-1938 ..... **TCLC 7; DAM DRAM**
See also CA 105; 153; DLB 9, 78

Galeano, Eduardo (Hughes) 1940- .... **CLC 72**
See also CA 29-32R; CANR 13, 32; HW

Galiano, Juan Valera y Alcala
See Valera y Alcala-Galiano, Juan

Gallagher, Tess 1943- **CLC 18, 63; DAM POET; PC 9**
See also CA 106; DLB 120

Gallant, Mavis 1922- **CLC 7, 18, 38; DAC; DAM MST; SSC 5**
See also CA 69-72; CANR 29; DLB 53; MTCW

Gallant, Roy A(rthur) 1924- .... **CLC 17**
See also CA 5-8R; CANR 4, 29, 54; CLR 30; MAICYA; SATA 4, 68

Gallico, Paul (William) 1897-1976 .... **CLC 2**
See also AITN 1; CA 5-8R; 69-72; CANR 23; DLB 9, 171; MAICYA; SATA 13

Gallo, Max Louis 1932- .... **CLC 95**
See also CA 85-88

Gallois, Lucien
See Desnos, Robert

Gallup, Ralph
See Whitemore, Hugh (John)

Galsworthy, John 1867-1933 .. **TCLC 1, 45; DA; DAB; DAC; DAM DRAM, MST, NOV; SSC 22; WLC 2**
See also CA 104; 141; CDBLB 1890-1914; DLB 10, 34, 98, 162; DLBD 16

Galt, John 1779-1839 .... **NCLC 1**
See also DLB 99, 116, 159

Galvin, James 1951- .... **CLC 38**
See also CA 108; CANR 26

Gamboa, Federico 1864-1939 .... **TCLC 36**

Gandhi, M. K.
See Gandhi, Mohandas Karamchand

Gandhi, Mahatma
See Gandhi, Mohandas Karamchand

Gandhi, Mohandas Karamchand 1869-1948 **TCLC 59; DAM MULT**
See also CA 121; 132; MTCW

Gann, Ernest Kellogg 1910-1991 .... **CLC 23**
See also AITN 1; CA 1-4R; 136; CANR 1

Garcia, Cristina 1958- .... **CLC 76**
See also CA 141

Garcia Lorca, Federico 1898-1936 **TCLC 1, 7, 49; DA; DAB; DAC; DAM DRAM, MST, MULT, POET; DC 2; HLC; PC 3; WLC**
See also CA 104; 131; DLB 108; HW; MTCW

Garcia Marquez, Gabriel (Jose) 1928- **CLC 2, 3, 8, 10, 15, 27, 47, 55, 68; DA; DAB; DAC; DAM MST, MULT, NOV, POP; HLC; SSC 8; WLC**
See also AAYA 3; BEST 89:1, 90:4; CA 33-36R; CANR 10, 28, 50; DLB 113; HW; MTCW

Gard, Janice
See Latham, Jean Lee

Gard, Roger Martin du
See Martin du Gard, Roger

Gardam, Jane 1928- .... **CLC 43**
See also CA 49-52; CANR 2, 18, 33, 54; CLR 12; DLB 14, 161; MAICYA; MTCW; SAAS 9; SATA 39, 76; SATA-Brief 28

Gardner, Herb(ert) 1934- .... **CLC 44**
See also CA 149

Gardner, John (Champlin), Jr. 1933-1982 **CLC 2, 3, 5, 7, 8, 10, 18, 28, 34; DAM NOV, POP; SSC 7**
See also AITN 1; CA 65-68; 107; CANR 33; DLB 2; DLBY 82; MTCW; SATA 40; SATA-Obit 31

Gardner, John (Edmund) 1926- .. **CLC 30; DAM POP**
See also CA 103; CANR 15; MTCW

Gardner, Miriam
See Bradley, Marion Zimmer

Gardner, Noel
See Kuttner, Henry

Gardons, S. S.
See Snodgrass, W(illiam) D(e Witt)

Garfield, Leon 1921-1996 **CLC 12**
See also AAYA 8; CA 17-20R; 152; CANR 38, 41; CLR 21; DLB 161; JRDA; MAICYA; SATA 1, 32, 76; SATA-Obit 90

Garland, (Hannibal) Hamlin 1860-1940 **TCLC 3; SSC 18**
See also CA 104; DLB 12, 71, 78, 186

Author Index

Garneau, (Hector de) Saint-Denys 1912-1943 **TCLC 13**
See also CA 111; DLB 88

Garner, Alan 1934- .. **CLC 17; DAB; DAM POP**
See also AAYA 18; CA 73-76; CANR 15, 64; CLR 20; DLB 161; MAICYA; MTCW; SATA 18, 69

Garner, Hugh 1913-1979 .... **CLC 13**
See also CA 69-72; CANR 31; DLB 68

Garnett, David 1892-1981 .... **CLC 3**
See also CA 5-8R; 103; CANR 17; DLB 34

Garos, Stephanie
See Katz, Steve

Garrett, George (Palmer) 1929- **CLC 3, 11, 51; SSC 30**
See also CA 1-4R; CAAS 5; CANR 1, 42, 67; DLB 2, 5, 130, 152; DLBY 83

Garrick, David 1717-1779 . **LC 15; DAM DRAM**
See also DLB 84

Garrigue, Jean 1914-1972 .... **CLC 2, 8**
See also CA 5-8R; 37-40R; CANR 20

Garrison, Frederick
See Sinclair, Upton (Beall)

Garth, Will
See Hamilton, Edmond; Kuttner, Henry

Garvey, Marcus (Moziah, Jr.) 1887-1940 . **TCLC 41; BLC; DAM MULT**
See also BW 1; CA 120; 124

Gary, Romain .... **CLC 25**
See also Kacew, Romain
See also DLB 83

Gascar, Pierre .... **CLC 11**
See also Fournier, Pierre

Gascoyne, David (Emery) 1916- .... **CLC 45**
See also CA 65-68; CANR 10, 28, 54; DLB 20; MTCW

Gaskell, Elizabeth Cleghorn 1810-1865**NCLC 5; DAB; DAM MST; SSC 25**
See also CDBLB 1832-1890; DLB 21, 144, 159

Gass, William H(oward) 1924-**CLC 1, 2, 8, 11, 15, 39; SSC 12**
See also CA 17-20R; CANR 30; DLB 2; MTCW

Gasset, Jose Ortega y
See Ortega y Gasset, Jose

Gates, Henry Louis, Jr. 1950- .... **CLC 65; DAM MULT**
See also BW 2; CA 109; CANR 25, 53; DLB 67

Gautier, Theophile 1811-1872**NCLC 1, 59; DAM POET; PC 18; SSC 20**
See also DLB 119

Gawsworth, John
See Bates, H(erbert) E(rnest)

Gay, Oliver
See Gogarty, Oliver St. John

Gaye, Marvin (Penze) 1939-1984 .... **CLC 26**
See also CA 112

Gebler, Carlo (Ernest) 1954- .... **CLC 39**
See also CA 119; 133

Gee, Maggie (Mary) 1948- .... **CLC 57**
See also CA 130

Gee, Maurice (Gough) 1931- .... **CLC 29**
See also CA 97-100; CANR 67; SATA 46

Gelbart, Larry (Simon) 1923- .... **CLC 21, 61**
See also CA 73-76; CANR 45

Gelber, Jack 1932- .... **CLC 1, 6, 14, 79**
See also CA 1-4R; CANR 2; DLB 7

Gellhorn, Martha (Ellis) 1908-1998 **CLC 14, 60**
See also CA 77-80; 164; CANR 44; DLBY 82

Genet, Jean 1910-1986**CLC 1, 2, 5, 10, 14, 44, 46; DAM DRAM**
See also CA 13-16R; CANR 18; DLB 72; DLBY 86; MTCW

Gent, Peter 1942- .... **CLC 29**
See also AITN 1; CA 89-92; DLBY 82

Gentlewoman in New England, A
See Bradstreet, Anne

Gentlewoman in Those Parts, A
See Bradstreet, Anne

George, Jean Craighead 1919- .... **CLC 35**
See also AAYA 8; CA 5-8R; CANR 25; CLR 1; DLB 52; JRDA; MAICYA; SATA 2, 68

George, Stefan (Anton) 1868-1933 .. **TCLC 2, 14**
See also CA 104

Georges, Georges Martin
See Simenon, Georges (Jacques Christian)

Gerhardi, William Alexander
See Gerhardie, William Alexander

Gerhardie, William Alexander 1895-1977**CLC 5**
See also CA 25-28R; 73-76; CANR 18; DLB 36

Gerstler, Amy 1956- .... **CLC 70**
See also CA 146

Gertler, T. .... **CLC 34**
See also CA 116; 121; INT 121

Ghalib .... **NCLC 39**
See also Ghalib, Hsadullah Khan

Ghalib, Hsadullah Khan 1797-1869
See Ghalib
See also DAM POET

Ghelderode, Michel de 1898-1962**CLC 6, 11; DAM DRAM**
See also CA 85-88; CANR 40

Ghiselin, Brewster 1903- .... **CLC 23**
See also CA 13-16R; CAAS 10; CANR 13

Ghose, Zulfikar 1935- .... **CLC 42**
See also CA 65-68; CANR 67

Ghosh, Amitav 1956- .... **CLC 44**
See also CA 147

Giacosa, Giuseppe 1847-1906 .... **TCLC 7**
See also CA 104

Gibb, Lee
See Waterhouse, Keith (Spencer)

Gibbon, Lewis Grassic .... **TCLC 4**
See also Mitchell, James Leslie

Gibbons, Kaye 1960- .... **CLC 50, 88; DAM POP**
See also CA 151

Gibran, Kahlil 1883-1931**TCLC 1, 9; DAM POET, POP; PC 9**
See also CA 104; 150

Gibran, Khalil
See Gibran, Kahlil

Gibson, William 1914-**CLC 23; DA; DAB; DAC; DAM DRAM, MST**
See also CA 9-12R; CANR 9, 42; DLB 7; SATA 66

Gibson, William (Ford) 1948-**CLC 39, 63; DAM POP**
See also AAYA 12; CA 126; 133; CANR 52

Gide, Andre (Paul Guillaume) 1869-1951**TCLC 5, 12, 36; DA; DAB; DAC; DAM MST, NOV; SSC 13; WLC**
See also CA 104; 124; DLB 65; MTCW

Gifford, Barry (Colby) 1946- .... **CLC 34**
See also CA 65-68; CANR 9, 30, 40

Gilbert, Frank
See De Voto, Bernard (Augustine)

Gilbert, W(illiam) S(chwenck) 1836-1911 **TCLC 3; DAM DRAM, POET**
See also CA 104; SATA 36

Gilbreth, Frank B., Jr. 1911- .... **CLC 17**
See also CA 9-12R; SATA 2

Gilchrist, Ellen 1935- . **CLC 34, 48; DAM POP; SSC 14**
See also CA 113; 116; CANR 41, 61; DLB 130; MTCW

Giles, Molly 1942- .... **CLC 39**
See also CA 126

Gill, Patrick
See Creasey, John

Gilliam, Terry (Vance) 1940- .... **CLC 21**
See also Monty Python
See also AAYA 19; CA 108; 113; CANR 35; INT 113

Gillian, Jerry
See Gilliam, Terry (Vance)

Gilliatt, Penelope (Ann Douglass) 1932-1993**CLC 2, 10, 13, 53**
See also AITN 2; CA 13-16R; 141; CANR 49; DLB 14

Gilman, Charlotte (Anna) Perkins (Stetson) 1860-1935 .... **TCLC 9, 37; SSC 13**
See also CA 106; 150

Gilmour, David 1949- .... **CLC 35**
See also CA 138, 147

Gilpin, William 1724-1804 .... **NCLC 30**

Gilray, J. D.
See Mencken, H(enry) L(ouis)

Gilroy, Frank D(aniel) 1925- .... **CLC 2**
See also CA 81-84; CANR 32, 64; DLB 7

Gilstrap, John 1957(?)- .... **CLC 99**
See also CA 160

Ginsberg, Allen 1926-1997 **CLC 1, 2, 3, 4, 6, 13, 36, 69, 109; DA; DAB; DAC; DAM MST, POET; PC 4; WLC 3**
See also AITN 1; CA 1-4R; 157; CANR 2, 41, 63; CDALB 1941-1968; DLB 5, 16, 169; MTCW

Ginzburg, Natalia 1916-1991 . **CLC 5, 11, 54, 70**
See also CA 85-88; 135; CANR 33; DLB 177; MTCW

Giono, Jean 1895-1970 .... **CLC 4, 11**
See also CA 45-48; 29-32R; CANR 2, 35; DLB 72; MTCW

Giovanni, Nikki 1943-**CLC 2, 4, 19, 64; BLC; DA; DAB; DAC; DAM MST, MULT, POET; PC 19; WLCS**
See also AAYA 22; AITN 1; BW 2; CA 29-32R; CAAS 6; CANR 18, 41, 60; CLR 6; DLB 5, 41; INT CANR-18; MAICYA; MTCW; SATA 24

Giovene, Andrea 1904- .... **CLC 7**
See also CA 85-88

Gippius, Zinaida (Nikolayevna) 1869-1945
See Hippius, Zinaida
See also CA 106

Giraudoux, (Hippolyte) Jean 1882-1944**TCLC 2, 7; DAM DRAM**
See also CA 104; DLB 65

Gironella, Jose Maria 1917- .... **CLC 11**
See also CA 101

Gissing, George (Robert) 1857-1903**TCLC 3, 24, 47**
See also CA 105; DLB 18, 135, 184

Giurlani, Aldo
See Palazzeschi, Aldo

Gladkov, Fyodor (Vasilyevich) 1883-1958**TCLC 27**

Glanville, Brian (Lester) 1931- .... **CLC 6**
See also CA 5-8R; CAAS 9; CANR 3; DLB 15, 139; SATA 42

Glasgow, Ellen (Anderson Gholson) 1873-1945 **TCLC 2, 7**
See also CA 104; 164; DLB 9, 12

Glaspell, Susan 1882(?)-1948 .... **TCLC 55**
See also CA 110; 154; DLB 7, 9, 78; YABC 2

Glassco, John 1909-1981 .... **CLC 9**
See also CA 13-16R; 102; CANR 15; DLB 68

Glasscock, Amnesia
See Steinbeck, John (Ernst)

Glasser, Ronald J. 1940(?)- .... **CLC 37**

Glassman, Joyce
See Johnson, Joyce

Glendinning, Victoria 1937- .... **CLC 50**
See also CA 120; 127; CANR 59; DLB 155

Glissant, Edouard 1928-**CLC 10, 68; DAM MULT**
See also CA 153

Gloag, Julian 1930- .... **CLC 40**
See also AITN 1; CA 65-68; CANR 10

Glowacki, Aleksander
See Prus, Boleslaw

Gluck, Louise (Elisabeth) 1943-CLC 7, 22, 44, 81; DAM POET; PC 16
See also CA 33-36R; CANR 40; DLB 5

Glyn, Elinor 1864-1943 .... TCLC 72
See also DLB 153

Gobineau, Joseph Arthur (Comte) de 1816-1882 NCLC 17
See also DLB 123

Godard, Jean-Luc 1930- .... CLC 20
See also CA 93-96

Godden, (Margaret) Rumer 1907- .... CLC 53
See also AAYA 6; CA 5-8R; CANR 4, 27, 36, 55; CLR 20; DLB 161; MAICYA; SAAS 12; SATA 3, 36

Godoy Alcayaga, Lucila 1889-1957
See Mistral, Gabriela
See also BW 2; CA 104; 131; DAM MULT; HW; MTCW

Godwin, Gail (Kathleen) 1937- CLC 5, 8, 22, 31, 69; DAM POP
See also CA 29-32R; CANR 15, 43; DLB 6; INT CANR-15; MTCW

Godwin, William 1756-1836 .... NCLC 14
See also CDBLB 1789-1832; DLB 39, 104, 142, 158, 163

Goebbels, Josef
See Goebbels, (Paul) Joseph

Goebbels, (Paul) Joseph 1897-1945 ..... **TCLC 68**
See also CA 115; 148

Goebbels, Joseph Paul
See Goebbels, (Paul) Joseph

Goethe, Johann Wolfgang von 1749-1832**NCLC 4, 22, 34; DA; DAB; DAC; DAM DRAM, MST, POET; PC 5; WLC 3**
See also DLB 94

Gogarty, Oliver St. John 1878-1957 .... **TCLC 15**
See also CA 109; 150; DLB 15, 19

Gogol, Nikolai (Vasilyevich) 1809-1852**NCLC 5, 15, 31; DA; DAB; DAC; DAM DRAM, MST; DC 1; SSC 4, 29; WLC**

Goines, Donald 1937(?)-1974**CLC 80; BLC; DAM MULT, POP**
See also AITN 1; BW 1; CA 124; 114; DLB 33

Gold, Herbert 1924- .... **CLC 4, 7, 14, 42**
See also CA 9-12R; CANR 17, 45; DLB 2; DLBY 81

Goldbarth, Albert 1948- .... **CLC 5, 38**
See also CA 53-56; CANR 6, 40; DLB 120

Goldberg, Anatol 1910-1982 .... **CLC 34**
See also CA 131; 117

Goldemberg, Isaac 1945- .... **CLC 52**
See also CA 69-72; CAAS 12; CANR 11, 32; HW

Golding, William (Gerald) 1911-1993CLC 1, 2, 3, 8, 10, 17, 27, 58, 81; DA; DAB; DAC; DAM MST, NOV; WLC
See also AAYA 5; CA 5-8R; 141; CANR 13, 33, 54; CDBLB 1945-1960; DLB 15, 100; MTCW

Goldman, Emma 1869-1940 .... TCLC 13
See also CA 110; 150

Goldman, Francisco 1954- .... CLC 76
See also CA 162

Goldman, William (W.) 1931- .... CLC 1, 48
See also CA 9-12R; CANR 29; DLB 44

Goldmann, Lucien 1913-1970 .... CLC 24
See also CA 25-28; CAP 2

Goldoni, Carlo 1707-1793 .... LC 4; DAM DRAM

Goldsberry, Steven 1949- .... CLC 34
See also CA 131

Goldsmith, Oliver 1728-1774 ... LC 2; DA; DAB; DAC; DAM DRAM, MST, NOV, POET; DC 8; WLC
See also CDBLB 1660-1789; DLB 39, 89, 104, 109, 142; SATA 26

Goldsmith, Peter
See Priestley, J(ohn) B(oynton)

Gombrowicz, Witold 1904-1969CLC 4, 7, 11, 49; DAM DRAM
See also CA 19-20; 25-28R; CAP 2

Gomez de la Serna, Ramon 1888-1963 .... CLC 9
See also CA 153; 116; HW

Goncharov, Ivan Alexandrovich 1812-1891NCLC 1, 63

Goncourt, Edmond (Louis Antoine Huot) de 1822-1896 .... NCLC 7
See also DLB 123

Goncourt, Jules (Alfred Huot) de 1830-1870 NCLC 7
See also DLB 123

Gontier, Fernande 19(?)- .... CLC 50

Gonzalez Martinez, Enrique 1871-1952TCLC 72
See also HW

Goodman, Paul 1911-1972 .... CLC 1, 2, 4, 7
See also CA 19-20; 37-40R; CANR 34; CAP 2; DLB 130; MTCW

Gordimer, Nadine 1923- CLC 3, 5, 7, 10, 18, 33, 51, 70; DA; DAB; DAC; DAM MST, NOV; SSC 17; WLCS
See also CA 5-8R; CANR 3, 28, 56; INT CANR-28; MTCW

Gordon, Adam Lindsay 1833-1870 ...... NCLC 21

Gordon, Caroline 1895-1981 CLC 6, 13, 29, 83; SSC 15
See also CA 11-12; 103; CANR 36; CAP 1; DLB 4, 9, 102; DLBY 81; MTCW

Gordon, Charles William 1860-1937
See Connor, Ralph
See also CA 109

Gordon, Mary (Catherine) 1949- .... **CLC 13, 22**
See also CA 102; CANR 44; DLB 6; DLBY 81; INT 102; MTCW

Gordon, N. J.
See Bosman, Herman Charles

Gordon, Sol 1923- .... **CLC 26**
See also CA 53-56; CANR 4; SATA 11

Gordone, Charles 1925-1995 .... **CLC 1, 4; DAM DRAM; DC 8**
See also BW 1; CA 93-96; 150; CANR 55; DLB 7; INT 93-96; MTCW

Gore, Catherine 1800-1861 .... **NCLC 65**
See also DLB 116

Gorenko, Anna Andreevna
See Akhmatova, Anna

Gorky, Maxim 1868-1936**TCLC 8; DAB; SSC 28; WLC**
See also Peshkov, Alexei Maximovich

Goryan, Sirak
See Saroyan, William

Gosse, Edmund (William) 1849-1928 .. **TCLC 28**
See also CA 117; DLB 57, 144, 184

Gotlieb, Phyllis Fay (Bloom) 1926- .... **CLC 18**
See also CA 13-16R; CANR 7; DLB 88

Gottesman, S. D.
See Kornbluth, C(yril) M.; Pohl, Frederik

Gottfried von Strassburg fl. c. 1210- . **CMLC 10**
See also DLB 138

Gould, Lois .... **CLC 4, 10**
See also CA 77-80; CANR 29; MTCW

Gourmont, Remy (-Marie-Charles) de 1858-1915 **TCLC 17**
See also CA 109; 150

Govier, Katherine 1948- .... **CLC 51**
See also CA 101; CANR 18, 40

Goyen, (Charles) William 1915-1983 . **CLC 5, 8, 14, 40**
See also AITN 2; CA 5-8R; 110; CANR 6; DLB 2; DLBY 83; INT CANR-6

Goytisolo, Juan 1931-**CLC 5, 10, 23; DAM MULT; HLC**
See also CA 85-88; CANR 32, 61; HW; MTCW

Gozzano, Guido 1883-1916 .... **PC 10**
See also CA 154; DLB 114

Gozzi, (Conte) Carlo 1720-1806 .... **NCLC 23**

Grabbe, Christian Dietrich 1801-1836 . **NCLC 2**
See also DLB 133

Grace, Patricia 1937- .... **CLC 56**

Gracian y Morales, Baltasar 1601-1658 .. **LC 15**

Gracq, Julien .... **CLC 11, 48**
See also Poirier, Louis
See also DLB 83

Grade, Chaim 1910-1982 .... **CLC 10**
See also CA 93-96; 107

Graduate of Oxford, A
See Ruskin, John

Grafton, Garth
See Duncan, Sara Jeannette

Graham, John
See Phillips, David Graham

Graham, Jorie 1951- .... **CLC 48**
See also CA 111; CANR 63; DLB 120

Graham, R(obert) B(ontine) Cunninghame
See Cunninghame Graham, R(obert) B(ontine)
See also DLB 98, 135, 174

Graham, Robert
See Haldeman, Joe (William)

Graham, Tom
See Lewis, (Harry) Sinclair

Graham, W(illiam) S(ydney) 1918-1986 **CLC 29**
See also CA 73-76; 118; DLB 20

Graham, Winston (Mawdsley) 1910- .... **CLC 23**
See also CA 49-52; CANR 2, 22, 45, 66; DLB 77

Grahame, Kenneth 1859-1932 ... **TCLC 64; DAB**
See also CA 108; 136; CLR 5; DLB 34, 141, 178; MAICYA; YABC 1

Grant, Skeeter
See Spiegelman, Art

Granville-Barker, Harley 1877-1946 ... **TCLC 2; DAM DRAM**
See also Barker, Harley Granville
See also CA 104

Grass, Guenter (Wilhelm) 1927- **CLC 1, 2, 4, 6, 11, 15, 22, 32, 49, 88; DA; DAB; DAC; DAM MST, NOV; WLC**
See also CA 13-16R; CANR 20; DLB 75, 124; MTCW

Gratton, Thomas
See Hulme, T(homas) E(rnest)

Grau, Shirley Ann 1929- ...... **CLC 4, 9; SSC 15**
See also CA 89-92; CANR 22; DLB 2; INT CANR-22; MTCW

Gravel, Fern
See Hall, James Norman

Graver, Elizabeth 1964- .... **CLC 70**
See also CA 135

Graves, Richard Perceval 1945- .... **CLC 44**
See also CA 65-68; CANR 9, 26, 51

Graves, Robert (von Ranke) 1895-1985 **CLC 1, 2, 6, 11, 39, 44, 45; DAB; DAC; DAM MST, POET; PC 6**
See also CA 5-8R; 117; CANR 5, 36; CDBLB 1914-1945; DLB 20, 100, 191; DLBY 85; MTCW; SATA 45

Graves, Valerie
See Bradley, Marion Zimmer

Gray, Alasdair (James) 1934- .... **CLC 41**
See also CA 126; CANR 47; DLB 194; INT 126; MTCW

Gray, Amlin 1946- .... **CLC 29**
See also CA 138

Gray, Francine du Plessix 1930- **CLC 22; DAM NOV**
See also BEST 90:3; CA 61-64; CAAS 2; CANR 11, 33; INT CANR-11; MTCW

Gray, John (Henry) 1866-1934 .... **TCLC 19**
See also CA 119; 162

Gray, Simon (James Holliday) 1936- **CLC 9, 14, 36**
See also AITN 1; CA 21-24R; CAAS 3; CANR 32; DLB 13; MTCW

Gray, Spalding 1941- **CLC 49; DAM POP; DC 7**
See also CA 128

Gray, Thomas 1716-1771 ... **LC 4, 40; DA; DAB; DAC; DAM MST; PC 2; WLC**
See also CDBLB 1660-1789; DLB 109

Grayson, David
See Baker, Ray Stannard

Grayson, Richard (A.) 1951- .... **CLC 38**
See also CA 85-88; CANR 14, 31, 57

Greeley, Andrew M(oran) 1928- . **CLC 28; DAM POP**
See also CA 5-8R; CAAS 7; CANR 7, 43; MTCW

Green, Anna Katharine 1846-1935 ..... **TCLC 63**
See also CA 112; 159

Green, Brian
See Card, Orson Scott

Green, Hannah
See Greenberg, Joanne (Goldenberg)

Green, Hannah 1927(?)-1996 .... **CLC 3**
See also CA 73-76; CANR 59

Green, Henry 1905-1973 .... **CLC 2, 13, 97**
See also Yorke, Henry Vincent
See also DLB 15

Green, Julian (Hartridge) 1900-
See Green, Julien
See also CA 21-24R; CANR 33; DLB 4, 72; MTCW

Green, Julien .... **CLC 3, 11, 77**
See also Green, Julian (Hartridge)

Green, Paul (Eliot) 1894-1981 .... **CLC 25; DAM DRAM**
See also AITN 1; CA 5-8R; 103; CANR 3; DLB 7, 9; DLBY 81

Greenberg, Ivan 1908-1973
See Rahv, Philip
See also CA 85-88

Greenberg, Joanne (Goldenberg) 1932- **CLC 7, 30**
See also AAYA 12; CA 5-8R; CANR 14, 32; SATA 25

Greenberg, Richard 1959(?)- .... **CLC 57**
See also CA 138

Greene, Bette 1934- .... **CLC 30**
See also AAYA 7; CA 53-56; CANR 4; CLR 2; JRDA; MAICYA; SAAS 16; SATA 8

Greene, Gael .... **CLC 8**
See also CA 13-16R; CANR 10

Greene, Graham (Henry) 1904-1991 **CLC 1, 3, 6, 9, 14, 18, 27, 37, 70, 72; DA; DAB; DAC; DAM MST, NOV; SSC 29; WLC**
See also AITN 2; CA 13-16R; 133; CANR 35, 61; CDBLB 1945-1960; DLB 13, 15, 77, 100, 162; DLBY 91; MTCW; SATA 20

Greene, Robert 1558-1592 .... **LC 41**
See also DLB 62, 167

Greer, Richard
See Silverberg, Robert

Gregor, Arthur 1923- .... **CLC 9**
See also CA 25-28R; CAAS 10; CANR 11; SATA 36

Gregor, Lee
See Pohl, Frederik

Gregory, Isabella Augusta (Persse) 1852-1932 **TCLC 1**
See also CA 104; DLB 10

Gregory, J. Dennis
See Williams, John A(lfred)

Grendon, Stephen
See Derleth, August (William)

Grenville, Kate 1950- .... **CLC 61**
See also CA 118; CANR 53

Grenville, Pelham
See Wodehouse, P(elham) G(renville)

Greve, Felix Paul (Berthold Friedrich) 1879-1948
See Grove, Frederick Philip
See also CA 104; 141; DAC; DAM MST

Grey, Zane 1872-1939 .... **TCLC 6; DAM POP**
See also CA 104; 132; DLB 9; MTCW

Grieg, (Johan) Nordahl (Brun) 1902-1943 **TCLC 10**
See also CA 107

Grieve, C(hristopher) M(urray) 1892-1978 **CLC 11, 19; DAM POET**
See also MacDiarmid, Hugh; Pteleon
See also CA 5-8R; 85-88; CANR 33; MTCW

Griffin, Gerald 1803-1840 .... **NCLC 7**
See also DLB 159

Griffin, John Howard 1920-1980 .... **CLC 68**
See also AITN 1; CA 1-4R; 101; CANR 2

Griffin, Peter 1942- .... **CLC 39**
See also CA 136

Griffith, D(avid Lewelyn) W(ark) 1875(?)-1948 **TCLC 68**
See also CA 119; 150

Griffith, Lawrence
See Griffith, D(avid Lewelyn) W(ark)

Griffiths, Trevor 1935- .... **CLC 13, 52**
See also CA 97-100; CANR 45; DLB 13

Griggs, Sutton Elbert 1872-1930(?) .... **TCLC 77**
See also CA 123; DLB 50

Grigson, Geoffrey (Edward Harvey) 1905-1985 **CLC 7, 39**
See also CA 25-28R; 118; CANR 20, 33; DLB 27; MTCW

Grillparzer, Franz 1791-1872 .... **NCLC 1**
See also DLB 133

Grimble, Reverend Charles James
See Eliot, T(homas) S(tearns)

Grimke, Charlotte L(ottie) Forten 1837(?)-1914
See Forten, Charlotte L.
See also BW 1; CA 117; 124; DAM MULT, POET

Grimm, Jacob Ludwig Karl 1785-1863 . **NCLC 3**
See also DLB 90; MAICYA; SATA 22

Grimm, Wilhelm Karl 1786-1859 .... **NCLC 3**
See also DLB 90; MAICYA; SATA 22

Grimmelshausen, Johann Jakob Christoffel von 1621-1676 .... **LC 6**
See also DLB 168

Grindel, Eugene 1895-1952
See Eluard, Paul
See also CA 104

Grisham, John 1955- .... **CLC 84; DAM POP**
See also AAYA 14; CA 138; CANR 47

Grossman, David 1954- .... **CLC 67**
See also CA 138

Grossman, Vasily (Semenovich) 1905-1964 **CLC 41**
See also CA 124; 130; MTCW

Grove, Frederick Philip .... **TCLC 4**
See also Greve, Felix Paul (Berthold Friedrich)
See also DLB 92

Grubb
See Crumb, R(obert)

Grumbach, Doris (Isaac) 1918- . **CLC 13, 22, 64**
See also CA 5-8R; CAAS 2; CANR 9, 42; INT CANR-9

Grundtvig, Nicolai Frederik Severin 1783-1872 **NCLC 1**

Grunge
See Crumb, R(obert)

Grunwald, Lisa 1959- .... **CLC 44**
See also CA 120

Guare, John 1938-**CLC 8, 14, 29, 67; DAM DRAM**
See also CA 73-76; CANR 21; DLB 7; MTCW

Gudjonsson, Halldor Kiljan 1902-1998
See Laxness, Halldor
See also CA 103; 164

Guenter, Erich
See Eich, Guenter

Guest, Barbara 1920- .... **CLC 34**
See also CA 25-28R; CANR 11, 44; DLB 5, 193

Guest, Judith (Ann) 1936-**CLC 8, 30; DAM NOV, POP**
See also AAYA 7; CA 77-80; CANR 15; INT CANR-15; MTCW

Guevara, Che .... **CLC 87; HLC**
See also Guevara (Serna), Ernesto

Guevara (Serna), Ernesto 1928-1967
See Guevara, Che
See also CA 127; 111; CANR 56; DAM MULT; HW

Guild, Nicholas M. 1944- .... **CLC 33**
See also CA 93-96

Guillemin, Jacques
See Sartre, Jean-Paul

Guillen, Jorge 1893-1984 **CLC 11; DAM MULT, POET**
See also CA 89-92; 112; DLB 108; HW

Guillen, Nicolas (Cristobal) 1902-1989 **CLC 48, 79; BLC; DAM MST, MULT, POET; HLC**
See also BW 2; CA 116; 125; 129; HW

Guillevic, (Eugene) 1907- .... **CLC 33**
See also CA 93-96

Guillois
See Desnos, Robert

Guillois, Valentin
See Desnos, Robert

Guiney, Louise Imogen 1861-1920 ...... **TCLC 41**
See also CA 160; DLB 54

Guiraldes, Ricardo (Guillermo) 1886-1927**TCLC 39**
See also CA 131; HW; MTCW

Gumilev, Nikolai (Stepanovich) 1886-1921 **TCLC 60**
See also CA 165

Gunesekera, Romesh 1954- .... **CLC 91**
See also CA 159

Gunn, Bill .... **CLC 5**
See also Gunn, William Harrison
See also DLB 38

Gunn, Thom(son William) 1929-**CLC 3, 6, 18, 32, 81; DAM POET**
See also CA 17-20R; CANR 9, 33; CDBLB 1960 to Present; DLB 27; INT CANR-33; MTCW

Gunn, William Harrison 1934(?)-1989
See Gunn, Bill
See also AITN 1; BW 1; CA 13-16R; 128; CANR 12, 25

Gunnars, Kristjana 1948- .... **CLC 69**
See also CA 113; DLB 60

Gurdjieff, G(eorgei) I(vanovich) 1877(?)-1949 **TCLC 71**
See also CA 157

Gurganus, Allan 1947- ...... **CLC 70; DAM POP**
See also BEST 90:1; CA 135

Gurney, A(lbert) R(amsdell), Jr. 1930- **CLC 32, 50, 54; DAM DRAM**
See also CA 77-80; CANR 32, 64

Gurney, Ivor (Bertie) 1890-1937 .... **TCLC 33**

Gurney, Peter
See Gurney, A(lbert) R(amsdell), Jr.

Guro, Elena 1877-1913 .... **TCLC 56**

Gustafson, James M(oody) 1925- .... **CLC 100**
See also CA 25-28R; CANR 37

Gustafson, Ralph (Barker) 1909- .... **CLC 36**
See also CA 21-24R; CANR 8, 45; DLB 88

Gut, Gom
See Simenon, Georges (Jacques Christian)

Guterson, David 1956- .... **CLC 91**
See also CA 132

Guthrie, A(lfred) B(ertram), Jr. 1901-1991 **CLC 23**
See also CA 57-60; 134; CANR 24; DLB 6; SATA 62; SATA-Obit 67

Guthrie, Isobel
See Grieve, C(hristopher) M(urray)

Guthrie, Woodrow Wilson 1912-1967
See Guthrie, Woody
See also CA 113; 93-96

Guthrie, Woody .... **CLC 35**
See also Guthrie, Woodrow Wilson

Guy, Rosa (Cuthbert) 1928- .... **CLC 26**
See also AAYA 4; BW 2; CA 17-20R; CANR 14, 34; CLR 13; DLB 33; JRDA; MAICYA; SATA 14, 62

Gwendolyn
See Bennett, (Enoch) Arnold

H. D. .... **CLC 3, 8, 14, 31, 34, 73; PC 5**
See also Doolittle, Hilda

H. de V.
See Buchan, John

Haavikko, Paavo Juhani 1931- .... **CLC 18, 34**
See also CA 106

Habbema, Koos
See Heijermans, Herman

Habermas, Juergen 1929- .... **CLC 104**
See also CA 109

Habermas, Jurgen
See Habermas, Juergen

Hacker, Marilyn 1942-**CLC 5, 9, 23, 72, 91; DAM POET**
See also CA 77-80; CANR 68; DLB 120

Haeckel, Ernst Heinrich (Philipp August) 1834-1919 .... **TCLC 80**
See also CA 157

Haggard, H(enry) Rider 1856-1925 ..... **TCLC 11**
See also CA 108; 148; DLB 70, 156, 174, 178; SATA 16

Hagiosy, L.
See Larbaud, Valery (Nicolas)

Hagiwara Sakutaro 1886-1942 **TCLC 60; PC 18**

Haig, Fenil
See Ford, Ford Madox

Haig-Brown, Roderick (Langmere) 1908-1976 **CLC 21**
See also CA 5-8R; 69-72; CANR 4, 38; CLR 31; DLB 88; MAICYA; SATA 12

Hailey, Arthur 1920- .. **CLC 5; DAM NOV, POP**
See also AITN 2; BEST 90:3; CA 1-4R; CANR 2, 36; DLB 88; DLBY 82; MTCW

Hailey, Elizabeth Forsythe 1938- .... **CLC 40**
See also CA 93-96; CAAS 1; CANR 15, 48; INT CANR-15

Haines, John (Meade) 1924- .... **CLC 58**
See also CA 17-20R; CANR 13, 34; DLB 5

Hakluyt, Richard 1552-1616 .... **LC 31**

Haldeman, Joe (William) 1943- .... **CLC 61**
See also CA 53-56; CAAS 25; CANR 6; DLB 8; INT CANR-6

Haley, Alex(ander Murray Palmer) 1921-1992 **CLC 8, 12, 76; BLC; DA; DAB; DAC; DAM MST, MULT, POP**
See also BW 2; CA 77-80; 136; CANR 61; DLB 38; MTCW

Haliburton, Thomas Chandler 1796-1865 **NCLC 15**
See also DLB 11, 99

Hall, Donald (Andrew, Jr.) 1928- **CLC 1, 13, 37, 59; DAM POET**
See also CA 5-8R; CAAS 7; CANR 2, 44, 64; DLB 5; SATA 23, 97

Hall, Frederic Sauser
See Sauser-Hall, Frederic

Hall, James
See Kuttner, Henry

Hall, James Norman 1887-1951 .... **TCLC 23**
See also CA 123; SATA 21

Hall, (Marguerite) Radclyffe 1886-1943 **TCLC 12**
See also CA 110; 150

Hall, Rodney 1935- .... **CLC 51**
See also CA 109

Halleck, Fitz-Greene 1790-1867 .... **NCLC 47**
See also DLB 3

Halliday, Michael
See Creasey, John

Halpern, Daniel 1945- .... **CLC 14**
See also CA 33-36R

Hamburger, Michael (Peter Leopold) 1924- **CLC 5, 14**
See also CA 5-8R; CAAS 4; CANR 2, 47; DLB 27

Hamill, Pete 1935- .... **CLC 10**
See also CA 25-28R; CANR 18

Hamilton, Alexander 1755(?)-1804 .... **NCLC 49**
See also DLB 37

Hamilton, Clive
See Lewis, C(live) S(taples)

Hamilton, Edmond 1904-1977 .... **CLC 1**
See also CA 1-4R; CANR 3; DLB 8

Hamilton, Eugene (Jacob) Lee
See Lee-Hamilton, Eugene (Jacob)

Hamilton, Franklin
See Silverberg, Robert

Hamilton, Gail
See Corcoran, Barbara

Hamilton, Mollie
See Kaye, M(ary) M(argaret)

Hamilton, (Anthony Walter) Patrick 1904-1962 **CLC 51**
See also CA 113; DLB 10

Hamilton, Virginia 1936- **CLC 26; DAM MULT**
See also AAYA 2, 21; BW 2; CA 25-28R; CANR 20, 37; CLR 1, 11, 40; DLB 33, 52; INT CANR-20; JRDA; MAICYA; MTCW; SATA 4, 56, 79

Hammett, (Samuel) Dashiell 1894-1961 **CLC 3, 5, 10, 19, 47; SSC 17**
See also AITN 1; CA 81-84; CANR 42; CDALB 1929-1941; DLBD 6; DLBY 96; MTCW

Hammon, Jupiter 1711(?)-1800(?) **NCLC 5; BLC; DAM MULT, POET; PC 16**
See also DLB 31, 50

Hammond, Keith
See Kuttner, Henry

Hamner, Earl (Henry), Jr. 1923- .... **CLC 12**
See also AITN 2; CA 73-76; DLB 6

Hampton, Christopher (James) 1946- .... **CLC 4**
See also CA 25-28R; DLB 13; MTCW

Hamsun, Knut .... **TCLC 2, 14, 49**
See also Pedersen, Knut

Handke, Peter 1942- **CLC 5, 8, 10, 15, 38; DAM DRAM, NOV**
See also CA 77-80; CANR 33; DLB 85, 124; MTCW

Hanley, James 1901-1985 .... **CLC 3, 5, 8, 13**
See also CA 73-76; 117; CANR 36; DLB 191; MTCW

Hannah, Barry 1942- .... **CLC 23, 38, 90**
See also CA 108; 110; CANR 43, 68; DLB 6; INT 110; MTCW

Hannon, Ezra
See Hunter, Evan

Hansberry, Lorraine (Vivian) 1930-1965 **CLC 17, 62; BLC; DA; DAB; DAC; DAM DRAM, MST, MULT; DC 2**
See also AAYA 25; BW 1; CA 109; 25-28R; CABS 3; CANR 58; CDALB 1941-1968; DLB 7, 38; MTCW

Hansen, Joseph 1923- .... **CLC 38**
See also CA 29-32R; CAAS 17; CANR 16, 44, 66; INT CANR-16

Hansen, Martin A. 1909-1955 .... **TCLC 32**

Hanson, Kenneth O(stlin) 1922- .... **CLC 13**
See also CA 53-56; CANR 7

Hardwick, Elizabeth 1916- **CLC 13; DAM NOV**
See also CA 5-8R; CANR 3, 32; DLB 6; MTCW

Haywood, Eliza (Fowler) 1693(?)-1756 .... **LC 1**

Hazlitt, William 1778-1830 .... **NCLC 29**
See also DLB 110, 158

Hazzard, Shirley 1931- .... **CLC 18**
See also CA 9-12R; CANR 4; DLBY 82; MTCW

Head, Bessie 1937-1986**CLC 25, 67; BLC; DAM MULT**
See also BW 2; CA 29-32R; 119; CANR 25; DLB 117; MTCW

Headon, (Nicky) Topper 1956(?)- .... **CLC 30**

Heaney, Seamus (Justin) 1939-**CLC 5, 7, 14, 25, 37, 74, 91; DAB; DAM POET; PC 18; WLCS**
See also CA 85-88; CANR 25, 48; CDBLB 1960 to Present; DLB 40; DLBY 95; MTCW

Hearn, (Patricio) Lafcadio (Tessima Carlos) 1850-1904 .... **TCLC 9**
See also CA 105; DLB 12, 78

Hearne, Vicki 1946- .... **CLC 56**
See also CA 139

Hearon, Shelby 1931- .... **CLC 63**
See also AITN 2; CA 25-28R; CANR 18, 48

Heat-Moon, William Least .... **CLC 29**
See also Trogdon, William (Lewis)
See also AAYA 9

Hebbel, Friedrich 1813-1863 .... **NCLC 43; DAM DRAM**
See also DLB 129

Hebert, Anne 1916- **CLC 4, 13, 29; DAC; DAM MST, POET**
See also CA 85-88; DLB 68; MTCW

Hecht, Anthony (Evan) 1923-**CLC 8, 13, 19; DAM POET**
See also CA 9-12R; CANR 6; DLB 5, 169

Hecht, Ben 1894-1964 .... **CLC 8**
See also CA 85-88; DLB 7, 9, 25, 26, 28, 86

Hedayat, Sadeq 1903-1951 .... **TCLC 21**
See also CA 120

Hegel, Georg Wilhelm Friedrich 1770-1831 **NCLC 46**
See also DLB 90

Heidegger, Martin 1889-1976 .... **CLC 24**
See also CA 81-84; 65-68; CANR 34; MTCW

Heidenstam, (Carl Gustaf) Verner von 1859-1940 **TCLC 5**
See also CA 104

Heifner, Jack 1946- .... **CLC 11**
See also CA 105; CANR 47

Heijermans, Herman 1864-1924 .... **TCLC 24**
See also CA 123

Heilbrun, Carolyn G(old) 1926- .... **CLC 25**
See also CA 45-48; CANR 1, 28, 58

Heine, Heinrich 1797-1856 .... **NCLC 4, 54**
See also DLB 90

Heinemann, Larry (Curtiss) 1944- .... **CLC 50**
See also CA 110; CAAS 21; CANR 31; DLBD 9; INT CANR-31

Heiney, Donald (William) 1921-1993
See Harris, MacDonald
See also CA 1-4R; 142; CANR 3, 58

Heinlein, Robert A(nson) 1907-1988**CLC 1, 3, 8, 14, 26, 55; DAM POP**
See also AAYA 17; CA 1-4R; 125; CANR 1, 20, 53; DLB 8; JRDA; MAICYA; MTCW; SATA 9, 69; SATA-Obit 56

Helforth, John
See Doolittle, Hilda

Hellenhofferu, Vojtech Kapristian z
See Hasek, Jaroslav (Matej Frantisek)

Heller, Joseph 1923- . **CLC 1, 3, 5, 8, 11, 36, 63; DA; DAB; DAC; DAM MST, NOV, POP; WLC**
See also AAYA 24; AITN 1; CA 5-8R; CABS 1; CANR 8, 42, 66; DLB 2, 28; DLBY 80; INT CANR-8; MTCW

Hellman, Lillian (Florence) 1906-1984**CLC 2, 4, 8, 14, 18, 34, 44, 52; DAM DRAM; DC 1**
See also AITN 1, 2; CA 13-16R; 112; CANR 33; DLB 7; DLBY 84; MTCW

Helprin, Mark 1947- .. **CLC 7, 10, 22, 32; DAM NOV, POP**
See also CA 81-84; CANR 47, 64; DLBY 85; MTCW

Helvetius, Claude-Adrien 1715-1771 .... **LC 26**

Helyar, Jane Penelope Josephine 1933-
See Poole, Josephine
See also CA 21-24R; CANR 10, 26; SATA 82

Hemans, Felicia 1793-1835 .... **NCLC 29**
See also DLB 96

Hemingway, Ernest (Miller) 1899-1961**CLC 1, 3, 6, 8, 10, 13, 19, 30, 34, 39, 41, 44, 50, 61, 80; DA; DAB; DAC; DAM MST, NOV; SSC 25; WLC**
See also AAYA 19; CA 77-80; CANR 34; CDALB 1917-1929; DLB 4, 9, 102; DLBD 1, 15, 16; DLBY 81, 87, 96; MTCW

Hempel, Amy 1951- .... **CLC 39**
See also CA 118; 137

Henderson, F. C.
See Mencken, H(enry) L(ouis)

Henderson, Sylvia
See Ashton-Warner, Sylvia (Constance)

Henderson, Zenna (Chlarson) 1917-1983**SSC 29**
See also CA 1-4R; 133; CANR 1; DLB 8; SATA 5

Henley, Beth **CLC 23; DC 6**
See also Henley, Elizabeth Becker
See also CABS 3; DLBY 86

Henley, Elizabeth Becker 1952-
See Henley, Beth
See also CA 107; CANR 32; DAM DRAM, MST; MTCW

Henley, William Ernest 1849-1903 **TCLC 8**
See also CA 105; DLB 19

Hennissart, Martha
See Lathen, Emma
See also CA 85-88; CANR 64

Henry, O. .... **TCLC 1, 19; SSC 5; WLC**
See also Porter, William Sydney

Henry, Patrick 1736-1799 .... **LC 25**

Henryson, Robert 1430(?)-1506(?) .... **LC 20**
See also DLB 146

Henry VIII 1491-1547 .... **LC 10**

Henschke, Alfred
See Klabund

Hentoff, Nat(han Irving) 1925- .... **CLC 26**
See also AAYA 4; CA 1-4R; CAAS 6; CANR 5, 25; CLR 1; INT CANR-25; JRDA; MAICYA; SATA 42, 69; SATA-Brief 27

Heppenstall, (John) Rayner 1911-1981 . **CLC 10**
See also CA 1-4R; 103; CANR 29

Heraclitus c. 540B.C.-c. 450B.C. .... **CMLC 22**
See also DLB 176

Herbert, Frank (Patrick) 1920-1986**CLC 12, 23, 35, 44, 85; DAM POP**
See also AAYA 21; CA 53-56; 118; CANR 5, 43; DLB 8; INT CANR-5; MTCW; SATA 9, 37; SATA-Obit 47

Herbert, George 1593-1633 . **LC 24; DAB; DAM POET; PC 4**
See also CDBLB Before 1660; DLB 126

Herbert, Zbigniew 1924-**CLC 9, 43; DAM POET**
See also CA 89-92; CANR 36; MTCW

Herbst, Josephine (Frey) 1897-1969 ..... **CLC 34**
See also CA 5-8R; 25-28R; DLB 9

Hergesheimer, Joseph 1880-1954 .... **TCLC 11**
See also CA 109; DLB 102, 9

Herlihy, James Leo 1927-1993 .... **CLC 6**
See also CA 1-4R; 143; CANR 2

Hermogenes fl. c. 175- .... **CMLC 6**

Hernandez, Jose 1834-1886 .... **NCLC 17**

Herodotus c. 484B.C.-429B.C. .... **CMLC 17**
See also DLB 176

Herrick, Robert 1591-1674 ... **LC 13; DA; DAB; DAC; DAM MST, POP; PC 9**
See also DLB 126

Herring, Guilles
See Somerville, Edith

Herriot, James 1916-1995 **CLC 12; DAM POP**
See also Wight, James Alfred
See also AAYA 1; CA 148; CANR 40; SA TA 86

Herrmann, Dorothy 1941- **CLC 44**
See also CA 107

Herrmann, Taffy
See Herrmann, Dorothy

Hersey, John (Richard) 1914-1993 **CLC 1, 2, 7, 9, 40, 81, 97; DAM POP**
See also CA 17-20R; 140; CANR 33; DLB 6, 185; MTCW; SATA 25; SATA-Obit 76

Herzen, Aleksandr Ivanovich 1812-1870 . **NCLC 10, 61**

Herzl, Theodor 1860-1904 .... **TCLC 36**

Herzog, Werner 1942- .... **CLC 16**
See also CA 89-92

Hesiod c. 8th cent. B.C.- .... **CMLC 5**
See also DLB 176

Hesse, Hermann 1877-1962 **CLC 1, 2, 3, 6, 11, 17, 25, 69; DA; DAB; DAC; DAM MST, NOV; SSC 9; WLC**
See also CA 17-18; CAP 2; DLB 66; MTCW; SATA 50

Hewes, Cady
See De Voto, Bernard (Augustine)

Heyen, William 1940- .... **CLC 13, 18**
See also CA 33-36R; CAAS 9; DLB 5

Heyerdahl, Thor 1914- .... **CLC 26**
See also CA 5-8R; CANR 5, 22, 66; MTCW; SATA 2, 52

Heym, Georg (Theodor Franz Arthur) 1887-1912 **TCLC 9**
See also CA 106

Heym, Stefan 1913- .... **CLC 41**
See also CA 9-12R; CANR 4; DLB 69

Heyse, Paul (Johann Ludwig von) 1830-1914 **TCLC 8**
See also CA 104; DLB 129

Heyward, (Edwin) DuBose 1885-1940 .. **TCLC 59**
See also CA 108; 157; DLB 7, 9, 45; SATA 21

Hibbert, Eleanor Alice Burford 1906-1993 **CLC 7; DAM POP**
See also BEST 90:4; CA 17-20R; 140; CANR 9, 28, 59; SATA 2; SATA-Obit 74

Hichens, Robert (Smythe) 1864-1950 .. **TCLC 64**
See also CA 162; DLB 153

Higgins, George V(incent) 1939- **CLC 4, 7, 10, 18**
See also CA 77-80; CAAS 5; CANR 17, 51; DLB 2; DLBY 81; INT CANR-17; MTCW

Higginson, Thomas Wentworth 1823-1911 **TCLC 36**
See also CA 162; DLB 1, 64

Highet, Helen
See MacInnes, Helen (Clark)

Highsmith, (Mary) Patricia 1921-1995 **CLC 2, 4, 14, 42, 102; DAM NOV, POP**
See also CA 1-4R; 147; CANR 1, 20, 48, 62; MTCW

Highwater, Jamake (Mamake) 1942(?)- **CLC 12**
See also AAYA 7; CA 65-68; CAAS 7; CANR 10, 34; CLR 17; DLB 52; DLBY 85; JRDA; MAICYA; SATA 32, 69; SATA-Brief 30

Highway, Tomson 1951- **CLC 92; DAC; DAM MULT**
See also CA 151; NNAL

Higuchi, Ichiyo 1872-1896 .... **NCLC 49**

Hijuelos, Oscar 1951- **CLC 65; DAM MULT, POP; HLC**
See also AAYA 25; BEST 90:1; CA 123; CANR 50; DLB 145; HW

Hikmet, Nazim 1902(?)-1963 .... **CLC 40**
See also CA 141; 93-96

Hildegard von Bingen 1098-1179 .... **CMLC 20**
See also DLB 148

Hildesheimer, Wolfgang 1916-1991 ...... **CLC 49**
See also CA 101; 135; DLB 69, 124

Hill, Geoffrey (William) 1932- **CLC 5, 8, 18, 45; DAM POET**
See also CA 81-84; CANR 21; CDBLB 1960 to Present; DLB 40; MTCW

Hill, George Roy 1921- .... **CLC 26**
See also CA 110; 122

Hill, John
See Koontz, Dean R(ay)

Hill, Susan (Elizabeth) 1942- **CLC 4; DAB; DAM MST, NOV**
See also CA 33-36R; CANR 29; DLB 14, 139; MTCW

Hillerman, Tony 1925- .... **CLC 62; DAM POP**
See also AAYA 6; BEST 89:1; CA 29-32R; CANR 21, 42, 65; SATA 6

Hillesum, Etty 1914-1943 .... **TCLC 49**
See also CA 137

Hilliard, Noel (Harvey) 1929- .... **CLC 15**
See also CA 9-12R; CANR 7

Hillis, Rick 1956- .... **CLC 66**
See also CA 134

Hilton, James 1900-1954 .... **TCLC 21**
See also CA 108; DLB 34, 77; SATA 34

Himes, Chester (Bomar) 1909-1984 **CLC 2, 4, 7, 18, 58, 108; BLC; DAM MULT**
See also BW 2; CA 25-28R; 114; CANR 22; DLB 2, 76, 143; MTCW

Hinde, Thomas .... **CLC 6, 11**
See also Chitty, Thomas Willes

Hindin, Nathan
See Bloch, Robert (Albert)

Hine, (William) Daryl 1936- .... **CLC 15**
See also CA 1-4R; CAAS 15; CANR 1, 20; DLB 60

Hinkson, Katharine Tynan
See Tynan, Katharine

Hinton, S(usan) E(loise) 1950- **CLC 30; DA; DAB; DAC; DAM MST, NOV**
See also AAYA 2; CA 81-84; CANR 32, 62; CLR 3, 23; JRDA; MAICYA; MTCW; SATA 19, 58

Hippius, Zinaida .... **TCLC 9**
See also Gippius, Zinaida (Nikolayevna)

Hiraoka, Kimitake 1925-1970
See Mishima, Yukio
See also CA 97-100; 29-32R; DAM DRAM; MTCW

Hirsch, E(ric) D(onald), Jr. 1928- .... **CLC 79**
See also CA 25-28R; CANR 27, 51; DLB 67; INT CANR-27; MTCW

Hirsch, Edward 1950- .... **CLC 31, 50**
See also CA 104; CANR 20, 42; DLB 120

Hitchcock, Alfred (Joseph) 1899-1980 .. **CLC 16**
See also AAYA 22; CA 159; 97-100; SATA 27; SATA-Obit 24

Hitler, Adolf 1889-1945 .... **TCLC 53**
See also CA 117; 147

Hoagland, Edward 1932- .... **CLC 28**
See also CA 1-4R; CANR 2, 31, 57; DLB 6; SATA 51

Hoban, Russell (Conwell) 1925- **CLC 7, 25; DAM NOV**
See also CA 5-8R; CANR 23, 37, 66; CLR 3; DLB 52; MAICYA; MTCW; SATA 1, 40, 78

Hobbes, Thomas 1588-1679 .... **LC 36**
See also DLB 151

Hobbs, Perry
See Blackmur, R(ichard) P(almer)

Hobson, Laura Z(ametkin) 1900-1986 **CLC 7, 25**
See also CA 17-20R; 118; CANR 55; DLB 28; SATA 52

Hochhuth, Rolf 1931- **CLC 4, 11, 18; DAM DRAM**
See also CA 5-8R; CANR 33; DLB 124; MTCW

Hochman, Sandra 1936- .... **CLC 3, 8**
See also CA 5-8R; DLB 5

Hochwaelder, Fritz 1911-1986 .... **CLC 36; DAM DRAM**
See also CA 29-32R; 120; CANR 42; MTCW

Hochwalder, Fritz
See Hochwaelder, Fritz

Hocking, Mary (Eunice) 1921- .... **CLC 13**
See also CA 101; CANR 18, 40

Hodgins, Jack 1938- .... **CLC 23**
See also CA 93-96; DLB 60

Hodgson, William Hope 1877(?)-1918 . **TCLC 13**
See also CA 111; 164; DLB 70, 153, 156, 178

Hoeg, Peter 1957- .... **CLC 95**
See also CA 151

Hoffman, Alice 1952- .... **CLC 51; DAM NOV**
See also CA 77-80; CANR 34, 66; MTCW

Hoffman, Daniel (Gerard) 1923- . **CLC 6, 13, 23**
See also CA 1-4R; CANR 4; DLB 5

Hoffman, Stanley 1944- .... **CLC 5**
See also CA 77-80

Hoffman, William M(oses) 1939- .... **CLC 40**
See also CA 57-60; CANR 11

Hoffmann, E(rnst) T(heodor) A(madeus) 1776-1822 **NCLC 2; SSC 13**
See also DLB 90; SATA 27

Hofmann, Gert 1931- .... **CLC 54**
See also CA 128

Howe, Tina 1937- .... **CLC 48**
See also CA 109

Howell, James 1594(?)-1666 .... **LC 13**
See also DLB 151

Howells, W. D.
See Howells, William Dean

Howells, William D.
See Howells, William Dean

Howells, William Dean 1837-1920**TCLC 7, 17, 41**
See also CA 104; 134; CDALB 1865-1917; DLB 12, 64, 74, 79, 189

Howes, Barbara 1914-1996 .... **CLC 15**
See also CA 9-12R; 151; CAAS 3; CANR 53; SATA 5

Hrabal, Bohumil 1914-1997 .... **CLC 13, 67**
See also CA 106; 156; CAAS 12; CANR 57

Hsun, Lu
See Lu Hsun

Hubbard, L(afayette) Ron(ald) 1911-1986**CLC 43; DAM POP**
See also CA 77-80; 118; CANR 52

Huch, Ricarda (Octavia) 1864-1947 ..... **TCLC 13**
See also CA 111; DLB 66

Huddle, David 1942- .... **CLC 49**
See also CA 57-60; CAAS 20; DLB 130

Hudson, Jeffrey
See Crichton, (John) Michael

Hudson, W(illiam) H(enry) 1841-1922 **TCLC 29**
See also CA 115; DLB 98, 153, 174; SATA 35

Hueffer, Ford Madox
See Ford, Ford Madox

Hughart, Barry 1934- .... **CLC 39**
See also CA 137

Hughes, Colin
See Creasey, John

Hughes, David (John) 1930- .... **CLC 48**
See also CA 116; 129; DLB 14

Hughes, Edward James
See Hughes, Ted
See also DAM MST, POET

Hughes, (James) Langston 1902-1967 **CLC 1, 5, 10, 15, 35, 44, 108; BLC; DA; DAB; DAC; DAM DRAM, MST, MULT, POET; DC 3; PC 1; SSC 6; WLC**
See also AAYA 12; BW 1; CA 1-4R; 25-28R; CANR 1, 34; CDALB 1929-1941; CLR 17; DLB 4, 7, 48, 51, 86; JRDA; MAICYA; MTCW; SATA 4, 33

Hughes, Richard (Arthur Warren) 1900-1976 **CLC 1, 11; DAM NOV**
See also CA 5-8R; 65-68; CANR 4; DLB 15, 161; MTCW; SATA 8; SATA-Obit 25

Hughes, Ted 1930- .... **CLC 2, 4, 9, 14, 37; DAB; DAC; PC 7**
See also Hughes, Edward James
See also CA 1-4R; CANR 1, 33, 66; CLR 3; DLB 40, 161; MAICYA; MTCW; SATA 49; SATA-Brief 27

Hugo, Richard F(ranklin) 1923-1982 **CLC 6, 18, 32; DAM POET**
See also CA 49-52; 108; CANR 3; DLB 5

Hugo, Victor (Marie) 1802-1885**NCLC 3, 10, 21; DA; DAB; DAC; DAM DRAM, MST, NOV, POET; PC 17; WLC**
See also DLB 119, 192; SATA 47

Huidobro, Vicente
See Huidobro Fernandez, Vicente Garcia

Huidobro Fernandez, Vicente Garcia 1893-1948 **TCLC 31**
See also CA 131; HW

Hulme, Keri 1947- .... **CLC 39**
See also CA 125; INT 125

Hulme, T(homas) E(rnest) 1883-1917 .. **TCLC 21**
See also CA 117; DLB 19

Hume, David 1711-1776 .... **LC 7**
See also DLB 104

Humphrey, William 1924-1997 .... **CLC 45**
See also CA 77-80; 160; CANR 68; DLB 6

Humphreys, Emyr Owen 1919- .... **CLC 47**
See also CA 5-8R; CANR 3, 24; DLB 15

Humphreys, Josephine 1945- .... **CLC 34, 57**
See also CA 121; 127; INT 127

Huneker, James Gibbons 1857-1921 ... **TCLC 65**
See also DLB 71

Hungerford, Pixie
See Brinsmead, H(esba) F(ay)

Hunt, E(verette) Howard, (Jr.) 1918- .... **CLC 3**
See also AITN 1; CA 45-48; CANR 2, 47

Hunt, Kyle
See Creasey, John

Hunt, (James Henry) Leigh 1784-1859 **NCLC 1; DAM POET**

Hunt, Marsha 1946- .... **CLC 70**
See also BW 2; CA 143

Hunt, Violet 1866-1942 .... **TCLC 53**
See also DLB 162

Hunter, E. Waldo
See Sturgeon, Theodore (Hamilton)

Hunter, Evan 1926- **CLC 11, 31; DAM POP**
See also CA 5-8R; CANR 5, 38, 62; DLBY 82; INT CANR-5; MTCW; SATA 25

Hunter, Kristin (Eggleston) 1931- **CLC 35**
See also AITN 1; BW 1; CA 13-16R; CANR 13; CLR 3; DLB 33; INT CANR-13; MAICYA; SAAS 10; SATA 12

Hunter, Mollie 1922- **CLC 21**
See also McIlwraith, Maureen Mollie Hunter
See also AAYA 13; CANR 37; CLR 25; DLB 161; JRDA; MAICYA; SAAS 7; SATA 54

Hunter, Robert (?)-1734 .... **LC 7**

Hurston, Zora Neale 1903-1960 . **CLC 7, 30, 61; BLC; DA; DAC; DAM MST, MULT, NOV; SSC 4; WLCS**
See also AAYA 15; BW 1; CA 85-88; CANR 61; DLB 51, 86; MTCW

Huston, John (Marcellus) 1906-1987 .... **CLC 20**
See also CA 73-76; 123; CANR 34; DLB 26

Hustvedt, Siri 1955- .... **CLC 76**
See also CA 137

Hutten, Ulrich von 1488-1523 .... **LC 16**
See also DLB 179

Huxley, Aldous (Leonard) 1894-1963**CLC 1, 3, 4, 5, 8, 11, 18, 35, 79; DA; DAB; DAC; DAM MST, NOV; WLC**
See also AAYA 11; CA 85-88; CANR 44; CDBLB 1914-1945; DLB 36, 100, 162, 195; MTCW; SATA 63

Huxley, T. H. 1825-1895 .... **NCLC 67**
See also DLB 57

Huysmans, Joris-Karl 1848-1907 ... **TCLC 7, 69**
See also CA 104; 165; DLB 123

Hwang, David Henry 1957-**CLC 55; DAM DRAM; DC 4**
See also CA 127; 132; INT 132

Hyde, Anthony 1946- .... **CLC 42**
See also CA 136

Hyde, Margaret O(ldroyd) 1917- .... **CLC 21**
See also CA 1-4R; CANR 1, 36; CLR 23; JRDA; MAICYA; SAAS 8; SATA 1, 42, 76

Hynes, James 1956(?)- .... **CLC 65**
See also CA 164

Ian, Janis 1951- .... **CLC 21**
See also CA 105

Ibanez, Vicente Blasco
See Blasco Ibanez, Vicente

Ibarguengoitia, Jorge 1928-1983 .... **CLC 37**
See also CA 124; 113; HW

Ibsen, Henrik (Johan) 1828-1906 **TCLC 2, 8, 16, 37, 52; DA; DAB; DAC; DAM DRAM, MST; DC 2; WLC**
See also CA 104; 141

Ibuse Masuji 1898-1993 .... **CLC 22**
See also CA 127; 141; DLB 180

Ichikawa, Kon 1915- .... **CLC 20**
See also CA 121

Idle, Eric 1943- **CLC 21**
See also Monty Python
See also CA 116; CANR 35

Ignatow, David 1914-1997 **CLC 4, 7, 14, 40**
See also CA 9-12R; 162; CAAS 3; CANR 31, 57; DLB 5

Ihimaera, Witi 1944- **CLC 46**
See also CA 77-80

Ilf, Ilya .... **TCLC 21**
See also Fainzilberg, Ilya Arnoldovich

Illyes, Gyula 1902-1983 .... **PC 16**
See also CA 114; 109

Immermann, Karl (Lebrecht) 1796-1840**NCLC 4, 49**
See also DLB 133

Inchbald, Elizabeth 1753-1821 .... **NCLC 62**
See also DLB 39, 89

Inclan, Ramon (Maria) del Valle
See Valle-Inclan, Ramon (Maria) del

Infante, G(uillermo) Cabrera
See Cabrera Infante, G(uillermo)

Ingalls, Rachel (Holmes) 1940- .... **CLC 42**
See also CA 123; 127

Ingamells, Rex 1913-1955 .... **TCLC 35**

Inge, William (Motter) 1913-1973 **CLC 1, 8, 19; DAM DRAM**
See also CA 9-12R; CDALB 1941-1968; DLB 7; MTCW

Ingelow, Jean 1820-1897 .... **NCLC 39**
See also DLB 35, 163; SATA 33

Ingram, Willis J.
See Harris, Mark

Innaurato, Albert (F.) 1948(?)- .... **CLC 21, 60**
See also CA 115; 122; INT 122

Innes, Michael
See Stewart, J(ohn) I(nnes) M(ackintosh)

Innis, Harold Adams 1894-1952 .... **TCLC 77**
See also DLB 88

Ionesco, Eugene 1909-1994**CLC 1, 4, 6, 9, 11, 15, 41, 86; DA; DAB; DAC; DAM DRAM, MST; WLC**
See also CA 9-12R; 144; CANR 55; MTCW; SATA 7; SATA-Obit 79

Iqbal, Muhammad 1873-1938 .... **TCLC 28**

Ireland, Patrick
See O'Doherty, Brian

Iron, Ralph
See Schreiner, Olive (Emilie Albertina)

Irving, John (Winslow) 1942- .. **CLC 13, 23, 38; DAM NOV, POP**
See also AAYA 8; BEST 89:3; CA 25-28R; CANR 28; DLB 6; DLBY 82; MTCW

Irving, Washington 1783-1859 **NCLC 2, 19; DA; DAB; DAM MST; SSC 2; WLC**
See also CDALB 1640-1865; DLB 3, 11, 30, 59, 73, 74, 186; YABC 2

Irwin, P. K.
See Page, P(atricia) K(athleen)

Isaacs, Susan 1943- .... **CLC 32; DAM POP**
See also BEST 89:1; CA 89-92; CANR 20, 41, 65; INT CANR-20; MTCW

Isherwood, Christopher (William Bradshaw) 1904-1986**CLC 1, 9, 11, 14, 44; DAM DRAM, NOV**
See also CA 13-16R; 117; CANR 35; DLB 15, 195; DLBY 86; MTCW

Ishiguro, Kazuo 1954-**CLC 27, 56, 59; DAM NOV**
See also BEST 90:2; CA 120; CANR 49; DLB 194; MTCW

Ishikawa, Hakuhin
See Ishikawa, Takuboku

Ishikawa, Takuboku 1886(?)-1912**TCLC 15; DAM POET; PC 10**
See also CA 113; 153

Iskander, Fazil 1929- .... **CLC 47**
See also CA 102

Isler, Alan (David) 1934- .... **CLC 91**
See also CA 156

Ivan IV 1530-1584 .... **LC 17**

Ivanov, Vyacheslav Ivanovich 1866-1949**TCLC 33**
See also CA 122

Ivask, Ivar Vidrik 1927-1992 .... **CLC 14**
See also CA 37-40R; 139; CANR 24

Ives, Morgan
See Bradley, Marion Zimmer

J. R. S.
See Gogarty, Oliver St. John

Jabran, Kahlil
See Gibran, Kahlil

Jabran, Khalil
See Gibran, Kahlil

Jackson, Daniel
See Wingrove, David (John)

Jackson, Jesse 1908-1983 .... **CLC 12**
See also BW 1; CA 25-28R; 109; CANR 27; CLR 28; MAICYA; SATA 2, 29; SATA-Obit 48

Jackson, Laura (Riding) 1901-1991
See Riding, Laura
See also CA 65-68; 135; CANR 28; DLB 48

Jackson, Sam
See Trumbo, Dalton

Jackson, Sara
See Wingrove, David (John)

Jackson, Shirley 1919-1965**CLC 11, 60, 87; DA; DAC; DAM MST; SSC 9; WLC**
See also AAYA 9; CA 1-4R; 25-28R; CANR 4, 52; CDALB 1941-1968; DLB 6; SATA 2

Jacob, (Cyprien-)Max 1876-1944 .... **TCLC 6**
See also CA 104

Jacobs, Harriet 1813(?)-1897 .... **NCLC 67**

Jacobs, Jim 1942- .... **CLC 12**
See also CA 97-100; INT 97-100

Jacobs, W(illiam) W(ymark) 1863-1943**TCLC 22**
See also CA 121; DLB 135

Jacobsen, Jens Peter 1847-1885 .... **NCLC 34**

Jacobsen, Josephine 1908- .... **CLC 48, 102**
See also CA 33-36R; CAAS 18; CANR 23, 48

Jacobson, Dan 1929- .... **CLC 4, 14**
See also CA 1-4R; CANR 2, 25, 66; DLB 14; MTCW

Jacqueline
See Carpentier (y Valmont), Alejo

Jagger, Mick 1944- .... **CLC 17**

Jahiz, Al- c. 776-869 .... **CMLC 25**

Jahiz, al- c. 780-c. 869 .... **CMLC 25**

Jakes, John (William) 1932-**CLC 29; DAM NOV, POP**
See also BEST 89:4; CA 57-60; CANR 10, 43, 66; DLBY 83; INT CANR-10; MTCW; SATA 62

James, Andrew
See Kirkup, James

James, C(yril) L(ionel) R(obert) 1901-1989 **CLC 33**
See also BW 2; CA 117; 125; 128; CANR 62; DLB 125; MTCW

James, Daniel (Lewis) 1911-1988
See Santiago, Danny
See also CA 125

James, Dynely
See Mayne, William (James Carter)

James, Henry Sr. 1811-1882 .... **NCLC 53**

James, Henry 1843-1916**TCLC 2, 11, 24, 40, 47, 64; DA; DAB; DAC; DAM MST, NOV; SSC 8; WLC**
See also CA 104; 132; CDALB 1865-1917; DLB 12, 71, 74, 189; DLBD 13; MTCW

James, M. R.
See James, Montague (Rhodes)
See also DLB 156

James, Montague (Rhodes) 1862-1936 . **TCLC 6; SSC 16**
See also CA 104

James, P. D. .... **CLC 18, 46**
See also White, Phyllis Dorothy James
See also BEST 90:2; CDBLB 1960 to Present; DLB 87

James, Philip
See Moorcock, Michael (John)

James, William 1842-1910 .... **TCLC 15, 32**
See also CA 109

James I 1394-1437 .... **LC 20**

Jameson, Anna 1794-1860 .... **NCLC 43**
See also DLB 99, 166

Jami, Nur al-Din 'Abd al-Rahman 1414-1492**LC 9**

Jammes, Francis 1868-1938 .... **TCLC 75**

Jandl, Ernst 1925- .... **CLC 34**

Janowitz, Tama 1957- .... **CLC 43; DAM POP**
See also CA 106; CANR 52

Japrisot, Sebastien 1931- .... **CLC 90**

Jarrell, Randall 1914-1965**CLC 1, 2, 6, 9, 13, 49; DAM POET**
See also CA 5-8R; 25-28R; CABS 2; CANR 6, 34; CDALB 1941-1968; CLR 6; DLB 48, 52; MAICYA; MTCW; SATA 7

Jarry, Alfred 1873-1907 .... **TCLC 2, 14; DAM DRAM; SSC 20**
See also CA 104; 153; DLB 192

Jarvis, E. K.
See Bloch, Robert (Albert); Ellison, Harlan (Jay); Silverberg, Robert

Jeake, Samuel, Jr.
See Aiken, Conrad (Potter)

Jean Paul 1763-1825 .... **NCLC 7**

Jefferies, (John) Richard 1848-1887 . **NCLC 47**
See also DLB 98, 141; SATA 16

Jeffers, (John) Robinson 1887-1962**CLC 2, 3, 11, 15, 54; DA; DAC; DAM MST, POET; PC 17; WLC**
See also CA 85-88; CANR 35; CDALB 1917-1929; DLB 45; MTCW

Jefferson, Janet
See Mencken, H(enry) L(ouis)

Jefferson, Thomas 1743-1826 .... **NCLC 11**
See also CDALB 1640-1865; DLB 31

Jeffrey, Francis 1773-1850 .... **NCLC 33**
See also DLB 107

Jelakowitch, Ivan
See Heijermans, Herman

Jellicoe, (Patricia) Ann 1927- .... **CLC 27**
See also CA 85-88; DLB 13

Jen, Gish .... **CLC 70**
See also Jen, Lillian

Jen, Lillian 1956(?)-
See Jen, Gish
See also CA 135

Jenkins, (John) Robin 1912- .... **CLC 52**
See also CA 1-4R; CANR 1; DLB 14

Jennings, Elizabeth (Joan) 1926- ..... **CLC 5, 14**
See also CA 61-64; CAAS 5; CANR 8, 39, 66; DLB 27; MTCW; SATA 66

Jennings, Waylon 1937- .... **CLC 21**

Jensen, Johannes V. 1873-1950 .... **TCLC 41**

Jensen, Laura (Linnea) 1948- .... **CLC 37**
See also CA 103

Jerome, Jerome K(lapka) 1859-1927 .. **TCLC 23**
See also CA 119; DLB 10, 34, 135

Jerrold, Douglas William 1803-1857 ... **NCLC 2**
See also DLB 158, 159

Jewett, (Theodora) Sarah Orne 1849-1909**TCLC 1, 22; SSC 6**
See also CA 108; 127; DLB 12, 74; SATA 15

Jewsbury, Geraldine (Endsor) 1812-1880 **NCLC 22**
See also DLB 21

Jhabvala, Ruth Prawer 1927- . **CLC 4, 8, 29, 94; DAB; DAM NOV**
See also CA 1-4R; CANR 2, 29, 51; DLB 139, 194; INT CANR-29; MTCW

Jibran, Kahlil
See Gibran, Kahlil

Jibran, Khalil
See Gibran, Kahlil

Jiles, Paulette 1943- .... **CLC 13, 58**
See also CA 101

Jimenez (Mantecon), Juan Ramon 1881-1958 **TCLC 4; DAM MULT, POET; HLC; PC 7**
See also CA 104; 131; DLB 134; HW; MTCW

Jimenez, Ramon
See Jimenez (Mantecon), Juan Ramon

Jimenez Mantecon, Juan
See Jimenez (Mantecon), Juan Ramon

Jin, Ha 1956- .... **CLC 109**
See also CA 152

Joel, Billy .... **CLC 26**
See also Joel, William Martin

Joel, William Martin 1949-
See Joel, Billy
See also CA 108

John, Saint 7th cent. - .... **CMLC 27**

John of the Cross, St. 1542-1591 .... **LC 18**

Johnson, B(ryan) S(tanley William) 1933-1973 **CLC 6, 9**
See also CA 9-12R; 53-56; CANR 9; DLB 14, 40

Johnson, Benj. F. of Boo
See Riley, James Whitcomb

Johnson, Benjamin F. of Boo
See Riley, James Whitcomb

Johnson, Charles (Richard) 1948-**CLC 7, 51, 65; BLC; DAM MULT**
See also BW 2; CA 116; CAAS 18; CANR 42, 66; DLB 33

Johnson, Denis 1949- .... **CLC 52**
See also CA 117; 121; DLB 120

Johnson, Diane 1934- .... **CLC 5, 13, 48**
See also CA 41-44R; CANR 17, 40, 62; DLBY 80; INT CANR-17; MTCW

Johnson, Eyvind (Olof Verner) 1900-1976**CLC 14**
See also CA 73-76; 69-72; CANR 34

Johnson, J. R.
See James, C(yril) L(ionel) R(obert)

Johnson, James Weldon 1871-1938 **TCLC 3, 19; BLC; DAM MULT, POET**
See also BW 1; CA 104; 125; CDALB 1917-1929; CLR 32; DLB 51; MTCW; SATA 31

Johnson, Joyce 1935- **CLC 58**
See also CA 125; 129

Johnson, Lionel (Pigot) 1867-1902 **TCLC 19**
See also CA 117; DLB 19

Johnson, Mel
See Malzberg, Barry N(athaniel)

Johnson, Pamela Hansford 1912-1981 **CLC 1, 7, 27**
See also CA 1-4R; 104; CANR 2, 28; DLB 15; MTCW

Johnson, Robert 1911(?)-1938 .... **TCLC 69**

Johnson, Samuel 1709-1784 .. **LC 15; DA; DAB; DAC; DAM MST; WLC**
See also CDBLB 1660-1789; DLB 39, 95, 104, 142

Johnson, Uwe 1934-1984 .... **CLC 5, 10, 15, 40**
See also CA 1-4R; 112; CANR 1, 39; DLB 75; MTCW

Johnston, George (Benson) 1913- .... **CLC 51**
See also CA 1-4R; CANR 5, 20; DLB 88

Johnston, Jennifer 1930- .... **CLC 7**
See also CA 85-88; DLB 14

Jolley, (Monica) Elizabeth 1923-**CLC 46; SSC 19**
See also CA 127; CAAS 13; CANR 59

Jones, Arthur Llewellyn 1863-1947
See Machen, Arthur
See also CA 104

Jones, D(ouglas) G(ordon) 1929- .... **CLC 10**
See also CA 29-32R; CANR 13; DLB 53

Jones, David (Michael) 1895-1974**CLC 2, 4, 7, 13, 42**
See also CA 9-12R; 53-56; CANR 28; CDBLB 1945-1960; DLB 20, 100; MTCW

Jones, David Robert 1947-
See Bowie, David
See also CA 103

Jones, Diana Wynne 1934- .... **CLC 26**
See also AAYA 12; CA 49-52; CANR 4, 26, 56; CLR 23; DLB 161; JRDA; MAICYA; SAAS 7; SATA 9, 70

Jones, Edward P. 1950- .... **CLC 76**
See also BW 2; CA 142

Jones, Gayl 1949- . **CLC 6, 9; BLC; DAM MULT**
See also BW 2; CA 77-80; CANR 27, 66; DLB 33; MTCW

Jones, James 1921-1977 .... **CLC 1, 3, 10, 39**
See also AITN 1, 2; CA 1-4R; 69-72; CANR 6; DLB 2, 143; MTCW

Jones, John J.
See Lovecraft, H(oward) P(hillips)

Jones, LeRoi .... **CLC 1, 2, 3, 5, 10, 14**
See also Baraka, Amiri

Jones, Louis B. .... **CLC 65**
See also CA 141

Jones, Madison (Percy, Jr.) 1925- .... **CLC 4**
See also CA 13-16R; CAAS 11; CANR 7, 54; DLB 152

Jones, Mervyn 1922- .... **CLC 10, 52**
See also CA 45-48; CAAS 5; CANR 1; MTCW

Jones, Mick 1956(?)- .... **CLC 30**

Jones, Nettie (Pearl) 1941- .... **CLC 34**
See also BW 2; CA 137; CAAS 20

Jones, Preston 1936-1979 **CLC 10**
See also CA 73-76; 89-92; DLB 7

Jones, Robert F(rancis) 1934- .... **CLC 7**
See also CA 49-52; CANR 2, 61

Jones, Rod 1953- .... **CLC 50**
See also CA 128

Jones, Terence Graham Parry 1942- ... **CLC 21**
See also Jones, Terry; Monty Python
See also CA 112; 116; CANR 35; INT 116

Jones, Terry
See Jones, Terence Graham Parry
See also SATA 67; SATA-Brief 51

Jones, Thom 1945(?)- .... **CLC 81**
See also CA 157

Jong, Erica 1942-**CLC 4, 6, 8, 18, 83; DAM NOV, POP**
See also AITN 1; BEST 90:2; CA 73-76; CANR 26, 52; DLB 2, 5, 28, 152; INT CANR-26; MTCW

Jonson, Ben(jamin) 1572(?)-1637 **LC 6, 33; DA; DAB; DAC; DAM DRAM, MST, POET; DC 4; PC 17; WLC**
See also CDBLB Before 1660; DLB 62, 121

Jordan, June 1936- **CLC 5, 11, 23; DAM MULT, POET**
See also AAYA 2; BW 2; CA 33-36R; CANR 25; CLR 10; DLB 38; MAICYA; MTCW; SATA 4

Jordan, Pat(rick M.) 1941- .... **CLC 37**
See also CA 33-36R

Jorgensen, Ivar
See Ellison, Harlan (Jay)

Jorgenson, Ivar
See Silverberg, Robert

Josephus, Flavius c. 37-100 .... **CMLC 13**

Josipovici, Gabriel 1940- .... **CLC 6, 43**
See also CA 37-40R; CAAS 8; CANR 47; DLB 14

Joubert, Joseph 1754-1824 .... **NCLC 9**

Jouve, Pierre Jean 1887-1976 .... **CLC 47**
See also CA 65-68

Jovine, Francesco 1902-1950 .... **TCLC 79**

Joyce, James (Augustine Aloysius) 1882-1941 **TCLC 3, 8, 16, 35, 52; DA; DAB; DAC; DAM MST, NOV, POET; PC 22; SSC 3, 26; WLC**
See also CA 104; 126; CDBLB 1914-1945; DLB 10, 19, 36, 162; MTCW

Jozsef, Attila 1905-1937 .... **TCLC 22**
See also CA 116

Juana Ines de la Cruz 1651(?)-1695 .... **LC 5**

Judd, Cyril
See Kornbluth, C(yril) M.; Pohl, Frederik

Julian of Norwich 1342(?)-1416(?) .... **LC 6**
See also DLB 146

Junger, Sebastian 1962- .... **CLC 109**
See also CA 165

Juniper, Alex
See Hospital, Janette Turner

Junius
See Luxemburg, Rosa

Just, Ward (Swift) 1935- .... **CLC 4, 27**
See also CA 25-28R; CANR 32; INT CANR-32

Justice, Donald (Rodney) 1925- **CLC 6, 19, 102; DAM POET**
See also CA 5-8R; CANR 26, 54; DLBY 83; INT CANR-26

Juvenal c. 55-c. 127 .... **CMLC 8**

Juvenis
See Bourne, Randolph S(illiman)

Kacew, Romain 1914-1980
See Gary, Romain
See also CA 108; 102

Kadare, Ismail 1936- .... **CLC 52**
See also CA 161

Kadohata, Cynthia .... **CLC 59**
See also CA 140

Kafka, Franz 1883-1924**TCLC 2, 6, 13, 29, 47, 53; DA; DAB; DAC; DAM MST, NOV; SSC 5, 29; WLC**
See also CA 105; 126; DLB 81; MTCW

Kahanovitsch, Pinkhes
See Der Nister

Kahn, Roger 1927- .... **CLC 30**
See also CA 25-28R; CANR 44; DLB 171; SATA 37

Kain, Saul
See Sassoon, Siegfried (Lorraine)

Kaiser, Georg 1878-1945 .... **TCLC 9**
See also CA 106; DLB 124

Kaletski, Alexander 1946- .... **CLC 39**
See also CA 118; 143

Kalidasa fl. c. 400- .... **CMLC 9; PC 22**

Kallman, Chester (Simon) 1921-1975 ..... **CLC 2**
See also CA 45-48; 53-56; CANR 3

Kaminsky, Melvin 1926-
See Brooks, Mel
See also CA 65-68; CANR 16

Kaminsky, Stuart M(elvin) 1934- .... **CLC 59**
See also CA 73-76; CANR 29, 53

Kane, Francis
See Robbins, Harold

Kane, Paul
See Simon, Paul (Frederick)

Kane, Wilson
See Bloch, Robert (Albert)

Kanin, Garson 1912- .... **CLC 22**
See also AITN 1; CA 5-8R; CANR 7; DLB 7

Kaniuk, Yoram 1930- .... **CLC 19**
See also CA 134

Kant, Immanuel 1724-1804 .... **NCLC 27, 67**
See also DLB 94

Kantor, MacKinlay 1904-1977 .... **CLC 7**
See also CA 61-64; 73-76; CANR 60, 63; DLB 9, 102

Kaplan, David Michael 1946- .... **CLC 50**

Kaplan, James 1951- .... **CLC 59**
See also CA 135

Karageorge, Michael
See Anderson, Poul (William)

Karamzin, Nikolai Mikhailovich 1766-1826 **NCLC 3**
See also DLB 150

Karapanou, Margarita 1946- .... **CLC 13**
See also CA 101

Karinthy, Frigyes 1887-1938 .... **TCLC 47**

Karl, Frederick R(obert) 1927- .... **CLC 34**
See also CA 5-8R; CANR 3, 44

Kastel, Warren
See Silverberg, Robert

Kataev, Evgeny Petrovich 1903-1942
See Petrov, Evgeny
See also CA 120

Kataphusin
See Ruskin, John

Katz, Steve 1935- .... **CLC 47**
See also CA 25-28R; CAAS 14, 64; CANR 12; DLBY 83

Kauffman, Janet 1945- .... **CLC 42**
See also CA 117; CANR 43; DLBY 86

Kaufman, Bob (Garnell) 1925-1986 .... **CLC 49**
See also BW 1; CA 41-44R; 118; CANR 22; DLB 16, 41

Kaufman, George S. 1889-1961 .. **CLC 38; DAM DRAM**
See also CA 108; 93-96; DLB 7; INT 108

Kaufman, Sue .... **CLC 3, 8**
See also Barondess, Sue K(aufman)

Kavafis, Konstantinos Petrou 1863-1933
See Cavafy, C(onstantine) P(eter)
See also CA 104

Kavan, Anna 1901-1968 .... **CLC 5, 13, 82**
See also CA 5-8R; CANR 6, 57; MTCW

Kavanagh, Dan
See Barnes, Julian (Patrick)

Kavanagh, Patrick (Joseph) 1904-1967 . **CLC 22**
See also CA 123; 25-28R; DLB 15, 20; MTCW

Kawabata, Yasunari 1899-1972 . **CLC 2, 5, 9, 18, 107; DAM MULT; SSC 17**
See also CA 93-96; 33-36R; DLB 180

Kaye, M(ary) M(argaret) 1909- .... **CLC 28**
See also CA 89-92; CANR 24, 60; MTCW; SATA 62

Kaye, Mollie
See Kaye, M(ary) M(argaret)

Kaye-Smith, Sheila 1887-1956 .... **TCLC 20**
See also CA 118; DLB 36

Author Index

Kincaid, Jamaica 1949- **CLC 43, 68; BLC; DAM MULT, NOV**
See also AAYA 13; BW 2; CA 125; CANR 47, 59; DLB 157

King, Francis (Henry) 1923- .. **CLC 8, 53; DAM NOV**
See also CA 1-4R; CANR 1, 33; DLB 15, 139; MTCW

King, Kennedy
See Brown, George Douglas

King, Martin Luther, Jr. 1929-1968 ..... **CLC 83; BLC; DA; DAB; DAC; DAM MST, MULT; WLCS**
See also BW 2; CA 25-28; CANR 27, 44; CAP 2; MTCW; SATA 14

King, Stephen (Edwin) 1947- **CLC 12, 26, 37, 61; DAM NOV, POP; SSC 17**
See also AAYA 1, 17; BEST 90:1; CA 61-64; CANR 1, 30, 52; DLB 143; DLBY 80; JRDA; MTCW; SATA 9, 55

King, Steve
See King, Stephen (Edwin)

King, Thomas 1943- **CLC 89; DAC; DAM MULT**
See also CA 144; DLB 175; NNAL; SATA 96

Kingman, Lee .... **CLC 17**
See also Natti, (Mary) Lee
See also SAAS 3; SATA 1, 67

Kingsley, Charles 1819-1875 .... **NCLC 35**
See also DLB 21, 32, 163, 190; YABC 2

Kingsley, Sidney 1906-1995 .... **CLC 44**
See also CA 85-88; 147; DLB 7

Kingsolver, Barbara 1955- **CLC 55, 81; DAM POP**
See also AAYA 15; CA 129; 134; CANR 60; INT 134

Kingston, Maxine (Ting Ting) Hong 1940- **CLC 12, 19, 58; DAM MULT, NOV; WLCS**
See also AAYA 8; CA 69-72; CANR 13, 38; DLB 173; DLBY 80; INT CANR-13; MTCW; SATA 53

Kinnell, Galway 1927- ..... **CLC 1, 2, 3, 5, 13, 29**
See also CA 9-12R; CANR 10, 34, 66; DLB 5; DLBY 87; INT CANR-34; MTCW

Kinsella, Thomas 1928- .... **CLC 4, 19**
See also CA 17-20R; CANR 15; DLB 27; MTCW

Kinsella, W(illiam) P(atrick) 1935- **CLC 27, 43; DAC; DAM NOV, POP**
See also AAYA 7; CA 97-100; CAAS 7; CANR 21, 35, 66; INT CANR-21; MTCW

Kipling, (Joseph) Rudyard 1865-1936 **TCLC 8, 17; DA; DAB; DAC; DAM MST, POET; PC 3; SSC 5; WLC**
See also CA 105; 120; CANR 33; CDBLB 1890-1914; CLR 39; DLB 19, 34, 141, 156; MAICYA; MTCW; YABC 2

Kirkup, James 1918- .... **CLC 1**
See also CA 1-4R; CAAS 4; CANR 2; DLB 27; SATA 12

Kirkwood, James 1930(?)-1989 .... **CLC 9**
See also AITN 2; CA 1-4R; 128; CANR 6, 40

Kirshner, Sidney
See Kingsley, Sidney

Kis, Danilo 1935-1989 .... **CLC 57**
See also CA 109; 118; 129; CANR 61; DLB 181; MTCW

Kivi, Aleksis 1834-1872 .... **NCLC 30**

Kizer, Carolyn (Ashley) 1925- . **CLC 15, 39, 80; DAM POET**
See also CA 65-68; CAAS 5; CANR 24; DLB 5, 169

Klabund 1890-1928 .... **TCLC 44**
See also CA 162; DLB 66

Klappert, Peter 1942- .... **CLC 57**
See also CA 33-36R; DLB 5

Klein, A(braham) M(oses) 1909-1972 ... **CLC 19; DAB; DAC; DAM MST**
See also CA 101; 37-40R; DLB 68

Klein, Norma 1938-1989 .... **CLC 30**
See also AAYA 2; CA 41-44R; 128; CANR 15, 37; CLR 2, 19; INT CANR-15; JRDA; MAICYA; SAAS 1; SATA 7, 57

Klein, T(heodore) E(ibon) D(onald) 1947- **CLC 34**
See also CA 119; CANR 44

Kleist, Heinrich von 1777-1811 **NCLC 2, 37; DAM DRAM; SSC 22**
See also DLB 90

Klima, Ivan 1931- .... **CLC 56; DAM NOV**
See also CA 25-28R; CANR 17, 50

Klimentov, Andrei Platonovich 1899-1951
See Platonov, Andrei
See also CA 108

Klinger, Friedrich Maximilian von 1752-1831 **NCLC 1**
See also DLB 94

Klingsor the Magician
See Hartmann, Sadakichi

Klopstock, Friedrich Gottlieb 1724-1803 **NCLC 11**
See also DLB 97

Knapp, Caroline 1959- .... **CLC 99**
See also CA 154

Knebel, Fletcher 1911-1993 .... **CLC 14**
See also AITN 1; CA 1-4R; 140; CAAS 3; CANR 1, 36; SATA 36; SATA-Obit 75

Knickerbocker, Diedrich
See Irving, Washington

Knight, Etheridge 1931-1991 **CLC 40; BLC; DAM POET; PC 14**
See also BW 1; CA 21-24R; 133; CANR 23; DLB 41

Knight, Sarah Kemble 1666-1727 .... **LC 7**
See also DLB 24

Knister, Raymond 1899-1932 .... **TCLC 56**
See also DLB 68

Knowles, John 1926- **CLC 1, 4, 10, 26; DA; DAC; DAM MST, NOV**
See also AAYA 10; CA 17-20R; CANR 40; CDALB 1968-1988; DLB 6; MTCW; SATA 8, 89

Knox, Calvin M.
See Silverberg, Robert

Knox, John c. 1505-1572 .... **LC 37**
See also DLB 132

Knye, Cassandra
See Disch, Thomas M(ichael)

Koch, C(hristopher) J(ohn) 1932- .... **CLC 42**
See also CA 127

Koch, Christopher
See Koch, C(hristopher) J(ohn)

Koch, Kenneth 1925- **CLC 5, 8, 44; DAM POET**
See also CA 1-4R; CANR 6, 36, 57; DLB 5; INT CANR-36; SATA 65

Kochanowski, Jan 1530-1584 .... **LC 10**

Kock, Charles Paul de 1794-1871 ...... **NCLC 16**

Koda Shigeyuki 1867-1947
See Rohan, Koda
See also CA 121

Koestler, Arthur 1905-1983 **CLC 1, 3, 6, 8, 15, 33**
See also CA 1-4R; 109; CANR 1, 33; CDBLB 1945-1960; DLBY 83; MTCW

Kogawa, Joy Nozomi 1935- **CLC 78; DAC; DAM MST, MULT**
See also CA 101; CANR 19, 62

Kohout, Pavel 1928- .... **CLC 13**
See also CA 45-48; CANR 3

Koizumi, Yakumo
See Hearn, (Patricio) Lafcadio (Tessima Carlos)

Kolmar, Gertrud 1894-1943 .... **TCLC 40**

Komunyakaa, Yusef 1947- .... **CLC 86, 94**
See also CA 147; DLB 120

Konrad, George
See Konrad, Gyoergy

Konrad, Gyoergy 1933- .... **CLC 4, 10, 73**
See also CA 85-88

Konwicki, Tadeusz 1926- .... **CLC 8, 28, 54**
See also CA 101; CAAS 9; CANR 39, 59; MTCW

Koontz, Dean R(ay) 1945- .. **CLC 78; DAM NOV, POP**
See also AAYA 9; BEST 89:3, 90:2; CA 108; CANR 19, 36, 52; MTCW; SATA 92

Kopit, Arthur (Lee) 1937- **CLC 1, 18, 33; DAM DRAM**
See also AITN 1; CA 81-84; CABS 3; DLB 7; MTCW

Kops, Bernard 1926- .... **CLC 4**
See also CA 5-8R; DLB 13

Kornbluth, C(yril) M. 1923-1958 .... **TCLC 8**
See also CA 105; 160; DLB 8

Korolenko, V. G.
See Korolenko, Vladimir Galaktionovich

Korolenko, Vladimir
See Korolenko, Vladimir Galaktionovich

Lamartine, Alphonse (Marie Louis Prat) de 1790-1869 .... **NCLC 11; DAM POET; PC 16**

Lamb, Charles 1775-1834 . **NCLC 10; DA; DAB; DAC; DAM MST; WLC**
See also CDBLB 1789-1832; DLB 93, 107, 163; SATA 17

Lamb, Lady Caroline 1785-1828 .... **NCLC 38**
See also DLB 116

Lamming, George (William) 1927- **CLC 2, 4, 66; BLC; DAM MULT**
See also BW 2; CA 85-88; CANR 26; DLB 125; MTCW

L'Amour, Louis (Dearborn) 1908-1988 **CLC 25, 55; DAM NOV, POP**
See also AAYA 16; AITN 2; BEST 89:2; CA 1-4R; 125; CANR 3, 25, 40; DLBY 80; MTCW

Lampedusa, Giuseppe (Tomasi) di 1896-1957 **TCLC 13**
See also Tomasi di Lampedusa, Giuseppe
See also CA 164; DLB 177

Lampman, Archibald 1861-1899 .... **NCLC 25**
See also DLB 92

Lancaster, Bruce 1896-1963 .... **CLC 36**
See also CA 9-10; CAP 1; SATA 9

Lanchester, John .... **CLC 99**

Landau, Mark Alexandrovich
See Aldanov, Mark (Alexandrovich)

Landau-Aldanov, Mark Alexandrovich
See Aldanov, Mark (Alexandrovich)

Landis, Jerry
See Simon, Paul (Frederick)

Landis, John 1950- .... **CLC 26**
See also CA 112; 122

Landolfi, Tommaso 1908-1979 .... **CLC 11, 49**
See also CA 127; 117; DLB 177

Landon, Letitia Elizabeth 1802-1838 .. **NCLC 15**
See also DLB 96

Landor, Walter Savage 1775-1864 ...... **NCLC 14**
See also DLB 93, 107

Landwirth, Heinz 1927-
See Lind, Jakov
See also CA 9-12R; CANR 7

Lane, Patrick 1939- .... **CLC 25; DAM POET**
See also CA 97-100; CANR 54; DLB 53; INT 97-100

Lang, Andrew 1844-1912 .... **TCLC 16**
See also CA 114; 137; DLB 98, 141, 184; MAICYA; SATA 16

Lang, Fritz 1890-1976 .... **CLC 20, 103**
See also CA 77-80; 69-72; CANR 30

Lange, John
See Crichton, (John) Michael

Langer, Elinor 1939- .... **CLC 34**
See also CA 121

Langland, William 1330(?)-1400(?) . **LC 19; DA; DAB; DAC; DAM MST, POET**
See also DLB 146

Langstaff, Launcelot
See Irving, Washington

Lanier, Sidney 1842-1881 **NCLC 6; DAM POET**
See also DLB 64; DLBD 13; MAICYA; SATA 18

Lanyer, Aemilia 1569-1645 .... **LC 10, 30**
See also DLB 121

Lao Tzu .... **CMLC 7**

Lapine, James (Elliot) 1949- .... **CLC 39**
See also CA 123; 130; CANR 54; INT 130

Larbaud, Valery (Nicolas) 1881-1957 .... **TCLC 9**
See also CA 106; 152

Lardner, Ring
See Lardner, Ring(gold) W(ilmer)

Lardner, Ring W., Jr.
See Lardner, Ring(gold) W(ilmer)

Lardner, Ring(gold) W(ilmer) 1885-1933 **TCLC 2, 14**
See also CA 104; 131; CDALB 1917-1929; DLB 11, 25, 86; DLBD 16; MTCW

Laredo, Betty
See Codrescu, Andrei

Larkin, Maia
See Wojciechowska, Maia (Teresa)

Larkin, Philip (Arthur) 1922-1985 **CLC 3, 5, 8, 9, 13, 18, 33, 39, 64; DAB; DAM MST, POET; PC 21**
See also CA 5-8R; 117; CANR 24, 62; CDBLB 1960 to Present; DLB 27; MTCW

Larra (y Sanchez de Castro), Mariano Jose de 1809-1837 .... **NCLC 17**

Larsen, Eric 1941- .... **CLC 55**
See also CA 132

Larsen, Nella 1891-1964 .. **CLC 37; BLC; DAM MULT**
See also BW 1; CA 125; DLB 51

Larson, Charles R(aymond) 1938- .... **CLC 31**
See also CA 53-56; CANR 4

Larson, Jonathan 1961-1996 .... **CLC 99**
See also CA 156

Las Casas, Bartolome de 1474-1566 .... **LC 31**

Lasch, Christopher 1932-1994 .... **CLC 102**
See also CA 73-76; 144; CANR 25; MTCW

Lasker-Schueler, Else 1869-1945 .... **TCLC 57**
See also DLB 66, 124

Laski, Harold 1893-1950 .... **TCLC 79**

Latham, Jean Lee 1902- **CLC 12**
See also AITN 1; CA 5-8R; CANR 7; MAICYA; SATA 2, 68

Latham, Mavis
See Clark, Mavis Thorpe

Lathen, Emma .... **CLC 2**
See also Hennissart, Martha; Latsis, Mary J(ane)

Lathrop, Francis
See Leiber, Fritz (Reuter, Jr.)

Latsis, Mary J(ane) 1927(?)-1997
See Lathen, Emma
See also CA 85-88; 162

Lattimore, Richmond (Alexander) 1906-1984 **CLC 3**
See also CA 1-4R; 112; CANR 1

Laughlin, James 1914-1997 .... **CLC 49**
See also CA 21-24R; 162; CAAS 22; CANR 9, 47; DLB 48; DLBY 96, 97

Laurence, (Jean) Margaret (Wemyss) 1926-1987 **CLC 3, 6, 13, 50, 62; DAC; DAM MST; SSC 7**
See also CA 5-8R; 121; CANR 33; DLB 53; MTCW; SATA-Obit 50

Laurent, Antoine 1952- .... **CLC 50**

Lauscher, Hermann
See Hesse, Hermann

Lautreamont, Comte de 1846-1870 **NCLC 12; SSC 14**

Laverty, Donald
See Blish, James (Benjamin)

Lavin, Mary 1912-1996 .... **CLC 4, 18, 99; SSC 4**
See also CA 9-12R; 151; CANR 33; DLB 15; MTCW

Lavond, Paul Dennis
See Kornbluth, C(yril) M.; Pohl, Frederik

Lawler, Raymond Evenor 1922- .... **CLC 58**
See also CA 103

Lawrence, D(avid) H(erbert Richards) 1885-1930 **TCLC 2, 9, 16, 33, 48, 61; DA; DAB; DAC; DAM MST, NOV, POET; SSC 4, 19; WLC**
See also CA 104; 121; CDBLB 1914-1945; DLB 10, 19, 36, 98, 162, 195; MTCW

Lawrence, T(homas) E(dward) 1888-1935 **TCLC 18**
See also Dale, Colin
See also CA 115; DLB 195

Lawrence of Arabia
See Lawrence, T(homas) E(dward)

Lawson, Henry (Archibald Hertzberg) 1867-1922 **TCLC 27; SSC 18**
See also CA 120

Lawton, Dennis
See Faust, Frederick (Schiller)

Laxness, Halldor .... **CLC 25**
See also Gudjonsson, Halldor Kiljan

Layamon fl. c. 1200- .... **CMLC 10**
See also DLB 146

Laye, Camara 1928-1980 **CLC 4, 38; BLC; DAM MULT**
See also BW 1; CA 85-88; 97-100; CANR 25; MTCW

Layton, Irving (Peter) 1912- .. **CLC 2, 15; DAC; DAM MST, POET**
See also CA 1-4R; CANR 2, 33, 43, 66; DLB 88; MTCW

Lazarus, Emma 1849-1887 .... **NCLC 8**

Lazarus, Felix
See Cable, George Washington

Lazarus, Henry
See Slavitt, David R(ytman)

Lea, Joan
See Neufeld, John (Arthur)

Leacock, Stephen (Butler) 1869-1944 .. **TCLC 2; DAC; DAM MST**
See also CA 104; 141; DLB 92

Lear, Edward 1812-1888 .... **NCLC 3**
See also CLR 1; DLB 32, 163, 166; MAICYA; SATA 18

Lear, Norman (Milton) 1922- .... **CLC 12**
See also CA 73-76

Leavis, F(rank) R(aymond) 1895-1978 .. **CLC 24**
See also CA 21-24R; 77-80; CANR 44; MTCW

Leavitt, David 1961- .... **CLC 34; DAM POP**
See also CA 116; 122; CANR 50, 62; DLB 130; INT 122

Leblanc, Maurice (Marie Emile) 1864-1941 **TCLC 49**
See also CA 110

Lebowitz, Fran(ces Ann) 1951(?)- ... **CLC 11, 36**
See also CA 81-84; CANR 14, 60; INT CANR-14; MTCW

Lebrecht, Peter
See Tieck, (Johann) Ludwig

le Carre, John .... **CLC 3, 5, 9, 15, 28**
See also Cornwell, David (John Moore)
See also BEST 89:4; CDBLB 1960 to Present; DLB 87

Le Clezio, J(ean) M(arie) G(ustave) 1940- **CLC 31**
See also CA 116; 128; DLB 83

Leconte de Lisle, Charles-Marie-Rene 1818-1894 **NCLC 29**

Le Coq, Monsieur
See Simenon, Georges (Jacques Christian)

Leduc, Violette 1907-1972 .... **CLC 22**
See also CA 13-14; 33-36R; CAP 1

Ledwidge, Francis 1887(?)-1917 .... **TCLC 23**
See also CA 123; DLB 20

Lee, Andrea 1953- . **CLC 36; BLC; DAM MULT**
See also BW 1; CA 125

Lee, Andrew
See Auchincloss, Louis (Stanton)

Lee, Chang-rae 1965- .... **CLC 91**
See also CA 148

Lee, Don L. .... **CLC 2**
See also Madhubuti, Haki R.

Lee, George W(ashington) 1894-1976 . **CLC 52; BLC; DAM MULT**
See also BW 1; CA 125; DLB 51

Lee, (Nelle) Harper 1926- **CLC 12, 60; DA; DAB; DAC; DAM MST, NOV; WLC**
See also AAYA 13; CA 13-16R; CANR 51; CDALB 1941-1968; DLB 6; MTCW; SATA 11

Lee, Helen Elaine 1959(?)- .... **CLC 86**
See also CA 148

Lee, Julian
See Latham, Jean Lee

Lee, Larry
See Lee, Lawrence

Lee, Laurie 1914-1997 **CLC 90; DAB; DAM POP**
See also CA 77-80; 158; CANR 33; DLB 27; MTCW

Lee, Lawrence 1941-1990 .... **CLC 34**
See also CA 131; CANR 43

Lee, Manfred B(ennington) 1905-1971 .. **CLC 11**
See also Queen, Ellery
See also CA 1-4R; 29-32R; CANR 2; DLB 137

Lee, Shelton Jackson 1957(?)- **CLC 105; DAM MULT**
See also Lee, Spike
See also BW 2; CA 125; CANR 42

Lee, Spike
See Lee, Shelton Jackson
See also AAYA 4

Lee, Stan 1922- .... **CLC 17**
See also AAYA 5; CA 108; 111; INT 111

Lee, Tanith 1947- .... **CLC 46**
See also AAYA 15; CA 37-40R; CANR 53; SATA 8, 88

Lee, Vernon .... **TCLC 5**
See also Paget, Violet
See also DLB 57, 153, 156, 174, 178

Lee, William
See Burroughs, William S(eward)

Lee, Willy
See Burroughs, William S(eward)

Lee-Hamilton, Eugene (Jacob) 1845-1907 **TCLC 22**
See also CA 117

Leet, Judith 1935- .... **CLC 11**

Le Fanu, Joseph Sheridan 1814-1873 **NCLC 9, 58; DAM POP; SSC 14**
See also DLB 21, 70, 159, 178

Leffland, Ella 1931- .... **CLC 19**
See also CA 29-32R; CANR 35; DLBY 84; INT CANR-35; SATA 65

Leger, Alexis
See Leger, (Marie-Rene Auguste) Alexis Saint-Leger

Leger, (Marie-Rene Auguste) Alexis Saint-Leger 1887-1975 .... **CLC 11; DAM POET**
See also Perse, St.-John
See also CA 13-16R; 61-64; CANR 43; MTCW

Leger, Saintleger
See Leger, (Marie-Rene Auguste) Alexis Saint-Leger

Le Guin, Ursula K(roeber) 1929- **CLC 8, 13, 22, 45, 71; DAB; DAC; DAM MST, POP; SSC 12**
See also AAYA 9; AITN 1; CA 21-24R; CANR 9, 32, 52; CDALB 1968-1988; CLR 3, 28; DLB 8, 52; INT CANR-32; JRDA; MAICYA; MTCW; SATA 4, 52

Lehmann, Rosamond (Nina) 1901-1990 ... **CLC 5**
See also CA 77-80; 131; CANR 8; DLB 15

Leiber, Fritz (Reuter, Jr.) 1910-1992 .... **CLC 25**
See also CA 45-48; 139; CANR 2, 40; DLB 8; MTCW; SATA 45; SATA-Obit 73

Leibniz, Gottfried Wilhelm von 1646-1716 **LC 35**
See also DLB 168

Leimbach, Martha 1963-
See Leimbach, Marti
See also CA 130

Leimbach, Marti .... **CLC 65**
See also Leimbach, Martha

Leino, Eino .... **TCLC 24**
See also Loennbohm, Armas Eino Leopold

Leiris, Michel (Julien) 1901-1990 .... **CLC 61**
See also CA 119; 128; 132

Leithauser, Brad 1953- .... **CLC 27**
See also CA 107; CANR 27; DLB 120

Lelchuk, Alan 1938- .... **CLC 5**
See also CA 45-48; CAAS 20; CANR 1

Lem, Stanislaw 1921- .... **CLC 8, 15, 40**
See also CA 105; CAAS 1; CANR 32; MTCW

Lemann, Nancy 1956- .... **CLC 39**
See also CA 118; 136

Lemonnier, (Antoine Louis) Camille 1844-1913 **TCLC 22**
See also CA 121

Lenau, Nikolaus 1802-1850 .... **NCLC 16**

L'Engle, Madeleine (Camp Franklin) 1918- **CLC 12; DAM POP**
See also AAYA 1; AITN 2; CA 1-4R; CANR 3, 21, 39, 66; CLR 1, 14; DLB 52; JRDA; MAICYA; MTCW; SAAS 15; SATA 1, 27, 75

Lengyel, Jozsef 1896-1975 .... **CLC 7**
See also CA 85-88; 57-60

Lenin 1870-1924
See Lenin, V. I.
See also CA 121

Lenin, V. I. .... **TCLC 67**
See also Lenin

Lennon, John (Ono) 1940-1980 .... **CLC 12, 35**
See also CA 102

Lennox, Charlotte Ramsay 1729(?)-1804 **NCLC 23**
See also DLB 39

Lentricchia, Frank (Jr.) 1940- .... **CLC 34**
See also CA 25-28R; CANR 19

Author Index

Mansfield, Katherine TCLC 2, 8, 39; DAB; SSC 9, 23; WLC
See also Beauchamp, Kathleen Mansfield
See also DLB 162

Manso, Peter 1940- .... **CLC 39**
See also CA 29-32R; CANR 44

Mantecon, Juan Jimenez
See Jimenez (Mantecon), Juan Ramon

Manton, Peter
See Creasey, John

Man Without a Spleen, A
See Chekhov, Anton (Pavlovich)

Manzoni, Alessandro 1785-1873 .... **NCLC 29**

Mapu, Abraham (ben Jekutiel) 1808-1867 **NCLC 18**

Mara, Sally
See Queneau, Raymond

Marat, Jean Paul 1743-1793 .... **LC 10**

Marcel, Gabriel Honore 1889-1973 .... **CLC 15**
See also CA 102; 45-48; MTCW

Marchbanks, Samuel
See Davies, (William) Robertson

Marchi, Giacomo
See Bassani, Giorgio

Margulies, Donald .... **CLC 76**

Marie de France c. 12th cent. - .... **CMLC 8**

Marie de l'Incarnation 1599-1672 .... **LC 10**

Marier, Captain Victor
See Griffith, D(avid Lewelyn) W(ark)

Mariner, Scott
See Pohl, Frederik

Marinetti, Filippo Tommaso 1876-1944 **TCLC 10**
See also CA 107; DLB 114

Marivaux, Pierre Carlet de Chamblain de 1688-1763 .... **LC 4; DC 7**

Markandaya, Kamala .... **CLC 8, 38**
See also Taylor, Kamala (Purnaiya)

Markfield, Wallace 1926- .... **CLC 8**
See also CA 69-72; CAAS 3; DLB 2, 28

Markham, Edwin 1852-1940 .... **TCLC 47**
See also CA 160; DLB 54, 186

Markham, Robert
See Amis, Kingsley (William)

Marks, J
See Highwater, Jamake (Mamake)

Marks-Highwater, J
See Highwater, Jamake (Mamake)

Markson, David M(errill) 1927- .... **CLC 67**
See also CA 49-52; CANR 1

Marley, Bob **CLC 17**
See also ~~Marley, Robert Nesta~~

Marley, Robert Nesta 1945-1981
See Marley, Bob
See also CA 107; 103

Marlowe, Christopher 1564-1593 ... **LC 22; DA; DAB; DAC; DAM DRAM, MST; DC 1; WLC**
See also CDBLB Before 1660; DLB 62

Marlowe, Stephen 1928-
See Queen, Ellery
See also CA 13-16R; CANR 6, 55

Marmontel, Jean-Francois 1723-1799 .... **LC 2**

Marquand, John P(hillips) 1893-1960 **CLC 2, 10**
See also CA 85-88; DLB 9, 102

Marques, Rene 1919-1979 **CLC 96; DAM MULT; HLC**
See also CA 97-100; 85-88; DLB 113; HW

Marquez, Gabriel (Jose) Garcia
See Garcia Marquez, Gabriel (Jose)

Marquis, Don(ald Robert Perry) 1878-1937 **TCLC 7**
See also CA 104; DLB 11, 25

Marric, J. J.
See Creasey, John

Marryat, Frederick 1792-1848 .... **NCLC 3**
See also DLB 21, 163

Marsden, James
See Creasey, John

Marsh, (Edith) Ngaio 1899-1982 **CLC 7, 53; DAM POP**
See also CA 9-12R; CANR 6, 58; DLB 77; MTCW

Marshall, Garry 1934- .... **CLC 17**
See also AAYA 3; CA 111; SATA 60

Marshall, Paule 1929-. **CLC 27, 72; BLC; DAM MULT; SSC 3**
See also BW 2; CA 77-80; CANR 25; DLB 157; MTCW

Marsten, Richard
See Hunter, Evan

Marston, John 1576-1634 .. **LC 33; DAM DRAM**
See also DLB 58, 172

Martha, Henry
See Harris, Mark

Marti, Jose 1853-1895 .. **NCLC 63; DAM MULT; HLC**

Martial c. 40-c. 104 .... **PC 10**

Martin, Ken
See Hubbard, L(afayette) Ron(ald)

Martin, Richard
See Creasey, John

Martin, Steve 1945- .... **CLC 30**
See also CA 97-100; CANR 30; MTCW

Martin, Valerie 1948- **CLC 89**
See also BEST 90:2; CA 85-88; CANR 49

Martin, Violet Florence 1862-1915 ..... **TCLC 51**

Martin, Webber
See Silverberg, Robert

Martindale, Patrick Victor
See White, Patrick (Victor Martindale)

Martin du Gard, Roger 1881-1958 ...... **TCLC 24**
See also CA 118; DLB 65

Martineau, Harriet 1802-1876 .... **NCLC 26**
See also DLB 21, 55, 159, 163, 166, 190; YABC 2

Martines, Julia
See O'Faolain, Julia

Martinez, Enrique Gonzalez
See Gonzalez Martinez, Enrique

Martinez, Jacinto Benavente y
See Benavente (y Martinez), Jacinto

Martinez Ruiz, Jose 1873-1967
See Azorin; Ruiz, Jose Martinez
See also CA 93-96; HW

Martinez Sierra, Gregorio 1881-1947 .. **TCLC 6**
See also CA 115

Martinez Sierra, Maria (de la O'LeJarraga) 1874-1974 .... **TCLC 6**
See also CA 115

Martinsen, Martin
See Follett, Ken(neth Martin)

Martinson, Harry (Edmund) 1904-1978 . CLC 14
See also CA 77-80; CANR 34

Marut, Ret
See Traven, B.

Marut, Robert
See Traven, B.

Marvell, Andrew 1621-1678 **LC 4; DA; DAB; DAC; DAM MST, POET; PC 10; WLC**
See also CDBLB 1660-1789; DLB 131

Marx, Karl (Heinrich) 1818-1883 ...... **NCLC 17**
See also DLB 129

Masaoka Shiki .... **TCLC 18**
See also Masaoka Tsunenori

Masaoka Tsunenori 1867-1902
See Masaoka Shiki
See also CA 117

Masefield, John (Edward) 1878-1967 **CLC 11, 47; DAM POET**
See also CA 19-20; 25-28R; CANR 33; CAP 2; CDBLB 1890-1914; DLB 10, 19, 153, 160; MTCW; SATA 19

Maso, Carole 19(?)- .... **CLC 44**

Mason, Bobbie Ann 1940- **CLC 28, 43, 82; SSC 4**
See also AAYA 5; CA 53-56; CANR 11, 31, 58; DLB 173; DLBY 87; INT CANR-31; MTCW

Mason, Ernst
See Pohl, Frederik

Mason, Lee W.
See Malzberg, Barry N(athaniel)

Mason, Nick 1945- .... **CLC 35**

Mason, Tally
See Derleth, August (William)

Mass, William
See Gibson, William

Masters, Edgar Lee 1868-1950 **TCLC 2, 25; DA; DAC; DAM MST, POET; PC 1; WLCS**
See also CA 104; 133; CDALB 1865-1917; DLB 54; MTCW

Masters, Hilary 1928- .... **CLC 48**
See also CA 25-28R; CANR 13, 47

Mastrosimone, William 19(?)- .... **CLC 36**

Mathe, Albert
See Camus, Albert

Mather, Cotton 1663-1728 .... **LC 38**
See also CDALB 1640-1865; DLB 24, 30, 140

Mather, Increase 1639-1723 .... **LC 38**
See also DLB 24

Matheson, Richard Burton 1926- .... **CLC 37**
See also CA 97-100; DLB 8, 44; INT 97-100

Mathews, Harry 1930- .... **CLC 6, 52**
See also CA 21-24R; CAAS 6; CANR 18, 40

Mathews, John Joseph 1894-1979 **CLC 84; DAM MULT**
See also CA 19-20; 142; CANR 45; CAP 2; DLB 175; NNAL

Mathias, Roland (Glyn) 1915- .... **CLC 45**
See also CA 97-100; CANR 19, 41; DLB 27

Matsuo Basho 1644-1694 .... **PC 3**
See also DAM POET

Mattheson, Rodney
See Creasey, John

Matthews, Greg 1949- .... **CLC 45**
See also CA 135

Matthews, William (Procter, III) 1942-1997 **CLC 40**
See also CA 29-32R; 162; CAAS 18; CANR 12, 57; DLB 5

Matthias, John (Edward) 1941- .... **CLC 9**
See also CA 33-36R; CANR 56

Matthiessen, Peter 1927- **CLC 5, 7, 11, 32, 64; DAM NOV**
See also AAYA 6; BEST 90:4; CA 9-12R; CANR 21, 50; DLB 6, 173; MTCW; SATA 27

Maturin, Charles Robert 1780(?)-1824 .... **NCLC 6**
See also DLB 178

Matute (Ausejo), Ana Maria 1925- **CLC 11**
See also CA 89-92; MTCW

Maugham, W. S.
See Maugham, W(illiam) Somerset

Maugham, W(illiam) Somerset 1874-1965 **CLC 1, 11, 15, 67, 93; DA; DAB; DAC; DAM DRAM, MST, NOV; SSC 8; WLC**
See also CA 5-8R; 25-28R; CANR 40; CDBLB 1914-1945; DLB 10, 36, 77, 100, 162, 195; MTCW; SATA 54

Maugham, William Somerset
See Maugham, W(illiam) Somerset

Maupassant, (Henri Rene Albert) Guy de 1850-1893 .. **NCLC 1, 42; DA; DAB; DAC; DAM MST; SSC 1; WLC**
See also DLB 123

Maupin, Armistead 1944- ... **CLC 95; DAM POP**
See also CA 125; 130; CANR 58; INT 130

Maurhut, Richard
See Traven, B.

Mauriac, Claude 1914-1996 .... **CLC 9**
See also CA 89-92; 152; DLB 83

Mauriac, Francois (Charles) 1885-1970 **CLC 4, 9, 56; SSC 24**
See also CA 25-28; CAP 2; DLB 65; MTCW

Mavor, Osborne Henry 1888-1951
See Bridie, James
See also CA 104

Maxwell, William (Keepers, Jr.) 1908- . **CLC 19**
See also CA 93-96; CANR 54; DLBY 80; INT 93-96

May, Elaine 1932- .... **CLC 16**
See also CA 124; 142; DLB 44

Mayakovski, Vladimir (Vladimirovich) 1893-1930 **TCLC 4, 18**
See also CA 104; 158

Mayhew, Henry 1812-1887 .... **NCLC 31**
See also DLB 18, 55, 190

Mayle, Peter 1939(?)- .... **CLC 89**
See also CA 139; CANR 64

Maynard, Joyce 1953- .... **CLC 23**
See also CA 111; 129; CANR 64

Mayne, William (James Carter) 1928- . **CLC 12**
See also AAYA 20; CA 9-12R; CANR 37; CLR 25; JRDA; MAICYA; SAAS 11; SATA 6, 68

Mayo, Jim
See L'Amour, Louis (Dearborn)

Maysles, Albert 1926- .... **CLC 16**
See also CA 29-32R

Maysles, David 1932- .... **CLC 16**

Mazer, Norma Fox 1931- .... **CLC 26**
See also AAYA 5; CA 69-72; CANR 12, 32, 66; CLR 23; JRDA; MAICYA; SAAS 1; SATA 24, 67

Mazzini, Guiseppe 1805-1872 .... **NCLC 34**

McAuley, James Phillip 1917-1976 .... **CLC 45**
See also CA 97-100

McBain, Ed
See Hunter, Evan

McBrien, William Augustine 1930- ..... **CLC 44**
See also CA 107

McCaffrey, Anne (Inez) 1926- .... **CLC 17; DAM NOV, POP**
See also AAYA 6; AITN 2; BEST 89:2; CA 25-28R; CANR 15, 35, 55; CLR 49; DLB 8; JRDA; MAICYA; MTCW; SAAS 11; SATA 8, 70

McCall, Nathan 1955(?)- .... **CLC 86**
See also CA 146

McCann, Arthur
See Campbell, John W(ood, Jr.)

McCann, Edson
See Pohl, Frederik

McCarthy, Charles, Jr. 1933-
See McCarthy, Cormac
See also CANR 42; DAM POP

McCarthy, Cormac 1933- .... **CLC 4, 57, 59, 101**
See also McCarthy, Charles, Jr.
See also DLB 6, 143

McCarthy, Mary (Therese) 1912-1989 **CLC 1, 3, 5, 14, 24, 39, 59; SSC 24**
See also CA 5-8R; 129; CANR 16, 50, 64; DLB 2; DLBY 81; INT CANR-16; MTCW

McCartney, (James) Paul 1942- ...... **CLC 12, 35**
See also CA 146

McCauley, Stephen (D.) 1955- .... **CLC 50**
See also CA 141

McClure, Michael (Thomas) 1932- ... **CLC 6, 10**
See also CA 21-24R; CANR 17, 46; DLB 16

McCorkle, Jill (Collins) 1958- .... **CLC 51**
See also CA 121; DLBY 87

McCourt, Frank 1930- .... **CLC 109**
See also CA 157

McCourt, James 1941- .... **CLC 5**
See also CA 57-60

McCoy, Horace (Stanley) 1897-1955 ... **TCLC 28**
See also CA 108; 155; DLB 9

McCrae, John 1872-1918 .... **TCLC 12**
See also CA 109; DLB 92

McCreigh, James
See Pohl, Frederik

McCullers, (Lula) Carson (Smith) 1917-1967 **CLC 1, 4, 10, 12, 48, 100; DA; DAB; DAC; DAM MST, NOV; SSC 9, 24; WLC**
See also AAYA 21; CA 5-8R; 25-28R; CABS 1, 3; CANR 18; CDALB 1941-1968; DLB 2, 7, 173; MTCW; SATA 27

McCulloch, John Tyler
See Burroughs, Edgar Rice

McCullough, Colleen 1938(?)- **CLC 27, 107; DAM NOV, POP**
See also CA 81-84; CANR 17, 46, 67; MTCW

McDermott, Alice 1953- .... **CLC 90**
See also CA 109; CANR 40

McElroy, Joseph 1930- .... **CLC 5, 47**
See also CA 17-20R

McEwan, Ian (Russell) 1948- **CLC 13, 66; DAM NOV**
See also BEST 90:4; CA 61-64; CANR 14, 41; DLB 14, 194; MTCW

McFadden, David 1940- .... **CLC 48**
See also CA 104; DLB 60; INT 104

McFarland, Dennis 1950- .... **CLC 65**
See also CA 165

McGahern, John 1934- ... **CLC 5, 9, 48; SSC 17**
See also CA 17-20R; CANR 29, 68; DLB 14; MTCW

McGinley, Patrick (Anthony) 1937- ..... **CLC 41**
See also CA 120; 127; CANR 56; INT 127

McGinley, Phyllis 1905-1978 .... **CLC 14**
See also CA 9-12R; 77-80; CANR 19; DLB 11, 48; SATA 2, 44; SATA-Obit 24

McGinniss, Joe 1942- .... **CLC 32**
See also AITN 2; BEST 89:2; CA 25-28R; CANR 26; DLB 185; INT CANR-26

McGivern, Maureen Daly
See Daly, Maureen

McGrath, Patrick 1950- .... **CLC 55**
See also CA 136; CANR 65

McGrath, Thomas (Matthew) 1916-1990 **CLC 28, 59; DAM POET**
See also CA 9-12R; 132; CANR 6, 33; MTCW; SATA 41; SATA-Obit 66

McGuane, Thomas (Francis III) 1939- **CLC 3, 7, 18, 45**
See also AITN 2; CA 49-52; CANR 5, 24, 49; DLB 2; DLBY 80; INT CANR-24; MTCW

McGuckian, Medbh 1950- **CLC 48; DAM POET**
See also CA 143; DLB 40

McHale, Tom 1942(?)-1982 .... **CLC 3, 5**
See also AITN 1; CA 77-80; 106

McIlvanney, William 1936- .... **CLC 42**
See also CA 25-28R; CANR 61; DLB 14

McIlwraith, Maureen Mollie Hunter
See Hunter, Mollie
See also SATA 2

McInerney, Jay 1955- .... **CLC 34; DAM POP**
See also AAYA 18; CA 116; 123; CANR 45, 68; INT 123

McIntyre, Vonda N(eel) 1948- .... **CLC 18**
See also CA 81-84; CANR 17, 34; MTCW

McKay, Claude ... TCLC 7, 41; BLC; DAB; PC 2
See also McKay, Festus Claudius
See also DLB 4, 45, 51, 117

McKay, Festus Claudius 1889-1948
See McKay, Claude
See also BW 1; CA 104; 124; DA; DAC; DAM MST, MULT, NOV, POET; MTCW; WLC

McKuen, Rod 1933- .... **CLC 1, 3**
See also AITN 1; CA 41-44R; CANR 40

McLoughlin, R. B.
See Mencken, H(enry) L(ouis)

McLuhan, (Herbert) Marshall 1911-1980 **CLC 37, 83**
See also CA 9-12R; 102; CANR 12, 34, 61; DLB 88; INT CANR-12; MTCW

McMillan, Terry (L.) 1951- .. **CLC 50, 61; DAM MULT, NOV, POP**
See also AAYA 21; BW 2; CA 140; CANR 60

McMurtry, Larry (Jeff) 1936- **CLC 2, 3, 7, 11, 27, 44; DAM NOV, POP**
See also AAYA 15; AITN 2; BEST 89:2; CA 5-8R; CANR 19, 43, 64; CDALB 1968-1988; DLB 2, 143; DLBY 80, 87; MTCW

McNally, T. M. 1961- .... **CLC 82**

McNally, Terrence 1939- **CLC 4, 7, 41, 91; DAM DRAM**
See also CA 45-48; CANR 2, 56; DLB 7

McNamer, Deirdre 1950- .... **CLC 70**

McNeile, Herman Cyril 1888-1937
See Sapper
See also DLB 77

McNickle, (William) D'Arcy 1904-1977 **CLC 89; DAM MULT**
See also CA 9-12R; 85-88; CANR 5, 45; DLB 175; NNAL; SATA-Obit 22

McPhee, John (Angus) 1931- .... **CLC 36**
See also BEST 90:1; CA 65-68; CANR 20, 46, 64; DLB 185; MTCW

McPherson, James Alan 1943- .... **CLC 19, 77**
See also BW 1; CA 25-28R; CAAS 17; CANR 24; DLB 38; MTCW

McPherson, William (Alexander) 1933- **CLC 34**
See also CA 69-72; CANR 28; INT CANR-28

Mead, Margaret 1901-1978 .... **CLC 37**
See also AITN 1; CA 1-4R; 81-84; CANR 4; MTCW; SATA-Obit 20

Meaker, Marijane (Agnes) 1927-
See Kerr, M. E.
See also CA 107; CANR 37, 63; INT 107; JRDA; MAICYA; MTCW; SATA 20, 61

Medoff, Mark (Howard) 1940- **CLC 6, 23; DAM DRAM**
See also AITN 1; CA 53-56; CANR 5; DLB 7; INT CANR-5

Medvedev, P. N.
See Bakhtin, Mikhail Mikhailovich

Meged, Aharon
See Megged, Aharon

Meged, Aron
See Megged, Aharon

Megged, Aharon 1920- .... **CLC 9**
See also CA 49-52; CAAS 13; CANR 1

Mehta, Ved (Parkash) 1934- .... **CLC 37**
See also CA 1-4R; CANR 2, 23; MTCW

Melanter
See Blackmore, R(ichard) D(oddridge)

Melikow, Loris
See Hofmannsthal, Hugo von

Melmoth, Sebastian
See Wilde, Oscar (Fingal O'Flahertie Wills)

Meltzer, Milton 1915- .... **CLC 26**
See also AAYA 8; CA 13-16R; CANR 38; CLR 13; DLB 61; JRDA; MAICYA; SAAS 1; SATA 1, 50, 80

Melville, Herman 1819-1891 **NCLC 3, 12, 29, 45, 49; DA; DAB; DAC; DAM MST, NOV; SSC 1, 17; WLC**
See also AAYA 25; CDALB 1640-1865; DLB 3, 74; SATA 59

Menander c. 342B.C.-c. 292B.C. **CMLC 9; DAM DRAM; DC 3**
See also DLB 176

Mencken, H(enry) L(ouis) 1880-1956 . **TCLC 13**
See also CA 105; 125; CDALB 1917-1929; DLB 11, 29, 63, 137; MTCW

Mendelsohn, Jane 1965(?)- .... **CLC 99**
See also CA 154

Mercer, David 1928-1980 .. **CLC 5; DAM DRAM**
See also CA 9-12R; 102; CANR 23; DLB 13; MTCW

Merchant, Paul
See Ellison, Harlan (Jay)

Meredith, George 1828-1909 **TCLC 17, 43; DAM POET**
See also CA 117; 153; CDBLB 1832-1890; DLB 18, 35, 57, 159

Meredith, William (Morris) 1919- **CLC 4, 13, 22, 55; DAM POET**
See also CA 9-12R; CAAS 14; CANR 6, 40; DLB 5

Merezhkovsky, Dmitry Sergeyevich 1865-1941 **TCLC 29**

Merimee, Prosper 1803-1870 **NCLC 6, 65; SSC 7**
See also DLB 119, 192

Merkin, Daphne 1954- .... **CLC 44**
See also CA 123

Merlin, Arthur
See Blish, James (Benjamin)

Merrill, James (Ingram) 1926-1995 **CLC 2, 3, 6, 8, 13, 18, 34, 91; DAM POET**
See also CA 13-16R; 147; CANR 10, 49, 63; DLB 5, 165; DLBY 85; INT CANR-10; MTCW

Merriman, Alex
See Silverberg, Robert

Merritt, E. B.
See Waddington, Miriam

Merton, Thomas 1915-1968 **CLC 1, 3, 11, 34, 83; PC 10**
See also CA 5-8R; 25-28R; CANR 22, 53; DLB 48; DLBY 81; MTCW

Merwin, W(illiam) S(tanley) 1927- **CLC 1, 2, 3, 5, 8, 13, 18, 45, 88; DAM POET**
See also CA 13-16R; CANR 15, 51; DLB 5, 169; INT CANR-15; MTCW

Metcalf, John 1938- .... **CLC 37**
See also CA 113; DLB 60

Mizoguchi, Kenji 1898-1956 .... **TCLC 72**

Mo, Timothy (Peter) 1950(?)- .... **CLC 46**
See also CA 117; DLB 194; MTCW

Modarressi, Taghi (M.) 1931- .... **CLC 44**
See also CA 121; 134; INT 134

Modiano, Patrick (Jean) 1945- .... **CLC 18**
See also CA 85-88; CANR 17, 40; DLB 83

Moerck, Paal
See Roelvaag, O(le) E(dvart)

Mofolo, Thomas (Mokopu) 1875(?)-1948**TCLC 22; BLC; DAM MULT**
See also CA 121; 153

Mohr, Nicholasa 1938-**CLC 12; DAM MULT; HLC**
See also AAYA 8; CA 49-52; CANR 1, 32, 64; CLR 22; DLB 145; HW; JRDA; SAAS 8; SATA 8, 97

Mojtabai, A(nn) G(race) 1938- **CLC 5, 9, 15, 29**
See also CA 85-88

Moliere 1622-1673**LC 28; DA; DAB; DAC; DAM DRAM, MST; WLC**

Molin, Charles
See Mayne, William (James Carter)

Molnar, Ferenc 1878-1952**TCLC 20; DAM DRAM**
See also CA 109; 153

Momaday, N(avarre) Scott 1934- **CLC 2, 19, 85, 95; DA; DAB; DAC; DAM MST, MULT, NOV, POP; WLCS**
See also AAYA 11; CA 25-28R; CANR 14, 34, 68; DLB 143, 175; INT CANR-14; MTCW; NNAL; SATA 48; SATA-Brief 30

Monette, Paul 1945-1995 .... **CLC 82**
See also CA 139; 147

Monroe, Harriet 1860-1936 .... **TCLC 12**
See also CA 109; DLB 54, 91

Monroe, Lyle
See Heinlein, Robert A(nson)

Montagu, Elizabeth 1917- .... **NCLC 7**
See also CA 9-12R

Montagu, Mary (Pierrepont) Wortley 1689-1762 **LC 9; PC 16**
See also DLB 95, 101

Montagu, W. H.
See Coleridge, Samuel Taylor

Montague, John (Patrick) 1929- ..... **CLC 13, 46**
See also CA 9-12R; CANR 9; DLB 40; MTCW

Montaigne, Michel (Eyquem) de 1533-1592**LC 8; DA; DAB; DAC; DAM MST; WLC**

Montale, Eugenio 1896-1981**CLC 7, 9, 18; PC 13**
See also CA 17-20R; 104; CANR 30; DLB 114; MTCW

Montesquieu, Charles-Louis de Secondat 1689-1755 .... **LC 7**

Montgomery, (Robert) Bruce 1921-1978
See Crispin, Edmund
See also CA 104

Montgomery, L(ucy) M(aud) 1874-1942**TCLC 51; DAC; DAM MST**
See also AAYA 12; CA 108; 137; CLR 8; DLB 92; DLBD 14; JRDA; MAICYA; YABC 1

Montgomery, Marion H., Jr. 1925- .... **CLC 7**
See also AITN 1; CA 1-4R; CANR 3, 48; DLB 6

Montgomery, Max
See Davenport, Guy (Mattison, Jr.)

Montherlant, Henry (Milon) de 1896-1972**CLC 8, 19; DAM DRAM**
See also CA 85-88; 37-40R; DLB 72; MTCW

Monty Python
See Chapman, Graham; Cleese, John (Marwood); Gilliam, Terry (Vance); Idle, Eric; Jones, Terence Graham Parry; Palin, Michael (Edward)
See also AAYA 7

Moodie, Susanna (Strickland) 1803-1885 **NCLC 14**
See also DLB 99

Mooney, Edward 1951-
See Mooney, Ted
See also CA 130

Mooney, Ted .... **CLC 25**
See also Mooney, Edward

Moorcock, Michael (John) 1939- **CLC 5, 27, 58**
See also CA 45-48; CAAS 5; CANR 2, 17, 38, 64; DLB 14; MTCW; SATA 93

Moore, Brian 1921-**CLC 1, 3, 5, 7, 8, 19, 32, 90; DAB; DAC; DAM MST**
See also CA 1-4R; CANR 1, 25, 42, 63; MTCW

Moore, Edward
See Muir, Edwin

Moore, George Augustus 1852-1933**TCLC 7; SSC 19**
See also CA 104; DLB 10, 18, 57, 135

Moore, Lorrie .... **CLC 39, 45, 68**
See also Moore, Marie Lorena

Moore, Marianne (Craig) 1887-1972**CLC 1, 2, 4, 8, 10, 13, 19, 47; DA; DAB; DAC; DAM MST, POET; PC 4; WLCS**
See also CA 1-4R; 33-36R; CANR 3, 61; CDALB 1929-1941; DLB 45; DLBD 7; MTCW; SATA 20

Moore, Marie Lorena 1957-
See Moore, Lorrie
See also CA 116; CANR 39

Moore, Thomas 1779-1852 .... **NCLC 6**
See also DLB 96, 144

Morand, Paul 1888-1976 .... **CLC 41; SSC 22**
See also CA 69-72; DLB 65

Morante, Elsa 1918-1985 .... **CLC 8, 47**
See also CA 85-88; 117; CANR 35; DLB 177; MTCW

Moravia, Alberto 1907-1990**CLC 2, 7, 11, 27, 46; SSC 26**
See also Pincherle, Alberto
See also DLB 177

More, Hannah 1745-1833 .... **NCLC 27**
See also DLB 107, 109, 116, 158

More, Henry 1614-1687 .... **LC 9**
See also DLB 126

More, Sir Thomas 1478-1535 .... **LC 10, 32**

Moreas, Jean .... **TCLC 18**
See also Papadiamantopoulos, Johannes

Morgan, Berry 1919- .... **CLC 6**
See also CA 49-52; DLB 6

Morgan, Claire
See Highsmith, (Mary) Patricia

Morgan, Edwin (George) 1920- .... **CLC 31**
See also CA 5-8R; CANR 3, 43; DLB 27

Morgan, (George) Frederick 1922- ...... **CLC 23**
See also CA 17-20R; CANR 21

Morgan, Harriet
See Mencken, H(enry) L(ouis)

Morgan, Jane
See Cooper, James Fenimore

Morgan, Janet 1945- .... **CLC 39**
See also CA 65-68

Morgan, Lady 1776(?)-1859 .... **NCLC 29**
See also DLB 116, 158

Morgan, Robin (Evonne) 1941- .... **CLC 2**
See also CA 69-72; CANR 29, 68; MTCW; SATA 80

Morgan, Scott
See Kuttner, Henry

Morgan, Seth 1949(?)-1990 .... **CLC 65**
See also CA 132

Morgenstern, Christian 1871-1914 ...... **TCLC 8**
See also CA 105

Morgenstern, S.
See Goldman, William (W.)

Moricz, Zsigmond 1879-1942 .... **TCLC 33**
See also CA 165

Morike, Eduard (Friedrich) 1804-1875 **NCLC 10**
See also DLB 133

Moritz, Karl Philipp 1756-1793 .... **LC 2**
See also DLB 94

Morland, Peter Henry
See Faust, Frederick (Schiller)

Morren, Theophil
See Hofmannsthal, Hugo von

Morris, Bill 1952- .... **CLC 76**

Morris, Julian
See West, Morris L(anglo)

Morris, Steveland Judkins 1950(?)-
See Wonder, Stevie
See also CA 111

Morris, William 1834-1896 **NCLC 4**
See also CDBLB 1832-1890; DLB 18, 35, 57, 156, 178, 184

Nabokov, Vladimir (Vladimirovich) 1899-1977 **CLC 1, 2, 3, 6, 8, 11, 15, 23, 44, 46, 64; DA; DAB; DAC; DAM MST, NOV; SSC 11; WLC**
See also CA 5-8R; 69-72; CANR 20; CDALB 1941-1968; DLB 2; DLBD 3; DLBY 80, 91; MTCW

Nagai Kafu 1879-1959 .... **TCLC 51**
See also Nagai Sokichi
See also DLB 180

Nagai Sokichi 1879-1959
See Nagai Kafu
See also CA 117

Nagy, Laszlo 1925-1978 .... **CLC 7**
See also CA 129; 112

Naidu, Sarojini 1879-1943 .... **TCLC 80**

Naipaul, Shiva(dhar Srinivasa) 1945-1985 . **CLC 32, 39; DAM NOV**
See also CA 110; 112; 116; CANR 33; DLB 157; DLBY 85; MTCW

Naipaul, V(idiadhar) S(urajprasad) 1932-**CLC 4, 7, 9, 13, 18, 37, 105; DAB; DAC; DAM MST, NOV**
See also CA 1-4R; CANR 1, 33, 51; CDBLB 1960 to Present; DLB 125; DLBY 85; MTCW

Nakos, Lilika 1899(?)- .... **CLC 29**

Narayan, R(asipuram) K(rishnaswami) 1906- **CLC 7, 28, 47; DAM NOV; SSC 25**
See also CA 81-84; CANR 33, 61; MTCW; SATA 62

Nash, (Frediric) Ogden 1902-1971 **CLC 23; DAM POET; PC 21**
See also CA 13-14; 29-32R; CANR 34, 61; CAP 1; DLB 11; MAICYA; MTCW; SATA 2, 46

Nashe, Thomas 1567-1601(?) .... **LC 41**
See also DLB 167

Nashe, Thomas 1567-1601 .... **LC 41**

Nathan, Daniel
See Dannay, Frederic

Nathan, George Jean 1882-1958 .... **TCLC 18**
See also Hatteras, Owen
See also CA 114; DLB 137

Natsume, Kinnosuke 1867-1916
See Natsume, Soseki
See also CA 104

Natsume, Soseki 1867-1916 .... **TCLC 2, 10**
See also Natsume, Kinnosuke
See also DLB 180

Natti, (Mary) Lee 1919-
See Kingman, Lee
See also CA 5-8R; CANR 2

Naylor, Gloria 1950-**CLC 28, 52; BLC; DA; DAC; DAM MST, MULT, NOV, POP; WLCS**
See also AAYA 6; BW 2; CA 107; CANR 27, 51; DLB 173; MTCW

Neihardt, John Gneisenau 1881-1973 **CLC 32**
See also CA 13-14; CANR 65; CAP 1; DLB 9, 54

Nekrasov, Nikolai Alekseevich 1821-1878 **NCLC 11**

Nelligan, Emile 1879-1941 .... **TCLC 14**
See also CA 114; DLB 92

Nelson, Willie 1933- .... **CLC 17**
See also CA 107

Nemerov, Howard (Stanley) 1920-1991 **CLC 2, 6, 9, 36; DAM POET**
See also CA 1-4R; 134; CABS 2; CANR 1, 27, 53; DLB 5, 6; DLBY 83; INT CANR-27; MTCW

Neruda, Pablo 1904-1973 **CLC 1, 2, 5, 7, 9, 28, 62; DA; DAB; DAC; DAM MST, MULT, POET; HLC; PC 4; WLC**
See also CA 19-20; 45-48; CAP 2; HW; MTCW

Nerval, Gerard de 1808-1855 **NCLC 1, 67; PC 13; SSC 18**

Nervo, (Jose) Amado (Ruiz de) 1870-1919 **TCLC 11**
See also CA 109; 131; HW

Nessi, Pio Baroja y
See Baroja (y Nessi), Pio

Nestroy, Johann 1801-1862 .... **NCLC 42**
See also DLB 133

Netterville, Luke
See O'Grady, Standish (James)

Neufeld, John (Arthur) 1938- .... **CLC 17**
See also AAYA 11; CA 25-28R; CANR 11, 37, 56; MAICYA; SAAS 3; SATA 6, 81

Neville, Emily Cheney 1919- .... **CLC 12**
See also CA 5-8R; CANR 3, 37; JRDA; MAICYA; SAAS 2; SATA 1

Newbound, Bernard Slade 1930-
See Slade, Bernard
See also CA 81-84; CANR 49; DAM DRAM

Newby, P(ercy) H(oward) 1918-1997 . **CLC 2, 13; DAM NOV**
See also CA 5-8R; 161; CANR 32, 67; DLB 15; MTCW

Newlove, Donald 1928- .... **CLC 6**
See also CA 29-32R; CANR 25

Newlove, John (Herbert) 1938- .... **CLC 14**
See also CA 21-24R; CANR 9, 25

Newman, Charles 1938- .... **CLC 2, 8**
See also CA 21-24R

Newman, Edwin (Harold) 1919- .... **CLC 14**
See also AITN 1; CA 69-72; CANR 5

Newman, John Henry 1801-1890 .... **NCLC 38**
See also DLB 18, 32, 55

Newton, Suzanne 1936- .... **CLC 35**
See also CA 41-44R; CANR 14; JRDA; SATA 5, 77

Nexo, Martin Andersen 1869-1954 ..... **TCLC 43**

Nezval, Vitezslav 1900-1958 .... **TCLC 44**
See also CA 123

Ng, Fae Myenne 1957(?)- .... **CLC 81**
See also CA 146

Ngema, Mbongeni 1955- .... **CLC 57**
See also BW 2; CA 143

Ngugi, James T(hiong'o) .... **CLC 3, 7, 13**
See also Ngugi wa Thiong'o

Ngugi wa Thiong'o 1938- . **CLC 36; BLC; DAM MULT, NOV**
See also Ngugi, James T(hiong'o)
See also BW 2; CA 81-84; CANR 27, 58; DLB 125; MTCW

Nichol, B(arrie) P(hillip) 1944-1988 ..... **CLC 18**
See also CA 53-56; DLB 53; SATA 66

Nichols, John (Treadwell) 1940- .... **CLC 38**
See also CA 9-12R; CAAS 2; CANR 6; DLBY 82

Nichols, Leigh
See Koontz, Dean R(ay)

Nichols, Peter (Richard) 1927-... **CLC 5, 36, 65**
See also CA 104; CANR 33; DLB 13; MTCW

Nicolas, F. R. E.
See Freeling, Nicolas

Niedecker, Lorine 1903-1970 **CLC 10, 42; DAM POET**
See also CA 25-28; CAP 2; DLB 48

Nietzsche, Friedrich (Wilhelm) 1844-1900 **TCLC 10, 18, 55**
See also CA 107; 121; DLB 129

Nievo, Ippolito 1831-1861 .... **NCLC 22**

Nightingale, Anne Redmon 1943-
See Redmon, Anne
See also CA 103

Nik. T. O.
See Annensky, Innokenty (Fyodorovich)

Nin, Anais 1903-1977 **CLC 1, 4, 8, 11, 14, 60; DAM NOV, POP; SSC 10**
See also AITN 2; CA 13-16R; 69-72; CANR 22, 53; DLB 2, 4, 152; MTCW

Nishiwaki, Junzaburo 1894-1982 .... **PC 15**
See also CA 107

Nissenson, Hugh 1933- .... **CLC 4, 9**
See also CA 17-20R; CANR 27; DLB 28

Niven, Larry .... **CLC 8**
See also Niven, Laurence Van Cott
See also DLB 8

Niven, Laurence Van Cott 1938-
See Niven, Larry
See also CA 21-24R; CAAS 12; CANR 14, 44, 66; DAM POP; MTCW; SATA 95

Nixon, Agnes Eckhardt 1927- .... **CLC 21**
See also CA 110

Nizan, Paul 1905-1940 .... **TCLC 40**
See also CA 161; DLB 72

Nkosi, Lewis 1936- **CLC 45; BLC; DAM MULT**
See also BW 1; CA 65-68; CANR 27; DLB 157

Nodier, (Jean) Charles (Emmanuel) 1780-1844 **NCLC 19**
See also DLB 119

O'Hara, John (Henry) 1905-1970 **CLC 1, 2, 3, 6, 11, 42; DAM NOV; SSC 15**
See also CA 5-8R; 25-28R; CANR 31, 60; CDALB 1929-1941; DLB 9, 86; DLBD 2; MTCW

O Hehir, Diana 1922- .... **CLC 41**
See also CA 93-96

Okigbo, Christopher (Ifenayichukwu) 1932-1967 **CLC 25, 84; BLC; DAM MULT, POET; PC 7**
See also BW 1; CA 77-80; DLB 125; MTCW

Okri, Ben 1959- .... **CLC 87**
See also BW 2; CA 130; 138; CANR 65; DLB 157; INT 138

Olds, Sharon 1942-**CLC 32, 39, 85; DAM POET; PC 22**
See also CA 101; CANR 18, 41, 66; DLB 120

Oldstyle, Jonathan
See Irving, Washington

Olesha, Yuri (Karlovich) 1899-1960 .... **CLC 8**
See also CA 85-88

Oliphant, Laurence 1829(?)-1888 ...... **NCLC 47**
See also DLB 18, 166

Oliphant, Margaret (Oliphant Wilson) 1828-1897 **NCLC 11, 61; SSC 25**
See also DLB 18, 159, 190

Oliver, Mary 1935- .... **CLC 19, 34, 98**
See also CA 21-24R; CANR 9, 43; DLB 5, 193

Olivier, Laurence (Kerr) 1907-1989 ..... **CLC 20**
See also CA 111; 150; 129

Olsen, Tillie 1913- **CLC 4, 13; DA; DAB; DAC; DAM MST; SSC 11**
See also CA 1-4R; CANR 1, 43; DLB 28; DLBY 80; MTCW

Olson, Charles (John) 1910-1970**CLC 1, 2, 5, 6, 9, 11, 29; DAM POET; PC 19**
See also CA 13-16; 25-28R; CABS 2; CANR 35, 61; CAP 1; DLB 5, 16, 193; MTCW

Olson, Toby 1937- .... **CLC 28**
See also CA 65-68; CANR 9, 31

Olyesha, Yuri
See Olesha, Yuri (Karlovich)

Ondaatje, (Philip) Michael 1943-**CLC 14, 29, 51, 76; DAB; DAC; DAM MST**
See also CA 77-80; CANR 42; DLB 60

Oneal, Elizabeth 1934-
See Oneal, Zibby
See also CA 106; CANR 28; MAICYA; SATA 30, 82

Oneal, Zibby .... **CLC 30**
See also Oneal, Elizabeth
See also AAYA 5; CLR 13; JRDA

O'Neill, Eugene (Gladstone) 1888-1953**TCLC 1, 6, 27, 49; DA; DAB; DAC; DAM DRAM, MST; WLC**
See also AITN 1; CA 110; 132; CDALB 1929-1941; DLB 7; MTCW

Onetti, Juan Carlos 1909-1994 **CLC 7, 10; DAM MULT, NOV; SSC 23**
See also CA 85-88; 145; CANR 32, 63; DLB 113; HW; MTCW

O Nuallain, Brian 1911-1966
See O'Brien, Flann
See also CA 21-22; 25-28R; CAP 2

Ophuls, Max 1902-1957 .... **TCLC 79**
See also CA 113

Opie, Amelia 1769-1853 .... **NCLC 65**
See also DLB 116, 159

Oppen, George 1908-1984 .... **CLC 7, 13, 34**
See also CA 13-16R; 113; CANR 8; DLB 5, 165

Oppenheim, E(dward) Phillips 1866-1946 **TCLC 45**
See also CA 111; DLB 70

Opuls, Max
See Ophuls, Max

Origen c. 185-c. 254 .... **CMLC 19**

Orlovitz, Gil 1918-1973 .... **CLC 22**
See also CA 77-80; 45-48; DLB 2, 5

Orris
See Ingelow, Jean

Ortega y Gasset, Jose 1883-1955 **TCLC 9; DAM MULT; HLC**
See also CA 106; 130; HW; MTCW

Ortese, Anna Maria 1914- .... **CLC 89**
See also DLB 177

Ortiz, Simon J(oseph) 1941- ...... **CLC 45; DAM MULT, POET; PC 17**
See also CA 134; DLB 120, 175; NNAL

Orton, Joe .... **CLC 4, 13, 43; DC 3**
See also Orton, John Kingsley
See also CDBLB 1960 to Present; DLB 13

Orton, John Kingsley 1933-1967
See Orton, Joe
See also CA 85-88; CANR 35, 66; DAM DRAM; MTCW

Orwell, George **TCLC 2, 6, 15, 31, 51; DAB; WLC**
See also Blair, Eric (Arthur)
See also CDBLB 1945-1960; DLB 15, 98, 195

Osborne, David
See Silverberg, Robert

Osborne, George
See Silverberg, Robert

Osborne, John (James) 1929-1994**CLC 1, 2, 5, 11, 45; DA; DAB; DAC; DAM DRAM, MST; WLC**
See also CA 13-16R; 147; CANR 21, 56; CDBLB 1945-1960; DLB 13; MTCW

Osborne, Lawrence 1958- .... **CLC 50**

Oshima, Nagisa 1932- .... **CLC 20**
See also CA 116; 121

Oskison, John Milton 1874-1947**TCLC 35; DAM MULT**
See also CA 144; DLB 175; NNAL

Ossoli, Sarah Margaret (Fuller marchesa d') 1810-1850
See Fuller, Margaret
See also SATA 25

Ostrovsky, Alexander 1823-1886 .. **NCLC 30, 57**

Otero, Blas de 1916-1979 .... **CLC 11**
See also CA 89-92; DLB 134

Otto, Whitney 1955- .... **CLC 70**
See also CA 140

Ouida .... **TCLC 43**
See also De La Ramee, (Marie) Louise
See also DLB 18, 156

Ousmane, Sembene 1923- .... **CLC 66; BLC**
See also BW 1; CA 117; 125; MTCW

Ovid 43B.C.-18(?) . **CMLC 7; DAM POET; PC 2**

Owen, Hugh
See Faust, Frederick (Schiller)

Owen, Wilfred (Edward Salter) 1893-1918**TCLC 5, 27; DA; DAB; DAC; DAM MST, POET; PC 19; WLC**
See also CA 104; 141; CDBLB 1914-1945; DLB 20

Owens, Rochelle 1936- .... **CLC 8**
See also CA 17-20R; CAAS 2; CANR 39

Oz, Amos 1939- . **CLC 5, 8, 11, 27, 33, 54; DAM NOV**
See also CA 53-56; CANR 27, 47, 65; MTCW

Ozick, Cynthia 1928-**CLC 3, 7, 28, 62; DAM NOV, POP; SSC 15**
See also BEST 90:1; CA 17-20R; CANR 23, 58; DLB 28, 152; DLBY 82; INT CANR-23; MTCW

Ozu, Yasujiro 1903-1963 .... **CLC 16**
See also CA 112

Pacheco, C.
See Pessoa, Fernando (Antonio Nogueira)

Pa Chin .... **CLC 18**
See also Li Fei-kan

Pack, Robert 1929- .... **CLC 13**
See also CA 1-4R; CANR 3, 44; DLB 5

Padgett, Lewis
See Kuttner, Henry

Padilla (Lorenzo), Heberto 1932- .... **CLC 38**
See also AITN 1; CA 123; 131; HW

Page, Jimmy 1944- .... **CLC 12**

Page, Louise 1955- .... **CLC 40**
See also CA 140

Page, P(atricia) K(athleen) 1916- .... **CLC 7, 18; DAC; DAM MST; PC 12**
See also CA 53-56; CANR 4, 22, 65; DLB 68; MTCW

Page, Thomas Nelson 1853-1922 .... **SSC 23**
See also CA 118; DLB 12, 78; DLBD 13

Pagels, Elaine Hiesey 1943- .... **CLC 104**
See also CA 45-48; CANR 2, 24, 51

Paget, Violet 1856-1935
See Lee, Vernon

See also CA 104

Paget-Lowe, Henry
See Lovecraft, H(oward) P(hillips)

Paglia, Camille (Anna) 1947- .... **CLC 68**
See also CA 140

Paige, Richard
See Koontz, Dean R(ay)

Paine, Thomas 1737-1809 .... **NCLC 62**
See also CDALB 1640-1865; DLB 31, 43, 73, 158

Pakenham, Antonia
See Fraser, (Lady) Antonia (Pakenham)

Palamas, Kostes 1859-1943 .... **TCLC 5**
See also CA 105

Palazzeschi, Aldo 1885-1974 .... **CLC 11**
See also CA 89-92; 53-56; DLB 114

Paley, Grace 1922-**CLC 4, 6, 37; DAM POP; SSC 8**
See also CA 25-28R; CANR 13, 46; DLB 28; INT CANR-13; MTCW

Palin, Michael (Edward) 1943- .... **CLC 21**
See also Monty Python
See also CA 107; CANR 35; SATA 67

Palliser, Charles 1947- .... **CLC 65**
See also CA 136

Palma, Ricardo 1833-1919 .... **TCLC 29**

Pancake, Breece Dexter 1952-1979
See Pancake, Breece D'J
See also CA 123; 109

Pancake, Breece D'J .... **CLC 29**
See also Pancake, Breece Dexter
See also DLB 130

Panko, Rudy
See Gogol, Nikolai (Vasilyevich)

Papadiamantis, Alexandros 1851-1911 **TCLC 29**

Papadiamantopoulos, Johannes 1856-1910
See Moreas, Jean
See also CA 117

Papini, Giovanni 1881-1956 .... **TCLC 22**
See also CA 121

Paracelsus 1493-1541 .... **LC 14**
See also DLB 179

Parasol, Peter
See Stevens, Wallace

Pardo Bazan, Emilia 1851-1921 .... **SSC 30**

Pareto, Vilfredo 1848-1923 .... **TCLC 69**

Parfenie, Maria
See Codrescu, Andrei

Parini, Jay (Lee) 1948- .... **CLC 54**
See also CA 97-100; CAAS 16; CANR 32

Park, Jordan
See Kornbluth, C(yril) M.; Pohl, Frederik

Park, Robert E(zra) 1864-1944 .... **TCLC 73**
See also CA 122; 165

Parker, Bert
See Ellison, Harlan (Jay)

Parker, Dorothy (Rothschild) 1893-1967**CLC 15, 68; DAM POET; SSC 2**
See also CA 19-20; 25-28R; CAP 2; DLB 11, 45, 86; MTCW

Parker, Robert B(rown) 1932- ... **CLC 27; DAM NOV, POP**
See also BEST 89:4; CA 49-52; CANR 1, 26, 52; INT CANR-26; MTCW

Parkin, Frank 1940- .... **CLC 43**
See also CA 147

Parkman, Francis, Jr. 1823-1893 ...... **NCLC 12**
See also DLB 1, 30, 186

Parks, Gordon (Alexander Buchanan) 1912-**CLC 1, 16; BLC; DAM MULT**
See also AITN 2; BW 2; CA 41-44R; CANR 26, 66; DLB 33; SATA 8

Parmenides c. 515B.C.-c. 450B.C. ...... **CMLC 22**
See also DLB 176

Parnell, Thomas 1679-1718 .... **LC 3**
See also DLB 94

Parra, Nicanor 1914- **CLC 2, 102; DAM MULT; HLC**
See also CA 85-88; CANR 32; HW; MTCW

Parrish, Mary Frances
See Fisher, M(ary) F(rances) K(ennedy)

Parson
See Coleridge, Samuel Taylor

Parson Lot
See Kingsley, Charles

Partridge, Anthony
See Oppenheim, E(dward) Phillips

Pascal, Blaise 1623-1662 .... **LC 35**

Pascoli, Giovanni 1855-1912 .... **TCLC 45**

Pasolini, Pier Paolo 1922-1975**CLC 20, 37, 106; PC 17**
See also CA 93-96; 61-64; CANR 63; DLB 128, 177; MTCW

Pasquini
See Silone, Ignazio

Pastan, Linda (Olenik) 1932- .... **CLC 27; DAM POET**
See also CA 61-64; CANR 18, 40, 61; DLB 5

Pasternak, Boris (Leonidovich) 1890-1960 **CLC 7, 10, 18, 63; DA; DAB; DAC; DAM MST, NOV, POET; PC 6; WLC**
See also CA 127; 116; MTCW

Patchen, Kenneth 1911-1972**CLC 1, 2, 18; DAM POET**
See also CA 1-4R; 33-36R; CANR 3, 35; DLB 16, 48; MTCW

Pater, Walter (Horatio) 1839-1894 .... **NCLC 7**
See also CDBLB 1832-1890; DLB 57, 156

Paterson, A(ndrew) B(arton) 1864-1941**TCLC 32**
See also CA 155; SATA 97

Paterson, Katherine (Womeldorf) 1932-**CLC 12, 30**
See also AAYA 1; CA 21-24R; CANR 28, 59; CLR 7; DLB 52; JRDA; MAICYA; MTCW; SATA 13, 53, 92

Patmore, Coventry Kersey Dighton 1823-1896 **NCLC 9**
See also DLB 35, 98

Paton, Alan (Stewart) 1903-1988 **CLC 4, 10, 25, 55, 106; DA; DAB; DAC; DAM MST, NOV; WLC**
See also CA 13-16; 125; CANR 22; CAP 1; MTCW; SATA 11; SATA-Obit 56

Paton Walsh, Gillian 1937-
See Walsh, Jill Paton
See also CANR 38; JRDA; MAICYA; SAAS 3; SATA 4, 72

Patton, George S. 1885-1945 .... **TCLC 79**

Paulding, James Kirke 1778-1860 .... **NCLC 2**
See also DLB 3, 59, 74

Paulin, Thomas Neilson 1949-
See Paulin, Tom
See also CA 123; 128

Paulin, Tom .... **CLC 37**
See also Paulin, Thomas Neilson
See also DLB 40

Paustovsky, Konstantin (Georgievich) 1892-1968 **CLC 40**
See also CA 93-96; 25-28R

Pavese, Cesare 1908-1950**TCLC 3; PC 13; SSC 19**
See also CA 104; DLB 128, 177

Pavic, Milorad 1929- .... **CLC 60**
See also CA 136; DLB 181

Payne, Alan
See Jakes, John (William)

Paz, Gil
See Lugones, Leopoldo

Paz, Octavio 1914-1998**CLC 3, 4, 6, 10, 19, 51, 65; DA; DAB; DAC; DAM MST, MULT, POET; HLC; PC 1; WLC**
See also CA 73-76; 165; CANR 32, 65; DLBY 90; HW; MTCW

p'Bitek, Okot 1931-1982 .. **CLC 96; BLC; DAM MULT**
See also BW 2; CA 124; 107; DLB 125; MTCW

Peacock, Molly 1947- .... **CLC 60**
See also CA 103; CAAS 21; CANR 52; DLB 120

Peacock, Thomas Love 1785-1866 ...... **NCLC 22**
See also DLB 96, 116

Peake, Mervyn 1911-1968 .... **CLC 7, 54**
See also CA 5-8R; 25-28R; CANR 3; DLB 15, 160; MTCW; SATA 23

Pearce, Philippa .... **CLC 21**
See also Christie, (Ann) Philippa
See also CLR 9; DLB 161; MAICYA; SATA 1, 67

Pearl, Eric
See Elman, Richard (Martin)

Pinsky, Robert 1940- . **CLC 9, 19, 38, 94; DAM POET**
See also CA 29-32R; CAAS 4; CANR 58; DLBY 82

Pinta, Harold
See Pinter, Harold

Pinter, Harold 1930-**CLC 1, 3, 6, 9, 11, 15, 27, 58, 73; DA; DAB; DAC; DAM DRAM, MST; WLC**
See also CA 5-8R; CANR 33, 65; CDBLB 1960 to Present; DLB 13; MTCW

Piozzi, Hester Lynch (Thrale) 1741-1821 **NCLC 57**
See also DLB 104, 142

Pirandello, Luigi 1867-1936 ... **TCLC 4, 29; DA; DAB; DAC; DAM DRAM, MST; DC 5; SSC 22; WLC**
See also CA 104; 153

Pirsig, Robert M(aynard) 1928- ... **CLC 4, 6, 73; DAM POP**
See also CA 53-56; CANR 42; MTCW; SATA 39

Pisarev, Dmitry Ivanovich 1840-1868 . **NCLC 25**

Pix, Mary (Griffith) 1666-1709 .... **LC 8**
See also DLB 80

Pixerecourt, (Rene Charles) Guilbert de 1773-1844 **NCLC 39**
See also DLB 192

Plaatje, Sol(omon) T(shekisho) 1876-1932 **TCLC 73**
See also BW 2; CA 141

Plaidy, Jean
See Hibbert, Eleanor Alice Burford

Planche, James Robinson 1796-1880 . **NCLC 42**

Plant, Robert 1948- .... **CLC 12**

Plante, David (Robert) 1940-**CLC 7, 23, 38; DAM NOV**
See also CA 37-40R; CANR 12, 36, 58; DLBY 83; INT CANR-12; MTCW

Plath, Sylvia 1932-1963 **CLC 1, 2, 3, 5, 9, 11, 14, 17, 50, 51, 62; DA; DAB; DAC; DAM MST, POET; PC 1; WLC**
See also AAYA 13; CA 19-20; CANR 34; CAP 2; CDALB 1941-1968; DLB 5, 6, 152; MTCW; SATA 96

Plato 428(?)B.C.-348(?)B.C. **CMLC 8; DA; DAB; DAC; DAM MST; WLCS**
See also DLB 176

Platonov, Andrei .... **TCLC 14**
See also Klimentov, Andrei Platonovich

Platt, Kin 1911- .... **CLC 26**
See also AAYA 11; CA 17-20R; CANR 11; JRDA; SAAS 17; SATA 21, 86

Plautus c. 251B.C.-184B.C. ...... **CMLC 24; DC 6**

Plick et Plock
See Simenon, Georges (Jacques Christian)

Plimpton, George (Ames) 1927- **CLC 36**
See also AITN 1; CA 21-24R; CANR 32; DLB 185; MTCW; SATA 10

Pliny the Elder c. 23-79 .... **CMLC 23**

Plomer, William Charles Franklin 1903-1973 **CLC 4, 8**
See also CA 21-22; CANR 34; CAP 2; DLB 20, 162, 191; MTCW; SATA 24

Plowman, Piers
See Kavanagh, Patrick (Joseph)

Plum, J.
See Wodehouse, P(elham) G(renville)

Plumly, Stanley (Ross) 1939- .... **CLC 33**
See also CA 108; 110; DLB 5, 193; INT 110

Plumpe, Friedrich Wilhelm 1888-1931 **TCLC 53**
See also CA 112

Po Chu-i 772-846 .... **CMLC 24**

Poe, Edgar Allan 1809-1849 **NCLC 1, 16, 55; DA; DAB; DAC; DAM MST, POET; PC 1; SSC 1, 22; WLC**
See also AAYA 14; CDALB 1640-1865; DLB 3, 59, 73, 74; SATA 23

Poet of Titchfield Street, The
See Pound, Ezra (Weston Loomis)

Pohl, Frederik 1919- .... **CLC 18; SSC 25**
See also AAYA 24; CA 61-64; CAAS 1; CANR 11, 37; DLB 8; INT CANR-11; MTCW; SATA 24

Poirier, Louis 1910-
See Gracq, Julien
See also CA 122; 126

Poitier, Sidney 1927- .... **CLC 26**
See also BW 1; CA 117

Polanski, Roman 1933- .... **CLC 16**
See also CA 77-80

Poliakoff, Stephen 1952- .... **CLC 38**
See also CA 106; DLB 13

Police, The
See Copeland, Stewart (Armstrong); Summers, Andrew James; Sumner, Gordon Matthew

Polidori, John William 1795-1821 ..... **NCLC 51**
See also DLB 116

Pollitt, Katha 1949- .... **CLC 28**
See also CA 120; 122; CANR 66; MTCW

Pollock, (Mary) Sharon 1936- ... **CLC 50; DAC; DAM DRAM, MST**
See also CA 141; DLB 60

Polo, Marco 1254-1324 .... **CMLC 15**

Polonsky, Abraham (Lincoln) 1910- ..... **CLC 92**
See also CA 104; DLB 26; INT 104

Polybius c. 200B.C.-c. 118B.C. .... **CMLC 17**
See also DLB 176

Pomerance, Bernard 1940-**CLC 13; DAM DRAM**
See also CA 101; CANR 49

Ponge, Francis (Jean Gaston Alfred) 1899-1988 **CLC 6, 18; DAM POET**
See also CA 85-88; 126; CANR 40

Pontoppidan, Henrik 1857-1943 .... **TCLC 29**

Poole, Josephine .... **CLC 17**
See also Helyar, Jane Penelope Josephine
See also SAAS 2; SATA 5

Popa, Vasko 1922-1991 .... **CLC 19**
See also CA 112; 148; DLB 181

Pope, Alexander 1688-1744 **LC 3; DA; DAB; DAC; DAM MST, POET; WLC**
See also CDBLB 1660-1789; DLB 95, 101

Porter, Connie (Rose) 1959(?)- .... **CLC 70**
See also BW 2; CA 142; SATA 81

Porter, Gene(va Grace) Stratton 1863(?)-1924 **TCLC 21**
See also CA 112

Porter, Katherine Anne 1890-1980 . **CLC 1, 3, 7, 10, 13, 15, 27, 101; DA; DAB; DAC; DAM MST, NOV; SSC 4**
See also AITN 2; CA 1-4R; 101; CANR 1, 65; DLB 4, 9, 102; DLBD 12; DLBY 80; MTCW; SATA 39; SATA-Obit 23

Porter, Peter (Neville Frederick) 1929- **CLC 5, 13, 33**
See also CA 85-88; DLB 40

Porter, William Sydney 1862-1910
See Henry, O.
See also CA 104; 131; CDALB 1865-1917; DA; DAB; DAC; DAM MST; DLB 12, 78, 79; MTCW; YABC 2

Portillo (y Pacheco), Jose Lopez
See Lopez Portillo (y Pacheco), Jose

Post, Melville Davisson 1869-1930 ...... **TCLC 39**
See also CA 110

Potok, Chaim 1929-**CLC 2, 7, 14, 26; DAM NOV**
See also AAYA 15; AITN 1, 2; CA 17-20R; CANR 19, 35, 64; DLB 28, 152; INT CANR-19; MTCW; SATA 33

Potter, (Helen) Beatrix 1866-1943
See Webb, (Martha) Beatrice (Potter)
See also MAICYA

Potter, Dennis (Christopher George) 1935-1994 **CLC 58, 86**
See also CA 107; 145; CANR 33, 61; MTCW

Pound, Ezra (Weston Loomis) 1885-1972 **CLC 1, 2, 3, 4, 5, 7, 10, 13, 18, 34, 48, 50; DA; DAB; DAC; DAM MST, POET; PC 4; WLC**
See also CA 5-8R; 37-40R; CANR 40; CDALB 1917-1929; DLB 4, 45, 63; DLBD 15; MTCW

Povod, Reinaldo 1959-1994 .... **CLC 44**
See also CA 136; 146

Powell, Adam Clayton, Jr. 1908-1972 ... **CLC 89; BLC; DAM MULT**
See also BW 1; CA 102; 33-36R

Powell, Anthony (Dymoke) 1905- **CLC 1, 3, 7, 9, 10, 31**
See also CA 1-4R; CANR 1, 32, 62; CDBLB 1945-1960; DLB 15; MTCW

Powell, Dawn 1897-1965 .... **CLC 66**
See also CA 5-8R; DLBY 97

Powell, Padgett 1952- .... **CLC 34**
See also CA 126; CANR 63

Power, Susan 1961- .... **CLC 91**

Powers, J(ames) F(arl) 1917- ... **CLC 1, 4, 8, 57; SSC 4**
See also CA 1-4R; CANR 2, 61; DLB 130; MTCW

Powers, John J(ames) 1945-
See Powers, John R.
See also CA 69-72

Powers, John R. .... **CLC 66**
See also Powers, John J(ames)

Powers, Richard (S.) 1957- .... **CLC 93**
See also CA 148

Pownall, David 1938- .... **CLC 10**
See also CA 89-92; CAAS 18; CANR 49; DLB 14

Powys, John Cowper 1872-1963 **CLC 7, 9, 15, 46**
See also CA 85-88; DLB 15; MTCW

Powys, T(heodore) F(rancis) 1875-1953 **TCLC 9**
See also CA 106; DLB 36, 162

Prado (Calvo), Pedro 1886-1952 .... **TCLC 75**
See also CA 131; HW

Prager, Emily 1952- .... **CLC 56**

Pratt, E(dwin) J(ohn) 1883(?)-1964 **CLC 19; DAC; DAM POET**
See also CA 141; 93-96; DLB 92

Premchand .... **TCLC 21**
See also Srivastava, Dhanpat Rai

Preussler, Otfried 1923- .... **CLC 17**
See also CA 77-80; SATA 24

Prevert, Jacques (Henri Marie) 1900-1977 **CLC 15**
See also CA 77-80; 69-72; CANR 29, 61; MTCW; SATA-Obit 30

Prevost, Abbe (Antoine Francois) 1697-1763 **LC 1**

Price, (Edward) Reynolds 1933- **CLC 3, 6, 13, 43, 50, 63; DAM NOV; SSC 22**
See also CA 1-4R; CANR 1, 37, 57; DLB 2; INT CANR-37

Price, Richard 1949- .... **CLC 6, 12**
See also CA 49-52; CANR 3; DLBY 81

Prichard, Katharine Susannah 1883-1969 **CLC 46**
See also CA 11-12; CANR 33; CAP 1; MTCW; SATA 66

Priestley, J(ohn) B(oynton) 1894-1984 **CLC 2, 5, 9, 34; DAM DRAM, NOV**
See also CA 9-12R; 113; CANR 33; CDBLB 1914-1945; DLB 10, 34, 77, 100, 139; DLBY 84; MTCW

Prince 1958(?)- .... **CLC 35**

Prince, F(rank) T(empleton) 1912- .... **CLC 22**
See also CA 101; CANR 43; DLB 20

Prince Kropotkin
See Kropotkin, Peter (Aleksieevich)

Prior, Matthew 1664-1721 .... **LC 4**
See also DLB 95

Prishvin, Mikhail 1873-1954 .... **TCLC 75**

Pritchard, William H(arrison) 1932- ... **CLC 34**
See also CA 65-68; CANR 23; DLB 111

Pritchett, V(ictor) S(awdon) 1900-1997 **CLC 5, 13, 15, 41; DAM NOV; SSC 14**
See also CA 61-64; 157; CANR 31, 63; DLB 15, 139; MTCW

Private 19022
See Manning, Frederic

Probst, Mark 1925- .... **CLC 59**
See also CA 130

Prokosch, Frederic 1908-1989 .... **CLC 4, 48**
See also CA 73-76; 128; DLB 48

Prophet, The
See Dreiser, Theodore (Herman Albert)

Prose, Francine 1947- .... **CLC 45**
See also CA 109; 112; CANR 46

Proudhon
See Cunha, Euclides (Rodrigues Pimenta) da

Proulx, Annie
See Proulx, E(dna) Annie

Proulx, E(dna) Annie 1935- **CLC 81; DAM POP**
See also CA 145; CANR 65

Proust, (Valentin-Louis-George-Eugene-) Marcel 1871-1922 **TCLC 7, 13, 33; DA; DAB; DAC; DAM MST, NOV; WLC**
See also CA 104; 120; DLB 65; MTCW

Prowler, Harley
See Masters, Edgar Lee

Prus, Boleslaw 1845-1912 .... **TCLC 48**

Pryor, Richard (Franklin Lenox Thomas) 1940- **CLC 26**
See also CA 122

Przybyszewski, Stanislaw 1868-1927 . **TCLC 36**
See also CA 160; DLB 66

Pteleon
See Grieve, C(hristopher) M(urray)
See also DAM POET

Puckett, Lute
See Masters, Edgar Lee

Puig, Manuel 1932-1990 ... **CLC 3, 5, 10, 28, 65; DAM MULT; HLC**
See also CA 45-48; CANR 2, 32, 63; DLB 113; HW; MTCW

Pulitzer, Joseph 1847-1911 .... **TCLC 76**
See also CA 114; DLB 23

Purdy, Al(fred Wellington) 1918- **CLC 3, 6, 14, 50; DAC; DAM MST, POET**
See also CA 81-84; CAAS 17; CANR 42, 66; DLB 88

Purdy, James (Amos) 1923- **CLC 2, 4, 10, 28, 52**
See also CA 33-36R; CAAS 1; CANR 19, 51; DLB 2; INT CANR-19; MTCW

Pure, Simon
See Swinnerton, Frank Arthur

Pushkin, Alexander (Sergeyevich) 1799-1837 **NCLC 3, 27; DA; DAB; DAC; DAM DRAM, MST, POET; PC 10; SSC 27; WLC**
See also SATA 61

P'u Sung-ling 1640-1715 .... **LC 3**

Putnam, Arthur Lee
See Alger, Horatio, Jr.

Puzo, Mario 1920- .. **CLC 1, 2, 6, 36, 107; DAM NOV, POP**
See also CA 65-68; CANR 4, 42, 65; DLB 6; MTCW

Pygge, Edward
See Barnes, Julian (Patrick)

Pyle, Ernest Taylor 1900-1945
See Pyle, Ernie
See also CA 115; 160

Pyle, Ernie 1900-1945 .... **TCLC 75**
See also Pyle, Ernest Taylor
See also DLB 29

Pym, Barbara (Mary Crampton) 1913-1980 **CLC 13, 19, 37**
See also CA 13-14; 97-100; CANR 13, 34; CAP 1; DLB 14; DLBY 87; MTCW

Pynchon, Thomas (Ruggles, Jr.) 1937- **CLC 2, 3, 6, 9, 11, 18, 33, 62, 72; DA; DAB; DAC; DAM MST, NOV, POP; SSC 14; WLC**
See also BEST 90:2; CA 17-20R; CANR 22, 46; DLB 2, 173; MTCW

Pythagoras c. 570B.C.-c. 500B.C. .... **CMLC 22**
See also DLB 176

Qian Zhongshu
See Ch'ien Chung-shu

Qroll
See Dagerman, Stig (Halvard)

Quarrington, Paul (Lewis) 1953- .... **CLC 65**
See also CA 129; CANR 62

Quasimodo, Salvatore 1901-1968 .... **CLC 10**
See also CA 13-16; 25-28R; CAP 1; DLB 114; MTCW

Quay, Stephen 1947- .... **CLC 95**

Quay, Timothy 1947- .... **CLC 95**

Queen, Ellery .... **CLC 3, 11**
See also Dannay, Frederic; Davidson, Avram; Lee, Manfred B(ennington); Marlowe, Stephen; Sturgeon, Theodore (Hamilton); Vance, John Holbrook

Queen, Ellery, Jr.
See Dannay, Frederic; Lee, Manfred B(ennington)

Queneau, Raymond 1903-1976 **CLC 2, 5, 10, 42**
See also CA 77-80; 69-72; CANR 32; DLB 72; MTCW

Quevedo, Francisco de 1580-1645 .... **LC 23**

Quiller-Couch, Sir Arthur Thomas 1863-1944 **TCLC 53**
See also CA 118; DLB 135, 153, 190

Quin, Ann (Marie) 1936-1973 .... **CLC 6**
See also CA 9-12R; 45-48; DLB 14

Quinn, Martin
See Smith, Martin Cruz

Quinn, Peter 1947- .... **CLC 91**

Quinn, Simon
See Smith, Martin Cruz

Quiroga, Horacio (Sylvestre) 1878-1937 . **TCLC 20; DAM MULT; HLC**
See also CA 117; 131; HW; MTCW

Quoirez, Francoise 1935- .... **CLC 9**
See also Sagan, Francoise
See also CA 49-52; CANR 6, 39; MTCW

Raabe, Wilhelm 1831-1910 .... **TCLC 45**
See also DLB 129

Rabe, David (William) 1940- **CLC 4, 8, 33; DAM DRAM**
See also CA 85-88; CABS 3; CANR 59; DLB 7

Rabelais, Francois 1483-1553 . **LC 5; DA; DAB; DAC; DAM MST; WLC**

Rabinovitch, Sholem 1859-1916
See Aleichem, Sholom
See also CA 104

Rachilde 1860-1953 .... **TCLC 67**
See also DLB 123, 192

Racine, Jean 1639-1699 **LC 28; DAB; DAM MST**

Radcliffe, Ann (Ward) 1764-1823 .... **NCLC 6, 55**
See also DLB 39, 178

Radiguet, Raymond 1903-1923 .... **TCLC 29**
See also CA 162; DLB 65

Radnoti, Miklos 1909-1944 .... **TCLC 16**
See also CA 118

Rado, James 1939- .... **CLC 17**
See also CA 105

Radvanyi, Netty 1900-1983
See Seghers, Anna
See also CA 85-88; 110

Rae, Ben
See Griffiths, Trevor

Raeburn, John (Hay) 1941- .... **CLC 34**
See also CA 57-60

Ragni, Gerome 1942-1991 .... **CLC 17**
See also CA 105; 134

Rahv, Philip 1908-1973 .... **CLC 24**
See also Greenberg, Ivan
See also DLB 137

Raimund, Ferdinand Jakob 1790-1836 **NCLC 69**
See also DLB 90

Raine, Craig 1944- .... **CLC 32, 103**
See also CA 108; CANR 29, 51; DLB 40

Raine, Kathleen (Jessie) 1908- .... **CLC 7, 45**
See also CA 85-88; CANR 46; DLB 20; MTCW

Rainis, Janis 1865-1929 .... **TCLC 29**

Rakosi, Carl 1903- .... **CLC 47**
See also Rawley, Callman
See also CAAS 5; DLB 193

Raleigh, Richard
See Lovecraft, H(oward) P(hillips)

Raleigh, Sir Walter 1554(?)-1618 ...... **LC 31, 39**
See also CDBLB Before 1660; DLB 172

Rallentando, H. P.
See Sayers, Dorothy L(eigh)

Ramal, Walter
See de la Mare, Walter (John)

Ramon, Juan
See Jimenez (Mantecon), Juan Ramon

Ramos, Graciliano 1892-1953 .... **TCLC 32**

Rampersad, Arnold 1941- .... **CLC 44**
See also BW 2; CA 127; 133; DLB 111; INT 133

Rampling, Anne
See Rice, Anne

Ramsay, Allan 1684(?)-1758 .... **LC 29**
See also DLB 95

Ramuz, Charles-Ferdinand 1878-1947 **TCLC 33**
See also CA 165

Rand, Ayn 1905-1982 **CLC 3, 30, 44, 79; DA; DAC; DAM MST, NOV, POP; WLC**
See also AAYA 10; CA 13-16R; 105; CANR 27; MTCW

Randall, Dudley (Felker) 1914- ... **CLC 1; BLC; DAM MULT**
See also BW 1; CA 25-28R; CANR 23; DLB 41

Randall, Robert
See Silverberg, Robert

Ranger, Ken
See Creasey, John

Ransom, John Crowe 1888-1974 **CLC 2, 4, 5, 11, 24; DAM POET**
See also CA 5-8R; 49-52; CANR 6, 34; DLB 45, 63; MTCW

Rao, Raja 1909- .... **CLC 25, 56; DAM NOV**
See also CA 73-76; CANR 51; MTCW

Raphael, Frederic (Michael) 1931- ... **CLC 2, 14**
See also CA 1-4R; CANR 1; DLB 14

Ratcliffe, James P.
See Mencken, H(enry) L(ouis)

Rathbone, Julian 1935- .... **CLC 41**
See also CA 101; CANR 34

Rattigan, Terence (Mervyn) 1911-1977 .. **CLC 7; DAM DRAM**
See also CA 85-88; 73-76; CDBLB 1945-1960; DLB 13; MTCW

Ratushinskaya, Irina 1954- .... **CLC 54**
See also CA 129; CANR 68

Raven, Simon (Arthur Noel) 1927- .... **CLC 14**
See also CA 81-84

Ravenna, Michael
See Welty, Eudora

Rawley, Callman 1903-
See Rakosi, Carl
See also CA 21-24R; CANR 12, 32

Rawlings, Marjorie Kinnan 1896-1953 . **TCLC 4**
See also AAYA 20; CA 104; 137; DLB 9, 22, 102; JRDA; MAICYA; YABC 1

Ray, Satyajit 1921-1992 **CLC 16, 76; DAM MULT**
See also CA 114; 137

Read, Herbert Edward 1893-1968 .... **CLC 4**
See also CA 85-88; 25-28R; DLB 20, 149

Read, Piers Paul 1941- .... **CLC 4, 10, 25**
See also CA 21-24R; CANR 38; DLB 14; SATA 21

Reade, Charles 1814-1884 .... **NCLC 2**
See also DLB 21

Reade, Hamish
See Gray, Simon (James Holliday)

Reading, Peter 1946- .... **CLC 47**
See also CA 103; CANR 46; DLB 40

Reaney, James 1926- **CLC 13; DAC; DAM MST**
See also CA 41-44R; CAAS 15; CANR 42; DLB 68; SATA 43

Rebreanu, Liviu 1885-1944 .... **TCLC 28**
See also CA 165

Rechy, John (Francisco) 1934- **CLC 1, 7, 14, 18, 107; DAM MULT; HLC**
See also CA 5-8R; CAAS 4; CANR 6, 32, 64; DLB 122; DLBY 82; HW; INT CANR-6

Redcam, Tom 1870-1933 .... **TCLC 25**

Reddin, Keith .... **CLC 67**

Redgrove, Peter (William) 1932- ...... **CLC 6, 41**
See also CA 1-4R; CANR 3, 39; DLB 40

Redmon, Anne .... **CLC 22**
See also Nightingale, Anne Redmon
See also DLBY 86

Reed, Eliot
See Ambler, Eric

Reed, Ishmael 1938- . **CLC 2, 3, 5, 6, 13, 32, 60; BLC; DAM MULT**
See also BW 2; CA 21-24R; CANR 25, 48; DLB 2, 5, 33, 169; DLBD 8; MTCW

Reed, John (Silas) 1887-1920 .... **TCLC 9**
See also CA 106

Reed, Lou .... **CLC 21**
See also Firbank, Louis

Reeve, Clara 1729-1807 .... **NCLC 19**
See also DLB 39

Reich, Wilhelm 1897-1957 .... **TCLC 57**

Reid, Christopher (John) 1949- .... **CLC 33**
See also CA 140; DLB 40

Reid, Desmond
See Moorcock, Michael (John)

Rosenstock, Sami
See Tzara, Tristan

Rosenstock, Samuel
See Tzara, Tristan

Rosenthal, M(acha) L(ouis) 1917-1996 .. **CLC 28**
See also CA 1-4R; 152; CAAS 6; CANR 4, 51; DLB 5; SATA 59

Ross, Barnaby
See Dannay, Frederic

Ross, Bernard L.
See Follett, Ken(neth Martin)

Ross, J. H.
See Lawrence, T(homas) E(dward)

Ross, Martin
See Martin, Violet Florence
See also DLB 135

Ross, (James) Sinclair 1908- .... **CLC 13; DAC; DAM MST; SSC 24**
See also CA 73-76; DLB 88

Rossetti, Christina (Georgina) 1830-1894**NCLC 2, 50, 66; DA; DAB; DAC; DAM MST, POET; PC 7; WLC**
See also DLB 35, 163; MAICYA; SATA 20

Rossetti, Dante Gabriel 1828-1882**NCLC 4; DA; DAB; DAC; DAM MST, POET; WLC**
See also CDBLB 1832-1890; DLB 35

Rossner, Judith (Perelman) 1935- **CLC 6, 9, 29**
See also AITN 2; BEST 90:3; CA 17-20R; CANR 18, 51; DLB 6; INT CANR-18; MTCW

Rostand, Edmond (Eugene Alexis) 1868-1918 **TCLC 6, 37; DA; DAB; DAC; DAM DRAM, MST**
See also CA 104; 126; DLB 192; MTCW

Roth, Henry 1906-1995 .... **CLC 2, 6, 11, 104**
See also CA 11-12; 149; CANR 38, 63; CAP 1; DLB 28; MTCW

Roth, Philip (Milton) 1933-**CLC 1, 2, 3, 4, 6, 9, 15, 22, 31, 47, 66, 86; DA; DAB; DAC; DAM MST, NOV, POP; SSC 26; WLC**
See also BEST 90:3; CA 1-4R; CANR 1, 22, 36, 55; CDALB 1968-1988; DLB 2, 28, 173; DLBY 82; MTCW

Rothenberg, Jerome 1931- .... **CLC 6, 57**
See also CA 45-48; CANR 1; DLB 5, 193

Roumain, Jacques (Jean Baptiste) 1907-1944 **TCLC 19; BLC; DAM MULT**
See also BW 1; CA 117; 125

Rourke, Constance (Mayfield) 1885-1941 **TCLC 12**
See also CA 107; YABC 1

Rousseau, Jean-Baptiste 1671-1741 .... **LC 9**

Rousseau, Jean-Jacques 1712-1778 .. **LC 14, 36; DA; DAB; DAC; DAM MST; WLC**

Roussel, Raymond 1877-1933 .... **TCLC 20**
See also CA 117

Rovit, Earl (Herbert) 1927- .... **CLC 7**
See also CA 5-8R; CANR 12

Rowe, Nicholas 1674-1718 .... **LC 8**
See also DLB 84

Rowley, Ames Dorrance
See Lovecraft, H(oward) P(hillips)

Rowson, Susanna Haswell 1762(?)-1824**NCLC 5, 69**
See also DLB 37

Roy, Arundhati 1960(?)- .... **CLC 109**
See also CA 163; DLBY 97

Roy, Gabrielle 1909-1983**CLC 10, 14; DAB; DAC; DAM MST**
See also CA 53-56; 110; CANR 5, 61; DLB 68; MTCW

Royko, Mike 1932-1997 .... **CLC 109**
See also CA 89-92; 157; CANR 26

Rozewicz, Tadeusz 1921-**CLC 9, 23; DAM POET**
See also CA 108; CANR 36, 66; MTCW

Ruark, Gibbons 1941- .... **CLC 3**
See also CA 33-36R; CAAS 23; CANR 14, 31, 57; DLB 120

Rubens, Bernice (Ruth) 1923- .... **CLC 19, 31**
See also CA 25-28R; CANR 33, 65; DLB 14; MTCW

Rubin, Harold
See Robbins, Harold

Rudkin, (James) David 1936- .... **CLC 14**
See also CA 89-92; DLB 13

Rudnik, Raphael 1933- .... **CLC 7**
See also CA 29-32R

Ruffian, M.
See Hasek, Jaroslav (Matej Frantisek)

Ruiz, Jose Martinez .... **CLC 11**
See also Martinez Ruiz, Jose

Rukeyser, Muriel 1913-1980 **CLC 6, 10, 15, 27; DAM POET; PC 12**
See also CA 5-8R; 93-96; CANR 26, 60; DLB 48; MTCW; SATA-Obit 22

Rule, Jane (Vance) 1931- .... **CLC 27**
See also CA 25-28R; CAAS 18; CANR 12; DLB 60

Rulfo, Juan 1918-1986 . **CLC 8, 80; DAM MULT; HLC; SSC 25**
See also CA 85-88; 118; CANR 26; DLB 113; HW; MTCW

Rumi, Jalal al-Din 1297-1373 .... **CMLC 20**

Runeberg, Johan 1804-1877 .... **NCLC 41**

Runyon, (Alfred) Damon 1884(?)-1946 **TCLC 10**
See also CA 107; 165; DLB 11, 86, 171

Rush, Norman 1933- .... **CLC 44**
See also CA 121; 126; INT 126

Rushdie, (Ahmed) Salman 1947-**CLC 23, 31, 55, 100; DAB; DAC; DAM MST, NOV, POP; WLCS**
See also BEST 89:3; CA 108; 111; CANR 33, 56; DLB 194; INT 111; MTCW

Rushforth, Peter (Scott) 1945- .... **CLC 19**
See also CA 101

Ruskin, John 1819-1900 .... **TCLC 63**
See also CA 114; 129; CDBLB 1832-1890; DLB 55, 163, 190; SATA 24

Russ, Joanna 1937- .... **CLC 15**
See also CA 25-28R; CANR 11, 31, 65; DLB 8; MTCW

Russell, George William 1867-1935
See Baker, Jean H.
See also CA 104; 153; CDBLB 1890-1914; DAM POET

Russell, (Henry) Ken(neth Alfred) 1927-**CLC 16**
See also CA 105

Russell, William Martin 1947- .... **CLC 60**
See also CA 164

Rutherford, Mark .... **TCLC 25**
See also White, William Hale
See also DLB 18

Ruyslinck, Ward 1929- .... **CLC 14**
See also Belser, Reimond Karel Maria de

Ryan, Cornelius (John) 1920-1974 .... **CLC 7**
See also CA 69-72; 53-56; CANR 38

Ryan, Michael 1946- .... **CLC 65**
See also CA 49-52; DLBY 82

Ryan, Tim
See Dent, Lester

Rybakov, Anatoli (Naumovich) 1911-**CLC 23, 53**
See also CA 126; 135; SATA 79

Ryder, Jonathan
See Ludlum, Robert

Ryga, George 1932-1987 .. **CLC 14; DAC; DAM MST**
See also CA 101; 124; CANR 43; DLB 60

S. H.
See Hartmann, Sadakichi

S. S.
See Sassoon, Siegfried (Lorraine)

Saba, Umberto 1883-1957 .... **TCLC 33**
See also CA 144; DLB 114

Sabatini, Rafael 1875-1950 .... **TCLC 47**
See also CA 162

Sabato, Ernesto (R.) 1911- ... **CLC 10, 23; DAM MULT; HLC**
See also CA 97-100; CANR 32, 65; DLB 145; HW; MTCW

Sacastru, Martin
See Bioy Casares, Adolfo

Sacher-Masoch, Leopold von 1836(?)-1895**NCLC 31**

Sachs, Marilyn (Stickle) 1927- .... **CLC 35**
See also AAYA 2; CA 17-20R; CANR 13, 47; CLR 2; JRDA; MAICYA; SAAS 2; SATA 3, 68

Sachs, Nelly 1891-1970 .... **CLC 14, 98**
See also CA 17-18; 25-28R; CAP 2

Sackler, Howard (Oliver) 1929-1982 ..... **CLC 14**
See also CA 61-64; 108; CANR 30; DLB 7

Sacks, Oliver (Wolf) 1933- .... **CLC 67**
See also CA 53-56; CANR 28, 50; INT CANR-28; MTCW

Sadakichi
See Hartmann, Sadakichi

Sade, Donatien Alphonse Francois Comte 1740-1814 .... **NCLC 47**

Sadoff, Ira 1945- .... **CLC 9**
See also CA 53-56; CANR 5, 21; DLB 120

Saetone
See Camus, Albert

Safire, William 1929- .... **CLC 10**
See also CA 17-20R; CANR 31, 54

Sagan, Carl (Edward) 1934-1996 .... **CLC 30**
See also AAYA 2; CA 25-28R; 155; CANR 11, 36; MTCW; SATA 58; SATA-Obit 94

Sagan, Francoise .... **CLC 3, 6, 9, 17, 36**
See also Quoirez, Francoise
See also DLB 83

Sahgal, Nayantara (Pandit) 1927- .... **CLC 41**
See also CA 9-12R; CANR 11

Saint, H(arry) F. 1941- .... **CLC 50**
See also CA 127

St. Aubin de Teran, Lisa 1953-
See Teran, Lisa St. Aubin de
See also CA 118; 126; INT 126

Saint Birgitta of Sweden c. 1303-1373 **CMLC 24**

Sainte-Beuve, Charles Augustin 1804-1869 **NCLC 5**

Saint-Exupery, Antoine (Jean Baptiste Marie Roger) de 1900-1944 **TCLC 2, 56; DAM NOV; WLC**
See also CA 108; 132; CLR 10; DLB 72; MAICYA; MTCW; SATA 20

St. John, David
See Hunt, E(verette) Howard, (Jr.)

Saint-John Perse
See Leger, (Marie-Rene Auguste) Alexis Saint-Leger

Saintsbury, George (Edward Bateman) 1845-1933 **TCLC 31**
See also CA 160; DLB 57, 149

Sait Faik .... **TCLC 23**
See also Abasiyanik, Sait Faik

Saki .... **TCLC 3; SSC 12**
See also Munro, H(ector) H(ugh)

Sala, George Augustus .... **NCLC 46**

Salama, Hannu 1936- .... **CLC 18**

Salamanca, J(ack) R(ichard) 1922 .. **CLC 4, 15**
See also CA 25-28R

Sale, J. Kirkpatrick
See Sale, Kirkpatrick

Sale, Kirkpatrick 1937- .... **CLC 68**
See also CA 13-16R; CANR 10

Salinas, Luis Omar 1937- **CLC 90; DAM MULT; HLC**
See also CA 131; DLB 82; HW

Salinas (y Serrano), Pedro 1891(?)-1951 **TCLC 17**
See also CA 117; DLB 134

Salinger, J(erome) D(avid) 1919- **CLC 1, 3, 8, 12, 55, 56; DA; DAB; DAC; DAM MST, NOV, POP; SSC 2, 28; WLC**
See also AAYA 2; CA 5-8R; CANR 39; CDALB 1941-1968; CLR 18; DLB 2, 102, 173; MAICYA; MTCW; SATA 67

Salisbury, John
See Caute, (John) David

Salter, James 1925- .... **CLC 7, 52, 59**
See also CA 73-76; DLB 130

Saltus, Edgar (Everton) 1855-1921 .... **TCLC 8**
See also CA 105

Saltykov, Mikhail Evgrafovich 1826-1889 **NCLC 16**

Samarakis, Antonis 1919- .... **CLC 5**
See also CA 25-28R; CAAS 16; CANR 36

Sanchez, Florencio 1875-1910 .... **TCLC 37**
See also CA 153; HW

Sanchez, Luis Rafael 1936- .... **CLC 23**
See also CA 128; DLB 145; HW

Sanchez, Sonia 1934- **CLC 5; BLC; DAM MULT; PC 9**
See also BW 2; CA 33-36R; CANR 24, 49; CLR 18; DLB 41; DLBD 8; MAICYA; MTCW; SATA 22

Sand, George 1804-1876 ... **NCLC 2, 42, 57; DA; DAB; DAC; DAM MST, NOV; WLC**
See also DLB 119, 192

Sandburg, Carl (August) 1878-1967 **CLC 1, 4, 10, 15, 35; DA; DAB; DAC; DAM MST, POET; PC 2; WLC**
See also AAYA 24; CA 5-8R; 25-28R; CANR 35; CDALB 1865-1917; DLB 17, 54; MAICYA; MTCW; SATA 8

Sandburg, Charles
See Sandburg, Carl (August)

Sandburg, Charles A.
See Sandburg, Carl (August)

Sanders, (James) Ed(ward) 1939- .... **CLC 53**
See also CA 13-16R; CAAS 21; CANR 13, 44; DLB 16

Sanders, Lawrence 1920-1998 **CLC 41; DAM POP**
See also BEST 89:4; CA 81-84; 165; CANR 33, 62; MTCW

Sanders, Noah
See Blount, Roy (Alton), Jr.

Sanders, Winston P.
See Anderson, Poul (William)

Sandoz, Mari(e Susette) 1896-1966 .... **CLC 28**
See also CA 1-4R; 25-28R; CANR 17, 64; DLB 9; MTCW; SATA 5

Saner, Reg(inald Anthony) 1931- .... **CLC 9**
See also CA 65-68

Sannazaro, Jacopo 1456(?)-1530 .... **LC 8**

Sansom, William 1912-1976 **CLC 2, 6; DAM NOV; SSC 21**
See also CA 5-8R; 65-68; CANR 42; DLB 139; MTCW

Santayana, George 1863-1952 .... **TCLC 40**
See also CA 115; DLB 54, 71; DLBD 13

Santiago, Danny .... **CLC 33**
See also James, Daniel (Lewis)
See also DLB 122

Santmyer, Helen Hoover 1895-1986 ...... **CLC 33**
See also CA 1-4R; 118; CANR 15, 33; DLBY 84; MTCW

Santoka, Taneda 1882-1940 .... **TCLC 72**

Santos, Bienvenido N(uqui) 1911-1996 . **CLC 22; DAM MULT**
See also CA 101; 151; CANR 19, 46

Sapper .... **TCLC 44**
See also McNeile, Herman Cyril

Sapphire 1950- .... **CLC 99**

Sappho fl. 6th cent. B.C.- **CMLC 3; DAM POET; PC 5**
See also DLB 176

Sarduy, Severo 1937-1993 .... **CLC 6, 97**
See also CA 89-92; 142; CANR 58; DLB 113; HW

Sargeson, Frank 1903-1982 .... **CLC 31**
See also CA 25-28R; 106; CANR 38

Sarmiento, Felix Ruben Garcia
See Dario, Ruben

Saroyan, William 1908-1981 **CLC 1, 8, 10, 29, 34, 56; DA; DAB; DAC; DAM DRAM, MST, NOV; SSC 21; WLC**
See also CA 5-8R; 103; CANR 30; DLB 7, 9, 86; DLBY 81; MTCW; SATA 23; SATA-Obit 24

Sarraute, Nathalie 1900- **CLC 1, 2, 4, 8, 10, 31, 80**
See also CA 9-12R; CANR 23, 66; DLB 83; MTCW

Sarton, (Eleanor) May 1912-1995 **CLC 4, 14, 49, 91; DAM POET**
See also CA 1-4R; 149; CANR 1, 34, 55; DLB 48; DLBY 81; INT CANR-34; MTCW; SATA 36; SATA-Obit 86

Sartre, Jean-Paul 1905-1980 . **CLC 1, 4, 7, 9, 13, 18, 24, 44, 50, 52; DA; DAB; DAC; DAM DRAM, MST, NOV; DC 3; WLC**
See also CA 9-12R; 97-100; CANR 21; DLB 72; MTCW

Sassoon, Siegfried (Lorraine) 1886-1967 .. **CLC 36; DAB; DAM MST, NOV, POET; PC 12**
See also CA 104; 25-28R; CANR 36; DLB 20, 191; MTCW

Satterfield, Charles
See Pohl, Frederik

Saul, John (W. III) 1942- **CLC 46; DAM NOV, POP**
See also AAYA 10; BEST 90:4; CA 81-84; CANR 16, 40; SATA 98

Saunders, Caleb
See Heinlein, Robert A(nson)

Saura (Atares), Carlos 1932- .... **CLC 20**
See also CA 114; 131; HW

Sauser-Hall, Frederic 1887-1961 .... **CLC 18**
See also Cendrars, Blaise
See also CA 102; 93-96; CANR 36, 62; MTCW

Saussure, Ferdinand de 1857-1913 ..... **TCLC 49**

Savage, Catharine
See Brosman, Catharine Savage

Savage, Thomas 1915-........................... **CLC 40**
See also CA 126; 132; CAAS 15; INT 132

Savan, Glenn 19(?)-.............................. **CLC 50**

Sayers, Dorothy L(eigh) 1893-1957 **TCLC 2, 15; DAM POP**
See also CA 104; 119; CANR 60; CDBLB 1914-1945; DLB 10, 36, 77, 100; MTCW

Sayers, Valerie 1952- .... **CLC 50**
See also CA 134; CANR 61

Sayles, John (Thomas) 1950- ...... **CLC 7, 10, 14**
See also CA 57-60; CANR 41; DLB 44

Scammell, Michael 1935-...................... **CLC 34**
See also CA 156

Scannell, Vernon 1922- .... **CLC 49**
See also CA 5-8R; CANR 8, 24, 57; DLB 27; SATA 59

Scarlett, Susan
See Streatfeild, (Mary) Noel

Schaeffer, Susan Fromberg 1941- **CLC 6, 11, 22**
See also CA 49-52; CANR 18, 65; DLB 28; MTCW; SATA 22

Schary, Jill
See Robinson, Jill

Schell, Jonathan 1943- .... **CLC 35**
See also CA 73-76; CANR 12

Schelling, Friedrich Wilhelm Joseph von 1775-1854 .... **NCLC 30**
See also DLB 90

Schendel, Arthur van 1874-1946 .... **TCLC 56**

Scherer, Jean-Marie Maurice 1920-
See Rohmer, Eric
See also CA 110

Schevill, James (Erwin) 1920- .... **CLC 7**
See also CA 5-8R; CAAS 12

Schiller, Friedrich 1759-1805 **NCLC 39, 69; DAM DRAM**
See also DLB 94

Schisgal, Murray (Joseph) 1926- .... **CLC 6**
See also CA 21-24R; CANR 48

Schlee, Ann 1934- .... **CLC 35**
See also CA 101; CANR 29; SATA 44; SATA-Brief 36

Schlegel, August Wilhelm von 1767-1845 **NCLC 15**
See also DLB 94

Schlegel, Friedrich 1772-1829 .... **NCLC 45**
See also DLB 90

Schlegel, Johann Elias (von) 1719(?)-1749 **LC 5**

Schlesinger, Arthur M(eier), Jr. 1917- **CLC 84**
See also AITN 1; CA 1-4R; CANR 1, 28, 58; DLB 17; INT CANR-28; MTCW; SATA 61

Schmidt, Arno (Otto) 1914-1979 .... **CLC 56**
See also CA 128; 109; DLB 69

Schmitz, Aron Hector 1861-1928
See Svevo, Italo
See also CA 104; 122; MTCW

Schnackenberg, Gjertrud 1953-........... **CLC 40**
See also CA 116; DLB 120

Schneider, Leonard Alfred 1925-1966
See Bruce, Lenny
See also CA 89-92

Schnitzler, Arthur 1862-1931 **TCLC 4; SSC 15**
See also CA 104; DLB 81, 118

Schoenberg, Arnold 1874-1951 .... **TCLC 75**
See also CA 109

Schonberg, Arnold
See Schoenberg, Arnold

Schopenhauer, Arthur 1788-1860 ...... **NCLC 51**
See also DLB 90

Schor, Sandra (M.) 1932(?)-1990 .... **CLC 65**
See also CA 132

Schorer, Mark 1908-1977 .... **CLC 9**
See also CA 5-8R; 73-76; CANR 7; DLB 103

Schrader, Paul (Joseph) 1946-.............. **CLC 26**
See also CA 37-40R; CANR 41; DLB 44

Schreiner, Olive (Emilie Albertina) 1855-1920 **TCLC 9**
See also CA 105; 154; DLB 18, 156, 190

Schulberg, Budd (Wilson) 1914- ...... **CLC 7, 48**
See also CA 25-28R; CANR 19; DLB 6, 26, 28; DLBY 81

Schulz, Bruno 1892-1942 . **TCLC 5, 51; SSC 13**
See also CA 115; 123

Schulz, Charles M(onroe) 1922- .... **CLC 12**
See also CA 9-12R; CANR 6; INT CANR-6; SATA 10

Schumacher, E(rnst) F(riedrich) 1911-1977 **CLC 80**
See also CA 81-84; 73-76; CANR 34

Schuyler, James Marcus 1923-1991 **CLC 5, 23; DAM POET**
See also CA 101; 134; DLB 5, 169; INT 101

Schwartz, Delmore (David) 1913-1966 **CLC 2, 4, 10, 45, 87; PC 8**
See also CA 17-18; 25-28R; CANR 35; CAP 2; DLB 28, 48; MTCW

Schwartz, Ernst
See Ozu, Yasujiro

Schwartz, John Burnham 1965- .... **CLC 59**
See also CA 132

Schwartz, Lynne Sharon 1939-............. **CLC 31**
See also CA 103; CANR 44

Schwartz, Muriel A.
See Eliot, T(homas) S(tearns)

Schwarz-Bart, Andre 1928- .... **CLC 2, 4**
See also CA 89-92

Schwarz-Bart, Simone 1938- .... **CLC 7**
See also BW 2; CA 97-100

Schwob, (Mayer Andre) Marcel 1867-1905 **TCLC 20**
See also CA 117; DLB 123

Sciascia, Leonardo 1921-1989 .... **CLC 8, 9, 41**
See also CA 85-88; 130; CANR 35; DLB 177; MTCW

Scoppettone, Sandra 1936- .... **CLC 26**
See also AAYA 11; CA 5-8R; CANR 41; SATA 9, 92

Scorsese, Martin 1942- .... **CLC 20, 89**
See also CA 110; 114; CANR 46

Scotland, Jay
See Jakes, John (William)

Scott, Duncan Campbell 1862-1947 **TCLC 6; DAC**
See also CA 104; 153; DLB 92

Scott, Evelyn 1893-1963 .... **CLC 43**
See also CA 104; 112; CANR 64; DLB 9, 48

Scott, F(rancis) R(eginald) 1899-1985 .. **CLC 22**
See also CA 101; 114; DLB 88; INT 101

Scott, Frank
See Scott, F(rancis) R(eginald)

Scott, Joanna 1960-............................... **CLC 50**
See also CA 126; CANR 53

Scott, Paul (Mark) 1920-1978 .... **CLC 9, 60**
See also CA 81-84; 77-80; CANR 33; DLB 14; MTCW

Scott, Walter 1771-1832 **NCLC 15, 69; DA; DAB; DAC; DAM MST, NOV, POET; PC 13; WLC**
See also AAYA 22; CDBLB 1789-1832; DLB 93, 107, 116, 144, 159; YABC 2

Scribe, (Augustin) Eugene 1791-1861 **NCLC 16; DAM DRAM; DC 5**
See also DLB 192

Scrum, R.
See Crumb, R(obert)

Scudery, Madeleine de 1607-1701 .... **LC 2**

Scum
See Crumb, R(obert)

Scumbag, Little Bobby
See Crumb, R(obert)

Seabrook, John
See Hubbard, L(afayette) Ron(ald)

Sealy, I. Allan 1951- .... **CLC 55**

Search, Alexander
See Pessoa, Fernando (Antonio Nogueira)

Sebastian, Lee
See Silverberg, Robert

Sebastian Owl
See Thompson, Hunter S(tockton)

Sebestyen, Ouida 1924- .... **CLC 30**
See also AAYA 8; CA 107; CANR 40; CLR 17; JRDA; MAICYA; SAAS 10; SATA 39

Secundus, H. Scriblerus
See Fielding, Henry

Sedges, John
See Buck, Pearl S(ydenstricker)

Sedgwick, Catharine Maria 1789-1867**NCLC 19**
See also DLB 1, 74

Seelye, John 1931- .... **CLC 7**

Seferiades, Giorgos Stylianou 1900-1971
See Seferis, George
See also CA 5-8R; 33-36R; CANR 5, 36; MTCW

Seferis, George .... **CLC 5, 11**
See also Seferiades, Giorgos Stylianou

Segal, Erich (Wolf) 1937-**CLC 3, 10; DAM POP**
See also BEST 89:1; CA 25-28R; CANR 20, 36, 65; DLBY 86; INT CANR-20; MTCW

Seger, Bob 1945- .... **CLC 35**

Seghers, Anna .... **CLC 7**
See also Radvanyi, Netty
See also DLB 69

Seidel, Frederick (Lewis) 1936- .... **CLC 18**
See also CA 13-16R; CANR 8; DLBY 84

Seifert, Jaroslav 1901-1986 .... **CLC 34, 44, 93**
See also CA 127; MTCW

Sei Shonagon c. 966-1017(?) .... **CMLC 6**

Selby, Hubert, Jr. 1928- **CLC 1, 2, 4, 8; SSC 20**
See also CA 13-16R; CANR 33; DLB 2

Selzer, Richard 1928- .... **CLC 74**
See also CA 65-68; CANR 14

Sembene, Ousmane
See Ousmane, Sembene

Senancour, Etienne Pivert de 1770-1846**NCLC 16**
See also DLB 119

Sender, Ramon (Jose) 1902-1982 .. **CLC 8; DAM MULT; HLC**
See also CA 5-8R; 105; CANR 8; HW; MTCW

Seneca, Lucius Annaeus 4B.C.-65**CMLC 6; DAM DRAM; DC 5**

Senghor, Leopold Sedar 1906- ... **CLC 54; BLC; DAM MULT, POET**
See also BW 2; CA 116; 125; CANR 47; MTCW

Serling, (Edward) Rod(man) 1924-1975 . **CLC 30**
See also AAYA 14; AITN 1; CA 162; 57-60; DLB 26

Serna, Ramon Gomez de la
See Gomez de la Serna, Ramon

Serpieres
See Guillevic, (Eugene)

Service, Robert
See Service, Robert W(illiam)
See also DAB; DLB 92

Service, Robert W(illiam) 1874(?)-1958**TCLC 15; DA; DAC; DAM MST, POET; WLC**
See also Service, Robert
See also CA 115; 140; SATA 20

Seth, Vikram 1952- .. **CLC 43, 90; DAM MULT**
See also CA 121; 127; CANR 50; DLB 120; INT 127

Seton, Cynthia Propper 1926-1982 .... **CLC 27**
See also CA 5-8R; 108; CANR 7

Seton, Ernest (Evan) Thompson 1860-1946**TCLC 31**
See also CA 109; DLB 92; DLBD 13; JRDA; SATA 18

Seton-Thompson, Ernest
See Seton, Ernest (Evan) Thompson

Settle, Mary Lee 1918- .... **CLC 19, 61**
See also CA 89-92; CAAS 1; CANR 44; DLB 6; INT 89-92

Seuphor, Michel
See Arp, Jean

Sevigne, Marie (de Rabutin-Chantal) Marquise de 1626-1696 .... **LC 11**

Sewall, Samuel 1652-1730 .... **LC 38**
See also DLB 24

Sexton, Anne (Harvey) 1928-1974 **CLC 2, 4, 6, 8, 10, 15, 53; DA; DAB; DAC; DAM MST, POET; PC 2; WLC**
See also CA 1-4R; 53-56; CABS 2; CANR 3, 36; CDALB 1941-1968; DLB 5, 169; MTCW; SATA 10

Shaara, Michael (Joseph, Jr.) 1929-1988**CLC 15; DAM POP**
See also AITN 1; CA 102; 125; CANR 52; DLBY 83

Shackleton, C. C.
See Aldiss, Brian W(ilson)

Shacochis, Bob .... **CLC 39**
See also Shacochis, Robert G.

Shacochis, Robert G. 1951-
See Shacochis, Bob
See also CA 119; 124; INT 124

Shaffer, Anthony (Joshua) 1926- **CLC 19; DAM DRAM**
See also CA 110; 116; DLB 13

Shaffer, Peter (Levin) 1926-**CLC 5, 14, 18, 37, 60; DAB; DAM DRAM, MST; DC 7**
See also CA 25-28R; CANR 25, 47; CDBLB 1960 to Present; DLB 13; MTCW

Shakey, Bernard
See Young, Neil

Shalamov, Varlam (Tikhonovich) 1907(?)-1982 **CLC 18**
See also CA 129; 105

Shamlu, Ahmad 1925- .... **CLC 10**

Shammas, Anton 1951- .... **CLC 55**

Shange, Ntozake 1948-**CLC 8, 25, 38, 74; BLC; DAM DRAM, MULT; DC 3**
See also AAYA 9; BW 2; CA 85-88; CABS 3; CANR 27, 48; DLB 38; MTCW

Shanley, John Patrick 1950- .... **CLC 75**
See also CA 128; 133

Shapcott, Thomas W(illiam) 1935- .... **CLC 38**
See also CA 69-72; CANR 49

Shapiro, Jane .... **CLC 76**

Shapiro, Karl (Jay) 1913- .... **CLC 4, 8, 15, 53**
See also CA 1-4R; CAAS 6; CANR 1, 36, 66; DLB 48; MTCW

Sharp, William 1855-1905 .... **TCLC 39**
See also CA 160; DLB 156

Sharpe, Thomas Ridley 1928-
See Sharpe, Tom
See also CA 114; 122; INT 122

Sharpe, Tom .... **CLC 36**
See also Sharpe, Thomas Ridley
See also DLB 14

Shaw, Bernard .... **TCLC 45**
See also Shaw, George Bernard
See also BW 1

Shaw, G. Bernard
See Shaw, George Bernard

Shaw, George Bernard 1856-1950**TCLC 3, 9, 21; DA; DAB; DAC; DAM DRAM, MST; WLC**
See also Shaw, Bernard
See also CA 104; 128; CDBLB 1914-1945; DLB 10, 57, 190; MTCW

Shaw, Henry Wheeler 1818-1885 .... **NCLC 15**
See also DLB 11

Shaw, Irwin 1913-1984 ...... **CLC 7, 23, 34; DAM DRAM, POP**
See also AITN 1; CA 13-16R; 112; CANR 21; CDALB 1941-1968; DLB 6, 102; DLBY 84; MTCW

Shaw, Robert 1927-1978 .... **CLC 5**
See also AITN 1; CA 1-4R; 81-84; CANR 4; DLB 13, 14

Shaw, T. E.
See Lawrence, T(homas) E(dward)

Shawn, Wallace 1943- .... **CLC 41**
See also CA 112

Shea, Lisa 1953- .... **CLC 86**
See also CA 147

Sheed, Wilfrid (John Joseph) 1930-**CLC 2, 4, 10, 53**
See also CA 65-68; CANR 30, 66; DLB 6; MTCW

Sheldon, Alice Hastings Bradley 1915(?)-1987
See Tiptree, James, Jr.

See also CA 108; 122; CANR 34; INT 108; MTCW

Sheldon, John
See Bloch, Robert (Albert)

Shelley, Mary Wollstonecraft (Godwin) 1797-1851 **NCLC 14, 59; DA; DAB; DAC; DAM MST, NOV; WLC**
See also AAYA 20; CDBLB 1789-1832; DLB 110, 116, 159, 178; SATA 29

Shelley, Percy Bysshe 1792-1822**NCLC 18; DA; DAB; DAC; DAM MST, POET; PC 14; WLC**
See also CDBLB 1789-1832; DLB 96, 110, 158

Shepard, Jim 1956- .... **CLC 36**
See also CA 137; CANR 59; SATA 90

Shepard, Lucius 1947- .... **CLC 34**
See also CA 128; 141

Shepard, Sam 1943-**CLC 4, 6, 17, 34, 41, 44; DAM DRAM; DC 5**
See also AAYA 1; CA 69-72; CABS 3; CANR 22; DLB 7; MTCW

Shepherd, Michael
See Ludlum, Robert

Sherburne, Zoa (Morin) 1912- .... **CLC 30**
See also AAYA 13; CA 1-4R; CANR 3, 37; MAICYA; SAAS 18; SATA 3

Sheridan, Frances 1724-1766 .... **LC 7**
See also DLB 39, 84

Sheridan, Richard Brinsley 1751-1816**NCLC 5; DA; DAB; DAC; DAM DRAM, MST; DC 1; WLC**
See also CDBLB 1660-1789; DLB 89

Sherman, Jonathan Marc .... **CLC 55**

Sherman, Martin 1941(?)- .... **CLC 19**
See also CA 116; 123

Sherwin, Judith Johnson 1936- .... **CLC 7, 15**
See also CA 25-28R; CANR 34

Sherwood, Frances 1940- .... **CLC 81**
See also CA 146

Sherwood, Robert E(mmet) 1896-1955 . **TCLC 3; DAM DRAM**
See also CA 104; 153; DLB 7, 26

Shestov, Lev 1866-1938 .... **TCLC 56**

Shevchenko, Taras 1814-1861 .... **NCLC 54**

Shiel, M(atthew) P(hipps) 1865-1947 .... **TCLC 8**
See also Holmes, Gordon
See also CA 106; 160; DLB 153

Shields, Carol 1935- .... **CLC 91; DAC**
See also CA 81-84; CANR 51

Shields, David 1956- .... **CLC 97**
See also CA 124; CANR 48

Shiga, Naoya 1883-1971 .... **CLC 33; SSC 23**
See also CA 101; 33-36R; DLB 180

Shilts, Randy 1951-1994 .... **CLC 85**
See also AAYA 19; CA 115; 127; 144; CANR 45; INT 127

Shimazaki, Haruki 1872-1943
See Shimazaki Toson
See also CA 105; 134

Shimazaki Toson 1872-1943 .... **TCLC 5**
See also Shimazaki, Haruki
See also DLB 180

Sholokhov, Mikhail (Aleksandrovich) 1905-1984 **CLC 7, 15**
See also CA 101; 112; MTCW; SATA-Obit 36

Shone, Patric
See Hanley, James

Shreve, Susan Richards 1939- .... **CLC 23**
See also CA 49-52; CAAS 5; CANR 5, 38; MAICYA; SATA 46, 95; SATA-Brief 41

Shue, Larry 1946-1985 ... **CLC 52; DAM DRAM**
See also CA 145; 117

Shu-Jen, Chou 1881-1936
See Lu Hsun
See also CA 104

Shulman, Alix Kates 1932- .... **CLC 2, 10**
See also CA 29-32R; CANR 43; SATA 7

Shuster, Joe 1914- .... **CLC 21**

Shute, Nevil .... **CLC 30**
See also Norway, Nevil Shute

Shuttle, Penelope (Diane) 1947- .... **CLC 7**
See also CA 93-96; CANR 39; DLB 14, 40

Sidney, Mary 1561-1621 .... **LC 19, 39**

Sidney, Sir Philip 1554-1586**LC 19, 39; DA; DAB; DAC; DAM MST, POET**
See also CDBLB Before 1660; DLB 167

Siegel, Jerome 1914-1996 .... **CLC 21**
See also CA 116; 151

Siegel, Jerry
See Siegel, Jerome

Sienkiewicz, Henryk (Adam Alexander Pius) 1846-1916 .... **TCLC 3**
See also CA 104; 134

Sierra, Gregorio Martinez
See Martinez Sierra, Gregorio

Sierra, Maria (de la O'LeJarraga) Martinez
See Martinez Sierra, Maria (de la O'LeJarraga)

Sigal, Clancy 1926- .... **CLC 7**
See also CA 1-4R

Sigourney, Lydia Howard (Huntley) 1791-1865 **NCLC 21**
See also DLB 1, 42, 73

Siguenza y Gongora, Carlos de 1645-1700 **LC 8**

Sigurjonsson, Johann 1880-1919 .... **TCLC 27**

Sikelianos, Angelos 1884-1951 .... **TCLC 39**

Silkin, Jon 1930- **CLC 2, 6, 43**
See also CA 5-8R; CAAS 5; DLB 27

Silko, Leslie (Marmon) 1948- **CLC 23, 74; DA; DAC; DAM MST, MULT, POP; WLCS**
See also AAYA 14; CA 115; 122; CANR 45, 65; DLB 143, 175; NNAL

Sillanpaa, Frans Eemil 1888-1964 .... **CLC 19**
See also CA 129; 93-96; MTCW

Sillitoe, Alan 1928- .... **CLC 1, 3, 6, 10, 19, 57**
See also AITN 1; CA 9-12R; CAAS 2; CANR 8, 26, 55; CDBLB 1960 to Present; DLB 14, 139; MTCW; SATA 61

Silone, Ignazio 1900-1978 .... **CLC 4**
See also CA 25-28; 81-84; CANR 34; CAP 2; MTCW

Silver, Joan Micklin 1935- .... **CLC 20**
See also CA 114; 121; INT 121

Silver, Nicholas
See Faust, Frederick (Schiller)

Silverberg, Robert 1935- ..... **CLC 7; DAM POP**
See also AAYA 24; CA 1-4R; CAAS 3; CANR 1, 20, 36; DLB 8; INT CANR-20; MAICYA; MTCW; SATA 13, 91

Silverstein, Alvin 1933- .... **CLC 17**
See also CA 49-52; CANR 2; CLR 25; JRDA; MAICYA; SATA 8, 69

Silverstein, Virginia B(arbara Opshelor) 1937- **CLC 17**
See also CA 49-52; CANR 2; CLR 25; JRDA; MAICYA; SATA 8, 69

Sim, Georges
See Simenon, Georges (Jacques Christian)

Simak, Clifford D(onald) 1904-1988 . **CLC 1, 55**
See also CA 1-4R; 125; CANR 1, 35; DLB 8; MTCW; SATA-Obit 56

Simenon, Georges (Jacques Christian) 1903-1989 **CLC 1, 2, 3, 8, 18, 47; DAM POP**
See also CA 85-88; 129; CANR 35; DLB 72; DLBY 89; MTCW

Simic, Charles 1938-**CLC 6, 9, 22, 49, 68; DAM POET**
See also CA 29-32R; CAAS 4; CANR 12, 33, 52, 61; DLB 105

Simmel, Georg 1858-1918 .... **TCLC 64**
See also CA 157

Simmons, Charles (Paul) 1924- .... **CLC 57**
See also CA 89-92; INT 89-92

Simmons, Dan 1948- .... **CLC 44; DAM POP**
See also AAYA 16; CA 138; CANR 53

Simmons, James (Stewart Alexander) 1933-**CLC 43**
See also CA 105; CAAS 21; DLB 40

Simms, William Gilmore 1806-1870 ... **NCLC 3**
See also DLB 3, 30, 59, 73

Simon, Carly 1945- .... **CLC 26**
See also CA 105

Simon, Claude 1913-1984**CLC 4, 9, 15, 39; DAM NOV**
See also CA 89-92; CANR 33; DLB 83; MTCW

Simon, (Marvin) Neil 1927-**CLC 6, 11, 31, 39, 70; DAM DRAM**
See also AITN 1; CA 21-24R; CANR 26, 54; DLB 7; MTCW

Simon, Paul (Frederick) 1941(?)- .... **CLC 17**
See also CA 116; 153

Simonon, Paul 1956(?)- .... **CLC 30**

Simpson, Harriette
See Arnow, Harriette (Louisa) Simpson

Simpson, Louis (Aston Marantz) 1923-**CLC 4, 7, 9, 32; DAM POET**
See also CA 1-4R; CAAS 4; CANR 1, 61; DLB 5; MTCW

Simpson, Mona (Elizabeth) 1957- .... **CLC 44**
See also CA 122; 135; CANR 68

Simpson, N(orman) F(rederick) 1919- . **CLC 29**
See also CA 13-16R; DLB 13

Sinclair, Andrew (Annandale) 1935- **CLC 2, 14**
See also CA 9-12R; CAAS 5; CANR 14, 38; DLB 14; MTCW

Sinclair, Emil
See Hesse, Hermann

Sinclair, Iain 1943- .... **CLC 76**
See also CA 132

Sinclair, Iain MacGregor
See Sinclair, Iain

Sinclair, Irene
See Griffith, D(avid Lewelyn) W(ark)

Sinclair, Mary Amelia St. Clair 1865(?)-1946
See Sinclair, May
See also CA 104

Sinclair, May .... **TCLC 3, 11**
See also Sinclair, Mary Amelia St. Clair
See also DLB 36, 135

Sinclair, Roy
See Griffith, D(avid Lewelyn) W(ark)

Sinclair, Upton (Beall) 1878-1968 **CLC 1, 11, 15, 63; DA; DAB; DAC; DAM MST, NOV; WLC**
See also CA 5-8R; 25-28R; CANR 7; CDALB 1929-1941; DLB 9; INT CANR-7; MTCW; SATA 9

Singer, Isaac
See Singer, Isaac Bashevis

Singer, Isaac Bashevis 1904-1991**CLC 1, 3, 6, 9, 11, 15, 23, 38, 69; DA; DAB; DAC; DAM MST, NOV; SSC 3; WLC**
See also AITN 1, 2; CA 1-4R; 134; CANR 1, 39; CDALB 1941-1968; CLR 1; DLB 6, 28, 52; DLBY 91; JRDA; MAICYA; MTCW; SATA 3, 27; SATA-Obit 68

Singer, Israel Joshua 1893-1944 .... **TCLC 33**

Singh, Khushwant 1915- .... **CLC 11**
See also CA 9-12R; CAAS 9; CANR 6

Singleton, Ann
See Benedict, Ruth (Fulton)

Sinjohn, John
See Galsworthy, John

Sinyavsky, Andrei (Donatevich) 1925-1997**CLC 8**
See also CA 85-88; 159

Sirin, V.
See Nabokov, Vladimir (Vladimirovich)

Sissman, L(ouis) E(dward) 1928-1976 **CLC 9, 18**
See also CA 21-24R; 65-68; CANR 13; DLB 5

Sisson, C(harles) H(ubert) 1914- .... **CLC 8**
See also CA 1-4R; CAAS 3; CANR 3, 48; DLB 27

Sitwell, Dame Edith 1887-1964**CLC 2, 9, 67; DAM POET; PC 3**
See also CA 9-12R; CANR 35; CDBLB 1945-1960; DLB 20; MTCW

Siwaarmill, H. P.
See Sharp, William

Sjoewall, Maj 1935- .... **CLC 7**
See also CA 65-68

Sjowall, Maj
See Sjoewall, Maj

Skelton, Robin 1925-1997 .... **CLC 13**
See also AITN 2; CA 5-8R; 160; CAAS 5; CANR 28; DLB 27, 53

Skolimowski, Jerzy 1938- .... **CLC 20**
See also CA 128

Skram, Amalie (Bertha) 1847-1905 .... **TCLC 25**
See also CA 165

Skvorecky, Josef (Vaclav) 1924-**CLC 15, 39, 69; DAC; DAM NOV**
See also CA 61-64; CAAS 1; CANR 10, 34, 63; MTCW

Slade, Bernard .... **CLC 11, 46**
See also Newbound, Bernard Slade
See also CAAS 9; DLB 53

Slaughter, Carolyn 1946- .... **CLC 56**
See also CA 85-88

Slaughter, Frank G(ill) 1908- .... **CLC 29**
See also AITN 2; CA 5-8R; CANR 5; INT CANR-5

Slavitt, David R(ytman) 1935- .... **CLC 5, 14**
See also CA 21-24R; CAAS 3; CANR 41; DLB 5, 6

Slesinger, Tess 1905-1945 .... **TCLC 10**
See also CA 107; DLB 102

Slessor, Kenneth 1901-1971 .... **CLC 14**
See also CA 102; 89-92

Slowacki, Juliusz 1809-1849 .... **NCLC 15**

Smart, Christopher 1722-1771 **LC 3; DAM POET; PC 13**
See also DLB 109

Smart, Elizabeth 1913-1986 .... **CLC 54**
See also CA 81-84; 118; DLB 88

Smiley, Jane (Graves) 1949- **CLC 53, 76; DAM POP**
See also CA 104; CANR 30, 50; INT CANR-30

Smith, A(rthur) J(ames) M(arshall) 1902-1980 **CLC 15; DAC**
See also CA 1-4R; 102; CANR 4; DLB 88

Smith, Adam 1723-1790 .... **LC 36**
See also DLB 104

Smith, Alexander 1829-1867 .... **NCLC 59**
See also DLB 32, 55

Smith, Anna Deavere 1950- .... **CLC 86**
See also CA 133

Smith, Betty (Wehner) 1896-1972 .... **CLC 19**
See also CA 5-8R; 33-36R; DLBY 82; SATA 6

Smith, Charlotte (Turner) 1749-1806 **NCLC 23**
See also DLB 39, 109

Smith, Clark Ashton 1893-1961 .... **CLC 43**
See also CA 143

Smith, Dave .... **CLC 22, 42**
See also Smith, David (Jeddie)
See also CAAS 7; DLB 5

Smith, David (Jeddie) 1942-
See Smith, Dave
See also CA 49-52; CANR 1, 59; DAM POET

Smith, Florence Margaret 1902-1971
See Smith, Stevie
See also CA 17-18; 29-32R; CANR 35; CAP 2; DAM POET; MTCW

Smith, Iain Crichton 1928- .... **CLC 64**
See also CA 21-24R; DLB 40, 139

Smith, John 1580(?)-1631 .... **LC 9**

Smith, Johnston
See Crane, Stephen (Townley)

Smith, Joseph, Jr. 1805-1844 .... **NCLC 53**

Smith, Lee 1944- .... **CLC 25, 73**
See also CA 114; 119; CANR 46; DLB 143; DLBY 83; INT 119

Smith, Martin
See Smith, Martin Cruz

Smith, Martin Cruz 1942-**CLC 25; DAM MULT, POP**
See also BEST 89:4; CA 85-88; CANR 6, 23, 43, 65; INT CANR-23; NNAL

Smith, Mary-Ann Tirone 1944- .... **CLC 39**
See also CA 118; 136

Smith, Patti 1946- .... **CLC 12**
See also CA 93-96; CANR 63

Smith, Pauline (Urmson) 1882-1959 ... **TCLC 25**

Smith, Rosamond
See Oates, Joyce Carol

Smith, Sheila Kaye
See Kaye-Smith, Sheila

Smith, Stevie .... **CLC 3, 8, 25, 44; PC 12**
See also Smith, Florence Margaret
See also DLB 20

Smith, Wilbur (Addison) 1933- .... **CLC 33**
See also CA 13-16R; CANR 7, 46, 66; MTCW

Smith, William Jay 1918- .... **CLC 6**
See also CA 5-8R; CANR 44; DLB 5; MAICYA; SAAS 22; SATA 2, 68

Squires, (James) Radcliffe 1917-1993 .. **CLC 51**
See also CA 1-4R; 140; CANR 6, 21

Srivastava, Dhanpat Rai 1880(?)-1936
See Premchand
See also CA 118

Stacy, Donald
See Pohl, Frederik

Stael, Germaine de 1766-1817
See Stael-Holstein, Anne Louise Germaine Necker Baronn
See also DLB 119

Stael-Holstein, Anne Louise Germaine Necker Baronn 1766-1817 .... **NCLC 3**
See also Stael, Germaine de
See also DLB 192

Stafford, Jean 1915-1979**CLC 4, 7, 19, 68; SSC 26**
See also CA 1-4R; 85-88; CANR 3, 65; DLB 2, 173; MTCW; SATA-Obit 22

Stafford, William (Edgar) 1914-1993 . **CLC 4, 7, 29; DAM POET**
See also CA 5-8R; 142; CAAS 3; CANR 5, 22; DLB 5; INT CANR-22

Stagnelius, Eric Johan 1793-1823 ..... **NCLC 61**

Staines, Trevor
See Brunner, John (Kilian Houston)

Stairs, Gordon
See Austin, Mary (Hunter)

Stannard, Martin 1947- .... **CLC 44**
See also CA 142; DLB 155

Stanton, Elizabeth Cady 1815-1902 ..... **TCLC 73**
See also DLB 79

Stanton, Maura 1946- .... **CLC 9**
See also CA 89-92; CANR 15; DLB 120

Stanton, Schuyler
See Baum, L(yman) Frank

Stapledon, (William) Olaf 1886-1950 .. **TCLC 22**
See also CA 111; 162; DLB 15

Starbuck, George (Edwin) 1931-1996 ... **CLC 53; DAM POET**
See also CA 21-24R; 153; CANR 23

Stark, Richard
See Westlake, Donald E(dwin)

Staunton, Schuyler
See Baum, L(yman) Frank

Stead, Christina (Ellen) 1902-1983 . **CLC 2, 5, 8, 32, 80**
See also CA 13-16R; 109; CANR 33, 40; MTCW

Stead, William Thomas 1849-1912 ..... **TCLC 48**

Steele, Richard 1672-1729 .... **LC 18**
See also CDBLB 1660-1789; DLB 84, 101

Steele, Timothy (Reid) 1948- .... **CLC 45**
See also CA 93-96; CANR 16, 50; DLB 120

Steffens, (Joseph) Lincoln 1866-1936 . **TCLC 20**
See also CA 117

Stegner, Wallace (Earle) 1909-1993 . **CLC 9, 49, 81; DAM NOV; SSC 27**
See also AITN 1; BEST 90:3; CA 1-4R; 141; CAAS 9; CANR 1, 21, 46; DLB 9; DLBY 93; MTCW

Stein, Gertrude 1874-1946**TCLC 1, 6, 28, 48; DA; DAB; DAC; DAM MST, NOV, POET; PC 18; WLC**
See also CA 104; 132; CDALB 1917-1929; DLB 4, 54, 86; DLBD 15; MTCW

Steinbeck, John (Ernst) 1902-1968 . **CLC 1, 5, 9, 13, 21, 34, 45, 75; DA; DAB; DAC; DAM DRAM, MST, NOV; SSC 11; WLC**
See also AAYA 12; CA 1-4R; 25-28R; CANR 1, 35; CDALB 1929-1941; DLB 7, 9; DLBD 2; MTCW; SATA 9

Steinem, Gloria 1934- .... **CLC 63**
See also CA 53-56; CANR 28, 51; MTCW

Steiner, George 1929- .... **CLC 24; DAM NOV**
See also CA 73-76; CANR 31, 67; DLB 67; MTCW; SATA 62

Steiner, K. Leslie
See Delany, Samuel R(ay, Jr.)

Steiner, Rudolf 1861-1925 .... **TCLC 13**
See also CA 107

Stendhal 1783-1842**NCLC 23, 46; DA; DAB; DAC; DAM MST, NOV; SSC 27; WLC**
See also DLB 119

Stephen, Adeline Virginia
See Woolf, (Adeline) Virginia

Stephen, SirLeslie 1832-1904 .... **TCLC 23**
See also CA 123; DLB 57, 144, 190

Stephen, Sir Leslie
See Stephen, SirLeslie

Stephen, Virginia
See Woolf, (Adeline) Virginia

Stephens, James 1882(?)-1950 .... **TCLC 4**
See also CA 104; DLB 19, 153, 162

Stephens, Reed
See Donaldson, Stephen R.

Steptoe, Lydia
See Barnes, Djuna

Sterchi, Beat 1949- .... **CLC 65**

Sterling, Brett
See Bradbury, Ray (Douglas); Hamilton, Edmond

Sterling, Bruce 1954- .... **CLC 72**
See also CA 119; CANR 44

Sterling, George 1869-1926 .... **TCLC 20**
See also CA 117; 165; DLB 54

Stern, Gerald 1925- .... **CLC 40, 100**
See also CA 81-84; CANR 28; DLB 105

Stern, Richard (Gustave) 1928- .... **CLC 4, 39**
See also CA 1-4R; CANR 1, 25, 52; DLBY 87; INT CANR-25

Sternberg, Josef von 1894-1969 .... **CLC 20**
See also CA 81-84

Sterne, Laurence 1713-1768 ... **LC 2; DA; DAB; DAC; DAM MST, NOV; WLC**
See also CDBLB 1660-1789; DLB 39

Sternheim, (William Adolf) Carl 1878-1942 **TCLC 8**
See also CA 105; DLB 56, 118

Stevens, Mark 1951- .... **CLC 34**
See also CA 122

Stevens, Wallace 1879-1955**TCLC 3, 12, 45; DA; DAB; DAC; DAM MST, POET; PC 6; WLC**
See also CA 104; 124; CDALB 1929-1941; DLB 54; MTCW

Stevenson, Anne (Katharine) 1933- .. **CLC 7, 33**
See also CA 17-20R; CAAS 9; CANR 9, 33; DLB 40; MTCW

Stevenson, Robert Louis (Balfour) 1850-1894 **NCLC 5, 14, 63; DA; DAB; DAC; DAM MST, NOV; SSC 11; WLC**
See also AAYA 24; CDBLB 1890-1914; CLR 10, 11; DLB 18, 57, 141, 156, 174; DLBD 13; JRDA; MAICYA; YABC 2

Stewart, J(ohn) I(nnes) M(ackintosh) 1906-1994 **CLC 7, 14, 32**
See also CA 85-88; 147; CAAS 3; CANR 47; MTCW

Stewart, Mary (Florence Elinor) 1916-**CLC 7, 35; DAB**
See also CA 1-4R; CANR 1, 59; SATA 12

Stewart, Mary Rainbow
See Stewart, Mary (Florence Elinor)

Stifle, June
See Campbell, Maria

Stifter, Adalbert 1805-1868 .. **NCLC 41; SSC 28**
See also DLB 133

Still, James 1906- .... **CLC 49**
See also CA 65-68; CAAS 17; CANR 10, 26; DLB 9; SATA 29

Sting
See Sumner, Gordon Matthew

Stirling, Arthur
See Sinclair, Upton (Beall)

Stitt, Milan 1941- .... **CLC 29**
See also CA 69-72

Stockton, Francis Richard 1834-1902
See Stockton, Frank R.
See also CA 108; 137; MAICYA; SATA 44

Stockton, Frank R. .... **TCLC 47**
See also Stockton, Francis Richard
See also DLB 42, 74; DLBD 13; SATA-Brief 32

Stoddard, Charles
See Kuttner, Henry

Stoker, Abraham 1847-1912
See Stoker, Bram
See also CA 105; DA; DAC; DAM MST, NOV; SATA 29

Stoker, Bram 1847-1912 .. **TCLC 8; DAB; WLC**
See also Stoker, Abraham

Tevis, Walter 1928-1984 .... **CLC 42**
See also CA 113

Tey, Josephine .... **TCLC 14**
See also Mackintosh, Elizabeth
See also DLB 77

Thackeray, William Makepeace 1811-1863**NCLC 5, 14, 22, 43; DA; DAB; DAC; DAM MST, NOV; WLC**
See also CDBLB 1832-1890; DLB 21, 55, 159, 163; SATA 23

Thakura, Ravindranatha
See Tagore, Rabindranath

Tharoor, Shashi 1956- .... **CLC 70**
See also CA 141

Thelwell, Michael Miles 1939- .... **CLC 22**
See also BW 2; CA 101

Theobald, Lewis, Jr.
See Lovecraft, H(oward) P(hillips)

Theodorescu, Ion N. 1880-1967
See Arghezi, Tudor
See also CA 116

Theriault, Yves 1915-1983 **CLC 79; DAC; DAM MST**
See also CA 102; DLB 88

Theroux, Alexander (Louis) 1939- .... **CLC 2, 25**
See also CA 85-88; CANR 20, 63

Theroux, Paul (Edward) 1941- **CLC 5, 8, 11, 15, 28, 46; DAM POP**
See also BEST 89:4; CA 33-36R; CANR 20, 45; DLB 2; MTCW; SATA 44

Thesen, Sharon 1946- .... **CLC 56**
See also CA 163

Thevenin, Denis
See Duhamel, Georges

Thibault, Jacques Anatole Francois 1844-1924
See France, Anatole
See also CA 106; 127; DAM NOV; MTCW

Thiele, Colin (Milton) 1920- .... **CLC 17**
See also CA 29-32R; CANR 12, 28, 53; CLR 27; MAICYA; SAAS 2; SATA 14, 72

Thomas, Audrey (Callahan) 1935-**CLC 7, 13, 37, 107; SSC 20**
See also AITN 2; CA 21-24R; CAAS 19; CANR 36, 58; DLB 60; MTCW

Thomas, D(onald) M(ichael) 1935-**CLC 13, 22, 31**
See also CA 61-64; CAAS 11; CANR 17, 45; CDBLB 1960 to Present; DLB 40; INT CANR-17; MTCW

Thomas, Dylan (Marlais) 1914-1953 **TCLC 1, 8, 45; DA; DAB; DAC; DAM DRAM, MST, POET; PC 2; SSC 3; WLC**
See also CA 104; 120; CANR 65; CDBLB 1945-1960; DLB 13, 20, 139; MTCW; SATA 60

Thomas, (Philip) Edward 1878-1917 **TCLC 10; DAM POET**
See also CA 106; 153; DLB 19

Thomas, Joyce Carol 1938- .... **CLC 35**
See also AAYA 12; BW 2; CA 113; 116; CANR 48; CLR 19; DLB 33; INT 116; JRDA; MAICYA; MTCW; SAAS 7; SATA 40, 78

Thomas, Lewis 1913-1993 .... **CLC 35**
See also CA 85-88; 143; CANR 38, 60; MTCW

Thomas, Paul
See Mann, (Paul) Thomas

Thomas, Piri 1928- .... **CLC 17**
See also CA 73-76; HW

Thomas, R(onald) S(tuart) 1913- **CLC 6, 13, 48; DAB; DAM POET**
See also CA 89-92; CAAS 4; CANR 30; CDBLB 1960 to Present; DLB 27; MTCW

Thomas, Ross (Elmore) 1926-1995 .... **CLC 39**
See also CA 33-36R; 150; CANR 22, 63

Thompson, Francis Clegg
See Mencken, H(enry) L(ouis)

Thompson, Francis Joseph 1859-1907 .. **TCLC 4**
See also CA 104; CDBLB 1890-1914; DLB 19

Thompson, Hunter S(tockton) 1939- **CLC 9, 17, 40, 104; DAM POP**
See also BEST 89:1; CA 17-20R; CANR 23, 46; DLB 185; MTCW

Thompson, James Myers
See Thompson, Jim (Myers)

Thompson, Jim (Myers) 1906-1977(?) .. **CLC 69**
See also CA 140

Thompson, Judith .... **CLC 39**

Thomson, James 1700-1748**LC 16, 29, 40; DAM POET**
See also DLB 95

Thomson, James 1834-1882**NCLC 18; DAM POET**
See also DLB 35

Thoreau, Henry David 1817-1862**NCLC 7, 21, 61; DA; DAB; DAC; DAM MST; WLC**
See also CDALB 1640-1865; DLB 1

Thornton, Hall
See Silverberg, Robert

Thucydides c. 455B.C.-399B.C. .... **CMLC 17**
See also DLB 176

Thurber, James (Grover) 1894-1961 . **CLC 5, 11, 25; DA; DAB; DAC; DAM DRAM, MST, NOV; SSC 1**
See also CA 73-76; CANR 17, 39; CDALB 1929-1941; DLB 4, 11, 22, 102; MAICYA; MTCW; SATA 13

Thurman, Wallace (Henry) 1902-1934 . **TCLC 6; BLC; DAM MULT**
See also BW 1; CA 104; 124; DLB 51

Ticheburn, Cheviot
See Ainsworth, William Harrison

Tieck, (Johann) Ludwig 1773-1853 **NCLC 5, 46**
See also DLB 90

Tiger, Derry
See Ellison, Harlan (Jay)

Tilghman, Christopher 1948(?)- .... **CLC 65**
See also CA 159

Tillinghast, Richard (Williford) 1940- . **CLC 29**
See also CA 29-32R; CAAS 23; CANR 26, 51

Timrod, Henry 1828-1867 .... **NCLC 25**
See also DLB 3

Tindall, Gillian (Elizabeth) 1938- .... **CLC 7**
See also CA 21-24R; CANR 11, 65

Tiptree, James, Jr. .... **CLC 48, 50**
See also Sheldon, Alice Hastings Bradley
See also DLB 8

Titmarsh, Michael Angelo
See Thackeray, William Makepeace

Tocqueville, Alexis (Charles Henri Maurice Clerel Comte) 1805-1859 .... **NCLC 7, 63**

Tolkien, J(ohn) R(onald) R(euel) 1892-1973**CLC 1, 2, 3, 8, 12, 38; DA; DAB; DAC; DAM MST, NOV, POP; WLC**
See also AAYA 10; AITN 1; CA 17-18; 45-48; CANR 36; CAP 2; CDBLB 1914-1945; DLB 15, 160; JRDA; MAICYA; MTCW; SATA 2, 32; SATA-Obit 24

Toller, Ernst 1893-1939 .... **TCLC 10**
See also CA 107; DLB 124

Tolson, M. B.
See Tolson, Melvin B(eaunorus)

Tolson, Melvin B(eaunorus) 1898(?)-1966 . **CLC 36, 105; BLC; DAM MULT, POET**
See also BW 1; CA 124; 89-92; DLB 48, 76

Tolstoi, Aleksei Nikolaevich
See Tolstoy, Alexey Nikolaevich

Tolstoy, Alexey Nikolaevich 1882-1945**TCLC 18**
See also CA 107; 158

Tolstoy, Count Leo
See Tolstoy, Leo (Nikolaevich)

Tolstoy, Leo (Nikolaevich) 1828-1910**TCLC 4, 11, 17, 28, 44, 79; DA; DAB; DAC; DAM MST, NOV; SSC 9, 30; WLC**
See also CA 104; 123; SATA 26

Tomasi di Lampedusa, Giuseppe 1896-1957
See Lampedusa, Giuseppe (Tomasi) di
See also CA 111

Tomlin, Lily .... **CLC 17**
See also Tomlin, Mary Jean

Tomlin, Mary Jean 1939(?)-
See Tomlin, Lily
See also CA 117

Tomlinson, (Alfred) Charles 1927- . **CLC 2, 4, 6, 13, 45; DAM POET; PC 17**
See also CA 5-8R; CANR 33; DLB 40

Tomlinson, H(enry) M(ajor) 1873-1958 **TCLC 71**
See also CA 118; 161; DLB 36, 100, 195

Tonson, Jacob
See Bennett, (Enoch) Arnold

Toole, John Kennedy 1937-1969 **CLC 19, 64**
See also CA 104; DLBY 81

Toomer, Jean 1894-1967 **CLC 1, 4, 13, 22; BLC; DAM MULT; PC 7; SSC 1; WLCS**
See also BW 1; CA 85-88; CDALB 1917-1929; DLB 45, 51; MTCW

Torley, Luke
See Blish, James (Benjamin)

Tornimparte, Alessandra
See Ginzburg, Natalia

Torre, Raoul della
See Mencken, H(enry) L(ouis)

Torrey, E(dwin) Fuller 1937- .... **CLC 34**
See also CA 119

Torsvan, Ben Traven
See Traven, B.

Torsvan, Benno Traven
See Traven, B.

Torsvan, Berick Traven
See Traven, B.

Torsvan, Berwick Traven
See Traven, B.

Torsvan, Bruno Traven
See Traven, B.

Torsvan, Traven
See Traven, B.

Tournier, Michel (Edouard) 1924-**CLC 6, 23, 36, 95**
See also CA 49-52; CANR 3, 36; DLB 83; MTCW; SATA 23

Tournimparte, Alessandra
See Ginzburg, Natalia

Towers, Ivar
See Kornbluth, C(yril) M.

Towne, Robert (Burton) 1936(?)- .... **CLC 87**
See also CA 108; DLB 44

Townsend, Sue .... **CLC 61**
See also Townsend, Susan Elaine
See also SATA 55, 93; SATA-Brief 48

Townsend, Susan Elaine 1946-
See Townsend, Sue
See also CA 119; 127; CANR 65; DAB; DAC; DAM MST

Townshend, Peter (Dennis Blandford) 1945-**CLC 17, 42**
See also CA 107

Tozzi, Federigo 1883-1920 .... **TCLC 31**
See also CA 160

Traill, Catharine Parr 1802-1899 ...... **NCLC 31**
See also DLB 99

Trakl, Georg 1887-1914 .... **TCLC 5; PC 20**
See also CA 104; 165

Transtroemer, Tomas (Goesta) 1931-**CLC 52, 65; DAM POET**
See also CA 117; 129; CAAS 17

Transtromer, Tomas Gosta
See Transtroemer, Tomas (Goesta)

Traven, B. (?)-1969 .... **CLC 8, 11**
See also CA 19-20; 25-28R; CAP 2; DLB 9, 56; MTCW

Treitel, Jonathan 1959- .... **CLC 70**

Tremain, Rose 1943- .... **CLC 42**
See also CA 97-100; CANR 44; DLB 14

Tremblay, Michel 1942-**CLC 29, 102; DAC; DAM MST**
See also CA 116; 128; DLB 60; MTCW

Trevanian .... **CLC 29**
See also Whitaker, Rod(ney)

Trevor, Glen
See Hilton, James

Trevor, William 1928-**CLC 7, 9, 14, 25, 71; SSC 21**
See also Cox, William Trevor
See also DLB 14, 139

Trifonov, Yuri (Valentinovich) 1925-1981 **CLC 45**
See also CA 126; 103; MTCW

Trilling, Lionel 1905-1975 .... **CLC 9, 11, 24**
See also CA 9-12R; 61-64; CANR 10; DLB 28, 63; INT CANR-10; MTCW

Trimball, W. H.
See Mencken, H(enry) L(ouis)

Tristan
See Gomez de la Serna, Ramon

Tristram
See Housman, A(lfred) E(dward)

Trogdon, William (Lewis) 1939-
See Heat-Moon, William Least
See also CA 115; 119; CANR 47; INT 119

Trollope, Anthony 1815-1882 .. **NCLC 6, 33; DA; DAB; DAC; DAM MST, NOV; SSC 28; WLC**
See also CDBLB 1832-1890; DLB 21, 57, 159; SATA 22

Trollope, Frances 1779-1863 .... **NCLC 30**
See also DLB 21, 166

Trotsky, Leon 1879-1940 .... **TCLC 22**
See also CA 118

Trotter (Cockburn), Catharine 1679-1749 . **LC 8**
See also DLB 84

Trout, Kilgore
See Farmer, Philip Jose

Trow, George W. S. 1943- .... **CLC 52**
See also CA 126

Troyat, Henri 1911- .... **CLC 23**
See also CA 45-48; CANR 2, 33, 67; MTCW

Trudeau, G(arretson) B(eekman) 1948-
See Trudeau, Garry B.
See also CA 81-84; CANR 31, SATA 35

Trudeau, Garry B. .... **CLC 12**
See also Trudeau, G(arretson) B(eekman)
See also AAYA 10; AITN 2

Truffaut, Francois 1932-1984 .... **CLC 20, 101**
See also CA 81-84; 113; CANR 34

Trumbo, Dalton 1905-1976 .... **CLC 19**
See also CA 21-24R; 69-72; CANR 10; DLB 26

Trumbull, John 1750-1831 .... **NCLC 30**
See also DLB 31

Trundlett, Helen B.
See Eliot, T(homas) S(tearns)

Tryon, Thomas 1926-1991 **CLC 3, 11; DAM POP**
See also AITN 1; CA 29-32R; 135; CANR 32; MTCW

Tryon, Tom
See Tryon, Thomas

Ts'ao Hsueh-ch'in 1715(?)-1763 .... **LC 1**

Tsushima, Shuji 1909-1948
See Dazai, Osamu
See also CA 107

Tsvetaeva (Efron), Marina (Ivanovna) 1892-1941 **TCLC 7, 35; PC 14**
See also CA 104; 128; MTCW

Tuck, Lily 1938- .... **CLC 70**
See also CA 139

Tu Fu 712-770 .... **PC 9**
See also DAM MULT

Tunis, John R(oberts) 1889-1975 .... **CLC 12**
See also CA 61-64; CANR 62; DLB 22, 171; JRDA; MAICYA; SATA 37; SATA-Brief 30

Tuohy, Frank .... **CLC 37**
See also Tuohy, John Francis
See also DLB 14, 139

Tuohy, John Francis 1925-
See Tuohy, Frank
See also CA 5-8R; CANR 3, 47

Turco, Lewis (Putnam) 1934- .... **CLC 11, 63**
See also CA 13-16R; CAAS 22; CANR 24, 51; DLBY 84

Turgenev, Ivan 1818-1883 . **NCLC 21; DA; DAB; DAC; DAM MST, NOV; DC 7; SSC 7; WLC**

Turgot, Anne-Robert-Jacques 1727-1781 **LC 26**

Turner, Frederick 1943- .... **CLC 48**
See also CA 73-76; CAAS 10; CANR 12, 30, 56; DLB 40

Tutu, Desmond M(pilo) 1931-**CLC 80; BLC; DAM MULT**
See also BW 1; CA 125; CANR 67

Tutuola, Amos 1920-1997 . **CLC 5, 14, 29; BLC; DAM MULT**
See also BW 2; CA 9-12R; 159; CANR 27, 66; DLB 125; MTCW

Twain, Mark **TCLC 6, 12, 19, 36, 48, 59; SSC 26; WLC**
See also Clemens, Samuel Langhorne
See also AAYA 20; DLB 11, 12, 23, 64, 74

Tyler, Anne 1941-**CLC 7, 11, 18, 28, 44, 59, 103; DAM NOV, POP**
See also AAYA 18; BEST 89:1; CA 9-12R; CANR 11, 33, 53; DLB 6, 143; DLBY 82; MTCW; SATA 7, 90

Veblen, Thorstein (Bunde) 1857-1929 . **TCLC 31**
See also CA 115; 165

Vega, Lope de 1562-1635 .... **LC 23**

Venison, Alfred
See Pound, Ezra (Weston Loomis)

Verdi, Marie de
See Mencken, H(enry) L(ouis)

Verdu, Matilde
See Cela, Camilo Jose

Verga, Giovanni (Carmelo) 1840-1922 . **TCLC 3; SSC 21**
See also CA 104; 123

Vergil 70B.C.-19B.C. **CMLC 9; DA; DAB; DAC; DAM MST, POET; PC 12; WLCS**

Verhaeren, Emile (Adolphe Gustave) 1855-1916 **TCLC 12**
See also CA 109

Verlaine, Paul (Marie) 1844-1896 . **NCLC 2, 51; DAM POET; PC 2**

Verne, Jules (Gabriel) 1828-1905 ... **TCLC 6, 52**
See also AAYA 16; CA 110; 131; DLB 123; JRDA; MAICYA; SATA 21

Very, Jones 1813-1880 .... **NCLC 9**
See also DLB 1

Vesaas, Tarjei 1897-1970 .... **CLC 48**
See also CA 29-32R

Vialis, Gaston
See Simenon, Georges (Jacques Christian)

Vian, Boris 1920-1959 .... **TCLC 9**
See also CA 106; 164; DLB 72

Viaud, (Louis Marie) Julien 1850-1923
See Loti, Pierre
See also CA 107

Vicar, Henry
See Felsen, Henry Gregor

Vicker, Angus
See Felsen, Henry Gregor

Vidal, Gore 1925- **CLC 2, 4, 6, 8, 10, 22, 33, 72; DAM NOV, POP**
See also AITN 1; BEST 90:2; CA 5-8R; CANR 13, 45, 65; DLB 6, 152; INT CANR-13; MTCW

Viereck, Peter (Robert Edwin) 1916- ..... **CLC 4**
See also CA 1-4R; CANR 1, 47; DLB 5

Vigny, Alfred (Victor) de 1797-1863 ... **NCLC 7; DAM POET**
See also DLB 119, 192

Vilakazi, Benedict Wallet 1906-1947 .. **TCLC 37**

Villaurrutia, Xavier 1903-1950 .... **TCLC 80**
See also HW

Villiers de l'Isle Adam, Jean Marie Mathias Philippe Auguste, Comte de 1838-1889 **NCLC 3; SSC 14**
See also DLB 123

Villon, Francois 1431-1463(?) .... **PC 13**

Vinci, Leonardo da 1452-1519 .... **LC 12**

Vine, Barbara .... **CLC 50**
See also Rendell, Ruth (Barbara)
See also BEST 90:4

Vinge, Joan D(ennison) 1948- **CLC 30; SSC 24**
See also CA 93-96; SATA 36

Violis, G.
See Simenon, Georges (Jacques Christian)

Visconti, Luchino 1906-1976 .... **CLC 16**
See also CA 81-84; 65-68; CANR 39

Vittorini, Elio 1908-1966 .... **CLC 6, 9, 14**
See also CA 133; 25-28R

Vizenor, Gerald Robert 1934- .. **CLC 103; DAM MULT**
See also CA 13-16R; CAAS 22; CANR 5, 21, 44, 67; DLB 175; NNAL

Vizinczey, Stephen 1933- .... **CLC 40**
See also CA 128; INT 128

Vliet, R(ussell) G(ordon) 1929-1984 ..... **CLC 22**
See also CA 37-40R; 112; CANR 18

Vogau, Boris Andreyevich 1894-1937(?)
See Pilnyak, Boris
See also CA 123

Vogel, Paula A(nne) 1951- .... **CLC 76**
See also CA 108

Voight, Ellen Bryant 1943- .... **CLC 54**
See also CA 69-72; CANR 11, 29, 55; DLB 120

Voigt, Cynthia 1942- .... **CLC 30**
See also AAYA 3; CA 106; CANR 18, 37, 40; CLR 13, 48; INT CANR-18; JRDA; MAICYA; SATA 48, 79; SATA-Brief 33

Voinovich, Vladimir (Nikolaevich) 1932-**CLC 10, 49**
See also CA 81-84; CAAS 12; CANR 33, 67; MTCW

Vollmann, William T. 1959-**CLC 89; DAM NOV, POP**
See also CA 134; CANR 67

Voloshinov, V. N.
See Bakhtin, Mikhail Mikhailovich

Voltaire 1694-1778**LC 14; DA; DAB; DAC; DAM DRAM, MST; SSC 12; WLC**

von Daeniken, Erich 1935- .... **CLC 30**
See also AITN 1; CA 37-40R; CANR 17, 44

von Daniken, Erich
See von Daeniken, Erich

von Heidenstam, (Carl Gustaf) Verner
See Heidenstam, (Carl Gustaf) Verner von

von Heyse, Paul (Johann Ludwig)
See Heyse, Paul (Johann Ludwig von)

von Hofmannsthal, Hugo
See Hofmannsthal, Hugo von

von Horvath, Odon
See Horvath, Oedoen von

von Horvath, Oedoen
See Horvath, Oedoen von

von Liliencron, (Friedrich Adolf Axel) Detlev
See Liliencron, (Friedrich Adolf Axel) Detlev von

Vonnegut, Kurt, Jr. 1922-**CLC 1, 2, 3, 4, 5, 8, 12, 22, 40, 60; DA; DAB; DAC; DAM MST, NOV, POP; SSC 8; WLC**
See also AAYA 6; AITN 1; BEST 90:4; CA 1-4R; CANR 1, 25, 49; CDALB 1968-1988; DLB 2, 8, 152; DLBD 3; DLBY 80; MTCW

Von Rachen, Kurt
See Hubbard, L(afayette) Ron(ald)

von Rezzori (d'Arezzo), Gregor
See Rezzori (d'Arezzo), Gregor von

von Sternberg, Josef
See Sternberg, Josef von

Vorster, Gordon 1924- .... **CLC 34**
See also CA 133

Vosce, Trudie
See Ozick, Cynthia

Voznesensky, Andrei (Andreievich) 1933-**CLC 1, 15, 57; DAM POET**
See also CA 89-92; CANR 37; MTCW

Waddington, Miriam 1917- .... **CLC 28**
See also CA 21-24R; CANR 12, 30; DLB 68

Wagman, Fredrica 1937- .... **CLC 7**
See also CA 97-100; INT 97-100

Wagner, Linda W.
See Wagner-Martin, Linda (C.)

Wagner, Linda Welshimer
See Wagner-Martin, Linda (C.)

Wagner, Richard 1813-1883 .... **NCLC 9**
See also DLB 129

Wagner-Martin, Linda (C.) 1936- .... **CLC 50**
See also CA 159

Wagoner, David (Russell) 1926- ... **CLC 3, 5, 15**
See also CA 1-4R; CAAS 3; CANR 2; DLB 5; SATA 14

Wah, Fred(erick James) 1939- .... **CLC 44**
See also CA 107; 141; DLB 60

Wahloo, Per 1926-1975 .... **CLC 7**
See also CA 61-64

Wahloo, Peter
See Wahloo, Per

Wain, John (Barrington) 1925-1994 . **CLC 2, 11, 15, 46**
See also CA 5-8R; 145; CAAS 4; CANR 23, 54; CDBLB 1960 to Present; DLB 15, 27, 139, 155; MTCW

Wajda, Andrzej 1926- .... **CLC 16**
See also CA 102

Wakefield, Dan 1932- .... **CLC 7**
See also CA 21-24R; CAAS 7

Author Index

Wakoski, Diane 1937-**CLC 2, 4, 7, 9, 11, 40; DAM POET; PC 15**
See also CA 13-16R; CAAS 1; CANR 9, 60; DLB 5; INT CANR-9

Wakoski-Sherbell, Diane
See Wakoski, Diane

Walcott, Derek (Alton) 1930-**CLC 2, 4, 9, 14, 25, 42, 67, 76; BLC; DAB; DAC; DAM MST, MULT, POET; DC 7**
See also BW 2; CA 89-92; CANR 26, 47; DLB 117; DLBY 81; MTCW

Waldman, Anne 1945- .... **CLC 7**
See also CA 37-40R; CAAS 17; CANR 34; DLB 16

Waldo, E. Hunter
See Sturgeon, Theodore (Hamilton)

Waldo, Edward Hamilton
See Sturgeon, Theodore (Hamilton)

Walker, Alice (Malsenior) 1944-**CLC 5, 6, 9, 19, 27, 46, 58, 103; BLC; DA; DAB; DAC; DAM MST, MULT, NOV, POET, POP; SSC 5; WLCS**
See also AAYA 3; BEST 89:4; BW 2; CA 37-40R; CANR 9, 27, 49, 66; CDALB 1968-1988; DLB 6, 33, 143; INT CANR-27; MTCW; SATA 31

Walker, David Harry 1911-1992 .... **CLC 14**
See also CA 1-4R; 137; CANR 1; SATA 8; SATA-Obit 71

Walker, Edward Joseph 1934-
See Walker, Ted
See also CA 21-24R; CANR 12, 28, 53

Walker, George F. 1947-**CLC 44, 61; DAB; DAC; DAM MST**
See also CA 103; CANR 21, 43, 59; DLB 60

Walker, Joseph A. 1935- **CLC 19; DAM DRAM, MST**
See also BW 1; CA 89-92; CANR 26; DLB 38

Walker, Margaret (Abigail) 1915- ..... **CLC 1, 6; BLC; DAM MULT; PC 20**
See also BW 2; CA 73-76; CANR 26, 54; DLB 76, 152; MTCW

Walker, Ted .... **CLC 13**
See also Walker, Edward Joseph
See also DLB 40

Wallace, David Foster 1962- .... **CLC 50**
See also CA 132; CANR 59

Wallace, Dexter
See Masters, Edgar Lee

Wallace, (Richard Horatio) Edgar 1875-1932 **TCLC 57**
See also CA 115; DLB 70

Wallace, Irving 1916-1990**CLC 7, 13; DAM NOV, POP**
See also AITN 1; CA 1-4R; 132; CAAS 1; CANR 1, 27; INT CANR-27; MTCW

Wallant, Edward Lewis 1926-1962 ..... **CLC 5, 10**
See also CA 1-4R; CANR 22; DLB 2, 28, 143; MTCW

Walley, Byron
See Card, Orson Scott

Walpole, Horace 1717-1797 .... **LC 2**
See also DLB 39, 104

Walpole, Hugh (Seymour) 1884-1941 .... **TCLC 5**
See also CA 104; 165; DLB 34

Walser, Martin 1927- .... **CLC 27**
See also CA 57-60; CANR 8, 46; DLB 75, 124

Walser, Robert 1878-1956 .... **TCLC 18; SSC 20**
See also CA 118; 165; DLB 66

Walsh, Jill Paton .... **CLC 35**
See also Paton Walsh, Gillian
See also AAYA 11; CLR 2; DLB 161; SAAS 3

Walter, Villiam Christian
See Andersen, Hans Christian

Wambaugh, Joseph (Aloysius, Jr.) 1937-**CLC 3, 18; DAM NOV, POP**
See also AITN 1; BEST 89:3; CA 33-36R; CANR 42, 65; DLB 6; DLBY 83; MTCW

Wang Wei 699(?)-761(?) .... **PC 18**

Ward, Arthur Henry Sarsfield 1883-1959
See Rohmer, Sax
See also CA 108

Ward, Douglas Turner 1930- .... **CLC 19**
See also BW 1; CA 81-84; CANR 27; DLB 7, 38

Ward, Mary Augusta
See Ward, Mrs. Humphry

Ward, Mrs. Humphry 1851-1920 .... **TCLC 55**
See also DLB 18

Ward, Peter
See Faust, Frederick (Schiller)

Warhol, Andy 1928(?)-1987 .... **CLC 20**
See also AAYA 12; BEST 89:4; CA 89-92; 121; CANR 34

Warner, Francis (Robert le Plastrier) 1937-**CLC 14**
See also CA 53-56; CANR 11

Warner, Marina 1946- .... **CLC 59**
See also CA 65-68; CANR 21, 55; DLB 194

Warner, Rex (Ernest) 1905-1986 .... **CLC 45**
See also CA 89-92; 119; DLB 15

Warner, Susan (Bogert) 1819-1885 ... **NCLC 31**
See also DLB 3, 42

Warner, Sylvia (Constance) Ashton
See Ashton-Warner, Sylvia (Constance)

Warner, Sylvia Townsend 1893-1978 **CLC 7, 19; SSC 23**
See also CA 61-64; 77-80; CANR 16, 60; DLB 34, 139; MTCW

Warren, Mercy Otis 1728-1814 .... **NCLC 13**
See also DLB 31

Warren, Robert Penn 1905-1989 **CLC 1, 4, 6, 8, 10, 13, 18, 39, 53, 59; DA; DAB; DAC; DAM MST, NOV, POET; SSC 4; WLC**
See also AITN 1; CA 13-16R; 129; CANR 10, 47; CDALB 1968-1988; DLB 2, 48, 152; DLBY 80, 89; INT CANR-10; MTCW; SATA 46; SATA-Obit 63

Warshofsky, Isaac
See Singer, Isaac Bashevis

Warton, Thomas 1728-1790 **LC 15; DAM POET**
See also DLB 104, 109

Waruk, Kona
See Harris, (Theodore) Wilson

Warung, Price 1855-1911 .... **TCLC 45**

Warwick, Jarvis
See Garner, Hugh

Washington, Alex
See Harris, Mark

Washington, Booker T(aliaferro) 1856-1915 **TCLC 10; BLC; DAM MULT**
See also BW 1; CA 114; 125; SATA 28

Washington, George 1732-1799 .... **LC 25**
See also DLB 31

Wassermann, (Karl) Jakob 1873-1934 .. **TCLC 6**
See also CA 104; DLB 66

Wasserstein, Wendy 1950-**CLC 32, 59, 90; DAM DRAM; DC 4**
See also CA 121; 129; CABS 3; CANR 53; INT 129; SATA 94

Waterhouse, Keith (Spencer) 1929- ..... **CLC 47**
See also CA 5-8R; CANR 38, 67; DLB 13, 15; MTCW

Waters, Frank (Joseph) 1902-1995 .... **CLC 88**
See also CA 5-8R; 149; CAAS 13; CANR 3, 18, 63; DLBY 86

Waters, Roger 1944- .... **CLC 35**

Watkins, Frances Ellen
See Harper, Frances Ellen Watkins

Watkins, Gerrold
See Malzberg, Barry N(athaniel)

Watkins, Gloria 1955(?)-
See hooks, bell
See also BW 2; CA 143

Watkins, Paul 1964- .... **CLC 55**
See also CA 132; CANR 62

Watkins, Vernon Phillips 1906-1967 .... **CLC 43**
See also CA 9-10; 25-28R; CAP 1; DLB 20

Watson, Irving S.
See Mencken, H(enry) L(ouis)

Watson, John H.
See Farmer, Philip Jose

Watson, Richard F.
See Silverberg, Robert

Waugh, Auberon (Alexander) 1939- .... **CLC 7**
See also CA 45-48; CANR 6, 22; DLB 14, 194

Waugh, Evelyn (Arthur St. John) 1903-1966**CLC 1, 3, 8, 13, 19, 27, 44, 107; DA; DAB; DAC; DAM MST, NOV, POP; WLC**
See also CA 85-88; 25-28R; CANR 22; CDBLB 1914-1945; DLB 15, 162, 195; MTCW

Waugh, Harriet 1944- .... **CLC 6**
See also CA 85-88; CANR 22

Wheatley (Peters), Phillis 1754(?)-1784 ... **LC 3; BLC; DA; DAC; DAM MST, MULT, POET; PC 3; WLC**
See also CDALB 1640-1865; DLB 31, 50

Wheelock, John Hall 1886-1978 .... **CLC 14**
See also CA 13-16R; 77-80; CANR 14; DLB 45

White, E(lwyn) B(rooks) 1899-1985 **CLC 10, 34, 39; DAM POP**
See also AITN 2; CA 13-16R; 116; CANR 16, 37; CLR 1, 21; DLB 11, 22; MAICYA; MTCW; SATA 2, 29; SATA-Obit 44

White, Edmund (Valentine III) 1940- ... **CLC 27; DAM POP**
See also AAYA 7; CA 45-48; CANR 3, 19, 36, 62; MTCW

White, Patrick (Victor Martindale) 1912-1990 **CLC 3, 4, 5, 7, 9, 18, 65, 69**
See also CA 81-84; 132; CANR 43; MTCW

White, Phyllis Dorothy James 1920-
See James, P. D.
See also CA 21-24R; CANR 17, 43, 65; DAM POP; MTCW

White, T(erence) H(anbury) 1906-1964 **CLC 30**
See also AAYA 22; CA 73-76; CANR 37; DLB 160; JRDA; MAICYA; SATA 12

White, Terence de Vere 1912-1994 .... **CLC 49**
See also CA 49-52; 145; CANR 3

White, Walter F(rancis) 1893-1955 .... **TCLC 15**
See also White, Walter
See also BW 1; CA 115; 124; DLB 51

White, William Hale 1831-1913
See Rutherford, Mark
See also CA 121

Whitehead, E(dward) A(nthony) 1933- .... **CLC 5**
See also CA 65-68; CANR 58

Whitemore, Hugh (John) 1936- .... **CLC 37**
See also CA 132; INT 132

Whitman, Sarah Helen (Power) 1803-1878**NCLC 19**
See also DLB 1

Whitman, Walt(er) 1819-1892 **NCLC 4, 31; DA; DAB; DAC; DAM MST, POET; PC 3; WLC**
See also CDALB 1640-1865; DLB 3, 64; SATA 20

Whitney, Phyllis A(yame) 1903- **CLC 42; DAM POP**
See also AITN 2; BEST 90:3; CA 1-4R; CANR 3, 25, 38, 60; JRDA; MAICYA; SATA 1, 30

Whittemore, (Edward) Reed (Jr.) 1919- .. **CLC 4**
See also CA 9-12R; CAAS 8; CANR 4; DLB 5

Whittier, John Greenleaf 1807-1892**NCLC 8, 59**
See also DLB 1

Whittlebot, Hernia
See Coward, Noel (Peirce)

Wicker, Thomas Grey 1926-
See Wicker, Tom
See also CA 65-68; CANR 21, 46

Wicker, Tom .... **CLC 7**
See also Wicker, Thomas Grey

Wideman, John Edgar 1941- **CLC 5, 34, 36, 67; BLC; DAM MULT**
See also BW 2; CA 85-88; CANR 14, 42, 67; DLB 33, 143

Wiebe, Rudy (Henry) 1934-**CLC 6, 11, 14; DAC; DAM MST**
See also CA 37-40R; CANR 42, 67; DLB 60

Wieland, Christoph Martin 1733-1813 **NCLC 17**
See also DLB 97

Wiene, Robert 1881-1938 .... **TCLC 56**

Wieners, John 1934- .... **CLC 7**
See also CA 13-16R; DLB 16

Wiesel, Elie(zer) 1928- ... **CLC 3, 5, 11, 37; DA; DAB; DAC; DAM MST, NOV; WLCS 2**
See also AAYA 7; AITN 1; CA 5-8R; CAAS 4; CANR 8, 40, 65; DLB 83; DLBY 87; INT CANR-8; MTCW; SATA 56

Wiggins, Marianne 1947- .... **CLC 57**
See also BEST 89:3; CA 130; CANR 60

Wight, James Alfred 1916-
See Herriot, James
See also CA 77-80; SATA 55; SATA-Brief 44

Wilbur, Richard (Purdy) 1921- **CLC 3, 6, 9, 14, 53; DA; DAB; DAC; DAM MST, POET**
See also CA 1-4R; CABS 2; CANR 2, 29; DLB 5, 169; INT CANR-29; MTCW; SATA 9

Wild, Peter 1940- .... **CLC 14**
See also CA 37-40R; DLB 5

Wilde, Oscar (Fingal O'Flahertie Wills) 1854(?)-1900**TCLC 1, 8, 23, 41; DA; DAB; DAC; DAM DRAM, MST, NOV; SSC 11; WLC**
See also CA 104; 119; CDBLB 1890-1914; DLB 10, 19, 34, 57, 141, 156, 190; SATA 24

Wilder, Billy .... **CLC 20**
See also Wilder, Samuel
See also DLB 26

Wilder, Samuel 1906-
See Wilder, Billy
See also CA 89-92

Wilder, Thornton (Niven) 1897-1975**CLC 1, 5, 6, 10, 15, 35, 82; DA; DAB; DAC; DAM DRAM, MST, NOV; DC 1; WLC**
See also AITN 2; CA 13-16R; 61-64; CANR 40; DLB 4, 7, 9; DLBY 97; MTCW

Wilding, Michael 1942- .... **CLC 73**
See also CA 104; CANR 24, 49

Wiley, Richard 1944- .... **CLC 44**
See also CA 121; 129

Wilhelm, Kate .... **CLC 7**
See also Wilhelm, Katie Gertrude
See also AAYA 20; CAAS 5; DLB 8; INT CANR-17

Wilhelm, Katie Gertrude 1928-
See Wilhelm, Kate
See also CA 37-40R; CANR 17, 36, 60; MTCW

Wilkins, Mary
See Freeman, Mary Eleanor Wilkins

Willard, Nancy 1936- .... **CLC 7, 37**
See also CA 89-92; CANR 10, 39, 68; CLR 5; DLB 5, 52; MAICYA; MTCW; SATA 37, 71; SATA-Brief 30

Williams, C(harles) K(enneth) 1936-**CLC 33, 56; DAM POET**
See also CA 37-40R; CAAS 26; CANR 57; DLB 5

Williams, Charles
See Collier, James L(incoln)

Williams, Charles (Walter Stansby) 1886-1945 **TCLC 1, 11**
See also CA 104; 163; DLB 100, 153

Williams, (George) Emlyn 1905-1987 .. **CLC 15; DAM DRAM**
See also CA 104; 123; CANR 36; DLB 10, 77; MTCW

Williams, Hugo 1942- .... **CLC 42**
See also CA 17-20R; CANR 45; DLB 40

Williams, J. Walker
See Wodehouse, P(elham) G(renville)

Williams, John A(lfred) 1925- **CLC 5, 13; BLC; DAM MULT**
See also BW 2; CA 53-56; CAAS 3; CANR 6, 26, 51; DLB 2, 33; INT CANR-6

Williams, Jonathan (Chamberlain) 1929-**CLC 13**
See also CA 9-12R; CAAS 12; CANR 8; DLB 5

Williams, Joy 1944- .... **CLC 31**
See also CA 41-44R; CANR 22, 48

Williams, Norman 1952- .... **CLC 39**
See also CA 118

Williams, Sherley Anne 1944- .. **CLC 89; BLC; DAM MULT, POET**
See also BW 2; CA 73-76; CANR 25; DLB 41; INT CANR-25; SATA 78

Williams, Shirley
See Williams, Sherley Anne

Williams, Tennessee 1911-1983**CLC 1, 2, 5, 7, 8, 11, 15, 19, 30, 39, 45, 71; DA; DAB; DAC; DAM DRAM, MST; DC 4; WLC**
See also AITN 1, 2; CA 5-8R; 108; CABS 3; CANR 31; CDALB 1941-1968; DLB 7; DLBD 4; DLBY 83; MTCW

Williams, Thomas (Alonzo) 1926-1990 . **CLC 14**
See also CA 1-4R; 132; CANR 2

Williams, William C.
See Williams, William Carlos

Williams, William Carlos 1883-1963**CLC 1, 2, 5, 9, 13, 22, 42, 67; DA; DAB; DAC; DAM MST, POET; PC 7**
See also CA 89-92; CANR 34; CDALB 1917-1929; DLB 4, 16, 54, 86; MTCW

Williamson, David (Keith) 1942- .... **CLC 56**
See also CA 103; CANR 41

Williamson, Ellen Douglas 1905-1984
See Douglas, Ellen

See also CA 17-20R; 114; CANR 39

Williamson, Jack .... **CLC 29**
See also Williamson, John Stewart
See also CAAS 8; DLB 8

Williamson, John Stewart 1908-
See Williamson, Jack
See also CA 17-20R; CANR 23

Willie, Frederick
See Lovecraft, H(oward) P(hillips)

Willingham, Calder (Baynard, Jr.) 1922-1995 **CLC 5, 51**
See also CA 5-8R; 147; CANR 3; DLB 2, 44; MTCW

Willis, Charles
See Clarke, Arthur C(harles)

Willy
See Colette, (Sidonie-Gabrielle)

Willy, Colette
See Colette, (Sidonie-Gabrielle)

Wilson, A(ndrew) N(orman) 1950- .... **CLC 33**
See also CA 112; 122; DLB 14, 155, 194

Wilson, Angus (Frank Johnstone) 1913-1991 **CLC 2, 3, 5, 25, 34; SSC 21**
See also CA 5-8R; 134; CANR 21; DLB 15, 139, 155; MTCW

Wilson, August 1945-**CLC 39, 50, 63; BLC; DA; DAB; DAC; DAM DRAM, MST, MULT; DC 2; WLCS**
See also AAYA 16; BW 2; CA 115; 122; CANR 42, 54; MTCW

Wilson, Brian 1942- .... **CLC 12**

Wilson, Colin 1931- .... **CLC 3, 14**
See also CA 1-4R; CAAS 5; CANR 1, 22, 33; DLB 14, 194; MTCW

Wilson, Dirk
See Pohl, Frederik

Wilson, Edmund 1895-1972 ... **CLC 1, 2, 3, 8, 24**
See also CA 1-4R; 37-40R; CANR 1, 46; DLB 63; MTCW

Wilson, Ethel Davis (Bryant) 1888(?)-1980 **CLC 13; DAC; DAM POET**
See also CA 102; DLB 68; MTCW

Wilson, John 1785-1854 .... **NCLC 5**

Wilson, John (Anthony) Burgess 1917-1993
See Burgess, Anthony
See also CA 1-4R; 143; CANR 2, 46; DAC; DAM NOV; MTCW

Wilson, Lanford 1937- ..... **CLC 7, 14, 36; DAM DRAM**
See also CA 17-20R; CABS 3; CANR 45; DLB 7

Wilson, Robert M. 1944- .... **CLC 7, 9**
See also CA 49-52; CANR 2, 41; MTCW

Wilson, Robert McLiam 1964- .... **CLC 59**
See also CA 132

Wilson, Sloan 1920- .... **CLC 32**
See also CA 1-4R; CANR 1, 44

Wilson, Snoo 1948- .... **CLC 33**
See also CA 69-72

Wilson, William S(mith) 1932- .... **CLC 49**
See also CA 81-84

Wilson, Woodrow 1856-1924 .... **TCLC 73**
See also DLB 47

Winchilsea, Anne (Kingsmill) Finch Counte 1661-1720
See Finch, Anne

Windham, Basil
See Wodehouse, P(elham) G(renville)

Wingrove, David (John) 1954- .... **CLC 68**
See also CA 133

Wintergreen, Jane
See Duncan, Sara Jeannette

Winters, Janet Lewis .... **CLC 41**
See also Lewis, Janet
See also DLBY 87

Winters, (Arthur) Yvor 1900-1968 **CLC 4, 8, 32**
See also CA 11-12; 25-28R; CAP 1; DLB 48; MTCW

Winterson, Jeanette 1959- **CLC 64; DAM POP**
See also CA 136; CANR 58

Winthrop, John 1588-1649 .... **LC 31**
See also DLB 24, 30

Wiseman, Frederick 1930- .... **CLC 20**
See also CA 159

Wister, Owen 1860-1938 .... **TCLC 21**
See also CA 108; 162; DLB 9, 78, 186; SATA 62

Witkacy
See Witkiewicz, Stanislaw Ignacy

Witkiewicz, Stanislaw Ignacy 1885-1939**TCLC 8**
See also CA 105; 162

Wittgenstein, Ludwig (Josef Johann) 1889-1951 **TCLC 59**
See also CA 113; 164

Wittig, Monique 1935(?)- .... **CLC 22**
See also CA 116; 135; DLB 83

Wittlin, Jozef 1896-1976 .... **CLC 25**
See also CA 49-52; 65-68; CANR 3

Wodehouse, P(elham) G(renville) 1881-1975**CLC 1, 2, 5, 10, 22; DAB; DAC; DAM NOV; SSC 2**
See also AITN 2; CA 45-48; 57-60; CANR 3, 33; CDBLB 1914-1945; DLB 34, 162; MTCW; SATA 22

Woiwode, L.
See Woiwode, Larry (Alfred)

Woiwode, Larry (Alfred) 1941- .... **CLC 6, 10**
See also CA 73-76; CANR 16; DLB 6; INT CANR-16

Wojciechowska, Maia (Teresa) 1927- **CLC 26**
See also AAYA 8; CA 9-12R; CANR 4, 41; CLR 1; JRDA; MAICYA; SAAS 1; SATA 1, 28, 83

Wolf, Christa 1929- **CLC 14, 29, 58**
See also CA 85-88; CANR 45; DLB 75; MTCW

Wolfe, Gene (Rodman) 1931-**CLC 25; DAM POP**
See also CA 57-60; CAAS 9; CANR 6, 32, 60; DLB 8

Wolfe, George C. 1954- .... **CLC 49**
See also CA 149

Wolfe, Thomas (Clayton) 1900-1938**TCLC 4, 13, 29, 61; DA; DAB; DAC; DAM MST, NOV; WLC**
See also CA 104; 132; CDALB 1929-1941; DLB 9, 102; DLBD 2, 16; DLBY 85, 97; MTCW

Wolfe, Thomas Kennerly, Jr. 1931-
See Wolfe, Tom
See also CA 13-16R; CANR 9, 33; DAM POP; DLB 185; INT CANR-9; MTCW

Wolfe, Tom .... **CLC 1, 2, 9, 15, 35, 51**
See also Wolfe, Thomas Kennerly, Jr.
See also AAYA 8; AITN 2; BEST 89:1; DLB 152

Wolff, Geoffrey (Ansell) 1937- .... **CLC 41**
See also CA 29-32R; CANR 29, 43

Wolff, Sonia
See Levitin, Sonia (Wolff)

Wolff, Tobias (Jonathan Ansell) 1945-**CLC 39, 64**
See also AAYA 16; BEST 90:2; CA 114; 117; CAAS 22; CANR 54; DLB 130; INT 117

Wolfram von Eschenbach c. 1170-c. 1220**CMLC 5**
See also DLB 138

Wolitzer, Hilma 1930- .... **CLC 17**
See also CA 65-68; CANR 18, 40; INT CANR-18; SATA 31

Wollstonecraft, Mary 1759-1797 .... **LC 5**
See also CDBLB 1789-1832; DLB 39, 104, 158

Wonder, Stevie .... **CLC 12**
See also Morris, Steveland Judkins

Wong, Jade Snow 1922- .... **CLC 17**
See also CA 109

Woodberry, George Edward 1855-1930 **TCLC 73**
See also CA 165; DLB 71, 103

Woodcott, Keith
See Brunner, John (Kilian Houston)

Woodruff, Robert W.
See Mencken, H(enry) L(ouis)

Woolf, (Adeline) Virginia 1882-1941 **TCLC 1, 5, 20, 43, 56; DA; DAB; DAC; DAM MST, NOV; SSC 7; WLC**
See also CA 104; 130; CANR 64; CDBLB 1914-1945; DLB 36, 100, 162; DLBD 10; MTCW

Woolf, Virginia Adeline
See Woolf, (Adeline) Virginia

Woollcott, Alexander (Humphreys) 1887-1943 **TCLC 5**
See also CA 105; 161; DLB 29

Woolrich, Cornell 1903-1968 .... **CLC 77**
See also Hopley-Woolrich, Cornell George

Wordsworth, Dorothy 1771-1855 .... **NCLC 25**
See also DLB 107

Author Index

Wordsworth, William 1770-1850 **NCLC 12, 38; DA; DAB; DAC; DAM MST, POET; PC 4; WLC**
See also CDBLB 1789-1832; DLB 93, 107

Wouk, Herman 1915- **CLC 1, 9, 38; DAM NOV, POP**
See also CA 5-8R; CANR 6, 33, 67; DLBY 82; INT CANR-6; MTCW

Wright, Charles (Penzel, Jr.) 1935- **CLC 6, 13, 28**
See also CA 29-32R; CAAS 7; CANR 23, 36, 62; DLB 165; DLBY 82; MTCW

Wright, Charles Stevenson 1932- **CLC 49; BLC 3; DAM MULT, POET**
See also BW 1; CA 9-12R; CANR 26; DLB 33

Wright, Jack R.
See Harris, Mark

Wright, James (Arlington) 1927-1980 **CLC 3, 5, 10, 28; DAM POET**
See also AITN 2; CA 49-52; 97-100; CANR 4, 34, 64; DLB 5, 169; MTCW

Wright, Judith (Arandell) 1915- **CLC 11, 53; PC 14**
See also CA 13-16R; CANR 31; MTCW; SATA 14

Wright, L(aurali) R. 1939- .... **CLC 44**
See also CA 138

Wright, Richard (Nathaniel) 1908-1960 **CLC 1, 3, 4, 9, 14, 21, 48, 74; BLC; DA; DAB; DAC; DAM MST, MULT, NOV; SSC 2; WLC**
See also AAYA 5; BW 1; CA 108; CANR 64; CDALB 1929-1941; DLB 76, 102; DLBD 2; MTCW

Wright, Richard B(ruce) 1937- .... **CLC 6**
See also CA 85-88; DLB 53

Wright, Rick 1945- .... **CLC 35**

Wright, Rowland
See Wells, Carolyn

Wright, Stephen 1946- .... **CLC 33**

Wright, Willard Huntington 1888-1939
See Van Dine, S. S.
See also CA 115; DLBD 16

Wright, William 1930- .... **CLC 44**
See also CA 53-56; CANR 7, 23

Wroth, Lady Mary 1587-1653(?) .... **LC 30**
See also DLB 121

Wu Ch'eng-en 1500(?)-1582(?) .... **LC 7**

Wu Ching-tzu 1701-1754 .... **LC 2**

Wurlitzer, Rudolph 1938(?)- .... **CLC 2, 4, 15**
See also CA 85-88; DLB 173

Wycherley, William 1641-1715 . **LC 8, 21; DAM DRAM**
See also CDBLB 1660-1789; DLB 80

Wylie, Elinor (Morton Hoyt) 1885-1928 **TCLC 8**
See also CA 105; 162; DLB 9, 45

Wylie, Philip (Gordon) 1902-1971 .... **CLC 43**
See also CA 21-22; 33-36R; CAP 2; DLB 9

Wyndham, John .... **CLC 19**
See also Harris, John (Wyndham Parkes Lucas) Beynon

Wyss, Johann David Von 1743-1818 .. **NCLC 10**
See also JRDA; MAICYA; SATA 29; SATA-Brief 27

Xenophon c. 430B.C.-c. 354B.C. .... **CMLC 17**
See also DLB 176

Yakumo Koizumi
See Hearn, (Patricio) Lafcadio (Tessima Carlos)

Yanez, Jose Donoso
See Donoso (Yanez), Jose

Yanovsky, Basile S.
See Yanovsky, V(assily) S(emenovich)

Yanovsky, V(assily) S(emenovich) 1906-1989 **CLC 2, 18**
See also CA 97-100; 129

Yates, Richard 1926-1992 .... **CLC 7, 8, 23**
See also CA 5-8R; 139; CANR 10, 43; DLB 2; DLBY 81, 92; INT CANR-10

Yeats, W. B.
See Yeats, William Butler

Yeats, William Butler 1865-1939 **TCLC 1, 11, 18, 31; DA; DAB; DAC; DAM DRAM, MST, POET; PC 20; WLC**
See also CA 104; 127; CANR 45; CDBLB 1890-1914; DLB 10, 19, 98, 156; MTCW

Yehoshua, A(braham) B. 1936- .... **CLC 13, 31**
See also CA 33-36R; CANR 43

Yep, Laurence Michael 1948- .... **CLC 35**
See also AAYA 5; CA 49-52; CANR 1, 46; CLR 3, 17; DLB 52; JRDA; MAICYA; SATA 7, 69

Yerby, Frank G(arvin) 1916-1991 . **CLC 1, 7, 22; BLC; DAM MULT**
See also BW 1; CA 9-12R; 136; CANR 16, 52; DLB 76; INT CANR-16; MTCW

Yesenin, Sergei Alexandrovich
See Esenin, Sergei (Alexandrovich)

Yevtushenko, Yevgeny (Alexandrovich) 1933- **CLC 1, 3, 13, 26, 51; DAM POET**
See also CA 81-84; CANR 33, 54; MTCW

Yezierska, Anzia 1885(?)-1970 .... **CLC 46**
See also CA 126; 89-92; DLB 28; MTCW

Yglesias, Helen 1915- .... **CLC 7, 22**
See also CA 37-40R; CAAS 20; CANR 15, 65; INT CANR-15; MTCW

Yokomitsu Riichi 1898-1947 .... **TCLC 47**

Yonge, Charlotte (Mary) 1823-1901 .... **TCLC 48**
See also CA 109; 163; DLB 18, 163; SATA 17

York, Jeremy
See Creasey, John

York, Simon
See Heinlein, Robert A(nson)

Yorke, Henry Vincent 1905-1974 .... **CLC 13**
See also Green, Henry
See also CA 85-88; 49-52

Yosano Akiko 1878-1942 .... **TCLC 59; PC 11**
See also CA 161

Yoshimoto, Banana .... **CLC 84**
See also Yoshimoto, Mahoko

Yoshimoto, Mahoko 1964-
See Yoshimoto, Banana
See also CA 144

Young, Al(bert James) 1939- **CLC 19; BLC; DAM MULT**
See also BW 2; CA 29-32R; CANR 26, 65; DLB 33

Young, Andrew (John) 1885-1971 .... **CLC 5**
See also CA 5-8R; CANR 7, 29

Young, Collier
See Bloch, Robert (Albert)

Young, Edward 1683-1765 .... **LC 3, 40**
See also DLB 95

Young, Marguerite (Vivian) 1909-1995 . **CLC 82**
See also CA 13-16; 150; CAP 1

Young, Neil 1945- .... **CLC 17**
See also CA 110

Young Bear, Ray A. 1950- **CLC 94; DAM MULT**
See also CA 146; DLB 175; NNAL

Yourcenar, Marguerite 1903-1987 **CLC 19, 38, 50, 87; DAM NOV**
See also CA 69-72; CANR 23, 60; DLB 72; DLBY 88; MTCW

Yurick, Sol 1925- .... **CLC 6**
See also CA 13-16R; CANR 25

Zabolotskii, Nikolai Alekseevich 1903-1958 **TCLC 52**
See also CA 116; 164

Zamiatin, Yevgenii
See Zamyatin, Evgeny Ivanovich

Zamora, Bernice (B. Ortiz) 1938- **CLC 89; DAM MULT; HLC**
See also CA 151; DLB 82; HW

Zamyatin, Evgeny Ivanovich 1884-1937 **TCLC 8, 37**
See also CA 105

Zangwill, Israel 1864-1926 .... **TCLC 16**
See also CA 109; DLB 10, 135

Zappa, Francis Vincent, Jr. 1940-1993
See Zappa, Frank
See also CA 108; 143; CANR 57

Zappa, Frank .... **CLC 17**
See also Zappa, Francis Vincent, Jr.

Zaturenska, Marya 1902-1982 .... **CLC 6, 11**
See also CA 13-16R; 105; CANR 22

Zeami 1363-1443 .... **DC 7**

Zelazny, Roger (Joseph) 1937-1995 ...... **CLC 21**
See also AAYA 7; CA 21-24R; 148; CANR 26, 60; DLB 8; MTCW; SATA 57; SATA-Brief 39

Zhdanov, Andrei A(lexandrovich) 1896-1948 **TCLC 18**
See also CA 117

Zhukovsky, Vasily 1783-1852 .... **NCLC 35**

Ziegenhagen, Eric .... **CLC 55**

Zimmer, Jill Schary
See Robinson, Jill

Zimmerman, Robert
See Dylan, Bob

Zindel, Paul 1936- **CLC 6, 26; DA; DAB; DAC; DAM DRAM, MST, NOV; DC 5**
See also AAYA 2; CA 73-76; CANR 31, 65; CLR 3, 45; DLB 7, 52; JRDA; MAICYA; MTCW; SATA 16, 58

Zinov'Ev, A. A.
See Zinoviev, Alexander (Aleksandrovich)

Zinoviev, Alexander (Aleksandrovich) 1922-**CLC 19**
See also CA 116; 133; CAAS 10

Zoilus
See Lovecraft, H(oward) P(hillips)

Zola, Emile (Edouard Charles Antoine) 1840-1902 **TCLC 1, 6, 21, 41; DA; DAB; DAC; DAM MST, NOV; WLC**
See also CA 104; 138; DLB 123

Zoline, Pamela 1941- .... **CLC 62**
See also CA 161

Zorrilla y Moral, Jose 1817-1893 .... **NCLC 6**

Zoshchenko, Mikhail (Mikhailovich) 1895-1958 **TCLC 15; SSC 15**
See also CA 115; 160

Zuckmayer, Carl 1896-1977 .... **CLC 18**
See also CA 69-72; DLB 56, 124

Zuk, Georges
See Skelton, Robin

Zukofsky, Louis 1904-1978**CLC 1, 2, 4, 7, 11, 18; DAM POET; PC 11**
See also CA 9-12R; 77-80; CANR 39; DLB 5, 165; MTCW

Zweig, Paul 1935-1984 .... **CLC 34, 42**
See also CA 85-88; 113

Zweig, Stefan 1881-1942 .... **TCLC 17**
See also CA 112; DLB 81, 118

Zwingli, Huldreich 1484-1531 .... **LC 37**
See also DLB 179

Literary Criticism Series Cumulative Topic Index

This index lists all topic entries in Gale's *Classical and Medieval Literature Criticism, Contemporary Literary Criticism, Literature Criticism from 1400 to 1800, Nineteenth-Century Literature Criticism,* and *Twentieth-Century Literary Criticism.*

CMLC Cumulative Nationality Index

CUMULATIVE INDEX TO TITLES

Title Index

Title Index

CMLC Cumulative Critic Index

Arnold, Edwin
Hesiod **5**:71
Iliad **1**:308
Odyssey **16**:208
Sappho **3**:384

Arnold, Mary
Poem of the Cid **4**:226

Arnold, Matthew
Aeneid **9**:316
Aristophanes **4**:54
Iliad **1**:300
Mabinogion **9**:146
The Song of Roland **1**:162
Sophocles **2**:311

Arnott, Geoffrey
Menander **9**:261

Arnott, W. G.
Menander **9**:253

Arnould, E. J.
Rolle, Richard **21**:350

Arnstein, Adolf
Meister Eckhart **9**:4

Arrowsmith, William
Aristophanes **4**:131

'Arudi, Nizami-i-
Avicenna **16**:147

Ascham, Roger
Cicero, Marcus Tullius **3**:186

Ashe, Geoffrey
Arthurian Legend **10**:2

Asquith, Herbert Henry
Demosthenes **13**:135

Astin, Alan E.
Cato, Marcus Porcius **21**:38

Aston, W. G.
Murasaki, Lady **1**:416
Sei Shonagon **6**:291

Athanasius
The Book of Psalms **4**:344

Atkins, J. W. H.
Aristophanes **4**:104
Longinus **27**:136

Atkinson, James C.
Mystery of Adam **4**:207

Auden, W. H.
Iliad **1**:347
Njals saga **13**:330

Auerbach, Erich
Augustine, St. **6**:79
Inferno **3**:72, 95
Mystery of Adam **4**:193
Odyssey **16**:221
Poem of the Cid **4**:251

Augustine, St.
Apuleius **1**:4
Augustine, St. **6**:4
Cicero, Marcus Tullius **3**:177
Epicurus **21**:79
Plato **8**:208
Seneca, Lucius Annaeus **6**:330

Aurobindo, Sri
Bhagavad Gita **12**:32

Austerlitz, Robert
Kalevala **6**:255

Austin, Scott
Parmenides **22**:242

Averroes
Plato **8**:212

Avery, Peter
Khayyam **11**:297

Axtell, Harold
Pliny the Elder **23**:318

Ayscough, Florence
Li Po **2**:132

Bachofen, J. J.
Aeschylus **11**:92
Sappho **3**:382

Bacon, Francis
Plato **8**:219

Bagley, F. R. C.
Khayyam **11**:283

Bailey, Cyril
Epicurus **21**:130

Baker, Donald C.
Beowulf **1**:154

Baldwin, Charles Sears
Sir Gawain and the Green Knight **2**:186

Baldwin, Spurgeon W., Jr.
Aesop **24**:29

Baljon, J. M. S.
The *Koran* **23**:274

Banks, Mary Macleod
Morte Arthure **10**:377

Barber, Richard
Sir Gawain and the Green Knight **2**:215

Barbera, Andre
Euclid **25**:205

Barbi, Michele
Inferno **3**:87

Barfield, Owen
Bhagavad Gita **12**:71
The Book of Psalms **4**:392

Bargen, Doris G.
Murasaki, Lady **1**:467

Baricelli, Jean-Pierre
Kalevala **6**:280

Barker, E. Phillips
Seneca, Lucius Annaeus **6**:375

Barker, William
Xenophon **17**:318

Barnes, Jonathan
Pythagoras **22**:319

Barney, Stephen A.
Romance of the Rose **8**:435

Barnstone, Willis
Llull, Ramon **12**:126
Sappho **3**:435

Barolini, Teodolinda
Sordello **15**:368

Barr, William
Juvenal **8**:86

Barron, W. R. J.
Layamon **10**:360
Sir Gawain and the Green Knight **2**:261

Barth, John
Arabian Nights **2**:43

Basgoz, Ilhan
Book of Dede Korkut **8**:108

Basore, John W.
Seneca, Lucius Annaeus **6**:374

Bassett, Samuel Eliot
Iliad **1**:329
Odyssey **16**:214

Bates, William Nickerson
Euripides **23**:115
Sophocles **2**:336

Batts, Michael S.
Gottfried von Strassburg **10**:293
Hartmann von Aue **15**:183

Bayerschmidt, Carl F.
Njals saga **13**:326
Wolfram von Eschenbach **5**:311

Beagon, Mary
Pliny the Elder **23**:363

Beare, W.
Terence **14**:343

Beaufret, Jean
Heraclitus **22**:147

Becher, Anne G.
Phaedrus **25**:386

Bede
Cædmon **7**:77

Beer, Frances
Hildegard von Bingen **20**:175

Bell, Aubrey F. G.
Poem of the Cid **4**:251

Bell, Richard
The *Koran* **23**:239, 267

Bennett, James O'Donnell
Arabian Nights **2**:27

Bennett, Josephine Waters
Mandeville, Sir John **19**:117

Benson, Eugene
Sordello **15**:33

Benson, Larry D.
Morte Arthure **10**:386
Sir Gawain and the Green Knight **2**:227

Bentwich, Norman
Josephus, Flavius **13**:199

Berggren, J. L.
Euclid **25**:258

Bergin, Thomas G.
Boccaccio, Giovanni **13**:74

Berkeley, George
Plato **8**:221

Berry, Francis
Sir Gawain and the Green Knight **2**:194

Berthoud, J. A.
Inferno **3**:116

Bespaloff, Rachel
Iliad **1**:343

Besserman, Lawrence
Sir Gawain and the Green Knight **2**:280

Bettelheim, Bruno
Arabian Nights **2**:53

Beye, Charles Rowan
Hesiod **5**:131

Bigg, Charles
Origen **19**:189

Bilde, Per
Josephus, Flavius **13**:302

Billson, Charles J.
Kalevala **6**:233

Bishop, Ian
Pearl **19**:339

Bittinger, J. B.
The Book of Psalms **4**:363

Bixby, James T.
Kalevala **6**:217
Lao Tzu **7**:118

Critic Index

Critic Index

Turunen, Aimo
Kalevala **6**:258

Twomey, Michael W.
Morte Arthure **10**:425

Tyrwhitt, Thomas
Layamon **10**:311

Uhland, Johann
Bertran de Born **5**:10

Uitti, Karl D.
Chretien de Troyes **10**:190
Romance of the Rose **8**:446
The Song of Roland **1**:243

Urwin, Kenneth
Mystery of Adam **4**:191

Usher, Stephen
Greek Historiography **17**:23

Uysal, Ahmet E.
Book of Dede Korkut **8**:98

Vaidya, C. V.
Mahabharata **5**:189

Valency, Maurice
Vita Nuova **18**:349

Valla, Lorenzo
Cato, Marcus Porcius **21**:4
Epicurus **21**:79

Van Antwerp, Margaret
Razon de Amor **16**:353

Van Buitenen, J. A. B.
Mahabharata **5**:267

Van Buskirk, William R.
Lao Tzu **7**:119

Van Doren, Mark
Aeneid **9**:366
The Book of Psalms **4**:425
Iliad **1**:336
Murasaki, Lady **1**:420
Odyssey **16**:231

Van Nooten, Barend A.
Mahabharata **5**:249

Vance, Eugene
The Song of Roland **1**:214

van Hamel, A. G.
Celtic Mythology **26**:80

Vannovsky, Alexander
Kojiki **21**:244

Vasiliev, A. A.
Anna Comnena **25**:41

Vellacott, Philip
Aeschylus **11**:207

Verdenius, W. J.
Plato **8**:296

Vergil
Aeneid **9**:312, 329

Versenyi, Laszlo
Hesiod **5**:137
Sappho **3**:455

Very, Jones
Homer **1**:292

Vigfusson, Gudbrand
Hrafnkel's Saga **2**:76

Vinaver, Eugene
Arthurian Legend **10**:81
Chretien de Troyes **10**:180
The Song of Roland **1**:234

Vittorini, Domenico
Vita Nuova **18**:346

Vivekananda, Swami
Bhagavad Gita **12**:5

Vlastos, Gregory
Socrates **27**:357

Voltaire, François-Marie Arouet
Aeneid **9**:314
Aristophanes **4**:41
The Book of Job **14**:123
Iliad **1**:288

von Fritz, Kurt
Polybius **17**:160

Vossler, Karl
Inferno **3**:51

Wa, Kathleen Johnson
Lao Tzu **7**:196
Vita Nuova **18**:329

Wailes, Stephen L.
Das Nibelungenlied **12**:231

Walbank, F. W.
Polybius **17**:167

Waldock, A. J. A.
Sophocles **2**:368

Waley, Arthur
Confucius **19**:17
Lao Tzu **7**:128
Li Po **2**:137
Murasaki, Lady **1**:421

Walhouse, Moreton J.
Sappho **3**:385

Waliszewski, K.
The Igor Tale **1**:479

Walker, Roger M.
Razon de Amor **16**:346

Walker, Warren S.
Book of Dede Korkut **8**:98

Wallace, David
Boccaccio, Giovanni **13**:87, 94

Wallace, William
Epicurus **21**:101

Wallace-Hadrill, Andrew
Pliny the Elder **23**:355

Wallacker, Benjamin E.
Po Chu-i **24**:366

Walpole, Horace
Arabian Nights **2**:3

Walsh, George B.
Euripides **23**:191
Hesiod **5**:166

Walsh, P. G.
Livy **11**:342, 350

Walshe, M. O'C.
Gottfried von Strassburg **10**:274
Das Nibelungenlied **12**:171
Wolfram von Eschenbach **5**:333

Warburton, William
Apuleius **1**:7

Ward, Benedicta
Bede **20**:102

Warmington, B. H.
Seneca, Lucius Annaeus **6**:395

Warton, Joseph
Inferno **3**:6

Watling, E. F.
Seneca, Lucius Annaeus **6**:387

Watson, Burton
Si Shih **15**:391

Watson, Nicholas
Rolle, Richard **21**:388

Webbe, Joseph
Terence **14**:296

Webbe, William
Ovid **7**:290

Webber, Ruth H.
Poem of the Cid **4**:286

Weber, Alfred
Bacon, Roger **14**:20

Webster, T. B. L.
Callimachus **18**:34
Menander **9**:246

Weigand, Hermann J.
Wolfram von Eschenbach **5**:315, 370

Weil, Simone
Iliad **1**:331

Weiler, Royal W.
Kalidasa **9**:113

Weinberg, Julius R.
Averroes **7**:44
Bacon, Roger **14**:94

Weinberg, S. C.
Layamon **10**:360

Weiss, Paul
The Book of Job **14**:157

Welch, Holmes
Lao Tzu **7**:141
Lieh Tzu **27**:104

Wellek, Rene
Pearl **19**:299

Wenley, R. M.
Socrates **27**:217

West, M. L.
Pindar **12**:333

Westcott, John Howell
Livy **11**:312

Westermann, Claus
The Book of Psalms **4**:428

Westlake, John S.
Anglo-Saxon Chronicle **4**:4

Weston, Jessie L.
Arthurian Legend **10**:28
Chretien de Troyes **10**:133
Gottfried von Strassburg **10**:247
Wolfram von Eschenbach **5**:300

Wetherbee, Winthrop
Romance of the Rose **8**:422

Wethered, H. N.
Pliny the Elder **23**:322

Wheeler, Arthur Leslie
Cattullus **18**:82

Whewell, William
Bacon, Roger **14**:3

Whibley, Charles
Apuleius **1**:15

Whigham, Peter
Catullus **18**:109

Whinfield, E. H.
Khayyam **11**:255
Rumi, Jalal al-Din **20**:338

Whitehead, Alfred North
Plato **8**:271

Whitelock, Dorothy
Beowulf **1**:101

Whitman, Cedric H.
Aristophanes **4**:133
Euripides **23**:177
Iliad **1**:350
Odyssey **16**:254
Sophocles **2**:362